Baseball Prospectus

2003

Jeff Bower
Will Carroll
Clay Davenport
Ted Fischer
Gary Gillette
Jeff Hildebrand
Gary Huckabay
Rany Jazayerli
Chris Kahrl
Jonah Keri
Mat Olkin
Doug Pappas
Dave Pease
Keith Scherer
Nate Silver
Michael Wolverton
Keith Woolner
Derek Zumsteg

Brassey's Sports

Brassey's
WASHINGTON, D.C.

sharon
382-2340

Tues. 8:30

ISBN 1-57488-561-8

Printed in the United States of America on acid-free paper that meets the American National Standards Institute Z39-48 Standard.

Brassey's, Inc.
22841 Quicksilver Drive
Dulles, Virginia 20166

Text design by Pen & Palette Unlimited

First Edition

10 9 8 7 6 5 4 3 2 1

Contents

Fungoes

Foreword

by Gary Huckabay

Thank you for purchasing *Baseball Prospectus 2003*. We're very grateful for the investment you've chosen to make with your time and money, and we hope you enjoy the book as much as we enjoy cranking it out every year, for you and for ourselves.

It's an extremely exciting time to be a baseball fan. The myth of a huge payroll being necessary for success has been beaten largely to death. There's no longer a cloud of an impending labor stoppage looming over the game, threatening to end the season and preventing people from emotionally investing in their teams. We're lucky enough to live in a time when baseball players are better than they've ever been in the history of the game, and we get to watch in awe, on a regular basis, as marvels like Randy Johnson, Pedro Martinez, Barry Bonds, Alex Rodriguez, and a dozen others play the game at a level simply never seen before. The days of East Coast fans suffering through a morning paper devoid of results from the West Coast are gone, replaced with immediate updates of everything in the baseball world on the Internet, down to individual pitches in every game.

It's also a time of tremendous change in the way baseball is presented. The mainstream media has moved toward quantitative analysis, with more attention given to things like on-base percentage, and greater exposure and acceptance for contributors like Baseball Prospectus, Rob Neyer at ESPN, or Lee Sinins and his tremendous *Sabermetric Baseball Encyclopedia*, among others. Many MLB clubs have identified the need to have a performance analysis component in the way they evaluate players and forecast their development, and have brought quantitative analysis in-house. Quantitative analysis has shown its value, and the mainstream has responded by moving toward it. There's still a long way to go, but the initial immobility within the industry has been overcome, replaced by an inexorable motion toward increased understanding and usage of serious analysis.

Baseball Prospectus 2003 also marks a major departure for the *Baseball Prospectus* book series. In the past, we've only used Clay Davenport's translated stats in the book; Clay's work normalizes player statistics relative to a particular league and ballpark, which tells you a lot about how to interpret what a player did on the field. Starting this year, we are presenting raw, untranslated stats for every player in the book. **You'll still see translated batting average, on base percentage, and slugging for hitters, and translated ERA for pitchers, but in addition to actual statistics, not just in lieu of them.**

Another big addition to this year's book is that we're very happy to introduce Nate Silver's forecasting system for hitters and pitchers, which we believe is the best system available anywhere. We hope you'll agree. Other new features you'll find making their debuts in this year's book are Doug Pappas's appreciation of the game's labor situation and Will Carroll's comprehensive explanation of player injuries.

Above and beyond the mechanical changes in the book, Baseball Prospectus is undergoing a number of exciting changes outside of these pages. We're very happy to be bringing Will Carroll aboard not just in this volume, but also as an on-line contributor specializing in player injuries, health, and rehabilitation, and finally, as the host of *Baseball Prospectus Radio*, launching this March across the USA. Will has been the driving force behind "Under the Knife," a fantastic daily newsletter and column at Fox Sports. More important, Will shares the passionate, unkillable love of baseball that readers and contributors of BP share. You know this feeling well: it's the kind of love for the game that gets you in trouble because you're secretly listening to a ball game in the back of the classroom.

We're very pleased to announce the introduction of Baseball Prospectus Premium on-line. It's a subscription-based service that will provide expanded content on a daily basis from spring training through the postseason, with weekly updates in the offseason. We'll be providing daily injury and health updates from Will Carroll, four pieces a week from Joe Sheehan, as well as expanded performance forecasts for hitters and pitchers, in depth interviews with ballplayers, front office executives, coaches, agents, and broadcasters, among others. The cost will be $39.95 annually, and while we understand that's not a small amount of money, but it comes out to less than a dime per article, and we wouldn't put our name on it if we didn't think it was well worth it. We hope you'll check out our trial period from February 15th through March 1st, and choose to support the endeavor. We'll be working hard to provide an even more informative and entertaining sidelight to your baseball season.

We should also take a moment to thank the tremendous amount of assistance we get to provide you with a perspective that is both aware of what's going on inside the game while remaining independent of it. At this point beyond count, we've had the good fortune to be able to talk to team executives, scouts, players, agents, journalists, other analysts, and not a few well-informed fans too, and get some of our questions answered as well as answer some that get posed to us. It's a way to indulge that most basic pleasure, talking about the game with the men and women who help make it something we all enjoy.

Perhaps the most important changes at BP have taken place behind the scenes, with the debut of Cedra Jazayerli and Sagan Woolner, both small by scouting standards. Sagan's listed at 1′ 8.5″, probably too diminutive even for the Astros to draft, and Cedra's more of a speedster, at a lithe 6 pounds, 15 ounces. There is already talk that the young Woolner's birth certificate may have been fudged, and that he may be as old as 4, as opposed to less than one month, as claimed by the Santa Clara County Recorder, an organization allegedly rife with inaccuracies and graft. Congratulations to Rany, Belsam, Keith, and Kathy on the very proximal births of their respective first children.

With all of the changes going on, two things aren't changing a bit—our focus on creating content that displays our abject, perhaps embarrassing love for the game, and our gratitude to all the readers and friends who make *Baseball Prospectus* possible. It is our sincere hope that this book finds you in good health and spirit, surrounded by friends, loved ones, mown grass, and the sounds of spring baseball. We could all use a little more of those things in our lives.

Gary Huckabay
Clayton, California
January 7, 2003

The New Alphabet Soup, or How to Use This Book

by Keith Woolner

This edition of Baseball Prospectus marks a substantial change in the way we present our analysis of players. For the past several years, we have been presenting entirely translated statistics, rather than actual unadjusted statistics. That is, a player's statistics were not identical to what you would find in other reference books, but had been modified to account for the league, level (MLB, Triple-A, Double-A, etc.), and park that they played in. **Starting this year, we will be presenting a combination of raw and adjusted data.** In part, we're doing this because we think it's more instructive to show you the raw stats and our own interpretive statistics, which in turn should help you know just that much more about player value through performance metrics.

In addition, we are introducing two measurements to the book that have been available at www.baseballprospectus.com for some time.

First, There's *Marginal Lineup Value (MLV)*

To calculate Marginal Lineup Value, we compute the change in expected run scoring between an average lineup, and a team with 8 average players and the batter in question. If we were to swap one of the nine average players for the 2002 vintage Barry Bonds, we would, naturally, expect them to score more runs. Similarly, if you replaced one such player with Neifi Perez, we would expect them to score fewer runs. For example:

Lineup A	Lineup B
Joe Average	Joe Average
Joe Average	Joe Average
Joe Average	Barry Bonds
Joe Average	Joe Average
Joe Average	Joe Average
Joe Average	Joe Average
Joe Average	Joe Average
Joe Average	Joe Average
Joe Average	Joe Average

If we expect Lineup A to score 750 runs, and Lineup B to score 900 runs, based on the offensive statistics of the individual players, then Barry Bonds' Marginal Lineup Value would be 900 – 750, or 150 runs. MLV can be expressed as a cumulative total over the course of a season or career, or as a rate of production (marginal runs per game). When using the rate of production, it is designated by an "r" at the end of the acronym, as in MLVr. In the case of Bonds and Perez, Bonds had an MLVr of 0.955 in 2002, while Neifi's MLVr was –0.317. Negative MLVr's are quite common, and an MLVr of exactly zero means the player performed at the league average.

In short, all above-average hitters have a positive MLVr, and all below-average hitters have a negative MLVr.

Next, There's *Value Over Replacement Player* (VORP)

Value Over Replacement Player, or VORP, uses MLV as a foundation, and builds on it to incorporate a player's position and playing time to estimate total player value. Replacement level is a concept discussed in great detail in "Understanding and Measuring Replacement Level," an article by Keith Woolner found in *Baseball Prospectus 2002*, so we will only briefly restate it here.

Metrics such as MLVr, that compare a player to league average offense are incomplete by themselves, because they fail to properly account for the value of having an average player healthy and in the lineup. Losing a starting player typically results in more starts given to bench players, who can be considerably below average. By comparing a player's production to the level of a typical bench player or Quadruple-A journeyman (guys which are cheaply available as **replacements,** hence the term), we recognize the value of a player's durability. We define replacement level as "the expected level of performance a major league team can receive from one or more of the best available players who substitute for a suddenly unavailable starting player at the same position and who are available with minimal expenditure of team resources."

And though we have been discussing it in terms of position players, VORP applies equally to pitchers. VORP has been available and updated daily during the season on the BP web site for a couple of years, and makes its first appearance in the book this year. However, there are a couple of minor differences between the way VORP is calculated on the web site and how it is presented here. First, all players are rated at their most frequently played position, rather than a weighted average across all positions they appeared at. Second, the park factors used for the in-season updates at www.baseballprospectus.com are calculated over the three previous seasons; in this book, we use five-year park factors for MLB and each of the minor leagues.

Tables 1 and 2 show what the stat lines look like for hitters and pitchers in *Baseball Prospectus 2003*.

Note: For everyone's convenience, keep in mind that all **translated stats** are presented with **gray shading**, and **unadjusted stats** are presented with **normal background**.

Table 1. Sample Hitter Statistics with Column Heads Legend

Nomar Garciaparra   SS   Born: 23-Jul-73   Age: 29   Bats: R   Throws: R

YEAR	TM	LG	AGE	AB	H	2B	3B	HR	BB	SO	SB	CS	AVG	OBP	SLG	MLVR	EQBA	EQOBP	EQSLG	EQMLVR	VORP	DEFENSE
2000	BOS	AL	26	529	197	51	3	21	61	50	5	2	.372	.439	.599	.484	.383	.443	.619	.549	101.9	130-SS 5
2001	BOS	AL	27	83	24	3	0	4	7	9	0	1	.289	.352	.470	.109	.301	.368	.494	.154	7.9	21-SS -1
2002	BOS	AL	28	635	197	56	5	24	41	63	5	2	.310	.358	.528	.233	.331	.378	.568	.310	83.8	150-SS 3
2003	BOS	AL	29	595	187	45	3	24	48	63	4	1	.314	.367	.521	.227	.321	.376	.546	.249	63.0	

Breakout: 5%   *Improve: 39%*   *Collapse: 16%*

YEAR, TM, LG, AGE: are the season, the team(s) the player was on, the league that team is in, and the player's age that season.

AB, H, 2B, 3B, HR, BB, SO, SB, CS: The actual, unadjusted totals compiled by the player with that team during the season.

BA: actual batting average.

OBP: actual on base percentage.

SLG: actual slugging average.

MLVr: Marginal Lineup Value rate. The increase (or decrease) in expected runs per game from substituting the player into an otherwise league average lineup. Adjusted for league and park, but not level. This enables the reader to discern whether a player was above or below average in his own league.

EqBA: EqOBP, EqSLG: translated batting average, on base percentage, and slugging average expected in the majors from a player posting the rates of production he did in his own league. This measures all players against the same standard—a neutral park in Major League Baseball. Naturally, most minor league players will not match up well with most major leaguers.

EqMLVr: translated Marginal Lineup Value rate. The increase (or decrease) in expected runs per game from substituting the player's major league translated performance into an otherwise major league average lineup.

VORP: Value Over Replacement Player. The cumulative full-season value of the player's major league translated performance at the player's most frequently played position. Note that most minor leagues typically have shorter seasons than the majors do, and as a result, even excellent translated rates of production may not produce as high a VORP as a player with the benefit of a 162 game schedule.

Defense: one or two entries that tell you Number of Games, Position, and Clay Davenport's Fielding Rating. Thus, "150-SS 3" means 150 games at shortstop, with a defensive performance 3 runs above average for shortstops.

2003: This is where we introduce our new projection system, Nate Silver's PECOTA. A full explanation of how it works can be found in Nate's essay about PECOTA (page 507).

Breakout, Improve, and Collapse: Explanations of what these mean in terms of what the PECOTA projection is predicting can be found in Nate Silver's essay.

Table 2. Sample Pitcher Statistics with Column Heads Legend

Pedro Martinez						Born: 25-Jul-71				Age: 31		Bats: R		Throws: R			
YEAR	TM	LG	AGE	G	GS	IP	H	BB	SO	HR	ERA	EQERA	EQH9	EQBB9	EQSO9	EQHR9	PERA	VORP	STF
2000	BOS	AL	28	29	29	217.0	128	32	284	17	1.74	1.53	5.1	1.1	11.5	0.6	1.45	95.8	58
2001	BOS	AL	29	18	18	116.7	84	25	163	5	2.39	2.12	6.1	1.8	11.7	0.3	2.10	43.9	57
2002	BOS	AL	30	30	30	199.3	144	40	239	13	2.26	2.48	6.5	1.7	10.5	0.5	2.27	67.0	48
2003	BOS	AL	31	29	28	195.3	150	40	212	17	2.44	2.42	6.7	1.7	9.4	0.8	2.33	74.1	41

Breakout: 23%   Improve: 59%   Collapse: 13%

YEAR, TM, LG, AGE: see table 1.

G, GS, IP, H, BB, SO, HR: the actual, unadjusted totals compiled by the pitcher during this stint.

ERA: actual, plain old unadjusted earned run average.

EqERA: translated ERA expected in the majors from a player based on his performance in the minors.

EqH9: major league translated hits allowed per 9 innings.

EqBB9: major league translated walks allowed per 9 innings.

EqSO9: major league equivalent strikeouts per 9 innings.

EqHR9: major league translated home runs allowed per 9 innings.

PERA: Peripheral ERA. The EqERA a pitcher would be expected to have given his EqH9, EqBB9, EqSO9, EqHR9. A PERA lower than his EqERA may indicate that he was somewhat unlucky, and could be expected to improve his EqERA next season even without substantial change in peripheral rates of production.

VORP: Value Over Replacement Pitcher.

STF: Stuff rating. We introduced "Stuff" in last year's edition. It is an attempt to evaluate a pitcher's performance for evidence of his pitching ability, both now and with a natural amount of growth figured in. It is a tool whose primary use is to do what the original Major League Equivalencies, and later the Davenport Translations, did for hitters, which is to identify the real prospects. Stuff is not a subjective measure of a pitcher's pitches, but is instead created by the statistical consequences of a pitcher's ability. To some extent, these statistical consequences are used to already produce Peripheral ERA, but Stuff does more than predict the number of runs a pitcher allows. It is designed to assess a pitcher's fitness to pitch in the majors for an extended period of time. The formula for stuff is:

$$\text{Stuff} = \left(6 \times \frac{K}{9}\right) - \left[1.333 \times \left(ERA + PERA\right)\right] - \left(5 \times \frac{HR}{9}\right) - \left(3 \times \frac{BB}{9}\right)$$

2003: This is where we introduce our new projection system, Nate Silver's PECOTA. A full explanation of how it works can be found in Nate's essay about PECOTA.

Breakout, Improve, and Collapse: Explanations of what these mean in terms of what the PECOTA projection is predicting can be found in Nate Silver's essay (page **507**).

You may notice that Equivalent Average, or EqA, is absent from this year's book, despite having figured prominently in every prior edition of BP. With the addition of MLV and VORP, EqA is now redundant. Both methods create an index of offensive production, adjusted for park, league, and level. Having EqMLVr allows you to quickly analyze situations and estimate the actual impact of a personnel change on a team. Your first baseman (0.209 EqMLVr) just got injured and will be out half the year. How much offense would we be expected to lose by promoting our Triple-A first baseman (-0.052 EqMLVr) to start for him in the meantime? The expected difference per game is roughly the difference in their MLVr's: [0.209 – (–0.052)] = .261 runs per game worse with the Triple-A first baseman. That means that .261 runs per game × 81 games = 21.14 runs. The team would be expected to score about 21 fewer runs over the next 81 games while the regular first baseman is unavailable, or, to make things really simple, it would hurt pretty badly. However, Equivalent Average is still an informative statistic, and you'll still be able to find Equivalent Average information and data on our web site, updated throughout the season, and for both the major leagues and the minors.

All of these changes are designed to tell you more about individual players, and will continue to be complemented year-round by content and analysis at:

www.baseballprospectus. com

We hope you enjoy the changes and find this year's book as interesting and entertaining as previous editions. Naturally, we'd love to hear whatever feedback you have on the subject, so feel free to contact us through the site. Take it as an opportunity to have a conversation about baseball, something I think we all agree you can't spend too much time doing.

Anaheim Angels

One of my favorite parts of Baseball Prospectus is being mammothly, enormously wrong, which means that on a regular basis, I get to be a pretty happy guy. At the start of the 2002 season, 100% of the buzz in the American League West was about whether or not the Rangers, with their acquisition of every misfit they could find, a new bullpen, and a shiny Chan Ho Park, would be strong enough to compete with the Ichiro-led 116-win Mariner juggernaut or the young, pitching-rich Athletics. Around the country, Baseball Prospectus hosted several Pizza Feeds, where literally hundreds of baseball fans came, shared their opinions with us, and talked about the great, brewing battle between the A's and Mariners; our readers tend to be pretty bright, so no one took Texas too seriously. Of the hundreds of people that came and filled out their prognostication forms, including every member of the Baseball Prospectus staff, and special guests that included baseball analysts, front office staff, and broadcasters, precisely one person picked the Angels to finish higher than fourth in the AL West. They picked them to finish third.

As we now know, the Mousemen did a wee bit better than that. Somewhere, Gene Autry is still gleefully jumping around, and one of baseball's stepsister franchises won it all in dramatic fashion, coming just a few outs from falling to Barry Bonds, Jeff Kent, and the 23 dwarves. The Angels did it in clichéd storybook fashion, with a whole bunch of guys making contributions, and no one individual being responsible for a disproportionate share of the win. The Angel front office, led by GM Bill Stoneman and Assistant GM Ken Forsch, put together an outstanding, balanced team, with few weaknesses (if any), and then Mike Scioscia and Bud Black led them to the promised land. It was a fantastic thing to watch.

So, having done all that, achieving what seemed impossible only last spring, can they do it again? Sure. But will they?

> ## Angels Prospectus
>
> **2002 record:** 99–63; Second place, AL West; Beat the Giants in the World Series 4–3
>
> **Pythagenport Record:** 102–60
>
> **Runs scored per game:** 5.3 (4th in AL)
>
> **Runs allowed per game:** 4.0 (1st in AL)
>
> **Team EqA:** .265 (5th in AL)
>
> **2002 Batters Age:** 28.8 (6th youngest in AL)
>
> **2002 Pitchers Age:** 30.3 (4th oldest in AL)
>
> **Ballpark:** Edison Field; slight hitters' park; Park Factor of 1.016
>
> **2002:** A great pen, a solid rotation, and a balanced attack works equally well over six months and in a postseason series.
>
> **2003:** Expect a letdown from the euphoria of Monkeymania.

There are a lot of reasons to like their chances to do it again. For one, this is not an old team. Of the starting position players, Tim Salmon is the old man at 34, and guys like Glaus, Eckstein, Kennedy, Spiezio, Anderson, Erstad, and most of the pitching staff are either at or near their primes. It's not like this is a team teetering on the brink of old age and collapse.

Even under the best of circumstances, repeating as a champion isn't easy. What's standing in the way of the Angels winning another World Series? First off, teams usually win championships because the players on the team have an exceptional year, and exceptional means that it doesn't happen too often. Almost every player on the Angels with significant playing time played at the top of the range of reasonable expectations in 2002. Just on the offensive side of the ball, let's take a look at the key performers in table 1.

"Reasonable expectations" are squishy here, in order to get to the point. Before we actually arrive there, let's take a look in table 2 at the ages of these guys, along with their defensive runs above average for the year.

Wow. One more thing before we get to that point. Let's look specifically at the bullpen real quick . . . table 3.

That's tasty, nasty, and vicious all at once. The pen is a structural strength of the team, and it doesn't even consider Francisco Rodriguez. The rotation had one stud in Washburn, and a solid supporting cast in Ortiz, Appier, and Lackey.

So why is it going to be so hard to repeat? Because pretty much everything that could go right did go right. Aaron Sele could have pitched better, but when he didn't, John Lackey stepped in and pitched great. The bullpen could protect the starters as needed. Almost everyone played just a little bit over their heads or their established career rates. That's not to say that it was necessarily luck. As far back as the late 1980s, people like Sherri Nichols talked about the virtues of

Table 1. Lineup Performance

Position/Player	2002 Performance
1B: Scott Spiezio	hit .285/.375/.436, an improvement over his established .257/.334/.452
2B: Adam Kennedy	hit .312/.348/.449, a big increase from his established .268/.313/.388
3B: Troy Glaus	hit .250/.356/.453, a significant drop from his established .267/.388/.594
SS: David Eckstein	hit .293/.368/.388, an improvement over his established .285/.356/.357
OF: Garret Anderson	hit .306/.337/.539, a large marginal improvement over his established .287/.314/.498
OF: Darin Erstad	hit .283/.315/.389, below his two-year average, and toward the bottom of reasonable expectations
OF: Tim Salmon	hit .286/.385/.503, a mild improvement over his established .258/.386/.472
DH: Brad Fullmer	hit .289/.359/.531, compared to an established .285/.337/.500

Table 2. Defensive Performance

Player	Age	Defensive Runs
Spiezio	29	+2
Kennedy	26	+16
Glaus	25	+12
Eckstein	27	+15
Anderson	30	+5
Erstad	28	+21
Salmon	33	-1

Table 3. Bullpen Performance

Player	IP	ERA
Percival	56.1	1.92
Donnelly	49.2	2.17
Shields	49.0	2.20
Weber	78.0	2.54
Pote	50.1	3.22
Levine	63.2	4.24

having an offense constructed around the idea of getting a bunch of guys at their peak ages, and living off the surprise seasons and multiplicative nature of offense. Stoneman went and did it, intentionally or not, and it paid off in spades.

Of course, all teams that win World Championships get a little lucky somewhere down the line, and the Angels are a team set up to take advantage of luck when it presents itself. The Angels are structured in a way that will allow them to be a strong contender for the next couple of years, as long as Stoneman and Forsch can keep the bullpen magic coming. "Numbers are part of it, and everyone loves velocity, but we've had good success with guys with tremendous movement on their pitches. It should be tough to pick up and track their pitches out of their hands. We look for movement," said Forsch, when asked about the source of the bullpen's success. Beyond keeping a constant eye out for relievers that fulfill that requirement, the Angels are in pretty good shape on both sides of the ball for the next season or two, provided everyone stays healthy.

The biggest immediate problem facing the Angels is something they have very little control over: the strength of their division. They're stuck in the Darwinian Campo Bello that is the AL West. The Mariners won 116 games two years ago and 93 games last year, and they're armed with a huge revenue base, loyal fans, and talent in the pipeline. They

aren't going to just go away. Oakland has been to the post-season for three straight years, and has a core that's even younger than the Angels, the best front office in the game, and a farm system that's stocked with talent. In Arlington, there's an opponent with a big budget, a bright new manager, probably the two best young hitters in the game, and a shortstop who may go down as the best player to ever put on a uniform. With that crowd of contenders, there's no time left to sit back and enjoy the trophy and the rings. That should be completed by now, and everyone at MausHaus should be focusing on the future.

The future doesn't look too bad, either. In addition to Francisco Rodriguez and the simple elegance of his vapor trail fastball, the Angels enter this season with a pretty decent portfolio of young talent. They'll have Lackey in his first full season in the rotation, Casey Kotchman looks like a B+ or better prospect at first base, and they've got a few scout-favored pitchers like Chris Bootcheck and Joe Torres. Most importantly in the short term, Disney has decided to spend more money on the payroll, authorizing a bump from the $60 million range to the $85 million range. That can be a good thing, or it may be a mixed blessing. One of the most common mistakes that champions make is that they become risk-averse. They overvalue the players on the championship team to the exclusion of others, and hang onto some players too tightly and for too long. When you're facing the increased expectations that naturally follow a championship season, it can be very dangerous to fall into that trap. With the Angels' lack of 36-year-old free agents, it's probably not a serious danger at this point.

The Angels' success in 2003 will depend heavily on the health of their starting rotation. That's true to a certain extent for every club, but the Angels don't have much depth there. An injury that causes the loss of Washburn, Appier, or Ortiz for an extended period of time could disturb a very delicately balanced pitching staff. Black and Scioscia were careful to allocate innings and workloads fairly carefully, and they were able to manage their way to one of the great bullpens in the history of the game. That bullpen was then used to support and protect the rotation starters. If one or two major parts of that staff end up collapsing, it can have a very dramatic and very negative impact, and the next thing you know, you've lost three of four to the Devil Rays. The Angels could use one more emergency starter above and beyond Schoeneweis. If they put Francisco Rodriguez in that role, they may be very pleasantly surprised. Seattle may have to begin a rebuilding process at the end of the 2004 season after being shut out of the playoffs yet again by the "surprising" Angels.

HITTERS

Alfredo Amezaga   SS   Born: 16-Jan-78   Age: 25   Bats: Throws: R

YEAR	TM	LG	AGE	AB	H	2B	3B	HR	BB	SO	SB	CS	AVG	OBP	SLG	MLVR	EQBA	EQOBP	EQSLG	EQMLVR	VORP	DEFENSE			
2000	LEL	CLF	22	420	117	13	4	4	63	70	73	21	.279	.378	.357	.034	.233	.301	.303	-.291	-8.2	91-2B	-1	14-SS	4
2001	ARK	TXS	23	285	89	10	5	4	22	55	24	15	.312	.370	.425	.125	.259	.307	.353	-.193	1.9	68-SS	3		
2001	SLC	PCL	23	200	50	5	4	1	14	45	9	6	.250	.309	.330	-.253	.207	.263	.278	-.416	-9.7	49-SS	-5		
2002	SLC	PCL	24	518	130	25	7	6	45	100	23	14	.251	.320	.361	-.146	.217	.278	.312	-.333	-14.8	128-SS	-6		
2002	ANA	AL	24	13	7	2	0	0	0	1	1	0	.538	.538	.692	1.044	.538	.538	.769	1.193	4.0				
2003	ANA	AL	25	161	39	7	1	2	13	29	5	3	.239	.297	.343	-.174	.243	.304	.354	-.198	-1.6				

Breakout: 39%   *Improve: 66%*   *Collapse: 20%*

Amezaga is a utility infielder with some promise. At one point or another, he's shown plate discipline, the ability to hit for a reasonable average, and the ability to play pretty good defense at both middle infield positions. If he does all of those things at once, he probably has a career as a pretty decent 24th man ahead of him.

Garret Anderson   LF   Born: 30-Jun-72   Age: 31   Bats: L   Throws: L

YEAR	TM	LG	AGE	AB	H	2B	3B	HR	BB	SO	SB	CS	AVG	OBP	SLG	MLVR	EQBA	EQOBP	EQSLG	EQMLVR	VORP	DEFENSE	
2000	ANA	AL	28	647	185	40	3	35	24	87	7	6	.286	.311	.519	.054	.295	.312	.537	.116	45.1	133-CF	7
2001	ANA	AL	29	672	194	39	2	28	27	100	13	6	.289	.316	.478	.057	.305	.334	.507	.119	34.6	145-LF	9
2002	ANA	AL	30	638	195	56	3	29	30	80	6	4	.306	.337	.539	.205	.322	.355	.573	.271	56.4	135-LF	5
2003	ANA	AL	31	553	159	36	2	24	27	75	5	3	.288	.321	.493	.096	.293	.328	.508	.092	19.2		

Breakout: 11%   *Improve: 43%*   *Collapse: 21%*

Just as he's been slightly underrated by analysts in the past, he was slightly overrated by the mainstream media this year. Anderson is what he is: a good defensive outfielder who can hit for a moderately good average and power, particularly against breaking stuff, but he walks approximately as often as Clarence Thomas deviates from Antonin Scalia. He's under contract through next season, and the forecast above looks about right.

Larry Barnes   1B   Born: 23-Jul-74   Age: 28   Bats: L   Throws: L

YEAR	TM	LG	AGE	AB	H	2B	3B	HR	BB	SO	SB	CS	AVG	OBP	SLG	MLVR	EQBA	EQOBP	EQSLG	EQMLVR	VORP	DEFENSE			
2000	EDM	PCL	25	397	102	22	11	7	48	81	3	6	.257	.337	.421	-.075	.225	.289	.364	-.235	-14.7	93-1B	-3		
2001	SLC	PCL	26	404	117	21	8	18	29	90	6	1	.290	.339	.515	.091	.248	.297	.434	-.105	-.9	81-1B	0		
2002	SLC	PCL	27	452	142	29	11	20	28	90	8	1	.314	.360	.560	.248	.271	.313	.481	.011	11.7	78-1B	3	21-RF	-2
2003	ANA	AL	28	166	42	8	2	5	13	36	2	2	.250	.306	.421	-.052	.254	.313	.434	-.067	-1.2				

Breakout: 24%   *Improve: 48%*   *Collapse: 25%*

Worse players have jobs. Barnes hits line drives, has some pop, and can play a corner outfield spot or first base well enough to hold a bench role. He's essentially the same player as John Mabry. He'll have to get lucky and be in the right training camp or on the right Triple-A team when an injury hits, or light up a September call-up as a pinch hitter if he's going to have a sustained career.

Michael Campo			LF		Born: 14-Nov-76					Age: 26			Bats: L			Throws: R	
YEAR	TM	LG	AGE	AB	H	2B	3B	HR	BB	SO	SB	CS	AVG	OBP	SLG	MLVR	EQBA	EQOBP	EQSLG	EQMLVR	VORP	DEFENSE

YEAR	TM	LG	AGE	AB	H	2B	3B	HR	BB	SO	SB	CS	AVG	OBP	SLG	MLVR	EQBA	EQOBP	EQSLG	EQMLVR	VORP	DEFENSE
2000	BUT	PIO	23	176	63	13	3	5	26	17	4	2	.358	.462	.551	.419	.224	.289	.341	-.267	-7.3	28-OF -7
2001	CDR	MDW	24	358	112	20	3	7	43	65	21	11	.313	.424	.444	.277	.247	.323	.350	-.174	-8.2	86-LF -7
2002	RCU	CLF	25	450	141	35	6	9	75	127	18	10	.313	.453	.478	.337	.249	.352	.377	-.080	1.0	89-LF -17
2003	*OAK*	*AL*	*26*	*154*	*38*	*8*	*1*	*3*	*15*	*34*	*3*	*2*	*.244*	*.321*	*.373*	*-.093*	*.252*	*.332*	*.390*	*-.093*	*-2.6*	

Breakout: 25%   Improve: 48%   Collapse: 31%

Campo went undrafted, so the Angels picked him up as a free agent, dropped him into the Pioneer League, and he simply started hitting . . . just like he did in college at Penn State. Not toolsy, but an exceptional batting eye, and it's hard to argue with the success he's had at every stop. His strikeout rate jumped a bit at Rancho, but there's nothing that says "This guy can't make the adjustments" in his record. When someone keeps popping out .420+ OBPs like Fox pops out demeaning, bland television shows, he deserves every chance to get to the bigs. He's old enough that he can't spend a year consolidating his gains. He needs to have one of those kick-ass years in Double- or Triple-A. Nabbed by the A's in the minor league portion of the Rule 5 draft.

Jeff DaVanon					Born: 08-Dec-73					Age: 29			Bats: B			Throws: R	

YEAR	TM	LG	AGE	AB	H	2B	3B	HR	BB	SO	SB	CS	AVG	OBP	SLG	MLVR	EQBA	EQOBP	EQSLG	EQMLVR	VORP	DEFENSE
2001	SLC	PCL	27	256	80	19	8	10	32	57	8	3	.313	.395	.566	.280	.265	.345	.470	.046	8.0	64-RF 0
2001	ANA	AL	27	88	17	2	1	5	11	29	1	3	.193	.283	.409	-.168	.205	.300	.420	-.151	-1.8	22-RF -1
2002	SLC	PCL	28	100	33	10	1	5	17	24	5	3	.330	.432	.600	.428	.280	.372	.510	.162	9.0	24-CF -3
2002	ANA	AL	28	30	5	3	0	1	2	6	1	0	.167	.219	.367	-.338	.167	.219	.400	-.358	-1.7	

DaVanon has yo-yoed between levels for a while now, trying desperately to pick up and hold onto a fourth outfielder job. Remember, Jeff—they can smell fear. DaVanon plays defense acceptably well, plus he has some pop and can hit for a decent average. It may come down to just being in the right place at the right time, or picking up a key hit that sticks in someone's mind. When it comes to the 25th man, there isn't a whole lot of rhyme or reason to whether you make it or not.

David Eckstein			SS		Born: 20-Jan-75					Age: 28			Bats: R			Throws: R	

YEAR	TM	LG	AGE	AB	H	2B	3B	HR	BB	SO	SB	CS	AVG	OBP	SLG	MLVR	EQBA	EQOBP	EQSLG	EQMLVR	VORP	DEFENSE	
2000	EDM	PCL	25	52	18	8	0	3	9	1	5	3	.346	.485	.673	.619	.294	.415	.549	.300	7.3	14-2B -4	
2000	PAW	INT	25	422	104	20	0	1	60	45	11	8	.246	.367	.301	-.118	.232	.334	.283	-.251	-4.2	114-2B 10	
2001	ANA	AL	26	582	166	26	2	4	43	60	29	4	.285	.356	.357	-.041	.305	.372	.383	.007	33.7	114-SS 4	12-2B 0
2002	ANA	AL	27	608	178	22	6	8	45	44	21	13	.293	.368	.388	.038	.319	.388	.423	.105	49.7	138-SS 15	
2003	*ANA*	*AL*	*28*	*551*	*145*	*26*	*3*	*5*	*48*	*49*	*15*	*3*	*.263*	*.333*	*.350*	*-.089*	*.268*	*.340*	*.361*	*-.106*	*9.0*		

Breakout: 3%   Improve: 22%   Collapse: 39%

Watching Eckstein play shortstop might be the most inspiring thing most people will ever see on a diamond. He visibly does not have the arm strength that scouts traditionally demand for the position. In order to field a ground ball and get the ball over to first, he goes through bizarre and intense contortions to get his entire 150 pounds behind the throw, then unleashes a toss in a frenetic ballet reminiscent of a bad martial arts film like *Kung Fu Cook*. It's great. He has a good approach at the plate, he's a good defender, and a joy to watch. Baseball doesn't get much better than this.

Darin Erstad			CF		Born: 04-Jun-74					Age: 29			Bats: L			Throws: L	

YEAR	TM	LG	AGE	AB	H	2B	3B	HR	BB	SO	SB	CS	AVG	OBP	SLG	MLVR	EQBA	EQOBP	EQSLG	EQMLVR	VORP	DEFENSE
2000	ANA	AL	26	676	240	39	6	25	64	82	28	8	.355	.412	.541	.334	.364	.414	.558	.392	80.2	136-LF 12
2001	ANA	AL	27	631	163	35	1	9	62	113	24	10	.258	.334	.360	-.096	.277	.351	.386	-.050	21.4	145-CF 12
2002	ANA	AL	28	625	177	28	4	10	27	67	23	3	.283	.315	.389	-.060	.301	.334	.414	-.022	24.2	143-CF 21
2003	*ANA*	*AL*	*29*	*574*	*161*	*31*	*4*	*12*	*40*	*74*	*17*	*5*	*.280*	*.330*	*.408*	*-.009*	*.285*	*.337*	*.421*	*-.019*	*14.4*	

Breakout: 6%   Improve: 43%   Collapse: 11%

He's probably the most underrated defender in baseball, and possibly the most overrated hitter. Erstad has one excellent season. One. That's it. Outside of that season, he's hit like a fourth outfielder. But because of his good defense, marquee value, and the perception that he's a scrappy, Pete Rose, hustling dude, Bill Stoneman saw fit to sign him to a contract for four years and $32 million. Granted, it's not one of those really dizzyingly bad Mike Hamptonesque signings, but it's not good. If you're going to pay that kind of money and take that kind of risk, it should be for a better player than this.

Chone Figgins — 2B — Born: 22-Jan-78 — Age: 25 — Bats: B — Throws: R

YEAR	TM	LG	AGE	AB	H	2B	3B	HR	BB	SO	SB	CS	AVG	OBP	SLG	MLVR	EQBA	EQOBP	EQSLG	EQMLVR	VORP	DEFENSE
2000	SLM	CRL	22	522	145	26	14	3	67	107	37	19	.278	.361	.398	.101	.226	.288	.328	-.286	-10.1	134-2B -19
2001	ARK	TXS	23	138	37	12	2	0	14	26	7	2	.268	.336	.384	-.022	.230	.291	.324	-.283	-2.5	34-2B -8
2001	CAR	SOU	23	332	73	14	5	2	40	73	27	8	.220	.307	.310	-.171	.196	.266	.282	-.409	-18.4	77-2B -3
2002	SLC	PCL	24	511	156	25	18	7	53	83	39	8	.305	.371	.466	.126	.266	.327	.406	-.075	18.1	117-2B 1
2002	ANA	AL	24	12	2	1	0	0	0	5	2	1	.167	.167	.250	-.590	.167	.167	.250	-.670	-1.5	
2003	*ANA*	*AL*	*25*	*206*	*52*	*10*	*2*	*3*	*20*	*37*	*8*	*5*	*.253*	*.320*	*.369*	*-.093*	*.257*	*.327*	*.380*	*-.110*	*2.4*	

Breakout: 30%   Improve: 62%   Collapse: 21%

Figgins is an incredibly speedy second baseman who basically served as a ballistic missile for the Angels during the second half of the 2002 season. Tim Salmon clogging the bases as the tying run in the 8th? No problem. Send Chone in. Figgins does have some skills beyond blazing speed, though. His defense is coming together nicely, he's shown a decent batting eye, and it's eye-popping to watch him take off when he slashes a ball into the gap. There's not really much of an opportunity for him in Anaheim right now, but under the right circumstances and with a little development, he could bring enough to the table to be a productive regular. That means 15 more hits and 10 more walks a year.

Brad Fullmer — DH — Born: 17-Jan-75 — Age: 28 — Bats: L — Throws: R

YEAR	TM	LG	AGE	AB	H	2B	3B	HR	BB	SO	SB	CS	AVG	OBP	SLG	MLVR	EQBA	EQOBP	EQSLG	EQMLVR	VORP	DEFENSE
2000	TOR	AL	25	482	142	29	1	32	30	68	3	1	.295	.344	.558	.169	.303	.345	.575	.235	42.9	
2001	TOR	AL	26	522	143	31	2	18	38	88	5	2	.274	.330	.444	.019	.287	.343	.468	.060	25.5	
2002	ANA	AL	27	429	124	35	6	19	32	44	10	3	.289	.359	.531	.212	.308	.373	.572	.280	40.8	21-1B 0
2003	*ANA*	*AL*	*28*	*400*	*111*	*26*	*2*	*17*	*33*	*54*	*8*	*2*	*.277*	*.338*	*.482*	*.098*	*.282*	*.345*	*.497*	*.094*	*14.8*	

Breakout: 1%   Improve: 26%   Collapse: 19%

On a team with inferior defense, he probably would have seen considerably more time in the field. Having elevated glove-work to a team fetish, Scioscia acted as if Fullmer was Robert Downey Jr., and his glove was Liza Minnelli's medicine cabinet—ne'er the twain should meet. Fullmer is a good enough hitter to help a championship club (obviously), but he needs a manager who can judiciously yank him out of the lineup from time to time. I don't believe a different manager would have been able to get as much out of him.

Benji Gil — SS — Born: 06-Oct-72 — Age: 30 — Bats: R — Throws: R

YEAR	TM	LG	AGE	AB	H	2B	3B	HR	BB	SO	SB	CS	AVG	OBP	SLG	MLVR	EQBA	EQOBP	EQSLG	EQMLVR	VORP	DEFENSE	
2000	ANA	AL	27	301	72	14	1	6	30	59	10	6	.239	.318	.352	-.217	.244	.317	.365	-.167	3.9	82-SS 1	
2001	ANA	AL	28	260	77	15	4	8	14	57	3	4	.296	.332	.477	.089	.310	.348	.506	.147	23.9	43-SS -9	17-2B 1
2002	SLC	PCL	29	24	10	5	1	2	1	4	0	2	.417	.440	.958	1.092	.333	.333	.792	.588	4.0		
2002	ANA	AL	29	130	37	8	1	3	5	33	2	1	.285	.311	.431	-.008	.305	.331	.466	.053	8.5	20-2B 3	11-SS 0
2003	*ANA*	*AL*	*30*	*150*	*38*	*9*	*1*	*4*	*10*	*33*	*2*	*2*	*.256*	*.304*	*.407*	*-.069*	*.261*	*.311*	*.419*	*-.085*	*1.5*		

Breakout: 5%   Improve: 24%   Collapse: 37%

It only seems like Gil has been around since the Eisenhower administration. He's a pretty good defender who can hit lefties well, and spell either Eckstein or Kennedy in case of nagging injuries. He really shouldn't be allowed to bat against right-handed pitching; he's south of a .600 OPS against it. Gil isn't a horrible guy to have around, but he is a replaceable talent, the type of player teams should be paying around the minimum for. Teams that win championships usually overvalue their roster composition, and having already re-signed him, it looks like the Angels are guilty as charged.

Troy Glaus — 3B — Born: 03-Aug-76 — Age: 26 — Bats: R — Throws: R

YEAR	TM	LG	AGE	AB	H	2B	3B	HR	BB	SO	SB	CS	AVG	OBP	SLG	MLVR	EQBA	EQOBP	EQSLG	EQMLVR	VORP	DEFENSE
2000	ANA	AL	23	563	160	37	1	47	112	163	14	11	.284	.405	.604	.328	.289	.404	.619	.370	85.2	153-3B 15
2001	ANA	AL	24	588	147	38	2	41	107	158	10	3	.250	.371	.531	.182	.266	.384	.569	.247	72.5	156-3B -3
2002	ANA	AL	25	569	142	24	1	30	88	144	10	3	.250	.356	.453	.071	.267	.372	.490	.123	48.2	147-3B 12
2003	*ANA*	*AL*	*26*	*547*	*143*	*30*	*2*	*35*	*94*	*135*	*11*	*4*	*.261*	*.372*	*.514*	*.177*	*.266*	*.381*	*.530*	*.179*	*47.7*	

Breakout: 10%   Improve: 51%   Collapse: 7%

Glaus is looking like the right-handed Darrell Evans, but with a much squarer jaw than Opie had. Glaus's performance is still very good but, overall, the trends are troubling. His platoon split has been all over the map, from brutal very early in his career to mild in 2001, and back to about 160 points of OPS in 2002. On the other hand, you can't shake the sense that he's fully capable of having a truly monster season at any given moment. Defensively, he's underrated; people have a hard time accepting that someone with Glaus's size can be so quick.

Nathan Haynes — CF Born: 07-Sep-79 Age: 23 Bats: L Throws: L

YEAR	TM	LG	AGE	AB	H	2B	3B	HR	BB	SO	SB	CS	AVG	OBP	SLG	MLVR	EQBA	EQOBP	EQSLG	EQMLVR	VORP	DEFENSE
2000	ERI	EAS	20	457	116	16	4	6	33	107	37	20	.254	.317	.346	-.112	.217	.264	.298	-.381	-24.3	111-CF -12
2001	ARK	TXS	21	316	98	11	5	5	32	65	33	15	.310	.379	.424	.137	.260	.319	.357	-.163	1.3	71-CF 0
2002	RCU	CLF	22	50	14	0	0	0	4	8	6	2	.280	.345	.280	-.124	.235	.271	.235	-.446	-3.3	11-CF -2
2002	SLC	PCL	22	283	80	14	6	2	12	53	10	10	.283	.314	.396	-.087	.243	.273	.339	-.289	-7.5	66-CF -5
2003	*ANA*	*AL*	*23*	*155*	*39*	*7*	*1*	*3*	*11*	*31*	*4*	*3*	*.250*	*.304*	*.374*	*-.115*	*.255*	*.311*	*.386*	*-.134*	*-.7*	

Breakout: 47%   Improve: 71%   Collapse: 14%

You only THINK he's been around forever. Haynes is still fast, but he's starting to develop a little pop. He still doesn't have much plate discipline, and hasn't learned enough about reading pitchers to effectively take advantage of his speed on the bases. Nevertheless, he's still young enough that he could develop one or two of these skills and have a career as an outfield spare. He'd better get to work on it pretty quick, because time's running out.

Gary Johnson — Born: 29-Oct-75 Age: 27 Bats: L Throws: L

YEAR	TM	LG	AGE	AB	H	2B	3B	HR	BB	SO	SB	CS	AVG	OBP	SLG	MLVR	EQBA	EQOBP	EQSLG	EQMLVR	VORP	DEFENSE
2000	LEL	CLF	24	266	90	20	2	13	41	59	13	6	.338	.434	.575	.479	.267	.335	.448	-.000	6.0	66-LF -9
2000	ERI	EAS	24	258	74	10	4	10	35	63	4	4	.287	.378	.473	.179	.241	.317	.398	-.123	-2.5	62-LF -8
2001	ARK	TXS	25	466	114	24	2	11	60	93	8	7	.245	.340	.376	-.042	.207	.286	.319	-.313	-28.9	101-LF -6
2002	SLC	PCL	26	143	38	9	3	5	15	49	1	1	.266	.348	.476	.067	.232	.309	.408	-.131	-2.0	36-RF -1

Johnson got a late start in 2002, but he made progress. Clubs can occasionally solve a problem by picking up a Gary Johnson from another organization, giving him a shot in spring training, and setting up a platoon. If things go right for him, he'll get that shot, but he's not as good a player as many other players that are freely available, like Billy McMillon or Ernie Young. You could do worse than picking him up to plug a gaping outfield hole, giving him 200 platoon at-bats, and living with the results. Okay, not a lot worse, perhaps only Derek Bell/Brady Anderson worse. Viva Operation Shutdown!

Adam Kennedy — 2B Born: 10-Jan-76 Age: 27 Bats: L Throws: R

YEAR	TM	LG	AGE	AB	H	2B	3B	HR	BB	SO	SB	CS	AVG	OBP	SLG	MLVR	EQBA	EQOBP	EQSLG	EQMLVR	VORP	DEFENSE
2000	ANA	AL	24	598	159	33	11	9	28	73	22	8	.266	.302	.403	-.156	.273	.302	.418	-.098	16.7	145-2B -2
2001	ANA	AL	25	478	129	25	3	6	27	71	12	7	.270	.324	.372	-.091	.288	.340	.401	-.040	21.1	123-2B 5
2002	ANA	AL	26	474	148	32	6	7	19	80	17	4	.312	.348	.449	.104	.335	.371	.486	.182	46.2	126-2B 16
2003	*ANA*	*AL*	*27*	*429*	*119*	*24*	*4*	*7*	*22*	*61*	*12*	*4*	*.278*	*.318*	*.405*	*-.034*	*.283*	*.325*	*.417*	*-.046*	*12.4*	

Breakout: 6%   Improve: 29%   Collapse: 26%

Kennedy is a great example of the Angels' blend of strengths and vulnerabilities. He's a good defensive player whose offensive production is highly dependent on his ability to hit for a very high batting average, much like Anderson, Erstad, and Fullmer. If he hits .312 and carries a great glove, he's an asset. If he hits .280 and the leather slips just a little, he's a problem. For the foreseeable future, he's a pretty good bet to be an asset, and he should exceed the forecast above.

Casey Kotchman — 1B Born: 22-Feb-83 Age: 20 Bats: L Throws: L

YEAR	TM	LG	AGE	AB	H	2B	3B	HR	BB	SO	SB	CS	AVG	OBP	SLG	MLVR	EQBA	EQOBP	EQSLG	EQMLVR	VORP	DEFENSE
2002	CDR	MDW	19	288	81	30	1	5	48	37	2	1	.281	.395	.444	.236	.221	.308	.356	-.211	-9.1	71-1B 3
2003	*ANA*	*AL*	*20*	*185*	*47*	*11*	*2*	*5*	*18*	*27*	*2*	*1*	*.255*	*.327*	*.412*	*-.026*	*.259*	*.334*	*.425*	*-.038*	*.2*	

Breakout: 46%   Improve: 71%   Collapse: 18%

What's not to love so far? Kotchman is a good defensive first baseman with a quick bat, a tremendous batting eye, and tremendous poise and baseball instincts. He'll be in Anaheim before too long, and he has a broad set of offensive skills to build off of. He's going to improve in at least one or two areas, and could be an elite first baseman in the AL before 2005. The key is going to be his ability to stay healthy.

Jeff Mathis — C Born: 31-Mar-83 Age: 20 Bats: R Throws: R

YEAR	TM	LG	AGE	AB	H	2B	3B	HR	BB	SO	SB	CS	AVG	OBP	SLG	MLVR	EQBA	EQOBP	EQSLG	EQMLVR	VORP	DEFENSE
2001	PRO	PIO	18	77	23	6	3	0	11	13	1	0	.299	.400	.455	.203	.205	.276	.308	-.349	-2.2	19-C -1
2002	CDR	MDW	19	491	141	41	3	10	40	75	7	4	.287	.351	.444	.182	.229	.275	.360	-.265	-3.8	77-C 3
2003	*ANA*	*AL*	*20*	*213*	*54*	*13*	*2*	*5*	*16*	*38*	*2*	*2*	*.253*	*.310*	*.404*	*-.065*	*.257*	*.317*	*.416*	*-.081*	*4.7*	

Breakout: 61%   Improve: 67%   Collapse: 19%

Scouts rave about Mathis's defense. His footwork is already good, his release is quick, and he's supposedly good at working with pitchers. (Isn't it strange to make that kind of assessment about a 19-year-old?) Mathis has a swing that's a bit long, but he has good command of the strike zone and the physical skills to translate his success thus far as he moves up the ladder. Joe Mauer and Victor Martinez may be getting all the prospect press, but Mathis isn't that far behind them, if he's behind them at all. As is, he and Jeremy Brown will be the next catching prospects people pay attention to. There will be a spot for him in Anaheim when he's ready.

Dallas McPherson   3B   Born: 23-Jul-80   Age: 22   Bats: L   Throws: R

YEAR	TM	LG	AGE	AB	H	2B	3B	HR	BB	SO	SB	CS	AVG	OBP	SLG	MLVR	EQBA	EQOBP	EQSLG	EQMLVR	VORP	DEFENSE
2001	PRO	PIO	20	124	49	11	0	5	12	22	1	0	.395	.449	.605	.604	.262	.302	.402	-.130	1.7	20-3B -3
2002	CDR	MDW	21	499	138	24	3	15	78	128	30	6	.277	.382	.427	.194	.221	.302	.347	-.235	-6.4	117-3B -9
2003	ANA	AL	22	197	47	9	1	6	19	51	4	4	.240	.314	.396	-.078	.244	.321	.408	-.094	1.3	

Breakout: 43%   *Improve: 65%*   *Collapse: 12%*

An athletic corner infielder who's shown flashes of greatness, McPherson is a selective hitter, with a quick bat and good speed. One Midwest League observer complained about his passivity at the plate, but it's hard to argue too much with the results for a 21-year-old. His defense is spotty but curable, so he has a good chance to make the majors as a third baseman instead of having to migrate over to the other side of the diamond or ending up as a tweener. McPherson could become an A-list prospect, depending on what he does in the California League next season.

Ransel Melgarejo   CF   Born: 28-Aug-81   Age: 21   Bats: R   Throws: R

YEAR	TM	LG	AGE	AB	H	2B	3B	HR	BB	SO	SB	CS	AVG	OBP	SLG	MLVR	EQBA	EQOBP	EQSLG	EQMLVR	VORP	DEFENSE
2002	CDR	MDW	20	427	101	14	5	2	53	71	19	12	.237	.337	.307	-.044	.194	.266	.252	-.451	-30.7	111-CF -7
2002	RCU	CLF	20	15	3	0	0	0	1	0	0	0	.200	.250	.200	-.444	.133	.187	.133	-.800	-2.5	
2003	ANA	AL	21	188	43	7	3	2	14	37	3	3	.227	.293	.330	-.205	.231	.299	.340	-.230	-5.5	

Breakout: 67%   *Improve: 82%*   *Collapse: 8%*

A fast runner with a name that gives you one more reason to miss Harry Caray. The possibilities boggle the mind. Melgarejo is a bit slow on the uptake in terms of tracking down balls hit in the gap. He's got the speed to be a legitimate center fielder, which would greatly improve his odds of having a big league career. He's going to need his glove, batting eye, and his legs to make the show.

Ben Molina   C   Born: 20-Jul-74   Age: 28   Bats: R   Throws: R

YEAR	TM	LG	AGE	AB	H	2B	3B	HR	BB	SO	SB	CS	AVG	OBP	SLG	MLVR	EQBA	EQOBP	EQSLG	EQMLVR	VORP	DEFENSE
2000	ANA	AL	25	473	133	20	2	14	23	33	1	0	.281	.323	.421	-.078	.291	.324	.437	-.015	24.8	123-C 10
2001	ANA	AL	26	317	80	10	0	6	16	50	0	1	.252	.305	.341	-.179	.268	.320	.366	-.143	7.3	83-C 2
2002	ANA	AL	27	428	105	18	0	5	15	34	0	0	.245	.277	.322	-.244	.265	.297	.349	-.214	2.2	110-C 14
2002	RCU	CLF	27	2	1	0	0	0	1	0	0	0	.500	.750	.500	.897	.500	.711	.500	.883	.7	
2003	ANA	AL	28	315	79	16	1	5	16	34	0	0	.251	.293	.355	-.160	.255	.299	.366	-.183	-1.1	

Breakout: 17%   *Improve: 52%*   *Collapse: 27%*

This is not a ballplayer you want to give 450 plate appearances to. On the bright side, it gives the Angels something they don't have: a problem that's fairly easy to fix. Molina hits like a defensive substitute, and few teams are good enough to absorb this kind of hit to their offensive production on a daily basis. He doesn't hit for average, doesn't hit for power, doesn't draw walks, and grounds into a ton of double plays. He does work well with the pitchers and he can throw, so they'll run him out there as long as things are pretty rosy. That's a mistake.

Jose Molina   C   Born: 03-Jun-75   Age: 28   Bats: R   Throws: R

YEAR	TM	LG	AGE	AB	H	2B	3B	HR	BB	SO	SB	CS	AVG	OBP	SLG	MLVR	EQBA	EQOBP	EQSLG	EQMLVR	VORP	DEFENSE
2000	IOW	PCL	25	248	58	9	0	1	23	61	1	4	.234	.299	.282	-.356	.206	.259	.250	-.463	-15.2	70-C 5
2001	SLC	PCL	26	213	64	11	1	5	14	49	1	2	.300	.349	.432	.003	.257	.304	.367	-.180	2.8	61-C 0
2002	SLC	PCL	27	290	89	14	2	4	12	60	0	3	.307	.343	.410	.004	.266	.301	.357	-.194	2.8	76-C 11
2002	ANA	AL	27	70	19	3	0	0	5	15	0	2	.271	.320	.314	-.161	.286	.342	.329	-.141	1.7	25-C 2
2003	ANA	AL	28	175	41	8	1	3	11	37	2	2	.234	.281	.344	-.204	.238	.287	.354	-.229	-2.8	

Breakout: 16%   *Improve: 42%*   *Collapse: 34%*

My God, there are two of them. Jose has a little more pop than Ben, which is among the faintest praise you'll read in this book. The Angels would be well served to go out and find a left-handed hitting catcher with some sock, just to bring off the bench and have a different option available. No, not Jorge Fabregas.

Tommy Murphy　　SS　Born: 27-Aug-79　Age: 23　Bats: R　Throws: R

YEAR	TM	LG	AGE	AB	H	2B	3B	HR	BB	SO	SB	CS	AVG	OBP	SLG	MLVR	EQBA	EQOBP	EQSLG	EQMLVR	VORP	DEFENSE	
2000	BOI	NWN	20	213	48	18	1	2	15	52	14	7	.225	.292	.347	-.076	.174	.207	.275	-.550	-16.6	43-SS	-3
2001	CDR	MDW	21	280	57	15	3	4	16	94	7	10	.204	.262	.321	-.206	.158	.199	.254	-.602	-27.2	71-SS	-24
2001	RCU	CLF	21	200	38	8	0	0	5	69	7	3	.190	.214	.230	-.470	.159	.173	.194	-.739	-25.7	47-SS	-1
2002	CDR	MDW	22	485	131	20	2	3	40	115	31	11	.270	.327	.338	-.002	.220	.262	.278	-.411	-23.8	123-SS	-8
2003	ANA	AL	23	180	41	10	1	3	12	49	4	7	.230	.284	.351	-.191	.234	.291	.361	-.216	-3.7		

Breakout: 83%　　Improve: 88%　　Collapse: 10%

The really interesting question here is why Mr. Murphy was promoted from level to level to begin with. "How'd he hit?" "Not well: .204, no power to speak of, struck out pretty much all the time. At the plate, he looks more lost than Tom Brokaw at a rave." "Defensively?" "Worse than we expected. The few balls he got to, he threw toward a random dugout, and, in one case, at a particularly surly peanut vendor." "Okay, promote him."

Mike Napoli　　C　Born: 31-Oct-81　Age: 21　Bats: R　Throws: R

YEAR	TM	LG	AGE	AB	H	2B	3B	HR	BB	SO	SB	CS	AVG	OBP	SLG	MLVR	EQBA	EQOBP	EQSLG	EQMLVR	VORP	DEFENSE	
2001	CDR	MDW	19	155	36	10	1	5	24	54	3	2	.232	.343	.406	.049	.180	.266	.311	-.378	-6.2	33-C	-3
2002	CDR	MDW	20	362	91	19	1	10	62	104	6	5	.251	.367	.392	.113	.199	.289	.315	-.317	-8.2	36-C	-4
2003	ANA	AL	21	180	40	7	1	6	20	54	2	3	.220	.302	.367	-.147	.224	.308	.378	-.168	-.3		

Breakout: 57%　　Improve: 69%　　Collapse: 16%

Stuck in Jeff Mathis's shadow, Napoli looks like a prospect in his own right. He's shown decent plate discipline to go with some power, and his glove isn't bad behind the plate. Considering Mathis is in this organization, he'll have to be a little lucky to get the playing time he'll need to develop. It wouldn't be surprising to see him moved to another organization before that actually happens.

Jose Nieves　　　　　　Born: 16-Jun-75　Age: 28　Bats: R　Throws: R

YEAR	TM	LG	AGE	AB	H	2B	3B	HR	BB	SO	SB	CS	AVG	OBP	SLG	MLVR	EQBA	EQOBP	EQSLG	EQMLVR	VORP	DEFENSE			
2000	CHC	NL	25	198	42	6	3	5	11	43	1	1	.212	.254	.348	-.364	.215	.245	.350	-.346	-8.1	28-3B	1	15-SS	-3
2001	SLC	PCL	26	258	85	15	4	11	8	36	8	7	.329	.357	.547	.210	.281	.308	.458	-.022	11.8	45-2B	-6	12-SS	-1
2001	ANA	AL	26	53	13	3	1	2	2	20	0	1	.245	.298	.453	-.045	.264	.310	.491	.013	3.0	10-2B	1		
2002	SLC	PCL	27	63	18	3	1	4	4	6	2	1	.286	.328	.556	.163	.242	.288	.468	-.078	.8				
2002	ANA	AL	27	97	28	2	0	0	2	14	1	1	.289	.303	.309	-.189	.309	.330	.330	-.147	1.6	13-2B	-4		

If you like an alternative skill set in your utility infielder, why not someone like Nieves? He's not a super slick glove man, and you certainly don't want him out there every day, but he can hit the ball out of the park with some regularity, and he won't kill you defensively at any position in the infield. If things break right, he can be someone like Luis Aguayo.

Alex Ochoa　　RF　Born: 29-Mar-72　Age: 31　Bats: R　Throws: R

YEAR	TM	LG	AGE	AB	H	2B	3B	HR	BB	SO	SB	CS	AVG	OBP	SLG	MLVR	EQBA	EQOBP	EQSLG	EQMLVR	VORP	DEFENSE	
2000	CIN	NL	28	244	77	21	3	13	24	27	8	4	.316	.384	.586	.300	.307	.368	.566	.263	22.9	62-LF	1
2001	CIN	NL	29	349	101	20	4	7	24	53	12	9	.289	.339	.430	.000	.284	.333	.420	-.029	4.4	80-RF	4
2001	COL	NL	29	187	47	10	3	1	21	23	5	4	.251	.333	.353	-.174	.235	.314	.332	-.224	-6.9	48-LF	2
2002	MIL	NL	30	215	55	9	0	6	32	30	8	5	.256	.357	.381	.018	.265	.360	.402	-.020	3.4	64-RF	1
2002	ANA	AL	30	65	18	7	0	2	10	5	2	2	.277	.373	.477	.152	.303	.395	.515	.230	5.4	22-RF	-3
2003	ANA	AL	31	249	65	14	2	6	25	34	7	2	.260	.331	.402	-.029	.265	.338	.414	-.042	-.8		

Breakout: 9%　　Improve: 37%　　Collapse: 29%

A good defensive corner outfielder who once had a gun for an arm, Ochoa is not going to kill you if he's a starter. He could even actually break out with some pretty good numbers. However, he's not going to hit like he did for those few weeks in Cincinnati a couple of years back, but he could be around or slightly above league average. The Angels decided league average wasn't enough, so they didn't offer him arbitration. He'll likely end up somewhere that harbors unreasonable expectations for his performance, and overpays him as another step in a franchise death spiral. But he could end up somewhere other than Baltimore, too.

Orlando Palmeiro RF Born: 19-Jan-69 Age: 34 Bats: Throws:

YEAR	TM	LG	AGE	AB	H	2B	3B	HR	BB	SO	SB	CS	AVG	OBP	SLG	MLVR	EQBA	EQOBP	EQSLG	EQMLVR	VORP	DEFENSE	
2000	ANA	AL	31	243	73	20	2	0	38	20	4	1	.300	.399	.399	.051	.312	.404	.412	.112	12.7	56-LF	1
2001	ANA	AL	32	230	56	10	1	2	25	24	6	6	.243	.326	.322	-.171	.260	.340	.346	-.138	-3.0	44-OF	-2
2002	ANA	AL	33	263	79	12	1	0	30	22	7	2	.300	.372	.354	.006	.317	.389	.377	.039	8.0	68-RF	-1
2003	*ANA*	*AL*	*34*	*189*	*53*	*11*	*1*	*1*	*21*	*17*	*3*	*1*	*.279*	*.353*	*.361*	*-.032*	*.284*	*.360*	*.372*	*-.044*	*-.1*		

Breakout: 19%   Improve: 53%   Collapse: 16%

Palmeiro has carved out a nice little career for himself in the Stan Javier mold. He can smack line drives from off the bench, fill in well anywhere in the outfield, and serve as the legs for an aging or tender outfielder. The Angels have opted not to offer him arbitration, but coming off of a season in which he got a ring, he should find a spot somewhere.

Julio Ramirez CF Born: 10-Aug-77 Age: 25 Bats: R Throws: R

YEAR	TM	LG	AGE	AB	H	2B	3B	HR	BB	SO	SB	CS	AVG	OBP	SLG	MLVR	EQBA	EQOBP	EQSLG	EQMLVR	VORP	DEFENSE	
2000	CLG	PCL	22	350	93	18	3	7	21	86	20	14	.266	.313	.394	-.184	.220	.255	.325	-.359	-15.9	90-CF	-8
2001	CHR	INT	23	319	69	11	1	8	20	80	15	6	.216	.267	.332	-.227	.202	.252	.315	-.389	-17.3	88-CF	-1
2002	SLC	PCL	24	139	38	3	5	2	4	31	8	3	.273	.299	.410	-.102	.241	.265	.358	-.279	-3.3	36-CF	-2
2002	ANA	AL	24	32	9	0	1	1	2	14	0	2	.281	.343	.438	.053	.281	.339	.469	.049	1.8	14-CF	-1
2003	*ANA*	*AL*	*25*	*165*	*39*	*7*	*1*	*4*	*10*	*39*	*5*	*4*	*.234*	*.283*	*.358*	*-.181*	*.238*	*.289*	*.369*	*-.206*	*-4.5*		

Breakout: 54%   Improve: 68%   Collapse: 17%

Pity Ramirez. He's a mediocre center fielder with nowhere near the bat to start in the major leagues. He got a quick look in Anaheim, and hit well enough so that he'll get another glance, but he's a long shot to have a career. He needs to improve his offense by about 20% just to hang on in the bigs, and with strikeout-to-walk ratios in the neighborhood of Terry Felton's ERA, that's just not that likely to happen.

Tim Salmon RF Born: 24-Aug-68 Age: 34 Bats: R Throws: R

YEAR	TM	LG	AGE	AB	H	2B	3B	HR	BB	SO	SB	CS	AVG	OBP	SLG	MLVR	EQBA	EQOBP	EQSLG	EQMLVR	VORP	DEFENSE	
2000	ANA	AL	31	568	165	36	2	34	104	139	0	2	.290	.406	.540	.249	.300	.409	.562	.314	59.3	116-RF	8
2001	ANA	AL	32	475	108	21	1	17	96	121	9	3	.227	.366	.383	-.026	.243	.379	.413	.015	12.4	118-RF	4
2002	ANA	AL	33	483	138	37	1	22	71	102	6	3	.286	.385	.503	.212	.306	.403	.540	.281	46.6	92-RF	-1
2003	*ANA*	*AL*	*34*	*357*	*91*	*20*	*2*	*16*	*58*	*84*	*4*	*2*	*.255*	*.362*	*.449*	*.076*	*.259*	*.370*	*.462*	*.071*	*9.1*		

Breakout: 2%   Improve: 43%   Collapse: 14%

It's your old buddy Lazarus! After a disastrous and ineffectual 2001, Salmon started the 2002 campaign looking like someone who should just hang 'em up and go home. On April 19th, he was hitting .135 and looking completely adrift in the batter's box, his timing more off than Yakov Smirnoff warming up a George Carlin crowd. The Angels, who had signed him to a four-year extension at about $9 million annually, were patient, and were rewarded with four months of Ragnarokesque thundering doom from Salmon's bat for the rest of the summer. He's still not a good bet to be worth the money of his extension, but if he continues his Jim Thome impression at the plate four months a year, the Angels will be pretty pleased.

Scott Spiezio 1B Born: 21-Sep-72 Age: 30 Bats: B Throws: R

YEAR	TM	LG	AGE	AB	H	2B	3B	HR	BB	SO	SB	CS	AVG	OBP	SLG	MLVR	EQBA	EQOBP	EQSLG	EQMLVR	VORP	DEFENSE			
2000	ANA	AL	27	297	72	11	2	17	40	56	1	2	.242	.338	.465	-.019	.251	.338	.485	.042	10.6	17-1B	-6		
2001	ANA	AL	28	457	124	29	4	13	34	65	5	2	.271	.329	.438	.008	.286	.343	.465	.055	17.7	91-1B	14	12-LF	-1
2002	ANA	AL	29	491	140	34	2	12	67	52	6	7	.285	.375	.436	.109	.309	.397	.473	.181	36.5	125-1B	2	13-3B	-2
2003	*ANA*	*AL*	*30*	*377*	*102*	*23*	*2*	*12*	*44*	*51*	*4*	*2*	*.271*	*.350*	*.440*	*.058*	*.276*	*.358*	*.453*	*.051*	*10.4*				

Breakout: 10%   Improve: 47%   Collapse: 14%

That was nice. First, Stoneman works his magic to excise the disaster that was Mo Vaughn from the club. Then Scott Spiezio steps up, plays good defense, draws a bunch of walks, stays healthy, and treats lefties like Sean Penn treats paparazzi, making him a good corner utility guy to have these days. The Angel infielders are all such good defenders that they can play out of position and not really hurt the team. If Eckstein had a minor injury, Scioscia could move Glaus over to shortstop, slip Spiezio over to third base, and have Fullmer fill in for a day at first base, albeit grudgingly. It's a nice managerial option to have.

Shawn Wooten   Born: 24-Jul-72   Age: 30   Bats: R   Throws: R

YEAR	TM	LG	AGE	AB	H	2B	3B	HR	BB	SO	SB	CS	AVG	OBP	SLG	MLVR	EQBA	EQOBP	EQSLG	EQMLVR	VORP		DEFENSE			
2000	ERI	EAS	27	191	56	12	2	9	17	30	4	1	.293	.357	.518	.215	.245	.297	.438	-.102	6.8		38-C	0		
2000	EDM	PCL	27	252	89	21	3	11	18	38	0	0	.353	.403	.591	.396	.306	.344	.516	.150	24.5		47-C	-2		
2001	ANA	AL	28	221	69	8	1	8	5	42	2	0	.312	.336	.466	.096	.326	.350	.493	.148	20.7		17-C	-1	15-1B	2
2002	RCU	CLF	29	18	4	3	0	0	4	4	0	0	.222	.364	.389	.016	.158	.273	.316	-.368	-1.2					
2002	SLC	PCL	29	42	11	2	0	0	0	11	0	0	.262	.279	.310	-.288	.220	.249	.268	-.452	-3.1					
2002	ANA	AL	29	113	33	8	0	3	6	24	2	0	.292	.333	.442	.052	.316	.354	.474	.116	7.0					

From the company that brought you Todd Greene, here's yet another right-handed basher with some isolated power and no interest in distinguishing balls from strikes. Like the original, Wooten is a considerably better hitter than anyone on the team named Molina. As a pinch hitter, backup first baseman, and emergency catcher, he should be able to carve out some sort of career, perhaps comparable to Greg Colbrunn if everything works out well.

PITCHERS

Steve Andrade   Born: 06-Feb-78   Age: 25   Bats: R   Throws: R

YEAR	TM	LG	AGE	G	GS	IP	H	BB	SO	HR	ERA	EQERA	EQH9	EQBB9	EQSO9	EQHR9	PERA	VORP	STF
2001	CDR	MDW	23	20	0	29.0	33	8	31	3	6.52	7.81	13.7	3.6	6.0	2.2	7.49	-7.8	-15
2002	CDR	MDW	24	46	0	54.3	30	16	93	1	1.16	2.55	7.1	3.6	9.6	0.5	2.84	17.1	23

Wow, how's that for a turnaround? Twenty-four is awfully old to be toiling in the Midwest League, but when you cut your ERA by 80% while striking out 15 guys per nine innings, giving up fewer hits than the season before, and all this while pitching twice as often . . . well, that has got to draw the attention of somebody in the organization. Geographically, I'd categorize the move from Cedar Rapids to Rancho Cucamonga as a lateral move.

Kevin Appier   Born: 06-Dec-67   Age: 35   Bats: R   Throws: R

YEAR	TM	LG	AGE	G	GS	IP	H	BB	SO	HR	ERA	EQERA	EQH9	EQBB9	EQSO9	EQHR9	PERA	VORP	STF
2000	OAK	AL	32	31	31	195.3	200	102	129	23	4.52	4.36	8.6	3.8	5.7	0.9	4.43	24.8	6
2001	NYM	NL	33	33	33	206.7	181	64	172	22	3.57	3.83	8.4	2.6	6.5	0.9	3.75	38.5	16
2002	ANA	AL	34	32	32	188.3	191	64	132	23	3.92	4.56	9.8	2.9	6.3	1.0	4.23	19.8	11
2003	ANA	AL	35	27	24	150.0	152	56	102	20	4.35	4.25	8.9	3.1	5.9	1.1	4.31	25.6	8

Breakout: 11%   Improve: 45%   Collapse: 16%

Ape certainly pitched better than I expected. People forget what dominating stuff Appier had when he came up with the Royals. He used to have nasty velocity and absolutely unfair movement on his pitches. The 1993 Royals had Appier's slurve or whateverthehellitwas, followed by a pre-injury Tom Gordon with a nasty fastball and curveball, followed by Jeff Montgomery dealing death by a thousand frisbees. Just thinking about it would make most hitters want to swallow their own bats. It was a wonder to watch, unless you happened to be Mike Devereaux or something. Appier deserves a lot of credit for being able to adapt to pitching without that kind of stuff; most guys never successfully make that adjustment. It was good to see him get a ring.

Chris Bootcheck   Born: 24-Oct-78   Age: 24   Bats: R   Throws: R

YEAR	TM	LG	AGE	G	GS	IP	H	BB	SO	HR	ERA	EQERA	EQH9	EQBB9	EQSO9	EQHR9	PERA	VORP	STF
2001	RCU	CLF	22	15	14	87.0	84	23	86	11	3.93	5.56	11.6	3.2	5.2	2.3	5.68	-0.6	2
2001	ARK	TXS	22	6	6	36.3	39	11	22	3	5.45	6.20	11.4	3.4	3.9	1.3	5.62	-2.8	-2
2002	ARK	TXS	23	19	19	116.0	130	35	90	11	4.81	5.99	12.5	3.3	5.4	1.8	6.06	-6.3	3
2002	SLC	PCL	23	9	9	58.0	64	16	38	5	3.88	4.57	10.6	2.9	4.6	1.0	4.72	6.0	5
2003	ANA	AL	24	15	10	62.3	72	23	41	10	5.31	5.19	10.2	3.1	5.7	1.3	5.00	4.8	-1

Breakout: 18%   Improve: 59%   Collapse: 14%

Bootcheck is a highly touted pitching prospect, and like a couple of the other Angel pitching prospects, the numbers don't necessarily jibe with the impressions of the scouts. Bootcheck has yet to post a strikeout rate or hit rate that jumps out at you. He'll begin the season at Triple-A, and have a chance to develop his breaking pitches and learn to set up hitters a little better. As it is now, he only projects to a back-of-the-rotation starter or swingman, despite being able to throw consistently in the low 90s.

Mickey Callaway | Born: 13-May-75 | Age: 28 | Bats: R | Throws: R

YEAR	TM	LG	AGE	G	GS	IP	H	BB	SO	HR	ERA	EQERA	EQH9	EQBB9	EQSO9	EQHR9	PERA	VORP	STF
2000	DUR	INT	25	26	20	117.3	151	50	64	11	5.29	6.96	13.0	3.9	4.2	1.1	6.83	-19.1	-13
2001	DUR	INT	26	29	21	129.0	131	24	81	9	3.07	4.61	10.9	2.0	4.5	0.9	4.53	12.6	0
2002	SLC	PCL	27	17	14	91.3	79	22	75	7	1.68	2.88	8.3	2.5	5.7	0.9	3.26	26.5	12
2002	ANA	AL	27	6	6	34.3	31	11	23	4	4.20	4.69	8.8	2.7	6.0	1.0	3.60	3.1	10
2003	*ANA*	*AL*	*28*	*16*	*12*	*78.7*	*89*	*27*	*48*	*11*	*4.98*	*4.87*	*9.9*	*2.9*	*5.3*	*1.1*	*4.70*	*9.2*	*2*

Breakout: 14%   Improve: 34%   Collapse: 22%

One of the game's definitive Quadruple-A starters. For years now, Callaway has been bouncing around, catching a start or two here or there. He's got mediocre stuff but does a reasonable job keeping hitters off balance, and his control has come around very nicely. He could end up with a #5 starter's job somewhere, turn in 160 good innings, and make a few bucks. There is one scout that believes that he learned to pitch in Salt Lake City last year, and will go on to have a right-handed Jamie Moyer-like career. It's possible, certainly, but I have to think the smart money is more along the lines of a right-handed Doug Johns.

Dennis Cook | Born: 04-Oct-62 | Age: 40 | Bats: L | Throws: L

YEAR	TM	LG	AGE	G	GS	IP	H	BB	SO	HR	ERA	EQERA	EQH9	EQBB9	EQSO9	EQHR9	PERA	VORP	STF
2000	NYM	NL	37	68	0	59.0	63	31	53	8	5.34	5.18	9.9	3.8	7.2	1.1	5.35	1.3	-3
2001	NYM	NL	38	43	0	36.0	28	10	34	6	4.25	4.01	7.3	2.4	7.3	1.4	3.58	5.5	4
2002	ANA	AL	39	37	0	24.0	21	10	13	2	3.38	3.77	8.6	3.6	4.9	0.7	3.53	4.3	-10

No one has offered Cook a contract yet, and he's coming off of a torn labrum and a season of reasonable contribution to a World Champion. This is probably the end of the line for him, but it wasn't a bad career, and not a bad finale.

Brendan Donnelly | Born: 04-Jul-71 | Age: 32 | Bats: R | Throws: R

YEAR	TM	LG	AGE	G	GS	IP	H	BB	SO	HR	ERA	EQERA	EQH9	EQBB9	EQSO9	EQHR9	PERA	VORP	STF
2000	IOW	PCL	29	9	0	16.7	25	6	14	3	7.54	8.88	14.6	3.2	6.2	2.1	8.37	-6.5	-19
2000	SYR	INT	29	37	0	42.7	47	27	34	5	5.48	7.33	11.5	5.8	6.2	1.3	6.29	-9.3	-20
2001	ARK	TXS	30	27	0	29.0	21	13	37	2	2.48	3.31	7.7	4.9	8.2	1.0	3.82	6.7	2
2001	SLC	PCL	30	29	0	41.3	38	8	50	4	2.40	2.92	8.6	2.0	7.8	1.0	3.45	11.3	12
2002	SLC	PCL	31	25	0	33.7	27	11	42	5	3.47	3.55	7.8	3.4	8.6	1.7	3.67	6.9	8
2002	ANA	AL	31	46	0	49.7	32	19	54	2	2.17	2.50	6.3	3.3	9.6	0.3	2.20	15.9	25
2003	*ANA*	*AL*	*31*	*46*	*0*	*56.7*	*55*	*24*	*53*	*7*	*4.01*	*3.92*	*8.5*	*3.5*	*8.1*	*1.0*	*4.14*	*12.3*	*8*

Breakout: 17%   Improve: 42%   Collapse: 24%

You could probably dislocate something just watching this guy pitch. Donnelly's motion resembles some sort of fast-forward Tai Chi regimen, with lots of jerky, angular motion. Assistant GM Ken Forsch says that they love bullpen guys with a lot of movement on their pitches, so obviously they love him. He throws a very nasty sinking pitch, which causes right-handers fits as they pound yet another ball to Eckstein. Righties hit a whopping .148 against him for the season, with no home runs in over 100 AB. He's a great guy to have in your pen, which isn't surprising to find on this team.

Matt Hensley | Born: 18-Aug-78 | Age: 24 | Bats: R | Throws: R

YEAR	TM	LG	AGE	G	GS	IP	H	BB	SO	HR	ERA	EQERA	EQH9	EQBB9	EQSO9	EQHR9	PERA	VORP	STF
2000	BUT	PIO	21	8	5	28.0	29	10	22	0	2.57	4.26	9.7	3.7	3.8	0.3	4.53	3.8	-5
2000	CDR	MDW	21	5	5	30.3	33	10	26	1	4.16	6.00	13.0	3.7	4.9	0.8	6.62	-1.7	5
2001	CDR	MDW	22	11	11	71.7	80	19	63	10	3.64	6.69	14.1	3.5	5.1	3.0	7.70	-9.4	-5
2001	RCU	CLF	22	14	12	68.3	85	24	58	4	5.93	8.03	14.3	4.3	4.5	1.1	7.41	-19.2	-8
2002	RCU	CLF	23	12	2	31.7	42	11	27	3	5.39	6.84	15.0	4.0	4.6	1.7	8.06	-5.0	-18
2002	SLC	PCL	23	19	18	117.7	132	39	106	16	4.97	5.55	10.8	3.4	6.2	1.5	5.40	-0.6	10
2003	*ANA*	*AL*	*24*	*15*	*10*	*60.0*	*70*	*25*	*40*	*9*	*5.46*	*5.33*	*10.2*	*3.4*	*5.7*	*1.2*	*5.18*	*3.8*	*-2*

Breakout: 18%   Improve: 57%   Collapse: 20%

Hensley doesn't get much ink, but he's got a shot to have a major league career. If he can get over his morbid curiosity about whether or not a particular hitter is expecting one of his thigh-high, middle-of-the-plate fastballs, he might be okay. He changes speeds well, doesn't have a great fastball, and he's going to have to spend some time learning how to get guys out with his slider, but he could help fill out a pitching staff two or three years down the road. He's one of the "one walk per nine innings away" guys.

Bobby Jenks Born: 14-Mar-81 Age: 22 Bats: R Throws: R

YEAR	TM	LG	AGE	G	GS	IP	H	BB	SO	HR	ERA	EQERA	EQH9	EQBB9	EQSO9	EQHR9	PERA	VORP	STF
2000	BUT	PIO	19	14	12	52.7	61	44	42	2	7.86	7.35	11.4	8.8	3.9	0.8	7.95	-10.8	-24
2001	CDR	MDW	20	21	21	99.0	90	64	98	10	5.27	7.42	11.4	8.7	5.8	2.2	7.41	-21.1	-12
2001	ARK	TXS	20	2	2	10.0	8	5	10	0	3.60	4.43	8.0	5.4	6.3	0.3	3.90	1.2	14
2002	RCU	CLF	21	11	10	65.3	50	46	64	4	4.82	5.39	8.4	8.1	5.2	1.1	5.22	0.8	-1
2002	ARK	TXS	21	10	10	58.0	49	44	58	2	4.66	5.70	8.9	8.2	6.9	0.6	5.45	-1.3	10
2003	ANA	AL	22	15	10	57.0	58	48	45	8	6.17	6.04	8.9	7.0	6.8	1.1	5.92	-2.8	-8

Breakout: 17%   Improve: 48%   Collapse: 12%

Velocity is nice and all, but it helps if it's in the vicinity of the strike zone. Scouts love Jenks and his ability to routinely throw 96, and they're even happier about his ability to rare back and bump it up a little bit from there. Hitters, on the other hand, are more than happy to simply let Jenks throw four balls and go to first base. Jenks doesn't have a reputation for being particularly coachable, so he may struggle for years before finding his control, and probably becoming a reliever in the process. It's more likely that he never finds it.

John Lackey Born: 23-Oct-78 Age: 24 Bats: R Throws: R

YEAR	TM	LG	AGE	G	GS	IP	H	BB	SO	HR	ERA	EQERA	EQH9	EQBB9	EQSO9	EQHR9	PERA	VORP	STF
2000	CDR	MDW	21	5	5	30.3	20	5	21	1	2.08	2.65	7.7	1.8	3.9	0.8	2.95	9.6	11
2000	LEL	CLF	21	15	15	100.7	94	42	74	9	3.40	5.81	11.5	4.2	4.3	1.9	5.86	-3.4	-2
2000	ERI	EAS	21	8	8	57.3	58	9	43	6	3.30	4.29	11.0	1.6	5.1	1.7	4.62	7.7	13
2001	ARK	TXS	22	18	18	127.3	106	29	94	11	3.46	4.10	8.9	2.5	4.8	1.3	3.86	19.9	9
2001	SLC	PCL	22	10	10	57.7	75	16	42	5	6.71	6.41	12.3	3.0	4.8	0.9	5.80	-5.8	4
2002	SLC	PCL	23	16	16	101.7	89	28	82	5	2.57	3.14	8.3	2.8	5.6	0.6	3.23	26.7	17
2002	ANA	AL	23	18	18	108.3	113	33	69	10	3.66	4.54	10.2	2.6	5.7	0.8	4.06	11.6	15
2003	ANA	AL	24	22	18	120.0	130	41	78	16	4.63	4.52	9.5	2.9	5.7	1.1	4.51	16.9	6

Breakout: 14%   Improve: 45%   Collapse: 15%

Lackey has a live fastball, and he's working on the other parts of his repertoire, but the fastball was live enough for him to get to and succeed at the major league level. He matured a lot in just one season, and if he can stay healthy, he looks to be a very good #2 starter for years to come. He could even compete for a Cy Young occasionally. He's pitched a lot of innings at a young age, but Scioscia is smart enough to lean on a good bullpen and not overwork him. If he can get his slider about 20% better, he could be well nigh unhittable.

Al Levine Born: 22-May-68 Age: 35 Bats: L Throws: R

YEAR	TM	LG	AGE	G	GS	IP	H	BB	SO	HR	ERA	EQERA	EQH9	EQBB9	EQSO9	EQHR9	PERA	VORP	STF
2000	ANA	AL	32	51	5	95.3	98	49	42	10	3.87	4.27	9.4	3.8	3.9	0.8	4.28	12.1	-15
2001	ANA	AL	33	64	1	75.7	71	28	40	7	2.38	3.42	8.7	3.2	4.5	0.8	3.70	16.5	-10
2002	ANA	AL	34	52	0	63.7	61	34	40	8	4.24	5.06	9.3	4.6	5.6	1.1	4.55	2.3	-12
2003	SLN	NL	35	38	1	48.7	52	25	31	5	4.69	5.10	10.0	4.0	5.1	0.9	5.27	3.4	-14

Breakout: 13%   Improve: 43%   Collapse: 30%

As veteran bullpen filler, Levine will be looking to round out a staff somewhere in 2003. Throughout his career, his ERA has been considerably better than his peripheral numbers would support. Whether this is an indictment of the use of ERA to evaluate relievers, a fluke, or a genuine skill that Levine has developed is left as an exercise for the reader.

Mark Lukasiewicz Born: 08-Mar-73 Age: 30 Bats: L Throws: L

YEAR	TM	LG	AGE	G	GS	IP	H	BB	SO	HR	ERA	EQERA	EQH9	EQBB9	EQSO9	EQHR9	PERA	VORP	STF
2000	SYR	INT	27	42	0	41.3	34	25	52	7	3.49	4.67	8.6	5.4	9.6	1.9	4.97	3.3	2
2001	SLC	PCL	28	20	0	30.3	12	2	41	4	1.49	1.30	3.8	0.7	8.7	1.3	1.08	13.7	25
2001	ANA	AL	28	24	0	22.3	21	9	25	6	6.05	5.81	8.4	3.4	9.5	2.2	5.01	-1.1	6
2002	SLC	PCL	29	35	0	43.0	46	17	48	6	3.98	5.34	10.3	4.1	7.7	1.6	5.32	0.2	-3
2002	ANA	AL	29	17	0	14.0	17	9	15	0	3.86	4.75	11.4	5.4	9.3	0.2	5.22	1.0	9

With slightly better control, Lukasiewicz would probably be a millionaire. He's always had good stuff, has always posted a strong strikeout rate, and has always given up the occasional hanging breaking ball that heads majestically into the night, often preceded by a walk or two. If he can lose one walk per nine innings, he could be a force to be reckoned with. The same can be said for a lot of guys, and most never manage to do so.

Bart Miadich   Born: 03-Feb-76   Age: 27   Bats: R   Throws: R

YEAR	TM	LG	AGE	G	GS	IP	H	BB	SO	HR	ERA	EQERA	EQH9	EQBB9	EQSO9	EQHR9	PERA	VORP	STF
2000	ERI	EAS	24	28	0	40.3	27	21	38	2	3.35	3.68	7.0	5.2	6.4	0.8	3.45	7.6	-2
2000	EDM	PCL	24	10	0	21.7	25	9	20	3	4.56	5.71	11.1	3.7	6.7	1.5	5.87	-0.8	-2
2001	SLC	PCL	25	55	0	59.0	40	29	73	4	2.44	3.04	6.5	5.2	8.1	0.7	2.95	15.3	7
2001	ANA	AL	25	11	0	10.0	6	8	11	2	4.50	4.23	5.5	6.8	9.4	1.6	4.00	1.3	4
2002	SLC	PCL	26	59	0	80.7	60	64	92	5	3.68	4.45	7.1	8.2	7.9	0.7	4.20	8.3	-7

Miadich didn't pitch too badly during a brief stint at the Ed, and he fits the Angel mold for semi-anonymous useful relievers, so he'll get a shot to stick in the bigs and slowly expand his role. If he can control his stuff a little better, he could be pretty good. We still really don't know why the Diamondbacks decided he wasn't worth the time and effort; a guy that can reach 94 and throw a slider like this is worth a little patience.

Ramon Ortiz   Born: 23-Mar-73   Age: 30   Bats: R   Throws: R

YEAR	TM	LG	AGE	G	GS	IP	H	BB	SO	HR	ERA	EQERA	EQH9	EQBB9	EQSO9	EQHR9	PERA	VORP	STF
2000	EDM	PCL	27	15	15	89.0	74	37	76	7	4.55	4.12	8.0	3.7	6.2	0.9	3.59	13.7	11
2000	ANA	AL	27	18	18	111.3	96	55	73	18	5.09	4.64	7.8	3.6	5.8	1.2	3.82	10.7	6
2001	ANA	AL	28	32	32	208.7	223	76	135	25	4.36	4.77	9.8	3.1	5.5	1.0	4.50	17.0	6
2002	ANA	AL	29	32	32	217.3	188	68	162	40	3.77	4.22	8.3	2.7	6.7	1.5	3.85	31.0	13
2003	*ANA*	*AL*	*30*	*29*	*27*	*175.0*	*175*	*62*	*121*	*26*	*4.38*	*4.28*	*8.8*	*2.9*	*6.0*	*1.2*	*4.27*	*28.6*	*10*

Breakout: 10%   Improve: 48%   Collapse: 10%

Although he had a few extra birthdays in the off-season, that's nothing so serious for a pitcher that it warrants much attention. Ortiz has matured into a middle-of-the-rotation starter, and thankfully, the comparisons to Pedro Martinez have come to a merciful end. He got some press for allowing a Blylevenesque 40 home runs during the season, and there were rumors that he had been tipping his pitches. He's signed to a long-term deal with the Angels, and will have some very good stretches during the course of the contract.

Troy Percival   Born: 09-Aug-69   Age: 33   Bats: R   Throws: R

YEAR	TM	LG	AGE	G	GS	IP	H	BB	SO	HR	ERA	EQERA	EQH9	EQBB9	EQSO9	EQHR9	PERA	VORP	STF
2000	ANA	AL	30	54	0	50.0	42	30	49	7	4.50	4.30	7.5	4.4	8.5	1.1	3.85	6.0	6
2001	ANA	AL	31	57	0	57.7	39	18	71	3	2.65	2.60	6.2	2.6	10.4	0.4	2.17	17.8	31
2002	ANA	AL	32	58	0	56.3	38	25	68	5	1.92	2.48	6.5	3.8	10.6	0.7	2.72	18.1	26
2003	*ANA*	*AL*	*33*	*54*	*0*	*50.0*	*43*	*21*	*51*	*6*	*3.36*	*3.28*	*7.5*	*3.5*	*8.8*	*1.0*	*3.60*	*14.6*	*13*

Breakout: 21%   Improve: 33%   Collapse: 35%

The days of sucking down six or eight cups of coffee 20 minutes before entering the game are gone, but apparently so are the days of anyone catching up with his fastball. Percival was damn near the perfect closer in 2002, and there's nothing in his record to suggest anything but continued success. You can be a great pitcher without being able to throw 97 mph high in the strike zone, but it's sure nice to be able to fall back on a fastball that even great hitters have to guess perfectly on to even touch.

Lou Pote   Born: 27-Aug-71   Age: 31   Bats: R   Throws: R

YEAR	TM	LG	AGE	G	GS	IP	H	BB	SO	HR	ERA	EQERA	EQH9	EQBB9	EQSO9	EQHR9	PERA	VORP	STF
2000	EDM	PCL	28	24	0	30.7	27	14	28	2	3.52	3.89	8.5	4.1	6.6	0.7	3.86	5.1	-1
2000	ANA	AL	28	32	1	50.3	52	17	44	4	3.40	3.90	9.4	2.5	7.7	0.6	3.63	8.3	12
2001	ANA	AL	29	44	1	86.7	88	32	66	11	4.15	4.34	9.3	3.1	6.5	1.0	4.29	10.1	0
2002	SLC	PCL	30	7	7	39.0	42	10	43	3	6.00	5.37	10.1	2.6	7.5	0.9	4.40	0.6	18
2002	ANA	AL	30	31	0	50.3	33	26	32	7	3.22	3.64	6.4	4.4	5.7	1.2	3.16	9.7	-7
2003	*ANA*	*AL*	*31*	*24*	*9*	*60.7*	*63*	*25*	*43*	*8*	*4.33*	*4.24*	*9.1*	*3.3*	*6.2*	*1.1*	*4.47*	*11.5*	*0*

Breakout: 15%   Improve: 48%   Collapse: 25%

Pote is a middle-of-the-bullpen guy with some upside. He's got the flexibility to work out of the pen, make the occasional spot start, and keep a team in a game for three innings if need be. A club that needs a 90 to 110-inning reliever should give him a shot. He was lucky in 2002 in terms of keeping batted balls from becoming hits, but he was also a little more wild in the zone than usual. The forecast is conservative.

Francisco Rodriguez   Born: 07-Jan-82   Age: 21   Bats: R   Throws: R

YEAR	TM	LG	AGE	G	GS	IP	H	BB	SO	HR	ERA	EQERA	EQH9	EQBB9	EQSO9	EQHR9	PERA	VORP	STF
2000	LEL	CLF	18	13	12	64.0	43	32	79	2	2.81	4.25	7.6	4.8	6.9	0.6	3.83	8.9	18
2001	RCU	CLF	19	20	20	113.7	127	55	147	13	5.38	7.14	13.4	5.9	6.9	2.1	7.60	-20.7	5
2002	ARK	TXS	20	23	0	41.3	32	15	61	2	1.96	3.51	8.2	3.8	9.9	0.9	3.70	8.6	31
2002	SLC	PCL	20	27	0	42.0	30	13	59	1	2.57	2.56	6.7	3.2	9.6	0.3	2.38	13.2	34
2002	ANA	AL	20	5	0	5.7	3	2	13	0	0.00	1.61	4.8	2.9	17.2	0.2	1.50	2.4	88
2003	ANA	AL	21	31	8	64.7	58	31	63	7	4.17	4.07	7.9	3.9	8.5	0.9	3.96	11.5	12

Breakout: 12%   Improve: 52%   Collapse: 2%

Roster shenanigans (or outright cheating) gave K-Rod a nice big postseason stage on which to make his national debut. He throws hard, hard enough to become a SoCal icon after only five regular season appearances, in which he made sure that people understood what "dominating" really means. Rodriguez is still very young, so it wouldn't be a bad idea to follow the Earl Weaver model with him, and giving him 80–100 innings in 30 or so games of long relief for a couple of years. Of course, that's some pretty expensive service time to pay for should it come to that. He's fun to watch, and gives the Angels a pair of very serious guns in a very strong bullpen.

Johan Santana   Born: 28-Nov-83   Age: 19   Bats: R   Throws: R

YEAR	TM	LG	AGE	G	GS	IP	H	BB	SO	HR	ERA	EQERA	EQH9	EQBB9	EQSO9	EQHR9	PERA	VORP	STF
2001	PRO	PIO	17	4	4	18.7	19	12	22	1	7.70	9.24	13.6	9.3	6.2	1.2	7.90	-7.8	-10
2002	CDR	MDW	18	27	27	147.0	133	48	146	10	4.16	6.71	13.1	4.4	6.0	1.9	5.80	-19.7	5

No relation to the Minnesota Twins hurler. Santana is a hard-throwing kid out of the Dominican Republic who's already figured out a little bit about how to pitch. He can reach 92 mph comfortably, and the Angels expect development of his breaking pitches to come along fairly quickly. He'll probably start the season in the California League, and if he continues to improve the command of his stuff, look out.

Scott Schoeneweis   Born: 02-Oct-73   Age: 29   Bats: L   Throws: L

YEAR	TM	LG	AGE	G	GS	IP	H	BB	SO	HR	ERA	EQERA	EQH9	EQBB9	EQSO9	EQHR9	PERA	VORP	STF
2000	ANA	AL	26	27	27	170.0	183	67	78	21	5.45	5.12	9.9	2.9	4.1	1.0	4.31	7.3	-1
2001	ANA	AL	27	32	32	205.3	227	77	104	21	5.09	5.04	10.3	3.2	4.4	0.8	4.60	10.6	0
2002	ANA	AL	28	54	15	118.0	119	49	65	17	4.88	5.22	9.8	3.6	4.9	1.2	4.59	3.0	-11
2003	ANA	AL	29	28	13	85.0	100	35	52	13	5.05	4.93	10.3	3.5	5.3	1.2	4.88	12.6	-7

Breakout: 19%   Improve: 48%   Collapse: 21%

Ineffectiveness and a large number of options cost Schoeneweis his spot in the rotation. His ERA dropped by two runs once he went to the pen, but he really didn't pitch as well as that suggests, allowing 23 hits, 9 walks, and 5 home runs in 27.2 innings of relief. He's asked to be traded to a team that will use him as a starter, but Stoneman has declined the request, so it looks like he'll man the situational reliever/emergency starter role in 2003. The Angels probably have considerably better options available for that role, but like most World Series winners, they'll probably play it a little too safe.

Aaron Sele   Born: 25-Jun-70   Age: 33   Bats: R   Throws: R

YEAR	TM	LG	AGE	G	GS	IP	H	BB	SO	HR	ERA	EQERA	EQH9	EQBB9	EQSO9	EQHR9	PERA	VORP	STF
2000	SEA	AL	30	34	34	211.7	221	74	137	17	4.51	4.17	9.4	2.6	5.7	0.6	3.90	31.4	12
2001	SEA	AL	31	34	33	215.0	216	51	114	25	3.60	4.45	10.0	2.1	4.7	1.0	4.12	25.2	5
2002	ANA	AL	32	26	26	160.0	190	49	82	21	4.89	5.48	11.5	2.6	4.6	1.1	5.07	0.4	0
2003	ANA	AL	33	25	22	140.0	160	43	75	19	4.82	4.71	10.0	2.6	4.6	1.1	4.68	16.5	1

Breakout: 14%   Improve: 45%   Collapse: 21%

Somehow, I think they were expecting a bit more than this. Sele signed a three-year deal before the 2002 season worth more than $20 million, and then had a rough season. He pitched badly for most of the year, with his patented knee-buckling curveball turning into a patented neck-turning curveball. To top it all off, he then tore his rotator cuff. There's no word yet on whether or not his car battery died or if he got stuck with jury duty as well. He'll return to the rotation for the start of next season, but may not be at full strength right off the bat.

Scot Shields | Born: 22-Jul-75 | Age: 27 | Bats: R | Throws: R

YEAR	TM	LG	AGE	G	GS	IP	H	BB	SO	HR	ERA	EQERA	EQH9	EQBB9	EQSO9	EQHR9	PERA	VORP	STF
2000	EDM	PCL	24	27	27	163.0	158	82	156	16	5.41	5.34	9.3	4.4	6.9	1.1	4.75	3.0	13
2001	SLC	PCL	25	21	21	137.7	141	31	104	24	4.97	5.19	9.8	2.4	5.0	1.8	4.75	4.8	2
2001	ANA	AL	25	8	0	11.0	8	7	7	0	0.00	1.64	6.8	5.4	5.4	0.2	2.89	4.6	-3
2002	SLC	PCL	26	28	1	47.0	39	6	50	5	3.06	3.16	7.9	1.3	7.3	1.2	2.94	11.7	11
2002	ANA	AL	26	29	1	49.0	31	21	30	4	2.20	2.72	6.3	3.7	5.5	0.7	2.50	14.5	-1
2003	*ANA*	*AL*	*27*	*32*	*5*	*55.7*	*56*	*22*	*40*	*8*	*4.12*	*4.02*	*8.8*	*3.2*	*6.2*	*1.2*	*4.25*	*11.7*	*-2*

Breakout: 19%   Improve: 48%   Collapse: 18%

Shields can look fantastic for ten pitches in a row, then throw a Jim Acker grapefruit right down the heart of the plate. He lives off of his slider, working mostly on the outside part of the plate to right-handers, while mixing in an average fastball that can get slightly above that from time to time. After some good numbers in 2002, he might have the glow that leads to a long career. This is exactly the sort of guy you pay the major league minimum to, to give him the last spot in the bullpen. He has some value and can help a team, but he's also replaceable.

Joe Torres | Born: 03-SEP-82 | Age: 20 | Bats: L | Throws: L

YEAR	TM	LG	AGE	G	GS	IP	H	BB	SO	HR	ERA	EQERA	EQH9	EQBB9	EQSO9	EQHR9	PERA	VORP	STF
2000	BOI	NWN	17	11	10	46.0	27	23	52	0	2.54	3.61	6.3	5.4	5.1	0.3	3.64	9.7	4
2001	PRO	PIO	18	9	8	31.3	32	15	39	2	4.03	7.37	13.4	6.8	6.4	1.5	7.19	-6.5	-5
2001	CDR	MDW	18	4	4	17.0	16	14	14	0	5.82	7.14	10.7	10.8	4.7	0.4	7.38	-3.1	-19
2002	CDR	MDW	19	25	25	133.0	125	66	87	7	3.52	7.50	13.7	6.8	4.0	1.5	6.73	-29.5	-14

Once again, the scouts love Torres's stuff and the movement he gets on the ball, but the performance metrics aren't there that say "This guy's going to be a good pitcher in the majors." Of course, Torres is barely 20 years old, so he's got lots of time to learn his craft, but right now, he's indistinguishable from a hundred other guys in the low minors. He's already had some shoulder soreness, but nothing out of the ordinary, and the Angels didn't call in Dallas Green to work with him on it. "Son, when you feel it pull and burn, you know it's getting stronger."

Jarrod Washburn | Born: 13-Aug-74 | Age: 28 | Bats: L | Throws: L

YEAR	TM	LG	AGE	G	GS	IP	H	BB	SO	HR	ERA	EQERA	EQH9	EQBB9	EQSO9	EQHR9	PERA	VORP	STF
2000	EDM	PCL	25	5	5	30.7	35	13	20	2	3.52	4.36	10.9	3.8	4.7	0.7	5.23	3.9	2
2000	ANA	AL	25	14	14	84.3	64	37	49	16	3.74	3.75	6.9	3.3	5.2	1.5	3.40	16.4	5
2001	ANA	AL	26	30	30	193.3	196	54	126	25	3.77	4.18	9.4	2.4	5.6	1.1	4.05	28.5	10
2002	ANA	AL	27	32	32	206.0	183	59	139	19	3.15	3.59	8.7	2.5	6.1	0.8	3.29	43.8	15
2003	*ANA*	*AL*	*28*	*29*	*27*	*174.7*	*182*	*53*	*112*	*22*	*4.14*	*4.04*	*9.1*	*2.5*	*5.6*	*1.0*	*4.13*	*33.7*	*10*

Breakout: 6%   Improve: 50%   Collapse: 13%

A solid starting pitcher, albeit one that doesn't inspire a ton of confidence going forward. Wasburn's stuff is fair for a starting pitcher, but nothing spectacular. He works the plate, sets hitters up effectively, and uses his entire repertoire very well. The bump in his strikeout rate is a good sign, but it's still not at a level that makes him a lock for a long string of successful seasons. The Angels don't have a traditional rotation ace; usually, when a team has pitching as a major strength, they've got at least one bone-crushing starter in the rotation. The Angels have no one like that, but have instead run out a rotation of solid #2 or #3 guys and a bullpen full of vicious, diverse, and most importantly effective freaks.

Ben Weber | Born: 17-Nov-69 | Age: 33 | Bats: R | Throws: R

YEAR	TM	LG	AGE	G	GS	IP	H	BB	SO	HR	ERA	EQERA	EQH9	EQBB9	EQSO9	EQHR9	PERA	VORP	STF
2000	FRE	PCL	30	38	3	78.0	72	20	66	7	2.42	3.13	8.3	2.2	6.1	1.0	3.47	19.7	3
2000	ANA	AL	30	10	0	14.7	12	2	8	0	1.84	2.74	7.8	1.0	4.9	0.2	1.83	4.3	5
2001	ANA	AL	31	56	0	68.3	66	31	40	4	3.43	3.85	9.0	3.9	5.0	0.5	3.84	11.6	-8
2002	ANA	AL	32	63	0	78.0	70	22	43	4	2.54	3.30	8.9	2.4	5.0	0.4	3.07	18.0	-2
2003	*ANA*	*AL*	*33*	*54*	*0*	*63.3*	*69*	*22*	*36*	*6*	*4.25*	*4.15*	*9.5*	*2.9*	*5.0*	*0.8*	*4.33*	*11.3*	*-8*

Breakout: 12%   Improve: 45%   Collapse: 22%

Weber has been quietly effective for several years, working off of a sinker and a stilted delivery. He's an extreme ground-ball pitcher, and when you've got a defense behind you that's got range and hands, it's a good situation for everyone. He posted a 3.66 ground ball/flyball ratio in 2002, and there's no reason to expect a change in performance going into 2003. He'll pop up somewhere as the #3 guy in a bullpen.

Matt Wise Born: 18-Nov-75 Age: 27 Bats: R Throws: R

YEAR	TM	LG	AGE	G	GS	IP	H	BB	SO	HR	ERA	EQERA	EQH9	EQBB9	EQSO9	EQHR9	PERA	VORP	STF
2000	EDM	PCL	24	19	19	124.3	122	26	82	10	3.69	3.74	9.5	1.9	4.8	0.9	3.76	24.4	11
2000	ANA	AL	24	8	6	37.3	40	13	20	7	5.55	5.07	9.7	2.6	4.7	1.4	4.60	1.8	0
2001	SLC	PCL	25	21	21	123.3	134	17	111	19	5.04	5.25	10.3	1.5	5.9	1.6	4.64	3.5	11
2001	ANA	AL	25	11	9	49.3	47	18	50	11	4.38	4.78	8.6	3.1	8.6	1.8	4.64	3.9	18
2002	SLC	PCL	26	16	16	78.0	102	15	76	12	5.42	5.96	12.5	2.0	6.7	1.7	6.14	-3.9	5
2002	ANA	AL	26	7	0	8.3	7	1	6	0	3.25	2.95	8.5	1.1	6.6	0.2	2.13	2.2	14

On a team with fewer options, Wise could be the best of a bad lot for the last spot in the pen. On the Angels, he's likely to see a lot of time in Triple-A. He doesn't have a whole lot to recommend him above and beyond a boatload of similar guys scrambling for jobs, except his mesmerizing renditions of the standards from *HMS Pinafore*.

Baltimore Orioles

Last year, the Baltimore Orioles went 67–95. And you know what? Their Double-A team, Bowie, was even worse, going 55–85. And their Triple-A team, Rochester, was even worse than that, going 55–89. And to finish this sad game of "can you top this?" their high-A team, Frederick, was even worse than that. At 47–92, Frederick had the worst record of any team in a full-season league in organized ball.

In the last ten years, no organization has come particularly close to that level of incompetence as shown in table 1.

The Diamondbacks are a special case in several ways, first because 1998 was their first season, and they didn't have a Double-A team yet, and that really played havoc with their prospect slotting. To get to four teams, we had to count their Midwest League farm team at South Bend, who were an awful 40–100. They are also the only organization on the list that has made the playoffs in the intervening years, which we have to stress was not done with homegrown talent. The Blue Jays reached 88 wins in 1998, missing the wild card by four games. The Rockies won 82 in 2000. None of the other teams

Orioles Prospectus

2002 record: 67–95; Fourth place, AL East

Pythagenport Records: 70–92

Runs scored per game: 4.1 (13th in AL)

Runs allowed per game: 4.8 (7th in AL)

Team EqA: .250 (10th in AL)

2002 Batters Age: 29.8 (5th oldest in AL)

2002 Pitchers Age: 28.3 (6th youngest in AL)

Ballpark: Oriole Park at Camden Yards; Moderate pitchers' park; Park Factor of .958

2002: Old front office rebuilds without a plan or talent, while Angelos fights to keep baseball out of DC.

2003: New front office will try and come up with a plan and find talent, while Angelos fights to keep baseball out of DC.

Table 1. Worst records by top four teams in system, 1993–2002:

1. Orioles 2002	224–361	.383
2. Marlins 1998	233–353	.398
Blue Jays 1995	232–334	.410
D'backs 1998	244–340	.418
Pirates 2001	247–335	.424
Tigers 1996	248–334	.426
Marlins 1999	247–331	.427
Rockies 1998	253–335	.430
Orioles 2001	252–333	.431
Brewers 2002	253–331	.433

have made it out of the 70s in wins since their own little annus horribilis.

Of course, for most of the year it looked as if the Orioles—who were already on the list by virtue of their 2001 season—were going to get out of the 70s themselves. They were usually just a little under .500, and kept making runs toward the .500 mark. They were 18–17 on May 10 before losing four in a row. By June 26 they had climbed to 37–38, but then they lost the next two. A win on July 7 got them to 42–43...and then they lost the next three. They got to 45–46 on the 16th, lost two more, won two to get back to one game under, and promptly lost three straight after that. It took until August 23rd, but on that night they finally won their fourth game in a row to make their record 63–63. With the celebration that followed this achievement, you could be forgiven for thinking that the season was over and the Orioles had won.

You would have been half right. After all of the buildup and energy expended trying to get to .500, the Orioles simply died. They lost ten straight games, broke the streak, lost eight more, went through a WLWLW series of games, and ended the season with a twelve-game losing flourish. Never before in Orioles' history had the team gone 4–32 over any stretch, not even the '88 team that started 0–21.

In fact, no team in history has ever finished the season so badly. The good people at Retrosheet put together (and made publicly available through their website, www.retrosheet. org) a log of every major league game played since 1900. Combing through that data to see who the worst finishers were, and table 2 (on page 22) shows what you'd find.

First the bad news...Baltimore teams have made this list twice before, and both times the franchise failed to survive the off-season. Can they survive this one?

Table 2.

Team	Finish	Final	Next	
1. 2002 Baltimore	4–32	67–95	???	
2. 1908 St Louis (NL)	6–30	49–105	54–98	+6
1914 Cincinnati	"	60–94	71–83	+11
1931 Boston (NL)	"	64–90	77–77	+13
1935 Boston (NL)	"	38–115	71–83	+32.5
1972 Texas	"	54–100	57–105	-1
3. 1902 Baltimore	7-29	50–87	72–62 (NY)	+23.5
1915 Baltimore (FL)	"	47–107	—	
1915 Philadelphia (AL)	"	43–109	36–117	-7.5
1928 Cleveland	"	62-92	81–71	+20
1939 Philadelphia (NL)	"	45–106	50–103	+4
1978 Oakland	"	69–93	54–108	-15

Assuming that we don't have a real-life version of *The Sum of All Fears* (the Affleck-ted film), then we should certainly think so, and there is some reason to hope. Most of the teams on this list improved the following year, by about eight games on average. Of course, several of them were so bad that they didn't have much room to sink any lower, and since the '02 Orioles have the second-best record of the bunch, they have room to sink lower. We also ran another list, which we won't reproduce here, looking at all the teams that finished the season 9–27 or worse since 1945. There were 20 teams on that list, counting last year's O's, and those teams improved an average of seven games the following year. One of them, the 2001 Angels, won the World Series the very next year.

What that means is that these teams' records before their terminal slide was more indicative of their futures than their final records. The teams in the above list had a .350 winning percentage for the season, and .403 before their late-season collapse. They played .407 ball the next year. An argument could be made that it is all regression to the mean. Actually, this is probably true of any team that has a long streak in either direction. Streaks are fluky things, and we're probably better off leaving them out of our thinking.

So what do the Orioles have to look forward to in 2003? Well, for the first time in 43 years, they won't be looking to Rochester for replacements. The Red Wings' owners have been complaining about the "talent" they were getting from Baltimore, as well as getting frustrated with their big league parent's refusal to fulfill requests from Rochester to sign popular minor league free agents. The Red Wings have finished last two years in a row, just had their worst record in 50 years, haven't had a winning season since 1998, and have seen their attendance drop 25% relative to the league since then. Looking at the players on Bowie and Frederick, it was pretty obvious that the Wings weren't going to get anything good

next year either. So they told the Orioles what to do with their affiliation, joined the Twins organization, and very nearly stuck the Orioles with Edmonton. In the end, Clan Angelos got Ottawa, the attendance doormats of the International League.

The second thing to look forward to is the replacement of Syd Thrift, who has been the de facto GM of the Orioles since after the 1999 season, and director of player personnel (read: in charge of the minor leagues) for four years before that. More than anyone else, Thrift built these Orioles and these Red Wings and these BaySox and these Keys into what they were in 2002. They were teams that couldn't hit: Baltimore scored 94 fewer runs than an average league team in the same number of plate appearances; Rochester was -49 in their league, Bowie was -67, and Frederick -41). They were also teams that couldn't pitch: Oriole pitchers were rated at -35 runs, Rochester -32, Bowie -39, and Frederick -72. At least the Orioles could field, earning a +43 mark and making the pitchers look average in the process. Sticking with the organizational playbook, however, the minor leaguers didn't throw the leather around any better than they hit or pitched: Rochester was -31, Bowie -46, and Frederick was -83, the third-worst mark in organized baseball last year.

As it stands now, there is no coherent Oriole Way that is taught from Bluefield to Baltimore. Under Thrift and his henchmen, every manager and every coach apparently has had a free hand to do it his way. What a player is taught at one level is what he's taught not to do at the next level. Promotions and demotions are virtually random, while others who clearly should move one way or the other stay put. The reports about lack of discipline and lack of teaching are too widespread to be dismissed, and resulted in the firing of Bowie's manager at mid-season, something that may be common enough in the majors, but is pretty rare in the minors. Players are floundering; the Orioles only had one player in the upper levels of the system who improved his translated equivalent run rate by as much as ten runs, while a half-dozen slid backward precipitously.

In Thrift's place, the Orioles have decided to go with a GM by mini-committee: Jim Beattie and Mike Flanagan. Flanagan, it seems, is Mr. Inside. He's been a part of the Orioles since the mid-1970s as a player, a coach, a roving minor league pitching instructor, and most recently as a broadcaster. During that time, he also became a confidant of Peter Angelos, someone that Angelos would actually talk to for advice on baseball matters. The feeling is that Flanny was the guy Angelos wanted in the GM seat, but there were worries that without any prior front office experience, he'd be overmatched for the job. Anyone remember Hawk Harrelson's reign of error in Chicago? However, unlike the Hawk, Flanagan has been a productive member of baseball society prior to this elevation to the front office.

Enter Mr. Outside. Jim Beattie, who has never had any connection to Baltimore, was the GM for the Expos in the mid-1990s and the Director of Player Development for the Mariners before that. He was brought in to be a mentor for Flanagan. He gets the fancier title—the Orioles still don't have a "general manager," they have a "vice-president of baseball operations." That's Flanagan. Beattie is the "executive vice-president of baseball operations," and he gets the bigger office, presumably the better parking space, and the task of running day-to-day operations. But he'll do it quietly; Flanagan looks like he'll be the public face of the team and in charge of the "vision thing."

Can it work? Yes, it has possibilities, but it requires a lot from both men as well as the cast around them. The papers are filled with notes about how neither Flanagan nor Beattie is ego-driven, which is a necessary condition for this arrangement. For the sake of argument, let's assume that it's true. The second thing needed will be clarity in the chain of command. Somebody has to have the last word, which for the Orioles has always been Peter Angelos. He needs to be available and open to suggestions from both of them, and not just to his old pal Mike. Otherwise, they're liable to be back into the Frank Wren/Syd Thrift situation of a few years ago, when only Mr. Inside had the boss's ear, while Wren wound up being undermined in the petty office politics scene before finally departing in disgust.

The third thing required for this arrangement to work is communication. Flanagan and Beattie have to know what the other one is doing, otherwise you've got duplication of effort or, even worse, working at cross-purposes. Fourth would be loyalty. Loyalties among staffers in baseball front offices are usually office politics at their worst, resting upon the individual that hired them rather than the team; every-body is somebody's protege. Even if Beattie and Flanagan are cordial and cooperative with each other, the staffs can split down the middle.

Let's suppose that they are able to overcome all of these hurdles. If it all works, it frees each of them to do those parts of the GM job at which they are best. Beattie has the experience of running a minor league system competently within the lifetimes of the players already in this system, and the Oriole system is in such bad shape that, even with the help of a minor league director, that itself will be a full-time job. Presumably, he understands the rules for transactions and roster management, and he knows the other GMs, neither of which is a small thing. He also ran the Expos under Brochu, so he is certainly used to taking orders from owners. That frees up Flanagan to pay more attention to the major league team, to learn all of the little things with a safety net, and to handle the press and public relations side of the job. At that, he should excel, as well as providing a safety blanket for Beattie, who was never regarded as a great communicator during his time running the Expos.

You can hope that it could be a productive, synergistic relationship. The opportunity is there for Beattie and Flanagan to create a productive relationship similar to the one between Brian Cashman and Mark Newman that has served the Yankees so well. However, you could also interpret the situation as one that has two men working under Angelos, one a close associate, just as Thrift was, and the other a hired gun without executive authority of his own, similar to what Wren was. What that means is that you still may not have the family out of the family-owned business, contributing to the mismanagement of an organization while at best providing golden years security for Syd Thrift and his ilk. On that level, hope in Baltimore is still dependent on family fiat.

HITTERS

Bryan Bass — SS — Born: 12-Apr-82 — Age: 21 — Bats: B — Throws: R

YEAR	TM	LG	AGE	AB	H	2B	3B	HR	BB	SO	SB	CS	AVG	OBP	SLG	MLVR	EQBA	EQOBP	EQSLG	EQMLVR	VORP	DEFENSE
2001	BLU	APL	19	71	23	6	1	5	10	17	0	0	.324	.407	.648	.509	.216	.275	.405	-.211	.1	17-SS -6
2002	DEL	SAL	20	457	101	20	7	6	40	146	15	2	.221	.302	.335	-.068	.184	.238	.286	-.467	-30.3	128-SS -16
2003	BAL	AL	21	190	43	8	2	6	14	60	3	6	.225	.287	.372	-.162	.236	.300	.395	-.154	-.8	

Breakout: 73%   Improve: 82%   Collapse: 10%

The Orioles' first pick from 2001, Bass went backward after a solid debut at Bluefield. The consensus is that he has the physical tools to succeed in pro baseball; the problems you hear about are mental. Some of those can be labeled as immaturity, and are common and usually curable, like errors that come from trying to make impossible plays. Some, such as a reported attitude that he can't miss and is just wasting his time in the sticks, aren't so easy to manage.

Tony Batista   3B   Born: 09-Dec-73   Age: 29   Bats: R   Throws: R

YEAR	TM	LG	AGE	AB	H	2B	3B	HR	BB	SO	SB	CS	AVG	OBP	SLG	MLVR	EQBA	EQOBP	EQSLG	EQMLVR	VORP	DEFENSE			
2000	TOR	AL	26	620	163	32	2	41	35	121	5	4	.263	.309	.519	.019	.268	.306	.534	.072	39.0	154-3B	10		
2001	TOR	AL	27	271	56	11	1	13	13	66	0	1	.207	.253	.399	-.229	.218	.264	.428	-.198	-.7	70-3B	-2		
2001	BAL	AL	27	308	82	16	5	12	19	47	5	1	.266	.309	.468	.027	.284	.329	.506	.087	21.9	28-3B	0	20-SS	5
2002	BAL	AL	28	615	150	36	1	31	50	107	5	4	.244	.312	.457	.015	.268	.335	.505	.080	43.7	153-3B	0		
2003	*BAL*	*AL*	*29*	*562*	*143*	*30*	*3*	*28*	*44*	*109*	*4*	*3*	*.254*	*.313*	*.466*	*.019*	*.266*	*.327*	*.494*	*.046*	*24.9*				

Breakout: 27%   Improve: 67%   Collapse: 7%

The token Oriole All-Star. Batista and fellow Blue Jays' discard Jay Gibbons combined to give the lineup what little threat of power it contained. It is still hard to believe that Toronto gave up on Batista so quickly in 2001; you just don't throw away major league–caliber bats. Of course, it was Gord Ash who did the tossing, and J. P. Ricciardi who then had to go out and get Hinske; interested parties should be happy that Ash has resurfaced in Milwaukee. Batista has added enough bulk over the last couple of years that talk of returning to shortstop should probably be dropped.

Larry Bigbie   RF   Born: 04-Nov-77   Age: 25   Bats: L   Throws: L

YEAR	TM	LG	AGE	AB	H	2B	3B	HR	BB	SO	SB	CS	AVG	OBP	SLG	MLVR	EQBA	EQOBP	EQSLG	EQMLVR	VORP	DEFENSE	
2000	FRD	CRL	22	201	59	11	0	2	23	34	7	3	.294	.366	.378	.096	.242	.296	.309	-.287	-11.4	54-RF	-4
2000	BOW	EAS	22	112	27	6	0	0	11	28	3	0	.241	.309	.295	-.189	.219	.270	.263	-.416	-9.6	30-LF	0
2001	BOW	EAS	23	262	77	13	3	8	40	54	10	7	.294	.387	.458	.213	.253	.338	.392	-.083	-.6	69-RF	-4
2001	BAL	AL	23	131	30	6	0	2	17	42	4	1	.229	.318	.321	-.182	.250	.340	.348	-.142	-1.9	32-OF	0
2002	ROC	INT	24	348	105	23	2	2	35	79	7	3	.302	.367	.397	.089	.283	.346	.377	-.067	1.9	69-OF	3
2002	BAL	AL	24	34	6	1	0	0	1	11	1	0	.176	.200	.206	-.569	.206	.229	.235	-.547	-3.5		
2003	*BAL*	*AL*	*25*	*192*	*47*	*10*	*1*	*4*	*18*	*43*	*3*	*2*	*.242*	*.311*	*.369*	*-.115*	*.254*	*.325*	*.391*	*-.102*	*-3.3*		

Breakout: 26%   Improve: 54%   Collapse: 26%

A capable enough fourth or fifth outfielder right now, Bigbie's future is going to be determined by how the Orioles handle all of their first basemen and DHs. Given his modest abilities, he's likely to be on a perpetual shuttle between Triple-A and the majors. He started 2002 as if he were angry to be in Rochester, hitting over .360 into June. Then his shoulder started acting up, and he sprained his ankle, and he barely slugged .300 after that.

Mike Bordick   SS   Born: 21-Jul-65   Age: 37   Bats: R   Throws: R

YEAR	TM	LG	AGE	AB	H	2B	3B	HR	BB	SO	SB	CS	AVG	OBP	SLG	MLVR	EQBA	EQOBP	EQSLG	EQMLVR	VORP	DEFENSE	
2000	BAL	AL	34	391	116	22	1	16	34	71	6	5	.297	.354	.481	.100	.313	.362	.510	.179	39.3	95-SS	-9
2000	NYM	NL	34	192	50	8	0	4	15	28	3	1	.260	.321	.365	-.161	.267	.315	.374	-.142	3.9	50-SS	0
2001	BAL	AL	35	229	57	13	0	7	17	36	9	3	.249	.317	.397	-.068	.277	.341	.442	.011	13.7	53-SS	1
2002	BAL	AL	36	367	85	19	3	8	35	63	7	4	.232	.304	.365	-.130	.261	.332	.415	-.057	15.9	112-SS	29
2003	*TOR*	*AL*	*37*	*247*	*61*	*13*	*1*	*6*	*19*	*44*	*6*	*2*	*.247*	*.304*	*.378*	*-.112*	*.250*	*.310*	*.388*	*-.136*	*2*		

Breakout: 20%   Improve: 43%   Collapse: 31%

Bordick had a remarkable year in the field, making just one official error all season and setting records for fewest errors and the longest errorless streak. Of course, once the streak got going, it was almost impossible for him to get charged with an error—and there were a few misplays that could have drawn the call, as there are in any streak like this. However, the Orioles' double play rate was dramatically higher when he was at short: .82 per nine innings, vs .47 for everyone else, and he did that despite missing six weeks with a broken kneecap.

    Would you have brought him back? My opinion was solidly no: even though there's no one in the system who can play short like Bordick, the Orioles aren't likely to contend unless they build a time machine and kidnap Cal Ripken and a half a dozen other guys from 1983. You may as well save the money for a player who might be able to contribute when you are ready to contend again. Apparently the new management agrees with me; after Bordick turned down a $1.5 million offer—a lot less than the $5 million he got in 2002—they refused arbitration and set him free. He then signed with the Blue Jays for less money to be their utility infielder, an appropriate role and price tag at this point of his career.

Raul Casanova   C   Born: 23-Aug-72   Age: 30   Bats: B   Throws: R

YEAR	TM	LG	AGE	AB	H	2B	3B	HR	BB	SO	SB	CS	AVG	OBP	SLG	MLVR	EQBA	EQOBP	EQSLG	EQMLVR	VORP	DEFENSE
2000	IND	INT	27	73	21	2	0	5	7	10	0	1	.288	.358	.521	.190	.260	.323	.466	-.003	4.4	18-C -1
2000	MIL	NL	27	231	57	13	3	6	26	48	1	2	.247	.333	.407	-.101	.245	.322	.403	-.104	8.2	58-C -2
2001	MIL	NL	28	192	50	10	0	11	12	29	0	0	.260	.307	.484	.010	.263	.309	.495	.016	13.2	46-C -2
2002	MIL	NL	29	87	16	1	0	1	10	18	0	0	.184	.276	.230	-.362	.193	.282	.250	-.421	-4.4	25-C -1
2002	IND	INT	29	43	12	4	0	0	3	8	0	0	.279	.326	.372	-.042	.256	.304	.349	-.206	-.8	
2003	BAL	AL	30	174	40	8	0	5	14	33	0	0	.229	.292	.364	-.163	.240	.305	.386	-.154	.6	

Breakout: 24%   Improve: 52%   Collapse: 24%

Once upon a time, Casanova was a touted prospect for his bat. As is distressingly common with catchers, it never happened. The Orioles claimed him off of waivers last September to give them catching depth down the stretch. "Having depth" doesn't automatically mean using it, though, as he just sat at the end of the bench every day. He'll be a waiver-wire pickup again in 2003.

Howie Clark   UT   Born: 13-Feb-74   Age: 29   Bats: L   Throws: R

YEAR	TM	LG	AGE	AB	H	2B	3B	HR	BB	SO	SB	CS	AVG	OBP	SLG	MLVR	EQBA	EQOBP	EQSLG	EQMLVR	VORP	DEFENSE	
2000	BOW	EAS	26	53	18	6	0	1	3	6	0	0	.340	.386	.509	.307	.283	.316	.453	-.013	1.6		
2000	ROC	INT	26	189	54	10	0	3	26	14	3	1	.286	.375	.386	.041	.267	.345	.361	-.103	5.7	25-2B -5	13-RF 0
2001	Yuc	MEX	27	493	164	42	7	5	43	47	5	4	.333	.388	.477	.235	.269	.316	.394	-.110	.0		
2002	ROC	INT	28	418	129	21	4	7	41	28	3	4	.309	.373	.428	.146	.288	.350	.406	-.015	6.8	66-RF -7	16-1B -2
2002	BAL	AL	28	53	16	5	0	0	3	6	0	0	.302	.362	.396	.066	.333	.386	.444	.144	3.8		
2003	TOR	AL	29	278	76	16	2	4	22	30	3	1	.272	.328	.389	-.043	.275	.334	.399	-.062	-2.3		

Breakout: 13%   Improve: 44%   Collapse: 25%

A couple of years ago, we took the Orioles to task for not giving Howie a cup of coffee when they were shorthanded. Since then he's spent another year in Rochester, a year in Mexico, then back to Rochester again, and this time, finally, he got his call and immediately homered. He's been one of the most popular players everywhere he's gone. Anybody who believes in clubhouse presence being important to winning should be chasing after him, not to mention they'd be getting a good utility player. The Jays obliged with a minor league contract.

Jeff Conine   1B   Born: 27-Jun-66   Age: 37   Bats: R   Throws: R

YEAR	TM	LG	AGE	AB	H	2B	3B	HR	BB	SO	SB	CS	AVG	OBP	SLG	MLVR	EQBA	EQOBP	EQSLG	EQMLVR	VORP	DEFENSE	
2000	BAL	AL	34	409	116	20	2	13	36	53	4	3	.284	.345	.438	.005	.299	.352	.466	.084	28.2	38-3B 2	37-1B 1
2001	BAL	AL	35	524	163	23	2	14	64	75	12	8	.311	.391	.443	.173	.342	.419	.487	.271	52.5	78-1B -4	36-LF 3
2002	BAL	AL	36	451	123	26	4	15	25	66	8	0	.273	.314	.448	.030	.296	.338	.491	.093	22.1	103-1B -3	
2003	BAL	AL	37	351	94	19	2	9	29	51	5	1	.267	.325	.410	-.023	.280	.340	.435	.000	4.8		

Breakout: 5%   Improve: 32%   Collapse: 26%

For the most part, last season looked the same as his last four years, 2001 excepted. Look closer, though, and the defense is slipping, the strikeouts are going up, and the walks were never there to begin with. He's a nice enough guy, but Father Time is catching up. The PECOTA numbers look about right: 2:1 odds that he declines, and with the chance of a big decline five times that of a big improvement.

Marty Cordova   LF   Born: 10-Jul-69   Age: 33   Bats: R   Throws: R

YEAR	TM	LG	AGE	AB	H	2B	3B	HR	BB	SO	SB	CS	AVG	OBP	SLG	MLVR	EQBA	EQOBP	EQSLG	EQMLVR	VORP	DEFENSE
2000	TOR	AL	30	200	49	7	0	4	18	35	3	2	.245	.317	.340	-.239	.256	.318	.352	-.175	-4.3	32-LF -4
2001	CLE	AL	31	409	123	20	2	20	23	81	0	3	.301	.350	.506	.160	.318	.366	.538	.232	32.3	101-LF 0
2002	BAL	AL	32	458	116	25	2	18	47	111	1	6	.253	.327	.434	.018	.282	.354	.487	.101	23.4	67-LF -4
2003	BAL	AL	33	320	80	15	1	12	27	71	1	2	.251	.314	.419	-.041	.263	.328	.445	-.020	1.0	

Breakout: 9%   Improve: 40%   Collapse: 26%

After being the team's biggest free agent signing of the off-season, the O's got the average Cordova, which has been a very rare beast indeed. He's been up and down his entire career, but rarely in the middle. He's not a bad player for this team to have around. I mean, he really is an outfielder, after all, not just thrown into the position out of desperation. The problem is that they committed to him through 2004, so that they pretty much assured themselves they would be buying into a declining talent over the life of the contract.

Mike Fontenot   2B   Born: 09-Jun-80   Age: 23   Bats: L   Throws: R

YEAR	TM	LG	AGE	AB	H	2B	3B	HR	BB	SO	SB	CS	AVG	OBP	SLG	MLVR	EQBA	EQOBP	EQSLG	EQMLVR	VORP	DEFENSE
2002	FRD	CRL	22	481	127	16	4	8	42	117	13	9	.264	.336	.364	.012	.214	.269	.304	-.364	-18.9	112-2B -12
2003	BAL	AL	23	180	40	7	1	4	13	49	3	4	.223	.281	.338	-.217	.234	.294	.358	-.215	-3.4	

Breakout: 59% Improve: 77% Collapse: 14%

The team's first pick in 2001, the Orioles thought it would be a good idea to challenge him by sending him straight to high-A. He was, after all, a star player at a major college (LSU). Keeping in mind it was his first season in the minors, he was a disappointment in virtually every phase of the game; his plate discipline was probably the worst surprise of all. Envisioned as a top-of-the-order guy, he struck out three times for every walk. Here's hoping that it was just the malaise hanging over everything related to Frederick last year that did him in.

Brook Fordyce   C   Born: 07-May-70   Age: 33   Bats: R   Throws: R

YEAR	TM	LG	AGE	AB	H	2B	3B	HR	BB	SO	SB	CS	AVG	OBP	SLG	MLVR	EQBA	EQOBP	EQSLG	EQMLVR	VORP	DEFENSE
2000	CWS	AL	30	125	34	7	1	5	6	23	0	0	.272	.316	.464	-.040	.274	.313	.476	.007	7.2	37-C 3
2000	BAL	AL	30	177	57	11	0	9	11	27	0	0	.322	.368	.537	.236	.335	.375	.568	.310	23.8	49-C -7
2001	BAL	AL	31	292	61	18	0	5	21	56	1	2	.209	.269	.322	-.285	.229	.290	.355	-.243	-.6	87-C -12
2002	BAL	AL	32	130	30	8	0	1	9	19	1	0	.231	.301	.315	-.202	.260	.328	.351	-.154	2.7	43-C -9
2003	BAL	AL	33	174	41	9	0	3	13	29	1	1	.236	.295	.349	-.173	.247	.308	.370	-.166	.2	

Breakout: 20% Improve: 50% Collapse: 26%

Fordyce made a great first impression on the Orioles in 2000, and suckered Angelos & Co. into a hefty contract. He then disappeared, and his bat is rumored to be living under an assumed name in Rio. His contract expires this year, and then he'll be free to rejoin his lumber on some distant shore.

Luis Garcia   RF   Born: 22-Sep-75   Age: 27   Bats: R   Throws: R

YEAR	TM	LG	AGE	AB	H	2B	3B	HR	BB	SO	SB	CS	AVG	OBP	SLG	MLVR	EQBA	EQOBP	EQSLG	EQMLVR	VORP	DEFENSE
2001	Mct	MEX	25	368	122	25	5	19	38	51	16	6	.332	.399	.582	.400	.264	.321	.473	.007	.1	
2002	ROC	INT	26	339	82	14	2	4	7	45	1	1	.242	.261	.330	-.220	.230	.253	.319	-.366	-24.1	77-RF 1
2002	BAL	AL	26	3	1	0	0	0	0	1	0	0	.333	.333	.333	-.051	.333	.333	.333	-.119	.0	
2003	BAL	AL	27	112	27	6	1	3	6	19	1	1	.241	.282	.382	-.148	.253	.295	.405	-.138	-3.5	

Breakout: 35% Improve: 51% Collapse: 31%

He's a survivor, we'll give him that. Garcia was originally drafted by the White Sox back in 1994, but never hit, and eventually returned to Mexico. He gave the Mexico City Tigers two seasons that look pretty good, but you have to remember that Mexico City is higher than Denver. The Orioles apparently didn't think about that.

Jay Gibbons   RF/1B   Born: 02-Mar-77   Age: 26   Bats: L   Throws: L

YEAR	TM	LG	AGE	AB	H	2B	3B	HR	BB	SO	SB	CS	AVG	OBP	SLG	MLVR	EQBA	EQOBP	EQSLG	EQMLVR	VORP	DEFENSE		
2000	TEN	SOU	23	474	152	38	1	19	61	67	3	1	.321	.409	.525	.343	.272	.340	.451	.017	14.2	92-1B -7		
2001	BAL	AL	24	225	53	10	0	15	17	39	0	1	.236	.301	.480	.003	.252	.319	.522	.061	8.8	28-LF 2		
2002	BAL	AL	25	490	121	29	1	28	45	66	1	3	.247	.313	.482	.052	.270	.335	.532	.120	25.7	84-RF 2	24-1B 0	
2003	BAL	AL	26	467	122	26	1	25	45	71	1	2	.262	.330	.481	.072	.274	.345	.510	.105	15.8			

Breakout: 23% Improve: 61% Collapse: 13%

Gibbons is one of the Oriole keepers, in that he can actually hit at the major league level. He did all this while playing with a sore wrist, actually a carryover from wrist surgery in 2001 that never healed quite right, and so he had surgery again last October. Given that, he's an even better candidate for a breakout season than that projection shows. Ideally, you'd play him at first base, maybe DH, but on the O's he's an outfielder until the graybeards in those roles finally die in their harnesses.

Geronimo Gil   C   Born: 07-Aug-75   Age: 27   Bats: R   Throws: R

YEAR	TM	LG	AGE	AB	H	2B	3B	HR	BB	SO	SB	CS	AVG	OBP	SLG	MLVR	EQBA	EQOBP	EQSLG	EQMLVR	VORP	DEFENSE		
2000	SAN	TXS	24	352	100	19	1	11	33	65	3	2	.284	.355	.438	.091	.247	.299	.382	-.175	5.6	75-C 2	12-RF -2	
2001	LVG	PCL	25	281	83	15	0	9	16	56	0	1	.295	.338	.445	-.007	.253	.294	.379	-.185	3.6	63-C 2	13-1B 1	
2001	ROC	INT	25	82	22	6	1	2	0	23	0	0	.268	.277	.439	-.023	.256	.271	.415	-.174	1.2	23-C -3		
2001	BAL	AL	25	58	17	2	0	0	5	7	0	0	.293	.369	.328	-.036	.322	.390	.356	.015	3.8	17-C -3		
2002	BAL	AL	26	422	98	19	0	12	21	88	2	2	.232	.270	.363	-.195	.256	.294	.404	-.147	9.5	116-C 1		
2003	BAL	AL	27	335	79	16	1	9	21	65	2	2	.237	.286	.369	-.162	.248	.298	.391	-.153	1.4			

Breakout: 24% Improve: 46% Collapse: 25%

Crouching behind the plate, Gil is very good at stopping the stolen base. That doesn't keep them at first, though, because he has trouble catching the ball, with 19 passed balls, six more than anyone else in the league, and there aren't even any knuckleballers on the staff to excuse it. Standing beside the plate, he's got a little power, but nothing to get excited about. He's a replacement-level catcher, maybe a little bit more, but to hold him as one of the shining examples of talent brought in by Syd Thrift is . . . you know, I was going to say silly, but actually it is pretty appropriate. Gil is one of Syd's best achievements.

Doug Gredvig   1B   Born: 25-Aug-79   Age: 23   Bats: R   Throws: R

YEAR	TM	LG	AGE	AB	H	2B	3B	HR	BB	SO	SB	CS	AVG	OBP	SLG	MLVR	EQBA	EQOBP	EQSLG	EQMLVR	VORP	DEFENSE
2000	DEL	SAL	20	186	41	12	0	6	35	48	3	5	.220	.347	.382	.043	.168	.264	.296	-.408	-16.4	11-1B -2
2001	FRD	CRL	21	484	123	35	2	20	37	125	2	3	.254	.314	.459	.135	.214	.263	.386	-.262	-21.9	126-1B -13
2002	BOW	EAS	22	465	128	22	1	14	46	94	2	3	.275	.346	.417	.064	.237	.296	.362	-.216	-15.2	125-1B -5
2003	BAL	AL	23	188	44	8	1	6	17	45	2	2	.233	.304	.383	-.116	.244	.318	.406	-.103	-3.3	

Breakout: 52%   Improve: 73%   Collapse: 9%

Although Gredvig isn't a tremendous prospect, he's a slugger who survived his initial leap into Double-A at 22, so he has a shot. He'll go as far as his bat takes him, although it hardly helps that first and DH will be clogged by Segui, Conine, and Cordova for the next couple of years.

Jerry Hairston Jr.   2B   Born: 29-May-76   Age: 27   Bats: R   Throws: R

YEAR	TM	LG	AGE	AB	H	2B	3B	HR	BB	SO	SB	CS	AVG	OBP	SLG	MLVR	EQBA	EQOBP	EQSLG	EQMLVR	VORP	DEFENSE
2000	ROC	INT	24	201	59	15	1	4	29	32	6	4	.294	.396	.438	.153	.271	.362	.404	-.009	11.3	52-2B -7
2000	BAL	AL	24	180	46	5	0	5	21	22	8	5	.256	.353	.367	-.104	.268	.358	.385	-.044	8.0	49-2B 6
2001	BAL	AL	25	532	124	25	5	8	44	73	29	11	.233	.307	.344	-.169	.258	.329	.385	-.106	15.2	154-2B 10
2002	BAL	AL	26	426	114	25	3	5	34	55	21	6	.268	.332	.376	-.041	.303	.363	.426	.050	29.9	116-2B 10
2003	BAL	AL	27	394	99	20	2	7	35	54	16	4	.252	.321	.369	-.093	.265	.335	.391	-.077	9.8	

Breakout: 10%   Improve: 46%   Collapse: 23%

For a few weeks right before the All-Star break, Hairston lost his job as the starting second baseman, thanks to a protracted slump and Brian Roberts's hot start in Rochester. After that, he finally started listening to his hitting coaches. Hairston's best asset is speed, and he was taking the same approach at the plate that Gibbons or Batista would. So he cut down his swing, aimed for more line drives and less loft, and had a solid second half, being one of the few Orioles who didn't go into the tank in September. His job should be safe for another year at least.

Luis Jimenez   LF   Born: 07-May-82   Age: 21   Bats: L   Throws: L

YEAR	TM	LG	AGE	AB	H	2B	3B	HR	BB	SO	SB	CS	AVG	OBP	SLG	MLVR	EQBA	EQOBP	EQSLG	EQMLVR	VORP	DEFENSE	
2002	BLU	APL	20	176	66	13	1	8	33	33	9	1	.375	.476	.597	.580	.237	.309	.373	-.176	-3.9	21-LF -1	16-1B -4
2003	BAL	AL	21	173	41	7	1	5	16	42	3	2	.234	.303	.372	-.131	.245	.316	.394	-.120	-4.0		

Breakout: 33%   Improve: 56%   Collapse: 18%

Is that finally a real prospect we see? Jimenez is a big slugger (6' 4" and considerably more than the 200 pounds he's listed at) who led the Appalachian League in batting average and slugging average while finishing second in OBP. That's the good news. The bad is that he doesn't have a real position, which is probably why *Baseball America* left him off of their top-10 prospect list for the league. He's got some emotional baggage; he was in the Oakland system, and they released him after he got into a fight with a trainer. There are questions about his work ethic, because he let himself get out of shape after Oakland cut him, and was almost cut by the Orioles before the season ever started. There are whispers about whether he was really 20 or not (he's Venezuelan, not Dominican), for what it's worth. At any age, he has terrific power and a clear approach to the plate, and so he stands out in the organization. I don't think I'd call him the best hitter in the system just yet, but he's close.

Tripper Johnson   3B   Born: 28-Apr-82   Age: 21   Bats: R   Throws: R

YEAR	TM	LG	AGE	AB	H	2B	3B	HR	BB	SO	SB	CS	AVG	OBP	SLG	MLVR	EQBA	EQOBP	EQSLG	EQMLVR	VORP	DEFENSE
2001	BLU	APL	19	157	41	6	1	2	11	37	4	0	.261	.318	.350	-.033	.181	.214	.244	-.575	-15.4	14-3B -2
2002	DEL	SAL	20	493	128	32	6	11	62	88	19	6	.260	.352	.416	.135	.210	.276	.340	-.303	-15.6	131-3B 9
2003	BAL	AL	21	215	50	10	2	4	17	46	4	4	.233	.296	.357	-.163	.244	.309	.378	-.155	-1.8	

Breakout: 63%   Improve: 80%   Collapse: 9%

Johnson was a sandwich pick in 2000 whose 2001 season was pretty much wiped out by a shoulder injury, so he just played his first full pro season. From Delmarva's point of view, he had a great year, leading the team in a half-dozen batting categories.

Tripper Johnson *(continued)*

From a prospect perspective his mediocre batting average is a big strike against him. He's an excellent all-around athlete with outstanding secondary offensive skills—walks, power, and speed—but he needs to show above-average improvement to make it to Baltimore.

Jose Leon   3B   Born: 08-Dec-76   Age: 26   Bats: R   Throws: R

YEAR	TM	LG	AGE	AB	H	2B	3B	HR	BB	SO	SB	CS	AVG	OBP	SLG	MLVR	EQBA	EQOBP	EQSLG	EQMLVR	VORP	DEFENSE			
2000	ARK	TXS	23	297	80	16	3	14	16	66	2	1	.269	.318	.485	.049	.229	.258	.411	-.225	-2.8	46-3B	-4	17-1B	-1
2000	BOW	EAS	23	68	17	1	0	1	4	13	5	2	.250	.311	.309	-.162	.217	.252	.275	-.437	-4.2	16-3B	1		
2001	BOW	EAS	24	95	34	9	1	4	8	21	1	1	.358	.413	.600	.499	.306	.356	.510	.161	9.0	21-3B	-5		
2001	ROC	INT	24	416	116	20	4	12	25	96	7	3	.279	.326	.433	.055	.264	.309	.413	-.100	9.5	107-3B	9		
2002	ROC	INT	25	312	87	16	1	8	18	54	0	0	.279	.322	.413	.021	.261	.304	.395	-.137	4.1	79-3B	9		
2002	BAL	AL	25	89	22	2	0	3	3	20	1	0	.247	.280	.371	-.157	.278	.307	.411	-.095	.0	15-1B	0		
2003	BAL	AL	26	200	49	10	1	6	13	40	2	1	.245	.294	.388	-.119	.257	.307	.411	-.106	.4				

Breakout: 27%   Improve: 50%   Collapse: 37%

Leon's biggest claim to fame, when his career is over, will be that he was once traded straight up for Will Clark. He's not really a prospect—he's too old and doesn't hit nearly enough—but he can back up at third in a pinch without embarrassing himself or the team too badly. The Orioles, however, primarily used him as a backup for whichever first baseman was injured that particular week. The fact that he was on the roster for three months and only got 90 at-bats is his future in a nutshell.

Luis Lopez   SS   Born: 04-Sep-70   Age: 32   Bats: B   Throws: R

YEAR	TM	LG	AGE	AB	H	2B	3B	HR	BB	SO	SB	CS	AVG	OBP	SLG	MLVR	EQBA	EQOBP	EQSLG	EQMLVR	VORP	DEFENSE			
2000	MIL	NL	29	201	53	14	0	6	9	35	1	2	.264	.312	.423	-.106	.261	.297	.424	-.109	5.6	36-SS	-7	15-2B	1
2001	MIL	NL	30	222	60	8	3	4	14	44	0	1	.270	.328	.387	-.080	.276	.329	.396	-.077	6.7	35-3B	-7	11-SS	-2
2002	IND	INT	31	22	5	0	0	0	0	4	0	0	.227	.261	.227	-.377	.227	.252	.227	-.501	-2.0				
2002	ROC	INT	31	68	22	6	0	3	3	11	0	0	.324	.361	.544	.301	.294	.340	.500	.108	5.5	14-2B	1		
2002	BAL	AL	31	109	23	6	0	2	3	20	1	0	.211	.232	.321	-.335	.236	.257	.364	-.289	-1.9	13-SS	0		
2003	COL	NL	32	124	33	7	1	3	7	22	1	1	.264	.310	.407	-.076	.245	.289	.370	-.201	-1.6				

Breakout: 14%   Improve: 34%   Collapse: 35%

Lopez started the year with the Brewers injured. They proceeded to string him out until June, using the maximum allowable time for a rehab assignment, and then the maximum time between the end of rehab and activation, all to try and avoid eating his contract. (Suggestion for new GMs: Backup infielders are spare parts. Never, ever commit future dollars and a multi-year contract to a spare part!) Lopez is a barely adequate utility infielder, since he can play three positions and can't hit a lick. So why did Hargrove use him, of all people, as a pinch hitter three times as often as anyone else, even though he was almost always a worse hitter than the man he replaced? He was released after the season, and will now be a similar nuisance to the Rockies.

Luis Matos   CF   Born: 30-Oct-78   Age: 24   Bats: R   Throws: R

YEAR	TM	LG	AGE	AB	H	2B	3B	HR	BB	SO	SB	CS	AVG	OBP	SLG	MLVR	EQBA	EQOBP	EQSLG	EQMLVR	VORP	DEFENSE	
2000	BOW	EAS	21	181	49	7	5	2	17	23	14	8	.271	.350	.398	.036	.230	.291	.344	-.255	-3.6	47-CF	0
2000	BAL	AL	21	182	41	6	3	1	12	30	13	4	.225	.284	.308	-.346	.242	.293	.330	-.264	-3.8	65-CF	0
2001	BAL	AL	22	98	21	7	0	4	11	30	7	0	.214	.300	.408	-.110	.232	.314	.455	-.058	3.2	27-CF	0
2002	BOW	EAS	23	218	60	14	2	9	32	45	14	4	.275	.373	.482	.191	.238	.320	.413	-.099	4.9	56-CF	-2
2002	BAL	AL	23	31	4	1	0	0	1	6	1	0	.129	.156	.161	-.731	.161	.188	.194	-.707	-4.4		
2003	BAL	AL	24	201	51	11	1	6	18	40	8	3	.252	.319	.417	-.034	.264	.334	.442	-.012	4.8		

Breakout: 38%   Improve: 75%   Collapse: 9%

You can't find a better example of the Orioles' bizarre slotting of players than by looking at Matos. Here's a guy who got 200 plate appearances in the majors two years ago, and the team has bounced him between Baltimore and Double-A Bowie—but not Triple-A—ever since. He's got speed, plays a pretty fair center field, and he's young, all qualities the team could use. Unfortunately for him, he's about as durable as a campaign promise, and hasn't been healthy for a full season since 1999.

Gary Matthews Jr.   RF   Born: 25-Aug-74   Age: 28   Bats: Throws:

YEAR	TM	LG	AGE	AB	H	2B	3B	HR	BB	SO	SB	CS	AVG	OBP	SLG	MLVR	EQBA	EQOBP	EQSLG	EQMLVR	VORP	DEFENSE	
2000	IOW	PCL	25	211	51	11	3	5	18	41	6	1	.242	.301	.393	-.183	.218	.263	.355	-.302	-6.9	57-CF	-2
2000	CHC	NL	25	158	30	1	2	4	15	28	3	0	.190	.264	.297	-.428	.194	.254	.306	-.402	-13.3	42-LF	-2
2001	CHC	NL	26	258	56	9	1	9	38	55	5	3	.217	.320	.364	-.160	.221	.322	.374	-.160	1.5	72-CF	-2
2001	PIT	NL	26	147	36	6	1	5	22	45	3	2	.245	.343	.401	-.059	.242	.339	.403	-.074	4.6	41-CF	-2
2002	BAL	AL	27	344	95	25	3	7	43	69	15	5	.276	.358	.427	.081	.311	.390	.483	.185	24.8	89-RF	-4
2003	*BAL*	*AL*	*28*	*308*	*75*	*15*	*2*	*8*	*37*	*63*	*9*	*4*	*.245*	*.328*	*.393*	*-.056*	*.257*	*.342*	*.417*	*-.036*	*1.9*		

Breakout: 19%   *Improve: 47%*   *Collapse: 18%*

Test #1 for the next Oriole GM will be what to do about center field. When you have a player who puts up Equivalent Averages of .220, .204, .237, and (at age 27) .291, you have two basic choices. Option one is give the player a chance in the spring to show you that this was no fluke, while being ready to move very quickly if (as is likely) his fairy godmother doesn't grant him an extension. Option two is to decide that it was no fluke and discard your backups on the assumption that he can handle the role full-time.

     The Orioles are pursuing the second option with a vengeance, having non-tendered Chris Singleton. In this special case, Option two may not be such a bad idea, but not because of the talents involved. I'd give 2–1 odds that Singleton outhits Matthews in 2003. The kicker is that the Orioles aren't going to contend in 2003, regardless of who's in center field. By the time they are ready to contend again, Singleton won't be a useful player, but Matthews could be, if 2002 wasn't a fluke. Matthews will be a lot cheaper than Singleton this year, plus there's Luis Matos and Darnell McDonald to fall back on if he crashes and burns. It's a risk a competitive team should not take, but for a down-and-out team it might just work.

Darnell McDonald   CF   Born: 17-Nov-78   Age: 24   Bats: R   Throws: R

YEAR	TM	LG	AGE	AB	H	2B	3B	HR	BB	SO	SB	CS	AVG	OBP	SLG	MLVR	EQBA	EQOBP	EQSLG	EQMLVR	VORP	DEFENSE	
2000	BOW	EAS	21	459	111	13	5	6	29	87	11	4	.242	.293	.331	-.167	.213	.249	.297	-.414	-39.4	102-RF	-6
2001	BOW	EAS	22	117	33	7	1	3	9	28	3	3	.282	.339	.436	.100	.242	.292	.383	-.191	-3.2	30-LF	-2
2001	ROC	INT	22	391	93	19	2	2	29	75	13	9	.238	.292	.312	-.189	.227	.279	.301	-.341	-16.5	101-CF	1
2002	BOW	EAS	23	144	42	9	1	4	22	27	9	3	.292	.393	.451	.195	.252	.338	.388	-.089	3.7	24-CF	1
2002	ROC	INT	23	332	96	21	6	6	32	78	11	3	.289	.355	.443	.121	.271	.335	.420	-.036	12.5	90-CF	3
2003	*BAL*	*AL*	*24*	*200*	*50*	*10*	*1*	*5*	*16*	*41*	*5*	*3*	*.249*	*.306*	*.384*	*-.101*	*.261*	*.320*	*.407*	*-.086*	*.8*		

Breakout: 35%   *Improve: 63%*   *Collapse: 12%*

Sometimes, you need patience. McDonald had given every indication of being a wasted draft pick, making no progress for four years after being taken in 1997's first round. And then, just when you're ready to give up on him, he starts taking a more patient approach at the plate, breaking the one walk per ten at-bats barrier (translated and real) for the first time in his career. Plus he starts getting pitches to drive, and breaks .100 in translated isolated power for the first time, and getting his translated batting average over .250 for the first time. He's back in center field, where he's supposed to be more comfortable. Assuming that these are lessons learned, he has a chance to make the Orioles in 2003 or 2004. If he can wait.

Melvin Mora   LF/SS   Born: 02-Feb-72   Age: 31   Bats: R   Throws: R

YEAR	TM	LG	AGE	AB	H	2B	3B	HR	BB	SO	SB	CS	AVG	OBP	SLG	MLVR	EQBA	EQOBP	EQSLG	EQMLVR	VORP	DEFENSE			
2000	NYM	NL	28	215	56	13	2	6	18	48	7	3	.260	.323	.423	-.069	.266	.318	.431	-.056	9.4	39-SS	-3	14-CF	-1
2000	BAL	AL	28	199	58	9	3	2	17	32	5	8	.291	.359	.397	-.020	.303	.364	.409	.028	12.4	52-SS	-2		
2001	BAL	AL	29	436	109	28	0	7	41	91	11	4	.250	.334	.362	-.083	.273	.354	.399	-.029	17.4	81-CF	1	41-SS	4
2002	BAL	AL	30	557	130	30	4	19	70	108	16	10	.233	.340	.404	-.013	.266	.366	.461	.072	24.6	104-LF	7	34-SS	-2
2003	*BAL*	*AL*	*31*	*442*	*109*	*23*	*3*	*12*	*46*	*84*	*9*	*5*	*.247*	*.326*	*.391*	*-.059*	*.259*	*.341*	*.415*	*-.040*	*7.4*				

Breakout: 6%   *Improve: 45%*   *Collapse: 21%*

Nobody gets less respect than Melvin Mora. You literally never hear a reference made to him without some statement about him being a natural backup who is stretched in a starting role. Yet this "backup" was second on the team in equivalent runs to Tony Batista and played four positions. At three of them (second, left, and center field) his fielding statistics were better than the regular's. At shortstop they weren't, and that's where a lot of the criticism comes in. He had real problems moving to short after Bordick broke his knee, and made six errors in his first 14 games there. Let the record show that he did adjust, and made only one in the next 22, but even then, he wasn't making the plays or turning the deuce like Mike. You can make a very good case for him being the Orioles' actual MVP of 2002.

Mike Moriarty   SS   Born: 08-Mar-74   Age: 29   Bats: R   Throws: R

YEAR	TM	LG	AGE	AB	H	2B	3B	HR	BB	SO	SB	CS	AVG	OBP	SLG	MLVR	EQBA	EQOBP	EQSLG	EQMLVR	VORP		DEFENSE			
2000	SLC	PCL	26	390	97	23	4	13	63	58	1	2	.249	.360	.428	-.051	.207	.304	.355	-.229	-1.0		121-SS	3		
2001	EDM	PCL	27	404	98	17	2	13	58	94	5	4	.243	.356	.391	-.064	.215	.317	.341	-.217	.1		123-SS	-5		
2002	BAL	AL	28	16	3	1	0	0	0	2	0	1	.188	.188	.250	-.530	.187	.187	.312	-.531	-1.5					
2002	ROC	INT	28	311	86	18	1	4	37	50	4	1	.277	.361	.379	.038	.263	.342	.364	-.107	9.3		51-SS	-9	38-3B	4
2003	BAL	AL	29	156	36	8	1	3	17	29	2	1	.228	.311	.351	-.148	.239	.325	.372	-.138	.9					

Breakout: 29%   Improve: 49%   Collapse: 33%

The Orioles wanted Brian Roberts to play every day, not sit on the end of the bench as seldom-used backup. So they got Mikey to try it, and he was outstanding, deftly getting water for players coming into the dugout, effortlessly guiding the batboys through the difficult re-shelving of lumber, and making dazzling stabs at rally caps at the end of lost games. He spent seven weeks in the majors, and got into eight games, but went back to Rochester for good when the Orioles decided to let Roberts play at Camden Yard. He's a better utility infielder to have around than Luis Lopez, but lacks that glossy veteran sheen.

Tim Raines Jr.   CF   Born: 31-Aug-79   Age: 23   Bats: B   Throws: R

YEAR	TM	LG	AGE	AB	H	2B	3B	HR	BB	SO	SB	CS	AVG	OBP	SLG	MLVR	EQBA	EQOBP	EQSLG	EQMLVR	VORP		DEFENSE	
2000	FRD	CRL	20	457	108	21	3	2	67	106	81	19	.236	.350	.309	-.051	.209	.290	.276	-.362	-23.1		123-CF	-5
2001	FRD	CRL	21	84	21	3	1	3	13	23	14	4	.250	.351	.417	.131	.213	.293	.360	-.240	-1.5		19-CF	-1
2001	BOW	EAS	21	254	74	14	1	4	34	60	29	10	.291	.381	.402	.131	.255	.335	.354	-.140	2.8		65-CF	-1
2001	ROC	INT	21	133	34	5	1	2	11	30	11	3	.256	.313	.353	-.089	.244	.301	.341	-.231	-1.8		34-CF	-4
2002	BOW	EAS	22	491	128	17	4	5	34	101	33	15	.261	.311	.342	-.104	.228	.269	.300	-.362	-23.9		113-CF	-6
2003	BAL	AL	23	156	35	6	1	4	13	36	5	4	.227	.292	.351	-.180	.238	.305	.372	-.174	-2.3			

Breakout: 44%   Improve: 69%   Collapse: 16%

This is definitely not your father's Tim Raines. Tim Sr. understood the value of taking pitches and getting on base to use your speed. Tim Jr. apparently thinks he's a power hitter, trying to launch balls at every opportunity—except that he doesn't have the strength to succeed that way. I think he was also sulking at being sent back to Bowie after seeing Rochester and Baltimore in 2001, and often played like he just didn't care anymore.

Keith Reed   RF   Born: 08-Oct-78   Age: 24   Bats: R   Throws: R

YEAR	TM	LG	AGE	AB	H	2B	3B	HR	BB	SO	SB	CS	AVG	OBP	SLG	MLVR	EQBA	EQOBP	EQSLG	EQMLVR	VORP		DEFENSE	
2000	DEL	SAL	21	269	78	16	1	11	25	56	20	4	.290	.361	.480	.240	.231	.281	.383	-.220	-10.1		65-RF	-4
2000	FRD	CRL	21	243	57	10	1	8	21	58	9	1	.235	.306	.383	-.026	.197	.245	.325	-.392	-20.1		61-RF	-7
2001	FRD	CRL	22	267	72	14	0	7	13	57	8	6	.270	.306	.401	.064	.223	.254	.343	-.334	-18.3		66-RF	-6
2001	BOW	EAS	22	67	17	3	0	1	6	10	2	2	.254	.315	.343	-.077	.217	.270	.304	-.360	-3.3		17-CF	0
2001	ROC	INT	22	74	23	7	1	2	5	14	1	1	.311	.354	.514	.238	.280	.325	.480	.039	2.2		18-RF	-3
2002	BOW	EAS	23	488	120	20	1	15	40	107	3	10	.246	.316	.383	-.051	.213	.268	.332	-.328	-33.0		97-RF	-3
2003	BAL	AL	24	156	36	7	1	4	11	35	2	2	.232	.288	.375	-.154	.243	.301	.397	-.145	-5.3			

Breakout: 57%   Improve: 77%   Collapse: 11%

A lot of teams like to have their farm clubs nearby, and there are some good reasons for that, but having them close to the big city isn't always a good idea. Bowie is about halfway between Washington and Baltimore, if it's not rush hour, you can get from there to either downtown in little more half an hour. Cities the size of Washington and Baltimore have a lot of things that cities like Bowie don't, like museums and symphony orchestras and monuments and cathedrals. And nightclubs. On and off the field, Keith has been known to chase a curve.

Chris Richard   DH   Born: 07-Jun-74   Age: 29   Bats: L   Throws: L

YEAR	TM	LG	AGE	AB	H	2B	3B	HR	BB	SO	SB	CS	AVG	OBP	SLG	MLVR	EQBA	EQOBP	EQSLG	EQMLVR	VORP		DEFENSE			
2000	MEM	PCL	26	375	104	24	0	16	50	70	9	3	.277	.368	.469	.094	.250	.325	.420	-.071	.4		84-RF	1	11-1B	-1
2000	BAL	AL	26	199	55	14	2	13	15	38	7	5	.276	.339	.563	.172	.291	.345	.593	.246	17.1		51-1B	1		
2001	BAL	AL	27	483	128	31	3	15	45	100	11	9	.265	.338	.435	.031	.290	.361	.476	.106	23.2		93-RF	5	16-1B	-1
2002	ROC	INT	28	53	17	6	0	6	6	14	0	0	.321	.410	.774	.666	.296	.382	.685	.437	8.2					
2002	BAL	AL	28	155	36	11	0	4	12	30	0	3	.232	.296	.381	-.124	.261	.320	.433	-.054	3.3					
2003	BAL	AL	29	253	62	14	1	10	25	52	3	2	.247	.320	.423	-.030	.259	.334	.448	-.008	2.2					

Breakout: 14%   Improve: 39%   Collapse: 29%

Richard tore his rotator cuff late in the 2001 season, and wasn't able to resume playing until August 2002. Even then, he couldn't play the field. He wasn't a bad outfielder before the surgery, and could even step into center without looking like an idiot, but it remains to be seen if he's going to be able to throw. He's never been able to hit lefties at all, so he has to be platooned, which makes him a sort of a luxury player that the Orioles can't really afford.

Brian Roberts   2B   Born: 09-Oct-77   Age: 25   Bats: B   Throws: R

YEAR	TM	LG	AGE	AB	H	2B	3B	HR	BB	SO	SB	CS	AVG	OBP	SLG	MLVR	EQBA	EQOBP	EQSLG	EQMLVR	VORP	DEFENSE
2000	FRD	CRL	22	163	49	6	3	0	27	24	13	10	.301	.403	.374	.150	.241	.319	.306	-.246	-1.3	42-SS -8
2001	BOW	EAS	23	81	24	7	0	1	9	12	10	0	.296	.374	.420	.145	.262	.330	.369	-.124	2.1	18-2B 2
2001	ROC	INT	23	161	43	4	1	1	28	22	23	3	.267	.376	.323	-.011	.259	.359	.313	-.146	3.3	44-SS -11
2001	BAL	AL	23	273	69	12	3	2	13	36	12	3	.253	.287	.341	-.200	.276	.311	.378	-.137	5.6	47-SS -5
2002	ROC	INT	24	313	86	9	7	3	40	46	22	4	.275	.362	.377	.036	.258	.341	.358	-.121	8.0	69-2B -12
2002	BAL	AL	24	128	29	6	0	1	15	21	9	2	.227	.313	.297	-.206	.254	.335	.331	-.172	1.5	25-2B 5
2003	BAL	AL	25	312	75	13	3	3	33	46	14	4	.241	.315	.331	-.157	.253	.329	.351	-.148	1.1	

Breakout: 13%   Improve: 43%   Collapse: 20%

Roberts's season was literally up and down. It started down in the minors so that he could play every day. But he was playing so well that in May he was called up and briefly took the second base job away from Hairston. He slumped after a hot start, so Hairston took the job back, and Roberts went back to Rochester at the All-Star break. A week later Bordick gets hurt, and they wanted Roberts to replace him, except that the Orioles were in Toronto at the time, and Roberts had left his passport at his mother's, so Luis Matos got called up instead. A few days later Chris Richard was supposed to be activated, only he hurt himself in pregame warmups, so now Roberts got his call, only to go back down four days later when Richard isn't really hurt. Then he got sick, played poorly through August and not at all in September, before turning around and being one of the top hitters in the Puerto Rican winter league. It would have been worth it to give him a full year at short to see what happens, but the Orioles have signed Deivi Cruz to man the position after Bordick's departure.

Ed Rogers   SS   Born: 29-Aug-78   Age: 24   Bats: R   Throws: R

YEAR	TM	LG	AGE	AB	H	2B	3B	HR	BB	SO	SB	CS	AVG	OBP	SLG	MLVR	EQBA	EQOBP	EQSLG	EQMLVR	VORP	DEFENSE
2000	DEL	SAL	21	332	91	14	5	5	22	63	27	6	.274	.319	.392	.051	.221	.251	.321	-.372	-13.0	80-SS -12
2001	FRD	CRL	22	292	76	20	3	8	14	47	18	6	.260	.312	.432	.104	.221	.261	.371	-.282	-4.9	73-SS -7
2001	BOW	EAS	22	191	38	10	1	0	6	40	10	2	.199	.231	.262	-.355	.182	.215	.240	-.579	-17.6	53-SS -3
2002	BOW	EAS	23	422	110	26	2	11	16	70	14	4	.261	.304	.410	-.025	.226	.258	.358	-.303	-9.2	111-SS -12
2002	BAL	AL	23	3	0	0	0	0	0	0	0	0	.000	.000	.000	-1.274	.333	.333	.333	-.119	.0	
2003	BAL	AL	24	162	37	8	1	4	8	31	4	3	.228	.270	.360	-.206	.239	.283	.381	-.202	-1.8	

Breakout: 55%   Improve: 77%   Collapse: 13%

Mea culpa. A year ago, I wrote about the Orioles' front office comparing Rogers to players like Jeter and Tejada and Guzman, and then I looked at what those players had done at the age of 19, and decided that they weren't necessarily off base. Well, Rogers wasn't 19 in 2001, he was 22, by far the most significant Oriole who used the Dominican birthday lottery. So now we know that Rogers had a translated OPS of .616 at age 23. By this time, Guzman's translated OPS was .718, Tejada's .830, and Jeter's .895. If he was still 20, you could reasonably expect him to make it to .750 during his career, which would be an average major league hitter. He'll be lucky now to reach major league replacement level.

David Segui   1B   Born: 19-Jul-66   Age: 36   Bats: B   Throws: L

YEAR	TM	LG	AGE	AB	H	2B	3B	HR	BB	SO	SB	CS	AVG	OBP	SLG	MLVR	EQBA	EQOBP	EQSLG	EQMLVR	VORP	DEFENSE
2000	CLE	AL	33	223	74	13	0	8	19	33	0	0	.332	.387	.498	.190	.336	.384	.509	.239	17.9	33-1B -1
2000	TEX	AL	33	351	118	29	1	11	34	51	0	1	.336	.395	.519	.233	.342	.393	.528	.288	33.3	38-1B 4
2001	BAL	AL	34	292	88	18	1	10	49	61	1	1	.301	.409	.473	.234	.328	.432	.517	.319	34.5	60-1B -10
2002	BAL	AL	35	95	25	4	0	2	11	22	0	0	.263	.340	.368	-.040	.292	.370	.406	.025	4.1	
2003	BAL	AL	36	221	58	11	1	5	26	44	0	0	.263	.341	.390	-.025	.276	.357	.413	-.002	2.4	

Breakout: 1%   Improve: 27%   Collapse: 37%

On April 26, Segui had his hand stepped on during a play at the plate. A week later, an MRI revealed a torn tendon, which would require surgery and a two-month layoff. You would expect him to at least go on the DL, but not on this team. The next day the Orioles announce that it's just a bruise, he won't need surgery at all—and in fact, they play him that day. Well, another

David Segui *(continued)*

ten days pass, his wrist still hurts, and he's 3–23 since it happened, so he decides to get a second MRI and an outside opinion, which returns to the original diagnosis of torn tendons and surgery and he should miss two months. Except then he didn't miss two months, he missed four, the entire rest of the season. Can he still hit? The bigger question is, how many plate appearances will he get before his contract runs out after 2004? Let the over-under start at 500.

Chris Singleton — CF — Born: 15-Aug-72 — Age: 30 — Bats: L — Throws: L

YEAR	TM	LG	AGE	AB	H	2B	3B	HR	BB	SO	SB	CS	AVG	OBP	SLG	MLVR	EQBA	EQOBP	EQSLG	EQMLVR	VORP	DEFENSE
2000	CWS	AL	27	511	130	22	5	11	35	85	22	7	.254	.303	.382	-.198	.260	.301	.394	-.145	4.2	145-CF 3
2001	CWS	AL	28	392	117	21	5	7	20	61	12	11	.298	.334	.431	.028	.309	.347	.449	.060	23.9	121-CF 5
2002	BAL	AL	29	466	122	30	6	9	21	83	20	2	.262	.299	.410	-.056	.287	.324	.450	.001	21.4	111-CF -4
2003	OAK	AL	30	385	101	21	4	8	20	63	12	6	.262	.302	.400	-.078	.271	.312	.419	-.076	4.5	

Breakout: 10%   Improve: 36%   Collapse: 22%

The Orioles seem to believe that Singleton was a huge disappointment, which leads you to wonder just what they were expecting. His translated rate stats for 1999–2001 total .291/.324/.451; his translated stats in Baltimore were .287/.324/.450. His fielding was a little worse than in the past, but on the whole he delivered exactly what his resume promised. PECOTA doesn't think he'll age well, and neither do we or the Orioles; he was non-tendered in December, then signed by Oakland to a one-year deal to patch over their scar in center.

PITCHERS

Jancy Andrade — Born: 29-Jun-78 — Age: 25 — Bats: R — Throws: R

YEAR	TM	LG	AGE	G	GS	IP	H	BB	SO	HR	ERA	EQERA	EQH9	EQBB9	EQSO9	EQHR9	PERA	VORP	STF
2000	DEL	SAL	22	29	19	114.0	121	43	99	7	5.37	7.71	13.8	4.8	4.7	1.6	7.41	-28.2	-13
2001	DEL	SAL	23	8	8	48.3	46	16	43	2	3.73	5.99	12.2	4.6	4.7	1.0	6.55	-2.6	-2
2001	FRD	CRL	23	20	13	75.0	80	28	57	6	4.44	7.81	14.2	5.2	4.5	1.9	7.39	-19.4	-19
2002	FRD	CRL	24	30	22	145.3	133	52	151	13	3.84	5.07	10.5	4.5	6.6	2.0	5.46	6.8	2

Andrade made one appearance for Bowie, on May Day appropriately enough, and he faced nine batters, yielding three walks and five hits, including two home runs, and a bus ride back to Frederick for the rest of the season. Until then, he'd been a reliever, but when he went back he moved into the rotation, and had a pretty good year for an absolutely awful team. Frederick was also one of the worst fielding teams in the minors, so he (like Hale) pitched better than the numbers look. But he was incensed at being returned to Frederick, and apparently grew angrier as he continued to pitch well without being recalled to Double-A. He swore he'd never, under any circumstances, re-sign with the Orioles as a pending six-year free agent.

Rick Bauer — Born: 10-Jan-77 — Age: 26 — Bats: R — Throws: R

YEAR	TM	LG	AGE	G	GS	IP	H	BB	SO	HR	ERA	EQERA	EQH9	EQBB9	EQSO9	EQHR9	PERA	VORP	STF
2000	BOW	EAS	23	26	23	129.0	154	39	87	16	5.30	7.20	13.8	3.1	4.8	2.1	6.85	-24.4	-7
2001	BOW	EAS	24	9	9	61.0	52	10	34	8	3.54	4.60	9.5	2.0	3.5	1.9	4.47	6.1	-3
2001	ROC	INT	24	19	18	113.3	119	28	89	10	3.89	4.79	9.9	2.6	5.5	1.1	4.98	9.0	9
2001	BAL	AL	24	6	6	33.0	35	9	16	7	4.64	5.32	9.5	2.3	4.2	1.8	5.10	0.7	-3
2002	BAL	AL	25	56	1	83.7	84	36	45	12	3.98	4.73	9.6	3.7	4.8	1.2	4.81	6.1	-13
2003	BAL	AL	26	36	4	57.7	65	24	36	9	5.18	5.41	10.2	3.5	5.3	1.2	5.38	3.0	-12

Breakout: 15%   Improve: 48%   Collapse: 20%

A career starter, Bauer was forced to learn how to pitch from the pen at the major league level, gradually becoming more of a long reliever as the season went on. He was pretty good in the role, except for a five-week stretch in May and June where his ERA topped ten; if you do the math, that means he had an ERA under 2.70 for the other 21 weeks of the season. He'll probably stay in that role in 2003, although he does have a chance at the rotation.

Steve Bechler   Born: 18-Nov-79   Age: 23   Bats: R   Throws: R

YEAR	TM	LG	AGE	G	GS	IP	H	BB	SO	HR	ERA	EQERA	EQH9	EQBB9	EQSO9	EQHR9	PERA	VORP	STF
2000	FRD	CRL	20	27	27	162.0	179	57	137	19	4.83	7.16	14.3	4.0	5.0	2.7	7.54	-29.8	-3
2001	FRD	CRL	21	13	13	83.3	73	22	71	3	2.27	4.52	10.8	3.5	4.8	0.8	4.99	9.1	8
2001	BOW	EAS	21	12	12	79.0	63	15	58	14	3.08	4.44	9.1	2.3	4.6	2.5	4.62	9.3	4
2002	BOW	EAS	22	4	4	23.7	28	6	13	2	3.42	5.05	12.5	2.8	3.8	1.3	6.08	1.2	-1
2002	ROC	INT	22	24	24	149.7	154	52	77	15	4.09	4.98	10.1	3.8	4.0	1.3	5.21	8.7	-1
2002	BAL	AL	22	3	0	4.7	6	4	3	3	13.40	12.17	11.3	7.0	5.5	5.3	11.24	-3.5	-43
2003	BAL	AL	23	13	9	54.3	64	24	32	8	5.50	5.74	10.6	3.7	5.0	1.2	5.76	0.7	-8

Breakout: 17%   *Improve: 66%*   *Collapse: 10%*

Bechler started the year in Bowie, but after a quick promotion to Rochester soon found himself in trouble. His control was off within the strike zone, and he was allowing 6.63 runs, 11.3 hits, and 1.5 home runs per nine innings. Then he settled down, and for the rest of the year cut those numbers to 3.59, 8.1, and 0.6. He's a horse of a pitcher with a temper to match (although he's getting better about that), with a good fastball, a very good knuckle-curve, and no third pitch. He figures to start for Ottawa in 2003, and be in line for replacement starts in Baltimore.

Erik Bedard   Born: 06-Mar-79   Age: 24   Bats: L   Throws: L

YEAR	TM	LG	AGE	G	GS	IP	H	BB	SO	HR	ERA	EQERA	EQH9	EQBB9	EQSO9	EQHR9	PERA	VORP	STF
2000	DEL	SAL	21	29	22	111.0	98	35	131	2	3.57	5.25	10.6	3.9	6.1	0.4	5.17	3.0	9
2001	FRD	CRL	22	17	17	96.3	68	26	130	4	2.15	3.94	8.7	3.6	7.5	0.9	3.90	16.7	25
2002	BOW	EAS	23	13	12	68.7	43	30	66	0	1.97	2.58	6.2	4.6	6.5	0.2	2.76	22.3	18
2002	BAL	AL	23	2	0	0.7	2	0	1	0	12.86	13.04	27.1	0.8	12.7	0.3	12.66	-0.6	30
2003	BAL	AL	24	13	11	70.3	70	34	57	8	4.48	4.67	9.0	4.0	6.8	0.9	4.66	10.5	10

Breakout: 12%   *Improve: 40%*   *Collapse: 24%*

Oriole medicine, part 2 (see David Segui for part 1). Bedard was, without a doubt, the best pitcher in the Oriole system at the start of 2002: left-handed, with an above-average fastball, a better curve, totally and completely unhittable by left-handed hitters (who were 2–37 against him in 2002). So the Orioles bring him to major league camp, and leave him there until mid-March, at which point he's thrown just 11 competitive innings. He starts the season on a 50-pitch limit, 25 behind the other Bowie starters. But no problem, he is just as dominating as ever, and even gets a quick little call-up to Baltimore. Still, he's tearing up the league, up until June 26. On that day, throwing a two-hitter, he went out for the eighth inning, even though he had already reached his pitch count. The manager thought it was just so much fun, and then *pop* goes the elbow. The MRI showed that he had a partially torn ligament. The Orioles' medical staff prescribed rest, hoping that the tear would heal on its own. Six weeks later, without taking another MRI to see if it had healed at all, they had Bedard resume throwing. The very next day, the pain was back, and Bedard was heading for surgery. He won't pitch in 2003; he's unlikely to be effective until the second half of 2004, if then. As you can see, that's a shame.

Lesli Brea   Born: 12-Oct-78   Age: 24   Bats: R   Throws: R

YEAR	TM	LG	AGE	G	GS	IP	H	BB	SO	HR	ERA	EQERA	EQH9	EQBB9	EQSO9	EQHR9	PERA	VORP	STF
2000	BIN	EAS	21	19	18	93.3	85	61	86	10	4.24	5.84	10.0	6.6	6.3	1.7	5.89	-3.5	2
2000	BOW	EAS	21	2	2	12.7	12	9	3	1	4.25	5.82	10.8	7.3	1.7	1.3	6.43	-0.4	-26
2000	ROC	INT	21	4	4	19.3	27	8	13	3	6.06	8.19	14.1	3.8	5.2	1.8	7.85	-5.8	-3
2001	ROC	INT	22	63	0	82.3	80	35	98	6	3.83	4.78	9.2	4.4	8.2	0.9	4.98	5.5	12
2002	ROC	INT	23	60	0	86.7	81	37	75	4	3.22	4.21	8.9	4.6	6.6	0.6	4.47	11.3	2
2003	TBY	AL	24	18	4	33.7	35	19	27	5	5.28	5.26	9.2	4.6	7.0	1.2	5.11	2.6	-4

Breakout: 18%   *Improve: 54%*   *Collapse: 18%*

Brea is that rarest of birds: a player whose age questions were all over the place before the 2002 visa scandal, and who managed to sail right through it with his claimed age intact. On top of that, he had the best season of his career, and is a legitimate, albeit marginal, candidate to work in the Devil Rays pen in 2003.

Chris Brock   Born: 05-Feb-71   Age: 32   Bats: R   Throws: R

YEAR	TM	LG	AGE	G	GS	IP	H	BB	SO	HR	ERA	EQERA	EQH9	EQBB9	EQSO9	EQHR9	PERA	VORP	STF
2000	PHI	NL	29	63	5	93.3	85	41	69	21	4.34	4.45	8.1	3.2	5.9	1.8	4.70	9.9	-9
2001	SWB	INT	30	13	13	78.7	75	16	56	9	3.55	4.88	10.8	2.2	5.2	1.5	4.56	5.5	4
2001	PHI	NL	30	24	0	32.7	35	15	26	6	4.13	5.09	10.3	3.9	6.2	1.5	5.67	1.1	-10
2002	BAL	AL	31	22	0	44.0	52	14	21	6	4.70	5.24	11.3	2.7	4.3	1.2	5.34	0.7	-14
2003	BAL	AL	32	31	8	65.0	71	22	36	11	4.66	4.86	9.9	2.8	4.7	1.3	5.05	6.4	-12

Breakout: 14%   Improve: 57%   Collapse: 18%

Brock missed two months with an inflamed right shoulder. When he did pitch, he was close to an all-or-nothing pitcher, either shutting out the side completely or giving up 3–4 runs at a time. Strictly filler for the back of a bullpen, he's a bad month away from retirement, and not really a good use of a 40-man roster spot in an organization that has to keep Albert Belle every winter.

Sean Douglass   Born: 28-Apr-79   Age: 24   Bats: R   Throws: R

YEAR	TM	LG	AGE	G	GS	IP	H	BB	SO	HR	ERA	EQERA	EQH9	EQBB9	EQSO9	EQHR9	PERA	VORP	STF
2000	BOW	EAS	21	27	27	160.7	155	55	118	17	4.03	5.39	11.1	3.5	5.1	1.8	5.31	2.1	5
2001	ROC	INT	22	27	27	162.3	160	61	156	13	3.49	4.53	9.3	3.9	6.7	1.0	4.97	17.6	18
2001	BAL	AL	22	4	4	20.3	21	11	17	3	5.32	5.10	9.1	4.5	7.0	1.2	5.27	0.9	14
2002	ROC	INT	23	14	13	66.7	66	35	71	4	4.72	5.31	9.6	5.7	8.2	0.8	5.21	1.4	16
2002	BAL	AL	23	15	8	53.3	58	35	44	10	6.08	6.62	10.1	5.5	7.2	1.6	6.23	-6.8	1
2003	BAL	AL	24	19	14	88.3	91	44	71	12	4.96	5.18	9.3	4.1	6.9	1.1	5.16	6.8	6

Breakout: 12%   Improve: 48%   Collapse: 18%

After four starts in Rochester, Douglass was called up when Jason Johnson broke his finger. After three bad starts, the Orioles hit a stretch where, due to schedule and rainouts, they didn't need a fifth starter for three weeks, so Douglass only pitched once. The rest didn't help, as he continued to pitch poorly, from the rotation and the pen, in Baltimore and Rochester. Since he doesn't have any one outstanding pitch, he's going to have to rely on his balance of mediocrity to fool hitters.

Travis Driskill   Born: 01-Aug-71   Age: 31   Bats: R   Throws: R

YEAR	TM	LG	AGE	G	GS	IP	H	BB	SO	HR	ERA	EQERA	EQH9	EQBB9	EQSO9	EQHR9	PERA	VORP	STF
2000	NWO	PCL	28	28	28	179.3	201	45	113	15	4.02	5.32	11.7	2.3	4.7	1.0	5.31	3.7	2
2001	NWO	PCL	29	28	28	178.7	175	33	145	21	3.78	4.84	10.3	2.0	5.5	1.3	4.70	13.2	7
2002	ROC	INT	30	4	4	22.0	17	1	15	1	1.64	2.85	7.3	0.5	5.2	0.6	2.48	6.5	17
2002	BAL	AL	30	29	19	132.7	150	48	78	21	4.95	5.43	10.8	3.1	5.2	1.4	5.36	0.8	-3
2003	BAL	AL	31	25	18	114.0	129	36	66	17	4.89	5.10	10.2	2.6	4.9	1.2	4.99	8.5	-2

Breakout: 13%   Improve: 50%   Collapse: 19%

There was a buzz around Driskill in June. It's not every day that a 30-year-old rookie goes 5–0, but ultimately the fairy tale came to an end and he was bounced from the rotation in September. He learned how to throw a split-fingered fastball while in Japan in 1998, but it took him five years to learn how to control it, and major league hitters about a month to learn to lay off it.

Eric DuBose   Born: 15-May-76   Age: 27   Bats: L   Throws: L

YEAR	TM	LG	AGE	G	GS	IP	H	BB	SO	HR	ERA	EQERA	EQH9	EQBB9	EQSO9	EQHR9	PERA	VORP	STF
2000	VIS	CLF	24	5	0	10.7	8	5	12	0	1.68	2.57	7.9	4.4	6.1	0.3	3.68	3.3	3
2000	MID	TXS	24	18	0	28.3	25	18	20	1	4.13	4.66	8.5	5.9	4.5	0.5	4.57	2.3	-16
2002	BOW	EAS	26	41	0	64.7	46	21	66	2	2.50	3.01	7.1	3.4	6.8	0.5	3.04	17.0	5
2002	BAL	AL	26	4	0	6.0	7	1	4	1	3.00	4.01	11.2	1.4	6.0	1.5	5.01	0.9	-1

Once upon a time, DuBose was a high-ranking starting pitcher prospect in the Oakland organization. Then he hurt his arm. He made a solid landing in Bowie, developed a good changeup to make up for the bite his fastball lost after surgery, and got a September call-up. This year, at least, lefties hit him better than right-handers did, so he may not be good LOOGY material (to borrow John Sickels's label for Lefty One-Out Guys).

Scott Erickson
Born: 02-Feb-68 · **Age: 35** · **Bats: R** · **Throws: R**

YEAR	TM	LG	AGE	G	GS	IP	H	BB	SO	HR	ERA	EQERA	EQH9	EQBB9	EQSO9	EQHR9	PERA	VORP	STF
2000	BAL	AL	32	16	16	92.7	127	48	41	14	7.86	6.46	11.5	3.7	3.8	1.2	6.50	-9.8	-11
2002	BAL	AL	34	29	28	160.7	192	68	74	20	5.54	5.98	11.5	3.6	4.1	1.1	5.64	-8.5	-8
2003	BAL	AL	35	22	20	123.3	146	50	60	18	5.50	5.74	10.7	3.4	4.1	1.2	5.65	-1.0	-8

Breakout: 3%   Improve: 45%   Collapse: 15%

Erickson looked like he was washed up in 2000, and after he missed all of 2001 following Tommy John surgery expectations couldn't have been much lower. Yet there he was in mid-July with an ERA barely over 4, allowing just around a hit per inning pitched, and scouts from contending teams checking him out for a deadline trade that never happened. It didn't happen because Erickson melted down. He was charged with assault following a fight with his girlfriend, during which he was bitten on the arm, and it took a month before charges were eventually dropped. During that time, he pitched in nine games, giving up 44 runs, 63 hits, and 8 home runs in only 32 innings before he was finally, mercifully shelved for the final month. It took until December, and yet another outside opinion, to discover that he had a torn labrum. Rest, not surgery, has been prescribed (a real shocker there, considering the team's handling of other injuries). Once again, expectations can't get much lower.

Buddy Groom
Born: 10-Jul-65 · **Age: 38** · **Bats: L** · **Throws: L**

YEAR	TM	LG	AGE	G	GS	IP	H	BB	SO	HR	ERA	EQERA	EQH9	EQBB9	EQSO9	EQHR9	PERA	VORP	STF
2000	BAL	AL	35	70	0	59.3	63	21	44	5	4.86	4.26	9.0	2.6	6.5	0.6	4.00	7.4	1
2001	BAL	AL	36	70	0	66.0	64	9	54	4	3.55	3.37	8.8	1.2	7.0	0.5	3.16	14.7	12
2002	BAL	AL	37	70	0	62.0	44	12	48	4	1.60	2.06	6.9	1.7	6.9	0.6	2.27	22.9	12
2003	BAL	AL	37	60	0	46.7	47	12	36	5	3.64	3.80	9.0	2.1	6.6	0.9	3.93	10.1	3

Breakout: 18%   Improve: 33%   Collapse: 27%

Another year, another 70 games for Groom. The more he pitches, the better he gets. That's seven years in a row now; Kent Tekulve had ten 70-game seasons between 1977 and 1988, but he never had seven in a row, and no one else in baseball history has ever had seven, so I guess that's a record. Groom could do little wrong in 2002, and was the best pitcher in one of the league's best bullpens.

Beau Hale
Born: 01-Dec-78 · **Age: 24** · **Bats: R** · **Throws: R**

YEAR	TM	LG	AGE	G	GS	IP	H	BB	SO	HR	ERA	EQERA	EQH9	EQBB9	EQSO9	EQHR9	PERA	VORP	STF
2001	FRD	CRL	22	5	5	34.0	30	4	30	1	1.32	3.87	10.6	1.5	4.9	0.7	4.35	6.2	14
2001	BOW	EAS	22	12	12	61.7	74	15	40	8	5.11	6.90	13.5	3.0	4.2	1.9	7.09	-9.6	-7
2002	FRD	CRL	23	22	22	131.0	157	27	79	8	5.02	6.09	13.0	2.6	3.8	1.4	6.57	-8.5	-4
2002	BOW	EAS	23	2	2	10.7	11	3	6	0	0.84	2.79	10.5	3.0	3.9	0.3	4.46	3.2	4

Hale came out of college with a flamethrower reputation, but he has never shown high velocity in the pros. Maybe that has something to do with 150-pitch starts at the University of Texas, and maybe not. He has worked hard on a changeup (his best pitch right now) and a curve, but has lost significant time to injuries: tendonitis in 2001, and an as-yet undisclosed shoulder injury in 2002. Expectations that he'd rocket through the system were premature.

Pat Hentgen
Born: 13-Nov-68 · **Age: 34** · **Bats: R** · **Throws: R**

YEAR	TM	LG	AGE	G	GS	IP	H	BB	SO	HR	ERA	EQERA	EQH9	EQBB9	EQSO9	EQHR9	PERA	VORP	STF
2000	STL	NL	31	33	33	194.3	202	89	118	24	4.72	4.79	9.7	3.4	4.9	1.0	4.71	15.4	1
2001	BAL	AL	32	9	9	62.3	51	19	33	7	3.47	3.34	7.4	2.6	4.5	1.0	3.28	15.0	5
2002	BAL	AL	33	4	4	22.0	31	10	11	6	7.77	8.10	13.3	3.9	4.4	2.4	7.93	-6.3	-19

Hentgen allegedly recovered from Tommy John surgery ahead of schedule, and he certainly did a number on the minor leaguers he faced during his rehab outings. Major league hitters handed him his head. Nevertheless, the Orioles saw enough to re-sign him, in one of Syd Thrift's last significant acts. His contract had a $6 million option for 2003; at least they bought that out and negotiated a deal for something less. Still, it's hard to imagine that he's going to be of much use to anybody in 2003.

Jason Johnson Born: 27-Oct-73 Age: 29 Bats: R Throws: R

YEAR	TM	LG	AGE	G	GS	IP	H	BB	SO	HR	ERA	EQERA	EQH9	EQBB9	EQSO9	EQHR9	PERA	VORP	STF
2000	ROC	INT	26	8	8	55.0	32	21	56	2	1.47	2.22	5.7	3.4	7.7	0.4	2.32	20.1	28
2000	BAL	AL	26	25	13	107.7	119	61	79	21	7.02	6.04	9.1	4.0	6.3	1.5	5.62	-6.8	-2
2001	BAL	AL	27	32	32	196.0	194	77	114	28	4.09	4.62	8.9	3.3	4.9	1.2	4.58	19.3	1
2002	BAL	AL	28	22	22	131.3	141	41	97	19	4.59	4.84	10.2	2.7	6.6	1.2	4.80	9.7	12
2003	BAL	AL	29	25	21	132.7	137	49	92	18	4.52	4.72	9.4	3.0	5.9	1.1	4.68	14.7	6

Breakout: 16%   Improve: 43%   Collapse: 17%

Johnson's season was considered a disappointment. It was loaded with injuries: a dead arm in April, a broken finger in May, elbow tendonitis in July, and another broken finger in September. In some respects, though, it was better than his "breakthrough" 2001, with more strikeouts and fewer walks. The big difference was that he allowed 14 fewer hits than expected, given his balls in play and the team's defense, in 2001, against 8 more than expected in 2002. Balance those out, and that leaves him as an average major league pitcher, and there's a lot of fates worse than that.

Jorge Julio Born: 03-Mar-79 Age: 24 Bats: R Throws: R

YEAR	TM	LG	AGE	G	GS	IP	H	BB	SO	HR	ERA	EQERA	EQH9	EQBB9	EQSO9	EQHR9	PERA	VORP	STF
2000	JUP	FSL	21	21	15	79.3	93	35	67	4	5.90	7.70	13.3	5.1	5.4	1.2	7.68	-19.5	-6
2001	BOW	EAS	22	12	0	12.3	5	2	14	0	0.73	1.22	4.1	1.9	6.8	0.2	1.32	5.7	18
2001	ROC	INT	22	34	0	43.3	39	19	48	4	3.74	5.02	8.5	4.6	7.7	1.1	4.78	1.7	7
2001	BAL	AL	22	18	0	21.3	25	9	22	2	3.80	5.15	10.4	3.5	8.6	0.8	5.21	0.5	17
2002	BAL	AL	23	67	0	68.0	55	27	55	5	1.99	3.21	7.7	3.4	7.2	0.6	3.26	16.4	11
2003	BAL	AL	24	47	1	63.7	64	27	51	8	4.36	4.55	9.1	3.6	6.8	1.0	4.65	9.7	-1

Breakout: 15%   Improve: 41%   Collapse: 25%

Julio was the sixth different pitcher to lead the Orioles in saves in the last six years, following Randy Myers, Armando Benitez, Mike Timlin, Ryan Kohlmeier, and Buddy Groom. What makes him different from the previous leaders? He's younger than any of the others, and has much better stuff than Kohlmeier or Timlin did. The job is clearly his in a way it never was for Groom, and he's still on the team. On the other hand, none of them pitched as poorly in the year prior to becoming the closer than Julio did—yes, even Kohlmeier had a better translated ERA than Julio did in 2001. The stats say Julio was a little on the lucky side in 2002, allowing eight fewer hits than expected, and four fewer runs than expected even after allowing for the hit shortage. Add in that Julio's strikeout rate, while good, was under what you expect from your elite closers, and you have a strong candidate for a sophomore slump.

Rommie Lewis Born: 02-Sep-82 Age: 20 Bats: L Throws: L

YEAR	TM	LG	AGE	G	GS	IP	H	BB	SO	HR	ERA	EQERA	EQH9	EQBB9	EQSO9	EQHR9	PERA	VORP	STF
2002	DEL	SAL	19	53	0	71.0	50	20	77	1	2.15	3.93	9.1	3.6	6.1	0.4	3.82	11.4	4

He's not supposed to be a closer, but that's what the Orioles might end up with. A fourth round pick in 2001 with a wicked-moving fastball, Lewis was supposed to be a starter at one of the short-season clubs; they just put him in Delmarva's bullpen to get his feet wet. But before they could follow that plan, he had established himself as the top relief pitcher on the staff, dominating Sally League hitters; he allowed only four runs after May. Have the Orioles hampered his development by keeping him in the closer role? Sending him down wouldn't make any sense, and Delmarva's starters were all doing fairly well, and I can fully appreciate not sending him up into the chamber of horrors that Frederick was last year, so I'm not sure they made a bad decision. What they do with him in 2003 is something else, however.

Rodrigo Lopez Born: 14-Dec-75 Age: 27 Bats: R Throws: R

YEAR	TM	LG	AGE	G	GS	IP	H	BB	SO	HR	ERA	EQERA	EQH9	EQBB9	EQSO9	EQHR9	PERA	VORP	STF
2000	LVG	PCL	24	20	20	109.3	123	45	100	9	4.69	4.78	10.1	3.6	6.5	0.9	4.93	8.8	12
2000	SDP	NL	24	6	6	24.7	40	13	17	5	8.74	8.64	15.5	3.9	5.6	1.7	8.97	-8.6	-11
2001	POR	PCL	25	11	8	52.3	45	15	37	7	3.44	4.34	9.0	3.1	4.8	1.5	4.25	6.7	-2
2002	BAL	AL	26	33	28	196.7	172	62	136	23	3.57	3.84	8.4	2.7	6.2	1.0	3.63	36.2	13
2003	BAL	AL	27	26	22	139.0	147	51	95	18	4.66	4.87	9.5	3.0	5.8	1.1	4.71	13.4	6

Breakout: 11%   Improve: 45%   Collapse: 17%

It is certainly possible that the Orioles' late swoon cost Lopez the Rookie of the Year award. However, he was part of the problem down the stretch, going 1–4 with a 5.80 ERA after going 14–5, 3.36 beforehand. More basically, where did he come from?

Mexico, and no, that's not a joke. San Diego released him after an injury-plagued 2001, even though he'd pitched well at Portland. He then had one of the best Winter League seasons of 2001, going 10–2 for Culiacan in the Mexican Pacific League, which doesn't reflect his 5–0 record in the playoffs. In all, Lopez threw about 110 innings in winter ball, followed by 197 more in the 2002 season, and simply wore out. He's not supposed to pitch for Culiacan this year, although he did pitch for the All-Star team in Japan.

Calvin Maduro — Born: 05-Sep-74 — Age: 28 — Bats: R — Throws: R

YEAR	TM	LG	AGE	G	GS	IP	H	BB	SO	HR	ERA	EQERA	EQH9	EQBB9	EQSO9	EQHR9	PERA	VORP	STF
2000	BAL	AL	25	15	2	23.3	29	16	18	8	9.66	7.85	10.0	4.8	6.5	2.5	7.72	-6.3	-19
2001	ROC	INT	26	12	11	67.0	61	22	48	9	4.03	4.71	8.7	3.5	5.0	1.6	4.84	5.9	-2
2001	BAL	AL	26	22	12	93.7	83	36	51	10	4.23	3.87	8.0	3.3	4.6	0.9	3.78	16.7	-1
2002	BAL	AL	27	12	10	56.7	64	22	29	12	5.56	5.95	10.7	3.3	4.6	1.8	5.83	-2.9	-11
2003	LAD	NL	28	18	12	81.3	82	37	51	12	4.67	5.42	9.6	3.6	4.9	1.3	5.42	2.0	-6

Breakout: 16%   Improve: 45%   Collapse: 27%

During the spring, Maduro suffered what was called a strained forearm. After taking two weeks off, he came back and pitched hideously for two months, then revealed that his elbow has been stiff and had never really cleared up. New tests showed a fractured elbow and bone chips, and the resulting surgery finished his season, although the Oriole medical staff, as ever, initially prescribed rest to take care of the problem. I could call this Oriole Medicine, part 3, but I'm going to give them a pass on this one, since it's pretty clear that the patient wasn't entirely forthcoming about his symptoms. He's been released.

John Maine — Born: 08-May-81 — Age: 22 — Bats: R — Throws: R

YEAR	TM	LG	AGE	G	GS	IP	H	BB	SO	HR	ERA	EQERA	EQH9	EQBB9	EQSO9	EQHR9	PERA	VORP	STF
2002	ABE	NYP	21	4	2	10.3	6	3	21	0	1.75	2.83	7.0	3.9	10.4	0.3	2.95	3.0	38
2002	DEL	SAL	21	6	5	33.0	21	4	39	0	1.36	3.17	8.0	1.5	6.5	0.3	2.70	8.5	29

In 2001, sophomore John Maine of UNC-Charlotte was the Conference USA Pitcher of the Year, and one of the top pitchers in the nation. He had to work hard to get there: 134 innings, 144 strikeouts, and 53 walks made the national (and not just conference) leader boards, and a rough estimate from his stat line numbers suggests that he averaged over a hundred pitches per game. Yes, we like to say that's a little rough for a 20-year-old. He struggled badly through his junior season, and instead of moving up into the first round, he fell to the Orioles in the sixth. Whatever problems he had in college disappeared in the pros. He completely overmatched New York-Penn league hitters, and wasn't much worse in the Sally. Few pitchers can manage a stuff score of 30 for any length of time, but Maine did. Staying healthy—that specter from college and the bugbear of this franchise—will be his biggest test.

Yorkis Perez — Born: 30-Sep-67 — Age: 35 — Bats: B — Throws: L

YEAR	TM	LG	AGE	G	GS	IP	H	BB	SO	HR	ERA	EQERA	EQH9	EQBB9	EQSO9	EQHR9	PERA	VORP	STF
2000	HOU	NL	32	33	0	22.7	25	14	21	4	5.15	5.81	9.2	4.3	7.1	1.3	5.77	-1.1	-8
2002	ROC	INT	34	28	0	40.3	42	20	44	4	3.80	5.17	10.2	5.4	8.4	1.3	5.75	0.9	-1
2002	BAL	AL	34	23	0	27.3	21	14	25	4	3.30	4.01	7.2	4.3	8.1	1.3	3.86	4.2	4
2003	BAL	AL	35	35	1	40.7	45	25	40	5	4.70	4.91	9.9	5.0	8.3	1.1	4.94	7.1	2

Breakout: 13%   Improve: 46%   Collapse: 28%

Originally signed just for Rochester, he earned a promotion and pitched well for two months before an appendectomy ended his season. If he was right-handed, his career would have already ended, but he is practically set for life as a LOOGY.

Sidney Ponson — Born: 02-Nov-76 — Age: 26 — Bats: R — Throws: R

YEAR	TM	LG	AGE	G	GS	IP	H	BB	SO	HR	ERA	EQERA	EQH9	EQBB9	EQSO9	EQHR9	PERA	VORP	STF
2000	BAL	AL	23	32	32	222.0	223	83	152	30	4.82	4.12	8.5	2.7	6.0	1.0	4.14	34.2	16
2001	BAL	AL	24	23	23	138.3	161	37	84	21	4.95	5.09	10.5	2.3	5.2	1.3	5.16	6.4	7
2002	BAL	AL	25	28	28	176.0	172	63	120	26	4.09	4.50	9.3	3.1	6.1	1.3	4.47	19.7	10
2003	BAL	AL	26	26	24	155.0	162	52	103	22	4.50	4.70	9.4	2.8	5.6	1.2	4.66	18.0	7

Breakout: 12%   Improve: 50%   Collapse: 14%

Fully recovered from his gateway injury of elbow tendonitis of 2001, Ponson advanced to the harder stuff—shoulder tendonitis—in 2002. Except that, as long as he was going off on this sort of bender to start off with, he chased the tendonitis with a partially torn labrum speedball. He pitched through it in September, apparently without incident, but everyone should be very wary of him in 2003. He's been a health risk for the last two years, and he's a much larger risk than PECOTA seems to indicate.

Matt Riley　　　　Born: 02-Aug-79　　Age: 23　　Bats: L　　Throws: L

YEAR	TM	LG	AGE	G	GS	IP	H	BB	SO	HR	ERA	EQERA	EQH9	EQBB9	EQSO9	EQHR9	PERA	VORP	STF
2000	BOW	EAS	20	19	14	74.0	74	49	66	9	6.08	7.54	11.6	6.8	6.2	2.1	6.94	-16.8	-6
2002	BOW	EAS	22	22	22	109.3	136	48	105	12	6.34	7.23	13.3	4.8	6.7	1.7	7.38	-20.9	3

Riley was an outrageously good pitcher with an outrageous personality before getting injured way back in June of 1999. Since then he's never been the same. Yes, he managed to finish the '99 season, and he even managed to pitch into August of 2000 before his elbow blew out completely, but by then he was a bad pitcher. All of 2001 was lost following his Tommy John surgery, and in 2002 he came back to Bowie, still a bad pitcher. And then a glimmer of life started to come back into his arm:

Stats	G	IP	H	R	BB	SO	RA	H/9	K/9
At Bowie thru 6/24	11	53.2	78	52	22	48	8.72	13.08	8.05
At Bowie after	11	55.2	58	32	26	57	5.17	9.38	9.22

I'm not saying that's good—a 5.17 ERA in Double-A is definitely not good—but the peripherals and age move him back onto the "prospect" side of the talent line. He might not be done just yet.

Willis Roberts　　　　Born: 19-Jun-75　　Age: 28　　Bats: R　　Throws: R

YEAR	TM	LG	AGE	G	GS	IP	H	BB	SO	HR	ERA	EQERA	EQH9	EQBB9	EQSO9	EQHR9	PERA	VORP	STF
2000	CHT	SOU	25	5	5	32.3	33	13	28	0	3.07	4.81	11.3	4.0	5.5	0.3	5.40	2.5	7
2000	LOU	INT	25	25	20	124.0	138	55	66	19	5.66	6.11	11.2	4.0	4.1	1.8	6.23	-8.5	-14
2001	BAL	AL	26	46	18	132.0	142	55	95	15	4.91	4.81	9.6	3.5	6.1	1.0	4.87	9.6	0
2002	BAL	AL	27	66	0	75.0	79	32	51	5	3.36	4.41	10.1	3.6	6.0	0.6	4.47	8.1	-3
2003	*BAL*	*AL*	*28*	*35*	*5*	*57.7*	*64*	*27*	*38*	*8*	*4.73*	*4.94*	*10.0*	*3.8*	*5.5*	*1.1*	*5.24*	*6.2*	*-11*

Breakout: 15%　　Improve: 44%　　Collapse: 29%

In 2001, Roberts was the golden child from the Caribbean, setting in between Jose Mercedes and Rodrigo Lopez for that honor. A sizzling April from the pen got him into the rotation, but he cooled off and was back in the pen by July. He took over as the closer in August, but blew three out of four chances in September, losing Hargrove's confidence. Julio beat him out for the closer's job in the spring. Though Roberts pitched well, Julio was sensational. Roberts wound up as the setup man, backup closer, and third wheel in a pen dominated by Julio and Groom, waiting for a stumble by Julio that never came.

B. J. Ryan　　　　Born: 28-Dec-75　　Age: 27　　Bats: L　　Throws: L

YEAR	TM	LG	AGE	G	GS	IP	H	BB	SO	HR	ERA	EQERA	EQH9	EQBB9	EQSO9	EQHR9	PERA	VORP	STF
2000	ROC	INT	24	14	4	24.7	23	9	28	4	4.74	4.93	9.3	3.3	8.7	1.9	4.94	1.4	10
2000	BAL	AL	24	42	0	42.7	36	31	41	7	5.90	4.78	6.9	5.2	8.2	1.2	4.55	2.8	4
2001	BAL	AL	25	61	0	53.0	47	30	54	6	4.25	4.60	7.8	4.7	8.5	0.9	4.33	4.6	7
2002	BAL	AL	26	67	0	57.7	51	33	56	7	4.68	4.72	8.3	4.8	8.5	1.0	4.43	4.2	3
2003	*BAL*	*AL*	*27*	*48*	*0*	*59.0*	*58*	*30*	*52*	*8*	*4.62*	*4.83*	*8.8*	*4.2*	*7.5*	*1.1*	*4.72*	*7.4*	*0*

Breakout: 16%　　Improve: 44%　　Collapse: 32%

A tall lefty with a funky motion and high socks, Ryan's career looks to be going down the LOOGY sidetrack. Unfortunately, that's not a very good place for him. First, his stuff is too good to be wasted in such a limited role. Second, his delivery works much better from the windup than the stretch; you want to make sure he can start the inning with the bases empty, and you certainly don't want to throw him into a fire that's already lit.

Rich Stahl　　　　Born: 11-Apr-81　　Age: 22　　Bats: R　　Throws: L

YEAR	TM	LG	AGE	G	GS	IP	H	BB	SO	HR	ERA	EQERA	EQH9	EQBB9	EQSO9	EQHR9	PERA	VORP	STF
2000	DEL	SAL	19	20	20	89.0	97	51	83	3	3.34	7.31	13.9	7.4	5.1	0.9	8.28	-17.8	-11
2001	DEL	SAL	20	6	6	33.7	24	15	31	3	2.67	5.56	9.9	6.4	4.9	2.1	5.71	-0.2	-5
2001	FRD	CRL	20	6	6	32.3	26	15	24	1	1.95	5.40	10.1	6.4	4.3	0.7	5.31	0.4	-4
2002	DEL	SAL	21	2	2	9.7	10	5	9	3	5.57	11.00	21.5	8.4	6.6	10.0	10.75	-5.9	-44

A former first round pick, high school pitcher, and recipient of big money to lure him away from Georgia Tech. Those are the sorts of things that should set off alarms in your head, since the punchline is pretty familiar: the Orioles have gotten three injury-shortened seasons and two shoulder surgeries. Stahl's potential continues to rate high with *Baseball America* and other publications, but we're not dealing with a Ryan Anderson, Matt Riley, or Eric Bedard here. Those players performed well before their turns under the knife, and Stahl hasn't. He's more like Bobby Seay.

John Stephens

Born: 15-Nov-79   Age: 23   Bats: R   Throws: R

YEAR	TM	LG	AGE	G	GS	IP	H	BB	SO	HR	ERA	EQERA	EQH9	EQBB9	EQSO9	EQHR9	PERA	VORP	STF
2000	FRD	CRL	20	20	20	118.0	119	22	121	5	3.05	4.79	11.8	2.0	5.8	0.9	5.28	9.4	17
2001	BOW	EAS	21	18	17	132.0	95	21	130	10	1.84	2.98	7.7	1.9	6.1	1.1	3.21	37.0	24
2001	ROC	INT	21	9	9	58.0	52	19	61	5	4.03	4.42	8.5	3.4	7.3	1.0	4.33	7.0	25
2002	ROC	INT	22	21	21	142.7	126	23	118	10	3.03	3.43	8.5	1.7	6.3	0.9	3.52	32.9	24
2002	BAL	AL	22	12	11	65.0	68	22	56	13	6.09	5.67	9.8	2.9	7.6	1.7	5.14	-1.2	20
2003	*BAL*	*AL*	*23*	*22*	*18*	*116.3*	*123*	*36*	*86*	*16*	*4.52*	*4.72*	*9.5*	*2.6*	*6.3*	*1.1*	*4.55*	*15.0*	*10*

Breakout: 6%   Improve: 40%   Collapse: 23%

My favorite pitcher in pro ball, getting hitters out on pitches that could be caught bare-handed. There was a time, way back when, that this Aussie was a hard thrower, but that was before a neck injury pinched a nerve in his shoulder that never really healed properly. But as a pitcher, he did, and even though the scouts always looked away, he kept succeeding at every level, until the Orioles finally had to call him up. When they did, he got lit up like a dry pine in Yellowstone . . . not that the squeezed strike zone he got from the home plate umpire that first night helped any. The Orioles stayed with him, and while he pitched better after the first two games, he had extraordinary trouble once runners got on base; that hasn't been a problem for him before. PECOTA shares the scouts' doubts, and history hasn't been kind to right-handed soft-tossers, but it's impossible to not root for the guy.

Josh Towers

Born: 26-Feb-77   Age: 26   Bats: R   Throws: R

YEAR	TM	LG	AGE	G	GS	IP	H	BB	SO	HR	ERA	EQERA	EQH9	EQBB9	EQSO9	EQHR9	PERA	VORP	STF
2000	ROC	INT	23	24	24	148.0	157	21	102	17	3.47	4.26	10.7	1.3	5.4	1.3	4.57	20.5	13
2001	ROC	INT	24	6	6	41.0	40	8	27	2	3.51	3.82	9.0	2.0	4.6	0.6	4.06	7.7	10
2001	BAL	AL	24	24	20	140.3	165	16	58	21	4.49	4.59	10.7	1.0	3.6	1.3	4.75	14.1	1
2002	ROC	INT	25	15	13	69.0	109	14	43	16	7.57	8.89	16.1	2.2	4.9	3.1	9.10	-26.0	-19
2002	BAL	AL	25	5	3	27.3	42	5	13	11	7.91	8.33	14.4	1.6	4.2	3.5	8.73	-8.6	-18
2003	*TOR*	*AL*	*26*	*11*	*8*	*48.0*	*65*	*13*	*25*	*8*	*5.96*	*5.77*	*11.9*	*2.2*	*4.6*	*1.3*	*5.54*	*1.9*	*-5*

Breakout: 12%   Improve: 38%   Collapse: 29%

Towers was the early edition of John Stephens, helping pave Stephens's way by showing that a soft-tossing control freak could have some success, winning Rookie of the Month in August 2001. Unfortunately, Towers never had Stephens's curve, and in 2002 he had nothing at all. It was BP (and we don't mean us) every time out, in Baltimore and Rochester, and he ran up a combined 0–12 record before his season mercifully ended. The Orioles dropped him from their 40-man, and the Jays scooped him up.

Boston Red Sox

Summer passed into fall and once again Boston fans are left looking to next year. Despite winning 93 games and finishing with the fifth-best record in the league, the 2002 season has to rank as a disappointment. Local expectations in spring training had Boston contending for the division crown against the Yankees, with the loser taking the wild card. While the predicted number of wins was not wildly different from what was actually achieved, fans were certain that the Sox would at the very least be in serious contention throughout September.

These high expectations were further fueled by a hot start. Fired by the early-season heroics of Shea Hillenbrand, the energy of free-agent acquisition Johnny Damon, and a 7–0 record from John Burkett, the Sox cruised to a 40–17 record on June 6. They had the best record in the league, held a 3.5 game lead over the hated Yankees, and were a full six games ahead of the Angels in the wild card race. What could possibly go wrong after a start like that? Fans calculated that they needed only a 60–45 record in their remaining games to reach a hundred wins for what seemed likely to be their first division title since 1995. In a collapse reminiscent of 1978, the Red Sox wilted in the summer heat while the other contenders surged. After losing two of three to the Yankees to begin September, the Red Sox were 8.5 games behind their division rival and 6.5 games behind the Angels for the wild card. Attitudes soured, the press turned ugly, and Boston sports fans turned to football for release.

The struggles in 2001 were comparatively easy to identify. Nomar Garciaparra's ill-timed wrist surgery cost him the first four months of the season, and hampered his offensive production after his return. Pedro Martinez missed twelve starts, straining the depth of both the rotation and the bullpen. Jason Varitek was lost for the second half of the season after breaking his right elbow, leaving the pitching staff

in the hands of backup backstops Doug Mirabelli and Scott Hatteberg. Finally, injuries and suspensions tripped up Carl Everett. In the face of all that, a second-place finish was perhaps understandable.

In 2002, you might think the Red Sox were going to reprise these sorts of difficulties. They lost their putative #2 starter, Dustin Hermanson, to a groin strained while pitching on a wet Fenway mound. He would pitch only 22 innings on the season. But the only other major injury was the broken left index finger suffered by Manny Ramirez on an ill-conceived "hustle" play when he slid headfirst into Dan Wilson's shin guard. This cost the Bosox cleanup hitter six weeks of play, during which the team nevertheless managed a winning record. Teams cannot expect a perfect bill of health over a full season; unlike 2001, injuries cannot be blamed for the collapse in 2002.

By at least one measure, the Red Sox played well enough to make the playoffs. As new owner John Henry pointed out during the season, "We lead the league in hitting. And we lead the league in pitching. So why aren't we in first place?" They finished the season second in runs scored and third in runs allowed (unadjusted for park factors). Using Pythagenports to translate this into an expected record, the Sox might have finished in a virtual tie with the Yankees for the division lead, with the loser qualifying for the wild card bid (see table 1).

If Boston scored as many runs as the other playoff contenders and their pitching was as effective as the other playoff contenders, why then did they fall six games short? You might initially guess that the run totals were inflated by blowouts against Tampa Bay (22 runs) and Texas (19 runs), while the runs allowed were inordinately influenced by 17 shutouts. There may be some truth to this, but neither mathematics nor experience supports the argument. A quick analy-

Red Sox Prospectus

2002 record: 93–69; Second place, AL East

Pythagenport Record: 100–62

Runs scored per game: 5.3 (2nd in AL)

Runs allowed per game: 4.1 (3rd in AL)

Team EqA: .271 (3rd in AL)

2002 Batters Age: 30.4 (3rd oldest in AL)

2002 Pitchers Age: 31.8 (2nd oldest in AL)

Ballpark: Fenway Park; Neutral park; Park Factor of .996

2002: Interim management came close with another odd blend of superstars and journeymen.

2003: Smart short-term patches will keep them in contention while they try to salvage a desolate farm system.

Table 1. What Could'a Been

Team	G	RS	RA	Est. Win%	Projected W-L	
Anaheim	162	851	644	0.629	102	60
Yankees	161	897	697	0.620	100	61
Boston	162	859	665	0.620	100	62
Oakland	162	800	654	0.594	96	66
Seattle	162	814	699	0.572	93	69
Minnesota	161	768	712	0.536	86	75

sis can be performed by probabilistically matching the distribution of runs scored against the distribution of runs allowed (breaking any ties evenly—a conservative assumption for a strong team). Calculating the projected record this way would merely lower the Sox total to 97 wins, still third in the league. One also observes that Oakland (with 19 shutouts) outperformed their Pythagenport projection by as much of a margin as the Red Sox missed by, so the number of shutouts would not seem to be the answer either.

A more significant factor might be Boston's record in one-run games. While experience suggests that a team's record in close games is generally closer to .500 than their overall record, the Red Sox finished the season with a dismal 13–23 record in one-run games. This is something the Red Sox had in common with the Devil Rays (17–28) and Royals (14–27), but not any of the contending teams. The success of the Twins (29–16) in one-run games was a component of their 13.5 game lead over the White Sox (15–21), while the A's (32–14) enjoyed their success in the close games, leaving Seattle (24–25) in the dust.

Though the record in close games is largely random, rookie manager Grady Little must shoulder some of the responsibility. Certainly the Red Sox had a weaker bullpen than any of the other contenders (reflected by the 4.25 ERA), but they still got nearly 250 quality relief innings from Embree, Urbina, Fossum, Banks, and Wakefield. With skilled management, these five pitchers could have played a larger role. Instead, Banks and Wakefield spent some of their best performances in mop-up situations, while less dependable pitchers worked in close games. Little also seemed to have difficulty taking advantage of offensive opportunities, as the Red Sox repeatedly failed to score in the late innings with the game on the line, and he appeared to be tactically overmatched at times. Nowhere was this more evident than the interleague games, in which the Red Sox finished with a 5–13 record despite only being outscored by a 70–63 margin.

Justice may have been served in the end, as the teams that made the playoffs clearly deserved to be there. Though Boston and New York had split their regular season series, the AL East champs had a clearly superior offense and greater pitching depth. Oakland had finished the regular sea-

son in impressive fashion after a slow start, while Anaheim was the strongest regular season team (by Pythagenport analysis), and made quick work of both of their AL opponents on their way to the World Series. Both AL West teams, of course, faced more difficult divisional matchups than the AL East contenders (who played 19 games each against Tampa Bay, Toronto, and Baltimore). Even had they made the playoffs, the Red Sox would not have been favored to advance.

This Red Sox team that fell short was the parting gift of erstwhile GM Dan Duquette. Over his eight-year tenure, the oft-vilified Duke assembled what could be the core of a championship team. Unfortunately, he struggled to turn that promise into reality, repeatedly overspending on a weak supporting cast while mismanaging relations with the players and the media. The change of ownership in February sealed his fate, as Duquette was replaced by vice-president of baseball operations Mike Port. To Duquette's credit, when he took over in 1994, he inherited a major league team coming off consecutive losing seasons that had a minor league system that was almost totally barren. The only remaining current Red Sox players to predate Duquette's reign are Trot Nixon and Lou Merloni. Allowing the stars of the previous regime to move on in a series of controversial decisions—marked by the controversial failures to re-sign Roger Clemens and Mo Vaughn—Duquette improved the team one piece at a time without entering a rebuilding phase. While this approach kept the Sox in regular contention, it may have limited the quality of the final product.

Most successful teams build their core through player development, investing wisely through the amateur draft and international signings. While Duquette publicly espoused this goal when he was hired, his actions did not consistently follow this philosophy. A strong 1994 draft produced Nomar Garciaparra and several lesser prospects, but it was followed by conservative drafting and a failure to sign high-profile talent (notably Mark Texiera in 1998). Strong teams that sign free agents do not receive many high draft picks. With only one pick since 1995 in the top half of the first round, the failure to ink the "hard sign" talents is particularly disturbing. Hoping to supplement weak drafts, the Red Sox invested heavily in Asian talent, acquiring Korean pitchers Jin-Ho Cho, Sun-Woo Kim, Sang-Hoon Lee, and Seung Song, as well as Japanese pitcher Tomokazu Ohka. Unfortunately, most of the imports flopped, and only Ohka and Song (both now Expos) remain as serious prospects.

As part consequence and part symptom of these failures, the Red Sox saw significant contributions (50+ innings or 200+ PA) from only five homegrown players last year. In addition to Trot Nixon and Lou Merloni (both drafted under Duquette's predecessor Lou Gorman), the only position players developed by the Sox in recent years are Nomar

Garciaparra (1997) and Shea Hillenbrand (2001). The pitching cupboard has been equally bare; Casey Fossum could become the first Sox draftee to record 150+ innings with the Red Sox since Aaron Sele. While a few more recent selections are working their way through the minors, the farm system is one of the weakest in baseball. It is clear that Duquette ultimately failed to revitalize the farm system.

This is not to say that the Red Sox system has been entirely unproductive. The Red Sox have developed several players who are now with other teams. In a futile attempt to patch a sinking ship over the last three years, the Sox have parted with nearly a dozen prospects to acquire a series of overpaid veterans and free-agent stopgaps. Not only did the Sox fail to make the playoffs in any of those seasons, few of the veterans acquired remain with the club, while several of the prospects given up are featured prominently in the plans of their new teams.

There were three particularly infuriating losses. During the 2000 season, while mediocrities such as Ed Sprague, Rico Brogna, and Izzy Alcantara graced the 40-man roster, David Eckstein was waived in August. Though his batting average that year was disappointing, Eckstein had cranked out good OBPs at every stop in the minors. The following spring the hustling infielder posted a respectable rookie season with the Angels, followed by an even better season in 2002. Meanwhile, the Red Sox have endured mediocrity from Mike Lansing and Rey Sanchez, spending nearly $8 million to cover the position that Eckstein could have filled for next to nothing.

That same season, the Sox traded Chris Reitsma for an aged Dante Bichette, the only DH in the league to hit like an adequate second baseman. Reitsma made his big league debut with the Reds in 2001, working 182 innings with a mediocre 5.29 ERA, and improving on that in 2002 with 21 starts totaling 138 innings and a 3.64 ERA. Meanwhile, the Red Sox paid Frank Castillo $4.5 million for a 4.22 ERA in 2001 and a 5.07 ERA in 2002. Little difference, you say? Keep in mind that Reitsma's career should continue to improve, while Castillo will leave the Red Sox with nothing but a lighter wallet for their troubles.

Finally, the Sox traded Tomokazu Ohka (and Rich Rundles) for Ugueth Urbina, an unexceptional closer, in an attempt to save the 2001 season. While this trade improved the bullpen and eventually allowed Derek Lowe to try his arm in the rotation, without Ohka the Sox still needed another starting pitcher in 2002. Thus they parted with two more prospects for Dustin Hermanson, a pitcher known primarily for his durability, but less and less of that while his performance kept sinking over the years. Hermanson broke down, while Ohka threw 193 innings of a 3.18 ERA and won 13 games. Between Urbina and Hermanson, the Red Sox ultimately spent over $13 million for a hundred mediocre

innings, while Ohka provided nearly twice the innings of quality pitching at a fraction of the price.

While some of the other traded prospects have already washed out, others are prominently featured with their new teams. The Padres are pleased with Dennis Tankersley, while Justin Duchsherer will figure in Texas. The Red Sox are likely to regret parting with Seung Song after having failed to retain Cliff Floyd. While Sun-Woo Kim, the other prospect in the deal, pitched impressively at the end of the season, it's Song that has the potential to become a top-of-the-rotation starter. If healthy, expect to see him in the majors as early as 2003, while the Sox continue their hunt for reliable pitching.

In the end, the Sox needed to buy frequently on the free agent market to build this team. Led by Manny Ramirez and Johnny Damon, the Sox have paid top dollar for offensive stars and depth in the rotation. As you might expect for any team spending heavily on aging veterans, this leaves the Sox prone to injuries and late-career declines. This season the goats included first basemen Jose Offerman and Tony Clark, who combined for over 600 PA of a composite performance that was 25 runs below replacement level, all for the low, low price of $11.5 million. Similarly, the Sox hoped for a better return on the $8 million spent on John Burkett and Frank Castillo. Teams relying heavily on veteran free agents will often be disappointed. Unless a team has the payroll and resources of the Yankees, this strategy will produce more second-place finishes than championships.

While Mike Port successfully managed the front office from Duquette's departure in February through the end of the season, it was clear that the owners had little faith in him over the long term. Their first choice for the job was Blue Jays GM J. P. Ricciardi, who instead signed a five-year contract extension. Seeking next to raid the Athletics' brain trust, the Red Sox wooed Billy Beane with a hefty raise. Once again, their candidate chose to stay put.

The intriguing name that kept popping up throughout the search was that of Assistant GM Theo Epstein. While the owners were initially wary of the reaction of the Boston press to his youth, the accolades Epstein received from both Beane and Ricciardi may have finally contributed to the decision to hand him the job. A lifetime Red Sox fan and analysis disciple, Epstein brings new energy to Yawkey Way. In his first few weeks, he's already initiated several innovations. Most curious is the use of statistical modeling to find the most improved players in the minor leagues, so that their *coaches* might be hired for the Red Sox system. Equally important to player development will be the "vertical integration of teaching," allowing the same fundamentals to be emphasized at every level of the system.

Epstein's hand will also be felt at the major league level and on the pitching staff, as he has already "suggested" that manager Grady Little try arrangements other than the standard setup/closer roles in the pen. In allowing Urbina to walk, Epstein seems to have accepted the idea that closers are overrated and overpaid, and with a mix including Bobby Howry and Alan Embree and imports Mike Timlin, Ramiro Mendoza, and the always-unpredictable Chad Fox, this year's pen should be a dramatic improvement on last year's. While it is too early to definitively assess Epstein's performance, it is encouraging to hear him speak out against conventional foolishness in his press conferences.

The offense features some returning stars, including Ramirez, Garciaparra, and Damon. Beyond that trio, the line-up is rife with uncertainty and change. Hillenbrand again frustrated fans, producing All-Star numbers in April and May but eating outs like Jim Corsi at a buffet throughout June, July, and September. Averaged over the year, Hillenbrand presents himself as one of the better offensive players on the team, but taken month by month, he frightens analysts who have no idea what to expect. Hillenbrand will be encouraged to improve his plate discipline this year, as he's being asked to watch video of at-bats he threw away through poor selectivity. After breakout seasons in 2001, both Varitek and Nixon regressed to their prior norms. Both remain respectable supporting players, yet neither produces consistently enough to serve in a key offensive role.

Addressing the remaining three positions in the lineup was the top priority for Epstein in the winter meetings. His first move was to trade A-ball prospects Tony Blanco and Josh Thigpen for Todd Walker to man second. Rey Sanchez gave the Red Sox exactly what they might reasonably have expected: consistent play at the keystone and light offensive contributions. Although Walker has limited defensive range, he can be counted on for at least league-average offense at the position. Acquired as a one-year stopgap, Walker may

give way to prospect Freddy Sanchez in 2004. With a year of Triple-A under his belt, this younger Sanchez may ultimately combine the best traits of his predecessors in a low-cost package.

Of greater impact was the acquisition of talented DH Jeremy Giambi for Josh Hancock. Giambi's power and patience makes him an offensive force to complement Manny Ramirez in the lineup. Though he has never been given more than 450 PA in a season, his recent development suggests that he is finally ready for a full-time role. Despite his defensive inadequacies, the Red Sox are likely to find a way to keep his bat in the lineup.

The Red Sox still have that hole at first base. While Brian Daubach filled the job capably, his difficulties with left-handed pitching and his rising salary led the team to look in other directions. Having traded prospect Luis Garcia and given up on heavyweights Juan Diaz and Calvin Pickering, Epstein is considering his options. Julio Zuleta is performing well in the Mexican Winter League and may have earned a look in spring training, and who knows what might happen with Derrek Lee's availability. One intriguing possibility is current third-base prospect Kevin Youkilis.

The core of this team is intact through 2004, giving these Red Sox at least two more shots at a ring. Epstein appears to be spending carefully, hopefully giving the Red Sox better balance and fewer offensive holes than they have suffered in the past. With roughly $10 million of payroll freed by the departure of Cliff Floyd, the Red Sox are well situated to pursue non-tendered free agents and salary-driven trade offers. If spent wisely, the club should be in position for 95 to 100 wins this year. If spent foolishly, or if injuries again rear their ugly head, the Sox could again finish below 90 wins.

HITTERS

Benny Agbayani   LF   Born: 28-Dec-71   Age: 31   Bats: R   Throws: R

YEAR	TM	LG	AGE	AB	H	2B	3B	HR	BB	SO	SB	CS	AVG	OBP	SLG	MLVR	EQBA	EQOBP	EQSLG	EQMLVR	VORP	DEFENSE
2000	NYM	NL	28	350	101	20	1	15	54	68	5	5	.289	.394	.480	.169	.293	.388	.487	.170	25.9	84-LF -1
2001	NYM	NL	29	296	82	14	2	6	36	73	4	5	.277	.365	.399	.025	.290	.373	.416	.043	11.3	66-LF -5
2002	COL	NL	30	117	24	5	0	4	10	35	1	0	.205	.268	.350	-.246	.197	.260	.342	-.339	-7.6	28-LF 1
2002	CSP	PCL	30	147	40	8	1	11	28	32	1	0	.272	.395	.565	.251	.231	.344	.463	.007	3.8	26-LF -1
2002	BOS	AL	30	37	11	1	0	0	6	5	0	0	.297	.395	.324	.014	.324	.432	.351	.090	1.8	13-LF -1
2003	BOS	AL	31	186	46	10	1	5	21	41	3	1	.246	.326	.392	-.059	.251	.334	.411	-.063	-1.4	

Breakout: 15%   Improve: 42%   Collapse: 35%

A useful role-player at his peak, Agbayani has fallen on hard times. Even Coors Field failed to make him look good, and with declining power and limited defensive skills, the hefty Hawaiian will be lucky to find a bench job. The Red Sox have re-signed him.

Shane Andrews   3B   Born: 28-Aug-71   Age: 31   Bats: R   Throws: R

YEAR	TM	LG	AGE	AB	H	2B	3B	HR	BB	SO	SB	CS	AVG	OBP	SLG	MLVR	EQBA	EQOBP	EQSLG	EQMLVR	VORP	DEFENSE			
2000	CHC	NL	28	192	44	5	0	14	27	59	1	1	.229	.330	.474	-.025	.232	.322	.474	-.018	9.2	46-3B	-1		
2001	MEM	PCL	29	193	42	9	1	9	33	63	2	0	.218	.341	.415	-.060	.199	.308	.372	-.203	-6.0	42-1B	-3	12-3B	0
2002	PAW	INT	30	390	100	19	1	22	52	123	1	1	.256	.348	.479	.136	.242	.328	.453	-.027	17.4	75-3B	-4	13-1B	0
2002	BOS	AL	30	13	1	1	0	0	1	3	0	0	.077	.200	.154	-.668	.077	.190	.154	-.777	-2.1				
2003	BOS	AL	31	163	36	8	0	7	19	49	2	2	.222	.309	.398	-.097	.227	.316	.416	-.104	.2				

Breakout: 21%   Improve: 49%   Collapse: 31%

Every year, Pawtucket gets stocked with enough unwanteds to fill a whole new island of misfit toys. This season, the Pawsox were a junkyard of prospects from the '90s: Andrews, Warren Morris, Michael Coleman, Jeff Abbott, Todd Erdos, Don Wengert; they even employed Jamie Brewington. It didn't really help, since Pawtucket finished over thirty games out of first. Andrews still has value as a platoon partner and backup in the infield corners, but that's short of growing up to be Jim Presley, as some had hoped.

Carlos Baerga   DH   Born: 04-Nov-68   Age: 34   Bats: B   Throws: R

YEAR	TM	LG	AGE	AB	H	2B	3B	HR	BB	SO	SB	CS	AVG	OBP	SLG	MLVR	EQBA	EQOBP	EQSLG	EQMLVR	VORP	DEFENSE	
2001	lgi	ATL	32	203	64	9	3	9	19	24	3	0	.315	.388	.522	.292	.259	.314	.429	-.072	.0		
2002	BOS	AL	33	182	52	11	0	2	7	20	6	0	.286	.319	.379	-.058	.306	.341	.404	-.019	8.7	12-2B	-3
2003	BOS	AL	34	230	66	14	1	3	10	26	7	2	.289	.321	.404	-.022	.295	.329	.423	-.021	4.3		

Breakout: 19%   Improve: 54%   Collapse: 20%

After showing he could still play in the Atlantic League, Baerga proved that he can still hit major league pitching as well as you can hope for from a chunky 34-year-old. Unfortunately, that wasn't his role on this team: he saw only 40 AB at 2B, spending most of his playing time at DH and as a PH. Baerga did make his presence felt on the bench, liberally distributing hugs to his teammates. Based on the season's disappointing finish, it is hard to attribute any positive effect to this.

Tony Blanco   Born: 10-Nov-81   Age: 21   Bats: R   Throws: R

YEAR	TM	LG	AGE	AB	H	2B	3B	HR	BB	SO	SB	CS	AVG	OBP	SLG	MLVR	EQBA	EQOBP	EQSLG	EQMLVR	VORP	DEFENSE	
2001	AUG	SAL	19	370	98	23	2	17	17	78	1	0	.265	.310	.476	.161	.213	.246	.379	-.305	-11.3	47-3B	-10
2002	SAR	FSL	20	244	54	13	2	6	6	70	2	0	.221	.252	.365	-.129	.190	.206	.316	-.486	-18.3	61-3B	-19
2003	CIN	NL	31	181	41	9	1	5	19	40	1	2	.227	.304	.361	-.171	.230	.304	.374	-.178	-.6		

Breakout: 41%   Improve: 63%   Collapse: 20%

Blanco suffered a broken wrist in spring training, then scuffled for the majority of the season. While he finished strong, his future as a prospect remains in doubt. Scouts say that Blanco has the tools to play in the majors; he has failed thus far to make an impression in A-ball. His plate discipline is very poor, leaving him a relatively easy strikeout target. Traded to Cincinnati along with Josh Thigpen in the Todd Walker deal, Blanco will get another chance to put his career back together.

Tony Clark   1B   Born: 15-Jun-72   Age: 31   Bats: B   Throws: R

YEAR	TM	LG	AGE	AB	H	2B	3B	HR	BB	SO	SB	CS	AVG	OBP	SLG	MLVR	EQBA	EQOBP	EQSLG	EQMLVR	VORP	DEFENSE	
2000	DET	AL	28	208	57	14	0	13	24	51	0	0	.274	.349	.529	.126	.285	.351	.556	.196	15.5	52-1B	4
2001	DET	AL	29	428	123	29	3	16	62	108	0	1	.287	.379	.481	.177	.308	.398	.521	.249	41.0	68-1B	8
2002	BOS	AL	30	275	57	12	1	3	21	57	0	0	.207	.266	.291	-.323	.231	.287	.325	-.289	-13.3	74-1B	5
2003	BOS	AL	31	240	60	14	1	8	25	52	0	0	.252	.323	.411	-.036	.258	.331	.430	-.038	.2		

Breakout: 22%   Improve: 50%   Collapse: 16%

When a young player fails in his first shot at the majors, the media pundits nod their heads sagely and talk about how you can never be certain how a prospect will fare in the majors. What they tend to ignore is that major league veterans also don't come with any guarantees. Tony Clark had been consistently valuable with Detroit, but then entirely fell apart this year. A prospect would have been returned to the minors by the end of April. As a highly paid veteran, Clark's performance was allowed to remain as a team millstone for the entire season.

Johnny Damon — CF — Born: 05-Nov-73 — Age: 29 — Bats: L — Throws: L

YEAR	TM	LG	AGE	AB	H	2B	3B	HR	BB	SO	SB	CS	AVG	OBP	SLG	MLVR	EQBA	EQOBP	EQSLG	EQMLVR	VORP	DEFENSE	
2000	KCR	AL	26	655	214	42	10	16	65	60	46	9	.327	.388	.495	.170	.327	.383	.497	.210	63.1	133-CF	5
2001	OAK	AL	27	644	165	34	4	9	61	70	27	12	.256	.325	.363	-.107	.274	.343	.390	-.061	19.3	154-CF	8
2002	BOS	AL	28	623	178	34	11	14	65	70	31	6	.286	.359	.443	.097	.307	.379	.477	.154	53.8	145-CF	2
2003	BOS	AL	29	556	159	33	6	11	58	61	23	5	.285	.355	.426	.058	.291	.363	.446	.065	27.6		

Breakout: 8%   Improve: 50%   Collapse: 9%

Since the Red Sox non-tendered Ellis Burks after 1992 out of fear of an excessive arbitration award, they have had trouble finding a quality center fielder. Otis Nixon could field and run, but was an offensive zero. Carl Everett wielded a passable bat, but his defense was weak and his powder-keg personality didn't win him any friends in Boston. The Red Sox may finally have their man in Damon. He's an excellent defender, a skilled baserunner, he can hit for average, and has line-drive power. Signed to a relatively modest four-year contract, Damon should thrill Sox fans for the foreseeable future.

Brian Daubach — 1B — Born: 11-Feb-72 — Age: 31 — Bats: L — Throws: R

YEAR	TM	LG	AGE	AB	H	2B	3B	HR	BB	SO	SB	CS	AVG	OBP	SLG	MLVR	EQBA	EQOBP	EQSLG	EQMLVR	VORP	DEFENSE			
2000	BOS	AL	28	495	123	32	2	21	44	130	1	1	.248	.317	.448	-.076	.256	.317	.465	-.018	9.5	73-1B	7		
2001	BOS	AL	29	407	107	28	3	22	53	108	1	0	.263	.355	.509	.142	.279	.369	.545	.204	32.7	101-1B	4	12-RF	0
2002	BOS	AL	30	444	118	24	2	20	51	126	2	1	.266	.351	.464	.094	.288	.370	.504	.158	29.5	50-1B	-1	38-LF	-1
2003	BOS	AL	31	349	89	20	1	15	41	94	2	1	.254	.336	.453	.039	.259	.345	.474	.044	7.5				

Breakout: 5%   Improve: 36%   Collapse: 28%

Over the last four years, Daubach has given the Red Sox average production at a bargain price. He is still a useful role-player, but in arbitration, he was likely to win an award more appropriate for a full-time starter. The acquisition of Jeremy Giambi, a similar player, was the death knell for Daubach's career with the Red Sox.

Cliff Floyd — OF — Born: 05-Dec-72 — Age: 30 — Bats: L — Throws: R

YEAR	TM	LG	AGE	AB	H	2B	3B	HR	BB	SO	SB	CS	AVG	OBP	SLG	MLVR	EQBA	EQOBP	EQSLG	EQMLVR	VORP	DEFENSE	
2000	FLA	NL	27	420	126	30	0	22	50	82	24	3	.300	.385	.529	.228	.304	.378	.534	.230	37.7	91-LF	-5
2001	FLA	NL	28	555	176	44	4	31	59	101	18	3	.317	.393	.578	.355	.324	.395	.590	.359	70.9	142-LF	-4
2002	FLA	NL	29	296	85	20	0	18	58	68	10	5	.287	.416	.537	.338	.296	.417	.562	.322	33.9	80-RF	0
2002	MON	NL	29	53	11	2	0	3	3	10	1	0	.208	.263	.415	-.139	.222	.262	.444	-.176	-.6		
2002	BOS	AL	29	171	54	21	0	7	15	28	4	0	.316	.378	.561	.315	.335	.397	.607	.400	21.4	23-LF	-1
2003	NYM	NL	30	490	139	31	2	26	64	97	15	4	.285	.371	.513	.180	.295	.378	.549	.227	34.9		

Breakout: 7%   Improve: 36%   Collapse: 17%

His development delayed by injuries, Floyd finally ranks among the top twenty major league hitters. Nevertheless, don't get carried away with the increase in his walk rate: in each of the last two years he received 19 intentionals. He may have difficulty sustaining that .370 OBP without those gifts. After dealing Seung Song to get him, the Red Sox could ill afford to lose Floyd's services. Floyd's medical history makes him a risky bet for a long-term deal, perhaps contributing to the lack of interest from other teams this winter. The offer he accepted from the Mets was ultimately no better than the one he initially refused from the Red Sox. A gambling man might instead have accepted the offer of arbitration from the Red Sox, giving himself the opportunity to put up some gaudy numbers in pursuit of a larger deal next year, but Steve Phillips seems to have worked his magic in convincing yet another free agent that this is the Mets' year.

Nomar Garciaparra — SS — Born: 23-Jul-73 — Age: 29 — Bats: R — Throws: R

YEAR	TM	LG	AGE	AB	H	2B	3B	HR	BB	SO	SB	CS	AVG	OBP	SLG	MLVR	EQBA	EQOBP	EQSLG	EQMLVR	VORP	DEFENSE	
2000	BOS	AL	26	529	197	51	3	21	61	50	5	2	.372	.439	.599	.484	.383	.443	.619	.549	101.9	130-SS	5
2001	BOS	AL	27	83	24	3	0	4	7	9	0	1	.289	.352	.470	.109	.301	.368	.494	.154	7.9	21-SS	-1
2002	BOS	AL	28	635	197	56	5	24	41	63	5	2	.310	.358	.528	.233	.331	.378	.568	.310	83.8	150-SS	3
2003	BOS	AL	29	595	187	45	3	24	48	63	4	1	.314	.367	.521	.227	.321	.376	.546	.249	63.0		

Breakout: 5%   Improve: 39%   Collapse: 16%

Is Garciaparra's wrist 100% recovered? In the two years prior to his injury, he was a significantly better hitter. In contrast, his 2002 season more closely approximates his line from 1998 at the age of 24. Nomar is unusual in that he has become less selective as he has matured, drawing only 41 walks last year while seeing only 3.06 pitches per plate appearance. He has also become more of a flyball hitter, dropping from a 1.25 G/F ratio in his youth to a 0.71 ratio last year. More so than Jeter, he remains an asset as a shortstop and as a hitting shortstop.

Rickey Henderson — LF — Born: 25-Dec-58 — Age: 44 — Bats: R — Throws: L

YEAR	TM	LG	AGE	AB	H	2B	3B	HR	BB	SO	SB	CS	AVG	OBP	SLG	MLVR	EQBA	EQOBP	EQSLG	EQMLVR	VORP	DEFENSE		
2000	NYM	NL	41	96	21	1	0	0	25	20	5	2	.219	.390	.229	-.223	.227	.389	.237	-.198	-3.3	20-LF	-2	
2000	SEA	AL	41	324	77	13	2	4	63	55	31	9	.238	.365	.327	-.146	.252	.371	.345	-.084	.4	83-LF	0	
2001	SDP	NL	42	379	86	17	3	8	81	84	25	7	.227	.367	.351	-.064	.242	.377	.373	-.042	5.5	81-LF	1	
2002	BOS	AL	43	179	40	6	1	5	38	47	8	2	.223	.371	.352	-.039	.243	.386	.392	.001	4.5	48-LF	-5	
2003	BOS	AL	44	205	49	9	3	3	52	49	17	0	.240	.396	.352	.009	.246	.406	.368	.010	5.6			

Breakout: 38%   Improve: 38%   Collapse: 25%

Even in the twilight of his career, Rickey Henderson remains a productive player. Despite the low batting average, his ability to draw walks and steal a base makes him an effective leadoff hitter. Unhappy with his playing time in Boston, he will not be returning.

Shea Hillenbrand — 3B — Born: 27-Jul-75 — Age: 27 — Bats: R — Throws: R

YEAR	TM	LG	AGE	AB	H	2B	3B	HR	BB	SO	SB	CS	AVG	OBP	SLG	MLVR	EQBA	EQOBP	EQSLG	EQMLVR	VORP	DEFENSE			
2000	TRN	EAS	24	529	171	35	3	11	19	39	3	3	.323	.356	.463	.190	.284	.305	.412	-.092	.5	65-1B	5	35-3B	-5
2001	BOS	AL	25	468	123	20	2	12	13	61	3	4	.263	.293	.391	-.123	.281	.311	.422	-.069	13.5	121-3B	-7		
2002	BOS	AL	26	634	186	43	4	18	25	95	4	2	.293	.332	.459	.081	.315	.352	.495	.142	51.0	150-3B	-6		
2003	BOS	AL	27	580	159	35	3	15	24	76	4	2	.275	.308	.423	-.030	.281	.315	.443	-.030	14.0				

Breakout: 9%   Improve: 32%   Collapse: 26%

Can he hit or not? Last year, we declared Hillenbrand to be a "total waste of the Red Sox' time." Unfazed, Shea did a passable imitation of an All-Star in April and May, earning him an invitation to the game. From June onward, he hit only 8 HR with 14 BB. The Sox can probably count on a .290 batting average, but without the secondary contributions you would normally expect from a corner infielder or that he gave them during his brief flirtation with excellence. Hillenbrand's defense at the hot corner has improved, but is still no better than average.

Steve Lomasney — C — Born: 29-Aug-77 — Age: 25 — Bats: R — Throws: R

YEAR	TM	LG	AGE	AB	H	2B	3B	HR	BB	SO	SB	CS	AVG	OBP	SLG	MLVR	EQBA	EQOBP	EQSLG	EQMLVR	VORP	DEFENSE	
2000	TRN	EAS	22	233	57	16	1	8	24	81	4	6	.245	.346	.425	.054	.215	.290	.376	-.223	.7	59-C	-12
2001	TRN	EAS	23	209	52	14	2	10	23	76	0	1	.249	.332	.478	.123	.219	.293	.419	-.156	4.5	50-C	-6
2001	PAW	INT	23	63	18	4	0	2	4	21	2	0	.286	.338	.444	.095	.266	.316	.422	-.072	2.7	17-C	-7
2002	TRN	EAS	24	338	71	17	3	8	55	133	5	5	.210	.336	.349	-.078	.187	.287	.310	-.333	-9.2	92-C	-14
2002	PAW	INT	24	30	2	1	0	0	2	15	0	0	.067	.152	.100	-.779	.100	.175	.133	-.832	-5.4		
2003	BOS	AL	25	127	28	7	1	4	13	46	2	3	.217	.297	.377	-.144	.222	.305	.394	-.156	.0		

Breakout: 45%   Improve: 62%   Collapse: 22%

Once touted as the catcher of the future, Lomasney's career has fallen into decline. He managed to avoid the freak injuries that stalled his development in 2000 and 2001, but once again, he failed to progress beyond Double-A. As a six-year free agent, he isn't likely to be re-signed, with Shoppach moving up to Trenton and veteran catchers likely to be hired to staff Pawtucket.

Lou Merloni — 2B — Born: 06-Apr-71 — Age: 32 — Bats: R — Throws: R

YEAR	TM	LG	AGE	AB	H	2B	3B	HR	BB	SO	SB	CS	AVG	OBP	SLG	MLVR	EQBA	EQOBP	EQSLG	EQMLVR	VORP	DEFENSE			
2000	YKO	JCL	29	94	20	4	0	1	7	15	0	0	.213	.275	.287	-.321	.213	.275	.287	-.376	-6.0				
2000	BOS	AL	29	128	41	11	2	0	4	22	1	0	.320	.346	.438	.025	.331	.351	.449	.089	8.3	34-3B	-2		
2001	PAW	INT	30	195	51	12	0	4	15	37	2	0	.262	.330	.385	-.015	.253	.313	.369	-.163	2.9	28-SS	-5	18-2B	-2
2001	BOS	AL	30	146	39	10	0	3	6	31	2	1	.267	.310	.397	-.082	.288	.330	.425	-.024	7.0	37-SS	1		
2002	BOS	AL	31	194	48	12	2	4	20	35	1	2	.247	.333	.392	-.043	.276	.355	.439	.031	12.3	52-2B	-4		
2003	BOS	AL	32	184	45	10	1	3	13	33	1	1	.244	.300	.353	-.154	.249	.307	.370	-.165	-0.9				

Breakout: 16%   Improve: 31%   Collapse: 43%

Fan favorite Lou Merloni again gave the Red Sox solid defense and adequate offensive production in a utility infielder role. Lou has consistently hit very well against LHP, averaging nearly a .900 OPS over the last four years. A platoon of Walker and Merloni at second base could be productive offensively, while minimizing Walker's defensive shortcomings, but Merloni will have to beat out free agent Damian Jackson for the job.

Doug Mirabelli   C   Born: 18-Oct-70   Age: 32   Bats: R   Throws: R

YEAR	TM	LG	AGE	AB	H	2B	3B	HR	BB	SO	SB	CS	AVG	OBP	SLG	MLVR	EQBA	EQOBP	EQSLG	EQMLVR	VORP	DEFENSE
2000	SFG	NL	29	230	53	10	2	6	36	57	1	0	.230	.340	.370	-.130	.239	.338	.385	-.103	8.7	65-C -2
2001	BOS	AL	30	141	38	8	0	9	17	36	0	0	.270	.364	.518	.175	.289	.377	.556	.243	17.8	44-C 3
2002	BOS	AL	31	151	34	7	0	7	17	33	0	0	.225	.316	.411	-.065	.243	.333	.447	-.025	8.2	41-C -1
2003	BOS	AL	32	179	41	9	0	7	23	45	0	0	.230	.323	.403	-.061	.235	.331	.422	-.065	4.8	

Breakout: 18%   *Improve: 40%*   *Collapse: 31%*

Mirabelli has an amazing platoon split, hitting for better than a 1.000 OPS against LHP over the last four years. Jason Varitek struggles against LHP with roughly a .700 OPS over that time. That ought to suggest some sort of ad hoc platoon, giving Varitek some much-needed rest while boosting the offensive production from the position. Instead, Grady Little designated Mirabelli to be Wakefield's caddy. Go figure.

Trot Nixon   RF   Born: 11-Apr-74   Age: 29   Bats: L   Throws: L

YEAR	TM	LG	AGE	AB	H	2B	3B	HR	BB	SO	SB	CS	AVG	OBP	SLG	MLVR	EQBA	EQOBP	EQSLG	EQMLVR	VORP	DEFENSE
2000	BOS	AL	26	427	118	27	8	12	63	85	8	1	.276	.372	.461	.067	.284	.373	.479	.125	22.3	106-RF 6
2001	BOS	AL	27	535	150	31	4	27	79	113	7	4	.280	.380	.505	.194	.297	.395	.537	.254	48.0	136-RF -1
2002	BOS	AL	28	532	136	36	3	24	65	109	4	2	.256	.342	.470	.080	.276	.360	.512	.140	30.3	146-RF 0
2003	BOS	AL	29	443	116	26	3	18	63	90	5	2	.263	.357	.460	.087	.268	.366	.481	.095	15.4	

Breakout: 5%   *Improve: 44%*   *Collapse: 14%*

At times, Nixon looks like a budding star. He practically carried the team in July, hitting .330/.392/.661 with 24 runs and 29 RBI. Nevertheless, two extended slumps kept his overall production well below the mark he set in 2001. Though he saw action in a career-high 152 games, essentially playing full-time, Nixon continues to hit very poorly against lefties. A platoon might make sense if the Red Sox could find a right-handed fourth outfielder with the necessary defensive range to handle Fenway's deep right field.

Calvin Pickering   Born: 29-Sep-76   Age: 26   Bats: L   Throws: L

YEAR	TM	LG	AGE	AB	H	2B	3B	HR	BB	SO	SB	CS	AVG	OBP	SLG	MLVR	EQBA	EQOBP	EQSLG	EQMLVR	VORP	DEFENSE
2000	ROC	INT	23	197	43	10	0	6	36	70	2	2	.218	.342	.360	-.097	.205	.314	.340	-.230	-7.4	56-1B 2
2001	ROC	INT	24	461	130	25	0	21	64	149	0	1	.282	.381	.473	.198	.265	.356	.447	.034	16.7	67-1B -6
2001	BOS	AL	24	50	14	1	0	3	8	13	0	0	.280	.379	.480	.160	.300	.407	.500	.227	4.5	11-1B 0
2003	BOS	AL	26	164	39	8	0	6	21	48	2	1	.238	.329	.396	-.054	.243	.337	.414	-.058	-.6	

Breakout: 5%   *Improve: 26%*   *Collapse: 25%*

Barry Bonds hits like a 600-pound gorilla, powering the middle of the Giants lineup; Calvin Pickering is merely 600 pounds. There is no denying his talent: he has good plate discipline and above-average power. Unfortunately, he has not shown any commitment to maintaining his physical fitness. After showing up to camp overweight, he promptly tore his right quadriceps. Following surgery to repair the injury, he missed the entire season. While he's dropped out of sight, there is still a chance that he might return to have a productive career. He should begin by working with a diet and fitness coach over the winter.

Hanley Ramirez   SS   Born: 23-Dec-83   Age: 19   Bats: B   Throws: R

YEAR	TM	LG	AGE	AB	H	2B	3B	HR	BB	SO	SB	CS	AVG	OBP	SLG	MLVR	EQBA	EQOBP	EQSLG	EQMLVR	VORP	DEFENSE
2002	LOW	NYP	18	97	36	9	2	1	4	14	4	3	.371	.408	.536	.460	.263	.290	.384	-.178	1.0	22-SS -6
2003	BOS	AL	19	119	32	7	1	2	6	19	1	0	.265	.300	.398	-.082	.271	.308	.416	-.087	2.3	

Breakout: 31%   *Improve: 66%*   *Collapse: 34%*

While Ramirez is still in the low minors, he looks like the real deal. His tremendous bat speed and line-drive power bode well for future success. He hammers heat and drives off speed stuff, so while patience isn't one of his virtues—yet—he has yet to meet a professional challenge he hasn't overcome. He's already exciting Red Sox Nation, and don't be surprised to see him in Fenway as early as 2004 at the tender age of 20.

Manny Ramirez　　　LF　　Born: 30-May-72　　Age: 31　　Bats: R　　Throws: R

YEAR	TM	LG	AGE	AB	H	2B	3B	HR	BB	SO	SB	CS	AVG	OBP	SLG	MLVR	EQBA	EQOBP	EQSLG	EQMLVR	VORP	DEFENSE	
2000	CLE	AL	28	439	154	34	2	38	86	117	1	1	.351	.460	.697	.610	.357	.461	.715	.669	85.6	73-RF	-2
2001	BOS	AL	29	529	162	33	2	41	81	147	0	1	.306	.406	.609	.397	.325	.423	.648	.482	82.4	53-LF	3
2002	BOS	AL	30	436	152	31	0	33	73	85	0	0	.349	.451	.647	.569	.372	.471	.698	.680	92.4	63-LF	-4
2003	BOS	AL	31	455	134	32	1	31	73	107	0	0	.295	.396	.571	.311	.302	.406	.598	.339	46.8		

Breakout: 4%　　Improve: 24%　　Collapse: 24%

Manny missed five weeks with a broken left index finger, struggled in his rehab assignment, then hit 14–63 with averages of .222/.329/.302 in the three weeks following his return. Despite this handicap, he finished the season as one of the team's top offensive performers. If he can stay healthy for an entire season, expect 45 HR and a bid for the league MVP. While he is frequently criticized by the Boston media for his baserunning mishaps, he's a true student of hitting and works as hard as anybody on this art.

Freddy Sanchez　　　SS　　Born: 21-Dec-77　　Age: 25　　Bats: R　　Throws: R

YEAR	TM	LG	AGE	AB	H	2B	3B	HR	BB	SO	SB	CS	AVG	OBP	SLG	MLVR	EQBA	EQOBP	EQSLG	EQMLVR	VORP	DEFENSE			
2000	LOW	NYP	22	132	38	13	2	1	9	16	2	4	.288	.347	.439	.196	.213	.242	.338	-.370	-5.2	33-SS	0		
2000	AUG	SAL	22	109	33	7	0	0	11	19	4	0	.303	.372	.367	.109	.241	.294	.295	-.311	-2.6	30-SS	0		
2001	SAR	FSL	23	280	95	19	4	1	22	30	5	3	.339	.391	.446	.267	.276	.314	.371	-.142	5.5	67-SS	-4		
2001	TRN	EAS	23	178	58	20	0	2	9	21	3	1	.326	.365	.472	.231	.286	.323	.412	-.057	7.5	41-SS	-4		
2002	TRN	EAS	24	311	102	23	1	3	37	45	19	3	.328	.408	.437	.237	.284	.351	.382	-.050	14.0	67-SS	-14	11-2B	-3
2002	PAW	INT	24	183	55	10	1	4	12	21	5	3	.301	.354	.432	.118	.281	.332	.411	-.046	8.2	35-SS	-4	11-2B	1
2002	BOS	AL	24	16	3	0	0	0	2	3	0	0	.188	.278	.188	-.440	.250	.333	.250	-.289	-.7				
2003	BOS	AL	25	204	55	12	1	3	14	29	4	2	.270	.321	.389	-.055	.276	.329	.407	-.057	5.5				

Breakout: 30%　　Improve: 57%　　Collapse: 25%

Despite an unimpressive September call-up and the acquisition of Todd Walker, Freddy Sanchez remains in the Sox plans. A .318 hitter in his rapid rise through the minors, Sanchez does little else to contribute offensively. He is nonetheless a respectable low-cost option for the next few years. In-season, he might get to replace Merloni and/or Damian Jackson as Walker's platoon mate and Nomar's backup, but he's optionable, and will almost certainly wait a shot at the full-time job at second in 2004.

Rey Sanchez　　　2B　　Born: 05-Oct-67　　Age: 35　　Bats: R　　Throws: R

YEAR	TM	LG	AGE	AB	H	2B	3B	HR	BB	SO	SB	CS	AVG	OBP	SLG	MLVR	EQBA	EQOBP	EQSLG	EQMLVR	VORP	DEFENSE	
2000	KCR	AL	32	509	139	18	2	1	28	55	7	3	.273	.316	.322	-.260	.274	.310	.325	-.217	.1	133-SS	26
2001	KCR	AL	33	390	118	14	5	0	11	34	9	1	.303	.325	.364	-.092	.312	.337	.376	-.063	14.9	93-SS	35
2001	ATL	NL	33	154	35	4	1	0	4	15	2	0	.227	.247	.266	-.436	.232	.252	.277	-.427	-8.5	45-SS	13
2002	BOS	AL	34	357	102	12	3	1	17	31	2	2	.286	.322	.345	-.102	.308	.344	.372	-.059	13.7	89-2B	12
2003	NYM	AL	35	271	67	11	2	0	11	27	3	1	.249	.281	.303	-.249	.262	.294	.325	-.241	-5.5		

Breakout: 0%　　Improve: 28%　　Collapse: 32%

The Red Sox got what they might reasonably have expected: solid defense but inadequate offensive production. Nevertheless, Grady Little was fooled by his high batting average, reputedly pushing for a new contract. Epstein showed greater restraint, declining to offer arbitration to Sanchez despite the lack of obvious alternatives at the time. Rey is best suited to a role as a utility infielder and defensive replacement, but will be the Mets' caretaker at shortstop until Jose Reyes is ready.

Kelly Shoppach　　　C　　Born: 29-Apr-80　　Age: 23　　Bats: R　　Throws: R

YEAR	TM	LG	AGE	AB	H	2B	3B	HR	BB	SO	SB	CS	AVG	OBP	SLG	MLVR	EQBA	EQOBP	EQSLG	EQMLVR	VORP	DEFENSE	
2002	SAR	FSL	22	414	112	35	1	10	59	112	2	1	.271	.370	.432	.160	.224	.300	.364	-.214	2.4	92-C	-4
2003	BOS	AL	23	182	42	9	1	5	17	52	2	3	.229	.303	.372	-.134	.234	.310	.390	-.144	.7		

Breakout: 39%　　Improve: 64%　　Collapse: 14%

What isn't there to like? Shoppach is considered a terrific defensive catcher, with a strong arm and good poise behind the plate. His offensive game could use a little more work, since he struck out 112 times in 479 PA at Sarasota, but he works the count well and shows the promise of future power. He'll begin the season at Double-A, but could step into a major league role as early as August if a trade opens up for Varitek.

Dernell Stenson LF Born: 17-Jun-78 Age: 25 Bats: L Throws: L

YEAR	TM	LG	AGE	AB	H	2B	3B	HR	BB	SO	SB	CS	AVG	OBP	SLG	MLVR	EQBA	EQOBP	EQSLG	EQMLVR	VORP	DEFENSE		
2000	PAW	INT	22	380	102	14	0	23	45	99	0	0	.268	.352	.487	.119	.248	.319	.449	-.044	5.3	65-1B -8	20-LF -1	
2001	PAW	INT	23	464	110	18	1	16	43	116	0	0	.237	.305	.384	-.076	.225	.289	.367	-.231	-17.8	115-LF -10		
2002	PAW	INT	24	368	92	20	1	9	37	96	4	3	.250	.322	.383	-.037	.236	.306	.367	-.191	-10.1	100-LF -5		
2003	BOS	AL	25	165	40	8	1	5	16	40	2	2	.243	.313	.400	-.072	.249	.321	.419	-.076	-2.1			

Breakout: 41%   Improve: 61%   Collapse: 22%

When a prospect makes it to Triple-A at the age of 21, people normally project steady progress and a rosy career. In stark contrast, Stenson's skills appear to be slowly slipping. A poor defensive first baseman, Stenson was moved to left in 2000. The results, both defensively and offensively, have been disappointing. Stenson should return to first base or DH to take one last crack at making the majors. Having worn out his welcome in Pawtucket, his best bet may be with another organization.

Jason Varitek C Born: 11-Apr-72 Age: 31 Bats: B Throws: R

YEAR	TM	LG	AGE	AB	H	2B	3B	HR	BB	SO	SB	CS	AVG	OBP	SLG	MLVR	EQBA	EQOBP	EQSLG	EQMLVR	VORP	DEFENSE
2000	BOS	AL	28	448	111	31	1	10	60	84	1	1	.248	.344	.388	-.110	.257	.347	.405	-.046	21.8	120-C -8
2001	BOS	AL	29	174	51	11	1	7	21	35	0	0	.293	.372	.489	.172	.309	.388	.520	.232	21.6	50-C 2
2002	BOS	AL	30	467	124	27	1	10	41	95	4	3	.266	.334	.392	-.030	.287	.353	.425	.017	29.9	121-C -2
2003	BOS	AL	31	328	82	19	1	9	32	64	3	1	.251	.323	.398	-.054	.257	.331	.416	-.057	9.8	

Breakout: 9%   Improve: 32%   Collapse: 32%

Like Nixon, Varitek achieved new heights in 2001. Unfortunately, Varitek also shared in the disappointment of 2002, as he hit .209 with only 2 HR in August and September. Varitek has a strong defensive reputation, but he's already 30, and at this point is unlikely to ever develop into an offensive star. However, he is set to earn $4.7 million in 2003 and $6.7 million in 2004. If Kelly Shoppach continues to progress in the minors, the Red Sox should consider shopping Varitek at the trading deadline, before the shine comes entirely off.

Kevin Youkilis 3B Born: 15-Mar-79 Age: 24 Bats: R Throws: R

YEAR	TM	LG	AGE	AB	H	2B	3B	HR	BB	SO	SB	CS	AVG	OBP	SLG	MLVR	EQBA	EQOBP	EQSLG	EQMLVR	VORP	DEFENSE		
2001	LOW	NYP	22	183	58	14	2	3	70	28	4	3	.317	.516	.464	.453	.223	.385	.335	-.085	6.1	58-3B 4		
2002	AUG	SAL	23	53	15	5	0	0	13	8	0	0	.283	.433	.377	.198	.214	.337	.286	-.250	-1.0	15-3B 1		
2002	SAR	FSL	23	268	79	16	0	3	49	37	0	2	.295	.431	.388	.207	.246	.349	.329	-.152	-4.4	40-1B -6	33-3B 0	
2002	TRN	EAS	23	160	55	10	0	5	31	18	5	4	.344	.464	.500	.416	.291	.393	.430	.099	13.1	44-3B -5		
2003	BOS	AL	24	207	52	11	1	5	28	33	3	1	.251	.346	.384	-.032	.256	.355	.402	-.034	3.8			

Breakout: 23%   Improve: 49%   Collapse: 20%

Youkilis has amply proven that he has a major league batting eye, even if he lacks the body of an athlete. Walking 93 times in 595 PA this year, his plate discipline has shown no signs of failing him as he climbs into the high minors. Most impressive, he showed signs at Trenton of turning some of his doubles power into home runs. The Red Sox haven't had a third-base prospect this promising since Jeff Bagwell, and before that, Wade Boggs. If he continues to clamber up this fast, he could step in at first or give Theo Epstein the freedom of action to accept some of the sillier offers made for Hillenbrand.

PITCHERS

Rolando Arrojo Born: 18-Jul-68 Age: 34 Bats: R Throws: R

YEAR	TM	LG	AGE	G	GS	IP	H	BB	SO	HR	ERA	EQERA	EQH9	EQBB9	EQSO9	EQHR9	PERA	VORP	STF
2000	BOS	AL	31	13	13	71.3	67	22	44	10	5.05	3.95	8.1	2.3	5.4	1.1	3.50	12.3	8
2000	COL	NL	31	19	19	101.3	120	46	80	14	6.04	5.37	10.1	3.3	6.2	1.0	4.85	1.5	6
2001	BOS	AL	32	41	9	103.3	88	35	78	8	3.48	3.14	7.2	2.8	6.3	0.6	3.17	26.4	7
2002	BOS	AL	33	29	8	81.3	83	27	51	7	4.98	4.45	9.2	2.8	5.5	0.7	4.07	9.0	0
2003	PIT	NL	34	26	11	71.0	74	26	53	7	4.43	4.62	9.4	2.9	6.0	1.0	4.49	8.4	1

Breakout: 14%   Improve: 45%   Collapse: 25%

With the much-anticipated departure of Arrojo, the last reminder of the disastrous 2000 stretch-drive trades will be gone. Between Sprague, Brogna, Bichette, Lansing, and Arrojo the Red Sox wasted nearly $20 million on below-replacement-level production. In recent years, Arrojo has been injured as often as he has been productive. He's been signed by the Pirates, probably to shore up the rotation, but don't count on him for anything.

Willie Banks Born: 27-Feb-69 Age: 34 Bats: R Throws: R

YEAR	TM	LG	AGE	G	GS	IP	H	BB	SO	HR	ERA	EQERA	EQH9	EQBB9	EQSO9	EQHR9	PERA	VORP	STF
2000	NOR	INT	31	9	9	51.3	56	25	20	5	5.09	6.10	11.4	4.5	3.1	1.1	5.88	-3.4	-17
2001	SYR	INT	32	24	23	146.7	151	53	121	12	3.25	4.76	10.4	3.9	5.8	1.0	5.06	12.1	5
2001	BOS	AL	32	5	0	10.7	5	4	10	0	0.84	1.90	3.9	3.2	8.0	0.2	1.37	4.1	21
2002	PAW	INT	33	6	4	26.0	20	9	15	2	4.50	4.38	7.7	3.8	4.5	1.0	3.63	3.2	-5
2002	BOS	AL	33	29	0	39.0	32	14	26	5	3.23	3.38	7.4	3.0	5.9	1.1	3.47	8.7	-2
2003	*BOS*	*AL*	*34*	*28*	*7*	*58.7*	*64*	*26*	*37*	*7*	*4.74*	*4.71*	*9.5*	*3.7*	*5.4*	*1.0*	*4.80*	*7.0*	*-8*

Breakout: 10%   Improve: 47%   Collapse: 21%

Banks has earned favorable reviews from us in the past, and he lived up to this billing in 2002, as he was the third-most effective reliever on the team. Despite this, Grady used Banks primarily in mop-up situations while a variety of clowns lost games in the seventh or eighth innings of tight games. He's been quietly re-signed by the Red Sox, and should play an increased role in 2003.

John Burkett Born: 28-Nov-64 Age: 38 Bats: R Throws: R

YEAR	TM	LG	AGE	G	GS	IP	H	BB	SO	HR	ERA	EQERA	EQH9	EQBB9	EQSO9	EQHR9	PERA	VORP	STF
2000	ATL	NL	35	31	22	134.3	162	51	110	13	4.89	5.03	11.2	2.8	6.6	0.8	5.13	6.9	8
2001	ATL	NL	36	34	34	219.3	187	70	187	17	3.04	3.57	8.4	2.7	6.7	0.6	3.35	47.1	19
2002	BOS	AL	37	29	29	173.0	199	50	124	25	4.53	4.76	10.3	2.4	6.3	1.2	5.01	14.3	11
2003	*BOS*	*AL*	*38*	*28*	*24*	*152.3*	*166*	*50*	*106*	*17*	*4.36*	*4.33*	*9.5*	*2.7*	*6.0*	*1.0*	*4.40*	*23.5*	*10*

Breakout: 13%   Improve: 36%   Collapse: 14%

Burkett pitched well for most of the year. His promised snub of the All-Star game (in protest of Czar Bud's various shenanigans) was not entirely ridiculous when it was first announced. Burkett had a 3.77 ERA through the end of July and a 2.76 ERA in September; in between fell a disastrous August, where he got pasted for 49 hits and 34 runs in 28 innings. While his career has been erratic, Burkett may yet have one more good season left in him.

Frank Castillo Born: 01-Apr-69 Age: 34 Bats: R Throws: R

YEAR	TM	LG	AGE	G	GS	IP	H	BB	SO	HR	ERA	EQERA	EQH9	EQBB9	EQSO9	EQHR9	PERA	VORP	STF
2000	TOR	AL	31	25	24	138.0	112	56	104	18	3.59	3.00	6.6	2.9	6.5	1.0	3.10	38.4	15
2001	BOS	AL	32	26	26	136.7	138	35	89	14	4.21	3.83	8.5	2.1	5.5	0.8	3.84	25.4	9
2002	BOS	AL	33	36	23	163.3	174	58	112	19	5.07	4.87	9.5	3.0	6.0	1.0	4.57	11.2	5
2003	*BOS*	*AL*	*34*	*29*	*21*	*124.3*	*131*	*43*	*79*	*15*	*4.53*	*4.49*	*9.2*	*2.9*	*5.5*	*1.1*	*4.38*	*17.2*	*2*

Breakout: 6%   Improve: 46%   Collapse: 16%

In the second half of a $4.5 million two-year deal, Castillo struggled from June through August. On his last legs as a Red Sock, he pitched well in September, earning himself an $800,000 contract and a shot at swinging between the fifth starter's role or mopping up. Castillo can still be effective when he has command of all his pitches, but that's true of everybody, and Castillo doesn't have it often enough to be a commodity.

Paxton Crawford Born: 04-Aug-77 Age: 25 Bats: R Throws: R

YEAR	TM	LG	AGE	G	GS	IP	H	BB	SO	HR	ERA	EQERA	EQH9	EQBB9	EQSO9	EQHR9	PERA	VORP	STF
2000	TRN	EAS	22	9	9	52.3	50	6	54	3	3.10	3.64	9.5	1.1	6.9	0.9	4.07	10.8	28
2000	PAW	INT	22	12	11	61.3	47	22	47	6	4.55	4.26	7.8	3.3	5.9	1.1	3.51	8.5	13
2000	BOS	AL	22	7	4	29.0	25	13	17	0	3.41	3.29	7.5	3.3	5.1	0.2	2.69	7.1	11
2001	PAW	INT	23	6	6	29.3	43	7	15	4	5.53	6.71	14.2	2.5	3.6	1.7	7.92	-3.9	-12
2001	BOS	AL	23	8	7	36.0	40	13	25	3	4.75	4.17	9.4	3.0	5.8	0.7	4.50	5.3	10
2002	PAW	INT	24	9	9	47.0	61	19	22	9	5.55	7.40	13.6	4.5	3.7	2.6	7.90	-9.9	-22

Crawford suffered through two surgeries this year, the first in February to repair a tendon in his shoulder that had separated from the bone and then another in August to fuse some bones in his lower spine. The back surgery was his second in two years. Crawford has demonstrated talent, but at this point he's a long shot to ever pitch again in the majors.

Jorge de la Rosa　　　　Born: 05-Apr-81　　Age: 22　　Bats: L　　Throws: L

YEAR	TM	LG	AGE	G	GS	IP	H	BB	SO	HR	ERA	EQERA	EQH9	EQBB9	EQSO9	EQHR9	PERA	VORP	STF
2001	SAR	FSL	20	12	0	29.7	13	12	27	0	1.21	2.16	4.2	4.2	5.3	0.2	2.19	10.6	6
2001	TRN	EAS	20	29	0	37.0	56	20	27	4	5.84	9.40	16.1	6.7	4.7	1.6	10.36	-16.5	-29
2002	SAR	FSL	21	23	23	120.7	105	52	95	10	3.65	5.15	11.0	5.1	5.2	1.8	5.38	4.8	0
2002	TRN	EAS	21	4	4	18.0	17	9	15	0	5.50	5.21	9.3	5.3	5.6	0.3	4.87	0.6	6

Purchased out of the Mexican League after the Snakes lost their initial rights to him, de la Rosa was a nice little find on Duquette's watch. He deals in the low-90s, and in 23 starts with Sarasota, de la Rosa compiled a 3.65 ERA with respectable peripheral stats. This earned the young left-hander another spin at Trenton, where he struggled again. He's young, and lefties who throw hard get twice as many chances as their more common soft-tossing brethren.

Manny Delcarmen　　　　Born: 16-Feb-82　　Age: 21　　Bats: R　　Throws: R

YEAR	TM	LG	AGE	G	GS	IP	H	BB	SO	HR	ERA	EQERA	EQH9	EQBB9	EQSO9	EQHR9	PERA	VORP	STF
2002	AUG	SAL	20	26	24	136.0	124	56	136	15	4.10	6.83	13.2	5.6	5.9	2.9	6.42	-20.1	-3

The Red Sox drafted Delcarmen out of West Roxbury High School in the second round of the 2000 draft. Despite initial criticism that he was drafted high, Delcarmen has shown steady progress. He features a mid-90s fastball and a good breaking ball, and the Sox are working on teaching him a change and when to use it. Expect him to spend a full season at Sarasota in 2003 alongside Dumatrait and Gamble, making for a nice cadre.

Phillip Dumatrait　　　　Born: 12-Jul-81　　Age: 21　　Bats: R　　Throws: L

YEAR	TM	LG	AGE	G	GS	IP	H	BB	SO	HR	ERA	EQERA	EQH9	EQBB9	EQSO9	EQHR9	PERA	VORP	STF
2001	LOW	NYP	19	2	2	10.3	9	4	15	0	3.50	5.71	11.1	5.2	7.5	0.3	5.88	-0.2	19
2002	AUG	SAL	20	22	22	120.3	109	47	108	5	2.77	5.18	11.8	5.2	5.2	1.1	5.55	4.3	3
2002	SAR	FSL	20	4	4	14.0	10	15	16	0	3.86	6.62	8.3	12.5	7.4	0.3	6.12	-1.7	-5

After Fossum, Dumatrait may be the best pitching prospect remaining in the Red Sox system. Working 22 starts with a 2.77 ERA at Augusta, Dumatrait featured a terrific 12–6 curve, complemented by low 90s heat. More importantly, the young pitcher managed to avoid the injuries that cost him most of the 2001 season. He struggled in four starts at Sarasota, which means he'll probably repeat the Florida State League to start.

Chris Elmore　　　　Born: 28-Apr-77　　Age: 26　　Bats: L　　Throws: L

YEAR	TM	LG	AGE	G	GS	IP	H	BB	SO	HR	ERA	EQERA	EQH9	EQBB9	EQSO9	EQHR9	PERA	VORP	STF
2000	LOW	NYP	23	15	10	71.3	55	14	46	0	1.89	4.07	10.0	2.4	3.3	0.3	4.07	11.2	-1
2001	SAR	FSL	24	17	5	59.7	58	12	40	1	2.41	4.17	10.0	2.1	3.9	0.4	4.70	8.5	-2
2001	TRN	EAS	24	14	13	78.7	76	19	56	4	2.29	4.23	9.6	2.9	4.4	0.7	4.85	11.1	3
2002	TRN	EAS	25	14	13	84.7	76	22	57	1	2.34	3.22	8.7	2.7	4.5	0.2	3.85	21.5	9
2002	PAW	INT	25	7	7	29.7	43	12	30	3	6.36	8.13	14.5	4.4	7.8	1.3	7.99	-8.7	2

A finesse lefty in the Blaise Illsley mold, Elmore led Trenton with a 2.34 ERA, but struggled after a promotion to Pawtucket. He has always been tough on lefties and isn't young, so a move to the bullpen may be in the cards.

Alan Embree　　　　Born: 23-Jan-70　　Age: 33　　Bats: L　　Throws: L

YEAR	TM	LG	AGE	G	GS	IP	H	BB	SO	HR	ERA	EQERA	EQH9	EQBB9	EQSO9	EQHR9	PERA	VORP	STF
2000	SFG	NL	30	63	0	60.0	62	25	49	4	4.95	4.71	9.9	3.1	6.6	0.6	4.47	4.5	0
2001	SFG	NL	31	22	0	20.0	34	10	25	7	11.25	11.16	15.9	4.2	9.5	2.9	10.89	-12.8	-14
2001	CWS	AL	31	39	0	34.0	31	7	34	7	5.03	4.51	8.0	1.7	8.5	1.7	3.86	3.3	10
2002	SDP	NL	32	36	0	28.7	23	9	38	2	0.94	2.73	7.3	2.5	10.4	0.7	3.35	8.5	27
2002	BOS	AL	32	32	0	33.3	24	11	43	4	2.97	2.98	6.4	2.7	11.2	1.0	2.86	8.9	31
2003	*BOS*	*AL*	*33*	*63*	*0*	*54.3*	*50*	*19*	*54*	*6*	*3.58*	*3.56*	*8.0*	*3.0*	*8.6*	*1.0*	*3.69*	*13.4*	*13*

Breakout: 16%　　　Improve: 44%　　　Collapse: 18%

Embree parlayed an excellent 2002 campaign into a $5.5 million two-year contract. While he has been wildly inconsistent over his career, the Sox clearly believe that the hard-throwing lefty has found his groove. He's been poised on this particular precipice for years, tilting between being Mike Stanton or Mark Guthrie for years. With the departure of Urbina, Embree is projected to share the save opportunities.

Casey Fossum　Born: 09-Jan-78　Age: 25　Bats: B　Throws: L

YEAR	TM	LG	AGE	G	GS	IP	H	BB	SO	HR	ERA	EQERA	EQH9	EQBB9	EQSO9	EQHR9	PERA	VORP	STF
2000	SAR	FSL	22	27	27	149.3	147	36	143	7	3.44	4.71	10.4	2.7	6.0	1.0	5.04	13.2	14
2001	TRN	EAS	23	20	20	117.7	102	28	130	5	2.83	3.81	8.5	2.8	6.7	0.6	4.12	22.2	22
2001	BOS	AL	23	13	7	44.3	44	20	26	4	4.88	4.25	8.3	3.7	4.9	0.7	4.23	6.0	0
2002	PAW	INT	24	5	3	25.0	34	6	28	1	3.96	6.13	13.3	2.6	8.5	0.5	6.33	-1.8	25
2002	BOS	AL	24	43	12	106.7	113	30	101	12	3.46	4.35	9.5	2.4	8.3	0.9	4.28	13.0	19
2003	*BOS*	*AL*	*25*	*30*	*15*	*97.0*	*100*	*31*	*75*	*10*	*4.16*	*4.12*	*9.0*	*2.6*	*6.7*	*0.9*	*4.07*	*18.0*	*9*

Breakout: 16%　Improve: 49%　Collapse: 17%

As a reliever, Fossum put up a 3.15 ERA. This earned him a shot at the rotation in late July. While his 3.65 ERA as a starter looks respectable, he also allowed 14 unearned runs, which means he was really allowing 5.54 runs per nine. He was also unusually ineffective in the middle innings, where opposing batters hit .348/.379/.523 against the young pitcher. Don't despair; he still has the obvious talent to be successful in the majors. With another year to build strength and develop a changeup, Fossum should be very effective at the bottom of the Red Sox rotation.

Jerome Gamble　Born: 05-Apr-80　Age: 23　Bats: R　Throws: R

YEAR	TM	LG	AGE	G	GS	IP	H	BB	SO	HR	ERA	EQERA	EQH9	EQBB9	EQSO9	EQHR9	PERA	VORP	STF
2000	AUG	SAL	20	15	15	78.7	69	32	71	1	2.52	4.94	10.9	5.1	4.8	0.3	5.38	4.9	3
2002	AUG	SAL	22	14	14	49.3	34	22	42	2	1.83	3.78	9.0	5.8	4.9	1.0	4.28	9.4	-5

Bouncing back from Tommy John surgery, Gamble was old for the Sally League, but his dominance was nevertheless impressive. He has great movement on heat in the low 90s, and alongside Delcarmen and Dumatrait, gives the organization a nice trio to watch as they move up to Sarasota. Sure, the odds are that at least one career will end on the surgeon's table and another will stall in Double-A, but one of them could end up being special. Snagged by the Reds in the Rule 5 Draft.

Rich Garces　Born: 18-May-71　Age: 32　Bats: R　Throws: R

YEAR	TM	LG	AGE	G	GS	IP	H	BB	SO	HR	ERA	EQERA	EQH9	EQBB9	EQSO9	EQHR9	PERA	VORP	STF
2000	BOS	AL	29	64	0	74.7	64	23	69	7	3.25	2.88	7.4	2.3	8.1	0.7	2.85	20.7	16
2001	BOS	AL	30	62	0	67.0	55	25	51	6	3.90	3.34	6.9	3.1	6.4	0.7	3.20	15.2	1
2002	BOS	AL	31	26	0	21.3	21	12	16	4	7.61	6.41	8.6	4.7	6.5	1.5	5.29	-2.4	-14

Last winter, Garces was hoping for a long-term deal. He'd lost 35 pounds since the end of the season and was reportedly in the best shape of his career. What happened to that? He was used very cautiously, throwing only one inning every second or third game, yet still struggling with his command. When he was finally demoted at the end of July, El Guapo had pitched only 21.3 innings. Garces has been an excellent reliever and a fan favorite in Boston, but sadly appears to have reached the end of the line. His collapse this year was a disappointment second only to that of Tony Clark.

Wayne Gomes　Born: 15-Jan-73　Age: 30　Bats: R　Throws: R

YEAR	TM	LG	AGE	G	GS	IP	H	BB	SO	HR	ERA	EQERA	EQH9	EQBB9	EQSO9	EQHR9	PERA	VORP	STF
2000	PHI	NL	27	65	0	73.7	72	35	49	6	4.40	4.33	9.0	3.5	5.3	0.7	4.11	8.6	-7
2001	PHI	NL	28	42	0	48.0	51	22	35	4	4.31	4.69	10.4	3.9	5.7	0.7	4.87	3.7	-8
2001	SFG	NL	28	13	0	15.0	21	7	17	3	8.40	8.08	13.4	3.9	8.8	1.7	7.95	-4.5	-3
2002	PAW	INT	29	42	0	71.7	61	28	54	8	2.64	4.34	8.7	4.3	5.9	1.5	4.48	8.3	-10
2002	BOS	AL	29	20	0	21.3	20	12	15	2	4.65	4.37	8.4	4.7	6.2	0.8	4.38	2.4	-7
2003	*BOS*	*AL*	*30*	*28*	*1*	*36.3*	*41*	*19*	*26*	*5*	*5.11*	*5.08*	*9.9*	*4.3*	*6.3*	*1.1*	*5.19*	*3.7*	*-8*

Breakout: 18%　Improve: 49%　Collapse: 26%

Knee problems in 2001 derailed his career, but Gomes picked up 19 saves with the Phillies in 1999, so he'll get kicked around for years to come. He's still as good as he ever was, with all that implies. With Ramiro Mendoza, Mike Timlin, and Chad Fox all signed for 2003, chances are that Gomes is out of the picture, but Fox's trick elbow could spring at any moment, and Gomes should be only a bus ride away.

Josh Hancock　　　Born: 11-Apr-78　　Age: 25　　Bats: R　　Throws: R

YEAR	TM	LG	AGE	G	GS	IP	H	BB	SO	HR	ERA	EQERA	EQH9	EQBB9	EQSO9	EQHR9	PERA	VORP	STF
2000	SAR	FSL	22	26	24	143.7	164	37	95	9	4.45	6.02	12.4	2.9	4.2	1.4	6.42	-8.3	-2
2001	TRN	EAS	23	24	24	130.7	138	37	119	8	3.65	4.79	10.6	3.4	5.6	0.9	5.69	10.4	8
2002	TRN	EAS	24	15	14	84.7	82	18	69	9	3.61	4.44	10.1	2.3	5.6	1.6	4.89	10.0	8
2002	PAW	INT	24	8	8	44.3	39	26	29	2	3.45	4.64	8.8	6.4	5.1	0.6	4.78	4.3	-2
2002	BOS	AL	24	3	1	7.3	5	2	6	1	3.70	3.05	6.2	2.3	7.3	1.2	2.67	2.0	15
2003	PHI	NL	25	15	11	68	71	28	48	8	4.65	5.1	9.7	3.2	5.6	1	4.97	4.1	1

Breakout: 23%　　Improve: 53%　　Collapse: 19%

The Bosox fifth round pick in 1998, Hancock has progressed through the minors without fanfare. After starting the season in Trenton, Hancock moved up to Pawtucket mid-season and got a cup of coffee with the big club in September. Featuring a low-90s fastball and an assortment of other average pitches, Hancock worked effectively at all three levels and might earn a spot in the bullpen with a strong spring training. Traded to Philadelphia for Jeremy Giambi, at best he might teach Ed Wade that solid relief pitching doesn't have to come with a seven-figure price tag.

Chris Haney　　　Born: 16-Nov-68　　Age: 34　　Bats: L　　Throws: L

YEAR	TM	LG	AGE	G	GS	IP	H	BB	SO	HR	ERA	EQERA	EQH9	EQBB9	EQSO9	EQHR9	PERA	VORP	STF
2000	BUF	INT	31	15	13	92.3	87	17	70	8	2.44	3.37	9.5	1.7	5.9	1.0	3.84	21.8	15
2001	FKU	JPL	32	7	7	31.3	34	12	16	7	5.74	6.52	10.7	3.2	4.0	1.9	6.27	-3.5	-17
2002	PAW	INT	33	25	0	29.0	27	10	31	1	2.79	3.82	9.1	3.7	8.2	0.5	4.14	5.0	9
2002	BOS	AL	33	24	0	30.0	32	10	15	2	4.20	4.06	9.6	2.8	4.4	0.6	4.17	4.4	-10
2003	ATL	NL	34	40	0	48.0	50	18	36	4	3.96	4.24	9.5	2.8	6.0	0.8	4.37	7.7	-3

Breakout: 17%　　Improve: 49%　　Collapse: 22%

What use is a soft-tossing lefty with a reverse platoon split in a big league bullpen? Haney isn't the worst pitcher in the league, but he isn't good enough to shoulder an important role, and at his age he's unlikely to improve. Haney saw some of the middle-relief situations that by rights should have gone to Willie Banks.

Dustin Hermanson　　　Born: 21-Dec-72　　Age: 30　　Bats: R　　Throws: R

YEAR	TM	LG	AGE	G	GS	IP	H	BB	SO	HR	ERA	EQERA	EQH9	EQBB9	EQSO9	EQHR9	PERA	VORP	STF
2000	MON	NL	27	38	30	198.0	226	75	94	26	4.77	4.70	9.8	2.7	3.8	1.0	5.03	17.5	-6
2001	STL	NL	28	33	33	192.3	195	73	123	34	4.45	5.29	10.0	3.3	5.0	1.5	5.05	4.6	-1
2002	PAW	INT	29	5	3	13.7	9	7	11	0	2.63	3.35	6.4	5.6	6.2	0.2	3.04	3.2	0
2002	BOS	AL	29	12	1	22.0	35	7	13	3	7.77	7.23	14.3	2.7	5.2	1.1	7.28	-4.5	-14
2003	STL	NL	30	24	9	63.7	67	25	40	8	4.48	4.88	9.8	1.2	3.0	5.0	5.05	4.4	-8

Breakout: 14%　　Improve: 47%　　Collapse: 19%

Acquired in the off-season for a trio of marginal offensive prospects, Hermanson injured his groin pitching from a wet mound in his first start for the Bosox, and then missing time with an infected elbow. When he finally returned to the team in August, he was merely ineffective. The Sox declined his $7.5 million option, but remain interested in negotiating something, but they'd do well to stay away. His peripherals haven't been headed in happy directions for years, and now he's damaged goods. Signed by the Cardinals as we went to press.

Jason Howell　　　Born: 25-May-79　　Age: 24　　Bats: L　　Throws: L

YEAR	TM	LG	AGE	G	GS	IP	H	BB	SO	HR	ERA	EQERA	EQH9	EQBB9	EQSO9	EQHR9	PERA	VORP	STF
2001	LOW	NYP	22	20	0	52.7	55	16	38	6	5.64	9.13	17.3	4.6	4.2	4.2	8.45	-22.0	-34
2002	AUG	SAL	23	40	0	76.7	73	16	47	3	2.11	5.12	12.3	2.7	3.5	1.0	5.09	2.2	-16

Signed as an undrafted free agent, Howell breezed through the Sally league with a 2.11 ERA in 76 IP as the Augusta closer. Howell doesn't strike out enough to be considered a prospect, but he's left-handed, and therefore worth keeping an eye on.

Bobby Howry   Born: 04-Aug-73   Age: 29   Bats: L   Throws: R

YEAR	TM	LG	AGE	G	GS	IP	H	BB	SO	HR	ERA	EQERA	EQH9	EQBB9	EQSO9	EQHR9	PERA	VORP	STF
2000	CWS	AL	26	65	0	71.0	54	29	60	6	3.17	2.75	6.5	3.0	7.4	0.6	2.66	20.7	10
2001	CWS	AL	27	69	0	78.7	85	30	64	11	4.69	4.61	9.5	3.2	6.9	1.1	4.75	6.7	-1
2002	CWS	AL	28	47	0	50.7	45	17	31	7	3.91	3.73	8.0	2.8	5.4	1.1	3.65	9.3	-6
2002	BOS	AL	28	20	0	18.0	22	4	14	2	5.00	5.84	11.0	1.9	6.9	0.9	4.92	-0.9	1
2003	BOS	AL	29	55	0	53.3	55	19	37	6	4.12	4.09	9.0	3.0	6.1	1.0	4.33	10.6	-4

Breakout: 17%   Improve: 46%   Collapse: 24%

Howry's struggles began in 2001, after off-season shoulder surgery, but he got save opportunities courtesy of Jerry Manuel's spat with Keith Foulke. After inking him to a midyear contract extension last year, the White Sox's affections quickly soured, and they traded him to the Red Sox for two unheralded minor leaguers. Despite his unimpressive beginning with the team, Boston is on the hook for $2 million this season and will give him every chance to succeed.

Mauricio Lara   Born: 02-Apr-79   Age: 24   Bats: B   Throws: L

YEAR	TM	LG	AGE	G	GS	IP	H	BB	SO	HR	ERA	EQERA	EQH9	EQBB9	EQSO9	EQHR9	PERA	VORP	STF
2000	LOW	NYP	21	15	14	85.0	70	21	83	0	2.12	4.19	10.6	3.0	5.0	0.3	4.66	12.4	12
2000	AUG	SAL	21	16	0	32.0	25	13	33	2	1.41	4.92	10.5	5.2	5.5	1.6	5.18	1.6	-7
2001	AUG	SAL	22	20	19	107.3	114	24	96	5	3.02	6.06	13.9	3.1	4.7	1.1	6.75	-6.6	0
2002	SAR	FSL	23	23	4	62.0	74	27	43	3	4.35	6.89	14.4	5.2	4.6	1.1	7.36	-10.1	-17

With a low-90s fastball and a good curve, Lara was considered one of the Sox top pitching prospects entering this season. He was unimpressive at Sarasota, with a 4.35 ERA in relief and is likely to repeat another season at that level, but again, hard-throwing lefties get more than their share of breaks.

Derek Lowe   Born: 01-Jun-73   Age: 30   Bats: R   Throws: R

YEAR	TM	LG	AGE	G	GS	IP	H	BB	SO	HR	ERA	EQERA	EQH9	EQBB9	EQSO9	EQHR9	PERA	VORP	STF
2000	BOS	AL	27	74	0	91.3	90	22	79	6	2.56	2.65	8.5	1.8	7.6	0.5	3.05	27.7	15
2001	BOS	AL	28	67	3	91.7	103	29	82	7	3.53	3.71	9.5	2.6	7.5	0.6	4.37	17.2	9
2002	BOS	AL	29	32	32	219.7	166	48	127	12	2.58	2.50	6.9	1.9	5.1	0.5	2.41	73.4	16
2003	BOS	AL	30	35	29	188.0	187	50	124	19	3.73	3.70	8.7	2.2	5.7	0.9	3.69	42.0	11

Breakout: 13%   Improve: 50%   Collapse: 11%

Coming into this season, analysts were uncertain how Lowe would fare in the starting rotation. Not only did he maintain the level of performance that he had established in the bullpen, he improved substantially in holding baserunners—formerly a weakness. Opposing batters hit only .211 against Lowe, a credit to the excellent infield defense. A repeat of 2002 might be a little much to expect, but there is every reason to believe he will again be among the top ten pitchers in the league if he's durable enough to maintain the workload; his age isn't a concern.

Second only to Randy Johnson among major league pitchers in VORP, he was the most deserving candidate for the AL Cy Young award. His park-adjusted Runs Allowed was the best mark in the league, nearly 70 points ahead of winner Barry Zito. Counting against Lowe was his weaker W–L record, a general preference of the voters for pitchers on playoff teams, and the invariably wacky pool of voters in the American League.

Anastacio Martinez   Born: 03-Nov-78   Age: 24   Bats: R   Throws: R

YEAR	TM	LG	AGE	G	GS	IP	H	BB	SO	HR	ERA	EQERA	EQH9	EQBB9	EQSO9	EQHR9	PERA	VORP	STF
2000	AUG	SAL	21	23	23	120.3	130	50	107	8	4.64	7.60	14.6	5.4	4.9	1.7	7.65	-28.0	-7
2001	SAR	FSL	22	25	24	145.0	130	39	123	12	3.35	4.69	10.2	2.9	5.1	1.9	5.09	13.1	5
2002	TRN	EAS	23	27	27	139.0	152	75	127	12	5.31	6.46	11.4	5.8	6.3	1.3	6.79	-14.7	0

After a 5.31 ERA at Trenton, this fireballing starter has lost some of his luster as a prospect. To continue his progress, Martinez would need to develop additional pitches for his arsenal, but since he turned out to be three years older than originally thought as one of the results of Visagate, he doesn't have quite as much time left. A future in the pen beckons.

Pedro Martinez — Born: 25-Jul-71 — Age: 31 — Bats: R — Throws: R

YEAR	TM	LG	AGE	G	GS	IP	H	BB	SO	HR	ERA	EQERA	EQH9	EQBB9	EQSO9	EQHR9	PERA	VORP	STF
2000	BOS	AL	28	29	29	217.0	128	32	284	17	1.74	1.53	5.1	1.1	11.5	0.6	1.45	95.8	58
2001	BOS	AL	29	18	18	116.7	84	25	163	5	2.39	2.12	6.1	1.8	11.7	0.3	2.10	43.9	57
2002	BOS	AL	30	30	30	199.3	144	40	239	13	2.26	2.48	6.5	1.7	10.5	0.5	2.27	67.0	48
2003	BOS	AL	31	29	28	195.3	150	40	212	17	2.44	2.42	6.7	1.7	9.4	0.8	2.33	74.1	41

Breakout: 23%   Improve: 59%   Collapse: 13%

When Martinez allowed seven earned runs in three innings on Opening Day, many fans were ready to throw in the towel. Certainly Pedro was not at his best in the first half of the year as he "only" managed a 2.72 ERA. His velocity was down a couple mph and at times he lacked the control on which he has built his dominance. The second half of the season sends a different message, as a 1.61 ERA exclaims to the world "Pedro is back!"

Pedro is nonetheless a different pitcher than you saw from 1997 through 2000. He is unlikely to again reach 250 strikeouts in a season, as he has come to rely less on his fastball. He still has a great chance to throw 210 IP with an ERA around 2.00. If Martinez can stay healthy for a few more years, he has a chance to be remembered as the best pitcher ever.

Rene Miniel — Born: 26-Apr-79 — Age: 24 — Bats: R — Throws: R

YEAR	TM	LG	AGE	G	GS	IP	H	BB	SO	HR	ERA	EQERA	EQH9	EQBB9	EQSO9	EQHR9	PERA	VORP	STF
2001	AUG	SAL	22	27	23	122.0	93	38	114	1	2.73	4.80	9.4	4.3	4.8	0.2	4.43	9.5	3
2002	SAR	FSL	23	26	26	127.7	125	39	78	11	4.51	5.95	12.3	3.6	4.0	1.9	5.66	-6.3	-10

Like Anastacio Martinez, Miniel aged rapidly last winter (born 4/26/79, and not 4/26/81). Miniel achieved only moderate success at Sarasota, with a 4.51 ERA over 127 IP. He may be promoted due to a lack of upper-minors talent, but he is a marginal prospect at best.

Greg Montalbano — Born: 24-Aug-77 — Age: 25 — Bats: L — Throws: L

YEAR	TM	LG	AGE	G	GS	IP	H	BB	SO	HR	ERA	EQERA	EQH9	EQBB9	EQSO9	EQHR9	PERA	VORP	STF
2000	LOW	NYP	22	2	2	10.3	4	4	15	0	1.75	3.09	4.9	4.6	7.1	0.3	2.32	2.8	24
2001	SAR	FSL	23	17	15	91.3	66	25	77	11	2.96	3.94	8.9	3.0	5.2	2.8	4.30	15.8	0
2001	TRN	EAS	23	10	10	48.0	50	14	45	8	4.50	5.60	11.1	3.5	5.9	2.4	6.65	-0.5	-1

Montalbano was the 2001 Pitcher of the Year for Trenton, but missed the entire 2002 season following shoulder surgery. He was a finesse lefty before surgery, so he won't have to worry about leaving much velocity on the surgeon's table. He tended to work high in the zone and rely on his delivery to help fool hitters, and he still merits some consideration within the organization.

Darren Oliver — Born: 06-Oct-70 — Age: 32 — Bats: R — Throws: L

YEAR	TM	LG	AGE	G	GS	IP	H	BB	SO	HR	ERA	EQERA	EQH9	EQBB9	EQSO9	EQHR9	PERA	VORP	STF
2000	TEX	AL	29	21	21	108.0	151	42	49	16	7.42	5.86	11.2	2.8	3.9	1.1	5.79	-4.3	-8
2001	TEX	AL	30	28	28	154.0	189	65	104	23	6.02	5.43	10.2	3.5	5.6	1.2	5.62	1.3	1
2002	BOS	AL	31	14	9	58.0	70	27	32	7	4.66	4.97	10.8	3.9	4.8	1.0	5.66	3.3	-7
2003	BOS	AL	32	18	11	61.7	75	31	39	8	5.63	5.59	10.6	4.2	5.4	1.1	5.70	1.4	-8

Breakout: 11%   Improve: 36%   Collapse: 31%

Texas demanded that the Red Sox take Oliver as penance for the Everett signing. Although he was surprisingly effective in April and contributed to the Sox hot start, he resumed his life as Darren Oliver in May, was banished to the bullpen in June, was released in July, and (presumably) retired in August. American League sluggers and bleacher creatures will miss him.

Shane Rhodes — Born: 19-Jan-80 — Age: 23 — Bats: L — Throws: L

YEAR	TM	LG	AGE	G	GS	IP	H	BB	SO	HR	ERA	EQERA	EQH9	EQBB9	EQSO9	EQHR9	PERA	VORP	STF
2001	LOW	NYP	21	15	14	71.7	62	25	58	2	2.89	5.78	11.8	4.9	4.3	0.9	6.02	-2.2	-5
2002	AUG	SAL	22	31	20	134.0	117	62	97	6	3.09	5.62	11.6	6.2	4.2	1.1	5.68	-2.0	-12

The Sox 11th round pick in 2001, Rhodes managed a 3.09 ERA in 134 innings at Augusta. Given his age and college experience, that doesn't mean much. He will need to repeat this success in Sarasota to really merit notice.

Josh Thigpen   Born: 27-Jun-82   Age: 21   Bats: R   Throws: R

YEAR	TM	LG	AGE	G	GS	IP	H	BB	SO	HR	ERA	EQERA	EQH9	EQBB9	EQSO9	EQHR9	PERA	VORP	STF
2002	AUG	SAL	20	25	9	82.7	76	45	87	5	3.92	6.76	12.4	7.3	6.2	1.6	6.53	-12.0	-7

Thigpen finished strong at Augusta this season, posting a 1.08 ERA in the final month. His fastball rides in the low to mid-90s, but his control has been unimpressive. He will need to develop additional pitches to make progress as a starter, but he has plenty of time to mature. It's no longer Boston's problem, as they traded him to Cincinnati along with Tony Blanco for Todd Walker.

Ugueth Urbina   Born: 15-Feb-74   Age: 29   Bats: R   Throws: R

YEAR	TM	LG	AGE	G	GS	IP	H	BB	SO	HR	ERA	EQERA	EQH9	EQBB9	EQSO9	EQHR9	PERA	VORP	STF
2001	MON	NL	27	45	0	46.7	42	21	57	8	4.24	4.27	7.8	3.7	9.1	1.3	4.42	5.8	10
2001	BOS	AL	27	19	0	20.0	16	3	32	1	2.25	2.08	6.8	1.2	13.4	0.4	2.27	7.3	53
2002	BOS	AL	28	61	0	60.0	44	20	71	8	3.00	3.02	6.5	2.8	10.3	1.1	3.02	15.7	24
2003	TEX	AL	29	65	0	62	52	25	68	8	3.49	3.34	7.3	3.2	9.5	1	3.4	17.5	18

Breakout: 15%   *Improve: 43%*   *Collapse: 24%*

Urbina is an effective enough reliever, but you can't help a bit of buyer's remorse and wonder if the Sox wouldn't be better off with Tomo Ohka. As one of the younger free-agent relievers on the market this year, Urbina might have expected a big pay-day, but he had to settle for a one-year deal with the Rangers. Is the market getting smarter? Sixty-inning closers simply are not worth that much, and certainly the Red Sox are better off applying the money to their offensive needs.

Tim Wakefield   Born: 02-Aug-66   Age: 36   Bats: R   Throws: R

YEAR	TM	LG	AGE	G	GS	IP	H	BB	SO	HR	ERA	EQERA	EQH9	EQBB9	EQSO9	EQHR9	PERA	VORP	STF
2000	BOS	AL	33	51	17	159.3	170	65	102	31	5.48	4.96	9.0	3.0	5.6	1.5	4.75	8.8	-4
2001	BOS	AL	34	45	17	168.7	156	73	148	13	3.89	3.71	7.8	3.6	7.3	0.6	3.75	32.8	13
2002	BOS	AL	35	45	15	163.3	121	51	134	15	2.81	2.89	6.6	2.6	7.2	0.8	2.77	46.5	16
2003	BOS	AL	36	38	19	119.3	116	44	96	15	4.06	4.03	8.4	3.1	6.9	1.1	4.10	23.9	7

Breakout: 19%   *Improve: 44%*   *Collapse: 14%*

In 2001, Wakefield pitched like an All-Star for the first half of the season before losing his grip, but in 2002, he kept his grip on the entire year. His peripheral stats have noticeably improved, with his strikeout rate in each of the last two seasons topping his previous best. Frequent baserunners, the bane of knuckleball pitchers, have not been a problem for Wakefield as opposing batters hit only .204/.275/.333 (think Gary DiSarcina in an off year). Earlier in his career, Wakefield seemed to be successful only in his first season in each league. His current streak of dominance has broken a pattern of mediocrity, which bodes well for this season. After pitching as a swingman in each of the last four seasons (with 45 to 51 appearances, 15–17 starts, and 140–170 innings each year), he was signed to a bargain deal (three years and $13 million), and will begin the season in the rotation behind Martinez and Lowe. If Wakefield can approach this success in a full-time role, the Red Sox could have starting pitchers win, place, *and* show in the AL ERA race.

Chicago White Sox

Although smart people with a working understanding of the mechanics of building a winning organization are slowly making their way into front offices around the majors, it's still easy to quickly come up with a list full of bad general managers. In Kansas City, Allard Baird has turned trading value for virtually nothing into an art form. Unless you're the world's biggest Wade Boggs fan, Chuck LaMar has been a failure in Tampa Bay. The Larry Beinfest era in Miami has the Marlins cornering the market in foot speed at the expense of players who can hit. Steve Phillips hasn't failed to offer a declining free-agent veteran 20% over market price in two years. In the 2002 off-season, Omar Minaya did the best job of waiting the market into oblivion since Bobby J. Jones in 2000.

But none of those guys had the cheap, talented, young organization White Sox general manager Kenny Williams inherited in October of 2000, and that's where he achieves separation from the pack. Going into year three of the Williams era on the South Side, the Sox have yet to sniff a pennant, and if the front office continues moving talent for inferior, expensive replacements, the team's enviable core will be dismantled faster than *Girls Club*.

It's amazing that it has come to this, because when Williams replaced general manager Ron Schueler, he looked like the perfect man for the job. He had the twin advantages of youth—he was 36 at the time—and experience, with seven years of employment in the White Sox front office. From 1997–2000, Williams was the club's vice president of player development, presiding over a system bursting with quality prospects. At the time of his promotion, there probably wasn't anyone on earth who knew the depth and talent that the White Sox system contained better than Williams.

At the major league level, Williams has shown a distressing tendency to mistrust the young pitchers he helped develop. In the David Wells acquisition, he got away with it because

the Ash Jays couldn't be bothered to schedule a physical for Mike Sirotka; with the Todd Ritchie deal, Williams went to the well once too often. He gave away two excellent pitching prospects for a veteran with a single above-average year under his belt, one that was coming off of a season in which he sported an awful 5.58 ERA on the road.

It isn't too much of a stretch to say Williams gave away the division in the Ritchie trade. The White Sox ended 2002 in second place, 13.5 games back of Minnesota. That's a lot of ground to cover, but swapping Kip Wells and Josh Fogg for Ritchie and Gary Glover would have done just that. Most of the white flag trades the organization made in July didn't make much difference, but holding on to second baseman Ray Durham all season would have had an impact. Most importantly, if it came down to a mid-season trade, the White Sox were far more able to address a need with a trade than the Twins, though Williams' inability to get value in a deal is what has the team in trouble to begin with. As it turned out, Wells and Fogg headed up the Pittsburgh rotation, Ritchie lit up the Chicago skyline, and Sox fans were left holding the bag.

In the abstract, Williams and manager Jerry Manuel's preference for veteran starters makes sense. Depending on a single young, inexperienced pitcher to take the ball every fifth day takes organizational leadership with a strong will, a slow temper, and an Antacid-of-the-Month club membership. But the unreal amount of internal options the Sox should have had to choose from make this a completely different situation. The team boasted an entire rotation's worth of starters with a record of success in at least the high minors in Wells, Fogg, Mark Buehrle, Jon Garland, and Jon Rauch. In a perfect world, each of these guys makes 30 starts and pitches well and the team gets to the World Series with a rotation that still gets carded at bars. Just as importantly, the Sox had several other pitchers with

---

White Sox Prospectus

2002 record: 81–81; Second place, AL Central

Pythagenport Record: 87–75

Runs scored per game: 5.3 (3rd in AL)

Runs allowed per game: 4.9 (8th in AL)

Team EqA: .265 (8th in AL)

2002 Batters Age: 29.3 (7th youngest in AL)

2002 Pitchers Age: 25.9 (youngest in AL)

Ballpark: New Comiskey Park; Severe hitters' park; Park Factor of 1.040

2002: Core talent gets let down by the front office again, missing another chance to compete or make progress.

2003: Kenny Williams will have to prove he can compete or make progress after wasting two years.

lesser pedigrees and upside, all at the right ages to make a performance spike a possibility, in Glover, Danny Wright, Rocky Biddle, and even Jim Parque. With these guys, you have a safety net for the inevitable problems that at least one of your starters will face, and as a bonus, you've got a non-zero chance of a John Snyderesque tumble. With this much depth and a crackerjack bullpen, Manuel and pitching coach Nardi Contreras could have played the hot hands in the rotation, given the backups plenty of innings in blowouts, and had a good chance of succeeding with what the organization had created on its own.

Back in reality, Todd Ritchie had a good first month but quickly reverted to form, Rauch pitched poorly early in the season and was demoted, and the Sox staff didn't have enough left to fill in the holes. The temps shuttling in experienced hard times, and the team's pitching took a face-plant in late June—in the three weeks prior to the All-Star break, the Sox held opposing teams to three runs or less only four times in 20 games. Things gradually improved as the season wore on, especially once Ritchie's quest for 20 losses came to an end with a trip to the DL in August. Rauch provided more good news by looking very strong in his return to the majors in September. The improvement didn't come quickly enough to save Contreras's job; he was unceremoniously dumped in late July, as Williams and Manuel scrounged for a scapegoat.

While the White Sox still retain some of the pitching that made them such a compelling team to watch over the last couple of years, Williams and Manuel need to resolve their issues with the youngsters in the rotation. Taking a page out of the team media guide might help; in 1993, the White Sox won their division and sported a league-best 3.70 ERA with a rotation comprised of Alex Fernandez (23 years old), Jack McDowell (27), Wilson Alvarez (23), Jason Bere (22), and a fifth spot paper-over duo of Kirk McCaskill and Tim Belcher. As good as that foursome was, 2003's rotation of Buherle, Garland, a completely healthy Rauch, and Wright might be even better. In the minors, Kris Honel is developing rapidly to add to the bounty, but the clown car full of pitching prospects the organization has boasted of in the last few years is now a thing of the past.

The pitching problems the Sox had in 2002 overshadowed a muscular performance by the team's offense. The team rebounded from a down 2001 with 856 runs scored—good for third in the league—and there is reason to expect continued improvement. The team endured another marginal season from Frank Thomas, but there's nothing physically wrong with his swing and he's still got another couple of years like 2000 left in him. Williams made an astute trade for second baseman D'Angelo Jimenez, and he should be an adequate top-of-the-order replacement for Durham. Left fielder Carlos Lee became the first Sox hitter other than Thomas to post more walks than strikeouts since 1995.

While the organization's pitching depth is drying up, the farm system is supplying a couple of blue chip hitting prospects. Third baseman Joe Crede was called up for good in August, and power-hitting outfielder Joe Borchard saw some late-season action with the Sox as well. With the departure of the execrable Royce Clayton, the Sox will be playing plus hitters everywhere in the infield in 2003, and if Borchard nabs the center field job out of spring training, the Sox could see 20+ home runs from seven lineup spots. Only Thomas and shortstop Jose Valentin are on the wrong side of 30 years old, and it wouldn't be a surprise for this offense to peak in 2003 and lead the league in production.

Despite the overall offensive quality, the Sox' attack still lacks a good lefty bat. As we noted last year, teams that skew too heavily toward one side of the plate run the risk of being marginalized by platoon splits in a short series. The lack of a left-handed threat hasn't escaped Williams's attention; he's talked about making a deal on this front all off-season. Two factors entering into the team's calculations on this front are the fear of how much Carlos Lee might make courtesy of arbitration, and how to stock second, short, and center field. If Lee's salary is onerous enough to force Williams to deal him, Joe Borchard might take over in left instead of center. Then there might be space to play both D'Angelo Jimenez and Willie Harris. Between the two of them and Jose Valentin—who has played center in winter ball—it's possible that you could see Harris at second, Valentin in center, and Jimenez at short, or Jimenez at second, Valentin at short, and Harris in center. Sorting through that mess will be a significant issue in camp for Jerry Manuel.

The Sox are a young team with a great core of talent, but the organization no longer has the monster depth that makes success with the homegrown talent a sure thing waiting to happen, especially in a division suddenly boasting a few threats. The no-longer-contractable Twins have good young players of their own and even more depth than the Sox used to boast, while the Indians are a year and an arm or two away from at least theoretical contention.

To ice the division for the next couple of seasons, the Sox will have to quickly address needs as they occur—a function most teams execute on the trade market. If Kenny Williams deals more talent for pennies on the dollar, the White Sox will fail. If he simply refuses any calls from Billy Beane or Dave Littlefield, the organization has a good chance to succeed just based on its in-house talent. If, by some strange development, Williams suddenly realizes what it takes to make a good trade—and it's the only thing he's missing as a general manager, because he's respected, well-liked, and looks great in a suit—the Sox have the resources to start a mini-dynasty. This club will go as far as their front office's ability to avoid being abused in trades develops.

HITTERS

Joe Borchard   CF   Born: 25-Nov-78   Age: 24   Bats: B   Throws: R

YEAR	TM	LG	AGE	AB	H	2B	3B	HR	BB	SO	SB	CS	AVG	OBP	SLG	MLVR	EQBA	EQOBP	EQSLG	EQMLVR	VORP	DEFENSE
2000	WNS	CRL	21	52	15	3	0	2	6	9	0	0	.288	.383	.462	.222	.241	.304	.389	-.160	-1.2	12-RF 0
2001	BIR	SOU	22	515	152	27	1	27	67	158	5	4	.295	.387	.509	.292	.262	.336	.449	-.001	24.7	133-CF -10
2002	CHR	INT	23	438	119	35	2	20	49	139	2	4	.272	.350	.498	.166	.251	.326	.463	-.009	20.6	115-CF -1
2002	CWS	AL	23	36	8	0	0	2	1	14	0	0	.222	.243	.389	-.236	.250	.270	.417	-.177	-.8	10-LF 0
2003	CWS	AL	24	231	61	13	2	10	24	61	3	3	.265	.338	.471	.073	.269	.346	.478	.059	9.8	

Breakout: 33%   Improve: 65%   Collapse: 16%

Borchard is a good prospect, but there are things to watch in 2003. His strikeout to walk ratio isn't good, and that becomes more of a concern as his playing time against major league pitchers increases. He may not be able to carry center field defensively, but the Sox don't have anywhere else to play him, so they'll give him every opportunity. A good spring could mean he's Chicago-bound for good.

Royce Clayton   SS   Born: 02-Jan-70   Age: 33   Bats: R   Throws: R

YEAR	TM	LG	AGE	AB	H	2B	3B	HR	BB	SO	SB	CS	AVG	OBP	SLG	MLVR	EQBA	EQOBP	EQSLG	EQMLVR	VORP	DEFENSE
2000	TEX	AL	30	513	124	21	5	14	42	92	11	7	.242	.303	.384	-.213	.244	.298	.389	-.170	6.2	138-SS 2
2001	CWS	AL	31	433	114	21	4	9	33	72	10	7	.263	.320	.393	-.078	.277	.334	.416	-.039	20.2	121-SS 15
2002	CWS	AL	32	342	86	14	2	7	20	67	5	1	.251	.299	.365	-.149	.268	.315	.391	-.117	8.8	100-SS 14
2003	MIL	NL	33	267	66	12	2	5	20	48	5	3	.247	.303	.361	-.162	.252	.305	.375	-.162	0.0	

Breakout: 19%   Improve: 49%   Collapse: 23%

Clayton was one of the worst players in the majors in 2002. That said, he is the kind of player you might take a chance on if you need leather at short and can deal with light offensive contributions. Clayton's last year was bad enough that he stood a chance of scaring that market away, leaving him the rare veteran bit player that comes cheap enough to make him worth the bother. It didn't happen this time; the Brewers will be paying him too much to start for them at short in 2003.

Joe Crede   3B   Born: 26-Apr-78   Age: 25   Bats: R   Throws: R

YEAR	TM	LG	AGE	AB	H	2B	3B	HR	BB	SO	SB	CS	AVG	OBP	SLG	MLVR	EQBA	EQOBP	EQSLG	EQMLVR	VORP	DEFENSE
2000	BIR	SOU	22	533	163	35	0	21	56	111	3	4	.306	.387	.490	.297	.276	.333	.447	.002	27.0	135-3B -16
2001	CHR	INT	23	463	128	34	1	17	46	88	2	1	.276	.351	.464	.125	.258	.328	.435	-.039	18.6	123-3B 6
2001	CWS	AL	23	50	11	1	1	0	3	11	1	0	.220	.278	.280	-.332	.240	.293	.300	-.307	-1.5	12-3B 0
2002	CHR	INT	24	359	112	21	0	24	26	48	0	1	.312	.365	.571	.325	.285	.337	.528	.133	30.9	92-3B 4
2002	CWS	AL	24	200	57	10	0	12	8	40	0	2	.285	.313	.515	.104	.303	.330	.547	.169	17.7	47-3B 0
2003	CWS	AL	25	373	101	21	1	18	28	65	2	2	.271	.326	.474	.064	.276	.334	.482	.050	17.1	

Breakout: 13%   Improve: 52%   Collapse: 20%

The Sox have been very patient with Crede, bordering on too patient, while running a series of temps out to third while he worked his way up the chain. They were rewarded in 2002, when he avoided the slow adjustment periods that have plagued younger, more heralded third-base prospects. He'll be poking line drives and manning the hot corner for the Sox for years.

Tony Graffanino   IF   Born: 06-Jun-72   Age: 31   Bats: R   Throws: R

YEAR	TM	LG	AGE	AB	H	2B	3B	HR	BB	SO	SB	CS	AVG	OBP	SLG	MLVR	EQBA	EQOBP	EQSLG	EQMLVR	VORP	DEFENSE	
2000	CWS	AL	28	148	40	5	1	2	21	25	7	4	.270	.365	.358	-.100	.274	.362	.363	-.063	5.9	17-SS 4	16-2B 2
2001	CWS	AL	29	145	44	9	0	2	16	29	4	1	.303	.377	.407	.072	.317	.392	.428	.117	11.9	23-3B -3	17-2B 2
2002	CWS	AL	30	229	60	12	4	6	22	38	2	1	.262	.332	.428	-.000	.278	.348	.457	.045	14.0	31-3B 1	19-2B 2
2003	CWS	AL	31	256	69	14	2	6	27	43	4	2	.269	.340	.409	.002	.274	.348	.416	-.015	8.8		

Breakout: 5%   Improve: 37%   Collapse: 26%

Like a channel surfer when there's nothing on, the White Sox flipped through a ton of different infield configurations in 2002. Supersub Graffanino was a main player in the drama until he tore his right ACL in August, but not before netting the most ABs he'd seen in a season since 1998. He should be ready for spring training, and remains one of the best utility infielders in the game.

Willie Harris　　2B　Born: 22-Jun-78　Age: 25　Bats: L　Throws: R

YEAR	TM	LG	AGE	AB	H	2B	3B	HR	BB	SO	SB	CS	AVG	OBP	SLG	MLVR	EQBA	EQOBP	EQSLG	EQMLVR	VORP	DEFENSE			
2000	DEL	SAL	22	474	130	27	10	6	89	89	38	15	.274	.399	.411	.191	.214	.308	.328	-.253	-5.1	106-2B	-5	19-CF	0
2001	BOW	EAS	23	525	160	27	4	9	46	71	54	16	.305	.366	.423	.144	.267	.323	.373	-.128	12.4	90-2B	-13	41-CF	0
2002	CHR	INT	24	360	102	16	5	5	33	61	32	14	.283	.347	.397	.038	.259	.322	.369	-.141	7.2	82-2B	-1		
2002	CWS	AL	24	163	38	4	0	2	9	21	8	0	.233	.273	.294	-.301	.245	.289	.313	-.294	-3.2	37-2B	0		
2003	*CWS*	*AL*	*25*	*284*	*71*	*14*	*2*	*5*	*27*	*47*	*11*	*5*	*.251*	*.317*	*.369*	*-.101*	*.255*	*.324*	*.375*	*-.125*	*2.6*				

Breakout: 26%　　Improve: 52%　　Collapse: 18%

Harris is a career second baseman, but the Sox tried playing him in center field in 2002. The official plan is to start Borchard in Triple-A, and since Rowand might not be back to start the season, Harris could be the Opening Day center fielder. Additional flexibility is critical for a player like Harris, who doesn't do enough things offensively to hold down a single position.

Tim Hummel　　SS/2B　Born: 18-Nov-78　Age: 24　Bats: R　Throws: R

YEAR	TM	LG	AGE	AB	H	2B	3B	HR	BB	SO	SB	CS	AVG	OBP	SLG	MLVR	EQBA	EQOBP	EQSLG	EQMLVR	VORP	DEFENSE			
2000	BUR	MDW	21	144	47	9	1	1	21	20	8	3	.326	.416	.424	.247	.250	.317	.324	-.220	-.1	36-SS	-6		
2000	WNS	CRL	21	98	32	7	0	1	13	12	1	1	.327	.416	.429	.254	.267	.333	.356	-.133	1.5	25-3B	-4		
2001	BIR	SOU	22	524	152	33	6	7	62	69	14	3	.290	.371	.416	.140	.262	.327	.378	-.117	13.7	91-2B	-11	35-SS	-9
2002	CHR	INT	23	523	136	33	0	4	51	95	6	5	.260	.337	.346	-.060	.244	.317	.330	-.215	.5	78-SS	0	53-2B	-2
2003	*CWS*	*AL*	*24*	*176*	*44*	*9*	*1*	*3*	*16*	*29*	*3*	*2*	*.248*	*.314*	*.370*	*-.106*	*.253*	*.321*	*.376*	*-.130*	*1.3*				

Breakout: 24%　　Improve: 45%　　Collapse: 23%

Hummel has been the second baseman of the future since he was drafted in 2000, but he hasn't progressed the way the Sox have hoped he would, and the arrival of Jimenez puts a dent in his future. He'll be at short for the Knights in 2003, as the Sox evaluate his ability to fill in there once Valentin moves on.

D'Angelo Jimenez　　2B/SS　Born: 21-Dec-77　Age: 25　Bats: B　Throws: R

YEAR	TM	LG	AGE	AB	H	2B	3B	HR	BB	SO	SB	CS	AVG	OBP	SLG	MLVR	EQBA	EQOBP	EQSLG	EQMLVR	VORP	DEFENSE			
2000	COH	INT	22	73	17	3	1	1	7	12	2	0	.233	.309	.342	-.177	.230	.286	.338	-.274	-1.1	12-2B	-8		
2001	COH	INT	23	214	56	11	1	5	24	31	5	6	.262	.339	.393	.012	.243	.317	.367	-.165	2.9	30-2B	-9	14-SS	3
2001	SDP	NL	23	308	85	19	0	3	39	68	2	3	.276	.357	.367	-.030	.288	.366	.380	-.021	17.4	85-SS	-1		
2002	SDP	NL	24	321	77	11	4	3	34	63	4	2	.240	.313	.327	-.125	.258	.326	.356	-.153	5.4	52-2B	1	31-3B	2
2002	CHR	INT	24	157	44	11	1	6	24	14	6	2	.280	.376	.478	.187	.256	.346	.450	.013	10.4	42-SS	-9		
2002	CWS	AL	24	108	31	4	3	1	16	10	2	1	.287	.384	.407	.081	.303	.396	.440	.129	10.2	16-2B	6		
2003	*CWS*	*AL*	*25*	*428*	*109*	*22*	*3*	*9*	*47*	*69*	*7*	*3*	*.254*	*.329*	*.383*	*-.060*	*.258*	*.336*	*.390*	*-.081*	*8.2*				

Breakout: 14%　　Improve: 39%　　Collapse: 20%

Teams ditch talented players all the time—for interpersonal problems because "they want to move in another direction," whatever—and there is no better opportunity to pick up a worthwhile prospect for nothing. The White Sox did just that with Jimenez. After an ugly start to the season in San Diego, he played well in a Sox uniform and in the Dominican League. He's the leading contender for the second-base job and leadoff slot with the Sox in 2003.

Mark Johnson　　C　Born: 12-Sep-75　Age: 27　Bats: L　Throws: R

YEAR	TM	LG	AGE	AB	H	2B	3B	HR	BB	SO	SB	CS	AVG	OBP	SLG	MLVR	EQBA	EQOBP	EQSLG	EQMLVR	VORP	DEFENSE	
2000	CWS	AL	24	213	48	11	0	3	27	40	3	2	.225	.315	.319	-.281	.232	.317	.327	-.226	.5	68-C	3
2001	CHR	INT	25	196	53	5	2	4	29	34	2	1	.270	.364	.378	.032	.255	.344	.355	-.121	6.2	47-C	-6
2001	CWS	AL	25	173	43	6	1	5	23	31	2	1	.249	.343	.382	-.059	.266	.360	.410	-.008	10.8	55-C	3
2002	CWS	AL	26	263	55	8	1	4	30	52	0	0	.209	.297	.293	-.269	.227	.314	.318	-.247	-.9	79-C	4
2003	*OAK*	*AL*	*27*	*221*	*52*	*10*	*1*	*4*	*26*	*41*	*1*	*1*	*.235*	*.318*	*.351*	*-.130*	*.243*	*.329*	*.367*	*-.133*	*2.2*		

Breakout: 37%　　Improve: 66%　　Collapse: 12%

Johnson isn't Piazza-in-waiting, but the Sox should have taken a chance on him instead of screwing around with Sandy Alomar Jr. last year. A lot of Johnson's offensive value comes from his strong plate discipline, which some teams don't value as much as others. It isn't surprising the A's nabbed him in the Foulke-Koch trade. He'll be backing up Ramon Hernandez in 2003, with his defense and patience giving him the opportunity to push into sharing the job.

Brooks Kieschnick — LF — Born: 06-Jun-72 — Age: 31 — Bats: L — Throws: R

YEAR	TM	LG	AGE	AB	H	2B	3B	HR	BB	SO	SB	CS	AVG	OBP	SLG	MLVR	EQBA	EQOBP	EQSLG	EQMLVR	VORP	DEFENSE			
2000	LOU	INT	28	440	122	35	0	25	38	107	2	1	.277	.336	.527	.158	.255	.303	.483	-.019	7.8	46-LF	-5	40-1B	2
2001	CSP	PCL	29	252	74	9	3	13	24	72	3	2	.294	.360	.508	.110	.250	.314	.423	-.088	-.8	39-RF	-2		
2002	CHR	INT	30	189	52	11	0	13	14	46	0	0	.275	.325	.540	.187	.253	.304	.500	.005	7.0				
2003	MIL	NL	31	125	30	6	1	6	12	35	1	1	.237	.306	.434	-.067	.242	.308	.451	-.064	-1.4				

Breakout: 29%   Improve: 55%   Collapse: 27%

Brooks Kieschnick — the Pitcher

YEAR	TM	LG	AGE	G	GS	IP	H	BB	SO	HR	ERA	EQERA	EQH9	EQBB9	EQSO9	EQHR9	PERA	VORP	STF
2002	CHR	INT	30	25	0	31.3	30	10	30	1	2.59	3.57	9.5	3.5	7.4	0.4	4.06	6.3	6

Kieschnick had a huge college career, both as a first baseman and as a pitcher, and was drafted in the first round by the Cubs to be a position player. Since then, he's been stuck with the reputation of a player with a Triple-A ceiling; his defensive mediocrity hurts him in any bid for a bench spot he might make. Similar players have stretched themselves defensively to add utility, but with the Knights, Kieschnick took the concept to its logical conclusion by joining the bullpen.

As baseball rosters become more and more specialized (or "LaRussaned"), Brooks Kieschnick might be the prototypical 25th man. He won't embarrass himself or his manager on the mound, and he's a better hitter than 90% of the bench players in the majors. The options for a player like this, especially in the NL, are fun to consider; letting Kieschnick bat for himself while pitching doesn't do the opposition any favors and saves a pinch hitter for later, and a double-switch with a guy who can pitch and play left is always a good time. The Brewers intend on letting Kieschnick play both roles in 2003, and if it works out look for more stalled players who were two-way stars to give this a try.

Paul Konerko — 1B — Born: 05-Mar-76 — Age: 27 — Bats: R — Throws: R

YEAR	TM	LG	AGE	AB	H	2B	3B	HR	BB	SO	SB	CS	AVG	OBP	SLG	MLVR	EQBA	EQOBP	EQSLG	EQMLVR	VORP	DEFENSE	
2000	CWS	AL	24	524	156	31	1	21	47	72	1	0	.298	.367	.481	.100	.305	.368	.494	.158	32.8	119-1B	0
2001	CWS	AL	25	582	164	35	0	32	54	89	1	0	.282	.352	.507	.146	.297	.366	.537	.207	46.7	141-1B	2
2002	CWS	AL	26	570	173	30	0	27	44	72	0	0	.304	.363	.498	.179	.319	.377	.529	.238	49.0	135-1B	-8
2003	CWS	AL	27	540	154	31	1	26	47	77	0	0	.284	.346	.488	.124	.290	.354	.496	.114	22.0		

Breakout: 7%   Improve: 36%   Collapse: 22%

Konerko started strong in 2002, but a mediocre second half returned him to his standard season. That's not something you want to see from your 27-year-old slugger, and at this point you have to ask yourself if Konerko merits the buzz and the shiny new contract he's got. A very popular player—he's seen in Chicago as the no-nonsense, blue-collar antidote to Frank Thomas's prima-donna act—but he's running out of time to make that step up to the pantheon of elite sluggers.

Carlos Lee — LF — Born: 20-Jun-76 — Age: 27 — Bats: R — Throws: R

YEAR	TM	LG	AGE	AB	H	2B	3B	HR	BB	SO	SB	CS	AVG	OBP	SLG	MLVR	EQBA	EQOBP	EQSLG	EQMLVR	VORP	DEFENSE	
2000	CWS	AL	24	572	172	29	2	24	38	94	13	4	.301	.347	.484	.074	.307	.346	.499	.130	30.1	140-LF	-3
2001	CWS	AL	25	558	150	33	3	24	38	85	17	7	.269	.322	.468	.032	.283	.337	.496	.086	25.1	121-LF	-1
2002	CWS	AL	26	492	130	26	2	26	75	73	1	4	.264	.364	.484	.127	.283	.380	.523	.196	38.5	124-LF	3
2003	CWS	AL	27	500	139	28	2	23	55	80	7	3	.278	.352	.481	.118	.283	.360	.488	.108	18.9		

Breakout: 17%   Improve: 47%   Collapse: 11%

The longer a hot streak gets, the harder it becomes to explain away, especially when it indicates a changing approach at the plate. Carlos Lee began the season up to his old tricks. He ended it with 65 walks in 326 at-bats from June on, tagging the league to the tune of a .394 OBP and .503 SLG over that period. Maybe it's the contrarian in me, but I'd rather take my chances with Lee than Konerko at this point.

Jeff Liefer   **1B**   **Born: 17-Aug-74**   **Age: 28**   **Bats: L**   **Throws: R**

YEAR	TM	LG	AGE	AB	H	2B	3B	HR	BB	SO	SB	CS	AVG	OBP	SLG	MLVR	EQBA	EQOBP	EQSLG	EQMLVR	VORP	DEFENSE			
2000	CHR	INT	25	445	125	29	1	32	53	107	2	3	.281	.360	.566	.244	.253	.322	.506	.045	17.0	61-1B	3	16-LF	-2
2001	CHR	INT	26	119	34	7	0	6	15	41	3	1	.286	.384	.496	.224	.264	.354	.463	.052	4.8	28-1B	4		
2001	CWS	AL	26	254	65	13	0	18	20	69	0	1	.256	.315	.520	.079	.268	.327	.551	.131	14.5	27-LF	1	11-3B	-3
2002	CWS	AL	27	204	47	8	0	7	19	60	0	0	.230	.296	.373	-.158	.249	.312	.400	-.124	-1.9	27-LF	0	23-1B	-4
2003	MON	NL	28	208	51	10	1	10	24	57	1	1	.246	.325	.445	-.015	.246	.322	.453	-.032	0.2				

Breakout: 22%   Improve: 51%   Collapse: 24%

Frank Thomas's re-signing should signal the end of Liefer's White Sox career. He's got cement hands and feet, so he'll be hard-pressed to hold down a defensive job, but he'd make a fair bat off the bench or DH for someone. Now that he's an Expo as a throw-in on the Colon deal, he could win the everyday job at first. He'll be easily mistaken for Lee Stevens.

Aaron Miles   **2B**   **Born: 15-Dec-76**   **Age: 26**   **Bats: B**   **Throws: R**

YEAR	TM	LG	AGE	AB	H	2B	3B	HR	BB	SO	SB	CS	AVG	OBP	SLG	MLVR	EQBA	EQOBP	EQSLG	EQMLVR	VORP	DEFENSE			
2000	KIS	FSL	23	295	86	20	1	2	28	29	11	6	.292	.353	.386	.079	.239	.287	.326	-.283	-5.4	71-2B	-5		
2001	BIR	SOU	24	343	89	16	3	8	26	35	3	5	.259	.315	.394	-.002	.233	.276	.355	-.267	-6.9	22-3B	-9	15-2B	-3
2002	BIR	SOU	25	531	171	39	1	9	40	45	25	16	.322	.372	.450	.244	.288	.321	.410	-.062	21.5	125-2B	-21		
2003	CWS	AL	26	191	49	10	1	4	12	21	4	1	.257	.305	.384	-.098	.262	.312	.390	-.122	1.8				

Breakout: 26%   Improve: 59%   Collapse: 20%

In his second campaign with the Barons, Miles led the Southern League with a .322 average, and he should open 2003 in Triple-A. He needs to master that level more quickly than he did Double-A to merit a major league call-up, and he's with the wrong organization in any case.

Miguel Olivo   **C**   **Born: 15-Jul-78**   **Age: 24**   **Bats: R**   **Throws: R**

YEAR	TM	LG	AGE	AB	H	2B	3B	HR	BB	SO	SB	CS	AVG	OBP	SLG	MLVR	EQBA	EQOBP	EQSLG	EQMLVR	VORP	DEFENSE	
2000	MOD	CLF	21	227	64	11	5	5	16	53	5	2	.282	.335	.441	.080	.227	.253	.354	-.317	-4.4	49-C	0
2000	MID	TXS	21	59	14	2	0	1	5	15	0	0	.237	.297	.322	-.266	.203	.242	.271	-.470	-3.3	13-C	-5
2001	BIR	SOU	22	316	82	23	1	14	37	62	6	3	.259	.350	.472	.157	.232	.304	.419	-.125	9.2	90-C	-9
2002	BIR	SOU	23	359	110	24	10	6	40	66	29	13	.306	.384	.479	.285	.272	.330	.434	-.025	20.6	98-C	-8
2002	CWS	AL	23	19	4	1	0	1	2	5	0	0	.211	.286	.421	-.126	.211	.286	.474	-.100	.2		
2003	CWS	AL	24	265	69	15	2	8	21	52	5	4	.260	.320	.427	-.015	.265	.327	.434	-.034	9.0		

Breakout: 28%   Improve: 54%   Collapse: 19%

The Sox are high on Olivo, who was the prize Kenny Williams got from Oakland in exchange for Chad Bradford. With the trade of Mark Johnson and the limp bat of Josh Paul, Olivo has next to nothing to hold him back. Olivo has a flashy arm but isn't otherwise known for his defense, so an Olivo/Paul offense/defense combo could be in the making, especially after they get the bones of Sandy Alomar out of the way.

Magglio Ordonez   **RF**   **Born: 28-Jan-74**   **Age: 29**   **Bats: R**   **Throws: R**

YEAR	TM	LG	AGE	AB	H	2B	3B	HR	BB	SO	SB	CS	AVG	OBP	SLG	MLVR	EQBA	EQOBP	EQSLG	EQMLVR	VORP	DEFENSE	
2000	CWS	AL	26	588	185	34	3	32	60	64	18	4	.315	.380	.546	.235	.321	.380	.560	.289	53.4	138-RF	0
2001	CWS	AL	27	593	181	40	1	31	70	70	25	7	.305	.383	.533	.254	.323	.400	.566	.331	65.5	132-RF	4
2002	CWS	AL	28	590	189	47	1	38	53	77	7	5	.320	.383	.597	.360	.341	.402	.639	.462	82.7	134-RF	2
2003	CWS	AL	29	554	168	37	2	31	58	71	10	2	.303	.371	.542	.247	.308	.379	.550	.245	38.8		

Breakout: 11%   Improve: 35%   Collapse: 15%

Ordonez started the season cold, with a bruised wrist and a sore back hampering his swing, and he ended it with a little silver bat. Over the last three years, only Bernie Williams and Manny Ramirez have been more productive outfielders, and Ramirez has played his share of DH. Maggs is everything people think Garret Anderson is, except he doesn't have a ring. Yet.

Josh Paul — C — Born: 19-May-75 — Age: 28 — Bats: R — Throws: R

YEAR	TM	LG	AGE	AB	H	2B	3B	HR	BB	SO	SB	CS	AVG	OBP	SLG	MLVR	EQBA	EQOBP	EQSLG	EQMLVR	VORP	DEFENSE	
2000	CHR	INT	25	168	40	5	1	4	13	38	6	2	.238	.301	.351	-.184	.225	.274	.331	-.310	-3.3	47-C	0
2000	CWS	AL	25	71	20	3	2	1	5	17	1	0	.282	.338	.423	-.052	.286	.342	.429	.002	4.1	23-C	3
2001	CHR	INT	26	75	21	4	0	4	7	18	0	0	.280	.341	.493	.152	.263	.325	.447	-.023	4.2	18-C	0
2001	CWS	AL	26	139	37	11	0	3	13	25	6	2	.266	.329	.410	-.036	.281	.346	.432	.009	9.0	46-C	-5
2002	CHR	INT	27	231	63	15	2	0	17	45	10	4	.273	.325	.355	-.061	.258	.307	.339	-.213	1.3	59-C	3
2002	CWS	AL	27	104	25	4	0	0	9	22	2	0	.240	.307	.279	-.254	.260	.329	.298	-.226	.2	31-C	-4
2003	*CWS*	*AL*	*28*	*226*	*56*	*12*	*1*	*5*	*18*	*47*	*6*	*3*	*.247*	*.305*	*.371*	*-.120*	*.252*	*.311*	*.377*	*-.146*	*1.3*		

Breakout: 23%   Improve: 52%   Collapse: 29%

The White Sox love Josh Paul, but even they are coming around to the realization that he's not going to hit. After a 2002 in which he was beaten out by Johnson and didn't see the majors until Alomar was traded. Although Paul is the incumbent for the starting job, even with the return of Sandy Alomar, expect Olivo to blow past him this year.

Guillermo Reyes — SS — Born: 29-Dec-81 — Age: 21 — Bats: B — Throws: R

YEAR	TM	LG	AGE	AB	H	2B	3B	HR	BB	SO	SB	CS	AVG	OBP	SLG	MLVR	EQBA	EQOBP	EQSLG	EQMLVR	VORP	DEFENSE			
2000	BRI	APL	18	257	76	10	2	3	22	24	21	10	.296	.356	.385	.066	.200	.234	.262	-.501	-18.8	42-2B	-4	21-SS	2
2001	KAN	SAL	19	280	78	8	5	0	27	30	29	8	.279	.346	.343	.052	.229	.283	.284	-.356	-11.1	70-SS	-10		
2001	WNS	CRL	19	216	45	4	1	0	14	33	16	4	.208	.272	.236	-.222	.190	.238	.217	-.559	-19.4	58-SS	-10		
2002	WNS	CRL	20	455	127	20	1	4	35	71	30	15	.279	.339	.354	.018	.231	.277	.296	-.350	-15.8	121-SS	-10		
2002	CHR	INT	20	13	4	0	0	0	0	1	2	0	.308	.308	.308	-.134	.308	.308	.308	-.224	-.3				
2003	*CWS*	*AL*	*21*	*205*	*50*	*9*	*1*	*3*	*15*	*32*	*5*	*3*	*.243*	*.299*	*.343*	*-.168*	*.247*	*.306*	*.349*	*-.197*	*-1.8*				

Breakout: 56%   Improve: 75%   Collapse: 6%

Reyes ended the season as one of the youngest players in the International League with the Knights, but don't expect to see him in the majors any time soon. After a hot start with Winston-Salem, his production deteriorated and he made a ton of errors at short. He still has plenty of time to make a career for himself.

Aaron Rowand — CF — Born: 29-Aug-77 — Age: 25 — Bats: R — Throws: R

YEAR	TM	LG	AGE	AB	H	2B	3B	HR	BB	SO	SB	CS	AVG	OBP	SLG	MLVR	EQBA	EQOBP	EQSLG	EQMLVR	VORP	DEFENSE	
2000	BIR	SOU	22	532	137	26	5	20	38	117	22	7	.258	.324	.438	.098	.239	.282	.408	-.177	-13.8	138-RF	-1
2001	CHR	INT	23	329	97	28	0	16	21	47	8	2	.295	.354	.526	.227	.274	.329	.491	.056	11.3	79-RF	0
2001	CWS	AL	23	123	36	5	0	4	15	28	5	1	.293	.387	.431	.115	.309	.401	.455	.163	8.4	46-OF	1
2002	CWS	AL	24	302	78	16	2	7	12	54	0	1	.258	.300	.394	-.104	.274	.314	.422	-.069	8.2	98-CF	-2
2003	*CWS*	*AL*	*25*	*301*	*80*	*18*	*2*	*11*	*18*	*53*	*3*	*2*	*.264*	*.313*	*.446*	*.002*	*.269*	*.320*	*.453*	*-.016*	*4.4*		

Breakout: 20%   Improve: 52%   Collapse: 29%

Rowand didn't get to play regularly until the Sox traded Kenny Lofton, and after a hot start, he tailed off down the stretch. He's in a precarious position, flanked by better bats and with Joe Borchard breathing down his neck. Unlike Borchard, there are no questions about Rowand's defense. He broke two ribs in a dirt biking accident in November, but is supposed to be healed up in time for spring training.

Frank Thomas — DH — Born: 27-May-68 — Age: 35 — Bats: R — Throws: R

YEAR	TM	LG	AGE	AB	H	2B	3B	HR	BB	SO	SB	CS	AVG	OBP	SLG	MLVR	EQBA	EQOBP	EQSLG	EQMLVR	VORP	DEFENSE	
2000	CWS	AL	32	582	191	44	0	43	112	94	1	3	.328	.441	.625	.459	.335	.442	.640	.511	94.5	30-1B	4
2001	CWS	AL	33	68	15	3	0	4	10	12	0	0	.221	.321	.441	-.043	.235	.333	.471	.001	2.5		
2002	CWS	AL	34	523	132	29	1	28	88	115	3	0	.252	.367	.472	.109	.270	.382	.506	.164	43.5		
2003	*CWS*	*AL*	*35*	*427*	*111*	*23*	*1*	*23*	*70*	*90*	*2*	*1*	*.260*	*.365*	*.479*	*.122*	*.265*	*.374*	*.486*	*.112*	*18.5*		

Breakout: 5%   Improve: 51%   Collapse: 8%

Thomas didn't give the White Sox what they needed in his first full season since his banner 2000 campaign, but to his credit he isn't resting on his laurels. Reports of a vigorous workout routine and batting practice with Walt Hriniak this off-season point toward a second revival for Thomas at the plate in 2003. He's campaigned for more playing time at first base, but he's still a menace to his own team with the glove.

Jose Valentin SS/3B Born: 12-Oct-69 Age: 33 Bats: L Throws: R

YEAR	TM	LG	AGE	AB	H	2B	3B	HR	BB	SO	SB	CS	AVG	OBP	SLG	MLVR	EQBA	EQOBP	EQSLG	EQMLVR	VORP	DEFENSE			
2000	CWS	AL	30	568	155	37	6	25	59	106	19	2	.273	.345	.491	.053	.281	.346	.508	.116	47.5	137-SS	3		
2001	CWS	AL	31	438	113	22	2	28	50	114	9	6	.258	.338	.509	.105	.271	.351	.542	.162	41.4	60-3B	-6	39-SS	1
2002	CWS	AL	32	474	118	26	4	25	43	99	3	3	.249	.314	.479	.026	.263	.327	.508	.066	31.4	83-3B	0	46-SS	-2
2003	CWS	AL	33	369	94	20	2	18	37	80	5	2	.256	.326	.468	.044	.261	.334	.475	.028	16.8				

Breakout: 18%   Improve: 52%   Collapse: 19%

Valentin has played all over the field the last two years, but he should be back at short to start 2003, where he'll quietly be one of the better shortstops in the league. Valentin's power bat is his calling card. He's not Royce Clayton defensively, but he still handles both shortstop and third base competently.

Anthony Webster Born: 10-Apr-83 Age: 20 Bats: L Throws: R

YEAR	TM	LG	AGE	AB	H	2B	3B	HR	BB	SO	SB	CS	AVG	OBP	SLG	MLVR	EQBA	EQOBP	EQSLG	EQMLVR	VORP	DEFENSE
2002	BRI	APL	19	244	86	7	3	1	38	38	16	7	.352	.451	.418	.275	.233	.299	.278	-.329	-8.9	57-CF -5

The .352 average as a first-year player gets him on every prospect list in the land. Webster was a mid-round find by the White Sox and is their only real hitting prospect in the low minors. He showed good patience for a tools prospect. His defense isn't good, but a lot of that will come with experience.

Edwin Yan 2B Born: 18-Feb-82 Age: 21 Bats: B Throws: R

YEAR	TM	LG	AGE	AB	H	2B	3B	HR	BB	SO	SB	CS	AVG	OBP	SLG	MLVR	EQBA	EQOBP	EQSLG	EQMLVR	VORP	DEFENSE		
2001	HIC	SAL	19	446	126	8	4	2	42	62	56	21	.283	.348	.332	.031	.227	.279	.268	-.387	-20.9	64-2B -13	50-SS -10	
2002	WNS	CRL	20	490	124	6	7	4	42	57	88	19	.253	.315	.318	-.081	.220	.268	.280	-.396	-23.6	126-2B -20		
2003	CWS	AL	21	203	50	7	2	2	15	30	10	5	.245	.302	.339	-.168	.249	.309	.344	-.196	-1.8			

Breakout: 58%   Improve: 77%   Collapse: 6%

Acquired from the Pirates in the Matt Guerrier trade, Yan literally hit the ground running in the Sox with a Winston-Salem record and minor league–leading 88 steals. Unfortunately, that's all he brings to the table; he's got zero power and limited defensive ability. If things break right, he'll be Vince Coleman someday.

PITCHERS

Jon Adkins Born: 30-Aug-77 Age: 25 Bats: L Throws: R

YEAR	TM	LG	AGE	G	GS	IP	H	BB	SO	HR	ERA	EQERA	EQH9	EQBB9	EQSO9	EQHR9	PERA	VORP	STF
2000	MOD	CLF	22	9	7	49.7	41	17	38	1	1.81	3.84	9.5	3.4	4.3	0.4	4.00	9.1	6
2001	MID	TXS	23	24	24	137.3	147	36	74	9	4.46	5.10	11.1	2.9	3.5	1.0	5.00	6.2	-3
2001	SAC	PCL	23	3	2	12.7	17	8	7	1	4.25	7.13	13.2	6.8	3.7	0.8	7.74	-2.3	-22
2002	SAC	PCL	24	20	20	97.0	139	33	76	9	6.03	6.64	13.4	3.5	5.4	1.1	7.38	-12.2	-2
2002	CHR	INT	24	8	7	46.3	47	12	31	4	3.69	4.61	10.3	2.8	5.2	1.1	4.62	4.6	7
2003	CWS	AL	25	13	9	51.7	60	20	31	7	5.05	4.92	10.4	3.2	5.1	1.0	4.88	6.4	-3

Breakout: 20%   Improve: 54%   Collapse: 18%

The swag from the Ray Durham trade, Adkins is a middling prospect who stepped up his game after coming over from the A's. The Sox added him to the 40-man roster and sent him to the AFL, where he was lit up like a Christmas tree. It'll take something very bad happening to multiple pitchers for Adkins to see daylight in the Sox system.

Wyatt Allen Born: 12-Apr-80 Age: 23 Bats: R Throws: R

YEAR	TM	LG	AGE	G	GS	IP	H	BB	SO	HR	ERA	EQERA	EQH9	EQBB9	EQSO9	EQHR9	PERA	VORP	STF
2001	KAN	SAL	21	12	11	62.7	60	16	45	4	3.16	6.70	13.8	3.7	3.9	1.5	6.23	-8.4	-6
2002	WNS	CRL	22	28	28	161.7	163	80	110	15	4.45	6.86	13.2	6.7	4.6	2.2	6.87	-24.3	-12
2002	CHR	INT	22	1	1	5.0	6	6	2	2	9.00	10.85	14.0	13.9	3.3	5.6	11.65	-3.0	-66

Allen is an advanced prospect and sandwich pick out of Tennessee who had some trouble with the competition at Winston-Salem. He's got all the size, the fastball, and the makeup to succeed, but he needs another pitch. Allen will start the season in Single-A, but he'll move up quickly if he has any success.

Lorenzo Barcelo   Born: 10-Aug-77   Age: 25   Bats: R   Throws: R

YEAR	TM	LG	AGE	G	GS	IP	H	BB	SO	HR	ERA	EQERA	EQH9	EQBB9	EQSO9	EQHR9	PERA	VORP	STF
2000	CHR	INT	22	17	17	99.3	114	17	62	20	4.26	5.81	12.5	1.6	5.0	2.4	5.72	-3.4	4
2000	CWS	AL	22	22	1	39.0	34	9	26	5	3.69	3.15	7.5	1.7	5.9	1.0	2.94	9.7	9
2001	CWS	AL	23	17	0	21.0	24	8	15	1	4.71	4.85	10.2	3.2	6.1	0.4	4.41	1.2	2
2002	CWS	AL	24	4	0	6.0	9	1	1	1	9.00	7.41	13.8	1.4	1.5	1.4	6.39	-1.4	-32
2002	CHR	INT	24	2	1	5.3	5	1	1	1	6.79	6.13	10.4	2.2	1.5	2.6	4.81	-0.4	-32

Barcelo's been blessed with a dominant fastball and cursed with Liz Taylor's health. He started the season with the Sox and was hammered, earning a quick demotion to Triple-A. Continuing problems with his shoulder shut him down soon enough, with the additional indignity of being whined about by Kenny Williams. Unsurprisingly, he was outrighted off of the 40-man roster in November.

Rocky Biddle   Born: 21-May-76   Age: 27   Bats: R   Throws: R

YEAR	TM	LG	AGE	G	GS	IP	H	BB	SO	HR	ERA	EQERA	EQH9	EQBB9	EQSO9	EQHR9	PERA	VORP	STF
2000	BIR	SOU	24	23	23	146.3	138	54	118	10	3.08	5.55	11.6	3.8	5.3	1.3	5.74	-0.7	2
2000	CWS	AL	24	4	4	22.7	31	8	7	5	8.33	7.28	11.6	2.6	2.7	1.7	6.26	-4.5	-15
2001	CWS	AL	25	30	21	128.7	137	52	85	16	5.38	5.19	9.5	3.4	5.6	1.0	4.64	4.3	1
2002	CHR	INT	26	2	2	7.0	4	1	9	0	1.29	1.63	5.5	1.5	9.6	0.2	1.60	3.0	39
2002	CWS	AL	26	44	7	77.7	72	39	64	13	4.05	4.58	8.2	4.2	7.2	1.4	4.50	7.3	-1
2003	*MON*	*NL*	*27*	*28*	*11*	*77.3*	*78*	*37*	*63*	*9*	*4.74*	*4.91*	*9.2*	*3.7*	*6.6*	*1.0*	*4.76*	*5.7*	*1*

Breakout: 17%   Improve: 44%   Collapse: 22%

In an eerily similar turn of events to 2001, Biddle started the season with Charlotte but was quickly called up to fill out an unsettled Sox pitching staff. Biddle got the job done, especially in seven spot starts in the second half, and he'll get a bunch of innings out of the swingman spot for the Sox in 2003. Wicked facial hair, man, and, hopefully, fans in Monteal will notice now that he's been packaged to the Expos to bring in Bartolo Colon.

Mark Buehrle   Born: 23-Mar-79   Age: 24   Bats: L   Throws: L

YEAR	TM	LG	AGE	G	GS	IP	H	BB	SO	HR	ERA	EQERA	EQH9	EQBB9	EQSO9	EQHR9	PERA	VORP	STF
2000	BIR	SOU	21	16	16	118.7	95	17	68	8	2.27	3.98	9.8	1.5	3.7	1.2	3.93	20.1	6
2000	CWS	AL	21	28	3	51.3	55	19	37	5	4.21	4.02	9.1	2.7	6.3	0.7	4.00	7.9	10
2001	CWS	AL	22	32	32	221.3	188	48	126	24	3.29	3.26	7.7	1.9	4.9	0.9	3.00	55.2	15
2002	CWS	AL	23	34	34	239.0	236	61	134	25	3.58	3.72	9.0	2.2	5.0	0.9	3.67	47.4	12
2003	*CWS*	*AL*	*24*	*33*	*31*	*198.7*	*212*	*55*	*119*	*28*	*4.35*	*4.23*	*9.5*	*2.3*	*5.2*	*1.0*	*4.21*	*34.4*	*8*

Breakout: 16%   Improve: 51%   Collapse: 18%

One of the best young pitchers in the league, but he was appreciably better in 2001 than 2002, and if he doesn't beat that projection he'll be quite a disappointment. Buehrle generates more ground balls than anyone in the Sox rotation, so if anyone's going to miss Ray Durham and Royce Clayton, it'll be him.

Jim Bullard   Born: 29-Dec-79   Age: 23   Bats: L   Throws: L

YEAR	TM	LG	AGE	G	GS	IP	H	BB	SO	HR	ERA	EQERA	EQH9	EQBB9	EQSO9	EQHR9	PERA	VORP	STF
2001	BRI	APL	21	4	4	20.7	20	1	31	4	3.04	7.74	16.3	0.7	6.5	5.1	6.90	-5.1	2
2001	KAN	SAL	21	8	8	45.3	45	6	26	4	2.98	6.26	14.6	1.9	3.1	2.1	6.21	-3.8	-7
2002	WNS	CRL	22	23	23	143.7	147	46	89	8	3.32	5.67	12.5	4.2	4.1	1.3	5.84	-2.6	-3
2002	BIR	SOU	22	3	3	20.0	21	4	12	1	4.50	5.74	12.8	2.0	4.2	1.0	5.47	-0.5	3

Everyone describes Bullard as "tall," which he is at 6′7″, but c'mon, he isn't Randy Johnson or Jon Rauch. Bullard is a finesse lefty with good breaking stuff and no fastball to speak of. The White Sox have a bunch of these guys in the low minors replacing the prospects who cook with gas. History is against them becoming successes, but keep in mind that's what they said about Mark Buehrle, too.

Felix Diaz   Born: 27-Jul-80   Age: 22   Bats: R   Throws: R

YEAR	TM	LG	AGE	G	GS	IP	H	BB	SO	HR	ERA	EQERA	EQH9	EQBB9	EQSO9	EQHR9	PERA	VORP	STF
2001	HAG	SAL	20	15	12	51.7	49	16	56	4	3.66	6.81	13.1	4.4	5.8	1.8	6.32	-7.6	-3
2002	SHV	TXS	21	12	12	60.0	54	23	48	1	2.70	4.27	9.7	4.1	5.5	0.3	4.47	8.2	11
2002	BIR	SOU	21	7	6	31.0	25	8	30	4	3.48	5.14	10.6	2.6	6.7	2.7	4.80	1.2	10

The reward for dealing Kenny Lofton to the Giants, Diaz has a chance to make an impact on the White Sox in short order. He could be the next Barcelo, since he's had trouble with a tender arm, but he has command of three pitches, including a plus fastball. He won't contend for a rotation spot early on, but he should be in the mix by September if the White Sox are out of contention.

Keith Foulke   Born: 19-Oct-72   Age: 30   Bats: R   Throws: R

YEAR	TM	LG	AGE	G	GS	IP	H	BB	SO	HR	ERA	EQERA	EQH9	EQBB9	EQSO9	EQHR9	PERA	VORP	STF
2000	CWS	AL	27	72	0	88.0	66	22	91	9	2.97	2.52	6.4	1.8	9.1	0.8	2.34	28.0	24
2001	CWS	AL	28	72	0	81.0	57	22	75	3	2.33	2.22	6.3	2.3	7.9	0.3	2.12	28.4	18
2002	CWS	AL	29	65	0	77.7	65	13	58	7	2.90	2.83	7.6	1.4	6.6	0.7	2.67	22.0	9
2003	OAK	AL	30	57	0	63.7	58	16	51	8	3.27	3.30	8.2	2.0	6.8	1.0	3.44	18.7	6

Breakout: 24%   *Improve: 42%*   *Collapse: 27%*

On May 29, both Keith Foulke and John Smoltz were having similarly bad starts to their seasons, though Smoltz's (5.93 ERA, 3 blown saves) was probably worse than Foulke's (5.56, 2). From that point on, they both pitched extremely well. The difference? Smoltz ended the season with 52 saves, and Foulke—the pitcher with the fireman pedigree of the two—was jerked around, pitching setup for inferior pitchers before finally winning his job back with a mid-season scoreless streak. It's got to be infuriating to know that despite years of success as a closer, you're only as good as your last 25 innings. Traded to Oakland, Foulke will be the closer for the A's in 2003. All of his peripherals remain solid, and he's a better bet for success than the man replacing him on the South Side.

Jon Garland   Born: 27-Sep-79   Age: 23   Bats: R   Throws: R

YEAR	TM	LG	AGE	G	GS	IP	H	BB	SO	HR	ERA	EQERA	EQH9	EQBB9	EQSO9	EQHR9	PERA	VORP	STF
2000	CHR	INT	20	16	16	103.7	99	32	63	3	2.26	3.46	10.1	2.9	4.8	0.3	3.73	23.6	14
2000	CWS	AL	20	15	13	69.7	82	40	42	10	6.46	5.73	9.8	4.1	5.2	1.1	5.41	-1.8	3
2001	CHR	INT	21	5	5	33.0	31	11	26	1	2.73	3.74	9.6	3.6	5.6	0.4	4.07	6.5	17
2001	CWS	AL	21	35	16	117.0	123	55	61	16	3.69	4.60	9.4	4.0	4.4	1.1	4.87	11.3	-3
2002	CWS	AL	22	33	33	192.7	188	83	112	23	4.58	4.56	8.8	3.6	5.1	1.0	4.21	20.2	8
2003	CWS	AL	23	29	25	150.3	162	65	97	20	4.92	4.78	9.5	3.6	5.6	1.0	4.73	16.9	3

Breakout: 16%   *Improve: 50%*   *Collapse: 18%*

Garland's first complete year in the majors was uneven but promising. He's got command of multiple pitches, frequently overpowering stuff, and youth in his favor. Garland also had a strong final couple of months of the season. Barring another disastrous Proven Starter™ trade, he'll be the #2 starter in 2003.

Matt Ginter   Born: 24-Dec-77   Age: 25   Bats: R   Throws: R

YEAR	TM	LG	AGE	G	GS	IP	H	BB	SO	HR	ERA	EQERA	EQH9	EQBB9	EQSO9	EQHR9	PERA	VORP	STF
2000	BIR	SOU	22	27	26	179.7	153	60	126	6	2.25	4.84	10.1	3.4	4.5	0.6	4.66	13.2	6
2001	CHR	INT	23	22	10	76.3	62	24	67	3	2.60	3.62	8.3	3.4	6.2	0.5	3.40	15.7	11
2001	CWS	AL	23	20	0	39.7	34	14	24	2	5.21	3.91	7.7	3.0	5.1	0.4	3.03	6.5	2
2002	CHR	INT	24	13	0	16.0	20	10	9	3	3.94	6.51	13.3	7.0	4.5	2.5	8.14	-2.0	-36
2002	CWS	AL	24	33	0	54.3	59	21	37	6	4.48	4.97	9.7	3.3	6.0	0.9	4.55	2.5	0
2003	CWS	AL	25	34	5	61.3	66	26	42	8	4.80	4.67	9.5	3.4	5.8	0.9	4.60	7.7	-5

Breakout: 18%   *Improve: 53%*   *Collapse: 17%*

Ginter had a heavy workload early on (he pitched 17 innings in May after being called up on the 3rd) and it may have affected him down the stretch, as he was hit hard several times to put an end to what had been a good season. He's got everything you look for from a setup man, and you should expect him to handily outperform that projection.

Gary Glover   Born: 03-Dec-76   Age: 26   Bats: R   Throws: R

YEAR	TM	LG	AGE	G	GS	IP	H	BB	SO	HR	ERA	EQERA	EQH9	EQBB9	EQSO9	EQHR9	PERA	VORP	STF
2000	SYR	INT	23	27	27	166.7	181	62	119	21	5.02	6.09	11.5	3.4	5.6	1.5	5.39	-10.8	6
2001	CHR	INT	24	6	6	38.3	21	5	29	3	1.88	2.20	5.8	1.4	5.4	0.9	1.91	14.1	20
2001	CWS	AL	24	46	11	100.3	98	32	63	16	4.94	4.69	8.7	2.7	5.3	1.3	4.20	8.4	-2
2002	CWS	AL	25	41	22	138.3	136	52	70	21	5.21	4.83	8.9	3.2	4.5	1.2	4.32	9.9	-7
2003	CWS	AL	26	32	14	94.7	104	36	57	16	5.28	5.13	9.7	3.2	5.2	1.2	4.85	6.6	-7

Breakout: 16%   *Improve: 38%*   *Collapse: 18%*

He wants to start, but his performance in the rotation doesn't make much of an argument for it. Obscured in his 2002 line are the four runs he allowed in 22.1 innings out of the pen, which suggest a future as a setup man. He'll get plenty of garbage time or better for the team in 2003, but he's probably and hopefully made his last non-emergency start.

Kris Honel   Born: 07-Nov-82   Age: 20   Bats: R   Throws: R

YEAR	TM	LG	AGE	G	GS	IP	H	BB	SO	HR	ERA	EQERA	EQH9	EQBB9	EQSO9	EQHR9	PERA	VORP	STF
2001	BRI	APL	18	8	8	46.0	41	9	45	4	3.13	6.13	13.9	3.0	4.2	2.3	5.73	-3.2	-2
2002	KAN	SAL	19	26	26	153.3	128	52	152	12	2.82	5.03	11.4	4.5	5.7	2.0	5.23	8.1	7
2002	WNS	CRL	19	1	1	5.3	3	3	8	0	1.70	3.92	6.5	7.2	9.7	0.3	3.29	0.9	35

Chicagoland native Honel had a promising first full season, racking up the third-most punchouts in the Sally League and making its All-Star team. He's got good mechanics and a potent, moving fastball, but a better third pitch than his middling change to supplement his knuckle-curve might become necessary as he moves up the chain. He's listed at 6′5″ and 180 pounds; putting on some weight of the non–Häagen-Dazs variety should be expected, and will improve his stamina.

Gary Majewski   Born: 26-Feb-80   Age: 23   Bats: R   Throws: R

YEAR	TM	LG	AGE	G	GS	IP	H	BB	SO	HR	ERA	EQERA	EQH9	EQBB9	EQSO9	EQHR9	PERA	VORP	STF
2000	BUR	MDW	20	22	22	134.7	83	68	137	8	3.07	4.17	7.7	5.5	5.7	1.4	4.00	20.0	9
2000	WNS	CRL	20	6	6	37.0	32	17	24	1	5.11	5.41	9.5	5.0	3.6	0.6	5.21	0.4	-2
2001	VRO	FSL	21	23	13	75.0	103	36	41	9	6.24	9.64	18.7	5.7	3.6	2.9	9.42	-34.7	-32
2001	WNS	CRL	21	9	6	43.0	42	10	31	3	2.93	5.33	12.7	3.2	4.2	1.6	5.86	0.8	-3
2002	BIR	SOU	22	57	1	74.7	61	34	75	3	2.65	4.97	9.6	4.5	6.7	0.8	4.83	3.5	1

The Sox reacquired Majewski in the James Baldwin trade, and he quickly proved that his poor performance in Vero Beach was an aberration. He's been converted to a reliever, where his slider-fastball combo is proving more effective, and he had a dominant campaign closing in the AFL. An astute Rule 5 pickup by the Blue Jays.

Corwin Malone   Born: 03-Jul-80   Age: 23   Bats: R   Throws: L

YEAR	TM	LG	AGE	G	GS	IP	H	BB	SO	HR	ERA	EQERA	EQH9	EQBB9	EQSO9	EQHR9	PERA	VORP	STF
2000	BUR	MDW	20	38	1	71.7	67	60	82	4	4.90	7.86	11.7	9.4	6.6	1.3	7.73	-19.7	-16
2001	KAN	SAL	21	18	18	112.3	83	44	119	2	2.00	4.51	10.0	5.5	5.6	0.4	4.67	12.4	11
2001	WNS	CRL	21	5	5	36.7	25	10	38	1	1.72	3.75	8.3	3.6	5.7	0.6	3.59	7.2	18
2001	BIR	SOU	21	4	4	19.3	8	12	20	2	2.33	3.33	4.8	6.5	6.3	1.6	3.58	4.7	7
2002	BIR	SOU	22	22	22	124.3	116	89	89	6	4.71	7.08	11.2	7.2	4.9	1.0	6.78	-21.8	-6

Malone had a setback season in 2002; hopefully, his uncharacteristic lack of command of the strike zone was related to the elbow pain that ended his season in August. Malone was added to the 40-man roster, and he'll be in major league camp in 2003. He'll make an immediate impression with his low-90s heat, which is always an eye-catcher from a lefty, but he needs to learn when to spot his curve, and improve his changeup.

Damaso Marte   Born: 14-Feb-75   Age: 28   Bats: L   Throws: L

YEAR	TM	LG	AGE	G	GS	IP	H	BB	SO	HR	ERA	EQERA	EQH9	EQBB9	EQSO9	EQHR9	PERA	VORP	STF
2001	NRW	EAS	26	23	0	36.0	29	7	36	3	3.50	4.35	8.7	2.4	6.2	1.2	4.03	4.1	-1
2001	PIT	NL	26	23	0	36.3	34	12	39	5	4.71	4.28	8.3	2.7	8.1	1.1	4.03	4.4	10
2002	CWS	AL	27	68	0	60.3	44	18	72	5	2.84	2.64	6.5	2.5	10.4	0.7	2.49	18.4	29
2003	CWS	AL	28	60	0	59.0	55	22	59	8	4.17	4.06	8.3	3.0	8.6	1.1	3.96	11.9	11

Breakout: 17%   *Improve: 37%*   *Collapse: 37%*

Matt Guerrier was a high price to pay for an ostensibly mediocre lefty, but Marte proceeded to have his finest year with the Sox in 2002. He was worked very hard: his 68 appearances were good for tenth in the league, but Manuel eased up on the workload after he complained of a tired arm.

Antonio Osuna   Born: 12-Apr-73   Age: 30   Bats: R   Throws: R

YEAR	TM	LG	AGE	G	GS	IP	H	BB	SO	HR	ERA	EQERA	EQH9	EQBB9	EQSO9	EQHR9	PERA	VORP	STF
2000	LAD	NL	27	46	0	67.3	57	35	70	7	3.74	3.99	7.9	3.8	8.3	0.9	4.03	10.4	9
2002	CWS	AL	29	59	0	67.7	64	28	66	1	3.86	3.70	8.5	3.5	8.5	0.1	3.31	12.6	16
2003	NYY	AL	30	42	0	51.7	51	23	48	7	4.58	4.62	8.9	3.8	7.9	1.0	4.46	7.3	5

Breakout: 10%   *Improve: 40%*   *Collapse: 33%*

The chief beneficiary of the organization's lack of confidence in Keith Foulke was Osuna, who notched 11 saves in 14 chances in the final two-thirds of the season. Osuna was healthy for the entire season, and his ability to go multiple innings made him an important member of the Sox pen in 2002. His appalling track record for staying healthy makes him a terrible risk, which the White Sox happily handed off to the Yankees in the Colon deal.

Jim Parque   Born: 08-Feb-76   Age: 27   Bats: L   Throws: L

YEAR	TM	LG	AGE	G	GS	IP	H	BB	SO	HR	ERA	EQERA	EQH9	EQBB9	EQSO9	EQHR9	PERA	VORP	STF
2000	CWS	AL	24	33	32	187.0	208	71	111	21	4.28	4.33	9.4	2.8	5.2	0.8	4.33	24.4	8
2001	CWS	AL	25	5	5	28.0	36	10	15	7	8.04	7.14	11.3	3.0	4.5	2.0	6.52	-5.1	-9
2002	CHR	INT	26	20	20	105.7	131	38	63	21	6.47	7.52	13.2	4.0	4.7	2.7	7.26	-23.7	-19
2002	CWS	AL	26	8	4	25.3	34	16	13	11	9.96	9.21	11.6	5.2	4.4	3.5	8.85	-10.5	-39
2003	CWS	AL	27	19	13	77.3	103	36	48	15	6.57	6.39	11.8	3.8	5.3	1.5	6.14	-2.6	-10

Breakout: 13%   *Improve: 38%*   *Collapse: 30%*

For Parque's sake, I hope he came back too early from a torn labrum. He was combustible everywhere he pitched in 2002, though if you ask Parque—an avowed fan of his own work—you'll hear about mistreatment, mismanagement, and how the Sox should have plugged him in the front of their rotation and left him alone. Expect him to be elsewhere in 2003.

Heath Phillips   Born: 24-Mar-82   Age: 21   Bats: L   Throws: L

YEAR	TM	LG	AGE	G	GS	IP	H	BB	SO	HR	ERA	EQERA	EQH9	EQBB9	EQSO9	EQHR9	PERA	VORP	STF
2001	KAN	SAL	19	14	12	71.7	74	18	54	1	3.64	6.99	14.1	3.6	4.1	0.3	6.24	-11.9	-2
2002	WNS	CRL	20	28	28	179.0	184	50	112	17	3.52	5.87	13.3	3.7	4.2	2.3	6.10	-7.3	-3

Phillips led the Carolina league in losses with a terrible Winston-Salem team, but he was the best starter on the staff and the only one with a K/BB ratio better than 2-1. Phillips's fastball is mediocre, and prospects with this profile usually wash out in Double-A; he'll have his chance there in 2003.

Mike Porzio   Born: 20-Aug-72   Age: 30   Bats: L   Throws: L

YEAR	TM	LG	AGE	G	GS	IP	H	BB	SO	HR	ERA	EQERA	EQH9	EQBB9	EQSO9	EQHR9	PERA	VORP	STF
2000	CAR	SOU	27	20	18	121.3	111	31	90	11	3.41	4.73	10.5	2.5	4.8	1.6	4.90	10.4	0
2000	CSP	PCL	27	6	6	26.0	39	20	26	7	10.04	9.18	13.5	6.6	7.1	2.8	9.49	-10.6	-21
2001	CHR	INT	28	31	23	134.3	138	55	107	14	4.36	5.77	10.7	4.4	5.7	1.3	5.44	-4.1	-5
2002	CHR	INT	29	14	13	75.7	83	29	59	9	4.52	5.87	11.3	4.2	6.1	1.6	5.80	-3.1	-1
2002	CWS	AL	29	32	0	43.0	40	23	33	10	4.81	5.03	8.2	4.5	6.7	1.9	5.07	1.7	-10
2003	CWS	AL	30	22	9	59.3	68	28	41	9	5.63	5.48	10.2	4.0	6.0	1.2	5.33	3.3	-6

Breakout: 18%   *Improve: 57%*   *Collapse: 24%*

Mike Porzio was signed to a minor league contract and almost made the team out of spring training with a solid effort. In two separate stints with the major league team, Porzio proved beyond a shadow of a doubt that he is, in fact, left-handed. Cripes, the White Sox had a boatload of lefty relievers last year.

Jon Rauch   Born: 27-SEP-78   Age: 24   Bats: R   Throws: R

YEAR	TM	LG	AGE	G	GS	IP	H	BB	SO	HR	ERA	EQERA	EQH9	EQBB9	EQSO9	EQHR9	PERA	VORP	STF
2000	WNS	CRL	21	18	18	110.0	102	33	124	10	2.86	5.06	11.1	3.3	6.4	2.0	5.57	5.4	14
2000	BIR	SOU	21	8	8	56.0	36	16	63	4	2.25	3.81	7.8	2.8	7.2	1.3	3.50	10.5	27
2001	CHR	INT	22	6	6	28.0	28	7	27	8	5.79	6.86	10.9	2.7	7.0	3.5	6.24	-4.2	4
2002	CHR	INT	23	19	19	109.3	91	42	97	14	4.28	4.99	8.7	4.2	6.9	1.7	4.34	6.3	13
2002	CWS	AL	23	8	6	28.7	28	14	19	7	6.59	6.37	8.6	4.1	5.8	2.0	5.26	-2.8	-3
2003	CWS	AL	24	22	13	78.0	83	35	67	15	5.71	5.56	9.4	3.7	7.4	1.5	5.06	2.2	4

Breakout: 16%   *Improve: 55%*   *Collapse: 13%*

Don't be fooled by Rauch's 2002. Initially, it looks disappointing, but his performance was skewed heavily toward the season's second half as he continued to get stronger after labrum surgery in 2001. He finished the year with two solid starts for the Sox, and he's on pace for an excellent season in 2003.

Todd Ritchie — Born: 07-Nov-71 — Age: 31 — Bats: R — Throws: R

YEAR	TM	LG	AGE	G	GS	IP	H	BB	SO	HR	ERA	EQERA	EQH9	EQBB9	EQSO9	EQHR9	PERA	VORP	STF
2000	PIT	NL	28	31	31	187.0	208	51	124	26	4.81	4.39	9.7	2.0	5.3	1.1	4.53	23.2	8
2001	PIT	NL	29	33	33	207.3	211	52	124	23	4.47	4.23	9.2	2.1	4.6	0.9	4.05	29.4	5
2002	CWS	AL	30	26	23	133.7	176	52	77	18	6.06	6.27	11.8	3.3	5.0	1.1	5.89	-11.4	-3
2003	MIL	NL	31	25	21	129.0	141	44	78	16	4.80	5.21	10.2	2.6	4.8	1.1	4.89	6.6	0

Breakout: 14%   Improve: 49%   Collapse: 23%

What now? Ritchie's been on increasingly shaky ground since his 1999 breakout year, and only Steve Sparks's tenacity kept Ritchie from being the worst starter in the majors in 2002. The pressure is off now, so look for marginally better things, but chances of a complete rebound are as a Brewer are slim.

David Sanders — Born: 29-Aug-79 — Age: 23 — Bats: L — Throws: L

YEAR	TM	LG	AGE	G	GS	IP	H	BB	SO	HR	ERA	EQERA	EQH9	EQBB9	EQSO9	EQHR9	PERA	VORP	STF
2000	WNS	CRL	20	51	0	48.3	39	39	50	4	5.22	7.13	9.7	8.9	5.9	1.8	6.83	-9.4	-22
2001	BIR	SOU	21	36	0	34.0	27	25	25	1	2.65	4.82	8.8	7.9	4.6	0.5	5.77	2.1	-19
2002	BIR	SOU	22	47	0	63.7	56	28	61	3	1.84	4.25	10.5	4.4	6.5	0.9	5.24	8.0	0

Being pigeonholed in relief hurts in more ways than one for a minor leaguer; Sanders has had much less in-game experience in his three years than most pitching prospects get in two. Despite that, he's performed well, and a dominant stint (24 IP, 0.75 ERA) in the AFL has raised his profile. He'll start the season at Triple-A.

Josh Stewart — Born: 05-Dec-78 — Age: 24 — Bats: L — Throws: L

YEAR	TM	LG	AGE	G	GS	IP	H	BB	SO	HR	ERA	EQERA	EQH9	EQBB9	EQSO9	EQHR9	PERA	VORP	STF
2000	BUR	MDW	21	25	25	138.0	157	58	82	14	4.57	7.26	15.1	4.9	3.6	2.5	7.92	-26.9	-17
2001	WNS	CRL	22	12	12	63.7	64	28	38	6	3.81	7.87	13.8	6.3	3.6	2.3	7.30	-16.7	-22
2001	BIR	SOU	22	16	16	82.3	110	42	47	7	6.67	9.09	15.6	5.7	3.7	1.4	9.25	-32.8	-20
2002	BIR	SOU	23	26	26	150.3	145	56	92	11	3.53	5.55	12.0	3.8	4.2	1.5	5.82	-0.8	-4

Despite the presence of the more heralded prospects Corwin Malone and Dennis Ulacia, Stewart was Birmingham's best pitcher last year. The usual caveats apply: it was his second look at Double-A hitters, he's not young for his league, and Stewart doesn't have overpowering stuff.

Dennis Ulacia — Born: 02-Apr-81 — Age: 22 — Bats: L — Throws: L

YEAR	TM	LG	AGE	G	GS	IP	H	BB	SO	HR	ERA	EQERA	EQH9	EQBB9	EQSO9	EQHR9	PERA	VORP	STF
2000	BUR	MDW	19	28	28	148.3	157	67	111	8	4.73	7.43	13.2	5.1	4.3	1.3	6.92	-31.7	-7
2001	KAN	SAL	20	15	15	89.0	68	36	93	6	2.43	4.94	11.1	5.8	5.6	1.6	5.42	5.6	4
2001	WNS	CRL	20	10	10	64.3	57	26	47	2	3.64	5.64	11.1	5.5	4.2	0.7	5.55	-1.0	-1
2001	BIR	SOU	20	3	3	20.0	11	5	18	1	2.25	3.22	6.0	2.6	5.5	0.8	2.70	5.1	19
2002	BIR	SOU	21	28	25	145.7	173	51	88	15	4.82	7.68	15.2	3.7	4.3	2.2	7.61	-35.3	-9

Ulacia couldn't follow up on his strong 2001 season. Home runs took their toll as he led the Southern League in losses in 2002, where he'll probably get a repeat engagement in 2003. A bottom-of-the-rotation starter looks like the upside here.

Joe Valentine — Born: 24-Dec-79 — Age: 23 — Bats: R — Throws: R

YEAR	TM	LG	AGE	G	GS	IP	H	BB	SO	HR	ERA	EQERA	EQH9	EQBB9	EQSO9	EQHR9	PERA	VORP	STF
2000	BRI	APL	20	19	0	25.0	14	12	30	1	2.88	4.43	8.0	6.4	5.7	1.0	3.56	2.6	-8
2001	KAN	SAL	21	30	0	30.7	21	10	33	0	2.93	4.49	9.1	4.5	5.6	0.3	3.84	3.0	-2
2001	WNS	CRL	21	27	0	44.7	18	27	50	0	1.01	2.69	5.0	8.1	6.3	0.3	2.96	13.4	0
2002	BIR	SOU	22	55	0	59.3	36	30	63	1	1.97	3.53	6.9	4.9	7.0	0.3	3.56	12.2	6
2003	OAK	AL	23	26	0	29	27	16	23	3	4.25	4.30	8.3	4.5	6.8	0.8	4.3	5.4	-3

Breakout: 24%   Improve: 58%   Collapse: 25%

Valentine failed to stick with the Tigers as their Rule 5 draftee in 2002, so he was returned to the White Sox and had another dominant season. He's the rare minor league closer that's worth keeping an eye on; his slider is good enough that he's not just blowing guys away with a fastball. Sent to Oakland in the Koch trade, so continue to keep an eye on him.

Ken Vining — Born: 05-Dec-74 — Age: 28 — Bats: L — Throws: L

YEAR	TM	LG	AGE	G	GS	IP	H	BB	SO	HR	ERA	EQERA	EQH9	EQBB9	EQSO9	EQHR9	PERA	VORP	STF
2000	BIR	SOU	25	43	0	46.3	36	18	41	2	4.08	5.52	9.2	3.9	5.7	0.8	4.47	-0.7	-9
2001	CHR	INT	26	41	0	46.0	35	19	47	2	1.96	2.96	7.8	4.4	7.3	0.5	3.46	12.4	3
2002	CHR	INT	27	44	0	47.0	37	25	35	4	2.87	3.84	8.2	5.9	5.8	1.1	4.25	8.0	-14
2003	HOU	NL	28	24	0	21.7	24	14	18	3	5.49	5.58	9.9	5.1	6.8	1.0	5.47	0.8	-10

Breakout: 15%   Improve: 41%   Collapse: 29%

He didn't make much of an impact with the Sox in 2002 when they were auditioning everyone but Hawk and Wimpy for the bullpen, but Vining had his second solid year in Charlotte and is a good bet to fill at least a situational lefty role with a major league team. Signed with Houston.

Danny Wright — Born: 14-Dec-77 — Age: 25 — Bats: R — Throws: R

YEAR	TM	LG	AGE	G	GS	IP	H	BB	SO	HR	ERA	EQERA	EQH9	EQBB9	EQSO9	EQHR9	PERA	VORP	STF
2000	WNS	CRL	22	21	21	132.3	135	50	106	4	3.74	5.41	11.4	4.1	4.5	0.6	6.00	1.4	2
2000	BIR	SOU	22	7	7	43.3	28	24	31	3	2.49	4.47	7.9	5.5	4.6	1.2	4.52	5.0	0
2001	BIR	SOU	23	20	20	134.0	112	41	128	6	2.82	4.48	9.2	3.2	5.9	0.7	4.48	15.3	14
2001	CWS	AL	23	13	12	66.3	78	39	36	12	5.70	5.95	10.4	4.9	4.6	1.5	6.15	-3.3	-7
2002	CWS	AL	24	33	33	196.3	200	71	136	32	5.18	4.97	9.1	3.0	6.1	1.3	4.52	11.7	11
2003	CWS	AL	25	31	28	176.3	190	68	118	25	4.83	4.70	9.5	3.2	5.8	1.1	4.66	19.9	6

Breakout: 10%   Improve: 53%   Collapse: 7%

Wright is another young Sox arm that ended the year on an up note, logging quality starts in 6 of his last 7 games. His control improved toward the end of the season, but he was still vulnerable to the long ball. Look for him to match that projection in 2003, with more room for improvement in the future.

Kelly Wunsch — Born: 12-Jul-72 — Age: 30 — Bats: L — Throws: L

YEAR	TM	LG	AGE	G	GS	IP	H	BB	SO	HR	ERA	EQERA	EQH9	EQBB9	EQSO9	EQHR9	PERA	VORP	STF
2000	CWS	AL	27	83	0	61.3	50	29	51	4	2.94	2.85	6.9	3.4	7.2	0.5	2.93	17.2	7
2001	CWS	AL	28	33	0	22.3	21	9	16	4	7.67	5.65	8.3	3.4	6.1	1.5	4.40	-0.7	-10
2002	CHR	INT	29	10	2	12.0	13	5	9	0	2.25	3.66	10.8	4.6	5.8	0.3	4.85	2.4	-6
2002	CWS	AL	29	50	0	31.7	26	19	22	3	3.41	3.55	7.4	5.1	6.1	0.8	3.78	6.4	-8
2003	CWS	AL	30	49	0	38.0	39	19	30	5	4.90	4.77	9.2	4.1	6.7	1.0	4.83	4.3	-6

Breakout: 13%   Improve: 50%   Collapse: 23%

Damaso Marte's strong start allowed the Sox to take their time with Wunsch's rehab, bringing him back from rotator cuff surgery in May after a rehab stint in Triple-A. Wunsch was a reliable performer for the team down the stretch, and lefty specialists generally have nine lives, so expect to see his name popping up in box scores for the next decade or so.

Cleveland Indians

The mood in Cleveland is resignation, driven by black-cloud local media coverage more usually found in the Boston newspapers, and reinforced by national publications and analysts. Cleveland's poor-mouthing about going broke certainly didn't help draw fans, so ticket sales suffered. Still, it's not easy to sell the product by coming out and saying "We're not going to win this year. We'll be pretty good in a couple of years. And to be honest, the players on the field this year aren't even the players who'll be part of the next division contender. Our stadium's still nice though, isn't it?" So to put it mildly, coming into the job, Mark Shapiro was handed a pretty tough assignment.

The successful Indians franchise that Shapiro inherited had been built up by a few good ideas that John Hart had several years ago. Hart's key decision was to develop and sign a core of young players to inexpensive long-term contracts, and then surround them with found parts to support playoff runs. Following that script, the Indians quickly climbed from traditional doormat to respectability in 1994, and then went on to win the division every year after that through 1999, finishing second once in 2000 with a 90–72 record before briefly returning to first in the wake of the White Sox's surprising implosion. The core of homegrown talent that Hart ruled the roost with was Manny Ramirez (1993–2000), Jim Thome (1991–2002), Albert Belle (1989–1996), and Carlos Baerga (1990–1996). But repeated near misses helped Hart lose the way. Rather than re-arm with internally developed talent, as the Braves have done for much of their long run, the Indians traded talent for supporting players (like dealing Brian Giles for Ricardo Rincon), the same kind of supporting players they'd been able to find lying around in guys like Paul Sorrento only years earlier.

It's appropriate then, that as John Hart left, taking his learned cash-burning, ageist, talent-neutral approach to

Texas, that his successor would have to walk that path in reverse. Instead of stripping down from the start, Shapiro started by lighting cigars with hundred dollar bills, signing 30-year-old Matt Lawton, a corner outfielder with a modest skills set, and 31-year-old Ricky Gutierrez, an easily replaceable infielder, to huge, multimillion dollar deals. Shapiro initially planned on running out an old, bad team, trying to contend in the same desperate vein that the last few Hart teams had tried.

When it didn't work, to Shapiro's credit, he promptly gutted it. For all of the talk about what a good guy Shapiro is, and how concerned about character he is, as the wreckage burned, he'd have traded his mother for a couple of blue-chip prospects. The Indians had an Opening Day payroll pegged at $79 million by ESPN. Of the 16 salaries that were over a million dollars, only six—Ellis Burks, Matt Lawton, Danys Baez, Ricky Gutierrez, Omar Vizquel, and Bob Wickman—will be back for 2003, and Vizquel might have been traded if he had been willing to waive his 10-and-5 veto power.

Here are the transaction highlights of last year: (1) Signed Mark Wohlers to a two-year, $4 million deal, (2) Signed and cut bait on Brady Anderson, (3) Signed Wil Cordero, and then tied him to a tree and abandoned him at a highway rest stop, (4) Traded strikeout king Russell Branyan to the Reds for Ben Broussard, (5) Traded Bartolo Colon to the Expos for Brandon Phillips, Grady Sizemore, Cliff Lee, and accepting Lee Stevens as the price of doing business, (6) Traded Chuck Finley to the Cardinals for Luis Garcia, eating some of the contract in the process, (7) Traded Paul Shuey to the Dodgers for Ricardo Rodriguez and Francisco Cruceta, and accepting Terry Mulholland as the price of doing business, and (8) Traded Ricardo Rincon to the A's for Marshall McDougall.

Beyond that, among the team's 2002 millionaires, Jim Thome's gone, lost to free agency, Charles Nagy and Jaret

---

Indians Prospectus

2002 record: 74–88; Third place, AL Central

Pythagenport Record: 71–91

Runs scored per game: 4.6 (10th in AL)

Runs allowed per game: 5.2 (10th in AL)

Team EqA: .249 (11th in AL)

2002 Batters Age: 30.9 (2nd oldest in AL)

2002 Pitchers Age: 28.4 (7th youngest in AL)

Ballpark: Jacobs Field; Slight hitters' park; Park Factor of 1.024

2002: Sports Commissar Shapiro purged all high-paid players as part of sweeping three-year master plan.

2003: Fans will get to see the newly acquired swag and the farm system pay its first dividends, but three years?

Wright won't be back, Travis Fryman retired, and Einar Diaz was dealt. Only Dave Burba, who's headed to arbitration to the surprise of almost everyone concerned, looks like an in-season addition that will make over a million dollars next year.

Overall, that's your basic mixed bag. The Colon trade is astounding. Shapiro had an opportunity to strip-mine the Expos of their organizational wealth, and he took it, taking nearly every good prospect that the Expos had. Trading Paul Shuey was also lucrative. As a result, the Indians are doing a good job of rebuilding by following the most conventional of methods, acquiring other people's good stuff. But while they're stocking their farm system with great prospects, Shapiro is spending too much money on fill-ins like Mark Wohlers. The instinct to pay a premium for certainty, especially in the bullpen, is part of what led Hart into darkness in the first place. The unnecessary Bob Wickman contract will serve as a grim reminder of that for years to come.

Shapiro seems to be learning quickly, though. Diaz only got one year into his contract, and dealt before his deal got too expensive. Shapiro sent him to Texas along with Ryan Drese for Travis Hafner and Aaron Myette, an outstanding deal that gives the Indians the two better players in the deal. Hafner might be the team's Opening Day first baseman, while Myette has an opportunity to win a job in the rotation, a job Drese would have been hard-pressed to earn. The question of whether the organization is really any smarter now than it was two years ago will be determined after the 2003 season, when we see if they can avoid making expensive mistakes on the free agent market while choosing which young players to commit playing time to, which ones to sign up to contract extensions, and which ones to cut bait on.

Shapiro has said he expected the team to be "in the middle of a long championship run, deep in dominant starting pitching and helped by an influx of position players." That's entirely possible. In two or three years, the Indians could field an interesting lineup:

C: Victor Martinez
1B: Travis Hafner
2B: Brandon Phillips
3B: Matt Whitney
SS: a cantankerous wheelchair-riding Omar Vizquel
LF: Grady Sizemore
CF: Bradley, Escobar, or the flycatcher-of-the-month
RF: Matt Lawton and the buzzards that will be circling him
DH: Ben Broussard or reasonable facsimile (Jason Cooper?)

That's a pencil sketch; Sizemore might stick in center if his arm doesn't force him to left. If Corey Smith develops, he could be playing right field, but what then gets done with Lawton? This gets even more fun if we figure Omar's going away after his contract ends in 2004. If Shapiro can get someone to take

Einar Diaz, you can have some hope that he'll find a buyer for Matt Lawton at some point.

There's no point in putting a rotation down; we're not insane. However, the Indians have more quality and quantity as far as young pitching than perhaps any other organization in the game. That doesn't mean many or any of them will pan out, but looking through this farm system is eye-opening. They have a ton of good guys, and fans in their minor league affiliates should be overjoyed, because they're likely to see these guys moving up in waves through their towns. For the short term, the Tribe is stocking the rotation with temps, adding veteran crumbs Jason Bere and Brian Anderson. However, it won't be long before they have a chance to go with four talented lefties—C. C. Sabathia, Brian Tallet, Cliff Lee, and Billy Traber—plus a righty or two from among Jason Davis, Aaron Myette, and Ricardo Rodriguez. It's a nice problem to have, but it won't really be an issue until several of these guys are ready to roll, probably no sooner than August.

Here's the problem: with young pitching, that doesn't always happen. It wasn't long ago that we looked at the Marlins system after their 1998 teardown and the huge swag of pitching talent that it yielded and saw a team that would compete for the NL East, starting in 2000 and for years afterward. No amount of potential talent is too great to not develop, be mismanaged, or fall prey to injuries. But no matter how low you set the bar for pitcher survival, a couple of these guys are going to get through and be good starting pitchers, and the Indians will be paying them next to nothing for the first few years. Where the Indians in their long run at success were often scraping to find enough pitching, soon they're going to be scrambling to find enough room for the pitching their system is about to start cranking out.

So generally speaking, the Indians have a bright long-term future. Baseball hit them in the head with the sledge-hammer of revenue sharing, punishing over and over an organization that had built their little market into one of the game's premier moneymaking machines through hard work and smarts. In the madness of yet another cockamamie Seligian scheme, baseball has taken the Indians' money and given it to incompetent teams like the Brewers and Phillies. The Indians have recoiled from the blows, and since the salary cap has been entirely payroll-based, that's what they've now slashed. When the team starts to win again, they'll win with a small payroll, and the money they make will only be going into the team's accounts.

After arbitration and filling their bullpen, the Indians could head into 2003 with a payroll of about $41 million if they scrape for minor league free agents and Burba only gets $2 million in arbitration, or somewhere in the area of $46–51 million if they decide they need more veteran presence. That's an amazing one-season turnaround: the Indians could drop from 9th in the major leagues in payroll to near the bottom of the list, down with the Padres and Marlins. Jack Welch would be proud. If you want to be particularly mercenary, just remember that while doing something like this, it's worthwhile to camouflage your activities by telling the standard fibs about the astounding financial losses you're suffering, especially if it means you can go to ground so quickly and start cultivating a more lucrative cash crop.

When the Indians field a winning young core, they'll have several assets to support it. First and foremost, they'll have their nice cash-cow stadium and a fan base that can't possibly erode that far in this brief retooling. However, when the time comes in another year or two, they'll enjoy an extra benefit that the Hart-grown teams did not have. Because of the salary cap, the middle class of baseball players is in the process of being destroyed. Supporting players, veterans, journeymen, the other half of a platoon, the second lefty out of the pen, these guys are going to get cheaper relative to total team payrolls as the new CBA devastates free agency, and as teams acclimate to a hot stove league where more guys get non-tendered than go to arbitration. So starting in 2004, the Indians will have a young, cheap core of starting pitching and position players, but they'll also be able to pick up the stopgap guys on the relative cheap. Where only a couple years ago an average guy at the hot corner would have run you a couple million, today a guy like David Bell—okay, so we're not quite all the way there just yet.

If the Indians are smart about it, they'll be very well positioned to be a dominant team under the salary cap. They have the money that they can pour into untaxed player development, which returns cheap players to help keep them under the cap. While other teams are almost certain to run over the cap for years to come, for reasons ranging to seeing payroll as an investment (like the Yankees) or charity (the Mets), the Indians may well take back all the revenue sharing they were forced to give up during the late Hart years and laugh all the way to the bank, winning division titles for some time to come. It won't start now, as the Tribe will have to gun for 75 wins now, keeping ahead of the far more pathetic Royals and Tigers, but the good times aren't too far off.

HITTERS

Josh Bard — C — Born: 30-Mar-78 — Age: 25 — Bats: B — Throws: R

YEAR	TM	LG	AGE	AB	H	2B	3B	HR	BB	SO	SB	CS	AVG	OBP	SLG	MLVR	EQBA	EQOBP	EQSLG	EQMLVR	VORP	DEFENSE
2000	SLM	CRL	22	309	88	17	0	2	32	33	3	1	.285	.354	.359	.044	.233	.284	.297	-.333	-8.1	89-C -1
2001	CAR	SOU	23	124	32	13	0	1	19	23	0	1	.258	.361	.387	.040	.227	.310	.344	-.220	.5	35-C 1
2001	AKR	EAS	23	194	54	11	0	4	16	27	0	0	.278	.340	.397	.053	.246	.303	.357	-.204	1.6	40-C 1
2002	BUF	INT	24	344	102	26	2	6	20	45	0	0	.297	.335	.436	.084	.277	.317	.413	-.074	14.1	93-C 1
2002	CLE	AL	24	90	20	5	0	3	4	13	0	0	.222	.255	.378	-.225	.233	.274	.400	-.208	.6	23-C 1
2003	CLE	AL	25	281	71	15	1	7	21	42	2	2	.252	.307	.391	-.089	.258	.315	.400	-.106	4.6	

Breakout: 24%   Improve: 65%   Collapse: 11%

I don't know about you, but I'm going to name my first kid "Josh" and teach him to be a backup catcher like Josh Paul and Josh Bard. Key drills will include smiling and "aw, shucks" interviews, playing baseball like it was meant to be played, calling a good game, being white, and hiring a good agent. I'll be retiring to Phoenix in about twenty years. So long, suckers!

Josh Bard's game-winning heroics during his call-up may lead the Indians to do something really stupid, like trade Victor Martinez or otherwise hold up Victor's development. In the short term, though, Bard will be the Indians' starting catcher next year unless he's awful in spring training, while Martinez starts throwing out baserunners.

Milton Bradley — CF — Born: 15-Apr-78 — Age: 25 — Bats: B — Throws: R

YEAR	TM	LG	AGE	AB	H	2B	3B	HR	BB	SO	SB	CS	AVG	OBP	SLG	MLVR	EQBA	EQOBP	EQSLG	EQMLVR	VORP	DEFENSE
2000	OTT	INT	22	342	104	20	1	6	45	56	10	15	.304	.387	.421	.119	.275	.347	.383	-.063	11.3	87-CF -3
2000	MON	NL	22	154	34	8	1	2	14	32	2	1	.221	.290	.325	-.321	.219	.279	.329	-.306	-5.4	35-CF 0
2001	MON	NL	23	220	49	16	3	1	19	62	7	4	.223	.287	.336	-.268	.221	.285	.333	-.288	-6.8	64-CF 2
2001	OTT	INT	23	136	37	7	2	2	23	30	14	1	.272	.385	.397	.103	.264	.366	.386	-.031	5.8	34-CF -1
2001	BUF	INT	23	114	29	3	0	5	19	31	9	2	.254	.361	.412	.064	.239	.341	.385	-.097	2.7	27-CF -2
2002	CLE	AL	24	325	81	18	3	9	32	58	6	3	.249	.317	.406	-.061	.269	.336	.440	-.008	14.8	86-CF -3
2003	CLE	AL	25	304	77	17	2	7	31	57	7	3	.253	.325	.392	-.056	.259	.333	.401	-.071	4.0	

Breakout: 18%   Improve: 45%   Collapse: 22%

Milton, Milton, Milton. Everyone loves Alex Escobar, and while Bradley's kept his attitude on a leash, no longer bumping umps or the like, having people in the front office who don't like you affects your opportunity. It means playing time flows to other players who they'd like to see succeed more. And there are enough people on enough teams that don't want to see

Milton Bradley *(continued)*

Bradley play for their organization, especially after seeing him do things like not sliding at second in double play situations, that it may make it harder for him to get traded if the team buries him, or get a shot at a job if he's released.

Bradley started to flash some of the walks he'd shown in the minors, but the power still hasn't shown up. He spent a lot of time on the DL for random nicks. What Bradley needs is a good, healthy season where he finally progresses, maybe takes up golf, cultivates some fans in high places, and at least establishes that he's worth putting up with. Otherwise, he'll lapse into obscurity as soon as the Indians can find a tolerable alternative like Crisp, and be remembered only by people who paid too much attention to the Bergeron-Bradley controversy in Montreal way back when there was a baseball team in Quebec.

Ben Broussard — LF/1B — Born: 24-Sep-76 — Age: 26 — Bats: L — Throws: L

YEAR	TM	LG	AGE	AB	H	2B	3B	HR	BB	SO	SB	CS	AVG	OBP	SLG	MLVR	EQBA	EQOBP	EQSLG	EQMLVR	VORP	DEFENSE		
2000	CHT	SOU	23	286	73	8	4	14	72	78	15	2	.255	.415	.458	.230	.226	.357	.405	-.049	3.5	66-LF -10	14-1B	-2
2001	MUD	CLF	24	102	25	5	0	5	16	31	0	0	.245	.369	.441	.131	.198	.291	.358	-.256	-4.5	30-1B 1		
2001	CHT	SOU	24	353	113	27	0	23	61	69	10	3	.320	.431	.592	.458	.268	.362	.490	.106	21.1	92-1B -7		
2002	BUF	INT	25	153	37	8	0	5	24	30	0	0	.242	.356	.392	.020	.231	.334	.378	-.125	-1.6	34-LF -2		
2002	LOU	INT	25	187	51	14	1	11	31	50	4	1	.273	.401	.535	.292	.251	.369	.497	.113	10.7	43-1B -2		
2002	CLE	AL	25	112	27	4	0	4	7	25	0	0	.241	.292	.384	-.140	.259	.313	.420	-.086	.0	25-LF -2		
2003	*CLE*	*AL*	*26*	*250*	*62*	*13*	*1*	*11*	*32*	*57*	*4*	*2*	*.250*	*.342*	*.443*	*.033*	*.256*	*.351*	*.453*	*.024*	*4.1*			

Breakout: 17%   Improve: 53%   Collapse: 18%

People within the Indians organization fought with Russ Branyan for years, trying to change him into something he wasn't, questioning his character, and when they didn't like what they saw, eventually got him traded. This trade made sense when it seemed the Indians were almost certain to lose Thome to free agency, and for a brief moment Broussard was penciled in somewhere to start. Picking up Travis Hafner throws it all open again. Broussard is not a left fielder, and pounding the square peg into the round hole's no good for the peg, the hole, or the hammer. He draws walks like crazy, and he hits for power, so what's not to like? Broussard's got a nice swing, but also does the hack-from-heels sometimes, which doesn't endear him to the ball-in-play crowd.

Ellis Burks — DH — Born: 11-Sep-64 — Age: 38 — Bats: R — Throws: R

YEAR	TM	LG	AGE	AB	H	2B	3B	HR	BB	SO	SB	CS	AVG	OBP	SLG	MLVR	EQBA	EQOBP	EQSLG	EQMLVR	VORP	DEFENSE
2000	SFG	NL	35	393	135	21	5	24	56	49	5	1	.344	.427	.606	.477	.350	.425	.618	.476	61.5	96-RF 0
2001	CLE	AL	36	439	123	29	1	28	62	85	5	1	.280	.375	.542	.229	.295	.389	.575	.295	44.9	14-LF 0
2002	CLE	AL	37	518	156	28	0	32	44	108	2	3	.301	.363	.541	.239	.319	.379	.576	.308	60.3	
2003	*CLE*	*AL*	*38*	*404*	*112*	*22*	*2*	*22*	*44*	*78*	*3*	*2*	*.278*	*.352*	*.507*	*.152*	*.285*	*.362*	*.518*	*.152*	*20.4*	

Breakout: 4%   Improve: 33%   Collapse: 10%

There are two constants here: Ellis Burks has bad knees and hits the cover off the ball. Everything else grows from that. He can't really play the field anymore, as he put on the leather only six times this year, but as long as he keeps hitting, there's a place for him as a DH somewhere. As long as the Indians are looking to cut payroll, the last year of his three-year, $20 million deal is going to look mighty attractive to punt elsewhere, especially now that they may want to get Broussard more DH time.

Jason Cooper — OF/DH — Born: 06-Dec-80 — Age: 22 — Bats: L — Throws: L

YEAR	TM	LG	AGE	AB	H	2B	3B	HR	BB	SO	SB	CS	AVG	OBP	SLG	MLVR	EQBA	EQOBP	EQSLG	EQMLVR	VORP	DEFENSE
2002	CGA	SAL	21	55	14	5	0	4	6	17	0	0	.255	.339	.564	.276	.193	.251	.421	-.251	-1.7	
2003	*CLE*	*AL*	*22*	*118*	*26*	*7*	*0*	*5*	*11*	*41*	*1*	*2*	*.223*	*.294*	*.419*	*-.095*	*.228*	*.301*	*.428*	*-.115*	*-2.8*	

Breakout: 54%   Improve: 71%   Collapse: 17%

Cooper was a huge power-hitting DH for Stanford that the Tribe drafted in the third round this summer. Washington's not known as a baseball powerhouse, and in part because of that Cooper wasn't signed out of high school despite being an All-American player before a blistering senior year. Then he was drafted, in 1999, just three spots behind high school teammate Ryan Doumit. Cooper has huge potential power, but it's not clear where he'll play, and the development record of pure bats is not cause for hope. From Moses Lake, Washington, Cooper may be swapping funny stories about growing up in white trash Washington backwaters with David Riske in a couple years. At least Riske could hang out in Seattle with a modest drive. Cooper had to beg rides into Yakima, or Spokane, which is about as exciting as what Riske could get by taking a long walk to Cascade Lanes for some bowling.

Coco Crisp

CF　　**Born: 01-Nov-79**　　**Age: 23**　　**Bats: B**　　**Throws: R**

YEAR	TM	LG	AGE	AB	H	2B	3B	HR	BB	SO	SB	CS	AVG	OBP	SLG	MLVR	EQBA	EQOBP	EQSLG	EQMLVR	VORP	DEFENSE	
2000	NWJ	NYP	20	134	32	5	0	0	11	22	25	3	.239	.301	.276	-.108	.201	.237	.230	-.539	-16.1	28-LF	-3
2000	PEO	MDW	20	98	27	9	0	0	16	15	7	3	.276	.377	.367	.101	.225	.301	.294	-.307	-6.1	22-LF	-1
2001	POT	CRL	21	530	162	23	3	11	52	64	39	21	.306	.369	.423	.188	.245	.301	.347	-.222	-19.8	133-LF	-10
2002	NHV	EAS	22	355	107	16	1	9	36	56	26	10	.301	.366	.428	.145	.262	.317	.378	-.136	4.0	80-CF	-1
2002	AKR	EAS	22	32	13	1	0	1	3	3	4	0	.406	.457	.531	.519	.344	.400	.438	.171	2.5		
2002	BUF	INT	22	21	5	1	0	0	0	2	1	0	.238	.238	.286	-.327	.238	.238	.286	-.439	-1.5		
2002	CLE	AL	22	127	33	9	2	1	11	19	4	1	.260	.319	.386	-.076	.281	.338	.422	-.020	5.3	32-CF	-1
2003	CLE	AL	23	345	88	17	2	8	28	56	10	5	.254	.312	.385	-.086	.260	.320	.394	-.103	.0		

Breakout: 29%　　Improve: 62%　　Collapse: 18%

Coco Crisp was the player to be named later in the Chuck Finley trade. The Indians see him as a leadoff hitter, and he's certainly capable of swiping bases, and his season line in the Eastern League was .310/.372/.437, so he's got the on-base skills as well. Looking over his minor league career though, he looks like another fourth outfielder in the making, and how many of those are floating around? If he develops some power and his defense improves, he'll be interesting, but there are more guys like this floating around than potential planets in the Kuiper Belt.

Einar Diaz

C　　**Born: 28-Dec-72**　　**Age: 30**　　**Bats: R**　　**Throws: R**

YEAR	TM	LG	AGE	AB	H	2B	3B	HR	BB	SO	SB	CS	AVG	OBP	SLG	MLVR	EQBA	EQOBP	EQSLG	EQMLVR	VORP	DEFENSE	
2000	CLE	AL	27	250	68	14	2	4	11	29	4	2	.272	.323	.392	-.135	.278	.322	.399	-.085	8.7	74-C	5
2001	CLE	AL	28	437	121	34	1	4	17	44	1	2	.277	.328	.387	-.062	.293	.340	.412	-.020	22.7	124-C	11
2002	CLE	AL	29	320	66	19	0	2	17	27	0	1	.206	.259	.284	-.350	.227	.279	.312	-.326	-7.4	96-C	-3
2003	TEX	AL	30	247	64	14	1	3	13	25	1	1	.258	.304	.359	-.132	.260	.308	.363	-.166	.2		

Breakout: 28%　　Improve: 46%　　Collapse: 21%

Einar was given the starting job, and responded by being the worst-hitting regular catcher in the majors. His defensive reputation skyrocketed, but fighting a cracked rib early in the season, he only threw out 36 of 82 baserunners, for a 30% gunnery rating. With Martinez charging onto the scene, Shapiro traded Diaz to Texas, where John Hart apparently saw a way to ... well, who knows what he saw.

Alex Escobar

OF　　**Born: 06-Sep-78**　　**Age: 24**　　**Bats: R**　　**Throws: R**

YEAR	TM	LG	AGE	AB	H	2B	3B	HR	BB	SO	SB	CS	AVG	OBP	SLG	MLVR	EQBA	EQOBP	EQSLG	EQMLVR	VORP	DEFENSE	
2000	BIN	EAS	21	437	126	25	7	16	57	114	24	5	.288	.379	.487	.198	.245	.319	.415	-.093	10.8	117-CF	-2
2001	NOR	INT	22	397	106	21	4	12	35	146	18	3	.267	.331	.431	.060	.255	.316	.416	-.090	9.9	104-CF	-4
2001	NYM	NL	22	50	10	1	0	3	3	19	1	0	.200	.245	.400	-.257	.216	.259	.412	-.231	-.7	13-CF	-1
2003	CLE	AL	24	158	39	9	1	5	15	40	4	1	.250	.319	.421	-.031	.256	.327	.431	-.045	0.2		

Breakout: 20%　　Improve: 41%　　Collapse: 27%

It's pointless now to speculate where Escobar should be placed on prospect lists. He's lost too much time to injuries, his minor league lines are cryptic and tainted by word that Mets coaches tinkering with his swing kept him confused and ill-at-ease. What do we know? Healthy, Escobar plays major league–quality defense in center field. He's walked in a little under 10% of his minor league PAs, and he strikes out about a quarter of the time. He hits for some power. And now he's 24 and has lost another year. Despite the pressure to see the once-⋄ prospect at the major league level, the Indians should let Escobar progress on his own, try to get him consistent hitting instruction, and see what happens.

Travis Fryman

3B　　**Born: 25-Mar-69**　　**Age: 34**　　**Bats: R**　　**Throws: R**

YEAR	TM	LG	AGE	AB	H	2B	3B	HR	BB	SO	SB	CS	AVG	OBP	SLG	MLVR	EQBA	EQOBP	EQSLG	EQMLVR	VORP	DEFENSE	
2000	CLE	AL	31	574	184	38	4	22	73	111	1	1	.321	.398	.516	.223	.326	.398	.527	.276	66.3	152-3B	3
2001	CLE	AL	32	334	88	15	0	3	30	63	1	2	.263	.330	.335	-.136	.278	.346	.353	-.105	7.1	83-3B	-10
2002	CLE	AL	33	397	86	14	3	11	40	82	0	0	.217	.292	.350	-.199	.233	.307	.381	-.171	1.8	103-3B	-3
2003	CLE	AL	34	276	69	13	1	7	28	56	1	1	.249	.322	.378	-.082	.254	.330	.387	-.099	2.2		

Breakout: 20%　　Improve: 43%　　Collapse: 23%

Retiring, finally. It's easy to forget, what with his awful performances and the attention paid to his massive contracts the last few years, that once upon a time, Travis Fryman wasn't always awful. For a while, he was downright okay, and the best young player on those final few Sparky teams in Detroit.

Karim Garcia　　RF　Born: 29-Oct-75　Age: 27　Bats: L　Throws: L

YEAR	TM	LG	AGE	AB	H	2B	3B	HR	BB	SO	SB	CS	AVG	OBP	SLG	MLVR	EQBA	EQOBP	EQSLG	EQMLVR	VORP	DEFENSE
2000	ROC	INT	24	270	75	17	1	13	34	70	3	3	.278	.363	.493	.159	.256	.329	.454	-.012	4.6	62-RF -1
2000	TOL	INT	24	155	46	6	2	15	11	32	2	1	.297	.355	.652	.381	.269	.315	.590	.168	14.1	39-CF -4
2001	BUF	INT	25	462	122	16	4	31	44	106	4	4	.264	.329	.517	.157	.245	.308	.482	-.020	6.9	110-RF -5
2002	COH	INT	26	288	78	16	3	12	20	48	1	5	.271	.318	.472	.083	.248	.297	.438	-.099	6.1	51-CF -1
2002	BUF	INT	26	91	36	7	2	3	9	14	0	1	.396	.450	.615	.601	.359	.416	.554	.382	13.6	16-CF -1
2002	CLE	AL	26	197	59	8	0	16	6	40	0	3	.299	.320	.584	.233	.313	.337	.621	.303	18.7	46-RF -1
2003	CLE	AL	27	335	88	18	1	17	26	69	3	3	.263	.318	.477	.048	.269	.326	.488	.039	7.5	

Breakout: 16%　　Improve: 48%　　Collapse: 21%

Karim debuted at the age of "19" with LA in 1995, back when the Dodgers were hyping Billy Ashley every week. Garcia's career line through 2001 was a paltry .223/.267/.397. He'd displayed little power, no batting eye, and struck out four times for every walk. So of course this is the year he plays out of his mind in limited use. The technical name for this kind of year is "fluke." It's like backup catchers: get 200 ABs per year for long enough and you'll eventually have that superficially good year that'll keep you employed until you're almost 40. At the same time, if you're the Tribe, why not play Garcia? It's not like the Indians don't have a year to fool around seeing if somebody can finally fulfill his promise.

Luis Garcia　　RF　Born: 05-Nov-78　Age: 24　Bats: R　Throws: R

YEAR	TM	LG	AGE	AB	H	2B	3B	HR	BB	SO	SB	CS	AVG	OBP	SLG	MLVR	EQBA	EQOBP	EQSLG	EQMLVR	VORP	DEFENSE
2000	AUG	SAL	21	493	128	27	5	20	51	112	8	1	.260	.330	.456	.136	.201	.253	.354	-.334	-30.3	115-1B -7
2001	SAR	FSL	22	267	81	14	1	12	18	61	2	2	.303	.350	.498	.251	.246	.279	.412	-.171	-5.1	54-1B -1
2001	TRN	EAS	22	229	71	20	1	14	28	68	0	1	.310	.385	.590	.399	.269	.338	.504	.085	11.5	57-1B -6
2002	NHV	EAS	23	308	82	16	1	12	32	59	3	2	.266	.337	.442	.089	.235	.292	.390	-.186	-9.0	73-RF -5
2002	AKR	EAS	23	166	48	9	0	6	13	27	1	0	.289	.344	.452	.125	.250	.298	.393	-.160	-3.0	22-LF 1
2003	CLE	AL	24	169	43	9	1	7	14	36	2	2	.256	.315	.442	-.006	.262	.323	.453	-.019	.1	

Breakout: 45%　　Improve: 77%　　Collapse: 16%

Luis Garcia's raw lines look good, but after his 2001 season, they've got to be seen as a disappointment. He's got a power stroke, and he can take a walk (though he should take more), but he needs to make contact more often. A former pitcher, Garcia shouldn't see his arm questioned any time soon. If you took the best parts of Coco Crisp and Luis Garcia, you'd have a top outfield prospect who would probably immediately suffer a season-ending injury and drop behind Alex Escobar on the depth charts.

Jody Gerut　　OF　Born: 18-Sep-77　Age: 25　Bats: L　Throws: L

YEAR	TM	LG	AGE	AB	H	2B	3B	HR	BB	SO	SB	CS	AVG	OBP	SLG	MLVR	EQBA	EQOBP	EQSLG	EQMLVR	VORP	DEFENSE
2000	CAR	SOU	22	362	103	32	3	3	76	54	18	11	.285	.411	.414	.192	.248	.351	.364	-.100	-1.3	89-LF -2
2002	AKR	EAS	24	256	72	15	2	9	34	30	17	8	.281	.368	.461	.166	.240	.313	.401	-.128	3.5	63-CF -3
2002	BUF	INT	24	183	59	7	2	1	23	20	3	5	.322	.401	.399	.160	.296	.372	.371	-.017	8.1	53-CF 3
2003	CLE	AL	25	184	48	11	1	4	20	26	4	2	.262	.336	.406	-.014	.268	.344	.416	-.026	4.3	

Breakout: 19%　　Improve: 54%　　Collapse: 22%

Gerut was acquired from the Rockies after 2000, and has unfortunately been nothing but injury-prone since. Despite the bad wheels, he's still playing center, but he broke down in August with a stress fracture in his leg. If he has a healthy season, he'll be up, but that's looking like a big if.

Ricky Gutierrez　　2B　Born: 23-May-70　Age: 33　Bats: R　Throws: R

YEAR	TM	LG	AGE	AB	H	2B	3B	HR	BB	SO	SB	CS	AVG	OBP	SLG	MLVR	EQBA	EQOBP	EQSLG	EQMLVR	VORP	DEFENSE
2000	CHC	NL	30	449	124	19	2	11	66	58	8	2	.276	.377	.401	.000	.277	.369	.400	.003	27.9	112-SS -5
2001	CHC	NL	31	528	153	23	3	10	40	56	4	3	.290	.351	.402	.001	.297	.355	.412	.010	33.6	137-SS -5
2002	CLE	AL	32	353	97	13	0	4	20	48	0	1	.275	.326	.346	-.106	.296	.345	.372	-.066	13.5	90-2B -3
2003	CLE	AL	33	315	80	15	1	5	24	39	1	1	.255	.315	.352	-.123	.261	.323	.360	-.142	1.2	

Breakout: 3%　　Improve: 25%　　Collapse: 43%

Ricky Gutierrez would have been a decent stopgap, but at three years and $11.5 million, he was a bad deal. Ricky didn't have that awful of a year when he could play, but then he had to have surgery to fuse three vertebrae in his neck in October. At press time, he's finishing up his time in a brace before attempting an aggressive three-month rehab to be ready for spring training. There's talk they may play him at third to replace Fryman, where he should be a marginal upgrade, as long as they're trying to maximize the value of the players they're committed to.

Greg LaRocca   2B/3B   Born: 10-Nov-72   Age: 30   Bats: R   Throws: R

YEAR	TM	LG	AGE	AB	H	2B	3B	HR	BB	SO	SB	CS	AVG	OBP	SLG	MLVR	EQBA	EQOBP	EQSLG	EQMLVR	VORP	DEFENSE			
2000	LVG	PCL	27	482	142	42	7	9	54	62	13	4	.295	.380	.467	.079	.253	.324	.399	-.100	10.8	105-3B	-5	19-2B	-2
2001	AKR	EAS	28	104	33	9	0	3	18	11	0	2	.317	.427	.490	.338	.266	.366	.422	.019	7.3	22-SS	-1		
2001	BUF	INT	28	216	67	12	1	12	12	35	2	1	.310	.363	.542	.284	.289	.340	.505	.110	16.8	47-3B	3		
2002	CLE	AL	29	52	14	3	1	0	6	6	1	0	.269	.367	.365	-.011	.288	.390	.385	.030	3.1	13-3B	-8		
2002	BUF	INT	29	382	112	28	2	7	48	48	17	4	.293	.404	.432	.185	.276	.375	.412	.030	22.7	47-3B	-1	29-2B	2
2003	*CLE*	*AL*	*30*	*225*	*58*	*14*	*1*	*6*	*21*	*33*	*4*	*2*	*.257*	*.327*	*.408*	*-.030*	*.263*	*.336*	*.417*	*-.043*	*5.5*				

Breakout: 4%   *Improve: 36%*   *Collapse: 34%*

LaRocca had another good year in Buffalo. He's an average defender at third, and if the team didn't have a logjam of large contracts at the major league level, he'd be perfect to fill the hole just left by Fryman. This off-season will bring a third ear surgery for LaRocca, the result of having punctured his eardrum with a Q-Tip way back when. Let this be a lesson to us all: do not insert in ear canal, just like the box says. A minor league free agent, LaRocca went to the AFL for no apparent reason as an Indian, which would seem to indicate he's still affiliated with the team.

Matt Lawton   RF   Born: 03-Nov-71   Age: 31   Bats: L   Throws: R

YEAR	TM	LG	AGE	AB	H	2B	3B	HR	BB	SO	SB	CS	AVG	OBP	SLG	MLVR	EQBA	EQOBP	EQSLG	EQMLVR	VORP	DEFENSE	
2000	MIN	AL	28	561	171	44	2	13	91	63	23	7	.305	.408	.460	.147	.309	.407	.468	.192	39.8	127-RF	-2
2001	MIN	AL	29	376	110	25	0	10	63	46	19	6	.293	.398	.439	.140	.308	.413	.464	.196	28.5	81-RF	0
2001	NYM	NL	29	183	45	11	1	3	22	34	10	2	.246	.352	.366	-.065	.262	.360	.390	-.038	2.0	44-RF	1
2002	CLE	AL	30	416	98	19	2	15	59	34	8	9	.236	.342	.399	-.035	.254	.357	.433	.008	9.7	108-RF	-4
2003	*CLE*	*AL*	*31*	*376*	*100*	*21*	*1*	*10*	*55*	*44*	*11*	*2*	*.265*	*.364*	*.409*	*.037*	*.271*	*.373*	*.418*	*.029*	*6.3*		

Breakout: 14%   *Improve: 46%*   *Collapse: 18%*

Lawton's headed into the second year of a four-year, $27 million deal. For an outfielder whose major attribute is his batting eye, that's a little pricey. He's coming off of an especially frustrating season that ended with surgery to remove a cyst in his shoulder that may push his return into the second half of the 2003 season. What they found in his shoulder was reportedly as gruesome as anything outside of Peter Jackson's horror classic *Bad Taste*. It took a team of medical specialists to revive the medical specialists who passed out after taking the first look into that abyss, unprepared for what would be staring back at them. Lawton's expected to be back and healthy eventually, but how many horror movies don't have sequels?

John McDonald   2B/SS   Born: 24-Sep-74   Age: 28   Bats: R   Throws: R

YEAR	TM	LG	AGE	AB	H	2B	3B	HR	BB	SO	SB	CS	AVG	OBP	SLG	MLVR	EQBA	EQOBP	EQSLG	EQMLVR	VORP	DEFENSE			
2000	BUF	INT	25	286	77	17	2	1	21	29	4	3	.269	.321	.353	-.115	.253	.295	.330	-.253	-2.5	68-SS	1		
2001	BUF	INT	26	410	100	17	1	2	33	72	17	10	.244	.310	.305	-.167	.231	.293	.292	-.323	-11.4	110-SS	8		
2002	CLE	AL	27	264	66	11	3	1	10	50	3	0	.250	.290	.326	-.214	.268	.307	.355	-.184	2.1	56-2B	7	17-SS	-4
2003	*CLE*	*AL*	*28*	*235*	*57*	*10*	*1*	*2*	*13*	*40*	*4*	*2*	*.242*	*.287*	*.319*	*-.221*	*.247*	*.295*	*.326*	*-.248*	*-5.4*				

Breakout: 17%   *Improve: 40%*   *Collapse: 31%*

With Gutierrez injured, McDonald saw a lot of time playing sure-handed defense at second while still not hitting. McDonald's going to play wherever they need him to play while they wait on their bumper crop of prospects, and then be pushed back into utility play or discarded.

Paul Shuey was the Indians union rep to start the season, and was traded. Ryan Drese, at the wise old age of 26, took over. He was demoted to Buffalo, so then McDonald took over. If he goes into 2003 still with the Indians, look for him to explode spontaneously while taking the field, forcing him to retire. I don't mean any disrespect to John McDonald, but why are union reps frequently young, marginal players? Is it a hazing thing, where the only way to get out of having to wear a dress on a cross-country flight is to sign up? Or do veterans prefer the hamster-like energy of the youngsters be channeled into something constructive like studying the history of collective bargaining, rather than getting into women, or men, or competitive Scrabble?

Marshall McDougall   INF   Born: 19-Dec-78   Age: 24   Bats: R   Throws: R

YEAR	TM	LG	AGE	AB	H	2B	3B	HR	BB	SO	SB	CS	AVG	OBP	SLG	MLVR	EQBA	EQOBP	EQSLG	EQMLVR	VORP	DEFENSE			
2000	VAN	NWN	21	102	28	4	2	0	18	19	5	3	.275	.383	.353	.128	.220	.292	.284	-.342	-3.6	24-2B	-1		
2001	VIS	CLF	22	534	137	43	7	12	46	110	14	2	.257	.324	.431	.027	.203	.253	.336	-.358	-22.4	75-3B	0	29-2B	-1
2002	MID	TXS	23	323	98	22	5	9	38	57	7	4	.303	.378	.486	.224	.252	.316	.408	-.103	7.1	36-3B	1	27-SS	-4
2003	TEX	AL	24	194	48	11	1	5	18	37	4	3	.250	.315	.400	-.066	.252	.320	.404	-.096	1.7				

Breakout: 41%   Improve: 70%   Collapse: 16%

McDougall came over from the A's in the Rincon trade. McDougall's performances haven't caught up to him yet. He's got a solid approach to hitting, drives the fastball, and he's taking some walks. He can also play every infield position, not that he's a good glove anywhere, but that versatility could be his ticket upward. Jeff Huson had a career, after all, and McDougall's already a much better hitter than Huson. Swiped by the Rangers in the Rule 5 draft, although it's hard to see him sticking with them.

Chris Magruder   OF   Born: 26-Apr-77   Age: 26   Bats: B   Throws: R

YEAR	TM	LG	AGE	AB	H	2B	3B	HR	BB	SO	SB	CS	AVG	OBP	SLG	MLVR	EQBA	EQOBP	EQSLG	EQMLVR	VORP	DEFENSE	
2000	SHV	TXS	23	496	140	33	3	4	67	75	18	10	.282	.377	.385	.031	.242	.312	.331	-.225	-6.4	123-CF	-3
2001	SHV	TXS	24	149	38	6	3	2	15	27	5	3	.255	.335	.376	-.033	.219	.283	.325	-.304	-9.3	39-RF	0
2001	FRE	PCL	24	214	60	7	1	10	18	45	3	1	.280	.356	.463	.044	.245	.312	.401	-.126	3.2	53-CF	1
2001	OKL	PCL	24	127	46	14	4	5	21	19	1	2	.362	.467	.654	.618	.312	.412	.562	.332	17.8	31-CF	0
2002	CLE	AL	25	258	56	15	1	6	15	55	2	0	.217	.263	.353	-.248	.232	.278	.382	-.226	-9.1	69-OF	-3
2002	BUF	INT	25	191	51	10	2	5	26	34	3	2	.267	.364	.419	.084	.247	.340	.397	-.077	.6	48-OF	-1
2003	CLE	AL	26	284	71	16	2	8	25	53	4	3	.248	.315	.401	-.064	.254	.324	.410	-.080	-1.8		

Breakout: 28%   Improve: 60%   Collapse: 28%

If Magruder had hit for more power in the minors and was two years younger he'd be as interesting as Coco Crisp. He didn't, so he isn't. He'll almost certainly be soldiering on for the Indians in the minors, hoping the major league team gets some sort of contagious, nonlethal temporarily disabling skin rash that allows him a chance to accumulate some more service time.

Victor Martinez   C   Born: 23-Dec-78   Age: 24   Bats: B   Throws: R

YEAR	TM	LG	AGE	AB	H	2B	3B	HR	BB	SO	SB	CS	AVG	OBP	SLG	MLVR	EQBA	EQOBP	EQSLG	EQMLVR	VORP	DEFENSE	
2000	CGA	SAL	21	70	26	9	1	2	11	6	0	0	.371	.463	.614	.595	.264	.341	.444	.002	4.6	20-C	0
2000	KIN	CRL	21	83	18	7	0	0	11	5	1	1	.217	.316	.301	-.118	.186	.259	.267	-.449	-4.9	25-C	-6
2001	KIN	CRL	22	420	138	33	2	10	39	60	3	3	.329	.396	.488	.343	.273	.328	.414	-.056	20.2	105-C	-6
2002	AKR	EAS	23	443	149	40	0	22	58	62	3	3	.336	.422	.576	.451	.283	.356	.487	.106	40.0	101-C	-4
2002	CLE	AL	23	32	9	1	0	1	3	2	0	0	.281	.343	.406	.009	.312	.371	.438	.090	1.9		
2003	CLE	AL	24	265	68	15	1	9	24	39	2	1	.257	.323	.420	-.022	.263	.331	.429	-.035	9.2		

Breakout: 11%   Improve: 34%   Collapse: 28%

That no one saw this coming contributed to Einar's four-year deal with a club option for 2005. Then Martinez won the Eastern League batting title and MVP after winning the Carolina League MVP the year before. Scouts say his defense makes him an incomplete package, but he has good receiving skills; the perceived deficiency is all in his arm strength. In his brief cup of coffee this year, Martinez didn't do anything to quell that concern, allowing 11 stolen bases and throwing out only 2 in his nearly 70 innings of work. The problem is whether there's much to do for him; there's a limit to how fast you can get rid of the ball after you've mastered your footwork, and if you can't get it screaming to second, the speedsters are going to be able to steal on him consistently.

Beyond that minor concern, check out that hitting line, which is why Martinez is as good a catching prospect as they come. He's not quite ready to take over the major league job, but he'll be ready before long.

Eddie Perez   Born: 04-May-68   Age: 35   Bats: R   Throws: R

YEAR	TM	LG	AGE	AB	H	2B	3B	HR	BB	SO	SB	CS	AVG	OBP	SLG	MLVR	EQBA	EQOBP	EQSLG	EQMLVR	VORP	DEFENSE	
2002	CLE	AL	34	117	25	9	0	0	5	25	0	0	.214	.252	.291	-.352	.231	.273	.316	-.330	-2.8	36-C	1

Some catchers have great defensive reputations, or are known for their ability to mentor young pitchers, or young catchers. Eddie Perez was once Greg Maddux's personal catcher. He's a free agent, and might bring his particular skill set to your town any day now. There's a secret society of backup catchers, who once they're out of the game take front office jobs and make sure that their younger members are never without a job. Anyone with a better explanation for Perez's longevity can drop us a line.

Brandon Phillips   SS/2B   Born: 28-Jun-81   Age: 22   Bats: R   Throws: R

YEAR	TM	LG	AGE	AB	H	2B	3B	HR	BB	SO	SB	CS	AVG	OBP	SLG	MLVR	EQBA	EQOBP	EQSLG	EQMLVR	VORP	DEFENSE
2000	CPF	SAL	19	484	117	17	8	11	38	97	23	8	.242	.309	.378	-.014	.188	.234	.297	-.458	-30.3	121-SS -11
2001	JUP	FSL	20	194	55	12	2	4	38	45	17	3	.284	.416	.428	.245	.240	.343	.373	-.108	6.2	55-SS -1
2001	HAR	EAS	20	265	79	19	0	7	12	42	13	6	.298	.338	.449	.116	.257	.295	.384	-.173	3.3	61-SS 2
2002	HAR	EAS	21	245	80	13	2	9	16	33	6	3	.327	.380	.506	.270	.276	.320	.427	-.050	10.3	53-SS -10
2002	OTT	INT	21	35	9	4	0	1	2	6	0	0	.257	.297	.457	.033	.257	.297	.429	-.105	.3	
2002	BUF	INT	21	223	63	14	0	8	14	39	8	2	.283	.328	.453	.083	.259	.308	.424	-.090	7.4	44-SS 7 11-2B 1
2002	CLE	AL	21	31	8	3	1	0	3	6	0	0	.258	.343	.419	.009	.290	.368	.452	.084	1.8	
2003	CLE	AL	22	314	79	15	2	10	25	55	7	4	.252	.314	.410	-.051	.258	.322	.420	-.066	7.8	

Breakout: 33%   Improve: 64%   Collapse: 15%

The Indians sent Phillips to the Arizona Fall League to keep working on becoming a second baseman because Omar's under contract for another two years. There's no reason to believe Phillips can't make the switch. It may even be for the best, since he's never been an outstanding defensive shortstop, although he has the arm for the position. However, because of his stick he's rightly regarded as one of the top infield prospects in baseball. If he doesn't stick at short, his value will go down a little, but the difference between a decent shortstop with a great stick and a good defensive second baseman with a good stick isn't that huge. The danger is more one of his risk of encountering more baserunners around the bag, because second basemen tend to have their careers altered by injury more often than shortstops. Nevertheless, his move across the keystone shouldn't take any luster off of his rising star.

Bill Selby   INF   Born: 11-Jun-70   Age: 33   Bats: L   Throws: R

YEAR	TM	LG	AGE	AB	H	2B	3B	HR	BB	SO	SB	CS	AVG	OBP	SLG	MLVR	EQBA	EQOBP	EQSLG	EQMLVR	VORP	DEFENSE
2000	BUF	INT	30	384	106	21	6	21	48	61	1	1	.276	.361	.526	.196	.255	.327	.485	.026	22.1	52-3B 3 26-LF -1
2001	LOU	INT	31	330	85	19	1	14	25	47	1	0	.258	.314	.448	.035	.243	.296	.425	-.124	7.9	35-2B 6 19-1B -3
2001	CIN	NL	31	92	21	7	1	2	5	13	0	0	.228	.276	.391	-.216	.226	.271	.398	-.221	-.1	17-2B 2
2002	BUF	INT	32	184	55	14	2	5	20	33	4	1	.299	.368	.478	.193	.274	.345	.446	.021	5.4	18-LF 0 17-2B 0
2002	CLE	AL	32	159	34	7	2	6	15	27	0	1	.214	.282	.396	-.159	.231	.297	.425	-.131	2.4	31-3B -6
2003	CLE	AL	33	189	46	10	1	6	19	35	2	1	.244	.315	.404	-.064	.250	.323	.413	-.080	.9	

Breakout: 21%   Improve: 55%   Collapse: 23%

Selby spent about four months on the major league roster and started 38 games in the field, but I can't remember seeing him. Maybe he's a Gray Man. There's got to be a reason he hung around—ah. His hitting and play at third base made Fryman look okay, which allowed Fryman to retire with some modicum of dignity.

Grady Sizemore   OF   Born: 02-Aug-82   Age: 20   Bats: L   Throws: L

YEAR	TM	LG	AGE	AB	H	2B	3B	HR	BB	SO	SB	CS	AVG	OBP	SLG	MLVR	EQBA	EQOBP	EQSLG	EQMLVR	VORP	DEFENSE
2001	CLN	MDW	18	451	121	16	4	2	81	92	32	11	.268	.384	.335	.038	.203	.294	.254	-.386	-26.2	113-CF -11
2002	BRV	FSL	19	256	66	15	4	0	36	41	9	9	.258	.354	.348	.039	.216	.290	.299	-.327	-17.9	65-LF -5
2002	KIN	CRL	19	172	59	9	3	3	33	30	14	7	.343	.451	.483	.398	.272	.365	.389	-.023	3.2	41-LF -5
2003	CLE	AL	20	208	50	9	3	4	21	41	5	3	.239	.312	.359	-.129	.244	.320	.367	-.150	-5.5	

Breakout: 33%   Improve: 65%   Collapse: 11%

Sizemore is a great prospect, and another example of why scouts aren't stupid to drool over guys with athletic tools. He controls the strike zone and powers line drives that are going to go for doubles and triples soon. His defense is good, and he could stick in center for at least a couple years, although we're a ways away from knowing if he'll get heavier and slower and have to move to a corner or not, or if he'll continue to be a greyhound at the major league level. He's young for his levels to boot. Strangely for a quarterback who turned down the University of Washington, where he would have played football and baseball, the consistent knock on Sizemore is that his arm is weak for center, but that didn't stop people like Willie Wilson, Brett Butler, or even Rudy Law.

Corey Smith   3B   Born: 15-Apr-82   Age: 21   Bats: R   Throws: R

YEAR	TM	LG	AGE	AB	H	2B	3B	HR	BB	SO	SB	CS	AVG	OBP	SLG	MLVR	EQBA	EQOBP	EQSLG	EQMLVR	VORP	DEFENSE
2000	BNC	APL	18	207	53	8	2	4	27	50	8	1	.256	.345	.372	.028	.178	.236	.252	-.520	-18.5	52-3B -12
2001	CGA	SAL	19	500	130	26	5	18	37	149	10	7	.260	.317	.440	.112	.203	.247	.345	-.357	-22.3	113-3B -20
2002	KIN	CRL	20	505	129	29	2	13	59	141	7	2	.255	.344	.398	.073	.212	.281	.337	-.296	-14.9	130-3B -15
2003	CLE	AL	21	206	47	8	1	6	17	57	3	3	.229	.293	.367	-.157	.235	.301	.375	-.179	-3.2	

Breakout: 51%   Improve: 70%   Collapse: 19%

Corey Smith (*continued*)

Corey Smith's hype is so wildly out of proportion to his demonstrated talent that he must have some sort of hypno-gaze superpower that he uses on scouts in the stands. He hit .255/.341/.398 at Akron, doubling his walk rate, and the doubles are up, but this is still not the performance of a third baseman. His defense is still a major source of concern after he committed 34 errors last season, which brings his three-year total up to 111, a lot considering one of those was in a short-season league. He's got bat speed and can hit fastballs, but he swings at anything. He's got a good arm, sure, but his fielding's still not any good. The acquisition of Marshall McDougall and later the Rule 5 pickup of Travis Chapman may mean Smith is no longer considered the heir to the hot corner.

Earl Snyder   3B/1B   Born: 06-May-76   Age: 27   Bats: R   Throws: R

YEAR	TM	LG	AGE	AB	H	2B	3B	HR	BB	SO	SB	CS	AVG	OBP	SLG	MLVR	EQBA	EQOBP	EQSLG	EQMLVR	VORP	DEFENSE			
2000	SLU	FSL	24	514	145	36	0	25	57	127	4	4	.282	.363	.498	.227	.227	.290	.403	-.178	-10.9	119-1B -9			
2001	BIN	EAS	25	405	114	35	2	20	58	111	4	2	.281	.377	.526	.248	.236	.322	.438	-.063	3.9	82-1B -12		13-3B	1
2002	BUF	INT	26	400	105	29	1	19	43	96	0	2	.263	.343	.482	.129	.244	.321	.454	-.037	16.2	62-3B -8		39-1B	-6
2002	CLE	AL	26	55	11	2	0	1	6	21	0	0	.200	.279	.291	-.308	.218	.295	.327	-.278	-2.7	12-1B -4			
2003	BOS	AL	27	246	59	14	1	9	25	61	2	3	.241	.316	.420	-.044	.246	.324	.440	-.046	2.2				

Breakout: 21%   Improve: 44%   Collapse: 21%

See, and here's another guy like LaRocca the Indians could plug in to play 3B and win some games, although his defense is bad and has never gotten better. A nice waiver snag by Boston, he might platoon at first or DH.

Lee Stevens   1B   Born: 10-Jul-67   Age: 36   Bats: L   Throws: L

YEAR	TM	LG	AGE	AB	H	2B	3B	HR	BB	SO	SB	CS	AVG	OBP	SLG	MLVR	EQBA	EQOBP	EQSLG	EQMLVR	VORP	DEFENSE			
2000	MON	NL	33	449	119	27	2	22	48	105	0	0	.265	.339	.481	.030	.263	.328	.480	.028	15.6	117-1B 12			
2001	MON	NL	34	542	133	35	1	25	74	157	2	1	.245	.341	.452	.004	.246	.340	.451	-.005	14.7	148-1B 4			
2002	MON	NL	35	205	39	6	1	10	39	57	1	0	.190	.320	.376	-.103	.197	.321	.394	-.151	-3.2	57-1B 4			
2002	CLE	AL	35	153	34	7	1	5	15	32	0	0	.222	.292	.379	-.158	.240	.308	.409	-.126	-1.2	24-1B -5		16-LF	0
2003	CLE	AL	35	275	63	13	1	10	35	67	1	1	.229	.316	.398	-.079	.234	.324	.407	-.096	-4.0				

Breakout: 16%   Improve: 49%   Collapse: 20%

Stevens was a throw-in for the Colon trade because Omar Minaya wasn't allowed to take on any salary during his strip-mining of the Expos' farm system. It must be annoying to be tossed in like that, but it's not as if Stevens is hitting enough to justify playing regularly. His contract is up after this year, after which he should be done.

Eddie Taubensee   Born: 31-Oct-68   Age: 34   Bats: L   Throws: R

YEAR	TM	LG	AGE	AB	H	2B	3B	HR	BB	SO	SB	CS	AVG	OBP	SLG	MLVR	EQBA	EQOBP	EQSLG	EQMLVR	VORP	DEFENSE
2000	CIN	NL	31	266	71	12	0	6	21	44	0	0	.267	.325	.380	-.151	.262	.313	.375	-.148	6.1	65-C -3
2001	CLE	AL	32	116	29	2	1	3	10	19	0	0	.250	.315	.362	-.136	.267	.335	.388	-.084	4.4	28-C -7

Taubensee's career's been dogged by a couple of degenerative discs in his back. This year they didn't respond to treatment, he spent the season on the DL, and in July he told the Indians he's not going to be able to return to baseball. Hopefully he'll be able to live a normal life.

Jim Thome   1B   Born: 27-Aug-70   Age: 32   Bats: L   Throws: R

YEAR	TM	LG	AGE	AB	H	2B	3B	HR	BB	SO	SB	CS	AVG	OBP	SLG	MLVR	EQBA	EQOBP	EQSLG	EQMLVR	VORP	DEFENSE
2000	CLE	AL	29	557	150	33	1	37	118	171	1	0	.269	.401	.531	.197	.274	.399	.547	.251	51.6	103-1B 3
2001	CLE	AL	30	526	153	26	1	49	111	185	0	1	.291	.418	.624	.409	.307	.433	.661	.490	87.6	142-1B -15
2002	CLE	AL	31	480	146	19	2	52	122	139	1	2	.304	.450	.677	.540	.325	.466	.730	.648	109.2	123-1B -2
2003	PHI	NL	32	483	132	25	2	38	121	152	3	1	.273	.421	.571	.313	.279	.424	.601	.345	55.7	

Breakout: 3%   Improve: 37%   Collapse: 10%

There wasn't an at-bat this year where Thome gave up, where he wasn't up there trying to work the pitcher, to get one on base one more time that day, no matter how far up or down the Indians were. While Thome was an immensely popular player and had said he'd be willing to make a deal, $22 million is a lot to leave on the table. It's surpising Cleveland offered as much as they did: there have been ugly incidents in recent years where free agents said they'd be willing to offer a hometown discount and the home team decided not to take any chances and tendered the player an insulting contract, forcing the issue. Look forward to seeing Thome back in a good-hitting offensive sequence again. Driving the ball, working the pitchers, seeing a lot of pitches; these are skills wasted in a lineup of light-hitting free-swingers.

Omar Vizquel — SS — Born: 24-Apr-67 — Age: 36 — Bats: B — Throws: R

YEAR	TM	LG	AGE	AB	H	2B	3B	HR	BB	SO	SB	CS	AVG	OBP	SLG	MLVR	EQBA	EQOBP	EQSLG	EQMLVR	VORP	DEFENSE
2000	CLE	AL	33	613	176	27	3	7	87	72	22	10	.287	.380	.375	-.039	.290	.377	.381	.002	34.1	149-SS -3
2001	CLE	AL	34	611	156	26	8	2	61	72	13	9	.255	.325	.334	-.152	.271	.342	.356	-.113	16.6	146-SS 2
2002	CLE	AL	35	582	160	31	5	14	56	64	18	10	.275	.347	.418	.026	.295	.365	.452	.083	46.8	146-SS -1
2003	CLE	AL	36	434	114	21	3	6	45	51	12	3	.262	.334	.366	-.068	.268	.343	.374	-.083	10.0	

Breakout: 14%   Improve: 42%   Collapse: 26%

If you haven't read his autobiography *Omar!*, let me save you the $24.95 hardcover price, making your purchase of BP2003 guaranteed profitable: "I went and tried something. I picked it up quickly and everyone was amazed. It turns out I'm naturally good at something. Let me tell you something about this player, followed by descriptions of various expensive things I own. It turns out I'm naturally good at owning things." Repeat. It's sort of a shame that Omar has become a 10-and-5 guy and wants to stick around in Cleveland. He's blocking Brandon Phillips, who can't possibly be as annoying as Omar has become.

Matt Whitney — 3B — Born: 13-Feb-84 — Age: 19 — Bats: R — Throws: R

YEAR	TM	LG	AGE	AB	H	2B	3B	HR	BB	SO	SB	CS	AVG	OBP	SLG	MLVR	EQBA	EQOBP	EQSLG	EQMLVR	VORP	DEFENSE
2002	BNC	APL	18	175	50	12	1	10	18	49	5	1	.286	.362	.537	.249	.188	.232	.341	-.401	-9.0	37-3B 0
2003	CLE	AL	19	175	32	7	0	3	19	57	3	4	.182	.267	.276	-.339	.187	.274	.282	-.375	-12.0	

Breakout: 77%   Improve: 81%   Collapse: 11%

You're probably saying "huh, that's weird. It's not often I see 19-year-olds in the Prospectus player comments. Must be a good reason." You bet your sweet ass there is. Whitney wants to put on some weight, add some power, and become Troy Glaus. This has led to endless cribs for "Troy Glaus potential" and "May not be on the level of Troy Glaus." Yeah, we don't know yet, but playing advanced rookie ball at Burlington fresh out of high school, he hit .286/.359/.537, and almost half of his hits (23 of 50) were for extra bases. What's more, Whitney's a smart kid: he knows what he needs to work on, he knows what he's going to have to do to get there, and he has the ability to make it happen. By the end of next season, Whitney could be one of the top prospects in baseball.

PITCHERS

Danny Baez — Born: 10-Sep-77 — Age: 25 — Bats: R — Throws: R

YEAR	TM	LG	AGE	G	GS	IP	H	BB	SO	HR	ERA	EQERA	EQH9	EQBB9	EQSO9	EQHR9	PERA	VORP	STF
2000	KIN	CRL	22	9	9	49.7	45	20	56	5	4.71	6.51	11.8	4.5	6.6	2.3	6.19	-5.5	5
2000	AKR	EAS	22	18	18	102.7	98	32	77	6	3.68	4.92	10.6	3.2	5.2	1.0	4.75	6.7	8
2001	BUF	INT	23	16	0	25.3	18	9	30	2	3.20	3.70	7.4	3.8	8.4	1.0	3.38	4.7	16
2001	CLE	AL	23	43	0	50.3	34	20	52	5	2.50	2.80	5.4	3.3	8.5	0.8	2.66	14.4	21
2002	CLE	AL	24	39	26	165.3	160	82	130	14	4.41	3.77	7.9	4.1	6.7	0.7	4.12	31.5	12
2003	CLE	AL	25	30	21	133.0	136	60	106	17	4.82	4.74	9.1	3.7	6.8	1.0	4.59	14.8	8

Breakout: 12%   Improve: 48%   Collapse: 11%

Here at Prospectus Labs, we initially greeted the news that Baez would be turned into a closer with a lot of gnashing and wailing. "Why would you use a good pitcher for fewer innings," we said. "Closers are overrated!" The problem is that Baez doesn't have the pitches. He's got two good pitches and that's it. If the Indians can turn him into an Established Closer and then flip him for some delicious talent, so much the better.

Dave Burba — Born: 07-Jul-66 — Age: 37 — Bats: R — Throws: R

YEAR	TM	LG	AGE	G	GS	IP	H	BB	SO	HR	ERA	EQERA	EQH9	EQBB9	EQSO9	EQHR9	PERA	VORP	STF
2000	CLE	AL	34	32	32	191.3	199	91	180	19	4.47	3.89	8.5	3.4	8.0	0.7	4.07	34.3	23
2001	CLE	AL	35	32	27	150.7	188	54	118	16	6.21	5.17	10.1	2.9	6.4	0.8	5.31	5.5	7
2002	TEX	AL	36	23	18	111.3	125	40	70	13	5.42	4.82	9.7	3.0	5.5	0.9	4.66	8.3	2
2002	CLE	AL	36	12	3	34.0	30	17	25	3	4.50	3.85	7.2	4.1	6.3	0.7	3.76	6.0	2
2003	CLE	AL	36	30	21	123.3	133	50	88	15	4.69	4.61	9.6	3.4	6.1	0.9	4.63	16.1	4

Breakout: 18%   Improve: 43%   Collapse: 15%

Dave Burba (*continued*)

"Hi, Dave Burba's agent here."

"This is Dave."

"Hey Dave, what's up?"

"Yeah, I just talked to Hart. The Rangers are releasing me. He said I just don't have the stuff to pitch in their rotation."

(long silence followed by sobbing)

Fortunately, the Indians gave Burba a minor league deal and promptly tossed him back in the fire. Burba's good for a 10–11 season almost any year, and the Indians bit, taking him to arbitration, where he'll probably get more than a floating free agent like Ismael Valdes would have cost.

Fernando Cabrera   Born: 16-Nov-81   Age: 21   Bats: R   Throws: R

YEAR	TM	LG	AGE	G	GS	IP	H	BB	SO	HR	ERA	EQERA	EQH9	EQBB9	EQSO9	EQHR9	PERA	VORP	STF
2000	BNC	APL	18	13	13	68.3	64	20	50	4	4.61	5.23	10.9	3.8	3.4	1.5	6.27	2.1	-9
2001	CGA	SAL	19	20	20	94.7	89	37	96	7	3.61	7.05	13.4	5.7	5.5	1.7	6.67	-16.3	-4
2002	KIN	CRL	20	21	21	110.0	83	40	107	7	3.52	5.10	9.8	4.7	6.4	1.5	4.42	5.0	11
2002	*AKR*	*EAS*	*20*	*7*	*4*	*27.0*	*26*	*12*	*29*	*1*	*5.33*	*6.28*	*11.3*	*4.9*	*7.6*	*0.6*	*5.08*	*-2.4*	*15*

Cabrera is starting to come together as a pitcher. His strikeout rates are climbing, though he's still dogged by hits and the long ball. This comes from his command issues: he'll nibble and then have to throw meatballs that get driven hard. Already throwing 94 with a power curve, if Cabrera's control gets a little finer and if he challenges hitters more, he'll blow through the rest of the minors quickly. Until then, he'll keep climbing the ladder.

Alberto Cruceta   Born: 04-Jul-81   Age: 22   Bats: R   Throws: R

YEAR	TM	LG	AGE	G	GS	IP	H	BB	SO	HR	ERA	EQERA	EQH9	EQBB9	EQSO9	EQHR9	PERA	VORP	STF
2002	SGA	SAL	21	20	20	112.7	98	34	111	7	2.80	5.27	11.9	4.0	5.7	1.6	5.48	2.9	7
2002	KIN	CRL	21	7	7	39.7	31	25	37	2	2.49	5.01	10.1	8.4	6.3	1.2	5.56	2.2	3

Ripped off from the Dodgers in the Shuey dump, Cruceta's an interesting project. His mechanics are messed up, with an entirely different arm slot for the fastball/change and the curve, which makes the curve easy to see coming. Still, he's consistently up to 94 with a fastball he's got good control of, and with a deceptive changeup, he's got a nice 1-2 punch. The Indians are going to work on getting him to use a single delivery, and while tinkering with mechanics is always a gamble, Cruceta's a player who could burst into the majors and make a few eyes pop.

Jason Davis   Born: 08-May-80   Age: 23   Bats: R   Throws: R

YEAR	TM	LG	AGE	G	GS	IP	H	BB	SO	HR	ERA	EQERA	EQH9	EQBB9	EQSO9	EQHR9	PERA	VORP	STF
2000	BNC	APL	20	10	10	45.0	48	16	35	5	4.40	6.26	13.8	4.8	3.7	3.0	8.47	-3.8	-21
2001	CGA	SAL	21	27	27	160.0	147	51	115	9	2.70	6.31	12.8	4.6	3.9	1.3	5.98	-14.3	-5
2002	KIN	CRL	22	17	17	99.7	107	31	68	7	4.15	7.43	13.9	4.1	4.6	1.7	6.50	-21.3	-4
2002	AKR	EAS	22	10	10	59.0	63	16	45	2	3.51	5.53	12.6	3.0	5.4	0.5	5.09	-0.2	12
2002	CLE	AL	22	3	2	14.7	12	4	11	1	1.84	1.96	6.7	2.3	6.5	0.6	2.74	5.8	25

If you like tall guys with heat, Davis is your man. He's 6'6" and throws a heavy fastball in the low 90s with good command. His other pitches, and his command with them, isn't good enough yet. Promoted from the Carolina League to Double-A Akron despite a rocky season, he did remarkably well. We'd like to see a consolidation season, giving Davis time to work on his repertoire, which would help out his walks and improve his strikeouts. He's expected to be in the mix for a rotation spot in spring training.

Dan Denham   Born: 24-Dec-82   Age: 20   Bats: R   Throws: R

YEAR	TM	LG	AGE	G	GS	IP	H	BB	SO	HR	ERA	EQERA	EQH9	EQBB9	EQSO9	EQHR9	PERA	VORP	STF
2001	BNC	APL	18	8	8	30.7	30	26	31	5	4.40	10.51	18.6	15.2	5.1	5.2	11.79	-17.1	-56
2002	CGA	SAL	19	28	28	124.7	123	65	109	7	4.76	7.19	13.0	7.0	5.1	1.4	6.86	-23.3	-10

Another piece of evidence that the Indians didn't really know what they were doing in John Hart's last couple of years. Nothing against Denham particularly, but they had two first-round picks in 2001 and took two right-handed high school pitchers. It's too early to draw any conclusions based on his bad seasons in the low minors. He's athletic, he's intense, he's got all those makeup and tools-type buzzwords, plus he threw 95 before he could buy cigarettes or be drafted, and his curveball's got double-take movement on it. What his stuff hasn't gotten him is a lot of strikeouts or plain old outs, and his problems with the long ball and walks add up to cause for concern. For now, he's another high-ceiling, high-risk project.

Jake Dittler — Born: 24-Nov-82 — Age: 20 — Bats: R — Throws: R

YEAR	TM	LG	AGE	G	GS	IP	H	BB	SO	HR	ERA	EQERA	EQH9	EQBB9	EQSO9	EQHR9	PERA	VORP	STF
2001	BNC	APL	18	6	5	22.0	25	12	20	0	3.68	9.02	17.1	8.8	4.1	0.5	9.37	-8.6	-25
2002	CGA	SAL	19	25	25	128.3	127	51	108	4	4.28	6.68	12.5	5.2	4.8	0.8	6.05	-16.8	-1

If this guy keeps it up, he'll be an ace! An ace, I tell you! Yeah, he was in the Sally League. I'm here to point Dittler out: he's showing rapid progress and is worth watching in a farm system chock-full of pitching prospects.

Ryan Drese — Born: 05-Apr-76 — Age: 27 — Bats: R — Throws: R

YEAR	TM	LG	AGE	G	GS	IP	H	BB	SO	HR	ERA	EQERA	EQH9	EQBB9	EQSO9	EQHR9	PERA	VORP	STF
2001	AKR	EAS	25	14	13	86.0	64	29	73	4	3.35	4.29	8.5	4.2	5.4	0.7	3.80	11.6	7
2001	BUF	INT	25	11	10	60.7	60	17	52	7	4.00	5.08	10.4	3.0	6.1	1.4	4.98	2.8	7
2001	CLE	AL	25	9	4	36.7	32	15	24	2	3.43	2.98	7.0	3.4	5.4	0.4	3.29	10.1	7
2002	BUF	INT	26	3	3	22.0	16	4	16	1	1.64	2.53	7.6	2.0	5.6	0.6	2.66	7.3	17
2002	CLE	AL	26	26	26	137.3	176	62	102	15	6.55	5.45	10.5	3.7	6.3	0.9	5.72	0.8	5
2003	TEX	AL	27	24	20	128.0	141	54	89	16	5.07	4.84	9.7	3.5	6.1	1.0	4.75	12.1	6

Breakout: 10%   Improve: 46%   Collapse: 16%

Drese got hit hard this year, but it was easy to watch, because he works fast. His stock was at its lowest at the end of July, when he was worked over like a tourist in a Hell's Kitchen alley. In three starts against the Yankees (1.1 IP, 8 ER, 8 H, 2 HR, 3 BB), Twins (5 IP, 5 ER, 10 H, 2 HR) and Yankees (1 IP, 8 ER, 7 H, 2 BB), he was likely more worried that he was going to get killed by a line drive than about his career.

He needs to throw his fastball for strikes like he can his breaking stuff. Scouts may rave about his makeup, but what Drese needs is consistent delivery and control. His fragility has really hurt him there: if he'd been healthy these last years, he might well have both. As it is, stick him in the rotation, let him take his lumps. Drese isn't going to be an ace, but seeing if he pans out into a mid-rotation guy would be worth it. He may not get the opportunity, now that he's been traded to the Rangers' Kingdom of Inflated Expectations along with Einar Diaz for Aaron Myette and Travis Hafner.

David Elder — Born: 23-Sep-75 — Age: 27 — Bats: R — Throws: R

YEAR	TM	LG	AGE	G	GS	IP	H	BB	SO	HR	ERA	EQERA	EQH9	EQBB9	EQSO9	EQHR9	PERA	VORP	STF
2000	TUL	TXS	24	33	21	116.7	121	88	104	9	4.94	6.53	10.6	7.1	5.8	1.1	6.84	-13.6	-13
2001	TUL	TXS	25	13	13	72.0	64	43	78	1	3.00	4.50	9.3	6.6	7.0	0.2	4.91	8.0	9
2001	OKL	PCL	25	15	8	57.7	54	43	56	4	4.99	5.84	9.5	8.2	6.5	0.8	5.63	-2.3	-8
2002	AKR	EAS	26	23	1	36.0	19	18	42	1	2.00	2.94	6.2	5.4	8.0	0.4	2.75	9.8	7
2002	BUF	INT	26	22	1	34.0	32	14	42	1	2.65	4.08	9.6	4.5	9.5	0.4	4.31	5.0	16
2002	CLE	AL	26	15	0	23.0	18	14	23	1	3.13	3.14	6.3	5.0	8.5	0.3	3.30	5.7	12
2003	CLE	AL	27	25	4	40.0	43	26	36	4	5.31	5.22	9.5	5.3	7.8	0.8	5.28	3.0	0

Breakout: 13%   Improve: 40%   Collapse: 26%

Elder has been throwing good stuff for two years now. He'll make a fine piece of a cheap and effective bullpen, and might be traded to patch someone else's problems at the cost of a prospect or two.

Travis Foley — Born: 11-Mar-83 — Age: 20 — Bats: R — Throws: R

YEAR	TM	LG	AGE	G	GS	IP	H	BB	SO	HR	ERA	EQERA	EQH9	EQBB9	EQSO9	EQHR9	PERA	VORP	STF
2001	BNC	APL	18	10	10	45.0	26	15	59	4	2.80	4.64	9.0	5.0	5.5	2.3	4.32	4.3	0
2002	CGA	SAL	19	26	26	137.3	108	44	138	9	2.82	4.49	10.3	4.2	5.7	1.6	4.60	15.5	8

John Sickels can definitely be annoying. A couple months into the season I was looking up this good guy I'd never heard about and there it was—"something tells me Foley is going to sneak up on people," Sickels wrote in the *STATS Minor League Scouting Notebook 2002* (also—if you've got $20 left over after buying this book, buy his new book). Thanks, John, yes, he did, and that was some quality gloating you got in so far in advance. You bastard.

Foley was a fourth round pick and so far he's quietly been much more effective than both J. D. Martin and Dan Denham, who were loudly drafted in the first round. Foley—and stop me if you've read this before in the book—has a sweet 90-something fastball and a quality curve he gets over for strikes, and his changeup is developing. He's improved at every level he's been at so far, and is the best of the 19–20 year-old pitching crop that the Indians are cultivating.

Alex Herrera   Born: 05-Nov-76   Age: 26   Bats: L   Throws: L

YEAR	TM	LG	AGE	G	GS	IP	H	BB	SO	HR	ERA	EQERA	EQH9	EQBB9	EQSO9	EQHR9	PERA	VORP	STF
2000	CGA	SAL	23	20	0	42.0	41	21	41	1	3.43	6.75	11.8	6.3	5.2	0.6	6.36	-6.4	-16
2000	KIN	CRL	23	17	0	31.0	28	19	40	1	2.32	5.24	10.7	6.7	7.3	0.7	6.37	0.5	-2
2001	KIN	CRL	24	28	0	59.7	36	18	83	1	0.60	2.55	7.4	3.9	7.7	0.4	3.33	18.8	14
2001	AKR	EAS	24	15	0	28.7	24	9	22	1	2.82	4.05	9.5	3.9	4.9	0.5	4.18	4.2	-6
2002	AKR	EAS	25	30	0	61.3	47	30	65	8	3.38	5.00	9.7	5.5	7.6	2.1	4.85	2.6	-5

Alex Herrera turned out to be three years older this year, which makes reading his minor league lines a whole new experience. That amazing season in Kinston last year, where he put up a 0.60 ERA in 60 relief innings, with an 18–83 walk to strikeout ratio, that was as a 25-year-old, and not quite so impressive. Yeah, Herrera had good stretches. But mostly he was bad. He's got a good fastball that runs way up into the 90s, and he's 5′11″, which makes for Billy Wagner comps . . . except Wagner has other pitches, which is why Wagner is good, and Herrera is not.

Cliff Lee   Born: 30-Aug-78   Age: 24   Bats: L   Throws: L

YEAR	TM	LG	AGE	G	GS	IP	H	BB	SO	HR	ERA	EQERA	EQH9	EQBB9	EQSO9	EQHR9	PERA	VORP	STF
2000	CPF	SAL	21	11	11	44.7	50	36	63	1	5.23	9.53	13.6	10.3	7.6	0.6	9.16	-20.0	-4
2001	JUP	FSL	22	21	20	109.7	78	46	129	13	2.79	5.23	10.3	4.8	7.5	2.9	5.06	3.3	9
2002	HAR	EAS	23	15	15	86.3	61	23	105	12	3.23	3.84	8.3	2.9	8.4	2.1	3.52	16.0	27
2002	AKR	EAS	23	3	3	16.7	11	10	18	1	5.39	5.86	8.1	6.7	7.7	1.0	4.02	-0.7	13
2002	BUF	INT	23	8	8	43.0	36	22	30	7	3.77	5.04	9.4	5.8	5.6	2.2	5.17	2.2	-3
2002	CLE	AL	23	2	2	10.3	6	8	6	0	1.75	1.88	4.6	6.3	4.9	0.2	2.64	4.1	5
2003	*CLE*	*AL*	*24*	*15*	*10*	*58.3*	*66*	*36*	*55*	*11*	*6.28*	*6.17*	*10.1*	*5.2*	*8.1*	*1.5*	*6.02*	*-0.8*	*3*

Breakout: 13%   Improve: 41%   Collapse: 24%

Mmmmmmm . . . left-handed. Lee has a variety of brutal pitches, from different fastballs he runs into the low 90s, a deceptive changeup that's just off 80, and two sweet breaking pitches, and he can throw all four for strikes. Which is not to say that he does throw them for strikes . . . but it happens. Lee is pure stuff at this point, with his control coming and going. He's a guy who could find consistent command and be a great pitcher, or he could be one of the majors' flakiest starters and would still be a guy I'd buy a ticket, and a OSHA-approved hardhat, to go see. With at least two rotation slots open, he has a shot to win a big league job in camp, and he'll have one before the season's out.

J. D. Martin   Born: 02-Jan-83   Age: 20   Bats: R   Throws: R

YEAR	TM	LG	AGE	G	GS	IP	H	BB	SO	HR	ERA	EQERA	EQH9	EQBB9	EQSO9	EQHR9	PERA	VORP	STF
2001	BNC	APL	18	10	10	45.7	26	11	72	3	1.38	3.25	8.4	3.5	6.4	1.7	3.59	11.5	14
2002	CGA	SAL	19	27	26	138.3	141	46	131	12	3.90	6.69	13.8	4.4	5.5	2.2	6.57	-18.2	0

Martin's projectable fastball hasn't projected yet and hasn't touched 90 yet on any honest gun. Still, he should fill out at some point—he's six-four and is listed at 170 pounds. Keith Woolner did some projections, and Martin collapsed, killing over two hundred people in Kuala Lumpur. He's still got five good pitches, and is known for his pitching instincts and mound presence. I was six-four and 170 at his age, and if Martin follows my development path in the next couple of years he'll put on thirty pounds, most of that muscle, drink heavily, and write for Prospectus. We'll save him a spot on the 2006 authors list—Bower can't desperately cling to life forever.

Dave Maurer   Born: 23-Feb-75   Age: 28   Bats: R   Throws: L

YEAR	TM	LG	AGE	G	GS	IP	H	BB	SO	HR	ERA	EQERA	EQH9	EQBB9	EQSO9	EQHR9	PERA	VORP	STF
2000	MOB	SOU	25	24	0	26.7	15	3	28	2	2.70	2.87	6.7	1.1	6.6	1.3	2.30	7.4	8
2000	LVG	PCL	25	35	0	44.3	47	15	44	5	3.25	3.85	9.6	3.0	7.1	1.2	4.56	7.5	2
2000	SDP	NL	25	14	0	14.7	15	5	13	2	3.67	4.70	9.8	2.5	7.2	1.2	4.66	1.1	4
2001	LOU	INT	26	18	0	21.7	18	7	23	4	4.15	5.13	8.8	3.4	7.5	2.2	4.74	0.6	-5
2001	POR	PCL	26	17	0	18.7	11	9	21	4	4.33	4.45	6.3	5.3	7.6	2.4	3.98	1.9	-9
2001	SAC	PCL	26	11	0	13.0	14	8	21	2	5.54	6.53	10.7	6.7	10.7	1.7	6.61	-1.7	3
2002	BUF	INT	27	36	3	68.3	50	24	73	6	2.90	4.02	7.8	3.9	8.3	1.2	3.45	10.5	9

Maurer had a nice little season in Triple-A. He's been throwing short relief in the minors for years now, with varied success. Still, he's left-handed, and as Terry Mulholland proves, that means he'll be getting spring training invites until he walks away. Maurer is best known for giving up two home runs to Luis Gonzalez, one in the fifth and the second in the sixth, during his stint with the Padres.

Terry Mulholland Born: 09-Mar-63 Age: 40 Bats: R Throws: L

YEAR	TM	LG	AGE	G	GS	IP	H	BB	SO	HR	ERA	EQERA	EQH9	EQBB9	EQSO9	EQHR9	PERA	VORP	STF
2000	ATL	NL	37	54	20	156.7	198	41	78	24	5.11	5.32	11.8	2.0	4.1	1.3	5.51	2.4	-11
2001	PIT	NL	38	22	1	36.3	38	10	17	5	3.72	3.81	9.4	2.3	3.6	1.1	4.46	6.4	-15
2001	LAD	NL	38	19	3	29.3	40	7	25	7	5.84	6.56	12.9	2.0	6.6	2.0	7.24	-3.7	-8
2002	LAD	NL	39	21	0	32.0	45	7	17	10	7.31	8.76	14.7	1.8	4.4	3.1	8.25	-12.0	-30
2002	CLE	AL	39	16	3	47.0	56	14	21	5	4.60	4.30	9.8	2.5	3.8	0.9	4.83	5.9	-9
2003	CLE	AL	40	40	6	68.3	86	19	36	12	5.22	5.13	11.2	2.3	4.5	1.3	5.27	5.6	-13

Breakout: 18%   Improve: 57%   Collapse: 7%

Mulholland's left-handed, which means somewhere, there are front offices picking up the phone to call his agent. Mulholland's only real skill at this point is his unreal ability to control runners. You'd almost want to use him as a bullpen pick-off specialist, except that he'd have to pitch at some point and, unfortunately, that's becoming uglier and uglier.

Because of his battles with injuries, and his slow move from starting to relief, Mulholland doesn't have impressive career marks like win totals, or saves. Mulholland's only had one year as a starter where he was really good (1993, with Philly). Yet every year, he's playing somewhere and getting traded. When the phone stops ringing for Terry, it'll probably be a relief: he can spend a full year in one place. The Indians offered him arbitration as part of their cunning plan to defeat the arbitration system by only pushing older pitchers with limited use before the panel.

Charles Nagy Born: 05-May-67 Age: 36 Bats: L Throws: R

YEAR	TM	LG	AGE	G	GS	IP	H	BB	SO	HR	ERA	EQERA	EQH9	EQBB9	EQSO9	EQHR9	PERA	VORP	STF
2000	BUF	INT	33	3	3	14.7	12	4	5	2	4.29	4.26	8.4	2.5	2.6	1.6	3.86	2.0	-13
2000	CLE	AL	33	11	11	57.0	71	21	41	15	8.21	6.30	10.1	2.6	6.2	1.9	5.90	-5.0	0
2001	BUF	INT	34	6	6	38.7	40	9	18	0	2.56	3.91	10.7	2.5	3.3	0.2	4.17	6.9	0
2001	CLE	AL	34	15	13	70.3	102	20	29	10	6.40	5.71	11.8	2.3	3.4	1.1	6.40	-1.6	-12
2002	BUF	INT	35	5	5	36.7	38	4	18	6	3.19	5.38	11.4	1.2	3.9	2.2	4.97	0.5	-5
2002	CLE	AL	35	19	7	48.7	76	13	22	10	8.87	7.25	12.9	2.2	3.9	1.7	7.28	-9.7	-21
2003	SDN	NL	36	20	12	78.0	85	22	40	9	4.38	5.08	10.3	2.2	4	1.2	5.03	4.2	-8

Breakout: 16%   Improve: 57%   Collapse: 20%

Nagy's bizarre trips on and off the DL this year, the strange talk about his career threatening muscle strains . . . look, he just can't pitch anymore. If everyone would just admit this, we could move on. Barring stunning medical advancements in cartilage and joint regeneration, Nagy won't make a team out of spring training if he's invited, and that'll be a career. The Padres are giving him a shot.

Chad Paronto Born: 28-Jul-75 Age: 27 Bats: R Throws: R

YEAR	TM	LG	AGE	G	GS	IP	H	BB	SO	HR	ERA	EQERA	EQH9	EQBB9	EQSO9	EQHR9	PERA	VORP	STF
2000	BOW	EAS	24	8	8	47.0	29	16	31	2	2.87	3.56	6.9	3.4	4.5	0.7	2.76	10.2	6
2000	ROC	INT	24	12	6	36.0	40	15	18	5	5.75	6.33	11.3	3.8	3.9	1.6	6.04	-3.4	-18
2001	ROC	INT	25	33	0	43.3	44	24	39	5	4.57	5.80	9.8	5.9	6.3	1.4	6.10	-2.0	-15
2001	BAL	AL	25	24	0	27.0	33	11	16	5	5.00	6.72	10.8	3.4	5.0	1.5	6.13	-4.0	-17
2002	BUF	INT	26	8	0	13.0	10	1	7	0	0.00	0.30	8.0	0.8	4.2	0.2	2.29	7.3	3
2002	CLE	AL	26	29	0	35.7	34	11	23	3	4.03	3.53	7.9	2.6	5.6	0.7	3.53	7.3	-1
2003	CLE	AL	27	41	0	43.3	50	17	27	6	5.17	5.08	10.3	3.2	5.4	1.1	4.92	4.3	-11

Breakout: 18%   Improve: 40%   Collapse: 25%

> You came close, but you never made it. And if you were going to make it, you would have made it before now.
> — Marsellus Wallace

For years, Paronto has posted bad ratios across the board in every one of his minor league stops. This year he had some arm trouble, too. Yeah, he's still only 27 and there's still some chance he might wake up tomorrow and throw an extra three miles faster with better control. Unfortunately for Paronto, it's not going to happen. Fortunately for the Indians, they have more replacements than they can count on both hands.

Jerrod Riggan — Born: 16-May-74 — Age: 29 — Bats: R — Throws: R

YEAR	TM	LG	AGE	G	GS	IP	H	BB	SO	HR	ERA	EQERA	EQH9	EQBB9	EQSO9	EQHR9	PERA	VORP	STF
2000	BIN	EAS	26	52	0	65.0	43	18	79	2	1.11	1.95	6.8	2.7	8.1	0.5	2.52	24.8	16
2001	NOR	INT	27	28	0	32.3	26	4	37	4	1.95	3.11	8.7	1.3	8.2	1.5	3.56	8.1	12
2001	NYM	NL	27	35	0	47.7	42	24	41	5	3.40	3.98	8.4	4.2	6.6	0.9	4.34	7.4	-2
2002	BUF	INT	28	27	0	45.3	40	11	37	3	2.38	3.52	9.3	2.7	6.4	0.9	3.75	9.4	2
2002	CLE	AL	28	29	0	33.0	53	18	22	3	7.64	6.64	13.1	4.4	5.6	0.7	7.48	-4.6	-16
2003	CLE	AL	29	35	5	59.3	65	24	44	7	4.40	4.33	9.8	3.4	6.4	0.9	4.68	10.6	-1

Breakout: 21%   Improve: 50%   Collapse: 21%

Riggan got promoted from Buffalo despite not posting any good ratios there, and was welcomed to the majors by being shelled, getting hit hard while walking guys. His stuff's still there, making him another replaceable bullpen widget, so he'll probably be picked off of waivers at some point by a team looking for incremental upgrades.

David Riske — Born: 23-Oct-76 — Age: 26 — Bats: R — Throws: R

YEAR	TM	LG	AGE	G	GS	IP	H	BB	SO	HR	ERA	EQERA	EQH9	EQBB9	EQSO9	EQHR9	PERA	VORP	STF
2001	BUF	INT	24	38	0	53.3	45	17	72	2	2.36	3.55	8.6	3.4	9.5	0.5	3.65	10.8	24
2001	CLE	AL	24	26	0	27.3	20	18	29	3	1.98	2.58	5.8	5.4	8.7	0.9	3.66	8.5	13
2002	CLE	AL	25	51	0	51.3	49	35	65	8	5.26	4.74	7.7	5.5	10.6	1.2	5.06	3.6	15
2003	CLE	AL	26	52	0	58.3	48	30	63	7	3.69	3.63	7.4	4.3	9.3	0.9	3.86	14.7	14

Breakout: 35%   Improve: 65%   Collapse: 13%

Riske went to Lindbergh High School, which was the next high school over from mine. He's one of the only success stories from our area, the others being two Kentridge Class of 1992 alumni: Ryan Geithman, who started Snowblind Studios and put out the hit video game "Baldur's Gate: Dark Alliance," and Evan Stoner, who placed second on *Jeopardy!* Riske's also one of the only pitchers to make a successful return to pre-injury effectiveness from a torn labrum, which must give hope to most of the Mariners farm system.

Riske has one astoundingly good pitch, that fastball that seems to accelerate mid-flight. Riske is one of the few relievers worth backing the tape up to see again. Attempts to give him a plus secondary pitch to set the fastball up haven't worked. If he manages it, though, he'll be a top-flight reliever. As it stands, he's still good. There are worse things than having one amazing pitch: ask Mariano Rivera.

Ricardo Rodriguez — Born: 21-May-78 — Age: 25 — Bats: R — Throws: R

YEAR	TM	LG	AGE	G	GS	IP	H	BB	SO	HR	ERA	EQERA	EQH9	EQBB9	EQSO9	EQHR9	PERA	VORP	STF
2000	GRF	PIO	22	15	15	95.7	66	23	129	2	1.88	2.96	8.2	2.6	6.8	0.5	2.60	27.1	28
2001	VRO	FSL	23	26	26	154.3	133	60	154	13	3.21	5.45	11.3	4.4	6.3	1.9	5.04	0.9	7
2002	JAX	SOU	24	11	11	68.0	56	13	44	4	1.99	4.40	11.0	2.0	4.5	1.2	3.71	8.3	7
2002	LVG	PCL	24	2	2	11.7	13	5	7	1	3.85	4.47	10.9	4.5	4.3	1.0	5.20	1.3	-3
2002	BUF	INT	24	4	4	25.0	26	7	14	1	3.60	4.70	10.9	3.1	4.4	0.5	4.55	2.2	4
2002	CLE	AL	24	7	7	41.3	40	18	24	5	5.67	4.29	7.9	3.6	5.0	1.0	4.21	5.6	5
2003	CLE	AL	25	17	13	83.0	97	32	54	12	5.49	5.40	10.4	3.2	5.6	1.1	5.17	4.1	1

Breakout: 23%   Improve: 49%   Collapse: 23%

"Hey, I've got the Dodgers on the phone. They want Paul Shuey. Who are we asking for?"

"Uh, tell them we want Ricardo Rodriguez or Francisco Cruceta."

"We want Ricardo Rodriguez and Francisco Cruceta."

"No! No! Wait, you'll piss them off . . ."

"They just said yes."

Rodriguez is regarded as an elite pitching prospect, and he certainly looks good. He's a tall lanky guy, throws a fast fastball with certain bloody-mindedness, picked up a changeup quickly, and flashes a nice curve. It turns out he's a year older than we'd thought, so the complaints that he unfairly beat up on the Pioneer League have merit. Despite his gaudy strikeout numbers in 2000 and 2001, he didn't do that much better than league averages last year. Still, Ricardo's a good pitcher and he's going to improve if he stays healthy, as one by one the young Indians pitchers take over the rotation.

C. C. Sabathia   Born: 21-Jul-80   Age: 22   Bats: L   Throws: L

YEAR	TM	LG	AGE	G	GS	IP	H	BB	SO	HR	ERA	EQERA	EQH9	EQBB9	EQSO9	EQHR9	PERA	VORP	STF
2000	KIN	CRL	19	10	10	56.0	48	24	69	4	3.54	5.26	10.7	4.7	7.1	1.6	5.62	1.5	15
2000	AKR	EAS	19	17	17	90.3	75	48	90	6	3.59	4.97	9.3	5.4	6.8	1.1	4.84	5.4	14
2001	CLE	AL	20	33	33	180.3	149	95	171	19	4.39	3.61	6.6	4.3	7.8	0.8	3.71	38.0	28
2002	CLE	AL	21	33	33	210.0	198	88	149	17	4.37	3.63	7.7	3.5	6.1	0.7	3.77	43.8	20
2003	CLE	AL	22	30	29	180.7	177	78	146	22	4.50	4.43	8.7	3.6	7.0	0.9	4.24	27.7	15

Breakout: 23%   Improve: 56%   Collapse: 9%

Worry about Sabathia. He's established that he's talented, and that his stuff is major league quality. However, his delivery is inconsistent, his mechanics are cause for injury concern, his mound presence, in both composure and intelligence, isn't there yet, and he may not have the makeup to cope with the burdens of stardom. Terry Mulholland was reported to have spent a lot of time working with Sabathia this season, and must surely have idly considered swapping brains and seeing how far veteran wiles, maturity, and experience can propel a million-dollar talent.

Carl Sadler   Born: 11-Oct-76   Age: 26   Bats: L   Throws: L

YEAR	TM	LG	AGE	G	GS	IP	H	BB	SO	HR	ERA	EQERA	EQH9	EQBB9	EQSO9	EQHR9	PERA	VORP	STF
2000	CGA	SAL	23	10	0	16.3	20	7	21	0	6.63	8.54	14.5	5.3	6.7	0.3	7.67	-5.7	-8
2001	KIN	CRL	24	27	2	62.3	51	18	78	2	1.88	4.79	10.4	3.9	7.1	0.7	4.81	4.3	5
2001	AKR	EAS	24	11	0	18.0	23	9	14	1	6.50	9.10	15.1	6.4	5.1	0.8	8.05	-7.4	-25
2002	AKR	EAS	25	21	0	46.3	39	12	37	0	2.33	3.59	9.9	2.9	5.6	0.7	3.44	9.2	2
2002	BUF	INT	25	12	0	18.7	19	8	13	1	1.93	4.76	10.7	4.7	5.4	0.7	5.03	1.3	-10
2002	CLE	AL	25	24	0	20.3	15	11	23	2	4.43	3.33	5.9	4.4	9.6	0.8	3.25	4.6	18
2003	CLE	AL	26	24	5	47.7	53	23	37	5	5.03	4.94	9.9	4.0	6.7	0.7	4.89	5.1	0

Breakout: 15%   Improve: 45%   Collapse: 30%

Sadler rose from obscurity to have a great year with the big club, striking out major league hitters while keeping his walks down and escaping with a pretty low hits per nine as well. You hope that performance doesn't mean the team is too attached to him: his minor league lines range from eye-popping bad to decent. He's done much better when he spends some time at a level. The big difference between Carl Sadler and Dave Maurer is that Maurer has bombed in his auditions.

Roy Smith   Born: 18-May-76   Age: 27   Bats: R   Throws: R

YEAR	TM	LG	AGE	G	GS	IP	H	BB	SO	HR	ERA	EQERA	EQH9	EQBB9	EQSO9	EQHR9	PERA	VORP	STF
2000	KIN	CRL	24	21	0	45.0	35	21	45	0	2.80	4.29	9.0	5.1	5.6	0.3	4.55	5.4	-4
2000	AKR	EAS	24	28	0	55.0	36	22	50	0	1.96	2.94	7.1	4.0	6.2	0.2	2.87	14.9	5
2001	BUF	INT	25	48	0	74.0	59	29	86	2	2.19	3.72	8.1	4.2	8.2	0.3	3.57	13.6	12
2001	CLE	AL	25	9	0	16.3	16	13	17	3	6.07	5.91	7.7	6.4	8.4	1.4	5.80	-1.0	-1
2002	BUF	INT	26	36	3	70.3	65	29	65	2	3.84	5.11	9.6	4.5	7.2	0.4	4.23	2.3	2

Roy Smith is a side-armer the Indians sold to the A's for cash. Recruited out of the independent Northern League, he can get guys out in multi-inning relief. The A's already have Chad Bradford as a right-handed specialist, and should be able to get good work out of Smith in a relief role.

Brian Tallet   Born: 21-Sep-77   Age: 25   Bats: L   Throws: L

YEAR	TM	LG	AGE	G	GS	IP	H	BB	SO	HR	ERA	EQERA	EQH9	EQBB9	EQSO9	EQHR9	PERA	VORP	STF
2000	MHV	NYP	22	6	6	15.7	10	3	20	0	1.15	2.64	8.3	2.3	6.3	0.3	2.98	5.0	14
2001	KIN	CRL	23	27	27	160.0	134	38	164	12	3.04	5.53	11.3	3.2	5.9	1.8	5.17	-0.4	8
2002	AKR	EAS	24	18	16	102.3	93	32	73	9	3.08	5.09	11.2	3.5	5.1	1.4	4.73	4.7	2
2002	BUF	INT	24	8	7	44.0	47	16	25	1	3.07	4.77	11.1	4.0	4.5	0.3	4.86	3.6	1
2002	CLE	AL	24	2	2	12.0	9	4	5	0	1.50	1.91	6.2	2.8	3.6	0.2	2.25	4.8	8
2003	CLE	AL	25	16	12	74.3	86	30	47	11	5.49	5.39	10.4	3.4	5.4	1.1	5.25	3.4	-2

Breakout: 16%   Improve: 54%   Collapse: 13%

Tallet confuses people. He's big (6′ 7″) and he's big (a stone over two hundred pounds). Drafted out of LSU, he drew raves for his know-how and smarts, and dominated in the low minors with a fastball that might touch 92 with a tailwind. He gets by mixing his fastball with a slider and a lower-gear changeup. You've got to cheer for guys like Tallet who have unexpected skill sets. It says a lot for an organization when they find roles for oddball prospects, rather than focusing on, say, their inability to hit three digits on the radar gun when closing. With a couple of rotation slots open and his nifty debut, he'll get a long look in camp, and should be in the rotation to stay by season's end.

Billy Traber   Born: 18-Sep-79   Age: 23   Bats: L   Throws: L

YEAR	TM	LG	AGE	G	GS	IP	H	BB	SO	HR	ERA	EQERA	EQH9	EQBB9	EQSO9	EQHR9	PERA	VORP	STF
2001	SLU	FSL	21	18	18	101.7	85	23	79	2	2.65	4.08	9.5	2.4	4.7	0.4	4.03	16.1	12
2001	BIN	EAS	21	8	8	42.7	50	13	45	4	4.43	6.24	12.4	3.7	6.6	1.3	6.37	-3.5	12
2002	AKR	EAS	22	18	17	107.7	99	20	82	8	2.76	4.55	11.1	2.1	5.4	1.2	4.22	11.4	14
2002	BUF	INT	22	9	9	54.7	58	12	33	3	3.29	4.73	11.1	2.4	4.7	0.7	4.58	4.7	10
2003	CLE	AL	23	16	12	69.0	84	22	43	10	5.29	5.20	10.8	2.6	5.4	1.1	5.07	5.6	0

Breakout: 10%   Improve: 46%   Collapse: 29%

Traber didn't headline the Alomar trade, but he may yet become the big return. He's recovered well from ligament damage sustained before he was drafted (cough Loyola Marymount cough). He's done well in the high-minors since his delayed debut, but since he's a big splitter man, the concern about his long-term health prospects isn't misplaced. Besides his 90ish fastball and the splitter, he's got a developing curveball and a changeup. He works down in the strike zone with good command. He'll be competing for a starting rotation spot next year, and the Indians should slot him in. The worst return is he's a good 4th or 5th starter for a couple years, and the upside is he develops into a #2 after he gets some experience.

Jake Westbrook   Born: 29-Sep-77   Age: 25   Bats: R   Throws: R

YEAR	TM	LG	AGE	G	GS	IP	H	BB	SO	HR	ERA	EQERA	EQH9	EQBB9	EQSO9	EQHR9	PERA	VORP	STF
2000	COH	INT	22	16	15	89.0	94	38	61	3	4.65	4.87	9.9	3.8	5.2	0.4	4.84	6.3	9
2001	BUF	INT	23	12	12	64.7	60	23	45	2	3.20	4.48	9.6	3.8	5.0	0.4	4.22	7.4	7
2001	CLE	AL	23	23	6	64.7	79	22	48	6	5.84	4.74	9.9	2.8	6.1	0.7	5.03	5.1	6
2002	AKR	EAS	24	3	3	15.0	13	1	8	0	4.80	4.76	10.2	0.7	3.8	0.2	2.96	1.2	6
2002	CLE	AL	24	11	4	41.7	50	12	20	6	5.83	4.97	9.9	2.4	4.1	1.2	5.10	2.3	-5
2003	CLE	AL	25	21	14	85.7	97	28	51	10	4.86	4.78	10.1	2.7	5.1	0.9	4.60	9.2	0

Breakout: 16%   Improve: 54%   Collapse: 11%

Westbrook struggled with his release point throughout the year, holding on too long and pushing the ball inside and into the dirt, or not long enough, leaving the ball up and out for left-handers, both results products of his perfect three-quarters delivery. He missed much of the season with a bone bruise, and will be back, healthy, and not particularly noticeable pitching long-relief and spot starts again next year.

Bob Wickman   Born: 06-Feb-69   Age: 34   Bats: R   Throws: R

YEAR	TM	LG	AGE	G	GS	IP	H	BB	SO	HR	ERA	EQERA	EQH9	EQBB9	EQSO9	EQHR9	PERA	VORP	STF
2000	MIL	NL	31	43	0	46.0	37	20	44	1	2.93	3.19	7.8	3.2	7.7	0.2	2.82	11.2	12
2000	CLE	AL	31	26	0	26.7	27	12	11	0	3.37	3.24	8.5	3.3	3.6	0.2	3.28	6.3	-12
2001	CLE	AL	32	70	0	67.7	61	14	66	4	2.39	2.29	7.3	1.7	8.1	0.5	2.89	23.2	19
2002	CLE	AL	33	36	0	34.3	42	10	36	3	4.46	4.58	10.1	2.4	8.9	0.7	4.79	3.0	15

Wickman's Tommy John surgery will keep him out for at least most of the 2003 season, after which he may return to be the not-especially effective closer we've come to know. There are a lot of bad feelings around Wickman, based on his three-year, $16 million deal, but it's not as if that's Wickman's fault. It's not as if he's Mike Armstrong, who paid himself millions while driving AT&T, one of the world's most known and trusted brands, into the ground. That somebody offered Wickman a tremendous amount of money to fill an overvalued position shouldn't reflect badly on our opinion of Wickman personally, or of any player who takes a team up on a similar offer.

Mark Wohlers   Born: 23-Jan-70   Age: 33   Bats: R   Throws: R

YEAR	TM	LG	AGE	G	GS	IP	H	BB	SO	HR	ERA	EQERA	EQH9	EQBB9	EQSO9	EQHR9	PERA	VORP	STF
2000	LOU	INT	30	17	2	20.7	30	9	16	4	6.09	8.94	14.5	4.0	6.0	2.2	8.52	-8.1	-25
2000	CIN	NL	30	20	0	28.0	19	17	20	3	4.50	3.89	6.5	4.4	5.7	0.8	3.17	4.6	-6
2001	CIN	NL	31	30	0	32.0	36	7	21	5	3.94	4.92	10.2	1.8	5.1	1.2	4.76	1.6	-9
2001	NYY	AL	31	31	0	35.7	33	18	33	3	4.54	4.22	7.9	4.2	7.8	0.7	4.13	4.6	4
2002	CLE	AL	32	64	0	71.3	71	26	46	6	4.80	3.86	8.2	3.0	5.6	0.7	3.89	12.0	-4
2003	CLE	AL	33	53	0	58.7	66	24	38	8	5.12	5.04	10.0	3.3	5.6	1.1	4.88	4.9	-10

Breakout: 13%   Improve: 39%   Collapse: 26%

One of the arguments made in defense of the Wohlers signing was that the Indians, dependent on attendance for their economic health, had to sign semi-famous names like Brady Anderson and Wohlers to drive up season ticket sales. Does anyone believe that fans, considering whether or not to invest their money, are swayed by the team spending millions to bring in players who had good years five years ago? Is this how Jose Offerman can find work next year, by shopping his 1998 performance to teams?

Wohlers' comeback has been anticlimactic. He lost his stuff, his career blew apart, he came back as a serviceable reliever with Cincinnati, and now he's just another aging right-handed arm, with deteriorating peripherals, except that Wohlers has been to the World Series four times.

Jaret Wright						Born: 29-Dec-75					Age: 27		Bats: R			Throws: R		
YEAR	TM	LG	AGE	G	GS	IP	H	BB	SO	HR	ERA	EQERA	EQH9	EQBB9	EQSO9	EQHR9	PERA	VORP	STF
2000	CLE	AL	24	9	9	51.7	44	28	36	6	4.70	3.63	6.9	3.9	6.0	0.9	3.52	10.8	12
2001	BUF	INT	25	7	7	28.7	25	13	28	3	4.70	5.75	9.2	4.9	7.0	1.3	4.80	-0.8	2
2001	CLE	AL	25	7	7	29.0	36	22	18	2	6.52	5.80	9.9	6.1	5.0	0.5	6.21	-1.0	-10
2002	BUF	INT	26	10	10	55.7	57	24	43	5	3.88	5.52	10.9	4.8	6.1	1.2	5.38	-0.1	0
2002	CLE	AL	26	8	6	18.3	40	19	12	3	15.74	12.71	17.5	8.2	5.4	1.3	12.30	-14.7	-43
2003	SDN	NL	27	17	10	62.0	63	37	48	6	5.02	5.82	9.6	4.6	6.0	0.9	5.53	-0.1	-4

Breakout: 23%   Improve: 46%   Collapse: 24%

You know spring has arrived when you read the first report out of spring training that says Jaret Wright is throwing like it's 1998. Since then his shoulder has never been right, it's been cracked and looked over more often than a supermarket *Sports Illustrated* Swimsuit Issue, and every year his comeback attempts flame out and crash. We've said it over and over: what Jaret Wright has needed is a year off to get healthy, and he never got it. Unfortunately for Jaret, the Indians declined his option and released him. He's signed with the Padres, who are entertaining the idea of moving him to the pen.

Detroit Tigers

On December 5, 2002, the Tigers announced that they were pulling in the left-center field fence at Comerica Park. The announcement was both routine—teams tinker with the dimensions of their home parks all the time—and expected, as everyone knew that the Tigers had been contemplating the move for some time. After all, the criticism from numerous batters over how difficult the ballpark was for power hitters was literally as old as the park itself.

The significance of this announcement, however, should not be overlooked. Changing the distance to the power alley in left-center is a tangible sign that the team's original grand strategy for returning to contention is being abandoned. It is also a clear admission of failure and a desperate attempt to put a little wind in the slack sails of the moribund franchise. The actual change in dimensions, of course, is not what people care about. But the consequences of that change in 2003— more home runs and higher scoring—are expected to make a difference.

The ugly truth is that the Tigers have been dead in the water for years, drifting aimlessly through baseball's equivalent of the horse latitudes, occasionally espying on the horizon other becalmed or sinking "small-market" craft, as well as bigger-market ships also going nowhere. Instead of carefully analyzing their predicament and making dramatic changes to address their problems, the Tigers have lurched from one crisis to another, leaving the Ilitch regime afflicted by crisis management of the worst kind.

Unfortunately, making Comerica less pitcher-friendly in an attempt to reverse the direction of the franchise (i.e., from losing to winning) may not represent enough of a change in the philosophy of the franchise. While things are not hopeless, there is more than sufficient reason for continued pessimism about the future, given that Detroit has pretty much struck out with its formerly loyal fan base.

Strike One: Putting a losing team on the field year after year, which is harmful enough. However, if the team has a solid fan base, and if the fans believe that the current losing club is an aberration, the damage can be quickly repaired with a return to contention. Except for the unwarranted optimism post–1997, Tigers' fans haven't believed that in quite a while.

Strike Two: Fielding a team that is perceived as boring by casual fans and that is simultaneously uninteresting to hard-core fans is devastating to the franchise's future. The lack of a true superstar, constant roster turnover, churlish or seemingly ungrateful veteran players all contribute to a downward spiral that normally takes years to reverse.

Strike Three: Asking the fans to have patience with a losing team when they have little hope for the future is a fatal blow. By far, the best kind of losing team to play is a young, inexpensive team that is hungry to prove itself and offers hope that the future will be better than the past.

Combine this bleak recap of recent Tigers' history with a misguided faith in the drawing power of a new ballpark and a huge miscalculation about what prices the local sports market would bear, and the result is the sad-sack 2002 Detroit Tigers.

In 2000, the average ticket price in Comerica was more than double what it had been the previous year in Tiger Stadium. The price of going to a game (as calculated by the Fan Cost Index) went up a wallet-busting 52 percent in the new park. The Tigers' brain trust was betting that Michigan fans would pay more to see a ball game than fans of every major league team except the Red Sox, the Mariners, and the defending World Champion Yankees. If the comparisons seem too remote for an industrial Midwestern city like Detroit, it's hard to imagine how anyone associated with the Tigers could have expected people to pay 21 percent more per ticket in Detroit than in nearby Cleveland. The 2000 Indians had won

---

Tigers Prospectus

2002 record: 55–106; Fifth place, AL Central

Pythagenport Record: 51–110

Runs scored per game: 3.6 (14th in AL)

Runs allowed per game: 5.4 (11th in AL)

Team EqA: .239 (14th in AL)

2002 Batters Age: 28.6 (4th youngest in AL)

2002 Pitchers Age: 28.6 (7th oldest in AL)

Ballpark: Comerica Park; Moderate pitchers' park; Park Factor of .974

2002: Dombrowski-led palace coup was timed to place blame for another failed season on the Smith regime.

2003: The well-regarded GM starts work on trying to build his third successful organization.

---

two AL pennants in the past five years, had been to the post-season for five consecutive years, and were the first club in baseball history to sell out every game, yet they didn't think their fans would pay prices like the Tigers were charging.

The recurring injuries, poor performance, and overall churlishness of Juan "Long Gone"-zalez became the enduring memory of the inaugural year at Comerica Park. Attendance in Comerica's first season (2,533,752) was good but hardly great, and complaints about price gouging at Comerica caused the Tigers to make a show of reducing some ticket prices in 2001. While ticket prices fell 3.7 percent, Detroit's Fan Cost Index *rose* by 4.4 percent. By then, however, the damage done by overpricing the market and enduring yet another losing team was tremendous. Attendance dropped 24 percent in the second year in Comerica, and an additional 22 percent last year.

The new moneymaking machine had increased the club's cash flow, but not nearly so much as had been expected. After Ilitch was unable to refinance his debt at a lower interest rate, a new round of salary purges was ordered so that the team could continue to service the debt the owner incurred in building the new ballpark. The departure of homegrown stars like Jeff Weaver and Robert Fick—players whom the fans were told represented the bright new future just three years ago—will drive even more fans away and continue to depress the franchise's attendance and TV ratings for a few more years, until and unless top young players like Pena and Bonderman become legitimate stars.

Detroit suffered through its ninth consecutive losing season last year, an embarrassing record for what was one of the flagship franchises in the mid-1980s, and now barely more than a laughingstock. Not only has contention eluded the new-look ComeriTigers in the last three years, but even mere respectability has escaped their grasp. Hired as president and CEO in January 1995, John McHale Jr. was the architect of the now-discredited strategy that has made Comerica Park a half-empty reminder of how revitalizing a downtrodden club requires more than a new pleasure palace. Comerica Park might as well have been named McHale's Folly.

McHale's background in baseball before arriving in Detroit was purely National League: three years as an Exec VP with the Rockies. With the differences between the leagues being reduced to triviality under Commissioner Selig's grand plan to restructure MLB, that background would no longer seem portentous. However, the older, deep-rooted psychology of the "Senior Circuit" made the NL and its pitching-and-defense style of play the "Superior League" in the minds of all NL executives as well as many AL personnel since the 1960s. The AL's traditional power-based game was so thoroughly disdained by veteran scouts, player development people, and front office employees that the insulting phrase "he's really an AL player" was considered damning. It

is clear now that Detroit management hasn't understood the ramifications of this unfounded but very pervasive bias against power-hitting teams. Scoring more runs results in winning more games and almost always results in higher attendance; of course, the best way to score more runs is to put more runners on base and hit more home runs. Nevertheless, slugging teams are frequently a public relations nightmare if they don't contend. Given half a chance, too many scribes, commentators, and broadcasters just *love* to maunder on endlessly about pitching and defense. Give some of these golden-tongued media hacks a losing team that scores lots of runs but has weak pitching and shaky defense, and they'll give that team a gift of millions of dollars of bad publicity—exactly the kind of incessant bad-mouthing that makes a losing situation seem even more hopeless.

The apathy Detroit fans felt toward the slugging but slow and pitcher-bereft Tigers for most of the 1990s was *not* a clarion call to create a new team based on speed and defense. The lesson that should have been learned was that the Tigers' estranged fan base wanted to see a winning team with identifiable superstars that also had better pitching. Stripping the new-look ComeriTigers of the club's historic power-centric character was exactly the wrong way to market the team. After all, whose steel sculptures adorn the new park? Hall of Famers Ty Cobb, Hank Greenberg, Charlie Gehringer, and Al Kaline, plus local favorite Willie Horton—sluggers all—and a single pitcher, Hal Newhouser.

In Colorado, McHale was in charge of the planning and development of Coors Field, a stunning success both aesthetically and financially that had the expansion Rockies hobnobbing with baseball's elite by their third year of play. McHale's mission in Motown was to do the same for the Tigers: put together a new ballpark deal, get a retro brick-and-steel money machine built, and give the team's baseball people the necessary money to put a contender on the field. Coors Field is the best hitters' park in major league history, a fact that has everything to do with its extreme altitude and the era in which it was built and almost nothing to do with its design. Regrettably, the slugfests that the mile-high park produced were instantly viewed as making a mockery of the game. Most of the 1990s retro ballparks were considered good hitters' parks—in some cases, erroneously.

In Detroit, given a free hand, John McHale Jr. set out to change that trend by designing Comerica to be the modern equivalent of the Astrodome. By hiring Randy Smith (who had spent his whole career with NL clubs) as GM, McHale committed the team to an NL-style game. When Smith hired Phil Garner to guide the club in its inaugural year in Comerica, he got a small-ball manager who had spent most of his playing career in the NL, much of it with Houston. None of the Tigers' troika of execs apparently understood that even in a good pitchers' park, the home run is the ultimate weapon.

When runs are hard to score, hitting the ball over the fence is even more important—not less important. While Detroit has had some legitimate power hitters since it moved into Comerica—Bobby Higginson, Tony Clark, Dean Palmer, Robert Fick—the team wasted precious time and money giving at-bats to non-power hitters like Brad Ausmus, Luis Polonia, Jose Macias, Wendell Magee, Roger Cedeno, and Brandon Inge, not to mention the folly of playing washed-up NL bozos like Gregg Jefferies and Hal Morris.

McHale and Smith and Garner tried mightily to make Detroit into a winning NL-style club in an NL-style ballpark, failing to understand that that was an impossible task in a power-based league in an era where power was at an all-time high. But, given their NL pedigrees, what could one expect?

What about Juan Gonzalez, you say? Getting a big-time power hitter to stick in the middle of the team's lineup was exactly the right idea; the problem was that Gonzo was exactly the wrong guy for the job. When Smith engineered the mega-deal for Gonzalez, he was desperate to save his job, which was hanging by a thread at the end of the 1999 season. On the cusp of moving to the new park, the Tigers hadn't made the expected progress that 1997's modest success had seemed to promise, and Smith needed a marquee name to show the public that the downtrodden Tigers' future would be different. Detroit's 1997 resurgence was really a mirage based on an especially miserable 1996 season. It gave false hope that the future was going to be bright, and it gave undue credibility to Smith's mode of operation.

Much of the criticism of the Gonzalez deal at the time focused on how much young talent Detroit had given up to acquire Gonzo. Less attention was paid to Gonzalez' many flaws: he was an overrated, malcontented, injury-prone, immobile slugger who would kill the team defensively if played in right field. The coup de grace was that Gonzalez had the leverage of impending free agency, and his gaudy Triple Crown stats and status as a two-time AL MVP meant that he would demand an enormous contract to stay in Detroit. If Gonzalez had had the brains to take the deal, Detroit would have been crippled for years by the combination of the surly slugger's enormous salary and the resulting fan backlash. That would have been reminiscent but even worse than what happened in the mid-1990s with Cecil Fielder, who was initially a fan favorite in Motown. The contract Fielder signed in January 1993 was a huge mistake. Rookie owner Ilitch, who had purchased the team only five months earlier, was in a seemingly no-win situation: he badly needed to show the

fans that he was committed to winning, unlike hated former owner Tom Monahan. Notwithstanding that need, giving the one-dimensional and ponderous Fielder a five-year $36 million contract nearly as lucrative as the one all-planet, five-tool superstar Barry Bonds was getting (a six-year, $44 million deal) was a mistake that would haunt the club. The parallels between the Fielder and Gonzalez situation were truly scary. Tigers' owner Mike Ilitch dodged more than a bullet when Gonzalez idiotically refused to sign the team's ridiculous $140 million offer in 2000—he dodged a high-velocity, armor-piercing, fin-stabilized, discarding sabot shell with a depleted uranium penetrator fired from a 120mm M1A2 Abrams tank cannon.

While McHale was able to check off the first two things on his to-do list before he fled to greener pastures in 2001, the third and most important item on that checklist remains undone. Unlike Denver, the new ballpark in Detroit was nowhere near the immediate success that the Tigers both expected and needed. Despite generally favorable reviews, Comerica has failed by a large margin to generate the requisite revenue for the Tigers to compete with the big boys in the AL again.

There are, of course, *some* reasons for optimism for those who seek silver linings. The new labor deal hammered out in 2002 will transfer more money from the wealthiest franchises to middle-revenue teams like the Tigers. Detroit remains a large, sports-crazy market where a winning baseball team should do well. The franchise's glory days aren't so remote that they are meaningless, as evidenced by the hiring of new manager Alan Trammell and bench coach Kirk Gibson. President/GM and putative savior Dave Dombrowski has now replaced both McHale and Smith. Dombrowski is not an incompetent like Randy Smith, but then again, very few thought apparent-savior Smith circa 1997 would become a thoroughly discredited and emasculated GM by 2002. Dombrowski has managed to rid the team of several burdensome contracts in the past year, though several huge millstones (particularly Higginson, Easley, and Palmer) remain.

The large amount of work that remains to be done to restore the Tigers to contention cannot be accomplished in a single year, or even two. The departure of beloved broadcaster Ernie Harwell at the end of 2002 caused many Tigers fans to say that listening to Ernie was the only thing that kept them following the team. Detroit's long summer of discontent is going to continue for some time.

HITTERS

Damion Easley 2B Born: 11-Nov-69 Age: 33 Bats: R Throws: R

YEAR	TM	LG	AGE	AB	H	2B	3B	HR	BB	SO	SB	CS	AVG	OBP	SLG	MLVR	EQBA	EQOBP	EQSLG	EQMLVR	VORP	DEFENSE
2000	DET	AL	30	464	120	27	2	14	55	79	13	4	.259	.351	.416	-.044	.269	.355	.436	.021	28.0	120-2B 18
2001	DET	AL	31	585	146	27	7	11	52	90	10	5	.250	.325	.376	-.088	.274	.346	.417	-.018	30.4	151-2B 8
2002	DET	AL	32	304	68	14	1	8	27	43	1	3	.224	.310	.355	-.140	.248	.328	.397	-.099	9.7	84-2B -8
2003	DET	AL	33	325	79	17	2	7	32	48	3	2	.242	.316	.366	-.111	.250	.328	.395	-.095	5.2	

Breakout: 24%   Improve: 54%   Collapse: 20%

In the understatement of the off-season, at the winter meetings new manager Alan Trammell said that he wouldn't promise Easley would keep his job in 2003. Easley recorded the seventh DL stint of his career in 2002, and the Tigers would have been better off if they'd left him on the bench for the rest of the season once he came back. Easley will probably bounce back, but unless he shows his 1997–1998 form, he shouldn't beat out Omar Infante for the starting job. The only reason to play Easley is to showcase him and hope another desperate team is foolish enough to make a deal.

David Espinosa 2B? Born: 16-Dec-81 Age: 21 Bats: B Throws: R

YEAR	TM	LG	AGE	AB	H	2B	3B	HR	BB	SO	SB	CS	AVG	OBP	SLG	MLVR	EQBA	EQOBP	EQSLG	EQMLVR	VORP	DEFENSE
2001	DYT	MDW	19	493	129	29	8	7	55	120	15	10	.262	.341	.396	.037	.196	.258	.300	-.401	-23.7	120-SS -29
2002	STO	CLF	20	367	90	13	7	7	62	104	26	17	.245	.357	.376	.034	.198	.286	.305	-.337	-12.3	94-2B -1
2003	DET	AL	21	190	45	8	2	4	19	48	4	5	.236	.310	.366	-.125	.244	.321	.395	-.111	1.7	

Breakout: 71%   Improve: 87%   Collapse: 6%

The Reds made the gangly young shortstop a first round pick in 2000, then dealt him to the Tigers in July to lasso Scuffy Moehler. After the deal, Espinosa spent the rest of the season on the DL in Lakeland. He has speed and patience, but struggles to make contact. The Reds briefly flirted with Espinosa as a second sacker; the Tigers see him as a second baseman or possibly a center fielder down the road.

Rob Fick 1B/RF Born: 15-Mar-74 Age: 29 Bats: L Throws: R

YEAR	TM	LG	AGE	AB	H	2B	3B	HR	BB	SO	SB	CS	AVG	OBP	SLG	MLVR	EQBA	EQOBP	EQSLG	EQMLVR	VORP	DEFENSE	
2000	TOL	INT	26	68	10	5	0	1	6	13	1	0	.147	.237	.265	-.461	.145	.219	.246	-.577	-8.1		
2000	DET	AL	26	163	41	7	2	3	22	39	2	1	.252	.344	.374	-.121	.265	.350	.395	-.048	2.0	24-1B -4	
2001	DET	AL	27	401	109	21	2	19	39	62	0	3	.272	.342	.476	.095	.290	.359	.512	.153	41.4	70-C -12	18-1B -2
2002	DET	AL	28	556	150	36	2	17	46	90	0	1	.270	.333	.433	.037	.295	.356	.476	.102	26.9	131-RF -2	
2003	ATL	NL	29	439	117	24	2	18	50	77	1	2	.266	.344	.449	.037	.270	.344	.466	.040	8.6		

Breakout: 15%   Improve: 43%   Collapse: 17%

The Tigers tried mightily to trade Fick during the winter meetings. Unable to do so, they non-tendered him since he was arbitration-eligible after being selected to the AL All-Star squad and posting career highs in most hitting categories in 2002. That's the proximate cause, but the deeper reason is that the Tigers have never understood what to do with him. Fick is a classic example of a guy who isn't going to be a superstar but who is a legitimate power hitter. Like many other guys who earn their keep with their bat and not their glove, he had no real position once he made the majors. The obvious solution was to figure out where to play him, give him some capable defensive tutoring to help him get up to speed, and let him learn a single position while enjoying his offensive production. Instead, the Tigers fiddled around, playing him at catcher and first base before moving him to the outfield, where he acquitted himself well enough while posting 21 assists. The crime is that Detroit didn't make this move three or four years ago to give Fick a chance to focus on his hitting and see what his ceiling really was.

Shane Halter UT Born: 08-Nov-69 Age: 33 Bats: R Throws: R

YEAR	TM	LG	AGE	AB	H	2B	3B	HR	BB	SO	SB	CS	AVG	OBP	SLG	MLVR	EQBA	EQOBP	EQSLG	EQMLVR	VORP	DEFENSE	
2000	DET	AL	30	238	62	12	2	3	14	49	5	2	.261	.304	.366	-.206	.270	.308	.384	-.139	2.9	38-3B -4	19-1B 1
2001	DET	AL	31	450	128	32	7	12	37	100	3	3	.284	.348	.467	.103	.305	.367	.503	.169	42.2	68-3B -2	60-SS -8
2002	DET	AL	32	410	98	22	6	10	39	92	0	4	.239	.311	.395	-.076	.261	.332	.435	-.029	21.4	79-SS -7	24-3B -1
2003	DET	AL	33	332	84	18	3	7	27	69	2	2	.252	.313	.393	-.076	.261	.324	.423	-.056	6.8		

Breakout: 12%   Improve: 41%   Collapse: 26%

The continued employment of Shane Halter would be the most comical element of the Tigers' 2002 season were it not for their continued employment of Craig Paquette. Perhaps the Tigers going into the season with Halter as their regular shortstop was

Shane Halter *(continued)*

the most tragic element of their 2002 season. In the end, Halter's year is a worthwhile cautionary tale about what can happen when you get too excited about your utility man. The fact that Halter's 29 hits in spring training and his .712 slugging average in Lakeland were both third among AL teams in the spring shows just how much value March numbers have—Halter started the regular season by going 1-for-25.

Jack Hannahan								3B			Born: 04-Mar-80			Age: 23			Bats: L		Throws: R	
YEAR	TM	LG	AGE	AB	H	2B	3B	HR	BB	SO	SB	CS	AVG	OBP	SLG	MLVR	EQBA	EQOBP	EQSLG	EQMLVR	VORP		DEFENSE
2001	WMI	MDW	21	170	54	11	0	1	26	39	4	2	.318	.411	.400	.222	.253	.326	.315	-.213	-1.1		45-3B	3
2002	LAK	FSL	22	246	67	11	1	6	36	44	9	3	.272	.367	.398	.116	.224	.299	.333	-.258	-4.8		63-3B	11
2002	ERI	EAS	22	226	54	12	1	3	21	50	2	1	.239	.309	.341	-.136	.202	.260	.294	-.402	-12.7		64-3B	11
2003	DET	AL	23	169	40	8	1	3	15	37	3	2	.236	.302	.360	-.146	.245	.312	.389	-.134	-.3		

Breakout: 63%   Improve: 77%   Collapse: 12%

After a fast start in 2001, Hannahan performed well in the Florida State League in the first half of 2002 before moving up to Double-A Erie. He struggled badly there, derailing any thoughts that he could be a solution to the Tigers' third-base problems in the near future. Hannahan's weak showing in the Arizona Fall League didn't help his prospects, but it did encourage the Tigers to get Travis Chapman from Cleveland in December.

Bobby Higginson								LF			Born: 18-Aug-70			Age: 32			Bats: L		Throws: R	
YEAR	TM	LG	AGE	AB	H	2B	3B	HR	BB	SO	SB	CS	AVG	OBP	SLG	MLVR	EQBA	EQOBP	EQSLG	EQMLVR	VORP		DEFENSE
2000	DET	AL	29	597	179	44	4	30	74	99	15	3	.300	.379	.538	.217	.313	.385	.563	.292	58.2		145-LF	4
2001	DET	AL	30	541	150	28	6	17	80	65	20	12	.277	.372	.445	.110	.299	.393	.485	.182	40.7		142-LF	6
2002	DET	AL	31	444	125	24	3	10	41	45	12	5	.282	.350	.417	.053	.313	.379	.467	.146	28.7		113-LF	-1
2003	DET	AL	32	420	115	25	3	12	49	53	9	3	.274	.351	.428	.046	.283	.364	.462	.079	13.3		

Breakout: 4%   Improve: 43%   Collapse: 15%

The biggest problem with Higginson, a career overachiever as well as a likeable and popular player, is the unbelievably fat contract he was given in April 2001 in the last, devastating salvo in Randy Smith's binge of excessive contracts that will hobble the club for years unless Dombrowski can work a miracle. With almost $30 million due for 2003–2005, Higginson will be untradable unless he boosts his power hitting substantially; his 2002 EqSLG was down almost 100 points from 2000. Higginson is slated to move back to right field in 2003 now that the Tigers have brought in the left field fences.

Omar Infante								SS/2B?			Born: 26-Dec-81			Age: 21			Bats: R		Throws: R	
YEAR	TM	LG	AGE	AB	H	2B	3B	HR	BB	SO	SB	CS	AVG	OBP	SLG	MLVR	EQBA	EQOBP	EQSLG	EQMLVR	VORP		DEFENSE
2000	LAK	FSL	18	259	71	11	0	2	20	29	11	5	.274	.329	.340	-.049	.221	.262	.279	-.409	-12.9		76-SS	2
2001	ERI	EAS	19	540	163	21	4	2	46	87	27	12	.302	.359	.367	.041	.262	.315	.316	-.228	-1.3		130-SS	3
2002	TOL	INT	20	436	117	16	8	4	28	49	19	15	.268	.313	.369	-.071	.245	.292	.341	-.248	-3.3		119-SS	7
2002	DET	AL	20	72	24	3	0	1	3	10	0	1	.333	.360	.417	.113	.370	.395	.452	.210	8.1		16-SS	-1
2003	DET	AL	21	389	100	17	3	4	27	52	10	4	.256	.308	.348	-.140	.265	.319	.375	-.127	3.8		

Breakout: 29%   Improve: 60%   Collapse: 7%

After a rough start to the season at Triple-A where he hit only .202 in April, Infante was disabled with a back strain and then diagnosed with spondylolysis. A program to strengthen his back muscles enabled him to return to the field, but his hitting didn't improve until he stopped trying to pull every pitch. Though Infante was voted best defensive shortstop in the International League by the loop's managers, Detroit tried him out at second base during his impressive September call-up. If the Tigers can unload Damion Easley, or have the guts to bench or release him, Infante might thrive at second base. He's very young and still somewhat raw, and would probably be overmatched by top-flight pitchers for a few years. However, having both him and Ramon Santiago in the lineup everyday would not only help Tigers' pitchers with good defense at both middle infield positions, it would help their chances of contending three years from now.

Brandon Inge   C   Born: 19-May-77   Age: 26   Bats: R   Throws: R

YEAR	TM	LG	AGE	AB	H	2B	3B	HR	BB	SO	SB	CS	AVG	OBP	SLG	MLVR	EQBA	EQOBP	EQSLG	EQMLVR	VORP	DEFENSE	
2000	JAX	SOU	23	298	77	25	1	6	26	73	10	3	.258	.318	.409	.043	.235	.279	.375	-.232	.2	69-C	4
2000	TOL	INT	23	190	42	9	3	5	15	51	2	1	.221	.282	.379	-.187	.204	.254	.356	-.327	-4.6	48-C	1
2001	TOL	INT	24	90	26	11	1	2	7	24	1	0	.289	.347	.500	.180	.264	.321	.462	-.008	5.2	25-C	-1
2001	DET	AL	24	189	34	11	0	0	9	41	1	4	.180	.217	.238	-.516	.201	.241	.270	-.475	-11.5	61-C	4
2002	TOL	INT	25	65	17	2	4	3	11	16	1	3	.262	.385	.554	.273	.227	.342	.485	.029	4.8	21-C	0
2002	DET	AL	25	321	65	15	3	7	24	101	1	3	.202	.266	.333	-.262	.229	.293	.378	-.205	2.6	93-C	-4
2003	DET	AL	26	256	59	15	2	6	21	66	3	4	.229	.291	.370	-.156	.237	.302	.399	-.145	1.1		

Breakout: 40%   Improve: 57%   Collapse: 25%

Inge is never going to hit enough to help, and his defensive worth is overvalued and overrated. For a supposedly terrific catcher, he had a very poor year behind the plate, throwing out only 13 of 57 base thieves. His struggles were exacerbated by the dislocated shoulder he suffered in mid-2001. Inge underwent arthroscopic surgery in early October to fix the shoulder problem, but there is no surgery that is going to fix his hitting. If he weren't a second round pick and the Tigers weren't so focused on the pitching-and-defense strategy, the club might have seen Inge for what he can be: a good reserve catcher with occasional power who would make a good caddy for a guy like Mike Rivera. Instead, Rivera was dealt to San Diego and Inge will be exposed as a woefully inadequate regular until someone wises up.

Damian Jackson   2B   Born: 16-Aug-73   Age: 29   Bats: R   Throws: R

YEAR	TM	LG	AGE	AB	H	2B	3B	HR	BB	SO	SB	CS	AVG	OBP	SLG	MLVR	EQBA	EQOBP	EQSLG	EQMLVR	VORP	DEFENSE			
2000	SDP	NL	26	470	120	27	6	6	62	108	28	6	.255	.346	.377	-.088	.266	.346	.393	-.057	21.3	83-SS	4	34-2B	5
2001	SDP	NL	27	440	106	21	6	4	44	128	23	6	.241	.318	.343	-.162	.256	.329	.365	-.136	9.8	115-2B	5		
2002	DET	AL	28	245	63	20	1	1	21	36	12	3	.257	.323	.359	-.089	.282	.347	.395	-.041	11.7	51-2B	-7		
2003	BOS	AL	29	275	68	15	2	4	27	54	12	4	.248	.319	.357	-.114	.253	.327	.374	-.122	2.6				

Breakout: 13%   Improve: 36%   Collapse: 33%

Released by the Tigers in November, Jackson was snarfed by the Red Sox and should be a serviceable utility infielder behind Todd "Stonehands" Walker. Among all the typical flaws of middle infielders, lack of willingness to take a walk has never been Jackson's problem. An excellent basestealer and baserunner as well as a capable bunter, Jackson has usually hit lefties well, making him a nifty spare part and backup to Walker.

Nook Logan   CF   Born: 28-Nov-79   Age: 23   Bats: B   Throws: R

YEAR	TM	LG	AGE	AB	H	2B	3B	HR	BB	SO	SB	CS	AVG	OBP	SLG	MLVR	EQBA	EQOBP	EQSLG	EQMLVR	VORP	DEFENSE	
2001	WMI	MDW	21	522	137	19	8	1	53	129	67	19	.262	.333	.335	-.025	.217	.271	.276	-.397	-29.9	126-CF	-10
2002	LAK	FSL	22	506	136	14	7	2	40	111	55	16	.269	.322	.336	-.033	.230	.269	.292	-.372	-25.5	122-CF	-5
2003	DET	AL	23	186	43	8	2	2	13	46	7	7	.231	.285	.325	-.223	.240	.295	.351	-.219	-5.4		

Breakout: 58%   Improve: 77%   Collapse: 13%

A fast switch-hitting center fielder who needs better plate discipline if he's going to hit much in the majors, Logan could get a chance in Detroit by 2004 if Torres and Kingsale don't cut the mustard. Already 23, he can't afford to lose a year due to injury or a bad slump if he is going to amount to anything more than a utility outfielder, organization player, or Eugene Kingsale.

George Lombard   CF   Born: 14-Sep-75   Age: 27   Bats: L   Throws: R

YEAR	TM	LG	AGE	AB	H	2B	3B	HR	BB	SO	SB	CS	AVG	OBP	SLG	MLVR	EQBA	EQOBP	EQSLG	EQMLVR	VORP	DEFENSE	
2000	RIC	INT	24	424	117	25	7	10	55	130	32	9	.276	.367	.439	.084	.255	.332	.407	-.072	1.8	103-LF	-10
2002	GRN	SOU	26	25	7	0	0	3	5	6	2	0	.280	.419	.640	.473	.231	.346	.500	.059	1.4		
2002	RIC	INT	26	39	12	4	1	1	5	12	2	0	.308	.400	.538	.329	.300	.374	.525	.206	3.7		
2002	DET	AL	26	241	58	11	3	5	20	78	13	2	.241	.302	.373	-.121	.263	.324	.412	-.074	6.9	62-CF	-2
2003	DET	AL	27	305	76	16	3	9	30	88	14	9	.250	.323	.414	-.034	.259	.334	.446	-.010	5.1		

Breakout: 14%   Improve: 40%   Collapse: 25%

Injury-prone and stuck behind better players in the Atlanta system, Lombard's career has gotten a late start. Freed from the Braves in June, he showed flashes of ability but had a disappointing season as he sagged down the stretch. Given his injury history and his defensive issues, it's unlikely he'll ever be an everyday center fielder, but the Tigers can't do much worse than another season of Wendell Magee. He'll compete with Torres and Kingsale for the job, but it's more likely he'll end up playing fairly often as a fourth outfielder.

Wendell Magee Jr.   CF   Born: 03-Aug-72   Age: 30   Bats: R   Throws: R

YEAR	TM	LG	AGE	AB	H	2B	3B	HR	BB	SO	SB	CS	AVG	OBP	SLG	MLVR	EQBA	EQOBP	EQSLG	EQMLVR	VORP	DEFENSE
2000	DET	AL	27	186	51	4	2	7	10	28	1	0	.274	.311	.430	-.086	.286	.316	.449	-.016	2.7	45-RF -3
2001	DET	AL	28	207	44	11	4	5	23	44	3	0	.213	.294	.377	-.167	.231	.313	.413	-.118	-1.6	60-OF -1
2002	DET	AL	29	347	94	19	1	6	10	64	2	4	.271	.293	.383	-.101	.297	.320	.426	-.033	13.1	91-CF 2
2003	CLE	AL	30	294	75	15	2	9	19	54	3	2	.257	.304	.409	-.066	.263	.312	.419	-.083	0.5	

Breakout: 20%   Improve: 49%   Collapse: 24%

How many fringe center fielders can one team have? A useful utility outfielder who mistakenly thinks he should play regularly, Magee doesn't have the patience at the plate to be a good hitter. However, he can play all three outfield positions and has no platoon split, so he should be able to play for years if he accepts a reserve role. The Indians have overreached by putting him on their 40-man.

Mitch Meluskey   DH   Born: 18-Sep-73   Age: 29   Bats: B   Throws: R

YEAR	TM	LG	AGE	AB	H	2B	3B	HR	BB	SO	SB	CS	AVG	OBP	SLG	MLVR	EQBA	EQOBP	EQSLG	EQMLVR	VORP	DEFENSE
2000	HOU	NL	26	337	101	21	0	14	55	74	1	0	.300	.404	.487	.177	.294	.392	.475	.162	37.6	91-C -8
2002	DET	AL	28	27	6	0	0	0	5	3	0	0	.222	.364	.222	-.204	.259	.408	.259	-.117	.1	
2003	OAK	AL	29	136	34	6	0	3	19	22	1	0	.248	.346	.355	-.070	.256	.357	.372	-.068	3.8	

Breakout: 10%   Improve: 31%   Collapse: 34%

"Mr. Personality" has now played exactly 135 games in the past four seasons, drawing most of his salary while on the DL. In 2002, the reason was a lower back injury that initially didn't seem that serious. Outrighted by Detroit after the season, Meluskey hooked on with Oakland for a minor league contract. If the pugnacious and pugilistic former catcher can stay healthy, he has exactly the right skills (power plus excellent plate discipline) to prosper in the Athletics' organization.

Craig Monroe   LF   Born: 27-Feb-77   Age: 26   Bats: R   Throws: R

YEAR	TM	LG	AGE	AB	H	2B	3B	HR	BB	SO	SB	CS	AVG	OBP	SLG	MLVR	EQBA	EQOBP	EQSLG	EQMLVR	VORP	DEFENSE
2000	TUL	TXS	23	464	131	34	5	20	64	91	12	13	.282	.372	.506	.185	.231	.302	.415	-.135	-6.9	113-RF -10
2001	OKL	PCL	24	410	115	25	5	20	46	85	10	8	.280	.360	.512	.156	.248	.322	.449	-.038	5.3	97-LF -2
2001	TEX	AL	24	52	11	1	0	2	6	18	2	0	.212	.293	.346	-.226	.231	.310	.365	-.189	-1.5	20-RF 0
2002	TOL	INT	25	358	115	30	4	10	35	57	7	3	.321	.385	.511	.276	.294	.357	.471	.095	17.2	78-LF -3
2002	DET	AL	25	25	3	1	0	1	0	5	0	2	.120	.154	.280	-.586	.160	.186	.320	-.537	-2.5	
2003	DET	AL	26	200	50	13	2	5	18	39	4	3	.251	.317	.410	-.047	.260	.329	.442	-.024	.0	

Breakout: 14%   Improve: 52%   Collapse: 31%

The Tigers claimed Monroe off of waivers from the Rangers in February, and he rewarded Detroit with a solid season in Toledo. The Tigers called him up five separate times, but he was given only 25 at-bats in 13 games to show what he could do. He's a bit long in the tooth, but has been kept on the 40-player winter roster. He has enough power to be a valuable reserve corner outfielder.

Eric Munson   1B   Born: 03-Oct-77   Age: 25   Bats: L   Throws: R

YEAR	TM	LG	AGE	AB	H	2B	3B	HR	BB	SO	SB	CS	AVG	OBP	SLG	MLVR	EQBA	EQOBP	EQSLG	EQMLVR	VORP	DEFENSE
2000	JAX	SOU	22	365	92	21	4	15	39	96	5	2	.252	.353	.455	.148	.233	.302	.418	-.130	-3.3	74-1B -4
2001	ERI	EAS	23	519	135	35	1	26	84	141	0	3	.260	.375	.482	.179	.222	.323	.407	-.113	-2.5	128-1B -12
2001	DET	AL	23	66	10	3	1	1	3	21	0	1	.152	.188	.273	-.539	.167	.203	.318	-.502	-6.7	15-1B 2
2002	TOL	INT	24	477	125	30	4	24	77	114	1	3	.262	.373	.493	.180	.241	.345	.456	.007	13.6	129-1B -8
2002	DET	AL	24	59	11	0	0	2	6	11	0	0	.186	.273	.288	-.317	.203	.297	.322	-.289	-2.6	
2003	DET	AL	25	311	75	18	2	11	37	72	3	3	.243	.328	.419	-.025	.251	.340	.452	.000	3.4	

Breakout: 29%   Improve: 72%   Collapse: 10%

Munson had a good but not great year in 2002, bookended by a slow April in Toledo and a miserable September in Motown. In between, he managed to restore his tattered reputation as a power prospect. The problem is that he has no position other than first base, and he isn't likely to push Carlos Pena out of a job. Like many young hitters with big power, he can hit almost any fastball, but he's pull-happy and has trouble with breaking pitches. The departure of Robert Fick bodes well for him, as it cleared up a potential logjam at DH. The Tigers need to give Munson 1,000 at-bats in the next two years to see if he can mature into the hitter they projected him to be when they drafted him with the #3 pick in 1999.

Dean Palmer   DH   Born: 27-Dec-68   Age: 34   Bats: R   Throws: R

YEAR	TM	LG	AGE	AB	H	2B	3B	HR	BB	SO	SB	CS	AVG	OBP	SLG	MLVR	EQBA	EQOBP	EQSLG	EQMLVR	VORP	DEFENSE
2000	DET	AL	31	524	134	22	2	29	66	146	4	2	.256	.343	.471	.017	.265	.345	.493	.078	36.0	105-3B -19 13-1B -3
2001	DET	AL	32	216	48	11	0	11	27	59	4	1	.222	.317	.426	-.055	.240	.333	.465	-.003	7.7	
2002	DET	AL	33	12	0	0	0	0	1	5	0	0	.000	.077	.000	-1.113	.083	.154	.083	-.946	-2.6	
2003	*DET*	*AL*	*34*	*208*	*43*	*9*	*1*	*7*	*26*	*63*	*2*	*1*	*.204*	*.295*	*.355*	*-.182*	*.212*	*.306*	*.383*	*-.175*	*-5.0*	

Breakout: 20%   *Improve: 44%*   *Collapse: 31%*

Palmer has been on the DL five times in the past two years; all were related to his shoulder problems. Another of the mega-buck millstones that Randy Smith hung around the neck of the club during his free-spending days as genius GM of the up-and-coming ComeriTigers, Palmer's contract has one more year to run. The Tigers will give him at-bats at DH if he's healthy, hoping against hope that he shows some of his previous home run power and that they can then hornswoggle some team to take him for the second half.

Craig Paquette   3B   Born: 28-Mar-69   Age: 34   Bats: R   Throws: R

YEAR	TM	LG	AGE	AB	H	2B	3B	HR	BB	SO	SB	CS	AVG	OBP	SLG	MLVR	EQBA	EQOBP	EQSLG	EQMLVR	VORP	DEFENSE
2000	STL	NL	31	384	94	24	2	15	27	83	4	3	.245	.298	.435	-.131	.243	.287	.432	-.130	5.9	60-3B -8 17-LF -2
2001	STL	NL	32	340	96	17	0	15	18	67	3	1	.282	.328	.465	.037	.288	.331	.471	.044	12.3	38-LF 1 20-3B 0
2002	DET	AL	33	252	49	14	1	4	10	53	1	0	.194	.225	.306	-.381	.217	.250	.344	-.344	-10.2	42-3B -5 11-1B -1
2003	*DET*	*AL*	*34*	*231*	*55*	*13*	*1*	*6*	*13*	*48*	*2*	*1*	*.238*	*.283*	*.378*	*-.154*	*.246*	*.293*	*.408*	*-.142*	*-3.0*	

Breakout: 38%   *Improve: 61%*   *Collapse: 22%*

It's one thing to keep a guy like Craig Paquette hanging around if you're a legend like Tony LaRussa and you can get away with playing guys out-of-position so that you can make numerous inscrutable lineup moves that confirm your genius. It's quite another thing entirely if you're an organization going nowhere and you have numerous marginal prospects that need a reasonable amount of playing time in order to be fairly evaluated. It's yet another thing to enter a season with someone like Paquette penciled in as a regular at a power position like third base.

Jarrod Patterson   3B   Born: 07-Sep-73   Age: 29   Bats: L   Throws: R

YEAR	TM	LG	AGE	AB	H	2B	3B	HR	BB	SO	SB	CS	AVG	OBP	SLG	MLVR	EQBA	EQOBP	EQSLG	EQMLVR	VORP	DEFENSE
2000	NAS	PCL	26	198	55	10	0	5	13	40	0	2	.278	.329	.404	-.071	.253	.290	.364	-.214	-1.3	45-3B 1
2000	OTT	INT	26	92	25	6	1	0	4	13	1	0	.272	.302	.359	-.140	.250	.274	.337	-.286	-2.4	24-3B -2
2001	ERI	EAS	27	70	28	5	1	7	11	11	0	0	.400	.481	.800	.868	.329	.402	.658	.472	12.9	20-3B -3
2001	TOL	INT	27	213	63	15	2	7	30	47	2	1	.296	.385	.484	.222	.275	.359	.450	.052	13.9	36-3B 0
2002	TOL	INT	28	447	132	34	6	13	46	71	3	1	.295	.366	.485	.190	.271	.339	.452	.016	24.0	68-3B 0 40-2B -6
2003	*KCR*	*AL*	*29*	*161*	*43*	*10*	*1*	*6*	*15*	*29*	*2*	*1*	*.268*	*.332*	*.450*	*.040*	*.264*	*.332*	*.446*	*-.011*	*4.9*	

Breakout: 16%   *Improve: 41%*   *Collapse: 37%*

For a team struggling just to compete, the Tigers' lack of confidence in Patterson is strange. While he's no spring chicken, he persevered and finally made it to the majors in 2001 in his ninth pro season, playing respectably in a handful of games. Last season he did his underappreciated thing at Toledo. Although Patterson shouldn't play regularly in the majors, he's a better and cheaper option than Chris Truby or Craig Paquette and won't look much worse than Joe Randa in Kansas City.

Carlos Pena   1B   Born: 17-May-78   Age: 25   Bats: L   Throws: L

YEAR	TM	LG	AGE	AB	H	2B	3B	HR	BB	SO	SB	CS	AVG	OBP	SLG	MLVR	EQBA	EQOBP	EQSLG	EQMLVR	VORP	DEFENSE
2000	TUL	TXS	22	529	158	36	2	28	101	108	12	0	.299	.419	.533	.313	.248	.346	.439	-.008	12.0	136-1B -16
2001	OKL	PCL	23	431	124	38	3	23	80	127	11	3	.288	.408	.550	.297	.256	.367	.483	.095	23.0	115-1B -2
2001	TEX	AL	23	62	16	4	1	3	10	17	0	0	.258	.361	.500	.125	.274	.375	.532	.191	4.8	16-1B 2
2002	OAK	AL	24	124	27	4	0	7	15	38	0	0	.218	.307	.419	-.080	.240	.325	.464	-.019	2.5	38-1B 9
2002	SAC	PCL	24	175	42	10	1	10	24	49	3	0	.240	.345	.480	.073	.220	.311	.429	-.108	-.5	40-1B 5
2002	DET	AL	24	273	69	13	4	12	26	73	2	2	.253	.322	.462	.042	.275	.343	.507	.104	15.0	70-1B 4
2003	*DET*	*AL*	*25*	*421*	*107*	*26*	*2*	*18*	*53*	*102*	*5*	*4*	*.255*	*.343*	*.451*	*.049*	*.264*	*.355*	*.486*	*.081*	*13.8*	

Breakout: 21%   *Improve: 56%*   *Collapse: 16%*

After a hot start in April (seven home runs and AL Rookie of the Month), Pena swooned in May and was sent down in the middle of a horrible slump as part of the Athletics' big shakeup when they were 10 games behind Seattle. Traded to Detroit on July 6, he got a second chance and did well. He is exactly what the Tigers need to generate some offense and excitement while they rebuild: a young, smooth-fielding, power-hitting first baseman. Scouts compare him defensively to Keith Hernandez

Carlos Pena (*continued*)

and Willie Montanez; he's also a decent baserunner, a smart ballplayer, and a good competitor. Comparisons to older ballplayers are frequently overdrawn, but invoking the name "Norm Cash" when talking about Pena isn't unreasonable at this point in his career. Confident to the point of being cocky, Pena is in the perfect situation to become a big star. Like most lefty power hitters, he gets his best hacks at pitches middle-in and low; pitchers can get him with cutters and sliders in and with sinkers and changeups away.

Mike Rivera C Born: 08-Sep-76 Age: 26 Bats: R Throws: R

YEAR	TM	LG	AGE	AB	H	2B	3B	HR	BB	SO	SB	CS	AVG	OBP	SLG	MLVR	EQBA	EQOBP	EQSLG	EQMLVR	VORP	DEFENSE
2000	LAK	FSL	23	243	71	19	4	11	16	45	2	0	.292	.338	.539	.250	.233	.267	.433	-.174	3.8	56-C 5
2000	JAX	SOU	23	150	29	8	1	2	7	30	0	0	.193	.229	.300	-.281	.183	.204	.288	-.533	-11.1	31-C -7
2001	ERI	EAS	24	415	120	19	1	33	44	96	2	2	.289	.371	.578	.319	.245	.319	.481	-.002	25.7	110-C -3
2002	TOL	INT	25	265	66	11	1	20	35	64	0	1	.249	.343	.525	.165	.228	.317	.485	-.015	15.7	62-C 3
2002	DET	AL	25	132	30	8	1	1	4	35	0	0	.227	.255	.326	-.279	.256	.282	.361	-.232	.1	37-C -5
2003	SDP	NL	26	258	61	13	1	11	24	63	2	3	.236	.307	.421	-.084	.247	.314	.456	-.041	8.2	

Breakout: 27% Improve: 60% Collapse: 20%

Traded to the Padres in mid-November for Gene Kingsale because the Tigers theoretically have a surplus of catching talent and a deficit of unproven speedy outfielders that can't hit, neither of which is true. Rivera isn't a blue-chip prospect, but he has real power and should easily replace the departed Tom Lampkin and resident floater Wiki Gonzalez as San Diego's regular backstop. While his defense is questionable, Bruce Bochy should be able to tutor Rivera to enable the team to benefit from his bat. Unfortunately for Rivera, too many teams refuse to start subpar defensive catchers who can thump the ball. In most cases, the best solution is to play the hitter and find a good catch-and-throw guy (they're easy to come by) as a reserve. By using the catch-and-throw receiver as a late-inning defensive replacement and spot-starting him against opponents who run a lot, a team can maximize its offensive production from the position while minimizing the defensive damage. Even assuming that Kingsale has value, they had other options in center and didn't have to give Rivera away. A Rivera/Inge "platoon" could have been a big plus for Detroit.

Cody Ross LF Born: 23-Dec-80 Age: 22 Bats: R Throws: L

YEAR	TM	LG	AGE	AB	H	2B	3B	HR	BB	SO	SB	CS	AVG	OBP	SLG	MLVR	EQBA	EQOBP	EQSLG	EQMLVR	VORP	DEFENSE
2000	WMI	MDW	19	434	116	17	9	7	55	83	11	3	.267	.361	.396	.122	.221	.283	.331	-.295	-25.4	120-RF 1
2001	LAK	FSL	20	482	133	34	5	15	44	96	28	5	.276	.343	.461	.158	.226	.273	.384	-.237	-18.8	125-LF -1
2002	ERI	EAS	21	400	112	28	3	19	44	86	16	2	.280	.356	.507	.186	.235	.299	.426	-.123	-3.7	102-LF -2
2003	DET	AL	22	203	52	11	1	6	16	43	4	4	.254	.315	.408	-.051	.263	.327	.440	-.029	-.3	

Breakout: 44% Improve: 66% Collapse: 9%

Ross continued to progress last year, though his small size means he is frequently downgraded by the tools-happy crowd despite his youth and broad base of offensive skills. An excellent baserunner with power who can also field and throw well, Ross is unlikely to get a chance to show what he can do in the majors unless he has a good year in Triple-A while the Tigers clear up their surplus of mediocre outfielders.

Ramon Santiago SS Born: 31-Aug-79 Age: 23 Bats: B Throws: R

YEAR	TM	LG	AGE	AB	H	2B	3B	HR	BB	SO	SB	CS	AVG	OBP	SLG	MLVR	EQBA	EQOBP	EQSLG	EQMLVR	VORP	DEFENSE
2000	WMI	MDW	20	379	103	15	1	1	34	60	39	12	.272	.351	.325	.014	.235	.281	.281	-.361	-13.9	75-SS 14
2001	LAK	FSL	21	429	115	15	3	2	54	60	34	8	.268	.364	.331	.016	.231	.300	.290	-.312	-20.6	
2002	ERI	EAS	22	75	21	0	2	1	3	12	6	0	.280	.333	.373	-.027	.253	.287	.333	-.264	-.9	20-SS -1
2002	TOL	INT	22	28	12	1	0	2	3	4	0	2	.429	.515	.679	.793	.357	.445	.607	.498	4.6	
2002	DET	AL	22	222	54	5	5	4	13	48	8	5	.243	.309	.365	-.118	.272	.333	.411	-.052	9.8	62-SS 3
2003	DET	AL	23	312	77	14	2	3	23	51	10	4	.247	.305	.342	-.157	.256	.316	.369	-.146	1.6	

Breakout: 17% Improve: 51% Collapse: 26%

Santiago jumped all the way from Lakeland in 2001 to Detroit in 2002, mostly because the Tigers unaccountably tried to live with Shane Halter at shortstop at the start of the season. Halter was a predictable bust, and Omar Infante was struggling, so Santiago made his debut on May 17 after only 31 games' experience in the high minors. His rookie season was disrupted by a broken hamate bone in his right hand, for which he underwent surgery in late July, as well as chronic looseness in his left shoulder, for which he underwent surgery in late September. His future doesn't look as bright now as it was before it was discovered that he was two years older than reported, but he has a decent chance of becoming a good player, especially if fixing his hand and shoulder problems improve his hitting.

Randall Simon   1B   Born: 26-May-75   Age: 28   Bats: L   Throws: L

YEAR	TM	LG	AGE	AB	H	2B	3B	HR	BB	SO	SB	CS	AVG	OBP	SLG	MLVR	EQBA	EQOBP	EQSLG	EQMLVR	VORP	DEFENSE	
2000	CLG	PCL	25	68	20	3	0	1	0	3	0	0	.294	.294	.382	-.215	.242	.242	.318	-.382	-4.6	13-1B	-3
2000	COH	INT	25	364	97	20	4	17	35	42	6	5	.266	.331	.484	.080	.245	.299	.447	-.085	1.0	73-1B	-3
2001	TOL	INT	26	222	75	13	0	10	21	21	0	3	.338	.400	.532	.347	.310	.369	.487	.154	14.5	50-1B	-9
2001	DET	AL	26	256	78	14	2	6	15	28	0	1	.305	.343	.445	.083	.322	.361	.477	.139	15.4	38-1B	4
2002	DET	AL	27	482	145	17	1	19	13	30	0	1	.301	.325	.459	.084	.324	.349	.497	.150	30.7	58-1B	-4
2003	PIT	NL	28	418	119	22	2	13	28	37	2	1	.285	.331	.440	.020	.285	.327	.454	.010	5.5		

Breakout: 4%   Improve: 25%   Collapse: 26%

Simon had a breakout year in the sense that he got to play almost every day, and it earned him a ticket from one disappointing and hopeless team in a new ballpark to another. However, his production last year was remarkably consistent in all three traditional batting aspects (AVG, OBP, SLG) with his half-season numbers in Atlanta in 1999 and in Detroit in 2001. Simon is a useful player when he can be platooned, but he shouldn't take at-bats away from Craig Wilson in Pittsburgh. Wilson's career numbers versus right-handers are about as good as Simon's. It would be a mistake for the Bucs to reduce Wilson to a part-time role by platooning him with Simon or Matt Stairs.

Andres Torres   CF   Born: 26-Jan-78   Age: 25   Bats: B   Throws: R

YEAR	TM	LG	AGE	AB	H	2B	3B	HR	BB	SO	SB	CS	AVG	OBP	SLG	MLVR	EQBA	EQOBP	EQSLG	EQMLVR	VORP	DEFENSE	
2000	LAK	FSL	22	398	118	11	11	3	63	82	65	16	.296	.399	.402	.155	.243	.325	.334	-.194	-1.7	104-CF	2
2000	JAX	SOU	22	54	8	0	0	0	5	14	2	0	.148	.220	.148	-.509	.179	.220	.179	-.654	-6.7	14-CF	-2
2001	ERI	EAS	23	252	74	16	3	1	36	50	19	11	.294	.392	.393	.123	.250	.336	.335	-.167	.8	55-CF	0
2002	TOL	INT	24	462	123	17	8	4	53	116	42	12	.266	.348	.364	-.020	.248	.326	.343	-.177	.2	112-CF	-8
2002	DET	AL	24	70	14	1	1	0	6	16	2	2	.200	.273	.243	-.369	.239	.306	.282	-.306	-2.4	18-CF	0
2003	DET	AL	25	292	73	14	3	3	32	62	11	7	.249	.327	.350	-.109	.258	.338	.377	-.094	2.2		

Breakout: 32%   Improve: 62%   Collapse: 22%

Though selected for the 2002 Futures Game, the Tigers showed their lack of confidence in Torres's future by trading for retread Gene Kingsale in the off-season. Torres will now have to beat out both Lombard and Kingsale, and Kingsale is reportedly a favorite of Trammell's from his coaching days in San Diego. A weak year in Toledo certainly didn't help Torres's stock. The organization also feels Torres muscled up too much in the mistaken assumption that he can add some power to his game. If it decreases his speed or his range, it will only hurt his chances.

Chris Truby   3B   Born: 09-Dec-73   Age: 29   Bats: R   Throws: R

YEAR	TM	LG	AGE	AB	H	2B	3B	HR	BB	SO	SB	CS	AVG	OBP	SLG	MLVR	EQBA	EQOBP	EQSLG	EQMLVR	VORP	DEFENSE			
2000	NWO	PCL	26	268	76	11	3	2	17	32	6	2	.284	.326	.369	-.107	.264	.295	.346	-.223	-2.4	62-3B	5		
2000	HOU	NL	26	258	67	15	4	11	10	56	2	1	.260	.300	.477	-.060	.258	.286	.469	-.066	7.9	67-3B	-3		
2001	NWO	PCL	27	321	100	25	6	12	24	66	10	5	.312	.367	.539	.268	.284	.336	.488	.073	23.5	54-3B	-1	27-1B	-3
2001	HOU	NL	27	136	28	6	1	8	13	38	1	2	.206	.280	.441	-.155	.204	.277	.438	-.171	.7	30-3B	-3		
2002	MON	NL	28	105	27	5	2	2	5	27	1	1	.257	.297	.400	-.067	.264	.303	.406	-.121	1.8	25-3B	-4		
2002	DET	AL	28	277	55	13	2	2	5	71	1	1	.199	.218	.282	-.425	.223	.244	.320	-.386	-14.0	87-3B	3		
2003	TBA	AL	29	271	66	14	2	6	15	61	3	3	.244	.288	.383	-.136	.250	.296	.400	-.146	-1.5				

Breakout: 26%   Improve: 57%   Collapse: 19%

Why the Tigers traded Jose Macias to get Truby is a puzzle. Probably the worst player in the AL last season, Truby had a scarcely believable .497 OPS, and the more he played, the worse he got. If the Tigers were truly desperate for a third baseman, they could have just brought Jarrod Patterson up from Toledo. Outrighted to Toledo after the season, and signed by Tampa Bay, appropriately enough.

Chris Wakeland   Born: 15-Jun-74   Age: 29   Bats: L   Throws: L

YEAR	TM	LG	AGE	AB	H	2B	3B	HR	BB	SO	SB	CS	AVG	OBP	SLG	MLVR	EQBA	EQOBP	EQSLG	EQMLVR	VORP	DEFENSE	
2000	TOL	INT	26	492	133	25	2	28	60	148	4	5	.270	.354	.500	.141	.248	.321	.456	-.031	6.1	123-RF	-15
2001	TOL	INT	27	547	155	33	3	23	39	126	7	8	.283	.340	.481	.139	.264	.317	.448	-.035	5.6	111-RF	-5
2002	TOL	INT	28	297	72	11	1	10	24	106	5	3	.242	.303	.387	-.080	.227	.286	.365	-.238	-12.4	48-RF	-1

Wakeland got his cuppajava in Detroit in 2001 after consecutive seasons in Triple-A. His 2002 numbers weren't so good. Given his age, he is unlikely to get another chance even though he signed a minor league deal with the Marlins in December. The same can be said about infielder Brian Rios, who had a very disappointing second year in Triple-A and who will probably toil

Chris Wakeland *(continued)*

for Toledo in 2003 unless a rash of injuries in Detroit create a vacancy. Despite all of the turmoil at the parent club in recent seasons, the Tigers' player development department didn't know what to do with either of these modestly talented guys. Phil Garner showed an excessive bias toward veterans, so they wouldn't have played much even if they were promoted.

Matt Walbeck — Born: 02-Oct-69 — Age: 33 — Bats: B — Throws: R

YEAR	TM	LG	AGE	AB	H	2B	3B	HR	BB	SO	SB	CS	AVG	OBP	SLG	MLVR	EQBA	EQOBP	EQSLG	EQMLVR	VORP	DEFENSE	
2000	ANA	AL	30	146	29	5	0	6	7	22	0	1	.199	.240	.356	-.393	.205	.237	.377	-.330	-3.3	37-C	2
2001	LOU	INT	31	197	45	7	0	3	23	26	1	0	.228	.309	.310	-.171	.215	.293	.295	-.327	-4.9	48-C	0
2001	SWB	INT	31	141	42	11	0	2	11	20	0	2	.298	.357	.418	.105	.280	.337	.399	-.055	6.6	37-C	1
2002	TOL	INT	32	75	16	3	0	1	4	10	0	0	.213	.253	.293	-.307	.200	.241	.280	-.461	-4.2	20-C	-2
2002	DET	AL	32	85	20	2	0	0	3	14	0	0	.235	.261	.259	-.355	.259	.284	.294	-.323	-1.9	25-C	-1

In his second go-round with the Tigers, Walbeck spent 2002 as Inge's caddy. He's failed as a hitter in several trials but has decent enough defensive skills to merit more big league bench time. Walbeck has already inked a Triple-A deal for 2003 with the club, and will probably win a backup job in the spring.

Dmitri Young — LF — Born: 11-Oct-73 — Age: 29 — Bats: B — Throws: R

YEAR	TM	LG	AGE	AB	H	2B	3B	HR	BB	SO	SB	CS	AVG	OBP	SLG	MLVR	EQBA	EQOBP	EQSLG	EQMLVR	VORP	DEFENSE			
2000	CIN	NL	26	548	166	37	6	18	36	80	0	3	.303	.349	.491	.089	.296	.333	.482	.071	22.7	84-LF	4	27-1B	-6
2001	CIN	NL	27	540	163	28	3	21	37	77	8	5	.302	.352	.481	.108	.299	.348	.475	.090	26.0	76-LF	-1	26-1B	1
2002	DET	AL	28	201	57	14	0	7	12	39	2	0	.284	.330	.458	.076	.305	.352	.502	.142	12.8	14-1B	-3		
2003	*DET*	*AL*	*29*	*361*	*99*	*23*	*2*	*9*	*24*	*58*	*3*	*1*	*.274*	*.323*	*.424*	*-.003*	*.284*	*.334*	*.458*	*.026*	*6.8*				

Breakout: 7%   Improve: 36%   Collapse: 26%

Signed to a four-year, $28.5 million deal in spring training that could expand to a five-year, $37 million deal if he plays regularly, Young spent most of 2002 on the DL with hernia problems, making his first year in Detroit a bust. While there was off-season talk about trying Young at third base in 2003, the Tigers will almost certainly move him to left field and hope he can reestablish his bona fides as a hitter there. Another long-term move by Randy Smith that could turn into a disaster, Dombrowski had to sign off on the deal and deserves some of the responsibility. Such is the enormous power of hitting the magic .300 number on a consistent basis.

PITCHERS

Juan Acevedo — Born: 05-May-70 — Age: 33 — Bats: R — Throws: R

YEAR	TM	LG	AGE	G	GS	IP	H	BB	SO	HR	ERA	EQERA	EQH9	EQBB9	EQSO9	EQHR9	PERA	VORP	STF
2000	MIL	NL	30	62	0	82.7	77	31	51	11	3.81	4.08	8.9	2.8	5.0	1.1	3.96	11.9	-8
2001	COL	NL	31	39	0	32.0	37	19	26	4	5.63	5.73	10.1	4.9	6.1	0.9	5.35	-1.2	-13
2001	FLA	NL	31	20	0	28.3	31	16	21	2	2.54	4.33	10.4	4.8	5.7	0.6	5.37	3.3	-9
2002	DET	AL	32	65	0	74.7	68	23	43	4	2.65	3.22	7.8	2.6	5.0	0.5	3.29	17.9	-3
2003	*DET*	*AL*	*33*	*48*	*0*	*54.0*	*59*	*21*	*32*	*5*	*4.27*	*4.40*	*9.6*	*3.2*	*5.2*	*1.0*	*4.67*	*8.1*	*-10*

Breakout: 17%   Improve: 45%   Collapse: 23%

In May, with Matt Anderson injured, Acevedo became the Tigers' closer by default. He did a decent job in the role, although he allowed 11 unearned runs, making his 2.65 ERA much less impressive. Acevedo is aggressive with his fastball but his motion gives hitters a good look at the pitch; his four-seamer is usually straight. Without a plus breaking pitch that can get him the strikeouts needed by a top closer, he's better suited for setup work. He'll be elsewhere in 2003.

Matt Anderson — Born: 17-Aug-76 — Age: 26 — Bats: R — Throws: R

YEAR	TM	LG	AGE	G	GS	IP	H	BB	SO	HR	ERA	EQERA	EQH9	EQBB9	EQSO9	EQHR9	PERA	VORP	STF
2000	DET	AL	23	69	0	74.3	61	45	71	8	4.72	3.96	6.8	4.3	8.2	0.8	3.62	11.7	13
2001	DET	AL	24	62	0	56.0	56	18	52	2	4.82	4.08	8.8	2.7	7.8	0.3	3.60	8.1	15
2002	DET	AL	25	12	0	11.0	17	8	8	1	9.00	8.32	13.2	5.9	6.2	0.7	7.96	-3.6	-19

The flame throwing righty missed almost all of the 2002 season with a torn muscle in his pitching shoulder. He was expected to have a big year after seemingly solving his control problems and saving 22 games in 2001. Anderson instead will start all over again in 2003. Given his shoulder injuries, Anderson is facing the same choice many other talented young pitchers do: ease up on his velocity and tighten his delivery for better command and to reduce the stress on his arm, or air it out and risk recurring injury. Reportedly not the most cerebral of pitchers, Anderson needs to apply himself physically and mentally to reviving his career. While his big four-seam fastball is renowned, it has little or no movement and he doesn't have a usable two-seamer.

Kenny Baugh   Born: 05-Feb-79   Age: 24   Bats: R   Throws: R

YEAR	TM	LG	AGE	G	GS	IP	H	BB	SO	HR	ERA	EQERA	EQH9	EQBB9	EQSO9	EQHR9	PERA	VORP	STF
2001	WMI	MDW	22	6	6	34.0	31	10	39	0	1.59	5.33	11.4	3.8	6.5	0.3	4.97	0.7	17
2001	ERI	EAS	22	5	5	30.3	23	6	30	5	2.97	5.04	8.7	2.4	6.2	2.3	4.12	1.6	13

The second stage of Baugh's rocket to stardom flamed out with a torn labrum in his pitching shoulder. After surgery to repair the injury in mid-June, he made good progress on his rehab and should be ready to go again in spring training. The pride of the Tigers pitching prospects finished 2001 on the DL with a strained right shoulder, showing that labrum tears aren't easy to diagnose, and that the choice of whether to heal them with rest and physical therapy isn't easy. At the very least, the injury will delay Baugh's development—the abuse heaped upon him in college clouds any future projections.

Adam Bernero   Born: 28-Nov-76   Age: 26   Bats: R   Throws: R

YEAR	TM	LG	AGE	G	GS	IP	H	BB	SO	HR	ERA	EQERA	EQH9	EQBB9	EQSO9	EQHR9	PERA	VORP	STF
2000	JAX	SOU	23	10	10	61.3	54	24	46	6	2.79	5.25	10.8	4.0	4.9	1.8	5.49	1.7	0
2000	TOL	INT	23	7	7	47.3	34	10	37	5	2.47	2.70	6.6	1.9	5.9	1.2	2.85	14.7	20
2000	DET	AL	23	12	4	34.3	33	13	20	3	4.20	3.67	8.1	2.8	5.1	0.7	3.53	6.8	3
2001	TOL	INT	24	26	25	140.3	172	54	99	13	5.13	6.26	12.0	4.1	5.0	1.1	6.53	-11.8	-3
2001	DET	AL	24	5	0	12.3	13	4	8	4	7.32	7.04	9.1	2.7	5.5	2.7	5.97	-2.3	-12
2002	TOL	INT	25	9	9	57.0	46	13	49	2	1.58	2.76	7.9	2.5	6.6	0.5	3.02	17.4	23
2002	DET	AL	25	28	11	101.7	128	31	69	17	6.19	5.55	10.8	2.5	5.9	1.4	5.80	-1.0	0
2003	DET	AL	26	26	15	96.7	104	34	66	11	4.74	4.89	9.4	3.0	5.9	1.1	4.65	9.2	1

Breakout: 18%   Improve: 48%   Collapse: 11%

Following his promotion from Triple-A in May after a hot streak in Toledo—being named Pitcher of the Week in the IL or PCL results in promotions way more often than it should—Bernero made 11 starts and was pounded for a 6.72 ERA. Shunted to the bullpen, he was only a little bit better (5.30 ERA). A finesse pitcher, Bernero has dropped off the prospect radar screen. He's the kind of pitcher that has enough experience and just enough stuff to get minor league hitters out, but not enough to get by in the majors.

Jason Beverlin   Born: 27-Nov-73   Age: 29   Bats: L   Throws: R

YEAR	TM	LG	AGE	G	GS	IP	H	BB	SO	HR	ERA	EQERA	EQH9	EQBB9	EQSO9	EQHR9	PERA	VORP	STF
2000	NRW	EAS	26	24	24	143.7	110	87	100	7	2.82	4.67	8.5	6.1	4.8	0.8	4.70	13.3	-6
2001	ARK	TXS	27	6	6	39.3	36	11	30	4	2.75	4.25	9.9	3.1	5.0	1.6	4.67	5.5	0
2001	SLC	PCL	27	19	12	83.0	82	29	74	9	4.23	4.50	9.4	3.7	5.8	1.1	4.42	9.1	1
2002	BUF	INT	28	23	20	118.7	107	39	106	11	3.87	4.87	9.6	3.6	7.0	1.2	4.33	8.3	9
2002	CLE	AL	28	4	0	7.3	9	4	9	1	7.40	6.29	10.1	4.5	10.4	1.1	5.88	-0.7	14
2002	TOL	INT	28	4	3	18.7	17	6	13	0	1.93	3.23	8.9	3.5	5.3	0.2	3.58	4.7	7
2002	DET	AL	28	3	3	12.3	18	5	7	2	9.51	7.92	12.7	3.4	5.0	1.4	7.09	-3.3	-12
2003	DET	AL	29	17	10	60.3	68	31	46	7	5.05	5.21	9.8	4.3	6.5	1.1	5.16	5.5	-1

Breakout: 21%   Improve: 41%   Collapse: 26%

Beverlin made his major league debut with Cleveland last year following eight years in the minors but only 22 games at Triple-A. Waived by the Tribe in August, he made three starts for the Tigers down the stretch, and was predictably hammered before being outrighted to Toledo at season's end. He's durable but nothing special.

Jeremy Bonderman   Born: 28-Oct-82   Age: 20   Bats: R   Throws: R

YEAR	TM	LG	AGE	G	GS	IP	H	BB	SO	HR	ERA	EQERA	EQH9	EQBB9	EQSO9	EQHR9	PERA	VORP	STF
2002	MOD	CLF	19	25	25	144.7	129	55	160	15	3.61	5.84	11.5	4.5	6.0	1.9	5.26	-5.4	8
2002	LAK	FSL	19	2	2	12.0	11	4	10	3	6.00	7.79	14.9	4.2	5.9	6.0	7.06	-3.0	-10

Oakland's first round pick in 2001, Bonderman is well-known for being the first high school player drafted before his senior year (even though he wasn't any younger than other high school graduates). He joined the Tigers in August 2002 as part of the three-cornered Weaver deal. Starting out in the advanced Class-A California League, Bonderman pitched very well, impressing with his fastball, slider, competitiveness, and relative maturity. Without any setbacks, he could realistically be in the Tigers' rotation by 2004.

Nate Cornejo   Born: 24-Sep-79   Age: 23   Bats: R   Throws: R

YEAR	TM	LG	AGE	G	GS	IP	H	BB	SO	HR	ERA	EQERA	EQH9	EQBB9	EQSO9	EQHR9	PERA	VORP	STF
2000	LAK	FSL	20	12	12	77.0	67	31	60	5	3.04	5.17	10.2	4.7	5.0	1.5	4.99	2.9	4
2000	JAX	SOU	20	16	16	91.7	91	43	60	6	4.61	6.42	11.8	4.7	4.3	1.2	6.27	-9.3	-3
2001	ERI	EAS	21	19	19	124.3	107	41	105	12	2.68	4.59	9.7	4.1	5.3	1.4	4.66	12.6	9
2001	TOL	INT	21	4	4	29.7	24	7	22	1	2.12	2.87	7.8	2.5	5.2	0.4	3.16	8.7	19
2001	DET	AL	21	10	10	42.7	63	28	22	10	7.38	7.74	12.7	5.5	4.3	1.9	8.49	-10.6	-15
2002	DET	AL	22	9	9	50.0	63	18	23	6	5.04	5.19	10.8	3.0	4.0	1.0	5.64	1.8	0
2002	TOL	INT	22	21	20	132.3	163	31	86	11	4.42	5.69	12.3	2.6	5.0	1.1	5.74	-2.7	7
2003	*DET*	*AL*	*23*	*18*	*15*	*91.0*	*109*	*37*	*57*	*11*	*5.30*	*5.46*	*10.5*	*3.4*	*5.4*	*1.2*	*5.42*	*4.1*	*-1*

Breakout: 11%   Improve: 50%   Collapse: 19%

A highly regarded, sinkerballing righty that has been too lightly compared to Kevin Brown, Cornejo began last year in the Tigers' rotation before being shipped out in mid-May. Command is still an issue for him, both on his two-seam fastball, which moves like crazy, and his slurvy breaking ball. He also needs a better changeup if he is to become a star, especially because of his problems with left-handed hitters.

Eric Eckenstahler   Born: 17-Dec-76   Age: 26   Bats: L   Throws: L

YEAR	TM	LG	AGE	G	GS	IP	H	BB	SO	HR	ERA	EQERA	EQH9	EQBB9	EQSO9	EQHR9	PERA	VORP	STF
2000	ONE	NYP	23	8	0	11.0	7	3	13	0	1.64	3.29	7.4	3.2	5.8	0.3	3.37	2.6	1
2000	WMI	MDW	23	10	3	18.7	21	11	22	4	5.78	11.45	20.5	7.6	7.9	6.2	10.80	-12.5	-37
2001	ERI	EAS	24	46	0	64.7	65	31	73	7	3.89	6.00	11.4	6.0	7.2	1.5	6.27	-4.5	-8
2002	TOL	INT	25	52	0	67.0	57	35	69	8	4.43	5.22	8.8	5.7	8.0	1.6	4.79	1.2	-2
2002	DET	AL	25	7	0	8.0	14	2	13	1	5.63	6.08	15.0	2.0	13.8	1.0	7.76	-0.6	41

In his third pro season, the 6′ 7″ lefty put in his claim for a situational role, fanning 13 in just eight innings. A 32nd round draft pick in 1999 as a college senior from Illinois State, he should face thin competition this spring for a southpaw relief job. Eckenstahler has an average fastball and a solid breaking pitch, which is enough, though his relative lack of pro experience (only 175.1 innings) means that he'll probably have an extended adjustment period in the majors. Fortunately for him, the Tigers aren't going anywhere soon, so they should have the time to let him learn the ropes.

Jeff Farnsworth   Born: 06-Oct-75   Age: 27   Bats: R   Throws: R

YEAR	TM	LG	AGE	G	GS	IP	H	BB	SO	HR	ERA	EQERA	EQH9	EQBB9	EQSO9	EQHR9	PERA	VORP	STF
2000	NHV	EAS	24	39	8	101.3	91	25	70	6	3.46	4.56	10.4	2.5	4.8	1.0	4.29	9.8	-4
2001	SAN	TXS	25	27	27	155.3	182	47	113	10	4.35	6.32	12.8	3.4	4.8	1.0	6.65	-14.1	-3
2002	DET	AL	26	44	0	70.0	100	29	28	6	5.79	5.59	12.3	3.4	3.5	0.7	6.42	-1.6	-22
2003	*DET*	*AL*	*27*	*33*	*6*	*58.7*	*75*	*23*	*30*	*7*	*5.16*	*5.32*	*11.1*	*3.2*	*4.4*	*1.1*	*5.51*	*3.7*	*-16*

Breakout: 18%   Improve: 50%   Collapse: 18%

A 2001 Rule 5 pick from Seattle, Farnsworth wasn't close to being ready for the majors, as evidenced by the fact that he allowed 100 hits in 70 innings and walked more hitters than he fanned. His development has been retarded after missing almost two whole seasons with an elbow injury, as well as spending a year in big league garbage time when he should have been starting every fifth day in Triple-A. It's highly unlikely he'll spend much time in Detroit this season after being outrighted to Toledo in November and performing poorly in the AFL.

Franklyn German   Born: 20-Jan-80   Age: 23   Bats: R   Throws: R

YEAR	TM	LG	AGE	G	GS	IP	H	BB	SO	HR	ERA	EQERA	EQH9	EQBB9	EQSO9	EQHR9	PERA	VORP	STF
2000	VAN	NWN	20	9	2	20.3	13	10	20	0	1.77	3.65	8.3	5.5	4.6	0.3	4.58	4.0	-7
2000	MOD	CLF	20	17	14	72.0	88	37	52	4	5.50	8.03	14.7	5.2	4.2	1.1	7.90	-20.3	-13
2001	VIS	CLF	21	53	0	63.3	67	31	93	7	3.98	6.06	11.9	5.8	7.7	1.9	7.11	-4.8	-2
2002	MID	TXS	22	37	0	41.3	28	27	59	0	3.05	3.61	6.9	6.9	9.6	0.3	3.64	8.1	19
2002	TOL	INT	22	23	0	22.7	15	7	31	0	1.59	2.16	6.4	3.3	10.3	0.2	2.34	8.1	36
2002	DET	AL	22	7	0	6.7	3	2	6	0	0.00	1.11	3.8	2.6	8.0	0.2	1.24	3.2	26
2003	*DET*	*AL*	*23*	*30*	*0*	*30.7*	*32*	*17*	*28*	*3*	*5.22*	*5.39*	*9.1*	*4.7*	*7.7*	*1.0*	*5.12*	*1.7*	*-2*

Breakout: 13%   Improve: 44%   Collapse: 31%

Part of the booty acquired from Oakland in the Jeff Weaver deal, German began his career as a starter before being converted to relief in 2001. Using mid-1990s heat, a splitter, and a subpar changeup, he blew away hitters in Toledo before earning a promotion to the Tigers in September, where he was likewise impressive. Color him "future closer," as German has a chance to fulfill the high expectations that were awaiting Matt Anderson in Motown for the past few years.

Seth Greisinger — Born: 29-Jul-75 — Age: 27 — Bats: R — Throws: R

YEAR	TM	LG	AGE	G	GS	IP	H	BB	SO	HR	ERA	EQERA	EQH9	EQBB9	EQSO9	EQHR9	PERA	VORP	STF
2002	ERI	EAS	26	4	4	21.0	12	9	21	1	1.29	2.24	6.0	4.6	6.8	0.7	2.60	7.6	14
2002	DET	AL	26	8	8	37.7	46	13	14	4	6.21	5.11	10.6	2.9	3.2	0.9	5.31	1.7	-11
2002	TOL	INT	26	3	3	15.3	15	7	11	0	4.12	4.86	9.7	5.0	5.6	0.2	4.36	1.1	2
2003	DET	AL	27	16	11	69.3	80	30	40	8	5.19	5.35	10.1	3.6	5.0	1.1	5.13	4.1	-5

Breakout: 17%   Improve: 42%   Collapse: 25%

After undergoing Tommy John surgery in 1999, Greisinger did not pitch in 2000 or 2001. Following just four starts in Double-A, he was recalled and made eight starts, six of them ineffective, with Detroit. In June, he went down with a sore shoulder, and with the exception of three Triple-A rehab starts, missed the remainder of the season. He signed a minor league deal with Detroit in December and will attempt to resurrect his star-crossed career.

Oscar Henriquez — Born: 28-Jan-74 — Age: 29 — Bats: R — Throws: R

YEAR	TM	LG	AGE	G	GS	IP	H	BB	SO	HR	ERA	EQERA	EQH9	EQBB9	EQSO9	EQHR9	PERA	VORP	STF
2000	NOR	INT	26	16	0	14.0	12	11	14	2	6.43	6.46	8.7	7.0	7.6	1.6	5.87	-1.7	-16
2001	NOR	INT	27	39	0	38.3	30	19	44	1	2.82	3.99	8.3	5.3	8.2	0.3	3.92	5.9	4
2002	TOL	INT	28	33	0	32.7	30	14	39	4	3.30	4.50	9.3	4.6	9.2	1.6	4.87	3.2	4
2002	DET	AL	28	30	0	28.0	19	15	23	5	4.50	3.66	5.6	4.4	7.1	1.5	3.64	5.4	-3
2003	DET	AL	29	43	0	36.0	38	23	33	4	5.30	5.46	9.1	5.4	8.0	1.1	5.11	3.2	-3

Breakout: 9%   Improve: 40%   Collapse: 26%

Once a highly touted prospect, Henriquez has bounced around a lot in the last few years. Landing in the Tigers bullpen in late June as a setup pitcher, he ultimately underwent an operation on September 20 to remove bone chips from his elbow. If he returns from the surgery without loss of velocity or command, he might have some future left as a middle reliever.

Tim Kalita — Born: 21-Nov-78 — Age: 24 — Bats: R — Throws: L

YEAR	TM	LG	AGE	G	GS	IP	H	BB	SO	HR	ERA	EQERA	EQH9	EQBB9	EQSO9	EQHR9	PERA	VORP	STF
2000	LAK	FSL	21	27	25	149.7	146	73	107	7	4.57	6.37	11.2	5.6	4.6	1.1	5.90	-14.4	-3
2001	ERI	EAS	22	30	29	200.0	190	49	147	25	3.83	5.46	10.8	3.0	4.7	1.8	5.17	1.0	2
2002	TOL	INT	23	15	15	87.7	93	22	47	10	4.93	5.77	10.8	2.8	4.2	1.5	5.07	-2.6	-1

After a terrific 2001 season at Double-A Erie in which he pitched a minor league-high 200 innings, Kalita struggled briefly at Toledo before a strained shoulder shelved him. He did pitch in Arizona in the fall. Kalita has a decent enough fastball and curve to be kept on the Detroit 40-player roster, but he struggles with his command. Assuming his shoulder problems don't become chronic, he should get at least another year in Toledo before being thrown into the fray in Detroit.

Preston Larrison — Born: 19-Nov-80 — Age: 22 — Bats: R — Throws: R

YEAR	TM	LG	AGE	G	GS	IP	H	BB	SO	HR	ERA	EQERA	EQH9	EQBB9	EQSO9	EQHR9	PERA	VORP	STF
2001	ONE	NYP	20	10	8	47.3	37	21	50	1	2.47	5.16	9.2	6.0	5.4	0.7	5.44	1.8	1
2002	LAK	FSL	21	21	19	120.3	86	45	92	6	2.39	4.22	9.3	4.4	5.0	1.1	3.90	17.1	7

A second round pick in 2001, Larrison made only 19 starts in Lakeland last year due to early season shoulder problems. Once he could pitch, he impressed by holding FSL hitters to a .199 batting average, becoming one of the Tigers' top prospects. Larrison depends on his sinking fastball and has a plus changeup but lacks the breaking pitch he'll need to get right-handed hitters out consistently. With only 31 pro games under his belt, it's best not to get too carried away by half a season of dominating a low minor league.

Jose Lima — Born: 30-Sep-72 — Age: 30 — Bats: R — Throws: R

YEAR	TM	LG	AGE	G	GS	IP	H	BB	SO	HR	ERA	EQERA	EQH9	EQBB9	EQSO9	EQHR9	PERA	VORP	STF
2000	HOU	NL	27	33	33	196.3	251	68	124	48	6.65	6.03	10.9	2.5	5.0	1.9	6.38	-11.5	-3
2001	DET	AL	28	18	18	112.7	120	22	43	23	4.71	4.69	9.3	1.7	3.3	1.7	4.78	10.2	-6
2001	HOU	NL	28	14	9	53.0	77	16	41	12	7.30	7.44	13.2	2.5	5.9	1.8	7.27	-11.5	-7
2002	DET	AL	29	20	12	68.3	86	21	33	12	7.77	6.11	10.8	2.6	4.2	1.5	5.88	-4.8	-13
2003	DET	AL	30	24	15	89.7	102	24	48	13	4.76	4.91	9.9	2.2	4.6	1.4	4.70	9.3	-6

Breakout: 31%   Improve: 67%   Collapse: 11%

There will be no more "Lima Time" in Motown, as the Tigers dumped the outspoken veteran in September. His second tour of duty in Detroit netted a 9–16 record in 38 games. The Tigers didn't really want Lima when they dealt for him in June 2001; the trade with Houston for Dave Mlicki was a classic "we'll dump our problem player/contract and hope the other team's problem player/contract will work out." Lima's career started as a good prospect but an underachiever, followed by his shooting star phase in Houston in a pitchers' park, followed by the big fall when the Astros moved into The Ballpark to Be Named Later.

Shane Loux — Born: 31-Aug-79 — Age: 23 — Bats: R — Throws: R

YEAR	TM	LG	AGE	G	GS	IP	H	BB	SO	HR	ERA	EQERA	EQH9	EQBB9	EQSO9	EQHR9	PERA	VORP	STF
2000	JAX	SOU	20	26	26	157.7	150	55	130	12	3.82	5.68	11.4	3.5	5.4	1.4	5.58	-3.1	8
2001	TOL	INT	21	28	27	151.0	203	73	72	22	5.78	7.46	13.5	5.2	3.4	1.8	8.09	-32.8	-16
2002	TOL	INT	22	26	26	158.3	196	38	87	11	4.72	5.91	12.3	2.6	4.3	0.9	5.69	-7.1	3
2002	DET	AL	22	3	3	14.0	19	3	7	4	9.00	7.59	11.7	1.8	4.3	2.4	6.91	-3.2	-7
2003	DET	AL	23	15	10	65.3	84	27	37	8	5.84	6.03	11.2	3.4	4.9	1.2	5.78	-0.8	-7

Breakout: 6%   Improve: 40%   Collapse: 21%

In 1997, Loux was the Tigers' second round pick. He's slowly worked his way up the ladder without impressing, losing some command due to elbow problems along the way, and finally making three poor starts for Detroit in September. His career minor league ERA is 4.52, and hitters have batted well over .300 against him in Triple-A, and those are the guys he's *supposed* to get out. Though Loux has disappointed in his two seasons in Toledo, he's young enough to learn how to pitch. There isn't much of an upside, however.

Mike Maroth — Born: 17-Aug-77 — Age: 25 — Bats: L — Throws: L

YEAR	TM	LG	AGE	G	GS	IP	H	BB	SO	HR	ERA	EQERA	EQH9	EQBB9	EQSO9	EQHR9	PERA	VORP	STF
2000	JAX	SOU	22	27	26	164.3	176	58	85	14	3.94	6.07	13.1	3.6	3.4	1.6	6.55	-10.3	-8
2001	TOL	INT	23	24	23	131.7	158	50	63	11	4.65	5.97	11.8	4.1	3.4	1.0	6.30	-6.8	-10
2002	TOL	INT	24	11	11	73.3	53	22	51	7	2.82	3.43	7.4	3.3	5.4	1.2	3.23	16.9	10
2002	DET	AL	24	21	21	128.7	136	36	58	7	4.48	3.82	9.1	2.4	3.9	0.5	3.91	24.1	6
2003	DET	AL	25	22	17	103.3	123	40	55	12	5.10	5.25	10.4	3.2	4.6	1.1	5.22	6.4	-5

Breakout: 10%   Improve: 42%   Collapse: 20%

In his second season at Triple-A, Maroth went 8–1 in 11 starts before getting the call to Detroit in early June. He spent the remainder of the year in the rotation. His velocity is the typical young finesse lefty average-minus, but his sinker cuts and runs nicely and he will use his cutter in on right-handed hitters. Maroth had a huge home/road split in Comerica in 2002 in the predictable direction. The Tigers were reportedly looking to trade him over the winter.

Jose Paniagua — Born: 20-Aug-73 — Age: 29 — Bats: R — Throws: R

YEAR	TM	LG	AGE	G	GS	IP	H	BB	SO	HR	ERA	EQERA	EQH9	EQBB9	EQSO9	EQHR9	PERA	VORP	STF
2000	SEA	AL	26	69	0	80.3	68	38	71	6	3.47	3.30	7.6	3.5	7.8	0.6	3.29	18.6	9
2001	SEA	AL	27	60	0	66.0	59	38	46	7	4.36	5.04	8.8	5.0	6.0	0.9	4.49	2.5	-10
2002	TOL	INT	28	12	0	15.7	10	4	13	1	1.15	1.94	6.4	2.7	6.3	0.8	2.49	6.0	4
2002	DET	AL	28	41	0	41.7	50	15	34	10	5.83	5.75	10.2	3.0	7.0	2.0	6.19	-1.7	-7
2003	DET	AL	29	41	0	45.7	49	19	35	5	4.28	4.41	9.4	3.5	6.5	1.1	4.72	7.9	-4

Breakout: 19%   Improve: 49%   Collapse: 22%

Not too long ago, Paniagua was one of the better unheralded relievers in the league, but he's lost a lot off his fastball in the last two years. Given an opportunity out of spring training to be the setup reliever in a very favorable environment (pitching in a pitchers' park on a non-contender), he was inconsistent and earned a demotion in July. Recalled in late August, he made five scoreless appearances, and was then racked on September 5 by the Yankees and released two days later. If there is no physical problem that is causing the loss of velocity, he could get another chance in a pitching-poor organization.

Danny Patterson Born: 17-Feb-71 Age: 32 Bats: R Throws: R

YEAR	TM	LG	AGE	G	GS	IP	H	BB	SO	HR	ERA	EQERA	EQH9	EQBB9	EQSO9	EQHR9	PERA	VORP	STF
2000	DET	AL	29	58	0	56.7	69	14	29	4	3.97	3.76	10.4	1.8	4.5	0.5	4.25	10.2	-6
2001	DET	AL	30	60	0	64.7	64	12	27	4	3.06	3.15	8.8	1.6	3.6	0.5	3.38	16.0	-9
2002	TOL	INT	31	5	1	5.0	1	0	3	0	0.00	0.41	2.0	0.5	4.6	0.2	0.39	2.8	7
2002	DET	AL	31	6	0	3.0	5	2	1	0	15.00	9.61	14.2	5.4	2.8	0.2	7.76	-1.4	-40

A torn medial collateral ligament destroyed Patterson's 2002 season, keeping him sidelined for all but six games. Reconstructive elbow surgery performed in late June could keep him out until 2004, the last year of his contract. Pitching on the edge even when he was effective, Patterson is not a good candidate for a comeback and Exhibit 4,782 in the case against long-term deals for fungible relievers.

Matt Perisho Born: 08-Jun-75 Age: 28 Bats: L Throws: L

YEAR	TM	LG	AGE	G	GS	IP	H	BB	SO	HR	ERA	EQERA	EQH9	EQBB9	EQSO9	EQHR9	PERA	VORP	STF
2000	TEX	AL	25	34	13	105.0	136	67	74	20	7.37	6.35	10.1	4.5	5.9	1.4	6.27	-10.4	-8
2001	TOL	INT	26	25	2	42.0	42	11	28	3	1.71	3.27	9.7	2.8	4.7	0.9	4.57	10.0	-8
2001	DET	AL	26	30	4	39.3	54	14	19	5	5.73	6.03	12.0	3.0	4.1	1.1	6.26	-2.7	-20
2002	TOL	INT	27	51	2	66.0	62	19	44	4	2.45	3.64	9.4	3.1	5.1	0.8	4.07	12.9	-7
2002	DET	AL	27	5	0	10.3	16	6	3	2	8.74	8.05	13.1	4.7	2.5	1.6	8.32	-3.1	-40
2003	*TBY*	*AL*	*28*	*24*	*3*	*36.0*	*44*	*17*	*23*	*6*	*5.65*	*5.63*	*10.7*	*3.9*	*5.4*	*1.3*	*5.54*	*2.4*	*-14*

Breakout: 18%   Improve: 42%   Collapse: 37%

In 86 major league games, Perisho has a 4–14 record and a 7.07 ERA, this despite a good arm and four solid pitches. He was converted to relief to try and salvage his career, but it may not work. Signed by Tampa Bay to a minor league deal in November, Perisho will get several more chances to realize his potential.

Adam Pettyjohn Born: 11-Jun-77 Age: 26 Bats: R Throws: L

YEAR	TM	LG	AGE	G	GS	IP	H	BB	SO	HR	ERA	EQERA	EQH9	EQBB9	EQSO9	EQHR9	PERA	VORP	STF
2000	JAX	SOU	23	8	8	50.3	43	12	45	4	3.40	4.62	10.2	2.4	5.8	1.4	4.53	4.9	13
2000	TOL	INT	23	7	7	39.0	45	22	23	5	6.69	6.69	10.7	5.0	4.5	1.4	6.61	-5.1	-8
2001	TOL	INT	24	17	17	107.3	107	26	78	9	3.44	4.51	9.7	2.6	5.1	1.0	4.58	11.9	8
2001	DET	AL	24	16	9	65.0	81	21	40	10	5.82	5.76	10.9	2.7	5.2	1.3	5.70	-2.0	-1

Once considered a good prospect, Pettyjohn underwent major surgery last spring to remove his colon after life-threatening complications with colitis and thus did not pitch at all last season. The Tigers outrighted him in November; it would be a major surprise if he were able to overcome this tragic development.

Brian Powell Born: 10-Oct-73 Age: 29 Bats: R Throws: R

YEAR	TM	LG	AGE	G	GS	IP	H	BB	SO	HR	ERA	EQERA	EQH9	EQBB9	EQSO9	EQHR9	PERA	VORP	STF
2000	NWO	PCL	26	18	18	103.7	103	41	57	9	4.95	5.40	10.4	3.6	4.1	1.1	5.08	1.2	-6
2000	HOU	NL	26	9	5	31.3	34	13	14	8	5.75	5.28	9.2	3.0	3.5	2.0	5.69	0.7	-20
2001	NWO	PCL	27	24	23	144.7	142	39	96	13	3.17	4.81	10.4	3.0	4.5	1.0	4.80	11.1	0
2002	TOL	INT	28	20	20	119.3	127	26	82	8	3.92	4.66	10.6	2.4	5.3	0.9	4.58	11.2	7
2002	DET	AL	28	13	9	57.7	64	21	30	11	4.84	4.82	9.5	3.0	4.5	1.6	5.40	4.3	-8
2003	*DET*	*AL*	*29*	*20*	*13*	*77.3*	*92*	*30*	*45*	*10*	*5.02*	*5.17*	*10.4*	*3.2*	*5.0*	*1.3*	*5.22*	*7.3*	*-6*

Breakout: 17%   Improve: 43%   Collapse: 27%

Originally a Tigers' farmhand, Powell spent three years in the Houston organization before returning as a free agent in November 2001. After going 10–3 in 20 starts at Toledo, the Tigers brought him up in late July, and he was bombed in six of his first nine big league starts. Sort of like Jason Beverlin, there are some minor league veterans who get that way for a reason. He has no future.

Mark Redman   Born: 05-Jan-74   Age: 29   Bats: L   Throws: L

YEAR	TM	LG	AGE	G	GS	IP	H	BB	SO	HR	ERA	EQERA	EQH9	EQBB9	EQSO9	EQHR9	PERA	VORP	STF
2000	MIN	AL	26	32	24	151.3	168	45	117	22	4.76	3.91	9.0	2.1	6.7	1.1	4.18	26.6	13
2001	TOL	INT	27	3	3	13.7	14	1	12	3	5.26	5.99	10.4	0.8	6.2	2.7	5.28	-0.7	1
2001	MIN	AL	27	9	9	49.0	57	19	29	6	4.22	4.80	10.3	3.3	5.0	1.0	5.02	3.8	0
2002	DET	AL	28	30	30	203.0	211	51	109	15	4.21	3.80	9.0	2.1	4.7	0.6	3.87	38.5	8
2003	FLO	NL	29	26	24	159.0	167	46	95	17	4.17	4.63	9.7	2.3	4.7	1.1	4.56	15.7	4

Breakout: 6%   Improve: 42%   Collapse: 18%

Perhaps the Tigers' only truly effective starter in 2002, Redman led the team in most categories and showed surprising ability in the first half. He fell apart beginning on August 12; in his last seven starts, he allowed 37 earned runs in 39.2 innings (8.39 ERA). Detroit claimed Redman had a tired arm. Even if that's so, Redman is a lefty with average velocity, good movement on his fastball, and a good turned-over change. If he can make the required adjustments, he might have a prosperous career somewhere else. Peddled to the Marlins, where he'll be the token grownup in the rotation.

Fernando Rodney   Born: 18-Mar-77   Age: 26   Bats: R   Throws: R

YEAR	TM	LG	AGE	G	GS	IP	H	BB	SO	HR	ERA	EQERA	EQH9	EQBB9	EQSO9	EQHR9	PERA	VORP	STF
2000	WMI	MDW	23	22	10	82.7	74	35	56	2	2.94	6.57	13.3	5.0	4.1	0.6	5.91	-10.1	-13
2001	LAK	FSL	24	16	9	55.3	53	19	44	2	3.42	5.83	11.8	3.8	4.9	0.8	5.29	-2.2	-6
2002	ERI	EAS	25	21	0	20.3	14	5	18	0	1.33	2.14	6.9	2.6	5.9	0.2	2.32	7.3	5
2002	TOL	INT	25	20	0	22.3	13	9	25	1	0.81	2.26	5.8	4.4	8.6	0.6	2.52	7.7	15
2002	DET	AL	25	20	0	18.0	25	10	10	2	6.00	6.44	12.0	4.6	4.8	0.9	6.81	-2.1	-20
2003	DET	AL	26	36	0	38.7	43	18	28	3	4.75	4.90	9.7	3.9	6.1	0.8	4.86	4.3	-7

Breakout: 20%   Improve: 53%   Collapse: 23%

Rodney throws up to 98, but the pitch has little movement, and he does have a slider and good changeup. Last year he was on the yo-yo, spending four separate stints with the Tigers, and predictably had problems with consistency. He pitched better in September, but his serious shortage of high-level experience (only 67 IP above A-ball) means he'll need at least another year before he can be expected to get big league hitters out.

Julio Santana   Born: 20-Jan-74   Age: 29   Bats: R   Throws: R

YEAR	TM	LG	AGE	G	GS	IP	H	BB	SO	HR	ERA	EQERA	EQH9	EQBB9	EQSO9	EQHR9	PERA	VORP	STF
2000	PAW	INT	27	12	12	65.0	61	23	55	7	4.71	4.82	9.5	3.2	6.5	1.2	4.49	4.9	9
2000	MON	NL	27	36	4	66.7	69	33	58	11	5.67	4.88	8.7	3.5	6.8	1.3	5.05	4.0	-2
2001	FRE	PCL	28	25	25	132.7	160	50	125	28	5.83	6.68	11.8	4.0	6.2	2.2	6.64	-17.3	-5
2002	TOL	INT	29	7	0	12.7	12	3	12	1	2.13	4.11	9.5	2.6	7.3	1.0	4.06	1.8	6
2002	DET	AL	29	38	0	57.0	49	28	38	8	2.84	3.20	7.3	4.1	5.8	1.2	4.14	13.8	-6
2003	DET	AL	29	26	4	45.7	50	22	33	6	4.73	4.88	9.5	4.0	6.3	1.3	5.15	5.7	-7

Breakout: 19%   Improve: 46%   Collapse: 23%

After pitching surprisingly well for the Tigers as a middle reliever, Santana began to decline in effectiveness in late July. A month later, he was officially shut down with a torn ulnar collateral ligament in his pitching elbow, which kept him out for the rest of the year even though he did not undergo surgery. Detroit designated him for assignment in December; the much-traveled Santana is probably finished as a big leaguer.

Steve Sparks   Born: 02-Jul-65   Age: 38   Bats: R   Throws: R

YEAR	TM	LG	AGE	G	GS	IP	H	BB	SO	HR	ERA	EQERA	EQH9	EQBB9	EQSO9	EQHR9	PERA	VORP	STF
2000	TOL	INT	35	16	14	90.7	86	41	44	8	3.77	4.55	8.7	4.0	3.7	1.0	4.70	9.6	-8
2000	DET	AL	35	20	15	104.0	108	29	53	7	4.07	3.66	8.9	2.1	4.5	0.5	3.49	21.2	6
2001	DET	AL	36	35	33	232.0	244	64	116	22	3.65	3.94	9.2	2.3	4.3	0.8	4.15	40.3	3
2002	DET	AL	37	32	30	189.0	238	67	98	23	5.52	5.37	10.9	3.0	4.5	1.0	5.64	2.8	-1
2003	DET	AL	37	26	22	137.0	162	46	69	15	4.84	4.99	10.4	2.8	4.4	1.1	5.02	11.7	-3

Breakout: 15%   Improve: 42%   Collapse: 14%

The aging knuckleballer took the ball when asked but was only sporadically effective, as he had 10 outings last year in which he allowed five or more earned runs. Still, even at this depressed level of performance, Sparks tied for the club lead in wins with eight, which tells you all about the '02 Bengals. Aside from the congenital problems of all knuckleballers (control and getting hit hard when his *mariposa* doesn't flutter), he has two specific problems: not much difference between his regular knuckler and his off-speed knuckler, and no slider to help out his minus fastball when he can't get his floater over the plate. Sparks has had two other seasons as bad as last year (1996 in Milwaukee and 1999 in Anaheim) and was able to bounce back both times.

Andy Van Hekken   Born: 31-Jul-79   Age: 23   Bats: R   Throws: L

YEAR	TM	LG	AGE	G	GS	IP	H	BB	SO	HR	ERA	EQERA	EQH9	EQBB9	EQSO9	EQHR9	PERA	VORP	STF
2000	WMI	MDW	20	26	25	158.0	139	37	126	3	2.45	5.23	12.7	2.7	4.8	0.5	4.87	4.8	11
2001	LAK	FSL	21	19	19	110.7	105	33	82	8	3.17	5.38	12.4	3.4	4.7	1.7	5.40	1.5	3
2001	ERI	EAS	21	8	8	48.0	63	8	29	5	4.69	7.04	14.7	2.1	3.9	1.5	7.08	-8.2	-1
2002	ERI	EAS	22	21	21	134.0	138	34	97	10	3.83	4.88	10.9	2.7	5.0	1.1	4.74	9.3	9
2002	TOL	INT	22	7	7	49.3	41	11	19	4	1.83	3.27	8.5	2.5	3.0	1.1	3.46	12.2	0
2002	DET	AL	22	5	5	30.0	38	6	5	2	3.00	3.85	11.0	1.7	1.5	0.6	4.83	5.5	-8
2003	DET	AL	23	19	16	93.0	116	31	49	11	5.31	5.47	10.9	2.8	4.6	1.2	5.45	3.5	-5

Breakout: 9%   *Improve: 47%*   *Collapse: 20%*

Van Hekken was recalled in September after spending most of the year in Erie and then posting a 5–0 record in seven Triple-A starts. He throws a below-average fastball that sinks and moves around effectively. His curve is sharp, but he doesn't always have command of it. After throwing a shutout in his major league debut, he was increasingly less effective as he faced more hitters. The Tigers piled a career-high 213.1 innings through three levels on his arm last year, and his velocity was down to the mid-80s or below at the end of the season. He should be able to make the changes he needs to be effective as he gains more experience in Triple-A and/or the majors, assuming no arm problems. That's a big assumption after a yearlong run at the Terry Francona School of Pitching Instruction.

Jamie Walker   Born: 01-Jul-71   Age: 32   Bats: L   Throws: L

YEAR	TM	LG	AGE	G	GS	IP	H	BB	SO	HR	ERA	EQERA	EQH9	EQBB9	EQSO9	EQHR9	PERA	VORP	STF
2000	OMA	PCL	29	24	15	101.7	138	25	52	25	5.22	6.89	14.5	2.3	3.9	2.9	7.69	-15.9	-23
2001	BUF	INT	30	38	8	93.0	104	27	51	12	3.87	5.61	11.9	3.2	4.0	1.6	5.95	-1.8	-20
2002	TOL	INT	31	10	0	13.7	7	3	9	2	1.97	2.39	5.6	2.4	5.2	1.9	2.34	4.6	-7
2002	DET	AL	31	57	0	43.7	32	9	40	9	3.71	3.17	6.2	1.7	8.0	1.7	3.16	10.7	9
2003	DET	AL	31	58	0	43.7	48	13	31	7	4.86	5.01	9.7	2.5	6.1	1.6	4.92	3.8	-8

Breakout: 16%   *Improve: 47%*   *Collapse: 24%*

The Tigers are his fifth organization. Walker pitched 57 times last year in relief after his promotion from Toledo, and he was surprisingly impressive. Lefties hit only .202 against him, but they did club seven home runs in just 89 at-bats, a vulnerability that he also displayed in Triple-A in the past. If Walker doesn't learn how to retire LHBs reliably, he's not going to acquire much more service time.

Kansas City Royals

So this is what the abyss looks like. After eight straight losing seasons, the Royals are still heading backward and downward. In 2002, the franchise reached depths not seen in Kansas City since the A's left town, as the highest-paid team in franchise history also became its first to lose a hundred games.

Only one man in the organization has the vision to turn things around. Only one man has shown the willingness to discard a team philosophy unchanged since the 1985 World Series even as it became more outdated than the waterbed. Only one man is willing to consider that the same ideas which have worked in Oakland and New York might apply in Kansas City as well.

That man is the same man who traded Jermaine Dye for Neifi Perez, who traded Johnny Damon for Roberto Hernandez, and oh-by-the-way tossed in Mark Ellis to seal the deal for Angel Berroa. The same man who stuck by Tony Muser longer than any other person of sound mind would have. The same man who guaranteed Brent Mayne $5 million over two years but who then found A. J. Hinch's $260,000 salary too pricey for his tastes.

You see the problem here.

Allard Baird is not the worst GM in baseball. On the contrary, he has shown flashes of insight unseen in a Kansas City front office since the days of Cedric Tallis. To quote Bill James, Baird "seems like a very sharp kind of guy." Like a five-tool talent who whets the scouts' appetite with his potential, Baird can make good things happen when he gets a hold of an idea.

Baird promised to make plate discipline a priority in his administration. In so doing, he was bucking a Kansas City tradition as enduring as barbecue. Between 1980 and 2001, the Royals finished among the bottom five teams in the AL in walks drawn every year but one (1989, when not coincidentally they won 92 games, their most in that span). They finished among the bottom three teams in walks 13 times in

those 22 years. In 2001, Baird's first full season at the helm, the Royals again finished dead last in walks, with just 406, their lowest full-season total since 1984. Last season, they increased their walk total to 524, eighth in the league, their second-best showing since the 1970s. And it wasn't a fluke. It was a direct mandate from Baird, a mandate that began tepidly in spring training when he stated, "We're going to have to run deeper counts, be willing to walk, add speed and utilize speed because we're not going to get a whole lot of three-run home runs." That philosophy was a decent rough draft, although linking the importance of OBP to speed on the base paths led to disastrous moves like the Chuck Knoblauch signing. As the season progressed, that emphasis on speed lessened even as the focus on reaching base intensified.

Complicating this about-face was the fact that the old guard, the cadre of coaches employed by the Royals for years, was reluctant to go along with the push for more patience at the plate. So Baird fired some of them, including hitting coach Lamar Johnson, at the end of the season. He then replaced Johnson with Jeff Pentland, the former Cubs' hitting coach widely credited with turning Sammy Sosa from a clueless hacker into the disciplined offensive machine he is today. As Baird said, "I think the compatibility of what Jeff Pentland brings and what we want—running deep counts, getting in good offensive counts, getting walks—his record speaks for itself." It certainly does: the Cubs, who before Pentland were almost as impatient as the Royals, finished in the top six in the NL in walks drawn in four of his five years there. The impact of Pentland's aggressive pitch to instill plate discipline cannot be underestimated. Flipping the Royals from the bottom third of the league in walks to the top third should be worth, conservatively, 50 to 75 runs, or five to seven wins. There aren't many ways a GM can improve his ball club more than that.

Royals Prospectus

2002 record: 62–100; Fourth place, AL Central

Pythagenport Record: 66–96

Runs scored per game: 4.5 (11th in AL)

Runs allowed per game: 5.5 (13th in AL)

Team EqA: .242 (13th in AL)

2002 Batters Age: 29.7 (6th oldest in AL)

2002 Pitchers Age: 27.9 (5th youngest in AL)

Ballpark: Kauffman Stadium; Severe hitters' park; Park Factor of 1.089

2002: They may not have bottomed out yet, but at least they'll be 100% Neifi-free.

2003: If nothing else, they should finally be taking a look at the talent they've developed.

Baird's other major contribution to the Royals has been his aggressive pursuit of talent on the "free" market, the dustbin of players available to any major league team for little more than the price of a waiver claim. Before the 2002 season, Baird signed Rontrez Johnson and Donzell McDonald as minor league free agents, and Tydus Meadows as a minor league Rule 5 pick; all three of them are outfielders with offensive skills unappreciated by their former teams, and all three might have a major league future. In the real Rule 5 draft, Baird snatched one of the clear prizes in Miguel Ascencio, whom Baseball America had ranked as the Phillies' #5 prospect, and who spent much of the season as the youngest starter in the American League. Baird also signed Aaron Guiel out of the Mexican League. He signed Darrell May out of Japan and gave him a guaranteed major league contract even though he hadn't pitched in the Western Hemisphere in five years. The Royals' international scouting efforts were beefed up to the point where they signed pitcher Barry Armitage out of that noted baseball hotbed, South Africa. Armitage made the South Atlantic League's All-Star team last year.

The acquisition of quality minor league free agents continued unabated this off-season, led by the signing of Jarrod Patterson, a candidate to play third for the Ken Phelps All-Star Team. Patterson could start for the Royals this year if Joe Randa is traded by the time you read this, and if things break his way, he could fit comfortably in the middle of the pack among AL third basemen. Baird also pulled another promising arm out of the Rule 5 draft this winter with the selection of Danny Carrasco. The Royals have also taken advantage of the untapped talent in their own farm system, converting Jeremy Hill from catcher to pitcher two winters ago. Their success with Hill, who is part of the team's bullpen plans for this year, emboldened the team to try no fewer than three other failed position player prospects on the mound last summer.

In comparison to the tenure of Herk Robinson, who in 10 years as GM never attended a minor league game, Baird's attention to scouting and development is refreshing.

So how did the Royals lose 100 games? Because, to finish Bill James's thought, "Allard Baird seems like a very sharp kind of guy to me. But it's like a very sharp knife that for some reason won't cut butter." Baird's moves are one part Marilyn vos Savant, two parts idiot savant. For every transaction in which he acquires a player for free, there's one in which he releases a more talented player for no reason. A. J. Hinch was the Royals' best catcher last season, and made barely one-tenth of Brent Mayne's salary. He wasn't even arbitration-eligible, yet he was released for the stated reason of making room on the 40-man roster, even though one of those open roster spots would have to go to a backup catcher anyway.

For every Miguel Ascencio that Baird grabs in the Rule 5 draft, he fails to protect a Corey Thurman, a more polished prospect who made the greatest contribution of any Rule 5 pick last season. For every player that benefits from Baird's newfound zeal for plate discipline, there's a better player that Baird trades away for peanuts. Raul Ibanez's maturation into a dangerous hitter can hardly make up for trading Johnny Damon for Roberto Hernandez. It certainly doesn't qualify as penance for trading Jermaine Dye for the scourge of modern civilization. (When an analyst who follows the Royals called Billy Beane the night before the Neifi Perez trade to discuss an unrelated issue, Beane told him to call back later. "I'm working on a trade right now," Beane said, "and when you hear about it, it's going to kill you.")

Yet Baird's trading record, as chilling as it is, is not the fault that most characterizes his administration. It's his inability to comprehend the fundamental principle of baseball economics. As Bill Veeck said decades ago, "It isn't the high price of stars that is expensive, it's the high price of mediocrity." Baird has spent as much money on mediocrity as any GM in baseball.

There's the money spent on Roberto Hernandez, who disregarding his thoroughly, predictably disappointing performance, was paid $12 million for 120 innings of work as a closer on a last-place team, which made him about as useful as a radar detector on a tricycle. There's the money spent on Neifi Perez, who earned almost as much in his time with the Royals as Dye would have. There's the $5.5 million over two years blown on Brent Mayne, the $5 million wasted on Michael Tucker, and the $2 million thrown at Chuck Knoblauch. That's $16.8 million last year alone, over a third of the Royals' payroll, that would have served the team better if they had lit the money on fire as part of a ballpark promotion.

As the Dodgers and Red Sox can attest, not even large-revenue teams can afford to flush 35% of their payroll down the toilet. For a team playing in the smallest metropolitan market in the league, spending 35% of your payroll on a bunch of stiffs is the quickest route from here to disaster.

But what was a disaster is now an opportunity for Baird to make amends. Owner David Glass's Scroogian insistence that the payroll be slashed to $37 million (less even than that of the ward of MLB, the Expos) may inadvertently prove a boon to the franchise. Baird, forced to make deep cuts to his squad, has found it a lot easier than he thought to separate all the fat on his roster from the flesh.

Hernandez was let go, without offer of arbitration. Knoblauch was not invited back. Perez was mercifully released. There's nothing that can be done about Mayne and Tucker for another year, but in the meantime the Royals have been exploring the trade market for Joe Randa, who while not nearly as useless as the other veterans shown the door, is nearly as overpaid. Even Jeff Suppan was expected to be cut if Paul Byrd had re-signed, and got cut anyway when Byrd fled to Atlanta.

The exodus of veterans not only diverts money to other, more deserving players. It also opens opportunities for them to perform, particularly on the pitching staff. Last year's Royals became just the third non-strike team since 1901 to go an entire season with just two pitchers winning five or more games. With Hernandez gone, Jason Grimsley is left to baby-sit a bullpen that might be the most inexperienced in base-ball, but also one with more promise than Royals pens of late. Rule 5'er Carrasco could be the soft-tosser by default in a bullpen that includes Hill, Ryan Bukvich, and Mike Mac-Dougal, a trio with 59 innings of combined major league experience who all throw 95 or more. The Royals could start the season with 22-year-old Miguel Ascencio, 23-year-old Jeremy Affeldt, and 24-year-old Runelvys Hernandez in the rotation. Add in Jimmy Gobble and Kyle Snyder, and by mid-season they could conceivably run with an entirely 25-and-under rotation.

Tony Pena can hardly be defended as the team's best choice to replace Tony Muser, not when Buck Showalter was there for the asking. But Pena's most obvious skill during his three years as a Triple-A manager was his ability to mold a collection of young hurlers into a workable pitching staff, sort of a poor man's Felipe Alou. The raw talent at his disposal this season is certainly comparable to some of Alou's finer staffs in Montreal.

The main obstacle keeping this youth movement from reaching full steam is that the Royals' predilection for pitch-ers in the draft—they haven't taken a hitter in the first round in seven years—has left the organization strapped of potential impact hitting prospects. The team is operating as if last sea-son's struggles never happened to Angel Berroa, all but hand-ing him the starting shortstop job before spring training opens. At least there's potential for improvement at shortstop; behind the plate, the Royals are content to go with Brent Mayne and a backup whose main qualification appears to be making Mayne look good by comparison.

The long-term contract negotiations with Carlos Beltran complicate everything. Beltran is the most talented all-around player the franchise has developed in a generation, and if there's any way to sign him past his initial free agency years, the Royals have to pursue it. Unfortunately, the Royals are becoming increasingly convinced that Beltran will have to sign over Scott Boras's dead body, and have begun to explore his trade value. Losing him would be a huge blow to the credi-bility of a franchise still struggling to live down the embarrass-ment of the Damon and Dye trades, but the potential to snag two or three top-tier hitting prospects and add afterburners to the team's youth movement cannot be ignored.

They say it is always darkest before the dawn. The prob-lem is that there's no way to tell whether now is that darkest hour, only that it's darker than it has ever been before. This year we'll see whether a thread of light appears on the hori-zon in the form of a full-blown, no-holds-barred youth move-ment—the kind the Royals should have engaged in years ago—or whether there's still another level of hopelessness that the Royals haven't reached yet.

HITTERS

Luis Alicea — 2B — Born: 29-Jul-65 — Age: 37 — Bats: B — Throws: R

YEAR	TM	LG	AGE	AB	H	2B	3B	HR	BB	SO	SB	CS	AVG	OBP	SLG	MLVR	EQBA	EQOBP	EQSLG	EQMLVR	VORP	DEFENSE			
2000	TEX	AL	34	540	159	25	8	6	59	75	1	3	.294	.369	.404	-.019	.297	.365	.410	.026	32.6	118-2B -13			
2001	KCR	AL	35	387	106	16	4	4	23	56	8	6	.274	.321	.367	-.115	.282	.329	.381	-.094	11.8	60-2B 1	13-3B -1		
2002	KCR	AL	36	237	54	8	2	1	32	34	2	3	.228	.322	.291	-.226	.241	.333	.312	-.210	-1.4	20-3B -4	28-2B 5		
2003	KCR	AL	37	187	47	9	1	2	18	29	2	1	.252	.321	.337	-.133	.249	.320	.334	-.189	-2.9				

Breakout: 28%   Improve: 52%   Collapse: 21%

A useful bench player at his peak, Alicea was decidedly off-peak during his two years with the Royals. He earned his keep by working with Carlos Beltran on a series of hitting drills—like swinging one-handed to gain bat control—that Beltran credits with his turnaround after the 2001 All-Star break. This is the kind of Latin influence the Royals need, not Neifi Perez distract-ing Carlos Febles with daily card games. After a nice 13-year career, Alicea has come to the end of the road.

Carlos Beltran — CF — Born: 24-Apr-77 — Age: 26 — Bats: B — Throws: R

YEAR	TM	LG	AGE	AB	H	2B	3B	HR	BB	SO	SB	CS	AVG	OBP	SLG	MLVR	EQBA	EQOBP	EQSLG	EQMLVR	VORP	DEFENSE
2000	KCR	AL	23	372	92	15	4	7	35	69	13	0	.247	.312	.366	-.223	.250	.307	.370	-.175	.4	86-CF 0
2001	KCR	AL	24	617	189	32	12	24	52	120	31	1	.306	.365	.514	.185	.317	.377	.537	.247	68.1	152-CF 4
2002	KCR	AL	25	637	174	44	7	29	71	135	35	7	.273	.350	.501	.119	.284	.360	.526	.168	58.3	148-CF 5
2003	KCR	AL	26	594	166	35	6	26	63	121	29	9	.279	.351	.488	.127	.276	.350	.484	.080	32.6	

Breakout: 6%   Improve: 43%   Collapse: 10%

One of the 10 most valuable commodities in baseball. Beltran let his batting average slip last year, but he set career highs in home runs (29), walks (71), and stolen bases (35). His career 87.2% stolen base percentage is the major league record (min: 100 attempts). He played in every game last year and has been on the DL once in his career. He quietly set the AL record for extra-base hits by a switch-hitter (80). In short, there's nothing he can't do. Only one switch-hitting center fielder in history hit more home runs before age 26 than Beltran: Mickey Mantle.

Signing Beltran to a long-term contract is absolutely the Royals' #1 priority this winter. To their credit, the Royals initiated discussion with Beltran's agent; unfortunately, that agent is Scott Boras, who responded with such a counteroffer (somewhere around 8 years, $130 million) intended to make it perfectly clear that Beltran has no intention of staying in KC a moment longer than he has to. Naturally, the Royals are now exploring offers for Carlos Beltran in trade. Given his youth, talent, and time until free agency, it's clear that Baird should fetch a considerable amount for Beltran. But the next time Baird gets fair value for one of his stars will be the first.

Brandon Berger — LF — Born: 21-Feb-75 — Age: 28 — Bats: R — Throws: R

YEAR	TM	LG	AGE	AB	H	2B	3B	HR	BB	SO	SB	CS	AVG	OBP	SLG	MLVR	EQBA	EQOBP	EQSLG	EQMLVR	VORP	DEFENSE
2000	WIL	CRL	25	379	108	18	4	15	40	71	12	4	.285	.378	.472	.242	.240	.302	.398	-.152	-6.5	100-LF -7
2000	WIC	TXS	25	86	14	2	0	3	7	27	6	1	.163	.242	.291	-.440	.149	.197	.264	-.596	-11.0	15-LF -1
2001	WIC	TXS	26	454	140	28	3	40	43	91	14	6	.308	.386	.648	.451	.258	.320	.531	.081	19.9	77-OF -5
2002	OMA	PCL	27	261	76	16	1	13	25	43	11	2	.291	.364	.510	.197	.263	.330	.454	-.004	5.6	52-LF 0
2002	KCR	AL	27	134	27	5	1	6	8	32	1	0	.201	.257	.388	-.237	.209	.262	.410	-.234	-5.3	30-RF 1
2003	*KCR*	*AL*	*28*	*215*	*55*	*12*	*1*	*9*	*16*	*45*	*4*	*3*	*.255*	*.314*	*.452*	*.003*	*.251*	*.314*	*.447*	*-.050*	*-1.0*	

Breakout: 15%   Improve: 51%   Collapse: 27%

Berger emerged from obscurity with a 40-home run season in the Texas League in 2001, and did his best last year to prove that his power surge wasn't a fluke, although difficulty making contact cost him at the major league level. His ability to mash lefties (career .508 SLG against southpaws) makes him a useful fifth outfielder. His upside is Shane Spencer.

Angel Berroa — SS — Born: 27-Jan-78 — Age: 25 — Bats: R — Throws: R

YEAR	TM	LG	AGE	AB	H	2B	3B	HR	BB	SO	SB	CS	AVG	OBP	SLG	MLVR	EQBA	EQOBP	EQSLG	EQMLVR	VORP	DEFENSE
2000	VIS	CLF	22	429	119	25	6	10	30	70	11	9	.277	.339	.434	.064	.218	.252	.343	-.341	-12.8	120-SS -27
2001	WIL	CRL	23	199	63	18	4	6	9	41	10	6	.317	.387	.538	.389	.262	.308	.456	-.042	9.0	51-SS -5
2001	WIC	TXS	23	304	90	20	4	8	17	55	15	6	.296	.376	.467	.180	.256	.312	.410	-.105	8.6	78-SS -2
2001	KCR	AL	23	53	16	2	0	0	3	10	2	0	.302	.339	.340	-.101	.321	.357	.358	-.045	2.3	12-SS 0
2002	OMA	PCL	24	297	64	11	4	8	15	84	6	4	.215	.279	.360	-.222	.199	.251	.330	-.372	-11.2	77-SS 1
2002	KCR	AL	24	75	17	7	1	0	7	10	3	0	.227	.301	.347	-.195	.240	.312	.373	-.168	1.0	20-SS 2
2003	*KCR*	*AL*	*25*	*320*	*80*	*18*	*2*	*7*	*18*	*63*	*8*	*5*	*.249*	*.297*	*.390*	*-.109*	*.246*	*.296*	*.386*	*-.166*	*-.4*	

Breakout: 32%   Improve: 61%   Collapse: 17%

Let's see: the Royals' best prospect entering the season injured his knee and missed two months, hit .215 in Omaha after he returned, showed vastly diminished range, and drew six walks by the end of July. On the plus side, he did celebrate three birthdays last year. No, it was not a good year for Berroa. His apologists argue that he continued to favor his knee when he got back, which hurt him both offensively and defensively. In their support, he looked much more comfortable both at bat and in the field during a September call-up. The Royals are determined to let him take over as the starting shortstop this season, and given that he turns 25 in April, they might as well see if he'll sink or swim. There's upside here, but right now Billy Beane wouldn't trade Mark Ellis for him straight up.

Dee Brown — LF — Born: 27-Mar-78 — Age: 25 — Bats: L — Throws: R

YEAR	TM	LG	AGE	AB	H	2B	3B	HR	BB	SO	SB	CS	AVG	OBP	SLG	MLVR	EQBA	EQOBP	EQSLG	EQMLVR	VORP	DEFENSE
2000	OMA	PCL	22	479	129	25	6	23	37	112	20	3	.269	.326	.491	.032	.243	.286	.439	-.122	-4.2	110-LF -8
2001	KCR	AL	23	380	93	19	0	7	22	81	5	3	.245	.288	.350	-.217	.253	.297	.367	-.196	-10.4	78-LF -2
2002	OMA	PCL	24	458	126	23	1	17	44	111	10	4	.275	.346	.441	.057	.249	.313	.399	-.124	-4.2	77-LF -3
2002	KCR	AL	24	51	12	3	1	1	4	20	0	0	.235	.291	.392	-.150	.255	.309	.412	-.108	.3	
2003	*KCR*	*AL*	*25*	*271*	*72*	*15*	*2*	*10*	*22*	*57*	*4*	*4*	*.266*	*.324*	*.447*	*.021*	*.263*	*.323*	*.442*	*-.031*	*-.2*	

Breakout: 42%   Improve: 64%   Collapse: 21%

Despite his pedigree and a veneer of self-assurance, Brown is plagued by insecurity. After he was sent to Omaha at the end of spring training, he seemed to give up on himself. He found himself in the second half of the season, hitting .315 and slugging

Dee Brown (*continued*)

558 from July 1st on. He has gone on record as saying that now that he is out of options and no longer has to worry about being demoted, he feels much more secure at the plate. He better hope that security will help him regain his plate discipline. In his breakout season of 1999, Brown walked 79 times; he hasn't walked even 50 times since.

David DeJesus   CF   **Born: 20-Dec-79**   **Age: 23**   **Bats: L**   **Throws: L**

YEAR	TM	LG	AGE	AB	H	2B	3B	HR	BB	SO	SB	CS	AVG	OBP	SLG	MLVR	EQBA	EQOBP	EQSLG	EQMLVR	VORP		DEFENSE
2002	WIL	CRL	22	334	99	22	6	4	48	42	15	6	.296	.405	.434	.236	.243	.328	.364	-.148	2.9		73-CF -4
2002	WIC	TXS	22	79	20	5	2	2	8	10	3	1	.253	.359	.443	.119	.225	.308	.387	-.167	.3		20-CF -2
2003	*KCR*	*AL*	*23*	*188*	*50*	*11*	*2*	*4*	*18*	*30*	*4*	*3*	*.265*	*.338*	*.411*	*-.003*	*.262*	*.337*	*.407*	*-.054*	*3.2*		

Breakout: 28%   Improve: 61%   Collapse: 17%

Call him Terry Wetzel's going-away present. Baird's first significant move after he was hired as GM in 2000 was to fire Wetzel as scouting director, even though Wetzel had presided over four productive drafts in a row. Drafted in the fourth round that year, DeJesus didn't make his pro debut until last April following a broken elbow and Tommy John surgery. He was so shook up by 18 months of inactivity that he posted a .400 OBP in hitter's hell at Wilmington, then moved up and hit well in the Texas League playoffs. He did wear down after a hot start in the AFL, but still finished with a .365 OBP. He's not particularly young, and some scouts worry that he's too small to hang in against major league pitching. But the Royals love his swing, and if he can build on his debut performance, he could quickly emerge as a leadoff hitter for a team that desperately needs one.

Carlos Febles   2B   **Born: 24-May-76**   **Age: 27**   **Bats: R**   **Throws: R**

YEAR	TM	LG	AGE	AB	H	2B	3B	HR	BB	SO	SB	CS	AVG	OBP	SLG	MLVR	EQBA	EQOBP	EQSLG	EQMLVR	VORP		DEFENSE
2000	KCR	AL	24	339	87	12	1	2	36	48	17	6	.257	.345	.316	-.220	.257	.338	.316	-.185	2.6		89-2B 5
2001	OMA	PCL	25	98	33	7	1	2	9	14	6	2	.337	.414	.490	.274	.296	.365	.439	.066	7.2		22-2B 3
2001	KCR	AL	25	292	69	9	2	8	22	58	5	2	.236	.292	.363	-.197	.244	.301	.381	-.175	3.0		69-2B 8
2002	OMA	PCL	26	54	12	2	1	1	4	5	2	1	.222	.288	.352	-.211	.204	.266	.315	-.360	-2.0		12-2B 2
2002	KCR	AL	26	351	86	16	4	4	41	63	16	5	.245	.336	.348	-.121	.256	.345	.368	-.101	10.7		100-2B 9
2003	*KCR*	*AL*	*27*	*258*	*65*	*12*	*2*	*5*	*25*	*45*	*8*	*3*	*.250*	*.322*	*.366*	*-.095*	*.247*	*.322*	*.363*	*-.149*	*.9*		

Breakout: 14%   Improve: 50%   Collapse: 25%

The enigma continues. For the first time in his career, Febles made it through a season without injury, which would be cause for celebration except that, after hitting just .245 with a .348 slugging average, it's an open question whether his frequent DL stints have permanently eroded his skills. For the second straight year, a strong finish has made it difficult for the Royals to give up on him entirely. He still plays good defense, still runs well, and there are still no ready alternatives in the system. The Royals could do a lot worse than to give Febles one more shot to regain his 1999 form, like moving Michael Tucker to second.

Alexis Gomez   CF   **Born: 06-Aug-80**   **Age: 22**   **Bats: L**   **Throws: L**

YEAR	TM	LG	AGE	AB	H	2B	3B	HR	BB	SO	SB	CS	AVG	OBP	SLG	MLVR	EQBA	EQOBP	EQSLG	EQMLVR	VORP		DEFENSE
2000	WIL	CRL	19	461	117	13	4	1	45	121	21	10	.254	.323	.306	-.079	.218	.266	.263	-.425	-30.3		119-CF -16
2001	WIL	CRL	20	169	51	8	2	1	11	43	7	3	.302	.348	.391	.140	.257	.299	.337	-.232	-2.4		47-CF -4
2001	WIC	TXS	20	342	96	15	6	4	27	70	16	10	.281	.340	.395	.012	.235	.285	.334	-.278	-8.7		83-CF -2
2002	WIC	TXS	21	461	136	21	8	14	45	84	36	24	.295	.361	.466	.189	.247	.302	.397	-.149	3.7		110-CF -8
2003	*KCR*	*AL*	*22*	*207*	*53*	*11*	*2*	*5*	*15*	*42*	*6*	*4*	*.258*	*.311*	*.403*	*-.061*	*.255*	*.311*	*.399*	*-.115*	*.1*		

Breakout: 43%   Improve: 70%   Collapse: 15%

Stop me if you've heard this one before: the Royals are enamored with a young, fleet-footed outfielder who is still more athlete than baseball player. Gomez gives reason to believe he'll eventually make the transition. Despite his obvious lack of refinement (he led the high minors with 24 caught stealings), his strikeout-to-walk ratio improved dramatically, and his 14 homers exceeded his previous career total. He needs a full year at Triple-A before we know what he can become. At 22, that could be almost anything.

Ruben Gotay — 2B — Born: 25-Dec-82 — Age: 20 — Bats: B — Throws: R

YEAR	TM	LG	AGE	AB	H	2B	3B	HR	BB	SO	SB	CS	AVG	OBP	SLG	MLVR	EQBA	EQOBP	EQSLG	EQMLVR	VORP	DEFENSE
2002	BUR	MDW	19	509	145	42	9	9	73	110	5	4	.285	.383	.456	.228	.222	.296	.360	-.229	-1.9	115-2B 0
2003	KCR	AL	20	226	57	12	3	6	19	52	3	3	.254	.318	.417	-.035	.251	.318	.413	-.089	3.4	

Breakout: 39%   Improve: 68%   Collapse: 20%

SLEEPER ALERT! Gotay didn't even make *Baseball America*'s list of the 20 top prospects in the Midwest League, so it's safe to say he's under the radar at the moment. That ought to change soon. Switch-hitting teenaged second baseman who can make the pivot, walk 72 times and swat 60 extra-base hits eventually get noticed. Right now he projects as the kind of player Carlos Febles was supposed to be, but with more power and less speed. He's two years away from generating serious buzz, but worth knowing about now.

Aaron Guiel — RF — Born: 05-Oct-72 — Age: 30 — Bats: L — Throws: R

YEAR	TM	LG	AGE	AB	H	2B	3B	HR	BB	SO	SB	CS	AVG	OBP	SLG	MLVR	EQBA	EQOBP	EQSLG	EQMLVR	VORP	DEFENSE
2000	OMA	PCL	27	258	74	15	2	13	35	54	6	0	.287	.389	.512	.192	.256	.340	.453	.006	5.7	70-RF 3
2001	OMA	PCL	28	442	118	27	3	21	51	92	6	4	.267	.360	.484	.101	.239	.322	.430	-.072	.5	112-RF -4
2002	OMA	PCL	29	215	76	11	1	9	29	34	8	1	.353	.448	.540	.436	.318	.400	.479	.204	15.8	54-RF 0
2002	KCR	AL	29	240	56	13	0	4	19	61	1	5	.233	.300	.338	-.205	.246	.310	.354	-.194	-7.3	55-RF -2
2003	KCR	AL	30	279	70	15	2	9	29	58	3	2	.251	.327	.415	-.026	.248	.326	.411	-.079	-4.6	

Breakout: 14%   Improve: 38%   Collapse: 33%

After seven pro seasons without sniffing the majors, Guiel was toiling in Mexico when the Royals picked him up in 2000. He was hitting .353 in Omaha last year when he became the third-oldest player ever to make his major league debut in a Royals uniform. (The Royals went back to that well again last July, signing ex-major leaguer Edwin Hurtado, who was leading the Mexican League with a 1.38 ERA.) Guiel has excellent bat speed and a line-drive stroke, so despite his disappointing debut, I don't think we've heard the last of him.

Ken Harvey — 1B — Born: 01-Mar-78 — Age: 25 — Bats: R — Throws: R

YEAR	TM	LG	AGE	AB	H	2B	3B	HR	BB	SO	SB	CS	AVG	OBP	SLG	MLVR	EQBA	EQOBP	EQSLG	EQMLVR	VORP	DEFENSE
2000	WIL	CRL	22	164	55	10	0	4	14	29	0	2	.335	.411	.470	.326	.278	.327	.391	-.087	.4	18-1B -6
2001	WIL	CRL	23	137	52	9	1	6	13	21	3	1	.380	.455	.591	.596	.310	.369	.497	.169	9.9	20-1B 1
2001	WIC	TXS	23	314	106	20	3	9	18	60	3	0	.338	.381	.506	.283	.283	.320	.430	-.039	4.5	52-1B 2
2002	OMA	PCL	24	488	135	30	1	20	42	87	8	3	.277	.344	.465	.087	.251	.311	.420	-.097	-.1	109-1B -4
2003	KCR	AL	25	201	55	12	1	7	15	34	3	2	.274	.330	.445	.034	.270	.329	.441	-.017	1.3	

Breakout: 21%   Improve: 51%   Collapse: 28%

I'm not sure what to make of Ken Harvey. On the one hand, he is coming off the greatest AFL season of all time, setting league records in batting average (.479), OBP (.537), and slugging average (.752). On the other hand, he uniformly failed to impress a legion of industry types who watched him play there. What I am sure of is that despite a .359 career minor league average, Harvey's lack of secondary skills convinced the Royals to completely overhaul his hitting style; that Harvey struggled with his new, Jeff Bagwell-like swing all season before catching fire in August, and that from the outset his new stance led to more power and walks than before. His AFL performance revives his prospectdom and guarantees a crowded DH situation in KC this year.

A. J. Hinch — C — Born: 15-May-74 — Age: 29 — Bats: R — Throws: R

YEAR	TM	LG	AGE	AB	H	2B	3B	HR	BB	SO	SB	CS	AVG	OBP	SLG	MLVR	EQBA	EQOBP	EQSLG	EQMLVR	VORP	DEFENSE
2000	SAC	PCL	26	417	111	23	2	6	45	67	5	5	.266	.348	.374	-.105	.236	.301	.332	-.249	-1.4	85-C -1
2001	OMA	PCL	27	168	54	14	0	10	11	33	1	0	.321	.367	.583	.313	.286	.328	.512	.096	14.2	24-C -3
2001	KCR	AL	27	121	19	3	0	6	8	26	1	1	.157	.227	.331	-.404	.165	.231	.355	-.397	-5.0	37-C -3
2002	KCR	AL	28	197	49	7	1	7	18	35	3	3	.249	.321	.401	-.076	.259	.329	.426	-.049	9.5	60-C -3
2003	CLE	AL	29	212	51	10	1	7	18	40	3	2	.241	.304	.388	-.104	.247	.312	.397	-.123	2.6	

Breakout: 29%   Improve: 50%   Collapse: 24%

Every time you think Allard Baird is starting to figure things out, he pulls a stunt like this. Hinch out-hit, out-hustled, and generally out-played Brent Mayne, at a salary less than the new major league minimum. His minor league track record raises hopes he could be a late bloomer, perhaps even a poor man's Mike Stanley. Whereupon he was released. Every time the Royals make a move that defies explanation, there's always a feeling that there must be more to the story. And every time, subsequent events reveal that there is no back-story; the Royals simply didn't know what they were doing.

Raul Ibanez   LF/1B   Born: 02-Jun-72   Age: 31   Bats: L   Throws: R

YEAR	TM	LG	AGE	AB	H	2B	3B	HR	BB	SO	SB	CS	AVG	OBP	SLG	MLVR	EQBA	EQOBP	EQSLG	EQMLVR	VORP	DEFENSE		
2000	SEA	AL	28	140	32	8	0	2	14	25	2	0	.229	.303	.329	-.276	.243	.307	.350	-.208	-4.6	43-RF	-2	
2001	KCR	AL	29	279	78	11	5	13	32	51	0	2	.280	.354	.495	.116	.288	.363	.514	.160	17.5	32-RF	-3	
2002	KCR	AL	30	497	146	37	6	24	40	76	5	3	.294	.349	.537	.185	.306	.361	.563	.246	42.6	45-LF	0	42-1B -4
2003	KCR	AL	31	382	105	24	3	16	35	66	3	2	.274	.337	.477	.086	.271	.336	.472	.037	6.9			

Breakout: 15%   *Improve: 49%*   *Collapse: 22%*

Sometimes the alien stays. There was nothing in Ibanez's major league or minor league record that suggested he was capable of slugging .495, as he did in 2001, let alone that he could improve on that performance and slug .537. Ibanez credits his performance to learning the value of plate discipline from Edgar Martinez and John Olerud while in Seattle. While his walks fell last season, Ibanez continued to take nearly four pitches per plate appearance, once again proving the saw that even when strike zone knowledge doesn't lead to more walks, it can lead to more hitter's counts.

Rontrez Johnson   CF   Born: 08-Dec-76   Age: 26   Bats: R   Throws: R

YEAR	TM	LG	AGE	AB	H	2B	3B	HR	BB	SO	SB	CS	AVG	OBP	SLG	MLVR	EQBA	EQOBP	EQSLG	EQMLVR	VORP	DEFENSE	
2000	TRN	EAS	23	524	141	21	2	6	55	73	30	19	.269	.345	.351	-.028	.235	.295	.310	-.292	-15.5	133-CF	-5
2001	TRN	EAS	24	255	72	15	1	10	22	40	17	7	.282	.360	.467	.178	.248	.314	.412	-.104	5.1	71-CF	-10
2001	PAW	INT	24	187	56	16	3	4	10	35	8	4	.299	.358	.481	.187	.280	.332	.450	.008	9.1	40-CF	-4
2002	OMA	PCL	25	403	121	27	4	9	50	51	31	11	.300	.403	.454	.193	.271	.360	.411	-.003	18.6	103-CF	0
2003	OAK	AL	26	169	42	9	1	4	15	26	6	2	.248	.318	.375	-.094	.257	.328	.392	-.094	1.7		

Breakout: 21%   *Improve: 44%*   *Collapse: 38%*

Johnson was signed away from the Red Sox, who were reluctant to take him seriously despite excellent production, and he had his best pro season. However, the Royals passed over him to call up fellow minor league veteran Donzell McDonald at mid-season, and he was once again freed as a minor league free agent. Johnson signed with the Rangers only to be assimilated by the A's in the Rule 5 draft, which should be enough to convince you that he has a future as a big league fourth outfielder.

Chuck Knoblauch   LF   Born: 07-Jul-68   Age: 35   Bats: R   Throws: R

YEAR	TM	LG	AGE	AB	H	2B	3B	HR	BB	SO	SB	CS	AVG	OBP	SLG	MLVR	EQBA	EQOBP	EQSLG	EQMLVR	VORP	DEFENSE	
2000	NYY	AL	32	400	113	22	2	5	46	45	15	7	.282	.368	.385	-.033	.294	.372	.405	.029	25.0	74-2B	-15
2001	NYY	AL	33	521	130	20	3	9	58	73	38	9	.250	.341	.351	-.089	.276	.362	.392	-.021	9.2	95-LF	1
2002	KCR	AL	34	300	63	9	0	6	28	32	19	3	.210	.286	.300	-.291	.223	.297	.323	-.277	-14.7	71-LF	1
2003	KCR	AL	34	287	72	14	2	4	30	37	15	4	.252	.329	.354	-.098	.249	.329	.350	-.152	-6.4		

Breakout: 20%   *Improve: 49%*   *Collapse: 23%*

That experiment didn't go very well. Knoblauch missed playing time with a sore right leg, a strained left elbow, a strained rib cage, and a sprained big toe. In between, he hit with less authority than Tom Ridge. Another example of the Kevin McReynolds Principle: never acquire a non–Hall-of-Fame hitter in his early 30s. No longer worth the roster spot, except as a pinch-runner and as someone who can lean into a curveball and pick up a cheap hit-by-pitch when you need it.

Alejandro Machado   SS/2B   Born: 26-Apr-82   Age: 21   Bats: R   Throws: R

YEAR	TM	LG	AGE	AB	H	2B	3B	HR	BB	SO	SB	CS	AVG	OBP	SLG	MLVR	EQBA	EQOBP	EQSLG	EQMLVR	VORP	DEFENSE			
2000	DNV	APL	18	217	74	6	2	0	53	29	30	12	.341	.482	.387	.295	.230	.334	.261	-.282	-4.1	59-2B	-1		
2001	BUR	MDW	19	109	26	5	0	0	10	16	5	2	.239	.314	.284	-.160	.189	.242	.225	-.540	-9.4	28-SS	7		
2001	MCN	SAL	19	306	83	6	3	1	34	56	20	13	.271	.368	.320	.050	.219	.288	.262	-.381	-14.2	60-2B	-3	12-SS	1
2002	WIL	CRL	20	325	102	9	1	2	27	43	20	6	.314	.387	.366	.136	.265	.319	.313	-.222	-.3	90-SS	-4		
2003	KCR	AL	21	208	53	9	2	2	16	32	6	2	.254	.318	.344	-.128	.251	.317	.341	-.184	-1.0				

Breakout: 36%   *Improve: 54%*   *Collapse: 18%*

More than a year after acquiring Machado and Brad Voyles from Atlanta for Rey Sanchez, the Royals still aren't entirely sure what they have in Machado. He adheres to the Luis Castillo weight-training regimen, having swatted a total of 12 extra-base hits all last season. Nevertheless, he hit .314 in one of America's toughest ballparks, and at age 20 there's still plenty of projection left. He could be anything from the next Max Bishop to the next Jackie Rexrode.

Brent Mayne   C   Born: 19-Apr-68   Age: 35   Bats: L   Throws: R

YEAR	TM	LG	AGE	AB	H	2B	3B	HR	BB	SO	SB	CS	AVG	OBP	SLG	MLVR	EQBA	EQOBP	EQSLG	EQMLVR	VORP	DEFENSE	
2000	COL	NL	32	335	101	21	0	6	47	48	1	3	.301	.389	.418	.010	.279	.362	.388	-.025	19.2	91-C	-5
2001	COL	NL	33	160	53	7	0	0	16	24	0	0	.331	.392	.375	.018	.314	.377	.358	-.012	9.6	43-C	4
2001	KCR	AL	33	166	40	4	1	2	10	17	1	2	.241	.288	.313	-.268	.248	.298	.327	-.254	-.8	45-C	-2
2002	KCR	AL	34	326	77	8	2	4	34	54	4	4	.236	.312	.310	-.217	.248	.324	.325	-.206	2.5	93-C	4
2003	KCR	AL	35	205	50	10	1	2	20	33	2	1	.244	.311	.333	-.161	.241	.310	.330	-.218	-2.5		

Breakout: 18%   Improve: 38%   Collapse: 24%

> It really was watching Brent Mayne play that broke my spirit, and caused me to abandon all hope for this organization. He's just awful; he is just frigging awful. He can' t hit, he can't throw, he doesn't hustle, he is slow as a tank rolling uphill, and he's now 34 years old. Why in the world they don't just release Brent Mayne and try to find somebody who can play at least a little bit is beyond me.

Two weeks after he wrote this, Bill James signed on with the Red Sox. Yep, even he's finally given up on his Royals. For a change, he's actually behind the curve on this one.

Tydus Meadows   LF   Born: 05-Sep-77   Age: 25   Bats: R   Throws: R

YEAR	TM	LG	AGE	AB	H	2B	3B	HR	BB	SO	SB	CS	AVG	OBP	SLG	MLVR	EQBA	EQOBP	EQSLG	EQMLVR	VORP	DEFENSE	
2000	DAY	FSL	22	167	52	11	2	6	17	36	11	4	.311	.388	.509	.294	.249	.306	.414	-.116	-1.2	42-LF	-4
2000	WTN	SOU	22	249	65	14	4	5	20	72	4	2	.261	.326	.410	.057	.238	.283	.379	-.217	-8.7	65-LF	-1
2001	WTN	SOU	23	197	53	10	3	10	40	57	0	2	.269	.412	.503	.285	.233	.351	.432	-.020	4.1	52-LF	-3
2002	WIL	CRL	24	339	100	19	4	11	54	83	13	3	.295	.405	.472	.283	.241	.329	.391	-.110	-2.1	68-LF	-3
2002	WIC	TXS	24	119	41	12	3	4	14	23	4	2	.345	.431	.597	.507	.289	.359	.504	.140	7.2	17-LF	-1
2003	KCR	AL	25	190	50	12	1	7	19	44	4	4	.265	.337	.455	.051	.262	.336	.450	.001	1.2		

Breakout: 20%   Improve: 52%   Collapse: 21%

A minor league Rule 5 pick from the Cubs, a draft that almost never yields talent at the major league level, Meadows anchored a strong Wilmington lineup most of the year before going nuts in August with a .345/.421/.597 performance in Wichita. Recent studies have shown that there's no inherent advantage to repeating a minor league level, and Meadows is certainly young enough to have major league relevance. More and more teams are realizing the principle of "free talent" that exists in the minor leagues; it's just surprising that the Royals are one of them.

Kit Pellow   3B/1B   Born: 28-Aug-73   Age: 29   Bats: R   Throws: R

YEAR	TM	LG	AGE	AB	H	2B	3B	HR	BB	SO	SB	CS	AVG	OBP	SLG	MLVR	EQBA	EQOBP	EQSLG	EQMLVR	VORP	DEFENSE			
2000	OMA	PCL	26	421	105	17	3	22	38	89	6	4	.249	.335	.461	-.014	.223	.290	.411	-.169	-8.0	114-1B	-8		
2001	OMA	PCL	27	484	141	15	0	20	37	101	4	3	.291	.358	.446	.067	.262	.322	.401	-.094	0.2	121-1B	4		
2002	OMA	PCL	28	402	116	25	2	27	21	82	4	2	.289	.353	.562	.249	.261	.313	.505	.036	22.0	78-3B	-6	22-1B	-4
2002	KCR	AL	28	63	15	1	0	1	9	21	1	1	.238	.342	.302	-.170	.254	.354	.317	-.153	.6	11-3B	-3		
2003	COL	NL	29	200	54	11	1	9	16	44	3	2	.271	.335	.469	.053	.251	.312	.427	-.080	0.6				

Breakout: 11%   Improve: 44%   Collapse: 30%

After seven seasons of mixing occasional home runs between strikeouts, Pellow was finally called up to KC because he increased the frequency of the former while decreasing the latter. He follows Phil Hiatt and Craig Paquette in the Royals' long-standing tradition of having all-or-nothing minor league sluggers at third base. He was waived and signed by the Rockies, where right-handed strikeout-prone sluggers thrive even more than the usual hitter. Makes a great reserve pick in a roto league for just that reason.

Neifi Perez   SS/Cancer   Born: 02-Jun-73   Age: 30   Bats: B   Throws: L

YEAR	TM	LG	AGE	AB	H	2B	3B	HR	BB	SO	SB	CS	AVG	OBP	SLG	MLVR	EQBA	EQOBP	EQSLG	EQMLVR	VORP	DEFENSE	
2000	COL	NL	27	651	187	39	11	10	30	63	3	6	.287	.319	.427	-.117	.269	.291	.399	-.149	11.3	159-SS	26
2001	COL	NL	28	382	114	19	8	7	16	49	6	2	.298	.327	.445	-.027	.283	.311	.425	-.063	15.2	87-SS	6
2001	KCR	AL	28	199	48	7	1	1	10	19	3	4	.241	.281	.302	-.297	.247	.290	.313	-.291	-3.6	44-SS	0
2002	KCR	AL	29	554	131	20	4	3	20	53	8	9	.236	.263	.303	-.317	.246	.275	.316	-.317	-13.4	135-SS	2
2003	SFG	NL	30	460	111	20	3	3	22	51	7	4	.241	.278	.317	-.269	.253	.284	.349	-.233	-8.3		

Breakout: 30%   Improve: 57%   Collapse: 16%

Lee Sinins, who runs a daily newsletter from www.baseballimmortals.net, uses a metric called "Runs Created Above Average"—adjusted for things like ballpark and league context—to evaluate ballplayers. By his metric, Neifi Perez is probably the worst hitter in major league history. Perez was -57 RCAA last year, the sixth-worst figure since 1900—but hardly worse than his usual

Neifi Perez *(continued)*

standards, which include -54 (1999), -52 (2000), and -48 (1998). Over the past five years, Perez has cost his team 243 runs offensively, which is a record. In fact, no other player has ever cost his team so many runs over a six-year span. Clearly, he's a special player. Put it this way: replacing Perez with a league-average hitter would help the Royals more than replacing Michael Tucker with Shawn Green would. Amazingly, the Giants signed him to a two-year contract, so we'll use the same analogy with say, J. T. Snow and Mike Sweeney in next year's book.

Mark Quinn   RF   Born: 21-May-74   Age: 29   Bats: R   Throws: R

YEAR	TM	LG	AGE	AB	H	2B	3B	HR	BB	SO	SB	CS	AVG	OBP	SLG	MLVR	EQBA	EQOBP	EQSLG	EQMLVR	VORP	DEFENSE	
2000	OMA	PCL	26	61	23	5	0	3	0	8	0	1	.377	.377	.607	.438	.339	.339	.525	.194	3.9	11-RF	1
2000	KCR	AL	26	500	147	33	2	20	35	91	5	2	.294	.344	.488	.050	.294	.337	.493	.092	21.8	77-LF	3
2001	KCR	AL	27	453	122	31	2	17	12	69	9	5	.269	.299	.459	-.032	.277	.307	.477	.000	8.5	95-RF	-2
2002	KCR	AL	28	76	18	4	0	2	5	15	2	1	.237	.301	.368	-.161	.250	.310	.395	-.134	-1.1	12-RF	0
2003	*KCR*	*AL*	*29*	*261*	*68*	*15*	*1*	*7*	*16*	*48*	*5*	*2*	*.261*	*.309*	*.416*	*-.045*	*.258*	*.309*	*.412*	*-.100*	*-4.5*		

Breakout: 18%   Improve: 49%   Collapse: 20%

One of the characteristics that separates winning organizations from losers is this: a winning organization would build on the strengths Mark Quinn showed in his rookie season (power, ability to hit for average), instead of allowing his weaknesses (strike zone judgment, defense) to eat him alive. That Quinn has become an injury-prone hackmaster instead of a top-tier left fielder is as much an indictment of the organization as any trade Allard Baird has made. He's likely to be forgotten after last year's washout, but there is still a 900 OPS waiting to be unleashed here.

Joe Randa   3B   Born: 18-Dec-69   Age: 33   Bats: R   Throws: R

YEAR	TM	LG	AGE	AB	H	2B	3B	HR	BB	SO	SB	CS	AVG	OBP	SLG	MLVR	EQBA	EQOBP	EQSLG	EQMLVR	VORP	DEFENSE	
2000	KCR	AL	30	612	186	29	4	15	36	66	6	3	.304	.349	.438	-.005	.305	.342	.442	.037	33.1	155-3B	2
2001	KCR	AL	31	581	147	34	2	13	42	80	3	2	.253	.310	.386	-.124	.263	.320	.401	-.097	13.5	133-3B	-4
2002	KCR	AL	32	549	155	36	5	11	46	69	2	1	.282	.348	.426	.026	.295	.359	.446	.064	35.7	125-3B	1
2003	*KCR*	*AL*	*33*	*442*	*121*	*25*	*3*	*10*	*32*	*55*	*2*	*1*	*.274*	*.326*	*.407*	*-.020*	*.271*	*.326*	*.403*	*-.073*	*5.4*		

Breakout: 12%   Improve: 48%   Collapse: 23%

Quietly, Randa benefited as much from the Royals' increased focus on plate discipline as anyone. While his walk rate increased almost imperceptibly, he set a career high by averaging 3.8 pitches per plate appearance, and the extra hitters' counts allowed him to keep the precipice at bay another year. Nevertheless, the end is near, and if the Royals can foist most of his contract on a contender, whatever they receive in return is just gravy.

Mike Sweeney   1B   Born: 22-Jul-73   Age: 29   Bats: R   Throws: R

YEAR	TM	LG	AGE	AB	H	2B	3B	HR	BB	SO	SB	CS	AVG	OBP	SLG	MLVR	EQBA	EQOBP	EQSLG	EQMLVR	VORP	DEFENSE	
2000	KCR	AL	26	618	206	30	0	29	71	67	8	3	.333	.415	.523	.261	.336	.411	.527	.308	62.6	108-1B	2
2001	KCR	AL	27	559	170	46	0	29	64	64	10	3	.304	.378	.542	.240	.314	.389	.562	.298	58.7	104-1B	2
2002	KCR	AL	28	471	160	31	1	24	61	46	9	7	.340	.422	.563	.375	.350	.431	.586	.439	67.7	100-1B	5
2003	*KCR*	*AL*	*29*	*509*	*160*	*35*	*2*	*23*	*62*	*56*	*7*	*2*	*.314*	*.390*	*.527*	*.268*	*.311*	*.390*	*.522*	*.226*	*36.9*		

Breakout: 5%   Improve: 35%   Collapse: 11%

He's the highest-paid player in Royals history, and he's underpaid. He might be the nicest guy in baseball, yet he attacks opposing pitchers without mercy. He took less than market value to stay loyal to a team that has finished under .500 in all eight of his major league seasons, but when it comes to demanding improvement he's the most vocal player in the clubhouse. The Royals aren't worthy of Mike Sweeney. I'm not sure any team is.

Mike Tonis   Born: 09-Feb-79   Age: 24   Bats: R   Throws: R

YEAR	TM	LG	AGE	AB	H	2B	3B	HR	BB	SO	SB	CS	AVG	OBP	SLG	MLVR	EQBA	EQOBP	EQSLG	EQMLVR	VORP	DEFENSE	
2000	CWV	SAL	21	100	20	8	0	0	9	22	1	0	.200	.273	.280	-.220	.165	.214	.233	-.597	-10.1	25-C	1
2001	WIL	CRL	22	123	31	8	0	3	15	34	0	0	.252	.343	.390	.099	.217	.293	.341	-.263	-1.0	31-C	1
2001	WIC	TXS	22	226	61	11	1	9	22	41	1	1	.270	.345	.447	.082	.228	.290	.382	-.206	1.7	58-C	2

The Royals' catcher of the future first has to find a way to stay healthy in the present. Tonis missed the AFL in 2001 with a knee injury, had rotator cuff surgery on his throwing arm last spring, then had his jaw broken by a fastball in his sixth game back and watched a wasted season whiz by. A planned trip to winter ball to make up for lost time fell through. His combination of defensive prowess and offensive sock when healthy still makes him an intriguing prospect, enough so that the Royals added him to the 40-man roster.

Michael Tucker — RF — Born: 25-Jun-71 — Age: 32 — Bats: L — Throws: R

YEAR	TM	LG	AGE	AB	H	2B	3B	HR	BB	SO	SB	CS	AVG	OBP	SLG	MLVR	EQBA	EQOBP	EQSLG	EQMLVR	VORP	DEFENSE
2000	CIN	NL	29	270	72	13	4	15	44	64	13	6	.267	.383	.511	.141	.258	.366	.494	.110	15.2	74-OF -1
2001	CIN	NL	30	231	56	10	1	7	23	55	12	5	.242	.314	.385	-.143	.240	.311	.378	-.163	-4.8	57-OF 1
2001	CHC	NL	30	205	54	9	7	5	23	47	4	3	.263	.341	.449	.025	.269	.344	.452	.023	6.5	51-OF 1
2002	KCR	AL	31	475	118	27	6	12	56	105	23	9	.248	.331	.406	-.052	.257	.339	.425	-.033	5.4	102-RF 5
2003	*KCR*	*AL*	*32*	*324*	*84*	*17*	*4*	*10*	*36*	*71*	*13*	*5*	*.260*	*.337*	*.426*	*.012*	*.257*	*.337*	*.422*	*-.039*	*1.1*	

Breakout: 20%   Improve: 43%   Collapse: 24%

While his salary-to-performance ratio pales in comparison to Perez and Roberto Hernandez, trading for a fourth outfielder guaranteed to make $5 million over two years ranks as one of Baird's most wasteful transactions. For the seventh time in eight seasons, he finished with an OPS in the 700s, a mark unbecoming a starting corner outfielder. The Royals are toying with the idea of moving him back to second base, where he starred in the minors. While their creativity is laudable, the Royals would do well to note that only one established outfielder in major league history ever successfully moved to second base. That player, Jimmy Johnston, died an old man in 1967.

PITCHERS

Jeremy Affeldt — Born: 06-Jun-79 — Age: 24 — Bats: L — Throws: L

YEAR	TM	LG	AGE	G	GS	IP	H	BB	SO	HR	ERA	EQERA	EQH9	EQBB9	EQSO9	EQHR9	PERA	VORP	STF
2000	WIL	CRL	21	27	26	147.3	158	59	92	7	4.09	6.86	13.2	4.5	3.7	1.1	6.95	-22.2	-9
2001	WIC	TXS	22	25	25	145.3	153	46	128	9	3.90	5.88	11.8	3.6	5.8	1.0	5.46	-6.1	10
2002	KCR	AL	23	34	7	77.7	85	37	67	8	4.63	4.33	9.3	3.9	7.4	0.8	4.55	9.5	11
2003	*KCR*	*AL*	*24*	*27*	*13*	*83.7*	*95*	*38*	*63*	*11*	*5.12*	*4.68*	*9.7*	*3.7*	*6.6*	*1.0*	*4.73*	*12.3*	*2*

Breakout: 14%   Improve: 54%   Collapse: 23%

Affeldt is that rarest of pitchers: the high school project turned major league phenom. His minor league performance didn't prepare anyone for his sudden emergence in spring training last year, when he unleashed a curveball that evoked, if not Sandy Koufax, at least Barry Zito. He endured the growing pains one would expect from a pitcher who skipped Triple-A, but had the best strikeout rate on the team. He continues to be dogged by a blister on his middle finger, a problem that cost him two months last summer and ended his winter league season prematurely. On the bright side, he totaled barely 80 innings in his age-23 season. If the blister heals up, he's the best candidate on the team and maybe the division to break out this season. You've been warned.

Miguel Ascencio — Born: 29-Sep-80 — Age: 22 — Bats: R — Throws: R

YEAR	TM	LG	AGE	G	GS	IP	H	BB	SO	HR	ERA	EQERA	EQH9	EQBB9	EQSO9	EQHR9	PERA	VORP	STF
2002	KCR	AL	21	31	21	123.3	136	64	58	17	5.11	4.79	9.4	4.3	4.1	1.1	4.98	9.6	-5
2003	*KCR*	*AL*	*22*	*22*	*15*	*94.0*	*109*	*48*	*54*	*16*	*5.85*	*5.34*	*9.9*	*4.2*	*5.1*	*1.27*	*5.18*	*5.7*	*-8*

Breakout: 14%   Improve: 48%   Collapse: 19%

The best "free talent" acquired by Baird, Ascencio was a Rule 5 pick who went into the rotation on May 21st and never left. The command and deception of his changeup borders on the preternatural. He reminds me of Johan Santana in 2000, who like Ascencio was a 21-year-old pitcher who struggled after he was plucked out of A-ball in the Rule 5 draft. Two years later, Santana might become one of the best young starters in the league. Ascencio is probably a year away from that kind of success himself, so the Royals would be well-advised to send him to Triple-A for at least a half-season to complete his minor league apprenticeship.

Jeff Austin   Born: 19-Oct-76   Age: 26   Bats: R   Throws: R

YEAR	TM	LG	AGE	G	GS	IP	H	BB	SO	HR	ERA	EQERA	EQH9	EQBB9	EQSO9	EQHR9	PERA	VORP	STF
2000	WIC	TXS	23	6	6	43.0	33	4	31	3	2.93	3.51	8.8	0.9	4.8	1.0	2.65	9.5	16
2000	OMA	PCL	23	23	19	126.7	150	35	57	16	4.48	6.15	12.4	2.5	3.4	1.5	5.71	-9.2	-7
2001	OMA	PCL	24	28	8	70.7	89	27	55	14	6.87	7.74	13.1	4.2	5.3	2.2	7.43	-18.0	-18
2001	KCR	AL	24	21	0	26.0	27	14	27	4	5.54	5.15	8.9	4.5	8.6	1.2	4.86	0.7	9
2002	OMA	PCL	25	39	0	52.3	54	15	44	2	3.27	4.46	10.4	3.0	5.9	0.5	4.36	5.3	-1
2002	KCR	AL	25	10	0	11.0	14	6	6	0	4.91	4.57	10.7	4.5	4.6	0.2	4.91	1.0	-12
2003	KCR	AL	26	31	1	42.0	50	17	28	6	5.25	4.79	10.2	3.3	5.9	1.0	4.87	5.0	-6

Breakout: 15%   Improve: 48%   Collapse: 18%

Since 1992, not one Royals' first round draft pick has established himself as a quality major league player. Austin, a Stanford graduate and Golden Spikes Award winner, should have been the safest bet of all, but he bombed miserably as a starter. His fastball and curveball have both improved dramatically in the bullpen, and while the Royals are deeper in relievers that at any other position, Austin would be nicely suited to front the flamethrowers in a long relief role.

Ryan Bukvich   Born: 13-May-78   Age: 25   Bats: R   Throws: R

YEAR	TM	LG	AGE	G	GS	IP	H	BB	SO	HR	ERA	EQERA	EQH9	EQBB9	EQSO9	EQHR9	PERA	VORP	STF
2000	CWV	SAL	22	11	0	14.3	6	7	17	0	1.89	2.56	4.9	5.8	6.0	0.3	2.47	4.5	0
2001	WIL	CRL	23	37	0	57.7	41	31	80	1	1.72	4.50	8.7	7.2	7.8	0.4	5.03	5.6	1
2002	WIC	TXS	24	23	0	34.3	17	15	47	0	1.31	2.75	5.5	4.6	9.3	0.2	2.37	10.0	22
2002	OMA	PCL	24	12	0	13.7	4	7	17	0	0.00	0.19	3.0	5.4	8.7	0.2	1.35	7.9	20
2002	KCR	AL	24	26	0	25.0	26	19	20	2	6.12	5.40	8.7	6.2	6.8	0.6	4.93	-0.1	-5
2003	KCR	AL	25	32	1	47.0	44	29	46	5	4.76	4.35	8.0	5.1	8.6	0.9	4.35	8.0	7

Breakout: 20%   Improve: 39%   Collapse: 31%

Welcome to The Closing Game! Reliever #1, tell us about yourself. "I dropped out of the University of Mississippi after posting ERAs above seven in both my collegiate seasons, but the Royals' area scout convinced the team to draft me in the 11th round, and I reached the majors in barely two years. I throw mid-90s heat and a good slider, and my career minor league ERA is 1.76." What would you describe as your biggest fault? "I need to throw more strikes." Thank you, reliever #1!

Paul Byrd   Born: 03-Dec-70   Age: 32   Bats: R   Throws: R

YEAR	TM	LG	AGE	G	GS	IP	H	BB	SO	HR	ERA	EQERA	EQH9	EQBB9	EQSO9	EQHR9	PERA	VORP	STF
2000	SWB	INT	29	3	3	26.0	20	6	10	2	1.73	3.03	8.5	2.2	3.1	0.9	3.13	7.2	0
2000	PHI	NL	29	17	15	83.0	89	35	53	17	6.51	5.91	9.7	3.1	5.1	1.6	5.33	-3.8	-5
2001	SWB	INT	30	5	5	37.0	34	7	35	4	3.65	5.17	10.3	2.1	6.9	1.4	4.24	1.4	15
2001	KCR	AL	30	16	15	93.3	110	22	49	11	4.05	4.29	10.4	2.0	4.5	0.9	4.46	12.6	3
2002	KCR	AL	31	33	33	228.3	224	38	129	36	3.90	3.67	8.4	1.4	4.9	1.3	3.55	46.5	9
2003	ATL	NL	32	29	27	175.0	177	43	106	24	4.04	4.31	9.3	1.9	4.8	1.2	4.22	23.6	6

Breakout: 13%   Improve: 44%   Collapse: 12%

The Steve Carlton comparisons were a little absurd, but Byrd did become the first pitcher to win 17 games for a 100-loss team since Ned Garver of the 1951 Browns. Byrd's success was strictly of the chuck-and-duck variety; he almost became the first American League pitcher ever to surrender more home runs (36) than walks (38). As it was, Rick Reed, with 32 home runs and 26 walks, got there first. He was extremely hit-lucky, giving up 33 fewer hits than expected, and regardless of how much success he finds under Leo Mazzone, he was unlikely to approach his 2002 performance again in a Royals' uniform. With an extra first round draft pick and all the money earmarked for Byrd tucked away, the Royals won't miss him nearly as much as they think they will.

Kiko Calero   Born: 09-Jan-75   Age: 28   Bats: R   Throws: R

YEAR	TM	LG	AGE	G	GS	IP	H	BB	SO	HR	ERA	EQERA	EQH9	EQBB9	EQSO9	EQHR9	PERA	VORP	STF
2000	WIC	TXS	25	28	25	153.7	141	66	130	16	3.63	5.24	10.6	4.2	5.7	1.5	4.86	4.4	0
2001	WIC	TXS	26	27	19	124.3	110	51	94	10	3.33	5.32	10.2	4.7	5.0	1.3	4.91	2.3	-8
2002	OMA	PCL	27	20	18	125.7	112	35	109	11	3.44	4.04	9.1	2.9	6.1	1.0	3.94	20.4	11
2003	SLN	NL	28	13	9	59.0	60	25	42	8	4.57	4.98	9.5	3.4	5.7	1.1	4.95	4.8	1

Breakout: 15%   Improve: 43%   Collapse: 24%

After spending parts of the last six seasons toiling in Wichita, Calero was finally paroled when the Royals traded him to Philadelphia, only to have him returned because he reported with a sore shoulder. From those inauspicious beginnings Calero went on to have his finest season, finally reaching Triple-A and recording a strikeout-to-walk ratio of better than 3 to 1. He signed with the Cardinals as a six-year minor leaguer; and given what St. Louis got out of Jason Simontacchi last season, don't be surprised if Calero earns a significant role on the Cardinals' staff this year.

Chad Durbin   Born: 03-Dec-77   Age: 25   Bats: R   Throws: R

YEAR	TM	LG	AGE	G	GS	IP	H	BB	SO	HR	ERA	EQERA	EQH9	EQBB9	EQSO9	EQHR9	PERA	VORP	STF
2000	OMA	PCL	22	12	12	72.7	75	22	53	10	4.46	4.98	10.8	2.8	5.4	1.6	4.96	4.2	9
2000	KCR	AL	22	16	16	72.3	91	43	37	14	8.22	6.86	10.6	4.3	4.4	1.4	5.93	-10.9	-7
2001	OMA	PCL	23	5	5	27.0	22	6	35	4	3.33	3.98	8.2	2.4	8.5	1.6	3.74	4.6	29
2001	KCR	AL	23	29	29	179.0	201	58	95	26	4.93	4.90	9.9	2.7	4.5	1.2	4.63	12.0	4
2002	KCR	AL	24	2	2	8.3	13	4	5	3	11.93	9.34	13.0	3.9	5.1	2.8	8.56	-3.5	-19
2002	WIC	TXS	24	3	1	5.3	5	4	6	1	5.09	8.39	12.2	8.4	8.0	3.6	7.76	-1.7	-23

In 2001, a 23-year-old Durbin was allowed to throw over 115 pitches on six different occasions, and twice went over the 130-pitch mark. In 2002, Durbin got bombed in two major league starts, didn't respond to a minor league demotion, and eventually underwent major arm surgery that will probably keep him out until 2004. As with Jose Rosado before him, Durbin is proof that while it may take years to develop a young pitcher, it only takes a few abusive starts to destroy one.

Ian Ferguson   Born: 23-Aug-79   Age: 23   Bats: R   Throws: R

YEAR	TM	LG	AGE	G	GS	IP	H	BB	SO	HR	ERA	EQERA	EQH9	EQBB9	EQSO9	EQHR9	PERA	VORP	STF
2000	SPO	NWN	20	15	15	71.3	76	16	66	6	3.28	7.26	16.4	2.8	4.8	2.9	7.06	-13.9	-6
2001	BUR	MDW	21	10	10	58.0	62	10	30	9	5.28	7.21	14.2	2.3	3.0	3.3	6.78	-11.0	-15
2001	WIL	CRL	21	18	18	96.3	85	27	72	5	3.83	6.03	11.2	3.8	4.3	1.2	5.53	-5.6	-1
2002	WIL	CRL	22	17	17	109.3	100	20	81	2	2.39	4.63	11.0	2.3	4.8	0.4	4.44	10.6	12
2002	WIC	TXS	22	11	11	76.0	60	17	60	7	2.61	4.07	9.7	2.5	5.6	1.8	3.91	12.1	13
2003	*KCR*	*AL*	*23*	*13*	*8*	*55.3*	*70*	*19*	*33*	*9*	*5.88*	*5.37*	*10.9*	*2.9*	*5.3*	*1.3*	*5.30*	*2.8*	*-3*

Breakout: 10%   *Improve: 51%*   *Collapse: 12%*

A 21st round pick out of Regis University, Ferguson has left his humble beginnings behind. He is 31–8 in the minors the last two years, which means nothing but ties a nice bow around his other numbers. Described as a "Brad Radke type" for a fastball that's a tick below-average, Ferguson made the jump to Double-A, which topples most finesse pitchers, without a hitch. As with any finesse pitcher, he needs a full year in the high minors to legitimize his prospect standing.

Chris George   Born: 16-Sep-79   Age: 23   Bats: L   Throws: L

YEAR	TM	LG	AGE	G	GS	IP	H	BB	SO	HR	ERA	EQERA	EQH9	EQBB9	EQSO9	EQHR9	PERA	VORP	STF
2000	WIC	TXS	20	18	18	97.3	92	51	80	5	3.14	4.94	10.6	5.0	5.5	0.7	4.92	6.1	7
2000	OMA	PCL	20	8	8	44.7	47	20	27	8	4.83	6.14	11.1	4.1	4.5	2.1	5.96	-3.2	-3
2001	OMA	PCL	21	20	20	117.3	103	51	84	14	3.53	4.72	9.2	4.8	4.8	1.3	4.62	10.2	4
2001	KCR	AL	21	13	13	74.0	83	18	32	14	5.59	5.10	9.9	2.1	3.7	1.5	4.71	3.3	0
2002	OMA	PCL	22	22	21	127.3	145	65	94	15	5.87	6.55	11.8	5.4	5.3	1.4	6.47	-14.8	-1
2002	KCR	AL	22	6	6	27.3	37	8	13	2	5.60	4.97	11.7	2.4	4.1	0.6	5.09	1.6	1
2003	*KCR*	*AL*	*23*	*14*	*12*	*72.0*	*91*	*37*	*46*	*12*	*6.32*	*5.76*	*10.9*	*4.2*	*5.7*	*1.3*	*5.64*	*2.0*	*-3*

Breakout: 11%   *Improve: 43%*   *Collapse: 27%*

The wheels have come off the Chris George train faster than Christina Aguilera's clothes. For a command pitcher, he showed no control, allowing more than a walk every two innings in Omaha. More ominously, his fastball lost a foot from the year before. He's still very young and has a good head on his shoulders, so assuming there isn't any structural reason for his decline, his bounce-back potential is pretty high.

Jimmy Gobble Born: 19-Jul-81 Age: 21 Bats: L Throws: L

YEAR	TM	LG	AGE	G	GS	IP	H	BB	SO	HR	ERA	EQERA	EQH9	EQBB9	EQSO9	EQHR9	PERA	VORP	STF
2000	CWV	SAL	18	25	25	145.0	144	34	115	10	3.66	6.04	12.8	3.0	4.2	1.7	5.89	-8.6	0
2001	WIL	CRL	19	27	27	162.3	134	33	154	8	2.55	4.86	10.3	2.7	5.3	1.1	4.74	11.6	12
2002	WIC	TXS	20	13	13	69.3	71	19	52	3	3.38	5.29	11.9	3.0	5.3	0.8	5.11	1.7	10

Gobble hasn't pitched in George's shadow—he *is* George's shadow, tailing his every step since he was drafted. Like George, Gobble is a left-hander drafted out of high school in the supplemental first round. Like George, he has excited the Royals with his poise and command, and had a very good season at Wilmington before his 21st birthday. However, Gobble throws harder than George, with a better curveball; George's only advantage is his ability to change speeds. Gobble had no problems with Double-A hitters, but major problems with his groin, suffering an injury that bothered him all season and eventually shut him down. He should be fully healed; he's the Royals' pitching prospect most likely to contribute this season.

Zack Greinke Born: 21-Oct-83 Age: 19 Bats: R Throws: R

YEAR	TM	LG	AGE	G	GS	IP	H	BB	SO	HR	ERA	EQERA	EQH9	EQBB9	EQSO9	EQHR9	PERA	VORP	STF
2002	WIL	CRL	18	1	0	2.0	1	0	0	0	0.00	1.65	6.5	0.7	0.0	0.2	1.53	0.8	-20

Ordinarily, we wouldn't write about a high school pitcher, even a #1 pick, with barely a dozen innings of minor league experience. But there is nothing ordinary about Greinke's first year as a professional. After the most statistically impressive performance of any warm-weather prep pitcher in at least a decade, Greinke became the first American high schooler ever to pitch in a Caribbean league game the winter after he was drafted. Barely 19 years old, he posted a 2.45 ERA in 26 innings, walking just two batters. The Royals are starting to whisper the "S" word—as in Saberhagen—when talking about him, and *Baseball America* already named him the organization's #1 prospect. His major league debut is still probably an arm injury away, but the potential for him to make a major league impact before he turns 21 is very real.

Colt Griffin Born: 29-Sep-82 Age: 20 Bats: R Throws: R

YEAR	TM	LG	AGE	G	GS	IP	H	BB	SO	HR	ERA	EQERA	EQH9	EQBB9	EQSO9	EQHR9	PERA	VORP	STF
2002	BUR	MDW	19	19	19	90.7	75	82	66	1	5.36	7.26	10.0	11.9	4.3	0.3	7.06	-17.7	-22

Say this about the man born to wear No. 45: he was exactly as advertised. Advertised as the first high schooler ever to hit 100 on the radar gun, with nearly as much sink as velocity on his fastball, Griffin allowed just 78 hits in 95 innings, and a single home run. He was also advertised as greener than the inside of the U.S. Mint, and sure enough, he gave up 87 walks and 29 wild pitches in those same 95 innings. Miss Cleo has as much chance of predicting which way his career is headed as any scout or analyst does.

Jason Grimsley Born: 07-Aug-67 Age: 35 Bats: R Throws: R

YEAR	TM	LG	AGE	G	GS	IP	H	BB	SO	HR	ERA	EQERA	EQH9	EQBB9	EQSO9	EQHR9	PERA	VORP	STF
2000	NYY	AL	32	63	4	96.3	100	42	53	10	5.05	4.38	8.8	3.2	4.8	0.8	4.23	10.9	-9
2001	KCR	AL	33	73	0	80.3	71	28	61	8	3.03	3.34	7.8	2.9	6.4	0.8	3.26	18.2	2
2002	KCR	AL	34	70	0	71.3	64	37	59	4	3.91	3.48	7.7	4.3	7.1	0.4	3.45	15.1	3
2003	*KCR*	*AL*	*35*	*56*	*0*	*58.0*	*57*	*27*	*46*	*6*	*4.11*	*3.75*	*8.5*	*3.8*	*7.0*	*0.8*	*3.95*	*14.0*	*1*

Breakout: 26% Improve: 60% Collapse: 13%

With the enormous influx of rookie relievers into KC, Grimsley may be the only man in the bullpen with significant major league experience. He hardly resembles the bottom-feeder who once bounced through six organizations in as many years. The Royals feel he doesn't have the makeup to be a closer, so he's likely to set up whichever rookie wins the closer's role. Given the importance of those outs in the 7th and 8th innings, that's not such a bad thing.

Roberto Hernandez Born: 11-Nov-64 Age: 38 Bats: R Throws: R

YEAR	TM	LG	AGE	G	GS	IP	H	BB	SO	HR	ERA	EQERA	EQH9	EQBB9	EQSO9	EQHR9	PERA	VORP	STF
2000	TBY	AL	35	68	0	73.3	76	23	61	9	3.19	3.61	8.8	2.3	7.2	0.9	3.81	14.4	7
2001	KCR	AL	36	63	0	67.7	69	26	46	7	4.12	4.15	9.0	3.2	5.8	0.8	4.01	9.3	-4
2002	KCR	AL	37	53	0	52.0	62	12	39	6	4.33	4.38	10.2	1.9	6.5	0.9	4.42	5.8	1
2003	*KCR*	*AL*	*38*	*43*	*0*	*40.0*	*43*	*13*	*28*	*5*	*4.28*	*3.91*	*9.2*	*2.6*	*6.2*	*1.0*	*4.12*	*8.9*	*-2*

Breakout: 27% Improve: 43% Collapse: 15%

Look at the bright side: few men have done more to disprove the myth of the importance of a closer more than Hernandez. The Royals went hard after Hernandez after the 2000 season because their bullpen became the first in history to blow more than half of their save opportunities. Even as Hernandez converted over 80% of his opportunities the past two years, the Royals still fell from 77 wins to 65 to 62. And for the privilege, the Royals shelled out $12 million, not to mention Johnny Damon. Even Allard Baird can learn this lesson: a closer is simply a reliever who gets to pitch the ninth inning. And there are better ways to spend $6 million a year than on a 70-inning pitcher.

Runelvys Hernandez				Born: 27-Apr-78			Age: 25		Bats: R		Throws: R					
YEAR	TM	LG	AGE	G	GS	IP	H	BB	SO	HR	ERA	EQERA	EQH9	EQBB9	EQSO9	EQHR9	PERA	VORP	STF
2001	BUR	MDW	23	17	17	100.7	94	29	100	5	3.40	5.18	11.1	3.7	5.6	1.0	5.10	3.6	8
2002	WIL	CRL	24	2	2	12.0	12	1	9	0	3.75	5.60	11.7	1.0	4.8	0.3	4.42	-0.1	12
2002	WIC	TXS	24	16	14	106.3	96	24	86	3	2.71	4.39	10.3	2.5	5.6	0.5	4.06	13.1	15
2002	KCR	AL	24	12	12	74.3	79	22	45	8	4.36	3.86	9.1	2.5	5.3	0.9	3.94	13.6	12
2003	KCR	AL	25	20	17	107.7	126	35	67	13	5.02	4.58	10.	2.7	5.5	1.	4.49	14.5	6

Breakout: 17%   Improve: 42%   Collapse: 17%

Sometimes, you just get lucky. This Hernandez needed three years to get out of the Dominican Summer League, but since coming stateside in 2001 he's risen faster than anyone this side of Theo Epstein. Like Berroa, he gained two years in the Age-Gate revelations, but as a pitcher that hardly changes his outlook—if anything, it just means he's probably less prone to breaking down. With Byrd gone, Hernandez has the inside track to start on Opening Day.

Jeremy Hill				Born: 08-Aug-77			Age: 25		Bats: R		Throws: R					
YEAR	TM	LG	AGE	G	GS	IP	H	BB	SO	HR	ERA	EQERA	EQH9	EQBB9	EQSO9	EQHR9	PERA	VORP	STF
2001	BUR	MDW	23	40	0	47.7	22	25	66	2	1.51	2.81	5.6	6.7	7.7	0.9	2.89	13.6	3
2001	WIL	CRL	23	9	0	12.3	10	8	13	0	0.73	3.92	10.1	9.0	6.1	0.3	6.10	2.0	-14
2002	WIC	TXS	24	56	0	76.3	61	32	80	4	2.36	4.39	9.3	4.6	7.3	1.0	4.31	8.4	2
2002	KCR	AL	24	10	0	9.3	8	8	7	1	3.87	3.89	7.2	7.0	6.4	0.8	4.52	1.5	-9

Reliever #2, tell us about yourself. "I spent five years as a good-throw, no-hit catcher before I moved to the mound in the 2000 instructional league. I can throw my fastball around 98, and I'm still working on perfecting my slider. My career minor league ERA is 1.91. Troy Percival is my hero." What would you describe as your biggest fault? "I need to throw more strikes." Thank you, reliever #2!

Mike MacDougal				Born: 05-Mar-77			Age: 26		Bats: B		Throws: R					
YEAR	TM	LG	AGE	G	GS	IP	H	BB	SO	HR	ERA	EQERA	EQH9	EQBB9	EQSO9	EQHR9	PERA	VORP	STF
2000	WIL	CRL	23	26	25	144.7	115	76	129	5	3.92	5.76	9.5	5.8	5.1	0.8	5.27	-4.1	-1
2001	OMA	PCL	24	28	27	144.3	144	76	110	13	4.68	5.90	10.4	5.8	5.2	1.0	5.40	-6.4	-5
2001	KCR	AL	24	3	3	15.3	18	4	7	2	4.71	5.06	10.5	2.2	3.9	1.1	4.60	0.8	-1
2002	WIC	TXS	25	4	4	17.7	11	24	14	1	3.05	7.56	7.7	15.3	5.7	1.1	6.84	-4.0	-38
2002	OMA	PCL	25	12	10	53.0	52	55	30	4	5.60	7.38	10.3	11.3	4.1	0.9	7.03	-11.1	-35

Reliever #3, tell us about yourself. "I'm a former first round pick and have spent almost my entire career as a starter. I was hit in the head by a bat while sitting in the dugout a year ago, and had trouble feeling my fingers all year, which is probably why I walked 92 batters in 91 innings. But I moved to the bullpen in September and pitched well, I keep the ball down, and I've been clocked as high as 102." What would you describe as your biggest fault? "I need to throw more strikes." Thank you, reliever #3!

Bet on reliever #3 to win The Closing Game. Given how hard he throws, and how heavy his fastball is (in two short major league trials, his G/F ratio is 3.75), his lack of relief experience is practically irrelevant. The Royals love him, and as of mid-December he was having a dominant season as a closer in the Puerto Rican winter league.

Darrell May				Born: 13-Jun-72			Age: 31		Bats: L		Throws: L					
YEAR	TM	LG	AGE	G	GS	IP	H	BB	SO	HR	ERA	EQERA	EQH9	EQBB9	EQSO9	EQHR9	PERA	VORP	STF
2000	YOM	JCL	28	24	24	155.3	123	40	165	19	2.95	3.63	7.4	2.4	8.0	1.1	3.66	32.4	25
2001	YOM	JCL	29	26	26	159.0	160	45	168	24	4.13	4.93	9.5	2.4	8.3	1.5	5.01	10.2	21
2002	KCR	AL	30	30	21	131.3	144	50	95	28	5.35	4.98	9.3	3.2	6.2	1.7	5.06	7.4	1

A worthwhile investment that hasn't paid dividends so far, May had pitched the four previous seasons in Japan, where he was one of the Central League's most consistent starting pitchers. He turned down a multimillion dollar offer to stay in Japan for the Royals' modest sum of $375,000. He's an extreme flyball pitcher working in the best home-run park in the AL. If he cuts his homers allowed in half—which could happen if the Royals move their fences out—he'll be an above-average starter.

Scott Mullen Born: 17-Jan-75 Age: 28 Bats: R Throws: L

YEAR	TM	LG	AGE	G	GS	IP	H	BB	SO	HR	ERA	EQERA	EQH9	EQBB9	EQSO9	EQHR9	PERA	VORP	STF
2000	WIC	TXS	25	33	1	73.3	65	26	61	5	3.19	4.25	10.1	3.4	5.6	1.0	4.11	9.3	-4
2000	OMA	PCL	25	16	0	20.7	15	8	21	1	3.04	3.72	7.4	3.5	7.5	0.6	2.89	3.8	9
2001	OMA	PCL	26	48	0	53.0	66	22	38	8	6.62	7.29	12.9	4.6	4.9	1.7	7.06	-11.2	-27
2002	OMA	PCL	27	19	1	31.0	32	9	21	0	2.61	3.99	10.4	3.0	4.8	0.2	4.10	4.8	-6
2002	KCR	AL	27	44	0	40.0	40	13	21	5	3.15	3.47	8.6	2.7	4.6	1.0	3.85	8.5	-10
2003	KCR	AL	28	35	0	41.7	54	18	24	6	5.58	5.09	11.1	3.6	5.1	1.1	5.38	4.1	-14

Breakout: 6%   Improve: 33%   Collapse: 34%

Mullen is a failed starter and not exactly a success as a reliever, but he has become the best one-out lefty in the organization by default. His ERA was helped greatly by his friends in the bullpen, who lopped nearly a full run off his ERA by stranding the baserunners he bequeathed. With just 21 strikeouts in 40 innings, and a similar track record of finesse in the minors, Mullen is a poor bet for any kind of sustained success.

Wes Obermueller Born: 22-Dec-76 Age: 26 Bats: R Throws: R

YEAR	TM	LG	AGE	G	GS	IP	H	BB	SO	HR	ERA	EQERA	EQH9	EQBB9	EQSO9	EQHR9	PERA	VORP	STF
2000	CWV	SAL	23	8	7	31.7	19	5	29	0	1.14	2.38	7.0	1.9	4.6	0.3	2.35	11.0	9
2001	WIL	CRL	24	20	6	38.0	38	16	28	3	3.08	6.35	13.4	5.9	4.4	1.9	7.41	-3.8	-29
2002	WIL	CRL	25	8	4	45.7	38	14	44	1	2.76	4.45	10.1	3.9	6.2	0.5	4.41	5.2	11
2002	WIC	TXS	25	17	17	105.7	98	40	65	6	2.89	4.95	11.0	4.2	4.4	1.1	5.03	6.5	-3
2003	KCR	AL	26	16	11	64.0	75	29	39	9	5.68	5.18	10.0	3.7	5.4	1.0	4.95	4.2	-3

Breakout: 14%   Improve: 49%   Collapse: 16%

Obermueller was drafted in the second round in 1999 after he moved from the outfield to the mound during his senior year of college, and was clocked at 97. Arm woes that eventually necessitated surgery limited his repetitions and dropped his fastball into the lower 90s, which makes it fairly impressive that he picked up the nuances of pitching so quickly, reaching Kansas City after barely 250 minor league innings. He still has a ways to go, and at age 26 it's a legitimate question whether he'll ever get there.

Dan Reichert Born: 12-Jul-76 Age: 26 Bats: R Throws: R

YEAR	TM	LG	AGE	G	GS	IP	H	BB	SO	HR	ERA	EQERA	EQH9	EQBB9	EQSO9	EQHR9	PERA	VORP	STF
2000	KCR	AL	23	44	18	153.3	157	91	94	15	4.70	4.54	8.8	4.3	5.3	0.7	4.18	15.7	1
2001	OMA	PCL	24	10	5	32.7	45	16	30	4	8.26	8.56	14.2	5.4	6.2	1.3	7.87	-11.2	-11
2001	KCR	AL	24	27	19	123.0	131	67	77	14	5.63	5.21	9.3	4.6	5.3	0.9	4.76	3.8	0
2002	KCR	AL	25	30	6	66.0	77	25	36	10	5.32	5.31	10.0	3.2	4.7	1.2	4.98	0.9	-10
2003	TBA	AL	26	29	10	71	79	34	45	8	5.24	5.21	9.8	3.9	5.5	0.9	5.03	4.0	-8

Breakout: 13%   Improve: 44%   Collapse: 15%

He's a former first round pick. He didn't let the onset of diabetes faze him. He has an excellent minor league track record. Scouts are biologically incapable of mentioning his slider without using the word "filthy." His 2.46 career groundball/flyball ratio is second only to Derek Lowe among AL pitchers. Despite all that, the Royals never got him to succeed at the major league level, and summarily released him in September. Reichert was immediately claimed on waivers by the Devil Rays; he would have been claimed by 28 other major league teams if they had the chance. Expect big things from Reichert in the coming years. Don't expect the Royals to learn anything from this debacle.

Shawn Sedlacek Born: 29-Jun-76 Age: 27 Bats: R Throws: R

YEAR	TM	LG	AGE	G	GS	IP	H	BB	SO	HR	ERA	EQERA	EQH9	EQBB9	EQSO9	EQHR9	PERA	VORP	STF
2000	WIC	TXS	23	35	16	140.3	153	43	81	10	3.66	5.54	12.5	3.0	3.9	1.0	5.21	-1.1	-7
2001	WIC	TXS	24	14	14	86.7	85	14	66	7	3.63	4.99	11.2	1.8	5.0	1.3	4.58	5.0	8
2001	OMA	PCL	24	14	13	81.0	98	22	44	13	5.00	6.34	12.6	3.0	3.7	1.8	6.42	-7.5	-10
2002	OMA	PCL	25	11	11	80.3	67	15	66	6	3.70	3.86	8.5	2.0	5.8	0.9	3.26	14.7	16
2002	KCR	AL	25	16	14	84.3	99	36	52	16	6.73	5.64	10.0	3.5	5.3	1.5	5.40	-1.3	-1
2003	KCR	AL	26	22	16	94.7	115	34	59	14	5.47	4.99	10.4	2.9	5.5	1.1	4.87	9.5	1

Breakout: 12%   Improve: 46%   Collapse: 16%

Statistically, this guy is all sorts of trouble. He's the kind of pitcher that's just good enough to be one of the worst pitchers in the major leagues over the next few years. But he's also the kind of pitcher that reaches the major leagues before it's discovered that he was born in 1976, not 1977, a clerical error usually seen in players that hail from the Dominican Republic, not from Cedar Rapids. And he's the kind of pitcher that, when asked about the error, puts on a look of feigned surprise that would make Gaylord Perry proud. I'm not saying that Sedlacek is the kind of pitcher that would do everything he can to grab an advantage. I'm just saying that if he isn't working on a greaseball this very moment, I'd almost be disappointed.

Kyle Snyder — Born: 09-Sep-77 — Age: 25 — Bats: B — Throws: R

YEAR	TM	LG	AGE	G	GS	IP	H	BB	SO	HR	ERA	EQERA	EQH9	EQBB9	EQSO9	EQHR9	PERA	VORP	STF
2002	WIL	CRL	24	15	15	48.3	49	11	48	1	2.98	5.44	12.1	2.9	6.4	0.5	5.28	0.3	6
2002	WIC	TXS	24	6	6	25.7	21	7	18	4	4.20	5.39	10.9	3.1	5.1	3.1	4.81	0.3	-9

Like Austin and Reichert, Snyder is also a collegiate player drafted in the top 10 overall. He was coveted by the A's, drafting two spots after Kansas City, who settled for Barry Zito instead. Snyder's biceps tendonitis in college festered into a Tommy John situation that he's only now fully recovered from. The Royals kept him on a very tight leash all season (try and find another pitcher that made 21 starts and threw just 74 innings). He continued to pitch well, three innings at a time, in the AFL. He's going to be a very good pitcher; it's just a question of whether he'll be starting games or finishing them.

Blake Stein — Born: 03-Aug-73 — Age: 29 — Bats: R — Throws: R

YEAR	TM	LG	AGE	G	GS	IP	H	BB	SO	HR	ERA	EQERA	EQH9	EQBB9	EQSO9	EQHR9	PERA	VORP	STF
2000	KCR	AL	26	17	17	107.7	98	57	78	19	4.68	4.15	7.7	3.8	6.3	1.3	4.00	16.2	8
2001	KCR	AL	27	36	15	131.0	112	79	113	20	4.74	4.42	7.4	5.0	7.2	1.2	4.16	15.2	3
2002	KCR	AL	28	27	2	46.7	59	27	42	6	7.90	6.30	10.6	4.7	7.6	1.0	5.82	-4.6	-2
2003	TBY	AL	29	22	8	53.0	59	31	45	7	5.26	5.23	9.7	4.8	7.3	1.1	5.14	6.2	0

Breakout: 19%   Improve: 45%   Collapse: 28%

The Blake Stein bandwagon is just about empty. He simply lacks the command—and the ability to prevent his high fastball from ending up in the seats—to succeed as anything more than a back-of-the-bullpen pitcher. His fastball will get him more chances, and if he ends up in a spacious ballpark, he might even take advantage of one of them.

Jeff Suppan — Born: 02-Jan-75 — Age: 28 — Bats: R — Throws: R

YEAR	TM	LG	AGE	G	GS	IP	H	BB	SO	HR	ERA	EQERA	EQH9	EQBB9	EQSO9	EQHR9	PERA	VORP	STF
2000	KCR	AL	25	35	33	217.0	240	84	128	36	4.94	4.50	9.5	2.8	5.2	1.2	4.46	24.2	5
2001	KCR	AL	26	34	34	218.3	227	74	120	26	4.37	4.39	9.2	2.9	4.7	1.0	4.09	27.0	3
2002	KCR	AL	27	33	33	208.0	229	68	109	32	5.32	4.77	9.4	2.7	4.5	1.2	4.53	17.0	0
2003	KCR	AL	28	29	26	163.7	189	56	94	23	5.18	4.73	9.9	2.8	5.1	1.1	4.61	18.2	3

Breakout: 14%   Improve: 48%   Collapse: 13%

He may be Greg Maddux Lite, but we're going to have to accept that he's never going to have a Greg Maddux Lite season. He has picture-perfect mechanics and hasn't missed a turn in the rotation in his four years with the Royals, and he has legitimate value to a contender needing a reliable innings-eater at the back of the rotation. The Royals fit that description like Anna Nicole Smith fits a size 4 dress. Unless they believe a breakthrough is imminent, at age 28, with a stagnant strikeout rate, the Royals need to cut bait and jettison his salary before he becomes a financial albatross. Done and done.

Brad Voyles — Born: 30-Dec-76 — Age: 26 — Bats: R — Throws: R

YEAR	TM	LG	AGE	G	GS	IP	H	BB	SO	HR	ERA	EQERA	EQH9	EQBB9	EQSO9	EQHR9	PERA	VORP	STF
2000	MYR	CRL	23	39	0	56.7	21	25	70	1	1.11	2.74	5.5	4.8	7.0	0.4	2.44	16.6	7
2001	GRN	SOU	24	15	0	16.7	11	10	25	0	1.08	2.72	7.0	6.3	9.1	0.3	3.49	4.9	14
2001	WIC	TXS	24	11	0	15.3	8	10	19	0	0.00	0.23	5.8	7.2	8.0	0.3	2.99	8.8	9
2002	OMA	PCL	25	26	0	32.3	29	22	34	2	4.18	4.84	9.2	7.2	7.4	0.7	5.09	1.9	-7
2002	KCR	AL	25	22	0	27.7	31	18	26	5	6.50	5.79	9.4	5.3	8.0	1.4	5.69	-1.3	-2
2003	KCR	AL	26	29	4	50.3	51	32	42	6	5.13	4.68	8.7	5.2	7.4	1.0	4.81	7.3	-2

Breakout: 14%   Improve: 45%   Collapse: 30%

Voyles is a one-trick pony, but unlike most pitchers with one dominant pitch, his bread-and-butter is a curveball that breaks hard and breaks late. When he throws it consistently for strikes, he's a bear to hit against. When he has trouble getting it over the plate, which is most of the time, it means baserunners galore. The five home runs he gave up with the Royals last season doubled his total in five professional seasons. A lot of minor league pitchers are one-walk-per-nine-innings away from major league success. Voyles is probably closer to two.

Kris Wilson Born: 06-Aug-76   Age: 26   Bats: R   Throws: R

YEAR	TM	LG	AGE	G	GS	IP	H	BB	SO	HR	ERA	EQERA	EQH9	EQBB9	EQSO9	EQHR9	PERA	VORP	STF
2000	WIC	TXS	23	21	15	102.7	99	21	69	12	3.51	5.20	11.3	2.0	4.6	1.7	4.46	3.3	0
2000	KCR	AL	23	20	0	34.3	38	11	17	3	4.20	3.82	9.6	2.4	4.4	0.6	3.76	5.9	-3
2001	OMA	PCL	24	6	5	29.0	31	6	18	2	2.79	3.89	10.9	2.2	4.1	0.7	4.54	5.2	1
2001	KCR	AL	24	29	15	109.3	132	32	67	26	5.19	5.78	10.5	2.5	5.2	1.9	5.59	-3.7	-4
2002	WIC	TXS	25	13	7	48.0	47	4	33	4	1.88	4.60	11.7	0.9	4.9	1.6	4.47	4.7	0
2002	OMA	PCL	25	8	3	26.3	38	1	17	0	3.08	4.40	14.5	0.4	4.5	0.3	5.62	3.1	3
2002	KCR	AL	25	12	0	18.7	29	5	10	7	8.18	7.75	13.1	2.2	4.6	3.0	8.04	-4.9	-25
2003	KCR	AL	26	18	9	61.0	78	15	35	11	5.61	5.12	11.0	2.0	5.1	1.4	4.96	4.5	-4

Breakout: 12%   Improve: 46%   Collapse: 22%

It's hard to ever write off a pitcher with Wilson's control; he's averaged just 1.62 walks per game in his minor league career, and last season walked just 6 batters in 84 innings. The problem is that while Wilson knows exactly where his fastball is going, so do the hitters. Lefties have hit a career .340 with a .644 slugging average against Wilson, a problem that no amount of control is going to fix. Like a lot of Royals' pitchers, he would benefit tremendously if the fences were moved back twenty feet. Extreme control pitchers in the Tewksbury/Rick Reed class don't usually peak before age 30, which gives Wilson time to have a career.

Minnesota Twins

Within the ranks of Baseball Prospectus, the Twins chapter is starting to earn a reputation as the space for all sorts of wild-eyed assertions, claims, and predictions. We've been excited if not downright wildly enthusiastic at times about the organization that's been drafted, assembled, and built over time, rarely shying away from the opportunity to sing the praises of what Terry Ryan and company have been slowly building up. Sometimes, that means we've jumped the gun in predicting success for the Twins. Sometimes, it also means that we've gotten pretty nasty toward Carl Pohlad's indifference to the organization that has thrived in the shadow of his malicious distaste for anything that doesn't involve lining his own pocket or stealing a stadium from the taxpayer's pockets. But in the shadow of the fighting and the lying about stadia and cities and shakedowns, the Twins have been in the process of building an organization the old-fashioned way. In today's game, that's even more notable, because as front offices get stocked with the rapacious competitors of the Beane Generation, the Twins make a fine case for the argument that there's more than one way to skin a cat.

Unfortunately, last year's bold position about the Twins was that we got negative about their outlook for 2003. Depending on how well you remember our premature claims for contention for this organization, it's sort of amusing that we're now guilty of souring at the wrong, penultimate moment. Sure, in a stathead sort of way, it was safe to look at Pythagenport projections for their actual wins (the 2001 Twins should have won only 82 games given their runs scored and allowed), consider the "Plexiglass Principle" (usually referred to less colorfully as regression to the mean), and claim that sliding backward was the most likely outcome. But as we know, it was also completely wrong, and it's worth identifying why.

> ## Twins Prospectus
>
> **2002 record:** 94–67; First place, AL Central; Lost to Angels in AL Championship Series
>
> **Pythagenport Records:** 87–75
>
> **Runs scored per game:** 4.8 (9th in AL)
>
> **Runs allowed per game:** 4.4 (6th in AL)
>
> **Team EqA:** .258 (8th in AL)
>
> **2002 Batters Age:** 27 (youngest in AL)
>
> **2002 Pitchers Age:** 29 (6th oldest in AL)
>
> **Ballpark:** Metrodome; Moderate hitters' park; Park Factor of 1.030
>
> **2002:** The team Selig and Pohlad almost destroyed romped in the game's weakest division, showing everyone how to do it.
>
> **2003:** They'll have to play the games, but the division should be theirs again.

First, it should have been worth recognizing the status of the other two semi-competitive franchises in the division going into last season. (These days, the Royals and Tigers only fulfill the very useful function of letting everyone else play a full schedule.) The Hart Indians made their final throw of the dice in 2001, and although Mark Shapiro generated the appropriate spin about how they were taking 2002 seriously, they hadn't added much in the way of significant talent to a decaying core. The White Sox have been expected to be at the top of the heap in the AL Central, but the continued front office hijinks on Chicago's South Side were nothing if not a blow in the name of competitive balance everywhere else in the division. At the very least, the Twins weren't implausible favorites by the time Opening Day rolled around, especially considering that their opportunity to win in 2001 had been hampered by the unfortunate Lawton/Reed deal that cost them their leadoff man while bringing in a fourth starter. Looking at the rest of the division, if you could win 85 games again, you'd have a shot at the division title in 2002.

To the Twins' credit, they didn't settle for that. It's interesting to look at this team and try to put together how they did it. Certainly, breakout seasons from Torii Hunter and Jacque Jones—at the ages that you can expect that sort of thing—helped. But that only reflects a reason for optimism: The 2001 Twins fielded the youngest lineup in the league, so if anybody's going to see hitters in their prime ages to break out, actually break out, it was the Twins. More significantly, the Twins remained in place relative to the league; offensively, they were eighth in the American League in both 2001 and 2002. Corey Koskie and Doug Mientkiewicz and Luis Rivas all had worse seasons, and Cristian Guzman had an especially disappointing year. So it wasn't the offense that got the Twins not just over the hump but nine games better than 2001.

Table 1. The Big Three

Year	GS	IP	ERA	WHIP	Support-Neutral Wins	Win-Loss
2001	101	680.1	3.80	1.22	14.4	47-31
2002	67	384.2	4.94	1.29	2.7	26-22

Moreover, you're talking about a team that saw its front three starters falter or break down. The trio of Eric Milton, Brad Radke, and Joe Mays were a significant reason why the Twins won 85 games in 2001, and were significantly worse in 2002 (see table 1).

Again, not many teams improve by nine games when the front of its rotation gives you 300 fewer innings. But nestled in there is what you might interpret as a hint, because it would be hard to envision the Twins being as successful in 2002 if Radke, Milton, and Mays had pitched as many starts and innings while coughing up an extra run per nine.

What the Twins had going for them more than any of their notional rivals in the AL Central was depth. And not just any kind of depth, but depth in quality that gave them the kind of flexibility you won't find in most organizations. That may not sound all that sexy in itself, but keep in mind, the Twins have nobody you'd consider a superstar, and arguably nobody about to turn into one currently on the active roster. The point is that nobody on the Twins is simultaneously famous, awful, and expensive. The Twins don't play Rey Ordonez. That might be because they have the good fortune not to be able to afford him or Joe Girardi or anybody named Brian Hunter. But that in turn makes it possible to give opportunities to the people who deserve to play, the guys an organization developed and drafted on their own.

Without the politically complicating factor of money, the decision of who plays has been, for the most part, a matter of who earns a job. As a team, the Twins are about as close as you can get to a real meritocracy within the game. When the question of who should replace Matt Lawton in right field had to be asked, new manager Ron Gardenhire could initially favor Brian Buchanan because he thought he needed power in his lineup. When that wasn't so much the case, he could plug in Bobby Kielty or Dustan Mohr. When rotation starters started breaking down, he could turn to Johan Santana or Matt Kinney or Kyle Lohse. After nabbing Santana through the Rule 5 draft (acquiring him from the Marlins, who made the pick, while giving up Jared Camp during his brief fling as a flavor of the moment) before the 2000 season, he gave good cause for the Twins to believe he's going to be a lot more than just a nice swingman or bullpen asset. Lohse rewarded a patience few organizations would have shown a pitcher who had an ERA over six through almost his first 40 starts in Double-A.

Certainly, experimentation with the rotation is a little easier when you've got one of the best defensive units in baseball. But an even more critical component of the Twins' success was that Gardenhire quickly mastered one of Tom Kelly's great skills in roster construction and player usage, which was assembling a good bullpen out of the talent he had at hand. The Angels won the World Series with a collection of unknowns in the bullpen behind closer Troy Percival, but the Twins went even further in demonstrating that great bullpens are dug up and slapped together, not bought. Bob Wells imploded, but the Twins more than adequately replaced him with their latest reclamation project, Tony Fiore. J. C. Romero and LaTroy Hawkins were once considered decent starting pitcher prospects earlier in their careers, but when they struggled in that role, both were turned into bullpen assets. And rather than get hung up on the mystique of the closer, Gardenhire just handed the role to Eddie Guardado and saw him thrive in it. The closest thing to a big-ticket reliever was veteran Mike Jackson, who fulfilled the situational right-hander role with aplomb. But with a bullpen filled with ex-starters and quality relievers capable of handling multi-inning outings, Gardenhire had the flexibility to avoid putting too much pressure on his makeshift rotation.

And with those assets, the Twins romped. They really only beat the bejeezus out of their weak AL Central brethren, going 50–25 against them while going 44–42 against everybody else. Once again, they had a better-than-expected record in one-run games, but with tactical advantages like a better bullpen than almost everybody else in the league, and a great defense, and a return of the Hefty Bag home field advantage (54–27 inside the Humpdome, and 19–5 in one-run games at home vs. 10–11 on the road), a better-than-expected record in one-run games doesn't seem so extraordinary. They squeaked by Oakland in the playoffs with some inspired hitting, great starts by Eric Milton and Brad Radke in the last two games, and some characteristically odd choices by Art Howe. Having fought their way to the ALCS, they then got chewed up by the postseason buzzsaw of the Angels' combination of relief pitching and death-by-a-thousand-monkey-cuts offense.

Unlike last year, we're not going to make any claims about backsliding this time around. The division has two patsies who might not have hit bottom yet, the Indians will be rebuilding for a couple of years yet, and Kenny Williams is still about as sensible as a hungry goat in a jalapeno patch. The Twins might have induced financial limitations that might hamper Terry Ryan's ability to go to arbitration with some players (David Ortiz was just shed to avoid a hearing, for example), but the tremendous amount of talent that's here and young or that is young and on the way up makes those sorts of losses relatively easy to absorb. At the start of the year, they'll be working Mike Cuddyer into the everyday lineup, and by the end of it, they'll have to decide who loses a job to Justin Morneau and what to do with Mike Restovich. In two years, the Twins will be wondering whether or not to move A. J. Pierzynski to make room for Joe Mauer. The rotation will be equally crowded, with somebody from among Brad Thomas, Johan Santana, and Juan Rincon leading a wave of arms which, after the inevitable casualties, will still provide the Twins with handy replacements for Rick Reed after 2003 and perhaps both Eric Milton and Brad Radke after 2004. As long as they're handicapped by their owner's parsimony, Terry Ryan and his crew simply need to avoid getting too tied up with long-term deals with mediocrities. That will mean avoiding any more than this year's arbitration fight with Doug Mientkiewicz, perhaps having to cut bait early with Luis Rivas, and making a relatively tough decision after 2004 on Cristian Guzman. But as long as the player development side of the organization gives Ryan choices, he can worry about getting creative on the financial side of things as the years progress. In the meantime, he should be able to look forward to being the favorite in the AL Central for the next two years.

On the more (or less) optimistic side of things, we could note that at least we were half right last year, by identifying that Carl Pohlad's latest stunt—his cynical participation in the contraction bogeyman scheme—was worth less than its weight in summer sausage. However, this was not altogether remarkable. After all, Pohlad's motives have always been pretty clearly communicated on these scores: he wants your money, he's always wanted your money, and he's going to do everything he can do to get your money. If he's ham-fisted and unsubtle about it, the only person really hurt by that has been himself, and perhaps his family to the extent that they may or may not want to operate a baseball franchise in the future.

This was merely the latest con in a long litany of bogus stunts aimed at extorting a stadium, this time targeted to coincide with negotiations over the latest Combined Bargaining Agreement as a means of simultaneously cowing the MLBPA and the citizens of Minnesota. At best, it was another self-inflicted black eye on the industry. State and local governments in Minnesota would be well within their rights if they refused to negotiate with baseball as long as Bud Selig or Carl Pohlad, considering their track records for misinformation and deceit, have anything to do with the future of baseball in the Twin Cities. After all, citizens and pols alike can point toward their track record of generating better attendance than most other big league markets, a track record that more than demonstrates the profitability of big league baseball in Minnesota. However, winning has a way of changing opinions of otherwise sensible people. One of the "dangers" of the success this franchise should enjoy over the next few years is that the good people of Minnesota might just give the Twins a stadium, Pohlads or no Pohlads.

HITTERS

Casey Blake — 3B — Born: 23-Aug-73 — Age: 29 — Bats: R — Throws: R

YEAR	TM	LG	AGE	AB	H	2B	3B	HR	BB	SO	SB	CS	AVG	OBP	SLG	MLVR	EQBA	EQOBP	EQSLG	EQMLVR	VORP	DEFENSE
2000	SYR	INT	26	106	23	6	1	2	8	23	0	3	.217	.291	.349	-.219	.196	.254	.318	-.384	-5.6	27-3B -1
2000	SLC	PCL	26	293	93	22	2	12	39	59	7	2	.317	.408	.529	.237	.268	.346	.443	.013	14.4	64-3B -8
2001	EDM	PCL	27	375	116	24	6	10	34	66	14	3	.309	.376	.485	.157	.273	.336	.424	-.027	15.3	82-3B -2
2002	EDM	PCL	28	482	149	25	3	19	54	78	24	9	.309	.386	.492	.212	.273	.343	.433	-.002	24.0	110-3B 4
2002	MIN	AL	28	20	4	1	0	0	2	7	0	0	.200	.273	.250	-.373	.200	.273	.300	-.369	-1.2	
2003	*CLE*	*AL*	*29*	*199*	*51*	*11*	*1*	*6*	*19*	*39*	*4*	*3*	*.257*	*.327*	*.417*	*-.019*	*.263*	*.335*	*.426*	*-.031*	*4.7*	

Breakout: 23%   *Improve: 45%*   *Collapse: 26%*

Blake isn't suited for a role as a platoon hitter. He kills junk from righties or lefties, but he can be overpowered. As managers like McCarthy, Stengel, and Weaver demonstrated, platooning doesn't have to be about righty-lefty splits, so Blake could have value as a spare part on a team that needs somebody who can put the hurt on Jamie Moyer or John Stephens with equal aplomb. He has a chance to be the Tribe's Opening Day third baseman.

Rob Bowen — C — Born: 24-Feb-81 — Age: 22 — Bats: B — Throws: R

YEAR	TM	LG	AGE	AB	H	2B	3B	HR	BB	SO	SB	CS	AVG	OBP	SLG	MLVR	EQBA	EQOBP	EQSLG	EQMLVR	VORP	DEFENSE
2000	ELZ	APL	19	73	21	3	0	4	11	18	0	0	.288	.381	.493	.257	.187	.256	.320	-.382	-3.0	18-C 5
2001	QUD	MDW	20	385	98	18	2	18	37	112	4	0	.255	.323	.452	.086	.193	.247	.341	-.368	-13.4	98-C -4
2002	QUD	MDW	21	21	4	1	0	0	2	4	0	0	.190	.261	.238	-.281	.182	.217	.182	-.655	-2.9	
2002	FTM	FSL	21	342	63	12	1	10	38	69	1	0	.184	.275	.313	-.165	.164	.230	.280	-.501	-24.9	83-C 2
2003	*MIN*	*AL*	*22*	*157*	*33*	*7*	*1*	*4*	*16*	*34*	*2*	*1*	*.208*	*.285*	*.332*	*-.228*	*.211*	*.290*	*.345*	*-.252*	*-3.2*	

Breakout: 90%   *Improve: 100%*   *Collapse: 0%*

Rob Bowen *(continued)*

Everybody likes catchers, and Bowen had a good first couple of years and he switch-hits, plus he's a good catcher with a strong arm. It's too easy to play make-believe and see Mickey Tettleton. Unfortunately, he just flopped in the Florida State League. He is the kind of player you'd expect to struggle in Florida: a power stroke with trouble making consistent contact. Bowen is young enough to bounce back, but Jeff Goldbach looked pretty good once upon a time, and young catchers are a risky bunch.

Jay Canizaro   **2B**   **Born: 04-Jul-73**   **Age: 30**   **Bats: R**   **Throws: R**

YEAR	TM	LG	AGE	AB	H	2B	3B	HR	BB	SO	SB	CS	AVG	OBP	SLG	MLVR	EQBA	EQOBP	EQSLG	EQMLVR	VORP	DEFENSE
2000	SLC	PCL	27	101	36	9	2	6	17	17	4	1	.356	.454	.663	.545	.306	.391	.561	.291	12.6	22-2B 5
2000	MIN	AL	27	346	93	21	1	7	24	57	4	2	.269	.318	.396	-.141	.274	.316	.408	-.086	11.0	77-2B -13
2002	MIN	AL	29	112	24	8	1	0	10	22	0	1	.214	.285	.304	-.275	.232	.305	.330	-.246	-.9	25-2B -1
2002	EDM	PCL	29	247	71	11	2	14	30	46	6	3	.287	.371	.518	.204	.254	.329	.460	-.006	13.9	57-2B -13
2003	*TBY*	*AL*	*29*	*258*	*64*	*14*	*1*	*8*	*24*	*49*	*3*	*2*	*.248*	*.315*	*.401*	*-.064*	*.254*	*.324*	*.419*	*-.069*	*5.5*	

Breakout: 23%   *Improve: 52%*   *Collapse: 24%*

Blowing out a knee in 2001 cost Canizaro any chance he might have had to hold onto the second base job. When he came back in 2002, he was still having knee problems, and since he can't really play anywhere but second, he doesn't have much value as a utility infielder. Signed as a NRI with the D-Rays, he might have a shot at Brent Abernathy's job.

Mike Cuddyer   **RF**   **Born: 27-Mar-79**   **Age: 24**   **Bats: R**   **Throws: R**

YEAR	TM	LG	AGE	AB	H	2B	3B	HR	BB	SO	SB	CS	AVG	OBP	SLG	MLVR	EQBA	EQOBP	EQSLG	EQMLVR	VORP	DEFENSE	
2000	NBR	EAS	21	490	129	30	8	6	55	93	5	4	.263	.352	.394	.037	.232	.301	.353	-.222	-4.4	137-3B -29	
2001	NBR	EAS	22	509	153	36	3	30	75	106	5	9	.301	.397	.560	.361	.257	.343	.472	.038	32.6	75-3B 1	53-1B -3
2002	EDM	PCL	23	330	102	16	9	20	36	79	12	7	.309	.382	.594	.348	.272	.338	.517	.106	16.0	74-RF -3	
2002	MIN	AL	23	112	29	7	0	4	8	30	2	0	.259	.314	.429	-.029	.277	.335	.464	.031	3.1	20-RF 0	
2003	*MIN*	*AL*	*24*	*249*	*66*	*15*	*2*	*9*	*25*	*55*	*4*	*4*	*.265*	*.336*	*.449*	*.042*	*.269*	*.342*	*.468*	*.039*	*5.7*		

Breakout: 11%   *Improve: 52%*   *Collapse: 18%*

Cuddyer almost won the job in right field in spring training, but being the last cut meant playing every day in Edmonton because he needed the at-bats. After recalling him later on, the Twins played him more and more often down the stretch, a sign of things to come. As an infielder, he had a great arm, which will hopefully carry over, because he's athletic enough to be an outstanding right fielder. The Twins have a nice problem as far as squeezing Cuddyer, Restovich, and later Morneau into the outfield corner/first base/DH mix. The Twins have already bumped David Ortiz; Doug Mientkiewicz should be next. Cuddyer's upside over the next six years is a lot better than this projection hints at.

Lew Ford   **CF**   **Born: 12-Aug-76**   **Age: 26**   **Bats: R**   **Throws: R**

YEAR	TM	LG	AGE	AB	H	2B	3B	HR	BB	SO	SB	CS	AVG	OBP	SLG	MLVR	EQBA	EQOBP	EQSLG	EQMLVR	VORP	DEFENSE
2000	AUG	SAL	23	514	162	35	11	9	52	83	52	4	.315	.391	.479	.294	.244	.298	.378	-.185	-.8	124-CF 6
2001	FTM	FSL	24	265	79	15	2	2	21	30	19	9	.298	.376	.392	.157	.260	.310	.344	-.199	-1.4	66-CF -4
2001	NBR	EAS	24	252	55	9	3	7	20	35	5	5	.218	.291	.361	-.115	.195	.256	.323	-.374	-12.9	55-CF -4
2002	NBR	EAS	25	373	116	27	2	15	49	47	17	5	.311	.402	.515	.312	.268	.342	.444	.008	19.1	92-CF -7
2002	EDM	PCL	25	193	64	11	2	5	13	21	11	1	.332	.392	.487	.238	.297	.350	.432	.030	10.3	46-CF 1
2003	*MIN*	*AL*	*26*	*182*	*47*	*11*	*1*	*4*	*16*	*28*	*5*	*2*	*.257*	*.321*	*.398*	*-.052*	*.261*	*.327*	*.415*	*-.063*	*3.1*	

Breakout: 33%   *Improve: 59%*   *Collapse: 29%*

Getting Ford for Hector Carrasco from the Red Sox in 2000 was a steal, but the clock is ticking. Ford is similar to Corey Koskie, because he didn't really start playing baseball until his junior year of college, which means he's a decent bet to fulfill the breakout potential PECOTA sees in him. His defense gets good reviews, and leading the minor leagues in runs scored (121) helps his rep as a leadoff type. He won't push past Hunter or Jones, and he's behind Cuddyer and Restovich, so for now his future is as a fourth outfielder or trade bait.

B. J. Garbe CF Born: 03-Feb-81 Age: 22 Bats: R Throws: R

YEAR	TM	LG	AGE	AB	H	2B	3B	HR	BB	SO	SB	CS	AVG	OBP	SLG	MLVR	EQBA	EQOBP	EQSLG	EQMLVR	VORP	DEFENSE
2000	QUD	MDW	19	476	111	12	3	5	63	91	14	7	.233	.335	.303	-.078	.187	.255	.245	-.486	-39.8	127-CF -16
2001	FTM	FSL	20	463	112	14	4	6	51	86	13	7	.242	.333	.328	-.028	.213	.275	.294	-.366	-35.2	127-RF -10
2002	FTM	FSL	21	427	102	13	2	5	36	89	18	6	.239	.309	.314	-.083	.211	.260	.281	-.416	-27.2	104-CF -3
2003	MIN	AL	22	166	37	7	1	3	13	36	3	3	.223	.286	.333	-.216	.226	.292	.346	-.239	-6.2	

Breakout: 60%   Improve: 73%   Collapse: 13%

After scuffling in Florida for a second year, prospect hounds are giving up on Garbe. Given his youth and his physical talent, he'll still keep getting chances, which could at least take him down the Shawn Abner career path, but even that won't be easy. He's gone backward as a hitter, getting less patient and losing power while ignoring instruction. If Garbe doesn't show something in the first half, he'll be in danger of being outrighted off of the 40-man roster.

Cristian Guzman SS Born: 21-Mar-78 Age: 25 Bats: B Throws: R

YEAR	TM	LG	AGE	AB	H	2B	3B	HR	BB	SO	SB	CS	AVG	OBP	SLG	MLVR	EQBA	EQOBP	EQSLG	EQMLVR	VORP	DEFENSE
2000	MIN	AL	22	631	156	25	20	8	46	101	28	10	.247	.300	.388	-.203	.252	.297	.397	-.154	10.0	146-SS -10
2001	MIN	AL	23	493	149	28	14	10	21	78	25	8	.302	.337	.477	.097	.316	.352	.501	.152	45.4	115-SS 0
2002	MIN	AL	24	623	170	31	6	9	17	79	12	13	.273	.294	.385	-.112	.290	.312	.411	-.076	21.8	141-SS 0
2003	MIN	AL	25	560	154	31	6	11	30	74	18	6	.275	.315	.409	-.035	.279	.321	.426	-.044	17.7	

Breakout: 8%   Improve: 53%   Collapse: 8%

A spray hitter with flashes of defensive excellence, you have to wonder about what's going to happen next with Guzman. His walk rate has gone from nearly adequate to ghastly, and his stolen base rates have gone from useful to ill-considered. In terms of performance, Guzman is somewhere between Greg Gagne and Gary Templeton; of the two, Templeton had better peak value, but ceased to be an asset by his 30th birthday. Gagne never really peaked as much as he had minor swings in his performance, retaining value but never mastering his faults. The Twins would be happier if Guzman gave them some of Templeton's flash, but if they settle for a Gagne-like blend of bat control, power, and basepath mayhem, that'll do. Either way, he'll be useful, but they can forego re-signing him after 2004 or 2005 if they don't see any progress.

Denny Hocking UT Born: 02-Apr-70 Age: 33 Bats: B Throws: R

YEAR	TM	LG	AGE	AB	H	2B	3B	HR	BB	SO	SB	CS	AVG	OBP	SLG	MLVR	EQBA	EQOBP	EQSLG	EQMLVR	VORP	DEFENSE
2000	MIN	AL	30	373	111	24	4	4	48	77	7	5	.298	.378	.416	.023	.302	.375	.421	.064	14.6	35-OF -1 32-2B -10
2001	MIN	AL	31	327	82	16	2	3	29	67	6	1	.251	.316	.339	-.167	.266	.331	.361	-.130	7.5	40-SS 2 12-2B -6
2002	MIN	AL	32	260	65	13	0	2	24	44	0	2	.250	.316	.323	-.172	.272	.338	.352	-.125	6.1	46-2B -7 18-SS -3
2003	MIN	AL	33	180	45	9	1	2	18	32	1	1	.249	.318	.347	-.128	.252	.324	.361	-.144	-.6	

Breakout: 20%   Improve: 49%   Collapse: 29%

Cookie Newman be damned, we got ourselves a new role model for hardworking scrubeenies. Hocking will play anywhere, although that flexibility costs the Twins a million bucks. However, if you have a guy on the roster who can play everywhere, that allows you to do things in-season like carry 12 pitchers or another platoon hitter or bring up a spot starter in an emergency. For that, Hocking is an asset for now, but he's close to the end of whatever use he had as a hitter.

Torii Hunter CF Born: 18-Jul-75 Age: 27 Bats: R Throws: R

YEAR	TM	LG	AGE	AB	H	2B	3B	HR	BB	SO	SB	CS	AVG	OBP	SLG	MLVR	EQBA	EQOBP	EQSLG	EQMLVR	VORP	DEFENSE
2000	SLC	PCL	24	209	77	17	2	18	11	28	11	3	.368	.408	.727	.601	.315	.345	.611	.303	22.8	48-CF -3
2000	MIN	AL	24	336	94	14	7	5	18	68	4	3	.280	.320	.408	-.111	.285	.318	.417	-.060	9.7	98-CF 5
2001	MIN	AL	25	564	147	32	5	27	29	125	9	6	.261	.306	.479	.010	.275	.319	.507	.063	34.1	147-CF 19
2002	MIN	AL	26	561	162	37	4	29	35	118	23	8	.289	.336	.524	.161	.307	.354	.562	.235	59.0	127-CF 5
2003	MIN	AL	27	498	139	30	3	23	33	103	16	7	.278	.328	.490	.093	.282	.334	.510	.094	27.7	

Breakout: 3%   Improve: 34%   Collapse: 19%

If the 2002 season was a coming-out party for the Twins, Hunter was the face most quickly identified with that success. He isn't really the AL's Andruw Jones, but he's a superb player nonetheless, sort of like a more athletic version of Tony Armas with better defense. The difficult question is deciding whether or not to give him a multiyear deal. He didn't really hit well on the road and he faded down the stretch, contributing to concerns that what you see is all you'll get. There's a real danger that he'll have a Grissomish slide into adequacy, just as Marquis Grissom had by his 30th birthday.

Jacque Jones   LF   Born: 25-Apr-75   Age: 28   Bats: L   Throws: L

YEAR	TM	LG	AGE	AB	H	2B	3B	HR	BB	SO	SB	CS	AVG	OBP	SLG	MLVR	EQBA	EQOBP	EQSLG	EQMLVR	VORP	DEFENSE
2000	MIN	AL	25	523	149	26	5	19	26	111	7	5	.285	.319	.463	-.028	.289	.315	.472	.019	13.5	139-LF 5
2001	MIN	AL	26	475	131	25	0	14	39	92	12	9	.276	.335	.417	-.012	.288	.348	.438	.027	14.1	126-LF 5
2002	MIN	AL	27	577	173	37	2	27	37	129	6	7	.300	.344	.511	.168	.319	.364	.547	.243	48.6	143-LF 10
2003	MIN	AL	28	472	129	29	2	17	36	99	6	5	.274	.327	.454	.041	.278	.333	.472	.038	8.6	

Breakout: 2%   Improve: 29%   Collapse: 26%

Gardenhire's decision to let Jones lead off and play every day worked, as Jones had his breakout season in a year where offense went down. He still didn't hit lefties (.213/.259/.331), and it seems doubtful he ever will. Maybe he busted out because he played every day, and maybe he busted out because playing for Ron Gardenhire was much more pleasant than playing for Tom Kelly. We can't really know, but the crush of outfielders in the system should start chewing into Jones's at-bats against lefties. In the meantime, he gives the team another center field–caliber glove in the outfield, and enough power to paste right-handers. Given his age and eventual free agency and the organization's depth, he shouldn't be a Twin after 2004.

Bobby Kielty   OF   Born: 05-Aug-76   Age: 26   Bats: B   Throws: R

YEAR	TM	LG	AGE	AB	H	2B	3B	HR	BB	SO	SB	CS	AVG	OBP	SLG	MLVR	EQBA	EQOBP	EQSLG	EQMLVR	VORP	DEFENSE
2000	NBR	EAS	23	451	118	30	3	14	98	109	6	4	.262	.399	.435	.163	.227	.342	.382	-.107	9.4	115-CF -13
2001	EDM	PCL	24	341	98	25	2	12	53	76	5	0	.287	.393	.478	.155	.251	.348	.415	-.035	13.2	94-CF 1
2001	MIN	AL	24	104	26	8	0	2	8	25	3	0	.250	.310	.385	-.118	.269	.326	.413	-.064	.6	28-OF -2
2002	MIN	AL	25	289	84	14	3	12	52	66	4	1	.291	.408	.484	.225	.309	.424	.519	.290	29.9	64-RF 2
2003	MIN	AL	26	346	93	20	2	12	51	76	5	2	.269	.367	.443	.088	.273	.374	.462	.088	14.6	

Breakout: 6%   Improve: 42%   Collapse: 23%

Kielty had a choice to sign wherever he pleased after being the Cape Cod League MVP in 1998, and he made a point of signing where he felt he'd get an opportunity. He obviously picked wisely, getting to the playoffs in his fourth year as a professional. He might get typecast as a fourth outfielder because he's a switch-hitter with power and patience who can handle center on a team that has Torii Hunter. That would be unfortunate, because Kielty's good enough to play every day, and he doesn't have any platoon issues.

Corey Koskie   3B   Born: 28-Jun-73   Age: 30   Bats: L   Throws: R

YEAR	TM	LG	AGE	AB	H	2B	3B	HR	BB	SO	SB	CS	AVG	OBP	SLG	MLVR	EQBA	EQOBP	EQSLG	EQMLVR	VORP	DEFENSE
2000	MIN	AL	27	474	142	32	4	9	77	104	5	4	.300	.402	.441	.104	.305	.401	.448	.150	42.6	131-3B 7
2001	MIN	AL	28	562	155	37	2	26	68	118	27	6	.276	.366	.488	.136	.293	.380	.520	.202	58.7	147-3B 18
2002	MIN	AL	29	490	131	37	3	15	72	127	10	11	.267	.371	.447	.099	.286	.387	.483	.156	46.4	133-3B 19
2003	MIN	AL	30	442	119	28	2	16	60	103	9	5	.270	.361	.451	.089	.274	.368	.470	.089	26.4	

Breakout: 4%   Improve: 43%   Collapse: 19%

Koskie is one of those guys you love to watch, because although he's not a masher with game-breaking power, he's an unselfish hitter (as in, somebody who works counts and gets on base), he's generally a smart baserunner, and he flashes good range at third. He's athletic enough to age well, but that would be the exception, not the rule. Appropriately enough, Koskie's under contract through 2004, or right up through the age where you should think twice about giving him big money.

Jason Kubel   RF   Born: 25-May-82   Age: 21   Bats: L   Throws: R

YEAR	TM	LG	AGE	AB	H	2B	3B	HR	BB	SO	SB	CS	AVG	OBP	SLG	MLVR	EQBA	EQOBP	EQSLG	EQMLVR	VORP	DEFENSE
2002	QUD	MDW	20	424	136	26	4	17	41	48	3	5	.321	.382	.521	.336	.245	.293	.401	-.161	-9.7	103-RF -6
2003	MIN	AL	21	211	53	10	2	6	15	32	2	1	.251	.305	.391	-.092	.255	.311	.407	-.106	-4.9	

Breakout: 38%   Improve: 58%   Collapse: 19%

The Twins might not be a stathead organization, but they're not afraid to take risks with different body types. Kubel is another one of the Twins' "short" outfielders who merely settles for hitting well. In his first full season, he made big strides with pitch identification, learning what he could drive and then hammering it. He's struggled against left-handed pitching, but the guys who hit right-handed pitching usually don't have to worry about getting noticed.

Matt LeCroy DH Born: 13-Dec-75 Age: 27 Bats: R Throws: R

YEAR	TM	LG	AGE	AB	H	2B	3B	HR	BB	SO	SB	CS	AVG	OBP	SLG	MLVR	EQBA	EQOBP	EQSLG	EQMLVR	VORP	DEFENSE			
2000	NBR	EAS	24	195	55	12	1	10	29	34	0	0	.282	.391	.508	.263	.245	.330	.445	-.032	10.9	42-C	-8		
2000	SLC	PCL	24	65	20	5	0	5	4	11	0	0	.308	.348	.615	.256	.266	.288	.516	.013	2.2				
2000	MIN	AL	24	167	29	10	0	5	17	38	0	0	.174	.258	.323	-.424	.175	.256	.331	-.374	-5.9	46-C	0		
2001	EDM	PCL	25	396	130	17	0	20	36	95	0	2	.328	.393	.523	.258	.287	.348	.452	.046	28.2	20-C	-2	10-1B	-1
2002	EDM	PCL	26	174	61	7	1	12	17	34	2	0	.351	.421	.609	.476	.310	.373	.534	.228	16.6				
2002	MIN	AL	26	181	47	11	1	7	13	38	0	2	.260	.309	.448	-.012	.275	.323	.478	.028	7.5				
2003	MIN	AL	27	285	74	16	1	11	23	58	2	2	.260	.320	.441	.003	.264	.327	.459	-.003	5.4				

Breakout: 10%   Improve: 32%   Collapse: 25%

Leg and knee injuries have crimped LeCroy's ability to catch, and that handicaps his prospects as long as Mientkiewicz is around. Could he still break out and become a good everyday DH? It's certainly possible, but the Twins' logjam of outfielders puts him in a precarious situation. Tactically, your third catcher isn't as helpful as you'd like if he's in the game as your DH. It would make the most sense if the Twins gave him a shot now at Mientkiewicz's expense, to see what he can do before Morneau arrives.

Brandon Marsters C Born: 14-Mar-75 Age: 28 Bats: R Throws: R

YEAR	TM	LG	AGE	AB	H	2B	3B	HR	BB	SO	SB	CS	AVG	OBP	SLG	MLVR	EQBA	EQOBP	EQSLG	EQMLVR	VORP	DEFENSE	
2000	FTM	FSL	25	407	126	25	4	7	31	61	2	1	.310	.364	.442	.198	.258	.299	.373	-.180	5.7	105-C	17
2001	NBR	EAS	26	349	77	16	1	9	29	75	2	1	.221	.286	.350	-.137	.197	.256	.312	-.388	-14.2	73-C	6
2002	NBR	EAS	27	76	18	8	0	2	7	18	0	0	.237	.318	.421	-.003	.208	.274	.364	-.275	-.8	22-C	2
2002	EDM	PCL	27	184	51	8	0	5	12	37	0	0	.277	.328	.402	-.038	.250	.293	.364	-.210	1.1	54-C	-1
2003	MIN	AL	28	115	28	6	1	3	8	24	1	1	.242	.295	.374	-.137	.245	.300	.390	-.154	0.5		

Breakout: 43%   Improve: 67%   Collapse: 21%

Marsters is your basic minor league soldier stumping for his union card with the International Brotherhood of Backup Catchers and Spot Welders. He throws well and isn't an offensive zero, which makes him a better player than guys like Alberto Castillo or Sandy Alomar Jr. for a fraction of the price, and he's a minor league free agent.

Joe Mauer C Born: 19-Apr-83 Age: 20 Bats: L Throws: R

YEAR	TM	LG	AGE	AB	H	2B	3B	HR	BB	SO	SB	CS	AVG	OBP	SLG	MLVR	EQBA	EQOBP	EQSLG	EQMLVR	VORP	DEFENSE			
2001	ELZ	APL	18	110	44	6	2	0	19	10	4	0	.400	.492	.491	.522	.274	.343	.333	-.141	3.3	19-C	-4		
2002	QUD	MDW	19	411	124	23	1	4	61	42	0	0	.302	.395	.392	.169	.236	.307	.311	-.266	-3.6	81-C	10	12-1B	0
2003	MIN	AL	20	195	49	10	2	3	19	24	2	1	.253	.324	.366	-.090	.256	.330	.381	-.104	3.6				

Breakout: 44%   Improve: 69%   Collapse: 17%

A tremendous prospect already, Mauer hasn't even learned how to pull the ball yet, mostly hammering pitches with authority to the opposite field. It's expected he'll soon master getting the bat around and hitting with more power. Behind the plate, he's nimble, flashing a strong arm and good release. There isn't really somebody you could compare him to: Dave Nilsson with a glove? A better Terry Kennedy? A lefty-batting Jason Kendall? None of those really work. He won't really be on the big league radar until late in 2004, but he's looking every bit the prospect the Twins thought they'd get when they signed him.

Doug Mientkiewicz 1B Born: 19-Jun-74 Age: 29 Bats: L Throws: R

YEAR	TM	LG	AGE	AB	H	2B	3B	HR	BB	SO	SB	CS	AVG	OBP	SLG	MLVR	EQBA	EQOBP	EQSLG	EQMLVR	VORP	DEFENSE			
2000	SLC	PCL	26	485	162	32	3	18	61	68	9	5	.334	.412	.524	.253	.281	.347	.439	.021	13.7	82-1B	5	36-3B	0
2001	MIN	AL	27	543	166	39	1	15	67	92	2	6	.306	.391	.464	.172	.324	.406	.493	.239	48.8	142-1B	21		
2002	MIN	AL	28	467	122	29	1	10	74	69	1	2	.261	.369	.392	.021	.281	.386	.421	.066	21.0	131-1B	8		
2003	MIN	AL	29	426	116	26	2	11	58	64	2	2	.273	.363	.423	.059	.277	.370	.440	.057	11.4				

Breakout: 8%   Improve: 41%   Collapse: 16%

Mientkiewicz might have a cool name and get good marks for his glovework and hustle. That's all well and good, but he's also not particularly young, and first basemen who don't put lots of runs on the board shouldn't keep their jobs. Minky had a season that wouldn't have kept Scott Stahoviak employed, division title or no. At the most, this should be his last season as a regular for the Twins.

Dustan Mohr OF Born: 19-Jun-76 Age: 27 Bats: R Throws: R

YEAR	TM	LG	AGE	AB	H	2B	3B	HR	BB	SO	SB	CS	AVG	OBP	SLG	MLVR	EQBA	EQOBP	EQSLG	EQMLVR	VORP	DEFENSE	
2000	FTM	FSL	24	370	98	19	2	11	35	65	7	4	.265	.341	.416	.092	.222	.277	.356	-.271	-17.8	89-LF	-5
2001	NBR	EAS	25	518	174	41	3	24	49	111	9	9	.336	.398	.566	.407	.287	.345	.481	.082	36.4	133-CF	-4
2001	MIN	AL	25	51	12	2	0	0	5	17	1	1	.235	.304	.275	-.284	.255	.321	.294	-.251	-2.3	18-RF	1
2002	MIN	AL	26	383	103	23	2	12	31	86	6	3	.269	.325	.433	.004	.288	.344	.468	.063	13.7	101-RF	3
2003	MIN	AL	27	378	100	23	2	12	32	81	6	4	.265	.326	.434	.008	.269	.332	.452	.002	3.2		

Breakout: 14%   Improve: 46%   Collapse: 20%

The Twins don't "just" get their talent from the draft, they also go shopping once in a while. They grabbed Mohr after his release by the Indians in spring training in 2000, eventually turning him into a useful spare outfielder. He did fall on his face over the last two months, and with his reputation as a mistake hitter, he probably just had the best season he's going to have.

Justin Morneau 1B Born: 15-May-81 Age: 22 Bats: L Throws: R

YEAR	TM	LG	AGE	AB	H	2B	3B	HR	BB	SO	SB	CS	AVG	OBP	SLG	MLVR	EQBA	EQOBP	EQSLG	EQMLVR	VORP	DEFENSE	
2001	QUD	MDW	20	236	84	17	2	12	26	38	0	0	.356	.426	.597	.514	.266	.322	.440	-.036	3.7	57-1B	2
2001	FTM	FSL	20	197	58	10	3	4	24	41	0	0	.294	.393	.437	.236	.249	.318	.380	-.141	-2.3	47-1B	-2
2002	NBR	EAS	21	494	147	31	4	16	42	88	7	0	.298	.360	.474	.182	.256	.308	.412	-.109	-1.7	124-1B	-13
2003	MIN	AL	22	205	50	11	2	6	17	43	2	2	.244	.306	.396	-.088	.247	.312	.413	-.102	-3.3		

Breakout: 25%   Improve: 51%   Collapse: 26%

Morneau's plus bat speed and sweet swing have produced solid offensive numbers at every level, generating comparisons to John Olerud. Considering his age, it's reasonable to expect a big power spike down the line. Defensively, he's merely service-able so far, but when you have a choice between Mark Grace Lite and somebody who could be the next Hrbek, you've got to go with the younger, better hitter. Assuming Morneau does fine in Rochester in 2003, he should be the everyday first base-man or DH by 2004.

David Ortiz DH Born: 18-Nov-75 Age: 27 Bats: L Throws: L

YEAR	TM	LG	AGE	AB	H	2B	3B	HR	BB	SO	SB	CS	AVG	OBP	SLG	MLVR	EQBA	EQOBP	EQSLG	EQMLVR	VORP	DEFENSE	
2000	MIN	AL	24	415	117	36	1	10	57	81	1	0	.282	.369	.446	.036	.289	.369	.457	.092	20.3	25-1B	0
2001	MIN	AL	25	303	71	17	1	18	40	68	1	0	.234	.326	.475	.017	.244	.338	.502	.059	15.8		
2002	MIN	AL	26	412	112	32	1	20	43	87	1	2	.272	.345	.500	.127	.287	.361	.531	.180	30.0	11-1B	0
2003	BOS	AL	27	391	105	26	1	18	46	83	1	1	.268	.346	.482	.102	.274	.355	.504	.112	16.0		

Breakout: 11%   Improve: 49%   Collapse: 14%

Welcome to the New Economics. We've warned for years that the benefits of arbitration shouldn't really trickle down to base-ball's middle class, because a smart organization can just non-tender or release a solid player rather than leave it to an arbi-trator to set his value; solid players can be replaced through player development and/or a sharp eye on the waiver wire. It would have made more sense to non-tender Mientkiewicz and go to arbitration with Ortiz, but Ortiz's annual struggle to stay healthy probably squelched that idea. Ortiz is a thoroughly useful DH, but this winter's market of free agents is flooded with useful DHs. As a Red Sock, he's every bit as nifty a pickup as Jeremy Giambi.

A. J. Pierzynski C Born: 30-Dec-76 Age: 26 Bats: L Throws: R

YEAR	TM	LG	AGE	AB	H	2B	3B	HR	BB	SO	SB	CS	AVG	OBP	SLG	MLVR	EQBA	EQOBP	EQSLG	EQMLVR	VORP	DEFENSE	
2000	NBR	EAS	23	228	68	17	2	4	8	22	0	0	.298	.347	.443	.124	.262	.293	.397	-.154	4.5	47-C	-6
2000	SLC	PCL	23	155	52	14	1	4	5	22	1	1	.335	.360	.516	.159	.285	.302	.437	-.060	6.1	38-C	-2
2000	MIN	AL	23	88	27	5	1	2	5	14	1	0	.307	.358	.455	.051	.310	.355	.471	.107	7.3	25-C	2
2001	MIN	AL	24	381	110	33	2	7	16	57	1	7	.289	.324	.441	.013	.299	.336	.462	.050	27.0	99-C	3
2002	MIN	AL	25	440	132	31	6	6	13	61	1	2	.300	.336	.439	.055	.317	.350	.468	.101	36.3	113-C	4
2003	MIN	AL	26	396	114	27	2	8	16	55	2	2	.288	.322	.433	.017	.292	.328	.450	.012	17.7		

Breakout: 14%   Improve: 43%   Collapse: 28%

One of the game's great carmine kiesters, A. J. Pierzynski is never going to win a popularity contest around the league, but he doesn't need to. Nobody liked Clint Courtney either, but 50 years later, everybody still talks about him. Pierzynski is a good catcher—his percentages throwing out runners aren't amazing, but the Twins control the running game as well as anybody—and as a guy who can make contact and drive the ball, he's a pest at the bottom of the order. As the man who holds the job until/if/when Joe Mauer is ready, he's the best placeholder in the game.

Tom Prince   C   Born: 13-Aug-64   Age: 38   Bats: R   Throws: R

YEAR	TM	LG	AGE	AB	H	2B	3B	HR	BB	SO	SB	CS	AVG	OBP	SLG	MLVR	EQBA	EQOBP	EQSLG	EQMLVR	VORP		DEFENSE
2000	PHI	NL	35	122	29	9	0	2	13	31	1	0	.238	.321	.361	-.196	.244	.315	.366	-.169	2.2		37-C 1
2001	MIN	AL	36	196	43	4	1	7	12	39	3	1	.219	.285	.357	-.219	.235	.297	.383	-.186	2.4		61-C 11
2002	MIN	AL	37	125	28	7	1	4	14	26	1	3	.224	.322	.392	-.088	.246	.337	.429	-.040	6.5		42-C 3
2003	MIN	AL	38	103	22	4	0	3	9	23	1	1	.211	.276	.336	-.236	.214	.281	.350	-.261	-2.6		

Breakout: 24%   Improve: 32%   Collapse: 51%

Why is Prince being kept around? To his credit, he can do things like work with Joe Mauer on catching technique, plus he still has a little bit of power and he can still field his position, so why not keep him around? There is something to be said for retaining veterans on the bench who take a mentoring role seriously.

Mike Restovich   RF   Born: 03-Jan-79   Age: 24   Bats: R   Throws: R

YEAR	TM	LG	AGE	AB	H	2B	3B	HR	BB	SO	SB	CS	AVG	OBP	SLG	MLVR	EQBA	EQOBP	EQSLG	EQMLVR	VORP		DEFENSE
2000	FTM	FSL	21	475	125	27	9	8	61	100	19	7	.263	.352	.408	.096	.220	.289	.349	-.259	-23.5		127-RF -9
2001	NBR	EAS	22	501	135	33	4	23	54	125	15	7	.269	.348	.489	.173	.236	.306	.424	-.112	-4.9		140-RF 0
2002	EDM	PCL	23	518	148	32	7	29	53	151	11	7	.286	.357	.542	.212	.252	.317	.474	-.009	10.8		120-OF -6
2002	MIN	AL	23	13	4	0	0	1	1	4	1	0	.308	.357	.538	.233	.308	.357	.615	.317	1.5		
2003	MIN	AL	24	220	58	13	2	8	20	54	5	3	.263	.328	.451	.031	.267	.335	.469	.027	3.4		

Breakout: 35%   Improve: 63%   Collapse: 17%

Restovich gets compared to the usual suspects in right field: Tim Salmon, Adam Dunn, and inevitably, Tom Brunansky. None of them really work. A guy with Brunansky's bat but not his glove sounds about right, since Restovich is more of a bruiser. He needs work on his defense, but it's expected that his athleticism will make him a good outfielder in time. He has options left, so he won't be the first choice to win a share of the right field or DH jobs, but if anyone falters, he'll be ready. He slugged nearly .700 against lefties in the PCL in 2002, so he could carve out a platoon role.

Luis Rivas   2B   Born: 30-Aug-79   Age: 23   Bats: R   Throws: R

YEAR	TM	LG	AGE	AB	H	2B	3B	HR	BB	SO	SB	CS	AVG	OBP	SLG	MLVR	EQBA	EQOBP	EQSLG	EQMLVR	VORP		DEFENSE
2000	NBR	EAS	20	328	82	23	6	3	36	41	11	4	.250	.332	.384	-.019	.222	.284	.344	-.274	-5.1		73-2B -2
2000	SLC	PCL	20	157	50	14	1	3	13	21	7	4	.318	.378	.478	.112	.273	.319	.409	-.080	5.0		32-2B 2
2000	MIN	AL	20	58	18	4	1	0	2	4	2	0	.310	.333	.414	-.051	.310	.322	.431	-.010	2.8		14-2B -7
2001	MIN	AL	21	563	150	21	6	7	40	99	31	11	.266	.322	.362	-.115	.281	.337	.382	-.079	19.7		144-2B -43
2002	MIN	AL	22	316	81	23	4	4	19	51	9	4	.256	.305	.392	-.096	.274	.322	.426	-.049	13.3		86-2B -10
2003	MIN	AL	23	389	104	24	3	6	29	55	14	4	.267	.322	.394	-.050	.271	.328	.410	-.060	10.7		

Breakout: 19%   Improve: 58%   Collapse: 17%

Luis Rivas is young enough that nobody's giving up hope just yet, but two years as a regular haven't helped him solidify his future. He hasn't hit nearly as well as expected, and his performance at second has left a lot to be desired, as he's shown little range and two left feet on the deuce. Some of that could be adapting to the position from his days as a shortstop, but if Rivas doesn't improve in some aspect of the game in 2003, he should lose his job to Luis Rodriguez or Jose Morban.

Luis Rodriguez   2B/SS   Born: 27-Jun-80   Age: 23   Bats: B   Throws: R

YEAR	TM	LG	AGE	AB	H	2B	3B	HR	BB	SO	SB	CS	AVG	OBP	SLG	MLVR	EQBA	EQOBP	EQSLG	EQMLVR	VORP		DEFENSE	
2000	QUD	MDW	20	342	77	11	2	0	40	29	4	5	.225	.315	.269	-.156	.184	.240	.220	-.553	-31.0		81-2B 3	14-SS 2
2001	FTM	FSL	21	463	127	21	3	4	82	42	11	8	.274	.390	.359	.117	.235	.323	.313	-.232	-1.7		68-SS 0	55-2B -4
2002	NBR	EAS	22	455	117	18	2	8	61	44	3	2	.257	.351	.358	-.016	.224	.301	.314	-.280	-7.8		119-SS 6	
2003	MIN	AL	23	178	44	9	1	3	17	22	2	1	.245	.317	.354	-.123	.249	.323	.368	-.139	1.1			

Breakout: 54%   Improve: 72%   Collapse: 11%

You already know that a middle infielder who draws walks is somebody we're quick to warm up to, but Rodriguez walks without being especially cautious at the plate, and he shows good power for someone who's young and not playing in hitter's paradise. What doesn't show up here is that his manager in 2002, Stan Cliburn, had him drop 32 sac bunts. How that helped Rodriguez develop is beyond me, unless he really needed to work on his bunting that badly, and nobody needs that much work on their bunting. A good first half and some more struggling by Rivas, and Rodriguez could nab the job at second.

Mike Ryan — LF — Born: 06-Jul-77 — Age: 26 — Bats: L — Throws: R

YEAR	TM	LG	AGE	AB	H	2B	3B	HR	BB	SO	SB	CS	AVG	OBP	SLG	MLVR	EQBA	EQOBP	EQSLG	EQMLVR	VORP	DEFENSE		
2000	NBR	EAS	23	481	133	23	8	11	34	79	4	3	.277	.327	.426	.051	.242	.280	.380	-.218	-16.0	104-LF	-11	16-2B -4
2001	EDM	PCL	24	527	152	36	7	18	52	121	1	6	.288	.355	.486	.100	.251	.316	.421	-.086	-1.3	87-RF	-6	36-2B -12
2002	EDM	PCL	25	540	141	36	6	31	55	124	4	5	.261	.332	.522	.119	.231	.296	.457	-.089	-.1	106-LF	-7	
2002	MIN	AL	25	11	1	0	0	0	0	2	0	0	.091	.091	.091	-.970	.182	.182	.182	-.730	-1.6			
2003	MIN	AL	26	199	51	12	1	7	17	41	3	2	.254	.315	.428	-.026	.258	.321	.445	-.035	-.3			

Breakout: 28%   Improve: 61%   Collapse: 20%

Tied for the minor league lead in extra-base hits in 2002, Ryan is one of those guys with a quick bat and no idea how to slow it down and thwack breaking stuff. That's not the end of the world; Earl Weaver would pinch-hit him against flamethrowing relievers and spot-start him against pitchers with weak off-speed repertoire. Ryan probably won't be the next John Lowenstein or Matt Stairs, but he could surprise you.

Ruben Salazar — 2B — Born: 16-Jan-78 — Age: 25 — Bats: R — Throws: R

YEAR	TM	LG	AGE	AB	H	2B	3B	HR	BB	SO	SB	CS	AVG	OBP	SLG	MLVR	EQBA	EQOBP	EQSLG	EQMLVR	VORP	DEFENSE	
2000	FTM	FSL	22	499	155	25	0	11	37	81	3	5	.311	.361	.427	.172	.256	.295	.358	-.211	.5	100-2B	-7
2001	NBR	EAS	23	530	158	29	2	10	37	77	6	1	.298	.352	.417	.110	.264	.313	.369	-.155	8.4	108-2B	-3
2002	NBR	EAS	24	371	103	24	2	4	27	72	4	0	.278	.332	.385	.001	.243	.288	.336	-.264	-4.8	48-2B	-11
2003	MIN	AL	25	151	37	8	1	3	10	27	2	1	.248	.296	.359	-.151	.251	.302	.374	-.170	-.6		

Breakout: 33%   Improve: 56%   Collapse: 23%

After a great winter season in 2001, there was some hope that Salazar would break out in 2002. It didn't happen, and his career has essentially stalled in Double-A after he got everyone's attention by hitting .401 in Elizabethton in 1999. He isn't a plus defender at second, and his core skill is hitting for average. If the majors still allowed 10-man pitching staffs and space on the bench for extra pinch hitters, he'd have hope, but we don't live in that world anymore.

Matt Scanlon — 3B — Born: 19-Jun-78 — Age: 25 — Bats: L — Throws: R

YEAR	TM	LG	AGE	AB	H	2B	3B	HR	BB	SO	SB	CS	AVG	OBP	SLG	MLVR	EQBA	EQOBP	EQSLG	EQMLVR	VORP	DEFENSE		
2000	QUD	MDW	22	439	113	29	5	7	39	61	5	4	.257	.344	.394	.067	.206	.256	.319	-.373	-21.2	53-3B	-6	19-2B -7
2001	FTM	FSL	23	348	88	12	2	3	43	67	2	1	.253	.340	.325	-.015	.221	.283	.290	-.351	-15.0	81-3B	-7	
2002	FTM	FSL	24	164	53	8	2	6	19	11	1	1	.323	.400	.506	.361	.269	.328	.427	-.041	6.7	37-3B	-5	
2002	NBR	EAS	24	197	38	6	2	3	16	39	4	1	.193	.274	.289	-.275	.175	.233	.270	-.503	-21.5	20-LF	-3	22-3B -2
2003	MIN	AL	25	150	36	8	1	3	11	25	2	1	.241	.301	.371	-.131	.245	.307	.387	-.147	-1.5			

Breakout: 60%   Improve: 75%   Collapse: 15%

A University of Minnesota alum, Scanlon started off the year with a huge April, smacking five of the nine home runs he'd hit on the year. At 24, he needed that kind of start if he's going to run up the ladder and have a career, but he flopped in New Britain. If there's a position where the Twins have no organizational depth, it's at third, where they have guys like Scanlon or Terry Tiffee, neither of whom can really play third. This could help Koskie's negotiating position later on.

Todd Sears — 1B — Born: 23-Oct-75 — Age: 27 — Bats: L — Throws: R

YEAR	TM	LG	AGE	AB	H	2B	3B	HR	BB	SO	SB	CS	AVG	OBP	SLG	MLVR	EQBA	EQOBP	EQSLG	EQMLVR	VORP	DEFENSE	
2000	CAR	SOU	24	299	90	21	0	12	72	76	12	3	.301	.440	.492	.339	.258	.374	.430	.039	12.5	80-1B	-12
2000	NBR	EAS	24	140	44	8	1	3	18	40	1	0	.314	.396	.450	.222	.273	.340	.399	-.055	1.6	33-1B	-4
2001	EDM	PCL	25	408	127	25	2	13	41	71	2	1	.311	.378	.478	.153	.271	.336	.416	-.040	5.8	103-1B	-2
2002	EDM	PCL	26	484	150	36	4	20	59	142	2	1	.310	.391	.525	.267	.274	.346	.463	.046	18.5	119-1B	-17
2002	MIN	AL	26	12	4	2	0	0	0	1	0	0	.333	.333	.500	.169	.333	.333	.583	.266	1.1		
2003	MIN	AL	27	171	43	10	1	5	17	40	3	2	.253	.325	.418	-.023	.257	.332	.435	-.031	.5		

Breakout: 9%   Improve: 35%   Collapse: 36%

Sears went into 2002 gunning to hit for more power, which he achieved at the cost of striking out much more. It paid off in terms of putting runs on the board and keeping him on the 40-man roster. If he has a window of opportunity, it's right now, should Mientkiewicz flop or get hurt, and before Morneau is ready. For whatever reason, his defense gets rave reviews; he's big and athletic, so he looks good out there, and he avoids errors.

James Tomlin   CF   Born: 12-Aug-82   Age: 20   Bats: R   Throws: R

YEAR	TM	LG	AGE	AB	H	2B	3B	HR	BB	SO	SB	CS	AVG	OBP	SLG	MLVR	EQBA	EQOBP	EQSLG	EQMLVR	VORP	DEFENSE
2001	ELZ	APL	18	237	71	14	4	1	21	33	15	7	.300	.376	.405	.174	.212	.259	.290	-.405	-15.7	60-CF -2
2002	QUD	MDW	19	427	116	17	1	3	34	58	18	13	.272	.337	.337	-.001	.215	.262	.268	-.428	-28.1	103-CF -5
2003	MIN	AL	20	183	43	8	2	3	12	30	3	2	.237	.290	.343	-.188	.240	.296	.357	-.209	-4.1	

Breakout: 65%   *Improve: 79%*   *Collapse: 9%*

Tomlin isn't the team's center fielder of the future yet, but he's young and he hasn't been overpowered so far, and 2002 was his introduction to full-season baseball. His glovework gets decent marks and he runs well, so as he fills out and matures physically, he could turn into something. I know, they say the same thing about Ben Affleck, but Tomlin should turn out better.

Javier Valentin   C   Born: 19-Sep-75   Age: 27   Bats: B   Throws: R

YEAR	TM	LG	AGE	AB	H	2B	3B	HR	BB	SO	SB	CS	AVG	OBP	SLG	MLVR	EQBA	EQOBP	EQSLG	EQMLVR	VORP	DEFENSE	
2000	SLC	PCL	24	140	50	16	2	7	9	27	1	0	.357	.400	.650	.454	.301	.334	.544	.169	12.9	23-C 1	
2001	EDM	PCL	25	431	121	29	2	17	47	108	0	1	.281	.357	.476	.082	.247	.319	.412	-.096	15.5	49-C 0	25-3B -5
2002	EDM	PCL	26	455	130	33	1	21	41	96	0	1	.286	.351	.501	.146	.253	.313	.442	-.060	20.8	68-C -3	
2003	MIL	NL	27	154	39	9	1	6	14	34	2	2	.252	.319	.424	-.048	.257	.321	.444	-.043	5.0		

Breakout: 22%   *Improve: 38%*   *Collapse: 29%*

The battles with Tom Kelly have been fought and lost, which along with a knee injury in 2000 helped cost Valentin three years he could have been in the majors. His lack of options finally forced the Twins to dump him on the Brewers, but he's still standing. His knees aren't the best, but he can hit, he's got a good arm, and he's still relatively young. He's better than several major league starters, let alone the Girardis of the world, so he could finally break out this year.

PITCHERS

Grant Balfour   Born: 30-Dec-77   Age: 25   Bats: R   Throws: R

YEAR	TM	LG	AGE	G	GS	IP	H	BB	SO	HR	ERA	EQERA	EQH9	EQBB9	EQSO9	EQHR9	PERA	VORP	STF
2000	FTM	FSL	22	35	10	89.0	91	34	90	8	4.25	6.75	13.4	4.6	6.8	2.2	6.77	-12.9	-4
2001	NBR	EAS	23	35	0	50.0	26	22	72	1	1.08	2.17	5.9	5.3	9.0	0.3	2.66	17.8	20
2001	EDM	PCL	23	11	0	16.3	18	10	17	2	5.52	6.12	10.4	6.5	6.8	1.3	6.36	-1.3	-9
2002	EDM	PCL	24	58	0	71.3	60	30	88	3	4.17	3.88	7.9	4.3	8.5	0.5	3.68	11.9	13
2003	MIN	AL	25	24	2	39.0	39	20	34	4	4.67	4.57	8.6	4.2	7.6	0.9	4.45	5.3	3

Breakout: 16%   *Improve: 51%*   *Collapse: 20%*

One of the organization's Australian assets, Balfour has slowly adapted to pitching after being a hitter down under. He throws in the low 90s and can overpower right-handed hitters, but he gets predictable with his slider, and that gets him in trouble against left-handed hitters. With veterans Bob Wells and Mike Jackson hitting the road, he's got a shot, but he'll be competing with teammate Kevin Frederick.

J. D. Durbin   Born: 24-Feb-82   Age: 21   Bats: R   Throws: R

YEAR	TM	LG	AGE	G	GS	IP	H	BB	SO	HR	ERA	EQERA	EQH9	EQBB9	EQSO9	EQHR9	PERA	VORP	STF
2001	ELZ	APL	19	8	7	33.7	23	17	39	2	1.87	6.01	11.3	8.0	5.1	1.6	5.52	-1.9	-11
2002	QUD	MDW	20	27	27	161.0	144	51	163	14	3.19	5.83	13.0	4.2	6.1	2.4	5.52	-5.8	8

The small-market Twins had what it took to keep Durbin from taking up a scholarship at Arizona State, and it's worked out well so far. Although he has had problems with elbow tendonitis, there's a lot to like. He's got a nifty sinker, works in the low 90s, sets up his change well, and polishes hitters off with a sharp slider. Nobody should get too excited about low A-ball pitchers, but Durbin looks good so far.

Willie Eyre — Born: 21-Jul-78 — Age: 24 — Bats: R — Throws: R

YEAR	TM	LG	AGE	G	GS	IP	H	BB	SO	HR	ERA	EQERA	EQH9	EQBB9	EQSO9	EQHR9	PERA	VORP	STF
2000	QUD	MDW	21	26	18	99.7	104	56	81	9	4.60	7.89	14.5	6.6	4.9	2.3	7.92	-26.6	-17
2001	QUD	MDW	22	17	0	22.3	19	2	21	1	2.42	3.88	10.7	1.2	5.3	0.9	3.78	3.7	1
2001	FTM	FSL	22	32	0	64.3	54	33	51	2	2.52	5.41	10.2	5.7	4.9	0.7	5.58	-0.2	-12
2002	FTM	FSL	23	19	0	33.7	28	13	25	0	2.40	3.99	10.0	4.5	4.8	0.3	4.57	5.2	-7
2002	NBR	EAS	23	28	0	50.0	40	21	43	1	3.24	4.02	8.4	4.5	5.9	0.3	3.81	7.6	0

Meet Willie Mays Eyre, straight out of Utah. Is this a great country or what? Anyway, he's been added to the 40-man roster, which was more of a scouty decision than anything else. The Twins already fretted in 2001 about losing Jon Pridie in the Rule 5 draft, and they didn't want to lose any of their fair-haired boys this winter. Eyre's got a good sinker-slider repertoire, and gets the usual kudos for moxie and fearlessness.

Tony Fiore — Born: 12-Oct-71 — Age: 31 — Bats: R — Throws: R

YEAR	TM	LG	AGE	G	GS	IP	H	BB	SO	HR	ERA	EQERA	EQH9	EQBB9	EQSO9	EQHR9	PERA	VORP	STF
2000	DUR	INT	28	53	1	75.0	62	38	39	3	2.28	3.38	8.2	4.6	4.0	0.5	3.98	16.7	-16
2000	TBY	AL	28	11	0	15.0	21	9	8	3	8.40	7.47	11.7	4.3	4.6	1.5	6.91	-3.5	-25
2001	DUR	INT	29	15	0	20.3	7	8	11	0	0.00	0.34	3.8	4.2	3.9	0.2	1.50	11.4	-7
2001	EDM	PCL	29	32	6	80.7	85	25	58	4	3.68	4.09	10.0	3.3	4.7	0.5	4.45	12.0	-6
2002	EDM	PCL	30	2	2	13.0	15	2	6	2	4.15	4.64	11.3	1.6	3.2	1.8	5.51	1.2	-7
2002	MIN	AL	30	48	2	91.0	74	43	55	10	3.16	3.36	7.5	4.0	5.3	0.9	3.50	20.6	-6
2003	MIN	AL	31	32	10	73.0	80	32	44	8	4.70	4.59	9.5	3.6	5.2	1.0	4.75	10.2	-8

Breakout: 15%   Improve: 50%   Collapse: 25%

One of the beautiful things about relief pitching is that what makes a useful relief pitcher is still baseball's equivalent of a dark continent as far as statheads are concerned. Sure, after the fact we can parse what a guy does well, as we can note with Fiore and his ability to pitch effectively from the stretch. Was he lucky? He gave up a lot fewer hits than you'd expect, particularly at home, and middle relievers who rely on their outfielders aren't usually the kinds of guys we endorse. Fiore was nevertheless an asset in 2002, soaking up two or three innings as needed, allowing the Twins to take pressure off of the rotation and letting Gardenhire keep his bullpen usage patterns stable. Where offenses today gun for winning the game in the sixth inning by beating an opponent's 10th, 11th, or 12th pitchers, the Twins had a 10th or 11th man who could hold the fort. Will he do it again? He's not a great bet, but before 1999, nobody took Bob Wells seriously, and after 1999 people still didn't take Bob Wells very seriously.

Joe Foote — Born: 30-Aug-79 — Age: 23 — Bats: R — Throws: R

YEAR	TM	LG	AGE	G	GS	IP	H	BB	SO	HR	ERA	EQERA	EQH9	EQBB9	EQSO9	EQHR9	PERA	VORP	STF
2000	QUD	MDW	20	25	25	146.0	152	43	128	13	3.88	6.93	14.2	3.4	5.2	2.2	6.63	-23.1	1
2001	QUD	MDW	21	13	8	55.7	64	10	46	7	5.17	8.11	15.9	2.4	4.9	2.8	7.24	-16.3	-7
2001	FTM	FSL	21	17	14	86.0	101	25	57	5	3.87	6.91	14.8	3.3	4.2	1.4	7.41	-13.5	-5
2002	FTM	FSL	22	26	23	144.7	141	35	92	9	3.11	5.53	12.5	2.9	4.2	1.4	5.56	-0.5	0

Foote was specifically charged with working on low strikes, and whether he was successful or just happier about pitching in the Florida State League, at least he made progress. In this organization, he's just another guy, but he's young, he's retained his health, and he throws strikes.

Kevin Frederick — Born: 04-Nov-76 — Age: 26 — Bats: L — Throws: R

YEAR	TM	LG	AGE	G	GS	IP	H	BB	SO	HR	ERA	EQERA	EQH9	EQBB9	EQSO9	EQHR9	PERA	VORP	STF
2000	QUD	MDW	23	27	0	46.0	34	23	51	1	2.35	4.61	9.2	5.5	6.3	0.5	4.59	3.9	-3
2000	FTM	FSL	23	19	0	30.0	20	14	37	0	2.70	4.30	7.8	5.3	7.8	0.3	3.75	3.6	9
2001	NBR	EAS	24	44	0	82.7	56	28	109	5	1.63	3.11	7.8	4.1	8.3	0.9	3.45	20.9	14
2002	EDM	PCL	25	46	2	55.0	63	21	47	8	4.58	5.47	11.1	4.0	5.9	1.7	6.15	-0.5	-13
2002	MIN	AL	25	8	0	11.7	13	10	5	3	10.00	8.28	10.0	7.2	3.7	2.1	7.13	-3.8	-41

A 34th rounder out of Creighton in 1998, Frederick was a first baseman who pitched occasionally. After missing 1999 with a torn labrum, he's been gaining command of a low 90s fastball and a hard slider. Can he be the next Felix Rodriguez? Sure, but like a lot of people, he could use better control. With Mike Jackson and Bob Wells gone, the opportunity is there for him to win a job in camp, but he'll be wrestling with whatever non-roster journeymen show up hoping to be the next Wells or Fiore.

Eddie Guardado Born: 02-Oct-70 Age: 32 Bats: R Throws: L

YEAR	TM	LG	AGE	G	GS	IP	H	BB	SO	HR	ERA	EQERA	EQH9	EQBB9	EQSO9	EQHR9	PERA	VORP	STF
2000	MIN	AL	29	70	0	61.7	55	25	52	14	3.94	3.47	7.1	2.9	7.2	1.7	4.01	13.1	1
2001	MIN	AL	30	67	0	66.7	47	23	67	5	3.51	2.96	6.3	2.9	8.5	0.6	2.46	17.9	17
2002	MIN	AL	31	68	0	67.7	53	18	70	9	2.92	2.95	7.1	2.2	9.1	1.1	2.94	18.3	19
2003	MIN	AL	32	59	0	56.7	48	18	54	7	3.13	3.06	7.4	2.7	8.3	1.1	3.28	17.4	13

Breakout: 29%   Improve: 58%   Collapse: 19%

Bless the Twins, Eddie Guardado had never been a closer per se, but did they care? They gave him the trophy stat, and while he didn't really pitch any better than he had the year before, he got a neato '45' in the saves column that will keep him gainfully employed until he's 40, or as long as he wants if he wants to go Orosco on us.

Latroy Hawkins Born: 21-Dec-72 Age: 30 Bats: R Throws: R

YEAR	TM	LG	AGE	G	GS	IP	H	BB	SO	HR	ERA	EQERA	EQH9	EQBB9	EQSO9	EQHR9	PERA	VORP	STF
2000	MIN	AL	27	66	0	87.7	85	32	59	7	3.39	2.95	7.9	2.6	5.8	0.6	3.31	23.7	1
2001	MIN	AL	28	62	0	51.3	59	39	36	3	5.96	5.62	10.2	6.3	5.9	0.5	5.57	-1.4	-16
2002	MIN	AL	29	65	0	80.3	63	15	63	5	2.13	2.52	7.3	1.6	6.9	0.5	2.36	25.5	13
2003	MIN	AL	30	58	0	62.7	62	21	47	5	3.55	3.47	8.5	2.7	6.5	0.7	3.68	16.4	3

Breakout: 23%   Improve: 59%   Collapse: 12%

After last season's meltdown, Hawkins started off the year mopping up, but after Mike Jackson's back injury and with Bob Wells sucking wind, Hawkins rose to the occasion and slipped into an important right-handed setup role. He's still got all of the pitches that made him a prospect, dialing up heat in the mid-90s, and mixing in a hard slider and extra-slow curve.

Brent Hoard Born: 03-Nov-76 Age: 26 Bats: R Throws: L

YEAR	TM	LG	AGE	G	GS	IP	H	BB	SO	HR	ERA	EQERA	EQH9	EQBB9	EQSO9	EQHR9	PERA	VORP	STF
2000	QUD	MDW	23	6	6	28.3	34	11	14	5	5.41	9.39	18.6	4.8	3.1	4.7	9.33	-12.2	-39
2000	FTM	FSL	23	19	18	92.0	98	44	55	6	4.30	7.67	13.8	5.8	4.0	1.6	7.30	-22.2	-18
2001	FTM	FSL	24	17	15	80.3	78	28	70	5	3.36	5.46	12.3	3.9	5.5	1.5	6.14	0.4	-2
2002	NBR	EAS	25	31	26	161.0	153	52	126	11	3.69	4.87	10.3	3.5	5.4	1.1	4.76	11.2	2
2003	MIN	AL	26	14	8	50.0	58	24	34	6	5.56	5.44	10.1	4.0	6.0	1.1	5.23	2.4	-3

Breakout: 17%   Improve: 49%   Collapse: 23%

Hoard was New Britain's staff ace, bouncing back after a 2001 season where he had some elbow trouble. He's your basic junkballer, working high in the strike zone, and not really a ground-ball pitcher. For a 3rd round pick in 1998 out of Stanford, he hasn't turned out quite as well as the Twins might have hoped, but you could say the same thing about Mark Redman before he finally broke through in 2000.

Ken Holubec Born: 01-Sep-78 Age: 24 Bats: L Throws: L

YEAR	TM	LG	AGE	G	GS	IP	H	BB	SO	HR	ERA	EQERA	EQH9	EQBB9	EQSO9	EQHR9	PERA	VORP	STF
2000	ELZ	APL	21	9	6	32.7	22	12	43	1	3.03	4.96	10.2	5.0	6.4	0.8	4.16	1.9	7
2001	QUD	MDW	22	27	22	134.0	107	63	129	7	3.22	5.50	10.6	6.3	5.6	1.1	5.07	-0.1	0
2002	FTM	FSL	23	26	24	111.7	93	44	125	8	3.22	5.21	10.8	4.6	7.4	1.6	5.26	3.6	9

An unheralded 9th round pick out of Northeast Louisiana University in 2000, Holubec is not your average lefty. He can get his heat into the low 90s and he'll buzz hitters with it, and he's been consistently tough on the leagues he's been in. The organization has quality lefties coming out of its ears, so they can afford to be patient and see if Holubec makes the jump to Double-A.

Mike Jackson Born: 22-Dec-64 Age: 38 Bats: R Throws: R

YEAR	TM	LG	AGE	G	GS	IP	H	BB	SO	HR	ERA	EQERA	EQH9	EQBB9	EQSO9	EQHR9	PERA	VORP	STF
2001	HOU	NL	36	67	0	69.0	68	22	46	14	4.70	4.60	8.9	2.7	5.1	1.6	4.76	6.0	-12
2002	MIN	AL	37	58	0	55.0	59	13	29	5	3.27	3.63	9.9	2.0	4.7	0.8	3.94	10.7	-7
2003	MIN	AL	38	54	0	45.3	54	13	26	6	4.49	4.39	10.4	2.3	5.0	1.2	4.64	8.7	-10

Breakout: 28%   Improve: 49%   Collapse: 23%

Do all relievers go to Valhalla, or just the really famous ones? Mike Jackson has been a reliever's reliever for 15 seasons, not counting the one spent on the DL, and he ranks 10th all-time in games pitched. He's been a top closer, a quality setup man, and way back when, a great long reliever. He's been traded for Phil Bradley and Kevin Mitchell, and outlasted both. A free agent, wherever he signs, he should pitch in his 1,000th game in 2003.

Adam Johnson | Born: 12-Jul-79 | Age: 23 | Bats: R | Throws: R

YEAR	TM	LG	AGE	G	GS	IP	H	BB	SO	HR	ERA	EQERA	EQH9	EQBB9	EQSO9	EQHR9	PERA	VORP	STF
2000	FTM	FSL	20	13	12	69.3	45	20	92	2	2.47	3.66	7.7	3.3	8.3	0.7	3.23	14.2	34
2001	NBR	EAS	21	18	18	113.0	105	39	110	10	3.82	5.57	10.9	4.3	6.2	1.3	5.26	-0.8	13
2001	EDM	PCL	21	4	4	23.7	19	10	25	0	5.70	4.11	7.5	4.5	6.9	0.2	3.11	3.7	25
2001	MIN	AL	21	7	4	25.0	32	13	17	6	8.28	7.57	11.1	4.3	5.7	1.9	6.81	-5.8	-3
2002	EDM	PCL	22	27	27	151.3	182	55	112	25	5.47	6.01	11.8	3.8	5.2	1.9	6.62	-8.5	0
2003	MIN	AL	23	13	9	57.3	66	26	39	8	5.41	5.29	10.0	3.7	5.9	1.3	5.19	4.0	-1

Breakout: 10%   Improve: 44%   Collapse: 23%

Johnson is one of those guys whose intensity on the mound is hard to miss. He wigged out after not making the club in spring training, and drew a suspension for beaning William Ortega in the PCL. His violent delivery creates some concern and encourages some observers to think he'll be better off in the pen, but the Twins still take him seriously as a starting pitcher. Although he struggled with command of his slider at times last summer, he gained better touch on his changeup. Between his flyball tendencies and a weak Edmonton outfield, it isn't hard to believe he'll do better once he gets up and has the benefit of pitching in front of the Twins' defense as either a starter or reliever.

Beau Kemp | Born: 31-Oct-80 | Age: 22 | Bats: R | Throws: R

YEAR	TM	LG	AGE	G	GS	IP	H	BB	SO	HR	ERA	EQERA	EQH9	EQBB9	EQSO9	EQHR9	PERA	VORP	STF
2000	ELZ	APL	19	17	0	20.7	12	6	28	2	2.17	4.38	10.0	4.0	6.7	2.7	3.79	2.3	-3
2001	QUD	MDW	20	31	0	43.0	29	15	46	4	2.51	4.77	9.4	4.6	6.2	2.0	4.09	2.9	-4
2002	FTM	FSL	21	59	0	68.3	49	18	49	0	0.66	3.07	8.5	3.0	4.6	0.3	3.39	17.5	-2

Kemp is another one of the Twins' relief "stars" from the minors, which tells you nothing about whether or not he has a future. The 0.66 ERA was a freak stat courtesy of only five earned runs among his 14 total. He's another short right-hander in an organization with the courage to give them a shot, he works in the low 90s, and he mixes in a curve now and again. Double-A in 2003 will be the real test of whether he'll pitch in the majors or be just another Curtis King.

Matt Kinney | Born: 16-Dec-76 | Age: 26 | Bats: R | Throws: R

YEAR	TM	LG	AGE	G	GS	IP	H	BB	SO	HR	ERA	EQERA	EQH9	EQBB9	EQSO9	EQHR9	PERA	VORP	STF
2000	NBR	EAS	23	15	15	86.3	74	35	93	7	2.71	3.62	8.3	4.0	7.1	1.3	4.71	18.1	18
2000	SLC	PCL	23	9	9	55.0	42	26	59	5	4.25	3.57	7.0	4.1	7.7	1.0	3.29	11.8	25
2000	MIN	AL	23	8	8	42.3	41	25	24	7	5.11	4.34	7.8	4.2	4.9	1.2	4.48	5.5	1
2001	EDM	PCL	24	29	29	161.7	178	74	146	25	5.06	5.77	10.5	4.9	5.9	1.6	6.10	-4.8	0
2002	EDM	PCL	25	5	5	27.3	42	4	21	9	8.90	8.93	15.3	1.5	5.4	3.8	9.27	-10.4	-14
2002	MIN	AL	25	14	12	66.0	78	33	45	13	4.64	5.57	10.7	4.2	6.0	1.6	5.98	-0.5	-2
2003	MIL	NL	26	19	13	80.7	82	41	65	12	4.86	5.27	9.5	3.9	6.4	1.3	5.36	3.8	1

Breakout: 15%   Improve: 46%   Collapse: 20%

Kinney suffered a major drop in velocity as the season progressed, which was eventually diagnosed as shoulder tendonitis. Happily, he was back up in the 90s in time for the PCL playoffs. The shortage of space on the 40-man roster forced the Twins' hand, as they dealt Kinney to the Brewers. Assuming last summer's shoulder woes weren't an indicator of future problems, he should be an asset in Milwaukee's rotation.

Kyle Lohse | Born: 04-Oct-78 | Age: 24 | Bats: R | Throws: R

YEAR	TM	LG	AGE	G	GS	IP	H	BB	SO	HR	ERA	EQERA	EQH9	EQBB9	EQSO9	EQHR9	PERA	VORP	STF
2000	NBR	EAS	21	28	28	167.0	196	55	124	23	6.04	6.28	11.9	3.3	5.0	2.3	7.08	-14.4	0
2001	NBR	EAS	22	6	6	38.0	32	4	32	5	2.37	3.84	9.9	1.3	5.3	1.9	4.19	7.0	13
2001	EDM	PCL	22	8	8	49.0	50	13	48	3	3.12	3.95	9.5	2.8	6.4	0.6	4.19	8.5	21
2001	MIN	AL	22	19	16	90.3	102	29	64	16	5.68	5.35	10.0	2.7	6.0	1.4	5.03	1.5	10
2002	MIN	AL	23	32	31	180.7	181	70	124	26	4.23	4.47	9.1	3.3	6.0	1.2	4.39	20.8	12
2003	MIN	AL	24	29	24	145.7	156	55	99	21	4.86	4.76	9.3	3.1	5.9	1.2	4.66	16.5	5

Breakout: 19%   Improve: 49%   Collapse: 16%

Not every organization would have stuck with a guy after that 2000 season, at which point Lohse had a 5.99 ERA at Double-A over 39 starts. But the key was that he was one of the youngest pitchers at the level. Given the opportunity to learn, he did, and as a result, the Twins got something they needed in 2002, which was as a fifth starter who could take his turn every fifth day while almost every other starter crashed or ached. On a particularly happy note, he got stronger as the season progressed: after July 1, he was 6–3 with a 2.83 ERA in 14 starts, nine of which were quality starts. I like his odds of becoming a solid third starter.

Joe Mays   Born: 10-Dec-75   Age: 27   Bats: B   Throws: R

YEAR	TM	LG	AGE	G	GS	IP	H	BB	SO	HR	ERA	EQERA	EQH9	EQBB9	EQSO9	EQHR9	PERA	VORP	STF
2000	MIN	AL	24	31	28	160.3	193	67	102	20	5.56	4.65	9.8	3.0	5.5	0.9	4.82	15.2	7
2001	MIN	AL	25	34	34	233.7	205	64	123	25	3.16	3.27	7.9	2.3	4.5	0.9	3.22	58.0	8
2002	MIN	AL	26	17	17	95.3	113	25	38	14	5.38	5.29	10.9	2.2	3.5	1.2	4.97	2.3	-6
2003	MIN	AL	27	21	16	103.7	122	33	54	14	4.74	4.64	10.1	2.6	4.5	1.2	4.75	13.2	-3

Breakout: 9%   *Improve: 44%*   *Collapse: 22%*

Well, everyone was worried about his 2001 workload, and for good reason, as elbow soreness had him on the DL by Tax Day (April 15). After rehab, he pitched adequately in the second half, but he clearly wasn't the workhorse of the previous season. He finally had surgery to remove a bone spur in his elbow at the end of November, and he should be ready to go in spring training. The question is whether or not he'll be able to fool hitters again, because he's not going to be a success trying to go down the Tewksbury career path.

Eric Milton   Born: 04-Aug-75   Age: 27   Bats: L   Throws: L

YEAR	TM	LG	AGE	G	GS	IP	H	BB	SO	HR	ERA	EQERA	EQH9	EQBB9	EQSO9	EQHR9	PERA	VORP	STF
2000	MIN	AL	24	33	33	200.0	205	44	160	35	4.86	3.98	8.3	1.6	6.9	1.3	3.77	33.9	23
2001	MIN	AL	25	35	34	220.7	222	61	157	35	4.32	4.23	8.9	2.3	6.0	1.3	4.16	31.2	13
2002	MIN	AL	26	29	29	171.0	173	30	121	24	4.84	4.38	9.3	1.5	6.3	1.2	3.80	21.4	16
2003	MIN	AL	27	29	25	159.7	167	37	106	23	4.24	4.14	9.1	1.9	5.8	1.3	4.03	29.4	10

Breakout: 12%   *Improve: 47%*   *Collapse: 15%*

There have been a lot of expectations loaded onto Milton, because we all keep thinking he's finally going to start posting ERAs under four and crank out that season that makes people start comparing him to John Tudor or Ron Guidry. Heck, it still works, Guidry didn't really have his first big season until he was 27. Milton had trouble with command of his fastball in June and July before breaking down with a knee injury in August. He hasn't gotten to the point that he's effective without his heat; he needs it to set up his curveball and make people bite on his changeup. It's still worth harboring great expectations.

Mike Nakamura   Born: 06-Sep-76   Age: 26   Bats: R   Throws: R

YEAR	TM	LG	AGE	G	GS	IP	H	BB	SO	HR	ERA	EQERA	EQH9	EQBB9	EQSO9	EQHR9	PERA	VORP	STF
2000	FTM	FSL	23	32	0	41.3	33	11	46	0	1.53	3.44	9.3	3.0	7.1	0.3	3.81	8.9	10
2001	NBR	EAS	24	48	1	86.3	75	24	109	3	1.77	3.58	9.8	3.4	7.9	0.5	4.14	17.3	13
2002	EDM	PCL	25	46	4	87.3	85	22	80	7	4.74	4.52	9.3	2.6	6.3	0.9	4.15	8.6	2
2003	MIN	AL	26	20	5	42.0	44	16	31	4	4.09	4.00	9.0	3.1	6.3	0.9	4.21	8.5	2

Breakout: 11%   *Improve: 48%*   *Collapse: 21%*

One of the three stalwarts of the Rock Cats bullpen in 2001 and another of the Twins' Aussie imports, Nakamura didn't succeed quite as well in the PCL. He doesn't throw hard, relying on a slider and change, which is why he didn't draw a look in the Rule 5 draft after he wasn't added to the 40-man roster. He's a year away from minor league free agency, and a longshot to win a relief job in camp, but could catch on as an 11th man somewhere.

Juan Padilla   Born: 17-Feb-77   Age: 26   Bats: R   Throws: R

YEAR	TM	LG	AGE	G	GS	IP	H	BB	SO	HR	ERA	EQERA	EQH9	EQBB9	EQSO9	EQHR9	PERA	VORP	STF
2000	QUD	MDW	23	32	0	33.0	24	9	40	0	1.91	3.08	8.8	3.0	6.8	0.3	3.40	8.4	8
2000	NBR	EAS	23	23	0	33.7	35	11	24	1	3.74	4.06	9.6	3.2	4.7	0.5	5.14	4.9	-7
2001	FTM	FSL	24	56	0	69.3	72	25	77	2	2.99	6.28	12.5	4.0	6.9	0.7	6.32	-6.9	-3
2002	NBR	EAS	25	54	0	65.3	69	18	52	2	3.31	4.75	11.1	3.0	5.5	0.5	4.91	4.6	-6
2003	MIN	AL	26	25	0	30.0	34	11	20	3	4.53	4.43	9.7	3.1	5.7	0.8	4.46	4.9	-5

Breakout: 18%   *Improve: 51%*   *Collapse: 19%*

The Twins did the Cardinals thing in 2002, tabbing individual relievers to be each minor league affiliate's "closer" and letting them rack up saves. Padilla's got good breaking stuff, but in the Rock Cats bullpen, he isn't any more of a prospect than Willie Eyre or Kevin Hodge or Jeromy Palki, he simply got the saves. As player usage patterns go, there's even less sense in making a guy a closer in the minors than there is in making somebody a situational lefty. You need to see what everybody can do to appreciate what they might be able to do in the majors, so why create specialized minor league bullpen roles?

Jon Pridie | Born: 07-Dec-79 | Age: 23 | Bats: R | Throws: R

YEAR	TM	LG	AGE	G	GS	IP	H	BB	SO	HR	ERA	EQERA	EQH9	EQBB9	EQSO9	EQHR9	PERA	VORP	STF
2000	QUD	MDW	20	45	8	97.0	89	42	91	5	3.43	5.95	12.0	4.9	5.5	1.2	5.90	-5.6	-7
2001	QUD	MDW	21	12	11	55.7	40	24	48	5	3.39	5.56	10.1	5.8	5.1	2.0	4.71	-0.4	-4
2001	FTM	FSL	21	14	9	57.0	54	37	42	3	4.58	6.96	12.0	7.4	4.7	1.3	7.25	-9.3	-14
2002	FTM	FSL	22	12	12	66.0	62	30	40	2	3.27	5.68	11.7	5.4	4.0	0.7	5.91	-1.3	-6
2002	NBR	EAS	22	16	15	94.0	95	46	70	6	5.07	5.68	10.9	5.3	5.2	1.0	5.73	-1.9	2

Pridie is on the 40-man roster, so we've got to say something. He's big, he's young, and he throws hard, so he might be anything from a fan favorite in the Northern League to a big league millionaire, or even both, over the next 15 years. Throwing in the mid-90s is a nice start, and he's got a good sinker, but his mastery of anything off-speed has been enough of a problem that there's talk of moving him into the bullpen.

Brad Radke | Born: 27-Oct-72 | Age: 30 | Bats: R | Throws: R

YEAR	TM	LG	AGE	G	GS	IP	H	BB	SO	HR	ERA	EQERA	EQH9	EQBB9	EQSO9	EQHR9	PERA	VORP	STF
2000	MIN	AL	27	34	34	226.7	261	51	141	27	4.45	3.78	9.5	1.6	5.4	0.9	4.01	43.5	12
2001	MIN	AL	28	33	33	226.0	235	26	137	24	3.94	3.80	9.4	1.0	5.2	0.9	3.52	42.8	14
2002	MIN	AL	29	21	21	118.3	124	20	62	12	4.72	4.27	9.7	1.4	4.7	0.8	3.70	16.2	7
2003	*MIN*	*AL*	*30*	*25*	*21*	*136.0*	*153*	*27*	*76*	*16*	*4.22*	*4.12*	*9.7*	*1.7*	*4.9*	*1.0*	*4.11*	*24.1*	*7*

Breakout: 20%   Improve: 50%   Collapse: 11%

Radke is the owner of one of the game's best changeups. At some point during the '90s it seemed like the changeup became the fashionable pitch, in the same way that the splitter was the pitch of the '80s. You could probably blame pitching coach Johnny Podres if you had to single out somebody, although nobody blamed the changeup for all of the flameouts in Philly in the late '80s and early '90s, and for good reason, considering the damaged goods the Phillies kept hauling in.

Radke suffered a groin pull last summer that cost him more than two months, with the Twins trying to rush him back at a couple of points. Throwing the changeup became physically difficult for him, aggravating the injury in August, but he was still able to notch a pair of quality starts in the playoffs. He should be fine in 2003, and that projection is a bit too modest.

Rick Reed | Born: 16-Aug-65 | Age: 37 | Bats: R | Throws: R

YEAR	TM	LG	AGE	G	GS	IP	H	BB	SO	HR	ERA	EQERA	EQH9	EQBB9	EQSO9	EQHR9	PERA	VORP	STF
2000	NYM	NL	34	30	30	184.0	192	34	121	28	4.11	4.23	9.9	1.4	5.4	1.3	4.32	26.1	10
2001	NYM	NL	35	20	20	134.7	119	17	99	16	3.47	3.47	8.5	1.1	5.8	1.0	3.35	30.5	17
2001	MIN	AL	35	12	12	67.7	92	14	43	12	5.18	5.77	12.0	1.7	5.4	1.4	5.85	-2.0	3
2002	MIN	AL	36	33	32	188.0	192	26	121	32	3.78	4.12	9.4	1.2	5.7	1.4	3.95	28.9	11
2003	*MIN*	*AL*	*37*	*25*	*20*	*126.0*	*146*	*25*	*72*	*20*	*4.34*	*4.25*	*10.0*	*1.6*	*5.0*	*1.4*	*4.43*	*23.2*	*4*

Breakout: 14%   Improve: 36%   Collapse: 17%

As much as it was a mistake to acquire Reed for the stretch drive in 2001, he came in handy in 2002. With the front three starters all fending off complaints both serious and minor, it was nice to have a known commodity making his starts every fifth day. The misfortune is when the Twins felt they had to start him in October. He's somebody you don't mind using in the regular season, but at this point counting on Reed against top offenses in the postseason shouldn't be anybody's first choice, and he was drubbed by both Oakland and Anaheim.

At what point will the MLBPA forgive and forget? Reed crossed the line in 1994 to pay medical bills that the union wasn't going to pay because Reed wasn't an active member at that point. True, the owners should go to the mat for the guys they got to cross, and the players should accept that they didn't live up to the promises they made in '94 to take care of minor league vets, and everyone should acknowledge that the whole thing was a big mistake. It's certainly more important to forgive and forget here than to give Pete Rose the time of day.

Juan Rincon — Born: 23-Jan-79 — Age: 24 — Bats: R — Throws: R

YEAR	TM	LG	AGE	G	GS	IP	H	BB	SO	HR	ERA	EQERA	EQH9	EQBB9	EQSO9	EQHR9	PERA	VORP	STF
2000	FTM	FSL	21	13	13	76.3	67	23	55	3	2.12	4.76	10.8	3.5	4.7	0.9	4.86	6.3	7
2000	NBR	EAS	21	15	15	89.0	96	39	79	9	4.65	5.53	10.7	4.3	5.9	1.7	6.51	-0.2	8
2001	NBR	EAS	22	29	23	153.3	130	57	133	9	2.88	4.80	9.9	4.6	5.6	0.9	4.59	11.8	7
2002	EDM	PCL	23	19	16	101.7	111	35	75	12	4.78	5.06	10.5	3.6	5.1	1.4	5.47	4.9	2
2002	MIN	AL	23	10	3	28.7	44	9	21	5	6.27	7.01	13.9	2.7	6.4	1.4	7.03	-5.0	1
2003	*MIN*	*AL*	*24*	*18*	*12*	*76.3*	*89*	*34*	*50*	*11*	*5.36*	*5.24*	*10.1*	*3.7*	*5.7*	*1.3*	*5.19*	*6.1*	*-3*

Breakout: 13%   Improve: 48%   Collapse: 25%

This might be the best time in the last 30 years for the under-six foot right-handed starter to make it in major league baseball. Rincon deals moving heat in the low 90s and throws four pitches for strikes, but at 5′11″, there are a lot of people in the game who couldn't care less. He's another candidate for the fifth starter's job, but with Bob Wells and Mike Jackson gone, he could slip into the pen and become another homegrown success story.

J. C. Romero — Born: 04-Jun-76 — Age: 27 — Bats: B — Throws: L

YEAR	TM	LG	AGE	G	GS	IP	H	BB	SO	HR	ERA	EQERA	EQH9	EQBB9	EQSO9	EQHR9	PERA	VORP	STF
2000	SLC	PCL	24	17	11	65.3	60	25	38	6	3.45	4.41	8.6	3.4	4.2	1.0	3.84	7.8	-4
2000	MIN	AL	24	12	11	57.7	72	30	50	8	7.02	5.75	10.0	3.7	7.4	1.0	5.40	-1.6	13
2001	EDM	PCL	25	12	10	63.7	67	24	55	4	3.67	4.62	9.9	4.0	5.7	0.7	4.76	6.2	5
2001	MIN	AL	25	14	11	65.0	71	24	39	10	6.23	5.54	9.7	3.1	5.1	1.2	4.83	-0.3	-1
2002	MIN	AL	26	81	0	81.0	62	36	76	3	1.89	2.34	7.0	3.8	8.2	0.3	2.76	27.4	14
2003	*MIN*	*AL*	*27*	*41*	*9*	*83.0*	*82*	*36*	*66*	*8*	*4.07*	*3.98*	*8.5*	*3.5*	*6.9*	*0.9*	*4.13*	*16.6*	*4*

Breakout: 16%   Improve: 51%   Collapse: 16%

With the wealth of alternatives the Twins have to choose from to stock the back end of the rotation, they had to find some way to put all of the quality arms they have knocking around to work. In Romero's case, they kept him as the third lefty, and he wound up being the rubber-armed strong man in one of the league's best pens. He's good with runners on base, keeps the ball low and in the infield, and squelches the running game. After a season like this, he may never go back to the rotation, making him a left-handed Keith Foulke in terms of what might have been, and the new Eddie Guardado in terms of what is.

Johan Santana — Born: 13-Mar-79 — Age: 24 — Bats: L — Throws: L

YEAR	TM	LG	AGE	G	GS	IP	H	BB	SO	HR	ERA	EQERA	EQH9	EQBB9	EQSO9	EQHR9	PERA	VORP	STF
2000	MIN	AL	21	30	5	86.0	102	54	64	11	6.49	5.24	9.5	4.4	6.3	0.9	5.34	1.8	5
2001	MIN	AL	22	15	4	43.7	50	16	28	6	4.74	4.95	10.2	3.1	5.4	1.1	4.97	2.4	1
2002	EDM	PCL	23	11	9	48.7	37	27	75	7	3.14	4.38	7.4	5.7	10.6	1.6	4.40	6.0	29
2002	MIN	AL	23	27	14	108.3	84	49	137	7	2.99	3.18	7.0	3.8	11.0	0.5	2.97	27.6	44
2003	*MIN*	*AL*	*24*	*27*	*20*	*124.0*	*112*	*60*	*124*	*12*	*3.90*	*3.81*	*7.8*	*4.0*	*8.7*	*0.9*	*3.96*	*27.0*	*21*

Breakout: 13%   Improve: 49%   Collapse: 10%

Santana was nabbed from the depths of the Midwest League out of the Astros' organization for the 2000 season, so you could expect him to get knocked around his first couple of years in the majors. Nevertheless, the Twins gave him game experience, and now they have his development as a starting pitcher as a reward. Although he's still wild, his climbing strikeout rate is reason to believe that the improvement will stick. He should be allowed to challenge Kyle Lohse for the fifth starter's job in camp, but Gardenhire has already said he'll have to settle for a long relief role until somebody gets hurt.

Brad Thomas · Born: 22-Oct-77 · Age: 25 · Bats: L · Throws: L

YEAR	TM	LG	AGE	G	GS	IP	H	BB	SO	HR	ERA	EQERA	EQH9	EQBB9	EQSO9	EQHR9	PERA	VORP	STF
2000	FTM	FSL	22	12	12	65.0	62	16	57	3	1.66	5.92	11.8	2.9	5.7	1.1	5.21	-3.0	10
2000	NBR	EAS	22	14	13	75.3	80	46	66	3	4.06	5.54	10.0	5.9	5.8	0.6	6.50	-0.3	3
2001	NBR	EAS	23	19	19	119.3	91	26	97	4	1.96	3.72	8.7	2.7	5.1	0.5	3.35	23.7	14
2001	MIN	AL	23	5	5	16.3	20	14	6	6	9.39	8.57	10.6	7.2	3.1	2.9	8.45	-5.6	-40
2002	EDM	PCL	24	28	27	152.0	175	54	97	20	5.74	6.12	11.2	3.7	4.5	1.5	6.00	-10.4	-6
2003	MIN	AL	25	13	9	57.0	66	25	33	7	5.37	5.25	10.1	3.6	5.1	1.2	5.15	3.8	-5

Breakout: 15%   Improve: 50%   Collapse: 16%

Amidst the wealth of ready or almost-ready pitching in the Twins' organization, Thomas might almost be forgotten. However, lefties who throw in the low 90s with a nifty curve tend to get remembered. Thomas is working on mastering his changeup, which will be the difference between his making it as a starting pitcher or merely being the next Mark Guthrie.

Bob Wells · Born: 01-Nov-66 · Age: 36 · Bats: R · Throws: R

YEAR	TM	LG	AGE	G	GS	IP	H	BB	SO	HR	ERA	EQERA	EQH9	EQBB9	EQSO9	EQHR9	PERA	VORP	STF
2000	MIN	AL	33	76	0	86.3	80	15	76	14	3.65	3.10	7.6	1.3	7.7	1.2	3.13	21.9	13
2001	MIN	AL	34	65	0	68.7	72	18	49	12	5.11	4.67	9.3	2.2	6.1	1.4	4.45	5.4	-4
2002	MIN	AL	35	48	0	58.0	78	16	30	8	5.90	5.99	12.3	2.3	4.6	1.1	5.73	-3.9	-15
2003	MIN	AL	36	47	0	56.0	62	15	34	8	4.24	4.14	9.5	2.2	5.4	1.2	4.38	9.8	-6

Breakout: 28%   Improve: 50%   Collapse: 6%

That projection is a wee bit optimistic. Wells is coming off of consecutive seasons where he's gotten belted around worse than Eleanor Clift on The McLaughlin Group. His plunging strikeout rate hints that he's gone around the league a few times too many, and the Twins reasonably chose not to pick up his option. He might be able to pull a Doug Jones and resurrect his career in the National League, but at his age, don't bet on it.

Brian Wolfe · Born: 29-Nov-80 · Age: 22 · Bats: R · Throws: R

YEAR	TM	LG	AGE	G	GS	IP	H	BB	SO	HR	ERA	EQERA	EQH9	EQBB9	EQSO9	EQHR9	PERA	VORP	STF
2000	QUD	MDW	19	31	18	123.3	148	34	91	13	4.74	7.62	16.9	3.3	4.5	2.7	7.98	-29.3	-13
2001	QUD	MDW	20	28	23	160.0	128	32	128	11	2.81	4.89	10.6	2.6	4.6	1.5	4.13	10.8	6
2002	FTM	FSL	21	25	23	132.0	160	34	85	17	4.64	7.94	16.9	3.2	4.5	3.1	8.13	-35.8	-10

In case we haven't mentioned often enough how the pitchers who move effortlessly upward are the exceptions, here's another example. Wolfe was touted last year because he had a nice repeat engagement in the Midwest League. He's got a good arm, with command of his fastball, slider, and change, and he gets good marks for his pitching savvy. He still got hammered in a pitcher's league the next rung up. Getting excited about a specific A-ball pitcher is a fool's errand, which is not to say Wolfe might not turn out okay, but don't get worked up about him in particular.

New York Yankees

Well, bollocks. The Yankees' vincibility has been pretty well established, and the postseason whammy that they held over much of the previous six years is gone. As a result of consecutive near misses in the postseason, they're now entering the most dangerous time a franchise can be in. See, it's these little setbacks that can get to you, creating a corrosive sense that you could claw your way back to where you were if you just spent something or got somebody or did something. They're already the most expensive team in baseball and the oldest, and those are two qualities that usually don't bode well for the future, especially now that the "Yankee exception" to big budget non-winners is so much historical flotsam.

Although the economic circumstances are very different than they were then, the scenario the Boss's minions have to work through is dangerously similar to life after 1964 or 1981. The last hurrahs of previous Yankee dynasties were notable for aging core talent that would retain its value into the future, but were nevertheless undermined by a deadly triangle of bad management decisions, weak supporting veterans, and the limitations of the next generation of Yankees. The Bronxmen are still the division's easy favorites, but the time is approaching when the greatest threat to the Yankees' place in the sun will no longer be themselves, but the Red Sox and the Blue Jays. With the sense that the clock is ticking, will that encourage the Yankees to make a big mistake or two? We'll revisit this theme and induce a few Horace Clarke flashbacks later on, because while the Yankees are currently run by a sharp group of front office types, all of that can change in a fit of Steinbrenner pique.

First, let's backtrack to review the problems the Yankees had to deal with after losing the World Series to the Snakes in 2001. With the last Combined Bargaining Agreement wind-

ing down, Brian Cashman and company went for broke in 2002, giving the Big Apple another year of vaunted acquisitions and big spending to support the homegrown crew that has given the Yankees their latest addition to their dynastic tradition. Although the off-season and in-season shopping sprees generated the usual whining from those predisposed to whine whenever the Yankees work at making themselves better, a lot of the activity was entirely necessary. After the 2001 World Series loss, Tino Martinez, Paul O'Neill, Chuck Knoblauch, and Scott Brosius became ex-Yankees, so almost half of the lineup needed replacing, and the cupboard really only had first baseman Nick Johnson to offer as an internal option to fill one of the slots. Characteristically, Cashman got creative, exchanging David Justice to the Mets for Robin Ventura, replacing Brosius while creating another hole between first base or DH.

Cashman could afford to, since he had the money to go hunting the winter's biggest big game. After Oakland's ownership had refused to sign off on the deal reached by Jason Giambi and Billy Beane the previous summer, Giambi was the prize on the free agent market. The Yankees correctly identified an opportunity to upgrade their offense after years of settling for Tino Martinez. In Giambi, they brought in an offensive star of a caliber worthy of the Jeter-Bernie-Posada core. To replace Knoblauch and O'Neill, they brought in Rondell White and John Vander Wal, while counting on Nick Johnson and Shane Spencer to cover the remaining at-bats between DH and the outfield corners. All in all, it was an elegant solution to the off-season problem of having to reshuffle the offense, and it resulted in baseball's best Bonds-less lineup.

Other changes of a more than cosmetic nature had to be made on the mound. To shore up an aging pitching staff and to plaster over the lack of big league–ready talent in the farm system, they brought in Steve Karsay, David Wells, and

Yankees Prospectus

2002 record: 103–58; First place AL East; Lost to Angels in Division Series 3–1

Pythagenport Record: 100–61

Runs scored per game: 5.6 (1st in AL)

Runs allowed per game: 4.3 (5th in AL)

Team EqA: .278 (1st in AL)

2002 Batters Age: 30.2 (4th oldest in AL)

2002 Pitchers Age: 33.2 (oldest in AL)

Ballpark: Yankee Stadium; Neutral park; Park Factor of 1.001

2002: Toyed with Boston for three months, then put them away, followed by another postseason disappointment.

2003: George broke out an even bigger checkbook to keep the aging Yankee juggernaut jugging.

Sterling Hitchcock. Karsay continued to be one of the best relievers in the league, Wells gave the rotation some of the breadth and depth that it needed, and Sterling Hitchcock...well, he cashed checks with the professionalism the Yankees should have expected.

Nevertheless, beyond overpaying to keep Hitchcock, the decisions were defensible. The need for pitching depth, both in the rotation and in middle relief, was fueled by failures on the farm among those guys who might have been ready or close to ready to be fifth starters or middle relievers. Christian Parker and Randy Keisler were both question marks going into spring training in 2002, and Adrian Hernandez had yet to post an ERA below four pitching in Double-A or higher. Even with the Famous Five of Clemens, Mussina, Pettitte, Wells, and El Duque, they only had Ted Lilly as insurance, after which you got down to hoping you wouldn't have to use Brandon Knight or Mike Thurman. And with only one starting pitcher under 30 among the front five, being concerned wasn't merely a sensible precaution, it's required when you're gunning for dominance.

It turned out they needed that pitching depth almost immediately. Andy Pettitte's elbow tweaked in April, and El Duque's back shelved him in May, and suddenly your New York Yankees weren't merely counting on Lilly as the fourth starter, they'd also had to stock the fifth starter's slot with all of their other grim alternatives. To make things even more interesting in the early going, the Red Sox frolicked to another early lead, inspiring the usual media love-ins about baseball in Beantown. When the Red Sox started cooling off, you might have been sanguine about the Yankees' prospects by the end of June. The Yankees were not. They'd gone 14–12 in June, and they had just slipped ahead of the Red Sox on the basis of a torrid 8–8 run. The Yankees were understandably nervous. Pettitte was back but had been roughed up in three starts before shutting out the Mets. The offense was granting Mike Mussina a lot of wins. The Rocket wasn't feeling so hot, and was about to slip onto the DL. The outfield hadn't worked out so well and Nick Johnson wasn't hitting in the early going, so even though the offense was cranking out runs by the bushel, the Yankees felt they had to do something about their rotation depth and one of their outfield corners.

The results were mixed. First, it appears team president Randy Levine decided to be "helpful," and helped orchestrate the deal to acquire Raul Mondesi from the Blue Jays for almost nothing on July 1. Unfortunately, Mondesi doesn't cost nothing, and offensively he wasn't an improvement over what they already had. As deals go, this might have felt superficially reassuring, but it didn't add quality. Quality did arrive four days later, when the Yankees made a good move for both the short- and long-term, acquiring Jeff Weaver in a three-way deal that cost them Ted Lilly, Jason Arnold, and John-Ford Griffin. Only 25 at the time of his acquisition,

Weaver is under contract through 2005 and is one of the best young veterans not pitching for the Cubs or Athletics. Beyond the practical considerations of the 2002 season, getting Weaver gives the Yankees somebody who can plausibly be at the front of the rotation over the life of his contract.

As it turned out, neither player was critical as the great pinstriped menace rolled to another AL East victory, which was instead fueled by a couple of reliable ingredients. First was the team's balance and depth. Although the pitching staff did not live up to exaggerated expectations, nobody important went Whitson when he pitched. The offense received contributions from so many regulars that it bordered on slump-proof, and they scored 182 runs in 25 July games, dusting the Red Sox in the process. Second, it's worth noting the advantage of playing in today's AL East. The Yankees get to play nearly a quarter of their schedule against the mismanaged patsies of their own division (the Orioles and Devil Rays), plus almost another quarter of their schedule against the weakest division in baseball, the AL Central. Clubbing your way to 55 wins in those 73 games was a nice head start to a hundred wins. Admittedly, Boston shares those advantages, and did just as well flogging the Orioles and D-Rays (although much of that was after the Red Sox became irrelevant in September). But the Red Sox didn't have the kind of depth in their rotation or lineup that allowed them to exploit all of the league's patsies to nearly the same extent.

The Yankees thus rolled into the playoffs again. But the first round match-up showed that while they might own the bad teams, the Yankees are hardly the perfect team. The Angels chewed up lefties all season long, and the Yankees had come down the stretch with Pettitte and Wells as their most reliable pitchers. Both got hammered by the Monkeymen (not that either Mussina or Clemens did well), and when the virtually unthinkable happened and Mike Stanton got hammered in a backbreaking Game Three loss, you were left with the specter of a Yankees team famed for its postseason pitching exploits falling short on the mound. Another contributing factor to their loss was the team's weak interior defense, a problem that can be less of an issue over 162 games against opponents of varying quality than it becomes in a short series against an opponent that can hit. So just like that, all of the maneuvering and spending and fretting had come to naught.

Where are the Yankees now? The economic system has changed radically, deliberately balanced in such a way as to stick it to the boys of the Bronx. Nobody's weeping for them, but it does create a unique and particularly dicey challenge for Cashman and the rest of the Yankees management team. Given a choice between trying to minimize the economic hit that they'll be taking, or going for broke, the Yankees are going for broke. Rather than let bad investments in players like Hitchcock or White or Mondesi affect them, they re-signed

Clemens, picked up Pettitte's option, and signed imports Hideki Matsui and Jose Contreras.

Admittedly, beyond a certain point, it hardly mattered what they did. No matter how creative they might have tried to be if they had tried to cut costs, they're screwed by the back-loading of contracts for Derek Jeter, Mussina, and Giambi. Those three alone will be making $54 million in 2006, and the way the new CBA works, that affects the Yankees right now. But beyond worthwhile expenditures to keep or acquire premium talent, the largesse of yesteryear adds up as well. Tossing money at goofy ideas like Drew Henson or Andy Morales or Hideki Irabu, those kinds of choices should be a thing of the past. It's always the price of mediocrity that kills you. The question is whether or not the decision-making will be merely economic in nature, or whether the Yankees' management team has noted that those were also bad ideas from the get-go. There's a real possibility that the Yankees could become a better-run team if it means avoiding the Hitchcocks or the Irabus.

On a certain level, this organization has been coasting on the strength of its core talent. Yes, Cashman and company have done a reasonably good job with the resources they've had at their disposal; we aren't talking about Kevin Malone or John Hart here. But what the Yankees have to keep doing is what the Braves have successfully accomplished over the past decade, which has been contending and rebuilding simultaneously. The Braves worked the Joneses in without missing a beat, they worked in Kevin Millwood, and they cobble together a bullpen year after year without making the kinds of commitments that make Ed Wade a punchline.

Yankees management has started to accept the challenge, and has done pretty well so far. Alfonso Soriano and Johnson are a good start, Weaver has the opportunity to turn his Tigers career into a historical footnote, and Juan Rivera should be next. Henson was supposed to be part of this particular script, but he's going to be in Ohio for at least another summer. Economically, it's a good idea to have quality big league–ready talent making fractions of what the veteran core is making. However, as much as the Yankees' farm system is credited with developing lots of goodies to barter with every July, not much of the talent is what you'd describe as big league–ready.

It's appropriate to credit Cashman and Mark Newman for the many things achieved in the last several seasons. The difficulty is that the Yankees are in an impossible situation: if they worry too much about having not won in 2000 or 2001, they could easily wind up making the Big Mistake that quickens pulses in Boston and gets Toronto into contention sooner rather than later. Matsui and Contreras could be those big mistakes, although both are expected to be solid major leaguers at the very least. Certainly, they were worth acquiring, because if the Yankees did nothing, they'd just get a little bit older, a little more expensive, and little less competitive.

The real problem is that if Levine can sail in and make a wacky suggestion that bleeds cash without adding talent, and if Cashman is held accountable for that and other choices he didn't make (like fighting arbitration scrums on orders that subsequently create bad precedents for pricey long-term contracts), it's worth asking whether or not we have a Boss-creep situation. One of the great happy accidents in Yankee history was George Steinbrenner's suspension, and how that created the breathing space that let Gene Michael and Buck Showalter and company put the Yankees back in the business of being a baseball operation.

But where the Yankees' compartmentalized management style has functioned well over the past decade, it's because the ghost in the machine has remained ghostly, at least by his own standards. The broad distribution of authority within the organization can quickly be transformed from a strength into a weakness if another season without a World Series produces disagreements between the chieftains about what has to be done next, because that invites an opportunity to let Steinbrenner make the final decisions or play favorites, undermining the authority of some while temporarily boosting others. The Boss is as well known for wearing out front office talent as he is for hiring it. There's a real danger that this team could go back to wacky ideas like getting Dave Collins and Ken Griffey Sr. to replace Reggie Jackson after falling short in 1981, if that hasn't happened already with the Mondesi and White pickups. The Yankees aren't going to crater this year, but the risk of it is mounting, especially since the talent in the system is less about providing the next great Yankee generation as it is about providing chits in trade to add veteran talent during stretch drives. If and when the Yankees go down, it'll be as historic as their previous letdowns, and it won't be gentle.

HITTERS

Erick Almonte   SS   Born: 01-Feb-78   Age: 25   Bats: R   Throws: R

YEAR	TM	LG	AGE	AB	H	2B	3B	HR	BB	SO	SB	CS	AVG	OBP	SLG	MLVR	EQBA	EQOBP	EQSLG	EQMLVR	VORP	DEFENSE
2000	NRW	EAS	22	454	123	18	4	15	35	129	12	2	.271	.327	.427	.052	.241	.282	.384	-.209	1.1	126-SS -25
2001	COH	INT	23	345	99	19	3	12	44	90	4	5	.287	.371	.464	.175	.266	.347	.436	.004	21.3	94-SS -10
2002	COH	INT	24	221	52	10	1	9	15	60	2	1	.235	.284	.412	-.080	.221	.270	.387	-.242	-1.4	60-SS -17
2002	NRW	EAS	24	187	45	7	0	8	30	59	10	2	.241	.346	.406	.033	.214	.304	.359	-.219	-.1	50-SS 9
2003	*NYY*	*AL*	*25*	*152*	*36*	*7*	*1*	*5*	*13*	*39*	*4*	*3*	*.236*	*.301*	*.400*	*-.097*	*.244*	*.311*	*.415*	*-.102*	*2.3*	

Breakout: 30%   *Improve: 64%*   *Collapse: 21%*

Prospects like Almonte are symbolic of a larger question we need to ask: what is the Yankee farm system for? Lately, it hasn't generated prospects the Yankees use themselves; instead, it provides talent designed to be dealt. Almonte illustrates the risk of holding onto some of it for too long. He has tools; he's got the great arm you like to see in a shortstop, and he has intriguing power for the position. But he's also expected to outgrow the position, and offensively, he doesn't hit well enough to be an asset as a regular at second or in the outfield. He hasn't learned how to handle breaking stuff, and earned a demotion back down to Double-A. He might carve out a career for himself, but it won't be as anything more than a spare part.

Robinson Cano   SS   Born: 22-Oct-82   Age: 20   Bats: L   Throws: R

YEAR	TM	LG	AGE	AB	H	2B	3B	HR	BB	SO	SB	CS	AVG	OBP	SLG	MLVR	EQBA	EQOBP	EQSLG	EQMLVR	VORP	DEFENSE	
2002	STA	NYP	19	87	24	5	1	1	4	8	6	1	.276	.308	.391	.059	.213	.231	.303	-.442	-5.0	18-2B 2	
2002	GRB	SAL	19	474	131	20	9	14	29	78	2	1	.276	.322	.445	.115	.212	.244	.343	-.360	-16.9	57-SS -10	54-2B -15
2003	*NYY*	*AL*	*20*	*215*	*48*	*8*	*2*	*6*	*13*	*41*	*2*	*3*	*.225*	*.273*	*.360*	*-.203*	*.233*	*.283*	*.373*	*-.216*	*-3.6*		

Breakout: 62%   *Improve: 74%*   *Collapse: 14%*

The Yankees' organization has a passel of touted young shortstops; most are touted merely for tout's sake. Deivi Mendez, Ferdin Tejeda, Almonte, they're all toolsy, and any one of them might grow up to be the next Alex Gonzalez (either edition). This year, the best of the bunch is Cano. Cano hit better than any of the others, and flashing lefty power at 19 makes him someone to follow. Although his footwork at shortstop needs work, he has the arm for the position.

Mike Cervenak   1B   Born: 17-Aug-76   Age: 26   Bats: R   Throws: R

YEAR	TM	LG	AGE	AB	H	2B	3B	HR	BB	SO	SB	CS	AVG	OBP	SLG	MLVR	EQBA	EQOBP	EQSLG	EQMLVR	VORP	DEFENSE	
2000	GRB	SAL	23	155	51	4	5	3	7	21	3	3	.329	.373	.477	.271	.255	.280	.369	-.225	-1.4	34-3B 2	
2001	NRW	EAS	24	463	127	37	1	11	44	75	2	4	.274	.349	.430	.111	.243	.308	.382	-.161	3.3	36-3B 3	30-1B -2
2002	NRW	EAS	25	492	136	34	1	21	30	78	5	2	.276	.331	.478	.133	.243	.285	.422	-.148	-6.8	60-1B -4	16-3B -1
2003	*SFG*	*NL*	*26*	*151*	*36*	*8*	*1*	*4*	*12*	*28*	*2*	*1*	*.239*	*.298*	*.377*	*-.154*	*.250*	*.306*	*.415*	*-.108*	*-1.9*		

Breakout: 32%   *Improve: 59%*   *Collapse: 29%*

Cervenak starred at shortstop and third at the University of Michigan before signing as an undrafted free agent in 2000. In addition to playing the infield corners, he has experience at second and short. If the Yankees ever take cost-cutting seriously, replacing the Coomers or the Zeiles with an organizational soldier like Cervenak would be an easy swap, while giving the Yankees' bench even better depth. A solid pick by the Giants in the minor league portion of the Rule 5 draft.

Ron Coomer   1B/3B   Born: 18-Nov-66   Age: 36   Bats: R   Throws: R

YEAR	TM	LG	AGE	AB	H	2B	3B	HR	BB	SO	SB	CS	AVG	OBP	SLG	MLVR	EQBA	EQOBP	EQSLG	EQMLVR	VORP	DEFENSE	
2000	MIN	AL	33	544	147	29	1	16	36	50	2	0	.270	.320	.415	-.108	.276	.318	.428	-.052	5.9	120-1B 13	
2001	CHC	NL	34	349	91	19	1	8	29	70	0	0	.261	.321	.390	-.095	.266	.324	.398	-.092	9.4	62-3B 1	19-1B 2
2002	NYY	AL	35	148	39	7	0	3	6	23	0	0	.264	.292	.372	-.134	.282	.310	.403	-.098	3.2	17-3B -2	
2003	*NYY*	*AL*	*36*	*151*	*36*	*7*	*0*	*3*	*9*	*23*	*0*	*0*	*.241*	*.285*	*.354*	*-.180*	*.249*	*.295*	*.367*	*-.191*	*-4.2*		

Breakout: 8%   *Improve: 36%*   *Collapse: 39%*

Coomer isn't really that much better than Scott Seabol or the Coolbaugh du jour. He can't really play third anymore, and he's not the platoon masher and caddy that the Yankees could really use for Ventura or Nick Johnson. They've signed Todd Zeile to fill the role. Coomer is better off as a spare part in the NL, but the Yankees inexplicably offered him arbitration.

Elvis Corporan 3B Born: 09-Jun-80 Age: 23 Bats: B Throws: R

YEAR	TM	LG	AGE	AB	H	2B	3B	HR	BB	SO	SB	CS	AVG	OBP	SLG	MLVR	EQBA	EQOBP	EQSLG	EQMLVR	VORP	DEFENSE
2000	STA	NYP	20	281	73	14	2	8	23	61	7	2	.260	.322	.409	.080	.188	.226	.307	-.460	-19.3	70-3B 5
2000	GRB	SAL	20	255	63	10	1	4	28	66	10	2	.247	.322	.341	-.045	.195	.249	.271	-.460	-18.2	61-3B -5
2001	GRB	SAL	21	484	109	25	6	15	35	124	15	8	.225	.282	.395	-.015	.179	.223	.311	-.465	-35.3	130-3B -14
2002	GRB	SAL	22	54	15	2	0	3	9	19	0	0	.278	.391	.481	.252	.196	.290	.357	-.260	-1.1	12-3B 2
2002	TAM	FSL	22	378	99	19	3	7	48	74	10	3	.262	.350	.384	.088	.225	.292	.339	-.263	-8.1	106-3B -14
2003	NYY	AL	23	182	42	8	1	5	16	45	3	3	.228	.293	.368	-.155	.236	.303	.382	-.165	-2.0	

Breakout: 64%   Improve: 82%   Collapse: 7%

In the same way that the Yankees have a small horde of shortstop suspects, they've got a bunch of non-Hensons floating around the organization at the hot corner. Corporan might be the one who works out. He's strong like bull, relatively young, and at times he's flashed power and improving patience. If he beats out Mitch Jones for the job at Norwich in 2003, he'll bear watching to see if he puts everything together and becomes a prospect.

Jason Giambi 1B Born: 08-Jan-71 Age: 32 Bats: L Throws: R

YEAR	TM	LG	AGE	AB	H	2B	3B	HR	BB	SO	SB	CS	AVG	OBP	SLG	MLVR	EQBA	EQOBP	EQSLG	EQMLVR	VORP	DEFENSE
2000	OAK	AL	29	510	170	29	1	43	137	96	2	0	.333	.482	.647	.564	.345	.487	.675	.630	104.3	121-1B 5
2001	OAK	AL	30	520	178	47	2	38	129	83	2	0	.342	.483	.660	.609	.362	.498	.705	.707	121.9	126-1B 11
2002	NYY	AL	31	560	176	34	1	41	109	112	2	2	.314	.439	.598	.448	.340	.458	.651	.554	101.4	86-1B 2
2003	NYY	AL	32	547	162	35	1	38	117	106	2	0	.297	.422	.572	.351	.307	.437	.594	.384	67.9	

Breakout: 0%   Improve: 27%   Collapse: 7%

It's unusually refreshing to see a big-ticket free agent come into the Big Apple, have a good year, not lead the team to the Promised Land, and not catch flack for it. He shared defensive responsibilities at first, which kept Nick Johnson from getting a rusty glove, although he did hit significantly better when he wasn't DHing. It isn't a Reggie-sized problem (.344/.461/.674 at first vs. .271/.397/.489 as a DH), but if it becomes an issue, given the financial commitment and Johnson's modest rookie season, you can understand the Yankees' willingness to dangle Johnson this winter.

Drew Henson 3B Born: 13-Feb-80 Age: 23 Bats: R Throws: R

YEAR	TM	LG	AGE	AB	H	2B	3B	HR	BB	SO	SB	CS	AVG	OBP	SLG	MLVR	EQBA	EQOBP	EQSLG	EQMLVR	VORP	DEFENSE
2000	CHT	SOU	20	64	11	8	0	1	4	25	2	0	.172	.221	.344	-.256	.154	.191	.308	-.546	-6.1	16-3B -3
2000	NRW	EAS	20	223	64	9	2	7	20	75	0	5	.287	.348	.439	.115	.247	.292	.388	-.180	.5	44-3B -5
2001	COH	INT	21	270	60	6	0	11	10	85	2	1	.222	.250	.367	-.199	.210	.241	.354	-.352	-11.2	66-3B -8
2002	COH	INT	22	471	113	30	4	18	37	151	2	1	.240	.304	.435	-.014	.224	.286	.411	-.176	1.5	124-3B -29
2003	NYY	AL	23	204	49	10	1	9	18	60	2	4	.241	.308	.426	-.050	.250	.318	.442	-.051	3.5	

Breakout: 62%   Improve: 81%   Collapse: 10%

You won't find a more controversial prospect in the game, not even Prince Fielder. The question is, can Henson learn how to play baseball? Nobody really knows. In four seasons, he hasn't really made any progress as a hitter, he has terrible problems getting the bat around, and he's an awful third baseman. In his favor, he's still very young, and should you hold it against him that he was raw to be up in Triple-A considering his game experience? At this point, the question isn't whether or not he'll grow into being a superstar, but whether or not he'll grow into being a big league regular. He's better than Josh Booty, but whether he becomes anything more than that is going to depend on his learning curve as a hitter, and so far, he hasn't shown that he has one.

Derek Jeter SS Born: 26-Jun-74 Age: 29 Bats: R Throws: R

YEAR	TM	LG	AGE	AB	H	2B	3B	HR	BB	SO	SB	CS	AVG	OBP	SLG	MLVR	EQBA	EQOBP	EQSLG	EQMLVR	VORP	DEFENSE
2000	NYY	AL	26	593	201	31	4	15	68	99	22	4	.339	.418	.481	.248	.356	.428	.506	.328	82.5	145-SS -27
2001	NYY	AL	27	614	191	35	3	21	56	99	27	3	.311	.378	.480	.198	.334	.398	.521	.277	79.4	142-SS -18
2002	NYY	AL	28	644	191	26	0	18	73	114	32	3	.297	.374	.421	.101	.320	.395	.456	.165	63.8	151-SS -30
2003	NYY	AL	29	593	173	32	4	16	61	95	22	4	.291	.362	.439	.092	.301	.374	.456	.104	44.1	

Breakout: 5%   Improve: 30%   Collapse: 20%

That's right, we've got a trend on our hands: Jeter is in his third year of losing slices of offensive value. That doesn't make him bad, any more than his consistently execrable defense makes him "bad." But these things do start adding up to become problems. The way the various third base suspects look, moving Jeter to the hot corner would make sense, or he could follow the

Derek Jeter *(continued)*

Yount career path and move out to center, letting Bernie Williams move to an outfield corner. The problem is, who do you replace Jeter with at short? As long as the choices are limited to the Almontes of the world, you can forgive the Yankees for ignoring the problem, although Jeter's glove killed the Yankees in the postseason. But if his offense keeps slipping while his contract escalates...A-Rod's contract looks like a bargain in comparison.

Nick Johnson   1B   Born: 19-Sep-78   Age: 24   Bats: L   Throws: L

YEAR	TM	LG	AGE	AB	H	2B	3B	HR	BB	SO	SB	CS	AVG	OBP	SLG	MLVR	EQBA	EQOBP	EQSLG	EQMLVR	VORP	DEFENSE
2001	COH	INT	22	359	92	20	0	18	81	105	9	2	.256	.412	.462	.213	.242	.382	.438	.052	16.0	109-1B -2
2001	NYY	AL	22	67	13	2	0	2	7	15	0	0	.194	.308	.313	-.232	.209	.321	.358	-.190	-1.7	11-1B -3
2002	NYY	AL	23	378	92	15	0	15	48	98	1	3	.243	.347	.402	-.009	.265	.365	.438	.038	13.3	62-1B 4
2003	NYY	AL	24	390	98	20	1	17	54	94	3	3	.250	.351	.439	.042	.259	.363	.455	.049	9.6	

Breakout: 27%   Improve: 60%   Collapse: 11%

Johnson was finally sort of healthy for most of a season, and he gave the Yankees enough of a year to almost make people forget Danny Pasqua. In part, you can blame a miserably cold start to the year, and you can blame his going onto the DL in August just when it looked like he was getting into the swing of things. Johnson was also pretty young, so it's far too early to give up. But a good sophomore season is a must if he wants to avoid growing up to be a Washington Expo.

Hideki Matsui   OF   Born: 12-Jun-74   Age: 29   Bats: L   Throws: R

YEAR	TM	LG	AGE	AB	H	2B	3B	HR	BB	SO	SB	CS	AVG	OBP	SLG	MLVR	EQBA	EQOBP	EQSLG	EQMLVR	VORP	DEFENSE
2000	YOM	JCL	26	474	150	32	1	42	106	108	5	2	.316	.443	.654	.527	.287	.412	.598	.451	86.8	
2001	YOM	JCL	27	481	160	23	3	36	120	96	3	—	.333	.466	.617	.547	.314	.441	.597	.517	95.2	
2002	YOM	JCL	28	500	167	27	1	50	114	104	3	—	.334	.458	.692	.636	.319	.447	.668	.533	84.2	
2003	NYY	AL	29	501	141	30	5	31	104	108	7	2	.281	.407	.547	.284	.290	.421	.567	.311	57.3	

Breakout: 1%   Improve: 39%   Collapse: 28%

That's right, the stats sing, PECOTA believes (up to a point, considering that collapse figure), and so do we. In the absence of any evidence to the contrary, Matsui looks like a worthwhile investment. Not all Japanese sluggers are created equal, and Matsui looks like one of the ones who can bop on any continent. He should take over in one of the outfield corners (probably right), and never look back.

We should take the time to nominate the Orioles for being the most considerate of suitors this off-season. By politely e-mailing him their interest, they gave Matsui the graceful option of clicking "delete," rather than forcing him to listen and smile politely through a particularly tedious come-on. And hey, it did let them publicize the fact that they'd tried. If you're feeling lonely, just tell your buddies that you're waiting to hear back from Nikki Cox on that marriage proposal.

Billy McMillon   OF   Born: 17-Nov-71   Age: 31   Bats: L   Throws: L

YEAR	TM	LG	AGE	AB	H	2B	3B	HR	BB	SO	SB	CS	AVG	OBP	SLG	MLVR	EQBA	EQOBP	EQSLG	EQMLVR	VORP	DEFENSE
2000	TOL	INT	28	380	131	30	1	13	71	65	3	1	.345	.450	.532	.404	.311	.406	.483	.213	32.9	100-LF -6
2000	DET	AL	28	123	37	7	1	4	19	19	1	0	.301	.399	.472	.158	.311	.400	.500	.226	9.8	13-RF -1
2001	OAK	AL	29	58	17	7	1	0	5	13	1	0	.293	.359	.448	.095	.310	.373	.483	.155	3.5	13-LF -1
2002	COH	INT	30	442	133	32	3	8	59	71	2	5	.301	.391	.441	.180	.278	.364	.412	.011	12.3	72-LF -4
2003	OAK	AL	31	127	32	7	1	3	15	25	2	1	.251	.332	.385	-.054	.260	.343	.403	-.051	-0.6	

Breakout: 11%   Improve: 29%   Collapse: 36%

McMillon has been a Ken Phelps All-Star for years, but he's also due to come off of that particular list. Like Warren Newson before him, his career has essentially been wasted. The particular misfortune was the time wasted in the Phillies organization, not that the Marlins gave him much of an opportunity. Could he still step in and give you a .350 OBP? Anywhere, any time. Matt Lawton got his big break; McMillon, with an almost identical skills set, did not.

Raul Mondesi   RF   Born: 12-Mar-71   Age: 32   Bats: R   Throws: R

YEAR	TM	LG	AGE	AB	H	2B	3B	HR	BB	SO	SB	CS	AVG	OBP	SLG	MLVR	EQBA	EQOBP	EQSLG	EQMLVR	VORP	DEFENSE
2000	TOR	AL	29	388	105	22	2	24	32	73	22	6	.271	.331	.523	.071	.275	.328	.535	.118	18.6	94-RF -5
2001	TOR	AL	30	572	144	26	4	27	73	128	30	11	.252	.343	.453	.033	.265	.356	.482	.082	24.0	140-RF -1
2002	TOR	AL	31	299	67	16	1	15	31	57	9	2	.224	.303	.435	-.065	.240	.318	.467	-.028	3.8	58-RF -1
2002	NYY	AL	31	270	65	18	0	11	28	46	6	4	.241	.317	.430	-.029	.265	.339	.471	.037	7.8	61-RF -2
2003	NYY	AL	32	447	113	24	2	22	48	94	14	7	.253	.330	.462	.040	.262	.341	.479	.047	8.8	

Breakout: 27%   Improve: 61%   Collapse: 16%

It isn't often that a guy is spectacularly overrated before he becomes a Yankee, but Buffalo is your man. He's also the only player who defended carrying his bat halfway to first on a home run trot because of his personal rivalry with the victims, the hapless Devil Rays. He had a Julio Franco-style slip-up, "mis-stating" his age, so he could very well be 36. He's threatened that this is his last year, which means the Yankees may not even reap the benefit of a draft choice when he goes away to the open-checkbook dummy of next winter. That was the most value he's going to give them.

Dave Parrish   C   Born: 13-Jun-79   Age: 24   Bats: R   Throws: R

YEAR	TM	LG	AGE	AB	H	2B	3B	HR	BB	SO	SB	CS	AVG	OBP	SLG	MLVR	EQBA	EQOBP	EQSLG	EQMLVR	VORP	DEFENSE
2000	STA	NYP	21	221	53	20	1	4	25	54	0	0	.240	.328	.394	.054	.175	.231	.298	-.469	-13.5	48-C 7
2001	TAM	FSL	22	367	93	25	0	6	54	88	2	1	.253	.357	.371	.068	.217	.293	.326	-.284	-5.0	99-C -10
2002	NRW	EAS	23	341	81	17	1	4	39	63	13	6	.238	.323	.328	-.109	.210	.280	.293	-.359	-11.8	99-C -12
2003	NYY	AL	24	157	35	8	1	3	15	36	2	2	.224	.294	.348	-.183	.231	.304	.361	-.195	-1.1	

Breakout: 53%   *Improve: 66%*   *Collapse: 22%*

Lance Parrish's son, and another Yankee who cut his teeth playing for Michigan in college. Parrish was the Yankees' 1st round pick in 2000, and it's looking like a wasted pick. His introduction to Double-A looks better than it was; after a hot first month, he was one of the worst hitters in the Eastern League. Although he has a strong arm, he's not a great receiver. Jorge Posada's future should be secure.

Andy Phillips   2B   Born: 06-Apr-77   Age: 26   Bats: R   Throws: R

YEAR	TM	LG	AGE	AB	H	2B	3B	HR	BB	SO	SB	CS	AVG	OBP	SLG	MLVR	EQBA	EQOBP	EQSLG	EQMLVR	VORP	DEFENSE
2000	TAM	FSL	23	478	137	33	2	13	46	98	2	0	.287	.352	.446	.160	.236	.287	.375	-.216	-3.6	125-3B -15
2001	TAM	FSL	24	288	87	17	4	11	25	55	3	3	.302	.364	.503	.292	.253	.296	.424	-.117	7.4	72-2B -10
2001	NRW	EAS	24	183	49	9	2	6	21	54	1	0	.268	.343	.437	.106	.238	.308	.386	-.159	2.8	46-2B -20
2002	NRW	EAS	25	272	83	24	2	19	33	56	4	3	.305	.386	.618	.431	.259	.328	.522	.083	22.7	72-2B 2
2002	COH	INT	25	205	54	11	1	9	10	46	0	1	.263	.298	.459	.026	.248	.282	.432	-.135	4.2	40-2B -5
2003	NYY	AL	26	187	46	11	1	7	15	42	3	2	.247	.305	.434	-.040	.255	.316	.450	-.040	5.3	

Breakout: 29%   *Improve: 54%*   *Collapse: 25%*

You might wonder why, in an organization as generally bereft of top-tier talent as the Yankees', a guy like Phillips doesn't get more press. After all, not everybody has a second baseman capable of popping 28 home runs. The reasons are pretty straightforward: he isn't much of a second baseman, he was old for his league, and he doesn't walk as much as we'd like. He's sort of like Kevin Jordan, in that he should make it to the majors, and give whoever he plays for some power and a decent average while playing anywhere but short in the infield. For the next three or four years he'd be a fine placeholder at the keystone for a team that's tired of futzing around with failed prospects.

Jorge Posada   C   Born: 17-Aug-71   Age: 31   Bats: B   Throws: R

YEAR	TM	LG	AGE	AB	H	2B	3B	HR	BB	SO	SB	CS	AVG	OBP	SLG	MLVR	EQBA	EQOBP	EQSLG	EQMLVR	VORP	DEFENSE
2000	NYY	AL	28	505	145	35	1	28	107	151	2	2	.287	.419	.527	.262	.303	.428	.559	.343	80.8	132-C 5
2001	NYY	AL	29	484	134	28	1	22	62	132	2	6	.277	.366	.475	.139	.301	.388	.520	.224	59.8	122-C -5
2002	NYY	AL	30	511	137	40	1	20	81	143	1	0	.268	.371	.468	.135	.290	.391	.509	.202	60.2	132-C 3
2003	NYY	AL	31	422	109	25	1	19	62	116	2	2	.260	.358	.459	.086	.268	.371	.476	.097	29.9	

Breakout: 5%   *Improve: 43%*   *Collapse: 17%*

There were major concerns about whether or not Posada's surgically repaired shoulder would be ready to go by Opening Day, but he was fully recovered in time, and logged another nifty season. It's hard not to be a little bittersweet about Posada; he had to waste time waiting for Joe Girardi to be moved aside, so like Ellie Howard, his career totals probably won't end up jumping off the charts. However, Posada didn't really start catching until 1992, converting in his second pro season. If that's saved his knees any wear and tear, he could age relatively gracefully. Physically, although he's got an old player skill set, he was once a pretty nimble second baseman. He'll be the league's best catcher for another couple of seasons, but I like his chances of retaining a lot of his value well into his 30s.

Kevin Reese — OF — Born: 11-Mar-78 — Age: 25 — Bats: L — Throws: L

YEAR	TM	LG	AGE	AB	H	2B	3B	HR	BB	SO	SB	CS	AVG	OBP	SLG	MLVR	EQBA	EQOBP	EQSLG	EQMLVR	VORP	DEFENSE
2000	IDA	PIO	22	201	72	14	4	2	43	30	12	3	.358	.478	.498	.414	.231	.317	.317	-.240	-7.9	42-RF -8
2001	FTW	MDW	23	459	151	30	6	13	54	62	30	10	.329	.405	.505	.349	.254	.313	.391	-.131	-6.9	121-RF -6
2002	NRW	EAS	24	514	149	24	6	4	77	87	22	14	.290	.387	.383	.104	.254	.335	.335	-.167	1.8	128-CF -10
2003	NYY	AL	25	182	46	10	1	4	19	32	3	2	.253	.327	.384	-.063	.262	.338	.398	-.064	1.6	

Breakout: 35%   Improve: 62%   Collapse: 21%

Acquired from the Padres for Bernabel Castro, Reese was an on-base machine in his Double-A debut, helping fuel Norwich's championship season. He showed a nice platoon split, posting a .400 OBP against right-handers. He can run and he has a good arm, so he has the makings of a nifty fourth or fifth outfielder in a Scott Pose mold. He's not young, so he can't miss a step, but his future looks very good so far.

Juan Rivera — OF — Born: 03-Jul-78 — Age: 25 — Bats: R — Throws: R

YEAR	TM	LG	AGE	AB	H	2B	3B	HR	BB	SO	SB	CS	AVG	OBP	SLG	MLVR	EQBA	EQOBP	EQSLG	EQMLVR	VORP	DEFENSE
2000	TAM	FSL	22	409	113	26	1	14	33	56	11	7	.276	.339	.447	.136	.228	.273	.376	-.247	-18.6	115-RF -3
2000	NRW	EAS	22	62	14	5	0	2	6	15	0	0	.226	.294	.403	-.068	.190	.250	.349	-.353	-4.5	13-RF -2
2001	NRW	EAS	23	316	101	18	3	14	15	50	5	7	.320	.356	.528	.294	.276	.311	.455	-.025	4.0	76-RF 2
2001	COH	INT	23	199	65	11	1	14	15	31	4	5	.327	.377	.603	.410	.297	.348	.550	.196	14.3	55-RF 0
2002	COH	INT	24	265	86	21	1	8	13	39	5	1	.325	.358	.502	.235	.297	.334	.466	.051	8.7	63-RF -5
2002	NYY	AL	24	83	22	5	0	1	6	10	1	1	.265	.315	.361	-.106	.286	.333	.393	-.066	.4	28-OF 0
2003	NYY	AL	24	292	77	17	1	11	20	46	4	3	.264	.315	.439	-.005	.273	.326	.455	-.002	1.2	

Breakout: 16%   Improve: 49%   Collapse: 18%

If the Yankees have a competitive advantage because of their revenue stream, it's that they can outspend their mistakes. If they can't peddle Rondell White or Raul Mondesi before Opening Day, they ought to cut bait, because they have a better alternative on hand who won't cost them anything by their standards. Rivera has the power and the arm strength you want from a right fielder, and while you'd like to see him walk more, that isn't his game. The upside is a poor man's Magglio Ordonez, but the Yankees might have to settle for the new Piniella. He has options, so he might get pushed back to Columbus.

Bronson Sardinha — SS or OF? — Born: 06-Apr-83 — Age: 20 — Bats: L — Throws: R

YEAR	TM	LG	AGE	AB	H	2B	3B	HR	BB	SO	SB	CS	AVG	OBP	SLG	MLVR	EQBA	EQOBP	EQSLG	EQMLVR	VORP	DEFENSE	
2002	GRB	SAL	19	342	90	13	0	12	34	78	15	6	.263	.340	.406	.079	.203	.259	.317	-.372	-13.7	63-SS -27	14-LF -2
2002	STA	NYP	19	124	40	8	0	4	24	36	4	1	.323	.436	.484	.374	.227	.317	.348	-.201	-4.1	31-LF -4	
2003	NYY	AL	20	203	45	7	2	7	17	54	3	5	.221	.285	.369	-.174	.228	.295	.383	-.185	-4.3		

Breakout: 61%   Improve: 73%   Collapse: 17%

A supplemental 1st rounder in 2001, there's very little doubt that Sardinha will hit. The question is where he'll wind up on the diamond; after 33 errors in 64 games as a shortstop at Greensboro, he was bumped out to left for everyone's safety. He doesn't have great lateral movement, so if he does go back to the infield, it would be to third, not short. But he hit well in the Sally League, and should move up to Double-A relatively quickly once they settle on a position.

Alfonso Soriano — 2B — Born: 07-Jan-78 — Age: 25 — Bats: R — Throws: R

YEAR	TM	LG	AGE	AB	H	2B	3B	HR	BB	SO	SB	CS	AVG	OBP	SLG	MLVR	EQBA	EQOBP	EQSLG	EQMLVR	VORP	DEFENSE	
2000	COH	INT	22	459	133	32	6	12	25	85	14	7	.290	.331	.464	.073	.269	.300	.432	-.085	15.3	65-SS -23	40-2B -9
2000	NYY	AL	22	50	9	3	0	2	1	15	2	0	.180	.196	.360	-.481	.180	.196	.380	-.421	-3.4		
2001	NYY	AL	23	574	154	34	3	18	29	125	43	14	.268	.307	.432	-.028	.288	.328	.466	.032	35.5	152-2B -21	
2002	NYY	AL	24	696	209	51	2	39	23	157	41	13	.300	.336	.547	.214	.324	.358	.593	.307	87.2	154-2B -23	
2003	NYY	AL	25	688	192	43	5	31	34	140	36	15	.279	.318	.490	.080	.289	.329	.509	.091	44.4		

Breakout: 6%   Improve: 48%   Collapse: 14%

The bigger, better, supercharged Juan Samuel for a new generation, with the tradeoff being that Soriano has a much worse glove but significantly more power, a tradeoff I'd take. Some insiders wonder why anybody ever throws Soriano a fastball or a strike, but so far, so good. The question is whether the Yankees can continue to make do with him at second. As Jeter has jokingly pointed out, Soriano can't jump, which makes a move to the outfield look unlikely, if not crabtastic. In general, the Yankees should only fret about moving Jeter or Soriano, not both.

Shane Spencer   RF   Born: 20-Feb-72   Age: 31   Bats: R   Throws: R

YEAR	TM	LG	AGE	AB	H	2B	3B	HR	BB	SO	SB	CS	AVG	OBP	SLG	MLVR	EQBA	EQOBP	EQSLG	EQMLVR	VORP	DEFENSE	
2000	NYY	AL	28	248	70	11	3	9	19	45	1	2	.282	.338	.460	.020	.296	.344	.486	.096	11.3	39-LF	3
2001	COH	INT	29	173	40	10	1	3	23	21	4	1	.231	.328	.353	-.077	.226	.313	.345	-.213	-6.0	32-LF	0
2001	NYY	AL	29	283	73	14	2	10	21	58	4	1	.258	.318	.428	-.023	.277	.336	.463	.031	8.7	68-LF	5
2002	NYY	AL	30	288	71	15	2	6	31	62	0	3	.247	.328	.375	-.076	.272	.351	.414	-.014	4.5	80-RF	0
2003	CLE	AL	31	233	57	12	1	6	21	45	2	1	.243	.310	.383	-.098	.249	.318	.392	-.117	-5.6		

Breakout: 11%   Improve: 35%   Collapse: 36%

Now a free agent with bad wheels, Spencer has had his Hank Bauer moments, and just as Bauer had to, Spencer gets to take the next step: the ignominy of playing baseball in the non-Yankee portion of the universe. He may not even have the bat speed to maim lefties anymore, so he's close to the end. Signed by Cleveland, where he should stick.

Marcus Thames   Born: 06-Mar-77   Age: 26   Bats: R   Throws: R

YEAR	TM	LG	AGE	AB	H	2B	3B	HR	BB	SO	SB	CS	AVG	OBP	SLG	MLVR	EQBA	EQOBP	EQSLG	EQMLVR	VORP	DEFENSE	
2000	NRW	EAS	23	474	114	30	2	15	50	89	1	5	.241	.318	.407	-.013	.211	.272	.360	-.282	-25.7	109-RF	-7
2001	NRW	EAS	24	520	167	43	4	31	73	101	10	4	.321	.412	.598	.461	.278	.361	.512	.144	46.7	133-CF	-4
2002	COH	INT	25	386	80	21	3	13	43	71	5	4	.207	.298	.378	-.118	.195	.280	.359	-.278	-10.5	104-CF	1
2002	NYY	AL	25	13	3	1	0	1	0	4	0	0	.231	.231	.538	-.035	.231	.231	.615	.025	.5		

In the Yankees' organization, Thames is a prospect because of his 2001 season, his third in Norwich. Unfortunately, that's the only year in the last four that he hit in. He'll take a walk and he has decent power, and defensively, he's got the arm for right and can fill in well enough anywhere. Considering his age, he could make a fine fifth outfielder on a team with plenty of left-handed power and an older slug in one of the corners.

Kevin Thompson   CF   Born: 18-Sep-79   Age: 23   Bats: R   Throws: R

YEAR	TM	LG	AGE	AB	H	2B	3B	HR	BB	SO	SB	CS	AVG	OBP	SLG	MLVR	EQBA	EQOBP	EQSLG	EQMLVR	VORP	DEFENSE	
2001	STA	NYP	21	260	68	11	4	6	36	48	11	5	.262	.362	.404	.117	.192	.263	.299	-.394	-14.9	64-CF	-6
2002	STA	NYP	22	139	42	5	2	4	17	24	6	3	.302	.378	.453	.250	.221	.280	.331	-.301	-4.7	25-CF	-3
2002	GRB	SAL	22	226	64	24	3	3	37	42	14	3	.283	.398	.456	.234	.217	.301	.353	-.231	-3.3	60-CF	-6
2002	TAM	FSL	22	87	16	5	0	0	13	15	11	1	.184	.304	.241	-.202	.176	.264	.231	-.491	-7.9	23-CF	-3
2003	NYY	AL	23	159	37	8	1	4	15	35	4	4	.232	.302	.364	-.143	.240	.313	.377	-.151	-1.7		

Breakout: 58%   Improve: 77%   Collapse: 18%

A Junior College All-Star drafted in the 31st round in 2000, Thompson is sort of this year's Mike Vento. A 40th round draft pick himself, Vento was the Florida State League MVP in 2001, but he flopped in Norwich in 2002. This year, Thompson rocketed past Shelley Duncan in Greensboro; when you've been drafted to be organizational filler, that sort of thing has to be nice. (You might wonder what Duncan's doing in the Sally League in his second season outside of the Pac-10, too.) Thompson isn't really a prospect, but he did do well with the opportunities he earned, and he's young enough to have a career. Shane Spencer was a 28th rounder, and he made it; all of these guys have to hope they get the same opportunity.

John Vander Wal   OF   Born: 29-Apr-66   Age: 37   Bats: L   Throws: L

YEAR	TM	LG	AGE	AB	H	2B	3B	HR	BB	SO	SB	CS	AVG	OBP	SLG	MLVR	EQBA	EQOBP	EQSLG	EQMLVR	VORP	DEFENSE			
2000	PIT	NL	34	384	115	29	0	24	72	92	11	2	.299	.413	.563	.299	.294	.399	.551	.277	39.1	72-RF	-3	27-1B	-3
2001	PIT	NL	35	313	87	22	3	11	42	84	7	4	.278	.365	.473	.102	.274	.361	.470	.083	14.7	57-RF	-3	11-1B	1
2001	SFG	NL	35	139	35	6	1	3	26	38	1	2	.252	.370	.374	-.008	.273	.385	.399	.029	4.4	35-RF	1		
2002	NYY	AL	36	219	57	17	1	6	23	58	1	1	.260	.331	.429	.009	.281	.351	.462	.060	7.6	45-RF	-2		
2003	NYY	AL	37	191	48	10	1	6	26	48	2	1	.250	.341	.406	-.014	.258	.353	.421	-.011	.8				

Breakout: 9%   Improve: 40%   Collapse: 31%

As far as temporary solutions go, you can understand the willingness to bring in John Vander Wal to give the Yankees some lefty sock in the outfield as part of the overall patch to cover up Paul O'Neill's retirement. However, Vander Wal is not young, and that 2000 season, while nifty, was something that came and went, not something to pay for and expect. Vander Wal might hang on by returning to a deluxe pinch-hitter role, and gun for the pinch-hit home run record; he needs three to tie Cliff Johnson for the all-time mark.

Robin Ventura   3B   Born: 14-Jul-67   Age: 35   Bats: L   Throws: R

YEAR	TM	LG	AGE	AB	H	2B	3B	HR	BB	SO	SB	CS	AVG	OBP	SLG	MLVR	EQBA	EQOBP	EQSLG	EQMLVR	VORP	DEFENSE	
2000	NYM	NL	32	469	109	23	1	24	75	91	3	5	.232	.341	.439	-.037	.238	.337	.448	-.021	22.6	120-3B	18
2001	NYM	NL	33	456	108	20	0	21	88	101	2	5	.237	.361	.419	.016	.248	.370	.439	.036	31.6	130-3B	11
2002	NYY	AL	34	465	115	17	0	27	90	101	3	1	.247	.372	.458	.106	.268	.390	.502	.171	46.3	127-3B	14
2003	NYY	AL	35	340	82	16	0	16	61	75	2	1	.239	.357	.433	.038	.248	.369	.450	.045	16.6		

Breakout: 23%   Improve: 58%   Collapse: 20%

The master plan was to get a nifty little year out of Ventura in what was supposed to be a single season engagement prior to the arrival of the stupendous Henson. A second season turned into a necessity after Henson floundered, which isn't going to kill the Yankees. Ventura's still an asset offensively and defensively, with a great first step around the bag, and the quick wrists to still get around on anybody and anything. His shot at the Hall of Fame probably depends on his willingness to stick around as long and as well as Graig Nettles and Darrell Evans did; since both have been overlooked so far, Ventura might have to settle for the Hall of the Really Very Good.

Rondell White   LF   Born: 23-Feb-72   Age: 31   Bats: R   Throws: R

YEAR	TM	LG	AGE	AB	H	2B	3B	HR	BB	SO	SB	CS	AVG	OBP	SLG	MLVR	EQBA	EQOBP	EQSLG	EQMLVR	VORP	DEFENSE	
2000	MON	NL	28	290	89	24	0	11	28	67	5	1	.307	.372	.503	.163	.305	.361	.497	.150	19.1	74-LF	1
2000	CHC	NL	28	67	22	2	0	2	5	12	0	2	.328	.392	.448	.141	.324	.376	.441	.114	3.6	18-LF	1
2001	CHC	NL	29	323	99	19	1	17	26	56	1	0	.307	.371	.529	.230	.311	.372	.537	.232	28.9	72-LF	0
2002	NYY	AL	30	455	109	21	0	14	25	86	1	2	.240	.291	.378	-.143	.260	.309	.413	-.103	-1.7	113-LF	11
2003	NYY	AL	31	348	91	19	1	13	24	64	2	1	.261	.313	.435	-.015	.270	.324	.451	-.012	1.8		

Breakout: 15%   Improve: 49%   Collapse: 22%

If you think everything goes the Yankees' way, just remember that they got almost a full season out of Rondell White, and he gave them a season that made them wish they hadn't. With Matsui signed and Rivera ready, White should be out of a job if he isn't dealt. At best, he might land Shane Spencer's role (which is fine, he is younger than Spencer), getting outfield and DH at-bats predominantly against lefties.

Chris Widger   Born: 21-May-71   Age: 32   Bats: R   Throws: R

YEAR	TM	LG	AGE	AB	H	2B	3B	HR	BB	SO	SB	CS	AVG	OBP	SLG	MLVR	EQBA	EQOBP	EQSLG	EQMLVR	VORP	DEFENSE	
2000	MON	NL	29	281	67	17	2	12	29	61	1	2	.238	.312	.441	-.100	.237	.301	.438	-.101	10.5	75-C	-7
2002	COH	INT	31	217	53	14	1	10	17	31	0	3	.244	.302	.456	.014	.225	.283	.427	-.159	4.4	51-C	-6
2002	NYY	AL	31	64	19	5	0	0	2	9	0	0	.297	.338	.375	-.023	.312	.359	.406	.022	3.9	16-C	0

Joe Torre has been the exceptional postseason manager of his generation, time and again outmaneuvering his opponent in the other dugout. But nobody's perfect, and one of Torre's annoying foibles is how he almost always seems to pick the worst available bodies to fill out the end of his bench. Case in point was last spring's selection of a backup catcher, where the options were Alberto Castillo, Bobby Estalella, Todd Greene, and Widger. Admittedly, the Yankees had concern about Posada's catching after his off-season shoulder surgery, but Castillo is a notoriously indifferent plate blocker with no offensive value. Anyway, the organization corrected the mistake once Widger had shown he had fully recuperated from the shoulder surgery that cost him 2001. He's a completely adequate backup.

Bernie Williams   CF   Born: 13-Sep-68   Age: 34   Bats: B   Throws: R

YEAR	TM	LG	AGE	AB	H	2B	3B	HR	BB	SO	SB	CS	AVG	OBP	SLG	MLVR	EQBA	EQOBP	EQSLG	EQMLVR	VORP	DEFENSE	
2000	NYY	AL	31	537	165	37	6	30	71	84	13	5	.307	.393	.566	.296	.321	.400	.596	.371	76.6	125-CF	9
2001	NYY	AL	32	540	166	38	0	26	78	67	11	5	.307	.401	.522	.287	.337	.427	.575	.402	86.0	141-CF	4
2002	NYY	AL	33	612	204	37	2	19	83	97	8	4	.333	.415	.493	.298	.356	.437	.532	.379	90.5	139-CF	2
2003	NYY	AL	34	517	153	31	2	20	68	79	8	2	.297	.381	.483	.180	.307	.394	.501	.200	45.1		

Breakout: 3%   Improve: 35%   Collapse: 18%

It's not easy to be The Underrated Yankee, but is Bernie Williams ever going to be remembered? At this rate, he's the super-charged Roy White or a more athletic Ken Singleton, a hitter who can reach base, thump, and basically do no wrong at the plate. But on a team that has Jeter and Giambi and famous pitchers and The Boss and the rest of the Yankees soap opera, Williams manages to barely register. Sixty years ago, his relative silence would be considered an admirable quality. His defensive work has slipped to the point that he's no longer a good center fielder, but it happened to Bonds too; he could be an outstanding left fielder for years to come.

Enrique Wilson

Born: 27-Jul-73   **Age: 29**   **Bats: B**   **Throws: R**

YEAR	TM	LG	AGE	AB	H	2B	3B	HR	BB	SO	SB	CS	AVG	OBP	SLG	MLVR	EQBA	EQOBP	EQSLG	EQMLVR	VORP	DEFENSE			
2000	CLE	AL	26	117	38	9	0	2	7	11	2	1	.325	.363	.453	.074	.328	.355	.466	.118	6.9				
2000	PIT	NL	26	122	32	6	1	3	11	13	0	1	.262	.323	.402	-.122	.260	.311	.398	-.121	2.2	14-3B	-3		
2001	PIT	NL	27	129	24	3	0	1	3	23	0	3	.186	.205	.233	-.594	.185	.203	.238	-.605	-13.3	23-SS	-2		
2001	NYY	AL	27	99	24	5	1	1	6	14	0	2	.242	.286	.343	-.208	.263	.311	.364	-.167	1.3	12-SS	-3	13-3B	4
2002	NYY	AL	28	105	19	2	2	2	8	22	1	1	.181	.239	.295	-.382	.200	.263	.324	-.356	-4.4	15-3B	-1		
2003	NYY	AL	29	90	21	4	1	1	6	16	1	1	.230	.280	.334	-.220	.238	.290	.347	-.235	-2.4				

Breakout: 47%   Improve: 67%   Collapse: 20%

One of Visagate's big losers, Enrique Wilson celebrated an extra couple of birthdays. As a result, he went from somebody you might argue could fill in at short for a year or two if they wanted to move Jeter to somebody who now isn't automatically worth a spot on the 40-man roster. He should have to fight for his job, but probably won't now that he's nearly old enough to be confused with Clay Bellinger.

PITCHERS

Jason Anderson

Born: 09-Jun-79   **Age: 24**   **Bats: L**   **Throws: R**

YEAR	TM	LG	AGE	G	GS	IP	H	BB	SO	HR	ERA	EQERA	EQH9	EQBB9	EQSO9	EQHR9	PERA	VORP	STF
2000	STA	NYP	21	15	15	80.3	84	25	73	1	4.03	7.47	14.5	4.0	4.8	0.5	6.50	-17.5	1
2001	STA	NYP	22	7	7	47.7	32	12	56	2	1.70	3.51	9.6	3.5	6.2	1.3	3.73	10.6	17
2001	GRB	SAL	22	23	19	124.3	127	40	101	9	3.77	7.22	14.1	4.7	4.4	1.7	7.04	-23.8	-9
2002	TAM	FSL	23	12	3	24.3	27	3	22	2	4.07	6.21	14.2	1.5	6.0	1.9	6.31	-2.1	-3
2002	NRW	EAS	23	16	0	19.3	14	5	21	1	0.93	1.98	7.8	2.8	7.4	0.8	3.21	7.3	14
2002	COH	INT	23	26	0	34.3	26	11	28	3	3.15	3.11	6.7	3.4	6.1	1.1	3.47	8.7	1

The Yankees get goofy at times with their young pitchers, hurling them up the chain after a brief taste of success. It really didn't work for Ryan Bradley, and it remains to be seen if it did Anderson any good. Drafted out of the University of Illinois (in case you haven't noticed, the organization has a thing for the Big 10), Anderson's tools in addition to his performance make you think he'll be the real deal. He's got good mechanics and throws strikes consistently in the mid-90s. He might earn a job in the back of the bullpen, although that really isn't the Yankees' style. As much as there might be no such thing as a pitching prospect and especially no such thing as a relief pitcher prospect, Anderson looks pretty good.

Andy Beal

Born: 31-Oct-78   **Age: 24**   **Bats: L**   **Throws: L**

YEAR	TM	LG	AGE	G	GS	IP	H	BB	SO	HR	ERA	EQERA	EQH9	EQBB9	EQSO9	EQHR9	PERA	VORP	STF
2000	STA	NYP	21	14	14	92.3	72	17	87	6	2.34	4.76	12.9	2.4	5.1	2.8	4.37	7.6	6
2001	GRB	SAL	22	2	2	10.3	10	3	6	0	0.00	2.97	12.5	4.1	3.1	0.3	5.66	2.9	-5
2001	TAM	FSL	22	17	17	99.0	101	30	72	6	3.00	6.32	12.4	3.4	4.5	1.4	6.30	-9.0	0
2002	TAM	FSL	23	10	10	54.3	59	13	37	0	2.65	4.88	12.9	2.8	4.4	0.3	5.80	3.8	4
2002	NRW	EAS	23	10	10	62.7	56	22	61	3	3.30	4.34	9.5	3.8	6.7	0.7	4.47	8.1	18
2002	COH	INT	23	8	8	44.7	50	21	31	6	6.04	6.23	10.2	5.0	5.3	1.7	6.43	-3.6	-3

The Yankees drafted a trio of lefties in 2000, Danny Borrell in the 2nd round out of Wake Forest, Beal in the 5th out of Vanderbilt, and Oklahoma State's Matt Smith in the 4th. Smith hit the wall at Double-A in 2002, but both Beal and Borrell are still standing. Beal is a finesse lefty of the standard mold, which means he's less a future Yankee than part of a package bound for Florida or Montreal.

Danny Borrell

Born: 24-Jan-79   **Age: 24**   **Bats: L**   **Throws: L**

YEAR	TM	LG	AGE	G	GS	IP	H	BB	SO	HR	ERA	EQERA	EQH9	EQBB9	EQSO9	EQHR9	PERA	VORP	STF
2000	STA	NYP	21	10	10	56.3	39	19	44	2	3.20	5.23	10.8	4.3	4.2	1.5	4.13	1.7	0
2001	TAM	FSL	22	22	20	111.0	109	38	84	6	3.97	5.96	11.8	3.8	4.7	1.3	6.11	-5.7	-2
2002	TAM	FSL	23	7	6	38.7	33	10	44	0	2.33	3.83	9.9	3.0	7.3	0.3	4.25	7.2	25
2002	NRW	EAS	23	21	20	128.3	116	39	91	5	2.31	3.89	9.6	3.3	4.9	0.6	4.31	23.0	9
2003	NYY	AL	24	14	11	69.0	77	27	45	10	5.17	5.21	10.1	3.3	5.6	1.1	5.02	5.8	1

Breakout: 15%   Improve: 50%   Collapse: 22%

Danny Borrell *(continued)*

The best of the trio of college lefties drafted high in 2000, Borrell throws the hardest most consistently and spots a good changeup. He's still working on his breaking stuff. He had to be shut down with shoulder problems in 2001, but didn't show any problems last year. He didn't pitch much in college, so the fact that he's moved up this quickly is promising. It also holds out hope that as he masters a curve or slider, his strikeout rates will improve.

Randy Choate — Born: 05-Sep-75 — Age: 27 — Bats: L — Throws: L

YEAR	TM	LG	AGE	G	GS	IP	H	BB	SO	HR	ERA	EQERA	EQH9	EQBB9	EQSO9	EQHR9	PERA	VORP	STF
2000	COH	INT	24	33	0	35.3	34	14	37	2	2.04	2.94	9.0	3.5	7.9	0.6	4.36	9.6	11
2000	NYY	AL	24	22	0	17.0	14	8	12	3	4.76	4.10	6.8	3.4	6.1	1.3	3.80	2.4	-3
2001	NYY	AL	25	37	0	48.3	34	27	35	0	3.35	3.02	6.0	4.7	6.1	0.2	2.75	12.7	1
2002	COH	INT	26	31	0	36.7	25	15	32	0	1.72	2.15	5.7	4.3	6.5	0.2	2.78	13.2	2
2002	NYY	AL	26	18	0	22.3	18	15	17	1	6.05	4.74	6.9	5.6	6.6	0.4	3.72	1.6	-4
2003	NYY	AL	27	31	3	44.7	45	23	33	5	5.02	5.06	9.1	4.3	6.4	0.9	4.81	3.8	-6

Breakout: 9%   Improve: 25%   Collapse: 29%

For whatever reason, Torre just doesn't seem to like Choate, which is unfortunate. He has value as a situational lefty, but Torre wouldn't use him as one regularly enough to keep him fresh, and then would do things like leave him out there to absorb a beating on a getaway day. Over the last three years, he's limited lefties to .168/.288/.248, which is the sort of thing that usually makes a situational reliever very wealthy. He might get taken a little more seriously now that Mike Stanton is gone. Or not, with Chris Hammond now on board.

Brandon Claussen — Born: 01-May-79 — Age: 24 — Bats: L — Throws: L

YEAR	TM	LG	AGE	G	GS	IP	H	BB	SO	HR	ERA	EQERA	EQH9	EQBB9	EQSO9	EQHR9	PERA	VORP	STF
2000	GRB	SAL	21	17	17	97.7	91	44	98	9	4.05	6.11	12.2	5.8	5.4	2.3	6.63	-6.6	-2
2000	TAM	FSL	21	9	9	52.3	49	17	44	1	3.10	5.24	10.7	3.7	5.4	0.4	5.03	1.5	11
2001	TAM	FSL	22	8	8	56.0	47	13	69	2	2.73	4.36	9.7	2.5	7.4	0.8	4.40	7.1	27
2001	NRW	EAS	22	21	21	131.0	101	55	151	6	2.13	3.92	8.3	5.1	7.2	0.7	4.33	23.1	21
2002	COH	INT	23	15	15	93.3	85	46	73	4	3.28	4.09	7.9	5.2	5.9	0.5	4.52	14.7	10

Claussen's already out for most of 2003 after Tommy John surgery, which is a damned shame, not that they have rotation spots to go around. The last couple of years have not been kind to Yankees farmhands. In the shoulder surgery bin, you've got Christian Parker, Todd Noel, and Chien-Ming Wang, and over in the elbow pile, you've got top fireballing lefty Sean Henn, 2001 supplemental 1st rounder Jon Skaggs, Randy Keisler, and now Claussen. This might sound extraordinary, but this is what happens with pitchers. Most of them are supposed to be healthy enough to pitch in 2003, with Claussen as the least likely to do anything before August. Nevertheless, he might still be the best bet to reach New York to stay, assuming his rehab goes well.

Roger Clemens — Born: 04-Aug-62 — Age: 40 — Bats: R — Throws: R

YEAR	TM	LG	AGE	G	GS	IP	H	BB	SO	HR	ERA	EQERA	EQH9	EQBB9	EQSO9	EQHR9	PERA	VORP	STF
2000	NYY	AL	37	32	32	204.3	184	84	188	26	3.70	3.61	7.6	3.0	8.0	1.0	3.65	43.0	24
2001	NYY	AL	38	33	33	220.3	205	72	213	19	3.51	3.48	8.0	2.7	8.1	0.7	3.66	49.6	27
2002	NYY	AL	39	29	29	180.0	172	63	192	18	4.35	3.94	8.2	2.9	9.2	0.8	3.87	31.3	31
2003	NYY	AL	40	26	23	145.7	138	59	140	16	3.91	3.94	8.5	3.4	8.2	0.9	3.71	36.8	23

Breakout: 15%   Improve: 54%   Collapse: 6%

An optimist would note that Clemens's peripherals were all better than his final ERA; a pessimist, his age, his worst ERA since his first year as a Yankee, and his first season without 30 starts since 1995. We're well into strange outlier territory in terms of what we might expect, but given Clemens's overall health, bringing him back to the tune of $10 million or so on a one-year deal seems sensible. The Rocket should win his 300th game in pinstripes, which, along with a couple of rings, should pretty much clinch the decision over whether or not he'll go to the Hall of Fame wearing a Blue Jays hat. The Clemens/Maddux/Pedro debate over which was the greatest right-handed pitcher of all time should make for good times on a bar stool near you.

Jose Contreras   Born: 12-Dec-71?   Age: 31?   Bats: R   Throws: R

The Cubano import should be something special, but you always have to wonder if he might just be the next Ariel Prieto or Rene Arocha. For all of the enthusiasm over El Duque, it's worth noting how very few of the Cuban imports have turned as well as wishcasted. Contreras is supposed to be the island's best, and he may well be. At $32 million spread over four years, he has to be.

What was interesting was the dance where Contreras defected to wherever he could become a free agent, while the commissioner's office tried to get him into the draft. So first he went to Mexico, except that the paperwork for his sudden residency in Mexico was considered improper. Then he discovered a bunch of friends in Nicaragua. Meanwhile, the industry tried to wangle a way to deflate his wages. No wonder they want to internationalize the draft.

Julio DePaula   Born: 27-Jul-79   Age: 23   Bats: R   Throws: R

YEAR	TM	LG	AGE	G	GS	IP	H	BB	SO	HR	ERA	EQERA	EQH9	EQBB9	EQSO9	EQHR9	PERA	VORP	STF
2000	ASH	SAL	20	28	27	155.0	151	62	187	16	4.70	6.35	12.4	5.0	6.4	2.4	6.20	-14.6	5
2001	GRB	SAL	21	8	8	55.7	35	21	67	2	2.75	4.32	8.2	5.2	6.2	0.8	3.91	7.3	15
2001	TAM	FSL	21	16	13	83.0	65	53	77	3	3.58	5.79	9.1	7.0	5.6	0.8	5.76	-2.7	1
2002	NRW	EAS	22	27	26	175.0	141	52	152	11	3.45	4.08	8.7	3.2	6.0	1.0	3.89	27.7	17
2003	NYY	AL	23	12	9	62.0	69	29	45	10	5.19	5.23	10.1	3.8	6.2	1.2	5.26	5.0	3

Breakout: 11%   Improve: 45%   Collapse: 23%

Nothing about the Yankees' preponderant revenue stream helped them get DePaula; the Rockies handed him over for Craig Dingman. Why anyone would acquire a wandering reliever for a guy who's consistently in the low 90s is beyond me. DePaula has gained polish on his slider and improved his changeup, and is arguably the best upper-level pitcher in the organization, although part of that is that he's one of the few that hasn't gotten hurt. There's already talk of moving him to the pen, but with Rivera and Karsay in place and Jason Anderson looking good, and considering how infrequently Torre turns to the bottom of the pen, it wouldn't make sense if it was intended to get DePaula up sooner. One way or another, he'll have a career.

Alex Graman   Born: 17-Nov-77   Age: 25   Bats: L   Throws: L

YEAR	TM	LG	AGE	G	GS	IP	H	BB	SO	HR	ERA	EQERA	EQH9	EQBB9	EQSO9	EQHR9	PERA	VORP	STF
2000	TAM	FSL	22	28	28	143.0	120	58	111	6	3.65	5.13	10.0	4.7	5.0	1.0	4.93	6.0	1
2001	NRW	EAS	23	28	28	166.3	174	60	138	10	3.52	5.64	11.4	4.4	5.2	0.9	6.05	-2.5	3
2002	NRW	EAS	24	8	8	50.0	46	13	31	2	2.88	4.04	9.8	2.8	4.3	0.6	4.26	8.1	5
2002	COH	INT	24	20	20	124.0	141	37	98	11	4.65	4.93	10.1	3.1	5.9	1.1	5.54	7.9	9
2003	NYY	AL	25	14	10	63.3	71	27	41	9	5.10	5.15	10.0	3.5	5.6	1.1	5.09	4.4	0

Breakout: 14%   Improve: 50%   Collapse: 15%

He's a little more likeable than the raw numbers suggest, since he generally does a good job of keeping the ball on the ground, but getting called up to an awful Columbus team didn't do him many favors. He's not a finesse pitcher, using legitimate 90-plus velocity and a forkball. Graman's sort of overlooked, but he's a half-step ahead of Borrell and Beal among the uninjured lefties, and should make for a nice bargaining chip come July.

Orlando Hernandez   Born: 11-Oct-69   Age: 33?   Bats: R   Throws: R

YEAR	TM	LG	AGE	G	GS	IP	H	BB	SO	HR	ERA	EQERA	EQH9	EQBB9	EQSO9	EQHR9	PERA	VORP	STF
2000	NYY	AL	30	29	29	195.7	186	51	141	34	4.51	3.90	8.1	1.9	6.3	1.3	3.79	34.9	15
2001	NYY	AL	31	17	16	94.7	90	42	77	19	4.85	4.54	8.1	3.7	6.8	1.6	4.94	10.1	7
2002	NYY	AL	32	24	22	146.0	131	36	113	17	3.64	3.37	7.7	2.1	6.7	1.0	3.44	34.6	20
2003	MON	NL	37	23	20	129.0	128	39	102	17	3.98	4.12	9.1	2.3	6.3	1.2	4.19	21.0	13

Breakout: 16%   Improve: 43%   Collapse: 15%

El Duque's 2002 season might have been his most impressive since his rookie season. Although a good lefty can still take him out of the yard, he dramatically improved his control against them. If that's something that sticks, he's considerably more valuable, since he could finally end up being a regular season ace instead of a postseason phenomenon. Because of his arbitration eligibility, he's perceived to be the starter on the bubble behind Clemens, Mussina, Pettitte, Contreras, and Wells. It would be easy to envision his being dealt to a near-contender, like the Phillies or Astros, but instead he's an Expo, partially paid for by others. Don't be surprised if he's in somebody else's uniform by August.

Adrian Hernandez Born: 25-Mar-75 Age: 28 Bats: R Throws: R

YEAR	TM	LG	AGE	G	GS	IP	H	BB	SO	HR	ERA	EQERA	EQH9	EQBB9	EQSO9	EQHR9	PERA	VORP	STF
2000	NRW	EAS	25	6	6	35.7	34	18	44	1	4.03	5.23	10.2	5.0	8.3	0.5	5.28	1.1	20
2000	COH	INT	25	5	5	30.7	24	18	29	2	4.40	4.47	7.3	5.2	7.1	0.7	4.08	3.5	14
2001	COH	INT	26	21	21	117.7	116	60	97	13	5.51	5.64	9.5	5.4	5.8	1.3	5.80	-1.8	-4
2001	NYY	AL	26	6	3	22.0	15	10	10	7	3.68	3.98	5.7	3.8	3.9	2.6	4.48	3.7	-19
2002	COH	INT	27	20	20	109.7	114	45	109	9	5.25	4.92	9.2	4.3	7.4	1.0	5.28	7.1	11
2002	NYY	AL	27	2	1	6.0	10	6	9	2	12.00	10.76	13.4	7.7	12.1	2.5	11.07	-3.5	-1
2003	*NYY*	*AL*	*28*	*15*	*11*	*62.3*	*67*	*34*	*51*	*10*	*5.23*	*5.28*	*9.6*	*4.5*	*6.9*	*1.2*	*5.32*	*4.7*	*2*

Breakout: 12%   Improve: 40%   Collapse: 27%

Hernandez has been an expensive disappointment so far, but the Yankees are being stubborn in trying to make him a starting pitcher. He doesn't throw especially hard, and he's no youngster, but he's the sort of guy who can go through a lineup once without getting into too much trouble. Significantly, he slipped off the 40-man roster after the season, and no other team gave thought to claiming him.

Sterling Hitchcock Born: 29-Apr-71 Age: 32 Bats: L Throws: L

YEAR	TM	LG	AGE	G	GS	IP	H	BB	SO	HR	ERA	EQERA	EQH9	EQBB9	EQSO9	EQHR9	PERA	VORP	STF
2000	SDP	NL	29	11	11	65.7	69	26	61	12	4.93	5.18	9.9	2.9	7.5	1.5	5.33	2.4	14
2001	SDP	NL	30	3	3	19.0	22	3	15	1	3.32	4.23	11.1	1.3	6.2	0.4	4.43	2.7	19
2001	NYY	AL	30	10	9	51.3	67	18	28	5	6.49	5.61	11.3	2.9	4.6	0.8	5.73	-0.6	-3
2002	NYY	AL	31	20	2	39.3	57	15	31	4	5.50	6.05	12.5	3.2	6.8	0.8	6.48	-2.8	-1
2003	*NYY*	*AL*	*32*	*18*	*9*	*54.7*	*67*	*19*	*36*	*8*	*5.14*	*5.19*	*11.0*	*2.9*	*5.6*	*1.1*	*5.23*	*4.8*	*-3*

Breakout: 8%   Improve: 40%   Collapse: 26%

Even the Yankees have brain cramps, and Hitchcock is among the worst in recent memory. He rushed back from his 2000 Tommy John surgery, barely spending the minimum 12 months recovering. A charitable interpretation is that he'll regain some command in 2003, but the Yankees should have expected him to struggle when they signed him, so why give him big money? Despite brave talk about how they're shopping him, he should have to continue to be a Yankee for the remainder of his contract. He hasn't been healthy since 1999, and at this point, must be keeping Dave LaPoint's seat warm.

Steve Karsay Born: 24-Mar-72 Age: 31 Bats: R Throws: R

YEAR	TM	LG	AGE	G	GS	IP	H	BB	SO	HR	ERA	EQERA	EQH9	EQBB9	EQSO9	EQHR9	PERA	VORP	STF
2000	CLE	AL	28	72	0	76.7	79	25	66	5	3.75	3.24	8.6	2.4	7.5	0.5	3.41	18.2	11
2001	CLE	AL	29	31	0	43.3	29	8	44	1	1.25	1.30	5.4	1.5	8.5	0.2	1.74	19.6	27
2001	ATL	NL	29	43	0	44.7	44	17	39	4	3.42	4.43	9.7	3.2	6.8	0.7	4.23	4.7	0
2002	NYY	AL	30	78	0	88.3	87	30	65	7	3.26	3.34	8.5	2.8	6.4	0.7	3.86	20.0	2
2003	*NYY*	*AL*	*31*	*57*	*0*	*63.7*	*65*	*22*	*49*	*7*	*3.84*	*3.87*	*9.2*	*2.8*	*6.6*	*0.9*	*4.18*	*14.7*	*1*

Breakout: 15%   Improve: 46%   Collapse: 30%

Karsay has been one of the game's great relievers over the previous three seasons, and as a Yankee, he did not disappoint. He's still due another $15 million or so for at least the next three years, but as the fireman who gets brought in with men on base in the middle innings and as a reliable substitute for Rivera, he's a luxury the Yankees need and can afford as their Vice-Closer.

Brandon Knight Born: 01-Oct-75 Age: 27 Bats: L Throws: R

YEAR	TM	LG	AGE	G	GS	IP	H	BB	SO	HR	ERA	EQERA	EQH9	EQBB9	EQSO9	EQHR9	PERA	VORP	STF
2000	COH	INT	24	28	28	184.7	172	61	138	21	4.43	4.57	8.9	3.0	5.7	1.3	4.45	19.2	10
2001	COH	INT	25	25	25	162.3	174	45	173	16	3.66	4.71	10.2	2.9	7.4	1.2	5.36	14.3	18
2002	COH	INT	26	36	7	80.7	67	37	81	6	3.90	3.95	7.3	4.9	7.5	0.9	4.19	13.3	2
2002	NYY	AL	26	7	0	8.7	11	5	7	2	11.38	8.67	10.7	4.7	6.9	1.9	7.09	-3.2	-17
2003	*NYY*	*AL*	*27*	*18*	*6*	*42.3*	*45*	*20*	*35*	*6*	*4.91*	*4.95*	*9.5*	*3.8*	*7.1*	*1.2*	*4.73*	*5.4*	*1*

Breakout: 20%   Improve: 48%   Collapse: 23%

It was a bit baffling why the Yankees didn't keep Knight around as a long reliever in 2002. Why have him on the 40-man or ship him off to his third year in Ohio if he can't beat out Jay Tessmer for the Opening Day roster? Knight throws four pitches for strikes but isn't overpowering; his future is as an 11th pitcher and spot starter. Sometimes those guys grow up to be Cory Lidle, but Knight will be pitching in Japan in 2003 after his contract was sold to the Fukuoka Daiei Hawks.

Charlie Manning   Born: 31-Mar-79   Age: 24   Bats: L   Throws: L

YEAR	TM	LG	AGE	G	GS	IP	H	BB	SO	HR	ERA	EQERA	EQH9	EQBB9	EQSO9	EQHR9	PERA	VORP	STF
2001	STA	NYP	22	14	14	80.0	73	21	87	4	3.49	6.15	13.2	3.7	5.9	1.6	5.66	-5.7	7
2002	TAM	FSL	23	17	16	100.0	82	31	85	4	3.24	5.04	10.0	3.6	5.5	0.9	4.62	5.1	9
2002	NRW	EAS	23	11	11	63.0	55	26	61	1	3.57	4.32	9.1	4.4	6.6	0.2	4.30	8.3	17

As the more famous and more talented pitchers in the organization broke down, opportunity arose for other guys. Manning is one of the ones who got that opportunity and ran with it. A bunch of unearned runs in Tampa (where he'd also pitched in college before being picked in the 9th round in 2001) superficially helped his stats, but he didn't embarrass himself in Double-A. Lefties with good strikeout rates and a talent for keeping the ball in the park bear watching.

Ramiro Mendoza   Born: 15-Jun-72   Age: 31   Bats: R   Throws: R

YEAR	TM	LG	AGE	G	GS	IP	H	BB	SO	HR	ERA	EQERA	EQH9	EQBB9	EQSO9	EQHR9	PERA	VORP	STF
2000	NYY	AL	28	14	9	65.7	66	20	30	9	4.25	3.80	8.6	2.2	4.0	1.1	3.94	12.3	-2
2001	NYY	AL	29	56	2	100.7	89	23	70	9	3.75	3.27	7.6	1.9	5.9	0.7	3.21	23.7	4
2002	NYY	AL	30	62	0	91.7	102	16	61	8	3.44	3.81	9.6	1.5	5.8	0.7	4.07	16.0	2
2003	BOS	AL	31	38	7	70.0	75	18	43	8	4.02	3.99	9.4	2.1	5.3	1.0	4.11	14.5	-3

Breakout: 18%   Improve: 44%   Collapse: 25%

Although he's been an asset in the past, his value has always been overstated by his being in pinstripes. Bought by the Red Sox as a gesture of that typically Beantown zesty blend of spite and envy. Mendoza hardly evens the score as far as the Yankees having Clemens and the Red Sox having . . . well, money they got to spend on guys like Troy O'Leary, plus the benefit of the exciting careers of compensation draft picks Mark Fischer and Aaron Capista. Once upon a time, there was this one friend who always argued that things even out in the end, but believe me, some things don't.

Mike Mussina   Born: 08-Dec-68   Age: 34   Bats: R   Throws: R

YEAR	TM	LG	AGE	G	GS	IP	H	BB	SO	HR	ERA	EQERA	EQH9	EQBB9	EQSO9	EQHR9	PERA	VORP	STF
2000	BAL	AL	31	34	34	237.7	236	46	210	28	3.79	3.35	8.5	1.4	7.8	0.9	3.46	56.9	28
2001	NYY	AL	32	34	34	228.7	202	42	214	20	3.15	3.01	7.6	1.5	7.9	0.7	3.07	63.4	30
2002	NYY	AL	33	33	33	215.7	208	48	182	27	4.05	3.69	8.3	1.9	7.3	1.0	3.74	43.5	23
2003	NYY	AL	34	30	29	190.3	188	44	151	24	3.77	3.80	8.8	1.9	6.8	1.0	3.69	42.3	20

Breakout: 8%   Improve: 45%   Collapse: 11%

Last year seemed worse than it was, because he got his wins before the All-Star Break, and did his best pitching down the stretch. But the Moose continued to roll along, giving the Yankees quality and quantity. He still spins one of the game's great curves, his peripheral numbers are all basically positive, and his physical reliability makes him about as safe a bet as you could ask for over the next few years.

Andy Pettitte   Born: 15-Jun-72   Age: 31   Bats: L   Throws: L

YEAR	TM	LG	AGE	G	GS	IP	H	BB	SO	HR	ERA	EQERA	EQH9	EQBB9	EQSO9	EQHR9	PERA	VORP	STF
2000	NYY	AL	28	32	32	204.7	219	80	125	17	4.35	4.09	9.2	2.9	5.3	0.6	4.11	32.2	9
2001	NYY	AL	29	31	31	200.7	224	41	164	14	3.99	4.01	9.7	1.7	6.9	0.6	4.10	33.3	22
2002	NYY	AL	30	22	22	134.7	144	32	97	6	3.27	3.50	9.3	2.0	6.3	0.4	3.75	30.0	20
2003	NYY	AL	31	26	24	152.0	159	41	100	15	3.95	3.99	9.4	2.2	5.6	0.7	3.98	29.4	12

Breakout: 13%   Improve: 45%   Collapse: 15%

Some guys are considered throwbacks because they look a certain way; Pettitte is a throwback to the deadball era because of what he does: he throws four pitches for strikes, he keeps the ball on the ground and in the infield, and he kills the running game with one of the best pickoff moves you'll ever see. But now that he's over 30, and his elbow's started twanging like a crunchy rubber band on a summer day, would you have picked up his option? Beyond 2003, Wells and Hitchcock will be gone, and Clemens might be gone, so Pettitte is probably one of the moving parts who will still be here.

Mariano Rivera Born: 29-Nov-69 Age: 33 Bats: R Throws: R

YEAR	TM	LG	AGE	G	GS	IP	H	BB	SO	HR	ERA	EQERA	EQH9	EQBB9	EQSO9	EQHR9	PERA	VORP	STF
2000	NYY	AL	30	66	0	75.7	58	25	58	4	2.85	2.52	6.6	2.4	6.7	0.4	2.44	24.1	9
2001	NYY	AL	31	71	0	80.7	61	12	83	5	2.34	2.31	6.5	1.2	8.7	0.5	2.29	27.5	25
2002	NYY	AL	32	45	0	46.0	35	11	41	3	2.74	2.59	6.5	2.0	7.7	0.5	2.51	14.3	15
2003	NYY	AL	33	50	0	54.3	51	14	43	5	3.39	3.42	8.5	2.1	6.8	0.8	3.38	14.2	7

Breakout: 21%　　Improve: 42%　　Collapse: 31%

The Deadly Skull was good when he was healthy, but he hit the DL three separate times with shoulder and groin strains. One of those things is more troubling than the other, but supposedly there won't be any lasting effects, and he'll be 100% in 2003. Perhaps the most inane spectacle at the start of last season was the speculation about who was more demoralized from the 2001 postseason, Mariano Rivera or Byung-Hyun Kim. It isn't like we were talking George Frazier or Mitch Williams here, folks. Rivera didn't seem to labor with any kind of baggage beyond his physical problems.

Brian Rogers Born: 13-Feb-77 Age: 26 Bats: R Throws: R

YEAR	TM	LG	AGE	G	GS	IP	H	BB	SO	HR	ERA	EQERA	EQH9	EQBB9	EQSO9	EQHR9	PERA	VORP	STF
2000	NRW	EAS	23	27	27	164.3	155	70	132	10	3.94	5.57	10.5	4.3	5.5	1.0	5.24	-1.2	6
2001	NRW	EAS	24	29	29	177.3	187	63	150	21	3.96	6.21	11.8	4.4	5.4	1.7	6.67	-13.9	-2
2002	NRW	EAS	25	13	11	68.3	69	16	48	4	2.77	4.56	10.9	2.5	4.8	0.9	4.86	7.1	3
2002	COH	INT	25	14	13	71.3	80	27	51	9	5.68	5.56	10.2	4.0	5.4	1.6	6.05	-0.5	-4

Big finesse right-handers aren't usually prospect maven favorites, so Rogers doesn't get a whole lot of attention. He's got a curve that he can set up effectively to freeze lefties, and a bunch of stuff that can get launched seatwards. He's essentially an organizational soldier who got sucked upward as the waves of injuries that beset the major and minor league staffs created opportunities.

Mike Stanton Born: 02-Jun-67 Age: 36 Bats: L Throws: L

YEAR	TM	LG	AGE	G	GS	IP	H	BB	SO	HR	ERA	EQERA	EQH9	EQBB9	EQSO9	EQHR9	PERA	VORP	STF
2000	NYY	AL	33	69	0	68.0	68	24	75	5	4.10	3.57	8.5	2.6	9.6	0.6	3.58	13.7	22
2001	NYY	AL	34	76	0	80.3	80	29	78	4	2.58	3.06	8.6	3.0	8.1	0.4	3.82	20.7	13
2002	NYY	AL	35	79	0	78.0	73	28	44	4	3.00	3.16	8.1	3.0	4.9	0.4	3.51	19.2	-5
2003	NYM	NL	36	62	0	56	54	21	40	5	3.40	3.59	8.6	3.2	6.0	0.7	3.99	15.0	-2

Breakout: 23%　　Improve: 63%　　Collapse: 19%

There was some public weeping and hand wringing on Stanton's behalf because of Cashman's "take it or leave it in the next 15 minutes" offer of $4.6 million over two years, but the only mistake made was including Chris Hammond and Mark Guthrie in the conversation. Of course Hammond or Guthrie is going to take that deal, at which point you've overpaid. Stanton's nice enough, but he's no spring chicken, and the drop in his strikeout rate is ominous. At $9 million over three years, the Mets overpaid and assumed a major risk as to whether Stanton will be worth it over the life of his contract. I guess competing with Ed Wade does that to you.

Mike Thurman Born: 22-Jul-73 Age: 29 Bats: R Throws: R

YEAR	TM	LG	AGE	G	GS	IP	H	BB	SO	HR	ERA	EQERA	EQH9	EQBB9	EQSO9	EQHR9	PERA	VORP	STF
2000	MON	NL	26	17	17	88.3	112	46	52	9	6.42	5.63	10.8	3.7	4.6	0.8	5.87	-1.2	-5
2001	MON	NL	27	28	26	147.0	172	50	96	21	5.33	5.06	10.5	2.9	5.0	1.1	5.31	7.2	0
2002	COH	INT	28	12	12	76.7	83	14	51	8	3.52	4.00	9.6	1.9	5.0	1.3	4.96	12.8	5
2002	NYY	AL	28	12	2	33.0	45	12	23	2	5.18	5.26	11.8	3.0	6.0	0.5	5.70	0.6	0
2003	CLE	AL	29	17	11	64.0	84	24	44	11	5.24	5.15	11.7	3.1	5.9	1.3	5.27	8.2	-1

Breakout: 18%　　Improve: 48%　　Collapse: 24%

Perhaps our most entertaining radio gig before the 2002 season was with a station in Oregon that wanted to talk to us about the Yankees. We were surprised, but sure, our guy goes on, and chats for five minutes about the Bronxians before the locals get to the point: "So, what about Mike Thurman?" Pause. "Mike Thurman. Ahem." It's good to know that Thurman's glory days at Oregon State University have not been forgotten. Tip your cap to his agent for putting him with the Tribe in 2003, where he could earn a big league rotation slot.

Dave Walling — Born: 12-Nov-78 — Age: 24 — Bats: R — Throws: R

YEAR	TM	LG	AGE	G	GS	IP	H	BB	SO	HR	ERA	EQERA	EQH9	EQBB9	EQSO9	EQHR9	PERA	VORP	STF
2000	TAM	FSL	21	9	9	58.7	48	12	45	1	1.99	3.67	9.3	2.3	4.9	0.4	3.77	12.0	16
2000	NRW	EAS	21	14	14	85.3	101	26	70	10	5.28	6.86	13.6	3.2	5.8	2.0	6.92	-12.8	6
2001	TAM	FSL	22	4	4	17.3	23	2	9	2	5.20	8.01	17.2	1.3	3.3	2.8	8.41	-4.8	-18
2001	NRW	EAS	22	5	5	31.7	44	4	24	1	5.39	7.34	14.8	1.5	4.7	0.5	7.20	-6.5	6
2002	COH	INT	23	11	11	67.3	73	11	46	8	4.55	4.52	9.7	1.7	5.1	1.5	5.02	7.4	9

So what would you have said about Mackey Sasser or Steve Blass (or Rick Ankiel nowadays) when nobody knew what would happen next? When he pitches, Walling gives you reasons to think he might be useful. Unfortunately, he's got a hang-up about baserunners—he'll get into ruts where he can't stop throwing over to first. The problem is serious enough that he had to be shut down in each of the last two years, even retiring briefly after 2001. When he does pitch, he's got moving heat in the low 90s and a nice changeup, but that could be little more than a rumor considering we're talking about somebody who's made 20 starts total in two years.

Chien-Ming Wang — Born: 31-Mar-80 — Age: 23 — Bats: R — Throws: R

YEAR	TM	LG	AGE	G	GS	IP	H	BB	SO	HR	ERA	EQERA	EQH9	EQBB9	EQSO9	EQHR9	PERA	VORP	STF
2000	STA	NYP	20	14	14	87.0	77	21	75	2	2.48	5.85	12.7	3.1	4.6	1.0	4.99	-3.3	6
2002	STA	NYP	22	13	13	78.3	63	14	64	2	1.72	4.63	11.3	2.6	4.5	0.9	4.30	7.6	8

Signed to a big-money bonus in 2000, Wang missed the 2001 season after shoulder surgery. He's still considered one of the system's best prospects on the strength of his low 90s heat and a nifty slider. Although the New York-Penn League is a long way from the majors, the hope is that Wang will move up quickly in 2003, potentially entering the big league picture by the end of 2004. Chinese prospects don't have the track record of disappointment that Koreans have had, but then there have been fewer of them.

Jeff Weaver — Born: 22-Aug-76 — Age: 26 — Bats: R — Throws: R

YEAR	TM	LG	AGE	G	GS	IP	H	BB	SO	HR	ERA	EQERA	EQH9	EQBB9	EQSO9	EQHR9	PERA	VORP	STF
2000	DET	AL	23	31	30	200.0	205	52	136	26	4.32	3.75	8.7	1.9	6.0	1.0	3.78	39.0	19
2001	DET	AL	24	33	33	229.3	235	68	152	19	4.08	3.99	9.0	2.5	5.6	0.7	3.98	38.6	14
2002	DET	AL	25	17	17	121.7	112	33	75	4	3.18	3.02	7.9	2.3	5.4	0.3	3.11	33.6	17
2002	NYY	AL	25	15	8	78.0	81	15	57	12	4.04	3.96	8.9	1.6	6.4	1.3	4.22	13.1	15
2003	NYY	AL	26	29	26	171.0	179	47	111	23	4.33	4.36	9.4	2.3	5.5	1.1	4.26	26.3	9

Breakout: 9%   Improve: 46%   Collapse: 15%

Barring a trade, Weaver is almost certain to wind up in the pen from among the seven starting pitchers on the roster after Clemens re-signed and Contreras was brought in. Weaver is also one of the guys that if the Yankees do deal a starter, they should hold onto. Jumbo Wells is ancient, Andy Pettitte is a risk, and El Duque's age and health record aren't exactly inspiring. Weaver won't grow up to be the next David Cone, but he should be an outstanding third starter for your 2004 Yankees. Hopefully; between his animated mound presence and his sweet slider, he can settle in and become a star.

David Wells — Born: 20-May-63 — Age: 40 — Bats: L — Throws: L

YEAR	TM	LG	AGE	G	GS	IP	H	BB	SO	HR	ERA	EQERA	EQH9	EQBB9	EQSO9	EQHR9	PERA	VORP	STF
2000	TOR	AL	37	35	35	229.7	266	31	166	23	4.11	3.58	9.6	1.0	6.3	0.8	3.73	49.1	21
2001	CWS	AL	38	16	16	100.7	120	21	59	12	4.47	4.69	10.7	1.8	5.0	1.0	4.67	9.1	7
2002	NYY	AL	39	31	31	206.3	210	45	137	21	3.75	3.75	8.8	1.8	5.8	0.8	3.83	40.2	14
2003	NYY	AL	40	29	28	183.7	196	41	113	22	4.19	4.23	9.6	1.9	5.3	0.9	4.10	30.9	10

Breakout: 17%   Improve: 55%   Collapse: 11%

The good news is that baseball's most famous gouty pitcher showed that 2001 was not the beginning of the end. As he's lost velocity, he's learned to adapt and rely more heavily on a cutter. Most of all, he gave the Yankees something they needed, a guy who could take the ball just about every fifth day and give the league's best offense a shot at a win. He should give them that in the last year of his deal as well, after which the Yankees can stop whistling past the graveyard. Was anyone else bemused by the idea that Brian Cashman had to give Wells the talking-to after Wells lost a couple of teeth in the diner slug-and-run incident? What's next, Orrin Hatch lecturing Nick Nolte on how to stay on the straight and narrow? "Behave yourself. It works for me."

Oakland Athletics

There's been a cottage industry in the baseball press that focuses on making excuses for teams without massive media contracts. After the A's started slowly in 2001, there was a tide of commentary about how the 2000 A's were a one-year fluke, and the reality of today's baseball is that only teams with huge payrolls can compete on regular basis. The A's were an anomaly, and while the work they had done was impressive, it was a passing fad.

Now, facing Jason Giambi's walk year, the A's would be faced with the horrible prospect of having a guy's imminent departure become a distraction and major story, and how the A's would have to deal him rather than "let him go to the Yankees for nothing." Jason walked, the A's took the draft compensation, looked at their stockpile of decent 1B options, got another one in Scott Hatteberg, and moved on to 2002.

Last year played out much like 2001, with the A's playing decently but not great in the first half, and playing like adults in a junior league in the second half, losing only 21 games after the All-Star break. The rotation was dependable for much of the year, and featured hot streaks by each of the top four starters, and solid work from Aaron Harang and Ted Lilly in the fifth spot. For a stretch in August, the A's rode a wave of timely hitting, great pitching, and the occasional defensive gem to an incredible 20-game winning streak, capped by a Hatteberg walk-off piece to win the final game of the streak over Kansas City. Despite the excitement of a prolonged winning streak, arguably the strongest rotation in baseball, and some inspired offensive performances, the A's were once again bounced in the first round of the postseason.

So the A's enter 2003 much like they entered 2001, facing the "walk year" of the AL MVP, and with the local media not understanding that the team is at least as strong as it was the previous season. A's GM Billy Beane said in 2000 that the A's

> ## Athletics Prospectus
>
> **2002 record:** 103–59; First place in AL West; Lost to Angels in Division Series
>
> **Pythagenport Record:** 96–67
>
> **Runs scored per game:** 4.9 (8th in AL)
>
> **Runs allowed per game:** 4 (2nd in AL)
>
> **Team EqA:** .266 (4th in AL)
>
> **2002 Batters Age:** 28.7 (5th youngest in AL)
>
> **2002 Pitchers Age:** 27.6 (3rd youngest in AL)
>
> **Ballpark:** Al Davis Reconfigurable Hole; Neutral park; Park Factor of .994
>
> **2002:** Another slow start and another blistering finish followed by another early postseason exit.
>
> **2003:** They're young, they're smart, and they're strong, and they'll be back in the playoffs again.

team on the field at that time was the worst team he'd field for the next five years, and he's stayed true to his word. The 2003 team is loaded for bear, and it didn't happen by accident. This is the best-run baseball organization in MLB, and as far as some other clubs have come over the past couple of years, the A's are still in the lead, and that lead's expanding over most of the teams in the league. In an environment where baseball's worst franchise tries to address its myriad of weaknesses by acquiring Rey Ordonez and paying him over a million bucks, the 100-win A's went out and did what they usually do—gather up a huge amount of underutilized and underrecognized talent and performance for a very low cost.

The A's front office is the best in the game. They know what information about players and performance is important, and what information isn't. There's a lot of results from this particular fact, not the least of which is that they believe they will "win" every transaction, so they make a lot of transactions to maximize their gain. And maximize they have. Let's take a quick look in table 1 at some of the changes in this off-season.

There are clubs in the league that don't have two hitters as good as McMillon and Meluskey; the A's picked them up for virtually nothing. Keith Foulke's one of the most underrated players in recent history, and has a performance profile that's a heck of a lot more indicative of future success than Koch's. Take a look at the similarities in the acquired players—light on items that don't matter as much as people think (defense), and heavy on the stuff that wins games—ability to get on base, and the ability to hit for extra bases. For pitchers? Check out the strikeout rate of those relievers. It's entirely possible that Kenny Williams, in his haste to acquire a "proven trustworthy closer," traded an unknown reliever who'll be better than the one he acquired. The A's are great at picking

Table 1.

Added:	Lost:
Erubiel Durazo	Billy Koch
Mitch Meluskey	Cory Lidle
Billy McMillon	John-Ford Griffin
Keith Foulke	Jason Arnold
Mark Johnson	Greg Myers
Joe Valentine	Ray Durham
Rontrez Johnson	
Buddy Hernandez	
Mike Neu	
Chris Singleton	

up value as throw-ins or through the scrap heap. While the Rangers will pay a fortune for Todd Van Poppel and Jay Powell, the A's will take their chances with Neu, Hernandez, and the likes of Chad Bradford. If you're going to be a kick-ass team on a limited budget, it's not enough to fill the back of your roster with cheap players—they have to be potentially great players who also happen to be cheap.

Just gathering underappreciated players without much service time isn't enough, even when you take Kenny Williams's generosity into account. A quick glance at the CBA and a little rudimentary arithmetic will demonstrate that the most cost-effective performers are players in the early stages of their career, pre-arbitration eligibility. That means that any team with constrained resources is going to have to be good at acquiring and developing talent through the draft. The A's have taken a careful look at the draft, and developed a strategy of talent acquisition that's been hugely successful. Over the past several years, the A's draft and development system has provided the A's with their impressive core of talent—Zito, Mulder, Hudson, Chavez, and Tejada. Additionally, the system's provided the necessary bargaining chips to go out and get players like Jermaine Dye and Ted Lilly. You have to bring great talent into the organization if you're going to win.

The key to the A's success in the draft? They stack the percentages in their favor, and let others take the expensive risks. It's always better to be the casino than the gambler. The A's don't take high school pitching early. Why should they? One of the biggest jokes in baseball is that franchises insist on flushing good money down the toilet by grabbing overworked 17-year-old kids with great fastballs. Beane et al. prefer to let colleges take on the risk of nurturing players through the ages of 18–21 or so, and take good gambles on Junior College players. The maturing process for a kid that age isn't easy, and the culture of minor league baseball isn't exactly conducive to social development. Colleges are. By drafting older players, the A's get several benefits. The risk that a player may just not turn out to be any good is absorbed by the college. The non-baseball risks associated with maturing are absorbed by the college. Development costs are absorbed by the college. Risks associated with player evaluation based on a slender performance record against spotty competition are mitigated. It's a good deal all around. So the A's have developed a tendency to draft college players, not to the exclusion of all high school players, but as a guideline, in an attempt to stack all the percentages in their favor. That's what all smart investors, business people, and ball clubs do.

Once the players are in the system, the A's pound the organizational philosophy. The strike zone is one of your weapons. Use it. You're a better hitter if you only swing at pitches in the zone, and teams need runners on base to score runs. Take the walks available to you, and crush the cookies that you're going to see as a result. The A's farm system is once again stocked with a number of prospects that represent the base of the club for the next several years, as some of the now-household names inevitably move on. Rich Harden looks like a potential #1 starter, Bobby Crosby looks like a potential star middle infielder, and Jeremy Brown could be the best prospect that no one's paid any attention to. There's also a portfolio of guys with some upside, and the A's minor leagues are loaded with guys that can step in and be very productive role-players at a moment's notice.

On the bench, Art Howe's gone, replaced with former bench coach Ken Macha. Local media decried the loss of Howe as some sort of indicator that the A's don't care about winning, and were trying to save money by not paying him a competitive salary. Well, that's one possible explanation, but it doesn't really hold water. The A's have made a habit of not spending money on investments that don't have a demonstrable promise of a great return. Howe did sign a hefty contract, but by no means is it clear that he's worth the money. The A's coaching staff is largely intact, and Macha's well thought of by the players and the community of MLB as a whole, as evidenced by Beane's refusal to let him interview for the Boston Red Sox job before the 2002 season. Howe's loss isn't any more surprising than Giambi's the year before, nor should it be any more of a concern. There is no organization in baseball that's better suited to manage and profit from change. Had the unthinkable happened and Billy Beane accepted the Boston Red Sox GM position during the off-season, Assistant GM Paul DePodesta would have been there to pick up the reins and move forward aggressively with a well-considered plan. Would Beane have been missed? Of course. But every team, no matter who they are, has to face the challenges of losing people, on and off the field, all the time. And the A's have a culture of moving on, not making excuses, and winning. It's a culture led by one man, and he's done it well enough so it can be led by another should the need arise.

Going into 2003, the A's are probably the favorite to repeat as champions of the AL West. Nobody in baseball can touch their rotation, and for a low payroll team, they'll have great depth, most of it stacked away in Sacramento. As Seattle ages, and Anaheim plays the role of the hunted, the A's are still the consistent, dominant force in baseball's toughest division. Even if Miguel Tejada leaves after the season, it's a trend that should continue past the 2003 season.

HITTERS

Matt Allegra   LF   Born: 10-Jul-81   Age: 21   Bats: R   Throws: R

YEAR	TM	LG	AGE	AB	H	2B	3B	HR	BB	SO	SB	CS	AVG	OBP	SLG	MLVR	EQBA	EQOBP	EQSLG	EQMLVR	VORP	DEFENSE
2001	VAN	NWN	19	273	60	16	2	11	30	104	5	6	.220	.308	.414	.044	.172	.233	.316	-.442	-19.2	70-CF -1
2001	MOD	CLF	19	153	32	3	2	2	21	61	3	1	.209	.320	.294	-.181	.166	.251	.236	-.515	-17.0	45-LF -3
2002	VIS	CLF	20	494	139	35	3	20	47	160	9	9	.281	.356	.486	.167	.220	.273	.374	-.255	-20.3	119-OF -6
2003	OAK	AL	21	209	46	10	2	6	18	67	3	5	.220	.290	.372	-.161	.227	.300	.389	-.168	-7.2	

Breakout: 60%   Improve: 75%   Collapse: 15%

Making some progress. Allegra's a great athlete with power and speed, but he's still got a ways to go as a ballplayer. He's going to need to bump that walk rate up a spot or two to get the attention of the people in the front office. Still, that's a pretty good line for a 20-year-old at Visalia. He'll have the opportunity to get better, and the A's would like nothing more than to come up with a great athlete who can play center field and hit a little.

Jeremy Brown   C   Born: 25-Oct-79   Age: 23   Bats: R   Throws: R

YEAR	TM	LG	AGE	AB	H	2B	3B	HR	BB	SO	SB	CS	AVG	OBP	SLG	MLVR	EQBA	EQOBP	EQSLG	EQMLVR	VORP	DEFENSE
2002	VAN	NWN	22	28	8	1	0	0	10	5	1	0	.286	.487	.321	.228	.226	.375	.258	-.201	-.6	
2002	VIS	CLF	22	187	58	14	0	10	44	49	1	1	.310	.446	.545	.402	.233	.348	.399	-.069	8.5	48-C -3
2003	OAK	AL	23	168	38	7	0	5	23	43	2	2	.225	.325	.364	-.108	.233	.336	.381	-.110	2.6	

Breakout: 15%   Improve: 45%   Collapse: 29%

Isn't on anyone's radar yet, but he should be. Brown's an Oakland-style hitter. Loads o' patience, some pop, and even a reasonable average. If Ramon Hernandez is suddenly gone in June, Brown's a large part of that calculus. Observers from other clubs have doubts about his ability to play catcher in the majors, but Brown's one of the unheralded catching prospects in the minors, along with Jeff Mathis of the Angels.

Eric Byrnes   LF   Born: 16-Feb-76   Age: 27   Bats: R   Throws: R

YEAR	TM	LG	AGE	AB	H	2B	3B	HR	BB	SO	SB	CS	AVG	OBP	SLG	MLVR	EQBA	EQOBP	EQSLG	EQMLVR	VORP	DEFENSE
2000	MID	TXS	24	259	78	25	2	5	43	38	21	11	.301	.403	.471	.173	.236	.320	.376	-.151	-4.9	66-RF -2
2000	SAC	PCL	24	243	81	23	1	9	31	30	12	5	.333	.413	.547	.332	.295	.362	.477	.113	12.0	50-LF -2
2001	SAC	PCL	25	415	120	23	2	20	33	66	25	3	.289	.349	.499	.119	.256	.313	.435	-.068	2.1	92-LF -4
2002	SAC	PCL	26	119	31	7	0	4	7	15	5	1	.261	.302	.420	-.067	.235	.272	.378	-.241	-4.3	30-LF -1
2002	OAK	AL	26	94	23	4	2	3	4	17	3	0	.245	.297	.426	-.070	.266	.320	.457	-.015	1.7	35-LF -4
2003	OAK	AL	27	119	30	7	1	4	10	20	3	2	.249	.308	.407	-.068	.257	.319	.426	-.065	-.8	

Breakout: 24%   Improve: 44%   Collapse: 33%

If you were confused by his appearance in Oakland, it's because he has above-average speed. Byrnes is a prototypical fourth outfielder. He can play CF if he has to, or he can cover a corner spot fairly well. Some power, but not enough to play a corner outfield spot on a regular basis. Often used as the legs for an old or recuperating outfielder, he'll probably have a similar role in 2003, depending on whether or not the A's Brain Trust can dig up a center fielder off the waiver wire or in the Rule 5 draft. We'll see what Rontrez Johnson can do, and we know what to expect from Chris Singleton.

Eric Chavez   3B   Born: 07-Dec-77   Age: 25   Bats: L Throws: R

YEAR	TM	LG	AGE	AB	H	2B	3B	HR	BB	SO	SB	CS	AVG	OBP	SLG	MLVR	EQBA	EQOBP	EQSLG	EQMLVR	VORP	DEFENSE
2000	OAK	AL	22	501	139	23	4	26	62	94	2	2	.277	.358	.495	.095	.288	.361	.519	.164	44.5	136-3B -8
2001	OAK	AL	23	552	159	43	0	32	41	99	8	2	.288	.342	.540	.186	.303	.357	.574	.252	60.7	146-3B 17
2002	OAK	AL	24	585	161	31	3	34	65	119	8	3	.275	.349	.513	.157	.292	.366	.548	.217	61.9	137-3B 10
2003	OAK	AL	25	541	154	33	3	31	60	104	7	2	.285	.359	.530	.198	.294	.372	.554	.224	50.5	

Breakout: 12%   Improve: 56%   Collapse: 11%

A better player than people think, because the Grey Wall of Despair keeps his stats from being overly gaudy. There's nothing Chavez can't do on the diamond. Defensively, he's improved dramatically over the past couple of years, and his approach at the plate has become more consistent. He was able to retain the increase in his walk rate, but 13 of those walks were intentional. Still very vulnerable to left-handed pitching; Chavez posted only a .623 OPS against lefties for the year. From a distance, his career path looks similar to Chipper Jones', but with less drama and better defense.

Bobby Crosby — SS — Born: 12-Jan-80 — Age: 23 — Bats: R — Throws: R

YEAR	TM	LG	AGE	AB	H	2B	3B	HR	BB	SO	SB	CS	AVG	OBP	SLG	MLVR	EQBA	EQOBP	EQSLG	EQMLVR	VORP	DEFENSE	
2002	MOD	CLF	22	280	86	17	2	2	33	43	5	0	.307	.394	.404	.149	.246	.312	.323	-.233	-1.1	70-SS	5
2002	MID	TXS	22	228	64	16	0	7	19	41	9	2	.281	.336	.443	.086	.239	.283	.383	-.210	.5	57-SS	-5
2003	OAK	AL	23	189	47	10	1	4	14	35	3	2	.252	.308	.385	-.094	.260	.319	.402	-.094	3.2		

Breakout: 38%   Improve: 63%   Collapse: 15%

He'll likely be the guy to have to fill Miguel Tejada's shoes should Tejada leave after the 2003 season. Crosby's a decent defender at short, has a quick stroke, a developing batting eye, and should develop some power as he matures. I'm sure Beane, DePodesta, and Forst would love for him to develop a little faster on all those fronts, but for now, Crosby's a solid prospect who should be ready to play middle infield in Oakland should the need arise after the 2003 season. Or, in a pinch, just before the trade deadline.

Ray Durham — 2B — Born: 30-Nov-71 — Age: 31 — Bats: B — Throws: R

YEAR	TM	LG	AGE	AB	H	2B	3B	HR	BB	SO	SB	CS	AVG	OBP	SLG	MLVR	EQBA	EQOBP	EQSLG	EQMLVR	VORP	DEFENSE	
2000	CWS	AL	28	614	172	35	9	17	75	105	25	13	.280	.365	.450	.036	.283	.361	.458	.074	45.0	142-2B	1
2001	CWS	AL	29	611	163	42	10	20	64	110	23	10	.267	.340	.466	.060	.281	.355	.493	.110	53.2	145-2B	11
2002	CWS	AL	30	345	103	20	2	9	49	59	20	5	.299	.393	.446	.156	.320	.412	.481	.229	41.8	89-2B	4
2002	OAK	AL	30	219	60	14	4	6	24	34	6	2	.274	.351	.457	.086	.299	.372	.502	.170	21.9	11-2B	2
2003	SFN	NL	31	499	134	28	5	11	65	85	21	6	.268	.356	.409	.005	.281	.364	.450	.063	28.4		

Breakout: 10%   Improve: 49%   Collapse: 12%

A dramatically underrated player, and a great acquisition for the Giants. Durham's going to end up having spent his best days in lousy hitters' parks, which will probably wipe out his HoF chances, but he's that good of a ballplayer. Plays defense at 2B pretty well, hits for average and power, has a good batting eye, and steals bases often and well. There's nothing wrong with Ray Durham as a ballplayer, and the fact that the Giants chose to sign him to a bargain deal rather than flush the money down a Jeff Kent-sized hole speaks well of their chances. Of course, their signing of Marquis Grissom speaks poorly of their chances, so who knows?

Jermaine Dye — RF — Born: 28-Jan-74 — Age: 29 — Bats: R — Throws: R

YEAR	TM	LG	AGE	AB	H	2B	3B	HR	BB	SO	SB	CS	AVG	OBP	SLG	MLVR	EQBA	EQOBP	EQSLG	EQMLVR	VORP	DEFENSE	
2000	KCR	AL	26	601	193	41	2	33	69	99	0	1	.321	.394	.561	.268	.323	.389	.567	.316	59.0	133-RF	-3
2001	KCR	AL	27	367	100	14	0	13	30	68	7	1	.272	.337	.417	-.020	.284	.347	.434	.016	8.7	84-RF	-1
2001	OAK	AL	27	232	69	17	1	13	27	44	2	0	.297	.373	.547	.255	.313	.389	.584	.328	24.3	56-RF	1
2002	OAK	AL	28	488	123	27	1	24	52	108	2	0	.252	.336	.459	.047	.271	.353	.497	.103	22.7	90-RF	0
2003	OAK	AL	29	502	136	29	2	23	53	99	3	1	.270	.343	.472	.087	.279	.355	.493	.103	16.3		

Breakout: 16%   Improve: 54%   Collapse: 8%

Didn't look good or fully healed during the first half of the season. Played much better down the stretch, with an .850 OPS in the second half, and should be healthy to begin the season next year. With the A's new lineup, he's going to be a big part of the right-handed balance, and remains the only Oakland outfielder who can actually show off his arm from time to time.

Mark Ellis — 2B — Born: 06-Jun-77 — Age: 26 — Bats: R — Throws: R

YEAR	TM	LG	AGE	AB	H	2B	3B	HR	BB	SO	SB	CS	AVG	OBP	SLG	MLVR	EQBA	EQOBP	EQSLG	EQMLVR	VORP	DEFENSE	
2000	WIL	CRL	23	484	146	27	4	6	78	72	25	7	.302	.406	.411	.214	.253	.331	.348	-.157	8.4	128-SS	-1
2001	SAC	PCL	24	472	129	38	0	10	54	78	21	7	.273	.354	.417	-.000	.243	.318	.368	-.161	6.9	129-SS	3
2002	SAC	PCL	25	84	25	10	1	0	6	13	4	0	.298	.372	.440	.117	.274	.333	.405	-.059	3.2	21-SS	3
2002	OAK	AL	25	345	94	16	4	6	44	54	4	2	.272	.361	.394	.021	.293	.379	.425	.069	25.9	83-2B	-10
2003	OAK	AL	26	381	97	19	2	7	39	60	7	3	.254	.328	.373	-.075	.262	.339	.390	-.074	8.6		

Breakout: 12%   Improve: 44%   Collapse: 22%

Mark Ellis *(continued)*

Ellis's swing is reminiscent of Terry Steinbach's. Kind of a stiff upper body that stays still and whips the bathead through the zone. He doesn't appear to be fully comfortable at second base, and has trouble taking an angle on ground balls to his right. Offensively, he's a nice middle infielder to have. Draws walks, hits for some average, and has enough power to keep defenses and opposing pitchers honest. Ellis is an underrated ballplayer, but he's going to have to light it up pretty quickly to keep Bobby Crosby off his back, on the off chance the A's decide to spend a bunch of dough on Tejada.

Esteban German 2B Born: 26-Jan-78 Age: 25 Bats: R Throws: R

YEAR	TM	LG	AGE	AB	H	2B	3B	HR	BB	SO	SB	CS	AVG	OBP	SLG	MLVR	EQBA	EQOBP	EQSLG	EQMLVR	VORP	DEFENSE
2000	VIS	CLF	22	428	113	14	10	2	61	86	78	8	.264	.362	.357	-.016	.216	.283	.297	-.344	-14.3	104-2B -17
2000	MID	TXS	22	75	16	1	0	1	18	21	5	3	.213	.379	.267	-.196	.171	.301	.224	-.423	-4.2	19-2B 1
2001	MID	TXS	23	335	95	20	3	6	63	66	31	11	.284	.415	.415	.143	.232	.342	.344	-.154	5.5	78-2B 2
2001	SAC	PCL	23	150	56	8	0	4	18	20	17	2	.373	.460	.507	.408	.333	.411	.453	.200	16.0	35-2B -3
2002	SAC	PCL	24	458	126	16	4	2	78	66	26	14	.275	.390	.341	-.003	.248	.350	.306	-.180	4.3	115-2B -13
2002	OAK	AL	24	35	7	0	0	0	4	11	1	0	.200	.300	.200	-.379	.229	.322	.229	-.350	-2.0	
2003	*OAK*	*AL*	*25*	*295*	*71*	*13*	*2*	*4*	*35*	*51*	*10*	*4*	*.239*	*.325*	*.340*	*-.130*	*.247*	*.336*	*.355*	*-.134*	*2.3*	

Breakout: 20%   Improve: 44%   Collapse: 24%

Probably the fastest guy in the upper minors, or one of them. German's an extreme slap hitter and speedster who's more than happy to take a free pass to first base. Defensively, he hasn't progressed particularly well, and with the bat, he tends to lack the power required to hit the ball out of most parks. His window of opportunity in Oakland will consist of the few days when Ellis goes on the DL—and that's a best-case scenario for German. He'll likely be moving on soon.

Jason Grabowski 3B Born: 24-May-76 Age: 27 Bats: L Throws: R

YEAR	TM	LG	AGE	AB	H	2B	3B	HR	BB	SO	SB	CS	AVG	OBP	SLG	MLVR	EQBA	EQOBP	EQSLG	EQMLVR	VORP	DEFENSE	
2000	TUL	TXS	24	493	135	33	5	19	88	106	8	7	.274	.388	.477	.162	.227	.319	.394	-.135	6.8	129-3B -9	
2001	TAC	PCL	25	394	117	32	3	9	61	94	7	4	.297	.394	.462	.173	.268	.359	.414	-.003	19.9	58-3B -4	20-LF -3
2002	SAC	PCL	26	265	78	22	3	12	39	56	6	4	.294	.387	.536	.268	.261	.346	.470	.045	8.2	34-RF -2	14-C -6
2002	OAK	AL	26	8	3	1	1	0	3	1	0	0	.375	.545	.750	.831	.375	.545	.875	.990	2.9		
2003	*OAK*	*AL*	*27*	*242*	*62*	*16*	*1*	*8*	*31*	*52*	*5*	*3*	*.258*	*.344*	*.431*	*.027*	*.267*	*.355*	*.450*	*.037*	*7.0*		

Breakout: 19%   Improve: 47%   Collapse: 16%

A pretty good ballplayer, and someone worthy of some admiration. Instead of falling down the defensive spectrum, Grabowski donned the mask and took over catcher for a few games in Sac. Grabowski can hit for average, has some power, a very good batting eye, and is clearly doing whatever he can to boost his team and career. What's not to like?

John-Ford Griffin LF Born: 19-Nov-79 Age: 23 Bats: L Throws: L

YEAR	TM	LG	AGE	AB	H	2B	3B	HR	BB	SO	SB	CS	AVG	OBP	SLG	MLVR	EQBA	EQOBP	EQSLG	EQMLVR	VORP	DEFENSE
2001	STA	NYP	21	238	74	17	1	5	40	41	10	4	.311	.416	.454	.284	.217	.299	.321	-.279	-12.4	60-LF -7
2002	TAM	FSL	22	255	68	16	1	3	29	45	1	0	.267	.348	.373	.075	.233	.293	.331	-.268	-12.9	46-LF -7
2002	MID	TXS	22	7	1	0	0	0	0	3	0	0	.143	.250	.143	-.510	.143	.201	.143	-.753	-1.0	
2002	NRW	EAS	22	67	22	3	0	5	8	13	0	1	.328	.400	.597	.448	.279	.347	.500	.105	3.6	17-LF -2
2003	*TOR*	*AL*	*23*	*171*	*42*	*9*	*1*	*5*	*16*	*35*	*2*	*2*	*.245*	*.314*	*.388*	*-.084*	*.248*	*.320*	*.398*	*-.106*	*-3.5*	

Breakout: 47%   Improve: 68%   Collapse: 15%

He's a stathead favorite, as we tend to fawn over anyone that has a "4" in the first digit of their OBP. Or, if you prefer the quote from Jerry Gimbel, "You had me at 5." Griffin's compared to Jeremy Giambi without either the defensive prowess or the baggage. A little good and a little bad there. He projects as a DH or 1B in the majors, but he might well develop the bat that would make him an asset at one of those positions. Traded to the Blue Jays, in what's becoming a two-way shuttle.

Scott Hatteberg 1B Born: 14-Dec-69 Age: 33 Bats: L Throws: R

YEAR	TM	LG	AGE	AB	H	2B	3B	HR	BB	SO	SB	CS	AVG	OBP	SLG	MLVR	EQBA	EQOBP	EQSLG	EQMLVR	VORP	DEFENSE
2000	BOS	AL	30	230	61	15	0	8	38	39	0	1	.265	.369	.435	.015	.273	.370	.454	.076	18.8	42-C -12
2001	BOS	AL	31	278	68	19	0	3	33	26	1	1	.245	.333	.345	-.123	.262	.348	.373	-.084	11.1	62-C -22
2002	OAK	AL	32	492	138	22	4	15	68	56	0	0	.280	.375	.433	.100	.300	.392	.468	.157	33.4	81-1B 17
2003	*OAK*	*AL*	*33*	*336*	*87*	*17*	*1*	*8*	*43*	*43*	*0*	*0*	*.257*	*.344*	*.389*	*-.025*	*.266*	*.355*	*.407*	*-.020*	*3.8*	

Breakout: 9%   Improve: 39%   Collapse: 23%

A fantastic low-risk, low-cost acquisition, much like this off-season's pickup of Mitch Meluskey. Hatteberg's a Rorschach test for an organization. Do they bitch about what he can't do, throw runners out as a catcher, then continue to run him out there, and get frustrated when he continues the same pattern? Or do they focus on what he CAN do, like hit righties, and let him focus on that, gaining the benefits for the team as a whole? Sometimes, it isn't rocket science. Hatteberg's likely to have the same role next year, have some moderate success, then find more lucrative pastures somewhere else while the A's dig up another guy from the fringes and get comparable production.

Ramon Hernandez — C — Born: 20-May-76 — Age: 27 — Bats: R — Throws: R

YEAR	TM	LG	AGE	AB	H	2B	3B	HR	BB	SO	SB	CS	AVG	OBP	SLG	MLVR	EQBA	EQOBP	EQSLG	EQMLVR	VORP	DEFENSE
2000	OAK	AL	24	419	101	19	0	14	38	64	1	0	.241	.315	.387	-.171	.252	.318	.405	-.104	13.5	120-C -1
2001	OAK	AL	25	453	115	25	0	15	37	68	1	1	.254	.319	.408	-.061	.269	.333	.438	-.016	24.9	127-C 12
2002	OAK	AL	26	403	94	20	0	7	43	64	0	0	.233	.315	.335	-.164	.252	.333	.365	-.131	10.9	119-C 13
2003	OAK	AL	27	308	75	16	1	8	30	49	0	0	.243	.316	.378	-.095	.252	.327	.396	-.095	6.0	

Breakout: 20%   Improve: 50%   Collapse: 20%

.241/.315/.387 in Oakland at age 24 is promising. So what happened? Hernandez just flat out hasn't developed, and really didn't look good at the plate all year. He looks his best when he's hitting balls hard to RF and RCF, usually pitches up and away. Anything else, he looks unbelievably slow with the bat. His batting eye got marginally better, but not by enough to be anything more than noise in the data. Other than that, he's been pretty much treading water for two years. With Beane's theft of Mark Johnson from the White Sox, he's going to have to do something with the bat in order to keep the lion's share of the playing time, despite his solid defense.

David Justice — LF — Born: 14-Apr-66 — Age: 37 — Bats: L — Throws: L

YEAR	TM	LG	AGE	AB	H	2B	3B	HR	BB	SO	SB	CS	AVG	OBP	SLG	MLVR	EQBA	EQOBP	EQSLG	EQMLVR	VORP	DEFENSE
2000	CLE	AL	34	249	66	14	1	21	38	49	1	1	.265	.362	.582	.197	.272	.361	.598	.256	21.8	43-OF -1
2000	NYY	AL	34	275	84	17	0	20	39	42	1	0	.305	.394	.585	.322	.319	.398	.619	.398	34.9	59-LF 4
2001	NYY	AL	35	381	92	16	1	18	54	83	1	2	.241	.336	.430	-.001	.260	.355	.466	.054	14.8	25-LF 2
2002	OAK	AL	36	398	106	18	3	11	70	66	4	1	.266	.377	.410	.065	.286	.394	.445	.117	22.6	67-LF 0
2003	OAK	AL	37	292	73	14	1	11	45	56	2	1	.251	.351	.421	.022	.260	.363	.440	.032	5.2	

Breakout: 20%   Improve: 53%   Collapse: 21%

Didn't have a great year, but it wasn't as bad as many seemed to think. Drew a ton of walks, occasionally parked a hanging curveball, and, sadly, appeared to be the best defensive outfielder the A's had on a few occasions. (Of course, this honor could also have been bestowed on several inanimate objects from time to time.) Justice had stated that this was his last year, but after the season, other players were supposedly trying to talk him into playing for one more year and a shot at a ring. We're still waiting to hear.

Graham Koonce — 1B — Born: 15-May-75 — Age: 28 — Bats: L — Throws: L

YEAR	TM	LG	AGE	AB	H	2B	3B	HR	BB	SO	SB	CS	AVG	OBP	SLG	MLVR	EQBA	EQOBP	EQSLG	EQMLVR	VORP	DEFENSE	
2000	RCU	CLF	25	475	140	40	3	18	107	105	0	0	.295	.428	.505	.315	.228	.330	.389	-.120	-3.1	132-1B -1	
2001	MOB	SOU	26	320	85	18	0	13	89	83	0	0	.266	.431	.444	.222	.226	.368	.378	-.063	3.4	50-1B -6	21-LF -4
2002	MID	TXS	27	470	129	28	0	24	133	117	2	0	.274	.444	.487	.292	.227	.373	.404	-.019	10.6	116-1B -8	
2003	OAK	AL	28	136	32	7	0	5	24	35	2	1	.233	.352	.401	-.013	.241	.364	.419	-.007	1.4		

Breakout: 24%   Improve: 55%   Collapse: 19%

Ok, so the implicit questions are:
1. How can the Atlanta Braves, a team that's been to the postseason every year since "The Simpsons" was funny, run a combination of Vinny Castilla, Julio Franco, and a Ghiberti statue out to first base every day when they could probably make two calls and acquire someone like Koonce? (This, of course, raises more implicit questions, many of which include phrases like "Kevin Young," "Eric Karros," and "Millions.")
2. When a guy in the minors has some subset of his stats that are just off the charts, like Koonce's walks, does that organization simply ignore those numbers, out of some sort of cognitive dissonance? I think that's what happened to Lavell Freeman, if memory serves.

Koonce isn't a worldbeater, and isn't going to be the next Jason Giambi or something. But he has some skills that might make him useful to a big league club, provided that club can recognize that it has a specific need. Why guys like Karros get long-term deals and guys like Koonce bounce around praying for a shot can be tough to explain.

Terrence Long | CF | Born: 29-Feb-76 | Age: 27 | Bats: L | Throws: L

YEAR	TM	LG	AGE	AB	H	2B	3B	HR	BB	SO	SB	CS	AVG	OBP	SLG	MLVR	EQBA	EQOBP	EQSLG	EQMLVR	VORP	DEFENSE
2000	SAC	PCL	24	60	24	6	0	3	4	4	0	3	.400	.438	.650	.623	.339	.371	.542	.270	6.2	14-CF -3
2000	OAK	AL	24	584	168	34	4	18	43	77	5	0	.288	.338	.452	.005	.298	.340	.472	.071	35.3	130-CF -3
2001	OAK	AL	25	629	178	37	4	12	52	103	9	3	.283	.338	.412	-.000	.298	.354	.436	.044	20.9	160-OF 0
2002	OAK	AL	26	587	141	32	4	16	48	96	3	6	.240	.300	.390	-.115	.259	.319	.425	-.068	16.4	161-CF 0
2003	OAK	AL	27	526	140	30	3	14	45	81	5	2	.267	.326	.417	-.013	.276	.337	.436	-.005	14.6	

Breakout: 20%   Improve: 52%   Collapse: 13%

Those aren't good trends. No matter what kind of spin you put on it, Long's been a bust. His offense has been absent or stagnant, and I don't know of a single observer that puts much stock in a defensive system that rates him as an average center fielder. But, hey, that's why we have numbers. He did have some strong defensive stretches, but he was unbelievably bad and unfocused at the plate all year. There are rumors that Long is suffering from some chronic eye problems that prevent him from playing well. His job is no longer safe—don't be surprised to see Beane find a CF before the season begins. Like, say, Rontrez Johnson and Chris Singleton. One noteworthy member of the media calls TLong "Magellan" because of his circuitous routes to the ball. Cold, mon.

John Mabry | 1B | Born: 17-Oct-70 | Age: 32 | Bats: L | Throws: R

YEAR	TM	LG	AGE	AB	H	2B	3B	HR	BB	SO	SB	CS	AVG	OBP	SLG	MLVR	EQBA	EQOBP	EQSLG	EQMLVR	VORP	DEFENSE			
2000	SDP	NL	29	123	28	8	0	7	5	38	0	0	.228	.258	.463	-.153	.240	.258	.480	-.117	-1.3	24-RF 0			
2000	SEA	AL	29	103	25	5	0	1	10	31	0	1	.243	.322	.320	-.241	.262	.334	.340	-.157	.8	12-3B -3	11-RF	0	
2001	FLA	NL	30	147	32	7	0	6	13	44	1	0	.218	.303	.388	-.155	.228	.307	.403	-.145	-2.8	26-RF -3			
2002	PHI	NL	31	21	6	0	0	0	1	5	0	0	.286	.318	.286	-.156	.286	.318	.286	-.251	-.6				
2002	OAK	AL	31	193	53	13	1	11	14	37	1	1	.275	.327	.523	.136	.294	.347	.557	.201	14.1	47-LF -1	17-1B	-5	
2003	SEA	AL	32	133	31	6	0	5	10	32	1	1	.233	.293	.394	-.121	.247	.309	.424	-.092	-2.0				

Breakout: 15%   Improve: 35%   Collapse: 32%

Wow. That was unexpected. Sometimes, small sample sizes can rock. Mabry was thought by many to be almost a punitive choice as compensation for Slidin' Jeremy, and A's fans figured they'd get the watered-down Hal Morris production Mabry'd put up over the years. Nope, instead, Mabry looked like a reborn hitter, working righties deep into counts, then drilling shots to right center field, many of which were surprisingly long home runs. If you take a look at Mabry's last three years, you get 25 HR in basically one full season. He's probably not as good of a hitter as he looked for Oakland in 2002, but it wouldn't be shocking to see some of the improvement stick for a couple of years.

Cody McKay | C | Born: 11-Jan-74 | Age: 29 | Bats: L | Throws: R

YEAR	TM	LG	AGE	AB	H	2B	3B	HR	BB	SO	SB	CS	AVG	OBP	SLG	MLVR	EQBA	EQOBP	EQSLG	EQMLVR	VORP	DEFENSE
2000	MID	TXS	26	427	136	35	2	5	67	54	1	5	.319	.423	.445	.185	.259	.341	.363	-.113	13.0	84-C -13
2000	SAC	PCL	26	58	13	4	0	1	5	14	0	0	.224	.297	.345	-.278	.190	.251	.310	-.405	-3.8	
2001	SAC	PCL	27	350	92	19	0	6	27	64	1	0	.263	.325	.369	-.133	.235	.294	.327	-.270	-3.1	77-C 0
2002	SAC	PCL	28	378	109	16	1	13	21	59	2	1	.288	.342	.439	.055	.262	.308	.399	-.123	10.0	71-C -4
2002	OAK	AL	28	3	2	0	0	0	0	1	0	0	.667	.667	.667	1.392	.667	.667	.667	1.435	1.1	
2003	MIL	NL	29	180	44	8	1	4	15	31	2	1	.245	.307	.360	-.157	.250	.309	.374	-.156	.7	

Breakout: 16%   Improve: 51%   Collapse: 22%

A favorite of Kathy DuVair and the staff of the River Cats up in Sacramento. McKay's a catch-and-throw guy who's going to need an injury and a hot streak to earn his "MLB Veteran" card, like one of the Molinas or something. Worse players have had long careers as backup catchers, but McKay's not going to light up the night or anything.

Frank Menechino | 2B | Born: 07-Jan-71 | Age: 32 | Bats: R | Throws: R

YEAR	TM	LG	AGE	AB	H	2B	3B	HR	BB	SO	SB	CS	AVG	OBP	SLG	MLVR	EQBA	EQOBP	EQSLG	EQMLVR	VORP	DEFENSE
2000	OAK	AL	29	145	37	9	1	6	20	45	1	4	.255	.349	.455	.002	.264	.350	.465	.047	9.7	39-2B 2
2001	OAK	AL	30	471	114	22	2	12	79	97	2	3	.242	.373	.374	-.015	.262	.386	.408	.035	31.9	131-2B 10
2002	SAC	PCL	31	314	78	12	0	6	46	58	10	3	.248	.359	.344	-.074	.227	.325	.312	-.233	-1.2	68-SS -11
2002	OAK	AL	31	132	27	7	0	3	20	32	0	0	.205	.314	.326	-.193	.226	.330	.361	-.159	2.0	27-2B 6
2003	OAK	AL	32	223	51	10	1	5	28	48	2	2	.228	.320	.352	-.130	.236	.331	.368	-.134	1.2	

Breakout: 14%   Improve: 38%   Collapse: 33%

The elbow injury and concomitant glitches that hit Menechino in the middle of 2001 basically robbed him of a chance at a sizable pension. Since the injury, he's hit something like Ozzie Guillen on codeine. He can't extend his arms, and only has batting eye remains as an offensive weapon. With the development of Ellis and Crosby, he's got no future in Oakland, and will likely be bouncing around some form of homestead looking for an opportunity come the spring.

Adam Morrissey 2B Born: 08-Jun-81 Age: 22 Bats: R Throws: R

YEAR	TM	LG	AGE	AB	H	2B	3B	HR	BB	SO	SB	CS	AVG	OBP	SLG	MLVR	EQBA	EQOBP	EQSLG	EQMLVR	VORP	DEFENSE			
2000	EUG	NWN	19	269	74	16	2	7	42	50	12	11	.275	.379	.428	.189	.203	.271	.320	-.344	-11.2	47-3B	-4	12-2B	2
2001	LNS	MDW	20	418	129	26	11	14	80	82	10	9	.309	.429	.524	.361	.226	.322	.382	-.146	8.0	44-2B	-9	31-OF	-3
2002	MOD	CLF	21	141	41	7	1	3	20	28	4	3	.291	.383	.418	.138	.229	.304	.326	-.255	-1.5	28-2B	-6		
2002	MID	TXS	21	302	71	15	1	2	38	71	4	2	.235	.323	.311	-.138	.202	.272	.270	-.411	-15.3	83-2B	-22		
2003	OAK	AL	22	172	40	8	1	4	17	36	2	2	.235	.306	.371	-.127	.242	.316	.388	-.130	.8				

Breakout: 46%   Improve: 64%   Collapse: 11%

Came over as a high-risk gamble from the Cubs in the Mark Bellhorn deal. Great batting eye, good pop, questionable defense in the middle infield. Hmmm. Apparently, Bellhorn was moved for a younger version of himself. Morrissey struggled early in the year, but appeared to get healthy as the season went on, and went down and pummeled the pitching in the Arizona Fall League, to the tune of .371/.496/.552. Morrissey's got some tough competition in the middle infield in this organization, but if he hits anywhere near what he did in Arizona, Beane and Macha will find a place for him.

Greg Myers C Born: 14-Apr-66 Age: 37 Bats: L Throws: R

YEAR	TM	LG	AGE	AB	H	2B	3B	HR	BB	SO	SB	CS	AVG	OBP	SLG	MLVR	EQBA	EQOBP	EQSLG	EQMLVR	VORP	DEFENSE	
2000	BAL	AL	34	125	28	6	0	3	8	29	0	0	.224	.271	.344	-.322	.240	.280	.368	-.237	-.1	26-C	0
2001	BAL	AL	35	74	20	2	0	4	8	17	0	0	.270	.341	.459	.075	.293	.361	.507	.152	5.7		
2001	OAK	AL	35	87	16	1	0	7	13	21	0	0	.184	.290	.437	-.124	.195	.307	.471	-.078	3.6	23-C	5
2002	OAK	AL	36	144	32	5	0	6	26	36	0	0	.222	.341	.382	-.063	.241	.360	.414	-.021	8.5	42-C	4
2003	TOR	AL	37	148	33	7	0	5	23	38	0	0	.222	.327	.379	-.089	.225	.333	.388	-.111	2.0		

Breakout: 17%   Improve: 58%   Collapse: 13%

Left-handed catcher with some pop and some patience. Nice guy to have late in a game as a home run threat against a hard throwing closer. With the acquisition of Mark Johnson, Myers became expendable. He'll ply his trade for the Blue Jays in 2003.

Adam Piatt RF Born: 08-Feb-76 Age: 27 Bats: R Throws: R

YEAR	TM	LG	AGE	AB	H	2B	3B	HR	BB	SO	SB	CS	AVG	OBP	SLG	MLVR	EQBA	EQOBP	EQSLG	EQMLVR	VORP	DEFENSE			
2000	SAC	PCL	24	254	72	15	0	8	26	57	3	2	.283	.359	.437	.023	.253	.315	.387	-.134	-3.5	20-RF	-3	21-3B	-5
2000	OAK	AL	24	157	47	5	5	5	23	44	0	1	.299	.392	.490	.170	.310	.396	.510	.232	12.4	20-RF	-1		
2001	SAC	PCL	25	109	28	9	0	1	11	27	2	0	.257	.341	.367	-.106	.229	.306	.330	-.246	-4.7	26-RF	-4		
2001	OAK	AL	25	95	20	5	1	0	13	26	0	0	.211	.306	.284	-.273	.221	.321	.305	-.254	-4.5	29-RF	0		
2002	SAC	PCL	26	234	69	15	0	8	35	30	4	3	.295	.389	.462	.171	.263	.350	.411	-.027	2.9	45-RF	-6		
2002	OAK	AL	26	137	32	8	0	5	12	33	2	1	.234	.305	.401	-.096	.254	.321	.435	-.055	1.2	37-LF	0		
2003	OAK	AL	27	191	46	9	1	6	19	40	3	2	.242	.314	.389	-.085	.250	.325	.407	-.085	-3.0				

Breakout: 18%   Improve: 42%   Collapse: 34%

Piatt was stricken with a nasty, energy-draining illness during the 2001 season, and it didn't look like he'd yet fully recovered. Piatt's numbers in the minors were gaudy, and he had committed to learning to play the outfield, as 3B in Oakland is sort of occupied. He's going to have to find somewhere, possibly Sacramento, to get a bunch of at-bats, and hit like he did a few years ago. If he can do that, he'll get another shot at playing time.

Olmedo Saenz 1B Born: 08-Oct-70 Age: 32 Bats: R Throws: R

YEAR	TM	LG	AGE	AB	H	2B	3B	HR	BB	SO	SB	CS	AVG	OBP	SLG	MLVR	EQBA	EQOBP	EQSLG	EQMLVR	VORP	DEFENSE			
2000	OAK	AL	29	214	67	12	2	9	25	40	1	0	.313	.402	.514	.235	.325	.407	.533	.298	26.0	15-3B	-3	14-1B	0
2001	OAK	AL	30	305	67	21	1	9	19	64	0	1	.220	.294	.384	-.162	.236	.306	.416	-.123	-2.0	21-1B	-1		
2002	OAK	AL	31	156	43	10	1	6	13	31	1	1	.276	.358	.468	.114	.299	.377	.503	.179	11.0	20-1B	0	15-3B	-4
2003	OAK	AL	32	174	43	9	1	5	15	35	1	1	.249	.320	.402	-.054	.257	.331	.421	-.051	.5				

Breakout: 6%   Improve: 29%   Collapse: 37%

Olmedo Saenz *(continued)*

A good, solid right-handed hitter who can play either corner, but is stretched a bit at third base. He hits the ball with authority. Should be able to find a job somewhere smacking lefties around. Properly spotted, he could post an .850 OPS in a couple of hundred plate appearances. He'll do it elsewhere in 2003, as the A's wisely declined his $1.2 million option. Saenz was picked up as a low-cost righty-basher because the A's understand that it doesn't make sense to pay $1.2 million for his skills.

Jorge Soto   C   Born: 14-Apr-78   Age: 25   Bats: R   Throws: R

YEAR	TM	LG	AGE	AB	H	2B	3B	HR	BB	SO	SB	CS	AVG	OBP	SLG	MLVR	EQBA	EQOBP	EQSLG	EQMLVR	VORP	DEFENSE		
2000	VIS	CLF	22	119	20	4	0	6	21	58	4	1	.168	.313	.353	-.163	.138	.232	.285	-.501	-12.9	32-1B -2		
2001	VAN	NWN	23	165	34	12	1	7	8	84	0	0	.206	.264	.418	-.026	.166	.198	.325	-.503	-11.1	23-C -9		
2001	MOD	CLF	23	55	11	2	1	3	12	31	0	0	.200	.343	.436	.031	.158	.273	.333	-.346	-3.8	11-1B -3		
2002	VIS	CLF	24	404	85	14	1	31	57	195	1	1	.210	.324	.480	.052	.167	.250	.365	-.345	-11.5	59-C -8	28-1B -3	
2003	OAK	AL	25	163	33	7	1	6	17	74	2	5	.203	.288	.377	-.169	.210	.297	.394	-.177	-2.2			

Breakout: 77% Improve: 86% Collapse: 8%

Despite the outcry of the religious right about cloning and genetic research, some labs have been clandestinely working to develop hybrid human beings. Their first experiment? A synthesis of Todd Hundley and Rob Deer. Instead of getting a chain smoker that drives a monster truck, they got a catcher that strikes out half the time, and occasionally hits a bomb. I understand the next project will be an attempt to fuse Ian Maxtone-Graham with Patton Oswalt, in an attempt to come up with at least one person with both a hyphenated name and some talent for comedy.

Larry Sutton   1B   Born: 14-May-70   Age: 33   Bats: L   Throws: L

YEAR	TM	LG	AGE	AB	H	2B	3B	HR	BB	SO	SB	CS	AVG	OBP	SLG	MLVR	EQBA	EQOBP	EQSLG	EQMLVR	VORP	DEFENSE		
2000	MEM	PCL	30	347	89	21	2	12	67	56	4	1	.256	.381	.432	.047	.229	.338	.384	-.111	-1.4	86-1B 17		
2001	EDM	PCL	31	147	37	7	3	3	23	32	0	1	.252	.357	.401	-.042	.223	.318	.351	-.197	-4.3	31-LF -2		
2001	MEM	PCL	31	99	26	5	0	2	21	16	1	1	.263	.392	.374	.018	.238	.358	.327	-.141	-1.3	25-1B 1		
2002	SAC	PCL	32	431	126	40	2	12	93	108	2	0	.292	.419	.478	.242	.258	.376	.422	.032	15.0	44-1B 0	46-LF -4	
2002	OAK	AL	32	19	2	0	0	1	1	8	0	0	.105	.150	.263	-.628	.105	.150	.316	-.642	-2.4			
2003	BOS	AL	33	182	43	10	1	5	28	41	2	1	.238	.340	.382	-.052	.243	.349	.400	-.055	-.6			

Breakout: 19% Improve: 53% Collapse: 26%

A perfect guy to have hanging around in your Triple-A club, and an excellent illustration of how a smart, financially challenged organization can compete. Sutton can cover either corner outfield spot, play first base, or be a solid PH off the bench. Here's a tip for all clubs: paying an overrated veteran to sit around on the big league roster and collect money and service time when he's easily replaced by someone like Sutton is a waste of time and money. No team can afford to do that.

Nick Swisher   CF   Born: 25-Nov-80   Age: 22   Bats: B   Throws: L

YEAR	TM	LG	AGE	AB	H	2B	3B	HR	BB	SO	SB	CS	AVG	OBP	SLG	MLVR	EQBA	EQOBP	EQSLG	EQMLVR	VORP	DEFENSE
2002	VAN	NWN	21	44	11	3	0	2	13	11	3	0	.250	.441	.455	.292	.188	.325	.354	-.200	-.3	12-CF -1
2002	VIS	CLF	21	183	44	13	2	4	26	48	3	1	.240	.341	.399	-.003	.187	.266	.305	-.383	-9.6	38-CF -4

He's all about the strike zone. First round pick of the A's in the June draft. He's got a long way to go, and I don't think anyone who's seen him thinks he's going to stick in center field. He'll likely start the season in Modesto or Midland.

Miguel Tejada   SS   Born: 25-May-76   Age: 27   Bats: R   Throws: R

YEAR	TM	LG	AGE	AB	H	2B	3B	HR	BB	SO	SB	CS	AVG	OBP	SLG	MLVR	EQBA	EQOBP	EQSLG	EQMLVR	VORP	DEFENSE
2000	OAK	AL	24	607	167	32	1	30	66	102	6	0	.275	.350	.479	.056	.285	.352	.501	.120	51.2	157-SS -4
2001	OAK	AL	25	622	166	31	3	31	43	89	11	5	.267	.327	.476	.055	.286	.344	.514	.126	53.2	159-SS -3
2002	OAK	AL	26	662	204	30	0	34	38	84	7	2	.308	.356	.508	.193	.328	.374	.543	.263	79.2	157-SS 2
2003	OAK	AL	27	624	175	34	2	29	48	89	6	2	.280	.335	.481	.094	.289	.347	.503	.111	44.2	

Breakout: 9% Improve: 38% Collapse: 19%

MVP? Not in any meaningful sense of the word. Damn great player? Absolutely. Athletic on defense, and powerfully built, something like a 30-year-old Rickey Henderson. Very strong, and capable of turning around even the very best fastball. Gets himself out fairly often through a lack of discipline at the plate. You'll hear a lot of local media griping about how Tejada's imminent departure after the 2003 season could be a distraction, and there will be some ephemeral pressure to trade him, but be serious. Clubs go through this all the time. The A's kept Giambi through his contract, and the "distraction" was nonexistent. The A's are a long shot to keep him after this season. He's going to demand somewhere north of five years and $12 million a season, and maybe he's worth it, but the A's will have better options available that won't be so constricting financially. There have been whispers that he's older than his listed age. Either way, that forecast looks low.

Mario Valdez													**Born: 19-Nov-74**			**Age: 28**		**Bats: L**		**Throws: R**			
YEAR	TM	LG	AGE	AB	H	2B	3B	HR	BB	SO	SB	CS	AVG	OBP	SLG	MLVR	EQBA	EQOBP	EQSLG	EQMLVR	VORP	DEFENSE	
2000	SLC	PCL	25	317	116	24	1	18	57	46	1	1	.366	.467	.618	.512	.305	.396	.513	.231	25.9	37-1B	-1
2000	SAC	PCL	25	61	14	3	0	2	9	13	0	0	.230	.347	.377	-.128	.197	.295	.328	-.288	-2.9	14-1B	-2
2001	OAK	AL	26	54	15	1	0	1	12	18	0	0	.278	.418	.352	.063	.296	.439	.370	.109	3.7		
2002	MOD	CLF	27	8	2	1	0	0	1	1	0	0	.250	.333	.375	-.031	.125	.222	.250	-.573	-.9		
2002	SAC	PCL	27	304	79	18	2	3	58	56	1	0	.260	.380	.362	-.003	.233	.343	.327	-.174	-6.3	39-1B -5	21-LF -3

Larry Sutton revisited, but better. Valdez is more than good enough to start for some major league clubs. He's not what you'd call gifted as an outfield defender, or even adequate, but his bat's enough to carry some difficulties. Contract wise, waiting for Billy.

Randy Velarde								**2B**					**Born: 24-Nov-62**			**Age: 40**		**Bats: R**		**Throws: R**		
YEAR	TM	LG	AGE	AB	H	2B	3B	HR	BB	SO	SB	CS	AVG	OBP	SLG	MLVR	EQBA	EQOBP	EQSLG	EQMLVR	VORP	DEFENSE
2000	OAK	AL	37	485	135	23	0	12	54	95	9	3	.278	.354	.400	-.047	.289	.358	.418	.018	28.2	114-2B 21
2001	TEX	AL	38	296	88	16	2	9	29	73	4	2	.297	.370	.456	.115	.314	.384	.483	.178	29.5	50-2B -5
2002	SAC	PCL	39	17	8	3	0	1	1	3	1	0	.471	.526	.824	1.116	.412	.462	.706	.748	3.6	
2002	OAK	AL	39	133	30	8	0	2	15	32	3	0	.226	.327	.331	-.152	.246	.340	.366	-.120	3.3	33-2B -6
2003	*OAK*	*AL*	*40*	*158*	*39*	*8*	*0*	*4*	*15*	*35*	*4*	*1*	*.245*	*.317*	*.369*	*-.104*	*.253*	*.327*	*.386*	*-.105*	*1.4*	

Breakout: 13%   Improve: 56%   Collapse: 40%

Retired, or at least giving it serious thought. Thanks for the exciting play, Randy.

PITCHERS

Jason Arnold								**Born: 02-May-79**			**Age: 24**		**Bats: R**		**Throws: R**	
YEAR	TM	LG	AGE	G	GS	IP	H	BB	SO	HR	ERA	EQERA	EQH9	EQBB9	EQSO9	EQHR9	PERA	VORP	STF
2001	STA	NYP	22	10	10	66.0	35	15	74	2	1.50	3.06	7.5	3.1	5.8	0.9	2.65	17.9	18
2002	TAM	FSL	23	13	13	80.0	64	22	83	2	2.48	4.10	9.4	3.1	6.6	0.6	4.20	12.5	21
2002	NRW	EAS	23	3	3	17.3	17	5	18	1	4.16	6.20	10.6	3.1	7.2	0.9	4.85	-1.3	19
2002	MID	TXS	23	10	10	58.0	42	24	53	2	2.33	3.67	7.5	4.4	6.2	0.6	3.40	11.8	15
2003	*TOR*	*AL*	*24*	*14*	*11*	*67.0*	*71*	*29*	*51*	*8*	*4.75*	*4.59*	*9.3*	*3.6*	*6.7*	*1.0*	*4.59*	*1.3*	*8*

Breakout: 10%   Improve: 38%   Collapse: 28%

Picked up from the Yankees in the Weaver/Pena deal, Arnold's an excellent prospect who's had some arm twinges, but after coming over and getting on the Oakland conditioning program, he pitched great. Decent control, good stuff, good performance metrics and peripheral numbers. A potential #1 starter fairly soon, unless he sticks with Oakland, where he could be a #5. Scary. Now with Toronto, he'll likely be more than that.

Heath Bost								**Born: 13-Oct-74**			**Age: 28**		**Bats: R**		**Throws: R**	
YEAR	TM	LG	AGE	G	GS	IP	H	BB	SO	HR	ERA	EQERA	EQH9	EQBB9	EQSO9	EQHR9	PERA	VORP	STF
2000	SLM	CRL	25	7	1	14.7	24	1	14	2	6.12	8.82	21.0	0.8	5.7	3.1	10.37	-5.6	-20
2000	CSP	PCL	25	7	0	11.0	8	4	7	1	4.91	3.78	6.4	3.2	4.5	0.9	2.68	2.0	-8
2001	CSP	PCL	26	45	2	75.0	82	23	64	13	4.32	4.26	9.4	3.2	5.5	1.7	5.24	9.5	-12
2002	SAC	PCL	27	52	0	78.0	67	19	69	8	3.35	3.47	8.0	2.5	6.1	1.2	3.72	16.6	-1

Interesting guy, and another example of using Triple-A for actual depth. Bost doesn't throw particularly hard, and was buried for a while in the Colorado organization, so it's not as if he's a hot prospect, but look at his peripherals. He's always been able to keep people from walking, and he strikes out enough guys that he's got a good chance of future success. He'll eventually get a cup of coffee, and if he's hot during that time, he could have a reasonable career as a righty out of the pen.

Micah Bowie　Born: 10-Nov-74　Age: 28　Bats: L　Throws: L

YEAR	TM	LG	AGE	G	GS	IP	H	BB	SO	HR	ERA	EQERA	EQH9	EQBB9	EQSO9	EQHR9	PERA	VORP	STF
2000	WTN	SOU	25	18	18	117.3	91	48	106	6	3.45	5.06	9.8	4.1	5.9	0.9	4.46	5.8	7
2000	IOW	PCL	25	9	9	45.3	59	31	35	9	7.95	8.27	12.6	6.1	5.6	2.2	8.48	-13.9	-18
2001	SAC	PCL	26	38	10	116.0	123	44	102	13	5.04	5.40	10.4	4.1	5.8	1.2	5.38	0.6	-7
2002	SAC	PCL	27	46	0	54.7	40	24	64	2	3.13	3.09	6.6	4.5	8.0	0.4	3.19	13.9	8
2002	OAK	AL	27	13	0	12.0	12	8	8	1	1.50	2.74	9.1	5.6	5.8	0.7	4.82	3.5	-10
2003	*OAK*	*AL*	*28*	*32*	*0*	*38.3*	*40*	*21*	*31*	*5*	*4.60*	*4.66*	*9.4*	*4.5*	*7.0*	*1.0*	*5.03*	*5.9*	*-4*

Breakout: 13%　　Improve: 47%　　Collapse: 25%

Veteran lefty who can fill in out of the pen or the rotation. He's got a shot to end up with a career as a situational lefty, but it'd have to be with the right organization. Nothing to distinguish him from several dozen other identical talents.

Chad Bradford　Born: 14-Sep-74　Age: 28　Bats: R　Throws: R

YEAR	TM	LG	AGE	G	GS	IP	H	BB	SO	HR	ERA	EQERA	EQH9	EQBB9	EQSO9	EQHR9	PERA	VORP	STF
2000	CHR	INT	25	55	0	53.7	38	12	42	2	1.51	3.08	7.6	2.1	6.1	0.4	2.35	13.7	6
2000	CWS	AL	25	12	0	13.7	13	1	9	0	1.97	2.22	8.3	0.5	5.8	0.2	2.16	4.8	12
2001	SAC	PCL	26	12	0	23.7	15	2	24	0	0.38	1.18	6.0	0.9	6.6	0.2	1.58	11.1	19
2001	OAK	AL	26	35	0	36.7	41	6	34	6	2.70	3.72	10.2	1.4	7.9	1.3	4.55	6.8	10
2002	OAK	AL	27	75	0	75.3	73	14	56	2	3.11	3.25	9.0	1.6	6.6	0.2	2.95	17.8	10
2003	*OAK*	*AL*	*28*	*47*	*0*	*66.0*	*69*	*16*	*46*	*7*	*3.53*	*3.57*	*9.3*	*2.1*	*5.9*	*0.9*	*3.92*	*18.5*	*1*

Breakout: 25%　　Improve: 42%　　Collapse: 25%

Yet another piece of evidence in Docket #32A47891, *Baseball Fans of Chicago vs. William Lamar Beane et al.* One of the best relievers in baseball, stolen from an organization that didn't like him because he didn't throw hard enough. That's something like not liking a car's velocity because it isn't burning enough fuel. Bradford has a nasty submarine delivery that looks like he's going to scrape the ground with each pitch. He shut down batters on both sides of the plate pretty well, and his consistent 3+ GB/FB ratio is well earned. In the future, as part of the Commissioner's strategy to speed up games, opposing right-handed batters will be permitted to simply throw a one-hopper down to Eric Chavez rather than actually execute their plate appearance against Bradford.

Bryce Florie　Born: 21-May-70　Age: 33　Bats: R　Throws: R

YEAR	TM	LG	AGE	G	GS	IP	H	BB	SO	HR	ERA	EQERA	EQH9	EQBB9	EQSO9	EQHR9	PERA	VORP	STF
2000	BOS	AL	30	29	0	49.3	57	19	34	5	4.56	4.58	9.9	2.8	6.0	0.8	4.45	4.4	-1
2001	TRN	EAS	31	6	1	11.0	5	6	17	0	1.64	2.92	4.3	6.4	9.3	0.2	2.57	3.1	14
2001	TOL	INT	31	10	0	11.7	14	13	10	1	6.15	7.61	11.9	12.0	6.1	1.1	8.90	-2.9	-42
2002	SAC	PCL	32	18	16	83.3	90	38	69	11	5.08	5.55	10.2	4.7	5.7	1.5	5.97	-0.5	-7

Tough SOB. Recovered nicely from that nasty comebacker, and showed flashes of the sinker that he'd used successfully in the past. He's going to need some time to get his legs back under him in terms of mechanics and timing, but he could make it back and be effective.

Aaron Harang　Born: 09-May-78　Age: 25　Bats: R　Throws: R

YEAR	TM	LG	AGE	G	GS	IP	H	BB	SO	HR	ERA	EQERA	EQH9	EQBB9	EQSO9	EQHR9	PERA	VORP	STF
2000	PCH	FSL	22	28	27	157.0	128	50	136	10	3.32	4.73	9.6	3.7	5.5	1.5	4.57	13.5	8
2001	MID	TXS	23	27	27	150.0	173	37	112	9	4.14	5.42	11.8	2.7	4.8	0.9	5.41	1.4	4
2002	MID	TXS	24	3	3	16.7	12	7	21	0	1.08	2.49	7.2	4.4	8.4	0.2	3.13	5.6	30
2002	SAC	PCL	24	8	8	38.7	41	9	39	1	3.26	3.76	9.6	2.4	6.8	0.3	4.19	7.5	20
2002	OAK	AL	24	16	15	78.3	78	45	64	7	4.83	4.79	9.1	4.8	7.1	0.7	4.56	6.2	12
2003	*OAK*	*AL*	*25*	*21*	*19*	*122.0*	*127*	*52*	*92*	*14*	*4.65*	*4.71*	*9.3*	*3.5*	*6.5*	*0.9*	*4.63*	*14.5*	*11*

Breakout: 16%　　Improve: 52%　　Collapse: 13%

Yes, the A's grabbing pitching from Texas. Harang's filled in nicely as a #5 starter, and with the trade of Cory Lidle, he'll get a crack at the rotation again. He's got a decent, slightly straight fastball, but he's really more of a work-the-strike-zone guy than an overpowering guy, despite his enormous 6′ 6″ frame. But hey, angles are angles. Harang's going to have to pitch well to hold off Harden.

Rich Harden — Born: 30-Nov-81 — Age: 21 — Bats: L — Throws: R

YEAR	TM	LG	AGE	G	GS	IP	H	BB	SO	HR	ERA	EQERA	EQH9	EQBB9	EQSO9	EQHR9	PERA	VORP	STF
2001	VAN	NWN	19	18	14	74.3	47	38	100	3	3.39	5.21	8.9	7.1	6.7	1.1	4.86	2.3	4
2002	VIS	CLF	20	12	12	67.7	49	24	85	4	2.92	3.88	8.3	4.0	6.6	1.0	3.55	12.2	19
2002	MID	TXS	20	16	16	85.3	67	52	102	2	2.95	4.17	8.1	6.5	8.1	0.4	4.29	12.7	24
2003	OAK	AL	21	15	12	69.0	64	44	62	7	4.71	4.76	8.3	5.3	7.7	0.9	4.81	7.7	9

Breakout: 23%   Improve: 47%   Collapse: 18%

Might be the best pitching prospect in baseball, with apologies to Foppert and Heilman. Harden has a plus fastball and a slider that makes right-handers beg for a quick and painless death. He knows how to work hitters, has put up great numbers, and lacks only perfect control. It'll be somewhat surprising if he's not in the A's rotation as a sub at some point during the 2003 season. He'll almost certainly be a mainstay of the A's rotation by the end of next season. Another part of the A's JuCo bounty.

Chad Harville — Born: 16-Sep-76 — Age: 26 — Bats: R — Throws: R

YEAR	TM	LG	AGE	G	GS	IP	H	BB	SO	HR	ERA	EQERA	EQH9	EQBB9	EQSO9	EQHR9	PERA	VORP	STF
2000	SAC	PCL	23	53	0	64.0	53	35	77	8	4.50	4.88	8.4	4.8	8.7	1.4	4.48	3.6	9
2001	SAC	PCL	24	33	0	40.7	35	12	55	5	3.98	4.28	8.3	3.1	8.8	1.3	3.99	5.0	14
2002	SAC	PCL	25	24	0	30.0	32	13	26	5	5.40	5.53	10.2	4.5	6.0	2.0	6.11	-0.5	-15

Once called "The Right-Handed Billy Wagner" because of his diminutive stature and vicious fastball, Harville's been struggling with injuries and mechanics. He needs to make the roster this season, and with the huge number of high-upside options the A's have, it's going to be tough to do. If his velocity's back in spring training, he'll have a shot.

Erik Hiljus — Born: 25-Dec-72 — Age: 30 — Bats: R — Throws: R

YEAR	TM	LG	AGE	G	GS	IP	H	BB	SO	HR	ERA	EQERA	EQH9	EQBB9	EQSO9	EQHR9	PERA	VORP	STF
2000	TOL	INT	27	46	0	70.7	67	20	81	3	3.44	3.68	8.6	2.5	8.6	0.5	3.75	13.4	17
2001	SAC	PCL	28	15	15	101.7	79	26	108	18	3.63	4.03	7.6	2.7	7.0	1.9	3.84	16.7	13
2001	OAK	AL	28	16	11	66.0	70	21	67	7	3.41	4.17	9.6	2.7	8.6	0.9	4.29	9.7	22
2002	SAC	PCL	29	9	6	37.7	54	15	30	3	7.64	7.05	13.5	4.1	5.5	0.9	7.47	-6.5	-9
2002	OAK	AL	29	9	9	45.7	52	21	29	11	6.50	6.46	10.3	3.9	5.6	2.0	6.04	-4.8	-7
2003	OAK	AL	30	19	14	82.3	92	34	61	14	5.04	5.10	10.0	3.4	6.4	1.4	5.17	8.2	3

Breakout: 13%   Improve: 37%   Collapse: 34%

Played the role of Aaron Harang in 2001, but just got lit up everywhere in 2002. Sometimes, you just have a rough year. It rains on you. Your car gets stolen. Someone uses your Social Security number. You miss the red lights by a fraction of a second. Nothing Hiljus did worked in 2002. He's got enough stuff to be successful in the majors, and he's been on the fringes of it. Maybe he'll be able to grab it out of the air again. The drop in the K rate isn't a good sign. There may have been some nagging injury or something.

Tim Hudson — Born: 14-Jul-75 — Age: 27 — Bats: R — Throws: R

YEAR	TM	LG	AGE	G	GS	IP	H	BB	SO	HR	ERA	EQERA	EQH9	EQBB9	EQSO9	EQHR9	PERA	VORP	STF
2000	OAK	AL	24	32	32	202.3	169	82	169	24	4.14	3.51	7.1	2.9	7.3	0.9	3.25	44.8	24
2001	OAK	AL	25	35	35	235.0	216	71	181	20	3.37	3.71	8.5	2.6	6.6	0.7	3.45	46.9	20
2002	OAK	AL	26	34	34	238.3	237	62	152	19	2.98	3.49	9.2	2.2	5.7	0.7	3.61	53.4	14
2003	OAK	AL	27	32	32	212.0	213	62	144	23	3.87	3.92	9.0	2.4	5.8	0.9	3.93	43.7	13

Breakout: 14%   Improve: 54%   Collapse: 13%

Hudson was great all year except in May, when he was collectively lit up by the AL East. His K rate hasn't been what it was in 2000–2001, which is a cause for some concern, but he is keeping his GB/FB ratio up above 2. He's a good bet to continue to be among the best pitchers in the game, but there is some mileage there, and lefties do hit him pretty hard—.283/.334/.448 in 2002.

Bill Koch — Born: 14-Dec-74 — Age: 28 — Bats: R — Throws: R

YEAR	TM	LG	AGE	G	GS	IP	H	BB	SO	HR	ERA	EQERA	EQH9	EQBB9	EQSO9	EQHR9	PERA	VORP	STF
2000	TOR	AL	25	68	0	78.7	78	18	60	6	2.63	2.74	8.2	1.7	6.7	0.6	3.09	23.1	11
2001	TOR	AL	26	69	0	69.3	69	33	55	7	4.81	4.51	8.8	4.0	6.7	0.8	4.31	6.7	-2
2002	OAK	AL	27	84	0	93.7	73	46	93	7	3.27	3.44	7.1	4.1	8.7	0.6	3.21	20.2	13
2003	CWS	AL	28	57	0	73.0	69	31	64	8	4.05	3.94	8.4	3.5	7.5	0.9	4.00	15.8	5

Breakout: 24%   Improve: 50%   Collapse: 24%

Rule of Commerce: Stock up on inexpensive goods that others overvalue. In the case of the A's, it's saves. Run Isringhausen's saves up, let him move along and be someone else's financial problem—we'll take the compensation. Run Billy Koch's saves up, and send him to an organization that can't even identify its own good relievers for Keith Foulke, Joe Valentine, and a patient catcher with some upside. It's a good plan, and as long as some GMs pay more attention to baseball's arcane accounting system than performance, someone will always overpay for a "proven closer."

Allen Levrault — Born: 15-Aug-77 — Age: 25 — Bats: R — Throws: R

YEAR	TM	LG	AGE	G	GS	IP	H	BB	SO	HR	ERA	EQERA	EQH9	EQBB9	EQSO9	EQHR9	PERA	VORP	STF
2000	IND	INT	22	21	18	108.3	98	46	78	9	4.24	4.85	9.4	3.9	5.6	1.0	4.30	7.8	8
2000	MIL	NL	22	5	1	12.0	10	7	9	0	4.50	4.13	8.0	4.3	6.0	0.2	3.21	1.7	7
2001	IND	INT	23	5	5	30.7	22	8	30	1	2.64	2.82	6.9	2.7	6.8	0.4	2.76	9.2	27
2001	MIL	NL	23	32	20	130.7	146	59	80	27	6.06	6.31	10.7	3.8	4.8	1.7	6.03	-12.0	-7
2002	SAC	PCL	24	24	23	111.3	145	45	81	15	6.39	6.79	12.3	4.2	5.0	1.6	7.18	-15.9	-9

Nice gamble, but it didn't pay off. Still, the cost was low, the potential gain sizable. Levrault looked pretty bad all year. His velocity was off, command suffered, and hitters seemed to know what was coming. He'll have to pull things together quickly to get another shot at a rotation, and it probably won't be in Oakland.

Cory Lidle — Born: 22-Mar-72 — Age: 31 — Bats: R — Throws: R

YEAR	TM	LG	AGE	G	GS	IP	H	BB	SO	HR	ERA	EQERA	EQH9	EQBB9	EQSO9	EQHR9	PERA	VORP	STF
2000	DUR	INT	28	9	9	50.0	52	8	44	3	2.52	3.49	10.3	1.4	6.8	0.7	4.14	11.2	21
2000	TBY	AL	28	31	11	96.7	114	29	62	13	5.03	4.67	10.1	2.2	5.6	1.0	4.54	8.5	1
2001	OAK	AL	29	29	29	188.0	170	47	118	23	3.59	3.82	8.3	2.1	5.4	1.0	3.49	35.2	11
2002	SAC	PCL	30	1	1	4.0	2	3	3	0	2.25	2.31	4.5	7.9	5.3	0.2	2.76	1.4	-6
2002	OAK	AL	30	31	30	192.0	191	39	111	17	3.89	3.89	9.3	1.7	5.1	0.7	3.51	34.4	12
2003	TOR	AL	31	28	25	155.3	174	42	89	19	4.59	4.44	9.7	2.3	5.0	1.0	4.32	22.9	5

Breakout: 5%   Improve: 52%   Collapse: 13%

Local sportscasters in the Bay Area are still surprised when the A's go get someone who's an inexpensive breakout candidate, he's successful at a low price for a couple years, and the A's let him go elsewhere and stock up on more good gambles. For those of you outside the SF Bay Area who don't get to enjoy the uninformed rantings of the likes of Ken Dito and Joe Starkey, consider yourself lucky. When Lidle left, the brief response was that the A's had given up trying to win, and were only interested in emulating the Calvin Griffith business model. Lidle was a great contributor, and he's still a good bet to be a reasonable starting pitcher, but the A's have better and less expensive options, like....

Ted Lilly — Born: 04-Jan-76 — Age: 27 — Bats: L — Throws: L

YEAR	TM	LG	AGE	G	GS	IP	H	BB	SO	HR	ERA	EQERA	EQH9	EQBB9	EQSO9	EQHR9	PERA	VORP	STF
2000	COH	INT	24	22	22	137.3	157	48	127	14	4.20	5.15	10.8	3.1	7.0	1.2	5.63	5.4	16
2001	COH	INT	25	5	5	25.3	16	8	30	2	2.85	3.15	5.9	3.3	8.2	0.9	2.90	6.6	25
2001	NYY	AL	25	26	21	120.7	126	51	112	20	5.37	5.13	8.9	3.5	7.7	1.4	5.09	4.9	13
2002	NYY	AL	26	16	11	76.7	57	24	59	10	3.40	3.05	6.3	2.6	6.7	1.1	3.01	20.8	15
2002	OAK	AL	26	6	5	23.3	23	7	18	5	4.64	4.60	8.9	2.5	6.7	1.8	4.60	2.3	5
2003	OAK	AL	27	22	16	101.7	102	38	81	15	4.43	4.48	9.0	3.1	6.8	1.2	4.36	15.9	10

Breakout: 7%   Improve: 43%   Collapse: 15%

When he came over from the Yankees, Lilly had a sore shoulder (similar to Jason Arnold), and went on the A's conditioning program. He fought through an inflamed shoulder and some later blister problems, and by and large, he looked pretty good. He'll start the season as the #4 starter, and he is an excellent candidate to break out and become one of the better pitchers in the league. Good control, good infield defense behind him, major pitchers' park, and a high, relatively stable K rate. The promise he showed in the Montreal system could manifest itself at any time.

Mike Magnante — Born: 17-Jun-65 — Age: 38 — Bats: L — Throws: L

YEAR	TM	LG	AGE	G	GS	IP	H	BB	SO	HR	ERA	EQERA	EQH9	EQBB9	EQSO9	EQHR9	PERA	VORP	STF
2000	OAK	AL	35	55	0	39.7	50	19	17	3	4.31	4.70	10.8	3.5	3.7	0.6	5.18	3.0	-19
2001	OAK	AL	36	65	0	55.3	50	13	23	7	2.77	3.70	8.4	2.0	3.6	1.1	3.48	10.3	-14
2002	LVG	PCL	37	7	0	6.0	5	2	4	1	3.00	4.21	8.1	3.4	4.6	1.8	3.96	0.8	-19
2002	OAK	AL	37	32	0	28.7	38	11	11	2	5.96	6.17	12.3	3.3	3.4	0.6	5.54	-2.5	-23

Magnante wanted his deal structured in such a way that the A's would have been crazy not to re-up him for the 2002 season. Well, they did, and Mike returned to the form that won him the moniker Mike "Magnum" Magnante in the old Binaca Blast Deep Drive Derby Contest. It's not that every pitch he threw went for a home run—most of them didn't have time to get elevated that high, or had excessive topspin. By July, he had more than earned his release, and was picked up by the Dodgers to be the Junior lefty specialist out of that pen, at least until Jesse the Aged took off two hours south along I-5.

Jim Mecir — Born: 16-May-70 — Age: 33 — Bats: B — Throws: R

YEAR	TM	LG	AGE	G	GS	IP	H	BB	SO	HR	ERA	EQERA	EQH9	EQBB9	EQSO9	EQHR9	PERA	VORP	STF
2000	OAK	AL	30	25	0	35.3	35	14	37	2	2.80	3.27	8.4	2.9	9.0	0.4	3.50	8.3	20
2000	TBY	AL	30	38	0	49.7	35	22	33	2	3.08	2.44	6.1	3.2	5.8	0.3	2.27	16.2	3
2001	OAK	AL	31	54	0	63.0	54	26	61	4	3.43	3.50	7.8	3.5	8.2	0.5	3.32	13.2	12
2002	OAK	AL	32	61	0	67.7	68	29	53	5	4.25	4.43	9.2	3.6	6.9	0.6	4.08	7.1	1
2003	*OAK*	*AL*	*33*	*47*	*0*	*55.7*	*56*	*23*	*41*	*6*	*3.89*	*3.94*	*8.9*	*3.5*	*6.4*	*0.8*	*4.24*	*11.8*	*-1*

Breakout: 11%   Improve: 44%   Collapse: 24%

Screwballing specialist had an off year. Gave up a lot of hits, K rate was down, and high-leverage situations that once might have gone to him went instead to Bradford or Rincon. He's still got lots of gas in the tank, and his performance record is promising. He'll be back in Oakland, unless the A's pick up a raftload of cheap, promising relievers, in which case it's possible he could be moved to another club. They did, so we'll see.

Mark Mulder — Born: 05-Aug-77 — Age: 25 — Bats: L — Throws: L

YEAR	TM	LG	AGE	G	GS	IP	H	BB	SO	HR	ERA	EQERA	EQH9	EQBB9	EQSO9	EQHR9	PERA	VORP	STF
2000	OAK	AL	22	27	27	154.0	191	69	88	22	5.44	5.37	10.5	3.2	4.9	1.1	5.46	2.3	5
2001	OAK	AL	23	34	34	229.3	214	51	153	16	3.45	3.49	8.7	1.9	5.7	0.6	3.21	51.3	20
2002	OAK	AL	24	30	30	207.3	182	55	159	21	3.47	3.54	8.1	2.3	6.8	0.8	3.22	45.3	23
2003	*OAK*	*AL*	*25*	*28*	*28*	*183.3*	*191*	*55*	*128*	*22*	*4.27*	*4.32*	*9.3*	*2.5*	*6.0*	*1.0*	*4.24*	*29.2*	*12*

Breakout: 10%   Improve: 30%   Collapse: 13%

The third leg of pitching's Iron Triangle. Mulder's a little more vulnerable than Zito—that K rate is good, but it's not outstanding. He's got a similar repertoire, with a slightly better fastball, and a different curveball than Zito. It's a good curve, but it's not quite as cartoonish as Zito's. He'll be back for the 2003 season, filling the #3 spot in the rotation with 200 solid innings and 17–22 wins.

Juan Pena — Born: 04-Dec-77 — Age: 25 — Bats: L — Throws: L

YEAR	TM	LG	AGE	G	GS	IP	H	BB	SO	HR	ERA	EQERA	EQH9	EQBB9	EQSO9	EQHR9	PERA	VORP	STF
2000	MOD	CLF	22	29	27	154.0	132	75	177	7	3.86	5.42	10.0	4.8	6.5	0.9	4.98	1.4	11
2001	MID	TXS	23	27	27	148.3	164	46	106	13	4.07	5.77	11.5	3.4	4.6	1.3	5.59	-4.4	0
2002	MOD	CLF	24	2	2	11.0	5	5	9	1	0.82	2.56	6.1	5.3	4.4	1.6	2.76	3.6	-2
2002	VIS	CLF	24	7	7	23.0	40	12	18	6	7.83	14.85	23.2	6.6	4.6	4.9	13.36	-23.9	-56
2002	*SAC*	*PCL*	*24*	*3*	*1*	*10.3*	*11*	*9*	*7*	*2*	*6.12*	*6.59*	*10.5*	*9.3*	*4.9*	*2.3*	*7.89*	*-1.3*	*-32*

Lives off his fastball and changeup. Pena actually pitched fairly well until the wheels came off in 2002. He's similar to ex-A and current Ranger farmhand Mario Ramos, in that neither of them is really a great prospect to be a good starting pitcher. Pena's got a better shot at a career as a situational lefty than as a starter, and if he's going to do that, he needs to develop and refine a nasty breaking pitch. That's going to take some time, and probably a change of scenery.

John Rheinecker Born: 29-May-79 Age: 24 Bats: L Throws: L

YEAR	TM	LG	AGE	G	GS	IP	H	BB	SO	HR	ERA	EQERA	EQH9	EQBB9	EQSO9	EQHR9	PERA	VORP	STF
2001	VAN	NWN	22	6	5	22.7	13	4	17	0	1.59	3.04	7.4	2.4	3.6	0.3	2.73	6.2	0
2001	MOD	CLF	22	2	2	10.0	10	5	5	1	6.30	7.09	12.1	6.1	2.7	1.8	6.73	-1.8	-25
2002	VIS	CLF	23	9	9	50.7	41	10	62	2	2.31	3.36	9.1	2.2	6.3	0.7	3.34	12.1	22
2002	MID	TXS	23	20	20	128.0	137	24	100	7	3.38	4.92	11.3	2.0	5.4	1.0	4.78	8.3	12
2003	OAK	AL	24	16	12	77.0	85	23	48	10	4.59	4.64	9.9	2.4	5.3	1.0	4.54	10.2	4

Breakout: 10%   Improve: 49%   Collapse: 23%

Lefty with more finesse than power. Has a full repertoire. Best pitch is probably slider or changeup, and he's had success at each level. He'll probably start the year at Sacramento, and he'll have to do something noteworthy to avoid the Quadruple-A pitcher career track, given the competition he has for future rotation slots. Control is excellent, and he's probably got a better path to the majors as a bullpen lefty than as a starter.

Ricardo Rincon Born: 13-Apr-70 Age: 33 Bats: L Throws: L

YEAR	TM	LG	AGE	G	GS	IP	H	BB	SO	HR	ERA	EQERA	EQH9	EQBB9	EQSO9	EQHR9	PERA	VORP	STF
2000	CLE	AL	30	35	0	20.0	17	13	20	1	2.70	2.91	6.9	4.6	8.5	0.4	3.37	5.5	10
2001	CLE	AL	31	67	0	54.0	44	21	50	3	2.83	2.59	6.5	3.2	7.7	0.4	2.97	16.7	11
2002	CLE	AL	32	46	0	35.7	36	8	30	3	4.79	3.73	8.3	1.8	7.2	0.7	3.55	6.5	8
2002	OAK	AL	32	25	0	20.3	11	3	19	1	3.10	2.10	5.1	1.3	8.3	0.4	1.36	7.4	23
2003	OAK	AL	33	74	0	62.7	57	18	51	6	3.12	3.15	8.1	2.4	7.0	0.8	3.33	18.6	7

Breakout: 13%   Improve: 53%   Collapse: 21%

Hmmm. I wonder if David Littlefield would take him for Brian Giles. Great situational lefty. He'll be back in a familiar role, with the same repertoire of familiar pitches in 2003. Nice thing to have in the pen—a reliable lefty that can be used on a regular basis. Nice setup tandem with Bradford and possibly one or two of the young guys that have been buried in other organizations, i.e., Mike Neu and Buddy Hernandez.

Bert Snow Born: 23-Mar-77 Age: 26 Bats: R Throws: R

YEAR	TM	LG	AGE	G	GS	IP	H	BB	SO	HR	ERA	EQERA	EQH9	EQBB9	EQSO9	EQHR9	PERA	VORP	STF
2000	MID	TXS	23	59	0	67.7	58	36	98	6	3.59	4.31	8.4	4.9	9.2	1.2	4.44	8.0	13
2002	VIS	CLF	25	12	1	18.0	8	7	25	1	1.00	1.63	5.1	4.3	7.1	0.9	2.14	7.6	5
2002	MID	TXS	25	24	0	21.7	21	11	29	1	4.98	5.46	10.1	5.4	9.1	0.8	5.21	-0.2	5

Beware the dreaded "Closer of the Future" label. At least we didn't put him on the cover or name him our #1 prospect. Snow missed the 2001 season with an elbow injury, and he's working his way back to full velocity and full command. If he can get those back, he's a pretty good relief prospect.

Jeff Tam Born: 19-Aug-70 Age: 32 Bats: R Throws: R

YEAR	TM	LG	AGE	G	GS	IP	H	BB	SO	HR	ERA	EQERA	EQH9	EQBB9	EQSO9	EQHR9	PERA	VORP	STF
2000	OAK	AL	29	72	0	85.7	86	23	46	3	2.63	2.91	8.8	2.0	4.8	0.3	3.12	23.5	-1
2001	OAK	AL	30	70	0	74.7	68	29	44	3	3.01	3.40	8.5	3.3	5.1	0.3	3.37	16.4	-5
2002	SAC	PCL	31	20	0	29.0	31	5	26	2	5.59	4.76	9.8	1.8	6.1	0.8	4.39	2.0	0
2002	OAK	AL	31	40	0	40.3	56	13	14	2	5.14	5.67	13.0	2.8	3.1	0.4	5.53	-1.3	-21
2003	TOR	AL	32	41	0	47.7	57	14	24	4	4.24	4.10	10.5	2.5	4.4	0.7	4.61	8.9	-11

Breakout: 21%   Improve: 44%   Collapse: 16%

"How long does it take to get to Sacramento on 80? About an hour, right?" Actually, it takes several really bad outings. Tam was horrible in 2002. His sinker usually didn't, his fastball wasn't, and get people out he couldn't. He's moved on to Toronto, so clearly, Ricciardi and Law think his troubles are behind him, at least for next year. I respectfully disagree, but their risk is pretty low.

Brad Weis — Born: 29-Nov-77 — Age: 25 — Bats: L — Throws: L

YEAR	TM	LG	AGE	G	GS	IP	H	BB	SO	HR	ERA	EQERA	EQH9	EQBB9	EQSO9	EQHR9	PERA	VORP	STF
2000	QUD	MDW	22	40	0	60.0	55	22	56	9	2.55	5.29	13.7	4.3	5.7	3.8	6.67	0.6	-19
2001	QUD	MDW	23	22	0	39.3	38	19	43	0	0.69	5.56	12.1	6.4	6.3	0.3	5.81	-0.8	-7
2001	FTM	FSL	23	17	0	20.7	20	10	26	1	2.61	5.97	12.0	5.4	7.8	1.2	6.54	-1.4	-1
2002	FTM	FSL	24	13	0	21.7	16	8	22	1	1.66	4.21	9.3	4.3	6.6	1.0	4.29	2.8	-1
2002	MOD	CLF	24	32	0	52.3	40	23	51	3	2.24	4.03	9.6	5.2	5.3	1.0	4.24	7.8	-11
2002	SAC	PCL	24	2	0	9.3	9	2	6	0	3.87	3.29	8.6	2.2	4.3	0.2	3.46	2.2	6

Been effective every step of the way, without eye-popping peripherals. He'll have a chance to make it as a situational lefty. That 2000 Quad Cities line is remarkable—9 home runs allowed in 60 innings, but only a 2.55 ERA? How many times you think he had to spring for dinner for the starter? "I'm sorry, dude."

Mike Wood — Born: 26-Apr-80 — Age: 23 — Bats: R — Throws: R

YEAR	TM	LG	AGE	G	GS	IP	H	BB	SO	HR	ERA	EQERA	EQH9	EQBB9	EQSO9	EQHR9	PERA	VORP	STF
2001	VAN	NWN	21	5	2	21.7	17	4	24	0	1.24	3.45	10.2	2.5	5.3	0.3	4.12	4.9	12
2001	MOD	CLF	21	10	9	58.3	46	10	52	6	3.09	3.99	9.3	2.0	4.6	1.8	3.90	9.8	8
2002	MOD	CLF	22	7	7	41.3	41	6	50	4	3.49	4.99	12.5	1.7	6.5	1.7	4.91	2.4	18
2002	MID	TXS	22	17	17	105.7	103	29	63	8	3.15	4.36	10.6	3.0	4.1	1.4	4.71	13.4	2

His splitter kept working. Scouts describe him as "similar to Mike Scott," and I can only presume they're not referring to alleged scuffing or spitters. Wood's been great at every stop, and he's got all the peripherals going for him except K rate. He's an underrated prospect, and one to keep an eye on in Sacramento this year. Not bad for a 10th round choice.

Barry Zito — Born: 13-May-78 — Age: 25 — Bats: L — Throws: L

YEAR	TM	LG	AGE	G	GS	IP	H	BB	SO	HR	ERA	EQERA	EQH9	EQBB9	EQSO9	EQHR9	PERA	VORP	STF
2000	SAC	PCL	22	18	18	101.7	88	45	91	4	3.19	4.00	8.7	4.0	6.6	0.4	3.72	17.0	20
2000	OAK	AL	22	14	14	92.7	64	45	78	6	2.72	2.52	5.9	3.5	7.3	0.5	2.53	30.7	30
2001	OAK	AL	23	35	35	214.3	184	80	205	18	3.49	3.66	7.8	3.2	8.1	0.7	3.35	43.9	31
2002	OAK	AL	24	35	35	229.3	182	78	182	24	2.75	3.13	7.3	2.9	7.0	0.9	3.07	60.5	23
2003	OAK	AL	25	35	33	218.0	203	76	175	25	3.78	3.83	8.3	2.9	6.9	0.9	3.84	46.7	18

Breakout: 15%   Improve: 49%   Collapse: 13%

Left-hander with broad repertoire and a curveball that sends lefties screaming into the night. Growing up, left-handed hitters of the future will be threatened with the appearance of Barry's curveball unless they eat their Candied Curried Brussel Sprouts. There's nothing here not to like, but there could be some improvement in control. Zito's the best pitcher on the staff, and there's no indication that that's going to change any time soon. In the second half of the season, Zito was Koufaxy, posting a 1.92 ERA. Nasty.

Seattle Mariers

Confident about their future, the most glaring issue the Mariners thought they faced to start 2002 was the complaining by batters that they couldn't see the ball during day games when center field was illuminated. They were apparently worried that they might be badly hurt if a ball got away from a pitcher and they couldn't see it. And if Edgar Martinez was killed by a fastball, you could probably count on rabid fans burning the stadium to the ground and stringing the front office from nearby lampposts, all of which would impede the team's ability to continue making dizzying amounts of money.

Unfortunately, instead of working out an effective, permanent solution to this problem, the Mariners screwed around all season. They repainted the walls with special super-expensive paint, they planted trees to block the glare off of the repainted walls and provide a better hitting background, and then they cut the trees down. They floated an idea for a Montgomery Burns-style moving sunshield that would extend off the stadium and blot out the sun. Eventually they swore off late afternoon weekday games, which was one of the most relaxing, fun things anyone could do in Seattle: get off work after a half-day, sit in the sunshine, watch a good ball game, and enjoy twelve ounces microbrew (at $6.50 a pop) with your sushi.

Even as they continued to struggle with the problem of sunlight, at mid-season the Mariners started to notice that they faced an even greater threat. They had a pitching rotation with Jamie Moyer and Joel Piniero, both of whom were performing well, an erratic Freddy Garcia, a fooling-nobody James Baldwin, and then the alternating platoon of John Halama and Ryan Franklin, taking turns where one would start and the other the long reliever to fill in when a starter was knocked out early. It was functional, but not quite the

quality the Mariners had gotten used to. On the bench, they only had Mark McLemore and two McLemore knock-offs. Their left field options ranged from bad to Ranger-quality. They were getting no production from new acquisition Jeff Cirillo, and not scoring enough runs in general.

All of which would have been fine, if the other teams in the division were playing dead, but they weren't. Anaheim, with their jumping monkey and run-and-gun offense, kept close on the heels of the Mariners all year, and Oakland was rallying back to contention again with yet another retooled team and the league's best rotation. The Mariners were in trouble if they stood pat, and the possibility of labor action loomed. Sure, it might not be a season-ender, but that was unlikely: the players had already caved on the major issues, and all that remained was to work out the gap in numbers. So to retain their place in the standings, bold action was required. An intern was sent for thai food, sleeves were rolled up, and brows were furrowed.

Unfortunately, the furrowing and the pondering came too late. Cliff Floyd, who would have solved two problems at once, was traded twice for prices the Mariners could have paid from among their bumper crop of young pitchers. Chuck Finley was traded for less than that. So was Scott Rolen. All kinds of other pitchers and outfielders changed hands in July. And what moves did the Mariners make? They added Doug Creek and Jose Offerman. The front office minions slapped each other on the back and congratulated themselves. They got Pagliacci to deliver some double-pepperoni pizza and celebrated.

For this lack of vision, the Angels and A's ran down the Mariners like they were the Pat Putnam Mariners of yore. The 2002 season might have been the last good chance the Mariners had to take their aging core to the postseason, and

---

Mariners Prospectus

2002 record: 93–69; Third place, AL West

Pythagenport Record: 93–69

Runs scored per game: 5 (6th in AL)

Runs allowed per game: 4.3 (4th in AL)

Team EqA: .275 (2nd in AL)

2002 Batters Age: 31.9 (oldest in AL)

2002 Pitchers Age: 30.6 (3rd oldest in AL)

Ballpark: Safeco Field; Severe pitchers' park; Park Factor of .937

2002: 116-win team came back down to earth, too far in the baseball's strongest division.

2003: The aging core is back for one more crack at it, but they're in the wrong division to start slipping in.

---

they decided to be bystanders. Apparently, the Mariners don't want to win the World Series, not really:

> The business model we are operating under now is wanting to field competitive teams on a consistent basis, and I think we are doing that. We don't believe in just going for it in any one particular year, but to try to have the discipline to work throughout the organization, both at the major-league and minor-league levels.
>
> — Howard Lincoln, Mariners CEO, in the *Seattle Post-Intelligencer*

Instead of taking advantage of the opportunities they have, the Mariners operate like an established movie studio. No movie studio ever wants to make *Titanic*, an awesome $300 million flick that makes $2 billion dollars in theaters alone, something that left people crying, amazed, and complaining. That's the Yankees' turf. The Mariners want to make *Miss Congeniality*, which costs $70M to make and market, will return $100M for sure, and leave people thinking "that was pretty good, I guess..." as they walk to their cars and wonder if they drank too much cola.

The Mariners don't want to build a dynasty. They have a sweetheart lease that requires them to sell just over forty Diamond Club season tickets to pay the year's rent ($700,000/year) on a beautiful new stadium. They sell nearly every ticket for every game, and they have lucrative broadcast deals because their games beat out hit prime-time dramas in the Seattle market. Their revenues are second only to the Yankees. They've done an awesome job of marketing their product here in the states and overseas. As successful business models go, they don't need to go to the World Series. If they stay in the race, keep interest and attendance up, they sit back and let the stadium do its job. It appears that they would rather do this as long as they can instead of taking a chance at playing in the World Series. For flavor, take that box-office philosophy, add one GM with a preference for plugging holes with veterans, and then stir in a crotchety manager who wants to win in the worst way to have a shot at a legacy of winning World Series pennants in both the American and National Leagues, and you've got an attention-getter.

It wasn't going to last forever. First, Lou Piniella and Pat Gillick didn't get along. They were both professional enough to keep it out of the press for the most part, but it was obvious. Piniella would wonder out loud what in the world Luis Ugueto was doing on his 25-man, and Gillick would pronounce that the team was committed to developing this budding star. Faced with daily sell-out crowds and a three-way pennant race, the ownership group decided to bank their good fortune and hope the team would make it to the postseason anyway, even though they'd gone to local groups in the preseason and said they'd budgeted on attendence much lower than what they were drawing, and if more people

turned out they should be able to spend more on payroll, renting potential free agent players like Cliff Floyd. Gillick was in every paper, talking about how because they were right against the budget—that low, start-of-the-season budget—and the door on trades was "more closed than open." Piniella has complained he needed another hitter all year, and the front office got him nothing. In fact, they got him less than that in the form of Jose Offerman.

After the debacle was over, and Gillick was convinced to come back for one more year, it didn't take long for Piniella's homesickness to get him to make a request to be released from his contract. The Mariners said they would do what they could. Gillick, having been on the opposite end of this stick while general manager of the Blue Jays and interested in hiring Piniella, knew what was up. An amicable split became bitter as Piniella's agent and the Mets waged war using the massive New York press machine, accusing the Mariners of asking unreasonable compensation, of not letting Piniella determine his own destiny, of using puppies in Safeco hot dogs; whatever they could come up with, they threw out there. Gillick was even said to be sabotaging Piniella's heart's desire for petty reasons: Pat wanted to get back at the Mets, who turned him in for tampering when John Olerud signed with Seattle. Between the actions of Piniella's agent and the Mets, there seems to be some truth in the rumors that they had already agreed to the basic terms of a new deal with the Mets. Spiteful to the last, the Mariners let Piniella sign a deal with Tampa Bay, picking up Randy Winn, and the dominant personality of the team had left.

Piniella was the best available manager back when the new owners needed a high-profile signing to bring respectability to the team. Piniella likes his teams just so, and every Mariner team was bent into becoming one of Piniella's teams. Piniella didn't like platoons, having resented it as a player, he didn't understand why pitchers couldn't get strikeouts all the time, he liked feisty scrappers who hustled, like he used to, and he always handed out an extra gold star for playing multiple positions. He hated having an unreliable bullpen, and usually didn't get along with many of his relievers. He fired a pitching coach almost every season.

And doing this his way, he won. Better yet, he learned, too. Piniella came to trust Bryan Price, a pitching coach who believed in pitch counts, workload monitoring, rotation planning, and all things related to pitching staff management that Piniella once regarded with disdain. As a result, Lou turned what had been one of his great weaknesses over to someone who could make it a team strength. Even handicapped much of the time by Woody Woodard, a GM who might charitably be called "okay," Piniella ran up an 840–711 record in his ten years with the Mariners, a .541 winning percentage. His teams became more and more fitted to his specifications, until he had an expensive all-veteran bullpen, a couple of switch-hitting super-subs, and regulars at every position.

The search for a replacement to lie in Piniella's bed revealed a lot about the Mariners management. They really weren't interested in putting together a team that could win in the playoffs, they were interested in getting another name, someone who knew how to glad-hand the press. They didn't care about ability, or record, when they made up their list. They interviewed guys as favors, or on whims. Besides cursory interviews with internal candidates like Tacoma manager Dan Rohn, third-base coach and Snelling Crippler Dave Myers, part-time coach Lee Elia, and M's pitching coach Byran Price, they flew in a who's who of managerial disappointments of the '90s: Don Baylor, Tony Muser, Jim Riggleman, Terry Francona, and Buddy Bell. There were also some interesting candidates: Willie Randolph, Ron Roenicke, and lastly Doug Melvin, who was added to the interview list on a whim. Melvin so impressed the Mariners in his initial interview that he was put on the short list for callbacks, and ended up winning the job over Sam Perlozzo, Buddy Bell, and Jim Riggleman. Do you think Earl Weaver or Billy Martin gave great interviews?

"Earl, if you were a tree, what kind of a tree would you be?"

"What the f^&k kind of bull$#it f^$&ing question is that? You want to win some motherf#^@&%ing ball games or are you a$$h*l@s just jerking me off here?"

"Thanks for stopping by, Mr. Weaver."

Managers don't necessarily have to have previous managerial experience, but seriously, given the choice between a guy with a killer resume and a proven record of doing the same job somewhere else, and a guy who's been around the job as it was done poorly, but has never really done the job in question, but hey, at least he's great in the interview, who's the better choice? This is not to suggest that Dan Rohn or Dave Myers would do a better job than Melvin might, but they've been managers before, and they've done a good job at it.

So what about Melvin? Typically, the bench coach is the strategist and sounding board for his manager. Since Bob Brenley's Diamondback teams have been known for their tactical ineptitude, poor lineup choices, and shallow bullpens, deficiencies only barely concealed by the Diamondbacks' World Series ring, you might find it strange that Melvin is regarded as a smart baseball man. However, Melvin has already made some smart comments: "I'd rather see a guy hit .260 with a .360 on-base percentage and doesn't run very well, than a guy who hits .300 with a .310 on-base percentage and runs well." I guess we know who he'd pick between Craig Counsell and Tony Womack, and the Mariners haven't made any move to re-sign Charles Gipson yet, so there's a chance that Piniella's super scrubs might finally be

phased out. Signing someone like Greg Colbrunn bodes well for a bench that might offer Melvin some tactical options, or potential matchup advantages, or even some platoons to cover up the more glaring weaknesses.

But what we haven't seen is any sort of large-scale changes. This off-season hinged on Edgar Martinez. If the heart of the lineup decided to return, it was going to be worth it to bring the graying team back for one last shot. If he retired or was unwilling to return, the team would almost certainly have torn down and slowly rebuilt on the backs of their bountiful pitching crop. But once Gillick was able to reach a deal with Edgar, they followed up by spreading the wealth to other members of the team's elderly core: John Olerud was re-signed for two years, and Slowest Pitching Ace in Baseball Jamie Moyer signed a three-year deal. Trickling down, players not key to the team's future were brought back enthusiastically: Dan Wilson was rewarded with a ridiculous two-year, $7 million for almost hitting an empty .300, and Shigethoshi Hasegawa had his option picked up at a cost of $1.5 million. Then, in a fit of buyer's remorse, the team explored saving money by trading Mike Cameron, who is due to make $7 million this coming season.

Perhaps it's just as well. Even before deciding to re-sign the old guard, they aren't poised to start a youth movement. They've got great pitching, but it's coming out of Double-A and high-A ball, and it isn't ready. In a few years, we should see an outfield of Shin-Soo Choo, Chris Snelling, and Jamal Strong, especially if Ichiro can't be retained. Unfortunately, the Mariners have few infield prospects they can look forward to ever seeing stick at the major league level. Shortstop Jose Lopez and second baseman Ismael Castro both have age questions, and they're the best the organization can boast. To make things worse, this year's draft was a disaster. They reached to pick high schooler John Mayberry Jr. with their first round choice, and then couldn't sign him. In the second round, they took a high school player known for his football skills. They drafted high school outfielder Eddy Martinez-Esteve in the third round and didn't sign him. They didn't take a college player until the seventh round, and seven of their first ten picks went to high schoolers, four of those to high school pitchers. There's not going to be much help from the minors until the next wave from last year's Double-A team arrives.

As a result, Doug Melvin starts his first season with the Mariners exactly where they were last year. They will field a strong veteran team in a tough division. They're looking for some good breaks, like the A's to have a rotation meltdown, the Angels to come down hard after their unexpected championship, and the Rangers to spend themselves to the cellar again. They're hoping they'll be in the running for the division, or at least the wild card, while they pocket even more money this year, as a new radio deal for around $10 million per year kicks in. They haven't made changes that would allow them to advance deep into the playoffs, but then, that's not really important. And they still haven't figured out how to keep their players from getting killed when the sun shines on center field.

HITTERS

Willie Bloomquist — UT — Born: 27-Nov-77 — Age: 25 — Bats: R — Throws: R

YEAR	TM	LG	AGE	AB	H	2B	3B	HR	BB	SO	SB	CS	AVG	OBP	SLG	MLVR	EQBA	EQOBP	EQSLG	EQMLVR	VORP	DEFENSE			
2000	LNC	CLF	22	256	97	19	6	2	37	27	22	12	.379	.457	.523	.421	.279	.339	.386	-.071	8.9	49-2B	2	11-SS	-1
2000	TAC	PCL	22	191	43	5	1	1	7	28	5	0	.225	.253	.277	-.456	.209	.226	.262	-.513	-13.7	50-2B	-1		
2001	SAN	TXS	23	491	125	23	2	0	28	55	34	9	.255	.296	.310	-.175	.229	.264	.281	-.398	-22.3	70-SS	-4	50-2B	3
2002	TAC	PCL	24	337	91	14	3	6	29	44	20	10	.270	.333	.383	-.046	.245	.302	.348	-.219	-12.0	34-LF	-2	26-2B	-5
2002	SEA	AL	24	33	15	4	0	0	5	2	3	1	.455	.526	.576	.743	.500	.575	.647	.934	9.9				
2003	*SEA*	*AL*	*25*	*245*	*61*	*12*	*1*	*3*	*16*	*32*	*7*	*3*	*.248*	*.296*	*.343*	*-.171*	*.262*	*.312*	*.370*	*-.148*	*-3.4*				

Breakout: 40%   Improve: 59%   Collapse: 22%

Pity poor Willie. Piniella always liked him, loved that scrappy play, and supported his call-up, which got Willie the chance to look good in a short trial, which almost certainly should have made Bloomquist next year's Gipson, the kind of guy Lou could play all over the place for no reason. Now Lou's gone, and for all the talk about Bloomquist's makeup, he's never hit well for long against good competition, and his glove isn't good enough to carry his bat. In the past, Piniella reached out to his previous organization to pluck his favorite young players, like Ayala and Wilson when he came to Seattle, but he's making noises about how he wants to fill the D-Rays' bench with veterans. It's more likely the helicopter extraction will be for McLemore than Bloomquist.

Bret Boone — 2B — Born: 06-Apr-69 — Age: 34 — Bats: R — Throws: R

YEAR	TM	LG	AGE	AB	H	2B	3B	HR	BB	SO	SB	CS	AVG	OBP	SLG	MLVR	EQBA	EQOBP	EQSLG	EQMLVR	VORP	DEFENSE	
2000	SDP	NL	31	463	116	18	2	19	50	97	8	4	.251	.330	.421	-.058	.261	.330	.439	-.027	24.0	121-2B	-4
2001	SEA	AL	32	623	206	37	3	37	40	110	5	5	.331	.379	.578	.365	.354	.402	.624	.458	103.8	151-2B	11
2002	SEA	AL	33	608	169	34	3	24	53	102	12	5	.278	.342	.462	.110	.307	.369	.515	.191	63.6	143-2B	5
2003	*SEA*	*AL*	*34*	*527*	*141*	*28*	*2*	*21*	*44*	*92*	*7*	*3*	*.267*	*.328*	*.450*	*.032*	*.283*	*.345*	*.485*	*.080*	*32.4*		

Breakout: 3%   Improve: 27%   Collapse: 24%

The Mariners signed him to a four-year, $24M deal as they went to arbitration, and while that's certainly more than they could have spent, they didn't have any internal options, and the free agent market last year for second basemen didn't offer better value. Going to the best-available replacement, Jermaine Clark, would have cost them 50 runs between the offensive and defensive drop-off. When you're that close to the playoffs, those 50 runs are easily worth an extra $8 million.

A former Mariner farmhand and friend of mine told me "someone needs to tell that dude he's 5'6" and not 6'5"." The league-wide scouting report on Boone reads "first pitch fastball up and out of the strikezone" Boone swung at that all year. Last year he came up with this weird Batista-esque two-strike stance, and this year we joked about it during his at-bats, betting on how many pitches it would take for him to go into the two-strike stance. Two? Three? I made a lot of money on two this year. What's the point of having a special two-strike stance if you go into that stance at some point every single at-bat? Why not just make that the regular stance?

Pat Borders — C — Born: 14-May-63 — Age: 40 — Bats: R — Throws: R

YEAR	TM	LG	AGE	AB	H	2B	3B	HR	BB	SO	SB	CS	AVG	OBP	SLG	MLVR	EQBA	EQOBP	EQSLG	EQMLVR	VORP	DEFENSE	
2000	DUR	INT	37	348	95	16	0	12	20	66	7	2	.273	.314	.422	-.022	.257	.289	.397	-.166	6.0	80-C	9
2001	DUR	INT	38	313	74	15	1	2	16	61	3	2	.236	.278	.310	-.216	.228	.268	.301	-.362	-10.2	39-C	3
2002	TAC	PCL	39	317	84	16	1	12	11	47	3	2	.265	.290	.435	-.054	.243	.266	.394	-.224	.9	78-C	8
2002	SEA	AL	39	4	2	1	0	0	0	1	0	0	.500	.500	.750	-1.000	.500	.500	.000	-.214	-1.0		
2003	*SEA*	*AL*	*40*	*81*	*18*	*4*	*0*	*2*	*4*	*16*	*1*	*1*	*.226*	*.266*	*.357*	*-.217*	*.240*	*.281*	*.385*	*-.199*	*-.9*		

Breakout: 47%   Improve: 57%   Collapse: 34%

Pat Borders *(continued)*

Some pitchers have personal catchers, but Pat Gillick might be the only GM with a personal catcher, Pat Borders. As long as Gillick is in a front office somewhere, Borders will have a job catching. When Gillick leaves front office work again and takes up coaching tee-ball, Pat Borders will be squatting down behind the little tykes, encouraging them to take a good swing. Like pitchers who were successful pitching complete games every other day, at this point it's certain that Pat Borders is some sort of freak of nature with super-human knees and pain resistance, or that he's had his knees cybernetically enhanced but at the same time passed up the opportunity for more powerful arms or kung-fu grip as being "too tacky."

Mike Cameron							CF		Born: 08-Jan-73			Age: 30		Bats: R		Throws: R		
YEAR	TM	LG	AGE	AB	H	2B	3B	HR	BB	SO	SB	CS	AVG	OBP	SLG	MLVR	EQBA	EQOBP	EQSLG	EQMLVR	VORP	DEFENSE
2000	SEA	AL	27	543	145	28	4	19	78	133	24	7	.267	.368	.438	.034	.281	.375	.465	.107	40.2	145-CF 2
2001	SEA	AL	28	540	144	30	5	25	69	155	34	5	.267	.360	.480	.133	.299	.388	.540	.249	60.5	144-CF 9
2002	SEA	AL	29	545	130	26	5	25	79	176	31	8	.239	.342	.442	.052	.276	.375	.515	.170	51.5	145-CF 6
2003	SEA	AL	30	515	129	27	4	22	68	149	21	10	.250	.342	.445	.035	.265	.360	.480	.081	29.3	

Breakout: 5%   Improve: 43%   Collapse: 15%

Why aren't teams more active in getting their players medical care? Cameron complained at the start of the year that he was having trouble picking up the spin and movement on pitches, and it took months for the team to get him help. It turned out that his right eye was badly messed up, having become a different shape than the left from an injury that might go back to a ball he took to the orbital bone years ago in the minors. Cameron's vision in that eye had deteriorated dramatically. He was fitted for a right-eye-only contact, but how long does it take to adjust to that kind of thing, mid-season, to really get to the point where you're seeing well? The difference between being a great hitter and a bad one is so very fine, and a player's sight so important, that it's hard to believe, months later, that it took as long as it did for the team to get him to a good optometrist.

Cameron needs to get traded. He hits so badly in Safeco, so far below even what park effects would predict, and has done so for so long, that it's obvious that it is just not his park. If he had played anywhere else this year, instead of calling him one of the season's biggest disappointments, he'd still be lauded as one of baseball's premier center fielders. Even with his home field and eye problems, he was still the 8th-best at the position offensively while playing his usual outstanding defense.

Having hit four home runs in the game, already tying the major league record, in his fifth at-bat, Cameron was up with a 3–0 count, and took a strike right down the middle. Faced with the choice between hacking at the pitch, which no one would have blamed him for, and playing the game, forsaking the record to get on base again, Cameron watched the pitch go by. You want an unselfish, giving player? Here he is.

Ismael Castro							2B		Born: 14-Aug-83			Age: 19		Bats: B		Throws: R		
YEAR	TM	LG	AGE	AB	H	2B	3B	HR	BB	SO	SB	CS	AVG	OBP	SLG	MLVR	EQBA	EQOBP	EQSLG	EQMLVR	VORP	DEFENSE
2002	EVE	NWN	18	284	89	26	1	9	16	41	13	2	.313	.359	.507	.309	.236	.263	.384	-.249	-2.4	64-2B -10
2002	SBR	CLF	18	20	3	2	0	0	1	9	0	1	.150	.261	.250	-.370	.150	.225	.200	-.623	-2.4	
2003	SEA	AL	19	211	50	10	2	5	11	40	4	4	.239	.281	.374	-.162	.253	.297	.403	-.137	.4	

Breakout: 54%   Improve: 65%   Collapse: 12%

Castro's here for a couple reasons: the Mariners are claiming that he's truly 19, no joke, and they're lying. Or mistaken. Or possibly blind. The age scandals aren't over, folks, and they may only have begun. While the Dominican might have been the hotbed of age-related chicanery, we haven't seen the end of the Dominican scandals, and when MLB opens validation offices in Venezuela or Mexico...oh, the fun has only started. If he's really 19, he's worth looking up next year to see how he's progressing. This is how far you have to go down in the Mariner system to find an infielder who might have a high ceiling.

Shin-Soo Choo							CF		Born: 13-Jul-82			Age: 20		Bats: L		Throws: L		
YEAR	TM	LG	AGE	AB	H	2B	3B	HR	BB	SO	SB	CS	AVG	OBP	SLG	MLVR	EQBA	EQOBP	EQSLG	EQMLVR	VORP	DEFENSE
2002	WIS	MDW	19	420	127	24	8	6	70	98	34	21	.302	.417	.440	.273	.231	.320	.345	-.197	-2.1	104-CF -6
2002	SBR	CLF	19	39	12	5	1	1	9	9	3	0	.308	.460	.564	.461	.244	.354	.463	.035	1.9	
2003	SEA	AL	20	210	50	9	2	4	21	55	6	6	.237	.314	.364	-.120	.251	.331	.392	-.092	1.0	

Breakout: 35%   Improve: 55%   Collapse: 16%

Choo is a Korean power pitcher converted to the outfield, and who is now already one of the best outfield prospects in baseball. He hit well at Wisconsin and then tore up the California League in limited exposure, but more importantly, his batting eye was just as good and his play just as smart against the higher-level competition. He'll be in Double-A before you know it, and his name will be on all the lists. If he can improve his defense as well—he's only been doing this for two years—he's a star in the making.

Ryan Christianson C Born: 21-Apr-81 Age: 22 Bats: R Throws: R

YEAR	TM	LG	AGE	AB	H	2B	3B	HR	BB	SO	SB	CS	AVG	OBP	SLG	MLVR	EQBA	EQOBP	EQSLG	EQMLVR	VORP	DEFENSE
2000	WIS	MDW	19	418	104	20	0	13	50	98	1	6	.249	.335	.390	.045	.194	.253	.310	-.398	-18.2	92-C 2
2001	SBR	CLF	20	528	131	42	5	12	53	112	3	2	.248	.323	.415	.010	.199	.256	.327	-.366	-17.6	108-C 7
2002	SBR	CLF	21	71	20	5	1	1	4	17	1	0	.282	.346	.423	.084	.236	.271	.347	-.286	-.9	17-C 1
2002	SAN	TXS	21	190	48	11	0	5	16	36	0	2	.253	.317	.389	.007	.231	.279	.359	-.257	-1.1	45-C -1
2003	SEA	AL	22	167	37	7	1	4	15	38	1	1	.220	.291	.344	-.195	.233	.307	.370	-.176	-.4	

Breakout: 51%   Improve: 70%   Collapse: 18%

Forgotten, but still a prospect. Christianson suffered some injuries after catching a whole lot of innings the last couple of years, but he did better in Double-A as the season went on. His power is for real, though he needs to work on his control of the strike zone and make contact more often. His defense is fine. Last year we said he'd start to put the package together, but injuries have pushed that back. This should be the year he puts the package together.

Jeff Cirillo 3B Born: 23-Sep-69 Age: 33 Bats: R Throws: R

YEAR	TM	LG	AGE	AB	H	2B	3B	HR	BB	SO	SB	CS	AVG	OBP	SLG	MLVR	EQBA	EQOBP	EQSLG	EQMLVR	VORP	DEFENSE
2000	COL	NL	30	598	195	53	2	11	67	72	3	4	.326	.399	.477	.132	.306	.372	.447	.099	45.5	151-3B 2
2001	COL	NL	31	528	165	26	4	17	43	63	12	2	.313	.370	.473	.098	.298	.355	.451	.067	35.7	136-3B 25
2002	SEA	AL	32	485	121	20	0	6	31	67	8	4	.249	.307	.328	-.156	.280	.335	.370	-.100	10.7	126-3B 13
2003	SEA	AL	33	386	99	19	1	6	27	51	5	2	.258	.311	.363	-.115	.273	.327	.391	-.085	4.5	

Breakout: 17%   Improve: 42%   Collapse: 24%

It looked like an expensive but good risk, trading for Jeff—his Milwaukee lines showed plate discipline, and Coors does strange things to batters. If it paid off, and that patient hitter showed up in Safeco, it would have been worth it. Optimism affects us all. Instead, Cirillo had a season in line with his career road splits with Colorado. It can't be easy to go from the weirdest hitting environment ever to one of baseball's best pitcher's parks, but that's ugly. Cirillo's said that the adjustment would take a year, that he's going to need to put on a lot of muscle, and train. He's a good guy; he's going to work his ass off trying to adjust, but that may not be enough.

Perhaps Cirillo's poor performance at home was due in large part to having Creed played as two of his three entrance themes. Who can hit after hearing such awfulness? Next year, he should try a course of Blackalicious and Jurassic 5. The current crop of faux metal complaint rockers, these jokers like Three Doors Down and Creed and Puddle of Mud, are beyond awful. In five years they'll only be played in elevators, their half-catchy generic riffs and inoffensive lyrics tapping the toes of junior employees unfortunate enough to have imprinted on "alternative" rock of the late 90s and early aughts.

Ben Davis C Born: 10-Mar-77 Age: 26 Bats: B Throws: R

YEAR	TM	LG	AGE	AB	H	2B	3B	HR	BB	SO	SB	CS	AVG	OBP	SLG	MLVR	EQBA	EQOBP	EQSLG	EQMLVR	VORP	DEFENSE
2000	LVG	PCL	23	221	58	16	1	7	38	43	5	2	.262	.373	.439	.001	.224	.319	.370	-.169	3.9	59-C -1
2000	SDP	NL	23	130	29	6	0	3	14	35	1	1	.223	.299	.338	-.260	.235	.299	.356	-.220	.5	34-C -1
2001	SDP	NL	24	448	107	20	0	11	66	112	4	4	.239	.342	.357	-.098	.253	.353	.380	-.071	21.4	120-C 5
2002	SEA	AL	25	228	59	10	1	7	18	58	1	1	.259	.319	.404	-.026	.289	.347	.448	.040	16.0	62-C 5
2003	SEA	AL	26	263	63	13	1	7	28	58	2	1	.240	.317	.380	-.094	.254	.334	.409	-.062	7.4	

Breakout: 13%   Improve: 47%   Collapse: 31%

Davis is dogged by word that pitchers don't like working with him, and that his work ethic sucks. However, he's better defensively than Wilson, his game-calling seems fine, so if he's goofing off with women or backgammon, it's not anything that affects his performance. Still, he's 26, and if this is as good as he gets, he's not a long-term solution at the position.

Greg Dobbs 3B Born: 02-Jul-78 Age: 25 Bats: L Throws: R

YEAR	TM	LG	AGE	AB	H	2B	3B	HR	BB	SO	SB	CS	AVG	OBP	SLG	MLVR	EQBA	EQOBP	EQSLG	EQMLVR	VORP	DEFENSE
2001	EVE	NWN	23	249	80	17	2	6	30	39	5	3	.321	.399	.478	.284	.230	.288	.344	-.261	-10.5	48-1B -12
2002	WIS	MDW	24	320	88	16	2	10	31	50	13	3	.275	.341	.431	.138	.215	.265	.342	-.318	-11.3	74-3B 1
2002	SAN	TXS	24	96	35	2	0	5	9	17	1	3	.365	.425	.542	.482	.313	.362	.475	.128	5.2	24-RF -2
2003	SEA	AL	25	166	40	8	1	4	13	32	3	2	.239	.297	.379	-.129	.253	.313	.409	-.101	-.3	

Breakout: 46%   Improve: 69%   Collapse: 19%

Sort of considered a power prospect after being a slugger at Oklahoma in college career, Dobbs is old enough that he'll have to move quickly to have any kind of career. As is, he hasn't been a dominant enough hitter to really justify his rep. Although error-prone at third, he's been able to handle the position well enough. If he can't play third, his hitting credentials won't carry him.

Michael Garciaparra   SS   Born: 02-Apr-83   Age: 20   Bats: R   Throws: R

YEAR	TM	LG	AGE	AB	H	2B	3B	HR	BB	SO	SB	CS	AVG	OBP	SLG	MLVR	EQBA	EQOBP	EQSLG	EQMLVR	VORP	DEFENSE
2002	EVE	NWN	19	31	5	2	0	0	4	15	0	1	.161	.257	.226	-.275	.125	.200	.188	-.700	-4.6	

A sandwich pick in the first round, the younger Garciaparra hit .275/.388/.383 in rookie ball, which is a weird line taken against his brother's. Promoted to Everett to help them out in their playoff hunt, he looks fine in the field for his age and level, but hitting, there's no power, no patience, he's hacking, and there's no plan there. He's really too young to pass judgment, so there's plenty of time.

Charles Gipson   UT   Born: 16-Dec-72   Age: 30   Bats: R   Throws: R

YEAR	TM	LG	AGE	AB	H	2B	3B	HR	BB	SO	SB	CS	AVG	OBP	SLG	MLVR	EQBA	EQOBP	EQSLG	EQMLVR	VORP	DEFENSE			
2000	TAC	PCL	27	214	53	6	6	1	31	38	16	7	.248	.351	.346	-.137	.223	.310	.312	-.266	-4.9	40-CF	1	16-3B	6
2001	SEA	AL	28	64	14	2	2	0	4	20	1	1	.219	.286	.313	-.258	.234	.305	.344	-.225	-2.2	22-LF	-1		
2002	SEA	AL	29	72	17	5	2	0	9	14	4	0	.236	.329	.361	-.078	.260	.356	.397	-.038	1.0	35-LF	-3		
2003	*SEA*	*AL*	*30*	*101*	*23*	*4*	*1*	*1*	*11*	*22*	*3*	*2*	*.231*	*.311*	*.321*	*-.183*	*.245*	*.327*	*.346*	*-.163*	*-3.0*				

Breakout: 14%   Improve: 40%   Collapse: 34%

Gipson was one of the many bad left-field options the Mariners tried this year. On fly balls, Gipson would tear off in a random direction, correct himself after about ten steps and rely on speed to get him there in time. This resulted in a lot of bizarre plays where, headed back late on a ball, Gipson would go too far left, then right, and the ball would drop in front of him to hit the wall to be scored as a double. His fielding is a lot like his base-stealing: all tools and not a lot of experience. Gipson was cheap and somewhat useful in indulging Piniella's in-game tactics, but the roster spot will be better spent on someone who actually has something tangible to offer.

Carlos Guillen   SS   Born: 30-Sep-75   Age: 27   Bats: B   Throws: R

YEAR	TM	LG	AGE	AB	H	2B	3B	HR	BB	SO	SB	CS	AVG	OBP	SLG	MLVR	EQBA	EQOBP	EQSLG	EQMLVR	VORP	DEFENSE			
2000	TAC	PCL	24	87	26	4	1	2	12	17	4	1	.299	.390	.437	.111	.276	.355	.391	-.036	3.5	13-3B	-1		
2000	SEA	AL	24	288	74	15	2	7	28	53	1	3	.257	.327	.396	-.113	.272	.335	.418	-.038	10.8	68-3B	-10	17-SS	-3
2001	SEA	AL	25	456	118	21	4	5	53	89	4	1	.259	.337	.355	-.079	.280	.359	.387	-.031	22.1	122-SS	9		
2002	SEA	AL	26	475	124	24	6	9	46	91	4	5	.261	.328	.394	-.021	.290	.355	.439	.043	32.2	125-SS	-16		
2003	*SEA*	*AL*	*27*	*425*	*107*	*21*	*3*	*8*	*44*	*79*	*5*	*3*	*.253*	*.326*	*.371*	*-.081*	*.268*	*.343*	*.400*	*-.048*	*12.3*				

Breakout: 10%   Improve: 37%   Collapse: 21%

At the start of the season, it looked like Guillen was breaking out. It didn't happen, as he sputtered and lost altitude fast as the season wore on. It is possible that last year's bout with tuberculosis wore him down quickly, and that ties into his drinking, which resulted in a DUI arrest. Certain TB medications have strange effects on the liver, and if Guillen's out drinking heavily, as it would seem he is, he could well have done himself some permanent damage. That doesn't explain his awful second half necessarily, but it's worth paying attention to.

Guillen's errors also went up, which is hard to do considering the Safeco scorer is as stingy with errors as Carl Pohlad with nickels. Guillen's reasonably cheap and average at his position, which offers the team flexibility in throwing money elsewhere.

Kenny Kelly   OF   Born: 26-Jan-79   Age: 24   Bats: R   Throws: R

YEAR	TM	LG	AGE	AB	H	2B	3B	HR	BB	SO	SB	CS	AVG	OBP	SLG	MLVR	EQBA	EQOBP	EQSLG	EQMLVR	VORP	DEFENSE	
2000	ORL	SOU	21	489	123	17	8	3	59	119	31	21	.252	.339	.337	-.030	.225	.291	.306	-.311	-18.1	122-CF	-5
2001	SAN	TXS	22	478	125	20	5	11	45	111	18	12	.262	.329	.393	.005	.230	.286	.346	-.262	-10.4	115-CF	-9
2002	TAC	PCL	23	391	97	13	10	11	26	93	11	3	.248	.298	.417	-.079	.226	.271	.382	-.244	-17.6	118-RF	-8
2003	*SEA*	*AL*	*24*	*161*	*37*	*7*	*1*	*4*	*12*	*38*	*3*	*3*	*.232*	*.290*	*.359*	*-.169*	*.246*	*.306*	*.387*	*-.146*	*-4.5*		

Breakout: 41%   Improve: 70%   Collapse: 16%

Swings more often then Rebecca Romijn-Stamos, but doesn't score nearly as often. Kelly is certainly a gifted athlete, but he may not become a baseball player. A truly mercenary GM might have swapped him after last year's solid AFL campaign, when there was debate over whether his promise was finally developing into performance. There's a good reason not to move him—pure tools guys with baseball skills can be invincible—but Kelly removed all doubt about what he was this year, when his at-bats were ugly piled on ugly.

Jose Lopez   SS   Born: 24-Nov-83   Age: 19   Bats: R   Throws: R

YEAR	TM	LG	AGE	AB	H	2B	3B	HR	BB	SO	SB	CS	AVG	OBP	SLG	MLVR	EQBA	EQOBP	EQSLG	EQMLVR	VORP	DEFENSE
2001	EVE	NWN	17	289	74	15	0	2	13	44	13	6	.256	.311	.329	-.078	.189	.223	.244	-.553	-23.2	61-SS 7
2002	SBR	CLF	18	522	169	39	5	8	27	45	31	13	.324	.363	.464	.206	.262	.289	.373	-.196	2.8	116-SS -18
2003	*SEA*	*AL*	*19*	*245*	*62*	*12*	*2*	*5*	*12*	*30*	*6*	*3*	*.251*	*.292*	*.382*	*-.126*	*.266*	*.308*	*.412*	*-.097*	*4.1*	

Breakout: 70%   Improve: 80%   Collapse: 7%

Assuming that he's really 19—a very big if—Lopez could grow into an improvement on Guillen. Even if he isn't the age he claims, he could grow up to be about as good as the Alex Gonzalezes. The major question is how much air will come out of his numbers when he moves out of the California League and into Double-A. If he makes that jump, he'll have a shot at the big league job by the end of 2004.

Mark McLemore   UT   Born: 04-Oct-64   Age: 38   Bats: B   Throws: R

YEAR	TM	LG	AGE	AB	H	2B	3B	HR	BB	SO	SB	CS	AVG	OBP	SLG	MLVR	EQBA	EQOBP	EQSLG	EQMLVR	VORP	DEFENSE	
2000	SEA	AL	35	481	118	23	1	3	81	78	30	14	.245	.355	.316	-.177	.257	.360	.333	-.118	12.3	123-2B 0	11-LF 0
2001	SEA	AL	36	409	117	16	9	5	69	84	39	7	.286	.389	.406	.102	.318	.418	.455	.201	32.2	38-LF 1	28-3B -2
2002	SEA	AL	37	337	91	17	2	7	61	63	18	10	.270	.383	.395	.086	.310	.418	.452	.190	26.3	77-LF 0	
2003	*SEA*	*AL*	*38*	*258*	*65*	*11*	*2*	*4*	*38*	*48*	*14*	*3*	*.254*	*.351*	*.353*	*-.061*	*.269*	*.370*	*.380*	*-.026*	*5.1*		

Breakout: 1%   Improve: 43%   Collapse: 33%

McLemore's defense in left wasn't spectacular. He's not the fastest to the ball, and he doesn't have the best arm, but at least he heads in the right direction. Despite being a switch-hitter, Piniella went to great lengths to keep him from getting many plate appearances against lefties. Unless the Mariners trade an outfielder, McLemore will be paid $3 million to be a super-utility player again, although Melvin may not take quite the shine to him that Piniella did.

Edgar Martinez   DH   Born: 02-Jan-63   Age: 40   Bats: R   Throws: R

YEAR	TM	LG	AGE	AB	H	2B	3B	HR	BB	SO	SB	CS	AVG	OBP	SLG	MLVR	EQBA	EQOBP	EQSLG	EQMLVR	VORP	DEFENSE
2000	SEA	AL	37	556	180	31	0	37	96	95	3	0	.324	.428	.579	.393	.340	.437	.611	.470	88.8	
2001	SEA	AL	38	470	144	40	1	23	93	90	4	1	.306	.430	.543	.366	.335	.453	.596	.467	78.8	
2002	SEA	AL	39	328	91	23	0	15	67	69	1	1	.277	.409	.485	.251	.310	.435	.548	.347	45.2	
2003	*SEA*	*AL*	*40*	*353*	*99*	*23*	*1*	*17*	*65*	*69*	*2*	*0*	*.280*	*.393*	*.493*	*.198*	*.296*	*.414*	*.531*	*.262*	*30.8*	

Breakout: 8%   Improve: 50%   Collapse: 27%

Age hasn't gotten to Edgar yet, but it's got fantastic box seats to the show. Edgar had to have a ruptured tendon removed this year, and recovery was slow and featured a setback when he twisted getting away from a pitch. That encouraged teams to come in on him, but his numbers after he came back were the same consistent Edgar we know and love. His injury also meant he didn't reach some career marks like 2000 hits or 300 home runs, that would have helped him make his Hall of Fame case if he had decided to retire after 2002.

Jose Offerman   Elsewhere   Born: 08-Nov-68   Age: 34   Bats: B   Throws: R

YEAR	TM	LG	AGE	AB	H	2B	3B	HR	BB	SO	SB	CS	AVG	OBP	SLG	MLVR	EQBA	EQOBP	EQSLG	EQMLVR	VORP	DEFENSE	
2000	BOS	AL	31	451	115	14	3	9	70	70	0	8	.255	.356	.359	-.122	.262	.357	.370	-.071	17.0	72-2B -1	31-1B 2
2001	BOS	AL	32	524	140	23	3	9	61	97	5	2	.267	.345	.374	-.049	.283	.362	.399	-.006	28.9	86-2B -2	38-1B 5
2002	BOS	AL	33	237	55	10	0	4	33	29	8	5	.232	.328	.325	-.148	.255	.350	.360	-.103	-.4	36-1B 8	
2002	SEA	AL	33	47	11	2	1	1	4	9	1	1	.234	.294	.383	-.115	.271	.327	.438	-.025	1.3		
2003	*SEA*	*AL*	*34*	*233*	*56*	*10*	*1*	*4*	*29*	*38*	*4*	*2*	*.242*	*.326*	*.343*	*-.123*	*.256*	*.344*	*.370*	*-.095*	*-1.4*		

Breakout: 29%   Improve: 58%   Collapse: 23%

Piniella complained about wanting a bat on his bench, and like an evil genie, Gillick granted his wish. Unfortunately, Piniella had never specified what kind of bat he wanted. Offerman hadn't hit in years, and because they dealt for a player who was otherwise bound for waivers, they had to pay him more than the minimum. Piniella responded by using Offerman to pinch-hit in crucial game situations, where he predictably failed, making Gillick look bad while Piniella got to shrug and say "hey, what am I going to do? I'm not up there swinging the bat. I'm just using the tools at hand." There are so many cheap, effective first-basemen who can hit better it will be a shock if Offerman is on an Opening Day roster or a 40-man roster when the season starts.

John Olerud — 1B — Born: 05-Aug-68 — Age: 34 — Bats: L — Throws: L

YEAR	TM	LG	AGE	AB	H	2B	3B	HR	BB	SO	SB	CS	AVG	OBP	SLG	MLVR	EQBA	EQOBP	EQSLG	EQMLVR	VORP	DEFENSE
2000	SEA	AL	31	565	161	45	0	14	102	96	0	2	.285	.398	.439	.105	.298	.405	.464	.173	40.6	152-1B 23
2001	SEA	AL	32	572	173	32	1	21	94	70	3	1	.302	.405	.472	.231	.329	.429	.517	.316	63.8	150-1B -1
2002	SEA	AL	33	553	166	39	0	22	98	66	0	0	.300	.410	.490	.280	.333	.438	.549	.378	73.5	146-1B 1
2003	SEA	AL	34	473	133	28	0	18	71	63	0	0	.282	.374	.455	.124	.299	.394	.491	.181	29.2	

Breakout: 2%   Improve: 40%   Collapse: 17%

Olerud has one of the prettiest swings in baseball. It's so effortless it doesn't attract attention. Olerud seems to swing through pitches, even the ones he drives 400 feet over a fence in dead-center field. It's a measure of his power stroke that Olerud, indisputably one of the slowest men in baseball, still manages to hit so many doubles every year. Like Cameron, Olerud is a huge guesser. He's willing to watch a pitch he didn't see coming all the way in for a strike so he can get another chance at it. Combined with his calm manner and easy swing, Olerud seems to be one of the most passive hitters in baseball, and idiots in the stands routinely yell for him to take the bat off his shoulders. Watch and learn: when the bat comes off the shoulder, the ball's pretty likely to go three hundred feet, and if you've been good, it'll keep going. You want to see your first baseman whiff at everything? Move to Pittsburgh.

Antonio Perez — 2B/SS — Born: 26-Jan-80 — Age: 23 — Bats: R — Throws: R

YEAR	TM	LG	AGE	AB	H	2B	3B	HR	BB	SO	SB	CS	AVG	OBP	SLG	MLVR	EQBA	EQOBP	EQSLG	EQMLVR	VORP	DEFENSE
2000	LNC	CLF	20	395	109	36	6	17	58	99	28	16	.276	.380	.527	.216	.202	.275	.384	-.249	-3.0	93-SS 1
2002	SAN	TXS	22	240	62	8	2	2	11	64	15	9	.258	.318	.333	-.064	.238	.277	.311	-.325	-6.6	58-2B -9
2003	TBY	AL	23	155	37	8	1	4	10	39	4	4	.238	.292	.373	-.144	.244	.300	.389	-.155	-0.4	

Last year, Perez got himself demoted from future superstar to someone who would be a good-to-very-good player. This year, the descent continued. Perez's star has fallen so far that he was a throw-in with Lou Piniella to the Devil Rays so that the Mariners could acquire Randy Winn. If there's anywhere Perez can regain his lost shine, it's Tampa Bay, where he'll get the high-quality coaching he needs to turn his still-evident physical abilities into . . . bwahahahahaha. I'm sorry, I couldn't keep a straight face. He's screwed.

Desi Relaford — INF — Born: 16-Sep-73 — Age: 29 — Bats: B — Throws: R

YEAR	TM	LG	AGE	AB	H	2B	3B	HR	BB	SO	SB	CS	AVG	OBP	SLG	MLVR	EQBA	EQOBP	EQSLG	EQMLVR	VORP	DEFENSE	
2000	PHI	NL	26	253	56	12	3	3	48	45	5	0	.221	.365	.328	-.162	.224	.355	.333	-.147	5.3	80-SS -13	
2000	SDP	NL	26	157	32	2	0	2	27	26	8	0	.204	.332	.255	-.318	.219	.334	.269	-.276	-2.6	40-SS 4	
2001	NYM	NL	27	301	91	27	0	8	27	65	13	5	.302	.369	.472	.157	.315	.378	.487	.175	33.2	44-2B -9	17-SS -1
2002	SEA	AL	28	329	88	13	2	6	33	51	10	3	.267	.345	.374	-.012	.299	.372	.421	.056	23.5	34-SS -1	26-3B -1
2003	KCR	AL	29	298	77	16	2	7	32	48	9	3	.260	.337	.393	-.031	.256	.337	.389	-.083	4.0		

Breakout: 3%   Improve: 16%   Collapse: 43%

Does anyone in baseball have cooler sideburns than Desi Relaford? Relaford got spot starts throughout the year, and Piniella eventually used him to replace Cirillo at third during September, another opportunity to tweak a high-level Gillick mistake. Relaford offers an average bat and glove in part-time duty, which makes him a strange bench player, since he's not strong as a pinch hitter or as a defensive replacement. Now a Royal, he may be their starting shortstop.

Ruben Sierra — DH — Born: 06-Oct-65 — Age: 37 — Bats: B — Throws: R

YEAR	TM	LG	AGE	AB	H	2B	3B	HR	BB	SO	SB	CS	AVG	OBP	SLG	MLVR	EQBA	EQOBP	EQSLG	EQMLVR	VORP	DEFENSE
2000	OKL	PCL	34	439	143	26	3	18	55	63	5	2	.326	.401	.522	.275	.291	.354	.465	.079	19.0	78-LF -4
2000	TEX	AL	34	60	14	0	0	1	4	9	1	0	.233	.281	.283	-.405	.233	.270	.300	-.357	-3.3	
2001	TEX	AL	35	344	100	22	1	23	19	52	2	0	.291	.328	.561	.184	.302	.341	.584	.240	26.5	28-RF -4
2002	SEA	AL	36	419	113	23	0	13	31	66	4	0	.270	.320	.418	.005	.298	.349	.462	.072	17.1	43-LF 0
2003	SEA	AL	37	298	76	15	1	10	23	49	3	1	.254	.307	.406	-.067	.269	.324	.438	-.031	.6	

Breakout: 8%   Improve: 39%   Collapse: 23%

Sierra started the season on fire, and did particularly well hitting while Edgar was out. Other than that, he pretty much sucked. He was also tough to watch in the field: he takes a step in on every fly ball before plodding to catch it on the bounce. I'm not saying you have to be a quality defender in left field, but seriously, until you know where you're running to, don't go anywhere. Better a correct late jump than moving in the wrong direction as the ball is hit.

Chris Snelling — LF — Born: 03-Dec-81 — Age: 21 — Bats: L — Throws: L

YEAR	TM	LG	AGE	AB	H	2B	3B	HR	BB	SO	SB	CS	AVG	OBP	SLG	MLVR	EQBA	EQOBP	EQSLG	EQMLVR	VORP		DEFENSE
2000	WIS	MDW	18	259	79	9	5	9	34	34	7	4	.305	.398	.483	.295	.235	.297	.377	-.195	-1.1		65-CF -8
2001	SBR	CLF	19	450	151	29	10	7	45	63	12	5	.336	.421	.491	.341	.266	.329	.389	-.095	-.8		103-LF -6
2002	SAN	TXS	20	89	29	9	2	1	12	11	5	1	.326	.429	.506	.393	.293	.376	.457	.108	4.8		23-OF 0
2002	SEA	AL	20	27	4	0	0	1	2	4	0	0	.148	.207	.259	-.491	.185	.241	.333	-.396	-1.8		
2003	SEA	AL	21	324	80	18	2	7	29	49	6	2	.248	.316	.382	-.087	.263	.333	.412	-.055	-.3		

Breakout: 7%   Improve: 37%   Collapse: 29%

When Chris Snelling was called up, I ordered a Snelling Mariners jersey. I had to have it custom-made, and by the time it turned up on my doorstop, Snelling had blown out his ACL trying to hold up rounding third after being waved in from second, waved in, waved in . . . STOP! The next two words third base coach Dave Meyers should have heard after Snelling went down were "you're fired." Snelling runs all-out, head down, and between Meyers's hesitation and Snelling's failure to keep his eye out if the signal changed, it cost him a year. Snelling is already injury prone, which may be a result of his rabid, Dykstra-esque style of play.

There's some dispute about what Snelling will become. Will his 5′10″ body develop improved power, or are his raw lines in the minors what we should expect: a .290/.350/.450 hitter with doubles power. He's a preternatural prospect, who has so far utterly defied those who say he is too small, or too slow, or not projectable enough. If Snelling's body doesn't come apart at the seams, the least valuable thing he'll become is a good outfielder. What he could become is something exciting and priceless.

Jamal Strong — CF — Born: 05-Aug-78 — Age: 24 — Bats: R — Throws: R

YEAR	TM	LG	AGE	AB	H	2B	3B	HR	BB	SO	SB	CS	AVG	OBP	SLG	MLVR	EQBA	EQOBP	EQSLG	EQMLVR	VORP		DEFENSE
2000	EVE	NWN	21	296	93	7	3	1	52	29	60	14	.314	.423	.368	.182	.244	.319	.287	-.270	-7.2		74-CF -3
2001	WIS	MDW	22	184	65	12	1	0	40	27	35	4	.353	.480	.429	.365	.269	.374	.326	-.093	4.6		46-CF -5
2001	SBR	CLF	22	331	103	11	2	0	51	60	47	8	.311	.411	.356	.124	.261	.339	.299	-.204	-2.2		80-CF -5
2002	SAN	TXS	23	503	140	16	5	1	62	87	46	16	.278	.369	.336	.036	.256	.328	.310	-.214	-4.7		123-CF -4
2003	SEA	AL	24	159	38	7	1	1	15	28	6	3	.238	.307	.316	-.192	.252	.324	.341	-.172	-1.8		

Breakout: 21%   Improve: 45%   Collapse: 25%

It looked as if the increased competition at Double-A had broken Strong, as he opened the season doing nothing right. At the half he looked like he might be no more, that he'd be unable to slap singles and draw walks against better pitching. But then Strong adapted, putting up huge numbers as the season went on to finish with a respectable season line. That in-season improvement is something to watch, and Strong could be for real. His defense in center is still weak, though, and he's not a good enough hitter to play the corners. What's that make him? A Chad Curtis that you'd invite to a dinner party?

Ichiro Suzuki — RF — Born: 22-Oct-73 — Age: 29 — Bats: L — Throws: R

YEAR	TM	LG	AGE	AB	H	2B	3B	HR	BB	SO	SB	CS	AVG	OBP	SLG	MLVR	EQBA	EQOBP	EQSLG	EQMLVR	VORP		DEFENSE
2000	ORX	JPL	26	395	153	22	1	12	54	36	21	1	.387	.466	.539	.496	.371	.435	.523	.381	52.7		
2001	SEA	AL	27	692	242	34	8	8	30	53	56	14	.350	.384	.457	.219	.381	.415	.499	.326	67.5		138-RF 9
2002	SEA	AL	28	647	208	27	8	8	68	62	31	15	.321	.390	.425	.179	.364	.429	.483	.305	64.8		140-RF 3
2003	SEA	AL	29	584	178	31	5	8	56	50	22	4	.306	.368	.419	.087	.324	.388	.451	.142	27.2		

Breakout: 0%   Improve: 31%   Collapse: 26%

Ichiro ran into a wall late in the season and had to get stitches in his knee. It affected his run-and-dash style, and he didn't beat out as many hits or steal as much. Don't believe the annual *Sports Illustrated* "pitchers will catch up to him" predictions: he'll be healthy and he'll have another good season. One of the uglier things baseball has ignored is the racism that's followed Ichiro around. In Oakland, for instance, fans shout Charlie Chan-style imitations, confusing their Chinese and Japanese racial taunts, asking him to do their laundry. "Ichiro Number One Strikeout Big Time!" I'm shocked that displays of racism go unchallenged in open society.

Luis Ugueto PR Born: 15-Feb-79 Age: 24 Bats: B Throws: R

YEAR	TM	LG	AGE	AB	H	2B	3B	HR	BB	SO	SB	CS	AVG	OBP	SLG	MLVR	EQBA	EQOBP	EQSLG	EQMLVR	VORP	DEFENSE			
2000	KNE	MDW	21	393	92	13	2	1	28	83	12	14	.234	.293	.285	-.163	.189	.222	.233	-.571	-36.1	113-SS	-2		
2001	BRV	FSL	22	392	103	12	5	3	38	96	22	7	.263	.331	.342	-.002	.230	.278	.301	-.341	-12.8	107-SS	0	14-2B	0
2002	TAC	PCL	23	51	13	1	0	0	3	13	2	1	.255	.296	.275	-.279	.235	.278	.235	-.432	-2.9	12-SS	3		
2002	SEA	AL	23	23	5	0	0	1	2	8	8	4	.217	.280	.348	-.199	.217	.280	.348	-.279	-.8				
2003	SEA	AL	24	59	13	2	0	1	4	14	4	1	.217	.268	.291	-.304	.230	.282	.314	-.298	-2.2				

Breakout: 50%   Improve: 63%   Collapse: 24%

A bizarre Rule 5 pickup by Pat Gillick, Ugueto wasn't a player Lou wanted, was totally redundant given the presence of no-hit Charles Gipson, and a source of constant friction between the GM and manager. After Ugueto spent the required amount of time for Rule 5 on the major league roster, he promptly got Rule 5 disease ("aggravated left index finger hangnail"), was thrown on the DL, went to the minors for a leisurely rehab where he exhibited no signs of being injured, and was called back up when rosters expanded. MLB roster transactions: they're fraudtastic!

Ugueto only started three games this year and almost scored more times (19) than he had at-bats (23), a product of being used frequently in late innings as pinch legs for Martinez or Olerud. We have no idea why Gillick thought Ugueto was worth drafting: while Ugueto can play some defense, he would have to be able to play two infield positions simultaneously to justify a spot on the major league roster. He'll return to the minor leagues this year, where his career will stall.

Dan Wilson C Born: 25-Mar-69 Age: 34 Bats: R Throws: R

YEAR	TM	LG	AGE	AB	H	2B	3B	HR	BB	SO	SB	CS	AVG	OBP	SLG	MLVR	EQBA	EQOBP	EQSLG	EQMLVR	VORP	DEFENSE	
2000	SEA	AL	31	268	63	12	0	5	22	51	1	2	.235	.293	.336	-.282	.250	.300	.362	-.200	2.3	75-C	2
2001	SEA	AL	32	377	100	20	1	10	20	69	3	2	.265	.306	.403	-.067	.287	.328	.437	-.011	20.6	103-C	4
2002	SEA	AL	33	359	106	16	1	6	18	81	1	0	.295	.332	.396	.016	.326	.362	.438	.087	28.6	99-C	1
2003	SEA	AL	34	261	66	12	1	6	15	54	2	1	.252	.296	.378	-.124	.267	.312	.407	-.095	4.7		

Breakout: 15%   Improve: 36%   Collapse: 30%

Wilson had his best offensive season in years during his walk year, but it's still all show: a hollow near-.300 batting average without walks or power. He's a great guy and all, but two more years on his contract will mean the Mariners have held on five years too long even before they set him up with his next contract. His contracts are partly a reflection of his popularity in Seattle, where he's well known for his good nature and selfless work with local charities. There are worse things to reward.

PITCHERS

Paul Abbott Born: 15-SEP-67 Age: 35 Bats: R Throws: R

YEAR	TM	LG	AGE	G	GS	IP	H	BB	SO	HR	ERA	EQERA	EQH9	EQBB9	EQSO9	EQHR9	PERA	VORP	STF
2000	SEA	AL	32	35	27	179.0	164	80	100	23	4.22	4.08	8.2	3.3	4.9	1.0	3.90	28.1	1
2001	SEA	AL	33	28	27	163.0	145	87	118	21	4.25	4.83	8.7	4.6	6.3	1.1	4.50	12.2	5
2002	SEA	AL	34	7	5	26.3	40	20	22	5	11.98	10.45	14.0	6.4	7.3	1.6	9.08	-14.5	-16

You read it here last year, and indeed, this season Abbott fessed up to having fought through a groin strain last year, and after continued ineffectiveness, it turned out he had a torn labrum all along. A torn labrum is a hard injury to come back from anyway. He could be effective if he comes back at full strength, but that could be as far away as next year, and he'll be 36 then. The Mariners released him.

Ryan Anderson Born: 12-Jul-79 Age: 23 Bats: L Throws: L

YEAR	TM	LG	AGE	G	GS	IP	H	BB	SO	HR	ERA	EQERA	EQH9	EQBB9	EQSO9	EQHR9	PERA	VORP	STF
2000	TAC	PCL	20	20	20	104.0	83	55	146	8	3.98	4.28	7.9	4.7	10.1	0.9	4.03	14.2	40

Another torn labrum victim, Anderson is making throws on flat ground at press time. Yeah, he was once a terrifying super-prospect, but injuries can turn the best pitching prospects into shells of their former potential. A torn labrum is not the career death sentence it once was, but no one can say what Anderson will become now. John Rauch's recovery gives us hope Anderson can come back to throw his eye-popping stuff in the majors.

James Baldwin | Born: 15-Jul-71 | Age: 31 | Bats: R | Throws: R

YEAR	TM	LG	AGE	G	GS	IP	H	BB	SO	HR	ERA	EQERA	EQH9	EQBB9	EQSO9	EQHR9	PERA	VORP	STF
2000	CWS	AL	28	29	28	178.0	185	59	116	34	4.65	4.27	8.7	2.4	5.7	1.4	4.39	24.4	8
2001	CWS	AL	29	17	16	95.7	109	38	42	15	4.61	5.13	10.2	3.4	3.7	1.3	5.24	4.0	-9
2001	LAD	NL	29	12	12	79.3	82	25	53	10	4.20	4.55	9.8	2.7	5.2	1.1	4.83	8.4	5
2002	SEA	AL	30	30	23	150.0	179	49	88	26	5.28	5.81	11.3	2.8	5.2	1.5	5.89	-5.3	-3
2003	SEA	AL	31	26	20	126.0	138	41	73	19	4.80	5.15	10.0	2.7	4.9	1.3	5.09	9.1	-2

Breakout: 10%   Improve: 47%   Collapse: 25%

Baldwin's a weird guy to watch. Despite his energy-saving zombie walk to and from the mound, he works quickly, he sprints to cover first on ground balls, and is an alert, athletic pitcher. He was a disaster in the rotation this year. He allowed at least a run an inning in six of his 23 starts, and only had four really good starts all year, and two of those came against Detroit and Tampa Bay. The Mariners paid $500,000 to avoid bringing him back for $4 million. Baldwin will be a gamble signing for some team not headed anywhere. If he can show the form of 1999–2000, or even the Dodgers portion of 2001, he'll have trade value to contenders with rotation problems. Still, there are better gambles out there, like three-card monte, or urgent e-mail requests for financial help from government officials in Nigeria.

Travis Blackley | Age: 20 | Throws: L

YEAR	TM	LG	AGE	G	GS	IP	H	BB	SO	HR	ERA	EQERA	EQH9	EQBB9	EQSO9	EQHR9	PERA	VORP	STF
2001	EVE	NWN	18	14	14	78.7	60	29	90	7	3.32	4.94	10.2	5.1	5.7	2.2	4.91	4.9	3
2002	SBR	CLF	19	21	20	121.3	102	44	152	11	3.49	4.89	10.4	4.2	6.7	1.6	4.83	8.3	16

Blackley's another of these ass-kicking Australian kids that the Mariners collect. He jumped from short-season Everett to high-A ball, where he was the youngest starter in the California league. His curveball is jaw-droppingly good, easily major league material, but his fastball only reaches the high 80s, and his changeup needs to come along. He's not a power pitcher yet, but the power may come; his delivery is still very raw, and if he gets that ironed out, he'll be a gem.

Norm Charlton | Born: 06-Jan-63 | Age: 40 | Bats: B | Throws: L

YEAR	TM	LG	AGE	G	GS	IP	H	BB	SO	HR	ERA	EQERA	EQH9	EQBB9	EQSO9	EQHR9	PERA	VORP	STF
2001	SEA	AL	38	44	0	47.7	36	11	48	4	3.02	3.45	7.4	2.0	8.7	0.7	2.70	10.2	19

Norm pushed his rehab aggressively, and suffered a series of setbacks that prevented him from pitching this season. Every competitive athlete wants to come back sooner than expected, but like the pitch-through-pain instinct, that's ultimately counterproductive. Healing takes time and no matter how badly a player wants to come back, willpower alone doesn't repair tissue. Charlton still wants to pitch and is still left-handed. He'll be bringing his tobacco-chewing, crotch-grabbing, gas-throwing pitching bonanza back to Seattle for one more try. Hide the children.

Doug Creek | Born: 01-Mar-69 | Age: 34 | Bats: L | Throws: L

YEAR	TM	LG	AGE	G	GS	IP	H	BB	SO	HR	ERA	EQERA	EQH9	EQBB9	EQSO9	EQHR9	PERA	VORP	STF
2000	TBY	AL	31	45	0	60.7	49	39	73	10	4.60	4.01	6.6	4.6	10.2	1.2	3.91	9.2	17
2001	TBY	AL	32	66	0	62.7	51	49	66	7	4.31	4.26	6.7	6.4	8.7	0.9	4.43	7.8	1
2002	TBY	AL	33	29	0	37.3	39	21	37	8	6.27	5.73	9.0	4.6	8.5	1.7	5.67	-1.5	-1
2002	SEA	AL	33	23	0	18.3	18	14	19	2	4.92	5.27	9.0	6.3	9.0	0.9	5.61	0.2	0
2003	TOR	AL	34	38	2	50.3	50	30	48	8	4.65	4.50	8.7	4.9	8.3	1.2	5.02	8.1	2

Breakout: 19%   Improve: 39%   Collapse: 32%

This is what having Norm Charlton out did to the Mariners. Gillick felt he had to get a left-handed reliever, so he picked up Creek from the Devil Rays for case after they had designated him for assignment. Piniella seemed to regard Creek as a one-inning mop-up man, possibly to make Gillick look bad, leaving him in regardless of who he'd face, including right-handers who tenderized him to the tune of a .277/.409/.492 line (lefties hit only .239/.333/.432). Now signed with the Blue Jays as a free agent, Creek will almost certainly be used as a LOOGY and turned into shiny prospects in a trade later this season.

Ryan Franklin   Born: 05-Mar-73   Age: 30   Bats: R   Throws: R

YEAR	TM	LG	AGE	G	GS	IP	H	BB	SO	HR	ERA	EQERA	EQH9	EQBB9	EQSO9	EQHR9	PERA	VORP	STF
2000	TAC	PCL	27	31	22	164.0	147	35	142	28	3.90	4.55	9.3	1.9	6.4	2.0	4.31	17.1	8
2001	SEA	AL	28	38	0	78.3	76	24	60	13	3.56	4.45	9.5	2.7	6.7	1.4	4.49	8.1	1
2002	SEA	AL	29	41	12	118.7	117	22	65	14	4.02	4.35	9.4	1.6	4.9	1.0	3.95	14.5	0
2003	SEA	AL	30	34	11	84.0	90	20	52	13	4.20	4.51	9.8	2.0	5.2	1.3	4.56	13.0	-4

Breakout: 17%   Improve: 44%   Collapse: 26%

For the first time in his career, Franklin made enough money last year that he didn't have to bag groceries or something like that in the off-season, and was able to concentrate on conditioning. As a result, he showed up to camp throwing a couple of miles faster. Regular work seems to suit him; given a steady rotation spot he's an average pitcher, but flipped between the rotation and the pen, he was unsteady. He's currently penciled in for a back-end rotation spot next year.

Freddy Garcia   Born: 10-Jun-76   Age: 27   Bats: R   Throws: R

YEAR	TM	LG	AGE	G	GS	IP	H	BB	SO	HR	ERA	EQERA	EQH9	EQBB9	EQSO9	EQHR9	PERA	VORP	STF
2000	SEA	AL	24	21	20	124.3	112	64	79	16	3.91	4.14	8.0	3.8	5.6	1.0	4.02	18.8	9
2001	SEA	AL	25	34	34	238.7	199	69	163	16	3.05	3.61	8.3	2.5	6.0	0.6	3.12	50.3	17
2002	SEA	AL	26	34	34	223.7	227	63	181	30	4.39	4.50	9.5	2.4	7.2	1.2	4.49	25.0	18
2003	SEA	AL	27	30	28	184.7	177	59	138	22	3.84	4.13	8.7	2.7	6.3	1.0	4.12	32.5	14

Breakout: 16%   Improve: 52%   Collapse: 12%

Garcia was helped greatly by the stellar Mariner defense of 2001, and its regression this year really tore him up. His head wasn't in games, he frequently got into feuds with umpires, and his famous game composure disappeared. This may have something to do with Freddy's postgame activities. Garcia was tangentially involved with the vile case of Darrell Russell drugging a woman so his friends could rape her while he videotaped it; Garcia was one of three men the woman said that she was dating at the same time, including Russell. Now whatever you want to say about the nature of relationships, that was probably a distraction.

John Halama   Born: 22-Feb-72   Age: 31   Bats: L   Throws: L

YEAR	TM	LG	AGE	G	GS	IP	H	BB	SO	HR	ERA	EQERA	EQH9	EQBB9	EQSO9	EQHR9	PERA	VORP	STF
2000	SEA	AL	28	30	30	166.7	206	56	87	19	5.07	5.28	11.1	2.5	4.6	0.9	5.04	4.2	0
2001	SEA	AL	29	31	17	110.3	132	26	50	18	4.73	6.03	11.8	2.1	4.0	1.4	5.47	-6.8	-12
2002	SEA	AL	30	31	10	101.0	112	33	70	9	3.56	4.44	10.5	2.8	6.2	0.8	4.79	11.4	4
2003	OAK	AL	31	27	14	86.0	99	28	52	10	4.71	4.76	10.3	2.7	5.1	1.0	4.80	10.1	-3

Breakout: 14%   Improve: 51%   Collapse: 27%

As a relief arm, Halama was far more effective than as a starter. His strikeouts were way up, while his other rates held steady. There are now two seasons of evidence supporting the Halama-as-ace-reliever-and-bad-starter theory, which is enough to start making decisions on. A full season of relief would make Halama look good enough to win a starting job, which would start this whole cycle over again. Halama seems to have the pitches for starting, but he's just not that good at it. For those of you are who fans of The Emperor's New Groove: when Halama comes in, turn to the guy next to you, clap your hands, and say "Yay, it's Halama again!" every time our boy comes in. Then look at your hands and go "oh."

Shigetoshi Hasegawa   Born: 01-Aug-68   Age: 34   Bats: R   Throws: R

YEAR	TM	LG	AGE	G	GS	IP	H	BB	SO	HR	ERA	EQERA	EQH9	EQBB9	EQSO9	EQHR9	PERA	VORP	STF
2000	ANA	AL	31	66	0	95.7	100	38	59	11	3.57	4.11	9.5	2.9	5.5	0.9	4.10	13.5	-5
2001	ANA	AL	32	46	0	55.7	52	20	41	5	4.04	4.13	8.7	3.1	6.3	0.7	3.62	7.7	0
2002	SEA	AL	33	53	0	70.3	60	30	39	4	3.20	3.53	8.1	3.7	4.9	0.5	3.59	14.5	-7
2003	SEA	AL	34	41	0	50.0	52	21	32	5	4.38	4.71	9.6	3.5	5.4	0.9	4.78	6.7	-10

Breakout: 13%   Improve: 47%   Collapse: 27%

Hasegawa sells his changeup better than almost any other pitcher in baseball. He seems to be reaching back for a little extra on his fastball, and you're bracing for it, and then it comes off of his hand and . . . nothing. Hasegawa started the season doing mop-up work; did so well at he started getting higher-leverage relief, an inning, two innings at a time, until a really bad August, when batters slapped him around for a .345/.429/.600 line, pushed him back on the depth charts. Hasegawa did okay by the team, but as many other teams have shown, you can assemble effective bullpens on the cheap. With Piniella gone, there's no need to stock the bullpen with expensive veterans for the sake of making the manager feel comfortable, so there was no need for the Mariners to bring Hasegawa back for a return engagement, which they've done anyway. Also, the "getting Shiggy with it" stuff was pretty annoying. For shame, Safeco music and scoreboard guys. For shame.

Jeff Heaverlo   Born: 13-Jan-78   Age: 25   Bats: R   Throws: R

YEAR	TM	LG	AGE	G	GS	IP	H	BB	SO	HR	ERA	EQERA	EQH9	EQBB9	EQSO9	EQHR9	PERA	VORP	STF
2000	LNC	CLF	22	27	27	155.7	170	52	159	18	4.22	5.94	13.2	3.4	5.9	2.2	6.05	-7.5	5
2000	TAC	PCL	22	2	2	13.0	14	6	4	2	4.85	5.56	11.1	4.2	2.3	1.8	6.19	-0.1	-17
2001	SAN	TXS	23	27	27	178.7	164	40	173	12	3.12	4.47	9.9	2.5	6.3	1.1	4.61	20.6	17

Another of the organization's torn labrums. Heaverlo had a good slider, a moving fastball that would run up past 90, and a developing change. This last year, needless to say, he didn't have anything. Like Anderson and Meche, Heaverlo's recovery will determine where he goes. I know, that's not the kind of insight you buy the book for, but what else am I going to tell you? Recoveries aren't scripted.

Rett Johnson   Born: 06-Jul-79   Age: 24   Bats: L   Throws: R

YEAR	TM	LG	AGE	G	GS	IP	H	BB	SO	HR	ERA	EQERA	EQH9	EQBB9	EQSO9	EQHR9	PERA	VORP	STF
2000	EVE	NWN	21	17	8	69.7	51	21	88	1	2.07	4.00	8.7	3.3	5.8	0.4	3.74	11.4	12
2001	WIS	MDW	22	16	16	99.3	92	30	96	4	2.27	4.82	11.6	4.0	5.5	0.9	5.23	7.6	11
2001	SBR	CLF	22	12	12	66.0	56	33	70	5	4.09	6.24	10.8	6.2	5.7	1.4	5.51	-5.4	2
2002	SBR	CLF	23	7	7	37.0	27	11	34	1	3.65	4.22	8.6	3.4	4.8	0.5	3.37	5.3	9
2002	SAN	TXS	23	21	21	117.0	107	53	104	5	3.62	6.02	10.9	5.0	6.3	0.9	5.34	-6.7	9

Johnson's command is improving, and he's got a good fastball that's already hitting the mid-90s, a nasty sinker that brutalizes hitters, and a power slider that's prime-time material. He needs to get the walks down, and his strikeouts will come up as his command becomes finer. Double-A was a test, and Johnson passed. He's officially a prospect as much as any pitcher is.

Justin Kaye   Born: 09-Jun-76   Age: 27   Bats: R   Throws: R

YEAR	TM	LG	AGE	G	GS	IP	H	BB	SO	HR	ERA	EQERA	EQH9	EQBB9	EQSO9	EQHR9	PERA	VORP	STF
2000	NHV	EAS	24	50	0	84.3	80	36	109	3	2.67	4.78	10.5	4.3	8.8	0.6	5.03	5.6	13
2001	TAC	PCL	25	56	0	77.0	51	46	107	5	2.92	3.73	6.9	6.5	9.3	0.7	3.67	14.1	10
2002	TAC	PCL	26	47	0	62.3	54	42	65	2	4.04	4.77	8.6	7.1	7.3	0.4	4.70	4.2	-7
2002	SEA	AL	26	3	0	3.0	6	1	3	0	12.00	10.18	18.1	2.7	8.5	0.2	8.83	-1.6	1

Kaye still has good stuff, with especially unreasonable movement on his pitches. He knew the clock was ticking on him, and took a minor league contract with Boston, who likely promised to give him a clean shot at a bullpen job. Hopefully now that Duquette is gone, the Sox won't give him the screwing they gave Mike Neill by sticking him in Pawtucket after promising big league opportunities.

Julio Mateo   Born: 02-Aug-77   Age: 25   Bats: R   Throws: R

YEAR	TM	LG	AGE	G	GS	IP	H	BB	SO	HR	ERA	EQERA	EQH9	EQBB9	EQSO9	EQHR9	PERA	VORP	STF
2000	WIS	MDW	22	36	1	68.7	63	23	73	12	4.19	7.01	14.4	4.0	6.5	4.5	6.92	-12.4	-16
2001	SBR	CLF	23	56	0	66.0	58	16	79	5	2.86	5.10	11.0	2.9	6.4	1.4	4.64	2.1	-2
2002	SAN	TXS	24	12	0	17.3	7	3	18	2	0.52	2.29	5.7	1.9	7.3	2.3	2.07	5.9	9
2002	TAC	PCL	24	20	0	31.0	39	7	23	2	4.06	5.11	12.6	2.4	5.2	0.8	5.76	0.9	-5
2002	SEA	AL	24	12	0	21.0	20	12	15	2	4.29	4.57	8.9	4.8	6.3	0.8	4.77	1.9	-2
2003	*SEA*	*AL*	*25*	*27*	*1*	*39.3*	*41*	*17*	*30*	*6*	*4.86*	*5.22*	*9.5*	*3.5*	*6.5*	*1.3*	*5.31*	*3.1*	*-6*

Breakout: 16%   *Improve: 48%*   *Collapse: 18%*

Mateo is not going to be a prospect until he starts getting some movement on his fastball. It's his bread-and-butter pitch, and regularly hits 94, but it also isn't striking a lot of batters out. I have also heard that having some off-speed stuff is good. Although Mateo is only 25, shouldn't he have developed one other pitch by now? When you've only got one pitch and it's not particularly good, that limits your ability to get major league hitters out. Mateo's audition was a patch; he came in during a difficult time for the M's bullpen. It's not that the team thought the added pressure would get his slider to break.

Gil Meche   Born: 08-Sep-78   Age: 24   Bats: R   Throws: R

YEAR	TM	LG	AGE	G	GS	IP	H	BB	SO	HR	ERA	EQERA	EQH9	EQBB9	EQSO9	EQHR9	PERA	VORP	STF
2000	SEA	AL	21	15	15	85.7	75	40	60	7	3.78	3.58	7.8	3.4	6.2	0.6	3.46	18.3	20
2002	SAN	TXS	23	25	13	65.0	68	32	56	8	6.51	8.16	13.6	5.7	6.3	2.5	7.19	-19.4	-15

Not to revive a dead horse for further beating, but when Meche complained about his shoulder and the organization thought he was exaggerating or didn't have the grittiness required to pitch, what did that do to his career? Meche was ostensibly put in Double-A for the warmer weather, and he did okay, considering it was essentially an extended rehab assignment. Meche's comeback included a stretch on the DL for soreness and "mental things" (seriously, that's what they said) related to Meche's problems with putting too much pressure on himself and being unable to pitch. He ended the season throwing in the 90s again, with his curveball breaking. Meche might win a rotation spot in spring training, but given his history, the Mariners would be wise to be extremely cautious with him. So they sent him to the Venezuela winter league, where he got a couple starts and looked really good. Is this the guy you want to be piling innings on, though?

Jamie Moyer   Born: 18-Nov-62   Age: 40   Bats: L   Throws: L

YEAR	TM	LG	AGE	G	GS	IP	H	BB	SO	HR	ERA	EQERA	EQH9	EQBB9	EQSO9	EQHR9	PERA	VORP	STF
2000	SEA	AL	37	26	26	154.0	173	53	98	22	5.49	5.17	10.0	2.5	5.6	1.1	4.71	5.7	7
2001	SEA	AL	38	33	33	209.7	187	44	119	24	3.43	3.96	8.9	1.8	5.0	1.0	3.47	36.0	9
2002	SEA	AL	39	34	34	230.7	198	50	147	28	3.32	3.53	8.1	1.9	5.7	1.1	3.45	50.6	13
2003	SEA	AL	40	30	28	188.3	182	49	109	21	3.59	3.86	8.8	2.2	4.9	1.0	3.94	38.0	7

Breakout: 9%   Improve: 66%   Collapse: 0%

Everyone knows that Moyer is flirting with disaster, and that he lives and dies on his control, wiles, and zealous preparation. The expectation is that at some point, age is supposed rob him of enough of his edge, and then he'll turn into the worst pitcher in baseball. And it never happens. At age 39, Moyer put up a season a lot like his 1998 performance, when people thought he was due to fall off that same tightrope.

    The Mariners re-signed Moyer, who represented himself in negotiations, to a unique three-year deal where the third year only guarantees $1.5 million, but can go to $7.5 million if he meets playing time incentives in the next two years. It's a creative compromise. As long as Jamie can hold it together, he'll be outstanding, but the drop should be a hell of a toboggan ride.

Clint Nageotte   Born: 25-Oct-80   Age: 22   Bats: R   Throws: R

YEAR	TM	LG	AGE	G	GS	IP	H	BB	SO	HR	ERA	EQERA	EQH9	EQBB9	EQSO9	EQHR9	PERA	VORP	STF
2001	WIS	MDW	20	28	26	152.3	141	50	187	10	3.13	5.58	11.9	4.3	7.0	1.4	5.58	-1.3	15
2002	SBR	CLF	21	29	29	164.7	153	68	214	10	4.54	6.11	11.3	4.8	7.0	1.1	5.35	-11.1	16

I'm so impressed with Clint Nageotte, I'm giving him my full endorsement. Clint is the kind of pitcher who is a couple of minor improvements away from being among the best pitching prospects in baseball. His control could be a little finer, his curve could improve, both of which might come from making his delivery more consistent. But look at this guy: he led the minor leagues in strikeouts, and it wasn't even close, and his stuff is undeniably great. That Nageotte was the pitcher smart teams were asking for when the Mariners went window-shopping in July is no coincidence. If you want a fantasy sleeper pick for a keeper league, Nageotte's your man. Please remember to cut me in on 10% of your winnings.

Jeff Nelson   Born: 17-Nov-66   Age: 36   Bats: R   Throws: R

YEAR	TM	LG	AGE	G	GS	IP	H	BB	SO	HR	ERA	EQERA	EQH9	EQBB9	EQSO9	EQHR9	PERA	VORP	STF
2000	NYY	AL	33	73	0	69.7	44	45	71	2	2.45	2.57	5.3	4.6	8.7	0.2	2.52	21.8	15
2001	SEA	AL	34	69	0	65.3	30	44	88	3	2.76	2.86	4.5	5.7	11.4	0.4	2.37	18.3	27
2002	SEA	AL	35	41	0	45.7	36	27	55	4	3.94	3.98	7.3	4.9	10.5	0.7	3.92	7.1	18
2003	SEA	AL	36	48	0	47.0	36	26	53	5	3.42	3.68	7.0	4.5	9.5	0.8	3.81	11.4	14

Breakout: 14%   Improve: 48%   Collapse: 17%

Nelson had some issues with bone chips in his elbow. He had surgery to remove them and then tried to sell them online for charity, but The Man shut him down. Apparently you're not allowed to sell body parts or medical waste. Sheesh. As scary as Nelson's come-and-go control can be normally, his on-the-job rehab this year was truly frightening. He had some terrifying outings that first month. Besides that, it's another typical Nelson year: crazy movement on his pitches, frequently dominant when healthy, and able to leave even the best hitters shaking their heads as they walk back to the dugout.

Joel Pineiro Born: 25-Sep-78 Age: 24 Bats: R Throws: R

YEAR	TM	LG	AGE	G	GS	IP	H	BB	SO	HR	ERA	EQERA	EQH9	EQBB9	EQSO9	EQHR9	PERA	VORP	STF
2000	NHV	EAS	21	9	9	52.3	42	12	43	6	4.13	4.86	9.7	2.4	5.8	2.0	4.10	3.7	13
2000	TAC	PCL	21	10	9	61.0	53	22	41	3	2.80	3.38	8.7	3.2	5.0	0.6	3.72	14.4	14
2000	SEA	AL	21	8	1	19.3	25	13	10	3	5.60	6.11	11.3	4.9	4.5	1.2	6.61	-1.5	-12
2001	TAC	PCL	22	18	10	77.0	68	33	64	8	3.62	4.53	9.3	4.7	5.6	1.2	4.67	8.1	3
2001	SEA	AL	22	17	11	75.3	50	21	56	2	2.03	2.83	6.7	2.4	6.5	0.2	2.14	22.2	24
2002	SEA	AL	23	37	28	194.3	189	54	136	24	3.24	3.89	9.2	2.4	6.2	1.1	4.19	34.6	16
2003	SEA	AL	24	34	27	169.3	165	55	118	21	3.85	4.14	8.9	2.7	5.9	1.0	4.23	30.3	8

Breakout: 20%   Improve: 54%   Collapse: 13%

If you have the chance to watch Pineiro pitch, don't miss it. Scientists have revealed that he throws ten different pitches for strikes. He's got a fastball, and then a fastball thrown exactly the same way that dives. He's got a great curve and a sweet changeup, and he can throw any pitch at any point in the count.

Piniella screwed around with jerking him from rotation to bullpen early, saying he thought Piniero was more valuable in long relief. The idea was basically sound: protect his arm and develop his stamina. Unfortunately, Lou somehow felt that coming in after Halama had given up five runs by the fourth inning was more important than having Pineiro give him five or six quality innings and then be relieved by Hasagawa. Fortunately, that idea was abandoned, and Pineiro clearly established himself as a top-flight pitcher and a joy to watch.

J. J. Putz Born: 22-Feb-77 Age: 26 Bats: R Throws: R

YEAR	TM	LG	AGE	G	GS	IP	H	BB	SO	HR	ERA	EQERA	EQH9	EQBB9	EQSO9	EQHR9	PERA	VORP	STF
2000	WIS	MDW	23	26	25	142.7	130	63	105	4	3.15	6.13	11.8	5.0	4.3	0.7	5.77	-9.9	-5
2001	SAN	TXS	24	27	26	148.0	145	59	135	11	3.83	5.65	10.8	4.5	6.0	1.2	5.78	-2.4	3
2002	SAN	TXS	25	15	15	84.0	84	28	60	7	3.64	6.02	12.5	3.8	5.2	1.7	5.83	-4.8	-3
2002	TAC	PCL	25	9	9	54.0	51	21	39	4	3.83	4.27	9.6	4.1	5.1	0.9	4.55	7.4	3

Putz is another example of the wisdom in the Mariners' approach to stockpiling pitching. With their top-of-the-line prospects tearing up their shoulders, the Mariners had a whole second tier who could have filled out rotation slots 3–5 despite the wide variation in their long-term potential: Anderson, Johnson, Nageotte, Putz . . . their whole Double-A rotation could have been promoted and not embarrassed themselves. That the Mariners exercised as much patience as they did is a credit to the organization.

Arthur Rhodes Born: 24-Oct-69 Age: 33 Bats: L Throws: L

YEAR	TM	LG	AGE	G	GS	IP	H	BB	SO	HR	ERA	EQERA	EQH9	EQBB9	EQSO9	EQHR9	PERA	VORP	STF
2000	SEA	AL	30	72	0	69.3	51	29	77	6	4.29	3.38	6.5	3.1	9.7	0.7	2.74	15.4	22
2001	SEA	AL	31	72	0	68.0	46	12	83	5	1.72	2.29	6.7	1.5	10.6	0.6	2.18	23.3	34
2002	SEA	AL	32	66	0	69.7	45	13	81	4	2.32	2.28	6.1	1.6	10.3	0.5	2.06	24.0	33
2003	SEA	AL	33	64	0	61.0	48	17	62	6	2.48	2.67	7.2	2.3	8.6	0.8	2.93	21.5	18

Breakout: 24%   Improve: 30%   Collapse: 34%

Rhodes did a little more long relief this year with the bullpen flexing around injuries and call-ups that Piniella didn't trust, but Rhodes was just as dominating working longer. Rhodes is a dominant pitcher, and he's got that intimidation stare down. He frequently makes it look as if he's still warming up while he's striking out batters. They might not even be standing in the box, for all the good it does them. They should spare themselves the trouble, head back to the dugout, and get some sunflower seeds. Maybe call their accountant, see how the tax return is going. I'm not exaggerating. Rhodes had only eight appearances this year where the opponent scored a run. Not earned run: any run at all. In 31 of his appearances no batter he faced reached base.

Kazuhiro Sasaki Born: 22-Feb-68 Age: 35 Bats: Throws: R

YEAR	TM	LG	AGE	G	GS	IP	H	BB	SO	HR	ERA	EQERA	EQH9	EQBB9	EQSO9	EQHR9	PERA	VORP	STF
2000	SEA	AL	32	63	0	62.7	42	31	78	10	3.16	3.22	5.8	3.6	10.7	1.2	3.08	15.0	24
2001	SEA	AL	33	69	0	66.7	48	11	62	6	3.24	3.14	7.2	1.4	8.1	0.8	2.42	16.6	17
2002	SEA	AL	34	61	0	60.7	44	20	73	6	2.52	3.31	6.8	2.8	10.6	0.9	2.97	14.0	27
2003	SEA	AL	35	59	0	56.7	48	21	58	7	3.35	3.60	7.7	3.1	8.7	1.1	3.61	15.4	13

Breakout: 10%   Improve: 25%   Collapse: 20%

Kazuhiro Sasaki *(continued)*

Kazu was clearly injured late in the season. The splitter disappeared from his arsenal and since that's his most deadly pitch, he became fair game for the league's hitters. When he did throw the forkball, he would frequently wince and clutch his arm. But he was fine, they'd tell us. After the season, it turned out he had a bone chip in his shoulder, and in late October he had surgery in Japan. He should be healthy in time for spring training. Given Sasaki's age, injury history, and make-the-fans-sweat style, his gaudy contract was probably not the wisest investment, but the team seems to run a second payroll for Japanese players. Other Mariners will talk after games about how since Kazu sweats a lot, he wants them to sweat as well, and they're joking, but their voices have a little terror in them, too.

Once, while drinking in the center field beer garden next to the M's bullpen, I saw three Japanese tourists looking through the fence. My Japanese is one step up from "worthless" so I didn't catch the full conversation, but they were wondering if Kazu was going to pitch that night. Kazu got up from the bench (which is right next to the fence and faces the field, and so ahead-and-to-the-right of the tourists), walked back, and explained that he had pitched two nights in a row so he wouldn't be coming out that night. And then he thanked them for coming to see the game, gave them a quick bow, they returned the bow, and he went back to the bench. How cool is that?

Wascar Serrano — Born: 02-Jun-77 — Age: 26 — Bats: R — Throws: R

YEAR	TM	LG	AGE	G	GS	IP	H	BB	SO	HR	ERA	EQERA	EQH9	EQBB9	EQSO9	EQHR9	PERA	VORP	STF
2000	MOB	SOU	23	20	20	112.3	93	42	112	11	2.80	4.64	9.9	3.7	6.4	1.7	4.88	10.8	10
2000	LVG	PCL	23	4	4	13.3	24	10	19	5	14.21	13.03	16.5	6.5	10.1	3.9	12.23	-11.1	-7
2001	POR	PCL	24	27	13	93.3	98	35	73	10	4.53	5.51	11.0	4.1	5.3	1.2	5.45	-0.4	-5
2001	SDP	NL	24	20	5	46.7	60	21	39	7	6.55	6.77	12.1	3.8	6.4	1.3	6.81	-6.9	-3
2002	TAC	PCL	25	41	3	71.3	85	30	56	6	6.31	6.55	12.1	4.5	5.6	1.0	6.22	-9.1	-14

Serrano came over in the Ben Davis trade and was the same bad pitcher the Padres saw in 2001. At this point, he's put up two great seasons in the minors and subsequently blown up, utterly failing to show the same promise at four different stops since then. Serrano denies that he's hurt, but he's lost a lot of velocity. Fess up, Wascar, get checked out, and maybe salvage a career. Otherwise, you're done.

Allan Simpson — Born: 26-Aug-77 — Age: 25 — Bats: R — Throws: R

YEAR	TM	LG	AGE	G	GS	IP	H	BB	SO	HR	ERA	EQERA	EQH9	EQBB9	EQSO9	EQHR9	PERA	VORP	STF
2000	LNC	CLF	22	46	0	52.0	34	27	67	1	2.08	3.30	7.2	5.0	7.1	0.4	3.09	12.0	7
2001	SBR	CLF	23	16	0	30.0	19	12	40	1	1.80	3.26	7.7	4.8	7.0	0.6	3.33	7.1	6
2001	SAN	TXS	23	22	0	38.7	25	15	37	1	1.86	2.73	6.7	4.3	6.1	0.4	3.25	11.4	4
2002	SAN	TXS	24	56	0	82.3	53	50	99	4	3.06	4.68	7.7	6.6	8.4	1.0	4.25	6.4	3

"Simpson, eh? Who is this strapping young lad?"

"Uh, Allan Simpson, sir, he's a middle reliever in section Double-A. He throws a good-looking fastball in the mid-90s and a quality slider."

"Excellent. Why isn't he pitching for the Isotopes yet?"

"Well sir, his control's not as good. He gives up a lot of walks."

"A free base! I've never given anything away for free in my life! Send this Simpson to my office, I want to have a stern chat with this young man about the value of parsimony."

Rafael Soriano — Born: 19-Dec-79 — Age: 23 — Bats: R — Throws: R

YEAR	TM	LG	AGE	G	GS	IP	H	BB	SO	HR	ERA	EQERA	EQH9	EQBB9	EQSO9	EQHR9	PERA	VORP	STF
2000	WIS	MDW	20	21	21	122.3	97	50	90	3	2.87	4.62	10.2	4.6	4.2	0.6	4.73	12.0	3
2001	SBR	CLF	21	15	15	89.0	49	39	98	4	2.53	3.63	6.9	5.3	5.8	0.8	3.09	18.5	14
2001	SAN	TXS	21	8	8	48.3	34	14	53	5	3.35	3.87	7.9	3.2	7.1	1.7	3.83	8.8	23
2002	SAN	TXS	22	10	8	46.7	32	15	52	6	2.31	3.93	9.1	3.6	8.0	2.6	4.13	8.1	18
2002	SEA	AL	22	10	8	47.3	45	16	32	8	4.57	4.71	8.9	2.9	6.0	1.5	4.60	4.1	10
2003	*SEA*	*AL*	*23*	*18*	*13*	*82.0*	*84*	*36*	*62*	*12*	*4.70*	*5.05*	*9.4*	*3.6*	*6.4*	*1.2*	*4.99*	*7.3*	*4*

Breakout: 12%   Improve: 46%   Collapse: 23%

Soriano was set up. Bryan Price and Lou Piniella would chart their rotation out over a month in advance (which is not to say the plan never changed), and Soriano was brought in to pitch to a series of no-offense clubs with the hopes that he'd rack up good numbers and wins, making himself into valuable trade bait in time for the end of July. If he failed, hey, no shine off his prospect status, and if he succeeded, his value would have gone through the roof. It sort of worked, except for the getting traded part. Soriano still badly needs a third pitch. He's got a great fastball in the upper 90s, his slider drops off the table, but without a change he doesn't fool his way through a lineup repeatedly. To his credit, he was showing a better changeup in the Texas League playoffs. He's battled shoulder soreness in each of the last two years, which in this organization has almost always led to discovering worse problems.

Aaron Taylor Born: 20-Aug-77 Age: 25 Bats: R Throws: R

YEAR	TM	LG	AGE	G	GS	IP	H	BB	SO	HR	ERA	EQERA	EQH9	EQBB9	EQSO9	EQHR9	PERA	VORP	STF
2000	EVE	NWN	22	15	14	63.0	76	37	57	5	7.43	9.65	17.0	7.1	4.6	2.6	9.51	-29.0	-27
2001	WIS	MDW	23	28	0	29.3	19	11	50	1	2.46	3.77	7.9	4.7	9.3	0.7	3.53	5.2	17
2002	SAN	TXS	24	61	0	77.0	51	34	93	5	2.34	4.29	8.1	4.8	8.5	1.3	3.90	9.3	7
2002	SEA	AL	24	5	0	5.0	8	0	6	2	9.00	8.77	15.3	0.7	10.9	3.6	8.70	-1.9	13

Taylor's old for his level, having spent five years making little to no progress in the Braves system before his 2001 conversion to relieving resulted in his breakout with the Mariners. Which shows that even the Braves fail sometimes. This year in Double-A, Taylor showed his turnaround is for real. He's got a scorching mid-90s fastball, a quality splitter, and he's developing a changeup. He'll start the year in Tacoma as part of the Mariners' strange plan to assemble a major league–quality bullpen in the Pacific Coast League.

Matt Thornton Born: 15-Sep-76 Age: 26 Bats: L Throws: L

YEAR	TM	LG	AGE	G	GS	IP	H	BB	SO	HR	ERA	EQERA	EQH9	EQBB9	EQSO9	EQHR9	PERA	VORP	STF
2000	WIS	MDW	23	26	17	103.3	94	72	88	2	4.01	7.10	11.7	7.9	5.0	0.5	6.84	-18.5	-15
2001	SBR	CLF	24	27	27	157.0	126	60	192	9	2.52	4.63	10.0	4.6	6.5	1.0	4.53	15.3	10
2002	SAN	TXS	25	12	12	62.0	52	29	44	3	3.63	5.62	10.2	5.2	5.1	1.0	4.97	-0.8	-5

A big lefty better known for his basketball play at Grand Valley State in Michigan, after three years of decreasing awfulness, Thornton finally started showing some results, taking a big step up in 2001 against good competition in high-A ball. To become a legitimate prospect, he needed two good years in a row. Instead, he got injured, out for the season and almost certainly 2003 as well. At this point, the best-case upside is a John Halama-style late debut at 28.

Ismael Valdes Born: 21-Aug-73 Age: 29 Bats: R Throws: R

YEAR	TM	LG	AGE	G	GS	IP	H	BB	SO	HR	ERA	EQERA	EQH9	EQBB9	EQSO9	EQHR9	PERA	VORP	STF
2000	CHC	NL	26	12	12	67.0	71	27	45	17	5.37	5.20	9.5	2.9	5.4	2.0	5.60	2.3	-2
2000	LAD	NL	26	9	8	40.0	53	13	29	5	6.08	6.20	12.8	2.4	5.9	1.1	6.11	-3.1	1
2001	ANA	AL	27	27	27	163.7	177	50	100	20	4.45	4.54	10.0	2.6	5.2	1.0	4.41	17.6	6
2002	TEX	AL	28	23	23	146.7	135	36	75	19	3.93	3.48	8.0	2.1	4.5	1.1	3.46	33.0	6
2002	SEA	AL	28	8	8	49.3	59	11	27	7	4.93	5.35	11.4	1.9	4.9	1.3	5.34	0.8	3
2003	*TEX*	*AL*	*29*	*27*	*24*	*150.7*	*174*	*43*	*87*	*23*	*4.92*	*4.70*	*10.1*	*2.3*	*5.0*	*1.2*	*4.68*	*17.6*	*4*

Breakout: 15%   Improve: 47%   Collapse: 16%

The Mariners responded to the failure of the James Baldwin Experiment by getting Baldwin's nonunion Mexican equivalent from the Rangers. Valdes was the best available roster patch, one that should have been made much earlier. Valdes and Balwin's major league careers have been almost parallel, although Valdes' career has been characterized by more nagging injuries, while Baldwin has only had that one shoulder surgery. Their park-adjusted rate stats are nearly identical, but Valdes is two years younger, and was clearly the better free agent choice going into the season. Had the Mariners chosen Valdes initially, they might well have made the postseason over the Angels. He's already back in Texas, still losing money to the perception that he's not a gamer.

Tampa Bay Devil Rays

Of all the major professional sports, achieving success in baseball is by far the most long-term affair. While a player can make an impact immediately after being drafted in the NFL or NBA, almost every baseball player—from the stars to the scrubs—has spent months upon months developing his skills in the minor leagues, toiling out of the spotlight and far away from their eventual major league employer. The best-laid plans for organizational direction can take years to come to fruition, and patience must be very high on the list of important attributes of a major league club owner. A Daniel Snyder-style ownership with a revolving-door-at-the-top policy will do even more damage to an MLB franchise than it does on to the Washington Redskins, and without some job security, any general manager will have scores of opportunities to make short-term oriented transactions—from trading a prospect for an established veteran to establishing heavy workloads for young pitchers on the squad—that hurt the long-term success of the team just to keep from getting fired.

As with any generally wise practice, an owner can take the mantra of patience too far. How do we explain Chuck LaMar's continued employment with the Tampa Bay Devil Rays?

LaMar is entering his ninth year of service as general manager of the Devil Rays organization, having been hired three years before the team's 1998 major league debut. During his tenure, the team has never escaped the basement, watching their expansion brethren in Arizona win division pennants and a World Series from their traditional October perch on the comfy couch in front of the TV. The team's five-year record stands at 318–490, which translates to a .394 winning percentage. That's not historically bad, but it's important to look at this in the framework of an expansion franchise in the 90s. These teams have had the advantages of a major league–wide (rather than league-wide) expansion

draft, effectively doubling the number of good players available, with a fully mature free agent market and better overseas scouting to help them become successful quickly. By way of comparison, the Diamondbacks have played .543 ball in their first five seasons. Of the 1993 expansion teams, Colorado had a .486 winning percentage and a trip to the playoffs in their first five years, while Florida finished at .475 and won the World Series in their fifth year of existence.

Like the Marlins, the Devil Rays paid big bucks for some free agent imports to put a charge into the franchise and its fan base, though the results couldn't have been more different. The Marlins' flag will fly forever, but Chunky A and the Slugging Ungulates put the Rays through seasons of payroll hell without the corresponding winning on the field. As the franchise goes into 2003 with the last of those big-ticket pickups, DH/OF Greg Vaughn, entering the final year of his contract, the team will again have money available to supplement their roster. Have LaMar and company learned their lesson?

If the off-season trade for Rey Ordonez is any indication, the answer is no. LaMar's big deal of the winter meetings was to sell off Steve Cox and Andy Sheets to Japan and then blow the windfall on a trade for Ordonez. We've been calling Ordonez overrated from the minute he arrived on U.S. soil, and the Mets have been trying to get out from under his contract for a couple of years, but LaMar didn't bat an eyelash in trading utility player Russ Johnson and marginal prospect Josh Pressley for Ordonez and $4.25 million to help cover Ordonez' $6.25 million contract in 2003. With the Rays netting $2 million in the Cox and Sheets sales, the team purportedly comes out even.

Unfortunately, they still have to play Rey Ordonez at short. Ordonez's flashy defense is his meal ticket, but he's the odds-on favorite to be the worst hitter in the major leagues in any given year, and he's not known to win friends and

---

Devil Rays Prospectus

2002 record: 55–106; Fifth place, AL East

Pythagenport Record: 57–104

Runs scored per game: 4.2 (12th in AL)

Runs allowed per game: 5.7 (14th in AL)

Team EqA: .244 (12th in AL)

2002 Batters Age: 27.5 (2nd youngest in AL)

2002 Pitchers Age: 27.5 (2nd youngest in AL)

Ballpark: Tropicana Field, Neutral park; Park Factor of 1.003

2002: Didn't seem to learn anything, and didn't get any better.

2003: Will they ever make some sort of progress? Or just win 70 games? Ever?

influence people off of the field: he called booing New York fans stupid in 2002, igniting unnecessary controversy with the Mets. Ordonez is a similar but decisively inferior player to Rey Sanchez, the shortstop that the Mets turned around and signed for less than $2 million to play for them in 2003. The Rays didn't get much from shortstop in 2002, but the organization could have played Andy Sheets there for close to free in 2003, or taken the defensive hit and given Johnson a try, or re-signed Chris Gomez, or signed Sanchez themselves and sold Cox and Sheets off to pay for him. The only reason a team trades for Rey Ordonez at this point in the game is if they are actively blowing the talent evaluation part of the job, and that's a dangerous indication of what LaMar and company will do next time they have some real money to spend.

The other large move the Rays made was hiring homesick two-time Manager of the Year Lou Piniella. Piniella moves from a very good organization to a very bad one, and while fans are hoping he'll catch lightning in a bottle with this year's Devil Rays team, there's no reason to think the Rays will see daylight in 2003. Piniella is as respected and accomplished a manager as you'll find in the game these days, and he's a local, so he'll be in town year-round. But expecting him to create the proverbial silk purse from a sow's ear is unfair to him and to this squad, especially considering that Piniella's $13 million, four-year contract looks like what teams will pay for real players in baseball's current economic climate. For Piniella's yearly salary, the Devil Rays could have signed both second baseman Frank Catalanotto and first baseman David Ortiz to short-term deals and grabbed a non–brand-name manager to run the show. Piniella's going to have to do some fancy managing to make that decision look like a no-brainer.

Ousted manager Hal McRae leaned heavily on his starting pitchers in 2002, though he saved the heaviest workload for since-departed Tanyon Sturtze. At 31, in the last year of his contract and bound for greener pastures, Sturtze was the perfect pitcher for this organization to overwork. Unfortunately, former Ray/ongoing riddle Paul Wilson and budding ace Joe Kennedy also toiled long and hard for McRae. In 2003, the Rays will field the youngest rotation in the league, with 2001 first round pick Dewon Brazelton a likely member of the cast of youngsters joining Kennedy as regulars. Whoever rounds out the staff, the young Devil Rays rotation will have Piniella popping Tums like Tic-Tacs this season. The Devil Rays endured seven separate losing streaks of five games or more in 2002, something that doesn't happen often to even the worst teams (the 1999 Twins were the last team to suffer a similar fate). Even though they're not close to winning anything, the marginal value of a Greg Maddux to the 2003 Devil Rays would be extremely high. He'd fill his usual role at the top of the rotation and be a potent antidote to the multigame losing streak; more importantly, he'd move Kennedy, Brazelton, and the rest of the rotation down a slot,

giving them valuable major league experience while shielding them from generally losing to the likes of Pedro Martinez, Roy Halladay, and Roger Clemens. Every team needs an ace, but an organization seriously considering Jorge Sosa for a spot in the rotation needs one just a little bit more obviously.

The bullpen produced a litany of disappointing performances in 2002. They are young and talented enough to produce better results this year, even—or especially, for those of you who watched as he blew chance after chance with this team—with Esteban Yan's departure to Texas. Piniella has had some great pitchers to work with in Seattle after years of chewing up the likes of Bobby Ayala and Heathcliff Slocumb, and how he modifies his usage patterns to account for the differences between his 2002 Sasaki-Rhodes-Hasegawa pen and the 2003 Carter-Harper-Lucky Season Ticket Holder model will be one of the interesting stories of the season.

Hal McRae's 2002 Rays squad was squarely below average at the plate, striking out with the ferocity of Tawny Kitaen and doing nothing save stealing a few bags with any sort of proficiency. This team sorely needed a middle-of-the-order threat for the first half of the season, when Father Time and Lady Luck were getting medieval on Greg Vaughn; luckily, DH Aubrey Huff stepped into the gap and had an excellent season. With Cox's departure, Huff will be at first base in 2003, and he'll be ably supported in the lineup by catcher Toby Hall. Ben Grieve may be done, but the Rays won't likely give up on him this quickly, and Vaughn will be doing his damnedest to return from his awful 2002. The up-the-middle defense will be fine with Ordonez and Brent Abernathy at short and second, but they're both threats to hit .220 with zero power, which will hurt.

Coming over from the Atlanta system that produced Tom Glavine, John Smoltz, and Chipper Jones, LaMar's theoretical strength was his player development background, and Vince Naimoli might be waiting on some of Tampa's high draft picks to take their bow in the majors. LaMar has presided over some high-risk drafts with the Devil Rays, as the team has invested heavily in first round high school players. Rocco Baldelli, Carl Crawford, Josh Hamilton, and 2002 draftees Wes Bankston and Jason Pridie look more like real players than future cringe-inducing high school outfielders (Chip Ambres, Choo Freeman, and Grand Poobah of Busted Picks Shawn Abner come to mind) but none of these guys is a sure thing as a major leaguer. The Devil Rays minor league system is full of young hitters with pathetic command of the strike zone, and this organization has not been successful at turning that type of player into a good major league hitter. Heralded shortstop B. J. Upton, the third overall pick in the 2002 draft, signed too late to play, but he fits the organizational pattern of picking high-upside high school players who are going to need a lot of instruction and development time to be successful.

Crawford has already made it to the majors, and with Baldelli's breakthrough in 2002, he's also a threat to stick with the team coming out of spring training. Both of these players are very young, and in 2002 they both hit consistent with what you'd expect from players of their respective ages. Unfortunately, like John Candy, neither of them sees anything cross the plate they don't like. That's a tendency that can kill careers more quickly than comedians. Itinerant hackers will beat the bushes for years looking for major league jobs, and even the relative "success stories" like Juan Samuel, Chuck Carr, and Pat Listach tend to have tough careers and flame out pretty early. Baldelli is a particularly worrisome case, walking only 23 times in 478 at-bats across three levels (and with no walks in 92 at-bats in Triple-A). There are players in the majors who achieve some level of success with that walk rate, but they're doing it against the best pitchers on the planet; Baldelli needs to have another serious performance spike to be a good major league regular next year. It's not impossible that Baldelli takes the majors by storm this year. It's not impossible for Jenna Jameson to win an Oscar this year, either. Baldelli is simply not an Adam Dunn in waiting. Dunn can fall back on his discipline when he hits a two-week cold streak, where Baldelli—or Crawford, or Hamilton—will do nothing at the plate when they hit theirs.

LaMar and scouting director Cam Bonifay need to hope that their young crop of outfielders are ready to take another quantum leap in performance in 2003. If they do, the Rays could put some runs on the board, surprise people, wrest fourth place from the cold dead hands of the Borioles, and have something to build upon in 2004. If they don't, they should both be looking for jobs, preferably in another field, by November. In the Billy Beane/J. P. Ricciardi/Theo Epstein era, there's no earthly reason a major league team should spend six straight years in the basement, and if there's such a thing as kismet, the fans in Tampa will have a front office that knows how to work the waiver wire and steer clear of the free agent boondoggles by the World Series.

HITTERS

Brent Abernathy   2B   Born: 23-Sep-77   Age: 25   Bats: R   Throws: R

YEAR	TM	LG	AGE	AB	H	2B	3B	HR	BB	SO	SB	CS	AVG	OBP	SLG	MLVR	EQBA	EQOBP	EQSLG	EQMLVR	VORP	DEFENSE
2000	SYR	INT	22	358	106	21	2	4	26	32	14	13	.296	.345	.399	.001	.265	.307	.360	-.179	3.5	89-2B 3
2000	DUR	INT	22	91	24	6	0	1	11	11	9	2	.264	.368	.363	-.018	.250	.337	.348	-.147	1.6	23-2B -9
2001	DUR	INT	23	252	76	20	0	4	16	23	11	4	.302	.348	.429	.107	.285	.330	.406	-.054	10.6	58-2B 8
2001	TBY	AL	23	304	82	17	1	5	27	35	8	3	.270	.329	.382	-.064	.289	.350	.410	-.008	16.7	78-2B -3
2002	TBY	AL	24	463	112	18	4	2	25	46	10	4	.242	.289	.311	-.234	.268	.314	.348	-.180	4.1	114-2B -5
2003	TBY	AL	25	450	117	23	3	6	30	47	10	3	.261	.312	.361	-.113	.267	.320	.377	-.121	4.8	

Breakout: 25%   Improve: 56%   Collapse: 17%

Abernathy is hanging on to the second-baseman-of-the-future mantle by a thread following a poor 2002 showing. His slow start made him a bit player in Hal McRae's strenuous lineup gymnastics during the second half, which didn't help. This year will be his last clean shot at making something positive happen as a starter.

Rocco Baldelli   CF   Born: 25-Sep-81   Age: 21   Bats: R   Throws: R

YEAR	TM	LG	AGE	AB	H	2B	3B	HR	BB	SO	SB	CS	AVG	OBP	SLG	MLVR	EQBA	EQOBP	EQSLG	EQMLVR	VORP	DEFENSE
2000	PRI	APL	18	232	50	9	2	3	12	56	11	3	.216	.269	.310	-.216	.150	.177	.214	-.706	-31.1	60-CF -3
2001	CSC	SAL	19	406	101	23	6	8	23	89	25	9	.249	.307	.394	.039	.201	.242	.321	-.401	-23.9	112-CF -7
2002	BAK	CLF	20	312	104	19	1	14	18	63	21	6	.333	.383	.535	.333	.262	.296	.422	-.112	5.1	63-CF -5
2002	ORL	SOU	20	70	26	3	1	2	5	11	3	2	.371	.429	.529	.455	.310	.348	.465	.086	4.9	13-CF -1
2002	DUR	INT	20	96	28	6	1	3	0	23	2	5	.292	.292	.469	.066	.260	.268	.438	-.142	.9	19-CF -2
2003	TBY	AL	21	238	56	11	2	6	15	53	6	6	.236	.290	.379	-.142	.242	.298	.395	-.153	-2.6	

Breakout: 40%   Improve: 61%   Collapse: 12%

A strong 2002 and recent first round pick pedigree make Rocco Baldelli a popular choice for the best prospect in the minors. Baldelli has the typical strengths and weaknesses of a toolsy high school draft pick, but his comparative lack of experience is a point in his favor. Despite having less experience than most prospects who can't legally buy a beer, Baldelli's outperforming almost all of them. He had a strong AFL campaign, and a good spring training will win him the starting job in center field in 2003.

Wesley Bankston   RF   Born: 23-Nov-83   Age: 19   Bats: R   Throws: R

YEAR	TM	LG	AGE	AB	H	2B	3B	HR	BB	SO	SB	CS	AVG	OBP	SLG	MLVR	EQBA	EQOBP	EQSLG	EQMLVR	VORP	DEFENSE
2002	PRI	APL	18	246	74	10	1	18	18	46	2	1	.301	.351	.569	.296	.196	.226	.355	-.388	-18.4	57-RF -8
2002	HUD	NYP	18	33	10	1	0	0	0	6	1	0	.303	.303	.333	-.006	.242	.242	.273	-.448	-2.5	
2003	TBY	AL	19	188	45	9	1	6	12	45	2	3	.237	.284	.390	-.139	.243	.292	.406	-.149	-6.9	

Breakout: 77%   Improve: 88%   Collapse: 12%

Squarely in the middle of the second wave of Tampa Bay outfield prospects, fourth round pick Bankston led the Appy league in home runs in 2002. Unlike most of the other outfielders in the system, he's not a good defensive player, and first base may be in his future. He'll be the right fielder for Charleston in 2003.

Jace Brewer   SS   Born: 06-Jun-79   Age: 24   Bats: R   Throws: R

YEAR	TM	LG	AGE	AB	H	2B	3B	HR	BB	SO	SB	CS	AVG	OBP	SLG	MLVR	EQBA	EQOBP	EQSLG	EQMLVR	VORP	DEFENSE
2000	CSC	SAL	21	137	30	7	2	0	6	28	3	0	.219	.257	.299	-.212	.173	.198	.245	-.611	-13.2	28-SS -2
2001	CSC	SAL	22	414	90	12	4	3	18	74	6	6	.217	.255	.287	-.186	.177	.206	.234	-.608	-42.0	99-SS -12
2002	BAK	CLF	23	378	114	17	2	6	11	62	8	2	.302	.327	.405	.032	.241	.255	.320	-.354	-12.3	89-SS -3
2002	ORL	SOU	23	153	33	5	0	1	4	27	2	0	.216	.250	.268	-.290	.206	.220	.258	-.532	-12.2	36-SS -4
2003	TBY	AL	24	177	41	8	1	2	7	32	2	2	.231	.265	.336	-.243	.237	.273	.350	-.263	-4.7	

Breakout: 83%   Improve: 85%   Collapse: 11%

Brewer is Exhibit A in the argument that a major league contract for a draftee isn't a good thing. The Rays inexplicably burned a 40-man spot on Brewer when they came to terms with him as a fifth round pick in 2000, and the resulting lack of roster flexibility had everything to do with them cutting him loose in late November. Brewer's no kind of prospect, although 16 walks in nearly 600 ABs of minor league and AFL playing time surely make him the Devil Rays' kind of hitter. The Rays need help up the middle, and Brewer's got a good defensive reputation, so he was in a good position after hitting over .300 in Double-A. Now, he'll have to catch on somewhere else and start all over.

Jorge Cantu   SS   Born: 30-Jan-82   Age: 21   Bats: R   Throws: R

YEAR	TM	LG	AGE	AB	H	2B	3B	HR	BB	SO	SB	CS	AVG	OBP	SLG	MLVR	EQBA	EQOBP	EQSLG	EQMLVR	VORP	DEFENSE	
2000	CSC	SAL	18	186	56	13	2	2	10	39	3	3	.301	.347	.425	.143	.233	.261	.333	-.328	-5.0	45-SS -1	
2000	STP	FSL	18	130	38	5	2	1	3	13	4	2	.292	.313	.385	.014	.238	.253	.323	-.355	-4.5	31-SS -7	
2001	ORL	SOU	19	512	131	26	3	4	17	93	4	9	.256	.291	.342	-.132	.226	.249	.305	-.396	-23.2	119-SS -26	
2002	ORL	SOU	20	512	124	31	1	3	23	74	2	6	.242	.280	.324	-.150	.219	.241	.298	-.426	-27.6	95-SS -4	33-3B -3
2003	TBY	AL	21	193	46	9	1	3	9	31	2	1	.241	.279	.346	-.202	.247	.286	.360	-.218	-2.9		

Breakout: 60%   Improve: 82%   Collapse: 6%

We get as tired of writing it as you probably do of reading it, but if Double-A pitchers abuse Cantu's propensity to swing at garbage, how is he ever going to make an impact in the majors? For every rule there are exceptions, but Alfonso Soriano has the advantage of a little more patience and a lot more power over Cantu. Pokey Reese minus most of the defense is the upside here.

Jason Conti   CF   Born: 27-Jan-75   Age: 28   Bats: L   Throws: R

YEAR	TM	LG	AGE	AB	H	2B	3B	HR	BB	SO	SB	CS	AVG	OBP	SLG	MLVR	EQBA	EQOBP	EQSLG	EQMLVR	VORP	DEFENSE
2000	TUC	PCL	25	383	117	20	5	11	23	57	11	3	.305	.353	.470	.045	.263	.298	.404	-.134	4.4	83-CF -6
2000	ARI	NL	25	91	21	4	3	1	7	30	3	0	.231	.293	.374	-.248	.228	.275	.380	-.237	-4.0	28-RF 0
2001	DUR	INT	26	157	48	12	0	5	9	31	3	1	.306	.347	.478	.177	.289	.330	.453	.017	8.0	35-CF -2
2001	TUC	PCL	26	362	120	23	6	9	33	54	2	5	.331	.405	.503	.229	.283	.351	.426	.011	18.2	85-CF -1
2002	TBY	AL	27	222	57	15	2	3	18	55	4	2	.257	.315	.383	-.082	.277	.333	.415	-.042	2.6	69-OF -4
2003	TBY	AL	28	249	64	14	2	5	19	52	4	3	.257	.313	.393	-.072	.264	.321	.410	-.077	-.7	

Breakout: 14%   Improve: 33%   Collapse: 35%

Conti's a handy player to have around; he can hit a little, he's a good fielder anywhere in the outfield, and he won't clog up the base paths. This is the minor league vet you want to sign to a minimum contract to play for your Triple-A team or man the bench as your fourth of fifth outfielder. On this team, if they turn to all of the rookies, he'll be a handy caddy.

Steve Cox   1B   Born: 31-Oct-74   Age: 28   Bats: L   Throws: L

YEAR	TM	LG	AGE	AB	H	2B	3B	HR	BB	SO	SB	CS	AVG	OBP	SLG	MLVR	EQBA	EQOBP	EQSLG	EQMLVR	VORP		DEFENSE			
2000	TBY	AL	25	318	90	19	1	11	46	47	1	2	.283	.380	.453	.076	.293	.383	.468	.135	17.9		53-RF	-4	18-1B	-5
2001	TBY	AL	26	342	88	22	0	12	24	75	2	2	.257	.324	.427	-.021	.274	.339	.458	.027	10.9		72-1B	3		
2002	TBY	AL	27	560	142	30	1	16	60	116	5	0	.254	.333	.396	-.034	.274	.352	.432	.014	16.3		108-1B	3		
2003	TBY	AL	28	406	105	23	1	14	44	80	3	1	.257	.333	.426	.004	.264	.342	.444	.005	5.1					

Breakout: 14%   Improve: 45%   Collapse: 21%

Cox has generated heat twice during his short career: in 1995 in the California League, and during the 2000 off-season, when he looked like a possible long-term solution for the Rays at first. His production since then has been mediocre, and he'll be playing in Japan in 2003. He can hope for a Lee Stevens-like comeback.

Carl Crawford   LF   Born: 05-Aug-81   Age: 21   Bats: L   Throws: L

YEAR	TM	LG	AGE	AB	H	2B	3B	HR	BB	SO	SB	CS	AVG	OBP	SLG	MLVR	EQBA	EQOBP	EQSLG	EQMLVR	VORP		DEFENSE	
2000	CSC	SAL	18	564	170	21	11	6	32	102	55	9	.301	.342	.410	.116	.234	.263	.323	-.338	-36.6		131-RF	-12
2001	ORL	SOU	19	537	147	24	3	4	36	90	36	20	.274	.324	.352	-.051	.239	.279	.311	-.320	-20.0		130-CF	-4
2002	DUR	INT	20	353	105	17	9	7	20	69	26	8	.297	.339	.456	.127	.275	.318	.433	-.046	12.1		82-CF	-4
2002	TBY	AL	20	259	67	11	6	2	9	41	9	5	.259	.292	.371	-.140	.284	.314	.406	-.084	.2		63-LF	5
2003	TBY	AL	21	424	109	22	4	9	26	74	17	9	.258	.305	.390	-.089	.265	.313	.406	-.095	-2.3			

Breakout: 31%   Improve: 58%   Collapse: 17%

Crawford's got youth on his side, and he's been pretty impressive thus far into his career. However, he's really only starting in the majors at 21 because the Rays are desperately lacking in outfield talent, sold about 10% of their position players to Japan, and need an inkling of excitement to get the fans to the park. The Rays will pay for their impatience in US legal tender; Crawford's not going to be a plus in his first year or two in the majors, but all that service time will make him an expensive 24-year-old.

Felix Escalona   2B   Born: 12-Mar-79   Age: 24   Bats: R   Throws: R

YEAR	TM	LG	AGE	AB	H	2B	3B	HR	BB	SO	SB	CS	AVG	OBP	SLG	MLVR	EQBA	EQOBP	EQSLG	EQMLVR	VORP		DEFENSE			
2000	MIC	MDW	21	251	65	14	1	6	22	49	7	0	.259	.329	.394	.038	.206	.247	.319	-.391	-11.1		51-2B	1	11-SS	-1
2000	KIS	FSL	21	143	36	5	1	0	9	21	5	3	.252	.323	.301	-.109	.214	.260	.262	-.441	-8.3		23-SS	-7	11-2B	-4
2001	LEX	SAL	22	536	155	42	2	16	30	85	46	12	.289	.345	.465	.204	.230	.271	.372	-.255	-5.3		109-2B	4	20-SS	-5
2002	TBY	AL	23	157	34	8	2	0	3	44	7	2	.217	.263	.293	-.321	.241	.280	.323	-.300	-3.1		19-SS	0	22-2B	-3
2003	TBY	AL	24	222	52	12	1	3	11	46	8	5	.233	.278	.343	-.211	.238	.286	.358	-.228	-4.2					

Breakout: 34%   Improve: 58%   Collapse: 23%

One of the trio of Rule 5 picks on the 2002 Rays, Escalona was drafted by the Astros from the Giants system and claimed off of waivers in March. He got the bulk of the playing time at second in August and September, which really helped make Brent Abernathy's case for the 2003 second base job. He's not a good bet to make the team or contribute much in 2003.

John Flaherty   C   Born: 21-Oct-67   Age: 35   Bats: R   Throws: R

YEAR	TM	LG	AGE	AB	H	2B	3B	HR	BB	SO	SB	CS	AVG	OBP	SLG	MLVR	EQBA	EQOBP	EQSLG	EQMLVR	VORP		DEFENSE	
2000	TBY	AL	32	394	103	15	0	10	20	57	0	0	.261	.297	.376	-.210	.270	.299	.390	-.147	8.5		100-C	0
2001	TBY	AL	33	248	59	17	1	4	10	33	1	0	.238	.270	.363	-.219	.254	.291	.387	-.178	3.5		70-C	-6
2002	TBY	AL	34	281	73	20	0	4	15	50	2	2	.260	.300	.374	-.120	.279	.320	.403	-.082	10.8		75-C	-1
2003	NYY	AL	35	205	49	10	0	4	11	36	1	1	.240	.278	.358	-.187	.248	.288	.371	-.199	-1.5			

Breakout: 16%   Improve: 41%   Collapse: 28%

The Rays failed to move Flaherty at the deadline for the second straight year, despite having Toby Hall hanging around and plenty of Flaherty-quality backups in the minors. Flash is a reliable defensive backstop. He lucked out, getting a NRI with the Yankees, where he might beat out Widger for the backup job.

Jonny Gomes   LF   Born: 22-Nov-80   Age: 22   Bats: R   Throws: R

YEAR	TM	LG	AGE	AB	H	2B	3B	HR	BB	SO	SB	CS	AVG	OBP	SLG	MLVR	EQBA	EQOBP	EQSLG	EQMLVR	VORP		DEFENSE	
2001	PRI	APL	20	206	60	11	2	16	33	73	15	4	.291	.449	.597	.481	.198	.292	.392	-.209	-1.7		59-CF	-10
2002	BAK	CLF	21	446	124	24	9	30	91	173	15	3	.278	.433	.574	.393	.217	.334	.432	-.063	3.1		117-LF	-12
2003	TBY	AL	22	231	54	11	2	9	26	79	4	8	.235	.323	.413	-.044	.241	.332	.431	-.047	-1.9			

Breakout: 24%   Improve: 46%   Collapse: 19%

A converted catcher, Gomes strikes out too much and is a project in the outfield, where he'll likely stick in left. He did everything else right, leading the Cal League in slugging and placing second in OBP in 2002. In many other systems Gomes would be a hot prospect, but thanks to expectations attached to the Rays' other, more heralded young outfielders, he faces an uphill battle for attention.

Chris Gomez   SS   Born: 16-Jun-71   Age: 32   Bats: R   Throws: R

YEAR	TM	LG	AGE	AB	H	2B	3B	HR	BB	SO	SB	CS	AVG	OBP	SLG	MLVR	EQBA	EQOBP	EQSLG	EQMLVR	VORP	DEFENSE
2001	SDP	NL	30	112	21	3	0	0	9	14	1	0	.188	.248	.214	-.511	.202	.260	.237	-.481	-8.0	25-SS -7
2001	DUR	INT	30	93	28	5	1	4	11	5	1	1	.301	.375	.505	.251	.274	.349	.474	.067	7.3	21-SS 3
2001	TBY	AL	30	189	57	16	0	8	8	24	3	0	.302	.337	.513	.158	.316	.352	.547	.220	21.0	51-SS -2
2002	TBY	AL	31	461	122	31	3	10	21	58	1	3	.265	.307	.410	-.055	.284	.326	.442	-.010	24.0	123-SS 8
2003	MIN	AL	32	388	101	21	2	8	24	50	2	1	.260	.305	.382	-.097	.263	.311	.398	-.111	4.8	

Breakout: 13%   Improve: 36%   Collapse: 28%

If you were expecting a bomb every 22 at-bats, you'd have been disappointed, but then if you were, you're probably more worried about your lucky numbers not translating into lottery winnings yet. Gomez was still the best shortstop the Rays had in 2002, and he'll be significantly better than Rey Ordonez for a fraction of the price in 2003. With Minnesota, he'll provide middle infield insurance if both starters continue to disappoint or get hurt.

Ben Grieve   RF   Born: 04-May-76   Age: 27   Bats: L Throws: R

YEAR	TM	LG	AGE	AB	H	2B	3B	HR	BB	SO	SB	CS	AVG	OBP	SLG	MLVR	EQBA	EQOBP	EQSLG	EQMLVR	VORP	DEFENSE
2000	OAK	AL	24	594	166	40	1	27	73	130	3	0	.279	.361	.487	.090	.290	.365	.508	.157	36.7	123-LF 3
2001	TBY	AL	25	542	143	30	2	11	87	159	7	1	.264	.374	.387	.021	.283	.390	.418	.071	22.5	110-RF -2
2002	TBY	AL	26	482	121	30	0	19	69	121	8	2	.251	.354	.432	.046	.273	.373	.470	.103	23.6	108-RF -4
2003	TBY	AL	27	487	127	28	2	19	70	121	7	3	.260	.356	.440	.060	.266	.366	.458	.065	12.0	

Breakout: 13%   Improve: 46%   Collapse: 16%

Chuck LaMar did everything right in trading for Grieve, and it's a tremendous disappointment that he hasn't gotten more positive reinforcement. Grieve has lost a lot of his aggressiveness at the plate, and even as a young man he had an old slugger's skills. A proactive hitting coach might be able to rescue him. Much will depend on whether Piniella decides Grieve is a project he can help personally, or someone he loses all patience with from the start, as he did with Jay Buhner when they were both Yankees.

Toby Hall   C   Born: 21-Oct-75   Age: 27   Bats: R   Throws: R

YEAR	TM	LG	AGE	AB	H	2B	3B	HR	BB	SO	SB	CS	AVG	OBP	SLG	MLVR	EQBA	EQOBP	EQSLG	EQMLVR	VORP	DEFENSE
2000	ORL	SOU	24	271	93	14	0	9	17	24	3	2	.343	.384	.494	.319	.299	.326	.439	-.001	16.8	55-C -13
2000	DUR	INT	24	184	56	15	0	7	3	19	0	0	.304	.323	.500	.134	.283	.296	.462	-.035	8.8	42-C 0
2001	DUR	INT	25	373	125	28	1	19	29	22	1	3	.335	.388	.568	.390	.311	.363	.529	.206	43.5	63-C 3
2001	TBY	AL	25	188	56	16	0	4	4	16	2	2	.298	.323	.447	.038	.317	.339	.476	.094	15.3	46-C -1
2002	DUR	INT	26	92	32	4	0	2	3	10	0	0	.348	.394	.457	.259	.323	.363	.430	.074	7.1	18-C -3
2002	TBY	AL	26	330	85	19	1	6	17	27	0	1	.258	.296	.376	-.125	.277	.316	.407	-.085	12.4	83-C -1
2003	TBY	AL	27	356	96	20	1	10	20	35	1	1	.269	.311	.410	-.046	.276	.319	.427	-.048	11.0	

Breakout: 13%   Improve: 33%   Collapse: 31%

Hall has a history with the bat that most catchers can't hope to match, and he's a good bet to be among the best hitting backstops in baseball in 2003. The Rays should be thinking longer-term than that, and there are risks that could make exploring Hall's value in trade reasonable. Hall's reputation as a top prospect comes in spite of his age (he's older than Ben Grieve), not because of it, and catchers who smoke the ball into their thirties are rare. He reported to camp out of shape in 2002, and even at his listed weight of 240 pounds he's putting a lot of pressure on his knees in every game. We'd love to have him on our team, but we're giving the long-term contract to someone else.

Josh Hamilton   CF   Born: 21-May-81   Age: 22   Bats: L   Throws: L

YEAR	TM	LG	AGE	AB	H	2B	3B	HR	BB	SO	SB	CS	AVG	OBP	SLG	MLVR	EQBA	EQOBP	EQSLG	EQMLVR	VORP	DEFENSE
2000	CSC	SAL	19	391	118	23	3	13	27	71	14	6	.302	.350	.476	.216	.229	.263	.364	-.282	-10.1	81-CF -6
2001	ORL	SOU	20	89	16	5	0	0	5	22	2	0	.180	.223	.236	-.430	.167	.202	.211	-.652	-11.0	22-CF -1
2002	BAK	CLF	21	211	64	14	1	9	20	46	10	1	.303	.364	.507	.234	.238	.282	.397	-.193	-3.2	
2003	TBY	AL	22	182	43	9	1	5	14	40	3	3	.234	.295	.383	-.130	.240	.303	.399	-.140	-1.1	

Breakout: 55%   Improve: 76%   Collapse: 12%

Josh Hamilton *(continued)*

It wasn't a supernova of self-destruction in the Toe Nash mode, but Hamilton has watched the organization's other outfield prospects blow by him as he continues to struggle with injuries. He alternated trips to the DL with pretty good production in his first year at high-A ball until surgery for an injured shoulder and bone spur knocked him out for the season. Hamilton has only totaled 702 at-bats over the last three seasons, and it's important that he get a full year of high-minors experience in 2003.

Paul Hoover　　　　　**C/UT**　**Born: 14-Apr-76**　**Age: 27**　**Bats: R**　**Throws: R**

YEAR	TM	LG	AGE	AB	H	2B	3B	HR	BB	SO	SB	CS	AVG	OBP	SLG	MLVR	EQBA	EQOBP	EQSLG	EQMLVR	VORP	DEFENSE			
2000	ORL	SOU	24	360	90	20	4	3	67	66	9	8	.250	.386	.353	.062	.226	.331	.324	-.206	-1.9	41-3B	0	26-LF	-1
2001	DUR	INT	25	293	63	18	4	3	11	66	5	3	.215	.260	.334	-.226	.207	.249	.325	-.379	-10.7	41-C	-5	15-3B	1
2002	DUR	INT	26	227	50	12	3	5	18	67	3	3	.220	.286	.366	-.138	.210	.274	.354	-.287	-3.1	48-C	0		
2002	TBY	AL	26	17	3	0	0	0	0	5	0	0	.176	.176	.176	-.663	.235	.235	.235	-.521	-1.6				
2003	FLO	NL	27	233	53	12	1	5	22	60	4	3	.229	.302	.353	-.186	.236	.304	.376	-.171	-.4				

Breakout: 52%　　Improve: 68%　　Collapse: 21%

The smart money was on Hoover to get some garbage time in the majors in 2002, but Tampa's inexplicable inability to move John Flaherty for anyone blew that plan. Hoover is your standard-issue Triple-A backstop: younger than many, reliable defensively, and not likely to make a team look like idiots for calling him up in a pinch. Signed with Florida, where Torborg likes to have a third catcher around, so he might stick.

Aubrey Huff　　　　　　**1B**　**Born: 20-Dec-76**　**Age: 26**　**Bats: L**　**Throws: R**

YEAR	TM	LG	AGE	AB	H	2B	3B	HR	BB	SO	SB	CS	AVG	OBP	SLG	MLVR	EQBA	EQOBP	EQSLG	EQMLVR	VORP	DEFENSE			
2000	DUR	INT	23	408	129	36	3	20	51	72	2	3	.316	.395	.566	.350	.291	.359	.519	.164	37.9	90-3B	-14		
2000	TBY	AL	23	122	35	7	0	4	5	18	0	0	.287	.320	.443	-.046	.298	.326	.455	.022	6.2	28-3B	-4		
2001	DUR	INT	24	66	19	6	0	3	5	7	0	0	.288	.338	.515	.196	.269	.319	.478	.015	3.5	16-3B	1		
2001	TBY	AL	24	411	102	25	1	8	23	72	1	3	.248	.288	.372	-.167	.267	.309	.400	-.116	7.6	68-3B	-3	17-1B	-4
2002	DUR	INT	25	126	41	9	0	3	12	13	0	0	.325	.388	.468	.246	.305	.368	.445	.088	6.2	25-1B	3		
2002	TBY	AL	25	454	142	25	0	23	37	55	4	1	.313	.366	.520	.236	.336	.387	.560	.318	48.8	44-1B	-6	14-3B	-2
2003	TBY	AL	26	496	142	32	1	20	42	73	4	2	.286	.344	.475	.106	.293	.354	.495	.116	23.6				

Breakout: 16%　　Improve: 49%　　Collapse: 13%

Huff has tremendous strength and can hit the ball a country mile. He's off to a late career start, and the Rays have decided that he can't play third base, where he could have been Jim Thome Lite. Huff is entrenched in the middle of the Rays' lineup, and will be hitting homers and displaying various cool peroxide stylings at the Trop for years.

Russ Johnson　　　　　　**INF**　**Born: 22-Feb-73**　**Age: 30**　**Bats: R**　**Throws: R**

YEAR	TM	LG	AGE	AB	H	2B	3B	HR	BB	SO	SB	CS	AVG	OBP	SLG	MLVR	EQBA	EQOBP	EQSLG	EQMLVR	VORP	DEFENSE			
2000	TBY	AL	27	185	47	8	0	2	25	30	4	1	.254	.346	.330	-.184	.262	.348	.344	-.124	3.2	32-3B	3	16-2B	3
2001	TBY	AL	28	248	73	19	2	4	34	57	2	2	.294	.382	.435	.120	.312	.398	.464	.173	24.9	31-3B	-3	31-2B	1
2002	ORL	SOU	29	43	12	5	0	0	8	7	1	0	.279	.392	.395	.140	.227	.333	.341	-.179	-.6				
2002	DUR	INT	29	33	9	0	1	2	4	5	1	0	.273	.351	.515	.203	.265	.324	.500	.051	2.1	10-3B	0		
2002	TBY	AL	29	111	24	5	0	1	16	22	5	2	.216	.320	.288	-.218	.241	.340	.330	-.171	.5	23-3B	0		
2003	NYM	NL	30	170	42	9	1	3	23	33	4	2	.244	.336	.355	-.115	.253	.341	.379	-.089	2.0				

Breakout: 18%　　Improve: 46%　　Collapse: 33%

Johnson has all of the ingredients to be a great bench player: he can play any infield position, and he has a good eye and some pop at the plate. He endured a tough year in 2002, including a three-week layoff for treatment of depression, and was sent to the Mets in the Rey Ordonez trade.

Pete LaForest　　　　　　**C**　**Born: 27-Jan-78**　**Age: 25**　**Bats: L**　**Throws: R**

YEAR	TM	LG	AGE	AB	H	2B	3B	HR	BB	SO	SB	CS	AVG	OBP	SLG	MLVR	EQBA	EQOBP	EQSLG	EQMLVR	VORP	DEFENSE	
2000	STP	FSL	22	474	128	28	7	14	56	108	2	4	.270	.354	.447	.142	.219	.284	.367	-.244	-1.2	58-C	-25
2002	ORL	SOU	24	359	97	18	1	20	60	94	9	6	.270	.378	.493	.239	.235	.319	.434	-.075	16.6	79-C	-21
2002	DUR	INT	24	66	17	3	0	3	3	28	0	1	.258	.290	.439	-.008	.242	.286	.409	-.165	1.2	13-C	-6
2003	TBY	AL	25	174	42	9	1	7	19	47	2	2	.240	.316	.426	-.037	.246	.325	.444	-.040	5.8		

Breakout: 52%　　Improve: 74%　　Collapse: 18%

From the studio that brought you *The Rookie* comes an inspirational film based on a true story. Pierre-Luc LaForest (Fred Savage), third baseman, Quebecer, and non-English speaker, thought his dream was over. Drafted by the Expos in 1995, his contract was voided after two games due to a misdiagnosed back injury. The Devil Rays signed him in 1997 and moved him behind the plate, only to have knee surgery for torn cartilage and bone chips wipe out his 2001 season. LaForest never gave up. Throwing caution to the wind, he came back with a vengeance in 2002, and was leading the league in homers for Orlando when he was called up to Durham. This heartfelt, uplifting story about not giving up on your dreams is a remarkable and affecting story that will have everyone cheering. And hey, this guy might even earn his shot at the big time.

Josh Pressley   1B   Born: 02-Apr-80   Age: 23   Bats: L   Throws: R

YEAR	TM	LG	AGE	AB	H	2B	3B	HR	BB	SO	SB	CS	AVG	OBP	SLG	MLVR	EQBA	EQOBP	EQSLG	EQMLVR	VORP	DEFENSE	
2000	CSC	SAL	20	488	148	44	0	6	49	61	2	1	.303	.372	.430	.186	.232	.281	.333	-.289	-24.3	80-1B	2
2001	ORL	SOU	21	111	31	2	1	1	6	22	0	0	.279	.316	.342	-.073	.248	.274	.310	-.326	-6.6	17-1B	-3
2002	ORL	SOU	22	342	104	19	0	4	42	47	5	6	.304	.382	.395	.143	.268	.326	.356	-.146	-4.7	54-1B	-11
2002	DUR	INT	22	47	7	1	0	0	8	6	0	1	.149	.273	.170	-.438	.167	.273	.188	-.531	-5.8	12-1B	-1
2003	*NYM*	*NL*	*23*	*181*	*44*	*9*	*1*	*4*	*17*	*29*	*2*	*1*	*.244*	*.310*	*.361*	*-.151*	*.253*	*.315*	*.386*	*-.127*	*-4.0*		

Breakout: 40%   Improve: 62%   Collapse: 18%

Pressley is the all-too-common prep home run king who hasn't been able to handle minor league pitching. At 6′ 6″, he should be generating a lot of torque, and he's shown some doubles power that could still turn into home runs as he matures. Traded to the Mets in the Rey Ordonez deal, where he goes from one organization with a poor track record converting tools into performance to another.

Jason Pridie   3B/CF   Born: 09-Oct-83   Age: 19   Bats: L   Throws: R

YEAR	TM	LG	AGE	AB	H	2B	3B	HR	BB	SO	SB	CS	AVG	OBP	SLG	MLVR	EQBA	EQOBP	EQSLG	EQMLVR	VORP	DEFENSE	
2002	PRI	APL	18	285	105	12	9	7	19	35	13	9	.368	.412	.547	.425	.242	.265	.356	-.281	-6.9	66-CF	0
2002	HUD	NYP	18	32	11	1	1	1	3	6	0	0	.344	.400	.531	.415	.242	.286	.394	-.187	-.4		
2003	*TBY*	*AL*	*19*	*202*	*51*	*10*	*3*	*4*	*10*	*35*	*3*	*3*	*.252*	*.293*	*.387*	*-.116*	*.258*	*.301*	*.404*	*-.125*	*-.5*		

Breakout: 58%   Improve: 77%   Collapse: 12%

Tampa's second round pick in 2002 had a memorable first season. His 105 hits tied Kirby Puckett's Appy League campaign in 1982 for second-most in league history. Pridie has shown speed and a live bat so far, and he's a popular player with the fans everywhere he's played. Due to the organization's outfield depth, he'll start at third for Charleston in 2003.

Damian Rolls   OF/2B   Born: 15-Sep-77   Age: 25   Bats: R   Throws: R

YEAR	TM	LG	AGE	AB	H	2B	3B	HR	BB	SO	SB	CS	AVG	OBP	SLG	MLVR	EQBA	EQOBP	EQSLG	EQMLVR	VORP	DEFENSE			
2000	ORL	SOU	22	51	13	5	0	0	7	6	1	1	.255	.356	.353	.018	.226	.299	.321	-.274	-2.0				
2001	TBY	AL	23	237	62	11	1	2	10	47	12	4	.262	.291	.342	-.193	.277	.309	.366	-.158	3.5	40-2B	-1	19-CF	-1
2002	ORL	SOU	24	7	3	0	1	0	1	0	0	1	.429	.500	.714	.865	.286	.375	.571	.257	.8				
2002	DUR	INT	24	244	65	6	4	6	21	43	15	0	.266	.337	.398	.020	.251	.319	.381	-.136	2.8	56-CF	-1		
2002	TBY	AL	24	89	26	6	1	0	3	16	2	5	.292	.330	.382	-.032	.311	.345	.411	.003	1.7	21-RF	-2		
2003	*TBY*	*AL*	*25*	*349*	*92*	*20*	*3*	*7*	*25*	*61*	*10*	*5*	*.265*	*.319*	*.392*	*-.057*	*.271*	*.328*	*.409*	*-.061*	*3.4*				

Breakout: 35%   Improve: 63%   Collapse: 17%

With the departure of Andy Sheets and Russ Johnson, the Rays are looking at Rolls for a utility job in 2003. Speed is his only real offensive asset, and he's not a great defensive player, so he'll have to have some good games while upper management is watching if he's going to get any kind of job security.

Jared Sandberg   3B   Born: 02-Mar-78   Age: 25   Bats: R   Throws: R

YEAR	TM	LG	AGE	AB	H	2B	3B	HR	BB	SO	SB	CS	AVG	OBP	SLG	MLVR	EQBA	EQOBP	EQSLG	EQMLVR	VORP	DEFENSE	
2000	ORL	SOU	22	244	63	15	1	5	33	55	5	3	.258	.351	.389	.060	.229	.301	.356	-.220	-2.2	60-3B	7
2001	DUR	INT	23	322	77	16	0	16	38	81	0	1	.239	.331	.438	.042	.229	.313	.421	-.108	7.0	89-3B	4
2001	TBY	AL	23	136	28	7	0	1	10	45	1	0	.206	.265	.279	-.359	.221	.283	.309	-.325	-4.8	38-3B	1
2002	DUR	INT	24	114	32	9	0	4	14	42	1	0	.281	.369	.465	.172	.267	.349	.440	.014	6.3	20-3B	-3
2002	TBY	AL	24	358	82	21	1	18	39	139	3	2	.229	.307	.444	-.036	.247	.323	.482	.008	18.6	96-3B	-2
2003	*TBY*	*AL*	*25*	*364*	*89*	*21*	*1*	*15*	*37*	*102*	*4*	*3*	*.244*	*.318*	*.433*	*-.021*	*.250*	*.327*	*.452*	*-.022*	*9.8*		

Breakout: 26%   Improve: 62%   Collapse: 14%

Jared Sandberg *(continued)*

The occasional four-bagger is basically Sandberg's entire offensive game. He made the most of that profile in 2002, ranking third in bombs with the Rays despite his abbreviated season. Sandberg isn't going to be a star, but he's got a shot at being an average—and cheap—third baseman offensively and in the field for the next couple of years. If everything breaks right, he might grow up to be a randomly generated Bell boy.

Andy Sheets   SS   Born: 19-Nov-71   Age: 31   Bats: R   Throws: R

YEAR	TM	LG	AGE	AB	H	2B	3B	HR	BB	SO	SB	CS	AVG	OBP	SLG	MLVR	EQBA	EQOBP	EQSLG	EQMLVR	VORP	DEFENSE				
2000	PAW	INT	28	281	64	9	3	8	38	48	4	2	.228	.322	.367	-.125	.211	.293	.342	-.266	-3.6	44-SS	-5	19-3B	0	
2001	DUR	INT	29	225	63	14	2	4	25	45	8	3	.280	.357	.413	.085	.265	.338	.396	-.069	9.2	59-SS	-10			
2001	TBY	AL	29	153	30	8	0	1	12	35	2	0	.196	.255	.268	-.400	.216	.277	.294	-.361	-5.7	47-SS	2			
2002	DUR	INT	30	374	110	25	6	14	28	72	7	2	.294	.348	.505	.205	.275	.329	.476	.036	21.9	51-3B	-2	22-2B	-4	
2002	TBY	AL	30	149	37	4	0	4	12	41	2	3	.248	.304	.356	-.143	.267	.325	.387	-.105	4.3	25-2B	3	11-SS	3	
2003	*TBY*	*AL*	*31*	*262*	*64*	*14*	*2*	*6*	*22*	*56*	*3*	*3*	*.244*	*.305*	*.376*	*-.115*	*.250*	*.314*	*.392*	*-.123*	*1.3*					

Breakout: 17%   Improve: 46%   Collapse: 30%

Sheets has the profile of a fine utility player. He's not a good shortstop, but he won't kill a team if they have to play him there every day, and he's significantly better than Rey Ordonez for a fraction of the price. Now a gaijin, he's been sold to the Hiroshima Carp in 2003.

Jason Smith   SS   Born: 24-Jul-77   Age: 25   Bats: L   Throws: R

YEAR	TM	LG	AGE	AB	H	2B	3B	HR	BB	SO	SB	CS	AVG	OBP	SLG	MLVR	EQBA	EQOBP	EQSLG	EQMLVR	VORP	DEFENSE	
2000	WTN	SOU	22	481	114	22	7	12	22	130	16	10	.237	.273	.387	-.070	.215	.237	.358	-.351	-16.8	113-SS	-14
2001	IOW	PCL	23	240	56	8	6	4	12	71	6	3	.233	.273	.367	-.255	.209	.249	.322	-.382	-10.3	67-SS	5
2002	DUR	INT	24	206	57	11	2	4	10	44	5	1	.277	.313	.408	.003	.261	.301	.391	-.149	3.7	46-SS	-1
2002	TBY	AL	24	65	13	1	2	1	2	24	3	0	.200	.224	.323	-.364	.215	.239	.369	-.331	-3.1		
2003	*TBY*	*AL*	*25*	*199*	*47*	*10*	*2*	*5*	*12*	*51*	*5*	*5*	*.233*	*.281*	*.367*	*-.174*	*.239*	*.289*	*.383*	*-.188*	*-2.3*		

Breakout: 36%   Improve: 66%   Collapse: 18%

The Rays gave Smith some time at shortstop when they were evaluating their 2003 options down the stretch, and they came away unimpressed. I can't blame them, but they should have noted that he's a reasonable alternative to Rey Ordonez for a fraction of the price.

Jason Tyner   LF   Born: 23-Apr-77   Age: 26   Bats: L   Throws: L

YEAR	TM	LG	AGE	AB	H	2B	3B	HR	BB	SO	SB	CS	AVG	OBP	SLG	MLVR	EQBA	EQOBP	EQSLG	EQMLVR	VORP	DEFENSE	
2000	NOR	INT	23	327	105	5	2	0	30	32	33	14	.321	.382	.349	.029	.300	.350	.324	-.123	4.8	78-CF	0
2000	TBY	AL	23	83	20	2	0	0	4	12	6	1	.241	.284	.265	-.412	.253	.288	.277	-.343	-5.2	26-LF	0
2001	DUR	INT	24	157	49	2	1	0	15	10	11	5	.312	.379	.338	.044	.294	.359	.319	-.117	2.6	37-CF	-1
2001	TBY	AL	24	396	111	8	5	0	15	42	31	6	.280	.312	.326	-.166	.302	.335	.350	-.113	-2.5	93-LF	0
2002	DUR	INT	25	351	102	12	4	0	34	27	20	7	.291	.363	.348	.015	.275	.344	.331	-.141	-5.0	82-LF	-3
2002	TBY	AL	25	168	36	2	1	0	7	19	7	1	.214	.250	.238	-.421	.237	.270	.266	-.403	-13.1	42-LF	1
2003	*TBY*	*AL*	*26*	*309*	*80*	*13*	*3*	*0*	*21*	*32*	*12*	*3*	*.259*	*.310*	*.323*	*-.166*	*.266*	*.319*	*.336*	*-.178*	*-9.0*		

Breakout: 17%   Improve: 43%   Collapse: 29%

Tyner is the exclamation point on the expletive that describes Tampa Bay's history of talent evaluation. Ignoring Tyner's entire professional career of doing nothing at the plate, the Rays gave him 694 plate appearances to discover what the Mets knew after a couple of weeks: Tyner will never hit enough to hold down an outfield job. That said, the Rays banished him to the minors early enough in the season that Jason Tyner Bobblehead Day was canceled, and somewhere those bobbleheads gather dust. With the logjam of outfielders in Tampa he'll be elsewhere next season.

Greg Vaughn   DH   Born: 03-Jul-65   Age: 38   Bats: R   Throws: R

YEAR	TM	LG	AGE	AB	H	2B	3B	HR	BB	SO	SB	CS	AVG	OBP	SLG	MLVR	EQBA	EQOBP	EQSLG	EQMLVR	VORP	DEFENSE	
2000	TBY	AL	35	461	117	27	1	28	80	128	8	1	.254	.366	.499	.088	.263	.368	.518	.150	30.0	72-LF	0
2001	TBY	AL	36	485	113	25	0	24	71	130	11	5	.233	.335	.433	-.013	.251	.352	.470	.047	18.2	57-LF	2
2002	TBY	AL	37	251	41	10	2	8	41	82	3	2	.163	.288	.315	-.272	.186	.307	.360	-.229	-9.8	31-LF	1
2003	*TBY*	*AL*	*37*	*221*	*47*	*10*	*1*	*9*	*33*	*70*	*4*	*2*	*.212*	*.318*	*.384*	*-.103*	*.217*	*.327*	*.400*	*-.111*	*-4.3*		

Breakout: 24%   Improve: 50%   Collapse: 25%

Vaughn had a season as brutal as his swing in 2002: despite regular playing time, he didn't hit his first home run until May 18. He hit the DL a month later with a deep shoulder bruise, and by the time he was activated after roster expansion, the Rays were using his playing time to evaluate their younger outfielders. With the salary correction that we've been hearing about for years finally taking effect en masse this off-season, there are plenty of better players taking less money than Vaughn makes to play in 2003. Still, it would be a bold move to cut him loose entirely, and the Rays are sensibly planning on DHing him regularly this year and hoping for a resurgence that makes him and his contract tradable by the end of July. It's not gonna happen, but you can't blame them for trying.

Randy Winn CF **Born: 09-Jun-74** **Age: 29** **Bats: B** **Throws: R**

YEAR	TM	LG	AGE	AB	H	2B	3B	HR	BB	SO	SB	CS	AVG	OBP	SLG	MLVR	EQBA	EQOBP	EQSLG	EQMLVR	VORP	DEFENSE
2000	DUR	INT	26	303	100	24	5	7	48	53	18	5	.330	.427	.512	.337	.303	.387	.472	.157	20.2	76-LF -4
2000	TBY	AL	26	159	40	5	0	1	26	25	6	7	.252	.364	.302	-.188	.255	.361	.306	-.154	-2.8	42-LF 0
2001	TBY	AL	27	429	117	25	6	6	38	81	12	10	.273	.340	.401	-.015	.290	.357	.432	.036	12.8	106-RF -2
2002	TBY	AL	28	607	181	39	9	14	55	109	27	8	.298	.362	.461	.137	.325	.387	.506	.227	64.5	138-CF 2
2003	SEA	AL	29	509	137	28	5	12	49	91	16	7	.269	.337	.410	-.003	.285	.355	.442	.040	19.6	

Breakout: 6% *Improve: 41%* *Collapse: 11%*

He was probably the best Devil Ray to choose for the All-Star Game in 2002, posting a .358 OBP, slugging .484, flashing speed and playing a respectable center field before the break. Winn's got everything you want in a fourth outfielder, but he shouldn't get regular playing time at either corner for a team that expects to contend, which the Mariners are planning on doing in 2003.

PITCHERS

Wilson Alvarez **Born: 24-Mar-70** **Age: 33** **Bats: L** **Throws: L**

YEAR	TM	LG	AGE	G	GS	IP	H	BB	SO	HR	ERA	EQERA	EQH9	EQBB9	EQSO9	EQHR9	PERA	VORP	STF
2001	ORL	SOU	31	5	5	20.3	24	6	18	2	4.43	6.03	13.5	3.2	5.6	1.5	6.75	-1.2	-7
2001	DUR	INT	31	4	4	18.0	20	6	16	2	3.00	5.57	11.9	3.6	6.4	1.4	5.98	-0.1	0
2002	ORL	SOU	32	2	2	8.0	6	2	7	0	1.13	2.23	8.1	2.4	5.7	0.2	3.08	2.9	12
2002	TBY	AL	32	23	10	75.0	80	36	56	13	5.28	5.14	9.3	4.0	6.5	1.4	5.26	2.7	-2
2003	LAD	NL	33	24	13	82.7	76	37	63	10	3.99	4.63	8.8	3.5	5.9	1.1	4.70	9.2	-1

Breakout: 18% *Improve: 47%* *Collapse: 19%*

Alvarez will be looking for a team to take a flyer on him, and he's not a bad risk if he comes cheap, which he surely will after his performance in this millennium. The critical object lesson for the Rays appears to have been learned: guys built like Sid Fernandez and Chris Bosio generally age about as well as Bosio and Fernandez did. Signed by the Dodgers, arguably out of nostalgia by ex-White Sox executive Dan Evans.

Nick Bierbrodt **Born: 16-May-78** **Age: 25** **Bats: L** **Throws: L**

YEAR	TM	LG	AGE	G	GS	IP	H	BB	SO	HR	ERA	EQERA	EQH9	EQBB9	EQSO9	EQHR9	PERA	VORP	STF
2000	ELP	TXS	22	7	7	35.3	37	24	36	1	7.14	6.07	9.7	6.2	6.4	0.4	5.39	-2.2	7
2000	TUC	PCL	22	4	3	18.7	13	14	11	3	4.81	4.43	6.8	6.7	4.3	1.7	4.27	2.2	-10
2001	ELP	TXS	23	4	4	19.7	13	6	18	1	1.37	1.59	5.9	3.3	5.7	0.7	2.50	8.6	15
2001	TUC	PCL	23	7	6	45.3	48	9	56	0	2.19	2.93	9.2	2.0	7.8	0.2	3.45	12.9	35
2001	ARI	NL	23	5	5	23.0	29	12	17	6	8.22	7.63	11.5	4.3	5.6	2.1	7.18	-5.4	-6
2001	TBY	AL	23	11	11	61.3	71	27	56	11	4.55	5.13	9.7	3.6	7.5	1.4	5.64	2.6	18

Expected to challenge for a rotation spot in camp after coming over in the Albie Lopez deal, Bierbrodt endured a trying spring training where he had trouble finding the plate. For three months he went through all sorts of off-field regimens and extended spring training to iron out his control. He had just begun pitching in A-ball when things went from bad to worse, as he was shot twice in a restaurant in Charleston on June 7. He spent the rest of the year rehabbing and is supposed to be ready to pitch in spring. Piniella has already said Bierbrodt will get a shot at the rotation if he's ready to go.

Dewon Brazelton — Born: 16-Jun-80 — Age: 23 — Bats: R — Throws: R

YEAR	TM	LG	AGE	G	GS	IP	H	BB	SO	HR	ERA	EQERA	EQH9	EQBB9	EQSO9	EQHR9	PERA	VORP	STF
2002	ORL	SOU	22	26	26	146.0	129	67	109	7	3.33	5.13	10.1	4.5	5.0	0.9	4.99	6.1	3
2002	DUR	INT	22	1	1	5.0	5	1	6	0	0.00	0.34	9.8	2.2	9.2	0.2	3.83	2.9	44
2002	TBY	AL	22	2	2	13.0	12	6	5	3	4.85	4.61	8.0	3.9	3.4	1.9	4.93	1.3	-7
2003	TBY	AL	23	14	10	65.3	76	34	43	9	5.69	5.66	10.2	4.3	5.7	1.2	5.47	2.7	-4

Breakout: 13%   Improve: 46%   Collapse: 30%

The third player selected in the 2001 draft, Brazelton was not pleased that he didn't make the Opening Day roster. There's an argument that he shouldn't pitch from a full windup, but after trying it the team's way to start 2002, he started to improve after he went back to doing what had worked for him. What sort of message does that convey about instruction in the organization from the player's perspective? Anyway, he got stronger as the season went on at Orlando, and solidified his status as a pitcher with some upside. The Rays will be rushing things if they don't send him to Durham to start 2003.

Lance Carter — Born: 18-Dec-74 — Age: 28 — Bats: R — Throws: R

YEAR	TM	LG	AGE	G	GS	IP	H	BB	SO	HR	ERA	EQERA	EQH9	EQBB9	EQSO9	EQHR9	PERA	VORP	STF
2000	OMA	PCL	25	34	6	76.3	88	18	51	13	4.95	5.81	12.1	2.2	5.0	2.0	5.74	-3.2	-12
2002	DUR	INT	27	33	18	132.0	111	12	90	15	2.80	3.54	8.7	1.0	5.3	1.5	3.52	28.4	5
2002	TBY	AL	27	8	0	20.3	15	5	14	2	1.33	1.80	6.5	2.1	6.0	0.8	2.56	8.1	9
2003	TBY	AL	28	21	11	75.0	82	15	46	11	4.24	4.22	9.6	1.6	5.3	1.2	4.17	12.8	3

Breakout: 26%   Improve: 52%   Collapse: 11%

The one-time Royals prospect was out of organized ball in 2001 (unless you count the Rock 'n Jock appearance he made with his N*Sync bandmates), but Carter had a damn good year for the Rays in 2002. An absurd 7.5-to-1 strikeout to walk ratio with Durham earned him a look with the Rays, and he'll be back as a reliever in 2003. He'll beat that projection.

Jesus Colome — Born: 23-Dec-77 — Age: 25 — Bats: R — Throws: R

YEAR	TM	LG	AGE	G	GS	IP	H	BB	SO	HR	ERA	EQERA	EQH9	EQBB9	EQSO9	EQHR9	PERA	VORP	STF
2000	MID	TXS	22	20	20	110.3	99	50	95	10	3.59	4.60	8.9	4.2	5.6	1.2	4.47	11.1	7
2000	ORL	SOU	22	3	3	14.7	18	7	9	2	6.73	9.11	16.0	5.1	4.2	2.5	8.41	-5.9	-20
2001	DUR	INT	23	13	0	17.3	22	6	18	1	6.24	7.43	13.5	3.8	7.5	0.7	6.51	-3.9	2
2001	TBY	AL	23	30	0	48.7	37	25	31	8	3.33	3.57	6.4	4.3	5.3	1.3	3.79	9.8	-5
2002	DUR	INT	24	18	0	29.0	18	13	30	1	2.17	3.00	6.2	4.8	7.9	0.5	2.93	7.7	12
2002	TBY	AL	24	32	0	41.3	56	33	33	6	8.28	7.67	11.7	6.6	6.8	1.2	7.45	-10.5	-13
2003	TBY	AL	25	33	7	63.7	68	36	50	8	5.37	5.34	9.4	4.7	6.7	1.1	5.22	3.5	-6

Breakout: 17%   Improve: 53%   Collapse: 17%

Colome was bitten by Agegate, instantly turning from a 22-year-old with years to put it together to a 25-year-old who still doesn't have a second pitch to go with his snapping fastball. He's not Brad Pennington yet, but that's where he's headed.

Luis de los Santos — Born: 01-Nov-77 — Age: 25 — Bats: R — Throws: R

YEAR	TM	LG	AGE	G	GS	IP	H	BB	SO	HR	ERA	EQERA	EQH9	EQBB9	EQSO9	EQHR9	PERA	VORP	STF
2002	DUR	INT	24	24	16	115.3	105	21	68	8	2.42	3.72	9.3	2.0	4.6	0.9	3.86	22.6	5
2003	TBY	AL	25	15	10	65.0	77	18	37	10	5.19	5.17	10.4	2.2	5.0	1.3	4.84	6.1	-1

Breakout: 17%   Improve: 46%   Collapse: 27%

There wasn't a more unlikely story in baseball than de los Santos, a former Yankee property with a serious injury history, taking the ERA crown in the International League last year. He can't dent bread with his fastball, and his control doesn't look good enough to overcome that at the major league level, but the Rays have worse options for their 2003 rotation.

Lee Gardner — Born: 16-Jan-75 — Age: 28 — Bats: R — Throws: R

YEAR	TM	LG	AGE	G	GS	IP	H	BB	SO	HR	ERA	EQERA	EQH9	EQBB9	EQSO9	EQHR9	PERA	VORP	STF
2000	ORL	SOU	25	36	0	45.0	34	14	48	0	3.40	4.28	8.8	3.1	6.8	0.3	3.40	5.5	5
2000	DUR	INT	25	21	0	18.7	12	9	8	1	3.37	3.33	6.5	4.4	3.3	0.6	3.06	4.3	-20
2001	DUR	INT	26	56	0	76.0	76	23	55	10	2.72	4.78	10.9	3.3	5.3	1.7	5.38	5.1	-15
2002	DUR	INT	27	45	0	49.7	50	15	52	1	2.35	3.69	9.9	3.3	8.0	0.3	4.37	9.3	10
2002	TBY	AL	27	12	0	13.3	12	8	8	3	4.06	5.82	7.8	5.0	5.2	1.9	5.16	-0.7	-22
2003	TBY	AL	28	32	0	40.7	45	18	30	5	4.87	4.85	9.6	3.6	6.4	1.0	4.73	4.6	-4

Breakout: 18%   Improve: 40%   Collapse: 28%

Gardner's a nice story—minor league closer finally makes it to the majors—and if there's one thing the Devil Rays are good at generating, it's nice stories. It came to a messy end when the Rays designated Gardner for assignment, and he became a free agent. Not a good bet for sustained major league success.

Travis Harper — Born: 21-May-76 — Age: 27 — Bats: L — Throws: R

YEAR	TM	LG	AGE	G	GS	IP	H	BB	SO	HR	ERA	EQERA	EQH9	EQBB9	EQSO9	EQHR9	PERA	VORP	STF
2000	ORL	SOU	24	9	9	51.3	49	11	33	1	2.63	4.61	11.4	2.2	4.2	0.3	4.41	5.1	6
2000	DUR	INT	24	17	17	104.0	98	26	48	15	4.24	4.72	9.7	2.3	3.6	1.7	4.59	9.1	-3
2000	TBY	AL	24	6	5	32.0	30	15	14	5	4.78	4.04	7.9	3.4	3.8	1.2	4.03	5.2	-3
2001	DUR	INT	25	25	25	155.7	140	38	115	25	3.70	5.05	9.9	2.7	5.3	2.0	4.80	7.9	2
2002	DUR	INT	26	4	4	19.3	31	3	17	5	6.99	8.71	17.2	1.7	7.0	3.5	9.50	-6.9	-9
2002	TBY	AL	26	37	7	85.7	101	27	60	14	5.46	5.15	10.4	2.6	6.1	1.4	5.27	2.7	-2
2003	TBY	AL	27	27	10	70.7	82	23	46	12	5.36	5.33	10.3	2.7	5.6	1.4	5.19	4.1	-6

Breakout: 16%   Improve: 47%   Collapse: 19%

Harper was used everywhere from starter to closer with the chaotic Rays staff in 2002. He pitched poorly in his emergency starts, but showed some of his 2001 form from the pen. Hopefully, a more defined role is in the cards for him in 2003.

Delvin James — Born: 03-Jan-78 — Age: 25 — Bats: R — Throws: R

YEAR	TM	LG	AGE	G	GS	IP	H	BB	SO	HR	ERA	EQERA	EQH9	EQBB9	EQSO9	EQHR9	PERA	VORP	STF
2000	STP	FSL	22	22	22	137.3	142	27	74	10	4.26	5.46	11.9	2.3	3.5	1.7	5.57	0.7	-3
2000	ORL	SOU	22	6	6	37.0	31	7	26	3	2.92	4.64	10.4	1.9	4.6	1.4	4.12	3.6	8
2001	ORL	SOU	23	7	7	43.7	25	9	31	1	1.65	2.20	6.2	2.2	4.3	0.3	2.23	16.0	14
2001	DUR	INT	23	31	9	84.3	99	27	51	8	4.80	6.59	12.7	3.5	4.4	1.2	6.20	-10.7	-12
2002	ORL	SOU	24	3	1	12.7	12	2	13	2	3.54	5.66	12.1	1.6	7.1	3.2	5.22	-0.3	5
2002	DUR	INT	24	7	7	34.3	41	4	26	4	3.94	5.12	12.2	1.3	5.8	1.6	5.65	1.5	8
2002	TBY	AL	24	8	6	34.3	40	15	17	5	6.56	5.62	10.3	3.7	4.3	1.2	5.45	-0.5	-7
2003	TBY	AL	25	17	11	67.3	80	22	41	10	5.26	5.24	10.5	2.7	5.2	1.2	5.07	5.3	-3

Breakout: 17%   Improve: 50%   Collapse: 22%

The Devil Rays blew the rest of MLB away with a 2.0 SPC (Starting Pitchers Capped) in 2002. Whatever else you might say about them, being a starter in this organization is not dull. James' recovery from a gunshot wound sustained in a Waffle House stickup on September 3 was swift, and he pitched in three games for the Rays later that month. He sports a great fastball but needs a backup pitch or a conversion to short relief.

Joe Kennedy — Born: 24-May-79 — Age: 24 — Bats: R — Throws: L

YEAR	TM	LG	AGE	G	GS	IP	H	BB	SO	HR	ERA	EQERA	EQH9	EQBB9	EQSO9	EQHR9	PERA	VORP	STF
2000	CSC	SAL	21	22	22	136.3	122	29	142	6	3.30	4.93	10.8	2.6	5.4	1.0	4.82	8.7	13
2001	ORL	SOU	22	7	7	47.0	29	3	52	0	0.19	1.35	6.5	0.7	6.7	0.2	1.88	21.7	36
2001	DUR	INT	22	4	4	26.0	22	9	23	2	2.42	3.95	9.1	3.7	6.4	1.0	4.15	4.5	18
2001	TBY	AL	22	20	20	117.7	122	34	78	16	4.44	4.12	8.8	2.4	5.6	1.1	4.29	18.1	14
2002	TBY	AL	23	30	30	196.7	204	55	109	23	4.53	4.37	9.2	2.4	4.9	1.0	4.14	24.8	9
2003	TBY	AL	24	28	27	173.7	188	53	110	23	4.64	4.62	9.5	2.5	5.5	1.1	4.49	21.9	8

Breakout: 12%   Improve: 54%   Collapse: 19%

On pace to pitch 235 innings by the break, Kennedy had a pedestrian second half, complaining of a tired arm in late August. It's tough to blame the coaching staff for using Kennedy the way they did; they had absolutely nothing else to work with. Still, both Kennedy and the organization would have been better off if he'd been handled more gently. He'll be the staff's ace in performance, if not role, in 2003.

Steve Kent — Born: 03-Oct-78 — Age: 24 — Bats: B — Throws: L

YEAR	TM	LG	AGE	G	GS	IP	H	BB	SO	HR	ERA	EQERA	EQH9	EQBB9	EQSO9	EQHR9	PERA	VORP	STF
2000	EVE	NWN	21	24	3	52.7	38	23	61	5	2.56	4.22	10.7	5.1	5.7	3.0	5.04	7.0	-10
2001	SBR	CLF	22	51	0	65.3	50	34	73	2	2.21	4.44	9.4	6.3	5.9	0.6	4.59	6.8	-6
2002	TBY	AL	23	34	0	57.3	67	38	41	6	5.65	5.76	10.2	5.5	6.2	0.9	5.82	-2.4	-5
2003	SEA	AL	24	24	6	50.0	51	29	39	8	5.36	5.76	9.4	4.8	6.6	1.3	5.58	1.2	-8

Breakout: 16%   Improve: 49%   Collapse: 21%

Steve Kent *(continued)*

Kent had never pitched above A-ball before the Angels nabbed him in the 2001 Rule 5 draft and then sold him to the Rays. He made the team, but was generally as much of a waste of time as your average Rule 5 player, and the Mariners grabbed him back off of waivers after the season ended. Kent might well turn into something down the road, but a year in the majors didn't do anything for his future.

Mark Malaska											Born: 17-Jan-78		Age: 25		Bats: L		Throws: L		
YEAR	TM	LG	AGE	G	GS	IP	H	BB	SO	HR	ERA	EQERA	EQH9	EQBB9	EQSO9	EQHR9	PERA	VORP	STF
2000	HUD	NYP	22	10	5	40.3	44	14	36	1	4.91	6.62	12.6	4.2	4.5	1.0	7.41	-5.1	-9
2001	CSC	SAL	23	25	25	157.0	153	35	152	11	2.92	5.82	12.7	3.1	5.1	1.6	6.17	-5.5	2
2001	BAK	CLF	23	3	3	17.7	14	5	13	1	4.07	4.48	9.3	3.4	3.9	1.0	3.92	2.0	0
2002	BAK	CLF	24	15	15	91.3	98	12	94	5	2.96	4.88	11.9	1.5	5.4	0.9	4.89	6.3	12
2002	ORL	SOU	24	12	11	70.7	82	28	49	4	3.69	6.23	13.4	4.0	4.7	1.1	6.66	-5.7	-3

A Cal League All-Star with the Blaze in 2002, Malaska saw his strikeouts plummet after his promotion to Double-A. He doesn't get the prospect watchers excited because he's fairly old for his competition and doesn't have a good fastball. That's the type of pitcher that Double-A eats alive, so next year will be pivotal, and he did pitch well in the AFL.

Seth McClung											Born: 07-Feb-81		Age: 22		Bats: R		Throws: R		
YEAR	TM	LG	AGE	G	GS	IP	H	BB	SO	HR	ERA	EQERA	EQH9	EQBB9	EQSO9	EQHR9	PERA	VORP	STF
2000	HUD	NYP	19	8	8	43.7	37	17	38	0	1.85	4.37	9.1	4.6	4.3	0.3	5.30	5.5	2
2000	CSC	SAL	19	6	6	31.0	30	19	26	0	3.19	5.96	11.6	7.7	4.5	0.3	6.75	-1.6	-8
2001	CSC	SAL	20	28	28	164.3	142	53	165	6	2.79	5.36	10.8	4.5	5.2	0.8	5.40	2.6	7
2002	BAK	CLF	21	7	7	37.0	35	11	48	1	2.92	4.25	10.2	3.3	6.7	0.5	4.44	5.2	21
2002	ORL	SOU	21	20	19	114.0	138	53	64	12	5.37	7.45	14.7	4.8	3.9	2.1	7.76	-24.7	-12

Here's a guy that sets scouts' hearts aflutter. McClung is built like a brick outhouse and has been clocked in the high 90s. He had a tough campaign at Orlando, and is working on improving the rest of his assortment during the off-season. Tampa Bay has pledged to take their time with him.

Travis Phelps											Born: 25-Jul-77		Age: 25		Bats: R		Throws: R		
YEAR	TM	LG	AGE	G	GS	IP	H	BB	SO	HR	ERA	EQERA	EQH9	EQBB9	EQSO9	EQHR9	PERA	VORP	STF
2000	ORL	SOU	22	21	21	108.0	85	46	106	5	3.00	4.76	9.4	4.2	6.3	0.8	4.37	8.9	13
2000	DUR	INT	22	6	6	29.7	29	16	21	6	4.85	5.86	10.0	4.9	5.5	2.4	6.29	-1.2	-4
2001	DUR	INT	23	9	0	15.7	11	1	12	0	0.00	0.34	7.5	0.7	5.5	0.2	2.08	8.8	15
2001	TBY	AL	23	49	0	62.0	53	24	54	6	3.48	3.50	7.2	3.2	7.3	0.8	3.42	13.0	11
2002	DUR	INT	24	27	0	31.0	29	14	34	2	4.35	4.96	9.5	4.9	8.4	0.9	4.82	1.4	7
2002	TBY	AL	24	26	0	37.7	30	27	36	7	4.77	4.47	6.8	5.9	8.2	1.5	4.68	3.8	2
2003	*TBY*	*AL*	*25*	*36*	*4*	*62.7*	*62*	*31*	*52*	*8*	*4.66*	*4.64*	*8.7*	*4.0*	*7.2*	*1.0*	*4.59*	*8.0*	*1*

Breakout: 16%   Improve: 55%   Collapse: 17%

In his third appearance of the year, Phelps was torched for three runs in a third of an inning by the Orioles. He was in the minors five days later. Was it to work on his sinker, or because the Rays didn't like being shown up by those Baltimore wiseacres? Phelps will be one of the better pitchers in the bullpen this year.

Ryan Rupe											Born: 31-Mar-75		Age: 28		Bats: R		Throws: R		
YEAR	TM	LG	AGE	G	GS	IP	H	BB	SO	HR	ERA	EQERA	EQH9	EQBB9	EQSO9	EQHR9	PERA	VORP	STF
2000	DUR	INT	25	5	5	19.3	24	7	18	3	6.53	7.30	12.6	3.3	7.2	1.8	6.82	-3.8	1
2000	TBY	AL	25	18	18	91.0	121	31	61	19	6.92	6.07	11.2	2.5	5.8	1.6	5.90	-5.7	2
2001	DUR	INT	26	2	2	11.0	3	1	17	0	0.82	0.77	2.9	1.0	10.8	0.2	0.72	5.8	57
2001	TBY	AL	26	28	26	143.3	161	48	123	30	6.59	5.58	9.4	2.8	7.1	1.7	5.38	-1.2	8
2002	TBY	AL	27	15	15	90.0	83	25	67	11	5.60	4.36	8.1	2.3	6.5	1.0	3.61	11.5	16
2003	*BOS*	*AL*	*28*	*18*	*16*	*108.3*	*113*	*33*	*77*	*15*	*4.78*	*4.74*	*9.1*	*2.6*	*6.2*	*1.2*	*4.35*	*12.3*	*11*

Breakout: 17%   Improve: 49%   Collapse: 16%

The Devil Rays' first homegrown player to make the majors became Theo Epstein's first waiver claim as the Red Sox GM. Rupe's got electric stuff, but he battled knee problems throughout 2002, and that kind of injury has broken pitchers much better than Rupe. The Sox are considering Rupe as a reliever or even closer, something Tampa Bay might have tried themselves if they weren't still waiting on Jesus Colome.

Jorge Sosa Born: 28-Apr-77   Age: 26   Bats: B   Throws: R

YEAR	TM	LG	AGE	G	GS	IP	H	BB	SO	HR	ERA	EQERA	EQH9	EQBB9	EQSO9	EQHR9	PERA	VORP	STF
2001	EVE	NWN	24	21	7	58.7	45	19	57	2	1.69	4.26	9.3	4.4	4.7	0.8	4.22	7.8	-9
2002	TBY	AL	25	31	14	99.3	88	54	48	16	5.53	4.75	7.8	4.6	4.2	1.3	4.48	7.9	-14
2003	TBY	AL	26	23	11	71.0	77	36	44	11	5.56	5.53	9.5	4.2	5.3	1.3	5.25	2.1	-10

Breakout: 12%   Improve: 44%   Collapse: 20%

Another in the Rays' parade of Rule 5 players, Sosa stuck with the team all year and even started 14 games. Most teams wouldn't blow a roster spot on a converted outfielder who has less pitching experience than your average Pony Leaguer, but the Devil Rays are nothing if not determined in their curiosity. Sosa has good stuff, but he's got a long way to go to harness it.

Jason Standridge Born: 09-Nov-78   Age: 24   Bats: R   Throws: R

YEAR	TM	LG	AGE	G	GS	IP	H	BB	SO	HR	ERA	EQERA	EQH9	EQBB9	EQSO9	EQHR9	PERA	VORP	STF
2000	STP	FSL	21	10	10	56.0	45	31	41	4	3.38	5.25	9.4	6.4	4.7	1.6	5.42	1.6	-4
2000	ORL	SOU	21	17	17	97.0	85	43	55	4	3.62	5.48	10.6	4.5	3.7	0.7	4.99	0.3	-2
2001	DUR	INT	22	20	20	102.3	130	50	48	13	5.28	7.91	14.0	5.4	3.5	1.6	7.71	-27.3	-19
2001	TBY	AL	22	9	1	19.3	19	14	9	5	4.66	4.93	8.2	6.0	3.9	2.1	6.21	1.0	-23
2002	DUR	INT	23	29	29	173.0	168	64	111	12	3.12	4.60	9.9	4.1	5.0	0.9	4.82	17.4	5
2002	TBY	AL	23	1	0	3.0	7	4	1	1	9.00	11.04	20.0	10.9	2.8	2.7	15.30	-1.9	-62
2003	TBY	AL	24	15	10	62.3	74	32	41	10	5.77	5.74	10.4	4.3	5.6	1.4	5.68	1.9	-7

Breakout: 16%   Improve: 49%   Collapse: 20%

Standridge took a step forward with Durham, improving his previously mediocre strikeout to walk ratio and keeping runners off base. Standridge has had problems challenging batters in the past, and with his fastball-curve combo he can still improve in that area. He's probably not ready for prime time, but he may be handed a starting job in 2003.

Tanyon Sturtze Born: 12-Oct-70   Age: 32   Bats: R   Throws: R

YEAR	TM	LG	AGE	G	GS	IP	H	BB	SO	HR	ERA	EQERA	EQH9	EQBB9	EQSO9	EQHR9	PERA	VORP	STF
2000	CWS	AL	29	10	1	15.7	25	15	6	4	12.04	10.23	12.7	6.6	3.2	1.8	9.32	-8.4	-49
2000	TBY	AL	29	19	5	52.7	47	14	38	4	2.56	2.54	7.7	2.0	6.3	0.6	2.78	17.0	12
2001	TBY	AL	30	39	27	195.3	200	79	110	23	4.42	4.06	8.7	3.4	4.7	1.0	4.44	31.0	0
2002	TBY	AL	31	33	33	224.0	271	89	137	33	5.18	5.29	10.7	3.3	5.3	1.2	5.56	5.4	1
2003	TOR	AL	32	29	28	172.0	202	67	103	26	5.38	5.20	10.2	3.2	5.2	1.2	5.21	9.3	1

Breakout: 9%   Improve: 37%   Collapse: 16%

Hal McRae rode him hard and put him away wet in an excruciating 2002, which saw Sturtze win the pitching Triple Raspberry, leading the league in hits, runs allowed, and losses. Sturtze's job was to pitch a ton of innings, and he did it with remarkable decorum for the Rays last season. Reunited with some of his ex-compadres from the Oakland organization in Toronto, where he'll be relied upon to be the third starter.

Jon Switzer Born: 13-Aug-79   Age: 23   Bats: L   Throws: L

YEAR	TM	LG	AGE	G	GS	IP	H	BB	SO	HR	ERA	EQERA	EQH9	EQBB9	EQSO9	EQHR9	PERA	VORP	STF
2001	HUD	NYP	21	5	0	14.3	9	2	20	0	0.63	2.84	7.5	1.8	6.9	0.3	2.70	4.0	21
2002	BAK	CLF	22	20	20	103.3	108	26	129	8	4.27	5.20	11.8	2.9	6.6	1.3	5.38	3.5	14

While we've got plenty of data on pitch counts for the pros, we don't have a lot of insight on the college game. Boyd Nation (http://www.boydsworld.com/) is applying our PAP^3 system to college players, and at Arizona State in 2001, Switzer racked up more PAP than any other college pitcher save Kenny Baugh and Pete Montrenes. Baugh missed all of 2002 after surgery to repair a shoulder tear, and Montrenes has yet to pitch professionally. Randy Johnson and Bartolo Colon were the only major leaguers with more PAP than Switzer in 2001. Switzer's workload might or might not have had something to do with a loss of velocity in his senior year, and he had to be shut down with elbow tendonitis in August 2002. He's changing his mechanics to put less stress on his arm, and he has shown a return to the low 90s velocity that excited scouts in the first place, but don't say you haven't been warned.

Doug Waechter　　　　　　　Born: 28-Jan-81　　Age: 22　　Bats: R　　Throws: R

YEAR	TM	LG	AGE	G	GS	IP	H	BB	SO	HR	ERA	EQERA	EQH9	EQBB9	EQSO9	EQHR9	PERA	VORP	STF
2000	HUD	NYP	19	14	14	72.7	53	37	58	2	2.35	3.87	8.4	6.1	4.0	1.1	5.25	13.2	-6
2001	CSC	SAL	20	26	26	153.3	179	38	107	14	4.34	7.86	15.8	3.6	3.8	2.2	8.16	-40.1	-10
2002	CSC	SAL	21	7	7	36.3	39	16	36	2	3.47	6.93	14.0	5.9	5.8	1.4	7.18	-5.7	0
2002	BAK	CLF	21	17	17	108.3	114	29	101	9	2.66	4.56	12.0	3.1	4.9	1.4	5.58	11.4	7
2002	ORL	SOU	21	4	4	18.0	27	13	18	4	9.00	11.96	19.7	7.7	7.2	4.6	11.80	-12.9	-19

Waechter put a grisly year at Charleston behind him, netting an early call-up to Bakersfield and quickly becoming the Blaze's best pitcher. He's an aggressive power pitcher with a football player's mentality, which isn't surprising considering he was a top prep quarterback. He'll start the season facing the toughest test by jumping up to Double-A.

Paul Wilson　　　　　　　　Born: 28-Mar-73　　Age: 30　　Bats: R　　Throws: R

YEAR	TM	LG	AGE	G	GS	IP	H	BB	SO	HR	ERA	EQERA	EQH9	EQBB9	EQSO9	EQHR9	PERA	VORP	STF
2000	SLU	FSL	27	5	5	25.7	22	4	19	0	1.40	4.02	9.7	1.8	4.7	0.3	3.56	4.2	8
2000	NOR	INT	27	15	13	83.0	85	25	56	7	4.23	4.82	10.6	2.8	5.3	1.0	4.71	6.3	4
2000	TBY	AL	27	11	7	51.0	38	16	40	1	3.35	2.46	6.5	2.3	6.9	0.1	2.02	17.1	23
2001	TBY	AL	28	37	24	151.3	165	52	119	21	4.88	4.67	9.2	2.9	6.6	1.1	4.73	13.7	6
2002	TBY	AL	29	30	30	193.7	219	67	111	29	4.83	4.84	10.0	2.9	5.0	1.2	5.03	14.3	1
2003	*CIN*	*NL*	*30*	*26*	*24*	*155*	*164*	*55*	*105*	*18*	*4.53*	*4.85*	*9.7*	*2.8*	*5.4*	*1.0*	*4.75*	*12.2*	*6*

Breakout: 12%　　Improve: 47%　　Collapse: 16%

Tampa Bay made attempts to trade Wilson at the deadline, but they didn't see an offer they liked. He may have been disheartened by the non-trade, because he ended the year on a note as ugly as the one he started off on in 2001. Wilson is a talented pitcher with mysterious streaks of god-awful that you want to put on the D-Rays. I'd like to see what Don Gullett or Joe Kerrigan would do with him, and happily enough, he signed with the Reds.

Esteban Yan　　　　　　　　Born: 22-Jun-75　　Age: 28　　Bats: R　　Throws: R

YEAR	TM	LG	AGE	G	GS	IP	H	BB	SO	HR	ERA	EQERA	EQH9	EQBB9	EQSO9	EQHR9	PERA	VORP	STF
2000	TBY	AL	25	43	20	137.7	158	42	111	26	6.21	5.08	9.7	2.2	7.0	1.4	4.77	6.0	8
2001	TBY	AL	26	54	0	62.3	64	11	64	7	3.90	3.88	8.7	1.5	8.6	0.9	3.73	10.4	17
2002	TBY	AL	27	55	0	69.0	70	29	53	10	4.30	4.34	8.9	3.5	6.7	1.2	4.62	8.0	-2
2003	*TBY*	*AL*	*28*	*37*	*5*	*63.0*	*66*	*22*	*47*	*8*	*4.47*	*4.45*	*9.2*	*2.9*	*6.5*	*1.1*	*4.38*	*9.5*	*0*

Breakout: 17%　　Improve: 48%　　Collapse: 17%

His stats aren't that bad, but the blown saves really stick out, as he's logged 41 saves against 17 blown saves over the last two seasons, and he's 42/26 over his career. Unsurprisingly, he lost the closer job in August, and Lou Piniella won't put up with this nonsense from his fireman, so the Rays will be actively courting closers this off-season. Yan escaped to Texas as a free agent, where he'll join the usual veteran middle relief shuffle that Hart seems to like to assemble.

Vic Zambrano　　　　　　　Born: 06-Aug-74　　Age: 28　　Bats: R　　Throws: R

YEAR	TM	LG	AGE	G	GS	IP	H	BB	SO	HR	ERA	EQERA	EQH9	EQBB9	EQSO9	EQHR9	PERA	VORP	STF
2000	DUR	INT	25	53	0	62.7	72	29	55	9	5.02	6.14	11.6	4.2	6.8	1.7	6.53	-5.3	-10
2001	DUR	INT	26	29	0	30.3	26	12	29	2	2.08	4.13	9.2	4.3	6.9	0.8	4.29	4.2	-2
2001	TBY	AL	26	36	0	51.3	38	18	58	6	3.16	3.00	6.2	2.9	9.4	0.9	2.93	13.6	21
2002	DUR	INT	27	10	0	14.0	9	4	15	2	1.93	3.22	6.8	3.1	8.2	1.9	3.28	3.4	7
2002	TBY	AL	27	42	11	114.0	120	68	73	15	5.53	5.32	9.2	5.0	5.5	1.1	5.25	1.6	-10
2003	*TBY*	*AL*	*28*	*33*	*10*	*74.7*	*81*	*41*	*55*	*11*	*5.39*	*5.36*	*9.5*	*4.5*	*6.4*	*1.2*	*5.40*	*3.4*	*-7*

Breakout: 7%　　Improve: 39%　　Collapse: 27%

Zambrano's 4.27 ERA as a starter in 2002 looks OK, but he allowed six unearned runs in only 65.1 innings, which make for much less pretty 5.10 RA per nine. He's been anointed a starter in 2003, but the Rays have better options, and they'll be utilizing them sooner rather than later.

Texas Rangers

It was another long summer in the Metroplex. For the third year in a row, the Rangers played themselves out of contention by the All-Star break. For the third year in a row, they were the highest-paid last place team in the majors. This would seem to be another story of an inept front office with deep pockets but no vision, spending like crazy but accumulating no talent—The Oriole Story, Part II. It would seem to be, except for one thing.

The Rangers just aren't all that bad.

Now wait, you say. The Rangers finished 72–90 last year, and 72–90 is a bad record, no matter what. And don't try to give us the old injury excuse. After all, the Rangers had an old team, with a bunch of regulars who visit the DL as often as Robert Downey Jr. visits Promises. Injuries are the rule on a team like that, not the exception.

All true. But even with the injuries, the Rangers were a far better team than their 72–90 record, for a couple of reasons. One reason is found in their run differential. Bill James showed us long ago that teams' win-loss records can be predicted fairly accurately from their runs scored and runs allowed totals, and that deviations from that prediction are generally a matter of luck. The Rangers scored 843 runs and allowed 882, which projects to a 77–85 record according to James's Pythagorean formula, as well as that of our own Clay Davenport's Pythagenports. In other words, the Rangers lost five more games than they "deserved" to, given the strength of their offense and defense.

The Rangers' bad luck with their run differential has gotten at least a little attention, with the topic showing up on ESPN.com and a few other places. But another source of bad luck has been almost completely ignored: the Rangers' brutal schedule. Thanks to the unbalanced schedule, the Rangers had to play 58 of their 162 games against the A's, Angels, and Mariners—three of the five best teams in the American League. By contrast, teams outside the AL West had to play those three fewer than half as many times.

The schedule was especially tough on the Rangers' hitting. On the surface, the high-priced Texas offense was a disappointment last year, finishing only fifth in the AL in run scoring despite playing half their games in the hitter-friendly Ballpark in Arlington. The EqA report on the Baseball Prospectus Web site, which adjusts for park, ranked the Ranger offense a mediocre seventh in the AL. But the Rangers' AL West opponents finished first, second, and fifth in the AL in ERA last year, a fact that could go a long way toward explaining their relatively meager output.

That's a fine argument for a fan's postseason finger-pointing—remember, all your team's problems are caused by the unbalanced schedule, Donald Fehr, and the Trilateral Commission—but we'd like to be a little more objective and quantitative here. Just how much of a difference can a tough schedule like the Rangers' make?

Let's look first at just the effect on the offense. We can measure the strength of schedule the offense faced pretty simply, by averaging the quality of pitching staffs faced weighted by the number of innings in which they faced them. (Here and below we'll use "pitching staff" as a shorthand for "total team defense.") Figuring out the quality of a pitching staff is a little more complicated, because we want to remove the distortions of the unbalanced schedule. So the quality of each pitching staff is going to depend on the mix of offenses it faces, which in turn will depend on the mix of pitching staffs they face, etc.; it's a circular problem. It isn't too hard to come up with a reasonable formulation of the problem (we'll skip the math here), which we can give to a computer to churn away until the results converge.

Table 1 shows the five toughest and five easiest schedules for offenses in the majors last year. The schedules are given in terms of percent over or under league average, so for example Minnesota's rating of +2.5% means the average pitching staff the Twins faced gave up runs at a rate 2.5%

Rangers Prospectus

2002 record: 72–90; Fourth place, AL West

Pythagenport Record: 77–85

Runs scored per game: 5.2 (5th in AL)

Runs allowed per game: 5.4 (12th in AL)

Team EqA: .265 (7th in AL)

2002 Batters Age: 29.6 (7th oldest in AL)

2002 Pitchers Age: 30.3 (4th oldest in AL)

Ballpark: The Ballpark in Arlington; Severe hitters' park; Park Factor of 1.049

2002: Following his old game plan, the new GM threw money at his problems, creating more problems.

2003: Weak pitching will again keep the Rangers from competing in the AL's toughest division; will they blame A-Rod or themselves?

Table 1.

1.	Rangers	-3.7%
2.	Padres	-2.4%
3.	Devil Rays	-2.2%
4.	Blue Jays	-1.9%
5.	Brewers	-1.3%
	. . .	
26.	Royals	+1.7%
27.	Astros	+1.8%
28.	Diamondbacks	+1.8%
29.	Twins	+2.5%
30.	Braves	+2.8%

higher than the league as a whole. All the numbers in tables 1 and 2 are park-adjusted.

The Rangers offense faced by far the toughest slate of pitching staffs in the majors last year, with the average Rangers opponent giving up 3.7% fewer runs than the league average. Not only did Texas hitters have to face a disproportionate number of Angels, A's, and Mariners hurlers, they were naturally enough also denied the opportunity of teeing off against their own subpar pitching staff. A figure of 3.7% isn't an overwhelming disadvantage, but it does make a difference. One way to look at it is that most of the benefit the Ranger hitters gain from playing half their games in their offense-inflating ballpark (five-year park factor: +4.9%) is wiped out by their offense-deflating schedule.

And how does adjusting for schedule change our assessment of various teams' hitting? Table 2 presents the top offenses in the AL after removing the schedule difficulty bias in the way described above. As before, offense strength is in terms of percent above or below league average. So the Yankees' schedule-adjusted rating of +16% means they scored 16% more runs than an average team would, playing their schedule in their park.

Without accounting for the schedule, the Ranger offense ranked 7th in the AL, behind the White Sox and A's among others. But after correcting for schedule disparities, Texas

Table 2.

Team	"Raw" Offense	Schedule-Adjusted Offense
Yankees	+16%	+16%
Mariners	+11%	+14%
Red Sox	+14%	+13%
Angels	+11%	+10%
Rangers	+4%	+9%
White Sox	+10%	+8%
Blue Jays	+4%	+6%
Athletics	+5%	+5%

hitters look much better: fifth best in the league, and not far behind fourth place Anaheim. That's still disappointing for a team that was pegged by some to score 1,000 runs, but the Ranger offense wasn't as mediocre as it looked.

Doing the same sort of analysis on the pitching side, we find that the unbalanced schedule wasn't nearly as tough on Ranger pitching as it was on their hitting. That's partly because their AL West opponents are built more on pitching than on hitting, and partly because Ranger pitchers didn't have to face their own team's solid offense. Still, the unbalanced schedule was tougher on Ranger pitching than it was on most teams. The average offense faced by the Rangers was 1% better than a league average offense, meaning the Ranger pitching staff was a little better than most pitching metrics (even the park-adjusted ones) give it credit for.

So what's the bottom line—how much difference did the Rangers' tough schedule make to the team overall? We can answer that by taking the schedule-adjusted offense and defense ratings described above and applying the Pythagorean formula to them to get a schedule-adjusted predicted win-loss record. The overall schedule difficulty would be the difference between their schedule-adjusted Pythagorean record and their regular Pythagorean record. Table 3 shows the teams that faced the five toughest and five easiest schedules in the majors in 2002.

The end result of this analysis is an eye-opener for the Rangers: When you remove the bias of the unbalanced schedule, the Rangers' 2002 performance (runs scored and runs allowed) was that of a .500 team. The Rangers played just about as well last year as the AL Central champion Minnesota Twins; they just played against a much tougher mix of opponents.

This may not be much of a consolation to Ranger fans. Yes, the analysis can be useful for assessing individual Ranger players. It's worth knowing that Ranger hitters are better than their park-adjusted numbers show, for example. It makes Miguel Tejada's MVP win over Alex Rodriguez seem

Table 3.

Team	Pyth W–L Pct	Pyth W–L Pct/SA	Diff
1. Rockies	.409	.438	+.029
2. Rangers	.477	.501	+.024
3. Orioles	.421	.445	+.024
4. Blue Jays	.489	.512	+.023
5. Devil Rays	.340	.363	+.023
. . .			
26. Cubs	.457	.442	-.015
27. Astros	.537	.520	-.017
28. White Sox	.534	.507	-.027
29. Cardinals	.601	.573	-.028
30. Twins	.542	.508	-.034

even more ludicrous, if that's possible. But does it offer much hope for the team going forward? After all, the Rangers aren't moving to the sorry AL Central anytime soon. They'll still face the same terrible trio from the AL West this year, right?

Yes and no. It's true that the AL West as a whole still looks pretty strong again this year. The A's, in particular, just get better and better, as Billy Beane continues his reign of terror over the rest of the league's GMs. But there are chinks in the armor of the Rangers' other two AL West opponents. The Mariners, who already felt some aches and pains from old age last year, are looking at an even older core in 2003. And the Angels are unlikely to put up another 99-win season while finishing 26th in the majors in walks and 21st in homers.

Meanwhile the Rangers have some reasons to hope for improvement. They have a strong collection of young players at or near the major league level in Kevin Mench, Hank Blalock, Mark Teixeira, Joaquin Benoit, and Colby Lewis. One or more of them could step up and make meaningful contributions this year. They have a shiny new bullpen that they're paying over $15 million for in 2003. That may not be our idea of good resource allocation, but at least the bullpen should

be an improvement over last year's dismal parade of journeymen. They have more than their share of veterans who underperformed last year and stand to improve, Chan Ho Park, Juan Gonzalez, and Carl Everett chief among them. And they have a new manager with a track record of success with two similar teams.

That's not to say the Rangers are a favorite for a playoff spot. They have to deal with the losses of Ivan Rodriguez, Kenny Rogers, and Frank Catalanotto—three big holes that haven't been adequately filled. They have a management team that at times seems directionless, saying the right things about giving youth a chance but then signing veterans like Herbert Perry and Doug Glanville who can only clog up the works for the youngsters. They have a starting rotation that doesn't exactly scream "contender," to put it mildly.

But this Rangers team is better and much closer to contention than people think. With reasonable progress from Teixeira et al. coupled with the rest of the division returning to earth, Texas could be a regular playoff contender in one or two more years. And if a few things break right for them this year... well, stranger things have happened.

HITTERS

Hank Blalock — 3B — Born: 21-Nov-80 — Age: 22 — Bats: L — Throws: L

YEAR	TM	LG	AGE	AB	H	2B	3B	HR	BB	SO	SB	CS	AVG	OBP	SLG	MLVR	EQBA	EQOBP	EQSLG	EQMLVR	VORP	DEFENSE
2000	SAV	SAL	19	512	153	32	2	10	62	53	31	8	.299	.380	.428	.206	.237	.296	.346	-.238	-7.0	134-3B 3
2001	PCH	FSL	20	237	90	19	1	7	26	31	7	4	.380	.443	.557	.524	.303	.352	.459	.078	17.1	62-3B 9
2001	TUL	TXS	20	272	89	18	4	11	39	38	3	3	.327	.415	.544	.375	.272	.349	.453	.036	16.3	66-3B -2
2002	TEX	AL	21	147	31	8	0	3	20	43	0	0	.211	.310	.327	-.205	.224	.325	.354	-.179	.4	39-3B -2
2002	OKL	PCL	21	387	119	32	1	8	34	61	2	1	.307	.365	.457	.144	.278	.330	.411	-.053	12.8	89-3B -8
2003	TEX	AL	22	321	87	20	1	11	32	54	4	2	.272	.340	.445	.050	.275	.346	.450	.026	13.4	

Breakout: 27%   Improve: 58%   Collapse: 23%

In one short year, Hank Blalock went from The Next George Brett to The Next Richie Hebner. He's still a very fine prospect, but his flopping at the major league level in April and his subsequent disappointing, injury-plagued showing in Oklahoma serve as a good reminder of how big the error bars are on predictions based mostly on a single season. Unfortunately, that's often all the evidence that's available. But the next time you hear the name George Brett (or even, for that matter, Richie Hebner) mentioned in conjunction with a 21-year-old, set your hype-detector on high.

Jason Botts — RF — Born: 26-Jul-80 — Age: 22 — Bats: B — Throws: R

YEAR	TM	LG	AGE	AB	H	2B	3B	HR	BB	SO	SB	CS	AVG	OBP	SLG	MLVR	EQBA	EQOBP	EQSLG	EQMLVR	VORP	DEFENSE
2001	SAV	SAL	20	392	121	24	2	9	53	88	13	7	.309	.417	.449	.313	.249	.328	.366	-.141	-5.2	57-1B -9 42-RF -5
2002	PCH	FSL	21	401	102	22	5	9	75	99	7	2	.254	.390	.401	.145	.214	.317	.342	-.217	-15.8	83-RF -4
2003	TEX	AL	22	198	48	10	2	5	22	50	3	3	.244	.331	.391	-.052	.247	.337	.395	-.081	-3.6	

Breakout: 36%   Improve: 58%   Collapse: 15%

Oakland asked for Hank Blalock as compensation for the Rangers' illegal negotiations with Grady Fuson—yeah, right—but reportedly they were actually hoping to end up with Botts. It's easy to see the attraction. Botts already has the batting eye Oakland likes, and he's the kind of player who very well could convert some doubles into homers and vault into the top prospects lists next year. One to watch.

Jason Bourgeois SS Born: 04-Jan-82 Age: 21 Bats: B Throws: R

YEAR	TM	LG	AGE	AB	H	2B	3B	HR	BB	SO	SB	CS	AVG	OBP	SLG	MLVR	EQBA	EQOBP	EQSLG	EQMLVR	VORP		DEFENSE	
2001	PUL	APL	19	251	78	12	2	7	26	47	21	7	.311	.389	.458	.252	.212	.266	.313	-.359	-9.3		61-2B -1	
2002	SAV	SAL	20	522	133	21	5	8	40	66	22	11	.255	.321	.360	.009	.207	.250	.296	-.417	-26.9		97-SS -25	20-2B 1
2003	TEX	AL	21	202	49	8	2	5	14	33	4	3	.245	.302	.375	-.122	.247	.306	.379	-.156	.1			

Breakout: 69%   Improve: 87%   Collapse: 3%

A second round draft pick in 2000, Bourgeois raised some eyebrows with a fine rookie league showing in 2001, but lowered them again with a mediocre full-season debut last year. His defense at short really is as raw as that 2002 rating suggests. It's a sad comment on the state of the Rangers' low minors that Bourgeois was the best player on the Sand Gnats last year.

Frank Catalanotto UT Born: 27-Apr-74 Age: 29 Bats: L Throws: R

YEAR	TM	LG	AGE	AB	H	2B	3B	HR	BB	SO	SB	CS	AVG	OBP	SLG	MLVR	EQBA	EQOBP	EQSLG	EQMLVR	VORP		DEFENSE	
2000	TEX	AL	26	282	82	13	2	10	33	36	6	2	.291	.377	.457	.068	.295	.374	.464	.116	23.6		38-2B -4	13-1B -4
2001	TEX	AL	27	463	153	31	5	11	39	55	15	5	.330	.392	.490	.229	.346	.406	.516	.296	44.6		86-LF -1	
2002	TEX	AL	28	212	57	16	6	3	25	27	9	5	.269	.367	.443	.083	.286	.381	.474	.134	12.3		18-LF -1	15-2B 2
2003	TOR	AL	29	318	89	19	3	6	31	40	9	3	.281	.351	.416	.038	.284	.358	.427	.025	8.8			

Breakout: 3%   Improve: 25%   Collapse: 37%

Ironically, the versatility that made Catalanotto so attractive to the Rangers when they acquired him may have played a role in his being dropped by the team three years later. Part of the rationale given for Catalanotto's being non-tendered in December was that he never established himself at any position. If he weren't so busy putting out fires all over the diamond, the Rangers might have allowed him to establish himself at second base, and in the process noticed he is a vastly superior player to Michael Young. If healthy and given a chance, he should easily beat the projection above. Toronto is a great place for him to thrive in a full-time or almost full-time role.

Jermaine Clark 2B Born: 29-Sep-76 Age: 26 Bats: L Throws: R

YEAR	TM	LG	AGE	AB	H	2B	3B	HR	BB	SO	SB	CS	AVG	OBP	SLG	MLVR	EQBA	EQOBP	EQSLG	EQMLVR	VORP		DEFENSE
2000	NHV	EAS	23	447	131	23	9	2	87	69	38	8	.293	.423	.398	.182	.260	.366	.360	-.068	18.4		127-2B -4
2001	TAC	PCL	24	216	54	7	3	1	27	39	13	2	.250	.341	.324	-.155	.229	.314	.294	-.279	-3.7		66-2B 0
2002	TAC	PCL	25	368	98	14	4	6	62	59	29	14	.266	.375	.375	.018	.241	.340	.337	-.162	5.8		97-2B -9
2002	OKL	PCL	25	57	17	2	1	1	7	11	6	2	.298	.375	.421	.102	.276	.344	.379	-.073	.9		
2003	TEX	AL	26	153	39	7	2	2	18	25	5	2	.255	.338	.374	-.056	.257	.343	.378	-.084	3.1		

Breakout: 26%   Improve: 54%   Collapse: 26%

Obtained from Seattle as part of the Ismael Valdes deal, Clark has little power, but his tremendous batting eye and speed make him an intriguing leadoff candidate. Texas has discussed moving him to center field, although it's tough to see why. He could make a decent platoon partner with Michael Young in Arlington.

Carl Everett CF Born: 03-Jun-71 Age: 32 Bats: B Throws: R

YEAR	TM	LG	AGE	AB	H	2B	3B	HR	BB	SO	SB	CS	AVG	OBP	SLG	MLVR	EQBA	EQOBP	EQSLG	EQMLVR	VORP		DEFENSE
2000	BOS	AL	29	496	149	32	4	34	52	113	11	4	.300	.376	.587	.276	.310	.378	.607	.340	64.5		116-CF 3
2001	BOS	AL	30	409	105	24	4	14	27	104	9	2	.257	.323	.438	-.011	.273	.336	.471	.039	22.5		84-CF -1
2002	TEX	AL	31	374	100	16	0	16	33	77	2	3	.267	.337	.439	.023	.285	.352	.469	.075	15.5		70-OF -4
2003	TEX	AL	32	314	83	17	2	14	30	71	4	2	.264	.335	.459	.052	.267	.340	.464	.029	8.4		

Breakout: 16%   Improve: 39%   Collapse: 28%

Last year was a relatively quiet one for Everett, off-field and on. You rarely saw the "cancer in the clubhouse" articles so common during his stay in Boston. Unfortunately, he was a cancer at the plate for much of the year. We saw a glimpse of the 1999–2000 Everett in his .327/.405/.524 second half. With his knee healthy again, expect to see more of it this year.

Juan Gonzalez RF Born: 16-Oct-69 Age: 33 Bats: R Throws: R

YEAR	TM	LG	AGE	AB	H	2B	3B	HR	BB	SO	SB	CS	AVG	OBP	SLG	MLVR	EQBA	EQOBP	EQSLG	EQMLVR	VORP		DEFENSE
2000	DET	AL	30	461	133	30	2	22	32	84	1	2	.289	.337	.505	.087	.301	.341	.532	.163	27.0		54-RF -2
2001	CLE	AL	31	532	173	34	1	35	41	94	1	0	.325	.380	.590	.349	.340	.395	.621	.424	67.2		106-RF -1
2002	TEX	AL	32	277	78	21	1	8	17	56	2	0	.282	.325	.451	.033	.295	.340	.478	.077	10.5		57-RF 3
2003	TEX	AL	33	353	100	22	1	15	24	66	2	1	.283	.332	.482	.094	.286	.337	.488	.073	8.4		

Breakout: 3%   Improve: 29%   Collapse: 24%

Gonzalez has suffered from nagging injuries so often and for so long it's hard to remember he's only 33. The right thumb problems that did him in last year go beyond "nagging," though. He hurt the thumb in the third game of the season, and it completely sapped him of his power all year. And it hasn't gone away—it derailed his plans for winter ball as well. Gonzalez was once considered a serious threat to Aaron's home run record, but with his thumb, his back, and plain old Father Time staring him in the face, he's now a long shot even to reach 500.

Todd Greene   C   Born: 08-May-71   Age: 32   Bats: R   Throws: R

YEAR	TM	LG	AGE	AB	H	2B	3B	HR	BB	SO	SB	CS	AVG	OBP	SLG	MLVR	EQBA	EQOBP	EQSLG	EQMLVR	VORP	DEFENSE			
2000	SYR	INT	29	91	27	3	0	7	6	16	1	0	.297	.340	.560	.221	.264	.302	.505	.020	2.6	11-LF	-1		
2000	TOR	AL	29	85	20	2	0	5	5	18	0	0	.235	.278	.435	-.185	.247	.281	.447	-.117	.3				
2001	COH	INT	30	131	33	8	0	6	4	19	3	2	.252	.279	.450	-.016	.242	.268	.432	-.166	2.3	27-C	-3		
2001	NYY	AL	30	96	20	4	0	1	3	21	0	0	.208	.240	.281	-.400	.229	.266	.312	-.350	-2.7	25-C	-3		
2002	LVG	PCL	31	125	44	12	0	11	3	21	0	0	.352	.382	.712	.537	.301	.322	.602	.236	13.6	24-C	1		
2002	OKL	PCL	31	152	46	9	0	6	9	27	2	0	.303	.346	.480	.140	.276	.315	.434	-.049	6.7	23-C	-5		
2002	TEX	AL	31	112	30	5	0	10	2	23	0	0	.268	.287	.580	.134	.277	.301	.616	.194	7.7	12-1B	0	13-C	-1
2003	TEX	AL	32	190	49	10	0	9	10	36	1	1	.256	.297	.452	-.023	.258	.301	.458	-.052	3.4				

Breakout: 29%   Improve: 54%   Collapse: 26%

On the one hand, having Todd Greene start 13 games at first base and DH would seem to be a sure-fire sign of a team with some problems. On the other hand, if he hits like this, why not? Twenty-seven homers and .583 slugging is a heck of a year, even if much of it was off Triple-A pitching. Despite his reputation and past use as a lefty masher, he's never shown much of a platoon split. Signed to a one-year deal by the Rangers, he stands to be the more productive end of a catching tandem with Einar Diaz.

Rusty Greer   LF   Born: 21-Jan-69   Age: 34   Bats: L   Throws: L

YEAR	TM	LG	AGE	AB	H	2B	3B	HR	BB	SO	SB	CS	AVG	OBP	SLG	MLVR	EQBA	EQOBP	EQSLG	EQMLVR	VORP	DEFENSE	
2000	TEX	AL	31	394	117	34	3	8	51	61	4	1	.297	.382	.459	.085	.300	.379	.468	.135	22.4	87-LF	1
2001	TEX	AL	32	245	67	23	0	7	27	32	1	2	.273	.348	.453	.054	.286	.361	.478	.105	12.1	59-LF	-5
2002	TEX	AL	33	199	59	9	2	1	19	17	1	0	.296	.358	.377	-.000	.315	.374	.400	.043	6.7	19-LF	-2

Greer is out for the year after surgery to repair a severe rotator cuff tear, and he's looking at three more significant surgeries on various body parts after that. With that dismal medical future, it's tempting to conclude that his playing days are over, and to use this space to write a tribute to the longtime BP favorite's career. But even though he's facing an uphill battle, Greer is not the kind of guy who's going to go soft on his rehab, especially since he's on the payroll for 2004. Here's hoping we see Greer in uniform again. But think about pulling up short of the wall next time, OK Rusty?

Travis Hafner   1B   Born: 03-Jun-77   Age: 26   Bats: L   Throws: R

YEAR	TM	LG	AGE	AB	H	2B	3B	HR	BB	SO	SB	CS	AVG	OBP	SLG	MLVR	EQBA	EQOBP	EQSLG	EQMLVR	VORP	DEFENSE			
2000	PCH	FSL	23	436	151	34	1	22	67	86	0	4	.346	.453	.580	.519	.272	.357	.462	.063	18.3	59-1B	-2	18-3B	-4
2001	TUL	TXS	24	323	91	25	0	20	59	82	3	1	.282	.399	.545	.305	.236	.336	.453	-.017	7.0	78-1B	-1		
2002	OKL	PCL	25	401	137	22	1	21	79	76	2	1	.342	.463	.559	.475	.306	.416	.498	.245	36.7	62-1B	-2		
2002	TEX	AL	25	62	15	4	1	1	8	15	0	1	.242	.329	.387	-.075	.258	.343	.419	-.033	1.6				
2003	CLE	AL	26	275	75	15	1	14	38	57	3	2	.272	.366	.483	.137	.278	.375	.494	.136	13.4				

Breakout: 19%   Improve: 56%   Collapse: 12%

Hafner must have felt like he was living in Bizarro World every time he heard the phrase "blocked by Mike Lamb" in 2002. It was clear all year that he was underappreciated by the Ranger brass, who claimed he had no place to play. (This while Lamb was getting 215 PAs at first base and DH.) Now that he's with an organization that's likely to give him a chance, he should do great things.

Jason Hart   LF/1B   Born: 05-Sep-77   Age: 25   Bats: R   Throws: R

YEAR	TM	LG	AGE	AB	H	2B	3B	HR	BB	SO	SB	CS	AVG	OBP	SLG	MLVR	EQBA	EQOBP	EQSLG	EQMLVR	VORP	DEFENSE			
2000	MID	TXS	22	546	178	44	3	30	67	112	4	0	.326	.405	.582	.360	.261	.323	.465	-.003	12.4	125-1B	2		
2001	SAC	PCL	23	494	122	26	1	19	57	102	3	3	.247	.330	.419	-.065	.220	.297	.367	-.218	-15.5	132-1B	1		
2002	OKL	PCL	24	514	135	32	1	25	68	122	1	0	.263	.358	.475	.115	.238	.323	.427	-.075	1.8	68-LF	-11	51-1B	13
2002	TEX	AL	24	15	4	3	0	0	2	7	0	0	.267	.353	.467	.087	.267	.353	.533	.149	1.1				
2003	TEX	AL	25	192	49	11	1	8	19	41	3	2	.252	.324	.447	.011	.255	.329	.452	-.015	1.0				

Breakout: 32%   Improve: 61%   Collapse: 15%

Jason Hart *(continued)*

The change in organizations did little to solve Hart's biggest problem: inability to hit off-speed stuff. In his repeat year at Triple-A after coming over from Oakland in the Carlos Pena deal, Hart's batting average stayed low, his strikeouts stayed high, and he looked totally overmatched against breaking pitches. A batting eye and an ability to tee off on fastballs will take you a long way in pro baseball, but not quite all the way. Hart's future as a major league regular is looking less and less likely.

Bill Haselman				**C**						**Born: 25-May-66**				**Age: 37**		**Bats: R**			**Throws: R**	
YEAR	TM	LG	AGE	AB	H	2B	3B	HR	BB	SO	SB	CS	AVG	OBP	SLG	MLVR	EQBA	EQOBP	EQSLG	EQMLVR	VORP	DEFENSE
2000	TEX	AL	34	193	53	18	0	6	15	36	0	1	.275	.330	.461	-.025	.277	.327	.466	.020	12.0	55-C 1
2001	TEX	AL	35	130	37	6	0	3	8	27	0	1	.285	.331	.400	-.038	.300	.344	.423	.009	7.7	38-C 1
2002	TEX	AL	36	179	44	7	0	3	11	25	0	0	.246	.297	.335	-.198	.263	.315	.358	-.168	3.0	50-C -3
2003	DET	AL	37	135	32	7	0	2	9	22	0	0	.241	.293	.345	-.177	.249	.304	.372	-.169	-0.1	

Breakout: 25%   Improve: 50%   Collapse: 22%

Haselman has always been a below average defender, and now his bat has pretty much disappeared as well. He can still paste lefties over the last three years (.325/.384/.476), so he could still make himself useful for another couple of seasons if he can find a lefty-hitting catcher to back up or platoon with. It doesn't look like he's found it by signing a minor league deal with Detroit, where right-handed Brandon Inge is the mainstay.

Scott Heard				**C**						**Born: 02-Sep-81**				**Age: 21**		**Bats: L**			**Throws: R**	
YEAR	TM	LG	AGE	AB	H	2B	3B	HR	BB	SO	SB	CS	AVG	OBP	SLG	MLVR	EQBA	EQOBP	EQSLG	EQMLVR	VORP	DEFENSE
2001	PUL	APL	19	114	34	6	1	5	12	31	3	1	.298	.365	.500	.265	.203	.248	.331	-.374	-4.1	28-C -4
2001	SAV	SAL	19	268	61	13	1	5	30	71	1	2	.228	.310	.340	-.023	.188	.249	.284	-.445	-16.1	65-C -11
2002	SAV	SAL	20	414	88	13	1	8	67	81	2	1	.213	.329	.307	-.070	.172	.258	.255	-.473	-27.5	74-C -14
2003	TEX	AL	21	177	39	7	1	5	16	40	1	1	.220	.288	.355	-.187	.222	.292	.359	-.225	-2.7	

Breakout: 75%   Improve: 84%   Collapse: 9%

A trip to Savannah's Grayson Stadium in 2002 often included a bonus seminar in drafting strategy. Many nights, you could see a lesson in why you don't use high picks on high school pitchers (David Mead, picked 47th overall in 1999), and then look 70 feet away and see a lesson in why you don't use high picks on high school catchers (Heard, picked 25th overall in 2000).

Todd Hollandsworth				**LF**						**Born: 20-Apr-73**				**Age: 30**		**Bats: L**			**Throws: L**	
YEAR	TM	LG	AGE	AB	H	2B	3B	HR	BB	SO	SB	CS	AVG	OBP	SLG	MLVR	EQBA	EQOBP	EQSLG	EQMLVR	VORP	DEFENSE
2000	LAD	NL	27	261	61	12	0	8	30	61	11	4	.234	.315	.372	-.175	.242	.314	.385	-.146	2.4	65-CF 2
2000	COL	NL	27	167	54	8	0	11	11	38	7	3	.323	.365	.569	.205	.297	.333	.527	.138	9.7	40-LF 0
2001	COL	NL	28	117	43	15	1	6	8	20	5	0	.368	.408	.667	.489	.345	.387	.621	.420	15.5	25-LF 0
2002	COL	NL	29	298	88	21	1	11	26	71	7	8	.295	.354	.483	.129	.282	.337	.466	.042	10.0	73-LF 0
2002	TEX	AL	29	132	34	6	0	5	14	27	1	0	.258	.329	.417	-.026	.273	.347	.439	.014	3.5	29-LF 0
2003	FLO	NL	30	327	86	19	2	11	30	74	7	4	.264	.327	.437	-.008	.271	.330	.465	.018	5.4	

Breakout: 11%   Improve: 43%   Collapse: 24%

The trade that brought Hollandsworth over from the Rockies wasn't about Hollandsworth. It was about dumping the last year of Gabe Kapler's contract (albeit not all the salary), and in that respect it was a good move. The deal put the frustrating Kapler behind them once and for all, and allowed them to give playing time to young outfielders with a strong upside who will play a key role on the club's long-term future. Like Doug Glanville. Signed by the Marlins. For his speed. Really.

Jason Jones				**1B**						**Born: 17-Oct-76**				**Age: 26**		**Bats: B**			**Throws: R**	
YEAR	TM	LG	AGE	AB	H	2B	3B	HR	BB	SO	SB	CS	AVG	OBP	SLG	MLVR	EQBA	EQOBP	EQSLG	EQMLVR	VORP	DEFENSE	
2000	SAV	SAL	23	466	125	34	6	9	65	97	9	5	.268	.363	.425	.154	.210	.280	.335	-.301	-26.6	95-1B 5	
2001	PCH	FSL	24	375	106	26	2	15	56	48	1	3	.283	.377	.483	.248	.231	.304	.401	-.151	-5.8	98-1B -1	
2001	TUL	TXS	24	107	23	6	0	2	3	17	0	0	.215	.243	.327	-.292	.187	.213	.280	-.525	-11.1	28-1B -7	
2002	TUL	TXS	25	471	139	33	2	13	87	97	12	7	.295	.405	.456	.237	.252	.346	.396	-.063	4.4	120-1B -13	14-LF -1
2003	TEX	AL	26	172	43	10	1	5	19	36	2	2	.250	.326	.412	-.033	.252	.331	.416	-.061	-.9		

Breakout: 37%   Improve: 69%   Collapse: 17%

Jones deserves a mention for being the seventh most productive player in the Texas League, according to Clay Davenport's minor league rankings, and for subsequently tearing up the Puerto Rican winter league as well. He was way too old to be in Double-A, and for that reason he's not a great prospect. But you can never completely rule out the possibility that a bat like his will eventually find its way to the majors.

Gerald Laird   C   Born: 13-Nov-79   Age: 23   Bats: R   Throws: R

YEAR	TM	LG	AGE	AB	H	2B	3B	HR	BB	SO	SB	CS	AVG	OBP	SLG	MLVR	EQBA	EQOBP	EQSLG	EQMLVR	VORP	DEFENSE
2000	VIS	CLF	20	103	25	3	0	0	14	27	7	2	.243	.339	.272	-.186	.200	.260	.229	-.492	-6.8	27-C -1
2001	MOD	CLF	21	443	113	13	5	5	48	101	10	9	.255	.341	.341	-.059	.202	.268	.268	-.421	-21.0	80-C 7
2002	TUL	TXS	22	442	122	21	4	11	45	95	8	6	.276	.350	.416	.086	.240	.299	.369	-.199	4.3	95-C 2
2003	TEX	AL	23	179	42	8	1	4	14	40	2	2	.232	.293	.366	-.157	.234	.297	.371	-.193	-1.1	

Breakout: 44%   Improve: 62%   Collapse: 22%

If I had told you last year at this time that Gerald Laird was the most promising player the Rangers received in the Carlos Pena deal, you would have nodded politely, backed away, and started phoning friends to perform the intervention. That Laird can now legitimately claim that distinction is only partly a reflection of the disappointing seasons of the other three. Laird broke through in the second half with a big power surge, while maintaining the plate discipline you'd expect from a former Oakland farmhand. And he continued to do excellent work behind the plate. He won't make anyone forget Pudge Rodriguez, but Ranger fans hope he can make them forget Einar Diaz. The sooner the better.

Mike Lamb   1B/3B   Born: 09-Aug-75   Age: 27   Bats: L   Throws: R

YEAR	TM	LG	AGE	AB	H	2B	3B	HR	BB	SO	SB	CS	AVG	OBP	SLG	MLVR	EQBA	EQOBP	EQSLG	EQMLVR	VORP	DEFENSE	
2000	OKL	PCL	24	55	14	5	1	2	5	6	2	1	.255	.317	.491	.006	.236	.288	.436	-.128	.8	12-3B -7	
2000	TEX	AL	24	493	137	25	2	6	34	60	0	2	.278	.330	.373	-.151	.283	.327	.379	-.100	10.6	125-3B -10	
2001	OKL	PCL	25	273	81	19	3	8	13	31	0	2	.297	.336	.476	.078	.265	.303	.423	-.096	6.2	69-3B -14	
2001	TEX	AL	25	284	87	18	0	4	14	27	2	1	.306	.350	.412	.029	.320	.363	.430	.071	17.9	67-3B -6	
2002	TEX	AL	26	314	89	13	0	9	33	48	0	0	.283	.357	.411	.034	.298	.371	.438	.077	14.0	42-1B -5	13-3B -4
2003	TEX	AL	27	275	75	15	1	6	22	36	1	1	.271	.327	.397	-.034	.273	.332	.402	-.062	1.2		

Breakout: 11%   Improve: 32%   Collapse: 32%

The Mike Lamb at catcher experiment was a bold move by the Rangers. Unfortunately, Lamb gave up on the idea after only three games, and forced the club to a retreat back into the conventional wisdom that catchers are born not made. Granted, Lamb's three appearances behind the plate were embarrassing. But he has the raw materials to be a catcher—specifically, a decent arm—and he spent a season behind the plate in college. And you can't tell me he couldn't learn (or relearn) to block pitches given some time and the right coaching. Catcher seems like the best option for him; he doesn't hit well enough to play first, and doesn't field well enough to play third.

Ryan Ludwick   CF   Born: 13-Jul-78   Age: 24   Bats: R   Throws: L

YEAR	TM	LG	AGE	AB	H	2B	3B	HR	BB	SO	SB	CS	AVG	OBP	SLG	MLVR	EQBA	EQOBP	EQSLG	EQMLVR	VORP	DEFENSE
2000	MOD	CLF	21	493	130	26	3	29	68	128	10	6	.264	.363	.505	.197	.209	.276	.396	-.226	-5.9	118-CF 2
2001	MID	TXS	22	443	119	23	3	25	56	113	9	10	.269	.360	.503	.157	.217	.294	.406	-.173	.7	114-CF -7
2001	SAC	PCL	22	57	13	3	0	1	2	16	2	0	.228	.254	.333	-.347	.211	.237	.298	-.438	-3.5	17-CF 2
2002	OKL	PCL	23	305	87	27	4	15	38	76	2	2	.285	.374	.548	.261	.256	.336	.490	.050	17.7	78-CF -5
2002	TEX	AL	23	81	19	6	0	1	7	24	2	1	.235	.295	.346	-.193	.247	.307	.370	-.177	.0	17-CF 0
2003	TEX	AL	24	300	79	18	1	14	29	69	5	3	.263	.332	.473	.065	.265	.337	.478	.042	12.4	

Breakout: 46%   Improve: 70%   Collapse: 13%

One of the most promising prospects in the system suddenly became a huge question mark in August when Ludwick underwent an unusual surgery to repair a deteriorating hip fracture. Before the injury, Ludwick had his best year yet, manhandling PCL pitching and showing an adequate if unspectacular glove in center. Now the guy who looked like a fair bet to solve the Rangers' long-standing center field problem may never be heard from again. Or he could be OK. This kind of injury is unusual enough that no one will have much idea until spring.

Ramon Martinez   2B   Born: 22-Feb-80   Age: 23   Bats: B   Throws: R

YEAR	TM	LG	AGE	AB	H	2B	3B	HR	BB	SO	SB	CS	AVG	OBP	SLG	MLVR	EQBA	EQOBP	EQSLG	EQMLVR	VORP	DEFENSE	
2000	SAV	SAL	20	164	51	9	0	1	2	29	6	5	.311	.331	.384	.088	.248	.258	.309	-.359	-5.7	38-SS -1	
2000	PCH	FSL	20	152	44	7	1	1	5	28	8	3	.289	.312	.368	-.012	.242	.256	.314	-.360	-5.1	41-SS -2	
2001	PCH	FSL	21	515	124	20	1	2	28	65	28	18	.241	.286	.295	-.156	.206	.236	.256	-.502	-38.2	94-2B -5	34-SS -6
2002	PCH	FSL	22	472	144	21	8	3	32	44	39	15	.305	.357	.403	.136	.257	.294	.344	-.232	-2.0	99-2B 13	13-SS 1
2003	TEX	AL	23	181	45	9	2	2	10	25	5	2	.250	.292	.356	-.160	.252	.297	.360	-.196	-1.7		

Breakout: 52%   Improve: 73%   Collapse: 14%

Ramon Martinez (continued)

Yes, there's another Ramon Martinez to keep track of. This one's a middle infielder in the Texas system. He got a little bit of attention last year because of decent numbers in Port Charlotte, but he was repeating the level at a relatively advanced age, so the numbers don't mean much. Unless he does something surprising, like break out at Frisco (the Rangers' new Double-A affiliate) this year, you don't need to keep track of him after all.

Kevin Mench								**RF**		**Born: 07-Jan-78**			**Age: 25**		**Bats: R**		**Throws: R**	
YEAR	TM	LG	AGE	AB	H	2B	3B	HR	BB	SO	SB	CS	AVG	OBP	SLG	MLVR	EQBA	EQOBP	EQSLG	EQMLVR	VORP	DEFENSE
2000	PCH	FSL	22	491	164	39	9	27	78	72	19	7	.334	.432	.615	.527	.265	.345	.489	.073	21.0	119-LF -4
2001	TUL	TXS	23	475	126	34	2	26	34	76	4	6	.265	.322	.509	.128	.224	.271	.427	-.182	-12.6	117-RF -3
2002	OKL	PCL	24	98	21	8	0	6	17	33	0	0	.214	.342	.480	.053	.200	.312	.430	-.119	-1.1	25-RF -1
2002	TEX	AL	24	366	95	20	2	15	31	83	1	1	.260	.331	.448	.020	.275	.344	.480	.068	13.3	94-RF 2
2003	TEX	AL	25	413	110	26	2	20	38	80	4	3	.267	.335	.486	.090	.269	.340	.492	.068	9.7	

Breakout: 34%   Improve: 68%   Collapse: 7%

It's fitting that a player who draws so many comparisons to Pete Incaviglia would become the first Ranger rookie since Inky to hit 15 homers. The left wrist that has bothered him off and on since he had surgery on it in February 2001 is now finally, according Mench, back to 100%. He'll be part of the Rangers left field mix going into the spring. If he gets the ABs, he's a very strong candidate for a breakout year.

Drew Meyer								**2B**		**Born: 29-Aug-81**			**Age: 21**		**Bats: L**		**Throws: R**	
YEAR	TM	LG	AGE	AB	H	2B	3B	HR	BB	SO	SB	CS	AVG	OBP	SLG	MLVR	EQBA	EQOBP	EQSLG	EQMLVR	VORP	DEFENSE
2002	SAV	SAL	20	214	52	5	4	1	10	53	7	6	.243	.277	.318	-.121	.197	.222	.257	-.534	-17.0	32-SS -5 19-2B -3

Early notices on John Hart's inaugural draft pick with the Rangers are not good, but it is still early. Many observers thought Meyer, a shortstop from the University of South Carolina, was a reach with the number 10 pick, but the Rangers felt he was the best college hitter available. He struggled with the bat and the glove in his half season in the Sally League. He's in the process of a position switch, moving from shortstop to second base for obvious reasons.

Laynce Nix								**CF**		**Born: 30-Oct-80**			**Age: 22**		**Bats: L**		**Throws: L**	
YEAR	TM	LG	AGE	AB	H	2B	3B	HR	BB	SO	SB	CS	AVG	OBP	SLG	MLVR	EQBA	EQOBP	EQSLG	EQMLVR	VORP	DEFENSE
2001	SAV	SAL	20	407	113	26	8	8	37	94	9	6	.278	.341	.440	.177	.222	.272	.354	-.284	-23.8	103-RF -8
2002	PCH	FSL	21	512	146	27	3	21	72	105	17	1	.285	.380	.473	.241	.235	.309	.395	-.147	4.4	116-CF -7
2003	TEX	AL	22	206	51	11	2	6	18	48	3	3	.248	.312	.404	-.066	.250	.317	.408	-.097	-.1	

Breakout: 33%   Improve: 62%   Collapse: 12%

Nix's star continued to rise with breakthrough improvements in power and batting eye in 2002. The 2000 fourth round draft pick was named the Florida State League's MVP by *Baseball America*. Clay Davenport's statistical player rating (Runs Above Replacement Position) pegged him as the second most productive position player in the league behind the Cubs' Jason Dubois. Nix's work in center has drawn some raves as well, although it hasn't translated into good defensive numbers. If he passes the all-important Double-A test this year, his arrival in the Arlington outfield could come as early as 2004.

Rafael Palmeiro								**1B**		**Born: 24-Sep-64**			**Age: 38**		**Bats: L**		**Throws: L**	
YEAR	TM	LG	AGE	AB	H	2B	3B	HR	BB	SO	SB	CS	AVG	OBP	SLG	MLVR	EQBA	EQOBP	EQSLG	EQMLVR	VORP	DEFENSE
2000	TEX	AL	35	565	163	29	3	39	103	77	2	1	.288	.401	.558	.246	.292	.399	.569	.299	59.5	103-1B -10
2001	TEX	AL	36	600	164	33	0	47	101	90	1	1	.273	.384	.563	.256	.285	.395	.593	.317	67.0	112-1B -6
2002	TEX	AL	37	546	149	34	0	43	104	94	2	0	.273	.395	.571	.291	.290	.409	.610	.367	70.5	88-1B 10
2003	TEX	AL	38	490	132	28	1	30	82	86	1	0	.269	.378	.514	.192	.272	.384	.520	.177	29.8	

Breakout: 1%   Improve: 39%   Collapse: 10%

There were plenty of naysayers when Doug Melvin inked the 34-year-old creaky-kneed Palmeiro to a five-year $45 million deal prior to the 1999 season. But Palmeiro has earned every penny of that contract, regardless of what he does in its final year this year. Only a handful of elite first basemen—Giambi, Bagwell, Delgado, Thome, and Helton—have out-hit Palmeiro over the course of that contract, and most of them not by much. Palmeiro won't last forever, but he hasn't shown many signs of slowing down yet; even his work at first was noticeably improved in 2002 when his knees permitted him to play there. When he hits his 500th home run this May or June, they might as well start engraving the Cooperstown plaque.

Herbert Perry   3B   Born: 15-Sep-69   Age: 33   Bats: R   Throws: R

YEAR	TM	LG	AGE	AB	H	2B	3B	HR	BB	SO	SB	CS	AVG	OBP	SLG	MLVR	EQBA	EQOBP	EQSLG	EQMLVR	VORP	DEFENSE	
2000	CWS	AL	30	383	118	29	1	12	22	68	4	1	.308	.360	.483	.102	.316	.360	.500	.164	32.4	101-3B	2
2001	CWS	AL	31	285	73	21	1	7	23	55	2	2	.256	.327	.411	-.046	.274	.343	.439	.007	14.6	58-3B	-3
2002	TEX	AL	32	450	124	24	1	22	34	66	4	2	.276	.335	.480	.082	.290	.349	.508	.130	36.1	105-3B	-6
2003	TEX	AL	33	330	91	19	1	12	24	54	3	1	.275	.330	.452	.044	.277	.335	.457	.020	11.9		

Breakout: 12%   Improve: 46%   Collapse: 19%

Herbert Perry's playing time should be a good reverse indicator of the Rangers' success over the next two years. If Perry is limited to spot starts and pinch hits against lefties, it'll most likely be because Blalock and Teixeira are entrenching themselves in the lineup and on their way to becoming stars. If Perry is the regular third baseman—or worse, the regular first baseman— it'll be because something went wrong. Perry's a good player, and would be a bargain for a lot of teams at two years and $3 million. But it's not clear he should be paid that kind of money by a team that hopes they don't have to use him much.

Ruben Rivera   CF   Born: 14-Nov-73   Age: 29   Bats: R   Throws: R

YEAR	TM	LG	AGE	AB	H	2B	3B	HR	BB	SO	SB	CS	AVG	OBP	SLG	MLVR	EQBA	EQOBP	EQSLG	EQMLVR	VORP	DEFENSE	
2000	SDP	NL	26	423	88	18	6	17	44	137	8	4	.208	.298	.400	-.186	.221	.297	.421	-.144	4.1	121-CF	1
2001	CIN	NL	27	263	67	13	1	10	21	83	6	3	.255	.322	.426	-.064	.253	.317	.423	-.080	7.1	72-CF	1
2002	TUL	TXS	28	205	64	17	4	10	23	46	4	3	.312	.395	.580	.403	.263	.329	.493	.048	12.5	58-CF	-2
2002	OKL	PCL	28	98	27	2	4	7	13	23	2	0	.276	.366	.592	.299	.242	.328	.525	.071	3.7	26-RF	1
2002	TEX	AL	28	158	33	4	0	4	17	45	4	2	.209	.306	.310	-.234	.228	.322	.335	-.208	-1.2	64-CF	0
2003	TEX	AL	29	239	60	12	2	9	22	63	5	3	.251	.322	.434	-.010	.253	.327	.439	-.037	4.2		

Breakout: 25%   Improve: 58%   Collapse: 19%

I had a Ruben Rivera comment, but I put it in Derek Jeter's locker, and now it's gone.

Alex Rodriguez   SS   Born: 27-Jul-75   Age: 27   Bats: R   Throws: R

YEAR	TM	LG	AGE	AB	H	2B	3B	HR	BB	SO	SB	CS	AVG	OBP	SLG	MLVR	EQBA	EQOBP	EQSLG	EQMLVR	VORP	DEFENSE	
2000	SEA	AL	24	554	175	34	2	41	100	121	15	4	.316	.427	.606	.420	.334	.438	.644	.509	107.4	145-SS	18
2001	TEX	AL	25	632	201	34	1	52	75	131	18	3	.318	.404	.622	.410	.331	.414	.653	.484	115.0	155-SS	5
2002	TEX	AL	26	624	187	27	2	57	87	122	9	4	.300	.394	.623	.384	.316	.408	.659	.464	113.6	156-SS	9
2003	TEX	AL	27	577	171	34	3	43	91	117	11	2	.296	.396	.590	.336	.299	.402	.597	.329	78.9		

Breakout: 3%   Improve: 43%   Collapse: 12%

The Rodriguez/Tejada MVP debate shows that, much as they like to claim that their passion is baseball, most sportswriters are really aspiring professional semanticists. Given an opportunity to wax poetic about one of the greatest seasons ever by a shortstop, evoking great names from baseball's past like Wagner, Vaughan, Banks, and Ripken, they instead subjected us to long-winded philosophical treatises on the meaning of "value," or how context affects value. The most frustrating thing is that, for all of those writers who are tempted to engage in Clintonian meaning-twisting to justify a vote for their pet player, the BBWAA spells it out: the instructions sent to all MVP voters state that "value" is equivalent to "strength of [a player's] offense and defense." Would anyone seriously claim that Tejada had stronger offense or defense than ARod?

Ivan Rodriguez   C   Born: 30-Nov-71   Age: 31   Bats: R   Throws: R

YEAR	TM	LG	AGE	AB	H	2B	3B	HR	BB	SO	SB	CS	AVG	OBP	SLG	MLVR	EQBA	EQOBP	EQSLG	EQMLVR	VORP	DEFENSE	
2000	TEX	AL	28	363	126	27	4	27	19	48	5	5	.347	.381	.667	.448	.347	.375	.675	.487	62.3	82-C	12
2001	TEX	AL	29	442	136	24	2	25	23	73	10	3	.308	.348	.541	.204	.321	.362	.568	.273	54.6	99-C	15
2002	TEX	AL	30	408	128	32	2	19	25	71	5	4	.314	.356	.542	.236	.330	.374	.575	.313	55.5	94-C	1
2003	TEX	AL	31	396	119	26	2	20	24	64	6	3	.300	.342	.530	.187	.302	.347	.536	.171	33.4		

Breakout: 6%   Improve: 50%   Collapse: 22%

Reports of Pudge's demise have been greatly exaggerated. Yes, the four significant injuries the past three seasons (broken thumb, bruised heel, knee surgery, and herniated disc) are a concern, but so far none of them have turned out to be chronic problems. Other than the missed time, he's shown virtually no signs that the injuries are affecting his on-field performance, and no tendency to aggravate old injuries. His hitting was as good as ever last year after recovering from his back woes, and his defense, even if it may have slipped a bit, is still strong. Even with an expected post-30 decline, he should still be one of the top catchers in the game over the next two or three years.

Mark Teixeira   3B   Born: 11-Apr-81   Age: 22   Bats: B   Throws: R

YEAR	TM	LG	AGE	AB	H	2B	3B	HR	BB	SO	SB	CS	AVG	OBP	SLG	MLVR	EQBA	EQOBP	EQSLG	EQMLVR	VORP	DEFENSE	
2002	PCH	FSL	21	150	48	10	2	9	21	24	2	0	.320	.414	.593	.470	.256	.331	.474	.019	8.4	36-3B	-8
2002	TUL	TXS	21	171	54	11	3	10	25	36	3	2	.316	.415	.591	.445	.263	.346	.497	.083	12.8	47-3B	1
2003	TEX	AL	22	235	63	12	2	10	23	51	3	2	.269	.341	.469	.078	.272	.346	.474	.056	11.3		

Breakout: 18%   Improve: 39%   Collapse: 25%

You'd be right to notice the many parallels between Hank Blalock in 2001 and Teixeira in 2002, and to wonder whether Teixeira could see his stock drop this year just as quickly as Blalock's did last year. But there's one important difference between the two: Teixeira was already highly regarded before his big pro year. He was College Player of the Year, a highly polished #5 draft pick, and number 10 on our Top 40 Prospects list before he had played an inning of pro ball. Blalock's resume had nothing close to that. There's been some preliminary talk and experimenting with position shifts for both Teixeira and Blalock, but for now the Rangers are wisely taking a wait-and-see attitude on the impending position collision. They're also being cautious about rushing him, so he may spend most of the year in Oklahoma City.

Michael Young   2B   Born: 19-Oct-76   Age: 26   Bats: R   Throws: R

YEAR	TM	LG	AGE	AB	H	2B	3B	HR	BB	SO	SB	CS	AVG	OBP	SLG	MLVR	EQBA	EQOBP	EQSLG	EQMLVR	VORP	DEFENSE	
2000	TEN	SOU	23	345	95	24	5	6	36	72	16	5	.275	.346	.426	.090	.238	.291	.377	-.204	1.0	89-2B	1
2000	TUL	TXS	23	188	60	13	5	1	17	28	9	3	.319	.376	.457	.158	.271	.312	.388	-.125	4.2	41-SS	1
2001	OKL	PCL	24	189	55	8	0	8	20	34	3	3	.291	.362	.460	.096	.258	.324	.405	-.088	6.3	43-2B	-2
2001	TEX	AL	24	386	96	18	4	11	26	91	3	1	.249	.301	.402	-.115	.260	.314	.421	-.082	12.6	102-2B	-5
2002	TEX	AL	25	573	150	26	8	9	41	112	6	7	.262	.311	.382	-.100	.277	.327	.408	-.063	21.8	142-2B	4
2003	TEX	AL	26	474	121	24	4	11	37	91	7	5	.256	.312	.391	-.078	.258	.317	.395	-.109	5.5		

Breakout: 14%   Improve: 49%   Collapse: 23%

Young led all major league second basemen in Zone Rating last year, after putting up an above-average rating the year before. While that kind of defense might make his .700 OPS a little more palatable, it doesn't solve the mystery of how he managed to get 373 plate appearances in the first two spots of the lineup. Young is not the kind of player a team should be comfortable playing every day.

PITCHERS

Juan Alvarez   Born: 09-Aug-73   Age: 29   Bats: L   Throws: L

YEAR	TM	LG	AGE	G	GS	IP	H	BB	SO	HR	ERA	EQERA	EQH9	EQBB9	EQSO9	EQHR9	PERA	VORP	STF
2000	EDM	PCL	26	44	0	38.3	30	19	27	3	2.82	3.09	7.5	4.4	5.1	0.9	3.59	9.7	-12
2001	SLC	PCL	27	48	1	67.3	68	27	44	13	4.95	5.59	9.8	4.3	4.3	2.0	5.42	-1.5	-26
2002	OKL	PCL	28	15	0	17.3	19	9	13	1	3.64	4.43	10.6	5.5	5.3	0.7	5.77	1.8	-17
2002	TEX	AL	28	52	0	39.7	35	21	30	7	4.76	4.37	7.5	4.4	6.5	1.4	4.38	4.5	-8
2003	TEX	AL	29	42	0	28.7	33	16	20	5	5.65	5.40	10.1	4.7	6.0	1.3	5.56	2.6	-15

Breakout: 24%   Improve: 46%   Collapse: 23%

This was as close as the Rangers came to having an effective lefty in the bullpen in 2002—i.e., not very. He walks too many guys to be a solid middle reliever, and he doesn't have the lefty-killing ability to be a good LOOGY. Released.

Rob Bell   Born: 17-Jan-77   Age: 26   Bats: R   Throws: R

YEAR	TM	LG	AGE	G	GS	IP	H	BB	SO	HR	ERA	EQERA	EQH9	EQBB9	EQSO9	EQHR9	PERA	VORP	STF
2000	LOU	INT	23	6	6	41.0	35	13	47	6	3.73	4.16	8.5	2.9	8.8	1.7	4.18	6.1	31
2000	CIN	NL	23	26	26	140.3	130	73	112	32	5.00	5.21	8.6	3.8	6.4	1.8	4.92	4.6	8
2001	LOU	INT	24	5	4	27.0	32	4	26	4	3.33	4.95	12.4	1.6	6.9	1.8	5.95	1.6	14
2001	CIN	NL	24	9	9	44.3	46	17	33	9	5.49	5.15	9.2	3.2	5.7	1.6	5.14	1.7	3
2001	TEX	AL	24	18	18	105.3	130	47	64	23	7.18	6.19	10.2	3.7	5.0	1.7	6.22	-8.0	-2
2002	OKL	PCL	25	12	11	75.3	70	25	55	10	4.06	4.34	9.0	3.5	5.1	1.6	4.74	9.7	1
2002	TEX	AL	25	17	15	94.0	113	35	70	16	6.22	5.60	10.3	3.1	6.4	1.4	5.46	-1.0	8
2003	TEX	AL	26	21	16	99.7	110	41	71	17	5.36	5.12	9.7	3.4	6.2	1.3	4.95	8.0	3

Breakout: 14%   Improve: 49%   Collapse: 22%

Bell's days with the Ranger organization may be numbered: he's out of options, and he's not a good bet to stick with the big club the whole year. But if so he would be a worthwhile gamble for another team willing to try to resurrect the fallen prospect's career. Last year's 6.22 ERA was brutal, but his peripherals paint a much brighter picture. His strikeout rate and strikeout-to-walk ratio were both better than league average, despite his pitching 60% of his innings in Arlington. He'd be especially well-suited to a team like the Tigers, where the home park would help him keep the homers down.

Joaquin Benoit   Born: 26-Jul-77   Age: 25   Bats: R   Throws: R

YEAR	TM	LG	AGE	G	GS	IP	H	BB	SO	HR	ERA	EQERA	EQH9	EQBB9	EQSO9	EQHR9	PERA	VORP	STF
2000	TUL	TXS	22	16	16	82.3	73	30	72	6	3.83	4.36	9.1	3.4	5.7	1.0	4.37	10.5	10
2001	TUL	TXS	23	4	4	21.7	23	6	23	1	3.32	4.47	11.1	3.0	6.8	0.7	5.08	2.5	18
2001	OKL	PCL	23	24	24	131.0	113	73	142	14	4.19	4.77	8.7	6.0	7.2	1.2	4.84	10.7	11
2002	OKL	PCL	24	16	16	98.7	74	37	103	8	3.56	3.52	7.2	3.9	7.2	1.0	3.48	21.8	21
2002	TEX	AL	24	17	13	84.7	91	58	59	6	5.31	4.88	9.2	5.7	6.0	0.6	5.04	5.8	3
2003	TEX	AL	25	20	18	114.7	122	59	88	15	5.13	4.90	9.3	4.2	6.7	1.0	4.87	11.0	9

Breakout: 16%   Improve: 47%   Collapse: 14%

Benoit conquered the command problems that plagued him in Triple-A in 2001, posting nearly a 3-to-1 K/BB ratio in Oklahoma last year. Unfortunately, those problems resurfaced with a vengeance in his 17 appearances in the big leagues, where he had the highest walk rate in the AL (minimum 50 innings). Benoit will try to prove once again that the second time is the charm for him in 2003, as the Rangers are very likely to put him in the rotation to start the year.

Jovanny Cedeno   Born: 25-Oct-79   Age: 23   Bats: R   Throws: R

YEAR	TM	LG	AGE	G	GS	IP	H	BB	SO	HR	ERA	EQERA	EQH9	EQBB9	EQSO9	EQHR9	PERA	VORP	STF
2000	SAV	SAL	20	24	22	130.3	95	53	153	1	2.42	4.78	9.8	5.1	6.2	0.2	4.34	10.4	15

This is why you shouldn't get excited about pitchers until they at least reach Double-A, no matter what they do before then. It was yet another year lost to a torn labrum for Cedeno, who had repeated setbacks and another exploratory surgery last September. Yet you still occasionally see notes in papers and Web sites speculating on Cedeno's timetable for return, and talking about his "unlimited potential," based mostly on a single year dominating low-A hitters. We propose a new rule: no more notices about Cedeno until he returns and pitches at least 50 professional innings. Same with Justin Thompson.

Francisco Cordero   Born: 11-May-75   Age: 28   Bats: R   Throws: R

YEAR	TM	LG	AGE	G	GS	IP	H	BB	SO	HR	ERA	EQERA	EQH9	EQBB9	EQSO9	EQHR9	PERA	VORP	STF
2000	TEX	AL	25	56	0	77.3	87	48	49	11	5.36	4.75	8.8	4.4	5.3	1.0	5.09	5.4	-11
2001	OKL	PCL	26	12	0	15.3	8	3	20	0	0.59	1.42	5.1	2.1	8.6	0.2	1.44	6.7	24
2002	OKL	PCL	27	11	1	12.3	15	7	21	2	5.85	8.63	11.9	5.8	11.7	1.9	7.50	-4.4	5
2002	TEX	AL	27	39	0	45.3	33	13	41	2	1.79	2.18	6.3	2.4	7.9	0.4	2.23	16.1	18
2003	TEX	AL	28	42	0	52.0	51	22	45	6	4.00	3.82	8.5	3.4	7.5	0.8	4.04	11.9	6

Breakout: 17%   Improve: 44%   Collapse: 24%

It took four months and a few amusing auditions (Hideki Irabu?), but the Rangers found themselves a closer. Recovered from the lower back stress fracture that cost him his 2001, Cordero finally made good on the promise he showed in the Tigers organization before coming over in the Juan Gonzalez trade. He found his command and boosted his K/BB ratio from a dismal 1:1 in 2000 to an outstanding 3:1 last year. He may not put up a 1.79 ERA again, but he should be the anchor the bullpen was missing in 2002, even if it's not in the 9th inning role just yet—he's lost his closer job for now with Ugueth Urbina's signing.

Doug Davis   Born: 21-Sep-75   Age: 27   Bats: R   Throws: L

YEAR	TM	LG	AGE	G	GS	IP	H	BB	SO	HR	ERA	EQERA	EQH9	EQBB9	EQSO9	EQHR9	PERA	VORP	STF
2000	OKL	PCL	24	12	12	69.7	62	34	53	8	2.84	4.24	8.7	4.4	5.6	1.3	4.66	9.8	4
2000	TEX	AL	24	30	13	98.7	109	58	66	14	5.38	4.51	8.7	4.2	5.7	1.0	4.90	10.5	0
2001	TEX	AL	25	30	30	186.0	220	69	115	14	4.45	4.39	9.9	3.1	5.1	0.6	4.72	23.0	7
2002	TEX	AL	26	10	10	59.7	67	22	28	7	4.97	4.71	9.7	3.1	4.1	1.0	4.70	5.3	-2
2002	OKL	PCL	26	9	9	61.3	70	11	48	7	4.99	5.20	11.0	1.9	5.4	1.3	5.32	2.1	6
2003	TEX	AL	27	18	14	88.7	102	33	53	12	4.89	4.67	10.1	3.1	5.2	1.0	4.80	10.9	1

Breakout: 13%   Improve: 43%   Collapse: 19%

Doug Davis (continued)

The mystifying May demotion of Davis to Oklahoma was more about sending a message than anything strictly baseball-related. Then-pitching coach Oscar Acosta cited Davis's lack of "a heartbeat." Maybe so, but this club could really use a corpse if it can put up a sub-5.00 ERA—it's the Rangers, after all. He's out of options, so the Rangers have less incentive to jerk him around again this year (not that it guarantees they won't). They can hope that the impressive control he demonstrated in Triple-A and the Dominican Winter League is a sign of things to come, and that the shoulder soreness that shortened his season isn't.

Ryan Dittfurth				Born: 18-Oct-79					Age: 23		Bats: R		Throws: R		
YEAR	TM	LG	AGE	G	GS	IP	H	BB	SO	HR	ERA	EQERA	EQH9	EQBB9	EQSO9	EQHR9	PERA	VORP	STF
2000	SAV	SAL	20	29	29	158.7	127	99	158	8	4.25	7.31	11.9	8.3	5.6	1.3	6.30	-31.8	-5
2001	PCH	FSL	21	27	24	147.3	123	66	134	9	3.48	5.46	10.6	5.0	5.7	1.4	5.22	0.7	5
2002	PCH	FSL	22	6	3	25.7	11	7	21	2	2.45	3.03	6.1	3.2	5.3	1.7	2.28	7.0	6
2002	TUL	TXS	22	9	9	41.3	42	23	32	1	5.67	6.90	11.2	6.1	5.4	0.5	5.87	-6.4	-2

The 2001 Rangers minor league pitcher of the year had his 2002 derailed by command problems and a shoulder injury that resulted in rotator cuff surgery in September. Even prior to last year, his strikeout and walk numbers weren't good enough for him to be considered a top prospect. He's a long way from the majors.

Travis Hughes				Born: 25-May-78					Age: 25		Bats: R		Throws: R		
YEAR	TM	LG	AGE	G	GS	IP	H	BB	SO	HR	ERA	EQERA	EQH9	EQBB9	EQSO9	EQHR9	PERA	VORP	STF
2000	PCH	FSL	22	39	14	126.3	122	54	96	9	4.42	6.43	11.6	5.0	4.9	1.7	6.17	-13.6	-11
2001	TUL	TXS	23	47	5	87.3	91	45	86	8	4.64	6.27	11.4	5.8	6.5	1.4	6.31	-8.3	-9
2002	TUL	TXS	24	26	26	143.3	139	82	137	11	3.52	5.83	11.3	6.3	6.8	1.5	6.11	-5.2	1

The 1997 19th round draft pick was sent back to Tulsa and moved into the starting rotation for 2002. His ERA improved, but his already shaky walk numbers got even worse. Hughes is listed by some analysts as one of the Rangers' top 10 prospects, but he doesn't deserve to be.

Danny Kolb				Born: 29-Mar-75					Age: 28		Bats: R		Throws: R		
YEAR	TM	LG	AGE	G	GS	IP	H	BB	SO	HR	ERA	EQERA	EQH9	EQBB9	EQSO9	EQHR9	PERA	VORP	STF
2000	OKL	PCL	25	13	0	18.3	11	8	18	0	0.98	2.45	5.6	3.8	7.0	0.2	2.22	6.0	9
2001	PCH	FSL	26	7	3	18.7	21	2	16	1	3.85	5.63	13.9	1.2	5.3	1.3	5.75	-0.3	-4
2001	OKL	PCL	26	12	0	19.0	13	4	21	1	1.42	2.00	6.8	2.3	7.3	0.6	2.43	7.1	13
2001	TEX	AL	26	17	0	15.3	15	10	15	2	4.71	4.37	8.0	5.3	8.0	1.0	4.89	1.7	0
2002	TEX	AL	27	34	0	32.0	27	22	20	1	4.22	3.91	7.3	5.7	5.4	0.3	3.67	5.2	-11
2003	TEX	AL	28	35	1	44.0	50	25	29	5	5.33	5.10	10.0	4.7	5.7	0.8	5.22	3.9	-12

Breakout: 16%   Improve: 36%   Collapse: 29%

Kolb returned from a rotator cuff tear in mid-season and once again impressed with his stuff if not his numbers. Despite all of his arm problems, he hasn't yet gone the junkballer route, still throwing a sinking fastball in the mid-90s and a vicious slider. Signed to a one-year contract, he's part of the Rangers middle relief picture for this year, at least until his next catastrophic arm breakdown. The over/under on that is May 15.

Ben Kozlowski				Born: 16-Aug-80					Age: 22		Bats: L		Throws: L		
YEAR	TM	LG	AGE	G	GS	IP	H	BB	SO	HR	ERA	EQERA	EQH9	EQBB9	EQSO9	EQHR9	PERA	VORP	STF
2000	MCN	SAL	19	15	14	77.0	76	39	67	6	4.21	8.02	13.6	6.6	4.8	2.0	7.15	-21.5	-12
2001	MCN	SAL	20	26	23	145.3	134	27	147	8	2.48	5.38	11.9	2.6	5.2	1.2	5.44	1.9	9
2002	PCH	FSL	21	21	12	79.0	63	25	76	2	2.05	4.75	9.9	3.7	6.2	0.6	4.11	6.4	12
2002	TUL	TXS	21	8	8	52.0	28	22	41	3	1.90	2.89	6.3	4.6	5.5	1.1	2.87	15.1	14
2003	TEX	AL	22	12	9	58.0	70	30	42	10	6.05	5.78	10.5	4.3	6.3	1.3	5.53	3.2	0

Breakout: 13%   Improve: 47%   Collapse: 32%

Stolen from the Braves for finesse artist Andy Pratt, Kozlowski is a big lefty with low-90s heat who's seen nothing but success in his two full seasons in the minors. His peripherals didn't really support the sub-2.00 ERA he put up in high-A and Double-A combined last year, but it was a fine showing regardless. Even though he saw a cup of coffee in the big leagues in September, he'll spend at least one more year in the high minors working on his command.

Colby Lewis

Born: 02-Aug-79 **Age: 23** **Bats: R** **Throws: R**

YEAR	TM	LG	AGE	G	GS	IP	H	BB	SO	HR	ERA	EQERA	EQH9	EQBB9	EQSO9	EQHR9	PERA	VORP	STF
2000	PCH	FSL	20	28	27	163.7	169	45	153	11	4.07	5.81	12.1	3.2	6.0	1.5	5.93	-5.6	12
2001	TUL	TXS	21	25	25	156.0	150	62	162	15	4.50	5.53	10.5	4.4	6.8	1.5	5.35	-0.4	15
2002	TEX	AL	22	15	4	34.3	42	26	28	4	6.30	6.11	10.3	6.2	6.9	0.9	6.29	-2.5	0
2002	OKL	PCL	22	20	20	106.7	100	28	99	4	3.63	3.79	8.8	2.7	6.4	0.4	3.80	20.3	21
2003	TEX	AL	23	17	12	77.7	88	34	61	11	5.14	4.91	9.9	3.7	6.8	1.1	4.98	9.7	7

Breakout: 13%   *Improve: 47%*   *Collapse: 25%*

There's plenty to like here. Lewis solidified his standing as the Rangers' best pitching prospect, and emerged as one of the best pitching prospects period, by conquering Triple-A with a dazzling K/BB ratio. His major league appearances were not as impressive, but even there he had some moments of brilliance amid the bouts of wildness. He throws a fastball that tops out in the high 90s, along with a wicked curve. The Rangers are bringing him along slowly, so there's a good chance he'll start 2003 back in Oklahoma.

Aaron Myette

Born: 26-Sep-77 **Age: 25** **Bats: R** **Throws: R**

YEAR	TM	LG	AGE	G	GS	IP	H	BB	SO	HR	ERA	EQERA	EQH9	EQBB9	EQSO9	EQHR9	PERA	VORP	STF
2000	BIR	SOU	22	3	3	15.3	11	8	21	1	3.53	5.19	8.6	5.1	8.6	1.2	4.76	0.5	23
2000	CHR	INT	22	19	18	111.7	103	56	85	18	4.35	5.46	9.9	4.6	6.0	1.9	5.19	0.5	6
2001	OKL	PCL	23	12	12	70.0	64	30	76	5	3.73	4.44	9.1	4.6	7.2	0.8	4.41	8.3	19
2001	TEX	AL	23	19	15	80.7	94	37	67	12	7.14	5.68	9.6	3.8	6.9	1.2	5.40	-1.7	9
2002	OKL	PCL	24	16	16	106.0	86	44	106	5	3.14	3.46	7.7	4.3	6.9	0.6	3.69	24.1	19
2002	TEX	AL	24	15	12	48.3	64	41	48	11	10.06	8.51	11.1	6.9	8.4	1.8	7.83	-16.2	-3
2003	CLE	AL	25	17	13	86.0	94	47	68	12	5.72	5.62	9.7	4.5	6.8	1.1	5.25	2.3	4

Breakout: 15%   *Improve: 45%*   *Collapse: 25%*

Ever notice how a minor leaguer's reputation will suddenly move up a notch when he's traded for a veteran? Aaron Myette is a good example. No one talked about him much when he was struggling with his control in the White Sox system. But once he started struggling with his control in the Rangers system, well, we had to talk about him, because he's "the guy who was traded for Royce Clayton." Granted, if he can ever manage to cut his walk rate down by two or so, he may become something special. The odds are against him, though; now he's probably destined to be talked about as "the guy who was traded with Travis Hafner."

Chan Ho Park

Born: 30-Jun-73 **Age: 30** **Bats: R** **Throws: R**

YEAR	TM	LG	AGE	G	GS	IP	H	BB	SO	HR	ERA	EQERA	EQH9	EQBB9	EQSO9	EQHR9	PERA	VORP	STF
2000	LAD	NL	27	34	34	226.0	173	124	217	21	3.27	3.64	7.2	4.0	7.6	0.8	3.66	46.8	20
2001	LAD	NL	28	36	35	234.0	183	91	218	23	3.50	3.63	7.3	3.3	7.2	0.8	3.55	48.7	19
2002	TEX	AL	29	25	25	145.7	154	78	121	20	5.74	5.05	9.0	4.4	7.1	1.1	4.98	7.4	10
2003	TEX	AL	30	25	23	148.3	153	72	121	19	4.77	4.56	9.0	4.0	7.1	1.0	4.58	21.4	13

Breakout: 13%   *Improve: 43%*   *Collapse: 17%*

Last off-season, we and many others pointed out the obvious danger in the Chan Ho Park signing: that the aptly named Park seemed to be a product of Dodger Stadium, and he wasn't a good bet to continue his success away from Chavez Ravine. The nightmare Park scenario was even worse: the hitter-friendly Ballpark at Arlington could act as an anti-Chavez, hurting Park just as much as Dodger Stadium had helped him. Guess what, boys and girls? Nightmares can come true. Park's road ERA in '02 was just about the same as it was the three previous years: 4.66 with the Rangers vs. 4.72 with the Dodgers. But his Arlington home ERA of 6.84 was more than double his 3.19 Dodger Stadium ERA. His peripherals and his second half performance show a small silver lining, though. He'll be better this year. Not $65 million better, but better.

Jesus Pena — Born: 08-Mar-75 — Age: 28 — Bats: L — Throws: L

YEAR	TM	LG	AGE	G	GS	IP	H	BB	SO	HR	ERA	EQERA	EQH9	EQBB9	EQSO9	EQHR9	PERA	VORP	STF
2000	BIR	SOU	25	23	0	21.3	19	6	25	2	3.38	5.25	11.0	2.8	7.6	1.7	5.23	0.3	0
2000	CHR	INT	25	21	0	17.3	10	10	19	1	3.12	3.33	6.1	5.2	8.4	0.7	2.83	3.9	8
2000	CWS	AL	25	20	0	23.3	25	16	19	6	5.41	5.95	8.7	4.9	6.9	1.9	6.00	-1.5	-10
2001	TRN	EAS	26	14	2	32.0	46	7	35	6	5.06	7.34	15.3	2.6	6.8	2.7	9.26	-6.8	-15
2001	PAW	INT	26	26	8	72.3	92	38	42	10	6.60	7.47	12.5	5.6	4.1	1.7	7.80	-16.2	-31
2002	TUL	TXS	27	17	0	22.0	24	5	15	2	3.27	5.28	12.8	2.5	4.8	1.7	5.72	0.2	-17
2002	OKL	PCL	27	29	5	57.0	73	45	57	7	7.26	7.82	12.6	8.3	7.0	1.5	8.43	-15.1	-24

John Hart traded soft-tossing prospect Justin Duchscherer to Oakland for flamethrower Luis Vizcaino during Spring Training, but then dealt Vizcaino less than a week later when the club decided to fill out its Opening Day bullpen with the likes of Dan Miceli and Rich Rodriguez. He ended up with Pena, a spare part lefty who pitched, well, like a spare part. The Vizcaino-Pena trade is perhaps an unfairly easy target—no one knew just how dominant Vizcaino would be in 2002, and it wouldn't have even been an issue if Hart hadn't made a shrewd move to acquire him in the first place. Still, Hart should have recognized that raw materials like Vizcaino's are worth trying to hold on to. In his desire to get something, anything, for Vizcaino, Hart ended up with nothing.

Jay Powell — Born: 09-Jan-72 — Age: 31 — Bats: R — Throws: R

YEAR	TM	LG	AGE	G	GS	IP	H	BB	SO	HR	ERA	EQERA	EQH9	EQBB9	EQSO9	EQHR9	PERA	VORP	STF
2000	HOU	NL	28	29	0	27.0	29	19	16	1	5.67	4.85	9.2	5.0	4.6	0.3	4.90	1.6	-17
2001	HOU	NL	29	35	0	36.3	41	19	28	4	3.72	4.79	10.3	4.4	5.9	0.9	5.41	2.4	-10
2001	COL	NL	29	39	0	38.7	34	12	26	5	2.79	3.57	7.8	2.6	5.1	1.0	3.29	7.8	-6
2002	TEX	AL	30	51	0	49.7	50	24	35	5	3.44	4.37	8.7	4.0	6.1	0.8	4.33	5.6	-6
2003	*TEX*	*AL*	*31*	*54*	*0*	*56.0*	*64*	*25*	*39*	*7*	*4.97*	*4.75*	*9.9*	*3.7*	*6.0*	*1.0*	*4.86*	*7.1*	*-8*

Breakout: 14%   Improve: 49%   Collapse: 28%

Powell's 3.44 ERA last year was deceptive—he gave up almost half as many unearned runs as earned (his RA: 5.07). He was still a decent arm out of the bullpen after the All-Star break. But he's never struck that many guys out, especially after the shoulder problems that cost him most of 2000, and that's not a great sign going forward. For the league minimum salary, 60 innings of Jay Powell would be an asset. For $3 million a year, when your team supposedly can't afford to keep Frank Catalanotto, he's a liability.

Erasmo Ramirez — Born: 29-Apr-76 — Age: 27 — Bats: L — Throws: L

YEAR	TM	LG	AGE	G	GS	IP	H	BB	SO	HR	ERA	EQERA	EQH9	EQBB9	EQSO9	EQHR9	PERA	VORP	STF
2000	SHV	TXS	24	39	2	58.7	80	21	46	7	6.44	8.06	15.8	3.5	5.4	1.8	7.82	-17.4	-19
2001	SJO	CLF	25	17	0	31.7	23	5	33	2	3.41	4.39	9.0	1.9	5.4	1.1	3.29	3.5	-2
2001	SHV	TXS	25	22	1	33.3	25	5	39	1	2.16	3.16	8.2	1.7	7.5	0.5	2.76	8.3	16
2001	TUL	TXS	25	12	0	16.3	17	5	18	3	4.42	5.71	11.9	3.5	7.2	2.9	6.34	-0.6	-10
2002	TUL	TXS	26	34	0	54.0	51	8	34	1	3.00	4.45	10.4	1.6	4.4	0.3	3.88	5.6	-6
2002	OKL	PCL	26	25	0	21.0	15	4	17	0	1.29	2.10	6.5	1.9	5.5	0.2	2.26	7.7	3

Rangers minor league authority Jamey Newberg (www.newbergreport.com) was banging the drum for Ramirez throughout the latter part of the season, and for good reason. Look at those translated walk numbers. Ramirez throws strikes, and he gets lefty hitters out. There's no excuse for more Rich Rodriguez-style reanimation experiments in 2003 while this guy is in the system.

Mario Ramos — Born: 19-Oct-77 — Age: 25 — Bats: L — Throws: L

YEAR	TM	LG	AGE	G	GS	IP	H	BB	SO	HR	ERA	EQERA	EQH9	EQBB9	EQSO9	EQHR9	PERA	VORP	STF
2000	MOD	CLF	22	26	24	152.0	131	50	134	6	2.90	4.40	10.1	3.3	5.0	0.8	4.35	18.6	10
2000	MID	TXS	22	4	4	27.3	24	6	19	0	1.32	2.28	8.4	2.0	4.5	0.2	2.92	9.8	16
2001	MID	TXS	23	15	15	93.7	71	28	68	7	3.07	3.67	7.9	3.3	4.7	1.1	3.36	19.1	7
2001	SAC	PCL	23	13	13	80.3	74	27	82	5	3.14	3.87	8.9	3.6	6.7	0.7	4.02	14.6	20
2002	OKL	PCL	24	34	19	121.7	162	53	75	20	7.40	7.64	13.2	4.6	4.3	2.0	7.88	-29.2	-21
2003	*TEX*	*AL*	*25*	*14*	*7*	*42.0*	*52*	*20*	*25*	*7*	*5.88*	*5.62*	*10.8*	*3.9*	*5.3*	*1.3*	*5.58*	*1.8*	*-10*

Breakout: 20%   Improve: 46%   Collapse: 23%

Ramos was never a grade-A pitching prospect, despite all the attention he got for being the centerpiece of the Carlos Pena deal. And his status as a grade-B or C prospect was always built on a shaky foundation—those relatively low strikeout numbers. But no one expected a collapse as complete as the one he experienced last year. One small bright note is that he showed good command in 39 Arizona Fall League innings. The Rangers will give him every opportunity to reestablish himself this year.

Dennys Reyes   Born: 19-Apr-77   Age: 26   Bats: R   Throws: L

YEAR	TM	LG	AGE	G	GS	IP	H	BB	SO	HR	ERA	EQERA	EQH9	EQBB9	EQSO9	EQHR9	PERA	VORP	STF
2000	CIN	NL	23	62	0	43.7	43	29	36	5	4.53	5.63	9.3	4.8	6.6	0.9	4.81	-1.2	-3
2001	LOU	INT	24	7	6	34.3	34	16	34	3	3.67	5.09	10.3	5.0	7.1	1.1	5.38	1.6	8
2001	CIN	NL	24	35	6	53.0	51	35	52	5	4.92	5.07	8.6	5.4	7.4	0.7	4.78	2.1	1
2002	COL	NL	25	43	0	40.3	43	24	30	1	4.24	4.20	9.4	4.7	5.8	0.2	4.39	5.3	-5
2002	TEX	AL	25	15	5	42.3	55	21	29	9	6.38	6.35	11.0	4.1	5.9	1.7	6.59	-4.2	-10
2003	TEX	AL	26	35	7	65.0	71	34	49	7	5.19	4.96	9.6	4.3	6.5	0.8	4.81	6.5	-3

Breakout: 19%   Improve: 49%   Collapse: 21%

Reyes's numbers are included here to represent all the generic lefties that passed through the Ranger's bullpen in 2002—John Rocker, Chris Michalak, Randy Flores, Rich Rodriguez, and C. J. Nitkowski—only because he's the one that stands the best chance of wearing a major league uniform in 2003. But don't count the other guys out either. As Tony Fossas, the patron saint of generic lefties, taught us, there are two ways to get a major league bullpen spot: be effective, or be left-handed.

Kenny Rogers   Born: 10-Nov-64   Age: 38   Bats: L   Throws: L

YEAR	TM	LG	AGE	G	GS	IP	H	BB	SO	HR	ERA	EQERA	EQH9	EQBB9	EQSO9	EQHR9	PERA	VORP	STF
2000	TEX	AL	35	34	34	227.3	257	78	127	20	4.55	3.83	9.1	2.5	4.8	0.6	3.99	42.3	7
2001	TEX	AL	36	20	20	120.7	150	49	74	18	6.19	5.53	10.3	3.4	5.1	1.2	5.65	-0.3	0
2002	TEX	AL	37	33	33	210.7	212	70	107	21	3.84	3.84	8.7	2.8	4.4	0.8	3.91	39.0	3
2003	TEX	AL	38	27	24	150.7	172	55	81	19	4.77	4.56	10.0	3.0	4.7	1.0	4.67	19.7	1

Breakout: 19%   Improve: 51%   Collapse: 14%

One of the more underrated pitchers of recent years. Rogers has gotten a bum rap in some circles because of some high-profile disappointments in New York, but overall he's had as good a run prevention record as more publicized lefties like Mike Hampton and Denny Neagle. The Rangers were smart not to give him the three-year contract he wants, though. Pitchers like Rogers tend not to make it much beyond age 37.

Derrick Van Dusen   Born: 06-Jun-81   Age: 22   Bats: L   Throws: L

YEAR	TM	LG	AGE	G	GS	IP	H	BB	SO	HR	ERA	EQERA	EQH9	EQBB9	EQSO9	EQHR9	PERA	VORP	STF
2000	EVE	NWN	19	4	2	15.0	17	5	24	1	3.60	8.60	15.4	3.9	7.9	2.1	7.45	-5.2	8
2001	WIS	MDW	20	18	18	96.0	82	24	103	6	3.19	5.09	10.9	3.3	6.1	1.3	4.70	4.4	13
2002	SBR	CLF	21	20	20	124.7	111	36	118	13	3.10	4.64	11.2	3.4	5.1	1.9	5.02	12.0	7
2002	SAN	TXS	21	5	4	25.0	31	12	17	4	7.20	9.53	16.7	5.7	5.1	3.4	8.87	-11.2	-16
2002	TUL	TXS	21	3	1	12.0	14	3	5	0	2.25	5.23	12.9	2.7	2.9	0.3	5.48	0.3	-8

A soft-tossing lefty who came over from Seattle in the Ismael Valdes trade, Van Dusen throws three pitches, including an above-average curve. He's put up low ERAs in Class-A ball the past two seasons, with good strikeout and walk numbers supporting them. He'll start the year in Frisco's rotation.

Todd Van Poppel   Born: 09-Dec-71   Age: 31   Bats: R   Throws: R

YEAR	TM	LG	AGE	G	GS	IP	H	BB	SO	HR	ERA	EQERA	EQH9	EQBB9	EQSO9	EQHR9	PERA	VORP	STF
2000	IOW	PCL	28	10	6	40.7	37	10	52	2	3.10	3.49	8.5	2.2	9.2	0.6	3.39	9.0	30
2000	CHC	NL	28	51	2	86.3	80	48	77	10	3.75	3.95	8.3	4.0	7.0	0.9	4.36	13.8	1
2001	CHC	NL	29	59	0	75.0	63	38	90	9	2.52	3.22	7.5	4.2	9.1	1.0	4.11	18.0	12
2002	TEX	AL	30	50	0	72.7	80	29	85	14	5.45	4.96	9.3	3.3	10.0	1.5	5.16	3.4	15
2003	TEX	AL	31	43	4	64.7	64	27	61	9	4.00	3.82	8.7	3.5	8.1	1.1	4.27	15.7	8

Breakout: 20%   Improve: 48%   Collapse: 24%

Van Poppel kept his strikeout rate the same as in his big 2001 with the Cubs, and he cut down significantly on his walks. So naturally his ERA more than doubled. That has more to do with his 2001, where his peripheral numbers just didn't support a 2.52 ERA, than his 2002. The story with Van Poppel is the same as with Powell: it's nice to have his 70 innings, but it'd be nicer to have $2.5 million to apply to a better player.

C. J. Wilson — Born: 18-Nov-80 — Age: 22 — Bats: L — Throws: L

YEAR	TM	LG	AGE	G	GS	IP	H	BB	SO	HR	ERA	EQERA	EQH9	EQBB9	EQSO9	EQHR9	PERA	VORP	STF
2001	PUL	APL	20	8	8	37.7	24	9	49	2	0.95	2.98	9.0	3.5	5.3	1.3	3.69	10.6	8
2001	SAV	SAL	20	5	5	34.0	30	9	26	2	3.18	5.12	11.3	3.7	4.0	1.4	5.82	1.5	0
2002	PCH	FSL	21	26	15	106.0	86	41	76	4	3.06	5.39	10.5	4.6	4.7	0.8	4.60	1.1	-1
2002	TUL	TXS	21	5	5	30.0	23	12	17	0	1.80	3.04	8.4	4.3	3.9	0.3	3.60	8.2	6

With finesse lefties suddenly playing a prominent role in the organization—Mario Ramos, Derrick Van Dusen, Wilson—the Rangers seem determined to find the next Tom Glavine or Jamie Moyer. I'll go out on a limb and predict Wilson won't become either of them. He's drawn raves from some analysts for the low ERAs in Charlotte and especially Tulsa, but the very low strikeout rates and relatively high walk rates suggest that those ERAs won't stay low for long.

Jeff Zimmerman — Born: 09-Aug-72 — Age: 30 — Bats: R — Throws: R

YEAR	TM	LG	AGE	G	GS	IP	H	BB	SO	HR	ERA	EQERA	EQH9	EQBB9	EQSO9	EQHR9	PERA	VORP	STF
2000	TEX	AL	27	65	0	69.7	80	34	74	10	5.29	4.59	9.0	3.4	8.9	1.0	4.81	6.1	10
2001	TEX	AL	28	66	0	71.3	48	16	72	10	2.40	2.19	5.6	1.9	8.5	1.1	2.39	25.3	18
2002	PCH	FSL	29	2	0	2.0	0	1	2	0	0.00	0.86	0.3	5.1	5.7	0.2	0.80	1.0	-1
2002	TUL	TXS	29	3	0	3.0	2	1	3	0	0.00	2.89	7.4	3.7	7.0	0.3	2.83	0.8	5

Of all the time lost due to injury the Rangers suffered in 2002, losing Zimmerman's 70 innings hurt the most. The injuries to position players like Gonzalez and Greer at least created opportunities for youngsters like Mench, Ludwick, and Hart to get their foot in the door. But Zimmerman's elbow problems not only robbed the Rangers of one of the best relievers in the game, it also contributed to the parade of Irabus, Telfords, and Woodards that did no one any good. After having reconstructive surgery in July, he's out until at least the All-Star Break.

Toronto Blue Jays

"**B**aseball isn't a game anymore, it's become a business" is a lament that has been repeated ad nauseum over the years. Some variation is inevitably trotted out whenever changes occur that run contrary to somebody's sepia-toned remembrances of the game when they were in grade school. In regards to professional baseball, such a statement hasn't been accurate since the first professional team, the Cincinnati Red Stockings, was formed in 1869. By definition, professional baseball has been a business ever since. The core product is the game played between individual business units.

Major League Baseball is indeed a very big business, with annual team revenues averaging nearly $115 million. Yet, despite the amount of money at stake and ownership groups that are wildly successful in other fields, decisions directly related to the product on the field are often made without applying rudimentary business principles. The lack of analysis and long-term planning, and subsequent misallocation of resources can lead to disastrous results.

Of course, this isn't a new phenomenon—it's a continuation of the way things have always worked in major league front offices. When ballplayers were little more than indentured servants, poor management decisions didn't pose as serious a problem to a franchise's future. Teams could retain their best players while offering them no pay raises or cutting their wages. Salaries skyrocketed after the dawn of free agency in 1975, but a corresponding explosion in baseball's popularity lifted all boats, allowing the operational status quo to continue. However, if owners are to be believed, nearly all of their 30 boats are now sinking in a sea of red ink. While that claim is certainly subject to debate, there are franchises in financial trouble, primarily teams that have made poor business decisions about their personnel for years on end.

Although the Blue Jays hadn't endured a decade of Brewers-style ineptitude, by the fall of 2001 they were staring at a payroll due to increase to $78 million and a won-loss record that had steadily fallen since 1998. Attendance at Skydome was less than half of its record-setting levels during their back-to-back championships in 1992 and 1993. The team's quick trip to the financial cliff was further accelerated by the weak Canadian exchange rate. It all added up to Rogers Communications, the team's parent company, announcing that the ball club lost $52.9 million (before revenue sharing) in 2001.

That was the backdrop when Blue Jays' CEO Paul Godfrey began interviewing candidates in November 2001 to find a replacement for fired general manager Gord Ash. One of eleven candidates, J. P. Ricciardi was little more than a name on the list when the process started. When it was over, he was Toronto's new GM. Ricciardi rose to the top of the heap because he presented Godfrey with something unique: a business strategy. Ricciardi laid out a comprehensive plan for the organization detailing how it could achieve the seemingly opposing goals of a greatly reduced payroll and a championship caliber team. He also had the experience of winning with a tight budget as the director of player personnel in Oakland. Since Godfrey is more a businessman than a baseball man, Ricciardi was an easy choice.

Since being hired, Ricciardi has clearly shown that he is going to run the ball club like a business, closely watching the bottom line while positioning the Blue Jays to beat the competition. To accomplish this, he isn't flying in motivational speakers or implementing passing fads like T-groups and Matrix Management. Ricciardi simply insists that decisions involving personnel be scrutinized from all angles on a risk/reward (cost/benefit) basis. The type of moves he has made consistently demonstrates this thinking:

Straight salary dumps: When somebody is making far more than he is contributing or ever likely to contribute, he won't be long for Toronto regardless of reputation. The Raul Mondesi, Alex Gonzalez, Brad Fullmer, and Pedro Borbon

---

Blue Jays Prospectus

2002 record: 78–84; Third place in AL East

Pythagenport Record: 80–82

Runs scored per game: 5.0 (6th in AL)

Runs allowed per game: 5.1 (9th in AL)

Team EqA: .258 (9th in AL)

2002 Batters Age: 27.6 (3rd youngest in AL)

2002 Pitchers Age: 27.7 (4th youngest in AL)

Ballpark: Skydome; moderate hitters' park; Park Factor of 1.030

2002: Under new management, some desperately overdue retooling takes its first encouraging steps.

2003: They'll top .500, making the AL East interesting while building up to contention in the years to come.

trades fall into this category. The Blue Jays will pay nearly half of Mondesi's salary in 2003 even if he spends the summer on a chaise lounge, but saved $12.5 million while at the same time making room for Josh Phelps. Ricciardi attempted to trade Homer Bush, but found no takers. Since Bush was blocking the path of better players, Ricciardi showed he understands the concept of sunk costs and just ate the contract.

Relievers as bright, shiny objects: The 2002 cash outlay for the projected seven-man bullpen that Ricciardi inherited was over $13 million, with only Bob File slated to make less than $1.65 million. Understanding that a brand-name reliever's perceived benefit is usually much higher than his actual worth, Ricciardi swapped most of those arms—Billy Koch, Paul Quantrill, Dan Plesac, and Borbon—for low-cost, high-upside players like Eric Hinske, Luke Prokopec, and Cliff Politte. Ricciardi has reversed the salary ratio in the bullpen; only Kelvim Escobar is due to make seven figures in 2003.

Extended test drives: By the first week of May, Toronto trailed Boston by 12 games and had already been erased from the playoff picture. Ricciardi saw the situation as an opportunity to evaluate fringe players at the major league level before the rosters expanded in September. Neither Joe Lawrence nor Dewayne Wise showed enough to retain their spots on the 40-man roster, but Chris Woodward and waiver wire refugee Pete Walker seized the moment and established themselves as useful contributors. While the players involved aren't going to be stars, roster spots are precious and the process had no downside risk in a non-contending season.

Albatross extinction: Ricciardi assumed nearly $10 million of liability in Esteban Loaiza and Steve Parris, and was delighted when he could push them out of the Blue Jays' nest after last season. Multiyear, big money commitments to journeymen starters are a thing of the past.

The team feels that the best example of risk/reward analysis, and the one that will yield the largest dividends in the future, is its focus on college players in the June first-year player draft. Ricciardi scooped some nice position prospects (Vernon Wells, Felipe Lopez, Josh Phelps, Orlando Hudson, Jayson Werth) from the top of the farm system he inherited, but there wasn't much cream rising below that layer. While Ash wasn't as myopic as Chuck LaMar in drafting prep players, he frequently spent high draft choices on raw-boned throwers. Not surprisingly, this strategy seldom paid off, and even those youngsters that show considerable promise— Dustin McGowan and Brandon League—are still at least two years from arriving in Toronto if everything breaks right. As a result, Ricciardi inherited an organization that was particularly thin in pitching at the upper levels.

Short of trading away building blocks already on the major league roster, drafting collegians is the quickest way to reload a farm system. However, that's just one of many benefits. College players carry less risk. Studies show that players drafted out of college, especially pitchers, have a greater chance of reaching the majors. In addition to the risk of suffering debilitating injury, those first few years after high school provide more information on a potential prospect— not just more data, but also better data. So why not watch from afar while players toil in college instead of spending millions on huge risks?

With improved competition and a more level playing field, statistical analysis can be included in the evaluation instead of relying almost solely on a scout's acumen in assessing a youngster's physical tools. The notion that teenagers yield a higher return if they reach the major leagues has been clearly demonstrated to not be true with pitchers. The evidence is muddier when it comes to position players, but if there is a performance benefit, it's small. And if there is an ARod-level talent out there, every team knows about it and he won't last.

A collegian also comes packaged with lower player development costs, since a large chunk of the financial burden is shifted to the university. Teams also improve their leverage in contract negotiations, because the clock starts to work against college players—they don't have as many palatable alternatives as high schoolers.

The Blue Jays followed the script very closely in the 2002 draft, selecting college players in 13 of the first 15 rounds. Though the final verdict won't be known for years, the initial returns were promising. Most choices signed quickly, and Russ Adams (1), David Bush (2), Justin Maureau (3), Chad Pleiness (5), Jason Perry (6), and Jordan DeJong (18) had particularly encouraging two-month stints in the minors. As many as eight members of the draft class have a good chance of being contributing major leaguers. Even *Baseball America,* which usually reserves its greatest gushing for toolsy teens, rated Toronto as having the best draft of any organization.

Focusing on college players also helped the ball club's bottom line by enabling it to reduce the scouting staff by over half. While the local fishwrap decried these firings as bordering on inhumane, the simple fact is that the Blue Jays' scouting department was bloated, and not as many eyes and miles are needed to evaluate college prospects. With all the various scouting bureaus, combines, player showcases, and availability of information today, the days of cloistering a Mickey Mantle away in the backwoods of Oklahoma are over. Toe Nash was an entertaining tale, but Peter Gammons reaped more benefit from him than any major league team ever will.

Ricciardi is also scaling back the Latin American program that the Blue Jays mined so successfully in the late-1970s and 1980s when they were one of the few organizations canvassing the area. The days of signing scores of prospects on the cheap are long gone and reminders of big-money investments—Jossephang Bernhardt, Glenn Williams, Diegomar Markwell, Guillermo Quiroz—still litter the system. The club will maintain a presence in the region, but won't take part in bidding wars that hand raw kids six- or seven-figure contracts.

On the field, Ricciardi is tearing pages from the sabermetric manifesto and papering the organization with them. Managers and coaches are expected to actively implement the principles or go find another job. While it isn't clear what Buck Martinez ever brought to the ball club except hairspray VOCs and media savvy, he obviously wasn't walking in step with the team's new philosophy. Consequently, he was fired as Blue Jays' manager in early June and replaced by long-time minor league skipper Carlos Tosca.

Toronto finished the 2002 campaign with six of nine spots in the lineup and three-fifths of the starting rotation filled by players with less than two years of major league service. Rather than fall back on the old saw that players should know how to play the game by the time they reach the majors, Ricciardi accepted the situation for what it is: a learning experience. By adding Tosca and third base/infield coach Brian Butterfield to the coaches already in place, the Blue Jays have the teaching staff that they will need for the next few years. Ricciardi acknowledges that the current staff may not be what the team needs when it's ready to contend, but realizes that you have to first get to the threshold before you can knock down the door.

The Blue Jays sprinted through the tape last year, finishing the season with 25 victories in their final 36 contests. However, 15 of those wins were against AL patsies Baltimore, Tampa Bay, and Detroit, indicating there are still many holes to fill to contend for the playoffs by Ricciardi's stated goal of 2005. The biggest voids are in the rotation. Short-term solutions (Cory Lidle) and stopgaps (Tanyon Sturtze) will man at least two of the slots this year, but Ricciardi needs to keep casting for young arms in the depleted waters caused by MLB's new economy and patiently wait for his first wave of draft choices to hit the beach.

Along with Billy Beane of Oakland and Theo Epstein of Boston, Ricciardi is one of the three most sabermetrically oriented general managers in the major leagues. Although Ricciardi has the lowest profile of the trio, he may well have the most influence in accelerating its acceptance in baseball's glacially slow-moving world. Beane is regarded as an aberration, seen as operating on a different level than his peers, while any success Theo Epstein has will be attributed in large measure to his payroll advantage. Ricciardi isn't viewed as a genius, and he is working with roughly half of the Red Sox budget, so the baseball establishment will have to acknowledge his success or invent a new excuse should he win in Toronto.

Can he reverse the team's fortunes and return the Blue Jays to the playoffs for the first time since 1993? It won't be easy with AL East heavyweights New York and Boston boasting larger payrolls and bright front offices. But at least the ball club is headed in the right direction with a comprehensive plan in place for both the team and the business. That's more than any major league franchise from Canada has been able to say in years.

HITTERS

Russ Adams — SS — Born: 30-Aug-80 — Age: 22 — Bats: L — Throws: R

YEAR	TM	LG	AGE	AB	H	2B	3B	HR	BB	SO	SB	CS	AVG	OBP	SLG	MLVR	EQBA	EQOBP	EQSLG	EQMLVR	VORP	DEFENSE	
2002	AUB	NYP	21	113	40	7	3	0	24	11	13	1	.354	.471	.469	.423	.256	.350	.339	-.130	2.8	30-SS	1
2002	DUN	FSL	21	147	34	4	2	1	18	17	5	2	.231	.323	.306	-.086	.197	.265	.263	-.437	-8.5	35-SS	-2
2003	TOR	AL	22	172	43	9	2	2	17	25	5	2	.247	.319	.355	-.116	.250	.325	.364	-.139	1.1		

Breakout: 56%   Improve: 75%   Collapse: 8%

Ricciardi would have swooned were Khalil Greene available when the club picked 14th in last year's June draft. When the Padres snared Greene at 13, the Blue Jays tabbed Adams. Adams doesn't have Greene's long ball power, but he can find the gaps with line drives and works pitchers until they drop. His arm may eventually force a move to second, but he'll stay on the left side of the keystone until he shows he can't handle shortstop. Adams lacks star power, but should be a Mark Ellis-type middle infielder with good on-base skills.

Jimmy Alvarez   2B   Born: 04-Oct-79   Age: 23   Bats: B   Throws: R

YEAR	TM	LG	AGE	AB	H	2B	3B	HR	BB	SO	SB	CS	AVG	OBP	SLG	MLVR	EQBA	EQOBP	EQSLG	EQMLVR	VORP	DEFENSE			
2000	QUD	MDW	20	134	30	7	2	4	19	38	3	1	.224	.329	.396	.025	.180	.254	.317	-.394	-6.6	33-2B	-7		
2000	HAG	SAL	20	155	36	5	1	3	25	44	12	5	.232	.346	.335	-.029	.180	.262	.261	-.453	-10.3	24-2B	1	23-SS	-7
2001	DUN	FSL	21	467	132	19	4	8	49	87	29	7	.283	.353	.392	.085	.234	.286	.333	-.278	-7.2	99-SS	-21	13-2B	2
2002	TEN	SOU	22	497	138	32	3	8	79	121	20	11	.278	.386	.402	.117	.237	.322	.351	-.181	4.5	109-2B	-2		
2003	TOR	AL	23	192	47	10	1	5	19	43	4	4	.245	.316	.385	-.086	.248	.322	.395	-.108	2.1				

Breakout: 44%   Improve: 64%   Collapse: 18%

Toronto churns out middle infield prospects as consistently as Chrysler launches ineffective ad campaigns. Alvarez actually came over from the Twins in a back page transaction a couple of years ago. He has always been willing to take a walk and has boosted his batting average and extra-base power since landing in the Blue Jays' nest. Alvarez is viewed as a future utilityman, but could develop into something more now that he's out from under the worst coaching staff in the system.

Dave Berg   IF   Born: 03-Sep-70   Age: 32   Bats: R   Throws: R

YEAR	TM	LG	AGE	AB	H	2B	3B	HR	BB	SO	SB	CS	AVG	OBP	SLG	MLVR	EQBA	EQOBP	EQSLG	EQMLVR	VORP	DEFENSE			
2000	FLA	NL	29	210	53	14	1	1	25	46	3	0	.252	.346	.343	-.151	.255	.340	.349	-.137	4.8	36-SS	-2		
2001	FLA	NL	30	215	52	12	1	4	14	39	0	1	.242	.294	.363	-.189	.252	.302	.381	-.168	2.8	29-2B	0	10-SS	-1
2002	TOR	AL	31	374	101	26	2	4	26	57	0	2	.270	.326	.382	-.061	.287	.342	.410	-.025	18.1	42-2B	1	17-3B	2
2003	TOR	AL	32	257	65	14	1	5	18	43	1	1	.252	.308	.372	-.111	.256	.313	.382	-.134	-.8				

Breakout: 21%   Improve: 36%   Collapse: 28%

Non-tendered by the Marlins, who were awash in utility players, Berg settled for a minor league deal with a team in need of his skills and proceeded to post the best season of his career. Berg can play six positions and contribute offensively without much of a platoon split. That's a handy package given the roster limitations caused by 11-man pitching staffs. There was mutual interest in him returning, resulting in a two-year contract last December.

Gary Burnham   1B   Born: 13-Oct-74   Age: 28   Bats: L   Throws: L

YEAR	TM	LG	AGE	AB	H	2B	3B	HR	BB	SO	SB	CS	AVG	OBP	SLG	MLVR	EQBA	EQOBP	EQSLG	EQMLVR	VORP	DEFENSE	
2000	REA	EAS	25	355	95	28	0	13	40	47	0	1	.268	.364	.456	.133	.233	.308	.400	-.143	-4.5	68-1B	4
2001	REA	EAS	26	371	118	25	2	15	35	43	1	2	.318	.393	.518	.314	.273	.339	.446	.009	10.8	76-1B	4
2002	SYR	INT	27	537	151	34	1	17	53	69	1	2	.281	.364	.443	.116	.259	.337	.416	-.048	6.8	126-1B	-9
2003	TOR	AL	28	144	36	8	1	5	14	22	1	1	.252	.322	.412	-.036	.255	.328	.423	-.055	-.5		

Breakout: 15%   Improve: 40%   Collapse: 28%

We babble at length about "freely available talent." When it was evident that Burnham was to be farmed out to Double-A for a fourth straight year, the Phillies allowed him to walk from their Clearwater complex to neighboring Dunedin without requesting compensation. That's "freely available." Unfortunately, he falls short of the mark in the "talent" department. Though Burnham was the SkyChiefs' MVP, he is too old and lacks the power or positional flexibility to be considered a prospect.

Kevin Cash   C   Born: 06-Dec-77   Age: 25   Bats: R   Throws: R

YEAR	TM	LG	AGE	AB	H	2B	3B	HR	BB	SO	SB	CS	AVG	OBP	SLG	MLVR	EQBA	EQOBP	EQSLG	EQMLVR	VORP	DEFENSE	
2000	HAG	SAL	22	196	48	10	1	10	22	54	5	3	.245	.324	.459	.102	.184	.242	.343	-.381	-7.7	49-C	9
2001	DUN	FSL	23	371	105	27	0	12	43	80	4	3	.283	.370	.453	.187	.232	.294	.376	-.204	3.0	77-C	6
2002	TEN	SOU	24	213	59	15	1	8	36	44	5	2	.277	.384	.469	.198	.234	.317	.404	-.120	6.4	36-C	0
2002	SYR	INT	24	236	52	18	0	10	25	72	0	1	.220	.300	.424	-.057	.202	.279	.395	-.227	.5	57-C	6
2003	TOR	AL	25	184	44	10	1	7	17	45	3	2	.239	.307	.418	-.062	.242	.313	.429	-.083	4.1		

Breakout: 48%   Improve: 68%   Collapse: 19%

It appears that the darkhorse has won the catching race, as the favorites heading into 2002 aren't suited for the rigors of the position. Ex-manager Buck Martinez was so taken with Cash in spring training that he wanted the converted third baseman to head north with the squad. Cooler heads prevailed, although Cash was pushed aggressively. He wasn't overmatched until his September sip in Toronto, showing excellent extra-base pop and a good eye in Double and Triple-A. He can put the clamps on the running game, too, gunning down nearly 45% of would-be basestealers. The team's current backstops are merely placeholders until Cash arrives sometime around the All-Star break. Think Jason Varitek.

Jose Cruz Jr. OF Born: 19-Apr-74 Age: 29 Bats: B Throws: R

YEAR	TM	LG	AGE	AB	H	2B	3B	HR	BB	SO	SB	CS	AVG	OBP	SLG	MLVR	EQBA	EQOBP	EQSLG	EQMLVR	VORP	DEFENSE
2000	TOR	AL	26	603	146	32	5	31	71	129	15	5	.242	.324	.466	-.050	.247	.322	.478	.001	27.7	155-CF -3
2001	TOR	AL	27	577	158	38	4	34	45	138	32	5	.274	.327	.530	.130	.289	.343	.566	.202	55.7	125-CF -4
2002	TOR	AL	28	466	114	26	5	18	51	106	7	1	.245	.319	.438	-.018	.261	.336	.468	.024	13.8	117-OF 5
2003	TOR	AL	29	453	118	25	3	21	51	105	11	3	.261	.338	.472	.071	.265	.344	.484	.060	15.8	

Breakout: 16%   Improve: 58%   Collapse: 7%

He failed to build on an encouraging 2001 campaign, virtually guaranteeing a ticket out of town thanks to a mediocre season and an indifferent attitude. Cruz is exactly what the new Blue Jays want to avoid: a slightly above-average player due to make big money simply because of major league service time. After marketing Cruz's pedigree and recent 30-homer seasons, Ricciardi non-tendered him when he didn't get any enticing nibbles. The money saved will be used to acquire pitching help.

Carlos Delgado 1B Born: 25-Jun-72 Age: 31 Bats: L Throws: R

YEAR	TM	LG	AGE	AB	H	2B	3B	HR	BB	SO	SB	CS	AVG	OBP	SLG	MLVR	EQBA	EQOBP	EQSLG	EQMLVR	VORP	DEFENSE
2000	TOR	AL	28	569	196	57	1	41	123	104	0	1	.344	.472	.664	.577	.351	.475	.683	.634	113.7	161-1B -18
2001	TOR	AL	29	574	160	31	1	39	111	136	3	0	.279	.409	.540	.279	.295	.422	.576	.348	71.6	159-1B -4
2002	TOR	AL	30	505	140	34	2	33	102	126	1	0	.277	.411	.549	.300	.298	.427	.592	.380	68.8	139-1B 8
2003	TOR	AL	31	486	137	32	1	32	93	114	1	0	.281	.400	.547	.276	.285	.408	.562	.279	44.3	

Breakout: 3%   Improve: 35%   Collapse: 11%

The grand prize winner in Gord Ash's Big Buck Bonanza after the 2000 season. While the new regime would love to move the remaining $36 million owed Delgado, the simple fact is that he is comfortable in Toronto and has a no-trade clause he won't waive. The good news is that he'll continue to be one of the top 15 hitters in the league over the final two years of the deal. Delgado has deteriorated against southpaws (.238/.325/.360 last year), to the point where Tosca should remove him from the lineup and spot Josh Phelps at first base once a week.

Jim Deschaine 3B/SS Born: 18-Sep-77 Age: 25 Bats: R Throws: R

YEAR	TM	LG	AGE	AB	H	2B	3B	HR	BB	SO	SB	CS	AVG	OBP	SLG	MLVR	EQBA	EQOBP	EQSLG	EQMLVR	VORP	DEFENSE	
2000	LNS	MDW	22	478	140	33	4	16	69	91	19	9	.293	.389	.479	.254	.223	.290	.369	-.227	-1.1	106-SS -3	
2001	DAY	FSL	23	485	140	26	2	21	62	103	6	10	.289	.374	.480	.238	.232	.297	.393	-.175	5.8	57-SS -13	48-3B -3
2002	TEN	SOU	24	405	91	13	0	16	51	85	3	3	.225	.317	.375	-.054	.194	.264	.329	-.350	-16.7	71-3B -5	23-SS -5
2003	TOR	AL	25	128	30	6	1	4	11	27	2	1	.237	.300	.399	-.099	.240	.306	.410	-.122	.5		

Breakout: 52%   Improve: 70%   Collapse: 15%

The unknown half of what came from the Cubs in exchange for Alex Gonzalez, Deschaine was the better half in many stat-heads' eyes. His minor league rap sheet was a carbon copy of Mark Bellhorn's: good eye, surprising power, and lots of whiffs while masquerading as a shortstop. The shine is off after a poor year offensively and defensively at Tennessee, and the overdue shift to third base lowers his value. Deschaine is at an age where he needs a quick rebound to have a shot at a career.

Shawn Fagan 1B/3B Born: 02-Mar-78 Age: 25 Bats: R Throws: R

YEAR	TM	LG	AGE	AB	H	2B	3B	HR	BB	SO	SB	CS	AVG	OBP	SLG	MLVR	EQBA	EQOBP	EQSLG	EQMLVR	VORP	DEFENSE	
2000	QUE	NYP	22	90	26	6	1	2	12	22	0	1	.289	.390	.444	.241	.204	.276	.333	-.316	-3.0	21-3B -3	
2000	HAG	SAL	22	172	48	8	1	2	18	28	5	1	.279	.351	.372	.052	.216	.268	.295	-.377	-8.7	43-3B -2	
2001	DUN	FSL	23	475	143	18	5	10	86	114	7	2	.301	.410	.423	.217	.242	.329	.348	-.168	2.7	113-3B -6	
2002	TEN	SOU	24	421	113	24	0	12	102	87	6	3	.268	.413	.411	.160	.226	.347	.353	-.136	-4.7	43-1B -3	44-3B 6
2003	TOR	AL	25	152	36	7	1	4	18	32	3	1	.239	.321	.373	-.095	.242	.327	.383	-.118	-1.2		

Breakout: 23%   Improve: 48%   Collapse: 23%

Prepare to be disappointed if you've been expecting the second coming of Eddie Yost. The Blue Jay brass loves Fagan's walk rates, but that's his only selling point. Although he has been chiseling a Fullmeresque body since leaving Penn State, his power numbers remain soft and the added bulk only hastens his slide to the left end of the defensive spectrum. With Eric Hinske and Josh Phelps already on the scene, Fagan is going to have to prove himself at every level.

Tyrell Godwin   OF   Born: 10-Jul-79   Age: 23   Bats: L   Throws: R

YEAR	TM	LG	AGE	AB	H	2B	3B	HR	BB	SO	SB	CS	AVG	OBP	SLG	MLVR	EQBA	EQOBP	EQSLG	EQMLVR	VORP	DEFENSE
2001	AUB	NYP	21	117	43	8	2	2	19	27	9	5	.368	.464	.521	.484	.260	.335	.374	-.109	2.3	19-CF -1
2002	CWV	SAL	22	185	52	8	5	0	20	23	10	2	.281	.364	.378	.096	.221	.280	.300	-.344	-12.4	47-LF -3
2003	TOR	AL	23	151	39	8	3	2	13	27	3	2	.260	.322	.387	-.063	.263	.328	.397	-.083	-1.8	

Breakout: 49%   Improve: 79%   Collapse: 12%

Godwin was a first round pick in 1997 and 2000 before the Blue Jays landed him in the third round in 2001. He has blazing speed and makes consistent contact, but is short on power and raw for a college player. He is also brittle, beginning last season with shoulder and hamstring problems and ending it with a broken hand. A Morehead Scholar, Godwin returned to Chapel Hill to finish his degree instead of signing with the Rangers after his junior year. Considering his age, lack of experience, and how far he has to climb, that sheepskin could come in handy.

Gabe Gross   RF   Born: 21-Oct-79   Age: 23   Bats: L   Throws: R

YEAR	TM	LG	AGE	AB	H	2B	3B	HR	BB	SO	SB	CS	AVG	OBP	SLG	MLVR	EQBA	EQOBP	EQSLG	EQMLVR	VORP	DEFENSE
2001	DUN	FSL	21	126	38	9	2	4	26	29	4	2	.302	.429	.500	.337	.237	.337	.397	-.090	-.5	34-RF -6
2002	TEN	SOU	22	403	96	17	5	10	53	71	8	2	.238	.334	.380	-.015	.209	.281	.338	-.296	-22.6	101-RF -1
2003	TOR	AL	23	159	39	8	1	4	16	33	2	2	.244	.319	.394	-.070	.247	.324	.404	-.091	-3.4	

Breakout: 48%   Improve: 71%   Collapse: 14%

After an auspicious 2001 debut, the Blue Jays were expecting more. However, like many Smokie hitters, Gross didn't heat up until the weather did, struggling (though maintaining his plate discipline) at .175/.280/.255 through mid-May before going .271/.351/.444 over the last 100 games. Gross faces a return engagement at Double-A to open the season, but will move up the minute he starts raking the ball. Don't be surprised if you see him in Toronto by August.

Eric Hinske   3B   Born: 05-Aug-77   Age: 25   Bats: L   Throws: R

YEAR	TM	LG	AGE	AB	H	2B	3B	HR	BB	SO	SB	CS	AVG	OBP	SLG	MLVR	EQBA	EQOBP	EQSLG	EQMLVR	VORP	DEFENSE
2000	WTN	SOU	22	436	113	21	9	20	78	133	14	5	.259	.375	.486	.224	.230	.321	.433	-.076	14.5	113-3B -5
2001	SAC	PCL	23	436	123	27	1	25	54	113	20	7	.282	.374	.521	.186	.249	.332	.454	-.013	19.8	114-3B -14
2002	TOR	AL	24	566	158	38	2	24	77	138	13	1	.279	.367	.481	.146	.296	.384	.516	.206	60.3	141-3B -11
2003	TOR	AL	25	550	148	33	3	27	72	132	14	7	.270	.357	.489	.130	.273	.364	.502	.123	37.9	

Breakout: 21%   Improve: 58%   Collapse: 10%

Ricciardi raised some eyebrows when he acquired Hinske from his old employers in his first player move as Blue Jays' GM. Hinske then went out and led American League rookies in most offensive categories. After making 15 errors in 50 games, many thought he couldn't handle the hot corner, but sessions with new coach Brian Butterfield solved his throwing problem and Hinske made only five errors the rest of the season. Eric Chavez and Troy Glaus will make All-Star appearances hard to come by, but Hinske will be rock-solid at third base for the next half dozen years.

Ken Huckaby   C   Born: 27-Jan-71   Age: 32   Bats: R   Throws: R

YEAR	TM	LG	AGE	AB	H	2B	3B	HR	BB	SO	SB	CS	AVG	OBP	SLG	MLVR	EQBA	EQOBP	EQSLG	EQMLVR	VORP	DEFENSE		
2000	TUC	PCL	29	243	67	11	1	4	10	30	2	2	.276	.310	.379	-.196	.234	.257	.322	-.351	-7.1	58-C 9		
2001	ELP	TXS	30	104	36	4	0	2	3	16	0	0	.346	.382	.442	.165	.284	.314	.363	-.147	-1.3	16-1B -1	11-C 1
2001	TUC	PCL	30	262	76	15	1	2	7	62	1	3	.290	.314	.378	-.150	.249	.275	.319	-.311	-5.0	35-C -3	22-1B -5
2002	SYR	INT	31	81	22	2	0	0	2	15	0	2	.272	.289	.296	-.212	.259	.277	.272	-.369	-2.6	19-C -3		
2002	TOR	AL	31	273	67	6	1	3	9	44	0	0	.245	.270	.308	-.280	.263	.289	.332	-.255	-1.4	77-C -3		
2003	TOR	AL	32	216	51	8	1	2	8	38	1	1	.234	.264	.311	-.277	.237	.268	.319	-.313	-7.8			

Breakout: 31%   Improve: 51%   Collapse: 35%

All the production of Alberto Castillo at just one-third the price! Huckaby couldn't scare a cat burglar with a bat in his hands, but the 11-year minor league veteran is a genuinely good defensive backstop with whom pitchers like to work. The Jays will continue the offense/defense job sharing arrangement with Tom Wilson to begin the year, but it'll come to a screeching halt the moment Kevin Cash is ready for The Show.

Orlando Hudson   2B   Born: 12-Dec-77   Age: 25   Bats: B   Throws: R

YEAR	TM	LG	AGE	AB	H	2B	3B	HR	BB	SO	SB	CS	AVG	OBP	SLG	MLVR	EQBA	EQOBP	EQSLG	EQMLVR	VORP	DEFENSE				
2000	DUN	FSL	22	358	102	16	2	7	37	42	9	5	.285	.355	.399	.076	.229	.282	.325	-.300	-10.3	80-3B	4	14-2B	-8	
2000	TEN	SOU	22	134	32	4	3	2	15	18	3	2	.239	.325	.358	-.052	.204	.269	.321	-.346	-5.5	39-3B	5			
2001	TEN	SOU	23	306	94	22	8	4	37	42	8	3	.307	.387	.471	.208	.260	.327	.399	-.089	10.1	66-2B	11	11-3B	3	
2001	SYR	INT	23	194	59	14	3	4	23	34	11	3	.304	.384	.469	.200	.279	.356	.437	.032	12.9	50-2B	12			
2002	SYR	INT	24	417	127	27	3	10	35	54	8	5	.305	.364	.456	.151	.279	.338	.422	-.021	20.7	97-2B	6			
2002	TOR	AL	24	192	53	10	5	4	11	27	0	1	.276	.322	.443	.018	.290	.337	.472	.058	13.2	52-2B	3			
2003	TOR	AL	25	361	97	22	3	7	30	50	5	3	.268	.327	.405	-.026	.271	.333	.416	-.043	10.2					

Breakout: 18%   Improve: 46%   Collapse: 21%

A non-stop chatterbox, the O-Dog livened up spring training with his comments about Ricciardi's pimpin' wardrobe. However, his 0-for-March hitting and unrefined play at second base were what sent him packing for Syracuse and kept him there four months despite the team's gaping wound at the keystone. The Jays still aren't completely sold on any aspect of Hudson's game, but from here it appears he could become the best non-Alomar second sacker in team history.

Reed Johnson   OF   Born: 08-Dec-76   Age: 26   Bats: R   Throws: R

YEAR	TM	LG	AGE	AB	H	2B	3B	HR	BB	SO	SB	CS	AVG	OBP	SLG	MLVR	EQBA	EQOBP	EQSLG	EQMLVR	VORP	DEFENSE	
2000	HAG	SAL	23	324	94	24	5	8	62	49	14	2	.290	.425	.469	.284	.219	.317	.355	-.196	-11.2	95-RF	-6
2000	DUN	FSL	23	133	42	9	2	4	14	27	3	2	.316	.424	.504	.333	.252	.330	.407	-.078	3.5	36-CF	-1
2001	TEN	SOU	24	554	174	29	4	13	45	79	42	12	.314	.384	.451	.183	.270	.324	.387	-.104	-2.2	128-LF	-4
2002	SYR	INT	25	159	37	8	3	2	12	23	1	4	.233	.318	.358	-.101	.219	.293	.338	-.266	-3.5	44-CF	1
2003	TOR	AL	26	120	29	7	1	2	10	19	2	1	.242	.307	.365	-.127	.245	.313	.374	-.152	-2.3		

Breakout: 20%   Improve: 42%   Collapse: 36%

Even in Toronto's enlightened atmosphere, the window of opportunity isn't held open long for aging, unheralded prospects sans great physical tools. While inferior peers and non-prospects were auditioning at SkyDome, Johnson spent most of last summer on the sidelines with an injured wrist. Johnson has a broad enough mix of skills to help a number of clubs as a reserve, but his chance for a try-out in Hollywood North has likely come and gone.

Joe Lawrence   2B/C   Born: 13-Feb-77   Age: 26   Bats: R   Throws: R

YEAR	TM	LG	AGE	AB	H	2B	3B	HR	BB	SO	SB	CS	AVG	OBP	SLG	MLVR	EQBA	EQOBP	EQSLG	EQMLVR	VORP	DEFENSE			
2000	DUN	FSL	23	375	113	32	1	13	69	74	21	7	.301	.416	.496	.300	.236	.330	.395	-.106	13.3	67-C	-13		
2000	TEN	SOU	23	133	35	9	0	0	30	27	7	1	.263	.410	.331	.059	.232	.352	.297	-.196	1.5	29-C	-2		
2001	SYR	INT	24	318	70	11	4	1	36	62	6	9	.220	.311	.289	-.204	.205	.289	.273	-.370	-11.4	75-C	-11	10-3B	0
2002	TOR	AL	25	150	27	4	0	2	16	38	2	1	.180	.268	.247	-.393	.200	.288	.280	-.365	-5.9	43-2B	-1		
2002	SYR	INT	25	108	18	4	1	2	14	23	3	0	.167	.262	.278	-.333	.156	.246	.266	-.490	-7.9	27-2B	3		
2003	MIL	NL	26	171	39	8	1	3	21	39	3	2	.226	.313	.337	-.187	.231	.315	.350	-.189	-1.5				

Breakout: 55%   Improve: 78%   Collapse: 16%

Lawrence's offensive vital signs took a nosedive when he was moved from shortstop to behind the plate after the 1999 season. Despite returning to the middle infield last spring, the former first-rounder has flat-lined and appeared set to leave the organization as a six-year minor league free agent. Successful conversions to catcher are rare, but long remembered. The failures should be, too. Lawrence signed a minor league deal with the Brewers, who want to try the catching experiment again.

Felipe Lopez   SS   Born: 12-May-80   Age: 23   Bats: B   Throws: R

YEAR	TM	LG	AGE	AB	H	2B	3B	HR	BB	SO	SB	CS	AVG	OBP	SLG	MLVR	EQBA	EQOBP	EQSLG	EQMLVR	VORP	DEFENSE			
2000	TEN	SOU	20	463	119	18	4	9	31	110	12	11	.257	.305	.371	-.053	.223	.257	.325	-.353	-15.7	122-SS	-23		
2001	TEN	SOU	21	72	16	2	1	2	9	23	4	4	.222	.309	.361	-.117	.178	.259	.288	-.424	-3.9	11-SS	-3		
2001	SYR	INT	21	358	100	19	7	16	30	94	13	5	.279	.340	.506	.160	.257	.315	.464	-.022	18.2	60-SS	-6	18-2B	6
2001	TOR	AL	21	177	46	5	4	5	12	39	4	3	.260	.307	.418	-.069	.271	.321	.441	-.032	6.9	44-3B	-3		
2002	TOR	AL	22	282	64	15	3	8	23	90	5	4	.227	.288	.387	-.153	.244	.305	.420	-.113	7.6	72-SS	-3		
2002	SYR	INT	22	173	55	11	2	3	29	37	13	0	.318	.419	.457	.248	.290	.386	.420	.072	13.9	43-SS	0		
2003	TOR	AL	23	372	96	21	3	12	34	86	11	7	.259	.324	.422	-.014	.262	.330	.434	-.031	11.9				

Breakout: 34%   Improve: 62%   Collapse: 13%

Felipe Lopez *(continued)*

Handed the shortstop job to open the season, Lopez punted it away with indifferent play and a lousy attitude. His physical tools rival those of any shortstop in the game, but he currently lacks the mental approach to succeed at the major league level. Lopez could be a special player if somebody can light a fire under him. The Blue Jays aren't convinced that's possible and dealt him to Cincinnati as part of the four-way trade that netted them Jason Arnold.

Josh Phelps — DH/1B — Born: 12-May-78 — Age: 25 — Bats: R — Throws: R

YEAR	TM	LG	AGE	AB	H	2B	3B	HR	BB	SO	SB	CS	AVG	OBP	SLG	MLVR	EQBA	EQOBP	EQSLG	EQMLVR	VORP	DEFENSE	
2000	DUN	FSL	22	113	36	7	0	12	12	34	0	0	.319	.389	.699	.552	.246	.304	.526	.035	7.9	16-C	1
2000	TEN	SOU	22	184	42	9	1	9	15	66	1	0	.228	.311	.435	.018	.202	.256	.383	-.287	-2.5	39-C	-11
2001	TEN	SOU	23	486	142	36	1	31	80	127	3	3	.292	.410	.562	.342	.241	.338	.460	-.000	31.0	67-C	-6
2002	SYR	INT	24	257	75	20	1	24	32	83	0	0	.292	.381	.658	.426	.262	.346	.592	.213	30.7	34-C	-9
2002	TOR	AL	24	265	82	20	1	15	19	82	0	0	.309	.362	.562	.276	.326	.378	.596	.344	32.3		
2003	*TOR*	*AL*	*25*	*387*	*101*	*23*	*2*	*23*	*41*	*108*	*3*	*4*	*.262*	*.339*	*.504*	*.114*	*.265*	*.345*	*.518*	*.106*	*18.3*		

Breakout: 14%   Improve: 47%   Collapse: 14%

While the Blue Jays were sifting through the contents of their 25-man roster the first half of the season, Phelps was honing his horsehide-mashing skills in Triple-A. After being recalled in early July, he wowed the coaching staff with his ability to make adjustments at the plate. Phelps's days of donning the tools of ignorance are over because of past surgery on both knees and a balky back, but his time as an imposing big league hitter has just begun. Over the next two years he'll be groomed to succeed Delgado at first base.

Guillermo Quiroz — C — Born: 29-Nov-81 — Age: 21 — Bats: R — Throws: R

YEAR	TM	LG	AGE	AB	H	2B	3B	HR	BB	SO	SB	CS	AVG	OBP	SLG	MLVR	EQBA	EQOBP	EQSLG	EQMLVR	VORP	DEFENSE	
2000	HAG	SAL	18	136	22	4	0	1	16	44	0	1	.162	.269	.213	-.330	.129	.201	.171	-.719	-17.9	40-C	1
2000	QUE	NYP	18	196	44	9	0	5	27	48	1	2	.224	.330	.347	-.001	.167	.236	.265	-.507	-14.0	54-C	7
2001	CWV	SAL	19	261	52	12	0	7	29	67	5	1	.199	.294	.326	-.090	.165	.234	.268	-.508	-20.5	79-C	0
2002	DUN	FSL	20	411	107	28	1	12	35	91	1	0	.260	.332	.421	.090	.218	.269	.358	-.286	-5.4	89-C	-3
2002	SYR	INT	20	45	10	4	0	1	3	14	0	0	.222	.271	.378	-.164	.200	.250	.356	-.338	-2.3		
2003	*TOR*	*AL*	*21*	*204*	*45*	*9*	*1*	*6*	*17*	*51*	*2*	*2*	*.221*	*.288*	*.367*	*-.170*	*.223*	*.294*	*.377*	*-.198*	*-1.7*		

Breakout: 66%   Improve: 78%   Collapse: 16%

Given $1.2 million to leave Venezuela at age 17, Quiroz looked for all the world to be just another big-bonus bust of the Blue Jays international operation. However, he clawed his way back to prospectdom after enjoying by far the best season of his pro career last year. Showing impeccable timing, it coincided with Phelps and Jayson Werth moving out from behind the dish. Quiroz has always been considered a strong catch-and-throw receiver. With his fair eye and good power, he could retrace the Mark Parent career path.

Dominic Rich — 2B — Born: 22-Aug-79 — Age: 23 — Bats: L — Throws: R

YEAR	TM	LG	AGE	AB	H	2B	3B	HR	BB	SO	SB	CS	AVG	OBP	SLG	MLVR	EQBA	EQOBP	EQSLG	EQMLVR	VORP	DEFENSE	
2000	QUE	NYP	20	236	62	11	4	0	38	33	10	4	.263	.376	.343	.079	.194	.271	.263	-.426	-13.3	66-2B	-15
2001	CWV	SAL	21	327	91	16	1	4	47	54	20	8	.278	.385	.370	.139	.223	.303	.301	-.295	-7.7	75-2B	-22
2002	DUN	FSL	22	377	130	14	5	8	57	49	8	6	.345	.440	.472	.369	.282	.358	.392	-.024	19.6	93-2B	5
2002	TEN	SOU	22	132	36	4	1	1	18	23	2	4	.273	.364	.341	.001	.231	.307	.291	-.296	-2.7	18-2B	-7
2003	*TOR*	*AL*	*23*	*192*	*49*	*9*	*2*	*4*	*20*	*30*	*3*	*2*	*.254*	*.328*	*.375*	*-.071*	*.257*	*.334*	*.385*	*-.092*	*3.3*		

Breakout: 30%   Improve: 60%   Collapse: 23%

Rich forced his way into the Blue Jays middle infield scramble with a breakout campaign, leading the Florida State League in batting average and on-base percentage. The club's second rounder in 2000 doesn't pack a lot of sock, but makes outstanding contact, striking out less than he walks. Actually, Rich is a very similar hitter to Russ Adams. With many scouts projecting Adams to eventually move to second base, Rich has to keep it up since he isn't as strong defensively and Adams will curry favor as the first player drafted by the new management group.

Alexis Rios · RF · Born: 18-Feb-81 · Age: 22 · Bats: R · Throws: R

YEAR	TM	LG	AGE	AB	H	2B	3B	HR	BB	SO	SB	CS	AVG	OBP	SLG	MLVR	EQBA	EQOBP	EQSLG	EQMLVR	VORP	DEFENSE
2000	HAG	SAL	19	74	17	3	1	0	2	14	2	3	.230	.260	.297	-.213	.176	.202	.216	-.642	-9.4	
2000	QUE	NYP	19	206	55	9	2	1	11	22	5	5	.267	.317	.345	.003	.200	.224	.267	-.514	-22.0	39-RF -4
2001	CWV	SAL	20	480	126	20	9	2	25	59	22	14	.263	.305	.354	-.005	.209	.242	.284	-.449	-48.8	124-RF -16
2002	DUN	FSL	21	456	139	22	8	3	27	55	14	8	.305	.348	.408	.129	.255	.285	.348	-.245	-19.3	108-RF -10
2003	TOR	AL	22	193	46	10	2	3	12	29	3	2	.237	.287	.350	-.184	.239	.292	.359	-.213	-9.8	

Breakout: 48%   Improve: 69%   Collapse: 15%

Rios and Miguel Negron have been linked since they were consecutive first round signability picks in 1999 and 2000, respectively. However, Rios is clearly starting to separate himself. Despite being a free-swinger, he makes hard contact and his power numbers could shoot up as his 6′ 5″ frame fills out. Rios is still very much a work in progress. His stay in the organization will be dictated by how much confidence the team has that his tools can be converted into skills.

Michael Rouse · SS/2B · Born: 25-Apr-80 · Age: 23 · Bats: L · Throws: R

YEAR	TM	LG	AGE	AB	H	2B	3B	HR	BB	SO	SB	CS	AVG	OBP	SLG	MLVR	EQBA	EQOBP	EQSLG	EQMLVR	VORP	DEFENSE	
2001	DUN	FSL	21	180	49	17	2	5	13	45	3	1	.272	.328	.472	.148	.224	.264	.393	-.243	-1.3	29-2B 4	23-SS -3
2002	TEN	SOU	22	231	60	11	0	9	29	47	7	6	.260	.347	.424	.076	.221	.288	.366	-.237	-1.1	57-SS -2	
2003	TOR	AL	23	167	41	9	1	5	13	38	3	3	.247	.306	.402	-.079	.250	.312	.413	-.100	2.2		

Breakout: 54%   Improve: 74%   Collapse: 12%

Toronto's fifth round pick in the 2001 draft opened some eyes by going from the Cal State Fullerton campus directly to high-A Dunedin and posting numbers above the league norm. He followed it up with a similar campaign last year at Tennessee. Rouse doesn't do any one thing exceptionally well, but is solid across the board and plays with intelligence beyond his years. His future with the Blue Jays was as a utilityman; the outlook hasn't changed after joining the Athletics as part of the payment for Cory Lidle.

Shannon Stewart · LF · Born: 25-Feb-74 · Age: 29 · Bats: R · Throws: R

YEAR	TM	LG	AGE	AB	H	2B	3B	HR	BB	SO	SB	CS	AVG	OBP	SLG	MLVR	EQBA	EQOBP	EQSLG	EQMLVR	VORP	DEFENSE
2000	TOR	AL	26	583	186	43	5	21	37	79	20	5	.319	.366	.518	.175	.326	.366	.535	.237	46.8	136-LF 1
2001	TOR	AL	27	640	202	44	7	12	46	72	27	10	.316	.372	.463	.150	.331	.386	.490	.209	47.7	138-LF -7
2002	TOR	AL	28	577	175	38	6	10	54	60	14	2	.303	.372	.442	.123	.322	.389	.471	.178	39.5	95-LF 1
2003	TOR	AL	29	548	165	35	5	12	45	61	14	3	.301	.358	.451	.108	.305	.364	.463	.100	20.3	

Breakout: 4%   Improve: 37%   Collapse: 22%

Stewart presents a dilemma. He's a solid leadoff hitter, owning a career on-base percentage of .369. He is also a free agent after the season and should draw considerable interest. However, if the owners keep squeezing free agents, it's not out of the question that the Blue Jays could re-sign him. More likely is that he'll be dangled at the trading deadline, with Ricciardi settling for draft choice compensation if he doesn't find a deal to his liking.

Pedro Swann · RF · Born: 27-Oct-70 · Age: 32 · Bats: L · Throws: R

YEAR	TM	LG	AGE	AB	H	2B	3B	HR	BB	SO	SB	CS	AVG	OBP	SLG	MLVR	EQBA	EQOBP	EQSLG	EQMLVR	VORP	DEFENSE
2000	RIC	INT	29	442	135	22	2	9	54	68	6	5	.305	.387	.425	.124	.281	.352	.393	-.035	5.0	100-RF -6
2001	RIC	INT	30	488	142	33	5	8	52	95	12	6	.291	.369	.428	.127	.274	.346	.406	-.033	5.9	124-RF 0
2002	SYR	INT	31	368	102	17	4	14	37	77	1	3	.277	.356	.459	.120	.253	.327	.429	-.053	3.4	77-OF -2
2003	TOR	AL	32	110	27	6	1	2	10	23	1	1	.249	.317	.378	-.090	.252	.323	.388	-.112	-2.3	

Breakout: 15%   Improve: 36%   Collapse: 38%

Triple-A has evolved into a level jam-packed with trigenarians waiting for somebody to get hurt so they can have a week of well-paid vacation in the major leagues. Blue-chip prospects might see a brief cameo, but frequently skip the rung entirely. Swann now has 2,383 Triple-A at-bats, or nearly enough to earn the title "Oriole." His bat has sufficient juice that he can keep touring America's small cities as long as he can tolerate the unrelenting fireworks promotions. There are worse jobs.

Vernon Wells   CF   Born: 08-Dec-78   Age: 24   Bats: R   Throws: R

YEAR	TM	LG	AGE	AB	H	2B	3B	HR	BB	SO	SB	CS	AVG	OBP	SLG	MLVR	EQBA	EQOBP	EQSLG	EQMLVR	VORP	DEFENSE	
2000	SYR	INT	21	493	120	31	7	16	48	88	23	4	.243	.316	.432	-.046	.226	.285	.399	-.193	-1.9	118-CF	0
2001	SYR	INT	22	413	116	27	4	12	29	68	15	11	.281	.334	.453	.083	.257	.310	.416	-.099	8.4	96-CF	-7
2001	TOR	AL	22	96	30	8	0	1	5	15	5	0	.313	.353	.427	.067	.323	.367	.448	.107	6.8	27-CF	-2
2002	TOR	AL	23	608	167	34	4	23	27	85	9	4	.275	.309	.457	.014	.295	.329	.493	.080	39.0	152-CF	3
2003	TOR	AL	24	502	137	31	3	18	34	79	10	5	.273	.322	.455	.034	.276	.328	.467	.020	17.3		

Breakout: 18%   Improve: 59%   Collapse: 15%

Wells's luster had faded after two uninspiring campaigns with Syracuse, but the sheen is back after a very promising season in Toronto. He is already an outstanding defensive center fielder and has the potential to be an offensive force if he learns to work the count consistently. He also has emerged as something of a clubhouse leader after serving as the Blue Jays' player rep. Although it seems like Wells's name has been on prospect lists forever, he's just 24 years old. He is in the right organization to blossom into an All-Star regular.

Jayson Werth   OF/C   Born: 20-May-79   Age: 24   Bats: R   Throws: R

YEAR	TM	LG	AGE	AB	H	2B	3B	HR	BB	SO	SB	CS	AVG	OBP	SLG	MLVR	EQBA	EQOBP	EQSLG	EQMLVR	VORP	DEFENSE			
2000	BOW	EAS	21	276	63	16	2	5	54	50	9	3	.228	.362	.355	-.026	.201	.309	.317	-.273	-3.0	79-C	-6		
2000	FRD	CRL	21	83	23	3	0	2	10	15	5	1	.277	.355	.386	.078	.233	.290	.326	-.281	-1.0	15-C	0		
2001	DUN	FSL	22	70	14	3	0	2	17	19	1	1	.200	.356	.329	-.037	.164	.291	.260	-.401	-5.4				
2001	TEN	SOU	22	369	105	23	1	18	63	93	12	3	.285	.393	.499	.232	.237	.329	.412	-.085	15.2	45-C	4	24-1B	0
2002	SYR	INT	23	443	114	25	2	18	67	125	24	7	.257	.360	.445	.093	.236	.334	.410	-.079	1.1	101-LF	-3	21-C	-5
2002	TOR	AL	23	46	12	2	1	0	6	11	1	0	.261	.346	.348	-.076	.283	.365	.370	-.041	.4	15-RF	1		
2003	TOR	AL	24	274	66	14	2	9	33	69	8	7	.243	.329	.410	-.033	.246	.335	.421	-.051	-.4				

Breakout: 28%   Improve: 61%   Collapse: 17%

Tossing aside the catching gear, Werth is officially an outfielder. A great athlete, he shines in either outfield corner and can even occasionally spell Wells in center. Hitting coach Mike Barnett wants to shorten his long swing in hopes of slicing his whiffs. Werth looks like he'll be one of those undervalued players that don't hit for a high batting average, but have strong secondary numbers. Given his huge platoon split, we might be looking at the next Gary Roenicke.

Tom Wilson   C   Born: 19-Dec-70   Age: 32   Bats: R   Throws: R

YEAR	TM	LG	AGE	AB	H	2B	3B	HR	BB	SO	SB	CS	AVG	OBP	SLG	MLVR	EQBA	EQOBP	EQSLG	EQMLVR	VORP	DEFENSE	
2000	COH	INT	29	330	91	20	0	20	73	114	2	2	.276	.411	.518	.262	.251	.373	.469	.083	30.3	76-C	-9
2001	SAC	PCL	30	259	73	15	1	8	49	62	0	1	.282	.404	.440	.131	.252	.363	.389	-.041	13.7	46-C	-8
2002	TOR	AL	31	265	68	10	0	8	28	79	0	0	.257	.339	.385	-.044	.274	.355	.417	-.001	16.2	51-C	-3
2003	TOR	AL	32	231	55	10	1	8	30	63	1	1	.237	.330	.391	-.060	.239	.336	.401	-.080	3.7		

Breakout: 16%   Improve: 42%   Collapse: 31%

A perennial member of the Ken Phelps All-Star Team, it was nice to see Wilson finally earn a full year of major league service time. A subpar defensive catcher who spent his best offensive years in places like Norwich and Durham, Wilson will be a useful contributor for another season, which is all the Blue Jays want.

Dewayne Wise   CF   Born: 24-Feb-78   Age: 25   Bats: L   Throws: L

YEAR	TM	LG	AGE	AB	H	2B	3B	HR	BB	SO	SB	CS	AVG	OBP	SLG	MLVR	EQBA	EQOBP	EQSLG	EQMLVR	VORP	DEFENSE	
2000	TEN	SOU	22	56	14	5	2	2	7	13	3	2	.250	.333	.518	.171	.207	.270	.431	-.191	-.2	15-CF	-4
2001	DUN	FSL	23	103	23	3	1	2	5	13	5	0	.223	.259	.330	-.171	.192	.215	.288	-.507	-8.3	25-CF	0
2001	TEN	SOU	23	351	84	13	6	8	21	58	13	5	.239	.284	.379	-.124	.206	.242	.325	-.393	-18.6	86-CF	-1
2002	TEN	SOU	24	340	101	21	4	10	29	49	15	8	.297	.354	.471	.177	.253	.293	.407	-.147	2.7	80-CF	-3
2002	TOR	AL	24	112	20	4	1	3	4	15	5	0	.179	.207	.313	-.426	.188	.222	.339	-.423	-9.6	33-RF	4
2003	TOR	AL	25	258	64	13	2	6	17	44	8	4	.249	.299	.391	-.103	.252	.305	.402	-.126	-2.8		

Breakout: 64%   Improve: 83%   Collapse: 13%

Wise has been clogging the 40-man roster since the previous administration had the brilliant idea of plucking him out of low-A ball in the 1999 Rule 5 draft. The new brain trust thought it was time to see exactly what they had and gave him a 40-game audition after the All-Star break. What they saw was a brilliant defensive outfielder who isn't yet worth stashing on the bench for an entire season. Wise is beginning to grasp the strike zone and someday could emerge as a decent reserve on another ball club.

Chris Woodward   SS   Born: 27-Jun-76   Age: 27   Bats: R   Throws: R

YEAR	TM	LG	AGE	AB	H	2B	3B	HR	BB	SO	SB	CS	AVG	OBP	SLG	MLVR	EQBA	EQOBP	EQSLG	EQMLVR	VORP	DEFENSE			
2000	SYR	INT	24	143	46	13	2	5	11	30	2	0	.322	.370	.545	.272	.287	.329	.490	.067	10.9	20-2B	3	11-3B	0
2000	TOR	AL	24	104	19	7	0	3	10	28	1	0	.183	.254	.337	-.406	.192	.250	.356	-.342	-3.2	19-SS	-3		
2001	TOR	AL	25	63	12	3	2	2	0	14	0	1	.190	.190	.397	-.357	.206	.206	.429	-.314	-1.5	13-2B	2	10-3B	-3
2001	SYR	INT	25	193	59	14	3	11	16	40	0	0	.306	.362	.580	.317	.277	.334	.528	.120	15.5	21-3B	3	12-SS	-1
2002	TOR	AL	26	312	86	13	4	13	26	72	3	0	.276	.337	.468	.077	.293	.354	.503	.135	28.3	79-SS	0		
2003	TOR	AL	27	407	107	23	3	16	34	88	4	3	.264	.323	.455	.029	.267	.329	.467	.015	17.3				

Breakout: 10%   Improve: 43%   Collapse: 18%

The Blue Jays had many pleasant performances from their recalls last year, but none was as unexpected as Woodward's, who did a fair impression of Rich Aurilia. Better yet, his minor league numbers don't suggest it was a fluke. The biggest question mark is his durability, as only once in eight years has he been healthy enough to play 100 games. Woodward is a good short-term solution until they see what Russ Adams is going to be when he grows up.

PITCHERS

Brian Bowles   Born: 18-Aug-76   Age: 26   Bats: R   Throws: R

YEAR	TM	LG	AGE	G	GS	IP	H	BB	SO	HR	ERA	EQERA	EQH9	EQBB9	EQSO9	EQHR9	PERA	VORP	STF
2000	TEN	SOU	23	49	0	81.7	64	36	72	1	2.97	3.94	8.2	4.3	5.5	0.2	3.89	13.1	-1
2001	SYR	INT	24	66	0	77.3	56	44	81	3	2.91	3.88	7.2	6.0	7.4	0.5	3.70	12.9	2
2002	SYR	INT	25	59	0	59.0	46	32	53	4	3.36	4.03	7.7	5.9	6.9	0.9	4.03	8.8	-5
2002	TOR	AL	25	17	0	20.0	13	14	19	0	4.05	3.47	5.7	5.8	8.2	0.2	2.73	4.2	10
2003	TOR	AL	26	37	0	40.0	39	24	33	4	4.73	4.57	8.5	4.9	7.1	0.8	4.64	5.8	-3

Breakout: 20%   Improve: 50%   Collapse: 24%

Bowles teases the organization with nasty stuff, but there are times when he simply can't throw a pitch in the box. Right now, the coaching staff isn't concerned with command, simply control. If Bowles can find it, he'll be more than bullpen filler. Sometimes guys like this pull a Brendan Donnelly. More often they enroll at a local community college before they turn 30.

Chris Carpenter   Born: 27-Apr-75   Age: 28   Bats: R   Throws: R

YEAR	TM	LG	AGE	G	GS	IP	H	BB	SO	HR	ERA	EQERA	EQH9	EQBB9	EQSO9	EQHR9	PERA	VORP	STF
2000	TOR	AL	25	34	27	175.3	204	83	113	30	6.26	5.17	9.4	3.4	5.5	1.3	5.19	6.3	2
2001	TOR	AL	26	34	34	215.7	229	75	157	29	4.09	4.44	9.4	2.9	6.2	1.1	4.50	25.5	10
2002	TOR	AL	27	13	13	73.3	89	27	45	11	5.28	5.18	10.6	3.1	5.3	1.2	5.46	2.6	1
2003	STL	NL	28	20	15	98.7	101	41	67	13	4.54	4.95	9.5	3.2	5.4	1.2	5.05	7.0	0

Breakout: 11%   Improve: 52%   Collapse: 20%

More nagging arm problems kept Carpenter from following up on a promising 2001 campaign. This time shoulder pain landed him on the disabled list three times before finally being diagnosed as a torn labrum. The tear was relatively minor and he should be back on the mound by mid-season. The Jays believe their 1993 first round pick could still emerge as a frontline pitcher and hoped to ink him to a minor league contract. Seeking a fresh start, Carpenter instead signed for the major league minimum with St. Louis, where he may thrive working with Dave Duncan.

Scott Cassidy   Born: 03-Oct-75   Age: 27   Bats: R   Throws: R

YEAR	TM	LG	AGE	G	GS	IP	H	BB	SO	HR	ERA	EQERA	EQH9	EQBB9	EQSO9	EQHR9	PERA	VORP	STF
2000	DUN	FSL	24	14	13	88.0	53	34	89	4	1.33	2.96	7.8	4.5	6.5	1.0	3.12	24.9	16
2000	TEN	SOU	24	8	7	42.7	48	15	39	7	5.90	7.19	13.3	3.6	6.0	2.8	7.08	-8.0	-5
2001	TEN	SOU	25	16	15	96.7	78	27	81	10	3.44	5.12	9.8	3.0	5.3	1.6	4.09	4.1	4
2001	SYR	INT	25	11	11	63.0	60	26	48	6	2.71	4.43	9.7	4.4	5.4	1.1	4.90	7.5	1
2002	TOR	AL	26	58	0	66.0	52	32	48	12	5.73	4.46	6.8	4.0	6.3	1.5	3.91	6.7	-7
2003	TOR	AL	27	34	2	45.7	50	22	34	7	5.24	5.07	9.5	4.0	6.4	1.3	4.91	5.1	-7

Breakout: 23%   Improve: 50%   Collapse: 28%

Scott Cassidy *(continued)*

That Cassidy spent nearly the entire season in first-class hotels and charter jets shows just how desperate the Blue Jays' pitching situation was last year. He was afraid to throw his middling stuff in the strike zone, a paranoia that produced the usual results: walks and home runs. Cassidy's best chance for a career is to learn a trick pitch or lead a grassroots movement to reinstate Eric Gregg. Outrighted to Syracuse.

Vinny Chulk   Born: 19-Dec-78   Age: 24   Bats: R   Throws: R

YEAR	TM	LG	AGE	G	GS	IP	H	BB	SO	HR	ERA	EQERA	EQH9	EQBB9	EQSO9	EQHR9	PERA	VORP	STF
2000	MED	PIO	21	14	13	68.7	75	20	51	5	3.80	5.65	14.1	3.3	3.9	1.7	5.99	-1.1	-6
2001	DUN	FSL	22	16	1	34.7	38	13	50	2	3.11	5.77	12.5	4.0	8.7	1.3	6.57	-1.4	13
2001	TEN	SOU	22	24	1	43.0	34	8	43	5	3.14	4.27	9.6	2.0	6.3	1.7	3.75	5.4	4
2002	TEN	SOU	23	25	24	152.0	133	53	108	12	2.96	4.38	10.2	3.5	4.8	1.5	4.51	19.0	4
2003	TOR	AL	24	14	10	58.7	70	25	39	9	5.64	5.46	10.4	3.5	5.8	1.3	5.26	3.0	-2

Breakout: 16%   Improve: 54%   Collapse: 18%

Chulk was the Southern League's Pitcher of the Year. Before sinking your kid's college fund in Chulk's trading cards though, bear in mind that tarot cards are as useful in forecasting future success as minor league hardware. Close to home, future journeyman Chris Baker took home the same honor with Tennessee two years ago. Although Chulk throws a little harder, he is cut from the same cloth, projecting as a middle reliever. If he has more success missing Triple-A bats than Baker, he could get a cup of coffee when the leaves turn—that is, if he's still around. Chulk may well be trade bait, since his value will never be higher.

Pasqual Coco   Born: 08-Sep-77   Age: 25   Bats: R   Throws: R

YEAR	TM	LG	AGE	G	GS	IP	H	BB	SO	HR	ERA	EQERA	EQH9	EQBB9	EQSO9	EQHR9	PERA	VORP	STF
2000	TEN	SOU	22	27	26	167.7	154	68	142	16	3.76	5.23	10.4	4.0	5.4	1.6	5.31	5.1	5
2001	SYR	INT	23	22	22	121.7	128	50	82	11	4.66	5.56	10.7	4.4	4.8	1.1	5.45	-0.7	0
2001	TOR	AL	23	7	1	14.3	12	6	9	0	4.41	3.64	7.4	3.5	5.3	0.2	2.79	2.8	3
2002	SYR	INT	24	30	23	141.0	145	57	98	17	4.98	5.81	10.3	4.4	5.4	1.6	5.40	-5.0	-3
2003	TOR	AL	25	15	9	57.0	67	28	37	8	5.61	5.43	10.2	4.0	5.6	1.2	5.41	2.8	-5

Breakout: 16%   Improve: 47%   Collapse: 17%

Coco only made the book because we tend to focus on upper-level prospects, and even then it's a stretch. He didn't progress at all in his efforts to master a third pitch, and the bullpen isn't a palatable alternative because although his changeup is terrific, his fastball is nothing special. Jayson Stark is salivating over the possibility of Coco facing Covelli Crisp.

Kelvim Escobar   Born: 11-Apr-76   Age: 27   Bats: R   Throws: R

YEAR	TM	LG	AGE	G	GS	IP	H	BB	SO	HR	ERA	EQERA	EQH9	EQBB9	EQSO9	EQHR9	PERA	VORP	STF
2000	TOR	AL	24	43	24	180.0	186	85	142	26	5.35	4.45	8.3	3.4	6.7	1.1	4.37	20.6	11
2001	TOR	AL	25	59	11	126.0	93	52	121	8	3.50	3.07	6.5	3.5	8.1	0.5	2.72	33.1	18
2002	TOR	AL	26	76	0	78.0	75	44	85	10	4.27	4.30	8.3	4.6	9.3	1.0	4.59	9.4	10
2003	TOR	AL	27	42	8	85.0	79	38	76	9	3.96	3.83	8.1	3.7	7.8	0.9	3.94	18.4	9

Breakout: 21%   Improve: 55%   Collapse: 17%

Like knighthood, the "closer" title is for life (see Exhibit A: Heathcliff Slocumb). The question is, after six months of white-knuckle ninth innings, has Escobar been so dubbed? Ricciardi certainly hopes so, and will be using Escobar's 38 saves as bait in the same trap that he put Billy Koch's. Escobar could improve significantly if he would dump his erratic curveball and go strictly with his fastball and splitter.

Bob File   Born: 28-Jan-77   Age: 26   Bats: R   Throws: R

YEAR	TM	LG	AGE	G	GS	IP	H	BB	SO	HR	ERA	EQERA	EQH9	EQBB9	EQSO9	EQHR9	PERA	VORP	STF
2000	TEN	SOU	23	36	0	34.7	29	13	40	1	3.11	4.92	8.9	3.6	7.2	0.5	4.08	1.8	6
2000	SYR	INT	23	20	0	19.3	14	2	10	1	0.93	1.71	7.8	1.0	4.1	0.6	2.18	7.9	0
2001	TOR	AL	24	60	0	74.3	57	29	38	6	3.27	3.07	6.9	3.3	4.4	0.7	2.91	19.1	-6
2002	SYR	INT	25	33	0	36.3	39	15	23	2	5.95	6.28	10.4	4.5	4.9	0.7	5.15	-3.6	-17
2003	TOR	AL	26	42	0	47.0	55	20	27	5	5.18	5.01	10.2	3.6	5.1	0.8	4.99	3.9	-13

Breakout: 13%   Improve: 47%   Collapse: 20%

File was penciled in to replace Paul Quantrill as the setup guy before straining an oblique muscle in late March. He finally returned two months later, but the hard, sinking stuff that made him effective out of the Blue Jays' bullpen in 2001 didn't show up all year, causing him to remain in Syracuse. When the SkyChiefs' season ended, File was told to just shut it down for the winter, but something is wrong. File has the ingredients to be a sturdy reliever, but that day may not come until after a surgical visit and a long rehab.

Matt Ford Born: 08-Apr-81 Age: 22 Bats: B Throws: L

YEAR	TM	LG	AGE	G	GS	IP	H	BB	SO	HR	ERA	EQERA	EQH9	EQBB9	EQSO9	EQHR9	PERA	VORP	STF
2000	HAG	SAL	19	18	14	83.7	81	36	86	5	3.87	6.10	12.1	5.4	5.5	1.4	6.30	-5.6	-1
2001	CWV	SAL	20	11	11	70.7	62	22	69	2	2.42	4.77	10.3	4.2	5.0	0.6	5.38	5.8	8
2001	DUN	FSL	20	13	12	60.0	67	37	48	8	5.85	7.99	14.3	7.1	5.1	3.1	8.63	-16.6	-18
2002	DUN	FSL	21	21	18	114.0	100	42	85	7	2.37	4.85	11.0	4.3	4.9	1.4	5.11	8.2	3

The Jays' third round pick out of a Florida high school in 1999, Ford made a return trip to the FSL last year and led the loop in ERA. That's impressive since Dunedin Stadium is a hitter's ballpark, but also deceiving, because nearly one-third of the runs he surrendered were unearned. Ford projects as a starter, as his fastball, curve, and changeup are all plus pitches and he is equally effective against lefties and righties. He has struggled whenever promoted a level, so the three-step leap to Milwaukee after being chosen in the Rule 5 draft should prove troublesome.

Roy Halladay Born: 14-May-77 Age: 26 Bats: R Throws: R

YEAR	TM	LG	AGE	G	GS	IP	H	BB	SO	HR	ERA	EQERA	EQH9	EQBB9	EQSO9	EQHR9	PERA	VORP	STF
2000	SYR	INT	23	11	11	73.7	85	21	38	10	5.50	6.22	12.4	2.7	4.1	1.6	5.58	-5.9	-2
2000	TOR	AL	23	19	13	67.7	107	42	44	14	10.64	8.46	12.5	4.3	5.4	1.5	7.87	-22.4	-10
2001	DUN	FSL	24	13	0	22.7	28	3	15	1	3.96	6.05	13.9	1.4	4.0	1.0	6.46	-1.7	-14
2001	TEN	SOU	24	5	5	34.0	25	6	29	2	2.12	3.41	8.8	1.9	5.3	0.9	2.99	7.9	15
2001	SYR	INT	24	2	2	14.0	12	0	13	2	3.21	3.56	9.0	0.7	6.7	1.8	3.36	3.0	23
2001	TOR	AL	24	17	16	105.3	97	25	96	3	3.16	3.08	8.2	2.0	7.7	0.2	2.84	28.3	34
2002	TOR	AL	25	34	34	239.3	223	62	168	10	2.93	3.11	8.2	2.2	6.1	0.3	3.06	63.7	21
2003	*TOR*	*AL*	*26*	*34*	*33*	*210.7*	*228*	*65*	*146*	*23*	*4.39*	*4.25*	*9.4*	*2.6*	*6.0*	*0.9*	*4.19*	*35.0*	*12*

Breakout: 10%   Improve: 40%   Collapse: 14%

Ace. Halladay led the American League in innings pitched, posting 24 quality starts in 34 tries, and has now strung together a year and a half of dazzling performances since returning from a complete overhaul after his 2000 meltdown. He's one of that rare and valuable species of ground ball pitchers who also rack up strikeouts. Halladay should be awarded the first long-term contract of the Ricciardi era.

Mark Hendrickson Born: 23-Jun-74 Age: 29 Bats: L Throws: L

YEAR	TM	LG	AGE	G	GS	IP	H	BB	SO	HR	ERA	EQERA	EQH9	EQBB9	EQSO9	EQHR9	PERA	VORP	STF
2000	DUN	FSL	26	12	12	51.3	63	29	38	7	5.61	9.12	17.4	7.2	5.2	3.4	9.01	-20.6	-37
2000	TEN	SOU	26	6	6	39.7	32	12	29	5	3.63	4.49	9.4	3.0	4.7	2.1	4.49	4.5	-3
2001	SYR	INT	27	38	6	73.3	80	18	33	13	4.67	5.94	11.4	2.7	3.2	2.2	5.86	-4.2	-28
2002	SYR	INT	28	19	14	92.0	90	22	68	12	3.52	4.34	9.8	2.6	5.7	1.7	4.62	11.8	2
2002	TOR	AL	28	16	4	36.7	25	12	21	1	2.45	2.28	6.0	2.8	5.0	0.2	2.13	12.9	3
2003	*TOR*	*AL*	*29*	*20*	*10*	*63.0*	*75*	*25*	*40*	*12*	*5.60*	*5.42*	*10.3*	*3.3*	*5.5*	*1.5*	*5.42*	*3.7*	*-7*

Breakout: 11%   Improve: 41%   Collapse: 35%

The ex-NBA hoopster shed the novelty tag and emerged as a genuine prospect last year. Hendrickson has outstanding command for a pitcher his size and learned to mix his diving high-80s heat with fair off-speed stuff to induce ground balls. Like grandma's Oldsmobile, his arm has low mileage despite its age. Hendrickson comes with the same caveat that Brandon Lyon did last year: more than half his MLB innings came against September rollovers Tampa Bay and Baltimore. However, unlike Lyon, Hendrickson has untapped upside and is still learning his craft. He'll be in the March mix for a spot at back of the rotation. If he gets it, expect some bumps along the way.

Felix Heredia   Born: 18-Jun-75   Age: 28   Bats: L   Throws: L

YEAR	TM	LG	AGE	G	GS	IP	H	BB	SO	HR	ERA	EQERA	EQH9	EQBB9	EQSO9	EQHR9	PERA	VORP	STF
2000	CHC	NL	25	74	0	58.7	46	33	52	6	4.75	3.92	7.0	4.1	7.0	0.8	3.60	9.5	1
2001	CHC	NL	26	48	0	35.0	45	16	28	6	6.17	6.50	11.6	3.8	6.1	1.4	6.70	-4.4	-15
2002	TOR	AL	27	53	0	52.3	51	26	31	5	3.61	4.35	8.5	4.2	5.2	0.8	4.26	6.0	-11
2003	CIN	NL	28	36	0	37.3	40	19	28	5	4.91	5.24	9.9	3.9	6.1	1.2	5.15	2.7	-10

Breakout: 15%   Improve: 39%   Collapse: 31%

When you think of situational left-handers, Heredia's name doesn't come to mind. Yet, his career average of .84 innings per appearance is fifth-lowest among pitchers with at least 350 career appearances, clearly indicating that has been his role. It shouldn't be, though. Heredia's platoon difference since 1999 is barely 90 points of OPS—not significantly better than a normal split. Heredia isn't any great shakes, but he's never even been used correctly, crammed into the LOOGY role at age 21.

Jason Kershner   Born: 19-Dec-76   Age: 26   Bats: L   Throws: L

YEAR	TM	LG	AGE	G	GS	IP	H	BB	SO	HR	ERA	EQERA	EQH9	EQBB9	EQSO9	EQHR9	PERA	VORP	STF
2000	REA	EAS	23	27	19	119.0	125	25	80	15	3.63	5.41	12.8	2.2	4.8	2.2	5.56	1.1	-3
2001	REA	EAS	24	26	19	123.7	147	26	70	18	4.80	7.15	14.0	2.6	3.7	2.1	7.03	-22.8	-16
2002	POR	PCL	25	31	12	86.0	65	26	83	8	3.03	3.88	8.5	3.2	6.9	1.2	3.51	15.1	7
2002	SDP	NL	25	15	0	18.7	15	10	11	2	5.78	5.05	7.3	4.3	4.7	1.0	4.33	0.7	-15
2002	TOR	AL	25	10	0	5.3	5	4	7	1	1.70	4.07	7.9	6.1	11.1	1.5	5.42	0.8	14
2003	TOR	AL	26	22	5	45.0	52	19	32	7	5.42	5.25	10.0	3.5	6.2	1.3	5.08	3.5	-5

Breakout: 17%   Improve: 50%   Collapse: 25%

Those of you with long memories may remember him as one of Piedmont's "Four Aces" back in 1996. Over the years, injuries and attrition has reduced the hand to a high-card six (David Coggin) and Kershner, who's about a three. Kershner's southpaw will allow him to play a few more rounds, but if he can't snuff out left-handed bats better than last year (.256/.383/.462), he'll be forced to fold, too.

Esteban Loaiza   Born: 31-Dec-71   Age: 31   Bats: R   Throws: R

YEAR	TM	LG	AGE	G	GS	IP	H	BB	SO	HR	ERA	EQERA	EQH9	EQBB9	EQSO9	EQHR9	PERA	VORP	STF
2000	TEX	AL	28	20	17	107.3	133	31	75	21	5.37	4.61	9.9	2.1	6.0	1.4	5.07	10.6	7
2000	TOR	AL	28	14	14	92.0	95	26	62	8	3.62	3.41	8.5	2.1	5.9	0.6	3.48	21.4	16
2001	TOR	AL	29	36	30	190.0	239	40	110	27	5.02	5.07	11.1	1.8	4.9	1.2	5.14	9.0	2
2002	TOR	AL	30	25	25	151.3	192	38	87	18	5.71	5.28	11.2	2.1	5.0	1.0	5.17	3.8	4
2003	TOR	AL	31	26	23	142.0	168	38	82	19	4.89	4.73	10.3	2.2	5.0	1.1	4.62	17.6	4

Breakout: 13%   Improve: 52%   Collapse: 20%

The $6 million paid to Loaiza in the final year of his contract would've been better spent on a government study on the health benefits of gerbilling. Loaiza's tenure in Toronto was no different than in any of his other stops: great stuff, inconsistent results, and bad karma. Tampa Bay is the usual suspect when you try to guess where a player like this will land; however, Loaiza even slammed that door, posting a 16.58 ERA in five starts against the Devil Fishies.

Brandon Lyon   Born: 10-Aug-79   Age: 23   Bats: R   Throws: R

YEAR	TM	LG	AGE	G	GS	IP	H	BB	SO	HR	ERA	EQERA	EQH9	EQBB9	EQSO9	EQHR9	PERA	VORP	STF
2000	QUE	NYP	20	15	13	60.3	43	6	55	1	2.39	4.13	9.6	1.2	4.6	0.7	3.22	9.2	8
2001	TEN	SOU	21	9	9	58.7	57	9	45	7	3.68	5.30	11.8	1.7	4.9	1.8	4.77	1.3	9
2001	SYR	INT	21	11	11	68.3	68	10	53	7	3.69	4.64	10.0	1.6	5.5	1.2	4.29	6.6	17
2001	TOR	AL	21	11	11	63.0	63	15	35	6	4.29	3.90	8.9	2.0	4.7	0.8	3.63	11.2	13
2002	TOR	AL	22	15	10	62.0	78	19	30	14	6.53	6.05	11.0	2.6	4.2	1.9	6.05	-3.9	-6
2002	SYR	INT	22	14	14	75.7	99	19	35	4	5.11	6.41	12.6	2.7	3.5	0.7	5.96	-7.6	-3
2003	BOS	AL	23	22	16	96.0	115	30	51	13	5.16	5.13	10.5	2.6	4.6	1.2	4.98	7.5	-5

Breakout: 7%   Improve: 46%   Collapse: 22%

Maybe the only thing as surprising as Lyon's meteoric rise through the system is that he left almost as quickly as he arrived. He was removed from the 40-man roster just 14 months after his Blue Jay debut and claimed by Boston. Lyon has decent command of hittable stuff, but nothing resembling an out pitch, and gets pasted the second time through an order. Though only 23 years old, he might not see the major leagues again.

Diegomar Markwell   Born: 08-Aug-80   Age: 22   Bats: L   Throws: L

YEAR	TM	LG	AGE	G	GS	IP	H	BB	SO	HR	ERA	EQERA	EQH9	EQBB9	EQSO9	EQHR9	PERA	VORP	STF
2000	QUE	NYP	19	14	13	73.7	59	31	66	2	3.05	5.70	11.5	5.3	4.7	1.1	5.41	-1.6	-1
2001	CWV	SAL	20	22	21	123.3	121	32	99	10	3.87	5.71	12.3	3.6	4.2	1.9	6.57	-2.8	-3
2001	DUN	FSL	20	5	5	33.7	27	13	26	4	3.20	4.51	10.3	4.3	4.8	2.7	5.20	3.7	0
2002	TEN	SOU	21	28	27	168.3	174	60	101	23	4.39	6.25	12.7	3.6	4.1	2.6	6.07	-14.0	-5

In 1992, Toronto signed a Brazilian youngster named Jose Pett to a $700,000 contract. At the time, many scouts called Pett the most refined 16-year-old pitcher ever. In 1996, the same year they shipped a floundering Pett to the Pirates, the club landed 16-year-old Diegomar Markwell out of Curacao for $750,000. After four years in rookie ball, Markwell finally started showing signs of life and reached Double-A last year. A league-average left-hander, Markwell will certainly never sniff the success of his cousin, Andruw Jones (who signed for a modest $46,000), but he could go one better than Pett and briefly don a major league uniform. Projecting high school hurlers is largely a guessing game; trying to project 16-year-old arms is a fool's errand.

Dustin McGowan   Born: 24-Mar-82   Age: 21   Bats: R   Throws: R

YEAR	TM	LG	AGE	G	GS	IP	H	BB	SO	HR	ERA	EQERA	EQH9	EQBB9	EQSO9	EQHR9	PERA	VORP	STF
2000	MED	PIO	18	8	8	25.0	26	25	19	2	6.48	8.87	13.9	11.6	4.1	1.9	9.04	-9.3	-39
2001	AUB	NYP	19	15	14	67.0	57	49	80	1	3.76	6.71	11.0	10.4	6.4	0.5	7.17	-9.0	-5
2002	CWV	SAL	20	28	28	148.3	143	59	163	10	4.19	6.41	12.8	5.3	6.4	1.7	6.25	-14.9	5

Of the scads of raw-boned teenage throwers Ash & Associates drafted, only McGowan and Brandon League show real promise, and they're at least three stops away from SkyDome. McGowan used smoke and a power curveball to pace the Sally League in strikeouts, averaging 10 every nine frames. Although he cut his walk rate by almost three a game from 2001, he needs to further hone his command. Against low-A hitters, McGowan could simply overpower hitters when he got behind in the count. There's a lot to like here, but we'd be remiss to omit the standard injury disclaimer for a pitcher this young.

Justin Miller   Born: 27-Aug-77   Age: 25   Bats: R   Throws: R

YEAR	TM	LG	AGE	G	GS	IP	H	BB	SO	HR	ERA	EQERA	EQH9	EQBB9	EQSO9	EQHR9	PERA	VORP	STF
2000	MID	TXS	22	18	18	87.0	74	41	82	8	4.55	4.51	8.4	4.4	6.1	1.2	4.26	9.6	8
2000	SAC	PCL	22	9	9	54.7	42	13	34	3	2.47	3.04	7.9	2.2	4.6	0.6	2.74	15.0	14
2001	SAC	PCL	23	29	28	165.0	174	64	134	26	4.75	5.52	10.4	4.2	5.4	1.7	5.78	-0.3	1
2002	SYR	INT	24	8	8	44.7	34	16	29	0	1.61	2.72	7.2	3.9	5.0	0.2	2.92	13.8	10
2002	TOR	AL	24	25	18	102.3	103	66	68	12	5.54	5.23	8.7	5.4	5.7	1.0	5.00	3.0	-1
2003	*TOR*	*AL*	*25*	*23*	*16*	*97.7*	*108*	*49*	*65*	*13*	*5.36*	*5.18*	*9.6*	*4.2*	*5.8*	*1.1*	*5.04*	*6.9*	*-2*

Breakout: 19%   *Improve: 50%*   *Collapse: 17%*

Miller arrived with Hinske from Sacramento and has the raw tools to make as big a splash. His two-seam fastball and slider combination is absolutely filthy, but it takes him a while to get his bearings, evidenced by a first inning ERA of 11.57 and 11 hit batters in just 102 innings. He went to the Instructional League after last season to work on a more consistent release point and an adequate off-speed pitch. Miller's progress will be a good litmus test of the teaching skills of the organization's pitching coaches.

Steve Parris   Born: 17-Dec-67   Age: 35   Bats: R   Throws: R

YEAR	TM	LG	AGE	G	GS	IP	H	BB	SO	HR	ERA	EQERA	EQH9	EQBB9	EQSO9	EQHR9	PERA	VORP	STF
2000	CIN	NL	32	33	33	192.7	227	71	117	30	4.81	5.27	11.3	2.8	4.9	1.3	5.22	5.0	0
2001	TOR	AL	33	19	19	105.7	126	41	49	18	4.60	5.14	10.5	3.3	3.9	1.4	5.55	4.3	-8
2002	TOR	AL	34	14	14	75.3	96	35	48	13	5.98	5.74	11.0	3.9	5.5	1.4	6.21	-2.0	-3
2003	*TBY*	*AL*	*35*	*18*	*14*	*84.0*	*104*	*33*	*47*	*13*	*5.35*	*5.33*	*10.9*	*3.2*	*4.8*	*1.3*	*5.55*	*5.2*	*-5*

Breakout: 7%   *Improve: 35%*   *Collapse: 31%*

Parris was a 10-year bush warrior before sticking with Cincinnati in 1998. Thirty months later, Gord Ash inked the very same player to a two-year deal worth $6 million. Even before Parris blew out his shoulder, how can you justify paying that amount for an essentially free commodity? Now 35, Parris could tack on a couple more years as a swingman, but like Internet stocks, his market has gone bust. Like alot of things gone bust, Parris has fled to Florida, where at least he'll accrue service time as a Devil Ray.

Chad Pleiness   Born: 05-Mar-80   Age: 23   Bats: R   Throws: R

YEAR	TM	LG	AGE	G	GS	IP	H	BB	SO	HR	ERA	EQERA	EQH9	EQBB9	EQSO9	EQHR9	PERA	VORP	STF
2002	AUB	NYP	22	16	9	74.3	48	32	70	2	2.42	4.84	9.6	6.3	5.3	0.9	4.32	5.3	-1

Part of the first wave of college hurlers that will land on the north beach of Lake Ontario over the next few years. Pleiness entered Central Michigan on a football scholarship, was honorable mention All-Mid-American Conference in basketball in 2001 and led the nation in strikeouts last year with 13.2 per nine innings. Not surprisingly, he blew away rookie league batters with his tailing 90-mph fastball and quick breaking slider. Team coaches think they'll find more in the tank after they iron out his mechanics. Pleiness has great mental toughness and should rise quickly.

Cliff Politte   Born: 27-Feb-74   Age: 29   Bats: R   Throws: R

YEAR	TM	LG	AGE	G	GS	IP	H	BB	SO	HR	ERA	EQERA	EQH9	EQBB9	EQSO9	EQHR9	PERA	VORP	STF
2000	SWB	INT	26	21	20	112.7	94	41	106	8	3.11	4.21	9.0	3.3	7.3	0.8	3.80	16.2	17
2000	PHI	NL	26	12	8	59.0	55	27	50	8	3.66	3.76	8.4	3.3	6.7	1.1	4.21	11.3	11
2001	PHI	NL	27	23	0	26.0	24	8	23	2	2.42	3.31	9.0	2.6	6.9	0.6	3.66	6.0	6
2002	PHI	NL	28	13	0	16.3	19	9	15	0	3.87	5.49	11.2	4.4	7.3	0.2	5.25	-0.2	0
2002	TOR	AL	28	55	0	57.3	38	19	57	5	3.61	2.77	5.8	2.8	8.6	0.7	2.37	16.6	18
2003	TOR	AL	29	31	5	56.0	54	21	47	6	3.84	3.72	8.4	3.2	7.2	0.9	3.86	12.9	6

Breakout: 26%   Improve: 46%   Collapse: 23%

Baseball men have been using Politte's height (5'9") against him his whole career. The Blue Jays used it to their advantage, stealing him from the Phillies when they unloaded Dan Plesac. Politte quickly emerged as the team's best reliever, mixing blazing mid-90s heat with a hard slider and nifty changeup. He'll probably be the closer this year, though Tosca should use him as game situations dictate rather than exclusively in the ninth inning, something Escobar complained about vehemently when they tried it with him.

Luke Prokopec   Born: 23-Feb-78   Age: 25   Bats: L   Throws: R

YEAR	TM	LG	AGE	G	GS	IP	H	BB	SO	HR	ERA	EQERA	EQH9	EQBB9	EQSO9	EQHR9	PERA	VORP	STF
2000	SAN	TXS	22	22	22	128.7	118	23	124	8	2.45	3.54	9.9	1.7	6.4	0.9	4.08	28.1	23
2000	LAD	NL	22	5	3	21.0	19	9	12	2	3.00	4.11	8.7	3.2	4.7	0.8	4.02	3.2	3
2001	LAD	NL	23	29	22	138.3	146	40	91	27	4.88	5.21	9.9	2.5	5.1	1.6	5.40	4.3	2
2002	TOR	AL	24	22	12	71.7	90	25	41	19	6.78	6.40	10.9	2.9	5.0	2.2	6.44	-7.3	-11

Canadians can be very provincial, so Prokopec was under the microscope from the moment Ricciardi bagged him for Ontarian Paul Quantrill. Things got worse when the games started. He was shelled every fifth day, not at all resembling the pitcher the team thought it was getting. In hindsight, he was likely damaged goods. Prokopec was on and off the disabled list the last four months of the season, before undergoing surgery for a torn labrum. Because he'll likely miss all of 2003, the Blue Jays took him off their 40-man roster. Prokopec re-signed with the Dodgers, then was bagged by Cincinnati in the Rule 5 draft. Whether Prokopec's electric stuff returns when he does is a huge question mark.

Chad Ricketts   Born: 12-Feb-75   Age: 28   Bats: R   Throws: R

YEAR	TM	LG	AGE	G	GS	IP	H	BB	SO	HR	ERA	EQERA	EQH9	EQBB9	EQSO9	EQHR9	PERA	VORP	STF
2000	ABQ	PCL	25	54	0	67.7	59	36	75	7	3.46	4.30	8.2	4.7	7.9	1.1	4.14	8.1	3
2001	LVG	PCL	26	48	0	58.7	49	25	70	5	2.91	3.48	7.6	4.5	7.7	0.9	3.60	12.4	3
2002	SYR	INT	27	15	0	16.7	15	7	19	3	3.23	4.64	9.2	4.6	8.8	2.3	5.17	1.4	-1

Ricketts is the type of throw-in that Ricciardi will snag in trades; guys who for some reason—too short, bad build, big ears—have managed to fly under the radar despite good numbers. Maybe with Ricketts it's the vitamin deficiency associated with his last name. In his past six minor league seasons, he has struck out 10.2 batters per nine innings while walking only 3.4. Ricketts had Tommy John surgery last May and is expected back around mid-season. When the command returns, he should claim a spot in Toronto's bullpen.

Francisco Rosario   Born: 28-Sep-80   Age: 22   Bats: R   Throws: R

YEAR	TM	LG	AGE	G	GS	IP	H	BB	SO	HR	ERA	EQERA	EQH9	EQBB9	EQSO9	EQHR9	PERA	VORP	STF
2001	MED	PIO	20	16	15	75.7	79	38	55	8	5.59	7.47	13.6	7.2	3.8	2.4	7.20	-16.6	-23
2002	CWV	SAL	21	13	13	66.7	50	14	78	5	2.56	4.16	10.0	2.7	6.6	1.8	4.01	10.0	17
2002	DUN	FSL	21	13	12	63.0	33	25	65	3	1.29	2.49	6.5	4.5	6.6	1.0	2.91	21.1	18

Rosario wasn't in anybody's sights entering the year, but arrived at camp with five more mph on his fastball and exploded onto the scene. Rosario had nearly a 4:1 K:BB ratio at two levels, mixing a sharp slider and baffling changeup with 95 mph octane gas. The Dominican was named a top-five prospect in both the South Atlantic and Florida State leagues. Rosario has everything you could want in a young pitcher and something you don't—a nearly complete tear of the ulnar collateral ligament suffered in the Arizona Fall League. Click your heels three times and repeat, "There is no such thing as a pitching prospect. There is no such thing . . ."

Mike Smith										**Born: 19-Sep-77**		**Age: 25**	**Bats: R**		**Throws: R**		
YEAR	TM	LG	AGE	G	GS	IP	H	BB	SO	HR	ERA	EQERA	EQH9	EQBB9	EQSO9	EQHR9	PERA	VORP	STF
2000	QUE	NYP	22	14	12	51.0	41	17	55	1	2.29	5.16	11.0	4.1	5.6	0.8	4.92	1.9	1
2001	CWV	SAL	23	14	14	94.3	78	21	85	2	2.10	4.04	9.4	3.0	4.5	0.5	4.55	15.3	8
2001	TEN	SOU	23	14	14	93.0	80	26	77	7	2.42	4.49	10.3	3.0	5.2	1.1	4.17	10.5	9
2002	SYR	INT	24	20	20	121.7	106	43	76	10	3.48	4.09	8.6	3.9	4.8	1.1	4.04	19.1	4
2002	TOR	AL	24	14	6	35.3	43	20	16	3	6.63	5.94	10.6	4.7	3.9	0.7	5.60	-1.9	-16
2003	TOR	AL	25	19	12	72.7	83	33	45	9	5.19	5.02	9.9	3.8	5.4	1.0	4.92	6.8	-4

Breakout: 21%   Improve: 47%   Collapse: 17%

A fifth round pick in the 2000 June draft, Smith is one of only three college hurlers selected that early during Gord Ash's last four drafts. That fondness for raw high school arms created a void of upper-level pitching, so Smith was rushed up the ladder and pressed into major league service last year. He clearly wasn't ready, nibbling at the edges of the plate instead of trusting his plus stuff. He will open the season in Syracuse and stay there until he returns to the aggressive style he flashed in 2001. The pieces are still there for a reliable fourth or fifth starter.

Corey Thurman										**Born: 05-Nov-78**		**Age: 24**	**Bats: R**		**Throws: R**		
YEAR	TM	LG	AGE	G	GS	IP	H	BB	SO	HR	ERA	EQERA	EQH9	EQBB9	EQSO9	EQHR9	PERA	VORP	STF
2000	WIL	CRL	21	19	19	115.7	97	46	96	6	2.26	4.24	10.3	4.4	4.8	1.2	5.21	16.3	5
2000	WIC	TXS	21	9	9	50.3	46	24	47	10	4.83	6.70	11.0	4.7	6.3	2.9	5.86	-6.7	3
2001	WIC	TXS	22	25	25	155.0	117	65	148	16	3.37	4.79	8.9	4.8	6.3	1.6	4.32	12.3	11
2002	TOR	AL	23	43	1	68.0	65	45	56	11	4.37	4.54	8.2	5.5	7.1	1.3	5.11	6.4	0
2003	TOR	AL	24	26	6	56.7	61	32	46	10	5.59	5.41	9.4	4.7	7.1	1.5	5.34	4.3	-5

Breakout: 17%   Improve: 48%   Collapse: 14%

The conditions weren't optimal, but at least the sad state of Toronto's pitching kept its Rule 5 pick from completely wasting a year of development. Although Thurman's offerings are somewhat raw, particularly his curveball, he has a great arm and the makings of a devastating changeup. Not surprisingly, one of the biggest battles he fought all season was with his nerves. The Blue Jays just want him to pitch, so he'll open the campaign in Syracuse.

Pete Walker										**Born: 08-Apr-69**		**Age: 34**	**Bats: R**		**Throws: R**		
YEAR	TM	LG	AGE	G	GS	IP	H	BB	SO	HR	ERA	EQERA	EQH9	EQBB9	EQSO9	EQHR9	PERA	VORP	STF
2000	CSP	PCL	31	58	0	73.3	64	30	61	3	3.07	2.99	7.6	3.6	5.9	0.4	3.16	19.5	0
2001	NOR	INT	32	26	26	168.3	145	46	106	12	2.99	4.29	9.3	3.0	4.5	0.9	4.00	22.7	2
2002	NOR	INT	33	2	2	9.0	9	1	6	1	3.00	3.97	10.2	1.2	5.1	1.5	4.47	1.5	3
2002	TOR	AL	33	37	20	139.3	143	51	80	18	4.33	4.26	9.0	3.1	5.0	1.1	4.38	18.8	-2
2003	TOR	AL	34	29	16	97.7	110	36	57	12	4.85	4.69	9.8	3.1	5.1	1.0	4.66	11.9	-4

Breakout: 7%   Improve: 51%   Collapse: 16%

Despite spending April collecting dust in the Mets system and mainly working out of the Jays bullpen until July, Walker trailed only Rodrigo Lopez in innings pitched among AL rookies. Like Steve Parris, Walker toiled for a decade as a minor league soldier; unlike Parris, he is financially compensated like one. Walker has fair stuff, throws strikes, and will help the club as a swingman for the next couple of years.

Scott Wiggins   Born: 24-Mar-76   Age: 27   Bats: L   Throws: L

YEAR	TM	LG	AGE	G	GS	IP	H	BB	SO	HR	ERA	EQERA	EQH9	EQBB9	EQSO9	EQHR9	PERA	VORP	STF
2000	TAM	FSL	24	28	15	100.7	106	46	68	4	4.11	6.89	12.5	5.4	4.4	0.9	6.68	-15.8	-16
2001	TAM	FSL	25	36	5	68.3	72	23	77	5	3.03	5.76	12.9	3.7	7.0	1.7	6.81	-2.6	-6
2002	NRW	EAS	26	24	0	27.7	19	9	26	1	2.27	3.06	7.3	3.5	6.4	0.6	3.12	7.1	0
2002	TEN	SOU	26	16	0	19.3	18	5	19	0	0.93	2.73	10.0	2.5	6.4	0.2	3.84	5.7	4
2002	SYR	INT	26	12	0	14.0	11	7	14	0	2.57	3.81	7.5	5.4	7.7	0.2	3.44	2.4	3
2003	TOR	AL	34	27	0	34.0	39	17	26	4	4.91	4.75	9.9	4.1	6.6	0.9	4.94	4.7	-4

Breakout: 24%   Improve: 53%   Collapse: 24%

Wiggins was the obligatory body Toronto got from the Yankees when they made Raul Mondesi into George Steinbrenner's problem. Having rid themselves of The Buffalo and saved $12.5 million to boot, they would have happily accepted Ralph Wiggum. Wiggins is one of dozens of soft-tossing lefties hoping for roster expansion or a waiver claim from St. Louis so they can be superfluous third lefty specialists in the bullpen.

Arizona Diamondbacks

So what now?

The plan was pretty simple: Ride the big two. Johnson and Schilling would pitch well enough to get to the playoffs, with a little help from a few lesser pitchers, a collection of relatively old but reliable offensive players, and a bunch of side-armers in the bullpen. It's a veteran team, and we can stay healthy enough to get through the marathon until we get to the sprint. Once we get to the postseason, no one's going to be able to beat Schilling and Johnson 3 out of 5 or 4 out of 7. It's a good plan. And Johnson and Schilling were up to the task, carrying the team through the regular season and to the postseason. But as has been demonstrated so many times in the past, the postseason's something of a crap shoot. It's fairly common for the best team not to win, and every year, only one team wins their final postseason game. In 2002, that team wasn't Arizona.

So right now, Joe Garagiola Jr. and his staff are looking at a new season with a year added on to the age of what was already a strikingly old team. The core of the team isn't just mature—it's venerable. Randy Johnson is 39 this season. Curt Schilling turned 36 in November. Luis Gonzalez will play this coming season at 35. Steve Finley? He'll play the 2003 season at 38. Matt Williams is no spring chicken. The core of the D-Backs is extremely old, but fortunately for Arizona fans, it's also extremely good. For pitchers, age isn't as much of a concern as health, and Schilling and Johnson are both prototypes of the pitcher that should be successful into his early 40s. So maybe the concept of a window isn't exactly the right one, when your senior citizens are likely to be kicking ass and taking names well into the decade.

So what do you do now, if you're Joe Jr.? Simple:

Let everyone else rebuild. This is the Oakland Raider model. Let's go get good players that are too old to be on cheap or rebuilding teams. Let's try to draft some young studs to bolster the old guys, and let's take some chances, and try to win now. Sometimes it works. We were an awfully good team last year, and it's not as if aging and its deleterious effects all happen at once, so let's see where we stand:

C	Chad Moeller	SS	Tony Womack
1B	Lyle Overbay	LF	Luis Gonzalez
2B	Junior Spivey	CF	Steve Finley
3B	Craig Counsell	RF	Danny Bautista

It's not great, but it's not bad, and there's some depth on the bench, with Matt Williams and Dave Dellucci available to come up and hit. It's an old bunch, and it'd be a considerably better squad if Joe Garagiola didn't give his best hitter away for a Quadruple-A starter, but hey, no one's perfect, and it's water under the bridge. We're not concentrating on the past. We're looking forward. And everyone (sweat) always needs starting pitching. You just can't have enough. Besides, Elmer Dessens was great last year. He's no Dave Fleming. (gulp)

The pitching fleshes out pretty nicely to say the least. We may even move BK into the rotation, now that he's a bit older and can handle a bigger workload. So let's see what we've got:

SP	Randy Johnson
SP	Curt Schilling
SP	Elmer Dessens
SP	Miguel Batista
SP	John Patterson

That's pretty shiny. No one in the division can get close to that, even if all those young kids in San Diego pan out and manage to keep their personal lives together. Patterson's a breakout candidate, and we can support the last three in the rotation with a pretty strong pen, thanks to the durability of the first two. Of course, if we hadn't acquired Dessens, Kim would probably have gotten that shot at the rotation that everyone was talking about, and we'd still have Erubiel Durazo on the club. After all, one of the few strengths of our farm system is relief prospects, with guys like Bevis and Belflower available, and maybe Mantei'd be healthy enough to close. I

Diamondbacks Prospectus

2002 record: 98–64; First place, NL West; Lost to Cardinals in Division Series

Pythagenport Record: 96–66

Runs scored per game: 5.1 (1st in NL)

Runs allowed per game: 4.2 (5th in NL)

Team EqA: .265 (4th in NL)

2002 Batters Age: 32.4 (2nd oldest in NL)

2002 Pitchers Age: 33 (oldest in NL)

Ballpark: Bank One Ballpark; Moderate hitters' park; Park Factor of 1.034

2002: The Big Two and some nice developments in the lineup fueled another run to the postseason.

2003: Aging, avoided for so long, will finally bring them low, and contingency planning doesn't seem to be something they're good at.

need a Pepcid. I digress. Durazo's gone, and Kim's in the pen, so we're good there, with:

RP Byung-Hyun Kim
RP Matt Mantei
RP Mike Koplove
RP Mike Myers
RP Greg Swindell

Maybe we mix in a Bret Prinz here or there. We're looking pretty good. Maybe good enough to show off and re-sign Mike Morgan. This is a good core. We can win with this. Is Oakland on the schedule? I want Johnson to start that game. Sombrero time, baby.

Might as well move forward with a win now strategy. Does the Durazo for Dessens swap match up with that strategy? We're forecasting Dessens and Durazo as both worth about 15 runs over a replacement player for the 2003 season. Of course, we're also forecasting Durazo for about 260 at-bats, and he'll clearly get considerably more than that in Oakland. Then again, the Snakes did lead the league in offense last year, and were fifth in runs allowed, so perhaps trading arguably your best hitter for Elmer Dessens makes some sense. Focusing just on 2003, it looks like a bad swap, and this is not a team that should be thinking in super long-time horizons unless seeking a state of profound depression.

The farm system isn't completely barren, but there are no Grade A prospects to speak of and not much of a portfolio of second-line prospects either. They're putting a lot of stock in people like Mike Gosling, a pitcher out of Stanford taken in the 2001 draft, a few bullpen candidates, the occasional project, and a few guys with some upside, like Scott Hairston, Lyle Overbay, and Jesus Cota. But youth doesn't necessarily mean prospects. John Patterson's young enough to take the big step forward, and there are some real signs of skill both in his performance record and in the eyes of the scouts. Byung-Hyun Kim is only 24 and it's not unusual for pitching prospects to take several years to really take a step forward. Additionally, there are a couple of other candidates for breakouts—guys like David Dellucci, who showed a great deal of promise years ago but has been battling health and opportunity issues for some time. If one or two of those guys pan out and do something special, there'll be time for the Diamondbacks to rebuild the farm system.

The Diamondbacks have bigger concerns than their aging talent base. If you're going to choose old players to have, the D-Backs have 'em. Pitchers with astronomical health records and K rates. Late-blooming hitters who still

retain young players' skills and have learned some plate discipline. The Diamondbacks' real problem is their decision, making process. Somewhere in the process, something's going haywire. Individual decisions can't work all the time. They just can't. But clubs need some sort of repeatable, tweakable system that guides their decision-making process, so the process can be improved, and everyone can get better at their jobs. The Diamondbacks don't have a system, or if they do, it's broken, and it needs to be fixed.

We know it needs to be fixed because of the symptoms. Cries of financial distress, even while successfully chasing down a World Series ring. A pattern of signing old players to expensive contracts because alternatives either haven't been adequately explored, or have been incompletely evaluated and found wanting. Failure to understand what performance metrics best forecast future success, illustrated by the acquisition of Elmer "Time Bomb" Dessens for Erubiel Durazo. All of these things point to a decision-making process that, at the very least, requires some major tweaking.

Parts of the process are in place. Probably the most important part is the feedback mechanism, where decisions are evaluated based on the results they produce. One of the worst decisions in franchise history was the decision to sign Matt Williams to a five-year, $45 million contract at the age of 32. Since then, the Diamondbacks have actually been more careful about signing veterans to those kinds of deals, while other clubs have jumped in with both feet—often to find very expensive peril, sometimes wearing the visage of Denny Neagle. So we know the franchise can pick up on major debacles and try to avoid them in the future.

But that's not enough. The Diamondback front office needs to do more. That doesn't necessarily mean having some big-ass, bureaucratic ISO 9000 compliant system. It means being honest with yourself and your organization about the repercussions of your actions. Did you sign a fragile, replacement level outfielder to a four-year deal worth $16 million? Recognize it, talk about how you can avoid doing that in the future, and execute on it. The Diamondbacks have actually been featured in venues like *CIO Magazine* for their progressive and intensive information technology programs. Here's a news flash—gathering information doesn't make you smarter. It needs to be used properly, or it's just another waste of money—a subject on which the D-Backs can speak from experience. The question is whether or not they'll learn from that experience. You can only ride Randy and Curt for so long.

HITTERS

Rod Barajas — C — Born: 05-Sep-75 — Age: 27 — Bats: R — Throws: R

YEAR	TM	LG	AGE	AB	H	2B	3B	HR	BB	SO	SB	CS	AVG	OBP	SLG	MLVR	EQBA	EQOBP	EQSLG	EQMLVR	VORP	DEFENSE			
2000	TUC	PCL	24	416	94	25	0	13	14	65	4	3	.226	.260	.380	-.327	.192	.214	.320	-.464	-24.0	83-C	6	12-1B	-1
2001	TUC	PCL	25	162	52	13	0	9	9	23	3	1	.321	.368	.568	.247	.277	.323	.484	.038	5.6	19-1B	0	17-C	-1
2001	ARI	NL	25	106	17	3	0	3	4	26	0	0	.160	.191	.274	-.579	.160	.191	.274	-.590	-9.7	26-C	-1		
2002	TUC	PCL	26	16	7	1	0	1	1	2	0	0	.438	.471	.688	.753	.375	.412	.562	.409	2.2				
2002	ARI	NL	26	154	36	10	0	3	10	25	1	0	.234	.293	.357	-.155	.239	.296	.361	-.216	.7	41-C	0		
2003	ARI	NL	27	176	42	9	0	5	11	30	2	1	.237	.286	.381	-.172	.236	.282	.386	-.200	-1.5				

Breakout: 28%   Improve: 46%   Collapse: 27%

Rany Jazayerli has a postulate that eventually, backup catchers will have a season in which they go Junior Ortiz on the league, and hit .300 as a fluke. If Barajas does that, he could actually have some value because unlike the Junior Ortizes of the world, he can occasionally pound a ball. He's 27 and his playing pattern will be strange, so maybe this is Rod's year.

Brian Barden — 3B — Born: 02-Apr-81 — Age: 22 — Bats: R — Throws: R

YEAR	TM	LG	AGE	AB	H	2B	3B	HR	BB	SO	SB	CS	AVG	OBP	SLG	MLVR	EQBA	EQOBP	EQSLG	EQMLVR	VORP	DEFENSE	
2002	YAK	NWN	21	15	5	1	0	0	1	1	0	0	.333	.412	.400	.250	.267	.327	.267	-.270	-.5		
2002	LNC	CLF	21	269	90	19	1	8	16	63	3	1	.335	.374	.502	.232	.252	.280	.376	-.217	-1.8	55-3B	4
2003	ARI	NL	22	182	44	9	2	4	12	43	3	3	.243	.295	.377	-.157	.242	.291	.382	-.184	-2.9		

Breakout: 29%   Improve: 55%   Collapse: 21%

As happy as the D-Backs are with Chad Tracy, Brian Barden may turn out to be better. He's got a quick stroke with a slight uppercut to it, and identifies pitches pretty well given his age. Defensively, he looks very solid, and fully capable of playing third base in the majors, which puts him way beyond the hordes of low-minors third basemen who end up as career tweeners at Triple-A. He's got to work on his plate discipline and learn to identify breaking pitches a little better, but he could turn into a real prospect as soon as this season.

Danny Bautista — RF — Born: 24-May-72 — Age: 31 — Bats: R — Throws: R

YEAR	TM	LG	AGE	AB	H	2B	3B	HR	BB	SO	SB	CS	AVG	OBP	SLG	MLVR	EQBA	EQOBP	EQSLG	EQMLVR	VORP	DEFENSE	
2000	FLA	NL	28	89	17	4	0	4	5	20	1	0	.191	.234	.371	-.378	.200	.234	.378	-.338	-5.9	26-LF	-1
2000	ARI	NL	28	262	83	16	7	7	20	30	5	2	.317	.372	.511	.173	.312	.357	.502	.158	16.5	68-RF	0
2001	ARI	NL	29	219	66	11	2	5	14	30	3	2	.301	.346	.438	.038	.299	.343	.434	.022	5.7	50-RF	1
2002	ARI	NL	30	154	50	5	2	6	11	21	4	2	.325	.370	.500	.233	.321	.361	.500	.171	9.6	33-RF	-1
2003	ARI	NL	31	279	80	15	3	7	20	39	4	2	.285	.335	.430	.011	.284	.330	.435	-.013	2.0		

Breakout: 6%   Improve: 26%   Collapse: 33%

Not a bad guy to have as a fourth outfielder. Bautista, like many of the Snakes, is overpaid, limiting the franchise's ability to invest in more strategically pressing areas, but he can help a club. His penchant for injuries is a little disturbing, especially given the advanced age of the club as a whole. He's expected to come to camp healthy, and fully rehabbed from surgery on his left shoulder. He'll be in the mix for at least 350 PA in right field.

Jay Bell — AARP — Born: 11-Dec-65 — Age: 37 — Bats: R — Throws: R

YEAR	TM	LG	AGE	AB	H	2B	3B	HR	BB	SO	SB	CS	AVG	OBP	SLG	MLVR	EQBA	EQOBP	EQSLG	EQMLVR	VORP	DEFENSE			
2000	ARI	NL	34	565	151	30	6	18	70	88	7	3	.267	.351	.437	-.019	.263	.338	.429	-.025	30.2	139-2B	-6		
2001	ARI	NL	35	428	106	24	1	13	65	79	0	1	.248	.352	.400	-.046	.249	.350	.400	-.053	19.9	69-2B	0	31-3B	-1
2002	ARI	NL	36	49	8	1	0	2	5	9	0	0	.163	.255	.306	-.326	.163	.253	.327	-.392	-3.3				

Good thing Joe Garagiola and friends decided to focus on signing good citizens and clubhouse guys, yes? For only $34 million, the D-Backs were able to get a player with declining skills and health. Bell's a free agent this off-season, and the new market sensibilities will probably bring his compensation more in line with his expected performance. Either that, or he'll be a Devil Ray.

Alex Cintron   SS   Born: 17-Dec-78   Age: 24   Bats: B   Throws: R

YEAR	TM	LG	AGE	AB	H	2B	3B	HR	BB	SO	SB	CS	AVG	OBP	SLG	MLVR	EQBA	EQOBP	EQSLG	EQMLVR	VORP	DEFENSE		
2000	ELP	TXS	21	522	157	30	6	4	29	56	9	9	.301	.340	.404	-.039	.241	.266	.325	-.325	-13.6	123-SS -23		
2001	TUC	PCL	22	425	124	24	3	3	15	48	9	6	.292	.319	.384	-.131	.249	.277	.325	-.298	-8.5	91-SS -20	13-2B	-1
2002	TUC	PCL	23	351	113	22	3	4	11	33	9	5	.322	.346	.436	.057	.280	.303	.382	-.143	6.4	47-SS -6	34-2B	-5
2002	ARI	NL	23	75	16	6	0	0	12	13	0	0	.213	.322	.293	-.197	.224	.322	.303	-.253	-.8	13-2B 0		
2003	ARI	NL	24	244	62	13	2	2	14	29	4	2	.256	.301	.356	-.167	.255	.296	.360	-.195	-2.2			

Breakout: 21%   Improve: 50%   Collapse: 21%

A Diamondback enthusiast who attended a California Pizza Feed asked me why I didn't include Cintron in my comments about promising young shortstops. After all, I had mentioned Jose Reyes, and he hadn't even had a cup of coffee yet. Well, the reasons are in black and white above. Cintron might have a career as a utility infielder or slap-hitting pinch hitter, but as a potential starter, he's a potential insurance salesman. Despite a swing that requires a great deal of effort, Cintron's a hacking slap hitter without tremendous defensive skills. He'll be fighting for roster spots for most of his career, hoping for the one fluke season where he hits .300 and earns the coveted "MLB Veteran" glow.

Greg Colbrunn   1B   Born: 26-Jul-69   Age: 33   Bats: R   Throws: R

YEAR	TM	LG	AGE	AB	H	2B	3B	HR	BB	SO	SB	CS	AVG	OBP	SLG	MLVR	EQBA	EQOBP	EQSLG	EQMLVR	VORP	DEFENSE
2000	ARI	NL	30	329	103	22	1	15	43	45	0	1	.313	.408	.523	.247	.307	.395	.511	.229	30.2	82-1B -4
2001	ARI	NL	31	97	28	8	0	4	9	14	0	0	.289	.373	.495	.151	.286	.365	.500	.142	7.3	
2002	ARI	NL	32	171	57	16	2	10	13	19	0	0	.333	.380	.626	.431	.329	.373	.630	.391	21.0	31-1B -2
2003	SEA	AL	33	219	61	13	1	9	20	30	0	0	.278	.343	.466	.086	.295	.362	.503	.141	11.1	

Breakout: 8%   Improve: 32%   Collapse: 28%

So, to recap—Mark Grace is signed on for another year. Colbrunn hasn't been a complicated player to manage. If there's a lefty on the mound, run him out there and let him mash. The only problem is that Colbrunn has not only been great against lefties, but righties as well, posting .398 OBP and .531 SLG against them over the last three years. Explain to me again why Mark Grace was brought in, much less re-signed? Colbrunn has been offered arbitration, but the Mariners inked him to a two-year deal, which isn't a bad signing in itself, except that it's going to cost Seattle a draft choice.

Jesus Cota   1B   Born: 07-Nov-81   Age: 21   Bats: L   Throws: R

YEAR	TM	LG	AGE	AB	H	2B	3B	HR	BB	SO	SB	CS	AVG	OBP	SLG	MLVR	EQBA	EQOBP	EQSLG	EQMLVR	VORP	DEFENSE	
2001	MSO	PIO	19	272	100	22	0	16	56	52	2	0	.368	.479	.625	.613	.234	.322	.394	-.124	-1.9	63-1B 3	
2002	LNC	CLF	20	540	151	33	3	16	38	121	0	1	.280	.329	.441	.032	.210	.248	.327	-.376	-36.4	70-1B -1	47-LF -5
2003	ARI	NL	21	183	42	8	1	5	16	43	2	2	.232	.298	.376	-.160	.231	.294	.381	-.187	-7.1		

Breakout: 40%   Improve: 63%   Collapse: 21%

Cota made quick work of the Pioneer League, but struggled against more advanced competition at Lancaster. He has quick hands at the plate, and shapes the L nicely on fastballs when he can get his arms extended. Changeups tend to cause him to completely bail out, but he's got a lot of time to figure out how to adjust. "He's going to be fine once he can pick up a pitch a little better," says one scout, "and he's going to have a nice bit of power." If he can rediscover half of his plate discipline, he might well hit himself into the Diamondbacks' plans, perhaps passing Lyle Overbay in the process.

Craig Counsell   INF   Born: 21-Aug-70   Age: 32   Bats: L   Throws: R

YEAR	TM	LG	AGE	AB	H	2B	3B	HR	BB	SO	SB	CS	AVG	OBP	SLG	MLVR	EQBA	EQOBP	EQSLG	EQMLVR	VORP	DEFENSE	
2000	TUC	PCL	29	198	69	14	3	3	22	20	4	1	.348	.416	.495	.236	.295	.351	.420	.013	10.5	19-3B 1	17-2B -1
2000	ARI	NL	29	152	48	8	1	2	20	18	3	3	.316	.402	.421	.094	.309	.389	.408	.077	12.5	17-2B -1	16-3B 4
2001	ARI	NL	30	458	126	22	3	4	61	76	6	8	.275	.363	.362	-.057	.272	.359	.356	-.079	18.0	46-SS 1	49-2B 8
2002	ARI	NL	31	436	123	22	1	2	45	52	7	5	.282	.351	.351	-.034	.283	.348	.356	-.093	10.8	94-3B 9	16-SS -2
2003	ARI	NL	32	343	91	17	2	3	38	45	5	3	.266	.340	.353	-.096	.264	.335	.357	-.121	1.8		

Breakout: 7%   Improve: 31%   Collapse: 33%

A gritty Tony Phillips Lite without the ability to smash the ball or exhibit multiple symptoms of bipolar disorder on a regular basis. Counsell is a very nice guy to have for the roster flexibility he gives you. You don't need to carry some glove wizard who couldn't hit his way out of the local pony league when you've got Counsell. Expected to be back and healthy to start spring training.

Brad Cresse   C   **Born: 31-Jul-78**   **Age: 24**   **Bats: R**   **Throws: R**

YEAR	TM	LG	AGE	AB	H	2B	3B	HR	BB	SO	SB	CS	AVG	OBP	SLG	MLVR	EQBA	EQOBP	EQSLG	EQMLVR	VORP	DEFENSE
2000	HDS	CLF	21	173	56	7	0	17	17	50	0	0	.324	.406	.659	.481	.240	.291	.480	-.058	7.5	35-C -4
2001	ELP	TXS	22	429	124	39	1	14	44	116	0	1	.289	.379	.483	.164	.236	.308	.393	-.151	9.2	91-C -12
2002	ELP	TXS	23	240	55	15	0	3	16	74	1	0	.229	.286	.329	-.189	.195	.238	.282	-.467	-13.9	42-C 3
2002	*TUC*	*PCL*	*23*	*126*	*34*	*10*	*0*	*2*	*4*	*38*	*0*	*0*	*.270*	*.308*	*.397*	*-.107*	*.240*	*.268*	*.352*	*-.283*	*-1.5*	*33-C 2*

Well, that was somewhat anticlimactic. Cresse's previously maligned defense took a step forward, particularly in terms of his mechanics behind the plate in blocking pitches and throwing to second, but unfortunately, his offense took a major hit. There were reports that he didn't react well to the acquisition of Chad Moeller and his resulting demotion to Double-A, but those are the kind of words that tend to float in the ether. He's still young, he's still got a batting eye, and he did take a step forward defensively. A year to consolidate, and he's good to go.

David Dellucci   RF   **Born: 31-Oct-73**   **Age: 29**   **Bats: L**   **Throws: L**

YEAR	TM	LG	AGE	AB	H	2B	3B	HR	BB	SO	SB	CS	AVG	OBP	SLG	MLVR	EQBA	EQOBP	EQSLG	EQMLVR	VORP	DEFENSE
2000	TUC	PCL	26	122	28	6	3	3	13	15	4	0	.230	.304	.402	-.208	.198	.260	.339	-.343	-8.7	27-RF -1
2000	ARI	NL	26	50	15	3	0	0	4	9	0	2	.300	.352	.360	-.103	.300	.340	.340	-.119	.2	
2001	ARI	NL	27	217	60	10	2	10	22	52	2	1	.276	.349	.479	.077	.274	.345	.475	.061	8.2	44-RF -2
2002	TUC	PCL	28	15	2	1	0	0	2	4	0	0	.133	.235	.200	-.574	.133	.235	.133	-.694	-2.3	
2002	ARI	NL	28	229	56	11	2	7	28	55	2	4	.245	.329	.402	-.028	.246	.324	.409	-.091	-.9	49-RF -4
2003	*ARI*	*NL*	*29*	*209*	*53*	*10*	*2*	*6*	*23*	*45*	*2*	*2*	*.252*	*.328*	*.407*	*-.055*	*.251*	*.323*	*.412*	*-.080*	*-3.1*	

Breakout: 24%   *Improve: 45%*   *Collapse: 31%*

A variety of injuries have robbed Mississippi standout Dellucci of his chance to be a surprise star, but he still has the capability to jump up with a .300/.380/.530 season. He's fragile, but he still covers enough ground and throws well enough to play a creditable right field, or share a job and get 400 productive PAs. Dellucci's one of those guys that has a rather dedicated fan base. You can keep up with David's life, in relatively creepy detail, at http://dellucci_girly.tripod.com/Gabys_David_Dellucci_site/.

Chris Donnels   PH   **Born: 21-Apr-66**   **Age: 37**   **Bats: L**   **Throws: R**

YEAR	TM	LG	AGE	AB	H	2B	3B	HR	BB	SO	SB	CS	AVG	OBP	SLG	MLVR	EQBA	EQOBP	EQSLG	EQMLVR	VORP	DEFENSE	
2000	ABQ	PCL	34	332	109	27	1	27	66	52	6	1	.328	.443	.660	.491	.274	.376	.542	.206	26.9	56-1B -5	21-3B -3
2001	LVG	PCL	35	137	32	5	0	7	21	24	0	1	.234	.335	.423	-.089	.197	.290	.358	-.258	-6.2	25-1B -2	
2001	LAD	NL	35	88	15	2	0	3	12	25	0	0	.170	.277	.295	-.348	.189	.283	.322	-.325	-3.5	11-3B -1	
2002	ARI	NL	36	80	19	4	1	3	10	14	0	0	.237	.322	.425	-.015	.247	.322	.432	-.063	2.6	11-3B -1	

He's riding out the tail end of a career. Donnels can still occasionally pop a ball, fill in at the corners, and once was good enough to deserve more of a shot than he actually got. He's a good guy, and may be a good coach down the road. For now, he's scrambling for NRI spots.

Erubiel Durazo   1B   **Born: 23-Jan-74**   **Age: 29**   **Bats: L**   **Throws: L**

YEAR	TM	LG	AGE	AB	H	2B	3B	HR	BB	SO	SB	CS	AVG	OBP	SLG	MLVR	EQBA	EQOBP	EQSLG	EQMLVR	VORP	DEFENSE
2000	ARI	NL	26	196	52	11	0	8	34	43	1	0	.265	.377	.444	.036	.255	.362	.429	.013	6.3	52-1B -6
2001	ARI	NL	27	175	47	11	0	12	28	49	0	0	.269	.376	.537	.193	.266	.371	.537	.183	14.1	31-1B -3
2002	ELP	TXS	28	14	7	3	0	2	4	1	0	0	.500	.611	1.143	1.547	.429	.529	.929	1.159	5.2	
2002	TUC	PCL	28	22	7	2	1	1	0	2	0	0	.318	.348	.636	.343	.273	.292	.545	.070	1.1	
2002	ARI	NL	28	222	58	12	2	16	49	60	0	1	.261	.399	.550	.280	.258	.392	.551	.229	20.7	50-1B -2
2003	*OAK*	*AL*	*29*	*267*	*68*	*14*	*2*	*15*	*44*	*64*	*1*	*1*	*.256*	*.363*	*.490*	*.128*	*.265*	*.375*	*.512*	*.147*	*13.8*	

Breakout: 14%   *Improve: 44%*   *Collapse: 20%*

Billy Beane's Great White Whale. Durazo's a great hitter, possibly even capable of competing for an MVP award, provided he finds a league without Barry Bonds or Alex Rodriguez in it. As much as we've run around waving Ruby's banner, it's hard to ignore his penchant for injuries. If he's healthy, he'll obliterate that projection. Now, it's over. Ahab finally got his whale, and Arizona got the shortest and pointiest end of the four-way stick, giving up Durazo for Elmer Dessens, whose numbers sure look an awful lot like that low ERA will be short-lived. If someone could stop by the Arizona Consulate in Los Angeles and let Joe Sheehan know that he can end his vigil, we'd really appreciate it. Erubiel Durazo is finally free.

Steve Finley   CF   Born: 12-Mar-65   Age: 38   Bats: L   Throws: L

YEAR	TM	LG	AGE	AB	H	2B	3B	HR	BB	SO	SB	CS	AVG	OBP	SLG	MLVR	EQBA	EQOBP	EQSLG	EQMLVR	VORP	DEFENSE
2000	ARI	NL	35	539	151	27	5	35	65	87	12	6	.280	.366	.544	.170	.274	.350	.530	.147	49.2	136-CF 2
2001	ARI	NL	36	495	136	27	4	14	47	67	11	7	.275	.339	.430	-.009	.272	.336	.424	-.028	20.4	124-CF 1
2002	ARI	NL	37	505	145	24	4	25	65	73	16	4	.287	.372	.499	.199	.286	.367	.501	.147	43.7	134-CF -1
2003	ARI	NL	38	334	90	18	2	11	39	51	9	2	.268	.346	.432	.020	.266	.341	.438	-.004	11.1	

Breakout: 9%   Improve: 42%   Collapse: 21%

Holding on nicely, thank you. Finley's been through the ringer a few times, but he can still track balls fairly well in center field, hit for a reasonable average, and stay healthy. If a team's looking for a very short-term center field solution, they could do worse than sign him. After flirting with a couple of West Coast teams, Finley re-upped with Arizona for two years at about $5.6 million annually. That's about as long as he should be signed for, and probably a little bit more money than he's worth, but nowhere near some of the other hideous signings in the Diamondback past.

Luis Gonzalez   LF   Born: 03-Sep-67   Age: 35   Bats: L Throws: R

YEAR	TM	LG	AGE	AB	H	2B	3B	HR	BB	SO	SB	CS	AVG	OBP	SLG	MLVR	EQBA	EQOBP	EQSLG	EQMLVR	VORP	DEFENSE
2000	ARI	NL	32	618	192	47	2	31	78	85	2	4	.311	.398	.544	.257	.304	.383	.532	.235	56.2	148-LF 0
2001	ARI	NL	33	609	198	36	7	57	100	83	1	1	.325	.432	.688	.541	.322	.425	.681	.526	108.9	149-LF 2
2002	ARI	NL	34	524	151	19	3	28	97	76	9	2	.288	.404	.496	.245	.286	.399	.501	.201	42.3	138-LF -4
2003	ARI	NL	35	478	140	27	3	25	79	70	6	2	.293	.396	.517	.230	.292	.391	.524	.211	32.4	

Breakout: 12%   Improve: 46%   Collapse: 14%

Another old, excellent player, which is the overriding trend in Phoenix. Gonzalez's season-ending injury should be healed up by the start of spring training. Gonzalez is entering the final year of a four-year deal, and will be able to test the free-agent waters at the end of the 2003 season. If only he can find a club that has a predilection for signing old ballplayers with good track records. Arizona's offense will be highly dependent on Gonzalez's ability to stay healthy and be productive, and his shoulder surgery has reportedly gone very well. The Snakes are betting on a lot of players on the late side of 30, but at least they're betting on talented old players, as opposed to the strategy several other teams are implementing.

Mark Grace   1B   Born: 28-Jun-64   Age: 39   Bats: L   Throws: L

YEAR	TM	LG	AGE	AB	H	2B	3B	HR	BB	SO	SB	CS	AVG	OBP	SLG	MLVR	EQBA	EQOBP	EQSLG	EQMLVR	VORP	DEFENSE
2000	CHC	NL	36	510	143	41	1	11	95	28	1	2	.280	.399	.429	.085	.279	.390	.429	.083	26.5	135-1B -1
2001	ARI	NL	37	476	142	31	2	15	67	36	1	0	.298	.389	.466	.150	.297	.386	.463	.137	31.7	122-1B -2
2002	ARI	NL	38	298	75	19	0	7	46	30	2	0	.252	.354	.386	-.003	.255	.351	.394	-.055	3.4	79-1B 1
2003	ARI	NL	39	216	59	13	1	4	29	21	2	1	.274	.363	.400	.011	.273	.358	.405	-.012	1.8	

Breakout: 17%   Improve: 51%   Collapse: 26%

Is it really a good signing if a guy does pretty much what you expect, and it's just not that impressive? Grace is now a sure-handed first baseman who can come off the bench and hit .270 with a few walks and the occasional gapper. That's not a bad thing, but when a guy like Grace takes even one plate appearance from the likes of Erubiel Durazo and Greg Colbrunn, it's just not good baseball. It's also pretty hard to swallow the "veteran proven winner" angle when he came over from the Cubs, of all places. Grace isn't a bad player by any means, but he belongs on a team with considerably fewer first-base options.

Scott Hairston   2B   Born: 25-May-80   Age: 23   Bats: R   Throws: R

YEAR	TM	LG	AGE	AB	H	2B	3B	HR	BB	SO	SB	CS	AVG	OBP	SLG	MLVR	EQBA	EQOBP	EQSLG	EQMLVR	VORP	DEFENSE	
2001	MSO	PIO	21	291	101	16	6	14	38	50	2	2	.347	.435	.588	.480	.228	.289	.376	-.216	-.1	62-2B 0	
2002	SBN	MDW	22	394	131	35	4	16	58	74	9	3	.332	.431	.563	.460	.251	.328	.424	-.060	17.1	94-2B -14	10-3B -3
2002	LNC	CLF	22	79	32	11	1	6	6	16	1	0	.405	.447	.797	.829	.295	.329	.564	.184	6.0		
2003	ARI	NL	23	226	60	13	2	8	23	48	4	3	.267	.339	.441	.019	.265	.334	.447	-.005	8.8		

Breakout: 31%   Improve: 57%   Collapse: 7%

It's feasible that Hairston could eventually stop hitting. Pestilence could strike, he could take up a different profession, or the D-Backs could hire Merv Rettenmund as a roving hitting instructor. There's nothing here not to like. Hairston hits for average and power, and has a great batting eye. The only things that can keep him from a very successful major league career are injuries and his defense. Scouts describe his defense as "spotty on a good day," and, more importantly, note that "he's going to get killed around the bag if he plays second base." Hairston needs a position, either by learning or moving, but he's going to be an outstanding hitter in the majors, possibly as soon as 2004.

Victor Hall   CF   Born: 16-Sep-80   Age: 22   Bats: L   Throws: L

YEAR	TM	LG	AGE	AB	H	2B	3B	HR	BB	SO	SB	CS	AVG	OBP	SLG	MLVR	EQBA	EQOBP	EQSLG	EQMLVR	VORP	DEFENSE
2000	MSO	PIO	19	241	74	7	9	3	77	38	47	14	.307	.483	.448	.302	.197	.328	.283	-.280	-6.7	67-CF -2
2000	SBN	MDW	19	164	38	4	5	2	13	41	12	5	.232	.296	.354	-.071	.185	.225	.286	-.493	-13.3	38-CF -7
2001	SBN	MDW	20	415	114	13	12	0	52	71	60	15	.275	.365	.364	.051	.220	.288	.290	-.342	-18.5	108-CF -12
2002	LNC	CLF	21	352	98	10	8	3	47	72	26	15	.278	.374	.378	.020	.206	.280	.280	-.379	-17.8	84-CF -3
2002	ELP	TXS	21	161	46	4	5	0	6	23	7	4	.286	.324	.373	-.037	.237	.267	.312	-.344	-10.0	32-LF -5
2003	HOU	NL	22	181	44	8	2	2	18	34	6	3	.245	.317	.338	-.168	.243	.312	.340	-.199	-4.4	

Breakout: 52%   Improve: 73%   Collapse: 11%

Hall's a quick outfielder with a great batting eye and creative routes to the ball. He has a fantastic first step on defense, often followed by five or six extra ones on the way to the ball. If he can work out his issues with tracking balls, he could have a nice Brett Butler–type career. He'll need to develop the ability to pull the ball at least a little bit to keep defenses honest against him, and maintain some semblance of a batting average as he moves up. Drafted by the Rockies in the Rule 5 draft, and traded to Houston, who must be hoping he'll be Brian (Speedy) Hunter insurance.

Felix Jose   OF   Born: 08-May-65   Age: 38   Bats: B   Throws: R

YEAR	TM	LG	AGE	AB	H	2B	3B	HR	BB	SO	SB	CS	AVG	OBP	SLG	MLVR	EQBA	EQOBP	EQSLG	EQMLVR	VORP	DEFENSE
2000	COH	INT	35	210	65	17	2	11	23	60	4	3	.310	.380	.567	.316	.280	.341	.512	.112	11.1	16-OF 0
2002	ARI	NL	37	19	5	0	0	2	4	8	0	0	.263	.391	.579	.306	.263	.391	.579	.269	2.2	

So, if Ruben Sierra and Felix Jose can vanish from organized ball for extended periods, then come back and play fairly well, how long until we see the first Jose Canseco comeback? Great story; most people who speak of Jose speak of him in high regard, and it's good to see someone bust their butt and have this kind of success coming back. If he can defeat his balky groin muscle, he'll battle for a roster spot somewhere in 2003.

Mark Little   OF   Born: 11-Jul-72   Age: 30   Bats: R   Throws: R

YEAR	TM	LG	AGE	AB	H	2B	3B	HR	BB	SO	SB	CS	AVG	OBP	SLG	MLVR	EQBA	EQOBP	EQSLG	EQMLVR	VORP	DEFENSE
2000	MEM	PCL	27	424	120	29	7	15	51	98	22	11	.283	.374	.491	.142	.250	.326	.434	-.050	14.1	103-CF -1
2001	COL	NL	28	85	29	6	0	3	1	20	5	2	.341	.378	.518	.201	.318	.350	.494	.141	4.9	19-OF 0
2002	COL	NL	29	105	21	5	2	0	13	28	2	1	.200	.311	.286	-.251	.190	.300	.276	-.350	-7.4	30-OF 0
2002	TUC	PCL	29	54	17	3	1	2	0	11	2	1	.315	.315	.519	.119	.264	.264	.434	-.152	.3	13-CF 1
2002	ARI	NL	29	22	6	0	1	0	2	5	0	0	.273	.429	.364	.110	.273	.417	.409	.102	1.3	

Minor league veteran who's deserved a shot gets one. He'll be in the mix for a job somewhere in 2003, and could end up as part of a very deep and experienced bench. I'm surprised he didn't end up playing center field for a team in the AL. Off the cuff—is this a time of unmatched scarcity of good outfielders in the AL?

Quinton McCracken   RF   Born: 16-Mar-70   Age: 33   Bats: B   Throws: R

YEAR	TM	LG	AGE	AB	H	2B	3B	HR	BB	SO	SB	CS	AVG	OBP	SLG	MLVR	EQBA	EQOBP	EQSLG	EQMLVR	VORP	DEFENSE
2000	DUR	INT	30	334	87	18	2	2	34	57	13	7	.260	.332	.344	-.109	.243	.304	.323	-.251	-14.1	81-OF -5
2001	EDM	PCL	31	361	122	27	4	4	21	54	8	10	.338	.376	.468	.161	.291	.332	.403	-.050	11.5	72-CF -4
2001	MIN	AL	31	64	14	2	2	0	5	13	0	1	.219	.275	.313	-.297	.234	.290	.328	-.277	-2.4	
2002	ARI	NL	32	349	108	27	8	3	32	68	5	4	.309	.371	.458	.163	.309	.366	.462	.112	16.8	89-RF 1
2003	ARI	NL	33	291	81	16	3	3	26	51	5	4	.277	.338	.385	-.050	.275	.333	.390	-.075	-1.9	

Breakout: 9%   Improve: 39%   Collapse: 37%

McCracken has built a nice little career as a fourth outfielder. He can run but not steal bases, play defense in CF well enough so you don't want to beat yourself repeatedly about the head and shoulders with a tire iron, covers the corner spots fairly well, and will hit the occasional gapper. Don't kid yourself, though—he's not going to hit like he did in 2002 on a regular basis.

Chad Moeller — C — Born: 18-Feb-75 — Age: 28 — Bats: R — Throws: R

YEAR	TM	LG	AGE	AB	H	2B	3B	HR	BB	SO	SB	CS	AVG	OBP	SLG	MLVR	EQBA	EQOBP	EQSLG	EQMLVR	VORP		DEFENSE
2000	SLC	PCL	25	167	48	13	1	5	9	45	0	1	.287	.324	.467	-.029	.244	.271	.396	-.211	.9		41-C -5
2000	MIN	AL	25	128	27	3	1	1	9	33	1	0	.211	.263	.273	-.464	.219	.259	.289	-.402	-5.3		40-C -2
2001	TUC	PCL	26	274	75	20	0	8	25	54	1	4	.274	.339	.434	-.036	.232	.296	.365	-.215	1.4		64-C -10
2001	ARI	NL	26	56	13	0	1	1	6	12	0	0	.232	.306	.321	-.248	.246	.306	.333	-.231	.1		15-C 0
2002	TUC	PCL	27	211	67	8	2	10	29	46	1	0	.318	.407	.517	.265	.271	.354	.443	.030	14.9		59-C 1
2002	ARI	NL	27	105	30	11	1	2	17	23	0	1	.286	.385	.467	.176	.283	.382	.462	.117	10.1		35-C -1
2003	ARI	NL	28	197	49	10	1	5	21	44	2	1	.249	.324	.395	-.079	.247	.320	.400	-.105	3.3		

Breakout: 20%   Improve: 45%   Collapse: 35%

Backup catcher with a bat. Moeller hasn't really ever had a chance to play full-time, and he may just bust out and put up some solid offensive numbers. He isn't heralded for his defense, but he doesn't have a reputation of a Scott Hatteberg or Mike Piazza, so what harm can it do? Considering this organization once rewarded Jorge Fabregas with a bigger contract than he asked for, this has to be seen as a quantum leap forward.

Corey Myers — 1B — Born: 05-Jun-80 — Age: 23 — Bats: R — Throws: R

YEAR	TM	LG	AGE	AB	H	2B	3B	HR	BB	SO	SB	CS	AVG	OBP	SLG	MLVR	EQBA	EQOBP	EQSLG	EQMLVR	VORP	DEFENSE	
2000	MSO	PIO	20	272	59	16	2	6	30	62	5	2	.217	.302	.357	-.201	.142	.186	.229	-.670	-31.9	55-3B -10	
2000	SBN	MDW	20	64	8	2	0	0	7	23	1	1	.125	.211	.156	-.502	.106	.169	.136	-.840	-11.1	19-3B -7	
2001	SBN	MDW	21	211	69	17	2	3	12	33	2	0	.327	.374	.469	.245	.249	.284	.362	-.231	-2.3	52-3B -2	
2001	LNC	CLF	21	183	52	13	1	5	15	49	0	0	.284	.338	.448	.062	.213	.254	.333	-.354	-7.3	41-3B -7	
2002	LNC	CLF	22	497	144	33	4	13	41	129	1	3	.290	.348	.451	.082	.216	.260	.335	-.337	-29.2	62-1B -4	58-3B -3
2003	ARI	NL	23	190	46	10	1	4	16	47	2	2	.240	.301	.377	-.148	.239	.297	.382	-.176	-5.3		

Breakout: 57%   Improve: 78%   Collapse: 10%

Another corner infielder that really isn't. Myers's defense at third base is more theoretical than anything else. He's got a long swing that generates some moderate power, and he's going to have to tighten it up considerably to have a shot at a career in the bigs. He needs to get to the point where he can hit enough to have only a first-base glove in his bag, which means more power and fewer strikeouts. Still young enough and promising enough to have a career.

Tim Olson — SS? — Born: 01-Aug-78 — Age: 24 — Bats: R — Throws: R

YEAR	TM	LG	AGE	AB	H	2B	3B	HR	BB	SO	SB	CS	AVG	OBP	SLG	MLVR	EQBA	EQOBP	EQSLG	EQMLVR	VORP	DEFENSE	
2000	SBN	MDW	21	261	57	14	2	2	15	49	15	3	.218	.282	.310	-.157	.184	.214	.262	-.549	-31.2	50-RF 1	19-3B -3
2001	LNC	CLF	22	239	69	12	4	6	14	49	13	9	.289	.336	.448	.061	.215	.251	.329	-.364	-8.3	33-SS -3	28-3B -3
2001	ELP	TXS	22	167	53	13	0	2	11	36	4	4	.317	.380	.431	.122	.265	.310	.355	-.180	1.6	46-SS -13	
2002	ELP	TXS	23	433	118	24	2	10	27	91	9	11	.273	.342	.406	.028	.226	.276	.346	-.284	-7.1	98-SS -7	20-CF -2
2003	ARI	NL	24	166	40	8	1	4	10	36	4	3	.240	.294	.372	-.168	.239	.289	.376	-.196	-2.0		

Breakout: 45%   Improve: 69%   Collapse: 13%

A great athlete, Olson has excellent speed, a quick first step, and a strong arm—if he has time to uncork the throw. The D-Backs don't know where he's going to end up defensively, and he might be able to fill in all over the diamond, increasing his chances of being able to make the bigs. A slightly improved batting eye would go a long way toward Olson having a career.

Lyle Overbay — 1B — Born: 28-Jan-77 — Age: 26 — Bats: L — Throws: L

YEAR	TM	LG	AGE	AB	H	2B	3B	HR	BB	SO	SB	CS	AVG	OBP	SLG	MLVR	EQBA	EQOBP	EQSLG	EQMLVR	VORP	DEFENSE	
2000	SBN	MDW	23	259	86	19	3	6	27	36	9	2	.332	.399	.498	.342	.256	.300	.391	-.154	-3.9	64-1B -2	
2000	ELP	TXS	23	244	86	16	2	8	28	39	3	2	.352	.423	.533	.328	.276	.332	.423	-.033	3.9	60-1B -6	
2001	ELP	TXS	24	532	187	49	3	13	67	92	5	4	.352	.429	.528	.357	.281	.349	.425	.005	13.8	106-1B -8	22-LF -6
2002	TUC	PCL	25	525	180	40	0	19	42	86	0	0	.343	.399	.528	.294	.297	.348	.455	.059	20.7	123-1B 1	
2002	ARI	NL	25	10	1	0	0	0	0	5	0	0	.100	.100	.100	-.898	.100	.100	.100	-1.040	-2.1		
2003	ARI	NL	26	185	51	11	1	5	17	33	2	1	.273	.338	.427	.005	.272	.333	.433	-.020	1.1		

Breakout: 16%   Improve: 38%   Collapse: 33%

The real question about Overbay is why he spent all of 2001 at El Paso. He's often compared to John Olerud by people who have no clue what they're talking about. Overbay's passable defensively, hits singles and line-drive gappers, and will be a solid hitter in the majors. If he can develop another 20 XBHs per season, he could be worth keeping around. Overbay is a Doug

Mientkiewicz–type hitter, but doesn't carry the Keith Hernandez or Olerud glove or bat that you need to hold a job and push a team toward a championship as a first baseman without huge power. All he needs is either a little more offense or defense, but he's already a considerably better option at first than Mark Grace at this point.

Junior Spivey 2B Born: 28-Jan-75 Age: 28 Bats: R Throws: R

YEAR	TM	LG	AGE	AB	H	2B	3B	HR	BB	SO	SB	CS	AVG	OBP	SLG	MLVR	EQBA	EQOBP	EQSLG	EQMLVR	VORP	DEFENSE
2000	TUC	PCL	25	117	33	8	4	3	11	17	3	1	.282	.344	.496	.044	.243	.293	.417	-.140	2.3	21-2B 0
2001	TUC	PCL	26	194	45	6	0	6	27	32	9	6	.232	.326	.356	-.196	.192	.281	.295	-.363	-7.9	50-2B 0
2001	ARI	NL	26	163	42	6	3	5	23	47	3	0	.258	.356	.423	-.000	.261	.357	.424	.002	10.1	44-2B -3
2002	ARI	NL	27	538	162	34	6	16	65	100	11	6	.301	.393	.476	.212	.299	.385	.481	.162	53.5	138-2B -9
2003	*ARI*	*NL*	*28*	*492*	*132*	*28*	*5*	*14*	*60*	*94*	*10*	*5*	*.267*	*.351*	*.428*	*.022*	*.266*	*.346*	*.433*	*-.001*	*20.4*	

Breakout: 8%   Improve: 38%   Collapse: 24%

How cool was that? Spivey rode the confluence of increased playing time, good health, and a shortened swing to become one of the most valuable players in the National League. If they can find a way to keep him in the lineup full-time, he can continue to be an outstanding contributor. If he can slide the angle he takes on ground balls to his right, he could even jack up his defensive value.

Luis Terrero CF Born: 18-May-80 Age: 23 Bats: R Throws: R

YEAR	TM	LG	AGE	AB	H	2B	3B	HR	BB	SO	SB	CS	AVG	OBP	SLG	MLVR	EQBA	EQOBP	EQSLG	EQMLVR	VORP	DEFENSE
2000	MSO	PIO	20	276	72	10	0	8	10	75	23	11	.261	.306	.384	-.120	.179	.190	.264	-.598	-32.7	68-RF -2
2000	HDS	CLF	20	79	15	3	1	0	3	16	5	5	.190	.229	.253	-.453	.139	.155	.190	-.789	-11.5	19-CF 0
2001	SBN	MDW	21	89	14	2	0	1	0	29	3	0	.157	.176	.213	-.516	.135	.142	.191	-.816	-16.1	22-RF -1
2001	LNC	CLF	21	71	32	9	1	4	1	14	5	0	.451	.466	.775	.895	.333	.338	.565	.246	6.7	17-CF -1
2001	ELP	TXS	21	147	44	13	3	3	4	45	9	2	.299	.331	.490	.111	.248	.271	.407	-.192	-.4	34-CF -4
2002	ELP	TXS	22	360	103	20	6	8	23	89	18	22	.286	.343	.442	.085	.228	.271	.358	-.276	-8.7	100-CF -2
2003	*ARI*	*NL*	*23*	*184*	*43*	*9*	*1*	*4*	*11*	*49*	*5*	*8*	*.237*	*.287*	*.372*	*-.182*	*.235*	*.283*	*.376*	*-.210*	*-6.0*	

Breakout: 48%   Improve: 71%   Collapse: 14%

Runs like he's been playing for Phil Garner as a manager for years. Terrero has plus speed, a reasonable arm, and a history of plate discipline of Guillenesque proportions. He made a concerted effort in 2002 to gain more control of the strike zone, and scouts thought he looked "tentative" and "passive" at the plate as a result. Personally, I don't know how a guy who walks 23 times in 360 at-bats can look passive, but the problems are clear enough. He can play a legitimate center field, and he's young enough to consolidate all his tools and develop a little power.

Chad Tracy 3B Born: 22-May-80 Age: 23 Bats: L Throws: R

YEAR	TM	LG	AGE	AB	H	2B	3B	HR	BB	SO	SB	CS	AVG	OBP	SLG	MLVR	EQBA	EQOBP	EQSLG	EQMLVR	VORP	DEFENSE
2001	SBN	MDW	21	215	73	11	0	4	19	19	3	0	.340	.398	.447	.259	.260	.307	.342	-.208	-1.1	52-3B -2
2002	ELP	TXS	22	514	177	39	5	8	38	51	2	3	.344	.394	.486	.269	.285	.326	.408	-.059	16.6	111-3B -9
2003	*ARI*	*NL*	*23*	*211*	*59*	*12*	*2*	*4*	*15*	*26*	*2*	*1*	*.278*	*.329*	*.411*	*-.030*	*.277*	*.324*	*.416*	*-.055*	*4.2*	

Breakout: 23%   Improve: 56%   Collapse: 18%

Tracy's a slashing contact hitter, and already very good at taking pitches away and slapping them with some authority back up the middle and to the left side. Arizona thinks he can handle third base well enough defensively, and he'll get his opportunity after he hits .325 or so at Tucson this year. He may be a good enough singles hitter to really contribute in the majors. With some luck, he could compete for a batting title or two in his career.

Matt Williams 3B Born: 28-Nov-65 Age: 37 Bats: R Throws: R

YEAR	TM	LG	AGE	AB	H	2B	3B	HR	BB	SO	SB	CS	AVG	OBP	SLG	MLVR	EQBA	EQOBP	EQSLG	EQMLVR	VORP	DEFENSE
2000	ARI	NL	34	371	102	18	2	12	20	51	1	2	.275	.317	.431	-.084	.271	.304	.424	-.087	9.9	92-3B 7
2001	ARI	NL	35	408	112	30	0	16	22	70	1	0	.275	.316	.466	-.000	.275	.316	.465	-.003	19.8	91-3B 9
2002	LNC	CLF	36	12	4	1	0	1	2	1	0	0	.333	.429	.667	.523	.250	.308	.500	.009	.4	
2002	TUC	PCL	36	15	3	0	0	1	0	0	0	0	.200	.200	.400	-.348	.200	.200	.400	-.372	-.9	
2002	ARI	NL	36	215	56	7	2	12	21	41	3	1	.260	.326	.479	.079	.263	.325	.484	.029	12.0	46-3B 4
2003	*ARI*	*NL*	*37*	*237*	*62*	*12*	*1*	*8*	*17*	*40*	*2*	*1*	*.261*	*.314*	*.422*	*-.051*	*.260*	*.309*	*.428*	*-.077*	*3.2*	

Breakout: 10%   Improve: 50%   Collapse: 17%

Matt Williams *(continued)*

One of the worst acquisitions in the history of baseball, and a colossal millstone around the neck of the franchise. It's interesting how the sports press has really picked up on how clubs get hamstrung by crappy, large contracts, yet no one seems to have the guts to point out lousy acquisitions and contracts when clubs execute them. Williams was given an enormous five-year deal (that will pay him $10 million in 2003) after his age 31 season, which followed two years of declining productivity and health. Understanding that such a contract was a bad gamble was simply a matter of due diligence on the part of the Arizona front office, and they didn't execute on it. There's simply no excuse for that kind of business practice when it comes to investments of this magnitude. Williams can still help a club in the right role—platoon at third and a right-handed bat off the bench. He's slugged .407 and gotten on base at a .302 clip against righties over the last three years, and can basically only hit a cookie from them. He can still punish lefties. For $10 million, he'd better.

Tony Womack — SS — Born: 25-Sep-69 — Age: 33 — Bats: L — Throws: R

YEAR	TM	LG	AGE	AB	H	2B	3B	HR	BB	SO	SB	CS	AVG	OBP	SLG	MLVR	EQBA	EQOBP	EQSLG	EQMLVR	VORP	DEFENSE
2000	ARI	NL	30	617	167	21	14	7	30	74	45	11	.271	.310	.384	-.171	.266	.296	.377	-.174	7.1	140-SS -7
2001	ARI	NL	31	481	128	19	5	3	23	54	28	7	.266	.308	.345	-.192	.264	.304	.342	-.211	.9	112-SS 0
2002	ARI	NL	32	590	160	23	5	5	46	80	29	12	.271	.328	.353	-.078	.272	.324	.356	-.147	10.7	139-SS -11
2003	ARI	NL	33	466	123	20	5	4	32	58	20	5	.264	.316	.352	-.140	.263	.311	.356	-.167	1.0	

Breakout: 10%   Improve: 44%   Collapse: 20%

Okay, what does it take to get an organization to realize they have a problem? Womack's drawn a tidy 99 walks over the last three years (Barry Bonds might call that August), and he's done exactly what any reasonable observer would have predicted since coming to the desert. He's hit for a league average BA, with no walks and no power, and stolen bases fairly effectively, all while playing a pedestrian shortstop. It's not abject failure and gaping holes in the roster that kill franchises—it's the unidentified drags. That being said, he should outperform that forecast by a little.

Ernie Young — Born: 08-Jul-69 — Age: 34 — Bats: R — Throws: R

YEAR	TM	LG	AGE	AB	H	2B	3B	HR	BB	SO	SB	CS	AVG	OBP	SLG	MLVR	EQBA	EQOBP	EQSLG	EQMLVR	VORP	DEFENSE
2000	MEM	PCL	31	453	119	16	0	35	66	117	11	1	.263	.361	.530	.155	.235	.318	.470	-.028	7.2	98-LF -1
2001	POR	PCL	32	409	112	21	2	20	38	115	0	3	.274	.356	.482	.108	.251	.323	.433	-.056	2.2	81-RF -4
2002	TUC	PCL	33	160	52	9	1	14	24	33	0	3	.325	.429	.656	.490	.277	.371	.547	.208	12.8	37-OF -1
2003	DET	AL	33	120	27	6	1	4	13	29	1	1	.228	.308	.396	-.095	.236	.319	.427	-.078	-1.4	

Breakout: 12%   Improve: 31%   Collapse: 38%

Young could help some clubs as a role-player, and he'll get a chance with the Tigers in 2003. In 2002, he had to go overseas to find an opportunity and make some bank, while a guy like Marquis Grissom can sign a two-year deal for over $4 million. It's kind of like Dolph Lundgren or Rob Schneider winning an Oscar as Willy Loman in David Mamet's remake of *Death of a Salesman*.

PITCHERS

Brian Anderson — Born: 26-Apr-72 — Age: 31 — Bats: B — Throws: L

YEAR	TM	LG	AGE	G	GS	IP	H	BB	SO	HR	ERA	EQERA	EQH9	EQBB9	EQSO9	EQHR9	PERA	VORP	STF
2000	ARI	NL	28	33	32	213.3	226	39	104	38	4.05	3.99	9.6	1.4	4.0	1.4	4.26	35.9	1
2001	ARI	NL	29	29	22	133.3	156	30	55	25	5.20	5.81	11.1	1.9	3.2	1.5	5.32	-4.7	-13
2002	ARI	NL	30	35	24	156.0	174	32	81	23	4.79	4.70	10.2	1.7	4.2	1.3	4.76	13.7	-4
2003	CLE	AL	31	29	19	119	145	28	57	21	5.28	5.19	10.9	2	4.1	1.3	5.1	8.5	-7

Breakout: 10%   Improve: 45%   Collapse: 21%

A fascinating pitcher to watch: Anderson makes hitters without a solid game plan and discipline look more frustrated than Bill O'Reilly without a mirror. He's a tough guy to root for, because he can go 15 hitters and look unhittable, give up a squib hit or two, and then leave a "breaking" ball at Sammy Sosa's thigh that goes souvenir at escape velocity. Nevertheless, he can be a solid back-of-the-rotation starter if healthy and affordable. The Indians nailed affordable and will hope for healthy.

Miguel Batista — Born: 19-Feb-71 — Age: 32 — Bats: R — Throws: R

YEAR	TM	LG	AGE	G	GS	IP	H	BB	SO	HR	ERA	EQERA	EQH9	EQBB9	EQSO9	EQHR9	PERA	VORP	STF
2000	OMA	PCL	29	18	1	28.3	35	7	27	6	6.04	6.70	13.0	2.3	7.1	2.5	6.61	-4.1	-8
2000	KCR	AL	29	14	9	57.0	66	34	30	17	7.74	6.84	9.6	4.3	4.5	2.2	6.18	-8.6	-19
2001	ARI	NL	30	48	18	139.3	113	60	90	13	3.36	3.63	7.7	3.7	5.0	0.8	3.45	28.3	-3
2002	ARI	NL	31	36	29	184.7	172	70	112	12	4.29	4.12	8.5	3.0	4.8	0.6	3.77	28.2	3
2003	ARI	NL	32	31	23	143.3	146	55	88	17	4.54	4.65	9.2	3.0	5.0	1.0	4.50	13.9	0

Breakout: 7%   Improve: 46%   Collapse: 11%

I'm always astonished when guys that can throw really hard, and have pretty good pitches to work off of other than their fastball, end up with generic or mediocre K rates, with concomitant middling performance. How is it that guys like Jamie Moyer, Bob Tewksbury, and Doug Jones pitch so well when EVERY BATTER knows that they're going to throw junk, down and away, and if they throw something that looks meaty, it's going to vanish? Meanwhile, someone like Batista has the stuff to just blow people away from time to time, and he can't consistently get people out. It's a mystery, and on some level, it's sort of a Zen thing.

Jay Belflower — Born: 12-Nov-79 — Age: 23 — Bats: R — Throws: R

YEAR	TM	LG	AGE	G	GS	IP	H	BB	SO	HR	ERA	EQERA	EQH9	EQBB9	EQSO9	EQHR9	PERA	VORP	STF
2001	LNC	CLF	21	27	0	29.0	15	6	24	1	0.62	1.47	5.1	2.4	4.1	0.6	1.65	12.6	-1
2002	LNC	CLF	22	16	0	18.7	17	3	14	0	3.85	3.65	9.8	1.8	3.9	0.3	3.08	3.6	-5
2002	ELP	TXS	22	36	0	55.7	67	14	53	5	4.04	5.57	12.7	2.7	6.5	1.6	5.95	-1.2	0

Belflower mixes a 92-mph fastball with a solid breaking pitch. He was drafted fairly late, put into a relief role and started mowing down opposing batters like so much dried chaff. His fastball appears to have lost a foot or so during the 2002 season, but there doesn't seem to be a serious underlying injury. Belflower will likely get a chance to work in the pen at El Paso and Tucson this year, and he'll be one of the candidates for closer a couple years down the road if he can find that missing velocity.

Chris Capuano — Born: 19-Aug-78 — Age: 24 — Bats: L — Throws: L

YEAR	TM	LG	AGE	G	GS	IP	H	BB	SO	HR	ERA	EQERA	EQH9	EQBB9	EQSO9	EQHR9	PERA	VORP	STF
2000	SBN	MDW	21	18	18	101.7	68	45	105	2	2.21	3.97	7.9	4.8	5.8	0.5	3.94	17.3	14
2001	ELP	TXS	22	28	28	159.3	184	75	167	13	5.31	5.56	10.7	5.0	6.5	1.1	6.11	-1.0	10
2002	TUC	PCL	23	6	6	36.3	30	11	29	1	2.73	3.09	8.2	3.2	5.6	0.3	2.90	9.7	18

He's hanging in the rotation, but realistically, Capuano's future is the Jesse Orosco role, coming in to nail down a lefty or two. He doesn't throw real hard, but keeps the ball down and away with a pretty good assortment of breaking pitches. It'll take a full year or so of Double-A to get a better read on whether or not he's going to have a major league career. He could still be in the minors six years from now and end up as a veteran Buddy Groom.

Mike Fetters — Born: 19-Dec-64 — Age: 38 — Bats: R — Throws: R

YEAR	TM	LG	AGE	G	GS	IP	H	BB	SO	HR	ERA	EQERA	EQH9	EQBB9	EQSO9	EQHR9	PERA	VORP	STF
2000	LAD	NL	35	51	0	50.0	35	25	40	7	3.24	3.38	6.5	3.7	6.4	1.2	3.53	11.1	-2
2001	LAD	NL	36	34	0	29.7	33	13	26	6	6.06	6.46	10.4	3.7	6.8	1.7	6.22	-3.6	-11
2001	PIT	NL	36	20	0	17.7	16	13	11	1	4.58	4.26	8.0	6.1	4.7	0.4	4.53	2.2	-19
2002	ARI	NL	37	33	0	24.7	28	19	24	1	5.10	5.94	10.1	6.0	7.5	0.4	5.74	-1.5	-6
2002	PIT	NL	37	32	0	30.3	25	18	29	3	3.27	4.10	7.8	4.7	7.5	0.9	4.10	4.3	0
2003	ARI	NL	38	49	0	40.3	36	21	35	4	4.11	4.21	8.1	4.0	7.0	0.8	4.32	5.4	-1

Breakout: 46%   Improve: 53%   Collapse: 12%

Puffy's still got a couple of years left in him. He basically works off of one pitch, which he's been throwing for a lot of years now. He'll be bouncing around, looking for a bullpen slot where he can collect a million bucks or so and induce a bunch of ground balls.

Edgar Gonzalez   Born: 23-Feb-83   Age: 20   Bats: R   Throws: R

YEAR	TM	LG	AGE	G	GS	IP	H	BB	SO	HR	ERA	EQERA	EQH9	EQBB9	EQSO9	EQHR9	PERA	VORP	STF
2002	SBN	MDW	19	23	23	151.3	141	34	110	4	2.91	4.76	10.8	2.8	4.1	0.7	4.81	12.5	6
2002	LNC	CLF	19	4	4	23.0	24	3	21	1	0.78	3.51	11.3	1.5	4.7	0.7	4.08	5.1	15

Gonzalez has great mechanics for a young guy. He throws well to spots, keeping hitters from waiting on a pitch in a particular zone. He's going to have an uphill battle to get through the minors without tremendous velocity, but he's got everything else, especially considering his age. Keeps the ball down, works the corners, keeps hitters off stride. Could have a bumpy couple of years before he finds his stride, but he's got time.

Mike Gosling   Born: 23-Sep-80   Age: 22   Bats: L   Throws: L

YEAR	TM	LG	AGE	G	GS	IP	H	BB	SO	HR	ERA	EQERA	EQH9	EQBB9	EQSO9	EQHR9	PERA	VORP	STF
2002	ELP	TXS	21	27	27	166.7	149	62	115	7	3.13	4.05	9.2	4.0	4.7	0.7	4.12	26.9	9
2003	ARI	NL	22	12	9	65.0	69	31	44	7	4.78	4.89	9.6	3.7	5.5	1.0	4.72	6.9	2

Breakout: 20%   *Improve: 43%*   *Collapse: 24%*

The Diamondbacks, their fans, and their scouts all absolutely love Gosling. Words like "composure," "poise," and "stuff" get thrown around a lot. Well, that's all well and good, and throwing 94 or 95 is very nice, but I'd rather hear words like "healthy" and "elbow" together. He did post a nice season—a 3.13 ERA at El Paso's not bad at all—but he didn't strike out enough guys to fill one with confidence, and the workload was a bit heavy for someone who had elbow tenderness to start the season. He's in the Snakes' plans for the rotation, probably as soon as late this year in case of injury. It won't be long until we hear the inevitable Mike Mussina comparisons.

Rick Helling   Born: 15-Dec-70   Age: 32   Bats: R   Throws: R

YEAR	TM	LG	AGE	G	GS	IP	H	BB	SO	HR	ERA	EQERA	EQH9	EQBB9	EQSO9	EQHR9	PERA	VORP	STF
2000	TEX	AL	29	35	35	217.0	212	99	146	29	4.48	3.82	7.8	3.3	5.8	1.0	3.89	40.6	9
2001	TEX	AL	30	34	34	215.7	256	63	154	38	5.17	4.91	9.8	2.4	5.9	1.4	5.22	14.3	7
2002	ARI	NL	31	30	30	175.7	180	48	120	31	4.51	4.62	9.3	2.2	5.4	1.6	4.70	17.3	5
2003	ARI	NL	32	29	26	165.3	169	52	111	23	4.29	4.39	9.3	2.4	5.4	1.2	4.38	20.7	7

Breakout: 11%   *Improve: 45%*   *Collapse: 18%*

The expectations for Helling were pretty simple: be a middle-of-the-rotation guy who chews up a bunch of innings and gives us a chance to win the ball game, without having to lean on our bullpen excessively. Mission accomplished. Aside from a mid-season bout with some ankle injuries, Helling was pretty much a generic starting pitcher. The D-Backs have decided they don't want to pay $6 million for a generic starting pitcher, so they've exercised their $1.5 million option, and might bring Helling back at a lower price. He'll end up somewhere as a #3 or #4 starter. Hopefully somewhere where the wind blows in.

Randy Johnson   Born: 10-Sep-63   Age: 39   Bats: R   Throws: L

YEAR	TM	LG	AGE	G	GS	IP	H	BB	SO	HR	ERA	EQERA	EQH9	EQBB9	EQSO9	EQHR9	PERA	VORP	STF
2000	ARI	NL	36	35	35	248.7	202	76	347	23	2.64	2.86	7.2	2.2	11.0	0.7	2.85	73.1	48
2001	ARI	NL	37	35	34	249.7	181	71	372	19	2.49	2.67	6.7	2.4	11.3	0.6	2.56	78.6	51
2002	ARI	NL	38	35	35	260.0	197	71	334	26	2.32	2.77	6.8	2.2	10.1	0.9	2.89	79.0	41
2003	ARI	NL	39	34	34	233.0	183	74	279	20	3.07	3.14	7.1	2.4	9.6	0.7	2.83	61.7	39

Breakout: 0%   *Improve: 45%*   *Collapse: 13%*

Johnson's one of the best few pitchers of all time, and arguably the most dominant ever. There's no reason to believe that 2003 is going to be any different than 2002 for him. Overlooked with Johnson because of his incredible stuff is that the guy works as hard as anyone in the game, physically and mentally. Yes, he'll play this season at age 39, but if he wants to keep pitching, he could end up making Nolan Ryan look like a premature retiree. If Jesse Orosco can be a situational lefty out of the pen at age 44 or 45, who's to say Johnson couldn't do that job until he was 50? The scary back problems of a few years ago are a distant memory.

Byung-Hyun Kim Born: 21-Jan-79 Age: 24 Bats: R Throws: R

YEAR	TM	LG	AGE	G	GS	IP	H	BB	SO	HR	ERA	EQERA	EQH9	EQBB9	EQSO9	EQHR9	PERA	VORP	STF
2000	ARI	NL	21	61	1	70.7	52	46	111	9	4.46	3.97	6.3	4.6	12.1	1.0	3.61	11.1	42
2001	ARI	NL	22	78	0	98.0	58	44	113	10	2.94	2.80	5.5	3.8	8.8	0.8	2.57	28.1	23
2002	ARI	NL	23	72	0	84.0	64	26	92	5	2.04	2.43	6.9	2.5	8.6	0.5	2.76	27.5	24
2003	ARI	NL	24	60	2	87.7	67	36	101	8	3.07	3.15	6.9	3.2	9.3	0.8	3.27	22.1	20

Breakout: 17%   Improve: 40%   Collapse: 16%

Originally, this space was filled with praise for the Diamondback front office for being willing to take a chance and move Kim to the rotation, against conventional wisdom. There was a mini-study to support the move, lots of praise for Kim, and a few comments suggesting some vision and masterful planning in terms of managing Kim's workload at a young age. Add to that the potential to really take advantage of his skills to a much greater extent than previously possible, since he's such a talented kid, and it seems so strange to not use him simply because of baseball's arcane system of accounting for wins, losses, and saves, which are kind of stupid constructs anyway. Now this space has something different in it.

Mike Koplove Born: 30-Aug-76 Age: 26 Bats: R Throws: R

YEAR	TM	LG	AGE	G	GS	IP	H	BB	SO	HR	ERA	EQERA	EQH9	EQBB9	EQSO9	EQHR9	PERA	VORP	STF
2000	HDS	CLF	23	20	0	25.3	14	10	31	0	1.42	1.38	5.1	3.6	6.5	0.2	1.95	11.2	9
2000	ELP	TXS	23	35	0	46.3	38	19	47	2	3.89	3.98	7.7	3.8	6.4	0.6	3.34	7.2	3
2001	ELP	TXS	24	34	0	44.0	44	19	43	3	2.66	3.79	9.1	4.6	6.1	1.0	4.90	7.8	-5
2001	TUC	PCL	24	17	0	22.3	17	10	22	1	2.83	2.67	6.7	4.7	6.3	0.4	3.04	6.7	2
2001	ARI	NL	24	9	0	10.0	8	9	14	1	3.60	5.43	7.2	7.3	10.3	0.8	4.73	-0.1	13
2002	TUC	PCL	25	23	0	30.7	21	4	31	1	1.17	1.75	6.7	1.4	7.0	0.4	1.85	12.4	17
2002	ARI	NL	25	55	0	61.7	47	23	46	2	3.35	3.04	6.9	3.0	5.9	0.3	2.78	16.0	3
2003	ARI	NL	26	47	1	64.7	58	28	52	6	3.77	3.86	8.2	3.3	6.4	0.8	3.89	11.3	0

Breakout: 12%   Improve: 44%   Collapse: 23%

One of Arizona's seemingly endless supply of guys that throw from funky angles. Anaheim loves bullpen guys with movement rather than velocity, Oakland loves scooping up the ubiquitous bargains from the Rule 5 draft and a snoozing Kenny Williams, and the Snakes love guys that look like they might release the ball near the fifth row of box seats. Koplove is a good bet to be successful in his role—a right-handed setup guy to come in and get righties out, despite the fact that lefties only hit .174 against him last season. He'll provide 60–80 innings of quality relief.

Matt Mantei Born: 07-Jul-73 Age: 30 Bats: R Throws: R

YEAR	TM	LG	AGE	G	GS	IP	H	BB	SO	HR	ERA	EQERA	EQH9	EQBB9	EQSO9	EQHR9	PERA	VORP	STF
2000	ARI	NL	27	47	0	45.3	31	35	53	4	4.57	3.81	5.9	5.4	9.0	0.7	3.48	7.9	9
2002	ARI	NL	29	31	0	26.7	28	12	26	3	4.72	4.82	9.4	3.6	7.6	1.0	4.87	1.7	1
2003	ARI	NL	29	42	0	47.0	44	25	47	5	4.14	4.24	8.4	4.1	8.0	1.0	4.35	7.5	5

Breakout: 12%   Improve: 39%   Collapse: 24%

Command was lacking after the extended layoff, but really, the command was lacking before the extended layoff. He's under contract for a minimum of one more year, and if healthy, could enter the mix as either a closer or setup guy, or anything in between. The Snakes have a lot of good options available in the pen, so Mantei will have to be nasty if he wants to regain and retain the closer position.

Mike Morgan Born: 08-Oct-59 Age: 43 Bats: R Throws: R

YEAR	TM	LG	AGE	G	GS	IP	H	BB	SO	HR	ERA	EQERA	EQH9	EQBB9	EQSO9	EQHR9	PERA	VORP	STF
2000	ARI	NL	40	60	4	101.7	123	40	56	10	4.87	4.63	10.9	2.9	4.4	0.8	5.04	8.7	-12
2001	ARI	NL	41	31	1	38.0	45	17	24	2	4.26	4.94	11.4	3.8	4.9	0.4	5.05	1.9	-11
2002	TUC	PCL	42	2	0	3.0	3	0	2	0	0.00	2.86	10.3	0.7	4.9	0.2	2.69	0.8	3
2002	ARI	NL	42	29	0	34.0	41	9	13	7	5.29	5.63	11.1	2.1	3.1	1.9	5.83	-0.9	-27

Well, he's filed for free agency. I don't know whether or not there's going to be much interest, but you have to admire the tenacity. Not even Charlie Finley could break Morgan's will to pitch. How many players have started their careers after Morgan, and have since been inducted into the Hall of Fame? I wonder if Steve Ontiveros is looking for a job this spring. He, Morgan, and Rickey Henderson can start ganging up on GMs at whatever homestead pops up in January.

Mike Myers · Born: 26-Jun-69 · Age: 34 · Bats: L · Throws: L

YEAR	TM	LG	AGE	G	GS	IP	H	BB	SO	HR	ERA	EQERA	EQH9	EQBB9	EQSO9	EQHR9	PERA	VORP	STF
2000	COL	NL	31	78	0	45.3	24	24	41	2	1.99	1.73	4.7	3.8	7.1	0.3	1.74	18.4	8
2001	COL	NL	32	73	0	40.0	32	24	36	2	3.60	3.36	7.1	5.0	6.8	0.4	3.20	9.0	-1
2002	ARI	NL	33	69	0	37.0	39	17	31	2	4.38	4.32	9.5	3.6	6.6	0.5	4.51	4.4	-2
2003	ARI	NL	34	84	0	46.3	44	23	36	4	3.90	3.95	8.5	3.8	6.2	0.7	4.22	8.0	-5

Breakout: 15%   Improve: 44%   Collapse: 35%

They liked him enough to pick up his 2003 option, so they must want the situational lefty back. It's not often that a pitcher leaves Coors Field and sees his ERA spike. He'll continue to fill the 80 appearance/50 inning role out of the pen for the Diamondbacks. What do advance scouts do when it comes to someone like this? Is there really an update to the scouting report that needs to be made?

Dustin Nippert · Born: 06-May-81 · Age: 22 · Bats: R · Throws: R

YEAR	TM	LG	AGE	G	GS	IP	H	BB	SO	HR	ERA	EQERA	EQH9	EQBB9	EQSO9	EQHR9	PERA	VORP	STF
2002	MSO	PIO	21	17	11	54.7	42	9	77	2	1.65	2.55	9.2	2.1	6.7	0.9	3.03	17.8	18

West Virginia University product who was simply too much for younger competition in Missoula. Nippert wasn't selected until the 15th round of the June draft, but his early performances are promising. He's not blessed with overpowering stuff, so he will need to figure some things out as he moves up, but late in the season, he was catching the eyes of a lot of scouts. Suffered arm spasms during the season, but did not suffer any structural arm damage.

Eddie Oropesa · Born: 23-Nov-71 · Age: 31 · Bats: L · Throws: L

YEAR	TM	LG	AGE	G	GS	IP	H	BB	SO	HR	ERA	EQERA	EQH9	EQBB9	EQSO9	EQHR9	PERA	VORP	STF
2000	SHV	TXS	28	59	2	76.3	70	40	76	6	3.07	5.30	10.3	5.0	6.6	1.2	5.14	0.8	-10
2001	SWB	INT	29	14	1	15.3	14	4	11	1	2.35	4.28	10.3	2.9	5.3	0.8	4.13	1.9	-8
2001	PHI	NL	29	30	0	19.0	16	17	15	1	4.74	4.88	8.1	7.5	6.0	0.4	4.83	1.1	-17
2002	TUC	PCL	30	29	0	25.7	23	13	26	2	3.85	4.18	9.0	5.3	7.1	0.9	4.20	3.4	-5
2002	ARI	NL	30	32	0	25.3	39	15	18	6	10.32	9.29	13.9	4.7	5.6	2.1	8.71	-11.0	-31
2003	ARI	NL	31	49	0	42.0	44	23	32	4	5.05	5.17	9.4	4.2	6.2	0.9	5.11	1.3	-9

Breakout: 19%   Improve: 52%   Collapse: 20%

Y'know, 32 games is quite a few to appear in when you're posting an ERA that would embarrass a Texas Ranger. Oropesa was awful. He stunk against lefties, was vile against righties, and just couldn't get anyone out. Anyone, that is, except the San Diego Padres, whom he held scoreless over six innings in five games. Bizarre. Not surprisingly, Oropesa was released by the Diamondbacks, so one assumes he'll end up with the Brewers or Devil Rays.

John Patterson · Born: 30-Jan-78 · Age: 25 · Bats: R · Throws: R

YEAR	TM	LG	AGE	G	GS	IP	H	BB	SO	HR	ERA	EQERA	EQH9	EQBB9	EQSO9	EQHR9	PERA	VORP	STF
2000	TUC	PCL	22	3	2	15.0	21	9	10	1	7.80	7.51	13.1	5.3	4.8	0.7	6.97	-3.4	-5
2001	ELP	TXS	23	5	5	25.3	30	9	19	2	4.27	4.99	10.8	3.8	4.7	1.1	5.87	1.4	-1
2001	TUC	PCL	23	13	12	67.7	82	31	40	9	5.85	5.94	10.9	4.9	3.9	1.3	6.22	-3.3	-11
2002	TUC	PCL	24	19	18	112.7	117	45	104	14	4.23	5.04	10.4	4.2	6.5	1.4	5.01	5.8	9
2002	ARI	NL	24	7	5	30.7	27	7	31	7	3.22	3.62	7.9	1.8	8.0	2.0	4.19	6.4	20
2003	ARI	NL	25	18	13	80.3	87	38	62	11	5.05	5.17	9.8	3.6	6.2	1.1	5.13	4.7	3

Breakout: 15%   Improve: 51%   Collapse: 18%

Disconnect. For months, scouts I talked to were raving about how healthy Patterson looked, how much movement he had on his stuff, how much velocity he had, and how impossible it was to hit him. Well, maybe, but the performance record just isn't that impressive. He's come off the major injury, surgery, and rehab, but the K rate that one wants to see for a forecast of future success just wasn't there before last season. Smarter people than I are raving about him, but until he shows that he can pitch 150 healthy innings, I think the skeptics have a better case here.

Beltran Perez — Born: 24-Oct-81 — Age: 21 — Bats: R — Throws: R

YEAR	TM	LG	AGE	G	GS	IP	H	BB	SO	HR	ERA	EQERA	EQH9	EQBB9	EQSO9	EQHR9	PERA	VORP	STF
2000	HDS	CLF	18	2	2	10.0	8	5	11	3	3.60	4.43	10.8	5.1	6.5	5.9	6.35	1.2	-8
2001	SBN	MDW	19	27	27	160.0	142	35	157	10	2.81	4.69	11.0	2.8	5.5	1.3	4.76	14.5	13
2002	LNC	CLF	20	5	5	32.3	31	3	30	1	2.51	3.37	10.3	1.0	4.8	0.5	3.35	7.7	19
2002	ELP	TXS	20	20	19	97.0	114	33	77	10	5.47	6.69	12.7	3.7	5.5	1.8	6.23	-12.8	1

Ah, learning experiences. Perez has apparently discovered that hitters in the Texas League are considerably better at picking up the telegraph on his changeup than hitters at two levels of A-ball. He's still got good stuff, but he's going to have to learn something to use in addition to his slider and fastball. He's got time.

Bret Prinz — Born: 15-Jun-77 — Age: 26 — Bats: R — Throws: R

YEAR	TM	LG	AGE	G	GS	IP	H	BB	SO	HR	ERA	EQERA	EQH9	EQBB9	EQSO9	EQHR9	PERA	VORP	STF
2000	ELP	TXS	23	53	0	60.7	71	16	69	6	3.56	4.05	11.2	2.4	7.3	1.3	5.25	9.0	6
2001	ARI	NL	24	46	0	41.0	33	19	27	4	2.63	3.25	7.6	3.9	5.1	0.8	3.54	9.7	-6
2002	LNC	CLF	25	5	0	7.0	2	1	6	0	0.00	0.44	3.0	1.5	4.3	0.2	0.42	3.8	3
2002	TUC	PCL	25	37	0	39.3	42	9	34	4	2.98	3.93	10.5	2.4	6.0	1.1	4.44	6.3	-2
2002	ARI	NL	25	20	0	13.3	23	10	10	1	9.47	8.86	15.2	5.8	5.7	0.7	8.94	-5.1	-23
2003	*ARI*	*NL*	*26*	*37*	*0*	*41.7*	*41*	*17*	*31*	*4*	*4.05*	*4.15*	*8.9*	*3.2*	*5.9*	*0.9*	*4.26*	*6.3*	*-5*

Breakout: 20%   Improve: 56%   Collapse: 11%

Prinz is erratic in a lot of ways. He's at least three or four different pitchers, depending on what's working for him on any given night. He's occasionally unhittable, throwing moving fastballs through a teacup, and then, boom, he's possessed by the spirit of Charlie Kerfeld or something, and starts leaving pitches in the middle of the plate. If anything's an interesting test of our new forecasting system, this is it.

Armando Reynoso — Born: 01-May-66 — Age: 37 — Bats: R — Throws: R

YEAR	TM	LG	AGE	G	GS	IP	H	BB	SO	HR	ERA	EQERA	EQH9	EQBB9	EQSO9	EQHR9	PERA	VORP	STF
2000	ARI	NL	34	31	30	170.7	179	52	89	22	5.27	4.44	9.4	2.2	4.2	1.0	4.21	20.2	0
2001	ARI	NL	35	9	9	46.7	58	13	15	13	5.97	6.35	11.7	2.4	2.5	2.3	6.53	-4.4	-22
2002	TUC	PCL	36	6	6	27.7	29	9	16	2	5.20	5.02	10.5	3.4	4.1	0.8	4.44	1.5	-7
2002	ARI	NL	36	2	0	1.7	3	1	2	0	10.59	9.10	15.9	4.6	9.2	0.2	8.28	-0.7	1

It's probably getting pretty tough for Armando's agent to make the "sample size" argument. Is he out of time? Maybe. He's been invited back as an NRI, and he's going to have to outpitch a bunch of youngsters that are just plain better than he is. The ride is probably over.

Curt Schilling — Born: 14-Nov-66 — Age: 36 — Bats: R — Throws: R

YEAR	TM	LG	AGE	G	GS	IP	H	BB	SO	HR	ERA	EQERA	EQH9	EQBB9	EQSO9	EQHR9	PERA	VORP	STF
2000	CLR	FSL	33	4	4	20.7	10	2	23	0	1.30	1.64	5.4	1.1	6.9	0.2	1.35	8.9	30
2000	ARI	NL	33	13	13	97.7	94	13	72	10	3.68	3.22	8.8	1.0	6.0	0.8	3.14	24.8	20
2000	PHI	NL	33	16	16	112.7	110	32	96	17	3.91	3.80	8.9	2.1	6.9	1.2	4.03	21.4	18
2001	ARI	NL	34	35	35	256.7	237	39	293	37	2.98	3.31	8.6	1.3	8.8	1.2	3.50	62.6	34
2002	ARI	NL	35	36	35	259.3	218	33	316	29	3.23	3.06	7.6	1.0	9.6	1.0	2.94	70.4	41
2003	*ARI*	*NL*	*36*	*32*	*32*	*225.7*	*201*	*47*	*232*	*26*	*3.00*	*3.07*	*8.1*	*1.6*	*8.3*	*1.0*	*3.12*	*62.6*	*32*

Breakout: 11%   Improve: 52%   Collapse: 14%

America's most famous Avalon Hill addict had another tremendous year, keeping up his half of the tremendous load. A rough September probably cost him the Cy Young, and advance scouting reports showed his velocity down toward the end of the season. If the D-Backs can find a way to give him 5% more rest, and maybe knock 20 innings off his season, there's no reason to believe that he can't continue to be a nostril-flaring, angry, viciously precise flamethrower for several seasons to come. An absolute blast to watch on the mound.

Todd Stottlemyre   Born: 20-May-65   Age: 38   Bats: L   Throws: R

YEAR	TM	LG	AGE	G	GS	IP	H	BB	SO	HR	ERA	EQERA	EQH9	EQBB9	EQSO9	EQHR9	PERA	VORP	STF
2000	ARI	NL	35	18	18	95.3	98	36	76	18	4.91	4.63	9.0	2.7	6.3	1.5	4.72	9.3	7
2002	ARI	NL	37	5	4	20.3	26	7	12	4	7.54	6.67	11.6	2.7	4.7	1.8	6.36	-2.6	-12

After fighting through rotator cuff problems, Stottlemyre returned and looked awful, primarily due to problems with his back. He's announced his retirement, probably saving the Royals from a very embarrassing signing.

Greg Swindell   Born: 02-Jan-65   Age: 38   Bats: L   Throws: L

YEAR	TM	LG	AGE	G	GS	IP	H	BB	SO	HR	ERA	EQERA	EQH9	EQBB9	EQSO9	EQHR9	PERA	VORP	STF
2000	ARI	NL	35	64	0	76.0	71	20	64	7	3.20	3.15	8.4	1.9	6.8	0.7	3.29	18.8	7
2001	ARI	NL	36	64	0	53.7	51	8	42	12	4.53	4.40	8.8	1.3	6.1	1.8	4.20	5.8	-3
2002	TUC	PCL	37	1	1	1.0	0	0	0	0	0.00	0.02	0.2	0.5	0.0	0.1	0.02	0.6	-18
2002	ARI	NL	37	34	0	33.0	38	5	23	9	6.27	5.78	10.5	1.2	5.5	2.5	5.68	-1.5	-13

Hey, since we're talking about back problems... Swindell's bulging disc problem, combined with shoulder tendonitis, put an end to a long run of reasonable relief. This being the Snakes, he's still under contract for another year, with a club option for 2004. You start to think they might have asked the Grove family if Lefty's estate would like a club option.

Jose Valverde   Born: 24-Jul-79   Age: 23   Bats: R   Throws: R

YEAR	TM	LG	AGE	G	GS	IP	H	BB	SO	HR	ERA	EQERA	EQH9	EQBB9	EQSO9	EQHR9	PERA	VORP	STF
2000	MSO	PIO	20	12	0	11.7	3	4	24	0	0.00	-0.34	3.0	3.5	10.0	0.3	0.62	7.4	37
2000	SBN	MDW	20	31	0	31.7	31	25	39	1	5.39	7.56	12.1	8.8	7.1	0.8	7.89	-7.7	-12
2001	ELP	TXS	21	39	0	41.3	36	27	72	1	3.92	3.98	7.8	6.9	10.7	0.3	4.49	6.4	26
2002	TUC	PCL	22	49	0	47.7	45	23	65	8	5.85	5.78	9.5	5.0	9.5	1.9	5.06	-2.1	12

After giving up three homers in over 110 innings to start his career, Valverde got lit up like Paul Williams at the Sambuca distillery. His fastball, once clocked as high as 98, was off considerably in 2002, which is particularly worrisome because of the strained elbow ligament that ended his 2001 season. If he's recovered, he can be part of a large coterie of promising relief prospects for the mix over the next couple of seasons. Watch his command early in the season.

Oscar Villarreal   Born: 22-Nov-81   Age: 21   Bats: L   Throws: R

YEAR	TM	LG	AGE	G	GS	IP	H	BB	SO	HR	ERA	EQERA	EQH9	EQBB9	EQSO9	EQHR9	PERA	VORP	STF
2000	SBN	MDW	18	13	5	32.7	37	17	30	0	4.40	7.04	13.8	5.8	5.3	0.3	7.50	-5.7	-9
2000	HDS	CLF	18	9	4	24.7	24	14	18	4	3.64	6.34	10.9	5.6	4.1	3.0	6.50	-2.4	-24
2001	ELP	TXS	19	27	27	140.7	154	63	108	10	4.41	5.22	10.0	4.8	4.8	1.0	5.58	4.5	0
2002	ELP	TXS	20	14	12	84.3	73	26	85	2	3.74	3.92	8.6	3.2	6.8	0.4	3.59	14.8	26
2002	TUC	PCL	20	10	10	64.0	68	22	40	8	4.36	5.01	10.7	3.6	4.4	1.4	4.99	3.5	3
2003	*ARI*	*NL*	*21*	*15*	*13*	*80.7*	*84*	*41*	*58*	*8*	*4.77*	*4.89*	*9.4*	*3.9*	*5.8*	*0.8*	*4.86*	*5.7*	*4*

Breakout: 6%   Improve: 48%   Collapse: 15%

Villareal has been touted as a top prospect, but so were a lot of guys. His strikeout rate has never been there, but the ERA's always been in the acceptable if not fantastic range. We'll know more after a year in the PCL, but right now, Villareal projects out as a middle-of-the-rotation starter if everything breaks his way, and it won't.

Atlanta Braves

It's over. Over the last dozen years, the Braves have enjoyed the most sustained run of excellence in the post-Messersmith era. They've had as good a twelve-year run as any team, of any era, has ever had. And now is the time to appreciate it, because it's over.

The Braves' dynasty, like all others, has been built around a handful of legitimately great players. Not "great" like Terry Pendleton in 1991, mind you; we're talking about players who consistently, predictably perform at a superstar-quality level year after year. With two or three of those to build around, it's quite possible to continually slot in enough quality players around them to keep a team on top for a period of years.

The Braves have done that fairly well, assembling a sufficiently strong supporting cast year after year. But now the challenge they face is completely different and a lot more serious. Their core of superstars has aged, eroded, and in one case, defected. Now it is almost gone. Over the last three years the gradual dissolution had been largely unfelt. Its effects had been masked, minimized and delayed by recent strokes of good fortune. Then Tom Glavine left.

As if that weren't bad enough, the club apparently painted itself into a corner when it took on Russ Ortiz's salary, signed Paul Byrd as a free agent, and offered arbitration to Greg Maddux, expecting him to reject it. When Maddux turned around and accepted arbitration, the club punched some numbers and suddenly decided it had a payroll crisis, so they dumped off Kevin Millwood for pennies on the dollar. Canadian pennies.

In any event, the problem the Braves faced was larger than merely getting maximum value out of their budgeted payroll. The club's off-season agenda was the same as it had been for years: to bring in more good players. This time, though, the remedy was insufficient, because the scope of the problem was completely different. To make up for the aging of Greg Maddux and John Smoltz and the loss of Tom

Braves Prospectus

2002 record: 101–59; First place, NL East; Lost to Giants in Division Series

Pythagenport Record: 96–64

Runs scored per game: 4.4 (7th in NL)

Runs allowed per game: 3.5 (1st in NL)

Team EqA: .260 (9th in NL)

2002 Batters Age: 31 (4th oldest in NL)

2002 Pitchers Age: 31.2 (3rd oldest in NL)

Ballpark: Turner Field; Neutral park; Park Factor of .996

2002: The ageless rotation, an instantly conjured great pen, and the usual offensive suspects triumphed over the four dwarves of the NL East.

2003: Several bad off-season decisions will bring their first second-place finish since 1994.

Glavine, it was not enough to merely get some more good players. To keep their dynasty from expiring, they needed to find some new foundation players around which to build.

Nobody—not even Tim McCarver—would find it necessary to point out that the Braves have always won on the strength of their starting pitching. During their dozen years at the top, their offense has not played a consistent role in their success. At times, it's been very good, as it was in 1991–92 and 1997–99; at other times it's been dead average, or worse, as it was in 1994–96 and from 2000 to the present. The bullpen has been a positive factor more often than not, but its impact has paled beside that of the team's starters.

Over the last ten years the Braves have had not just one, but two of the most consistently durable and effective pitchers of all time, Greg Maddux and Tom Glavine. For most of that time they were joined by John Smoltz, who also gave them both quality and quantity, year in and year out. To illustrate how big an edge this gave the club every year, we present in table 1 the yearly breakdown of the runs saved by each of the members of the starting rotation (runs saved over 20 in **bold**).

(Runs saved is simply the number of runs a league-average pitcher would have allowed in the number of innings the pitcher pitched, minus the number of runs the pitcher actually allowed. For Atlanta-Fulton County Stadium, a hitter's park, runs allowed were deflated 3%; for Turner Field, a neutral park, no adjustment was made.)

In most years, the combined efforts of Maddux, Glavine, and Smoltz alone saved the Braves over 100 runs, enough to move the club 18–20 games over .500 even if the rest of the roster was average.

The troika was reduced to a duo in 2000 when Smoltz's elbow unraveled. It cost them, but few noticed, for two reasons. First, Maddux and Glavine each were able to pick up

Table 1.

1991	Leibrandt	0	Glavine	32	Smoltz	7	Avery	9	Smith	-11
1992	Leibrandt	5	Glavine	18	Smoltz	19	Avery	8	Bielecki	8
1993	Maddux	51	Glavine	31	Smoltz	21	Avery	33	Smith	0
1994	Maddux	61	Glavine	11	Smoltz	2	Avery	9	Mercker	13
1995	Maddux	70	Glavine	28	Smoltz	25	Avery	0	Mercker	3
1996	Maddux	45	Glavine	34	Smoltz	42	Avery	0	Schmidt	-17
1997	Maddux	61	Glavine	37	Smoltz	34	Neagle	32	Wade	-10
1998	Maddux	53	Glavine	50	Smoltz	28	Neagle	17	Millwood	3
1999	Maddux	18	Glavine	14	Smoltz	33	Perez	-11	Millwood	46
2000	Maddux	48	Glavine	33	Burkett	-4	Mulholland	-9	Millwood	4
2001	Maddux	36	Glavine	23	Burkett	32	Marquis	6	Millwood	3
2002	Maddux	32	Glavine	26	Moss	9	Marquis	-9	Millwood	24

some of the slack by bouncing back from 1999 seasons that were below their established levels. Second, when a club wins 95 games and successfully defends its division title, few people pick nits like: "the team won eight fewer games than the year before," or "the team won five more games than it should have, given its runs scored and allowed."

Smoltz's absence from the rotation continued to be felt, but the club kept winning, through increasingly unlikely means. In 2001, it was John Burkett, who seemingly stole a season from Mike Mussina and cut-and-pasted it into his own career, placing third in the National League in ERA. (Those who would ascribe Burkett's success to the genius of pitching coach Leo Mazzone should be reminded that this was not Burkett's first season in Atlanta. He'd posted a more representative 4.89 ERA for the Braves the year before.)

Last year, things got even more bizarre. The bullpen came to the rescue, posting a cumulative 2.60 ERA—the best mark by any team in over a decade. Chris Hammond and Darren Holmes were exhumed from Steven King's Journeyman Reliever Sematary and combined for a stranger-than-fiction 1.31 ERA in 130 2/3 innings.

Like a dying TV series, the Braves will have to continue to rely on such improbable plot twists just to stay where they're at. Glavine is gone, leaving only Maddux, who's now 37 and no longer the sure thing he once was. Last year he was bothered by an inflamed nerve in his back, a strained calf, and a strained muscle in his side. As a result, he failed to pitch 200 innings for the first time since 1987.

So the rotation ain't what it used to be. Can the offense make up for that? Not likely. Having Chipper Jones and Gary Sheffield is a great start, but they were around last year and the Braves still scored fewer runs than the average National League team. Four positions—catcher, first base, second base, and third base—featured either vast uncertainty or proven mediocrity. Maddux's decision to accept the Braves' offer of arbitration limited the amount of money left over to

address the club's offensive holes, although the club was able to nab Robert Fick for $1 million, hopefully fixing first base.

It's safe to say the bullpen won't repeat last year's magic. Mike Remlinger has been replaced by Ray King; if they're very lucky they'll almost break even on that swap. Tim Spooney-barger has been traded. Hammond is gone, but Holmes remains, and if he reverts to form he doubtlessly will get a lot more second chances than pitchers of his caliber are usually afforded.

So, despite the state of the rotation, for the Braves to get back into the playoffs, the game plan must remain the same. The starting pitchers must once again be good enough to get the team there without too much help from the rest of the roster. And for that to happen, a lot of things will have to break right.

First, Maddux must avoid the slippage in effectiveness and durability to which pitchers his age inevitably succumb. He might be able to do that for at least one more year, but last year's aches and pains raise legitimate concerns.

Second, Mike Hampton must get it back. Not just some of it—all of it. In other words, he must get back to being every bit the pitcher he was at his peak. What the Braves need from him (in terms of the chart above) is a 20–30-run season. Hampton was at that level only in 1999 (40) and 2000 (27); he wasn't even close in 1995–98, when the Astrodome's effects are taken into account. Still, to get him back even to his 1995–98 level would be a lot to ask. Darryl Kile's example shows that it's possible, but that's all. It doesn't mean that it's likely.

Those two pitchers must be what Maddux and Glavine used to be. That's the bare minimum, because there is no potential Smoltz in the rest of the rotation. Their chances of getting a star-caliber performance out of any of their other starters—Russ Ortiz, Paul Byrd, or Jason Marquis—are pretty slim.

John Schuerholz might disagree, but Ortiz and Byrd really are nothing to get excited about. Ortiz has put up decent superficial numbers, with the help of one of the best offenses in baseball and perhaps the most pitcher-friendly park in the league. He hasn't been any more than 16 runs better than average in any of his four seasons as a full-time starter. Byrd, having his career year last season, was at 23. Their one starter who had the potential to be an ace, Kevin Millwood, has been donated to their chief divisional rival.

The Braves no longer have any starting pitchers they can reasonably expect to pitch like superstars. The foundation is gone. As a result, the NL East is wide open. The Braves might still win the division, but it's a division where 85–90 wins might be enough. The Phillies don't have many holes beyond their collection of white elephants in the bullpen, and the Mets are throwing the usual wads of cash at their problems while finally expelling Rey Ordonez. If the Marlins or Expos took themselves seriously, this would be a very interesting division indeed. We no longer live in the Braves' New World, but in a brave new world.

HITTERS

Wilson Betemit · SS · Born: 02-Nov-81 · Age: 21 · Bats: B · Throws: R

YEAR	TM	LG	AGE	AB	H	2B	3B	HR	BB	SO	SB	CS	AVG	OBP	SLG	MLVR	EQBA	EQOBP	EQSLG	EQMLVR	VORP	DEFENSE
2000	JAM	NYP	18	269	89	15	2	5	30	37	3	4	.331	.400	.457	.302	.238	.286	.336	-.271	-3.7	68-SS -16
2001	MYR	CRL	19	318	88	20	1	7	23	71	8	5	.277	.327	.412	.140	.240	.284	.363	-.236	-1.5	83-SS 1
2001	GRN	SOU	19	183	65	14	0	5	12	36	6	2	.355	.398	.514	.336	.297	.332	.438	.006	11.2	46-SS -2
2002	RIC	INT	20	343	84	17	1	8	34	82	8	5	.245	.315	.370	-.075	.231	.297	.352	-.232	-1.3	87-SS -20
2003	ATL	NL	21	194	50	10	1	6	18	41	4	2	.257	.321	.407	-.062	.260	.321	.423	-.063	4.9	

Breakout: 44%   Improve: 66%   Collapse: 12%

Betemit fell well down the prospect charts last year, but in hindsight, he was almost certain to fall short of expectations even if he'd stayed healthy. His super 2001 season, which he capped by hitting .355 in two months at Double-A, put him a step away from the majors in the minds of many, including Braves GM John Schuerholz. It was easy to get swept up in it all. Still, few 20-year-olds are able to make the jump to the majors after playing only a few months above A-ball. We weren't ready to promote him as a Rookie of the Year candidate last year, but we aren't about to write him off now either. Last year, he struggled, he got hurt, and he hit better—but not anywhere close to .355—when he got back. He's still young, and he's still got very good offensive potential, even if he has to move to third base. We like his future.

Gregor Blanco · LF · Born: 12-Dec-83 · Age: 19 · Bats: L · Throws: L

YEAR	TM	LG	AGE	AB	H	2B	3B	HR	BB	SO	SB	CS	AVG	OBP	SLG	MLVR	EQBA	EQOBP	EQSLG	EQMLVR	VORP	DEFENSE
2002	MCN	SAL	18	468	127	14	9	7	85	120	40	16	.271	.393	.385	.140	.210	.302	.302	-.302	-28.9	122-LF -16
2003	ATL	NL	19	209	50	9	5	5	25	58	6	7	.238	.325	.394	-.087	.241	.325	.408	-.089	-3.9	

Breakout: 62%   Improve: 74%   Collapse: 17%

They say you can't walk off the island, but they never said you can't walk out of Venezuela. Blanco's a young Venezuelan outfielder with speed, and he actually takes walks. If he can hit for a decent average, that will make for a great combination at the top of the lineup. He handled the low-A Sally League last year at age 18.

Henry Blanco · C · Born: 29-Aug-71 · Age: 31 · Bats: R · Throws: R

YEAR	TM	LG	AGE	AB	H	2B	3B	HR	BB	SO	SB	CS	AVG	OBP	SLG	MLVR	EQBA	EQOBP	EQSLG	EQMLVR	VORP	DEFENSE
2000	MIL	NL	28	284	67	24	0	7	36	60	0	3	.236	.322	.394	-.149	.234	.311	.392	-.148	6.8	81-C 17
2001	MIL	NL	29	314	66	18	3	6	34	72	3	1	.210	.291	.344	-.249	.217	.296	.355	-.239	-.3	96-C 7
2002	ATL	NL	30	221	45	9	1	6	20	51	0	2	.204	.273	.335	-.227	.214	.278	.353	-.278	-2.5	63-C 2
2003	ATL	NL	31	181	41	9	1	4	19	40	1	2	.227	.304	.361	-.172	.230	.304	.374	-.178	-.6	

Breakout: 41%   Improve: 63%   Collapse: 21%

If this doesn't prove that Greg Maddux is beyond help in controlling the running game, nothing does. Blanco is one of the two or three best-throwing catchers in the game (which is kind of obvious from his offensive numbers). The Braves acquired Blanco and made him Maddux's personal catcher, but Maddux still allowed 24 stolen bases in 28 attempts; only two National League pitchers allowed more steals. The Braves traded Kevin Millwood for (gulp) Johnny Estrada, another catcher, so Blanco's days may be numbered.

Darren Bragg   RF   Born: 07-SEP-69   Age: 33   Bats: L   Throws: R

YEAR	TM	LG	AGE	AB	H	2B	3B	HR	BB	SO	SB	CS	AVG	OBP	SLG	MLVR	EQBA	EQOBP	EQSLG	EQMLVR	VORP	DEFENSE	
2000	COL	NL	30	149	33	7	1	3	17	41	4	1	.221	.301	.342	-.315	.203	.276	.311	-.346	-10.3	29-LF	-1
2001	COH	INT	31	199	58	11	2	7	27	51	3	2	.291	.379	.472	.202	.275	.356	.446	.041	7.2	27-LF	0
2001	NOR	INT	31	99	33	4	0	4	23	22	5	2	.333	.468	.495	.409	.308	.430	.471	.234	10.2	20-OF	-1
2001	NYM	NL	31	57	15	6	0	0	4	23	3	2	.263	.323	.368	-.107	.276	.331	.379	-.098	-.2	11-OF	0
2002	RIC	INT	32	75	22	5	0	1	20	15	4	2	.293	.442	.400	.208	.269	.406	.372	.030	2.5	21-RF	1
2002	ATL	NL	32	212	57	15	2	3	24	52	5	2	.269	.349	.401	.032	.278	.352	.417	-.004	4.1	50-RF	-2
2003	*ATL*	*NL*	*33*	*173*	*44*	*9*	*1*	*4*	*25*	*43*	*4*	*2*	*.257*	*.353*	*.394*	*-.028*	*.260*	*.352*	*.408*	*-.027*	*.7*		

Breakout: 18%   Improve: 45%   Collapse: 29%

Dave Martinez was the Braves' fourth outfielder in 2001. When Martinez had season-ending knee surgery in spring training, the club asked Darren Bragg to step in. He did his best Martinez impression:

Player	YEAR	G	AB	R	H	2B	3B	HR	RBI	BB	SO	SB	CS	BA	OBP	SLG	OPS
Martinez	2001	120	237	33	68	11	3	2	20	21	44	3	3	.287	.347	.384	.731
Bragg	2002	109	212	34	57	15	2	3	15	24	52	5	2	.269	.347	.401	.748

Rich Little must be sweating. Hey, Darren, can you do a little George W. for us?

Vinny Castilla   3B   Born: 04-Jul-67   Age: 36   Bats: R   Throws: R

YEAR	TM	LG	AGE	AB	H	2B	3B	HR	BB	SO	SB	CS	AVG	OBP	SLG	MLVR	EQBA	EQOBP	EQSLG	EQMLVR	VORP	DEFENSE	
2000	TBY	AL	33	331	73	9	1	6	14	41	1	2	.221	.259	.308	-.413	.230	.259	.323	-.348	-12.9	82-3B	8
2001	TBY	AL	34	93	20	6	0	2	3	22	0	0	.215	.247	.344	-.302	.226	.263	.376	-.267	-1.9	24-3B	1
2001	HOU	NL	34	445	120	28	1	23	32	86	1	4	.270	.323	.492	.044	.267	.319	.488	.028	25.8	121-3B	1
2002	ATL	NL	35	543	126	23	2	12	22	69	4	1	.232	.271	.348	-.196	.242	.275	.365	-.249	-8.2	136-3B	-1
2003	*ATL*	*NL*	*35*	*332*	*78*	*15*	*1*	*8*	*18*	*52*	*2*	*2*	*.235*	*.277*	*.358*	*-.220*	*.238*	*.276*	*.371*	*-.227*	*-8.2*		

Breakout: 14%   Improve: 40%   Collapse: 24%

Maybe Schuerholz figured, "I signed a slick-fielding third baseman (Pendleton) and he became an MVP, and I signed an ex-Rockies power hitter (Galarraga) and he hit 44 home runs, so if I sign a slick-fielding third baseman who's *also* an ex-Rockies power hitter... (evil cackling)." Castilla supposedly played with a bad wrist most of the year, so for the sake of argument, let's ignore his offense for a second. What was the impact of his defense? Clay Davenport's analysis says it was about one run above average. Chipper Jones had been 11 runs below average the year before, so the net gain was 12 runs. In other words, Castilla's glovework probably helped the Braves gain all of one game in the standings. Now do you want to talk about offense?

Ramon Castro   SS   Born: 23-Oct-79   Age: 23   Bats: R   Throws: R

YEAR	TM	LG	AGE	AB	H	2B	3B	HR	BB	SO	SB	CS	AVG	OBP	SLG	MLVR	EQBA	EQOBP	EQSLG	EQMLVR	VORP	DEFENSE			
2000	MYR	CRL	20	385	97	20	3	5	44	76	13	5	.252	.347	.358	.042	.221	.285	.318	-.309	-9.7	90-SS	9		
2001	GRN	SOU	21	261	80	19	5	6	25	56	5	8	.307	.386	.487	.234	.257	.320	.408	-.092	9.2	58-SS	-1		
2001	RIC	INT	21	135	30	8	2	1	7	30	1	2	.222	.266	.333	-.217	.213	.255	.324	-.365	-5.3	27-SS	3		
2002	GRN	SOU	22	210	68	17	2	5	39	44	14	8	.324	.450	.495	.371	.273	.372	.426	.041	15.6	42-SS	-1		
2002	RIC	INT	22	121	28	7	1	6	14	22	4	3	.231	.340	.455	.066	.220	.316	.431	-.096	4.0	18-2B	3	16-SS	-1
2003	*ATL*	*NL*	*23*	*207*	*53*	*12*	*1*	*5*	*22*	*41*	*5*	*3*	*.254*	*.334*	*.402*	*-.049*	*.258*	*.334*	*.417*	*-.049*	*6.0*				

Breakout: 20%   Improve: 53%   Collapse: 13%

That can't be his real age, can it? If he hit like that, and he really was that young, they wouldn't keep moving him around like an unwanted piece of furniture, would they? He began the year at Triple-A, played six games, and was demoted. He then became Greenville's starting shortstop and leadoff hitter batting .370 through mid-May. They then promoted him back to Richmond, where he hit .253 and slugged .515 in 33 games between second base and shortstop. Then they demoted him again. He hit .288 the rest of the way while playing short and a little third.

Mark DeRosa SS Born: 02-Feb-75 Age: 28 Bats: R Throws: R

YEAR	TM	LG	AGE	AB	H	2B	3B	HR	BB	SO	SB	CS	AVG	OBP	SLG	MLVR	EQBA	EQOBP	EQSLG	EQMLVR	VORP		DEFENSE				
2000	RIC	INT	25	370	108	22	3	3	38	36	13	4	.292	.363	.392	.025	.272	.331	.363	-.123	9.5		89-SS	3			
2001	RIC	INT	26	186	55	18	0	2	17	22	7	3	.296	.358	.425	.109	.275	.337	.402	-.055	8.5		24-SS	1	17-3B	0
2001	ATL	NL	26	164	47	8	0	3	12	19	2	1	.287	.354	.390	-.015	.295	.357	.398	-.008	9.6		39-SS	3			
2002	RIC	INT	27	55	14	3	0	0	5	2	2	0	.255	.339	.309	-.106	.250	.317	.304	-.248	-1.7						
2002	ATL	NL	27	212	63	9	2	5	12	24	2	3	.297	.344	.429	.084	.302	.344	.447	.045	14.0		28-2B	6	16-SS	3
2003	ATL	NL	28	277	74	14	1	4	23	31	4	2	.266	.328	.370	-.095	.270	.327	.384	-.097	3.6						

Breakout: 8%   Improve: 25%   Collapse: 38%

After the Braves soured on Marcus Giles, they gave DeRosa a look at second base, and he didn't do anything to dissuade them from letting him stay there. He seems to be on track to become the Braves' Placido Polanco—someone who's overqualified to be a reserve and might be just good enough to hold a regular job.

Carlos Duran CF Born: 27-Dec-82 Age: 20 Bats: L Throws: L

YEAR	TM	LG	AGE	AB	H	2B	3B	HR	BB	SO	SB	CS	AVG	OBP	SLG	MLVR	EQBA	EQOBP	EQSLG	EQMLVR	VORP		DEFENSE
2002	MCN	SAL	19	534	144	22	10	7	29	80	23	17	.270	.313	.388	.029	.207	.238	.304	-.430	-34.5		122-CF -14
2003	ATL	NL	20	200	48	10	4	3	13	37	4	4	.239	.291	.369	-.176	.242	.291	.383	-.182	-3.5		

Breakout: 72%   Improve: 83%   Collapse: 10%

This is the Braves' *other* speedy Venezuelan left-handed–hitting outfield prospect who played at Macon last year. Duran is the one who *doesn't* take walks—that's how you can tell the two apart.

Julio Franco 1B Born: 23-Aug-58 Age: 44 Bats: R Throws: R

YEAR	TM	LG	AGE	AB	H	2B	3B	HR	BB	SO	SB	CS	AVG	OBP	SLG	MLVR	EQBA	EQOBP	EQSLG	EQMLVR	VORP		DEFENSE	
2001	MCT	MEX	42	407	178	34	5	18	50	56	15	6	.437	.504	.678	.816	.343	.402	.549	.334	.4			
2001	ATL	NL	42	90	27	4	0	3	10	20	0	0	.300	.376	.444	.113	.304	.377	.457	.120	5.6		22-1B	2
2002	ATL	NL	43	338	96	13	1	6	39	75	5	1	.284	.360	.382	.036	.294	.364	.395	.000	8.7		80-1B	-6
2003	ATL	NL	43	256	69	14	1	5	31	52	4	1	.268	.349	.394	-.026	.271	.349	.409	-.025	1.6			

Breakout: 13%   Improve: 28%   Collapse: 43%

Julio did a decent job for a man rumored to be his age, and will come to camp on a minor league contract to see if he'll get the chance to do it again. It's hard to believe he got to do it once; the only reason it happened is the Braves probably planned to address the first base problem in-season, and then built a big lead so quickly that they never had to.

Matt Franco 1B Born: 19-Aug-69 Age: 33 Bats: L Throws: R

YEAR	TM	LG	AGE	AB	H	2B	3B	HR	BB	SO	SB	CS	AVG	OBP	SLG	MLVR	EQBA	EQOBP	EQSLG	EQMLVR	VORP		DEFENSE			
2000	NOR	INT	30	51	7	1	0	0	3	10	0	0	.137	.185	.157	-.704	.154	.185	.173	-.744	-8.0					
2000	NYM	NL	30	134	32	4	0	2	21	22	0	0	.239	.342	.313	-.205	.250	.342	.324	-.170	-2.9		12-1B	-2	11-3B	-2
2001	NOR	INT	31	433	106	25	1	8	52	72	5	2	.245	.329	.363	-.049	.237	.315	.352	-.193	-.6		78-3B	-3	34-1B	0
2002	RIC	INT	32	173	50	11	0	6	14	19	1	0	.289	.353	.457	.134	.269	.327	.434	-.033	3.0		32-1B	0		
2002	ATL	NL	32	205	65	15	4	6	27	31	1	0	.317	.397	.517	.303	.321	.396	.531	.273	20.6		40-1B	-7		
2003	ATL	NL	33	213	53	10	1	5	25	34	2	1	.250	.331	.374	-.094	.254	.330	.388	-.097	-2.3					

Breakout: 15%   Improve: 41%   Collapse: 34%

He had a fine season, and we enjoyed the all-Franco platoon as much as anyone else, but when your first baseman against right-handed pitchers is Matt Franco, your GM has got to get his hands back on the wheel.

Jeff Francoeur CF Born: 08-Jan-84 Age: 19 Bats: R Throws: R

YEAR	TM	LG	AGE	AB	H	2B	3B	HR	BB	SO	SB	CS	AVG	OBP	SLG	MLVR	EQBA	EQOBP	EQSLG	EQMLVR	VORP		DEFENSE
2002	DAN	APL	18	147	48	12	1	8	15	34	8	5	.327	.400	.585	.413	.211	.252	.374	-.302	-4.5		36-CF 5
2003	ATL	NL	19	191	47	11	1	7	17	55	4	4	.246	.311	.424	-.065	.250	.311	.440	-.067	2.2		

Breakout: 70%   Improve: 76%   Collapse: 14%

Selected by the Braves with the 23rd overall pick in the 2002 draft, Francoeur got a $2.2 million bonus, the biggest the Braves had ever given. He then went to the Appy League and tore it up, inspiring comparisons to Dale Murphy. We'll have to see more before we'll sign on to something like that, but he hasn't yet ruled it out.

Rafael Furcal　　　SS　Born: 24-Oct-77　Age: 25　Bats: B　Throws: R

YEAR	TM	LG	AGE	AB	H	2B	3B	HR	BB	SO	SB	CS	AVG	OBP	SLG	MLVR	EQBA	EQOBP	EQSLG	EQMLVR	VORP	DEFENSE			
2000	ATL	NL	22	455	134	20	4	4	73	80	40	14	.295	.395	.382	.022	.290	.384	.376	.008	29.9	94-SS	-4	24-2B	2
2001	ATL	NL	23	324	89	19	0	4	24	56	22	6	.275	.327	.370	-.102	.280	.328	.377	-.103	10.3	77-SS	6		
2002	ATL	NL	24	636	175	31	8	8	43	114	27	15	.275	.324	.387	-.024	.282	.326	.398	-.075	23.3	142-SS	20		
2003	ATL	NL	25	532	143	26	5	8	48	86	27	7	.270	.333	.382	-.067	.273	.332	.397	-.068	15.1				

Breakout: 10%　　Improve: 35%　　Collapse: 19%

He didn't reach base like he did as a rookie, but it wasn't all bad. The shoulder dislocation that ended his 2001 season didn't affect him, and he showed nice improvement in the field. Now if they could only get him to start taking walks again, he'd be back to being one of the league's best all-around shortstops.

Marcus Giles　　　2B　Born: 18-May-78　Age: 25　Bats: R　Throws: R

YEAR	TM	LG	AGE	AB	H	2B	3B	HR	BB	SO	SB	CS	AVG	OBP	SLG	MLVR	EQBA	EQOBP	EQSLG	EQMLVR	VORP	DEFENSE			
2000	GRN	SOU	22	458	133	28	2	17	72	71	25	5	.290	.389	.472	.228	.252	.331	.414	-.067	19.7	121-2B	0		
2001	RIC	INT	23	252	84	19	1	6	22	48	13	5	.333	.391	.488	.279	.307	.363	.455	.095	21.8	60-2B	0		
2001	ATL	NL	23	244	64	10	2	9	28	37	2	5	.262	.338	.430	-.007	.266	.341	.431	-.014	14.1	57-2B	6		
2002	RIC	INT	24	115	37	6	0	3	13	15	3	0	.322	.391	.452	.215	.299	.364	.427	.050	8.5	13-2B	-1	13-3B	3
2002	ATL	NL	24	213	49	10	1	8	25	41	1	1	.230	.317	.399	-.051	.236	.317	.417	-.101	6.5	47-2B	2		
2003	ATL	NL	25	317	82	17	1	9	35	52	5	3	.259	.337	.409	-.032	.263	.337	.424	-.031	10.3				

Breakout: 12%　　Improve: 45%　　Collapse: 24%

Giles is in danger of becoming the new Warren Morris, except with an even more rapid descent into oblivion. A year ago, we liked him as much as anyone, and we stand by what we wrote about him at the time. Since then, however, the Braves have gotten a closer look at him and have decided, for whatever reason, that they didn't like what they saw. As he was coming through the minors, it always was assumed that if anything would be his undoing, it would be his glove, but apparently it was more than that. He got hurt in May, and again in June. While he was on rehab, Bobby Cox announced that when he returned he'd be tried at third base and in the outfield. In light of the fact that the Braves already had an established starter at third base and all three outfield positions, it didn't take much reading between the lines to see what Cox was saying. At the time, Keith Lockhart was playing second and batting below .200. Mark DeRosa, who had about 15 games of pro experience at second, was being given a crash course at the keystone while rehabbing an ankle injury. The premature birth and eventual death of Giles's infant daughter might have played a part, and we don't mean to minimize its possible effect on Giles and his play. Still, when Giles was activated in early August and apparently was ready to play, Cox hardly used him. Then, at the winter meetings the Braves shopped Giles extensively. There's something going on here, and until it comes to light, we can't endorse him.

Nick Green　　　2B　Born: 10-Sep-78　Age: 24　Bats: R　Throws: R

YEAR	TM	LG	AGE	AB	H	2B	3B	HR	BB	SO	SB	CS	AVG	OBP	SLG	MLVR	EQBA	EQOBP	EQSLG	EQMLVR	VORP	DEFENSE	
2000	MCN	SAL	21	339	83	19	4	11	22	75	10	4	.245	.301	.422	.027	.191	.227	.330	-.424	-17.4	83-SS	-12
2000	MYR	CRL	21	91	22	6	0	1	10	23	3	2	.242	.337	.341	-.003	.211	.275	.305	-.352	-3.4	13-SS	-8
2001	MYR	CRL	22	297	79	18	1	10	32	70	9	2	.266	.351	.434	.192	.232	.299	.385	-.182	2.8	69-2B	-2
2002	GRN	SOU	23	355	85	16	2	15	36	92	2	5	.239	.323	.423	.036	.210	.270	.376	-.265	-4.7	75-2B	-7
2003	ATL	NL	24	156	37	8	1	5	13	38	3	2	.236	.301	.392	-.132	.239	.300	.407	-.136	.6		

Breakout: 51%　　Improve: 73%　　Collapse: 14%

Green's somewhat intriguing because he has above-average power for a second baseman. The downside is that he doesn't do anything else particularly well, and he's a little old for a guy who's just reaching Triple-A. He's a converted shortstop, so if he can still get by there he might eventually be a useful reserve middle infielder.

Wes Helms　　　1B/3B　Born: 12-May-76　Age: 27　Bats: R　Throws: R

YEAR	TM	LG	AGE	AB	H	2B	3B	HR	BB	SO	SB	CS	AVG	OBP	SLG	MLVR	EQBA	EQOBP	EQSLG	EQMLVR	VORP	DEFENSE			
2000	RIC	INT	24	539	155	27	7	20	27	92	0	6	.288	.329	.475	.081	.265	.297	.437	-.086	14.2	123-3B	-13		
2001	ATL	NL	25	216	48	10	3	10	21	56	1	1	.222	.294	.435	-.113	.228	.298	.443	-.107	-.6	53-1B	-6		
2002	ATL	NL	26	210	51	16	0	6	11	57	1	1	.243	.290	.405	-.080	.249	.291	.423	-.131	-1.8	33-1B	-3	15-3B	-3
2003	MIL	NL	27	228	56	12	1	9	17	54	2	2	.247	.302	.430	-.070	.253	.304	.447	-.067	0.0				

Breakout: 17%　　Improve: 46%　　Collapse: 27%

The Brewers apparently were quite happy to land Helms, whom they variously mischaracterized as "young" and "talented." They think he might be their third baseman; last year he could have been the right-handed–hitting half of the Braves' first-base platoon, but he was beaten out by an undead Julio Franco.

Mike Hessman   **3B**   **Born: 05-Mar-78**   **Age: 25**   **Bats: R**   **Throws: R**

YEAR	TM	LG	AGE	AB	H	2B	3B	HR	BB	SO	SB	CS	AVG	OBP	SLG	MLVR	EQBA	EQOBP	EQSLG	EQMLVR	VORP	DEFENSE			
2000	GRN	SOU	22	437	80	23	1	19	37	178	3	1	.183	.259	.371	-.163	.168	.220	.336	-.443	-30.2	123-3B	-12		
2001	GRN	SOU	23	478	110	23	2	26	39	124	2	4	.230	.298	.450	-.009	.198	.252	.384	-.296	-14.3	109-3B	-7	16-LF	-1
2002	RIC	INT	24	484	127	28	1	26	34	107	1	5	.262	.324	.486	.104	.244	.303	.454	-.069	15.5	114-3B	-5	12-1B	0
2003	ATL	NL	25	195	46	10	1	9	18	52	2	3	.236	.307	.428	-.075	.239	.306	.444	-.077	2.3				

Breakout: 53%   Improve: 75%   Collapse: 15%

Boy, just when you get rid of one Wes Helms, here comes another one. Like Helms, Hessman is a right-handed–hitting third baseman with decent power and little else of interest. With Wilson Betemit set to move to third, Hessman is on track to be an organizational player. What he needs is for a clueless organization to become infatuated with him. Hey, don't laugh, it happened to Helms.

Kelly Johnson   **SS**   **Born: 22-Feb-82**   **Age: 21**   **Bats: L**   **Throws: R**

YEAR	TM	LG	AGE	AB	H	2B	3B	HR	BB	SO	SB	CS	AVG	OBP	SLG	MLVR	EQBA	EQOBP	EQSLG	EQMLVR	VORP	DEFENSE	
2001	MCN	SAL	19	415	120	22	1	23	71	111	25	6	.289	.405	.513	.341	.226	.316	.397	-.137	10.0	109-SS	-22
2002	MYR	CRL	20	482	123	21	5	12	51	105	12	15	.255	.328	.394	.062	.212	.271	.335	-.318	-13.3	118-SS	2
2003	ATL	NL	21	187	45	7	1	5	20	47	3	3	.239	.317	.376	-.123	.242	.316	.390	-.126	1.5		

Breakout: 49%   Improve: 70%   Collapse: 13%

It wasn't a huge year, but it was better than it looked. One big thing was that Johnson improved his glovework significantly, cutting his errors nearly in half. His power numbers fell off, but part of that was his tough home park; he hit nine of his 12 homers on the road. He's still very much on track. One of the things he still must learn to do is hang in against southpaws.

Andruw Jones   **CF**   **Born: 23-Apr-77**   **Age: 26**   **Bats: R**   **Throws: R**

YEAR	TM	LG	AGE	AB	H	2B	3B	HR	BB	SO	SB	CS	AVG	OBP	SLG	MLVR	EQBA	EQOBP	EQSLG	EQMLVR	VORP	DEFENSE	
2000	ATL	NL	23	656	199	36	6	36	59	100	21	6	.303	.369	.541	.211	.301	.357	.537	.197	67.2	161-CF	14
2001	ATL	NL	24	625	157	25	2	34	56	142	11	4	.251	.316	.461	-.015	.257	.319	.470	-.007	30.2	161-CF	14
2002	ATL	NL	25	560	148	34	0	35	83	135	8	3	.264	.369	.512	.206	.270	.369	.532	.177	55.0	153-CF	8
2003	ATL	NL	26	577	156	32	3	32	74	125	11	4	.271	.357	.500	.128	.274	.357	.519	.135	40.2		

Breakout: 14%   Improve: 58%   Collapse: 8%

OK, he hit 35 homers, drew a career-high 83 walks, and won another Gold Glove, but . . . is something else going on here? His putouts dropped to 404, 57 fewer than the year before and his lowest total in a full season since moving to center field. His stolen bases dropped from 11 to 8, after having dropped from 21 to 11 the year before. He grounded into a career-high 14 double plays, and he didn't hit a single triple all year. Has he lost a step or two? Is it a bit unsettling that we have to ask, when he'll be only 26 this year?

Chipper Jones   **LF**   **Born: 24-Apr-72**   **Age: 31**   **Bats: B**   **Throws: R**

YEAR	TM	LG	AGE	AB	H	2B	3B	HR	BB	SO	SB	CS	AVG	OBP	SLG	MLVR	EQBA	EQOBP	EQSLG	EQMLVR	VORP	DEFENSE	
2000	ATL	NL	28	579	180	38	1	36	95	64	14	7	.311	.410	.566	.323	.306	.398	.558	.298	81.8	145-3B	-1
2001	ATL	NL	29	572	189	33	5	38	98	82	9	10	.330	.430	.605	.452	.332	.429	.603	.437	109.0	141-3B	-11
2002	ATL	NL	30	548	179	35	1	26	107	89	8	2	.327	.438	.536	.397	.330	.437	.549	.373	72.9	140-LF	-1
2003	ATL	NL	31	544	167	33	2	28	97	83	11	3	.306	.411	.531	.281	.310	.411	.550	.294	54.6		

Breakout: 9%   Improve: 48%   Collapse: 10%

In the second half he batted .353 with 17 homers—which is pretty damn impressive, even by his standards—but what really caught our eye is this: 61 walks versus only 33 strikeouts. He hasn't had a ratio that impressive in any half-season since the second half of 1999, a three-month stretch that won him the NL MVP. It's possible that the conversion to left field was a distraction over the first half last year, and that his second-half numbers are more representative of how he'll do this year. Scary.

Ryan Langerhans OF Born: 20-Feb-80 Age: 23 Bats: L Throws: L

YEAR	TM	LG	AGE	AB	H	2B	3B	HR	BB	SO	SB	CS	AVG	OBP	SLG	MLVR	EQBA	EQOBP	EQSLG	EQMLVR	VORP		DEFENSE	
2000	MYR	CRL	20	392	83	14	7	6	32	104	25	11	.212	.286	.329	-.114	.188	.237	.296	-.453	-39.9		88-RF	-6
2001	MYR	CRL	21	450	129	30	3	7	55	104	22	13	.287	.374	.413	.212	.246	.316	.365	-.167	-12.0		121-RF	-1
2002	GRN	SOU	22	391	98	23	2	9	68	83	10	5	.251	.370	.389	.069	.219	.314	.346	-.214	-3.9		106-CF	-2
2003	ATL	NL	23	183	45	9	1	4	20	42	4	3	.244	.323	.377	-.108	.247	.323	.391	-.111	-1.3			

Breakout: 38%   Improve: 67%   Collapse: 12%

Langerhans bats left-handed, runs well, plays a good center field, and draws a decent amount of walks. With any luck, his bat will develop enough to make him a Mike Kinger or Darren Bragg type of player, and he could turn out to be quite a bit better.

Adam LaRoche 1B Born: 06-Nov-79 Age: 23 Bats: L Throws: L

YEAR	TM	LG	AGE	AB	H	2B	3B	HR	BB	SO	SB	CS	AVG	OBP	SLG	MLVR	EQBA	EQOBP	EQSLG	EQMLVR	VORP		DEFENSE	
2000	DNV	APL	20	201	62	13	3	7	24	46	4	1	.308	.388	.507	.296	.205	.258	.332	-.352	-13.3		36-1B	-1
2001	MYR	CRL	21	471	118	31	0	7	30	108	10	8	.251	.308	.361	.029	.220	.265	.324	-.341	-31.4		119-1B	-4
2002	MYR	CRL	22	250	84	17	0	9	27	37	0	2	.336	.409	.512	.402	.273	.332	.427	-.030	4.6		64-1B	-7
2002	GRN	SOU	22	173	50	9	0	4	19	38	1	1	.289	.363	.410	.114	.250	.307	.364	-.183	-4.1		45-1B	5
2003	ATL	NL	23	195	49	10	1	6	18	42	2	2	.251	.318	.395	-.087	.255	.318	.410	-.089	-2.5			

Breakout: 50%   Improve: 65%   Collapse: 11%

LaRoche jumped over low-A to Myrtle Beach in 2001 and didn't do much. The Braves sent him back there in 2002, and he went crazy-go-nuts. It earned him a mid-season promotion to Double-A, where he lost a little power but kept his average up nicely. If he pans out? Oh, hell, we'll say it: Steve Cox. His given name is David—yes, that's right, the father of "LaLob" is his father as well, longtime reliever Dave LaRoche.

Richard Lewis 2B Born: 29-Jun-80 Age: 23 Bats: R Throws: R

YEAR	TM	LG	AGE	AB	H	2B	3B	HR	BB	SO	SB	CS	AVG	OBP	SLG	MLVR	EQBA	EQOBP	EQSLG	EQMLVR	VORP		DEFENSE	
2001	JAM	NYP	21	285	69	7	1	4	20	50	16	4	.242	.301	.316	-.083	.185	.224	.247	-.549	-25.4		69-2B	-12
2002	MYR	CRL	22	484	135	23	4	2	55	80	31	10	.279	.362	.355	.079	.241	.305	.312	-.266	-6.8		124-2B	-4
2003	ATL	NL	23	181	43	9	2	2	15	38	5	4	.236	.300	.343	-.197	.239	.300	.355	-.204	-2.5			

Breakout: 53%   Improve: 72%   Collapse: 17%

Does the whole Jewish-neurotic shtick, turns his therapy sessions into monologues, has a chronic case of Basset Hound eyes . . . oh, wait—wrong Richard Lewis. This Richard Lewis was a supplemental first round pick (and the 40th overall selection) in the 2001 draft. He's got speed and on-base skills, but it remains to be seen if he has enough to make it. He'll need to move quickly, but he has college experience and may be able to.

Keith Lockhart 2B Born: 10-Nov-64 Age: 38 Bats: L Throws: R

YEAR	TM	LG	AGE	AB	H	2B	3B	HR	BB	SO	SB	CS	AVG	OBP	SLG	MLVR	EQBA	EQOBP	EQSLG	EQMLVR	VORP		DEFENSE			
2000	ATL	NL	35	275	73	12	3	2	29	31	4	1	.265	.336	.353	-.159	.267	.328	.354	-.145	5.3		60-2B	3	14-3B	0
2001	ATL	NL	36	178	39	6	0	3	16	22	1	2	.219	.291	.303	-.299	.228	.297	.311	-.290	-3.8		33-2B	1		
2002	ATL	NL	37	296	64	13	3	5	27	50	0	1	.216	.284	.331	-.205	.223	.287	.347	-.263	-3.7		69-2B	18		
2003	ATL	NL	38	166	39	8	1	2	15	24	1	1	.235	.301	.330	-.213	.238	.301	.343	-.220	-3.0					

Breakout: 33%   Improve: 60%   Collapse: 29%

Lockhart hasn't been around forever, and he still looks like a paperboy (Ed. note: perhaps a wrinkly one you've left out in the sun), so it's easy to forget he's 38. He's been dropping subtle hints to remind us, like batting .219 and .216 the last two years. Hopefully Mark DeRosa will take the second base job and Lockhart no longer will be asked to do much more than pinch-hit.

Javy Lopez C Born: 05-Nov-70 Age: 32 Bats: R Throws: R

YEAR	TM	LG	AGE	AB	H	2B	3B	HR	BB	SO	SB	CS	AVG	OBP	SLG	MLVR	EQBA	EQOBP	EQSLG	EQMLVR	VORP		DEFENSE	
2000	ATL	NL	29	481	138	21	1	24	35	80	0	0	.287	.340	.484	.061	.287	.330	.485	.062	38.3		119-C	-3
2001	ATL	NL	30	438	117	16	1	17	28	82	1	0	.267	.326	.425	-.034	.273	.327	.432	-.032	24.4		113-C	-2
2002	ATL	NL	31	347	81	15	0	11	26	63	0	1	.233	.302	.372	-.110	.241	.303	.392	-.158	6.8		92-C	6
2003	ATL	NL	32	269	66	12	0	8	20	48	0	1	.244	.302	.385	-.133	.248	.302	.400	-.137	2.2			

Breakout: 11%   Improve: 42%   Collapse: 33%

Lopez strained his right shoulder in July, and it bothered him the rest of the way. On the other hand, he wasn't exactly going great guns while he was still healthy. He might bounce back a little—a *little*, mind you—if the presence of Johnny Estrada helps him get more days off.

Andy Marte   3B   Born: 21-Oct-83   Age: 19   Bats: R   Throws: R

YEAR	TM	LG	AGE	AB	H	2B	3B	HR	BB	SO	SB	CS	AVG	OBP	SLG	MLVR	EQBA	EQOBP	EQSLG	EQMLVR	VORP	DEFENSE
2001	DNV	APL	17	125	25	6	0	1	20	45	3	0	.200	.310	.272	-.153	.136	.214	.189	-.666	-16.7	37-3B 1
2002	MCN	SAL	18	488	137	32	4	21	41	114	2	1	.281	.344	.492	.216	.214	.261	.379	-.275	-11.2	121-3B -10
2003	ATL	NL	19	225	54	11	2	7	22	62	2	3	.240	.312	.405	-.093	.243	.311	.421	-.096	1.6	

Breakout: 81%   Improve: 88%   Collapse: 11%

Marte, a Dominican third baseman, led the Sally league in RBI and was second in home runs. If his age is to be believed, he did this at the age of 18, which would make him a tremendous prospect. We have no reason to be skeptical of Marte in particular. Just a reminder that the usual caveat to Dominican ages applies. If he unexpectedly stagnates, as many of the later-exposed birthday frauds have done, that's a tip-off.

Gary Sheffield   RF   Born: 18-Nov-68   Age: 34   Bats: R   Throws: R

YEAR	TM	LG	AGE	AB	H	2B	3B	HR	BB	SO	SB	CS	AVG	OBP	SLG	MLVR	EQBA	EQOBP	EQSLG	EQMLVR	VORP	DEFENSE
2000	LAD	NL	31	501	163	24	3	43	101	71	4	6	.325	.442	.643	.526	.332	.440	.652	.520	91.2	119-LF -6
2001	LAD	NL	32	515	160	28	2	36	94	67	10	4	.311	.421	.583	.408	.321	.427	.602	.420	81.0	121-LF -3
2002	ATL	NL	33	492	151	26	0	25	72	53	12	2	.307	.407	.512	.301	.315	.409	.530	.286	49.2	114-RF 2
2003	ATL	NL	34	454	135	25	1	23	74	57	9	2	.298	.399	.513	.233	.302	.399	.532	.245	34.2	

Breakout: 3%   Improve: 44%   Collapse: 8%

If our estimation of Atlanta's outlook proves accurate, no Brave would be more affected than Sheffield. If the club falls out of contention, they probably aren't going to want to keep carrying his salary, and he very well might want to relocate himself. He's been stuck in pitchers' parks for years, so the right move could make a difference if it happens before age takes its toll.

B. J. Surhoff   OF/1B   Born: 04-Aug-64   Age: 38   Bats: L   Throws: R

YEAR	TM	LG	AGE	AB	H	2B	3B	HR	BB	SO	SB	CS	AVG	OBP	SLG	MLVR	EQBA	EQOBP	EQSLG	EQMLVR	VORP	DEFENSE
2000	BAL	AL	35	411	120	27	0	13	29	46	7	2	.292	.342	.453	.030	.305	.346	.478	.097	19.0	102-LF 3
2000	ATL	NL	35	128	37	9	2	1	12	12	3	0	.289	.355	.414	-.015	.287	.342	.419	-.012	2.7	27-LF 0
2001	ATL	NL	36	484	131	33	1	10	38	48	9	3	.271	.325	.405	-.060	.277	.330	.411	-.053	4.7	108-LF 1
2002	ATL	NL	37	75	22	5	0	0	9	5	1	3	.293	.369	.360	.029	.289	.365	.368	-.039	1.9	

Coming off a torn ACL in his right knee that wiped out most of his 2002 season, Surhoff is a free agent and looking for work. He won't play regularly again, but his left-handed bat and ability to play a few different positions would make him a fine bench player. It's up to him whether he'd accept that kind of work, and that kind of pay.

Scott Thorman   1B   Born: 06-Jan-82   Age: 21   Bats: L   Throws: R

YEAR	TM	LG	AGE	AB	H	2B	3B	HR	BB	SO	SB	CS	AVG	OBP	SLG	MLVR	EQBA	EQOBP	EQSLG	EQMLVR	VORP	DEFENSE
2002	MCN	SAL	20	470	138	38	3	16	51	83	2	2	.294	.371	.489	.259	.225	.281	.376	-.234	-17.5	121-1B -21
2003	ATL	NL	21	205	48	10	2	5	19	45	2	2	.236	.304	.373	-.151	.239	.303	.387	-.156	-6.3	

Breakout: 30%   Improve: 56%   Collapse: 21%

When the Braves took Thorman with the 30th overall pick in 2000, Canadian papers trumpeted that he was the second-highest Canadian selection in the draft's history. (Of course, they kind of played down the fact that the only one taken higher was shortstop Kevin Nicholson, who batted .216 for the Padres in 2000 and has been kicking around the minors ever since.) Thorman missed all of 2001 with a shoulder injury that forced him to be moved across the diamond from third to first. He had hit .227 with only one home run in 29 games in the Gulf Coast League in 2000, so there was some concern about jumping him over advanced rookie ball, but he put those fears to rest convincingly.

PITCHERS

Ray Aguilar — Born: 18-Jan-80 — Age: 23 — Bats: B — Throws: L

YEAR	TM	LG	AGE	G	GS	IP	H	BB	SO	HR	ERA	EQERA	EQH9	EQBB9	EQSO9	EQHR9	PERA	VORP	STF
2001	JAM	NYP	21	2	2	12.0	7	3	16	1	1.50	4.48	9.7	3.5	7.2	2.7	3.53	1.4	19
2002	MYR	CRL	22	35	6	106.7	82	28	114	1	1.60	3.76	9.3	3.3	6.8	0.2	3.92	19.8	15

He is believed to be a different person than Nebraska State Senator Ray Aguilar. But who knows for sure? If Senator Fred Thompson can star on *Law & Order* while still in office, hell, anything's possible. Aguilar was drafted and signed by the Rockies in 1999, but was unable to pitch, so they voided his contract a few weeks later. He then went to Cypress College, led California's Orange Empire Conference in strikeouts in 2001, and got signed by the Braves. Since then he's been taking advantage of low-level hitters while waiting to be advanced to the level he deserves (note to Braves: He hasn't reached it yet). Aguilar pounds the strike zone but isn't overpowering.

Matt Belisle — Born: 06-Jun-80 — Age: 23 — Bats: B — Throws: R

YEAR	TM	LG	AGE	G	GS	IP	H	BB	SO	HR	ERA	EQERA	EQH9	EQBB9	EQSO9	EQHR9	PERA	VORP	STF
2000	MCN	SAL	20	15	15	102.3	79	18	97	7	2.38	4.44	10.2	2.2	5.0	1.6	3.97	12.1	11
2000	MYR	CRL	20	12	12	78.7	72	11	71	5	3.43	6.25	13.8	1.6	5.5	1.6	5.10	-6.5	13
2002	GRN	SOU	22	26	26	159.3	162	39	123	18	4.35	5.86	12.3	2.5	5.3	2.2	5.41	-6.3	5

Surgery for a ruptured disc in his back cost Belisle the 2001 season and knocked him off the upper tier of many prospect lists. He pitched better than his record, notching 13 quality starts but getting only five wins. His ERA was uglified by a nine-run pounding and two sevens.

Jung Bong — Born: 15-Jul-80 — Age: 22 — Bats: L — Throws: L

YEAR	TM	LG	AGE	G	GS	IP	H	BB	SO	HR	ERA	EQERA	EQH9	EQBB9	EQSO9	EQHR9	PERA	VORP	STF
2000	MCN	SAL	19	20	19	112.7	119	45	90	4	4.23	7.18	13.6	5.1	4.3	0.9	6.72	-21.0	-4
2000	MYR	CRL	19	7	6	41.3	33	7	37	1	2.18	5.19	11.5	1.9	5.3	0.6	4.04	1.4	17
2001	MYR	CRL	20	28	28	168.0	151	47	145	7	3.00	5.77	11.6	3.8	5.0	1.0	5.87	-4.9	6
2002	GRN	SOU	21	27	17	122.0	136	45	107	6	3.25	5.66	12.6	3.7	5.9	0.9	5.92	-2.4	8

His overall numbers were less than thrilling, but he made good progress last year. After a few bad starts in May, Bong was bumped to the bullpen for a couple of months. He returned to the rotation in August and was superb the rest of the way. An extreme ground-baller, he's someone who might make the big club this spring and contribute out of the pen.

Daniel Curtis — Born: 03-Nov-79 — Age: 23 — Bats: R — Throws: R

YEAR	TM	LG	AGE	G	GS	IP	H	BB	SO	HR	ERA	EQERA	EQH9	EQBB9	EQSO9	EQHR9	PERA	VORP	STF
2000	MCN	SAL	20	7	6	45.7	35	7	45	4	1.97	3.52	10.5	1.9	5.2	2.1	4.01	10.0	12
2000	MYR	CRL	20	8	8	50.3	48	15	34	5	2.68	6.58	15.3	3.6	4.3	2.5	6.52	-6.0	-5
2002	MYR	CRL	22	17	17	117.3	106	18	99	10	2.53	4.86	12.3	2.0	5.6	2.1	5.08	8.4	10
2002	GRN	SOU	22	10	10	54.3	61	18	29	7	4.81	6.27	13.9	3.4	3.7	2.6	6.61	-4.6	-12

Curtis missed 2001 to have his elbow re-strung. He always had been a pitcher who succeeded with pinpoint control rather than velocity, and he was no different when he returned last year. At Class-A, he seemingly was able to put two strikes past each hitter before they could react, but Double-A hitters proved harder to set up. We'll see.

Joey Dawley — Born: 19-Sep-71 — Age: 31 — Bats: R — Throws: R

YEAR	TM	LG	AGE	G	GS	IP	H	BB	SO	HR	ERA	EQERA	EQH9	EQBB9	EQSO9	EQHR9	PERA	VORP	STF
2001	MYR	CRL	29	5	0	10.0	4	0	16	0	1.80	1.50	4.8	0.7	8.7	0.2	1.53	4.3	30
2001	GRN	SOU	29	22	21	127.3	95	46	130	15	3.04	4.25	8.5	3.9	6.3	1.8	4.12	17.7	5
2002	RIC	INT	30	24	23	140.3	113	36	136	10	2.63	3.43	8.2	2.8	7.5	0.9	3.42	32.3	22
2003	*ATL*	*NL*	*31*	*15*	*11*	*67.7*	*65*	*26*	*58*	*9*	*4.06*	*4.34*	*8.8*	*3.0*	*6.8*	*1.2*	*4.48*	*10.2*	*10*

Breakout: 11% *Improve: 41%* *Collapse: 31%*

Leo Mazzone and Bobby Cox have always had good success turning underappreciated veteran minor leaguers into useful major league relievers, from Kevin Gryboski, to Kerry Ligtenberg, to Greg McMichael, to Mike Cather. Dawley easily could be the next name in that progression. He was terrific at Double-A in 2001, and just as impressive in Triple-A last year.

John Ennis   Born: 17-Oct-79   Age: 23   Bats: R   Throws: R

YEAR	TM	LG	AGE	G	GS	IP	H	BB	SO	HR	ERA	EQERA	EQH9	EQBB9	EQSO9	EQHR9	PERA	VORP	STF
2000	MCN	SAL	20	18	16	98.7	77	25	105	5	2.55	4.61	10.1	3.2	5.6	1.2	4.17	9.8	12
2001	MYR	CRL	21	25	25	138.3	111	45	144	12	3.58	6.10	11.2	4.5	6.1	2.2	5.82	-9.1	5
2002	GRN	SOU	22	26	26	148.7	131	62	103	7	4.18	5.24	10.0	4.1	4.6	0.9	4.63	4.4	3
2002	ATL	NL	22	1	1	4.0	5	3	1	0	4.50	5.85	13.1	6.3	2.1	0.2	6.19	-0.2	-24
2003	ATL	NL	23	13	9	59.3	65	29	42	8	4.97	5.32	10.0	3.8	5.7	1.2	5.39	2.9	-2

Breakout: 12%   Improve: 47%   Collapse: 21%

The numbers lie—Ennis pitched well almost all year, save for a bad three-start stretch in May and an eight-run, 1 1/3 inning fiasco in his final start of the season. A big guy with good stuff and good upside, he could surface sometime this season.

Brett Evert   Born: 23-Oct-80   Age: 22   Bats: L   Throws: R

YEAR	TM	LG	AGE	G	GS	IP	H	BB	SO	HR	ERA	EQERA	EQH9	EQBB9	EQSO9	EQHR9	PERA	VORP	STF
2000	JAM	NYP	19	15	15	77.3	92	19	64	6	3.38	8.49	18.3	3.3	4.6	3.5	8.45	-25.6	-12
2000	MCN	SAL	19	7	7	42.7	53	9	29	7	4.64	8.51	18.6	2.9	3.9	4.3	8.76	-14.3	-17
2001	MCN	SAL	20	6	6	36.3	25	3	34	0	0.74	2.43	8.2	1.1	4.6	0.3	2.89	12.4	20
2001	MYR	CRL	20	13	13	72.3	63	15	75	4	2.24	5.23	11.4	2.8	5.9	1.3	5.45	2.2	13
2002	MYR	CRL	21	10	10	57.7	53	21	51	3	3.74	6.47	12.1	4.8	5.9	1.3	5.76	-6.2	7
2002	GRN	SOU	21	16	15	93.7	94	35	84	15	4.90	6.60	12.7	3.8	6.2	3.1	6.26	-11.4	4

Evert started the year at Double-A Greenville and pitched fairly well for the first six weeks, but then dropped seven of eight decisions and was demoted to Class-A Myrtle Beach in early July. It wasn't necessarily an overreaction; he was only 21, and they had jumped him to Double-A after he'd spent only a partial season at Myrtle Beach the year before. He throws hard and he throws strikes, and chances are he'll have better success with upper-level hitters the second time around.

John Foster   Born: 17-May-78   Age: 25   Bats: L   Throws: L

YEAR	TM	LG	AGE	G	GS	IP	H	BB	SO	HR	ERA	EQERA	EQH9	EQBB9	EQSO9	EQHR9	PERA	VORP	STF
2000	MYR	CRL	22	38	0	48.7	48	14	46	2	1.85	5.55	14.4	3.4	5.8	1.0	6.06	-0.9	-5
2001	GRN	SOU	23	50	0	68.7	71	33	63	6	3.01	5.43	11.6	5.2	5.7	1.3	6.10	-0.4	-12
2002	RIC	INT	24	55	0	62.0	67	28	48	5	4.21	5.40	11.0	5.0	6.0	1.1	5.69	-0.1	-10

The Braves packaged Foster off to Milwaukee with Wes Helms for Ray King. For the Brewers, Foster gives them a cheap potential lefty specialist to replace King. Foster might be able to do it; he was tough on lefties last year but not so tough the year before.

Tom Glavine   Born: 25-Mar-66   Age: 37   Bats: L   Throws: L

YEAR	TM	LG	AGE	G	GS	IP	H	BB	SO	HR	ERA	EQERA	EQH9	EQBB9	EQSO9	EQHR9	PERA	VORP	STF
2000	ATL	NL	34	35	35	241.0	222	65	152	24	3.40	3.51	8.6	2.0	5.1	0.8	3.45	53.4	11
2001	ATL	NL	35	35	35	219.3	213	97	116	24	3.57	4.35	9.6	3.8	4.2	0.9	4.52	28.1	-2
2002	ATL	NL	36	36	36	224.7	210	78	127	21	2.96	4.18	9.7	2.9	4.6	0.9	4.01	33.1	3
2003	NYM	NL	37	30	26	161.3	164	58	94	17	4.05	4.58	9.5	2.8	4.6	1.0	4.70	17.9	0

Breakout: 15%   Improve: 43%   Collapse: 14%

There's no mystery here; Glavine remains effective only as long as he's able to throw his changeup within three inches of the outside corner. Jamie Moyer, who employs the same modus operandi, just turned 40, and he's still doing it. Glavine should have a few more good years in him as long as he stays healthy, and as you know, injuries never have been a problem for him.

Kevin Gryboski   Born: 15-Nov-73   Age: 29   Bats: R   Throws: R

YEAR	TM	LG	AGE	G	GS	IP	H	BB	SO	HR	ERA	EQERA	EQH9	EQBB9	EQSO9	EQHR9	PERA	VORP	STF
2000	NHV	EAS	26	16	0	18.0	15	8	20	0	2.50	3.75	9.1	4.4	7.5	0.3	4.09	3.3	3
2000	TAC	PCL	26	31	0	41.0	45	23	35	3	4.83	5.54	11.1	5.0	6.3	0.9	5.90	-0.7	-12
2001	TAC	PCL	27	58	0	60.0	64	19	50	8	3.90	5.42	11.2	3.5	5.6	1.5	5.64	-0.3	-15
2002	ATL	NL	28	57	0	51.7	50	37	33	6	3.48	4.82	9.8	5.8	5.1	1.1	5.46	3.2	-21
2003	ATL	NL	29	48	0	40.7	44	24	28	4	4.80	5.13	10.0	4.6	5.5	1.0	5.66	3.3	-16

Breakout: 21%   Improve: 44%   Collapse: 21%

Kevin Gryboski *(continued)*

Those who are into trends should note Gryboski's first- and second-half ERAs: 1.54 and 7.56. At that rate, his ERA in the first half of 2003 should be either 13.58 or 37.11, depending on whether the progression is arithmetic or geometric. Seriously, batters reached base against him at a .388 clip, so he didn't have any right to be within shouting distance of a sub-4.00 ERA.

Chris Hammond   Born: 21-Jan-66   Age: 37   Bats: L   Throws: L

YEAR	TM	LG	AGE	G	GS	IP	H	BB	SO	HR	ERA	EQERA	EQH9	EQBB9	EQSO9	EQHR9	PERA	VORP	STF
2001	BUF	INT	35	28	4	51.7	53	20	54	5	3.31	5.08	10.7	4.2	7.5	1.2	5.41	2.0	-1
2001	RIC	INT	35	21	0	30.7	32	4	29	0	2.35	3.54	10.4	1.4	6.6	0.2	3.83	6.3	9
2002	ATL	NL	36	63	0	76.0	53	31	63	1	0.95	2.52	7.2	3.3	6.7	0.1	2.59	24.2	8
2003	NYY	AL	37	54	0	60.3	61	25	48	5	3.60	3.65	9.1	3.5	6.8	0.7	4.24	15.8	2

Breakout: 20%   Improve: 37%   Collapse: 31%

Left-handers who pitched in the majors last year include Chris Haney, Donovan Osborne, Kent Mercker, Terry Mulholland, Andrew Lorraine, Ed Vosberg, and (the even worse) Bobby Jones. Thank you, Chris Hammond, for ensuring that future generations of baseball fans will continue to be subjected to recycled Greg Cadarets. Hammond said he owed his success to the prayers of his friends back home; if Judge Landis were still around he'd have hauled the Almighty into his office on a game-fixing charge.

Buddy Hernandez   Born: 03-Mar-79   Age: 24   Bats: R   Throws: R

YEAR	TM	LG	AGE	G	GS	IP	H	BB	SO	HR	ERA	EQERA	EQH9	EQBB9	EQSO9	EQHR9	PERA	VORP	STF
2000	JAM	NYP	21	12	0	23.0	17	7	35	0	1.57	3.47	8.9	3.6	7.5	0.3	4.08	4.9	15
2001	MCN	SAL	22	7	0	14.0	13	1	29	1	3.21	6.06	11.9	1.0	10.5	1.6	5.04	-1.1	32
2001	MYR	CRL	22	34	0	53.7	28	18	77	1	1.17	2.77	6.4	4.4	7.9	0.4	3.27	15.6	15
2002	GRN	SOU	23	40	0	59.0	36	23	81	0	1.22	2.64	6.5	3.7	8.8	0.2	2.65	18.0	23
2003	OAK	AL	24	20	5	46.7	42	20	45	4	3.60	3.66	8.0	3.5	8.2	0.7	3.78	11.1	14

Breakout: 21%   Improve: 33%   Collapse: 21%

Hernandez has an ERA of 1.44 in 149 $^2/_3$ pro innings. Opponents have hit .176 off him, with a total of two home runs. He has struck out 222 of the 593 batters he's faced (37.4%). We could go on. The Braves left him exposed in the Rule 5 draft, though, apparently because he's short. The Padres took him, and Oakland GM Billy Beane worked out a deal for him. He'll pitch middle relief for the A's this year, probably with good success. But chances are he always will be short.

Trey Hodges   Born: 29-Jun-78   Age: 25   Bats: R   Throws: R

YEAR	TM	LG	AGE	G	GS	IP	H	BB	SO	HR	ERA	EQERA	EQH9	EQBB9	EQSO9	EQHR9	PERA	VORP	STF
2000	JAM	NYP	22	13	2	19.7	22	12	13	3	5.94	9.82	21.9	9.1	4.1	7.6	10.68	-9.6	-67
2001	MYR	CRL	23	26	26	173.0	156	18	139	13	2.76	5.37	12.0	1.4	4.6	1.8	5.44	2.6	4
2002	RIC	INT	24	28	28	172.3	158	56	116	9	3.19	4.11	9.3	3.6	5.2	0.7	4.10	26.7	9
2002	ATL	NL	24	4	0	11.7	16	2	6	2	5.38	6.39	14.2	1.4	4.3	1.7	6.30	-1.3	-10
2003	ATL	NL	25	15	10	59.0	67	25	41	9	5.27	5.63	10.4	3.3	5.5	1.3	5.42	1.6	-4

Breakout: 16%   Improve: 51%   Collapse: 25%

Hodges could be this year's Damian Moss if the Braves need him to be. They jumped him from high-A to Triple-A last year, and he led the International League in wins, the second year in a row he'd been his circuit's top winner. Unlike Moss, he is not overpowering, relying instead on changing speeds.

Darren Holmes   Born: 25-Apr-66   Age: 37   Bats: R   Throws: R

YEAR	TM	LG	AGE	G	GS	IP	H	BB	SO	HR	ERA	EQERA	EQH9	EQBB9	EQSO9	EQHR9	PERA	VORP	STF
2000	MEM	PCL	34	9	0	14.7	10	3	8	0	2.45	2.57	7.5	1.9	4.1	0.2	2.02	4.6	-2
2002	ATL	NL	36	55	0	54.7	41	12	47	3	1.81	2.63	7.8	1.8	7.0	0.5	2.56	16.7	12
2003	ATL	NL	37	58	0	50.3	50	15	41	5	3.43	3.67	9.1	2.2	6.5	0.8	3.95	11.0	3

Breakout: 22%   Improve: 47%   Collapse: 27%

Back problems bothered Holmes on and off for several years before he had surgery and missed all of 2001. Whatever that surgery was, there probably are a bunch of pitchers who'd take two of 'em. Obviously, his odds of repeating a season like 2002 are remote.

Kerry Ligtenberg   Born: 11-May-71   Age: 32   Bats: R   Throws: R

YEAR	TM	LG	AGE	G	GS	IP	H	BB	SO	HR	ERA	EQERA	EQH9	EQBB9	EQSO9	EQHR9	PERA	VORP	STF
2000	ATL	NL	29	59	0	52.3	43	24	51	7	3.61	3.55	7.4	3.3	7.7	1.1	3.70	10.6	5
2001	ATL	NL	30	53	0	59.7	50	30	56	4	3.02	3.69	8.2	4.3	7.3	0.6	3.71	11.2	3
2002	ATL	NL	31	52	0	66.7	52	33	51	6	2.97	3.79	8.0	4.0	6.2	0.8	3.66	11.8	-3
2003	BAL	AL	32	44	0	55.7	54	24	43	7	4.02	4.20	8.7	3.6	6.6	1.0	4.48	9.7	-2

Breakout: 18%   *Improve: 42%*   *Collapse: 22%*

The Braves' record in games in which Ligtenberg appeared was 18–34; they were 83–25 in all other games. Eight of the 18 wins weren't really close—the Braves won by five runs or more. In the remaining 10 games, Ligtenberg pitched to two batters or less in four of them. Also, seven of the 10 came after July 19, by which time the club had opened up a 12 1/2-game lead, and one other came in the last week of the season, after they'd clinched. It isn't difficult to get hitters out when they're more interested in getting the game over with than scoring runs. The Orioles are about to put him on the spot in tougher situations.

Albie Lopez   Born: 18-Aug-71   Age: 31   Bats: R   Throws: R

YEAR	TM	LG	AGE	G	GS	IP	H	BB	SO	HR	ERA	EQERA	EQH9	EQBB9	EQSO9	EQHR9	PERA	VORP	STF
2000	TBY	AL	28	45	24	185.3	199	70	96	24	4.13	4.06	9.2	2.8	4.5	1.0	4.23	29.2	-2
2001	TBY	AL	29	20	20	124.7	152	51	67	16	5.34	5.34	10.3	3.4	4.5	1.0	5.52	2.3	-2
2001	ARI	NL	29	13	13	81.0	74	24	69	10	4.00	3.92	8.6	2.5	6.6	1.0	3.74	14.3	16
2002	ATL	NL	30	30	4	55.7	66	18	39	1	4.36	5.21	12.2	2.7	5.8	0.2	4.65	1.3	0
2003	KCR	AL	31	26	10	66.0	81	25	40	9	5.33	4.87	10.5	3.1	5.4	1.0	4.80	8.6	-5

Breakout: 14%   *Improve: 44%*   *Collapse: 27%*

For anyone who considers the Braves infallible when it comes to pitchers, consider Lopez. The Braves signed him to a one-year, $4 million deal in the hopes that Leo Mazzone's influence (and his leaving Tampa Bay) could turn him into a decent starter. Lopez went on the DL with a strained groin after two appearances, and Damian Moss took his spot. Lopez came back, made two starts—Two! Decent ones! Against Houston and St. Louis!—but someone had to go to the bullpen to make room for Jason Marquis, and Moss had outpitched him. Cox mumbled something about being unable to change the fact that Lopez was a high fastball pitcher; Lopez was given a mop and was rarely used the rest of the way. It was an odd excuse; Turner Field isn't exactly a fly-ball pitcher's graveyard, and the Braves do have a guy named Andruw Jones to run balls down. Whether that was the real reason or not, the Braves simply threw in the towel on Lopez after 17 innings. He'll get a shot at jump-starting his career in the Royals' rotation.

Gonzalo Lopez   Born: 06-Oct-83   Age: 19   Bats: R   Throws: R

YEAR	TM	LG	AGE	G	GS	IP	H	BB	SO	HR	ERA	EQERA	EQH9	EQBB9	EQSO9	EQHR9	PERA	VORP	STF
2002	MCN	SAL	18	28	27	157.0	134	51	130	11	3.10	5.44	11.4	4.3	4.8	1.8	5.17	1.1	0

Lopez, a Nicaraguan right-hander, was only 18 last year, but more than held his own in the low-A South Atlantic League. His youth showed, as he lacked stamina, both over the course of a game and the season. He's the darkhorse in the wave of pitching talent in the lower levels of the Braves' system; his name hasn't been bandied about with those of Macay McBride and Adam Wainwright, but he's young enough and advanced enough to catch up, if he stays healthy.

Greg Maddux   Born: 14-Apr-66   Age: 37   Bats: Throws:

YEAR	TM	LG	AGE	G	GS	IP	H	BB	SO	HR	ERA	EQERA	EQH9	EQBB9	EQSO9	EQHR9	PERA	VORP	STF
2000	ATL	NL	34	35	35	249.3	225	42	190	19	3.00	3.03	8.5	1.3	6.2	0.6	2.94	68.6	22
2001	ATL	NL	35	34	34	233.0	220	27	173	20	3.05	3.50	9.4	1.0	5.9	0.7	3.27	51.9	19
2002	ATL	NL	36	34	34	199.3	194	45	118	14	2.62	3.81	10.1	1.9	4.9	0.7	3.69	37.5	9
2003	ATL	NL	37	28	23	151.3	149	40	96	16	3.58	3.83	9.1	2.0	5.1	0.9	3.85	29.2	8

Breakout: 21%   *Improve: 47%*   *Collapse: 24%*

Apparently the projection system thinks Maddux's minor physical ailments are going to grow less minor. It's perfectly logical to predict that for a 38-year-old pitcher, but this is Greg Maddux. He's the rarest of animals—the starting pitcher who misses hardly any starts, ever. There aren't too many of those, so it's hard to predict how long he'll hold up. He'll be pitching for a new contract, so the Braves might toss caution to the wind and stop handling him with kid gloves. If that happens, he could break down, or he could throw 260 great innings.

Jason Marquis Born: 21-Aug-78 Age: 24 Bats: L Throws: R

YEAR	TM	LG	AGE	G	GS	IP	H	BB	SO	HR	ERA	EQERA	EQH9	EQBB9	EQSO9	EQHR9	PERA	VORP	STF
2000	GRN	SOU	21	11	11	68.0	68	23	49	10	3.57	6.15	12.6	3.5	4.8	2.6	6.16	-4.9	0
2000	RIC	INT	21	6	6	20.0	26	13	18	2	9.00	7.95	12.0	5.7	6.7	1.1	7.48	-5.4	0
2000	ATL	NL	21	15	0	23.3	23	12	17	4	5.02	5.33	8.9	3.7	5.8	1.4	4.96	0.1	-1
2001	ATL	NL	22	38	16	129.3	113	59	98	14	3.48	4.37	8.6	3.9	5.9	0.9	4.04	15.7	6
2002	ATL	NL	23	22	22	114.3	127	49	84	19	5.04	5.93	11.3	3.5	6.0	1.6	5.69	-5.4	5
2003	ATL	NL	24	26	20	124.0	123	53	95	14	4.41	4.71	9.1	3.3	6.1	1.0	4.64	12.9	6

Breakout: 18%   Improve: 56%   Collapse: 14%

One of the unavoidable drawbacks of the way Bobby Cox handles his starting rotation is that it makes it very hard for a young starter like Jason Marquis to establish himself. As the fifth starter, Marquis had his start skipped many, many times last year, regardless of how he'd been pitching. Whenever Cox could keep Maddux and Glavine on a five-day schedule, he would, even if it meant Marquis would have to go eight days between starts. Very, very few young pitchers have been able to thrive serving as Cox's fifth starter.

Macay McBride Born: 24-Oct-82 Age: 20 Bats: L Throws: L

YEAR	TM	LG	AGE	G	GS	IP	H	BB	SO	HR	ERA	EQERA	EQH9	EQBB9	EQSO9	EQHR9	PERA	VORP	STF
2002	MCN	SAL	19	25	25	157.3	119	48	138	6	2.12	4.07	9.5	3.9	4.9	0.9	4.13	25.1	9

McBride is a young Billy Wagner, a southpaw who throws in the mid-90s despite standing less than six feet tall. At the age of 19 he led the Sally League in ERA and gave up more than four earned runs only once all year. We constantly harp on the inherent risks of pitchers drafted out of high school, but if you're going to have one, McBride is one of the first ones you'd take.

Dan Meyer Born: 03-Jul-81 Age: 22 Bats: R Throws: L

YEAR	TM	LG	AGE	G	GS	IP	H	BB	SO	HR	ERA	EQERA	EQH9	EQBB9	EQSO9	EQHR9	PERA	VORP	STF
2002	DAN	APL	21	13	13	65.7	47	18	77	4	2.74	3.85	9.9	3.5	5.8	1.4	3.54	12.1	12

The Braves took Dan Meyer with the 34th overall pick in the 2002 draft, gave him a $1.1 million bonus, and sent him to Danville. (Dan arrived and probably quipped, "Hey, this is my kind of town.") He went on to rank third in the Appalachian League in strikeouts, and fifth in ERA. He's a left-hander with college experience who throws in the low 90s, so he could move quickly.

Kevin Millwood Born: 24-Dec-74 Age: 28 Bats: R Throws: R

YEAR	TM	LG	AGE	G	GS	IP	H	BB	SO	HR	ERA	EQERA	EQH9	EQBB9	EQSO9	EQHR9	PERA	VORP	STF
2000	ATL	NL	25	36	35	212.7	213	62	168	26	4.65	4.28	9.3	2.2	6.4	1.0	4.02	28.9	17
2001	ATL	NL	26	21	21	121.0	121	40	84	20	4.31	5.02	9.8	2.8	5.4	1.4	4.73	6.5	3
2002	ATL	NL	27	35	34	217.0	186	65	178	16	3.24	3.84	8.8	2.5	6.7	0.7	3.36	40.1	19
2003	PHI	NL	28	31	28	183.3	173	55	144	19	3.7	4.04	8.8	2.3	6.2	0.9	3.93	29.7	15

Breakout: 10%   Improve: 57%   Collapse: 9%

From June 8 through the end of the season Millwood went 15–3 with a 2.51 ERA in 22 starts. He also got significantly more ground balls last year, and induced 20 double plays, more than he had in the previous two seasons combined. Thirdly, he threw only 96 pitches per start, six fewer than he averaged during his first big season, 1999. We're optimistic he'll be able to repeat this time, even in Philly.

Zachary Miner Born: 12-Mar-82 Age: 21 Bats: R Throws: R

YEAR	TM	LG	AGE	G	GS	IP	H	BB	SO	HR	ERA	EQERA	EQH9	EQBB9	EQSO9	EQHR9	PERA	VORP	STF
2001	JAM	NYP	19	15	15	90.7	76	16	68	6	1.89	5.04	13.1	2.6	4.1	2.2	4.92	4.7	0
2002	MCN	SAL	20	29	28	159.0	143	51	131	10	3.28	5.57	11.8	4.2	4.7	1.6	5.41	-1.2	0

In his first full pro season, Miner had a respectable but unspectacular season. He's shaping up as a pitcher who will rely more on the ground ball than the strikeout. That's not necessarily a bad thing, but the Braves do prefer pure power pitchers, and they have more than enough to keep them occupied.

Damian Moss   Born: 24-Nov-76   Age: 26   Bats: R   Throws: L

YEAR	TM	LG	AGE	G	GS	IP	H	BB	SO	HR	ERA	EQERA	EQH9	EQBB9	EQSO9	EQHR9	PERA	VORP	STF
2000	RIC	INT	23	29	28	160.7	130	106	123	14	3.14	3.90	7.4	5.8	5.7	1.0	4.57	28.6	5
2001	RIC	INT	24	17	16	88.7	75	38	94	10	3.15	4.37	8.9	4.6	7.6	1.4	4.60	11.2	14
2002	ATL	NL	25	33	29	179.0	140	89	111	20	3.42	4.39	8.1	4.1	5.0	1.1	3.83	22.1	1
2003	SFG	NL	26	25	19	118.0	111	61	88	13	4.46	5.21	8.8	4.0	5.8	1.1	5.03	6.1	0

Breakout: 13%   Improve: 37%   Collapse: 26%

Moss might have broken through in 2001 if he hadn't come down with a blood clot in his shoulder in mid-season. He'd come to camp with 20 extra pounds of muscle, and had gotten off to a terrific start at Triple-A before his fingers started tingling. Last year, he not only stayed healthy, but lucked into a rotation spot when both Jason Marquis and Albie Lopez got hurt. He pitched well, but was wildly inconsistent, allowing one run or less in 12 of 29 starts, five runs or more in nine other starts. He had *six* starts in which he pitched six-plus innings and allowed two hits or less (including his seven no-hit, seven-walk innings on May 3). As hard as he was to hit, he had more than five strikeouts only three times all season. He could have a very good year at Pac Bell Park, where the effects of his walks will be minimized.

Bubba Nelson   Born: 26-Aug-81   Age: 21   Bats: R   Throws: R

YEAR	TM	LG	AGE	G	GS	IP	H	BB	SO	HR	ERA	EQERA	EQH9	EQBB9	EQSO9	EQHR9	PERA	VORP	STF
2001	MCN	SAL	19	25	24	151.0	144	57	154	16	3.93	6.81	13.4	5.5	5.5	2.5	7.21	-21.9	-2
2002	MYR	CRL	20	23	23	135.7	98	44	105	4	1.72	4.09	9.2	4.2	5.1	0.7	4.06	21.3	10

Nelson led the minors in ERA last year. He missed most of June with a sore hip, then came back and had a near-impossible 1.18 ERA in 12 starts the rest of the way. He's a big, hard thrower, and could reach the bigs as quickly as Adam Wainwright.

Andy Pratt   Born: 27-Aug-79   Age: 23   Bats: L   Throws: L

YEAR	TM	LG	AGE	G	GS	IP	H	BB	SO	HR	ERA	EQERA	EQH9	EQBB9	EQSO9	EQHR9	PERA	VORP	STF
2000	PCH	FSL	20	16	16	92.7	68	26	95	8	2.72	4.30	9.0	3.2	6.6	2.0	4.08	12.4	17
2000	TUL	TXS	20	11	11	52.3	66	33	42	7	7.23	8.38	13.3	6.0	5.3	1.9	8.39	-16.7	-10
2001	TUL	TXS	21	27	26	168.0	175	57	132	18	4.61	5.97	11.5	3.8	5.2	1.7	5.78	-8.7	4
2002	GRN	SOU	22	20	18	93.0	92	44	67	5	4.26	6.00	11.3	4.7	4.8	1.0	5.57	-5.2	-3
2002	RIC	INT	22	6	6	40.7	35	9	36	2	3.10	3.70	8.6	2.4	6.8	0.6	3.43	8.2	26

Pratt was acquired from Texas for Ben Kozlowski in early April, a trade that later proved embarrassing for Atlanta when Kozlowski rocketed through the minors. Easily overlooked was the fact that Pratt also showed impressive development over the course of the season. He had some sort of arm problem early on, but from mid-May on he pitched quite well. Promoted to Triple-A Richmond, he had a 3.10 ERA in six starts and struck out 36 men in 40 2/3 innings. He's a year older than Kozlowski, but he also has more experience at the higher levels and is closer to the majors. It's too early to render a verdict on the trade.

Mike Remlinger   Born: 23-Mar-66   Age: 37   Bats: L   Throws: L

YEAR	TM	LG	AGE	G	GS	IP	H	BB	SO	HR	ERA	EQERA	EQH9	EQBB9	EQSO9	EQHR9	PERA	VORP	STF
2000	ATL	NL	34	71	0	72.7	55	37	72	6	3.47	3.30	6.9	3.7	7.9	0.7	3.22	16.8	8
2001	ATL	NL	35	75	0	75.0	67	23	93	9	2.76	3.53	8.6	2.6	9.6	1.0	3.75	15.4	19
2002	ATL	NL	36	73	0	68.0	48	28	69	3	1.99	2.87	7.2	3.4	8.2	0.4	2.80	19.0	14
2003	CHC	NL	37	62	0	56.7	49	23	59	5	3.18	3.51	8.1	3.2	8.2	0.8	3.87	13.3	11

Breakout: 31%   Improve: 48%   Collapse: 39%

The Cubs, on one hand, swap two years of one bad contract (Todd Hundley) for one year of two bad contracts (Eric Karros and Mark Grudzielanek). The logical conclusion is that in 2003 they'll retrench and gear up for another run in 2004, right? Then, on the other hand, they sign Mike Remlinger to a multiyear deal—a guy who'll be 37 this year and has a much better chance of pitching well *this* year than he does *next* year. Remlinger's a fine pitcher, but it seems like the thing they like best about him is the fact that he *isn't* Kyle Farnsworth or Antonio Alfonseca.

John Smoltz   Born: 15-May-67   Age: 36   Bats: R   Throws: R

YEAR	TM	LG	AGE	G	GS	IP	H	BB	SO	HR	ERA	EQERA	EQH9	EQBB9	EQSO9	EQHR9	PERA	VORP	STF
2001	ATL	NL	34	36	5	59.0	53	10	57	7	3.36	3.71	8.8	1.5	7.6	1.0	3.39	11.2	13
2002	ATL	NL	35	75	0	80.3	59	24	85	4	3.25	3.37	7.5	2.4	8.5	0.5	2.66	17.9	18
2003	ATL	NL	36	59	0	73.7	59	22	75	6	2.80	2.99	7.3	2.3	8.1	0.7	2.91	20.0	16

Breakout: 27%   Improve: 70%   Collapse: 9%

The eight-run shellacking he absorbed in April tacked nearly a full run onto his season ERA. Understandably, his final mark of 3.25 doesn't do him justice. He pitched much better than that—brilliantly, in fact. His elbow never was a problem, and there were even rumblings that he wanted to return to the rotation at some point in the future. It's impossible to speculate over whether Smoltz really would want that, or whether the Braves would let him do it, or what would happen if they butted heads over it. All we can say is that he obviously is one of the best closers around, and is perfectly capable of remaining so for several more years.

Tim Spooneybarger   Born: 21-Oct-79   Age: 23   Bats: R   Throws: R

YEAR	TM	LG	AGE	G	GS	IP	H	BB	SO	HR	ERA	EQERA	EQH9	EQBB9	EQSO9	EQHR9	PERA	VORP	STF
2000	MYR	CRL	20	19	6	49.7	18	19	57	0	0.91	2.59	5.3	4.2	6.5	0.3	2.11	15.8	14
2001	GRN	SOU	21	15	0	21.0	20	4	24	1	5.14	5.08	10.2	2.0	6.9	0.7	4.13	0.7	12
2001	RIC	INT	21	42	0	50.7	33	21	58	1	0.71	1.90	6.6	4.4	8.1	0.2	2.85	19.6	20
2002	RIC	INT	22	18	0	20.0	13	8	21	1	0.90	1.92	6.5	4.3	8.0	0.7	2.93	7.7	16
2002	ATL	NL	22	51	0	51.3	38	26	33	4	2.63	3.53	7.6	4.1	5.2	0.7	3.43	10.5	-3
2003	FLO	NL	23	43	1	60.7	54	29	50	5	3.74	4.16	8.3	3.7	6.5	0.8	4.33	9.0	-1

Breakout: 11%   Improve: 41%   Collapse: 22%

Spooneybarger had a fine rookie year, and now will be thrown into the Marlins' closer mix, along with Braden Looper and Vladimir Nunez. None of the three is head-and-shoulders above the others, and Jeff Torborg's propensity to ride the hot hand should give pause to anyone who speculates on getting too many saves out of any one of them.

Adam Wainwright   Born: 30-Aug-81   Age: 21   Bats: R   Throws: R

YEAR	TM	LG	AGE	G	GS	IP	H	BB	SO	HR	ERA	EQERA	EQH9	EQBB9	EQSO9	EQHR9	PERA	VORP	STF
2000	DNV	APL	18	6	6	29.3	28	2	39	3	3.69	6.06	14.9	0.9	6.6	2.8	5.47	-1.8	13
2001	MCN	SAL	19	28	28	164.7	144	48	184	9	3.77	6.17	11.4	4.1	5.8	1.2	5.55	-12.2	9
2002	MYR	CRL	20	28	28	163.3	149	66	167	7	3.31	5.81	11.8	5.3	6.8	1.1	5.78	-5.5	14
2003	ATL	NL	21	18	13	77	79	42	65	8	4.70	5.02	9.4	4.3	6.7	0.9	5.21	5.0	5

Breakout: 9%   Improve: 58%   Collapse: 15%

Of all the Braves' young power arms, Wainwright is both the most dominant at present, and the most promising for the future. Not only does he throw in the low-90s consistently, he's also got three plus pitches, and he throws them for strikes. Now it's on to Double-A, and possibly the majors before the year's out. It seems only an injury could stop him; to paraphrase Waylon Jennings, someday the surgeons might get him but the bats never will.

Chicago Cubs

At long last, the nightmare is over. Willingly maneuvered into hiring Don Baylor in a dance that placed Baylor in Chicago and Davey Lopes in Milwaukee, the Cubs finally moved beyond the limp political correctness that got two bad managers hired and retained long beyond the point when they became liabilities. Rich in talent and armed with one of the game's biggest stars, on Baylor's three-plus-year watch the Cubs put up two seasons with wins in the sixties and profits in the tens of millions. The third season, 2001, was the high point, where they managed to blow an opportunity to win the division by dragging their feet on acquiring reinforcements and misdiagnosing what ailed the team. It was a lost opportunity in which Baylor had played an important part.

Managers have discretion in a few areas: pitching staff management, roster selection, and in-game tactics. It would be hard to identify what Baylor did well on any of those fronts during his term. On the pitching side of the ledger, Baylor had the rule of the roost after running off pitching coach Oscar Acosta in 2001. The pen basically imploded in 2002, falling from 12th-best in baseball in 2001 to the worst unit in the majors. Part of the problem was unsurprising: you're surprised when Flash Gordon breaks down? You can attribute the failures to Acosta's absence, or Baylor's incompetence, or chalk it up as just one of those things that just happens, but other managers have managed pens effectively through injuries and roster turnover. Left to his own devices, Baylor made as much of a hash of it as he had in 2000.

Roster selection was always a problem. Rather than make space for people with talent, Baylor would make bizarre low-yield, high-risk roster choices, favoring mediocre to awful veterans like Donovan Osborne or Jesus Sanchez. Who expects to contend with cast-offs like Delino DeShields or Darren Lewis or three catchers who can't play? Worse yet, the grating, almost resentful way Baylor treated almost every prospect

during his watch was astounding, as if there was something wrong with the hope hard-wired into being a baseball fan in general, or a Cubs fan in particular. Like the petty principal in *Ferris Buehler's Day Off*, Baylor seemed to live for the opportunity to put a dent in somebody's future.

Was he at least an inspirational leader? Baylor had stomped in claiming everything was going to change under his watch, from the Sosa retinue to the music in the clubhouse to the team's attitude to the brand of baseball that got played in Wrigley. Having issued his edicts while the cameras were on, he spent the next three years hiding in the manager's office or the interview room. Sometimes, you had to wonder if he was on the same continent as his players, who usually had to wait and see his complaints about them in print. That's a great way to get held in high esteem by guys on the beat, but it's a consistently lousy way to run a ball club.

Baylor's addiction to a fundamental, unimaginative, and uninspired brand of baseball was undoubtedly ideal in the tin-eared world of major league management today. Members of the media, especially the print media, will rarely criticize managers who operate conservatively. Bunting in a world populated by those "dull" big offenses seems popular with beat writers searching for proofs of their passion for puerile purism as some sort of equally dopey initiation rite. As he had for years, Baylor played to his audience: at the rate they were going with Baylor at the helm, the Cubs would have finished second in the NL in sacrifice bunts (behind les Expos), Baylor's lowest ranking in his three years as Cubs manager. Perhaps he was adapting to having a thunderstick in the lineup like Alex Gonzalez instead of Rickey Gutierrez and Eric Young, but he was still a bunting fool in a competitive environment that doesn't reward easily surrendered outs.

Having excused Baylor, the Cubs went whole hog for crazy, inviting Bruce Kimm to do his best Ditka impression

---

Cubs Prospectus

2002 record: 67–95; Fifth place, NL Central

Pythagenport Record: 75–87

Runs scored per game: 4.4 (11th in NL)

Runs allowed per game: 4.7 (11th in NL)

Team EqA: .261 (6th in NL)

2002 Batters Age: 30.9 (5th oldest in NL)

2002 Pitchers Age: 27.7 (4th youngest in NL)

Ballpark: Wrigley Field; Moderate pitchers' park; Park Factor of .955

2002: The youth movement didn't pay off, but enough things went wrong that they finally got to ditch Don Baylor.

2003: Will they let the youth movement pay off, or will Dusty get all Cubby and turn to the veteran mediocrities?

---

over the last three months. Kimm yammered about guts and determination and manliness and professionalism and letting the players play and the pitchers pitch and the sun rise and the moon set and that girl from Ipanema, and by the end of three months, you just wanted the constant cacophony to stop, so that maybe the Cubs could get back in the baseball business. Open mike night finally ended with the season, and Kimm was informed that sometimes "interim" means that tomorrow never comes.

The question that matters going forward is whether or not Baylor was a symptom or the disease. Itching to get back into contention, the Cubs looked at last year's failures, and have identified four big problems that needed fixing: the manager, the bullpen, the catchers, and offensive strikeouts.

Fixing the first was done effectively by the Cubs' decision to hire Dusty Baker. Baker may not be a stathead's idea of a tactical genius, but he is an effective communicator and a dominant clubhouse personality. As we discuss in the Giants' essay, he has a tremendous track record of getting good work out of veteran players in particular, and hitters in general. On a team with aging vets like Sammy Sosa, Moises Alou or even mediocre ones like Alex Gonzalez or Damian Miller, that's not an unimportant consideration. However, with guys like Eric Karros and Mark Grudzielanek now on board, it might be worth choosing discretion over faith in Dusty's abilities.

Moreover, Baker's handling of his pitching staffs shouldn't be a source of concern. His rotations usually roll along without breaking down, and since he's being handed the talented trio of Kerry Wood, Mark Prior, and Matt Clement, that's a very big deal. Supported by old Baker ace Shawn Estes as the token lefty, and backed by Carlos Zambrano or Juan Cruz in the fifth slot, that's one of the best rotations in the game. The Cubs should be able to look forward to some great match-ups against the Astros' Roy Oswalt, Wade Miller, and Carlos Hernandez with an almost unique sense of confidence that they can take that series, even if all of the games were pitching duels.

The one source of worry is whether or not Baker can really work with young players at the start of their careers. With the Giants, he favored veterans and generally had useful ones to work with. With the Cubs, he's going to control the destinies of Hee Choi, Corey Patterson, and Bobby Hill. All three should be in the lineup in 2003, but with Karros and Grudzielanek around, there will be a temptation to mix and match. Certainly, Baker successfully broke in Rich Aurilia, Marvin Benard, and Armando Rios while running a Giants team that was always flirting with contention. The only danger is that the Cubs are expected to contend right now, and while Choi, Patterson, and Hill all have the talent to be key players on a contender, Baker, GM Jim Hendry, and president Andy MacPhail might not have the patience to let them work

their way into that kind of importance if they struggle at any point in 2003.

The team's second problem was equally important to address. A worthwhile bullpen is something worth investing time, effort, and sometimes money to acquire and use. Unfortunately, they're borrowing the page from Ed Wade's playbook. Rather than learn something from the success they've had with guys like Todd Van Poppel or Joe Borowski, or just from watching the Angels' no-name pen do its part to win a World Series, the Cubs decided to throw a bunch of cash at Mike Remlinger and Dave Veres and Antonio Alfonseca. This is a time when most organizations are coming to terms with the idea that a bullpen is where you don't have to spend big money to get quality pitching. Rather than invest more time in scouting to dig up the next Van Poppel (and discard him before he gets expensive), the Cubs are lazily throwing money at the problem. Unfortunately, Veres and Alfonseca have never been particularly consistent or all that great, while Remlinger is young only if you're counting his age in Orosco years. Far more important will be getting Kyle Farnsworth back on track, but the Cubs seem to be giving up on him. Add in Borowski, a last-chancin' Rod Beck, and some lefty to be named later, and you've got a bullpen you could call professional, if falling well short of the Nasty Boys or last year's Angels.

The third problem was the team's catching situation. Joe Girardi's good citizenship was the team's only asset in shin-guards the last two years. Todd Hundley might have sparred with Baylor and might have profited from more consistent playing time, but nothing he did on a diamond inspired any reason to really believe that. Good guy antics aside, Girardi hasn't been a significant defensive asset, and offensively he was worthless. While Pudge Rodriguez's free agency offered one big ticket solution this winter, the Cubs have so far done the opposite of what they did to address their bullpen concerns, picking up an arbitration-eligible Damian Miller, and trading for Paul Bako. In case either get injured, they've signed Triple-A veteran Keith McDonald to start at Iowa; McDonald would have started for last year's team. You might argue that it would have made more sense to pool the money spent on relievers to sign Pudge, and then spend less to get some bullpen help, but the Cubs have acquired depth that should prevent them from enduring anything like the horror of the last two seasons.

The other "issue" shows how far some teams still have to go. See, the Cubs are fretting about strikeouts in general, and Mark Bellhorn's strikeouts in particular. Perhaps you can take the Baylor out of the Cubs, but you can't dig out the mentality that approved of his value system. Offensively, the Cubs led the league in home runs and were third in unintentional walks drawn, so it probably shouldn't be too surprising that they led the league in the third leg of the Three True

Outcomes, finishing first in strikeouts by almost 100. (It could have been worse, if only they had had to face their own power rotation.) Certainly, fixing some things, like replacing Hundley, will go far to help end this crisis. But it isn't like Sammy Sosa or Alex Gonzalez will stop striking out; it's in their natures. Swapping out Fred McGriff for Hee Choi shouldn't lower total strikeouts. Unfortunately, beyond obvious candidates like Hundley or Rosie Brown, the search for fewer strikeouts could end up targeting two players who need to play every day: Corey Patterson and Mark Bellhorn. Patterson has to improve across the board, but the only way he's going to improve is through repetition and playing time. Bellhorn was one of the team's few bright points on offense, so getting cranky with him because he's a Three True Outcomes hitter is equally self-defeating.

It's easy to get cranky about this sort of nit-natty stuff in the same way that you can get overly frustrated with Kenny Williams on the South Side. Like the White Sox, the Cubs organization has done an outstanding job of assembling talent. But where the White Sox don't seem to have done as well in their last couple of seasons, the Cubs have had outstanding drafts in each of the last two years. Beyond domestic player acquisition, they're both among the most aggressive and most successful franchises in baseball when it comes to

acquiring talent in the Far East, and they remain involved in the Caribbean. They're not perfect, but they scout the Midwest extensively, show a balanced appreciation for college and high school and foreign and domestic players, and don't shy away from expense when it comes to player development. As far as organizational philosophy, it's hard to see where they could improve. In terms of young pitching talent, the Cubs are more loaded than a New Orleans convention, and as far as young hitting, they've got the trio of Hill, Patterson, and Choi who should start, and third baseman Brendan Harris and (some infield or outfield corner to be named later) Dave Kelton looking good on the way up. Sammy Sosa's finest seasons may have been wasted, but there's a very good chance he'll get to spend his golden years getting help from some homegrown friends.

The Cubs can contend, starting now. They've made some bold moves, not all of them inspired, but all of them generally aimed at putting a team on the field that should support the team's core talent: that rotation and Sammy. The Astros and Cardinals aren't going to just roll up and go away, but by eliminating some of their old problems, the Cubs can look forward to 2003 and beyond knowing they've positioned themselves to contend.

HITTERS

Moises Alou LF Born: 03-Jul-66 Age: 37 Bats: R Throws: R

YEAR	TM	LG	AGE	AB	H	2B	3B	HR	BB	SO	SB	CS	AVG	OBP	SLG	MLVR	EQBA	EQOBP	EQSLG	EQMLVR	VORP	DEFENSE			
2000	HOU	NL	34	454	161	28	2	30	52	45	3	3	.355	.423	.623	.468	.346	.408	.610	.435	62.4	99-RF	-5		
2001	HOU	NL	35	513	170	31	1	27	57	57	5	1	.331	.401	.554	.322	.329	.397	.550	.311	55.4	108-RF	0		
2002	CHC	NL	36	484	133	23	1	15	47	61	8	0	.275	.339	.419	.058	.287	.345	.444	.029	15.0	111-LF	0		
2003	*CHC*	*NL*	*36*	*386*	*110*	*21*	*1*	*13*	*41*	*47*	*4*	*1*	*.285*	*.354*	*.447*	*.064*	*.293*	*.357*	*.469*	*.087*	*12.1*				

Breakout: 10%   Improve: 35%   Collapse: 19%

What do you think is more remarkable, that Alou was terribly disappointing, or that as a guy who's going to turn 37 this year, there might only be less than a one-in-five chance that he craters? The Cubs like to note his slow start in April and May, but you're still talking about a left fielder that hit only 13 home runs over the season's last four months. His projection seems about right.

Mark Bellhorn UT Born: 23-Aug-74 Age: 28 Bats: B Throws: R

YEAR	TM	LG	AGE	AB	H	2B	3B	HR	BB	SO	SB	CS	AVG	OBP	SLG	MLVR	EQBA	EQOBP	EQSLG	EQMLVR	VORP	DEFENSE			
2000	SAC	PCL	25	436	116	17	11	24	94	121	20	5	.266	.402	.521	.202	.233	.352	.453	.009	22.7	90-3B	-5	10-2B	3
2001	SAC	PCL	26	156	42	6	0	12	22	60	3	0	.269	.374	.538	.197	.236	.332	.471	-.000	3.6	14-OF	-1	16-2B	4
2001	OAK	AL	26	74	10	1	2	1	7	37	0	0	.135	.210	.243	-.546	.149	.222	.284	-.518	-7.2				
2002	CHC	NL	27	445	115	24	4	27	76	144	7	5	.258	.374	.512	.221	.272	.380	.544	.214	53.7	63-2B	3	24-3B	-5
2003	*CHC*	*NL*	*28*	*355*	*85*	*17*	*3*	*18*	*59*	*111*	*6*	*5*	*.240*	*.353*	*.457*	*.041*	*.247*	*.356*	*.480*	*.060*	*18.4*				

Breakout: 17%   Improve: 49%   Collapse: 21%

Now that was fun! Skip the Tony Phillips comparisons, he *is* Tony Phillips, back from an exotic Swedish race change operation. Nobody envisioned that kind of power spike, but we've been hoping Bellhorn would get 500 at-bats for a while, and he didn't disappoint. The shame of it is that the Cubs seem determined to stick Bellhorn in the role Billy Beane originally envisioned for

Mark Bellhorn (continued)

him, using him as a multi-positional rover, instead of letting him fix their third base problem. If they had a third baseman, it would be understandable, but they don't. They don't even have somebody as good as Steve Buechele or Keith Moreland as an alternative. They've got Kevin Orie, Mark Grudzielanek, and Ramon Martinez. If Bellhorn loses a start to any of those people, it's a mistake.

Roosevelt Brown — LF — Born: 03-Aug-75 — Age: 27 — Bats: L — Throws: R

YEAR	TM	LG	AGE	AB	H	2B	3B	HR	BB	SO	SB	CS	AVG	OBP	SLG	MLVR	EQBA	EQOBP	EQSLG	EQMLVR	VORP	DEFENSE	
2000	IOW	PCL	24	363	112	32	0	12	37	60	10	3	.309	.383	.496	.181	.271	.333	.438	-.015	6.0	86-RF -7	
2000	CHC	NL	24	91	32	8	0	3	4	22	0	1	.352	.385	.538	.294	.348	.368	.543	.278	8.5	20-LF 0	
2001	IOW	PCL	25	364	126	34	1	22	14	67	3	5	.346	.383	.626	.436	.307	.344	.546	.195	26.7	75-LF 0	
2001	CHC	NL	25	83	22	6	1	4	7	12	0	0	.265	.330	.506	.086	.274	.336	.512	.098	4.3	12-LF -1	
2002	CHC	NL	26	204	43	12	0	3	23	50	2	2	.211	.300	.314	-.191	.226	.308	.337	-.234	-7.9	43-LF -3	
2003	*CHC*	*NL*	*27*	*205*	*53*	*12*	*1*	*7*	*17*	*42*	*3*	*2*	*.261*	*.323*	*.429*	*-.028*	*.269*	*.326*	*.450*	*-.011*	*1.6*		

Breakout: 18%   Improve: 41%   Collapse: 30%

Already sold off to Japan, and replaced with Troy O'Leary. O'Leary has none of Brown's potential as an offensive asset as a semi-regular, but he will almost certainly be more comfortable with the job of backing up Alou and pinch-hitting in a way that Brown clearly was not. A year in Japan, and Brown will be ready to be a Royal.

Hee Choi — 1B — Born: 16-Mar-79 — Age: 24 — Bats: L — Throws: L

YEAR	TM	LG	AGE	AB	H	2B	3B	HR	BB	SO	SB	CS	AVG	OBP	SLG	MLVR	EQBA	EQOBP	EQSLG	EQMLVR	VORP	DEFENSE	
2000	DAY	FSL	21	345	102	25	6	15	37	78	4	1	.296	.374	.533	.292	.234	.295	.426	-.131	-3.1	83-1B -1	
2000	WTN	SOU	21	122	37	9	0	10	25	38	3	1	.303	.422	.623	.498	.258	.358	.531	.146	9.0	35-1B 3	
2001	IOW	PCL	22	266	61	11	0	13	34	67	5	1	.229	.317	.417	-.102	.205	.288	.369	-.243	-11.0	68-1B 4	
2002	IOW	PCL	23	478	137	24	3	26	95	119	3	2	.287	.411	.513	.271	.257	.370	.457	.066	21.9	127-1B -10	
2002	CHC	NL	23	50	9	1	0	2	7	15	0	0	.180	.281	.320	-.234	.196	.293	.353	-.260	-2.2	14-1B -1	
2003	*CHC*	*NL*	*24*	*235*	*58*	*11*	*1*	*11*	*34*	*59*	*3*	*3*	*.249*	*.348*	*.444*	*.022*	*.256*	*.351*	*.466*	*.041*	*5.3*		

Breakout: 37%   Improve: 64%   Collapse: 16%

What would you have if you had Nick Johnson without as many annoying injuries? Choi's power potential is daunting. There's a bit of chauvinism about him, with whispers he can't handle inside pitches (he does), or might be soft (he isn't). He's shortened his swing, but as you can see, it didn't lead to more contact, less power, or fewer strikeouts; it was intended to squelch the complaints about hitting the inside pitch. Although Karros is here to caddy or platoon for him, Choi manhandled lefties in the PCL, slugging almost .550 against them vs. .501 against right-handers. He's as ready to take over at first as he's ever going to be, and should be primed for a nice six-year run.

Kevin Collins — 1B — Born: 06-May-81 — Age: 22 — Bats: L — Throws: L

YEAR	TM	LG	AGE	AB	H	2B	3B	HR	BB	SO	SB	CS	AVG	OBP	SLG	MLVR	EQBA	EQOBP	EQSLG	EQMLVR	VORP	DEFENSE
2002	BOI	NWN	21	187	64	18	2	13	14	52	0	2	.342	.403	.668	.598	.249	.288	.472	-.066	1.4	23-1B -2
2003	*CHC*	*NL*	*22*	*172*	*41*	*9*	*1*	*6*	*12*	*56*	*1*	*3*	*.238*	*.297*	*.418*	*-.101*	*.245*	*.300*	*.439*	*-.089*	*-2.6*	

Breakout: 21%   Improve: 49%   Collapse: 29%

This wasn't really Collins's professional debut: he was a Florida high schooler drafted in 1999, and spent the next two seasons on the Cubs' Arizona complex team. He led the Northwest League in slugging and average. The Cubs have a bunch of college hitters at first above him in the chain, and 2002 draftee Brian Dopirak behind him, so Collins will have to push if he doesn't want to spend a year of his life in the Midwest League.

Jason Dubois — RF — Born: 26-Mar-79 — Age: 24 — Bats: R — Throws: R

YEAR	TM	LG	AGE	AB	H	2B	3B	HR	BB	SO	SB	CS	AVG	OBP	SLG	MLVR	EQBA	EQOBP	EQSLG	EQMLVR	VORP	DEFENSE	
2001	LNS	MDW	22	443	131	28	9	24	46	120	1	2	.296	.380	.562	.334	.222	.283	.412	-.182	-12.1	85-RF -8	13-1B -4
2002	DAY	FSL	23	361	116	25	1	20	57	95	6	2	.321	.426	.562	.437	.256	.339	.451	.002	7.7	83-RF -6	
2003	*TOR*	*AL*	*24*	*187*	*48*	*10*	*2*	*7*	*19*	*52*	*2*	*3*	*.254*	*.329*	*.437*	*.008*	*.257*	*.335*	*.448*	*-.008*	*0.0*		

Breakout: 26%   Improve: 55%   Collapse: 19%

A college hitting star at Virginia Commonwealth drafted in 2000, Dubois was an organizational player in the making with a Cubs organization that was never really not that curious about whether his bat is for real; see, he's not a "National League" player because all he does is hit. He also missed two months with a broken wrist in the middle of the season. He was rescued by the Blue Jays in the third round of the Rule 5 draft, a thoughtful selection considering their need for outfielders. It beats kicking Pedro Swann around, and the wrist creates a handy excuse to have him spend extended time on the DL and rehabbing.

Angel Echevarria								**RF**			**Born: 25-May-71**			**Age: 32**		**Bats: R**		**Throws: R**		
YEAR	TM	LG	AGE	AB	H	2B	3B	HR	BB	SO	SB	CS	AVG	OBP	SLG	MLVR	EQBA	EQOBP	EQSLG	EQMLVR	VORP		DEFENSE
2000	CSP	PCL	29	284	95	23	2	7	26	44	1	1	.335	.400	.504	.193	.279	.333	.424	-.028	3.5		50-RF 0 13-1B -2
2001	MIL	NL	30	133	34	11	0	5	8	29	0	1	.256	.313	.451	-.031	.259	.312	.459	-.033	2.0		16-LF -2
2002	IOW	PCL	31	217	64	12	3	13	17	48	0	0	.295	.357	.558	.255	.266	.320	.495	.038	6.3		49-RF 1
2002	CHC	NL	31	98	30	7	0	3	8	17	0	0	.306	.364	.469	.194	.320	.375	.490	.179	6.5		18-RF 0
2003	*CHC*	*NL*	*32*	*177*	*46*	*10*	*1*	*6*	*15*	*35*	*1*	*1*	*.263*	*.324*	*.435*	*-.016*	*.270*	*.328*	*.457*	*.001*	*1.1*		

Breakout: 21%   Improve: 47%   Collapse: 26%

Called up in late June to be reunited with his old manager, which lasted all of two weeks. He'd make a good spare part on a team like the Angels or Cardinals, spot-starting against lefties and pinch-hitting, but he's joining Rosie Brown as a Nippon Ham Fighter.

Nate Frese											**Born: 10-Jul-77**			**Age: 25**		**Bats: R**		**Throws: R**		
YEAR	TM	LG	AGE	AB	H	2B	3B	HR	BB	SO	SB	CS	AVG	OBP	SLG	MLVR	EQBA	EQOBP	EQSLG	EQMLVR	VORP	DEFENSE
2000	DAY	FSL	22	425	126	24	5	7	64	84	10	6	.296	.396	.426	.182	.237	.318	.348	-.193	2.9	107-SS 26
2001	WTN	SOU	23	233	42	5	1	4	38	62	0	1	.180	.308	.262	-.239	.169	.268	.248	-.462	-16.6	69-SS 6
2002	WTN	SOU	24	230	52	10	1	2	23	59	4	3	.226	.302	.304	-.148	.208	.261	.288	-.405	-11.1	60-SS -1

Frese is something of an organizational favorite, since he's a converted pitcher who can throw the leather at short. However, Frese has not passed the Double-A test, and deserves comparisons to the White Sox's Jason Dellaero, another shortstop who can't hit but might be able to pitch and field. Who says your 11th or 12th pitcher only has to pitch mop-up?

Joe Girardi								**C**			**Born: 14-Oct-64**			**Age: 38**		**Bats: R**		**Throws: R**		
YEAR	TM	LG	AGE	AB	H	2B	3B	HR	BB	SO	SB	CS	AVG	OBP	SLG	MLVR	EQBA	EQOBP	EQSLG	EQMLVR	VORP	DEFENSE
2000	CHC	NL	35	363	101	15	1	6	32	61	1	0	.278	.342	.375	-.105	.279	.333	.377	-.095	13.5	96-C 3
2001	CHC	NL	36	229	58	10	1	3	21	50	0	1	.253	.316	.345	-.171	.259	.320	.353	-.168	4.3	60-C 4
2002	CHC	NL	37	234	53	10	1	1	16	35	1	0	.226	.276	.291	-.258	.244	.289	.311	-.297	-3.7	67-C -2
2003	*STL*	*NL*	*38*	*134*	*29*	*5*	*1*	*1*	*11*	*22*	*1*	*1*	*.216*	*.275*	*.289*	*-.324*	*.221*	*.277*	*.301*	*-.329*	*-5.6*	

Breakout: 6%   Improve: 18%   Collapse: 43%

If all dogs go to heaven, all weak-hitting paesano backstops go to St. Louis to die. Girardi's as nice a guy as they come, but he's the antithesis of the kind of backup Mike Matheny needs. He's so done, they'll have to bury him with the fork.

Jeff Goldbach								**C**			**Born: 20-Dec-79**			**Age: 23**		**Bats: R**		**Throws: R**		
YEAR	TM	LG	AGE	AB	H	2B	3B	HR	BB	SO	SB	CS	AVG	OBP	SLG	MLVR	EQBA	EQOBP	EQSLG	EQMLVR	VORP	DEFENSE
2000	DAY	FSL	20	420	84	15	1	10	31	76	6	5	.200	.268	.312	-.223	.165	.213	.261	-.561	-34.7	95-C -15
2001	DAY	FSL	21	145	28	5	1	4	15	28	0	0	.193	.278	.324	-.162	.168	.225	.282	-.506	-10.6	27-C -4
2001	WTN	SOU	21	98	20	4	1	3	9	17	1	0	.204	.278	.357	-.159	.190	.247	.320	-.399	-4.4	26-C -6
2002	DAY	FSL	22	272	71	17	0	11	30	43	0	0	.261	.343	.445	.131	.218	.279	.371	-.249	-1.0	31-C -10
2003	*CHC*	*NL*	*23*	*175*	*40*	*7*	*1*	*5*	*16*	*35*	*2*	*1*	*.228*	*.296*	*.365*	*-.181*	*.234*	*.299*	*.383*	*-.173*	*-.2*	

Breakout: 62%   Improve: 78%   Collapse: 17%

Far-removed from a golden 1999 in the Midwest League, Goldbach is finally hitting again, but his catching skills have seriously deteriorated. He's young enough that he could still make it, the way Tyler Houston or Derk Parks did, or hang on as a first baseman who catches once in a while, like Alan Zinter.

Alex Gonzalez								**SS**			**Born: 08-Apr-73**			**Age: 30**		**Bats: R**		**Throws: R**		
YEAR	TM	LG	AGE	AB	H	2B	3B	HR	BB	SO	SB	CS	AVG	OBP	SLG	MLVR	EQBA	EQOBP	EQSLG	EQMLVR	VORP	DEFENSE
2000	TOR	AL	27	527	133	31	2	15	43	113	4	4	.252	.314	.404	-.148	.258	.312	.417	-.093	16.3	137-SS -8
2001	TOR	AL	28	636	161	25	5	17	43	149	18	11	.253	.308	.388	-.113	.267	.322	.412	-.075	22.9	151-SS 22
2002	CHC	NL	29	513	127	27	5	18	46	136	5	3	.248	.313	.425	.001	.258	.319	.449	-.035	24.5	139-SS -10
2003	*CHC*	*NL*	*30*	*484*	*119*	*24*	*3*	*14*	*42*	*119*	*7*	*5*	*.245*	*.310*	*.396*	*-.105*	*.252*	*.313*	*.415*	*-.092*	*8.4*	

Breakout: 15%   Improve: 49%   Collapse: 14%

Alex Gonzalez *(continued)*

The Alex Gonzalez Sweepstakes are still waiting for their first winner not named Alex Gonzalez. Gord Ash played, paid, and lost, and the Cubs found out why. Gonzalez is thoroughly adequate, but he always gives you little hints of hope and mystery. This year, he plugged five home runs in the final month, and some people think that means he's going to finally break out. Don't hold your breath; like the Cubs, at the end of the day, you need to realize that if you have Gonzalez, you settled.

Ryan Gripp 3B Born: 20-Apr-78 Age: 25 Bats: R Throws: R

YEAR	TM	LG	AGE	AB	H	2B	3B	HR	BB	SO	SB	CS	AVG	OBP	SLG	MLVR	EQBA	EQOBP	EQSLG	EQMLVR	VORP	DEFENSE	
2000	LNS	MDW	22	498	166	36	0	20	68	86	4	0	.333	.419	.526	.389	.250	.313	.399	-.123	8.7	121-3B	1
2001	DAY	FSL	23	241	71	19	0	5	27	57	6	5	.295	.382	.436	.195	.243	.305	.364	-.192	-.2	60-3B	-4
2001	WTN	SOU	23	255	58	19	0	8	25	60	2	0	.227	.314	.396	-.034	.206	.270	.363	-.285	-6.8	62-3B	-8
2002	WTN	SOU	24	380	88	24	2	10	46	85	4	2	.232	.323	.384	-.008	.210	.276	.355	-.282	-9.4	82-3B	1
2003	MIL	NL	25	152	37	8	1	5	14	33	2	2	.246	.314	.404	-.086	.251	.316	.420	-.083	1.9		

Breakout: 49%   Improve: 73%   Collapse: 15%

Gripp was sort of a Hendry guy, in that he was a Creighton product. He played some outfield and first in the AFL, although there was little explanation as to why he got assigned there. Since clobbering the Midwest League as a man among boys in 2000, he's made no real progress at the plate. His glovework at third has improved slightly, and since he's been dealt to the Brewers (for Paul Bako), he might surface somehow.

Brendan Harris 3B Born: 26-Aug-80 Age: 22 Bats: R Throws: R

YEAR	TM	LG	AGE	AB	H	2B	3B	HR	BB	SO	SB	CS	AVG	OBP	SLG	MLVR	EQBA	EQOBP	EQSLG	EQMLVR	VORP	DEFENSE			
2001	LNS	MDW	20	113	31	5	1	4	17	26	5	1	.274	.379	.442	.162	.207	.291	.328	-.291	-2.3	11-2B	5		
2002	DAY	FSL	21	425	140	35	6	13	43	57	16	4	.329	.396	.532	.372	.265	.317	.432	-.057	14.6	59-3B	1	54-2B	2
2002	WTN	SOU	21	53	17	4	1	2	2	5	1	1	.321	.345	.547	.328	.278	.291	.481	-.021	1.5				
2003	CHC	NL	22	220	57	13	2	7	20	39	4	3	.261	.326	.428	-.025	.268	.329	.449	-.008	7.1				

Breakout: 41%   Improve: 66%   Collapse: 14%

Ballplayer. He's not devoid of tools, he just has the ones that matter: he fields what he reaches, and he's a complete hitter. Having played some second and some short, now that the Cubs have settled on playing him in at third, he has the opportunity to move up quickly. He's tightly wound to the point that he had a red-ass rep before he turned 21.

Chad Hermansen CF Born: 10-Sep-77 Age: 25 Bats: R Throws: R

YEAR	TM	LG	AGE	AB	H	2B	3B	HR	BB	SO	SB	CS	AVG	OBP	SLG	MLVR	EQBA	EQOBP	EQSLG	EQMLVR	VORP	DEFENSE	
2000	NAS	PCL	22	294	66	12	1	11	25	89	16	4	.224	.305	.384	-.190	.206	.267	.351	-.308	-17.1	73-OF	-3
2000	PIT	NL	22	108	20	4	1	2	6	37	0	0	.185	.228	.296	-.514	.183	.212	.303	-.496	-8.8	22-CF	-1
2001	NAS	PCL	23	447	110	22	6	17	41	154	22	5	.246	.316	.436	-.051	.224	.290	.393	-.193	-13.0	113-OF	-2
2002	NAS	PCL	24	56	11	2	0	4	8	23	1	0	.196	.318	.446	-.035	.193	.295	.404	-.190	-.2	13-CF	-1
2002	PIT	NL	24	194	40	11	1	7	17	68	7	5	.206	.274	.381	-.169	.209	.272	.393	-.238	-3.1	50-CF	0
2002	CHC	NL	24	43	9	3	0	1	5	14	0	0	.209	.292	.349	-.162	.227	.306	.364	-.201	-1.3	11-OF	-3
2003	LAD	NL	25	180	41	9	1	7	17	56	6	6	.225	.297	.404	-.130	.237	.305	.435	-.093	-.7		

Breakout: 47%   Improve: 71%   Collapse: 11%

What do you do with Hermansen? He kills fastballs, but from the bench he goes stale faster than an open bag of chips, so he's not cut out for the pinch-hitting duties a reserve outfielder is supposed to handle. He can play center and give you some pop, but there seems to be a preference for lower-wattage hitters like Tsuyoshi Shinjo, who seem so athletic they must be bringing you other bits of little goodness. Spliced into Jim Tracy's platoons, he has a chance to be an asset as a part-time player.

Bobby Hill 2B Born: 03-Apr-78 Age: 25 Bats: B Throws: R

YEAR	TM	LG	AGE	AB	H	2B	3B	HR	BB	SO	SB	CS	AVG	OBP	SLG	MLVR	EQBA	EQOBP	EQSLG	EQMLVR	VORP	DEFENSE	
2000	NWK	ATL	22	394	120	16	6	11	90	49	66	9	.305	.437	.459	.237	.253	.363	.379	-.053	.7		
2001	WTN	SOU	23	209	63	8	1	3	32	39	20	8	.301	.399	.392	.151	.263	.345	.346	-.126	5.4	49-2B	-6
2002	IOW	PCL	24	354	99	23	3	8	49	66	29	5	.280	.384	.429	.110	.257	.347	.394	-.061	14.6	88-2B	0
2002	CHC	NL	24	190	48	7	2	4	17	42	6	1	.253	.327	.374	-.040	.268	.335	.397	-.071	7.2	45-2B	0
2003	CHC	NL	25	323	83	16	3	7	39	62	11	6	.256	.340	.387	-.059	.263	.343	.406	-.044	9.9		

Breakout: 23%   Improve: 46%   Collapse: 23%

Another victim of Baylor's ability to blow hot and cold and go planless. Despite a great spring training, Baylor wouldn't keep him, preferring Delino DeShields. Hill got a shot in May, but he slumped and Baylor soured. With the Cubs already 10 games out, they could have ridden it out, but Mueller was back and Bellhorn hitting, so good future or no, Hill went back down. For a guy who worked through the Boras holdout ploy, Hill is already getting high marks for being a gamer, with particular accolades going to his glovework and his willingness to hang tough on the deuce. He's old to really fulfill a Knoblauch comparison, but he does all of the things Knoblauch could do in his prime.

Todd Hundley   C   Born: 27-May-69   Age: 34   Bats: B   Throws: R

YEAR	TM	LG	AGE	AB	H	2B	3B	HR	BB	SO	SB	CS	AVG	OBP	SLG	MLVR	EQBA	EQOBP	EQSLG	EQMLVR	VORP	DEFENSE
2000	LAD	NL	31	299	85	16	0	24	45	69	0	1	.284	.382	.579	.290	.289	.377	.592	.292	45.2	77-C -11
2001	CHC	NL	32	246	46	10	0	12	25	89	0	0	.187	.270	.374	-.263	.193	.273	.386	-.256	-1.5	63-C -8
2002	CHC	NL	33	266	56	8	0	16	32	80	0	0	.211	.302	.421	-.049	.221	.307	.450	-.086	10.6	71-C -8
2003	*LAD*	*NL*	*34*	*199*	*45*	*8*	*0*	*10*	*25*	*56*	*0*	*1*	*.225*	*.317*	*.419*	*-.077*	*.236*	*.325*	*.451*	*-.038*	*6.9*	

Breakout: 37%   Improve: 77%   Collapse: 11%

There are all sorts of explanations, some of them printable, for why Hundley was even worse as a Cub than anyone had any right to expect. Certainly an unsympathetic manager didn't help, so Hundley had a hard time getting regular playing time, but some of the issues go beyond anything a manager is supposed to fix. Theoretically, getting away from a day baseball routine and back to L.A. could help Hundley get focused and productive.

Nic Jackson   Born: 25-Sep-79   Age: 23   Bats: L   Throws: R

YEAR	TM	LG	AGE	AB	H	2B	3B	HR	BB	SO	SB	CS	AVG	OBP	SLG	MLVR	EQBA	EQOBP	EQSLG	EQMLVR	VORP	DEFENSE
2000	EUG	NWN	20	294	75	12	7	6	22	64	25	3	.255	.309	.405	.053	.202	.229	.321	-.427	-25.6	73-RF -5
2001	DAY	FSL	21	503	149	30	6	19	39	96	24	10	.296	.359	.493	.242	.242	.284	.409	-.169	1.3	129-CF -7
2002	WTN	SOU	22	131	38	9	1	3	6	23	8	2	.290	.331	.443	.129	.263	.285	.406	-.155	.8	27-CF -4
2003	*CHN*	*NL*	*23*	*167*	*41*	*8*	*1*	*4*	*12*	*35*	*4*	*2*	*.245*	*.302*	*.383*	*-.135*	*.252*	*.305*	*.402*	*-.124*	*-0.9*	

Breakout: 27%   Improve: 57%   Collapse: 20%

Jackson hurt himself twice on foul balls, driving one into his shin and another into his foot, which derailed his entire season. He's running okay in the Mexican winter league. He's got a machine-tooled physique, and gets good marks for his aptitude and coachability. The Cubs think he can handle center, but the rap is that his arm is weak for the position. But if he's healthy and has a good camp, those persistent Corey Patterson trade rumors might get less implausible.

Dave Kelton   1B, 3B or LF   Born: 17-Dec-79   Age: 23   Bats: R   Throws: R

YEAR	TM	LG	AGE	AB	H	2B	3B	HR	BB	SO	SB	CS	AVG	OBP	SLG	MLVR	EQBA	EQOBP	EQSLG	EQMLVR	VORP	DEFENSE
2000	DAY	FSL	20	523	140	30	7	18	38	120	7	8	.268	.320	.455	.089	.214	.254	.367	-.306	-15.5	96-3B -17
2001	WTN	SOU	21	224	70	9	4	12	24	55	1	3	.313	.382	.549	.346	.268	.325	.468	.011	12.4	50-3B -9
2002	WTN	SOU	22	498	130	28	6	20	52	129	12	6	.261	.333	.462	.133	.231	.283	.417	-.168	-9.3	120-1B -8
2003	*CHC*	*NL*	*23*	*189*	*48*	*9*	*1*	*7*	*19*	*48*	*4*	*3*	*.253*	*.326*	*.432*	*-.026*	*.260*	*.329*	*.453*	*-.009*	*2.3*	

Breakout: 45%   Improve: 71%   Collapse: 10%

The Cubs keep hedging, wondering if they could get Kelton to hit and play third adequately at the same time. He's playing third in Mexico this winter, so they're still not giving up on it just yet. He's coming off of a year where he was named the best hitting prospect in the Southern League. With Brendan Harris scrambling up the chain, Kelton's position will have to be chosen this spring, after which he'll be able to settle into mashing, the thing he'll do more and more if his discipline continues to improve. He won't be the next Konerko, but he could be Alou's eventual replacement.

Yoon-Min Kweon   Born: 22-Jan-79   Age: 24   Bats: R   Throws: R

YEAR	TM	LG	AGE	AB	H	2B	3B	HR	BB	SO	SB	CS	AVG	OBP	SLG	MLVR	EQBA	EQOBP	EQSLG	EQMLVR	VORP	DEFENSE
2000	EUG	NWN	21	145	37	9	1	5	22	29	5	3	.255	.372	.434	.174	.192	.269	.325	-.347	-4.3	39-C 3
2001	LNS	MDW	22	326	88	15	1	6	15	44	0	0	.270	.312	.377	-.025	.204	.235	.287	-.462	-18.1	81-C 3
2002	DAY	FSL	23	300	66	11	0	5	23	34	1	4	.220	.289	.307	-.149	.186	.233	.264	-.506	-20.8	69-C 2

We're happy to tout Leon Lee's Asian recruiting successes, but so far, Kweon has to be counted as one of the failures. He's a nimble receiver, but he was flattened by the Florida State League after a mediocre year in the Midwest League.

Fred McGriff   1B   Born: 31-Oct-63   Age: 39   Bats: L   Throws: L

YEAR	TM	LG	AGE	AB	H	2B	3B	HR	BB	SO	SB	CS	AVG	OBP	SLG	MLVR	EQBA	EQOBP	EQSLG	EQMLVR	VORP	DEFENSE	
2000	TBY	AL	36	566	157	18	0	27	91	120	2	0	.277	.377	.452	.065	.286	.379	.469	.123	33.6	142-1B	-8
2001	TBY	AL	37	343	109	18	0	19	40	69	1	1	.318	.389	.536	.290	.336	.408	.571	.366	43.1	73-1B	-4
2001	CHC	NL	37	170	48	7	2	12	26	37	0	1	.282	.387	.559	.271	.289	.389	.566	.276	18.9	46-1B	-3
2002	CHC	NL	38	523	143	27	2	30	63	99	1	2	.273	.356	.505	.198	.282	.359	.529	.168	37.3	127-1B	-10
2003	LAD	NL	39	387	99	18	1	19	50	83	1	1	.256	.344	.455	.036	.269	.353	.489	.085	13.2		

Breakout: 11%   Improve: 42%   Collapse: 8%

McGriff is perceived as consistent, but the 30 home runs can mask a lot. The dip in his OBP isn't a good sign, his defense has regressed to statuesque, and who else treats running down the line as optional and doesn't catch flak for it? He's not a menace, but he's workmanlike, in both the positive "does his job" sense of the word, and its damning-with-faint-praise meaning. For the Dodgers, he's an improvement on Karros, but so's Sealboy from your local freak show. McGriff is an improvement, but not as much as you might think.

Jackson Melian   RF   Born: 07-Jan-80   Age: 23   Bats: R   Throws: R

YEAR	TM	LG	AGE	AB	H	2B	3B	HR	BB	SO	SB	CS	AVG	OBP	SLG	MLVR	EQBA	EQOBP	EQSLG	EQMLVR	VORP	DEFENSE	
2000	NRW	EAS	20	290	73	8	4	9	18	69	17	1	.252	.302	.400	-.041	.228	.262	.367	-.281	-7.4	78-CF	-5
2001	CHT	SOU	21	426	101	22	0	16	36	95	10	7	.237	.311	.401	-.036	.207	.264	.353	-.310	-25.8	109-OF	-13
2002	HUN	SOU	22	184	41	6	1	6	35	63	10	3	.223	.367	.364	.026	.204	.312	.340	-.235	-8.4	53-RF	-1
2002	WTN	SOU	22	234	72	17	0	4	17	62	10	6	.308	.379	.432	.196	.276	.323	.393	-.093	-1.0	56-RF	-3
2003	CHC	NL	23	186	45	8	1	6	18	50	5	4	.241	.315	.396	-.099	.248	.318	.416	-.087	-3.1		

Breakout: 52%   Improve: 71%   Collapse: 14%

Melian has been labeled a failure, but he's still listed as 23 and has considerable Double-A experience, so he's still a fringe prospect and not Mario Encarnacion. Although previous employers have complained about his work habits, the Cubs think he's coachable, and at different points he's shown power, patience, and the ability to hit for average.

Luis Montanez   SS   Born: 15-Dec-81   Age: 21   Bats: R   Throws: R

YEAR	TM	LG	AGE	AB	H	2B	3B	HR	BB	SO	SB	CS	AVG	OBP	SLG	MLVR	EQBA	EQOBP	EQSLG	EQMLVR	VORP	DEFENSE			
2001	LNS	MDW	19	499	127	33	6	5	34	121	20	7	.255	.317	.375	-.031	.196	.239	.291	-.452	-29.1	112-SS	-20		
2002	DAY	FSL	20	487	129	21	5	4	44	89	14	8	.265	.337	.353	.008	.222	.275	.301	-.352	-16.8	97-SS	-29	21-2B	-1
2003	CHC	NL	21	205	47	9	2	3	16	47	3	4	.228	.290	.331	-.236	.235	.293	.347	-.231	-4.1				

Breakout: 56%   Improve: 75%   Collapse: 10%

Montanez is generally considered the franchise's shortstop of the future. He's athletic, and offensively there's little he doesn't do. Unfortunately, although the Cubs thought he'd be fine at short, 23 errors in his first 50 games in 2002 had to create some concern. The time at second base is not supposed to mean he's done at short. Gonzalez is under contract through 2004, by which time Montanez will have survived the jump to Double-A or not, and the Cubs will know whether they've grown a very Gonzalez-like player on the farm.

Augie Ojeda   SS   Born: 20-Dec-74   Age: 28   Bats: B   Throws: R

YEAR	TM	LG	AGE	AB	H	2B	3B	HR	BB	SO	SB	CS	AVG	OBP	SLG	MLVR	EQBA	EQOBP	EQSLG	EQMLVR	VORP	DEFENSE			
2000	IOW	PCL	25	396	111	23	2	8	33	27	16	6	.280	.346	.409	-.042	.251	.302	.367	-.188	3.2	99-SS	5		
2000	CHC	NL	25	77	17	3	1	2	10	9	0	1	.221	.310	.364	-.223	.218	.299	.359	-.227	-.2	21-SS	3		
2001	CHC	NL	26	144	29	5	1	1	12	20	1	0	.201	.272	.271	-.389	.212	.279	.281	-.376	-7.6	20-3B	-1	24-SS	-3
2002	CHC	NL	27	70	13	4	0	0	5	5	1	0	.186	.250	.243	-.388	.197	.258	.268	-.444	-4.1	14-SS	1		
2002	IOW	PCL	27	291	67	20	4	1	31	30	5	3	.230	.323	.337	-.160	.208	.289	.307	-.323	-7.9	68-SS	4		
2003	CHC	NL	28	205	49	10	1	3	22	25	3	2	.237	.315	.339	-.174	.244	.318	.356	-.166	-.5				

Breakout: 45%   Improve: 66%   Collapse: 15%

With Grudzielanek and Ramon Martinez in the fold, and Bobby Hill awaiting Dusty Baker's judgment, Ojeda's pretty well walled off from the big leagues as a Cub. He can bunt and run a little, and he's a sweet fielder. If Luis Lopez and Miguel Cairo can hang around, so can he.

Kevin Orie   3B   Born: 01-Sep-72   Age: 30   Bats: R   Throws: R

YEAR	TM	LG	AGE	AB	H	2B	3B	HR	BB	SO	SB	CS	AVG	OBP	SLG	MLVR	EQBA	EQOBP	EQSLG	EQMLVR	VORP	DEFENSE
2000	OMA	PCL	27	175	49	11	2	5	28	24	3	3	.280	.394	.451	.109	.246	.342	.400	-.070	5.7	52-3B -3
2000	COH	INT	27	149	43	13	0	4	12	28	1	0	.289	.354	.456	.099	.267	.318	.427	-.061	4.9	38-3B 0
2001	SWB	INT	28	509	149	34	2	13	77	63	11	6	.293	.395	.444	.194	.273	.369	.421	.029	30.9	132-3B -6
2002	IOW	PCL	29	294	88	16	3	20	25	40	0	1	.299	.358	.578	.291	.268	.321	.512	.066	19.1	71-3B 3
2002	CHC	NL	29	32	9	3	0	0	1	4	0	0	.281	.324	.375	-.024	.303	.321	.424	-.029	.8	
2003	*CHC*	*NL*	*30*	*205*	*52*	*12*	*1*	*6*	*22*	*32*	*3*	*1*	*.254*	*.329*	*.406*	*-.054*	*.261*	*.332*	*.426*	*-.039*	*5.1*	

Breakout: 9%   Improve: 43%   Collapse: 35%

At this rate, Orie's pursuit of the Cubs' third-base job is a setup for his being featured as the heavy in *Ace Ventura 4: Lauren Holly's Alimony Comes Due*. His grievances would be just, because he could still be a very creditable temp at the hot corner: he can field the position, hit for a bit of power, and he'll take a free pass.

Corey Patterson   CF   Born: 13-Aug-79   Age: 23   Bats: L   Throws: R

YEAR	TM	LG	AGE	AB	H	2B	3B	HR	BB	SO	SB	CS	AVG	OBP	SLG	MLVR	EQBA	EQOBP	EQSLG	EQMLVR	VORP	DEFENSE
2000	WTN	SOU	20	444	116	26	5	22	45	115	27	14	.261	.343	.491	.188	.233	.291	.438	-.122	7.0	118-CF 6
2001	IOW	PCL	21	367	93	22	3	7	29	65	19	8	.253	.310	.387	-.139	.226	.280	.341	-.284	-10.3	83-CF -2
2001	CHC	NL	21	131	29	3	0	4	6	33	4	0	.221	.271	.336	-.291	.227	.273	.348	-.287	-3.8	37-CF -1
2002	CHC	NL	22	592	150	30	5	14	19	142	18	3	.253	.286	.392	-.085	.266	.293	.417	-.122	8.3	129-CF -3
2003	*CHC*	*NL*	*23*	*517*	*133*	*26*	*4*	*16*	*36*	*109*	*17*	*9*	*.257*	*.310*	*.415*	*-.072*	*.265*	*.313*	*.435*	*-.057*	*8.6*	

Breakout: 27%   Improve: 68%   Collapse: 13%

Before the season, the Cubs said they wanted 10 to 20 home runs, and they wanted to see him stick in the 7th or 8th slot all year. Baylor didn't wait until the end of April before kyboshing all of that, leading Patterson off throughout May and into June, and it worked. At the All-Star break, Patterson was hitting .275/.320/.415. Unfortunately, once Bobby Hill came up, they tried to bat Patterson second, and the inevitable distractions there as well as some fatigue undermined what had been a nice little year. There's some concern that the Cubs have already soured on him because of the strikeouts and the ugly walk rate, but he was only 22. He might be like Devon White, in that he's just going to have to bat leadoff, and you take the bad with the good.

Ray Sadler   CF   Born: 19-Sep-80   Age: 22   Bats: R   Throws: R

YEAR	TM	LG	AGE	AB	H	2B	3B	HR	BB	SO	SB	CS	AVG	OBP	SLG	MLVR	EQBA	EQOBP	EQSLG	EQMLVR	VORP	DEFENSE
2001	LNS	MDW	20	378	129	27	3	10	22	58	18	7	.341	.382	.508	.312	.258	.290	.387	-.177	-8.3	89-LF -13
2002	DAY	FSL	21	462	132	31	1	11	27	91	30	12	.286	.333	.429	.115	.236	.270	.362	-.267	-10.2	105-CF -10
2002	WTN	SOU	21	30	2	1	0	0	5	5	2	0	.067	.263	.100	-.515	.097	.238	.129	-.699	-4.7	
2003	*CHC*	*NL*	*22*	*178*	*44*	*9*	*1*	*5*	*12*	*39*	*5*	*5*	*.244*	*.299*	*.386*	*-.138*	*.251*	*.302*	*.405*	*-.128*	*-1.5*	

Breakout: 51%   Improve: 68%   Collapse: 14%

A 1999 draft-and-follow, Sadler isn't as toolsy as Mike Mallory or J. J. Johnson, so he doesn't get the prospect press of either of those two. However, a guy who hits everywhere he goes and who makes Double-A at 21 is worth noticing. He could use better patience, but power in the FSL isn't easy to generate. He bears watching.

Brandon Sing   LF?   Born: 13-Mar-81   Age: 22   Bats: R   Throws: R

YEAR	TM	LG	AGE	AB	H	2B	3B	HR	BB	SO	SB	CS	AVG	OBP	SLG	MLVR	EQBA	EQOBP	EQSLG	EQMLVR	VORP	DEFENSE	
2000	EUG	NWN	19	218	50	11	1	9	35	75	4	5	.229	.341	.413	.088	.171	.246	.307	-.428	-14.1	28-3B -8	
2001	LNS	MDW	20	417	102	27	2	16	46	109	3	5	.245	.331	.434	.059	.185	.249	.324	-.392	-22.0	50-3B -16	52-1B -4
2002	DAY	FSL	21	440	109	18	5	18	64	96	5	7	.248	.351	.434	.118	.202	.282	.357	-.272	-22.0	80-LF -9	14-1B -4
2003	*CHC*	*NL*	*22*	*178*	*41*	*8*	*2*	*6*	*20*	*50*	*2*	*3*	*.228*	*.312*	*.386*	*-.125*	*.235*	*.316*	*.405*	*-.114*	*-3.6*		

Breakout: 61%   Improve: 80%   Collapse: 8%

Like Sadler, Sing is going to be very interesting to watch to see how he adapts to Double-A. He has the power and he'll take a walk. He doesn't really have a position yet, so he's sort of a Kelton Lite in Kelton's organizational wake. If he makes enough contact in Double-A, he could have a career, but even then, he could wind up like Chris Haas, hoping to catch on as a bench player somewhere someday.

    A year ago, it looked like the Cubs were stocked with third basemen, but Kelton and Sing can't really handle the position that well, Gripp has been dealt, and both Blair Barbier and Corey Slavik flopped in 2002. Ron Santo doesn't really have a vengeful goat, does he?

Sammy Sosa RF Born: 12-Nov-68 Age: 34 Bats: R Throws: R

YEAR	TM	LG	AGE	AB	H	2B	3B	HR	BB	SO	SB	CS	AVG	OBP	SLG	MLVR	EQBA	EQOBP	EQSLG	EQMLVR	VORP	DEFENSE	
2000	CHC	NL	31	604	193	38	1	50	91	168	7	4	.320	.410	.634	.432	.316	.399	.627	.407	81.9	148-RF	-7
2001	CHC	NL	32	577	189	34	5	64	116	153	0	2	.328	.445	.737	.647	.331	.445	.742	.647	130.5	160-RF	0
2002	CHC	NL	33	556	160	19	2	49	103	144	2	0	.288	.402	.594	.395	.296	.405	.618	.379	72.4	145-RF	-6
2003	CHC	NL	34	480	137	26	2	36	81	124	3	2	.285	.390	.570	.281	.293	.394	.598	.314	43.9		

Breakout: 6%   Improve: 50%   Collapse: 10%

That's right, at 34, we're saying that Sammy isn't only not going to flirt with 50, he may drop below 40 home runs. Try not to string up your nearest BP writer, Cubs fans. Even with fewer than 40 home runs, Sammy's a considerable asset. He'll still take his walks, and although he's starting to lumber around in right, he isn't running gingerly on the bases. He's aging much more gracefully than Dawson did, basically. Don't worry about the cost: Sammy's a core media asset for *Tribune* broadcasting. The question is whether they've essentially wasted another great player's career without building a real team around him.

Chris Stynes UT Born: 19-Jan-73 Age: 30 Bats: R Throws: R

YEAR	TM	LG	AGE	AB	H	2B	3B	HR	BB	SO	SB	CS	AVG	OBP	SLG	MLVR	EQBA	EQOBP	EQSLG	EQMLVR	VORP	DEFENSE			
2000	CIN	NL	27	380	127	24	1	12	32	54	5	2	.334	.389	.497	.200	.328	.374	.488	.183	37.2	66-3B	5		
2001	BOS	AL	28	361	101	19	2	8	20	56	4	5	.280	.323	.410	-.031	.296	.340	.439	.021	18.9	39-3B	-3	39-2B	3
2002	CHC	NL	29	195	47	9	1	5	21	29	1	1	.241	.318	.374	-.062	.256	.327	.397	-.095	4.8	28-3B	-6	12-2B	2
2003	COL	NL	30	194	56	12	1	5	17	27	2	1	.288	.349	.444	.055	.267	.325	.403	-.076	3.0				

Breakout: 6%   Improve: 32%   Collapse: 38%

One of the truly cranky players in the game, but leave it to Cubby sweetness to cover up for the fact that he treats the Fourth Estate with considerably less respect than Barry Bonds does. By one account, in one fine infield practice he flung a half-dozen throws at a beat writer from one of Chicago's big four papers, and he wasn't missing. But you see, he's not famous, so why write about that? And this is the Cubs, so why suspend him? As a player, he's a multi-positional asset, but he signed with the Rockies hoping to get plenty of playing time at third.

Julio Zuleta LF/1B Born: 28-Mar-75 Age: 28 Bats: R Throws: R

YEAR	TM	LG	AGE	AB	H	2B	3B	HR	BB	SO	SB	CS	AVG	OBP	SLG	MLVR	EQBA	EQOBP	EQSLG	EQMLVR	VORP	DEFENSE			
2000	IOW	PCL	25	392	122	25	1	26	31	77	5	4	.311	.375	.579	.295	.275	.326	.509	.077	17.9	83-1B	-12	18-LF	-1
2000	CHC	NL	25	68	20	8	0	3	2	19	0	1	.294	.342	.544	.162	.290	.325	.551	.152	4.3	10-1B	-3		
2001	CHC	NL	26	106	23	3	0	6	8	32	0	1	.217	.291	.415	-.149	.224	.293	.430	-.137	-1.2	27-1B	-7		
2001	IOW	PCL	26	146	45	13	0	7	7	33	3	1	.308	.353	.541	.212	.276	.318	.483	.027	4.7	20-1B	-2		
2002	IOW	PCL	27	444	130	21	0	31	43	106	0	1	.293	.364	.550	.253	.262	.326	.487	.034	14.0	44-LF	-8		
2003	BOS	AL	28	162	41	9	0	7	12	38	1	1	.253	.311	.443	-.014	.258	.319	.464	-.013	0.9				

Breakout: 16%   Improve: 45%   Collapse: 30%

After never really getting on Baylor's good side and catching a break with the Cubs, Zuleta has already signed with Boston. He'll make an outstanding option to man first base or do some spot duty in left or at DH, depending on how Manny Ramirez's hamstring feels that day. He's not as patient as you'd like, but he hammers both right- and left-handed pitching, and he's replacing Tony Clark. He could easily be more valuable to the Red Sox than McGriff will be for the Dodgers.

PITCHERS

Antonio Alfonseca   Born: 16-Apr-72   Age: 31   Bats: R   Throws: R

YEAR	TM	LG	AGE	G	GS	IP	H	BB	SO	HR	ERA	EQERA	EQH9	EQBB9	EQSO9	EQHR9	PERA	VORP	STF
2000	FLA	NL	28	68	0	70.0	82	24	47	7	4.24	4.54	11.0	2.5	5.4	0.8	4.99	6.5	-6
2001	FLA	NL	29	58	0	61.7	68	15	40	6	3.06	4.02	10.6	2.1	5.1	0.8	4.62	9.3	-6
2002	CHC	NL	30	66	0	74.3	73	36	61	5	4.00	4.13	8.8	3.8	6.4	0.6	4.63	10.3	-2
2003	CHC	NL	31	48	0	56.7	58	24	43	5	4.00	4.42	9.6	3.3	5.9	0.8	4.82	7.4	-5

Breakout: 18%   Improve: 47%   Collapse: 26%

Ahhh, Pulpo, baseball's 12-fingered menace. If you look at his ERA, Equivalent ERA, and Peripheral ERA columns, what stands out? That 2001 ERA, which after his 45-save 2000 made him seem like an asset to some people. He got predictable against lefties, missing with his slider and curve, and his fastball doesn't have enough movement to fool everybody most of the time. He's supposed to be in shape for the first time in two or three years, and mixed with Remlinger and Dave Veres, could be an asset as part of a closer-by-committee.

Rod Beck   Born: 03-Aug-68   Age: 34   Bats: R   Throws: R

YEAR	TM	LG	AGE	G	GS	IP	H	BB	SO	HR	ERA	EQERA	EQH9	EQBB9	EQSO9	EQHR9	PERA	VORP	STF
2000	BOS	AL	31	34	0	40.7	34	12	35	2	3.10	2.67	7.2	2.2	7.5	0.4	2.48	12.3	15
2001	BOS	AL	32	68	0	80.7	77	28	63	15	3.90	4.12	8.0	2.9	6.5	1.5	4.41	11.3	-2

H. P. Lovecraft wrote about this, I'm sure. *The Creeping Horror? It Came From Beyond? Maid in Manhattan?* Who knows, something involving eldritch terror. At any rate, Beck is back, trying to recover from Tommy John surgery that cost him 2002. He's very popular in Chicago, and if Darren Holmes can keep going, why not The Shooter?

Francis Beltran   Born: 29-Nov-79   Age: 23   Bats: R   Throws: R

YEAR	TM	LG	AGE	G	GS	IP	H	BB	SO	HR	ERA	EQERA	EQH9	EQBB9	EQSO9	EQHR9	PERA	VORP	STF
2000	EUG	NWN	20	25	0	43.7	28	20	52	1	2.68	4.51	8.5	5.2	5.7	0.7	4.09	4.2	-3
2000	LNS	MDW	20	16	0	17.7	24	19	16	0	9.66	12.78	16.8	12.3	5.4	0.4	11.49	-14.6	-40
2001	DAY	FSL	21	21	18	95.3	93	40	72	10	5.01	6.72	12.2	4.7	4.7	2.4	6.49	-12.9	-9
2002	WTN	SOU	22	39	0	41.7	28	19	43	2	2.59	3.85	7.8	4.5	6.8	0.9	3.73	7.1	3
2002	CHC	NL	22	11	0	12.0	14	16	11	2	7.50	8.28	10.0	10.0	6.8	1.5	9.03	-3.9	-21
2003	CHC	NL	23	38	0	42.3	42	29	35	5	5.09	5.62	9.3	5.4	6.5	1.0	5.82	0.1	-12

Breakout: 13%   Improve: 60%   Collapse: 18%

The Cubs' pen is already crowded with the various veterans being hauled in or kept around, but Beltran may still get a shot. Not many people throw in the mid-90s, and can support it with a mid-80s slider or the occasional forkball. Among relief prospects (almost an oxymoron), Beltran's stock is probably only behind that of K-Rod and Franklyn German.

Alan Benes   Born: 21-Jan-72   Age: 31   Bats: R   Throws: R

YEAR	TM	LG	AGE	G	GS	IP	H	BB	SO	HR	ERA	EQERA	EQH9	EQBB9	EQSO9	EQHR9	PERA	VORP	STF
2000	MEM	PCL	28	9	8	39.3	45	21	26	7	5.95	7.63	12.5	4.9	5.0	2.1	7.00	-9.3	-20
2000	STL	NL	28	30	0	46.0	54	23	26	7	5.67	5.99	10.9	3.7	4.5	1.2	5.74	-3.1	-19
2001	MEM	PCL	29	25	25	142.0	164	51	96	13	3.55	5.36	11.7	3.9	4.5	1.0	5.89	2.3	-5
2002	IOW	PCL	30	28	19	113.0	130	53	85	17	5.65	6.63	11.8	5.0	5.3	1.8	6.70	-14.3	-16
2002	CHC	NL	30	7	7	39.3	42	12	32	3	4.35	4.49	9.7	2.4	6.4	0.7	4.58	4.4	14
2003	CHC	NL	31	19	11	72.3	78	36	50	9	5.06	5.59	10.1	3.8	5.5	1.1	5.44	0.9	-5

Breakout: 22%   Improve: 58%   Collapse: 24%

Yes, another Creighton guy, so where else was Alan Benes supposed to get another shot but playing for ex-Creighton coach and Zugmeister Jim Hendry? He's been slapped around in the PCL for two straight seasons, so health isn't the issue. He isn't even fooling right-handed hitters the way he used to. However, the spirit is still willing, and he gave the Cubs a game seven starts at the end. He might make it as the fifth starter, but he won't keep the job.

Jason Bere   Born: 26-May-71   Age: 32   Bats: R   Throws: R

YEAR	TM	LG	AGE	G	GS	IP	H	BB	SO	HR	ERA	EQERA	EQH9	EQBB9	EQSO9	EQHR9	PERA	VORP	STF
2000	MIL	NL	29	20	20	115.0	115	63	98	19	4.93	5.07	9.3	4.0	6.8	1.3	5.02	5.6	7
2000	CLE	AL	29	11	11	54.3	65	26	44	6	6.63	5.16	9.7	3.4	6.9	0.8	4.90	2.1	10
2001	CHC	NL	30	32	32	188.0	171	77	175	24	4.31	4.28	8.2	3.4	7.1	1.0	4.24	25.6	15
2002	CHC	NL	31	16	16	85.7	98	28	65	13	5.67	5.73	10.4	2.6	6.0	1.4	5.64	-2.1	3
2003	CLE	AL	32	21	17	106.0	119	40	73	16	5.27	5.18	10	3.1	6	1.2	4.97	7.2	4

Breakout: 4%   Improve: 43%   Collapse: 22%

It came a year late, but eventually, Bere made the Cubs eat the bitter herbs of regret. He missed most of the last three months of the season with a strained groin and a knee injury. You already know the basics: if he's at the top of his game, he's an adequate fourth starter. If he isn't, he's Losing Pitcher Mulcahy. For the Indians, he joins Brian Anderson as a token "already has a baseball card" guy to get slapped around in the front end of the rotation.

Joe Borowski   Born: 04-May-71   Age: 32   Bats: R   Throws: R

YEAR	TM	LG	AGE	G	GS	IP	H	BB	SO	HR	ERA	EQERA	EQH9	EQBB9	EQSO9	EQHR9	PERA	VORP	STF
2001	IOW	PCL	30	39	12	110.0	87	26	131	10	2.62	3.37	8.1	2.5	7.9	1.0	3.26	25.4	15
2002	CHC	NL	31	73	0	95.7	84	29	97	10	2.73	3.21	7.9	2.4	8.0	1.0	3.81	23.1	12
2003	CHC	NL	32	55	0	71.0	66	24	68	8	3.47	3.83	8.7	2.7	7.5	1.0	4.10	13.8	7

Breakout: 13%   Improve: 39%   Collapse: 25%

You can always scare up a perfectly good reliever out of the bushes and pay him next to nothing. The Angels' pen was built on this, the Braves dragged Hammond and Holmes out of their fresh graves, and the Cubs hauled in Borowski. He's a true middleman, durable and throwing strikes, and he can be handed leads or tight situations. Sort of like Dave Weathers or Bob Wells, he's had years where he's gotten a lot of experience throwing from the stretch, so he's familiar with coping with runners on base. Alfonseca, Veres, and Remlinger will handle the 8th and 9th innings, but Borowski should still own the 6th and 7th.

Matt Bruback   Born: 12-Jan-79   Age: 24   Bats: R   Throws: R

YEAR	TM	LG	AGE	G	GS	IP	H	BB	SO	HR	ERA	EQERA	EQH9	EQBB9	EQSO9	EQHR9	PERA	VORP	STF
2000	LNS	MDW	21	9	9	55.3	49	19	36	2	2.93	4.90	10.9	3.8	3.7	0.8	4.97	3.7	0
2000	DAY	FSL	21	18	18	89.0	101	50	69	6	4.85	7.76	14.0	6.7	5.2	1.6	7.66	-22.3	-9
2001	DAY	FSL	22	14	14	84.0	70	21	87	3	3.00	4.18	9.3	2.7	6.2	0.8	4.10	12.4	20
2001	WTN	SOU	22	9	9	38.0	58	20	43	3	9.00	11.06	17.4	5.8	7.2	1.3	10.08	-23.5	-3
2002	WTN	SOU	23	28	28	174.0	157	48	158	9	3.16	4.57	10.5	2.7	6.1	1.0	4.48	18.1	16
2003	CHC	NL	24	14	11	72.7	76	29	58	8	4.49	4.96	9.8	3.1	6.3	1.0	4.90	5.9	8

Breakout: 16%   Improve: 49%   Collapse: 18%

Although it wasn't his first exposure to Double-A, Bruback clearly mastered the level. He led the Southern League in strikeouts, lefties didn't hit him particularly well, and right-handed hitters slugged all of .286 against him. He didn't get the publicity of the Cubs' Latins or top-shelf college picks, but he's another one of the organization's big flamethrowers. Draft enough of these guys, and odds are that some of them, and any from among them, will make it. Bruback has gone from sleeper to one of the better-established young pitchers in the organization, but that was always within his power. The failure is when people like Ben Christensen get more attention than the people pitching.

Wilton Chavez   Born: 13-Jun-78   Age: 25   Bats: R   Throws: R

YEAR	TM	LG	AGE	G	GS	IP	H	BB	SO	HR	ERA	EQERA	EQH9	EQBB9	EQSO9	EQHR9	PERA	VORP	STF
2000	EUG	NWN	22	15	15	90.3	69	25	103	0	1.69	4.11	9.8	3.1	5.4	0.3	3.95	14.0	16
2001	LNS	MDW	23	8	8	47.0	38	27	60	4	4.02	5.36	9.6	7.5	7.2	1.8	5.76	0.8	4
2001	DAY	FSL	23	17	16	89.7	96	30	59	8	4.11	6.06	13.0	3.8	4.1	2.1	6.66	-5.6	-10
2002	DAY	FSL	24	8	6	24.7	30	12	25	2	4.74	7.62	14.2	5.7	6.6	1.8	8.15	-5.8	-12
2002	WTN	SOU	24	18	18	103.0	97	39	86	7	3.76	5.31	11.1	3.8	5.6	1.3	5.27	2.2	4

One of the bigger losers in Agegate, as it turned out Chavez was nearly three years older than he claimed, taking almost as much blush off his rose as removing the gauze from the lens of every camera on Diane Sawyer's set. Think about it: he was 21 in Rookie-ball in 1999, when he got lit up for a 5.88 ERA. Think he'd have been so readily touted with that on his resume? Whatever his age, he still owns a nasty slider, but the Cubs understandably want to push him now, to see if he's ever going to amount to anything.

Scott Chiasson   Born: 14-Aug-77   Age: 25   Bats: R   Throws: R

YEAR	TM	LG	AGE	G	GS	IP	H	BB	SO	HR	ERA	EQERA	EQH9	EQBB9	EQSO9	EQHR9	PERA	VORP	STF
2000	VIS	CLF	22	31	23	156.0	146	57	150	17	3.06	4.73	11.3	3.7	5.5	2.2	5.51	13.2	2
2001	WTN	SOU	23	52	0	61.3	43	20	62	2	1.76	3.07	7.5	3.4	6.1	0.5	3.42	15.7	3
2001	IOW	PCL	23	11	0	12.0	11	0	14	1	2.25	2.95	9.5	0.7	7.8	0.9	3.12	3.2	20
2002	CHC	NL	24	4	0	4.7	11	6	3	2	22.98	18.97	21.0	9.9	4.9	3.9	17.24	-7.1	-73
2002	IOW	PCL	24	27	0	28.3	34	13	26	9	7.95	8.52	12.7	4.9	6.6	3.8	8.41	-9.9	-26

Chiasson struggled early on, then got demoted from Iowa to West Tenn to work with Alan Dunn, his pitching coach from his successful 2001 season as the co-closer there. It didn't matter, his elbow was scragged, and he needed Tommy John surgery. He won't be a factor in 2003 before August or September, if then.

Ben Christensen   Born: 07-Feb-78   Age: 25   Bats: R   Throws: R

YEAR	TM	LG	AGE	G	GS	IP	H	BB	SO	HR	ERA	EQERA	EQH9	EQBB9	EQSO9	EQHR9	PERA	VORP	STF
2000	DAY	FSL	22	10	10	64.3	43	15	63	6	2.10	3.50	8.7	2.7	6.3	2.1	3.36	14.3	17
2000	WTN	SOU	22	7	7	42.3	36	15	42	2	2.77	5.32	10.6	3.6	6.5	0.8	4.68	0.9	17
2001	WTN	SOU	23	3	3	16.7	20	9	9	2	6.47	7.94	13.8	5.9	3.4	1.9	8.36	-4.5	-23
2002	WTN	SOU	24	12	12	64.0	73	35	36	6	6.33	8.05	13.9	5.6	3.9	1.9	7.55	-18.1	-21

So far, Christensen has had shoulder tendonitis wreck his 2000, "minor" shoulder surgery end his 2001 season early, and then he had to have Tommy John surgery last July. Considering Anthony Molina's fate at Christensen's hands, sometimes bad things keep happening to the right people.

Matt Clement   Born: 12-Aug-74   Age: 28   Bats: R   Throws: R

YEAR	TM	LG	AGE	G	GS	IP	H	BB	SO	HR	ERA	EQERA	EQH9	EQBB9	EQSO9	EQHR9	PERA	VORP	STF
2000	SDP	NL	25	34	34	205.0	194	125	170	22	5.14	5.19	8.9	4.4	6.6	0.9	4.87	7.2	10
2001	FLA	NL	26	31	31	169.3	172	85	134	15	5.05	5.08	9.6	4.2	6.1	0.7	4.89	8.0	5
2002	CHC	NL	27	32	32	205.0	162	85	215	18	3.60	3.47	7.0	3.3	8.2	0.8	3.59	46.4	25
2003	*CHC*	*NL*	*28*	*29*	*28*	*184.3*	*163*	*76*	*165*	*18*	*3.84*	*4.24*	*8.3*	*3.2*	*7.0*	*0.9*	*4.07*	*25.6*	*17*

Breakout: 14%   *Improve: 53%*   *Collapse: 11%*

Tip your cap to Hendry and company, this looks like an old-fashioned breakout. His strikeout rate jumped, his walk rate dropped, and he was much more durable, seemingly putting the strange liver problem he was diagnosed as having in 2001 completely behind him. But how much of his improvement was just allowing fewer hits, i.e., getting good defensive support? The difference in his OBP and his BA allowed between 2001 and 2002 is almost entirely because fewer balls in play dropped for hits, and there's a good dose of luck involved in that, as it would be with any pitcher. Nevertheless, the big jump in his strikeout rate is the true sign that he's made gains that should stick. He's definitely the third starter behind Wood and Prior, but he could be one of the league's best third starters.

Juan Cruz   Born: 15-Oct-78   Age: 24   Bats: R   Throws: R

YEAR	TM	LG	AGE	G	GS	IP	H	BB	SO	HR	ERA	EQERA	EQH9	EQBB9	EQSO9	EQHR9	PERA	VORP	STF
2000	LNS	MDW	21	17	17	96.0	75	60	106	6	3.28	5.85	10.0	7.0	6.3	1.5	5.68	-3.7	5
2000	DAY	FSL	21	8	7	44.3	30	18	54	5	3.25	5.08	9.1	4.8	7.9	2.6	4.21	2.1	18
2001	WTN	SOU	22	23	23	121.3	107	60	137	6	4.01	5.10	9.6	5.2	6.9	0.8	5.26	5.5	14
2001	CHC	NL	22	8	8	44.7	40	17	39	4	3.22	3.38	8.2	3.2	6.7	0.7	3.83	10.6	22
2002	CHC	NL	23	45	9	97.3	84	59	81	11	3.98	4.66	7.7	4.8	6.5	1.0	4.72	8.4	1
2003	*CHC*	*NL*	*24*	*30*	*10*	*73.7*	*69*	*41*	*67*	*9*	*4.65*	*5.13*	*8.8*	*4.3*	*7.2*	*1.0*	*5.07*	*4.7*	*1*

Breakout: 10%   *Improve: 50%*   *Collapse: 16%*

Cruz isn't a disappointment as much as he was sort of left hanging. Baylor quit on him in mid-May, bumping him into the pen. By the time Kimm was hired, Zambrano had established himself, and when Lieber went down, they wanted to take a look at Smyth. So he spent much of the year in the pen as the forgotten man. He spent two weeks on the DL with a strained arm, but he pitched a whopping 31 innings after the All-Star break despite posting a 2.32 ERA. Previously noted for his poise, he was generally in control with men on base, throws three good pitches and has good velocity. What does he need to do? Some feel he could add bulk and thus endurance, but basically, he looks like a guy who can pitch, and should be allowed to. He could win the fifth slot in the rotation in camp, but he'll have to contend with Dusty's preference for the aged as well as Carlos Zambrano.

Will Cunnane　　Born: 24-Apr-74　　Age: 29　　Bats: R　　Throws: R

YEAR	TM	LG	AGE	G	GS	IP	H	BB	SO	HR	ERA	EQERA	EQH9	EQBB9	EQSO9	EQHR9	PERA	VORP	STF
2000	LVG	PCL	26	17	17	97.3	96	26	97	7	3.98	3.61	8.9	2.3	7.1	0.8	3.64	20.5	21
2000	SDP	NL	26	27	3	38.3	35	21	34	2	4.23	4.42	8.7	4.0	7.1	0.4	4.11	4.2	3
2001	MIL	NL	27	31	1	51.7	66	22	37	6	5.40	6.12	12.4	3.6	5.6	1.0	6.10	-4.2	-11
2002	IOW	PCL	28	43	0	73.7	67	23	69	3	2.20	3.39	9.0	3.2	6.5	0.5	3.81	16.3	3
2002	CHC	NL	28	16	0	26.3	27	13	30	5	5.48	5.39	9.1	3.8	8.8	1.7	5.79	-0.0	4
2003	CHC	NL	29	25	7	60.0	59	25	52	6	3.84	4.24	9.2	3.2	6.8	0.9	4.47	8.7	4

Breakout: 24%　　Improve: 48%　　Collapse: 22%

Cunnane does all the things you think should work, keeping the ball on the ground, striking people out, showing good control. But in the majors, he seems to flounder in these 11th pitcher roles. Lefties hammer him, and he falls apart with men on base. Will he finally become something? People have been asking the same thing about Keanu Reeves for twice as long.

Courtney Duncan　　Born: 09-Oct-74　　Age: 28　　Bats: L　　Throws: R

YEAR	TM	LG	AGE	G	GS	IP	H	BB	SO	HR	ERA	EQERA	EQH9	EQBB9	EQSO9	EQHR9	PERA	VORP	STF
2000	WTN	SOU	25	61	0	73.3	57	33	72	2	3.07	5.22	9.6	4.5	6.3	0.5	4.41	1.3	-5
2001	CHC	NL	26	36	0	42.7	42	25	49	5	5.06	4.86	8.9	4.8	8.7	0.9	5.08	2.5	5
2002	IOW	PCL	27	55	0	67.7	67	33	64	6	3.99	5.06	10.0	5.1	6.7	1.1	5.23	2.4	-9
2002	CHC	NL	27	2	0	2.3	2	1	1	0	0.00	3.04	7.4	3.3	3.3	0.2	3.41	0.6	-14

If there was a weird decision about the team's bullpen last summer, it was the choice to turn their backs on Duncan, who had done reasonably well at the bottom of the 2001 pen. Why you'd use Pat Mahomes instead is unfathomable, especially in a pen stocked with graybeards like Alfonseca and Fassero and Borowski. Duncan isn't a prospect as much as a guy who could be useful, versus a guy with nearly 300 big league games that tell you he isn't.

Kyle Farnsworth　　Born: 14-Apr-76　　Age: 27　　Bats: R　　Throws: R

YEAR	TM	LG	AGE	G	GS	IP	H	BB	SO	HR	ERA	EQERA	EQH9	EQBB9	EQSO9	EQHR9	PERA	VORP	STF
2000	IOW	PCL	24	22	0	25.3	24	18	22	1	3.20	4.03	8.8	6.2	6.2	0.4	5.05	3.8	-7
2000	CHC	NL	24	46	5	77.0	90	50	74	14	6.43	6.21	10.3	4.6	7.5	1.4	6.34	-6.8	-1
2001	CHC	NL	25	76	0	82.0	65	29	107	8	2.74	2.99	7.1	2.9	9.9	0.8	3.29	21.8	25
2002	CHC	NL	26	45	0	46.7	53	24	46	9	7.32	7.24	10.2	4.0	7.7	1.8	6.48	-9.7	-8
2003	CHC	NL	27	39	2	57.0	53	25	54	6	4.03	4.45	8.6	3.4	7.5	1.0	4.26	7.2	5

Breakout: 23%　　Improve: 53%　　Collapse: 19%

Some people have all sorts of talent, and lose the popularity contests anyway, and because Farnsworth seems to wear his heart on his sleeve, people quit on him pretty quickly when the going gets tough. Did it matter that Farnsworth had been successful in 2001? No, as soon as he got into a rut, missing early with his breaking stuff and then getting predictable with his heat, the Cubs didn't merely get frustrated, they got resentful. How disappointed are they? Rod Beck's making a comeback, for god's sakes.

Angel Guzman　　Born: 14-Dec-81　　Age: 21　　Bats: R　　Throws: R

YEAR	TM	LG	AGE	G	GS	IP	H	BB	SO	HR	ERA	EQERA	EQH9	EQBB9	EQSO9	EQHR9	PERA	VORP	STF
2001	BOI	NWN	19	14	14	76.7	68	19	63	2	2.23	5.14	11.7	3.4	4.1	0.7	4.86	3.1	2
2002	LNS	MDW	20	9	9	62.0	42	16	49	3	1.89	4.06	9.5	3.3	4.6	1.3	3.50	10.0	8
2002	DAY	FSL	20	16	15	94.0	99	33	74	2	2.39	4.49	11.4	4.0	5.0	0.5	5.79	10.6	8

Touted as the next Chavez or Cruz or Cubs Latin hurler du jour, Guzman has a big-breaking sinker that he supports with an adequate curve and change. Although he has yet to be really checked by any level he's pitched at, he didn't ride over hitters in Florida the way he did in the Midwest League, so he probably shouldn't go straight to Double-A. Nevertheless, he'll get every opportunity to keep rocketing through the system.

Aaron Krawiec　　Born: 17-Mar-79　　Age: 24　　Bats: L　　Throws: L

YEAR	TM	LG	AGE	G	GS	IP	H	BB	SO	HR	ERA	EQERA	EQH9	EQBB9	EQSO9	EQHR9	PERA	VORP	STF
2000	EUG	NWN	21	14	14	78.0	59	26	99	4	2.54	4.75	10.7	3.8	6.2	1.6	4.63	6.5	12
2001	LNS	MDW	22	27	26	153.3	183	51	170	15	4.58	7.28	14.0	4.3	6.2	2.0	7.77	-30.3	2
2002	DAY	FSL	23	28	28	169.3	159	48	128	8	4.09	4.93	10.4	3.2	4.8	1.0	4.98	10.8	5

Krawiec is 6′6″ and throws in the low 90s. A product of Villanova, you might expect him to dominate a little more than he has, but he's made progress as he gets more consistent with his mechanics. He just needs repetition and continued good health, which will help him survive the jump to Double-A.

Beyond their large brood of flamethrowing right-handed pitching scattered at every level of the organization, the Cubs also have a penchant for grooming huge lefties. Further down the chain, they've got the even larger Andrew Sisco (6′9″), and he throws even harder, but Boise's a long way from the majors.

Jon Lieber												Born: 02-Apr-70		Age: 33		Bats: L		Throws: R	
YEAR	TM	LG	AGE	G	GS	IP	H	BB	SO	HR	ERA	EQERA	EQH9	EQBB9	EQSO9	EQHR9	PERA	VORP	STF
2000	CHC	NL	30	35	35	251.0	248	54	192	36	4.41	4.02	9.1	1.6	6.2	1.2	3.87	41.4	15
2001	CHC	NL	31	34	34	232.3	226	41	148	25	3.80	3.70	9.0	1.5	4.9	0.9	3.75	46.6	10
2002	CHC	NL	32	21	21	141.0	153	12	87	15	3.70	3.88	10.0	0.7	5.0	1.0	4.23	25.5	11

Lieber is a free agent, and thinks he'll be able to pitch in the second half after the minimum of 12 months' recovery time after his Tommy John surgery. It might turn out well, but keep in mind, not everybody recovers in a year, and almost nobody has good command in the first year after he comes back. And then there's Sterling Hitchcock. You want Lieber to make it back, because he's one of the game's real pleasures to watch work, but that doesn't mean you have to share his optimism.

Pat Mahomes												Born: 09-Aug-70		Age: 32		Bats: R		Throws: R	
YEAR	TM	LG	AGE	G	GS	IP	H	BB	SO	HR	ERA	EQERA	EQH9	EQBB9	EQSO9	EQHR9	PERA	VORP	STF
2000	NYM	NL	29	53	5	94.0	96	66	76	15	5.46	5.74	9.3	5.1	6.4	1.3	5.84	-3.4	-11
2001	TEX	AL	30	56	4	107.3	115	55	61	17	5.70	5.04	8.9	4.2	4.7	1.3	5.18	4.3	-16
2002	IOW	PCL	31	44	5	72.3	57	20	70	11	3.49	3.91	8.0	2.9	6.8	1.8	3.87	12.1	-1
2002	CHC	NL	31	16	2	32.7	36	17	23	3	3.85	4.55	10.0	4.1	5.5	0.9	5.57	3.2	-8
2003	*CHC*	*NL*	*32*	*29*	*4*	*49.7*	*49*	*25*	*39*	*6*	*4.51*	*4.98*	*9.3*	*3.9*	*6.1*	*1.1*	*5.06*	*3.4*	*-7*

Breakout: 17%   *Improve: 44%*   *Collapse: 19%*

In the MacPhail tradition of recycling Twins castoffs, you knew it was only a matter of time before Pat Mahomes wandered into Wrigleyville. He relieved in only three winning efforts, and gave up runs in two of them. As a mop-up man and emergency starter, you could probably do worse, but you'd have to dig down to the bottom of the toy box.

Will Ohman												Born: 13-Aug-77		Age: 25		Bats: L		Throws: L	
YEAR	TM	LG	AGE	G	GS	IP	H	BB	SO	HR	ERA	EQERA	EQH9	EQBB9	EQSO9	EQHR9	PERA	VORP	STF
2000	WTN	SOU	22	59	0	71.3	53	36	85	3	1.89	4.29	9.2	5.0	7.7	0.7	4.52	8.6	7
2001	IOW	PCL	23	40	1	51.0	51	18	66	9	4.06	5.21	10.3	3.8	8.6	1.9	5.50	1.0	8
2001	CHC	NL	23	11	0	11.7	14	6	12	2	7.69	6.71	10.8	4.3	7.8	1.4	6.41	-1.7	1

Reminders territory: Ohman had Tommy John surgery (in January 2002), and missed the entire season, as did one-time prospect lefty Phil Norton. They're both supposed to be ready in 2003. With Mike Remlinger's arrival, Ohman should be first in line for the job of second lefty in the pen, but he'll have to prove he's healthy and pitch consistently first.

Mark Prior												Born: 07-Sep-80		Age: 22		Bats: R		Throws: R	
YEAR	TM	LG	AGE	G	GS	IP	H	BB	SO	HR	ERA	EQERA	EQH9	EQBB9	EQSO9	EQHR9	PERA	VORP	STF
2002	WTN	SOU	21	6	6	34.7	26	10	55	0	2.59	4.10	8.1	2.7	10.2	0.2	3.19	5.4	50
2002	IOW	PCL	21	3	3	16.3	13	8	24	1	1.66	4.73	7.9	5.1	10.1	0.7	3.88	1.4	40
2002	CHC	NL	21	19	19	116.7	98	38	147	14	3.32	3.49	7.5	2.6	9.8	1.1	3.78	26.1	46
2003	*CHC*	*NL*	*22*	*23*	*21*	*138.3*	*117*	*52*	*145*	*15*	*3.59*	*3.96*	*7.9*	*2.9*	*8.3*	*1.0*	*3.81*	*25.4*	*26*

Breakout: 10%   *Improve: 43%*   *Collapse: 26%*

And like Athena, Prior sprang into action fully formed. He's got it all, the 12-6 curve, the mid-90s heat, you name it. The comparisons to a young Clemens proved warranted, and the claims that he's the greatest college pitcher ever don't look too shabby. Was he worth the $4 million bonus or the 40-man roster slot? Certainly. Is he ready to dominate the league? Absolutely. Is he the best starter on this team? At this rate, he will be, but on that score at least, there's less certainty, because Wood seems primed and Clement is no slouch.

Jae-Kuk Ryu   Born: 30-May-83   Age: 20   Bats: R   Throws: R

YEAR	TM	LG	AGE	G	GS	IP	H	BB	SO	HR	ERA	EQERA	EQH9	EQBB9	EQSO9	EQHR9	PERA	VORP	STF
2002	BOI	NWN	19	10	10	53.0	45	25	56	1	3.57	6.79	11.9	6.3	5.6	0.6	5.89	-7.6	2
2002	LNS	MDW	19	5	4	19.0	26	8	21	1	7.11	10.52	19.1	5.8	6.9	1.5	9.28	-10.6	-4

Another product of Leon Lee's heralded Asian acquisitions program, Ryu can deal strikes three different ways, starting off with a mid-90s heater, a big-breaking splitter, a nice curve; he's learning to throw a changeup. Like the Koreans that filled the Red Sox organization, he's relatively polished for someone so young, but the majority of the Korean Red Sox flamed out or became Expos. Ryu seems more promising.

Jesus Sanchez   Born: 11-Oct-74   Age: 28   Bats: L   Throws: L

YEAR	TM	LG	AGE	G	GS	IP	H	BB	SO	HR	ERA	EQERA	EQH9	EQBB9	EQSO9	EQHR9	PERA	VORP	STF
2000	FLA	NL	25	32	32	182.0	197	76	123	32	5.34	5.33	9.9	3.1	5.4	1.4	5.32	3.5	2
2001	CLG	PCL	26	16	11	75.7	61	33	58	4	3.21	3.11	6.9	4.6	4.9	0.5	3.22	20.0	0
2001	FLA	NL	26	16	9	62.7	61	31	46	7	4.74	4.74	9.2	4.2	5.7	0.9	4.82	5.2	-2
2002	CHC	NL	27	8	0	8.3	15	10	6	4	13.01	13.11	16.0	9.2	5.5	4.3	14.40	-7.1	-68
2002	IOW	PCL	27	26	24	125.0	144	65	94	27	5.90	7.12	12.0	5.6	5.4	2.6	7.47	-22.5	-20
2003	HOU	NL	28	13	7	44.7	49	27	31	7	5.77	5.88	10.0	4.7	5.7	1.3	5.89	-0.4	-10

Breakout: 19%   Improve: 45%   Collapse: 24%

The Cubs acquired Sanchez for Nate Teut, a deal that didn't really help either club. It also didn't actively hurt either club. Since both were basically lefty-flavored Quadruple-A hangers-on, it was about as random as Woody Harrelson's career path. Now that he's with the Astros, he might hang on as a second lefty in the pen or get some spot starts if Carlos Hernandez isn't healthy, but he's basically treading water.

Steve Smyth   Born: 03-Jun-78   Age: 25   Bats: L   Throws: L

YEAR	TM	LG	AGE	G	GS	IP	H	BB	SO	HR	ERA	EQERA	EQH9	EQBB9	EQSO9	EQHR9	PERA	VORP	STF
2000	DAY	FSL	22	24	23	138.3	134	57	100	9	3.25	5.73	11.9	4.9	4.8	1.5	5.80	-3.5	-2
2001	WTN	SOU	23	18	18	120.3	110	40	93	9	2.54	4.20	10.2	3.6	4.8	1.2	5.10	17.4	4
2002	WTN	SOU	24	11	11	73.0	62	18	74	7	3.58	4.86	10.3	2.5	6.9	1.9	4.41	5.2	15
2002	IOW	PCL	24	6	6	31.0	35	10	25	4	5.81	6.09	11.4	3.4	5.7	1.5	5.85	-2.0	1
2002	CHC	NL	24	8	7	26.0	34	10	16	9	9.35	8.45	12.0	3.1	4.9	3.3	8.19	-8.5	-21
2003	CHC	NL	25	18	11	69.3	76	30	52	11	5.24	5.79	10.3	3.3	5.9	1.4	5.47	0.8	-3

Breakout: 18%   Improve: 49%   Collapse: 27%

You want a rough way to break into the majors? Called up to replace Lieber, in his first game, Smyth had to face Barry Bonds and the Giants, pitch in Coors in his second start, and then face Curt Schilling in his third. He has good velocity for a lefty, and throws four pitches for strikes. There are worse options as your fifth starter, but he's not a great bet to beat out Zambrano, Benes, and Cruz, and since signing Estes, he's no longer their token lefty starter. He might stick as the second lefty in the pen.

John Webb   Born: 23-May-79   Age: 24   Bats: R   Throws: R

YEAR	TM	LG	AGE	G	GS	IP	H	BB	SO	HR	ERA	EQERA	EQH9	EQBB9	EQSO9	EQHR9	PERA	VORP	STF
2000	LNS	MDW	21	21	21	134.7	125	40	108	4	2.47	4.80	11.3	3.3	4.6	0.7	5.00	10.6	8
2000	DAY	FSL	21	4	2	17.0	17	3	18	1	4.76	6.31	11.9	2.0	6.8	1.3	4.94	-1.6	16
2001	DAY	FSL	22	5	4	20.0	23	7	20	0	5.40	6.63	12.6	3.8	6.0	0.3	6.34	-2.5	5
2002	DAY	FSL	23	10	10	57.7	43	23	65	3	3.43	4.03	8.3	4.5	7.1	1.1	4.19	9.5	17
2002	WTN	SOU	23	11	11	61.7	52	22	45	5	4.52	5.34	10.2	3.6	5.0	1.6	4.69	1.1	1

This past year was Webb's first back from the Tommy John surgery he had to have early in 2001. It wasn't too shabby a season, as he flashed the live arm that led the Cubs to convert him from shortstop in the first place. He's a sinker-slider guy, with a good changeup, and he shows great touch for someone without a ton of pitching experience.

Todd Wellemeyer Born: 30-Aug-78 Age: 24 Bats: R Throws: R

YEAR	TM	LG	AGE	G	GS	IP	H	BB	SO	HR	ERA	EQERA	EQH9	EQBB9	EQSO9	EQHR9	PERA	VORP	STF
2000	EUG	NWN	21	15	15	76.0	62	33	85	3	3.67	5.79	11.3	5.0	5.5	1.3	5.43	-2.4	2
2001	LNS	MDW	22	27	27	147.0	165	74	167	14	4.16	6.72	13.3	6.6	6.5	2.0	7.98	-19.8	-1
2002	DAY	FSL	23	14	14	73.7	63	19	87	7	3.79	4.54	10.1	2.9	7.5	2.0	4.73	7.9	17
2002	WTN	SOU	23	8	8	46.0	33	18	37	2	4.70	4.79	8.3	3.9	5.4	0.8	3.74	3.7	8
2003	CHN	NL	24	14	9	56.3	59	30	51	8	5.14	5.68	9.8	4.1	7.1	1.2	5.50	0.7	3

Breakout: 18%   Improve: 52%   Collapse: 20%

One of the final cuts from last year's book, Wellemeyer more than earned the write-up this year. He's been accused of being almost too fine with his control and for taking extended periods to test what works and what doesn't, but he's got good heat and a humiliating changeup, and he's flinging an improved slider. On the heels of an outstanding AFL and having made his Double-A debut, he could surface in a relief role by the end of 2003, or start challenging for a rotation spot in 2004. He won't come by one easily, considering how full the big league rotation already is, and how many other prospects are ahead of him, but he's got plenty of promise.

Kerry Wood Born: 16-Jun-77 Age: 26 Bats: R Throws: R

YEAR	TM	LG	AGE	G	GS	IP	H	BB	SO	HR	ERA	EQERA	EQH9	EQBB9	EQSO9	EQHR9	PERA	VORP	STF
2000	CHC	NL	23	23	23	137.0	112	87	132	17	4.80	4.31	7.2	4.5	7.5	1.0	4.10	18.2	21
2001	CHC	NL	24	28	28	174.3	127	92	217	16	3.36	3.41	6.5	4.4	9.4	0.7	3.45	40.6	34
2002	CHC	NL	25	33	33	213.7	169	97	217	22	3.66	3.66	7.0	3.6	7.9	1.0	3.82	43.8	23
2003	CHC	NL	26	30	28	191.7	154	82	197	19	3.43	3.78	7.5	3.3	8.1	0.9	3.74	36.6	24

Breakout: 26%   Improve: 63%   Collapse: 10%

We've seen good stuff, but things look like they're about to get better. The Cubs were careful with Wood in 2002, watching his pitch counts. He responded by giving them his first full season since 1997, making a professional career-high 33 starts. Wood had quality starts in 23 of his 33 starts (blowing one in the 7th inning), which is an outstanding rate. He's doing a much better job of freezing lefties with his curve, so they don't hammer him for extra-base hits like they used to. He's good and getting better, and poised for a breakout season.

Mike Wuertz Born: 15-Dec-78 Age: 24 Bats: R Throws: R

YEAR	TM	LG	AGE	G	GS	IP	H	BB	SO	HR	ERA	EQERA	EQH9	EQBB9	EQSO9	EQHR9	PERA	VORP	STF
2000	DAY	FSL	21	28	28	171.3	166	64	142	15	3.78	5.82	12.2	4.4	5.5	2.0	5.85	-6.0	4
2001	WTN	SOU	22	27	27	160.0	160	58	135	20	3.99	5.78	11.5	3.9	5.3	2.0	6.28	-4.9	1
2002	IOW	PCL	23	28	27	154.0	185	69	131	24	5.55	6.82	12.3	4.7	6.0	1.9	6.98	-22.5	0
2003	CHC	NL	24	15	10	61.0	64	29	47	8	4.93	5.45	9.7	3.7	6.1	1.2	5.43	0.8	-1

Breakout: 16%   Improve: 60%   Collapse: 8%

Wuertz might be moving up the chain, but he isn't making much progress. He throws in the low 90s, but nothing else really works, and although he's been durable, he hasn't improved as he's moved up. With his limited repertoire, he might eventually move into the pen, but the big league staff is pretty full for 2003. He'll almost certainly repeat at Iowa.

Carlos Zambrano Born: 01-Jun-81 Age: 22 Bats: B Throws: R

YEAR	TM	LG	AGE	G	GS	IP	H	BB	SO	HR	ERA	EQERA	EQH9	EQBB9	EQSO9	EQHR9	PERA	VORP	STF
2000	WTN	SOU	19	9	9	60.3	39	21	43	2	1.34	3.48	8.1	3.5	4.6	0.6	3.34	13.6	11
2000	IOW	PCL	19	34	0	56.7	54	40	46	3	3.97	4.73	8.9	6.2	5.8	0.6	5.19	4.1	-4
2001	IOW	PCL	20	26	25	150.7	124	68	155	9	3.88	4.50	8.5	4.9	6.9	0.6	3.89	16.8	20
2002	IOW	PCL	21	3	3	9.0	2	6	11	0	0.00	0.19	2.2	7.0	8.6	0.2	1.45	5.3	27
2002	CHC	NL	21	32	16	108.3	94	63	93	9	3.66	4.19	7.7	4.6	6.7	0.8	4.45	15.4	12
2003	CHC	NL	22	26	14	85.7	83	49	78	9	4.79	5.28	9.0	4.5	7.1	0.9	5.10	4.8	3

Breakout: 17%   Improve: 41%   Collapse: 33%

There are some comments that are just hopelessly generic, but Zambrano's yet another flamethrower who could use a sharper breaking pitch, in this case, his slider. Where the Cubs plan to use him is still a bit up in the air: he could be the fifth starter, or he could wind up in the bullpen in long relief if Benes or Smyth sneak past him. He should be the favorite, however. In his half-season in the rotation (essentially replacing Bere), he logged nine quality starts (one subsequently blown) in 16 starts.

Cincinnati Reds

In April 1999, Carl Lindner headed a group of three limited partners that agreed to pay Marge Schott $67 million for 5.5 of her 6.5 shares in the Cincinnati Reds. Schott's departure had many obvious benefits. The Ohio Valley was spared any more reflected embarrassment caused by her all-too-public racist remarks. Freed from Schott's demeaning treatment, the organization could hire and retain quality people. Less penny-pinching meant increased spending on player development to rebuild a farm system ravaged by years of neglect. These changes were set in motion when Major League Baseball indefinitely suspended Schott and forced her to relinquish day-to-day operations of the team in June 1996. The sale signified the official end of her reign.

But did the Reds actually gain much from the change in ownership?

Lindner is portrayed as a reluctant owner, one not really interested in having a baseball team in his portfolio. Like Schott, he claims to have become the majority owner simply to keep an out-of-town ownership group from buying the franchise. Unlike Schott, who prided herself on Cincinnati having a winning team, Linder wants only to ensure the Reds remain in the Queen City and that he doesn't sacrifice any personal wealth (estimated at $650 million last year) while owning the ball club. Given MLB's unique accounting methods and Commissioner Bud Selig's persistent claim that most teams lose money, that's not encouraging news for Reds' fans.

In contrast to his statements about merely not wanting to lose money on the Reds, Lindner actually stands to gain substantially. Under the standard extortion of teams leaving town because they can't compete financially, in March 1996 the voters of Hamilton County approved a half-cent increase in their sales tax to build new stadiums for the Reds and the NFL Bengals. Schott didn't like either of the competing stadium sites—"the Wedge" and Broadway Commons—and dragged her feet for over two years approving a deal. Ulti-

mately, Lindner used his warm relationship with Schott to help convince her to sign off on "the Wedge" site, even though construction costs at Broadway Commons would have run at least $30 million less and placed the ballpark in a neighborhood instead of a parking lot. Companies controlled by Lindner own prime real estate directly north of "the Wedge", property that will increase in value with a new baseball stadium just a few hundred yards away.

Within a month of signing the agreement to buy a controlling interest in the team, the new group had signed a 30-year lease on the new ballpark. It is one of the best deals of any team in Major League Baseball. The Reds will only pay out about $80 million total in today's dollars for construction and rent, while receiving all revenue generated by the stadium. Of course, the majority of their costs will be paid for by selling the name for a building that they don't even own. Lindner's Great American Insurance Company bought those naming rights for $75 million over 30 years. Although the price paid isn't out of line with the going rate, when a company owned by an individual awards a contract to another business he owns, questions of impropriety should arise.

Local seamheads didn't notice Lindner's questionable ethics; indeed, they couldn't seem to find any negatives associated with the new ownership group—certainly not when compared to the previous regime. The honeymoon continued when Lindner brought native son Ken Griffey Jr. home in February 2000 with a long-term contract at a below-market price. Although Lindner was reluctant to open his wallet, his advisers finally convinced him that with increased attendance and better local radio and television contracts, Griffey would pay for himself.

As shown by Billy Bob Thornton and Angelina Jolie's divorce, even the most sugary of relationships can go sour. Reds fans' infatuation with Lindner took a turn for the worse in July 2000 when he went against his baseball people and

---

Reds Prospectus

2002 record: 78–84; Third place, NL Central

Pythagenport Record: 74–88

Runs scored per game: 4.4 (10th in NL)

Runs allowed per game: 4.8 (13th in NL)

Team EqA: .256 (13th in NL)

2002 Batters Age: 28.1 (2nd youngest in NL)

2002 Pitchers Age: 29.2 (7th oldest in NL)

Ballpark: Cinergy Field; Severe hitters' park; Park Factor of 1.042

2002: Kearns and Dunn arrived, and the usual collection of retread starters inspired hope briefly.

2003: A young and improving team, they will contend if the rotation ever gets stable.

---

extended Barry Larkin's contract for three years at $27 million. While bad from an on-field standpoint, ensuring that a local icon finishes his career in his hometown could have been a public relations coup, except that the team at the same time announced it would be raising ticket prices to cover the cost of Larkin's contract.

Perhaps it was the public backlash that followed the announcement, or the realization that unlike other businesses, increased costs can't be immediately passed onto the consumer. Or maybe it was because the 2000 Reds won 11 fewer games than the overachieving 1999 squad despite adding Griffey and substantially increasing its payroll. Whatever the case, one huge negative about Lindner has since emerged loud and clear: he no longer intends to invest in his product.

Near the end of the 2000 season, the Reds set about slashing their payroll, and had whittled it down from $60 million to $45 million by last season. Taken alone, that isn't necessarily a bad thing, especially if a club is in the midst of a rebuilding phase. Cincinnati wasn't. With nearly 40% of its payroll consumed by Griffey and Larkin, the team scaled back to the bone in other areas. The salaries for last year's opening day rotation (Hamilton, Reitsma, Acevedo, Dessens, Haynes) summed to but $3.35 million. There were only three teams in baseball that didn't have at least one individual starter making more than that. In fact, last year's payroll was less than the club's payroll in 1995, despite a 110% surge in revenue over the same time period. Marge Schott may not have paid for scouts to have their laundry washed while on the road, but she did spend money to try to acquire quality major league players.

Lindner's tightfistedness has also impacted Cincinnati's farm system. It all stems from general manager Jim Bowden overextending himself by nearly $2 million to sign Alejandro Diaz out of Japan in 1999. Lindner refused to see the signing as a one-time hit to the player development budget, and Bowden has been borrowing from Peter to pay Paul ever since. In lieu of large signing bonuses, 2000 draftees David Espinosa and Dane Sardinha were instead given major league contracts. Bowden didn't get Dustin Moseley's signature on a deal until the new fiscal year began that November. The lunacy reached new heights in 2001 when the Reds spent their first-round selection in the June draft on Jeremy Sowers, knowing full well that they had no chance of signing him. Though it seemed that the Sowers fiasco should have straightened out the budget mess, apparently it didn't. Last year's picks in rounds two through five weren't signed until November, either.

In addition to the obvious damage inflicted by tossing away a first round pick, harm to the Reds' player development program has been felt in other subtler ways. The inability to sign draftees until November limits the pool of players from which the club can select. Prospects signing that late also lose nearly half a season of development time. Doling

out major league contracts to entice players to sign burns precious spaces on the 40-man roster and usually forces youngsters to the majors before they are ready. The overall effect has been dramatic. A Reds farm system that had rebuilt itself into one of the 10 best in baseball in 1999 has slid back to the bottom 10, with no clear impact players in sight.

Lindner also ties Bowden's hands with his old-fashioned ideals when it comes to player contracts. He won't swallow a contract or any portion of one, even if it would improve the team on the field. As a result, Sean Casey becomes an immovable object at first base, and Kelly Stinnett and Juan Castro will likely wear Reds colors this year, though better options are readily available.

While the aforementioned penny-pinching hurts both the short- and long-term outlook for the Reds in the NL Central, it pales compared to the fallout caused last fall when the team let slip that its payroll wouldn't grow very much as it moves into Great American Ball Park in 2003.

Following the tried-and-true method, the Reds used their supposed inability to acquire and retain higher-priced players as the primary reason for needing a new ballpark. As the club shed salary in its final years at Cinergy Field, chief operating officer John Allen pointed to the future and tossed out $15 million as the anticipated payroll bump when the team entered its new digs. Then last November, Allen admitted the payroll wouldn't increase much in 2003, while at the same time stating that the team anticipates $25 million in new revenue (a conservative estimate, based on previous stadium debuts).

The timing of the announcement couldn't have been much worse, since any local benefit from the self-imposed sales tax hike had already been reduced to hoping to field a better baseball team. After picking up an additional $51 million of cost overruns on $458 million Paul Brown Stadium, the Bengals rewarded Cincinnati with three more seasons of suckiness. Property tax reductions that were to be funded by the half-cent stadium tax were the first thing slashed by Hamilton County commissioners when stadium costs were higher than expected and tax collections fell short of projections. The Reds themselves had just finished disappointing the city by refusing to add salary during the 2002 stretch drive, causing a team that was in first place as late as July 1 to stagger to the finish line 19 games behind the division-winning Cardinals.

Consequently, Cincinnatians weren't in any mood to listen to management's excuses for its sudden reversal after years of promises. The team continued shooting itself in the foot by blaming its fiscal constraints on the revenue-sharing provisions of the new collective bargaining agreement. This after Lindner had aligned himself closely with Selig during talks between owners and the players' association to ensure that the final agreement would benefit his small-market team.

Along with destroying whatever trust remained between the team and the city, Lindner has pissed away any chance of taking full advantage of the new ballpark with his shortsighted stinginess. He should have looked past the bottom lines in the year or two leading up to the opening of Great American Ball Park and positioned the team for success, similar to what the Indians did heading into Jacobs Field and what the Phillies are doing as they prepare to move into their new stadium in 2004. Putting an exciting, competitive team on the field for the first few post-Cinergy seasons would have maximized revenue streams and established a strong following for years to come. Instead, Lindner has aligned himself with Selig again, following the Brewers "plan" of making money hand over fist in Year One, as curiosity seekers eyeball the new structure, then disappear after satisfying their curiosity and realizing there's no greater reason to head out to the ballpark.

Contrary to the grousing used to extort their new home and help ramrod the latest CBA down the players' throats, Cincinnati is a strong baseball town. Only a handful of clubs can match the Reds' tradition and passionate following, and the team has little competition for the local sports dollar. Prior to the last five years, the Reds consistently ranked far higher in attendance than would be expected with a market size that places 22nd out of 30 teams.

Even as Lindner fritters away opportunities in his beloved Queen City, there is still a solid foundation in place to push the organization to the next level. Jim Bowden may not be the discriminating stathead's GM of choice, but he has demonstrated that he can assemble playoff-caliber teams with deft trades and free-agent signings, and can build a productive

farm system when provided the resources. Sometimes he seems to lack a clear strategy and confuses motion with progress; however, it's tough to formulate and execute a plan when the club's financial parameters are a wildly moving target. Bowden and his front office staff look at things from different angles, unafraid to challenge conventional thinking. As a result, last year's closer, Danny Graves, becomes this year's starter, and the return of the four-man rotation might not be that far off.

Closer to the playing field, pitching coach Don Gullett is the closest thing there is to an alchemist in baseball today. His knack for turning other teams' castoff arms into reliable rotation members allows the team to dedicate more resources to other areas. The Reds also control Adam Dunn, Griffey, and Austin Kearns for at least the next five years. If Griffey can get healthy, and Dunn and Kearns develop as anticipated, Cincinnati will have the best outfield since Rickey Henderson, Dwayne Murphy, and Tony Armas chased flies in the Oakland Coliseum in the early-1980s.

These positives make the 90-win barrier attainable if the injury bug stays away and a few players have surprise seasons. In other words, the Reds can land in the playoffs this year if pretty much everything breaks their way. Despite the recent posturing about more than half the teams in baseball lacking hope and faith, there aren't a whole lot of clubs that can't state the same thing. The Reds need commitment from their ownership if they are to separate themselves from the pack and emerge as a consistent postseason contender. Old dogs don't change easily, so until Carl Lindner leaves the picture, it's unlikely we'll see that commitment in Cincinnati.

HITTERS

Andy Beattie — UT — Born: 28-Feb-78 — Age: 25 — Bats: B — Throws: R

YEAR	TM	LG	AGE	AB	H	2B	3B	HR	BB	SO	SB	CS	AVG	OBP	SLG	MLVR	EQBA	EQOBP	EQSLG	EQMLVR	VORP	DEFENSE	
2000	CLN	MDW	22	398	124	30	4	4	44	58	18	7	.312	.381	.437	.213	.244	.292	.345	-.243	-2.6	85-SS -16	
2001	MUD	CLF	23	227	71	17	0	7	28	50	11	2	.313	.395	.480	.283	.252	.317	.385	-.133	2.8	37-CF -6	11-2B -4
2001	CHT	SOU	23	169	45	12	0	3	21	30	4	2	.266	.351	.391	.033	.230	.297	.345	-.242	-1.3	29-2B -3	
2002	STO	CLF	24	350	101	21	2	15	53	88	26	5	.289	.387	.489	.267	.239	.315	.398	-.129	4.8	74-CF -3	
2002	CHT	SOU	24	166	41	9	1	6	18	30	2	2	.247	.321	.422	.043	.218	.273	.376	-.254	-3.2	35-CF -6	
2003	CIN	NL	25	178	44	10	1	5	18	37	4	3	.250	.322	.397	-.080	.253	.321	.411	-.084	2.0		

Breakout: 36%   Improve: 64%   Collapse: 20%

The Reds' high-A Stockton club played .636 baseball en route to winning the Cal League championship, which could make you think they had a lineup chock full of prospects. On the contrary, for the most part it was a collection of minor league soldiers-to-be, Beattie included. He had nothing to prove in Mudville, but was sent down so the good people of Chattanooga could continue to bask in the glory of Tom Nevers. Beattie is built like Chris Stynes and has an outside shot at a similar career as a utilityman.

Aaron Boone   2B/3B   Born: 09-Mar-73   Age: 30   Bats: R   Throws: R

YEAR	TM	LG	AGE	AB	H	2B	3B	HR	BB	SO	SB	CS	AVG	OBP	SLG	MLVR	EQBA	EQOBP	EQSLG	EQMLVR	VORP	DEFENSE			
2000	CIN	NL	27	291	83	18	0	12	24	52	6	1	.285	.360	.471	.061	.281	.345	.462	.049	18.3	82-3B	9		
2001	CIN	NL	28	381	112	26	2	14	29	71	6	3	.294	.356	.483	.109	.294	.351	.478	.095	29.3	101-3B	-1		
2002	CIN	NL	29	606	146	38	2	26	56	111	32	8	.241	.315	.439	-.007	.242	.311	.444	-.070	18.6	144-3B	12	13-SS	-3
2003	CIN	NL	30	493	132	29	3	18	45	92	18	7	.268	.335	.449	.024	.271	.335	.465	.025	21.4				

Breakout: 19%   *Improve: 62%*   *Collapse: 11%*

After four assorted surgeries the two previous years, the coach's kid stayed away from the injury bug, playing the full 162-game slate. Wedged between a ghastly start (.194/.269/.274 on May 24) and a gasping finish were four months of sturdy offense and occasionally spectacular glovework. Boone's range allows him to fill in at shortstop and may prompt a position switch when Barry Larkin retires. For now he'll start at second base on Opening Day, with Brandon Larson moving to third, Larkin hogging short and newly acquired Felipe Lopez eating pine. Given an occasional breather, Boone could be an All-Star this season.

Russell Branyan   LF/1B/3B   Born: 19-Dec-75   Age: 27   Bats: L   Throws: R

YEAR	TM	LG	AGE	AB	H	2B	3B	HR	BB	SO	SB	CS	AVG	OBP	SLG	MLVR	EQBA	EQOBP	EQSLG	EQMLVR	VORP	DEFENSE			
2000	BUF	INT	24	229	56	9	2	21	28	93	1	1	.245	.332	.576	.188	.225	.302	.519	.002	11.7	35-3B	-2	19-LF	-1
2000	CLE	AL	24	193	46	7	2	16	22	76	0	0	.238	.329	.544	.060	.241	.326	.560	.114	9.7	31-LF	-1		
2001	CLE	AL	25	315	73	16	2	20	38	132	1	1	.232	.320	.486	.022	.244	.334	.514	.068	21.2	61-3B	-8	23-LF	-3
2002	CLE	AL	26	161	33	4	0	8	17	65	1	2	.205	.281	.379	-.189	.222	.296	.420	-.147	-2.5	36-LF	-1		
2002	CIN	NL	26	217	53	9	1	16	34	86	3	1	.244	.352	.516	.152	.245	.346	.523	.102	11.3	20-LF	-1	18-1B	6
2003	CIN	NL	27	256	60	12	1	15	33	93	2	3	.233	.323	.463	-.005	.236	.322	.480	-.005	3.4				

Breakout: 11%   *Improve: 40%*   *Collapse: 28%*

Bowden's penchant for monster mashers put Branyan behind the wheel careening down I-71 last June. While Branyan was only too happy to put Indians' hitting coach Eddie Murray in the rearview mirror, the road to Cincinnati ended in more part-time work. Since Bob Boone likes Branyan's power off the bench, that'll be his role in 2003. It's maddening to see a valuable player underutilized simply because he too frequently carries his own bat back to the dugout after making an out. It makes as much sense as keeping an Esperante parked in the driveway out of fear the paint will get chipped. Branyan underwent surgery to repair a torn labrum in his right shoulder last December and is expected to miss all of spring training.

Sean Casey   1B   Born: 02-Jul-74   Age: 29   Bats: L   Throws: R

YEAR	TM	LG	AGE	AB	H	2B	3B	HR	BB	SO	SB	CS	AVG	OBP	SLG	MLVR	EQBA	EQOBP	EQSLG	EQMLVR	VORP	DEFENSE	
2000	CIN	NL	26	480	151	33	2	20	52	80	1	0	.315	.390	.517	.208	.308	.374	.507	.189	37.0	122-1B	-2
2001	CIN	NL	27	533	165	40	0	13	43	63	3	1	.310	.371	.458	.114	.309	.368	.455	.106	29.4	124-1B	2
2002	CIN	NL	28	425	111	25	0	6	43	47	2	1	.261	.336	.362	-.058	.265	.334	.370	-.113	-1.9	103-1B	1
2003	CIN	NL	28	387	109	23	1	9	38	49	2	1	.280	.348	.418	.012	.284	.347	.433	.013	5.8		

Breakout: 6%   *Improve: 39%*   *Collapse: 21%*

Six home runs from your starting first baseman in the year 2002? Casey is on his way to becoming Wes Parker without the mantel lined with Gold Gloves and a failed acting career. Yes, Casey played much of the season with a torn muscle in his left shoulder, but his power has now declined for three consecutive seasons. Casey is very popular around town and in the clubhouse, where he leads the Reds' postgame victory dance. However, you'll know the organization is serious about winning when they move his hefty contract and reinvest it at a position where good help is harder to find.

Juan Castro   SS/2B   Born: 20-Jun-72   Age: 31   Bats: R   Throws: R

YEAR	TM	LG	AGE	AB	H	2B	3B	HR	BB	SO	SB	CS	AVG	OBP	SLG	MLVR	EQBA	EQOBP	EQSLG	EQMLVR	VORP	DEFENSE			
2000	LOU	INT	28	60	19	5	1	2	12	12	0	1	.317	.431	.533	.349	.295	.394	.475	.166	6.5	14-SS	-1		
2000	CIN	NL	28	224	54	12	2	4	14	33	0	2	.241	.286	.366	-.266	.236	.271	.360	-.268	-2.9	41-SS	7	18-2B	-1
2001	CIN	NL	29	242	54	10	0	3	13	50	0	0	.223	.263	.302	-.367	.225	.262	.303	-.373	-9.9	29-SS	-5	21-2B	-2
2002	CIN	NL	30	82	18	3	0	2	7	18	0	0	.220	.281	.329	-.222	.229	.281	.337	-.285	-1.4	13-SS	-2		
2003	CIN	NL	31	106	24	5	0	2	8	21	0	1	.231	.286	.328	-.246	.234	.285	.339	-.256	-2.9				

Breakout: 35%   *Improve: 55%*   *Collapse: 24%*

Early last season, the Reds gave Castro a two-year, $1.7 million contract extension. This move was designed to give the team some cost certainty as it moved into the new ballpark. The problem is that slick-fielding, banjo-hitting backup middle infielders like Castro are the very definition of cost certainty—they're called "minor league free agents."

Bobby Darula — LF — Born: 29-Oct-74 — Age: 28 — Bats: L — Throws: R

YEAR	TM	LG	AGE	AB	H	2B	3B	HR	BB	SO	SB	CS	AVG	OBP	SLG	MLVR	EQBA	EQOBP	EQSLG	EQMLVR	VORP	DEFENSE	
2000	BLT	MDW	25	237	91	18	3	3	44	25	16	2	.384	.497	.523	.529	.290	.376	.400	.026	7.1	24-RF	-1
2000	HUN	SOU	25	117	28	7	0	1	14	17	3	1	.239	.336	.325	-.055	.223	.296	.306	-.302	-7.4	25-RF	-3
2001	HUN	SOU	26	65	18	2	1	2	4	7	1	1	.277	.329	.431	.064	.242	.281	.379	-.218	-2.3	10-LF	-1
2001	HDS	CLF	26	254	77	10	6	2	42	26	15	4	.303	.420	.413	.157	.230	.323	.312	-.236	-9.7	21-LF	-5
2002	CHT	SOU	27	323	105	17	4	4	43	27	10	3	.325	.414	.440	.261	.287	.354	.393	-.027	5.3	77-LF	-13
2002	LOU	INT	27	49	12	1	0	0	7	4	0	0	.245	.339	.265	-.166	.240	.321	.260	-.305	-2.8	12-LF	0
2003	CIN	NL	28	149	39	8	1	1	17	17	3	1	.262	.341	.361	-.087	.265	.340	.373	-.090	-2.2		

Breakout: 20%   Improve: 42%   Collapse: 32%

Darula makes the book because he led the Southern League in batting average. Period. He couldn't crack the Brewers' 40-man roster after six years of trying, packs the power of an Atari 400, and plays left field like the converted catcher he is. Does an entry in *BP2003* qualify as 15 minutes of fame?

Gookie Dawkins — SS/2B — Born: 12-May-79 — Age: 24 — Bats: R — Throws: R

YEAR	TM	LG	AGE	AB	H	2B	3B	HR	BB	SO	SB	CS	AVG	OBP	SLG	MLVR	EQBA	EQOBP	EQSLG	EQMLVR	VORP	DEFENSE			
2000	CHT	SOU	21	368	85	20	6	6	40	71	22	10	.231	.311	.367	-.051	.208	.267	.335	-.328	-11.3	53-SS	-3	38-2B	1
2001	CHT	SOU	22	394	89	16	3	8	32	88	14	4	.226	.287	.343	-.160	.200	.248	.304	-.414	-20.9	95-SS	-5		
2002	CHT	SOU	23	155	42	10	1	1	25	28	5	5	.271	.372	.368	.065	.237	.315	.325	-.230	-.5	24-SS	0	14-2B	-6
2002	LOU	INT	23	167	42	5	2	0	12	34	2	3	.251	.306	.305	-.172	.238	.292	.292	-.321	-4.3	46-SS	5		
2002	CIN	NL	23	48	6	2	0	0	6	21	2	1	.125	.222	.167	-.572	.125	.222	.188	-.653	-5.6	12-SS	-3		
2003	CIN	NL	24	178	43	9	1	3	17	38	4	3	.241	.310	.354	-.163	.244	.309	.367	-.170	-.5				

Breakout: 56%   Improve: 76%   Collapse: 14%

Since a fluke 1999 campaign, Dawkins has been idling in neutral and occasionally rolling backward. Even so, he could have left Sarasota as either the Reds' utility infielder or had a shot at the starting second baseman's job before the club settled its Boone-Larkin-Larson-Lopez mess. If Castro and Lopez both make the team, Dawkins is staring at a fifth season in Appalachia, a streak that's beginning to approach Arnold Ziffel's memorable run in the late 1960s.

Adam Dunn — LF/1B — Born: 09-Nov-79 — Age: 23 — Bats: L — Throws: R

YEAR	TM	LG	AGE	AB	H	2B	3B	HR	BB	SO	SB	CS	AVG	OBP	SLG	MLVR	EQBA	EQOBP	EQSLG	EQMLVR	VORP	DEFENSE			
2000	DYT	MDW	20	420	118	29	1	16	100	101	24	5	.281	.432	.469	.289	.211	.325	.354	-.187	-11.9	115-LF	-13		
2001	CHT	SOU	21	140	48	9	0	12	24	31	6	3	.343	.449	.664	.600	.283	.372	.545	.213	12.4	39-LF	-2		
2001	LOU	INT	21	210	69	13	0	20	38	51	5	1	.329	.443	.676	.581	.301	.409	.616	.388	28.8	54-LF	-1		
2001	CIN	NL	21	244	64	18	1	19	38	74	4	2	.262	.371	.578	.230	.259	.363	.571	.209	20.2	63-RF	3		
2002	CIN	NL	22	535	133	28	2	26	128	170	19	9	.249	.402	.454	.157	.245	.394	.454	.096	29.1	104-LF	-4	40-1B	-8
2003	CIN	NL	23	504	134	27	2	30	101	136	18	7	.265	.391	.502	.178	.268	.390	.520	.184	31.9				

Breakout: 20%   Improve: 67%   Collapse: 9%

He fell considerably short of Hidalgo depths, but you can chalk Dunn up as another casualty of the dreaded BP cover jinx. Although his 128 walks broke the major league record by players under 23 years of age, Dunn struggled with the strike zone all season long. He was tentative at the plate, too often passing on meatballs early in the count. Feeling that his natural position is first base, Boone gave him plenty of on-the-job training when Casey was hurt. Right now, as a first baseman he makes a better left fielder. Dunn has too much drive and natural talent not to bounce back this season.

Edwin Encarnacion — 3B/SS — Born: 07-Jan-83 — Age: 20 — Bats: R — Throws: R

YEAR	TM	LG	AGE	AB	H	2B	3B	HR	BB	SO	SB	CS	AVG	OBP	SLG	MLVR	EQBA	EQOBP	EQSLG	EQMLVR	VORP	DEFENSE			
2001	BIL	PIO	18	211	55	8	2	5	15	29	8	1	.261	.310	.389	-.087	.171	.205	.252	-.587	-20.0	51-3B	-5		
2001	SAV	SAL	18	170	52	9	2	4	12	34	3	3	.306	.359	.453	.240	.247	.287	.365	-.222	-1.6	44-3B	-11		
2002	DYT	MDW	19	518	146	32	4	17	40	108	25	7	.282	.342	.458	.168	.219	.262	.357	-.301	-15.0	116-3B	-12	15-SS	-5
2003	CIN	NL	20	219	53	10	2	6	17	46	5	4	.240	.299	.384	-.143	.243	.298	.398	-.148	-1.3				

Breakout: 67%   Improve: 75%   Collapse: 16%

Included in the Rob Bell-for-Ruben Mateo trade at the insistence of special assistant Al Goldis, Encarnacion could end up as the best player in the deal. He possesses tape measure power, but must curb his aggressiveness to display it more often. Although the organization knows the importance of plate discipline, they need to be more consistent in emphasizing it. Defensively, Encarnacion's tools are so good that last year's trial at shortstop will be extended into this season. The Reds have an impressive block of clay in their hands; it's up to them to fashion it into something useful.

Ken Griffey Jr.   CF   Born: 21-Nov-69   Age: 33   Bats: L   Throws: L

YEAR	TM	LG	AGE	AB	H	2B	3B	HR	BB	SO	SB	CS	AVG	OBP	SLG	MLVR	EQBA	EQOBP	EQSLG	EQMLVR	VORP	DEFENSE
2000	CIN	NL	30	520	141	22	3	40	94	117	6	4	.271	.392	.556	.220	.265	.377	.541	.198	56.3	136-CF 10
2001	CIN	NL	31	364	104	20	2	22	44	72	2	0	.286	.369	.533	.191	.283	.364	.527	.175	36.5	74-CF 1
2002	CIN	NL	32	197	52	8	0	8	28	39	1	2	.264	.364	.426	.073	.266	.361	.432	.024	10.9	40-CF -1
2003	CIN	NL	33	238	60	11	1	10	32	49	2	1	.253	.345	.430	.005	.256	.345	.446	.005	7.9	

Breakout: 4%   Improve: 39%   Collapse: 19%

As the condition of Griffey's legs has regressed from fair to critical, his place in the mind of baseball fans has gone from being a member of the All-Century Team to an afterthought. It's likely that his rehab and training regimen this past off-season will prove to be the most important factor toward a return to his old form. The playing surface at Great American Park should help, too, because while Cinergy's AstroTurf was gone when Griffey arrived, the grass that replaced it was too spongy. Mickey Mantle's career ended prematurely due to bad legs. Let's hope the same thing doesn't happen to another Hall of Fame center fielder four decades later. A healthy Griffey in the lineup for 145 games is worth five games in the standings.

Jose Guillen   RF   Born: 17-May-76   Age: 27   Bats: R   Throws: R

YEAR	TM	LG	AGE	AB	H	2B	3B	HR	BB	SO	SB	CS	AVG	OBP	SLG	MLVR	EQBA	EQOBP	EQSLG	EQMLVR	VORP	DEFENSE
2000	TBY	AL	24	316	80	16	5	10	18	65	3	1	.253	.320	.430	-.094	.260	.319	.448	-.035	3.2	84-RF 1
2001	TBY	AL	25	135	37	5	0	3	6	26	2	3	.274	.319	.378	-.084	.289	.335	.407	-.040	1.2	36-RF 2
2001	DUR	INT	25	119	35	9	0	7	3	28	0	0	.294	.311	.546	.207	.275	.293	.517	.033	3.2	27-RF -1
2002	ARI	NL	26	131	30	4	0	4	7	25	3	4	.229	.279	.351	-.191	.227	.275	.348	-.283	-6.7	29-RF 0
2002	CSP	PCL	26	17	7	3	0	0	1	2	0	1	.412	.474	.588	.553	.353	.375	.529	.274	1.6	
2002	LOU	INT	26	29	9	4	0	2	0	5	0	0	.310	.310	.655	.370	.276	.276	.621	.161	2.0	
2002	CIN	NL	26	109	27	3	0	4	7	18	1	1	.248	.299	.385	-.099	.245	.296	.391	-.170	-2.6	22-RF 0
2003	CIN	NL	27	236	62	13	1	9	15	44	3	2	.264	.315	.443	-.019	.267	.314	.459	-.020	-.1	

Breakout: 19%   Improve: 55%   Collapse: 27%

Guillen collected unemployment for three weeks last summer before agreeing to a minor league deal to be a RiverBat. As usual, he crushed Triple-A pitching (.345/.384/.631 career in Triple-A). But when promoted to stand in for Austin Kearns in September, he flailed like he did as a rushed, 21-year-old Pirates' rookie. Guillen's biggest contribution to the franchise will be playing the role of Wily Mo Pena when Bowden is visited by the Ghost of Redlegs' Future.

Austin Kearns   RF   Born: 20-May-80   Age: 23   Bats: R   Throws: R

YEAR	TM	LG	AGE	AB	H	2B	3B	HR	BB	SO	SB	CS	AVG	OBP	SLG	MLVR	EQBA	EQOBP	EQSLG	EQMLVR	VORP	DEFENSE
2000	DYT	MDW	20	484	148	37	2	27	90	93	18	5	.306	.422	.558	.408	.233	.318	.419	-.099	-3.0	130-RF -13
2001	CHT	SOU	21	205	55	11	2	6	26	43	7	5	.268	.367	.429	.111	.232	.309	.374	-.178	-5.9	52-RF -5
2002	CHT	SOU	22	41	11	2	0	5	9	9	1	0	.268	.434	.683	.536	.233	.350	.581	.174	2.9	10-RF -2
2002	CIN	NL	22	372	117	24	3	13	54	81	6	3	.315	.410	.500	.281	.313	.404	.501	.236	31.7	102-RF 2
2003	CIN	NL	23	483	140	31	2	22	62	95	10	4	.291	.375	.501	.175	.294	.375	.519	.182	26.8	

Breakout: 30%   Improve: 63%   Collapse: 11%

Kearns went AWOL when sent to Chattanooga near the end of the spring training. Three weeks later he was in Cincinnati and on his way to being the Reds' best hitter last season. Kearns is solidly above average in all phases of the game, combining outstanding knowledge of the strike zone with a vicious line drive stroke like a modern-day Al Kaline. Bowden took Kearns and Dunn with the club's top two picks in June 1998, a duo that will be regarded as the best one-two pairing in the history of the amateur draft within a few years. With Dunn, Griffey, and Kearns patrolling the outfield, the Reds will be perennial playoff contenders if the rest of the team is merely average.

Barry Larkin   SS   Born: 28-Apr-64   Age: 39   Bats: R   Throws: R

YEAR	TM	LG	AGE	AB	H	2B	3B	HR	BB	SO	SB	CS	AVG	OBP	SLG	MLVR	EQBA	EQOBP	EQSLG	EQMLVR	VORP	DEFENSE
2000	CIN	NL	36	396	124	26	5	11	48	31	14	6	.313	.389	.487	.163	.305	.373	.476	.141	38.8	94-SS -5
2001	CIN	NL	37	156	40	12	0	2	27	25	3	2	.256	.373	.372	-.039	.253	.368	.367	-.060	7.3	39-SS -8
2002	CIN	NL	38	507	124	37	2	7	44	57	13	4	.245	.309	.367	-.110	.246	.306	.373	-.175	5.6	121-SS 3
2003	CIN	NL	39	267	71	15	1	5	29	33	7	1	.265	.339	.382	-.060	.268	.338	.396	-.062	7.7	

Breakout: 22%   Improve: 43%   Collapse: 20%

Barry Larkin (*continued*)

Individual career paths generally resemble a jagged mountain, starting low, rising rapidly, and then slowly retreating. Although nagged by minor injuries, Larkin was able to play in 145 games last season. However, his performance returned to sea level, a virtual dead ringer of his first full season in 1987. Here's hoping that Larkin's upcoming retirement causes Reds rooters to stop beating the drum for Dave Concepcion's entrance into the Hall of Fame and take up the banner for a truly deserving shortstop candidate.

Brandon Larson　3B　Born: 24-May-76　Age: 27　Bats: R　Throws: R

YEAR	TM	LG	AGE	AB	H	2B	3B	HR	BB	SO	SB	CS	AVG	OBP	SLG	MLVR	EQBA	EQOBP	EQSLG	EQMLVR	VORP	DEFENSE
2000	CHT	SOU	24	427	116	26	0	20	31	122	15	5	.272	.333	.473	.149	.242	.282	.425	-.150	4.4	106-3B -22
2000	LOU	INT	24	63	18	7	1	2	4	16	0	0	.286	.328	.524	.150	.270	.303	.476	-.015	2.7	16-3B 3
2001	LOU	INT	25	424	108	22	2	14	24	123	5	6	.255	.313	.415	-.012	.239	.293	.391	-.180	.9	109-3B 16
2002	LOU	INT	26	297	101	20	1	25	24	70	1	1	.340	.395	.667	.531	.310	.365	.607	.320	38.6	64-3B -3
2002	CIN	NL	26	51	14	2	0	4	6	10	1	0	.275	.362	.549	.237	.269	.343	.558	.169	4.1	
2003	CIN	NL	27	245	63	13	1	11	20	63	3	4	.257	.319	.457	.001	.260	.318	.474	.001	6.9	

Breakout: 10%　Improve: 39%　Collapse: 22%

Anybody who tells you they saw that coming is lying. No team in baseball did, since the Reds took their 1997 first round pick off the 40-man roster in December 2001 and he went unclaimed. Laser eye surgery that enabled Larson to pick up the spin on a slider is credited for much of his progress. While batters with low walk and high strikeout totals aren't good bets to succeed, they're also the group most likely to have dramatic jumps in performance. At 27, we may have already seen the peak, but even if Larson gives a third of his improvement back, he still can help a team. To try to find a space for him in the lineup, the Reds had him work out at second base in the Florida Instructional League. They settled on handing Larson the third-base job, letting him settle in at his natural position.

Jason LaRue　C　Born: 19-Mar-74　Age: 29　Bats: R　Throws: R

YEAR	TM	LG	AGE	AB	H	2B	3B	HR	BB	SO	SB	CS	AVG	OBP	SLG	MLVR	EQBA	EQOBP	EQSLG	EQMLVR	VORP	DEFENSE
2000	LOU	INT	26	307	78	22	1	14	22	52	3	2	.254	.320	.469	.030	.236	.290	.437	-.123	8.7	71-C -5
2000	CIN	NL	26	98	23	3	0	5	5	19	0	0	.235	.299	.418	-.170	.232	.280	.424	-.163	1.8	30-C 2
2001	CIN	NL	27	364	86	21	2	12	27	106	3	3	.236	.305	.404	-.138	.237	.300	.406	-.147	8.6	94-C 11
2002	CIN	NL	28	353	88	17	1	12	27	117	1	2	.249	.326	.405	-.028	.252	.321	.417	-.081	13.9	98-C -1
2003	CIN	NL	29	304	72	15	1	10	25	81	2	3	.238	.303	.391	-.128	.241	.303	.405	-.134	2.4	

Breakout: 10%　Improve: 43%　Collapse: 23%

BP's 2001 Golden Gun winner hauled home the far less-coveted lead glove last year by allowing 20 passed balls, five more than any other NL team. Jared Fernandez wasn't the sole culprit, since LaRue caught less than half of the knuckleballer's 50 innings. Naturally, the miscues didn't sit well with his seven-time Gold Glove–winning manager. Either LaRue or Kelly Stinnett will be leaving town to make room for Corky Miller. The Reds would prefer to keep LaRue, who is Stinnett's equal offensively, but younger and cheaper.

Donny Leon　3B　Born: 07-May-76　Age: 27　Bats: B　Throws: R

YEAR	TM	LG	AGE	AB	H	2B	3B	HR	BB	SO	SB	CS	AVG	OBP	SLG	MLVR	EQBA	EQOBP	EQSLG	EQMLVR	VORP	DEFENSE
2000	TAM	FSL	24	79	17	6	0	1	6	23	0	0	.215	.279	.329	-.158	.175	.228	.275	-.506	-7.8	
2000	COH	INT	24	204	51	10	1	9	20	49	3	3	.250	.323	.441	-.006	.233	.293	.408	-.161	1.5	58-3B 4
2001	NRW	EAS	25	436	111	26	2	15	19	115	0	2	.255	.293	.427	.004	.228	.264	.379	-.260	-7.8	60-3B -12
2002	CHT	SOU	26	408	116	29	1	19	46	97	14	8	.284	.365	.500	.240	.247	.307	.439	-.080	11.5	98-3B -13
2002	LOU	INT	26	68	17	5	0	3	2	10	0	0	.250	.282	.456	-.013	.235	.265	.441	-.164	-.5	
2003	CIN	NL	27	174	41	9	1	6	15	44	3	3	.238	.303	.405	-.109	.241	.303	.419	-.114	.4	

Breakout: 34%　Improve: 55%　Collapse: 23%

Cincinnati signed Leon as a minor league free agent after he wore out his welcome in the Yankees' chain. For six weeks he set fire to the South like Sherman before cooling off and finishing exactly where you would have expected. He won't be back with the Reds after being suspended from Chattanooga for undisclosed reasons. Attitude problems can bring a quick end to the career of a marginal player. If Leon wants any shot at the major league minimum, he needs to realize that guys with his skill set aren't much tougher to find than a good plumber.

Ruben Mateo RF Born: 10-Feb-78 Age: 25 Bats: R Throws: R

YEAR	TM	LG	AGE	AB	H	2B	3B	HR	BB	SO	SB	CS	AVG	OBP	SLG	MLVR	EQBA	EQOBP	EQSLG	EQMLVR	VORP	DEFENSE	
2000	TEX	AL	22	206	60	11	0	7	10	34	6	0	.291	.339	.447	-.015	.294	.334	.456	.033	10.4	49-CF	1
2001	TEX	AL	23	129	32	5	2	1	9	28	1	0	.248	.326	.341	-.149	.264	.333	.364	-.124	-1.5	31-RF	-2
2001	LOU	INT	23	251	63	16	4	2	13	45	2	0	.251	.309	.371	-.080	.241	.292	.360	-.224	-9.5	58-RF	-5
2002	LOU	INT	24	209	63	14	0	9	11	40	6	2	.301	.345	.498	.188	.276	.322	.467	.011	4.5	42-RF	-5
2002	CIN	NL	24	86	22	6	0	2	6	20	0	0	.256	.319	.395	-.047	.264	.317	.414	-.084	-.2	16-RF	0
2003	CIN	NL	25	243	63	14	1	7	17	45	4	2	.261	.316	.409	-.067	.264	.315	.423	-.070	-2.4		

Breakout: 18%   Improve: 46%   Collapse: 28%

Mateo's career path isn't what would have been predicted three years ago, but he lost almost two years of critical development time shaking the effects of a broken femur suffered in 2000. The Reds have a very crowded outfield situation and can use the time bought by Wily Mo Pena's hamstring woes to sift through the field of candidates. Mateo is clearly a better option as the first outfielder off the bench than Reggie Taylor, but the club isn't sold on his ability to handle center field. Barring a major injury, somebody will be leaving town due to the roster crunch. Mateo probably still has the most trade value and could be sent packing.

Corky Miller C Born: 18-Mar-76 Age: 27 Bats: R Throws: R

YEAR	TM	LG	AGE	AB	H	2B	3B	HR	BB	SO	SB	CS	AVG	OBP	SLG	MLVR	EQBA	EQOBP	EQSLG	EQMLVR	VORP	DEFENSE	
2000	CHT	SOU	24	317	74	18	0	9	41	51	5	8	.233	.374	.375	.057	.213	.309	.348	-.225	.9	100-C	7
2001	CHT	SOU	25	170	47	12	0	9	25	32	1	2	.276	.425	.506	.300	.240	.353	.440	-.000	11.5	54-C	8
2001	LOU	INT	25	144	50	11	0	7	10	19	2	0	.347	.434	.569	.455	.322	.396	.534	.279	19.3	41-C	7
2002	CIN	NL	26	114	29	10	0	3	9	20	0	0	.254	.331	.421	.005	.252	.325	.426	-.062	5.1	35-C	3
2002	LOU	INT	26	134	31	5	0	6	16	21	1	2	.231	.340	.403	-.000	.221	.318	.382	-.157	2.8	39-C	-2
2003	CIN	NL	27	241	58	12	1	8	25	44	3	2	.241	.325	.398	-.080	.244	.324	.412	-.084	5.6		

Breakout: 13%   Improve: 29%   Collapse: 32%

Catchers can come from anywhere. Miller wasn't even drafted out of college, but made The Show just three years after signing a pro contract. Last season, he had played his way into the majority of the starts, but was farmed out to Louisville when Stinnett was activated because he had options left. Miller is an outstanding receiver, pitchers love working with him and he even has fair offensive potential. He'll be on the Reds roster this year, probably as the starter. Cool fact: Corky is his given name.

Rainer Olmedo SS Born: 31-May-81 Age: 22 Bats: B Throws: R

YEAR	TM	LG	AGE	AB	H	2B	3B	HR	BB	SO	SB	CS	AVG	OBP	SLG	MLVR	EQBA	EQOBP	EQSLG	EQMLVR	VORP	DEFENSE			
2000	DYT	MDW	19	369	94	19	1	4	30	70	17	11	.255	.313	.344	-.053	.199	.234	.273	-.486	-25.0	92-SS	-1	15-2B	4
2001	MUD	CLF	20	536	131	23	4	0	24	121	38	17	.244	.287	.302	-.195	.205	.234	.255	-.508	-38.7	126-SS	-5		
2002	CHT	SOU	21	478	118	21	1	3	53	86	15	16	.247	.331	.314	-.084	.219	.281	.282	-.367	-18.6	107-SS	-16	21-2B	0
2003	CIN	NL	22	194	45	8	1	3	16	37	4	3	.233	.296	.334	-.219	.236	.295	.346	-.228	-3.5				

Breakout: 64%   Improve: 78%   Collapse: 11%

Since the moment Larkin signed his final contract, the Reds have known they were going to need a new shortstop in 2004. Prior to acquiring Felipe Lopez, Olmedo was the best the system had to offer. He draws obligatory comparisons to fellow Venezuelan Omar Vizquel at the same age, and they are very alike. However, Vizquel always knew how to coax a walk from bush league tossers while Olmedo is only now learning that skill. More importantly, the shortstop landscape has changed dramatically in the past 15 years. There used to be one mountain on the horizon, but now there is an entire range with many peaks equal or higher than Mt. Ripken. While Vizquel's bat was inadequate when he broke in, Olmedo's looks like it will be unacceptable.

Wily Mo Pena OF Born: 23-Jan-82 Age: 21 Bats: R Throws: R

YEAR	TM	LG	AGE	AB	H	2B	3B	HR	BB	SO	SB	CS	AVG	OBP	SLG	MLVR	EQBA	EQOBP	EQSLG	EQMLVR	VORP	DEFENSE	
2000	STA	NYP	18	73	22	1	2	0	2	23	2	0	.301	.354	.370	.099	.233	.258	.288	-.398	-3.9	19-CF	-1
2000	GRB	SAL	18	249	51	7	1	10	18	91	6	5	.205	.272	.361	-.118	.161	.205	.283	-.549	-23.5	56-CF	-6
2001	DYT	MDW	19	511	135	25	5	26	33	177	26	10	.264	.330	.485	.139	.203	.248	.368	-.323	-18.5	127-CF	-2
2002	CHT	SOU	20	388	99	23	1	11	36	126	8	0	.255	.333	.405	.044	.227	.282	.369	-.240	-15.1	95-OF	-11
2003	CIN	NL	21	214	49	9	2	7	18	71	4	7	.228	.295	.385	-.157	.230	.294	.399	-.163	-6.6		

Breakout: 50%   Improve: 78%   Collapse: 14%

Wily Mo Pena *(continued)*

Ready or not (and he's not), here he is. Pena ruptured a hamstring tendon in the Arizona Fall League and underwent the same new procedure Edgar Martinez had last summer. Since Edgar is twice Pena's age and returned in 10 weeks, Pena should be 100% by spring training. Nonetheless, he'll almost certainly need "extended rehab" in Louisville. At some point the roster peek-a-boo will have to stop, and that's when the trouble starts. Keep in mind this isn't a Rule 5 situation where the pain lasts just one season—it's year one of an annual transgression that will ultimately strip away any chance of Pena's skills catching up with his enormous tools. It's why you don't give a major league contract to a 16-year-old kid.

Dane Sardinha — C — Born: 08-Apr-79 — Age: 24 — Bats: R — Throws: R

YEAR	TM	LG	AGE	AB	H	2B	3B	HR	BB	SO	SB	CS	AVG	OBP	SLG	MLVR	EQBA	EQOBP	EQSLG	EQMLVR	VORP	DEFENSE	
2001	MUD	CLF	22	422	99	24	2	9	12	97	0	1	.235	.261	.365	-.159	.193	.212	.296	-.501	-27.6	109-C	7
2002	CHT	SOU	23	394	81	20	0	4	14	114	0	2	.206	.237	.287	-.294	.190	.204	.270	-.556	-30.8	100-C	2
2003	*CIN*	*NL*	*24*	*137*	*29*	*6*	*1*	*3*	*6*	*38*	*1*	*2*	*.212*	*.244*	*.326*	*-.332*	*.214*	*.244*	*.338*	*-.345*	*-6.2*		

Breakout: 72%   Improve: 77%   Collapse: 12%

Defensively, Sardinha may well be the best catching prospect in the minors. Offensively, not so much. Don't be deceived by Sardinha's AFL mirage, his bat has less starch than Chris Kahrl's cotton oxfords. Like Pena, Sardinha holds a major league contract, with this the last option year. While the Reds could elect to expose the retro set to an updated version of Bill Plummer, unless Sardinha's hitting improves radically, Bowden should outright him this fall and hope that another club bites on the remaining three years of his deal.

Chris Sexton — IF — Born: 03-Aug-71 — Age: 31 — Bats: R — Throws: R

YEAR	TM	LG	AGE	AB	H	2B	3B	HR	BB	SO	SB	CS	AVG	OBP	SLG	MLVR	EQBA	EQOBP	EQSLG	EQMLVR	VORP	DEFENSE			
2000	LOU	INT	28	389	126	19	1	7	63	45	8	4	.324	.418	.432	.201	.296	.380	.398	.036	27.0	81-SS	8	15-2B	-4
2000	CIN	NL	28	100	21	4	0	0	13	12	4	2	.210	.313	.250	-.390	.208	.297	.248	-.386	-4.6	14-SS	-2		
2001	LOU	INT	29	409	114	25	3	2	40	57	5	5	.279	.344	.369	-.003	.260	.325	.347	-.166	5.8	91-SS	-2		
2002	LOU	INT	30	414	131	29	5	6	42	41	3	2	.316	.381	.454	.197	.294	.358	.427	.035	24.0	42-3B	-3	33-SS	0
2003	*SDP*	*NL*	*31*	*145*	*36*	*7*	*1*	*1*	*14*	*19*	*2*	*1*	*.247*	*.317*	*.331*	*-.177*	*.259*	*.324*	*.359*	*-.143*	*.2*				

Breakout: 3%   Improve: 29%   Collapse: 41%

In an unconventional defensive alignment, the Reds stationed their best utility infielder 100 miles down the Ohio River for the second straight season. Sexton can handle any infield position with aplomb and added extra-base power to his resume once he turned 30. The native Cincinnatian had hoped for a real opportunity with his hometown nine, but instead signed with San Diego as a minor league free agent.

Steve Smitherman — LF — Born: 01-Sep-78 — Age: 24 — Bats: R — Throws: R

YEAR	TM	LG	AGE	AB	H	2B	3B	HR	BB	SO	SB	CS	AVG	OBP	SLG	MLVR	EQBA	EQOBP	EQSLG	EQMLVR	VORP	DEFENSE	
2000	BIL	PIO	21	301	95	16	5	15	23	67	14	1	.316	.376	.551	.294	.209	.235	.361	-.354	-18.0	59-LF	-6
2001	DYT	MDW	22	497	139	45	2	20	43	113	16	7	.280	.349	.499	.197	.212	.263	.374	-.280	-24.5	125-LF	-8
2002	STO	CLF	23	482	151	36	1	19	39	126	17	2	.313	.372	.510	.301	.257	.299	.413	-.124	-4.4	118-LF	-5
2003	*CIN*	*NL*	*24*	*194*	*49*	*11*	*1*	*7*	*14*	*48*	*5*	*4*	*.251*	*.307*	*.421*	*-.071*	*.254*	*.307*	*.436*	*-.074*	*-2.4*		

Breakout: 54%   Improve: 78%   Collapse: 14%

Smitherman is the best outfield prospect in the system, although it's not clear the Reds recognize it. Despite being old for the Cal League and posting outstanding numbers in the best pitcher's park in the loop, he wasn't given a mid-season promotion to Chattanooga. A tremendous athlete, Smitherman fell to the 23rd round in 2000 in large part because he is diabetic. He needs to improve his pitch recognition and plate discipline in order to cross Double-A off his to-do list. We're more optimistic than we probably should be.

Kelly Stinnett — C — Born: 4-Feb-70 — Age: 33 — Bats: R — Throws: R

YEAR	TM	LG	AGE	AB	H	2B	3B	HR	BB	SO	SB	CS	AVG	OBP	SLG	MLVR	EQBA	EQOBP	EQSLG	EQMLVR	VORP	DEFENSE	
2000	ARI	NL	30	240	52	7	0	8	19	56	0	1	.217	.291	.346	-.301	.215	.275	.343	-.297	-4.1	70-C	1
2001	CIN	NL	31	187	48	11	0	9	17	61	2	2	.257	.335	.460	.008	.259	.330	.460	.001	12.1	52-C	-10
2002	LOU	INT	32	86	17	6	0	0	3	24	0	0	.198	.225	.267	-.395	.198	.225	.267	-.513	-5.8	22-C	0
2002	CIN	NL	32	93	21	5	0	3	15	25	2	0	.226	.333	.376	-.067	.223	.330	.383	-.131	2.7	29-C	-4
2003	*CIN*	*NL*	*33*	*158*	*36*	*8*	*0*	*4*	*15*	*42*	*2*	*1*	*.226*	*.300*	*.354*	*-.189*	*.229*	*.299*	*.366*	*-.197*	*-1.2*		

Breakout: 23%   Improve: 55%   Collapse: 30%

Stinnett's saga makes you wonder if sometimes anybody is driving the Big Red bus. The career backup was given a two-year, $2.55 million contract extension a month into his first season with the Reds in 2001. Not even a year later, he was placed on waivers to try to dump that contract. When nobody bit, the Reds put him on the DL with simple elbow tendonitis and didn't reinstate him for three (!) months. Then, instead of being showcased for a possible trade, he saw limited action the rest of the season. Stinnett will be a reliable, if overpaid, reserve wherever he ends up.

Reggie Taylor — CF — Born: 12-Jan-77 — Age: 26 — Bats: L — Throws: R

YEAR	TM	LG	AGE	AB	H	2B	3B	HR	BB	SO	SB	CS	AVG	OBP	SLG	MLVR	EQBA	EQOBP	EQSLG	EQMLVR	VORP	DEFENSE
2000	SWB	INT	23	422	116	10	8	15	21	87	23	12	.275	.312	.443	.009	.256	.284	.414	-.151	3.0	97-CF -2
2001	SWB	INT	24	464	122	20	9	7	24	94	31	15	.263	.303	.390	-.048	.249	.289	.371	-.209	-3.5	107-CF -4
2002	CIN	NL	25	287	73	15	4	9	14	79	11	8	.254	.294	.429	-.046	.255	.289	.431	-.118	4.3	77-CF -3
2003	CIN	NL	26	251	63	12	3	6	16	57	10	7	.250	.299	.389	-.129	.253	.299	.403	-.134	-2.7	

Breakout: 18%   Improve: 51%   Collapse: 29%

The failed Phillies' first-rounder has found a niche on the banks of the Ohio River. Taylor accepts his backup role and isn't without uses. He can pinch run, play good defense anywhere in the outfield, and won't kill a team in an occasional start against a right-handed hurler. However, Boone is too willing to put Taylor and his sub-300 OBP in the lineup for extended stretches when a regular is sidelined, a common recent occurrence with Griffey's bad wheels.

Todd Walker — 2B — Born: 25-May-73 — Age: 30 — Bats: L — Throws: R

YEAR	TM	LG	AGE	AB	H	2B	3B	HR	BB	SO	SB	CS	AVG	OBP	SLG	MLVR	EQBA	EQOBP	EQSLG	EQMLVR	VORP	DEFENSE
2000	MIN	AL	27	77	18	1	0	2	7	10	3	0	.234	.298	.325	-.308	.237	.301	.329	-.252	-.7	17-2B -9
2000	SLC	PCL	27	249	81	14	1	2	32	32	8	3	.325	.402	.414	.068	.275	.340	.352	-.120	5.8	59-2B 0
2000	COL	NL	27	171	54	10	4	7	20	19	4	1	.316	.391	.544	.202	.296	.363	.509	.161	17.2	43-2B -4
2001	COL	NL	28	290	86	18	2	12	25	40	1	3	.297	.352	.497	.086	.280	.338	.471	.049	20.4	71-2B -2
2001	CIN	NL	28	261	77	17	0	5	26	42	0	5	.295	.361	.418	.028	.292	.355	.413	.008	16.1	60-2B -5
2002	CIN	NL	29	612	183	42	3	11	50	81	8	5	.299	.355	.431	.092	.300	.352	.436	.042	40.5	147-2B 2
2003	BOS	NL	30	524	144	29	3	10	50	73	6	3	.274	.339	.402	-.027	.277	.338	.419	-.027	17.8	

Breakout: 12%   Improve: 37%   Collapse: 25%

Walker has left Tom Kelly in his wake and planted himself in the top third of second sackers, but there are a myriad of reasons why the team needs to trade him. As a 30-year-old second baseman he's going to get worse, not better. He's owed at least $3.4 million in the final year of his contract. He's due to be a free agent, and with much of his value stored in his batting average, he's likely to command more money than he's worth. The only fly in the ointment is that Bowden will have to find an outside replacement because the Reds upper-level middle infielders aren't going to make anybody forget Pokey Reese. Mission accomplished: Walker was dealt to the Red Sox, and Felipe Lopez was brought in from Toronto.

PITCHERS

Jose Acevedo — Born: 18-Dec-77 — Age: 25 — Bats: R — Throws: R

YEAR	TM	LG	AGE	G	GS	IP	H	BB	SO	HR	ERA	EQERA	EQH9	EQBB9	EQSO9	EQHR9	PERA	VORP	STF
2000	DYT	MDW	22	25	23	141.0	135	53	123	16	3.89	6.00	12.5	4.3	5.1	2.7	6.55	-7.8	-4
2001	CHT	SOU	23	16	11	78.0	68	25	82	6	3.69	4.57	9.3	3.4	6.4	1.1	4.67	8.0	11
2001	CIN	NL	23	18	18	96.0	101	34	68	17	5.44	5.06	9.4	3.0	5.4	1.4	4.94	4.7	6
2002	CIN	NL	24	6	5	23.7	28	12	14	8	7.22	7.53	10.8	4.0	4.6	3.0	7.33	-5.4	-20
2002	LOU	INT	24	23	23	154.7	146	34	128	16	3.20	4.15	9.5	2.4	6.4	1.4	4.30	23.3	16
2003	CIN	NL	25	16	10	65.7	71	27	50	9	5.00	5.34	10.0	3.2	6.0	1.3	5.19	3.2	0

Breakout: 18%   Improve: 44%   Collapse: 27%

Hammered in two brief early season stints, the Reds exiled Acevedo to Louisville for the rest of the year. Although the demotion smacked more of disgust than player development, it was the proper tonic for Acevedo's disorders. He tightened his command and began thinking of pitching as a craft instead of mere physical activity. That Acevedo wasn't recalled when the rosters expanded indicates that the organization has soured on him. He's ready to help someone at the major league level.

Ricardo Aramboles   Born: 04-Dec-81   Age: 21   Bats: R   Throws: R

YEAR	TM	LG	AGE	G	GS	IP	H	BB	SO	HR	ERA	EQERA	EQH9	EQBB9	EQSO9	EQHR9	PERA	VORP	STF
2000	GRB	SAL	18	25	25	137.7	150	47	150	12	4.31	6.94	13.9	4.3	5.8	2.1	7.29	-22.0	1
2001	TAM	FSL	19	12	11	68.7	72	19	59	5	4.06	6.26	12.9	3.1	5.3	1.7	6.52	-5.8	5
2001	COH	INT	19	4	4	23.7	26	4	14	2	3.04	4.45	10.3	1.8	4.1	1.0	5.05	2.8	7
2001	DYT	MDW	19	4	4	19.7	23	4	9	2	3.65	6.04	15.1	2.7	2.7	2.2	7.14	-1.2	-16
2002	CHT	SOU	20	4	4	23.0	22	8	22	0	3.13	3.90	9.8	3.3	6.2	0.3	4.49	4.1	21

Aramboles tore a thumb ligament in April and followed that up with a scope job on his wonky elbow in August. For someone who has barely worked 50 innings since joining the organization in June 2001, the Reds remain very high on him, likening him to Francisco Rodriguez. Anything is possible, but right now the most accurate part of the comparison is that Aramboles will have to move to the bullpen if he can't learn to throw a pitch with a wrinkle. He'll open the season as a Lookout and probably be unveiled in Great American Ballpark in September if he can stay healthy.

Bobby Basham   Born: 07-Mar-80   Age: 23   Bats: R   Throws: R

YEAR	TM	LG	AGE	G	GS	IP	H	BB	SO	HR	ERA	EQERA	EQH9	EQBB9	EQSO9	EQHR9	PERA	VORP	STF
2001	BIL	PIO	21	6	6	29.7	36	17	37	2	4.85	9.25	16.8	8.4	6.6	1.6	8.72	-12.4	-6
2002	DYT	MDW	22	13	13	87.7	64	9	97	4	1.64	3.40	9.0	1.3	6.2	1.1	3.21	20.5	24
2003	CIN	NL	23	15	13	82.0	85	27	62	10	4.37	4.67	9.6	2.6	6.0	1.0	4.53	9.0	9

Breakout: 17%   Improve: 47%   Collapse: 19%

Where did that come from? Basham showed good stuff and poor control in a brief stint at Billings in 2001, but returned from winter classes at the University of Richmond a different pitcher. While it's not unusual for college hurlers to dominate low-A ball, his numbers with Dayton were Schillingesque and he backed it up with a similar showing in the AFL. Basham now finds the target with all the bullets in his holster: a low-90s fastball, tight-breaking 12-6 yakker and his best pitch, a true major league slider. With Cincinnati hunting for quality arms ready to step in and help, Basham should rise very rapidly.

Bruce Chen   Born: 19-Jun-77   Age: 26   Bats: B   Throws: L

YEAR	TM	LG	AGE	G	GS	IP	H	BB	SO	HR	ERA	EQERA	EQH9	EQBB9	EQSO9	EQHR9	PERA	VORP	STF
2000	ATL	NL	23	22	0	39.7	35	19	32	4	2.49	3.51	8.1	3.5	6.4	0.8	3.84	8.2	6
2000	PHI	NL	23	15	15	94.3	81	27	80	14	3.63	3.44	7.8	2.1	6.8	1.2	3.46	21.6	24
2001	PHI	NL	24	16	16	86.3	90	31	79	19	5.01	5.57	9.8	3.0	7.1	1.8	5.48	-0.6	11
2001	NYM	NL	24	11	11	59.7	56	28	47	10	4.67	5.26	8.9	4.0	6.1	1.4	5.01	1.6	6
2002	MON	NL	25	15	5	37.3	47	23	43	9	7.00	7.14	11.4	4.8	8.9	2.2	7.51	-7.0	1
2002	CIN	NL	25	39	1	39.7	37	20	37	7	4.31	5.10	8.5	4.0	7.3	1.6	4.86	1.3	-2
2003	CIN	NL	26	31	10	77.7	72	36	68	10	4.29	4.59	8.5	3.5	7.0	1.2	4.57	8.0	3

Breakout: 16%   Improve: 56%   Collapse: 19%

Having worn the colors of four NL East teams in less than 21 months, the next logical stop for Chen was Florida. Instead, he hung a right out of Montreal and landed in Cincinnati last June. Chen showed some improvement after arriving, but still hasn't approached the promise he flashed as a Braves' farmhand. There's a reason that a player with his raw talent is traded so often, and it usually has more to do with attitude than ability. Chen will be fighting for a spot in the rotation when camp opens. With Don Gullett in his corner, this might be his last best chance for success.

Lance Davis   Born: 01-Sep-76   Age: 26   Bats: R   Throws: L

YEAR	TM	LG	AGE	G	GS	IP	H	BB	SO	HR	ERA	EQERA	EQH9	EQBB9	EQSO9	EQHR9	PERA	VORP	STF
2000	CHT	SOU	23	25	16	115.7	96	52	98	4	2.18	4.38	9.3	4.4	5.4	0.6	4.68	14.2	4
2000	LOU	INT	23	5	5	32.0	32	8	14	4	3.38	5.07	10.1	2.3	3.4	1.4	4.67	1.5	-2
2001	LOU	INT	24	13	13	79.7	81	15	47	7	3.05	4.50	10.6	2.0	4.2	1.1	4.60	8.9	4
2001	CIN	NL	24	20	20	106.3	124	34	53	12	4.74	4.78	10.7	2.7	3.8	0.9	4.97	8.6	-1
2002	LOU	INT	25	11	11	62.0	78	17	27	9	4.50	5.89	12.9	3.0	3.4	1.9	6.72	-2.7	-14
2002	CHT	SOU	25	12	11	65.3	72	17	51	5	3.58	5.64	12.2	2.6	5.2	1.5	5.79	-1.0	0

You can slap a spoiler, tinted windows, and chrome alloy wheels on a Kia Sephia, but at the end of the day it's still a Kia Sephia. Davis has a similar problem. The little southpaw comes loaded with accessories—sharp command, terrific fielder, slick pick-off move—but simply doesn't have enough horsepower under the hood. He's a six-year free agent and will be looking for a greener pasture than the bluegrass of Louisville's Slugger Field.

Ryan Dempster — Born: 03-May-77 — Age: 26 — Bats: R — Throws: R

YEAR	TM	LG	AGE	G	GS	IP	H	BB	SO	HR	ERA	EQERA	EQH9	EQBB9	EQSO9	EQHR9	PERA	VORP	STF
2000	FLA	NL	23	33	33	226.3	210	97	209	30	3.66	3.98	8.5	3.1	7.4	1.1	4.22	38.3	23
2001	FLA	NL	24	34	34	211.3	218	112	171	21	4.94	5.13	9.8	4.5	6.2	0.8	5.14	8.8	10
2002	FLA	NL	25	18	18	120.3	126	55	87	12	4.79	4.95	9.8	3.7	5.7	0.9	5.09	7.4	7
2002	CIN	NL	25	15	15	88.7	102	38	66	16	6.19	5.92	10.6	3.4	5.9	1.6	5.77	-4.1	3
2003	CIN	NL	26	30	29	188.3	187	77	144	21	4.28	4.58	9.1	3.2	6.1	1.0	4.60	19.8	10

Breakout: 16%   Improve: 57%   Collapse: 13%

Swags don't get much sweeter than Bowden's mid-season flip of $2.4 million worth of Juan Encarnacion and Wilton Guerrero for a legitimate power arm. Dempster's mechanics were a mess when he arrived from Jeff Torborg's Chamber of Slag. By the end of the season, Gullett had lowered his leg kick and lengthened his delivery, which helped keep his fastball down and put some bite back on his slider. The Reds aren't always penurious with their money; although Dempster is eligible for arbitration, they're committed to seeing if he can be the top-of-the-rotation starter they desperately need.

Elmer Dessens — Born: 13-Jan-71 — Age: 32 — Bats: R — Throws: R

YEAR	TM	LG	AGE	G	GS	IP	H	BB	SO	HR	ERA	EQERA	EQH9	EQBB9	EQSO9	EQHR9	PERA	VORP	STF
2000	LOU	INT	28	4	4	22.7	24	7	14	1	3.17	4.33	10.4	2.8	4.7	0.5	4.53	3.0	4
2000	CIN	NL	28	40	16	147.3	170	43	85	10	4.28	4.52	11.3	2.2	4.8	0.6	4.25	15.4	0
2001	CIN	NL	29	34	34	205.0	221	56	128	32	4.48	4.39	9.7	2.3	4.8	1.2	4.69	25.4	3
2002	CIN	NL	30	30	30	178.0	173	49	93	24	3.03	3.83	9.1	2.2	4.2	1.2	4.11	33.1	1
2003	CIN	NL	31	27	23	142.3	155	45	82	18	4.40	4.70	10.0	2.4	4.6	1.1	4.71	15.4	0

Breakout: 10%   Improve: 50%   Collapse: 17%

Dessens is a nifty number-four starter miscast as a leading man. He doesn't have the stamina to devour fistfuls of innings, only once pitching beyond the seventh stanza last year. Despite leading the staff with 18 quality starts, Dessens was credited with only seven wins (none after July 21st) because of poor run support. That imprecise gauge of a starting pitcher's effectiveness might keep his price tag low enough for the Reds to re-sign him. It didn't, so he'll now be properly slotted at the back of the Diamondbacks' rotation.

Scott Dunn — Born: 23-May-78 — Age: 25 — Bats: R — Throws: R

YEAR	TM	LG	AGE	G	GS	IP	H	BB	SO	HR	ERA	EQERA	EQH9	EQBB9	EQSO9	EQHR9	PERA	VORP	STF
2000	CLN	MDW	22	26	26	147.7	123	89	159	9	3.96	6.04	10.6	6.7	6.2	1.5	6.10	-8.8	1
2001	MUD	CLF	23	10	10	59.7	45	31	73	2	2.11	4.26	9.4	6.3	6.5	0.6	4.71	8.3	11
2001	CHT	SOU	23	17	17	98.3	96	71	87	10	4.12	6.22	10.8	7.8	5.5	1.6	7.21	-7.8	-8
2002	CHT	SOU	24	37	12	110.3	99	54	114	10	3.92	5.23	10.0	4.8	6.8	1.7	5.46	2.7	-1
2003	CIN	NL	25	12	6	41.3	44	27	38	6	5.57	5.95	9.7	5.0	7.3	1.2	5.80	-0.3	-1

Breakout: 16%   Improve: 44%   Collapse: 21%

Last year's reassignment to the bullpen was unavoidable, but starting work two hours later didn't significantly boost Dunn's productivity. While his control improved, he's still wild as a wounded wolverine. What color is his parachute? Without question, Dunn has big league caliber stuff. On the other hand, the only minor league pitcher who issued more free passes in 2001 now heaves pigskin for Jerry Jones. And there is always the allure of that rodeo clown school in Branson, Missouri.

Shawn Estes — Born: 18-Feb-73 — Age: 30 — Bats: R — Throws: L

YEAR	TM	LG	AGE	G	GS	IP	H	BB	SO	HR	ERA	EQERA	EQH9	EQBB9	EQSO9	EQHR9	PERA	VORP	STF
2000	SFG	NL	27	30	30	190.3	194	108	136	11	4.26	4.68	9.7	4.2	5.7	0.5	4.80	17.4	6
2001	SFG	NL	28	27	27	159.0	151	77	109	11	4.02	4.45	9.2	4.1	5.3	0.6	4.55	18.6	4
2002	NYM	NL	29	23	23	132.7	133	66	92	12	4.54	4.96	9.6	4.0	5.5	0.9	5.07	8.0	2
2002	CIN	NL	29	6	6	28.0	38	17	17	1	7.71	6.88	12.6	4.8	4.8	0.3	6.31	-4.3	-8
2003	CHC	NL	30	26	22	135.3	136	65	98	12	4.23	4.67	9.4	3.7	5.7	0.8	4.87	13.3	4

Breakout: 16%   Improve: 48%   Collapse: 9%

Has anybody ever milked more mileage out of six good months than Estes's 1997? Since then he has lost five miles off of his fastball and logged one season that could even be considered average. In an act of desperation last August, Cincinnati surrendered four Grade C prospects to the Mets for six pre-paid weeks of Estes's services. The relationship quickly deteriorated to where Boone skipped Estes's final three turns in the rotation. Estes is a free agent and neither he nor the Reds have any interest in trying to rekindle the flames. The Cubs will pay him $3 million in 2003, as Estes continues to deceive his employers, but he's back to pitching for Dusty.

Jared Fernandez   Born: 02-Feb-72   Age: 31   Bats: R   Throws: R

YEAR	TM	LG	AGE	G	GS	IP	H	BB	SO	HR	ERA	EQERA	EQH9	EQBB9	EQSO9	EQHR9	PERA	VORP	STF
2000	PAW	INT	28	31	9	113.3	103	36	65	10	3.02	4.29	9.3	2.9	4.5	1.0	4.08	14.6	-5
2001	LOU	INT	29	33	28	196.3	218	54	118	24	4.13	5.82	11.7	3.0	4.3	1.5	5.76	-7.0	-6
2002	LOU	INT	30	26	18	128.3	151	31	80	14	3.93	5.34	11.8	2.6	4.8	1.4	5.80	2.1	-4
2002	CIN	NL	30	14	8	50.7	59	24	36	5	4.44	5.40	10.7	3.8	5.6	0.9	5.39	0.5	-3
2003	HOU	NL	31	20	12	73.0	85	30	44	10	5.03	5.12	10.5	3.2	4.8	1.1	5.18	4.8	-7

Breakout: 24%   Improve: 53%   Collapse: 25%

Fernandez is unique among his species in that he puts his knuckles, not fingertips, on the ball, enabling him to throw a "hard knuckleball." When Joey Hamilton's tightrope act began regularly ending in disaster, Fernandez was recalled to rescue an overworked bullpen. He actually pitched fairly well, but wasn't allowed to work late in games and eventually returned to Louisville because Boone was scared to use him in tight situations. In an era when managers are afraid of being second-guessed, anything unconventional becomes increasingly rare. One of the last of a dying breed, the Reds released Fernandez to make room for the three damaged pitchers Bowden lassoed in the Rule 5 draft. He signed a minor league contract with the Astros.

David Gil   Born: 01-Oct-78   Age: 24   Bats: R   Throws: R

YEAR	TM	LG	AGE	G	GS	IP	H	BB	SO	HR	ERA	EQERA	EQH9	EQBB9	EQSO9	EQHR9	PERA	VORP	STF
2000	DYT	MDW	21	4	4	26.7	20	11	15	1	2.70	4.66	8.8	4.5	3.2	0.9	4.42	2.5	-4
2000	CHT	SOU	21	6	3	25.0	15	13	25	1	2.16	3.46	6.7	5.1	6.3	0.7	3.59	5.6	12
2001	DYT	MDW	22	2	2	11.7	11	3	15	0	0.77	2.28	11.0	3.3	7.1	0.3	4.54	4.2	28
2001	CHT	SOU	22	11	10	61.0	65	30	55	4	3.10	5.07	11.5	5.3	5.6	1.0	6.53	2.9	3
2002	CHT	SOU	23	18	18	110.7	102	36	103	16	3.66	4.87	10.9	3.2	6.3	2.8	5.50	7.8	6
2002	LOU	INT	23	9	4	21.3	29	11	18	8	8.87	9.89	15.0	5.8	6.7	5.1	10.10	-10.5	-29

Most of the Reds' pitching prospects are command freaks who could grow up to be #4 or #5 starters if they make the necessary adjustments. Gil's season shows how difficult that is to do. The Reds' third round pick in 2000 went back to Chattanooga to focus on throwing more strikes. He did, but negated any positive effect by frequently catching too much of the plate, which caused his home run rate to skyrocket. Gil still needs to conquer Double-A and likely won't be ready for a spin in Cincinnati until next year.

Danny Graves   Born: 07-Aug-73   Age: 29   Bats: R   Throws: R

YEAR	TM	LG	AGE	G	GS	IP	H	BB	SO	HR	ERA	EQERA	EQH9	EQBB9	EQSO9	EQHR9	PERA	VORP	STF
2000	CIN	NL	26	66	0	91.3	81	42	53	8	2.56	3.45	8.6	3.4	4.7	0.7	3.59	19.6	-8
2001	CIN	NL	27	66	0	80.3	83	18	49	7	4.15	3.99	9.5	1.9	4.7	0.7	3.83	12.4	-5
2002	CIN	NL	28	68	4	98.7	99	25	58	7	3.19	3.58	9.4	2.1	4.7	0.6	3.75	20.0	-4
2003	CIN	NL	29	49	2	72.0	76	22	44	7	3.84	4.11	9.7	2.4	4.9	0.9	4.34	12.2	-7

Breakout: 15%   Improve: 47%   Collapse: 21%

One of the more interesting stories to follow this year is Graves's move into the rotation. Unlike most firemen, Graves wasn't a starter in the minor leagues. However, he took to it like a cat to warm milk in a September test run, posting a 1.89 ERA in four starts. There are plenty of reasons for optimism: he has never been strictly a one-inning closer, he has a four-pitch repertoire and he is economical with his pitches. If Graves can adjust to the new workload, the experiment will be a success. Here's hoping that other teams follow the Reds' lead.

Chris Gruler   Born: 11-Sep-83   Age: 19   Bats: R   Throws: R

YEAR	TM	LG	AGE	G	GS	IP	H	BB	SO	HR	ERA	EQERA	EQH9	EQBB9	EQSO9	EQHR9	PERA	VORP	STF
2002	BIL	PIO	18	4	4	16.7	11	6	11	1	1.08	2.95	9.9	4.9	3.4	1.6	3.37	4.7	-10
2002	DYT	MDW	18	7	7	27.3	23	16	31	2	5.60	7.21	11.3	7.7	6.8	2.0	6.22	-5.2	-4

The Reds ensured they would sign their June first-rounder to a standard contract for the first time since 1999 by reaching a pre-draft agreement with Gruler. They then fast-tracked their highest pick since Kurt Stilwell (1983), debuting him in the Pioneer League and promoting him to Dayton after just four starts. Many scouts said the prepster had the cleanest delivery in the draft, but it didn't prevent him from being shut down with a frayed rotator cuff in the Instructional League. It looks like he'll avoid surgery, but it's not an auspicious way to start a career.

Josh Hall — Born: 16-Dec-80 — Age: 22 — Bats: R — Throws: R

YEAR	TM	LG	AGE	G	GS	IP	H	BB	SO	HR	ERA	EQERA	EQH9	EQBB9	EQSO9	EQHR9	PERA	VORP	STF
2001	DYT	MDW	20	22	22	132.3	117	39	122	4	2.65	4.79	10.6	3.8	5.2	0.6	4.62	10.5	11
2002	STO	CLF	21	7	7	43.7	31	13	51	1	2.27	3.94	9.1	3.5	6.3	0.4	3.56	7.6	22
2002	CHT	SOU	21	22	22	132.0	140	50	116	7	3.75	5.58	11.4	3.7	5.8	1.0	5.76	-1.1	12

Hall has rapidly climbed the ladder despite missing almost two years following arm and shoulder surgery that threatened to end his career. His fastball is only a tick above average, but has good sinking action and is backed up by a knee-buckling 12-6 yellow hammer. That's where Hall separates himself from the majority of other mound hopefuls in the Reds' system: he has a true out pitch instead of a collection of slightly above-average offerings. Hall needs to sharpen his command and gain consistency, but has shown that he can overcome much larger obstacles.

Joey Hamilton — Born: 09-Sep-70 — Age: 32 — Bats: R — Throws: R

YEAR	TM	LG	AGE	G	GS	IP	H	BB	SO	HR	ERA	EQERA	EQH9	EQBB9	EQSO9	EQHR9	PERA	VORP	STF
2000	SYR	INT	29	6	6	39.3	41	12	17	1	3.66	4.70	11.0	2.8	3.4	0.3	4.14	3.5	-1
2000	TOR	AL	29	6	6	33.0	28	12	15	3	3.55	2.80	7.0	2.6	4.0	0.7	2.93	9.9	3
2001	TOR	AL	30	22	22	122.3	170	38	82	17	5.89	6.03	12.2	2.6	5.6	1.1	6.07	-7.1	3
2001	CIN	NL	30	4	4	17.3	23	6	10	3	6.24	5.96	12.0	2.9	4.4	1.4	6.29	-0.9	-10
2002	CIN	NL	31	39	17	124.7	136	50	85	11	5.27	5.12	10.1	3.2	5.4	0.8	4.73	4.8	-2
2003	*STL*	*NL*	*32*	*27*	*17*	*104.3*	*110*	*41*	*67*	*11*	*4.5*	*4.95*	*9.8*	*3.0*	*5.1*	*1.0*	*4.85*	*6.4*	*-3*

Breakout: 12%   Improve: 45%   Collapse: 23%

Hamilton has never fully recovered from 1999 rotator cuff surgery. Though he poured gasoline all over himself last spring, no team lit a match until his eighth start. From that point on infernos raged until he was shifted to the bullpen, where he showed he could still dial up his old hard, sinking fastball for brief stretches. Although the Reds were interested in signing Hamilton to a modest free agent contract to pitch in relief, he's signed on with the Cardinals in their drive to mass-acquire every struggling veteran starting pitcher in his thirties.

Jimmy Haynes — Born: 05-Sep-72 — Age: 30 — Bats: R — Throws: R

YEAR	TM	LG	AGE	G	GS	IP	H	BB	SO	HR	ERA	EQERA	EQH9	EQBB9	EQSO9	EQHR9	PERA	VORP	STF
2000	MIL	NL	27	33	33	199.3	228	100	88	21	5.33	5.50	11.0	3.7	3.6	0.9	5.21	0.1	-8
2001	MIL	NL	28	31	29	172.7	182	78	112	20	4.85	5.18	10.2	3.9	5.1	1.0	5.01	6.2	0
2002	CIN	NL	29	34	34	196.7	210	81	126	21	4.12	4.59	9.9	3.3	5.1	1.0	4.78	20.0	2
2003	*CIN*	*NL*	*30*	*29*	*25*	*158.7*	*170*	*65*	*103*	*16*	*4.50*	*4.81*	*9.8*	*3.2*	*5.2*	*0.9*	*4.90*	*13.0*	*3*

Breakout: 9%   Improve: 51%   Collapse: 10%

It would be easy, but wrong, to lump Haynes among Gullett's greatest reclamation projects. The only difference between last year and his 17-loss campaign in 2001 with Milwaukee is that he walked half a batter less per game. All his other rates stayed the same. A half a walk reduction could be expected to lower a pitcher's ERA by about a quarter of a run. The other half run of Haynes's drop in ERA was luck, which combined with good run support to produce a 15–9 record. Haynes is a reliable fixture at the back end of a rotation, but if Cincinnati re-signed him expecting a rebuilt frontline starter, they'll be disappointed.

Ty Howington — Born: 04-Nov-80 — Age: 22 — Bats: B — Throws: L

YEAR	TM	LG	AGE	G	GS	IP	H	BB	SO	HR	ERA	EQERA	EQH9	EQBB9	EQSO9	EQHR9	PERA	VORP	STF
2000	DYT	MDW	19	27	26	141.7	150	86	119	7	5.27	7.19	12.8	6.8	4.8	1.2	7.71	-26.6	-8
2001	DYT	MDW	20	6	6	39.0	15	9	47	0	1.15	1.81	4.5	2.9	6.5	0.2	1.35	16.0	31
2001	MUD	CLF	20	7	7	37.0	33	20	44	2	2.43	6.15	11.3	6.7	6.4	1.0	5.97	-2.7	6
2001	CHT	SOU	20	7	7	41.3	36	24	38	3	3.27	5.04	9.4	6.2	5.7	1.1	5.64	2.1	5
2002	CHT	SOU	21	15	15	65.0	65	33	51	5	5.12	5.91	11.0	5.0	5.2	1.5	6.10	-2.9	-2
2002	STO	CLF	21	2	2	11.7	7	4	9	1	3.08	5.11	8.4	4.1	4.3	1.6	3.59	0.5	1

Howington cooks with white gas, so there was anxiety when his velocity only kissed 90 in the 2001 Arizona Fall League. Those fears were valid, as Howington spent all of last year battling shoulder problems that limited him to 17 starts. The big southpaw has the highest ceiling of any pitcher in the organization when he's throwing free and easy, boasting a 92–94 mph fastball, a tight curveball, and a fair changeup. Thus far he's avoided the surgical table, but if a winter of strengthening and conditioning doesn't have him pegging the needle this spring, it's probably inevitable.

Luke Hudson   Born: 02-May-77   Age: 26   Bats: R   Throws: R

YEAR	TM	LG	AGE	G	GS	IP	H	BB	SO	HR	ERA	EQERA	EQH9	EQBB9	EQSO9	EQHR9	PERA	VORP	STF
2000	SLM	CRL	23	19	19	110.0	101	34	80	9	3.27	5.09	11.3	3.4	4.2	1.8	5.52	5.1	-3
2001	CAR	SOU	24	29	28	165.0	159	68	145	19	4.20	5.75	10.8	4.4	5.5	1.8	5.86	-4.5	-1
2002	LOU	INT	25	30	17	117.7	102	57	129	6	4.51	4.84	8.5	5.2	8.4	0.7	4.32	8.4	14
2003	*CIN*	*NL*	*26*	*16*	*10*	*61.7*	*63*	*34*	*54*	*8*	*5.06*	*5.41*	*9.3*	*4.3*	*6.9*	*1.1*	*5.25*	*1.4*	*2*

Breakout: 13%   Improve: 49%   Collapse: 22%

Essentially a throw-in from Colorado when Bowden dumped Pokey Reese's contract, Hudson immediately displayed the best arm in the upper reaches of the Reds' system. He looks a bit like Mark Prior on the mound, with moving mid-90s heat exploding from a silky delivery. While improving, Hudson's pitchability isn't so similar, even though he has pared his repertoire down to a fastball and curve. Eight overpowering weeks in the Arizona Fall League has led to speculation that he could go Williamson on the NL this summer. There are always plenty of relief innings to go around with Bob Boone at the helm, and Hudson enters camp as the front-runner to absorb some of the excess. However, wait for some early returns before checking his name for Rookie of the Year on your IBA ballot.

John Koronka   Born: 03-Jul-80   Age: 23   Bats: L   Throws: L

YEAR	TM	LG	AGE	G	GS	IP	H	BB	SO	HR	ERA	EQERA	EQH9	EQBB9	EQSO9	EQHR9	PERA	VORP	STF
2000	CLN	MDW	20	20	18	104.0	123	38	74	7	4.33	7.40	15.2	4.2	4.2	1.6	7.82	-21.9	-9
2001	DYT	MDW	21	5	5	24.0	23	8	25	0	0.75	5.59	11.4	4.3	5.9	0.3	4.99	-0.2	10
2001	MUD	CLF	21	12	12	71.0	78	39	66	10	4.94	8.23	15.1	7.1	5.3	2.8	8.57	-21.5	-12
2001	CHT	SOU	21	9	9	55.0	62	28	44	7	5.73	7.23	12.6	5.5	5.0	2.0	7.62	-10.5	-4
2002	STO	CLF	22	12	12	73.3	59	35	69	4	3.07	5.95	10.8	5.8	5.2	1.0	5.18	-3.6	3
2002	CHT	SOU	22	16	15	95.7	109	52	69	10	4.98	6.50	12.9	5.4	4.9	2.0	7.44	-10.6	-4

The slender southpaw gained national attention thanks to a pristine 11–0 record at Stockton before returning to Double-A. He draws the inevitable comparisons to Jamie Moyer because of his build, mediocre fastball, and a tailing changeup that makes him more effective against right-handers. However, Koronka needs to make three walks a contest go away to approach Moyer's command. It's not worth investing too many team resources on that steep a long shot paying off. Selected by Texas in the Rule 5 draft.

Brian Moehler   Born: 31-Dec-71   Age: 31   Bats: R   Throws: R

YEAR	TM	LG	AGE	G	GS	IP	H	BB	SO	HR	ERA	EQERA	EQH9	EQBB9	EQSO9	EQHR9	PERA	VORP	STF
2000	DET	AL	28	29	29	178.0	222	40	103	20	4.50	4.32	10.6	1.6	5.1	0.9	4.62	23.4	9
2002	TOL	INT	30	4	4	24.0	28	3	7	3	4.88	5.88	11.9	1.4	2.3	1.6	5.36	-1.0	-13
2002	DET	AL	30	3	3	19.7	17	2	13	3	2.28	2.43	7.4	0.9	5.8	1.3	3.14	6.7	18
2002	CIN	NL	30	10	9	43.3	61	11	18	8	6.03	6.75	13.2	2.1	3.3	1.7	6.61	-6.0	-17
2003	*HOU*	*NL*	*31*	*21*	*17*	*103.0*	*126*	*27*	*51*	*17*	*5.23*	*5.32*	*11.1*	*2.0*	*4.0*	*1.4*	*5.22*	*5.6*	*-7*

Breakout: 15%   Improve: 38%   Collapse: 32%

Picking up Moehler in late July on the premise that he was going to help the team catch St. Louis was silly, not even allowing for the fact that they knew he wasn't close to 100% following 2001 shoulder surgery. Bowden compounded the gaffe by using David Espinosa, the organization's only semi-legitimate middle infield prospect, as bait. Even at full strength, Moehler is little more than a journeyman starter. With slim pickings on the free agent market, he's taking a shot at pitching in Houston.

Dustin Moseley   Born: 26-Dec-81   Age: 21   Bats: R   Throws: R

YEAR	TM	LG	AGE	G	GS	IP	H	BB	SO	HR	ERA	EQERA	EQH9	EQBB9	EQSO9	EQHR9	PERA	VORP	STF
2001	DYT	MDW	19	25	25	148.0	158	42	108	10	4.20	6.65	13.4	3.8	4.2	1.4	6.32	-18.8	-2
2002	STO	CLF	20	14	14	88.7	60	21	80	3	2.74	3.90	8.8	2.8	4.9	0.6	3.25	15.8	14
2002	CHT	SOU	20	13	13	80.7	91	37	52	5	4.13	6.07	12.3	4.5	4.3	1.2	6.63	-5.1	-1

Moseley has supplanted Howington as the team's top pitching hope. While his improving three-pitch mix doesn't dramatically stand out from his peers, he understands his craft and has poise and makeup that are off the charts. The Reds have been promoting him faster than warranted by his performance, but he will revisit Chattanooga to begin 2003. Barring massive injury, Moseley will be a solid big league hurler. Toward that end, the development folks need to remember how young he is and exercise more restraint with his workload. Allusions to Brad Radke aren't far-fetched.

Mike Neu — Born: 09-Mar-78 — Age: 25 — Bats: B — Throws: R

YEAR	TM	LG	AGE	G	GS	IP	H	BB	SO	HR	ERA	EQERA	EQH9	EQBB9	EQSO9	EQHR9	PERA	VORP	STF
2000	CLN	MDW	22	58	0	69.0	47	52	95	5	3.13	5.10	8.8	8.3	7.9	1.7	5.74	2.1	-6
2001	MUD	CLF	23	53	0	64.7	50	30	102	3	2.36	4.50	9.5	5.6	8.3	0.9	4.71	6.3	6
2002	CHT	SOU	24	21	0	27.0	22	9	38	0	1.33	2.41	8.3	3.2	9.0	0.2	3.59	8.9	22
2002	LOU	INT	24	40	0	40.3	35	18	47	4	4.02	4.65	8.7	4.9	9.0	1.3	4.57	3.3	9
2003	OAK	AL	25	28	0	33	30.9	18.2	30	4	4.53	4.58	8.3	4.6	7.8	1	4.57	4.3	2

Breakout: 16%   Improve: 51%   Collapse: 17%

Scouts aren't keen on Neu because of two numbers: 70 and 90. The former is his height in inches, the latter his best velocity in mph. Meanwhile, they choose to ignore his killer changeup and figures like 11.4 K/9 and a 2.94 ERA in Double- and Triple-A last season. Neu is hoping that somebody with a little clout in the organization remembers Doug Jones. Billy Beane once owned Yosemite Sam, and snagged Neu in the Rule 5 draft; he has a good chance of being part of Oakland's 2003 bullpen.

Luis Pineda — Born: 17-Oct-74 — Age: 28 — Bats: R — Throws: R

YEAR	TM	LG	AGE	G	GS	IP	H	BB	SO	HR	ERA	EQERA	EQH9	EQBB9	EQSO9	EQHR9	PERA	VORP	STF
2000	LAK	FSL	25	18	0	26.7	23	19	42	3	3.37	6.00	10.8	8.3	10.2	2.6	6.64	-1.8	-5
2001	ERI	EAS	26	16	12	85.7	68	28	92	8	3.05	4.39	8.9	4.0	6.7	1.3	4.20	10.5	8
2001	DET	AL	26	16	0	18.3	16	14	13	2	4.92	4.55	7.5	6.4	5.9	0.9	4.78	1.7	-14
2002	CIN	NL	27	26	2	32.3	25	24	31	4	4.18	4.40	7.0	5.8	7.5	1.1	4.39	3.6	-4
2002	LOU	INT	27	3	3	12.7	9	4	12	1	4.25	3.87	7.2	3.4	7.3	1.0	3.18	2.3	13
2003	CIN	NL	28	26	5	45.7	43	29	43	6	4.66	4.98	8.6	4.9	7.4	1.1	5.18	3.7	-2

Breakout: 15%   Improve: 42%   Collapse: 27%

Caught in the Agegate sting, Pineda grew almost four years longer in the tooth overnight. As a middle reliever, the damage was minimal in his case. His ERA stood at 2.14 in late-May before he inexplicably altered his delivery. The explanation turned out to be tears in the labrum and rotator cuff. Before the injury, Pineda pumped high octane fuel from his thin frame, regularly working in the upper 90s. While elbow surgery has become fairly cookbook, shoulder procedures remain dicey, so what will be left of Pineda when he returns this year is pure speculation.

Chris Reitsma — Born: 31-Dec-77 — Age: 25 — Bats: R — Throws: R

YEAR	TM	LG	AGE	G	GS	IP	H	BB	SO	HR	ERA	EQERA	EQH9	EQBB9	EQSO9	EQHR9	PERA	VORP	STF
2000	SAR	FSL	22	11	11	64.0	57	17	47	3	3.66	4.31	9.4	3.0	4.6	1.0	4.53	8.5	6
2000	TRN	EAS	22	14	14	90.7	78	21	58	7	2.58	3.28	8.7	2.3	4.3	1.3	4.12	22.4	7
2001	CIN	NL	23	36	29	182.0	209	49	96	23	5.29	5.10	10.5	2.3	4.1	1.0	4.82	8.0	0
2002	CIN	NL	24	32	21	138.3	144	45	84	17	3.64	4.61	9.7	2.6	4.9	1.1	4.51	13.5	1
2002	LOU	INT	24	3	3	21.0	17	8	13	2	3.86	4.38	8.2	4.2	4.8	1.3	4.04	2.6	2
2003	CIN	NL	25	24	18	115.3	122	39	71	14	4.58	4.89	9.7	2.6	4.9	1.1	4.70	9.5	0

Breakout: 15%   Improve: 43%   Collapse: 17%

A young pitcher with options had as much chance of logging a full year of service in Cincinnati last year as Chico Escuela. Reitsma won't become the ace that management once envisioned, but he needs better nurturing than Bob Boone's whimsy for a fair assessment of how far short of the mark he's going to fall. Reitsma's sparkling September in relief could cause a blind squirrel/acorn scenario where Boone has him in the bullpen to open the season and slides him into the rotation later in the year.

John Riedling — Born: 29-Aug-75 — Age: 27 — Bats: R — Throws: R

YEAR	TM	LG	AGE	G	GS	IP	H	BB	SO	HR	ERA	EQERA	EQH9	EQBB9	EQSO9	EQHR9	PERA	VORP	STF
2000	LOU	INT	24	53	0	75.0	63	30	75	7	2.52	3.49	8.3	3.6	7.6	1.1	3.98	15.7	8
2000	CIN	NL	24	13	0	15.3	11	8	18	1	2.35	3.50	6.8	3.8	9.3	0.5	2.84	3.2	22
2001	CIN	NL	25	29	0	33.7	22	14	23	1	2.40	2.28	6.0	3.5	5.3	0.2	2.32	11.6	0
2002	LOU	INT	26	7	0	9.7	10	4	10	0	4.64	5.32	10.0	4.5	7.9	0.2	4.62	0.1	4
2002	CIN	NL	26	33	0	46.7	39	26	30	2	2.70	3.37	7.7	4.4	5.1	0.4	3.63	10.4	-7
2003	CIN	NL	27	34	3	53.7	52	26	40	5	4.11	4.40	8.9	3.7	5.9	0.8	4.56	6.7	-5

Breakout: 15%   Improve: 44%   Collapse: 24%

John Riedling (*continued*)

It's odd that teams go to great lengths to find lefty getters for their bullpen, but most don't perform similar due diligence to identify righty killers even though right-handed hitters collect 60% of all at-bats. While we're not pushing for more specialization, Riedling could become a card-carrying member of the Steve Reed Society. Righties have yet to take him deep in the major leagues, compiling a three-year line of .168/.275/.207. He should inherit much of the setup work Scott Williamson leaves behind.

Jose Rijo   Born: 13-May-65   Age: 38   Bats: R   Throws: R

YEAR	TM	LG	AGE	G	GS	IP	H	BB	SO	HR	ERA	EQERA	EQH9	EQBB9	EQSO9	EQHR9	PERA	VORP	STF
2001	LOU	INT	36	6	4	14.0	16	5	7	2	5.14	6.70	12.1	3.9	3.6	1.8	6.44	-1.9	-28
2001	CIN	NL	36	13	0	17.0	19	9	12	2	2.12	3.97	10.2	4.4	5.4	0.9	5.37	2.7	-12
2002	CIN	NL	37	31	9	77.0	89	20	38	13	5.14	5.37	10.9	2.1	4.0	1.5	5.23	0.7	-15
2003	CIN	NL	38	30	8	63.0	74	19	32	8	4.75	5.08	10.8	2.3	4.0	1.1	5.19	3.6	-14

Breakout: 11%   Improve: 37%   Collapse: 23%

Rijo's right elbow was nearly declared a Ligament-Free Zone sometime between the third and fifth time it was operated on. Nonetheless, the winner of the 2002 Tony Conigliaro Award showed signs of being something more than an inspirational story until Boone asked him to throw 110 pitches in a start in early May. Rijo wants to pitch again this season, which forces the Reds to decide whether his contributions off the mound will exceed someone else's on it.

Scott Sullivan   Born: 13-Mar-71   Age: 32   Bats: R   Throws: R

YEAR	TM	LG	AGE	G	GS	IP	H	BB	SO	HR	ERA	EQERA	EQH9	EQBB9	EQSO9	EQHR9	PERA	VORP	STF
2000	CIN	NL	29	79	0	106.3	87	38	96	14	3.47	3.59	7.8	2.6	7.3	1.1	3.27	21.1	7
2001	CIN	NL	30	79	0	103.3	94	36	82	10	3.31	3.57	8.2	2.9	6.1	0.8	3.65	20.8	0
2002	CIN	NL	31	71	0	78.7	93	31	78	15	6.06	6.28	10.8	3.1	7.8	1.7	5.89	-7.9	-2
2003	CIN	NL	32	53	0	69.0	68	25	58	8	4.08	4.36	9.0	2.8	6.7	1.1	4.40	9.3	1

Breakout: 17%   Improve: 42%   Collapse: 21%

Sullivan's unprecedented four-year run of leading the majors in relief innings ended last year. He didn't succumb to the workload, but pitching through a Richie Sexson line drive off the elbow caused gopher balls and subsequent rotator cuff tendonitis. The Reds have already declined his 2004 option, so expect Boone to return to a no-holds-barred usage pattern. Sullivan's sidearming motion may allow him to dodge an arm blowout of Duane Ward proportions.

Gabe White   Born: 20-Nov-71   Age: 31   Bats: L   Throws: L

YEAR	TM	LG	AGE	G	GS	IP	H	BB	SO	HR	ERA	EQERA	EQH9	EQBB9	EQSO9	EQHR9	PERA	VORP	STF
2000	COL	NL	28	67	0	83.0	62	14	82	5	2.17	1.90	6.6	1.2	7.9	0.5	1.81	32.1	22
2001	COL	NL	29	69	0	67.7	70	26	47	18	6.25	5.41	8.9	3.2	5.3	2.0	5.15	-0.2	-17
2002	CIN	NL	30	62	0	54.3	49	10	41	3	2.98	3.09	8.5	1.5	6.1	0.5	2.99	13.8	5
2003	CIN	NL	31	58	0	50.7	50	14	39	6	3.71	3.97	9.1	2.1	6.2	1.1	4.01	9.1	-1

Breakout: 12%   Improve: 47%   Collapse: 26%

Example #382 of using a bazooka to kill a fly: When White returned to the Queen City after two Jekyll and Hyde seasons at altitude, Boone initially used him successfully in multi-inning stretches. White was unexpectedly lights out against lefties in those stints, so Boone happily changed his job description to a one-out lefty, greatly reducing his value to the ball club. White is too pricey ($3.15 million in 2003) and too good to pigeonhole in such a narrow role.

Scott Williamson   Born: 17-Feb-76   Age: 27   Bats: R   Throws: R

YEAR	TM	LG	AGE	G	GS	IP	H	BB	SO	HR	ERA	EQERA	EQH9	EQBB9	EQSO9	EQHR9	PERA	VORP	STF
2000	CIN	NL	24	48	10	112.0	92	75	136	7	3.29	3.70	7.7	4.8	9.5	0.5	3.66	21.6	23
2002	CIN	NL	26	63	0	74.0	46	36	84	5	2.92	2.96	5.7	3.8	8.9	0.6	2.63	19.9	16
2003	CIN	NL	27	37	7	76.0	62	38	80	6	3.41	3.64	7.4	3.9	8.4	0.7	3.76	15.6	13

Breakout: 20%   Improve: 39%   Collapse: 32%

The Reds cautiously eased Williamson back after April 2001 Tommy John surgery. His progress is clearly evident in his seasonal splits: 4.86 ERA in 33.1 innings before the All-Star break, 1.33 ERA in 40.2 innings afterward. Williamson still would prefer to be a starter, but as the heir to Graves's job as finisher, he'll close instead. Mindless prattle aside, a closer's makeup is only as good as his stuff and location. Williamson has plenty of both.

Colorado Rockies

Without better pitching and more road wins, the Rockies will never win the pennant. This summer, the SABR convention will be in Denver for the purpose of exploring how the Rockies should adapt to their environment and try to win "at altitude."

They'll be flogging the wrong dead horse. The Rockies already win at altitude. Their home field advantage is well above the norm. A typical home winning percentage is about .540. The Rockies have been winning home games at a .560 clip over the past three years. Even last year, when they had one of the worst teams in baseball, they won 47 home games.

Their problem is and always has been that they don't win on the road. Everyone knows this, but no one talks much about it. The Rockies don't need Coors hitters and Coors pitchers, or different lineups for home and road games. They don't need unique baseballs, humidors, or an extra roster spot. They need a team that can win anywhere. To make that happen they need what all bad teams need: better ballplayers.

It's not the first time the eggheads have gotten the Rockies into trouble. Following the advice of a prominent sabermetrician, two years ago the Rockies hatched a plan to win at altitude. They were persuaded that the changeup was the most effective Coors pitch, so they committed $172 million to Mike Hampton and Denny Neagle. It will be remembered as the blunder that ruined the Rockies' decade.

For general manager Dan O'Dowd, epistemological endeavors have been nettlesome. For 10 years the Rockies have been concerned about winning at altitude; since taking over, O'Dowd has been obsessed with it. He has a new theory every other year, but never sticks with one long enough to see if it works. This winter he did it again. Doubly. He gave up on Hampton and Neagle, and then conceded that his plan to win with speed, pitching, and defense has failed.

If the test of a first-rate intelligence is the ability to hold two opposed ideas in the mind at the same time without losing the ability to function, O'Dowd must be a genius—a spaz genius. It seems as though he simultaneously believes several mutually exclusive theories. It's a problem of confidence, not intelligence. He's thoughtful and inquisitive, but he changes his mind too often, as insubstantial data chase him off one notion and onto another. He knows just enough Greek to get himself into trouble.

Experience is a better guide than reason, and baseball doesn't have to be this difficult. O'Dowd doesn't realize it, but he was right to focus on run prevention. In almost every case throughout baseball's history, teams playing in extreme hitters' parks have won pennants only when they have led their league in pitching. Rarely have they led their league in hitting. Nearly 20 years ago, Pete Palmer and John Thorn demonstrated this in *The Hidden Game of Baseball* using the Linear Weights System and nothing has happened since then to disprove their argument.

Is it impossible for the Rockies to lead the National League in pitching? Based on raw numbers, probably. Coors is one of the most pitching-hostile environments in baseball history. But Palmer and Thorn's conclusion was based on data that had been adjusted to account for park effects. If we take out the exaggerations of Coors and give the Rockies' pitchers a level playing field, it's not unfair to ask them to do what like teams before them have done.

Last year they won when they got ordinary pitching, and when they didn't they lost. From April 26 through May 26 the Rockies had three home stands covering 20 games. They went 17–3. They won with pitching, allowing only 63 runs. Their pitching became the lead story on *Baseball Tonight*. The dominance didn't last long, but throughout the season they won whenever they got decent pitching.

Rockies Prospectus

2002 record: 73–89; Fourth place, NL West

Pythagenport Record: 70–92

Runs scored per game: 4.8 (4th in NL)

Runs allowed per game: 5.5 (16th in NL)

Team EqA: .247 (15th in NL)

2002 Batters Age: 29.2 (6th youngest in NL)

2002 Pitchers Age: 28.9 (8th oldest in NL)

Ballpark: Coors Field; Crazy-insane hitters' park; Park Factor of 1.180

2002: Rookie of the Year Jason Jennings had success winning in Coors, but the team still hasn't figured out the secret yet.

2003: Is there a solution? And if they knew, would the team stick with the plan long enough?

At home, the Rockies' ERA was 5.47. They went 33–7 (.825) when they allowed 5 runs or less. They went 14–27 in all other games (.341).

Away from home their ERA was 4.92. When they allowed four runs or less they were 21–18 (.538). In all other games they went 5–37 (.119).

They don't need to do as well as they did in that early homestand and they don't need to have an ERA like the Braves'. If they can merely get to ordinary more often, they're going to win the pennant.

Most theories about winning at altitude focus on hitting. One popular argument is that the Rockies need to forget about pitching, speed, and defense and focus instead on putting together a lineup that would score 1,100 runs. The pitching might suffer but this squad of goons would win by hitting clusters of three-run homers.

Unlike the visiting teams, the Rockies would have to play 81 games like that. Over the course of a season this would place an unbearable strain on the Rockies' players, especially their pitchers, with collateral damage to the minor leagues as players got rushed to cover holes blown through the major league roster. In this scenario, the Rockies would win games by kegball scores of 20–18, 15–12, 11–10. Over the last three years the Rockies have allowed 10 or more runs 40 times. They won just three of those games.

A corollary to the "1,100-run lineup" argument is the notion that the Rockies have an inherent advantage in home slugfests. Since they have a disproportionately high winning percentage in slugfests, they should try to get into as many of them as possible. You do this by improving the offense. Given the Rockies' resources, they couldn't spend on pitching and hitting, so they would have to choose. Instead of spending your free agent money on the best pitchers, you spend it on A-Rod, Piazza, and Ramirez. The pitching would suffer, but it wouldn't be a problem since you don't mind if the teams combine to score a lot of runs. All you care about is getting the score up.

The argument borrows from Bill James to define a slugfest as a game in which the teams combine to score at least 12 runs. But is it fair to treat all 12-run games alike? A 12-run game at PacBell is not the same as a 12-run game at Coors. Twelve combined runs was an average game at Coors last season. To be valid, the argument would have to adjust for the park effect, especially since Coors is such an extraordinary case. If we use the park effect, a Coors slugfest would be between 17 and 19 combined runs, depending on the year. This cuts way down on the number of slugfests at Coors, reducing the sample to a size that makes the study worthless.

The Rockies do not have an advantage in slugfests. Compared to how they do in non-slugfests at Coors, they're worse when the score gets that high. Over the past three seasons the Rockies' home winning percentage has been .560 in all games. In park-adjusted slugfests it has been .540. The perceived advantage is illusory.

And not all slugfests are alike, even within the same park. When teams combine to score a lot of runs, some games will be competitive and some will be blowouts. If a team wins 12–0 it's a blowout. And you could get your games to 12 easily by making your pitching as bad as possible. It would be disingenuous to lump blowouts—when a team wins by at least five runs—in with the slugfests. If the Rockies went for hitters only and tanked their pitching, they wouldn't be running up 17 runs all by themselves. Take out the Coors blowout slugfests and the number of competitive slugfests drops to 23 over the three years. In those games the Rockies' winning percentage was .563, a meaningless gain over their usual success.

One more problem: If the Rockies did manage to increase their number of home slugfests, they'd get into more of them on the road as well. As even the proponents of the argument acknowledge, in most years the Rockies have a distinct disadvantage in road slugfests. They would give back whatever gain they got at home and then some. This is hardly an argument that would justify an organizational overhaul.

Rather than obsess over winning at altitude, the Rockies need to develop a team that can win in any park. They have the lowest road-game park factor in baseball, and no team plays more road games in extreme pitchers' parks. A team skewed so severely to take advantage of Coors will necessarily be unsuited to games in San Diego, San Francisco, and Los Angeles. Slow-footed, flyball hitters who open their swing once they start playing half their games at Coors would have a hard time on a cold night at PacBell Park. What they need is a consistent approach to hitting—not based on park quirks—that can withstand the environmental torque their schedule causes.

Every year Colorado does much better at home than on the road. Over the last three years they have won an average of 31 road games. Last year they celebrated their diamond anniversary by winning fewer road games than ever. They were 21 games worse than at home. In 2001, they were nine games worse on the road and 14 games worse in 2000.

If the Rockies did even better at home, they still wouldn't win the pennant. A team that wins 92 games by going 61–29 at home and 31–50 on the road is not the model of a championship team. From 2000 to 2002, 21 of the 24 playoff teams had winning road records and no playoff team had fewer than 39 road wins. The Rockies have never won more than 36. The average spread between a playoff team's home and road wins was less than five games. This is where the Rockies need to improve. Yes, if they won 92 games that way they would still make the playoffs, and if they made the playoffs they would stand a puncher's chance of winning the pennant. It's not that it can't happen that way. It just never does for teams like this. And would you bet on the Rockies as the team that could pull it off?

Their goal should be to minimize the spread between home and road performance, not to maximize home wins. Historically, this has been the key to winning—especially for teams in extreme hitter's parks. As Palmer and Thorn pointed out, pennant winners from extreme hitters' parks won more than 60% of their road games and typically did better on the road than at home.

Every year we offer ideas on how the Rockies could play better at home, but what kind of team do they need if they're going to be better on the road? Not that he believes it this week, but last winter O'Dowd told Salon.com that a good, balanced team that can win on the road will win anywhere, which of course is true. Occam's razor: The Rockies need better players.

Like most teams, they need to do a better job evaluating talent, both at the major league level and in the draft. More than anything, they need to be better at preventing runs. But they also have only two impact hitters, Larry Walker and Todd Helton. Their lineup needs to improve if they're going to play better on the road. If they want to borrow from Earl Weaver, they need all three legs of the stool—power, pitching, and defense—not just power. The ability to get on base is always paramount, but what else? Speed plays everywhere, and it goes together with defense. Speed and defense aren't as susceptible to park effects as batting factors are, so emphasizing those qualities over raw slugging would help. And better defense would bring down the staff ERA, which is what the Rockies need most if they're going to win anything.

In 2002, the Rockies had the worst ERA in the league, a feat they have accomplished eight times in their 10-year history. That will change by 2005. The organization is already deep in pitching talent. If O'Dowd has a pronounced talent it's for putting together bullpens that are among the league's best every year. The rotation is getting better. Eliminating Hampton was addition by subtraction. Jason Jennings won the Rookie of the Year Award, and Aaron Cook is a credible threat to win it in 2003. Chin-Hui Tsao is one of the game's best pitching prospects and he'll be ready for a call-up by late summer of 2004. In last June's amateur draft the Rockies selected Jeffrey Francis, the best pitcher ever to come out of Canada.

A small story but a crucial factor in their likelihood of success was the hiring of Duane Espy as the Rockies' hitting coach. Espy was with the Padres in 2001, when they were the best road-scoring team in baseball. That this was a factor in hiring him suggests that the Rockies are catching on in spite of their fixation with winning at Coors. Having spent time in the West, Espy knows the division's pitchers and extreme parks, including Coors. He knows what it takes to score at altitude and sea level.

A pervasive belief is that Coors screws up hitters. The hitting environment fosters habits helpful in Coors but harmful everywhere else, so that the Rockies always take a long time to adjust when they go on the road. The organization believes it and so do the players, but Rany Jazayerli and Michael Wolverton destroyed that myth last summer in a short essay we put up on www.baseballprospectus.com. Their conclusion was that too many of the Rockies' hitters simply suck. Occam's razor. It's easier than they make it seem.

But Espy hasn't joined the company caterwaul, at least not yet:

> I realize it's more difficult when you're in there 80-some days during the season...But what I'll be trying to get across is, to me, hitting is about finding your best swing and repeating it as much as you can. If we have good, solid fundamentals and a consistent day-in, day-out swing, that's a format to be a good offense anywhere.
> — quoted at MLB.com

Behind Todd Helton and Larry Walker there isn't much talent in the lineup, but if the batters take Espy's advice, the Rockies will improve their run production both at home and on the road—without giving up on pitching. Having a team that can play anywhere will be the key to the Rockies' success. With a consistent approach to hitting and a crew of good young pitchers arriving in twos, they're in position to become the team they need to be.

Not that they realize it. The Rockies under O'Dowd have become too clever by half. Their fascination with winning at altitude has led them into financial traps they can't escape, limiting the flexibility they'll need to finish off their roster when the homegrown talent ripens in 2005. Like the Devil Rays, the Rockies have seemed more like a gimmick than a baseball club. This isn't a polemic against fancy book learnin'— many of the theories about what would win at Coors make good sense. But that misses the point, since the Rockies already do well enough at home. It might help if they stopped tinkering all the damn time. They need to develop a plan and see it through a three-to-five-year run, for better or worse. They need pitching, road wins, and better players. What they don't need is the distraction of a convention in their own backyard, speculating about what it would take to win even more games at altitude, but that's what 2003 is going to bring them. Here comes more trouble.

HITTERS

Sandy Alomar Jr.   C   Born: 18-Jun-66   Age: 37   Bats: R   Throws: R

YEAR	TM	LG	AGE	AB	H	2B	3B	HR	BB	SO	SB	CS	AVG	OBP	SLG	MLVR	EQBA	EQOBP	EQSLG	EQMLVR	VORP	DEFENSE	
2000	CLE	AL	34	356	103	16	2	7	16	41	2	2	.289	.327	.404	-.096	.295	.325	.414	-.043	15.8	88-C	-6
2001	CWS	AL	35	220	54	8	1	4	12	17	1	2	.245	.291	.345	-.207	.264	.309	.368	-.164	4.0	61-C	1
2002	CWS	AL	36	167	48	10	1	7	5	14	0	0	.287	.312	.485	.065	.299	.327	.515	.113	14.3	47-C	-2
2002	COL	NL	36	116	31	4	0	0	4	19	0	0	.267	.292	.302	-.234	.259	.283	.293	-.326	-2.6	32-C	-1
2003	CWS	AL	37	179	45	9	1	4	8	20	0	0	.251	.287	.370	-.150	.256	.293	.376	-.179	-0.4		

Breakout: 23%   Improve: 37%   Collapse: 21%

The Rocks can't afford to be paying for the little things that don't show up in the box scores. They lost in clusters, with nine losing streaks of at least four games. They were 33–56 in games following a loss. They got blown out once every five road games, and in those games they averaged two runs, scoring one or none eight times. They need run producers, not the "veteran leadership" Kenny Williams finds so irresistible. Alomar will once again bring his slowing bat and glacial receiving skills to the White Sox for the inspirational value of watching a once-good player play out the string.

Garrett Atkins   3B   Born: 12-Dec-79   Age: 23   Bats: R   Throws: R

YEAR	TM	LG	AGE	AB	H	2B	3B	HR	BB	SO	SB	CS	AVG	OBP	SLG	MLVR	EQBA	EQOBP	EQSLG	EQMLVR	VORP	DEFENSE			
2000	POR	NWN	20	251	76	12	0	7	45	48	2	0	.303	.413	.434	.281	.229	.305	.338	-.237	-10.0	35-1B	1	13-3B	-2
2001	SLM	CRL	21	465	151	43	5	5	74	98	6	4	.325	.426	.471	.346	.263	.347	.390	-.062	4.7	125-1B	-7		
2002	CAR	SOU	22	510	138	27	3	12	59	77	6	6	.271	.349	.406	.074	.234	.293	.363	-.223	-4.5	119-3B	-17		
2003	COL	NL	23	188	51	10	1	6	21	34	3	1	.274	.352	.440	.045	.254	.328	.400	-.085	1.3				

Breakout: 26%   Improve: 50%   Collapse: 18%

Atkins is not the answer to their perennial problem at third, although within the next year people will start erroneously comparing him to Jeff Cirillo and Kevin Seitzer. Atkins has decent strike zone judgment and developing gap power. Early on, when he'd get jammed he'd try to inside-out the ball to right field, but as the season progressed he learned to turn on those pitches. He hit .353 in the AFL, but without power, walks, or zone control. They need him to be a third baseman but it's not working out; he has bad range and an erratic arm. There's also concern that because he starred at UCLA, Atkins has a California attitude about his press clippings. Atkins might survive for a while if his defense improves but he won't be a breakout player.

John Barnes   OF   Born: 24-Apr-76   Age: 27   Bats: R   Throws: R

YEAR	TM	LG	AGE	AB	H	2B	3B	HR	BB	SO	SB	CS	AVG	OBP	SLG	MLVR	EQBA	EQOBP	EQSLG	EQMLVR	VORP	DEFENSE	
2000	SLC	PCL	24	441	161	37	6	13	57	48	7	6	.365	.446	.565	.403	.304	.375	.470	.135	33.3	111-CF	-4
2001	EDM	PCL	25	311	91	21	2	8	27	28	3	2	.293	.370	.450	.081	.258	.328	.394	-.096	-.6	73-OF	-3
2002	CSP	PCL	26	269	77	20	2	6	18	16	5	4	.286	.340	.442	.012	.242	.293	.374	-.202	-1.5	60-CF	-3
2003	PIT	NL	27	119	31	7	1	2	12	12	2	1	.262	.334	.395	-.053	.262	.330	.408	-.065	1.3		

Breakout: 25%   Improve: 51%   Collapse: 32%

Barnes led the PCL in batting average just a couple years ago, when he hit .365/.446/.565. His EqBA has dropped from .304 to .242 since then. Twice last year on the eve of being promoted he pulled up lame with hamstring troubles. He's gone from being somebody you argue for to a nice flyer to pick up. Invited to the Pirates' camp, he might finally stick as a reserve.

Gary Bennett   C   Born: 17-Apr-72   Age: 31   Bats: R   Throws: R

YEAR	TM	LG	AGE	AB	H	2B	3B	HR	BB	SO	SB	CS	AVG	OBP	SLG	MLVR	EQBA	EQOBP	EQSLG	EQMLVR	VORP	DEFENSE	
2000	SWB	INT	28	317	97	24	0	12	40	44	1	0	.306	.396	.495	.247	.283	.360	.461	.076	26.5	73-C	-2
2000	PHI	NL	28	74	18	5	0	2	13	15	0	0	.243	.371	.392	-.051	.253	.362	.400	-.027	4.4	25-C	1
2001	PHI	NL	29	75	16	3	1	1	9	19	0	0	.213	.298	.320	-.264	.213	.298	.333	-.267	-.7	22-C	-2
2001	COL	NL	29	55	15	3	0	1	3	5	0	0	.273	.322	.382	-.143	.255	.303	.364	-.188	.7	14-C	-1
2002	COL	NL	30	291	77	10	2	4	15	45	1	3	.265	.314	.354	-.128	.256	.299	.348	-.217	1.3	78-C	-3
2003	SDP	NL	31	243	57	11	1	5	19	41	1	1	.235	.296	.342	-.207	.246	.303	.371	-.174	-0.4		

Breakout: 15%   Improve: 36%   Collapse: 29%

In April, one pitcher said that Bennett "takes control of a game." The coaches said he's "definitely a gamer." No, perception is not reality. It's debatable whether a catcher's contribution to ERA can be measured accurately, but the tools we have tell us the pitching's worse when he catches. They admit now that he was overextended. Though "he's tough and durable and cares a lot about our pitchers" they non-tendered him, and he's signed on with the Padres, potentially as a glovely backup to Mike Rivera.

Cliff Brumbaugh — OF — Born: 21-Apr-74 — Age: 29 — Bats: R — Throws: R

YEAR	TM	LG	AGE	AB	H	2B	3B	HR	BB	SO	SB	CS	AVG	OBP	SLG	MLVR	EQBA	EQOBP	EQSLG	EQMLVR	VORP	DEFENSE			
2000	OKL	PCL	26	454	126	28	4	10	85	72	9	12	.278	.393	.423	.069	.244	.344	.369	-.109	-2.6	69-OF	3	44-1B	-3
2001	OKL	PCL	27	202	62	11	3	8	33	41	3	3	.307	.409	.510	.265	.270	.367	.441	.050	7.0	50-RF	3		
2001	CSP	PCL	27	208	69	18	1	3	34	52	5	3	.332	.426	.471	.209	.273	.366	.385	-.026	3.6	31-OF	-4	18-3B	-7
2002	CSP	PCL	28	505	148	36	2	16	57	107	6	2	.293	.365	.467	.093	.248	.316	.394	-.126	-4.9	72-OF	-10	32-1B	0

Has just enough power and patience to be useful, especially if they would platoon him at third with Norton. Listed as an outfielder, he also plays the infield corners and was drafted as an All-American third baseman out of the University of Delaware. He wouldn't have to play third often if he was platooned—it's a cheap solution that would complement the bench, but of course it won't happen. When the season ended, the organization named him Sky Sox MVP and cut him loose.

Kevin Burford — 1B — Born: 07-Nov-77 — Age: 25 — Bats: L — Throws: L

YEAR	TM	LG	AGE	AB	H	2B	3B	HR	BB	SO	SB	CS	AVG	OBP	SLG	MLVR	EQBA	EQOBP	EQSLG	EQMLVR	VORP	DEFENSE			
2000	SLM	CRL	22	465	136	40	4	16	58	79	11	4	.292	.383	.499	.272	.236	.302	.401	-.151	-8.0	61-LF	-8	16-1B	-3
2001	CAR	SOU	23	363	105	21	4	6	45	79	4	1	.289	.380	.419	.133	.252	.323	.367	-.147	-5.3	76-1B	-12		
2002	CAR	SOU	24	266	75	23	1	3	48	51	2	6	.282	.399	.410	.160	.241	.334	.361	-.141	-3.3	72-1B	0		
2003	*COL*	*NL*	*25*	*167*	*47*	*11*	*1*	*5*	*20*	*31*	*3*	*2*	*.279*	*.359*	*.455*	*.080*	*.259*	*.335*	*.414*	*-.051*	*-.4*				

Breakout: 27%   Improve: 59%   Collapse: 20%

Burford draws a lot of walks and controls the strike zone. At the least, he could be a valuable bench player, but he has lost a lot of time to injuries, and at 25 with Hawpe coming up on him he needs to bloom. Petrick, Ortiz, Uribe, and Cust let them down, but this one won't. He gets to play in Colorado Springs this year, where he'll probably be the team's MVP. He'll have a better career as a Rockie than Hawpe.

Brent Butler — INF — Born: 11-Feb-78 — Age: 25 — Bats: R — Throws: R

YEAR	TM	LG	AGE	AB	H	2B	3B	HR	BB	SO	SB	CS	AVG	OBP	SLG	MLVR	EQBA	EQOBP	EQSLG	EQMLVR	VORP	DEFENSE			
2000	CSP	PCL	22	438	128	35	1	8	44	46	1	3	.292	.362	.432	-.018	.245	.303	.361	-.199	1.9	95-2B	-15	24-SS	-1
2001	CSP	PCL	23	272	91	20	3	7	15	26	4	2	.335	.378	.507	.181	.286	.328	.429	-.024	13.1	50-2B	-9		
2001	COL	NL	23	119	29	7	1	1	7	7	1	1	.244	.291	.345	-.269	.227	.274	.328	-.313	-3.0	19-2B	-4		
2002	CSP	PCL	24	105	35	9	1	2	6	12	0	0	.333	.375	.495	.186	.282	.325	.417	-.050	4.4	16-SS	1		
2002	COL	NL	24	344	89	18	4	9	10	40	2	6	.259	.290	.413	-.094	.249	.275	.403	-.189	2.2	62-2B	-1		
2003	*COL*	*NL*	*25*	*349*	*100*	*20*	*3*	*9*	*22*	*38*	*4*	*2*	*.288*	*.334*	*.436*	*.021*	*.266*	*.311*	*.396*	*-.111*	*3.5*				

Breakout: 16%   Improve: 44%   Collapse: 25%

Seasons run long in Colorado, players get tired, and there are a million pitching changes. You need a 12-man staff and a bench of guys who give you a variety of options in-game. You can't waste slots on two guys who do the same thing. If Ozuna starts at second, they'll keep either Butler or Romano, but not both.

J. D. Closser — C — Born: 15-Jan-80 — Age: 23 — Bats: B — Throws: R

YEAR	TM	LG	AGE	AB	H	2B	3B	HR	BB	SO	SB	CS	AVG	OBP	SLG	MLVR	EQBA	EQOBP	EQSLG	EQMLVR	VORP	DEFENSE	
2000	SBN	MDW	20	331	74	19	1	8	60	61	6	2	.224	.348	.360	.009	.179	.266	.288	-.409	-16.2	70-C	-9
2001	LNC	CLF	21	468	136	26	6	21	65	106	6	7	.291	.379	.506	.205	.214	.287	.367	-.242	-.8	91-C	-7
2002	CAR	SOU	22	315	89	27	1	13	44	69	9	3	.283	.370	.498	.236	.242	.313	.435	-.079	13.0	64-C	-9
2003	*COL*	*NL*	*23*	*191*	*50*	*11*	*1*	*8*	*23*	*42*	*3*	*3*	*.264*	*.348*	*.457*	*.052*	*.244*	*.325*	*.415*	*-.078*	*4.4*		

Breakout: 36%   Improve: 59%   Collapse: 20%

Because of the extraordinary pitching rigors, it's difficult to break in a catcher in Coors. The organization generally prefers to wait until he's ready. Closser's defense isn't as stagnant as it looks. His footwork is slow but improving, and he has a strong arm. Like Petrick, he has trouble returning the ball to the mound. He won't do it from a crouch or from his knees. He insists on standing up and striding the box. Petrick had the same quirk, but it started only after he drilled a batter in the head on one of his throws. This could be a silly extrapolation, but maybe this hesitancy indicates a degree of Closser's discomfort with the position.

Jack Cust · DH · Born: 16-Jan-79 · Age: 24 · Bats: L · Throws: R

YEAR	TM	LG	AGE	AB	H	2B	3B	HR	BB	SO	SB	CS	AVG	OBP	SLG	MLVR	EQBA	EQOBP	EQSLG	EQMLVR	VORP	DEFENSE
2000	ELP	TXS	21	447	131	32	6	20	117	150	12	9	.293	.442	.526	.285	.225	.355	.399	-.061	3.5	120-LF -13
2001	TUC	PCL	22	442	123	24	2	27	102	160	6	3	.278	.419	.525	.230	.233	.365	.432	.006	10.7	105-RF -10
2002	CSP	PCL	23	359	95	24	0	23	83	121	6	3	.265	.409	.524	.215	.223	.357	.432	-.016	7.4	87-LF -8
2002	COL	NL	23	65	11	2	0	1	12	32	0	1	.169	.299	.246	-.334	.154	.286	.231	-.452	-6.7	13-LF -1
2003	COL	NL	24	221	61	12	2	14	42	66	4	4	.276	.394	.530	.227	.255	.367	.482	.089	6.8	

Breakout: 28%   Improve: 57%   Collapse: 17%

Not a flight risk. Wouldn't it be nice if he actually hit .276/.394/.530? He won't. He got no boost from playing at altitude. That projection assumes his static performance is just a case of the Triple-A blues and that he'll get over it right now. It took Jeremy Giambi a while, and it would be unusual for a hitter this good not to make it, but if his raw stats don't improve substantially this year you can write him off as a potential star.

Bobby Estalella · C · Born: 23-Aug-74 · Age: 28 · Bats: R · Throws: R

YEAR	TM	LG	AGE	AB	H	2B	3B	HR	BB	SO	SB	CS	AVG	OBP	SLG	MLVR	EQBA	EQOBP	EQSLG	EQMLVR	VORP	DEFENSE
2000	SFG	NL	25	299	70	22	3	14	57	92	3	0	.234	.360	.468	.049	.243	.359	.484	.071	27.0	94-C 1
2001	COH	INT	26	171	44	10	1	10	21	45	0	2	.257	.345	.503	.161	.246	.324	.474	-.002	10.9	34-C -2
2001	SFG	NL	26	93	19	5	1	3	11	28	0	0	.204	.295	.376	-.182	.221	.307	.400	-.154	2.1	26-C 2
2002	CSP	PCL	27	79	23	9	0	6	11	20	0	0	.291	.378	.633	.332	.244	.330	.513	.060	6.2	20-C 3
2002	COL	NL	27	112	23	8	0	8	14	33	0	1	.205	.294	.491	-.026	.196	.286	.473	-.113	3.7	34-C -1
2003	COL	NL	28	170	45	10	1	11	26	45	1	2	.264	.365	.535	.179	.245	.340	.486	.040	9.4	

Breakout: 30%   Improve: 55%   Collapse: 24%

They're bringing Estalella back as the caddy for Charles Johnson. Generally speaking, you want a catcher who's durable, but Estalella has had surgery on both shoulders, and has never had more than 299 at-bats in a season. He's cheap, but if Johnson breaks down again this probably isn't a guy who can take over and take the daily pounding behind the plate.

Choo Freeman · CF · Born: 20-Oct-79 · Age: 23 · Bats: R · Throws: R

YEAR	TM	LG	AGE	AB	H	2B	3B	HR	BB	SO	SB	CS	AVG	OBP	SLG	MLVR	EQBA	EQOBP	EQSLG	EQMLVR	VORP	DEFENSE
2000	SLM	CRL	20	429	114	18	7	5	37	104	16	8	.266	.330	.375	.017	.219	.264	.312	-.360	-20.5	122-CF -10
2001	SLM	CRL	21	517	124	16	5	8	31	108	19	7	.240	.294	.337	-.052	.204	.247	.292	-.430	-34.9	120-CF -10
2002	CAR	SOU	22	430	125	18	6	12	64	101	15	13	.291	.401	.444	.213	.248	.333	.389	-.100	9.0	117-CF -9
2003	COL	NL	23	192	52	10	2	6	19	43	4	3	.270	.343	.437	.023	.250	.320	.397	-.105	.6	

Breakout: 43%   Improve: 62%   Collapse: 16%

Dave Collins has been brought back largely because of the work he did with their outfielders, especially Juan Pierre and Freeman. Freeman takes good routes to the ball, but his arm is iffy and it takes him a long time to deliver his throws. However, he doubled his walk rate in 2002, which might make him the rare tools player who's developing his skills. Collins can't teach him to be fast enough to play center in Coors, so think of Freeman as another right-handed corner.

Brad Hawpe · 1B/OF · Born: 22-Jun-79 · Age: 24 · Bats: L · Throws: L

YEAR	TM	LG	AGE	AB	H	2B	3B	HR	BB	SO	SB	CS	AVG	OBP	SLG	MLVR	EQBA	EQOBP	EQSLG	EQMLVR	VORP	DEFENSE	
2000	POR	NWN	21	205	59	19	2	7	40	51	2	0	.288	.409	.502	.351	.216	.299	.381	-.198	-6.5	24-LF -1	25-1B -1
2001	ASH	SAL	22	393	105	22	3	22	59	113	7	4	.267	.371	.506	.242	.198	.281	.366	-.265	-20.9	47-RF -9	52-1B -3
2002	SLM	CRL	23	450	156	38	2	22	81	84	1	1	.347	.448	.587	.523	.269	.356	.461	.057	19.3	121-1B 11	
2003	COL	NL	24	203	56	11	1	10	28	47	3	3	.274	.366	.496	.139	.253	.341	.451	.003	2.0		

Breakout: 28%   Improve: 58%   Collapse: 18%

Hell of a year, but where to now? This winter they sent Hawpe to Venezuela to get him some games in the outfield. It's a dead end for him because he's slower than Jack Cust—he'd make left field in Coors seem twice as expansive as it already is. Trade him before the league catches on.

Todd Helton   1B   Born: 20-Aug-73   Age: 29   Bats: L   Throws: L

YEAR	TM	LG	AGE	AB	H	2B	3B	HR	BB	SO	SB	CS	AVG	OBP	SLG	MLVR	EQBA	EQOBP	EQSLG	EQMLVR	VORP	DEFENSE
2000	COL	NL	26	580	216	59	2	42	103	61	5	3	.372	.470	.698	.605	.345	.439	.647	.529	100.9	152-1B 26
2001	COL	NL	27	587	197	54	2	49	98	104	7	5	.336	.435	.685	.506	.318	.417	.646	.462	93.6	153-1B 13
2002	COL	NL	28	553	182	39	4	30	99	91	5	1	.329	.435	.577	.398	.315	.419	.557	.339	67.4	153-1B 13
2003	COL	NL	29	527	176	39	3	33	93	85	6	2	.334	.434	.608	.443	.309	.405	.552	.288	47.9	

Breakout: 7%   Improve: 43%   Collapse: 5%

If the Rockies didn't have bad luck, it seems like they'd have no luck at all. They need hitters, but two of their three best prospects are blocked by their having an already-great first baseman. Two years ago an infield of Helton, Ortiz, and Uribe was exciting, but now it looks as though Helton, like Walker, will waste his prime losing 85 games a year. He's had a couple of off-season issues, having surgery to remove bone spurs from his elbow, and then the doctors found a benign tumor (which they removed), plus he's been seeing a back specialist. He's not going away, but these are the kinds of things that start cropping up as you reach 30.

Gabe Kapler   OF   Born: 31-Aug-75   Age: 27   Bats: R   Throws: R

YEAR	TM	LG	AGE	AB	H	2B	3B	HR	BB	SO	SB	CS	AVG	OBP	SLG	MLVR	EQBA	EQOBP	EQSLG	EQMLVR	VORP	DEFENSE
2000	TEX	AL	24	444	134	32	1	14	42	57	8	4	.302	.362	.473	.074	.304	.359	.478	.118	32.7	113-CF -1
2001	TEX	AL	25	483	129	29	1	17	61	70	23	6	.267	.353	.437	.036	.280	.365	.462	.084	33.1	124-CF 1
2002	TEX	AL	26	196	51	12	1	0	8	30	5	2	.260	.289	.332	-.208	.276	.307	.352	-.182	-4.5	56-OF 0
2002	COL	NL	26	119	37	4	3	2	8	23	6	2	.311	.359	.445	.100	.303	.346	.437	.035	3.4	31-RF 2
2003	COL	NL	27	281	82	18	2	8	26	42	10	3	.294	.355	.452	.082	.272	.331	.411	-.051	1.6	

Breakout: 9%   Improve: 23%   Collapse: 40%

Not exactly a "WTF?" season. Kapler was bothered by injuries all year, the most nagging of which was a sore left wrist. He has the arm strength and range to cut down the size of the outfield so he'll get 400 at-bats. He opened his swing when he got to Coors, as a lot of hitters do, but needs to close it. If he regains his patience, he'll revive his career. As Ron Shandler likes to say, once a player establishes a skill he owns it, so Kapler's not dead yet. He'll outdo that projection. If they play him, Payton, and Walker they'll wind up with one of the best defensive outfields in the league.

Adam Melhuse   C   Born: 27-Mar-72   Age: 31   Bats: B   Throws: R

YEAR	TM	LG	AGE	AB	H	2B	3B	HR	BB	SO	SB	CS	AVG	OBP	SLG	MLVR	EQBA	EQOBP	EQSLG	EQMLVR	VORP	DEFENSE	
2000	ABQ	PCL	28	108	37	9	0	1	22	21	4	2	.343	.454	.454	.238	.283	.382	.377	.001	6.8	14-C 0	10-1B 1
2000	CSP	PCL	28	140	39	5	1	3	21	35	2	3	.279	.373	.393	-.064	.232	.312	.326	-.238	-5.6	23-LF 0	
2001	CSP	PCL	29	184	49	10	1	7	31	42	0	1	.266	.378	.446	.035	.224	.328	.372	-.149	4.4	35-C -3	
2001	COL	NL	29	71	13	2	0	1	6	18	1	0	.183	.247	.254	-.506	.169	.234	.239	-.545	-5.9	16-C -5	
2002	IOW	PCL	30	226	66	19	0	7	28	47	2	3	.292	.370	.469	.150	.259	.332	.417	-.056	10.7	45-C -4	11-3B -2
2002	CSP	PCL	30	115	40	10	1	6	16	23	2	1	.348	.427	.609	.437	.292	.370	.504	.162	12.0	25-C -1	
2003	OAK	NL	31	115	27	6	0	3	14	27	2	1	.230	.317	.372	-.133	.235	.319	.387	-.131	1.1		

Breakout: 19%   Improve: 37%   Collapse: 34%

He's Corky Miller without the defense, which makes him a lot like Scott Hatteberg. Melhuse batted .348/.427/.609 for the Sky Sox, and he gets on base, and hits for power and average. He can stand at third or first, so the Rocks should have been a good organization for him. Although he's 31, there has to be a place for him somewhere as backup to a defensive specialist. In their wisdom, the Cubs thought they had no use for him, since neither of their catchers were defensive specialists. They weren't hitters either, so . . .

Greg Norton   3B   Born: 06-Jul-72   Age: 31   Bats: B   Throws: R

YEAR	TM	LG	AGE	AB	H	2B	3B	HR	BB	SO	SB	CS	AVG	OBP	SLG	MLVR	EQBA	EQOBP	EQSLG	EQMLVR	VORP	DEFENSE	
2000	CHR	INT	28	97	28	4	0	5	24	23	1	0	.289	.439	.485	.265	.255	.395	.439	.087	8.0	24-3B 4	
2000	CWS	AL	28	201	49	6	1	6	26	47	1	0	.244	.336	.373	-.154	.251	.338	.387	-.092	5.0	34-3B -7	12-1B 0
2001	COL	NL	29	225	60	13	2	13	19	65	1	0	.267	.324	.516	.036	.254	.313	.487	.004	5.5	11-LF -1	15-3B -3
2002	COL	NL	30	168	37	8	1	7	24	52	2	3	.220	.318	.405	-.084	.208	.304	.393	-.178	.5	18-3B -6	
2003	COL	NL	30	116	28	6	1	5	15	32	2	1	.246	.336	.437	-.008	.227	.313	.398	-.133	-1.3		

Breakout: 24%   Improve: 46%   Collapse: 30%

Greg Norton *(continued)*

They could just give the job at third base to Norton. They're already paying him, he hits right-handers just fine, and he knows how to get on base. He moves well laterally and has a strong arm, which allows him to play deep. His defense isn't what it used to be but it's a lot better than Zeile's. Norton can manage third and first, and frighten the children in left. They think he's more valuable on their bench, where his versatility would come in handy if they didn't have Helton and four good outfielders.

Jose Ortiz   2B   Born: 13-Jun-77   Age: 26   Bats: R   Throws: R

YEAR	TM	LG	AGE	AB	H	2B	3B	HR	BB	SO	SB	CS	AVG	OBP	SLG	MLVR	EQBA	EQOBP	EQSLG	EQMLVR	VORP		DEFENSE	
2000	SAC	PCL	23	518	182	34	5	24	47	64	22	9	.351	.409	.575	.392	.311	.357	.506	.163	46.2	74-2B	2	48-SS -10
2001	SAC	PCL	24	256	70	16	4	7	25	50	7	4	.273	.345	.449	.028	.242	.310	.391	-.146	4.5	53-2B	-9	
2001	COL	NL	24	204	52	8	1	13	14	36	3	1	.255	.315	.495	-.016	.245	.301	.471	-.048	8.9	45-2B	3	
2002	COL	NL	25	192	48	7	1	1	16	30	2	0	.250	.318	.313	-.184	.245	.308	.302	-.271	-2.8	48-2B	-5	
2002	CSP	PCL	25	111	37	9	2	6	4	13	1	1	.333	.357	.613	.325	.284	.310	.514	.067	7.6	14-SS	4	

From top prospect to baffled *gaijin* in two years. Ortiz is yet another hitter expected to bloom at Coors who didn't. His career in the U.S. is probably over. He had one good year. Let him go.

Jay Payton   CF   Born: 22-Nov-72   Age: 30   Bats: R   Throws: R

YEAR	TM	LG	AGE	AB	H	2B	3B	HR	BB	SO	SB	CS	AVG	OBP	SLG	MLVR	EQBA	EQOBP	EQSLG	EQMLVR	VORP	DEFENSE	
2000	NYM	NL	27	488	142	23	1	17	30	60	5	11	.291	.336	.447	.017	.295	.330	.451	.020	25.6	128-CF	1
2001	NYM	NL	28	361	92	16	1	8	18	52	4	3	.255	.299	.371	-.154	.264	.306	.387	-.143	3.6	94-CF	0
2002	NYM	NL	29	275	78	6	3	8	21	34	4	1	.284	.337	.415	.062	.298	.346	.440	.035	15.5	65-CF	3
2002	COL	NL	29	170	57	14	4	8	8	20	3	3	.335	.376	.606	.365	.324	.360	.588	.303	16.5	40-LF	3
2003	COL	NL	30	349	103	21	2	12	24	43	4	2	.295	.343	.472	.090	.273	.320	.429	-.047	5.1		

Breakout: 8%   Improve: 30%   Collapse: 34%

At the time, the John Thomson trade was, as Ned Flanders might say, a real noodle-scratcher. Thomson had a history of injury and off-field problems, his success in 2001 was exaggerated by late-season starts against weak lineups, and his one-year deal was going to expire after the season. So O'Dowd traded him at high value. Going from Coors to Shea, Thomson was expected to flourish but he flopped, and the Mets chose not to bring him back for 2003. Meanwhile, Payton hit .335 for the Rockies. He's at peak value now, so dealing him between now and the end of July to some AL near-contender with a weak outfield would make sense.

Ben Petrick   LF   Born: 07-Apr-77   Age: 26   Bats: R   Throws: R

YEAR	TM	LG	AGE	AB	H	2B	3B	HR	BB	SO	SB	CS	AVG	OBP	SLG	MLVR	EQBA	EQOBP	EQSLG	EQMLVR	VORP	DEFENSE			
2000	CSP	PCL	23	248	78	22	3	9	32	40	7	2	.315	.393	.536	.208	.264	.333	.446	-.009	14.8	55-C	-7		
2000	COL	NL	23	146	47	10	1	3	20	33	1	2	.322	.411	.466	.133	.299	.379	.438	.092	12.9	40-C	-6		
2001	COL	NL	24	244	58	15	3	11	31	67	3	3	.238	.331	.459	-.049	.225	.316	.430	-.093	9.5	66-C	-9		
2002	CSP	PCL	25	265	85	18	4	16	40	77	10	6	.321	.412	.600	.371	.267	.355	.492	.096	13.0	55-LF	-4		
2002	COL	NL	25	95	20	3	1	5	9	33	0	1	.211	.286	.421	-.123	.200	.275	.411	-.214	-3.1	11-LF	-1	14-C	-2
2003	COL	NL	26	242	69	16	2	11	32	60	6	4	.283	.369	.507	.167	.262	.344	.461	.029	8.1				

Breakout: 27%   Improve: 60%   Collapse: 20%

He won't play catcher for this team, so roto owners can give up on that. And have you noticed how he's never mentioned when the Rockies talk about their outfield depth? It's not as if he has lacked for chances. He's a Quadruple-A outfielder now, counting the time until he either gets dropped from the 40-man or qualifies for free agency and a shot to go Fick.

Jorge Piedra   LF   Born: 17-Apr-79   Age: 24   Bats: L   Throws: L

YEAR	TM	LG	AGE	AB	H	2B	3B	HR	BB	SO	SB	CS	AVG	OBP	SLG	MLVR	EQBA	EQOBP	EQSLG	EQMLVR	VORP	DEFENSE	
2000	DAY	FSL	21	139	48	11	1	1	6	15	8	4	.345	.372	.460	.240	.281	.301	.374	-.158	.7	34-CF	1
2000	VRO	FSL	21	360	102	11	6	6	29	57	21	5	.283	.345	.397	.052	.231	.276	.331	-.302	-11.6	91-CF	-6
2001	WTN	SOU	22	441	108	26	6	8	37	80	12	5	.245	.315	.385	-.034	.221	.273	.347	-.292	-24.5	114-OF	-6
2002	WTN	SOU	23	60	10	3	1	0	3	11	2	0	.167	.219	.250	-.385	.164	.198	.246	-.613	-7.8	17-LF	-1
2002	SLM	CRL	23	392	118	37	12	13	37	55	10	2	.301	.373	.556	.348	.242	.297	.446	-.093	-.5	99-LF	-5
2003	COL	NL	24	183	52	12	2	6	16	31	4	3	.281	.343	.461	.063	.260	.320	.419	-.070	-1.3		

Breakout: 29%   Improve: 58%   Collapse: 18%

The Cubs gave up on him, too. After coming to the Rockies' organization, he cut down on the strikeouts, led his league in triples, and finished on the leader boards for average and doubles. He missed the league lead for extra-base hits by one. He's about to turn 24, so they're going to push him to Triple-A to see if he's wasting their time.

Juan Pierre   CF   Born: 14-Aug-77   Age: 25   Bats: L   Throws: L

YEAR	TM	LG	AGE	AB	H	2B	3B	HR	BB	SO	SB	CS	AVG	OBP	SLG	MLVR	EQBA	EQOBP	EQSLG	EQMLVR	VORP	DEFENSE	
2000	CAR	SOU	22	439	143	16	4	0	33	26	46	12	.326	.379	.380	.132	.293	.330	.347	-.133	5.4	103-CF	1
2000	COL	NL	22	200	62	2	0	0	13	15	7	6	.310	.355	.320	-.186	.288	.325	.293	-.225	-2.4	47-CF	-1
2001	COL	NL	23	617	202	26	11	2	41	29	46	17	.327	.379	.415	.046	.309	.359	.392	-.001	28.7	146-CF	-1
2002	COL	NL	24	592	170	20	5	1	31	52	47	12	.287	.332	.343	-.098	.280	.320	.336	-.178	.2	138-CF	5
2003	FLO	NL	25	518	143	22	5	0	33	39	32	5	.275	.323	.337	-.141	.283	.326	.359	-.123	3.6		

Breakout: 8%   Improve: 32%   Collapse: 30%

It isn't all doom and gloom, Pierre has improved substantially as a center fielder. He has a Rudy Law popgun, but he covered the gaps in Coors, so he'll manage Pro Player. He'll get to more balls than Preston Wilson. As a batter Pierre goes from the penthouse to the outhouse, but leaving Coors should hurt him less than it hurts others. The projection is right on. Jeff Torborg is going to love this guy, and never mind that he won't put runs on the board.

Rene Reyes   RF   Born: 21-Feb-78   Age: 25   Bats: B   Throws: R

YEAR	TM	LG	AGE	AB	H	2B	3B	HR	BB	SO	SB	CS	AVG	OBP	SLG	MLVR	EQBA	EQOBP	EQSLG	EQMLVR	VORP	DEFENSE			
2001	ASH	SAL	23	484	156	27	2	11	28	80	53	12	.322	.374	.455	.227	.243	.282	.347	-.260	-23.1	58-RF	-7	57-1B	-2
2002	CAR	SOU	24	455	133	33	4	14	29	69	10	11	.292	.342	.475	.175	.249	.282	.416	-.157	-9.2	66-RF	-8	37-1B	2
2003	COL	NL	25	205	58	13	2	6	13	33	4	4	.283	.328	.456	.035	.262	.306	.415	-.099	-4.5				

Breakout: 36%   Improve: 58%   Collapse: 16%

It's kind of like winning a tallest midget contest, but among their prospects, Reyes is their best athlete and most promising hitter. He was used to being the best player in whatever league he was in, but last year changed that, as Double-A so often does. His stolen bases dropped way off because he got caught a few times early in the year and realized he couldn't read the pitchers. He needs to double his walk rate if he's going to make it.

Jason Romano   2B/CF   Born: 24-Jun-79   Age: 24   Bats: R   Throws: R

YEAR	TM	LG	AGE	AB	H	2B	3B	HR	BB	SO	SB	CS	AVG	OBP	SLG	MLVR	EQBA	EQOBP	EQSLG	EQMLVR	VORP	DEFENSE			
2000	TUL	TXS	21	535	145	35	2	8	56	84	25	10	.271	.347	.389	-.034	.230	.285	.331	-.285	-9.1	123-2B	-13		
2001	TUL	TXS	22	186	45	9	1	1	16	31	8	3	.242	.305	.317	-.179	.207	.261	.277	-.421	-9.7	42-2B	-10		
2001	OKL	PCL	22	149	47	6	1	4	20	28	3	4	.315	.396	.450	.167	.273	.351	.393	-.043	6.9	18-2B	2	12-CF	0
2002	OKL	PCL	23	196	53	8	1	4	19	41	10	3	.270	.335	.383	-.045	.244	.304	.345	-.220	-2.0	30-CF	2	17-2B	-4
2002	TEX	AL	23	54	11	4	0	0	4	13	2	0	.204	.259	.278	-.366	.222	.276	.296	-.357	-3.6	14-LF	0		
2002	CSP	PCL	23	129	40	7	2	0	6	27	8	3	.310	.341	.395	-.033	.268	.295	.339	-.230	-1.6	18-CF	-1		
2002	COL	NL	23	37	12	0	1	0	3	11	4	1	.324	.375	.378	.046	.324	.375	.351	-.019	1.1				
2003	COL	NL	24	181	49	10	1	4	17	34	6	3	.269	.332	.403	-.041	.249	.310	.367	-.165	-1.8				

Breakout: 20%   Improve: 46%   Collapse: 27%

Romano is perceived to be better than Butler, and people seem to have higher expectations for him, but it's hard to see why. Neither of them draw all that many walks, Butler has more power and he's the better infielder, which could come in handy if Uribe's evil twin returns.

Terry Shumpert   UT   Born: 16-Aug-66   Age: 36   Bats: R   Throws: R

YEAR	TM	LG	AGE	AB	H	2B	3B	HR	BB	SO	SB	CS	AVG	OBP	SLG	MLVR	EQBA	EQOBP	EQSLG	EQMLVR	VORP	DEFENSE			
2001	COL	NL	34	242	70	14	5	4	15	44	14	3	.289	.338	.438	-.024	.274	.323	.419	-.057	10.0	26-2B	-1	21-LF	0
2002	COL	NL	35	234	55	12	1	6	21	41	4	1	.235	.309	.372	-.131	.226	.297	.363	-.220	-.3	46-2B	-5		
2000	COL	NL	33	263	68	11	7	9	28	40	8	4	.259	.343	.456	-.054	.241	.318	.421	-.090	-.1	31-LF	-2	15-2B	-3
2003	LAD	NL	36	127	29	5	1	2	11	25	3	1	.231	.295	.343	-.210	.242	.302	.369	-.181	-1.6				

Breakout: 13%   Improve: 42%   Collapse: 29%

Earl Weaver used defensive specialists differently than most managers use them today. Instead of using them in the late innings to preserve a lead, he would start his best defensive players so he could get the most innings out of his starting pitchers. If he needed to, he'd pinch-hit for the glovemen. To make this work he couldn't have a bench of Gashouse Gorillas. He

Terry Shumpert (continued)

could carry a couple of those but he also needed guys who could substitute passably in the field when the frame flipped over. Shumpert is a decent hitter with some speed who could play adequately at several positions, so he would have been ideal for a team like that. He found his niche with the Rockies because Coors games are so exhausting. With Tracy's Dodgers, he'll be a nifty bit part for late inning machinations.

Rob Stratton								**RF**		**Born: 07-Oct-77**			**Age: 25**		**Bats: R**		**Throws: R**	
YEAR	TM	LG	AGE	AB	H	2B	3B	HR	BB	SO	SB	CS	AVG	OBP	SLG	MLVR	EQBA	EQOBP	EQSLG	EQMLVR	VORP	DEFENSE
2000	SLU	FSL	22	381	87	18	4	29	60	180	3	5	.228	.345	.525	.191	.184	.275	.416	-.218	-14.8	93-RF -9
2001	BIN	EAS	23	483	120	30	1	29	53	201	9	5	.248	.333	.495	.118	.211	.287	.415	-.178	-13.9	106-RF -6
2002	NOR	INT	24	256	63	8	0	20	18	84	6	3	.246	.308	.512	.113	.232	.291	.486	-.056	1.3	70-RF 0
2002	CSP	PCL	24	80	17	2	1	7	6	42	0	1	.212	.308	.525	.006	.177	.261	.443	-.214	-2.8	21-RF -1
2003	FLO	NL	25	160	35	7	1	8	17	64	2	4	.218	.301	.425	-.102	.224	.304	.452	-.082	-3.7	

Breakout: 39%   Improve: 71%   Collapse: 14%

Stratton is a beneficiary of unrealistic expectations. The Rockies weren't the only ones seduced by the idea of what his power might produce in Colorado—either for the Sky Sox or Rockies—but altitude doesn't make bad hitters good. Stratton cut his strikeout rate a little last year, but for the first time he drew walks in less than 10% of his plate appearances. His big chance was to make it as a publicity stunt. Now with the Marlins, he's gator bait.

Juan Uribe								**SS**		**Born: 22-Jul-79**			**Age: 23**		**Bats: R**		**Throws: R**	
YEAR	TM	LG	AGE	AB	H	2B	3B	HR	BB	SO	SB	CS	AVG	OBP	SLG	MLVR	EQBA	EQOBP	EQSLG	EQMLVR	VORP	DEFENSE
2000	SLM	CRL	20	485	124	22	7	13	38	100	22	5	.256	.315	.410	.035	.214	.253	.345	-.338	-15.2	131-SS -5
2001	CSP	PCL	21	281	87	27	7	7	12	43	11	8	.310	.342	.530	.128	.258	.292	.440	-.097	8.5	73-SS -6
2001	COL	NL	21	273	82	14	11	8	8	55	3	0	.300	.325	.520	.077	.287	.311	.493	.041	17.9	66-SS -2
2002	COL	NL	22	566	136	25	7	6	34	120	9	2	.240	.289	.341	-.201	.233	.278	.335	-.292	-10.5	150-SS 25
2003	COL	NL	23	479	130	28	5	12	33	83	9	5	.272	.321	.423	-.029	.252	.300	.385	-.156	.6	

Breakout: 16%   Improve: 48%   Collapse: 24%

Too thick-headed to be a star? Uribe hasn't taken the time to learn English and it's hindering his progress. He's supporting a huge extended family on his minimum salary, and on the trip to Shea last year he'd bought tickets for dozens of friends and family members, and then spent the series trying to prove he could hit 600-foot homers. He wound up hitting 3-for-20 with no extra-base bits. He's fast enough to steal a lot more bases than this. Hurdle stuck by him at first, but started to lose patience by season's end. They're done screwing around with him. They forced him to train all winter and had him report to Denver in January to work on "the mental and physical aspects of the game" with the new coaching staff. Not that anyone noticed, but he doubled his walk rate last year. Espy can work with that. Now that Rey Sanchez and Orlando Cabrera have their historic seasons behind them, Uribe's the best fielding shortstop in the National League.

Larry Walker								**RF**		**Born: 01-Dec-66**			**Age: 36**		**Bats: L**		**Throws: R**	
YEAR	TM	LG	AGE	AB	H	2B	3B	HR	BB	SO	SB	CS	AVG	OBP	SLG	MLVR	EQBA	EQOBP	EQSLG	EQMLVR	VORP	DEFENSE
2000	COL	NL	33	314	97	21	7	9	46	40	5	5	.309	.412	.506	.178	.285	.382	.469	.128	17.5	82-RF 4
2001	COL	NL	34	497	174	35	3	38	82	103	14	5	.350	.455	.662	.522	.333	.437	.626	.482	79.0	119-RF 3
2002	COL	NL	35	477	161	40	4	26	65	73	6	5	.338	.424	.602	.425	.323	.407	.581	.363	56.5	112-RF 5
2003	COL	NL	36	414	132	27	4	22	60	67	7	3	.320	.409	.567	.339	.296	.381	.516	.190	23.2	

Breakout: 2%   Improve: 32%   Collapse: 21%

Baseball's meal on a bun, and one of those guys worth the price of admission. Despite all of the injuries, Walker is still the best baserunner in the league. One of Dave Collins's duties will be baserunning coach, a job he held with the Brewers last year when Milwaukee ran themselves into more costly baserunning outs than any other team. Most studies conclude that luck determines a team's record in one-run games and that luck tends to even out over time. But when Bill James studied the issue, he found that there seems to be a persistent tendency of certain teams to play poorly in one-run games. In 2001, the Brewers had the major league's second-worst record in one-run games, an ignominious distinction they earned again last year. If a team continues to lose so many of these games from one year to the next, isn't it fair to think there might be a fundamental problem with the coaching staff? And how many of the Brewers' one-run losses last year can we hang on Collins? Does Walker need to shield Uribe from him?

Todd Zeile   3B/1B   Born: 09-Sep-65   Age: 37   Bats: R   Throws: R

YEAR	TM	LG	AGE	AB	H	2B	3B	HR	BB	SO	SB	CS	AVG	OBP	SLG	MLVR	EQBA	EQOBP	EQSLG	EQMLVR	VORP	DEFENSE
2000	NYM	NL	34	544	146	36	3	22	74	85	3	4	.268	.358	.467	.066	.274	.355	.475	.079	26.8	142-1B 6
2001	NYM	NL	35	531	141	25	1	10	73	102	1	0	.266	.361	.373	-.026	.278	.369	.389	-.011	13.4	143-1B 14
2002	COL	NL	36	506	138	23	0	18	66	92	1	1	.273	.358	.425	.042	.264	.345	.416	-.029	21.6	133-3B -13
2003	NYY	AL	37	324	78	16	1	9	35	61	1	1	.241	.315	.373	-.104	.249	.326	.387	-.109	-0.5	

Breakout: 6%   Improve: 42%   Collapse: 29%

Emblematic of what's wrong with the Rockies and 20 other teams. Why pay Zeile $6.5 million when you have no chance to compete and Adam Piatt could have been had for Jack Cust? That was the rumored deal, but the Rocks say they never gave it serious consideration. Instead, they pursued John Valentin and David Bell before settling on Zeile, who hadn't played third since 1999. This winter they brought in Chris Stynes, another player who makes little or no sense for a team at this stage of the development cycle. O'Dowd's too smart to keep doing this. The Yankees have mercifully changed Zeile's position to "batter."

PITCHERS

Kip Bouknight   Born: 16-Nov-78   Age: 24   Bats: R   Throws: R

YEAR	TM	LG	AGE	G	GS	IP	H	BB	SO	HR	ERA	EQERA	EQH9	EQBB9	EQSO9	EQHR9	PERA	VORP	STF
2001	TRI	NWN	22	15	15	81.0	69	19	86	3	2.78	5.11	11.4	3.2	5.2	1.0	5.32	3.6	6
2002	SLM	CRL	23	27	27	166.7	156	48	120	13	3.35	5.63	12.0	3.8	4.8	1.8	5.41	-2.3	0

Bouknight's college career included a College World Series championship and the Golden Spikes Award in 2000. He was tagged as a non-prospect because he's 6' 0" and his fastball tops out at 85. As a senior he was throwing breaking pitches much more often than the fastball, afraid of what aluminum would do to it. He spent this season regaining confidence in the pitch and learning to locate it out of harm's way. We know the Rockies favor the changeup but when the Braves come to town, Mazzone has his pitchers throw fastballs 80% of the time, telling them to throw strikes, work ahead, and avoid the three-run homer. That goes for Maddux, too, another guy who is 6' 0" with a mid-80s fastball. Bouknight threw a no-hitter in August. If he doesn't do well he'll be an exception. Other winners of the Golden Spikes Award between 1997 and 2001: Mark Prior, Jason Jennings, Pat Burrell, J. D. Drew.

Chris Buglovsky   Born: 22-Nov-79   Age: 23   Bats: L   Throws: R

YEAR	TM	LG	AGE	G	GS	IP	H	BB	SO	HR	ERA	EQERA	EQH9	EQBB9	EQSO9	EQHR9	PERA	VORP	STF
2000	POR	NWN	20	14	12	65.0	50	32	50	5	2.63	6.16	12.1	6.0	3.9	2.7	6.16	-4.8	-17
2001	ASH	SAL	21	26	26	143.3	158	32	119	14	4.08	6.87	14.2	3.1	4.4	2.1	6.93	-21.7	-4
2002	SLM	CRL	22	27	27	164.7	161	58	126	12	3.11	5.69	12.5	4.6	5.1	1.7	5.92	-3.4	0

A converted infielder quickly learning how to pitch well. Buglovsky has numbers similar to Bouknight's, but his fastball gets into the low-90s, territory Bouknight's will never reach. The plan is to have him skip Double-A and go directly to Colorado Springs.

Ryan Cameron   Born: 13-Sep-77   Age: 25   Bats: R   Throws: R

YEAR	TM	LG	AGE	G	GS	IP	H	BB	SO	HR	ERA	EQERA	EQH9	EQBB9	EQSO9	EQHR9	PERA	VORP	STF
2000	SLM	CRL	22	26	26	160.3	152	78	168	9	3.59	5.89	11.2	5.3	6.0	1.2	6.22	-6.9	6
2001	CAR	SOU	23	18	13	89.7	112	45	74	10	5.22	7.73	14.1	5.5	5.2	1.7	8.09	-22.3	-11
2002	CAR	SOU	24	37	15	118.7	84	55	139	9	3.26	4.14	7.5	4.4	7.6	1.4	4.02	17.5	9

In another case of stunning improvement as a Double-A repeater, Cameron raised his strikeout rate from 7.4 to 10.6. In the AFL, he jacked it up to 14.6. His fastball tops out in the high 80s, but he has one of the best changeups in the minors. He throws it 70% of the time but doesn't always know where it's going. He gives it a lot of arm action, which causes the strikeouts. They're going to give him a chance. He and Elarton could make a great spot/long tandem.

Shawn Chacon Born: 23-Dec-77 Age: 25 Bats: R Throws: R

YEAR	TM	LG	AGE	G	GS	IP	H	BB	SO	HR	ERA	EQERA	EQH9	EQBB9	EQSO9	EQHR9	PERA	VORP	STF
2000	CAR	SOU	22	27	27	173.7	151	85	172	10	3.16	4.76	9.6	4.8	6.3	1.0	5.19	14.4	12
2001	CSP	PCL	23	4	4	24.0	18	7	28	3	2.25	2.26	6.4	3.0	7.5	1.2	2.98	8.7	27
2001	COL	NL	23	27	27	160.0	157	87	134	26	5.06	4.77	8.5	4.5	6.3	1.2	4.63	13.1	11
2002	CSP	PCL	24	4	4	20.7	23	10	15	3	4.78	4.66	9.6	4.9	4.9	1.6	5.69	1.9	-5
2002	COL	NL	24	21	21	119.3	122	60	67	25	5.73	5.56	9.1	4.0	4.4	1.8	5.21	-0.7	-6
2003	COL	NL	25	20	19	120.3	139	64	86	21	5.76	4.99	10.0	4.0	6.0	1.2	4.90	12.0	5

Breakout: 17%   Improve: 54%   Collapse: 19%

Beyond the normal problem of learning to love home when it's called Coors, Chacon's delivery is unclean and he gets out of sync too easily. They claim he pitches better from behind, but the stats don't really bear it out. He's correctly projected to stagnate at about the level you can live with from a fifth starter; his days in Denver are numbered.

Aaron Cook Born: 08-Feb-79 Age: 24 Bats: R Throws: R

YEAR	TM	LG	AGE	G	GS	IP	H	BB	SO	HR	ERA	EQERA	EQH9	EQBB9	EQSO9	EQHR9	PERA	VORP	STF
2000	ASH	SAL	21	21	21	142.7	130	23	118	10	2.96	4.35	11.1	2.0	4.3	1.6	4.42	18.3	7
2000	SLM	CRL	21	7	7	43.0	52	12	37	4	5.44	7.99	15.0	3.1	5.1	2.1	7.67	-11.9	0
2001	SLM	CRL	22	27	27	155.0	157	38	122	4	3.08	5.73	11.8	3.3	4.4	0.6	5.79	-3.9	2
2002	CAR	SOU	23	14	14	95.0	73	19	58	4	1.42	2.72	7.8	1.9	4.0	0.8	3.24	29.4	9
2002	CSP	PCL	23	10	10	64.3	67	18	32	6	3.78	4.02	8.7	2.8	3.3	1.0	4.25	10.6	0
2002	COL	NL	23	9	5	35.7	41	13	14	4	4.54	4.53	10.3	2.9	3.1	1.0	4.76	3.8	-9
2003	COL	NL	24	19	14	82.3	102	31	45	13	5.64	4.89	10.7	2.9	4.6	1.1	4.80	7.9	-5

Breakout: 11%   Improve: 48%   Collapse: 25%

The drop in strikeouts was semi-intentional. Cook used to blow hitters away with 98-mph heat, but Bob McClure got hold of him and taught him to emphasize placement over power. Cook never gets rattled, and induces a lot of ground balls and fouls off the batter's body. He threw back-to-back shutouts before his promotion to Triple-A. On May 5, Mark Prior came to town and had a good day but Cook outpitched him. You wouldn't know it based on what he did in the majors last year, and Coors will mask his talent for a while, but he's going to be good.

Mark Difelice Born: 23-Aug-76 Age: 26 Bats: R Throws: R

YEAR	TM	LG	AGE	G	GS	IP	H	BB	SO	HR	ERA	EQERA	EQH9	EQBB9	EQSO9	EQHR9	PERA	VORP	STF
2000	CAR	SOU	23	23	22	133.0	152	19	98	15	3.59	5.33	13.3	1.4	4.8	2.0	6.18	2.6	3
2001	CAR	SOU	24	19	18	123.0	108	23	98	13	3.15	4.18	9.8	2.0	4.9	1.6	4.37	18.1	7
2001	CSP	PCL	24	8	8	46.0	56	8	43	11	5.28	5.23	10.5	1.8	5.9	2.3	6.02	1.4	6
2002	TRI	NWN	25	6	1	17.0	18	0	13	2	5.29	7.99	18.1	1.1	4.4	3.8	6.11	-4.8	-23
2002	SLM	CRL	25	6	6	35.3	40	5	21	3	2.80	5.35	14.4	1.9	3.9	2.0	6.26	0.6	-6

Difelice doesn't have Bouknight's pedigree, but the Rockies say that when he's on, he has the best command in the organization. He needs it, because he only throws 85 mph. He made it as far as Colorado Springs before an injury sent him back to Start. They like him and he'll be pushed to Triple-A this year. Suddenly this kind of pitcher is all the rage.

Scott Dohmann Born: 13-Feb-78 Age: 25 Bats: R Throws: R

YEAR	TM	LG	AGE	G	GS	IP	H	BB	SO	HR	ERA	EQERA	EQH9	EQBB9	EQSO9	EQHR9	PERA	VORP	STF
2000	POR	NWN	22	5	4	23.0	14	5	23	0	0.78	2.45	7.7	2.4	4.7	0.3	2.98	7.8	11
2000	ASH	SAL	22	7	7	32.7	43	8	36	3	6.06	8.07	16.3	3.1	5.9	2.1	7.93	-9.3	-1
2001	ASH	SAL	23	28	28	173.0	165	33	154	27	4.32	6.14	13.1	2.7	4.7	3.4	6.26	-12.2	-6
2002	SLM	CRL	24	28	28	170.3	149	53	131	22	4.23	6.04	12.2	4.2	5.2	3.1	5.59	-10.1	-7

Dohmann's ratios make him look a lot like fellow collegians Bouknight and Buglovsky, and his fastball rides right between theirs at about 88 mph. It's the gopheritis that sets him apart. It'll catch up to him when he gets to Colorado Springs—the Rockies won't let him give up 50 home runs there before deciding he isn't worth it. Like most pitchers drafted out of college, he has good makeup and instincts. He's a bit ripe to be giving up so many bombs to 20-year-olds.

Scott Elarton   Born: 23-Feb-76   Age: 27   Bats: R   Throws: R

YEAR	TM	LG	AGE	G	GS	IP	H	BB	SO	HR	ERA	EQERA	EQH9	EQBB9	EQSO9	EQHR9	PERA	VORP	STF
2000	HOU	NL	24	30	30	192.7	198	84	131	29	4.81	4.54	8.8	3.1	5.3	1.2	4.69	20.7	7
2001	HOU	NL	25	20	20	109.7	126	49	76	26	7.14	6.50	10.3	3.7	5.3	1.9	6.23	-12.1	-5
2001	COL	NL	25	4	4	23.0	20	10	11	8	6.65	5.54	7.4	3.6	3.6	2.6	5.08	-0.1	-15

In 1999, we said it was imperative that you GET SCOTT ELARTON. Well, some days you get the bear and some days the bear gets you. He's healthy and he's the one pitcher who's actually grateful to be with the Rockies. As the last man in a good bullpen on a team that has nothing to lose, he's in the right place to work his way back. He's guaranteed to make $300,000 this year but he'll jack that up to $1.5 million if he proves to be as good as we said he was.

Cam Esslinger   Born: 28-Dec-76   Age: 26   Bats: R   Throws: R

YEAR	TM	LG	AGE	G	GS	IP	H	BB	SO	HR	ERA	EQERA	EQH9	EQBB9	EQSO9	EQHR9	PERA	VORP	STF
2000	ASH	SAL	23	47	2	64.7	55	23	84	2	3.06	4.20	9.7	4.3	6.6	0.7	4.39	8.6	0
2001	CAR	SOU	24	40	0	42.0	32	31	51	0	4.93	5.50	8.1	7.8	7.4	0.3	4.74	-0.6	-5
2002	CSP	PCL	25	29	0	32.0	30	17	23	2	6.19	4.76	7.9	5.4	4.9	0.7	4.23	2.2	-16

Esslinger throws hard but not for strikes. He got mashed in his second season in the AFL, with a 7.16 ERA. Ignore the 96-mph fastball. It's the only reason he's still on the periphery of prospect status.

Jeff Francis   Born: 08-Jan-81   Age: 22   Bats: L   Throws: L

YEAR	TM	LG	AGE	G	GS	IP	H	BB	SO	HR	ERA	EQERA	EQH9	EQBB9	EQSO9	EQHR9	PERA	VORP	STF
2002	TRI	NWN	21	4	3	10.7	5	4	16	0	0.00	0.31	6.5	4.8	7.6	0.3	2.47	6.2	21
2002	ASH	SAL	21	4	4	20.0	16	4	23	2	1.80	3.70	10.3	2.6	6.5	2.3	4.04	4.0	14

A physics major, Francis was the Rockies' first round pick in the 2002 draft. He had posted an ERA under 1.00 as a sophomore, and faced wooden bats in summer leagues in Alaska, so he was ready to adapt quickly. He already has equivalencies better than most pitchers in their system. He gets ahead quickly, and works with four finished pitches. Big body. Fast track. Think Mulder.

Brian Fuentes   Born: 09-Aug-75   Age: 27   Bats: L   Throws: L

YEAR	TM	LG	AGE	G	GS	IP	H	BB	SO	HR	ERA	EQERA	EQH9	EQBB9	EQSO9	EQHR9	PERA	VORP	STF
2000	NHV	EAS	24	26	26	139.7	127	70	152	7	4.51	5.93	10.3	5.1	7.5	0.9	5.21	-6.6	12
2001	TAC	PCL	25	35	0	52.0	35	25	70	4	2.94	3.70	7.0	5.2	9.0	0.8	3.44	9.7	11
2001	SEA	AL	25	10	0	11.7	6	8	10	2	4.62	4.28	5.0	5.8	7.3	1.4	3.40	1.4	-3
2002	CSP	PCL	26	41	0	48.7	44	32	61	0	3.70	3.66	7.5	6.6	8.4	0.2	3.95	9.3	3
2002	COL	NL	26	31	0	26.7	25	13	38	4	4.72	4.35	8.1	3.8	10.9	1.3	4.28	3.1	20
2003	*COL*	*NL*	*27*	*31*	*1*	*40.7*	*43*	*24*	*42*	*6*	*5.36*	*4.64*	*9.0*	*4.5*	*8.7*	*1.0*	*4.67*	*5.0*	*7*

Breakout: 17%   *Improve: 41%*   *Collapse: 33%*

Improbably, Fuentes cut his walks when he got called up, posting a 25:7 strikeout-to-walk ratio at Coors, with a 3.31 ERA. Over his last 16 innings he struck out 22 and walked only 3. Alongside Darensbourg, he gives the Rockies a nifty pair of lefties in the pen, arguably among the best in the league.

Mike Hampton   Born: 09-Sep-72   Age: 30   Bats: R   Throws: L

YEAR	TM	LG	AGE	G	GS	IP	H	BB	SO	HR	ERA	EQERA	EQH9	EQBB9	EQSO9	EQHR9	PERA	VORP	STF
2000	NYM	NL	27	33	33	217.7	194	99	151	10	3.14	3.56	8.4	3.4	5.6	0.4	3.63	47.0	11
2001	COL	NL	28	32	32	203.0	236	85	122	31	5.41	5.34	10.2	3.5	4.6	1.1	5.09	3.7	-2
2002	COL	NL	29	30	30	178.7	228	91	74	24	6.14	6.16	11.3	4.0	3.2	1.2	5.94	-13.0	-14
2003	*ATL*	*NL*	*30*	*27*	*24*	*148.7*	*160*	*66*	*86*	*14*	*4.63*	*4.95*	*9.9*	*3.4*	*4.6*	*0.9*	*4.95*	*11.8*	*-2*

Breakout: 13%   *Improve: 56%*   *Collapse: 14%*

When the Rockies sin, they sin boldly. In the three years before moving to Colorado, Hampton put up walk rates of 3.5, 3.8, and 4.1 with a strikeout-to-walk ratio under 2.0 each year. He managed low home run rates but he had been pitching in two of baseball's best pitchers' parks. Buyer's remorse set in quickly. By last year his strikeout rate had fallen to half of what it was at his peak, and he walked more than he whiffed. Don't blame it all on Coors. Last year his ERA was better there than on the road. In 2001 his road ERA was a little better than at home but it was still 5.10. Does Coors cause permanent disability? Plenty of others have recovered once they escaped. Now he's back in a pitcher's park. If he flops, don't blame it on an altitude-sickness hangover. He was oversold to begin with.

Pete Harnisch — Born: 23-Sep-66 — Age: 36 — Bats: R — Throws: R

YEAR	TM	LG	AGE	G	GS	IP	H	BB	SO	HR	ERA	EQERA	EQH9	EQBB9	EQSO9	EQHR9	PERA	VORP	STF
2000	CIN	NL	33	22	22	131.0	133	46	71	23	4.74	4.98	9.8	2.6	4.4	1.4	4.51	7.6	-1
2001	CIN	NL	34	7	7	35.3	48	17	17	9	6.37	7.06	12.1	4.0	3.7	2.0	7.46	-6.1	-22

Another lost season, this time due to Tommy John surgery, and arguably his just desserts for blowing off the Reds after their considerable patience with him. He's slunk back to Cincinnati for a minor league deal, and once he's physically sound by June or so, he might have a shot at the rotation.

Jason Jennings — Born: 17-Jul-78 — Age: 24 — Bats: L — Throws: R

YEAR	TM	LG	AGE	G	GS	IP	H	BB	SO	HR	ERA	EQERA	EQH9	EQBB9	EQSO9	EQHR9	PERA	VORP	STF
2000	SLM	CRL	21	22	22	150.3	136	42	133	6	3.47	4.85	10.5	3.0	5.0	0.9	4.87	10.9	10
2000	CAR	SOU	21	6	6	36.7	32	11	33	4	3.43	5.17	10.1	3.0	5.8	1.9	4.95	1.4	11
2001	CAR	SOU	22	4	4	25.0	25	8	24	1	2.88	4.37	10.8	3.4	5.9	0.6	5.03	3.2	16
2001	CSP	PCL	22	22	22	131.7	145	41	110	9	4.72	4.32	9.3	3.2	5.3	0.7	4.46	17.3	12
2001	COL	NL	22	7	7	39.3	42	19	26	2	4.58	4.27	9.6	4.0	5.1	0.4	4.12	5.4	9
2002	COL	NL	23	32	32	185.3	201	70	127	26	4.52	4.67	9.6	3.0	5.4	1.2	4.66	17.2	9
2003	*COL*	*NL*	*24*	*26*	*24*	*151.3*	*170*	*59*	*106*	*22*	*5.04*	*4.36*	*9.7*	*2.9*	*5.9*	*1.0*	*4.39*	*21.1*	*9*

Breakout: 15%   Improve: 49%   Collapse: 14%

Notice that Jennings is still younger than most of their prospects? He's good, but he doesn't have an ace's strikeout rate. The park shaves some strikeouts over the course of a season, but Jennings's translated rates have been steadily under six. Consistent equivalencies say he's not likely to flake out this year. What is worrisome is that Jennings's home run rate spiked in 2002. His combined 2001 numbers are similar to last year, so the Rookie of the Year shouldn't have been that shocking.

Jose Jimenez — Born: 07-Jul-73 — Age: 30 — Bats: R — Throws: R

YEAR	TM	LG	AGE	G	GS	IP	H	BB	SO	HR	ERA	EQERA	EQH9	EQBB9	EQSO9	EQHR9	PERA	VORP	STF
2000	COL	NL	27	72	0	70.7	63	28	44	4	3.18	2.95	7.9	2.9	5.0	0.4	2.88	19.1	-4
2001	COL	NL	28	56	0	55.0	56	22	37	6	4.09	4.06	9.0	3.3	5.1	0.8	4.05	8.1	-9
2002	COL	NL	29	74	0	73.3	76	11	47	7	3.56	3.73	9.3	1.2	5.1	0.8	3.49	13.4	-2
2003	*COL*	*NL*	*29*	*58*	*0*	*56.0*	*63*	*16*	*36*	*7*	*4.28*	*3.71*	*9.7*	*2.2*	*5.5*	*0.9*	*3.98*	*11.8*	*-3*

Breakout: 15%   Improve: 45%   Collapse: 25%

The Rockies find good relievers and they're usually stuck with them. Too many GMs can't see past the superficial scarring Coors can inflict on an ERA. For example, when the Rockies released Rick White in August, he cleared waivers. GMs took one look at his 6.20 ERA and blanched. But he had been very successful for the Rockies in 2001 and had been rated as one of the most underrated relievers in the league. His 4.11 road ERA in 2002 indicated he was still useful, but a bad showing at Coors blew up his overall numbers. Those who understand the Coors effect can pretend they don't and then use the inflated numbers to drive down the Rockies' asking price until they have no choice but to get burned in the deal, release the player, or play him. The good news is that if their hitters ever come around, they'll have a championship bullpen. Like Fuentes, Jimenez was much better at home last year. Of course exceptions don't prove rules; they disprove them. People just make far too much of the Coors effect.

Todd Jones — Born: 24-Apr-68 — Age: 35 — Bats: R — Throws: R

YEAR	TM	LG	AGE	G	GS	IP	H	BB	SO	HR	ERA	EQERA	EQH9	EQBB9	EQSO9	EQHR9	PERA	VORP	STF
2000	DET	AL	32	67	0	64.0	67	25	67	6	3.52	3.57	8.8	2.8	9.0	0.7	3.97	12.9	17
2001	DET	AL	33	45	0	48.7	60	22	39	6	4.62	5.40	10.7	3.8	6.7	1.0	5.78	-0.1	-5
2001	MIN	AL	33	24	0	19.3	27	7	15	3	3.26	4.73	12.2	3.0	6.5	1.2	6.32	1.4	-6
2002	COL	NL	34	79	0	82.3	84	28	73	10	4.70	4.27	9.1	2.7	7.0	1.0	4.10	10.2	2
2003	*COL*	*NL*	*35*	*58*	*0*	*60.3*	*67*	*24*	*53*	*9*	*4.64*	*4.02*	*9.5*	*3.1*	*7.4*	*1.0*	*4.26*	*11.3*	*4*

Breakout: 21%   Improve: 47%   Collapse: 22%

The Rockies understand that when the goal is the World Series, there's no difference between 75 wins and 25. A 75-team doesn't really need a closer, so why keep two of them? In 2002, the Rockies' attendance dropped below three million for the first time. In most cities the illusion of competitiveness has value, so this is a losing team that sees value in every one of its victories, but it has yet to be explained how a nondescript reliever is supposed to convince people to pony up for a season ticket.

Ryan Kibler — Born: 17-Sep-80 — Age: 22 — Bats: R — Throws: R

YEAR	TM	LG	AGE	G	GS	IP	H	BB	SO	HR	ERA	EQERA	EQH9	EQBB9	EQSO9	EQHR9	PERA	VORP	STF
2000	ASH	SAL	19	26	26	155.0	173	67	110	9	4.41	7.34	13.6	5.5	3.8	1.4	6.96	-31.6	-10
2001	ASH	SAL	20	10	10	61.3	50	27	59	3	2.94	5.12	10.2	6.1	5.0	1.1	5.20	2.6	2
2001	SLM	CRL	20	11	11	75.7	53	16	61	0	1.55	3.27	7.8	2.7	4.4	0.3	3.32	18.8	13
2001	CAR	SOU	20	8	8	47.0	38	19	41	0	2.11	3.82	8.5	4.3	5.3	0.3	3.85	8.8	14
2002	CAR	SOU	21	25	25	143.0	158	64	59	6	4.91	6.08	11.4	4.4	2.7	0.8	6.21	-9.1	-11

The organization blamed Kibler's bad year on a secret injury. Unfortunately, it wasn't really that secret. Early in the season one of his teammates hit a home run. Kibler was the lead runner and didn't know it had gone out, so he hauled ass and injured his pitching thumb sliding into the plate. His real problem was that he lost his focus when other prospects passed him by. He has been promoted to Triple-A, so they're not babying him. Is it ever a good idea for a pitcher to slide headfirst?

Chandler Martin — Born: 23-Oct-73 — Age: 29 — Bats: R — Throws: R

YEAR	TM	LG	AGE	G	GS	IP	H	BB	SO	HR	ERA	EQERA	EQH9	EQBB9	EQSO9	EQHR9	PERA	VORP	STF
2000	POR	NWN	26	3	3	16.0	15	1	14	0	2.81	4.42	12.2	0.7	4.2	0.3	4.57	1.9	6
2000	SLM	CRL	26	7	7	45.7	41	12	25	1	3.54	4.45	10.2	2.9	3.1	0.5	4.61	5.4	-4
2000	CAR	SOU	26	4	4	23.0	27	11	10	1	3.91	5.71	13.2	4.8	2.8	0.8	7.10	-0.5	-19
2001	TRI	NWN	27	4	4	18.0	14	1	11	3	3.00	4.93	12.9	0.8	3.2	4.7	5.32	1.2	-26
2001	ASH	SAL	27	2	2	13.7	10	5	8	1	1.31	2.91	9.4	5.1	3.1	1.6	4.55	4.0	-14
2001	SLM	CRL	27	9	9	57.0	68	14	32	5	4.74	7.59	15.1	3.4	3.3	2.1	7.86	-13.2	-21
2002	CSP	PCL	28	8	6	28.0	39	21	14	1	7.07	6.42	11.7	7.5	3.4	0.4	7.28	-2.9	-30
2002	CAR	SOU	28	19	19	113.3	109	34	82	8	3.18	4.33	10.2	2.9	4.8	1.3	4.94	14.8	0

Martin has spent quite a while returning from injury. Far too old for Double-A in any case, he's not under contract now, but he did have a healthy season, ending with a great August, where he posted a 2.57 ERA and a 27:2 strikeout-to-walk ratio in 28 innings. It's hard to believe he couldn't make it as an 11th man on some staff, at minimum cost.

Kent Mercker — Born: 01-Feb-68 — Age: 35 — Bats: L — Throws: L

YEAR	TM	LG	AGE	G	GS	IP	H	BB	SO	HR	ERA	EQERA	EQH9	EQBB9	EQSO9	EQHR9	PERA	VORP	STF
2000	ANA	AL	32	21	7	48.3	57	29	30	12	6.52	6.29	10.3	4.4	5.4	1.9	6.26	-4.5	-17
2002	CSP	PCL	34	2	0	1.7	3	2	0	2	21.18	19.30	21.0	14.5	0.0	15.5	20.34	-2.6	-19
2002	COL	NL	34	58	0	44.0	55	22	37	12	6.14	6.49	10.9	3.9	6.5	2.3	6.70	-5.4	-17
2003	*CIN*	*NL*	*35*	*41*	*0*	*38.7*	*40*	*19*	*30*	*5*	*4.71*	*5.04*	*9.4*	*3.8*	*6.3*	*1.2*	*5.17*	*3.3*	*-9*

Breakout: 19%   Improve: 62%   Collapse: 16%

So Mercker "thrived" as a lefty specialist? What bull. He wiped out the intended platoon advantage by posting a grotesquely reversed split. He faced more righties than lefties—they almost always do—and it offset some of the damage, but right-handers still slugged .433 against him. Just as worthless on the road as at Coors. The Reds have taken a flyer, sparing everyone else the risk.

Denny Neagle — Born: 13-Sep-68 — Age: 34 — Bats: L — Throws: L

YEAR	TM	LG	AGE	G	GS	IP	H	BB	SO	HR	ERA	EQERA	EQH9	EQBB9	EQSO9	EQHR9	PERA	VORP	STF
2000	CIN	NL	31	18	18	117.7	111	50	88	15	3.52	3.95	9.0	3.1	6.0	1.0	4.01	20.3	11
2000	NYY	AL	31	16	15	91.3	99	31	58	16	5.82	4.85	9.2	2.5	5.5	1.3	4.68	6.6	5
2001	COL	NL	32	30	30	170.7	192	60	139	29	5.38	4.98	9.8	2.9	6.2	1.3	4.82	10.0	7
2002	COL	NL	33	35	28	164.3	170	63	111	26	5.26	4.87	9.2	3.0	5.3	1.4	4.56	11.4	0
2003	*COL*	*NL*	*34*	*28*	*21*	*126.3*	*141*	*49*	*89*	*20*	*5.10*	*4.42*	*9.6*	*2.9*	*6.0*	*1.1*	*4.37*	*17.5*	*6*

Breakout: 12%   Improve: 46%   Collapse: 13%

There was an officer who got kicked out of the Air Force for saying publicly that his boss was "a duck with ears," except he didn't say "duck." What does Neagle have to do to get out of Denver? He sucks only relative to what he's getting paid. In his

Denny Neagle *(continued)*

two seasons with the Rockies his home ERA has been 5.41 over 168 innings. Here's how some of his predecessors have done in Coors:

Pitcher	IP	ERA
Pedro Astacio	404	7.24
Marvin Freeman	128.2	6.92
Bobby M. Jones	143.1	6.59
Darryl Kile	218.1	6.76
Armando Reynoso	155.1	5.48
Kevin Ritz	233	6.22
Bill Swift	100.1	5.56
John Thomson	266.2	6.14

Neagle's two-year road ERA of 5.25 is the problem. There are a few dozen minor league free agent pitchers who could do at least that well, and they'd play for peanuts. The Diamondbacks spend $13 million on Randy Johnson. It's OK to spend that kind of money on a pitcher, so long as you give it to a bona fide star. You don't spread it around to the understudies.

Matt Roney — Born: 10-Jan-80 — Age: 23 — Bats: R — Throws: R

YEAR	TM	LG	AGE	G	GS	IP	H	BB	SO	HR	ERA	EQERA	EQH9	EQBB9	EQSO9	EQHR9	PERA	VORP	STF
2000	POR	NWN	20	15	15	80.3	75	44	85	6	3.14	6.76	14.4	6.7	5.4	2.6	7.81	-11.2	-9
2001	ASH	SAL	21	23	23	121.0	131	43	115	16	4.98	7.48	14.7	5.1	5.1	3.0	7.75	-26.6	-9
2002	ASH	SAL	22	14	14	82.7	82	25	88	7	3.48	5.44	12.3	3.9	6.0	2.0	5.62	0.6	7
2002	CAR	SOU	22	13	13	70.7	73	33	61	6	6.11	6.39	11.1	4.5	5.7	1.6	6.17	-7.0	2

Roney has the prospecty things you like to hear: 1st round pick in 1998, 6′ 4″, 230 pounds, throws 95 to 98 mph. Unfortunately, so far, he's been uncoachable. They exposed him to the Rule 5 draft, where the Pirates took him off of their hands. It won't come back to haunt the Rockies.

Justin Speier — Born: 06-Nov-73 — Age: 29 — Bats: R — Throws: R

YEAR	TM	LG	AGE	G	GS	IP	H	BB	SO	HR	ERA	EQERA	EQH9	EQBB9	EQSO9	EQHR9	PERA	VORP	STF
2000	BUF	INT	26	13	0	13.0	13	3	12	0	4.15	4.07	9.8	2.1	7.0	0.2	3.64	1.9	8
2000	CLE	AL	26	47	0	68.3	57	28	69	9	3.29	3.00	6.8	2.9	8.7	1.0	3.18	18.1	16
2001	CSP	PCL	27	11	0	12.3	10	7	16	0	1.46	1.89	6.8	5.8	8.2	0.2	3.23	4.8	7
2001	CLE	AL	27	12	0	20.7	24	8	15	5	6.96	5.65	9.3	3.2	6.0	1.9	5.95	-0.6	-11
2001	COL	NL	27	42	0	56.0	47	12	47	8	3.70	3.24	7.4	1.8	6.4	1.1	2.94	13.3	5
2002	CSP	PCL	28	12	0	14.0	20	3	14	2	3.86	4.68	12.2	2.1	6.6	1.5	6.54	1.1	-4
2002	COL	NL	28	63	0	62.3	51	19	47	9	4.33	3.71	7.3	2.4	6.0	1.3	3.23	11.6	-2
2003	*COL*	*NL*	*29*	*51*	*0*	*55.0*	*56*	*20*	*44*	*9*	*4.43*	*3.84*	*8.9*	*2.7*	*6.7*	*1.1*	*4.00*	*10.4*	*1*

Breakout: 19%   Improve: 44%   Collapse: 25%

Speier was one of the most underrated relievers in baseball last year, and the best at preventing inherited runners from scoring. All the damage occurred at home, where his ERA was 6.40. In spite of the ERA, his ratios at Coors were good. He is one of at least five high-caliber relievers in their bullpen. We have long argued for an unconventional (egghead) approach to bullpen management when the Rockies play at Coors. One component of the argument is that they need to stretch out the length of relief appearances, eschewing one-out specialists and single-inning appearances. The Rockies were the only team in baseball to average less than an inning per relief appearance. It's 180 degrees from the way we'd do it, but their bullpen has done just fine without our help.

Denny Stark — Born: 27-Oct-74 — Age: 28 — Bats: R — Throws: R

YEAR	TM	LG	AGE	G	GS	IP	H	BB	SO	HR	ERA	EQERA	EQH9	EQBB9	EQSO9	EQHR9	PERA	VORP	STF
2000	NHV	EAS	25	8	8	49.3	31	17	42	1	2.19	3.06	7.0	3.5	5.8	0.3	2.80	13.4	16
2001	TAC	PCL	26	24	24	151.7	124	41	130	12	2.37	3.70	8.5	2.9	5.7	0.9	3.59	30.4	11
2001	SEA	AL	26	4	3	14.7	21	4	12	5	9.18	9.04	13.6	2.3	7.0	2.9	8.13	-5.8	-9
2002	CSP	PCL	27	7	7	37.7	35	14	38	4	3.82	3.70	7.9	3.7	6.8	1.1	3.99	7.6	11
2002	COL	NL	27	32	20	128.3	108	64	64	25	4.00	4.40	7.5	4.0	3.9	1.7	4.23	15.5	-14
2003	*COL*	*NL*	*28*	*23*	*15*	*91.3*	*102*	*43*	*58*	*16*	*5.70*	*4.94*	*9.7*	*3.6*	*5.3*	*1.2*	*4.82*	*7.4*	*-4*

Breakout: 8%   Improve: 42%   Collapse: 22%

He's excitable, and when it gets the best of him, he gets very wild. He gives up a lot of walks. His strikeout rate is mediocre. Not many pitchers can survive with a 1:1 strikeout to walk ratio, especially when they give up so many homers. Stark gave up 1.9 home runs per 9 innings at home, and even if that's in Coors, that's dangerous. Although he works down in the zone, those home runs accounted for 18 of his 30 earned runs at home. He was a much worse pitcher on the road. A potential time bomb, though the Rockies think he's fine.

Chin-Hui Tsao   Born: 02-Jun-81   Age: 22   Bats: R   Throws: R

YEAR	TM	LG	AGE	G	GS	IP	H	BB	SO	HR	ERA	EQERA	EQH9	EQBB9	EQSO9	EQHR9	PERA	VORP	STF
2000	ASH	SAL	19	24	24	145.0	119	40	187	8	2.73	4.16	9.7	3.3	6.6	1.2	4.11	21.7	21
2001	SLM	CRL	20	4	4	17.3	23	5	18	1	4.68	8.15	16.3	4.0	6.0	1.3	8.69	-5.1	0
2002	TRI	NWN	21	3	3	11.0	6	2	16	0	0.00	2.57	7.4	2.3	7.3	0.3	2.23	3.6	27
2002	SLM	CRL	21	9	9	47.3	34	12	45	3	2.09	3.75	9.0	3.2	6.1	1.5	3.71	9.2	15

The organization's lone power pitcher. Tsao is healthy again after Tommy John surgery in 2001. Culture shock is wearing off as his grasp of English improves. A forgotten man, once he shakes off the rust he could return to being one of the most promising young prospects in the game. We don't have to keep saying "assuming he stays healthy," do we?

Cory Vance   Born: 20-Jun-79   Age: 24   Bats: L   Throws: L

YEAR	TM	LG	AGE	G	GS	IP	H	BB	SO	HR	ERA	EQERA	EQH9	EQBB9	EQSO9	EQHR9	PERA	VORP	STF
2000	POR	NWN	21	7	3	24.3	11	8	26	1	1.11	2.87	6.6	3.7	5.1	1.3	2.78	7.0	3
2001	SLM	CRL	22	26	26	154.0	129	65	142	9	3.10	5.40	10.3	5.7	5.3	1.3	5.62	1.8	0
2002	CAR	SOU	23	25	25	150.3	142	76	114	8	3.77	4.89	9.8	4.9	5.0	1.0	5.46	10.3	1
2002	COL	NL	23	2	1	4.0	4	4	1	2	6.75	7.30	8.6	7.7	1.9	4.2	8.53	-0.8	-57
2003	COL	NL	24	13	10	64.0	76	38	44	11	6.26	5.42	10.2	4.5	5.8	1.2	5.43	2.8	-2

Breakout: 9%   Improve: 55%   Collapse: 23%

Vance had a poor work ethic between starts when the year began, but it got better. He then became Carolina's ace by default when Cook and Young left. He runs up high pitch counts when he loses track of his fastball, often busting the 100-pitch threshold by the fifth inning. If you're a sadist, the PCL will be a good test for those bad equivalencies.

Jason Young   Born: 28-Sep-79   Age: 23   Bats: R   Throws: R

YEAR	TM	LG	AGE	G	GS	IP	H	BB	SO	HR	ERA	EQERA	EQH9	EQBB9	EQSO9	EQHR9	PERA	VORP	STF
2001	SLM	CRL	21	17	17	104.7	104	28	91	8	3.44	5.87	12.4	3.6	5.0	1.8	6.29	-4.2	3
2002	CAR	SOU	22	14	14	88.7	71	30	76	1	2.64	3.32	7.9	3.2	5.5	0.2	3.62	21.5	18
2002	CSP	PCL	22	13	13	79.7	87	38	74	10	4.97	4.82	9.4	4.8	6.3	1.3	5.38	6.1	10
2003	COL	NL	23	12	9	59.7	71	30	46	10	5.76	4.99	10.2	3.9	6.4	1.1	5.01	5.4	5

Breakout: 11%   Improve: 45%   Collapse: 22%

Young needed to jack up his strikeout rate, and he did. He has command of several pitches, and the fastball hits 92 to 94. He also has presence or mound moxie, whatever it is the White Sox wish Jon Garland had. Young projects to be the same in Denver as he was in Colorado Springs; the team's Triple-A park is the minor league equivalent of Coors and a good proving ground for future Rockies. Young's professionalism was considered a good influence on Vance. The quartet of Jennings, Cook, Young, and Vance gives the Rockies an extremely underrated young pitching base, but that's what the environment does to perception: it creates blind spots.

Florida Marlins

In just about any facet you care to consider, Jeffrey Loria's ownership of the Expos was a failure. Loria's handpicked front-office staff not only failed to meaningfully market the team, they couldn't even figure out how to *give away* the Expos' broadcast rights. They made their share of asinine trades; getting a more expensive analog to what they gave often appeared to be the team's player acquisition strategy. The team's free-agent signings were frequently regrettable, with multimillionaire lefty specialist/angry man Graeme Lloyd taking the Bizarro crown here. The minor league system was run in an essentially random fashion, with promising former first round draft pick Donnie Bridges enduring a complete slagging in 2000 in an attempt to prove that he was the real deal. The organization's attempts at securing public funding of a new stadium were ham-handed and clumsy, rubbing raw a fan base and municipality already irritated by former owner Claude Brochu's frequent bleating. The product on the field was by all accounts awful, and the team's attendance continued to slide toward REO Speedwagon/Foghat double bill territory.

The Loria era in Montreal hurt the Expos, and it hurt their fans. But considering Jeffrey Loria left Montreal considerably better off than he arrived when Major League Baseball agreed to purchase the Expos for $120 million in 2002, lots of amusing cloak-and-dagger, evil-genius scenarios occurred to the paranoid mind. Loria bought into the Expos in 1999, slowly consolidated his power within the franchise with cash calls the other owners were unwilling to meet, and sold for a handsome profit just three years later. Perhaps Loria knew what he was doing all along by deepening the funk Montreal baseball was in. Maybe he'd anticipated the blood money MLB would throw his way, and he was willing to take it and disappear. It takes an economic climate rife with Enron/WorldCom-style debacles to make such a scenario worth thinking about, but a Loria scorched-earth campaign against his own franchise to make a buck was a cunning plan that would make Ken Lay green with envy.

Unless Loria has a line on a used large-market franchise, he and his organization have put the conspiracy theories to rest after they swapped and negotiated their way into Florida and operated the Marlins in 2002. Presumably, these guys are doing their best; realistically, they still don't have a clue how to run a franchise.

In fairness, baseball in Miami has problems that would prove daunting for the best of organizations. Former Marlins owner Wayne Huizenga still owns the NFL's Miami Dolphins and Pro Player Stadium, and he continues to bleed the Marlins with regressive lease terms. We touched on the similarities to the Twins' deal with the Metrodome in last year's book, but this is actually a fairly widespread problem. In San Diego, the Padres run into a similar issue with their lease to play in Qualcomm Stadium, which allows the Chargers to sell all the advertising in the stadium, take most of the proceeds, and leech the luxury box revenues from baseball games. In multisport venues with football and baseball tenants, the NFL—where franchise relocation is as easy as renting a U-Haul—has significant leverage over Major League Baseball, and football teams don't let stadium owners forget it. When the stadium owner happens to own the football team as well, it's obvious the baseball team is going to get jobbed, but this happens even when the stadium is owned by a third party, and it's a significant problem for several major league franchises.

The Padres will be getting a new stadium in 2004, but the Marlins are stuck with their situation for the foreseeable future. Former owners John Henry and Huizenga unsuccessfully demanded, begged, and pleaded for a baseball-only facility in Miami for the better part of a decade. Meanwhile, the Marlins haven't been successful since their bald-faced fire sale following the 1997 World Series. Attendance has fallen

---

Marlins Prospectus

2002 record: 79–83; Fourth place, NL East

Pythagenport Record: 74–88

Runs scored per game: 4.3 (12th in NL)

Runs allowed per game: 4.7 (12th in NL)

Team EqA: .265 (5th in NL)

2002 Batters Age: 29 (5th youngest in NL)

2002 Pitchers Age: 26.4 (youngest in NL)

Ballpark: Pro Player Stadium; Moderate pitchers' park; Park Factor of .966

2002: Young talent squandered, bad trades made, bad baseball played, another Loria operation.

2003: Never underestimate the ability of bad management to get between a talented team and success.

---

precipitously since that year's team, and in 2002, the Marlins outdrew only Montreal in the National League and failed to reach one million tickets sold for the first time in franchise history, a bad sign for any effort on the team's part to secure public support and financing. (The Marlins would have finished last behind Montreal but for an anonymous benefactor—wink, wink—who purchased more than 15,000 unused tickets on the last day of the season to ensure they didn't finish last.) Frankly, it's tough to blame most Miamians for being fed up with the entire situation, and unless the Marlins somehow come up with the cash for a stadium themselves, the team will have to play its 2003 home games in a 75,000-seat mausoleum half an hour from downtown Miami.

Loria and stepson/club president David Samson assumed control of the Marlins on February 15, giving them a late start on building their organization for the 2002 run. In large part, they simply hired away many of the people they had assembled with the Expos, with general manager Larry Beinfest heading up the front office and Jeff Torborg donning teal and white as the Marlins manager. The new regime placed their stamp on the club early, trading closer Antonio Alfonseca and starter Matt Clement to the Cubs for Julian Tavarez and three minor leaguers. One of the imports, pitching prospect Dontrelle Willis, had an excellent season and established himself as one of the better pitching prospects in the low minors, but Clement finally blossomed in Chicago and became the frontline starter that the Marlins were sorely missing in 2002.

The Marlins started the season hot, and were in first place in the NL East in the middle of May. But the team's bad luck with injuries to its rotation began to take its toll as Tavarez, Josh Beckett, and Brad Penny were all placed on the DL before the end of May and the team began to slide from contention. The Marlins pulled into the All-Star break in third place, only two games above .500 and 12 games behind the division-leading Braves. Accepting their also-ran status quickly, by the trading deadline, slugging outfielder Cliff Floyd and starting pitcher Ryan Dempster were both gone, and the team limped to a disappointing fourth-place finish in the NL East.

To be fair, not many teams have the depth required to make up for the starts the Marlins lost early in the season, but the most worrisome developments with the pitching staff occurred elsewhere. A 25-year-old starter, A. J. Burnett, was turning in an excellent performance as the Marlins fell out of contention, but manager Torborg didn't exactly throttle back with Burnett's usage patterns. Before he made his own trip to the DL with a "deep bone bruise" on August 19, Burnett had made as many 120-pitch outings as Randy Johnson and Curt Schilling combined. The heavy usage meshed seamlessly with a pattern Torborg had exhibited in previous stints with the Chicago White Sox and New York Mets, where he wrung plenty of work out of his better starters.

Unfortunately, the best Marlins starting pitchers are all very young; the team will run with the now-26-year-old Burnett, Beckett (23), and Penny (25) at the front of the rotation in 2003. These are three very good young pitchers, and while there's something to be said for letting your good pitchers pitch when you're in a pennant race, giving one of these guys 593 pitches over five starts without being in shouting distance of the division leader (as Burnett got in late July and early August) probably isn't the risk-averse strategy Torborg should be taking with the team's strength.

The Marlins' pitcher abuse has hurt in other ways as well. A reported three-way, off-season deal with Cincinnati and Montreal that would have brought in Bartolo Colon for Brad Penny and prospects was on the verge of being quashed after the ugly details of Penny's frayed pitching shoulder—largely the result of Penny being trotted out to pitch with a bum elbow—came to light. Whether or not you agree with the idea of chucking a big chunk out of your future for a one-year rental of Colon, in Penny the Marlins now find themselves with a talented, young pitcher too injured to help the club and too injured to trade.

Offensively, the Marlins got ink-friendly, fluke-hitting streaks of 35 games from second baseman Luis Castillo and 25 from outfielder Kevin Millar. But Cliff Floyd was the engine of the team's hitting attack, and they missed him when he was traded. On the bright side, the Marlins were able to swap out light-hitting shortstop Alex Gonzalez for the slightly more threatening Andy Fox after Gonzalez's season-ending shoulder dislocation in late May. Eric Owens's playing time plummeted after the team acquired Juan Encarnacion, while Millar slugged his way into more at-bats toward the end of the year. The team ended the season with an above-average offense.

That may not be in the cards for 2003. The off-season trade of Charles Johnson and Preston Wilson for Tim Spooneybarger and Juan Pierre gives the team the top two basestealers in the NL in 2002 and solidifies Beinfest's commitment to team speed. But the quality of the Marlins' hitting attack in 2002 didn't have a lot to do with their leading the league in steals, and if the front office assembles its 2003 roster with speed as their top priority, they'll be making a mistake. Beinfest made matters worse when he signed Tin Man Todd Hollandsworth to play the outfield while letting Millar bolt for greener pastures, most likely Japan. Hollandsworth isn't necessarily that much worse a player than Millar, but he's as likely to stay healthy for 550 at-bats as Jeffrey Hammonds chaperoning for a troop of pox-ridden Boy Scouts.

With Millar and Floyd gone and Mike Lowell rumored to be on the trading block, the Marlins will miss their power no matter how many bases their likely replacements steal. Pierre, in particular, creates a lineup construction problem for this team. He has everything you look for in a leadoff hitter except the all-important ability to get on base regularly. Batting him leadoff for the 2003 team puts an out machine at the top of the lineup, and his lack of power makes him a bad choice for the second spot in the order as well. With the other options this team has, Pierre should be batting in the bottom of the order—steals be damned—but that's not a conclusion Torborg will reach.

With their relative youth and most of their divisional foes taking steps back in the off-season, the Marlins have another 80-win season squarely in their sights, but without a serious marketing push, that's not likely to impress the natives. The team has announced several promotions—reduced price hot dogs being one of them—that will have a minimal effect at best where the turnstiles are concerned. The Marlins could do a much better job at staffing the stadium and making sure people are able to spend their money there. A fan having to walk halfway around the stadium to buy a program on game day is not a difficult problem to address.

The rash of negative comments Loria's players have made about his front offices isn't a plus in the public relations department either. While a little grumbling in the clubhouse isn't out of the ordinary, and nobody likes a white flag trade, the Marlins took a lot of flak in the media from their roster in 2002. Derrek Lee's complaints about being lied to by the organization were particularly damaging, because of Lee's generally long and successful Marlins career and there not being any obvious sour grapes involved. Trading for Graeme Lloyd was actually kind of a funny thing to do, unless you're Graeme Lloyd, and he had plenty to say about Loria's sense of humor.

The organization's treatment of the Mike Hampton trades will be the single most important indicator of how Loria and company intend to run this club in the long-term.

The Marlins saved themselves $52 million in player salaries through 2005 that were due to Johnson and Wilson, and they picked up $6.5 million in cash in the deal. However, to ship Hampton to the Braves, the Marlins had to agree to pay $30 million of his salary over the next three seasons. Worst-case, the team will claim poverty for paying a player $10 million a season to pitch for a division rival, a claim with no merit when accounting for the salaries the Marlins don't have to pay as part of the bargain. Using the conspicuous eight-digit payments to the Braves as evidence of "how the economics of baseball don't work, especially without our own ballpark," the team will pare payroll and flounder at the bottom of the division, alienating home fans even further. Paid admissions in Miami can't get too much lower before the team's viability becomes a legitimate question, if it isn't already. After 2003, the lease at Pro Player is up, with the Marlins holding a series of one-year options. Loria has entered negotiations with the Orange Bowl to give himself some leverage, and while it might not exactly be an improvement, it would cut ties with Huizenga, and there's some hope that it would give all concerned a better read on the Miami market.

Alternately, the team might cop to saving a bunch of cash, make a legitimate attempt to spend some of it wisely, and reinforce the solid core and numerous exciting players in the Marlins farm system with some free agent fill-ins. Treating local government and ticket-buying fans with a modicum of respect will cause spit-takes throughout the county, and can only help ticket sales. With the Keystone Kop routine Loria and his front office have specialized in throughout his time in Montreal, that's an unlikely scenario at best, but there would be nothing better for the future of Major League Baseball in South Florida.

HITTERS

Chip Ambres   CF   Born: 19-Dec-79   Age: 23   Bats: R   Throws: R

YEAR	TM	LG	AGE	AB	H	2B	3B	HR	BB	SO	SB	CS	AVG	OBP	SLG	MLVR	EQBA	EQOBP	EQSLG	EQMLVR	VORP	DEFENSE
2000	KNE	MDW	20	320	74	16	3	7	52	72	26	8	.231	.344	.366	.017	.183	.263	.293	-.407	-20.6	81-CF -4
2001	KNE	MDW	21	377	100	26	8	5	53	81	19	15	.265	.372	.416	.126	.203	.283	.318	-.323	-14.1	90-CF -8
2002	JUP	FSL	22	509	120	25	7	9	57	98	23	8	.236	.323	.365	.008	.206	.271	.323	-.338	-21.3	119-CF -10
2003	FLO	NL	23	167	39	8	1	3	18	39	4	4	.236	.315	.359	-.150	.243	.318	.382	-.134	-.9	

Breakout: 63%   Improve: 82%   Collapse: 12%

For as much as Ambres has been a disappointment, it's worth noting he just turned 23, he had a good AFL campaign, and he'll take a free pass. Could he develop into a prospect, instead of somebody on prospect lists? He's in an organization that will keep giving him opportunities to find out.

Brian Banks 　　1B/OF/C　Born: 28-Sep-70　Age: 32　Bats: B　Throws: R

YEAR	TM	LG	AGE	AB	H	2B	3B	HR	BB	SO	SB	CS	AVG	OBP	SLG	MLVR	EQBA	EQOBP	EQSLG	EQMLVR	VORP		DEFENSE			
2000	DAI	JWL	29	157	42	6	0	7	26	1	3	23	.268	.372	.439	-.016	.230	.314	.385	-.155	-.2					
2000	FKU	JPL	29	74	11	2	0	0	8	23	0	0	.149	.241	.176	-.551	.147	.219	.187	-.655	-10.0					
2001	CLG	PCL	30	357	104	27	4	23	32	97	5	4	.291	.355	.583	.201	.244	.305	.480	-.029	6.3		72-1B	7		
2002	CLG	PCL	31	439	136	38	3	19	73	77	10	5	.310	.415	.540	.286	.261	.359	.452	.043	17.4		67-1B	2	43-LF	1
2002	FLA	NL	31	28	9	1	0	1	1	6	0	0	.321	.345	.464	.168	.345	.345	.483	.146	1.9					
2003	FLO	NL	32	142	35	8	1	5	19	33	2	2	.245	.338	.414	-.034	.252	.341	.441	-.010	1.2					

Breakout: 25%　　Improve: 50%　　Collapse: 28%

Banks's last season in the majors was as a multi-positional threat with the Brewers in 1999. He didn't hit much, but he played first base, the outfield corners, and 40 games behind the plate. Banks isn't young, but his two-year power spike and ability to catch make him an excellent choice for a major league bench. It doesn't hurt that the manager, a former backstop himself, seems to like having three catchers on the roster.

Homer Bush 　　　　　　Born: 12-Nov-72　Age: 30　Bats: R　Throws: R

YEAR	TM	LG	AGE	AB	H	2B	3B	HR	BB	SO	SB	CS	AVG	OBP	SLG	MLVR	EQBA	EQOBP	EQSLG	EQMLVR	VORP		DEFENSE	
2000	TOR	AL	27	297	64	8	0	1	18	60	9	4	.215	.272	.253	-.471	.223	.272	.260	-.415	-14.4		75-2B	8
2001	TOR	AL	28	271	83	11	1	3	8	50	13	4	.306	.340	.387	-.016	.321	.356	.410	.030	16.1		74-2B	16
2002	TOR	AL	29	78	18	2	0	1	2	12	2	0	.231	.268	.295	-.308	.256	.289	.321	-.276	-1.1		20-2B	0
2002	FLA	NL	29	54	12	0	0	0	3	13	2	1	.222	.263	.222	-.378	.236	.276	.236	-.434	-4.1			
2003	SDP	AL	23	120	29	5	1	1	7	19	4	1	.240	.288	.310	-.233	.255	.303	.337	-.212	-1.3			

Breakout: 20%　　Improve: 43%　　Collapse: 26%

Bush's defining characteristic is that he's got a great baseball name, and he looks great in a baseball uniform—especially when you see those things associated with the opposing team. He signed a minor league contract with San Diego, where he's a long shot to make the team as a pinch runner and defensive sub.

Miguel Cabrera 　　　3B　Born: 18-Apr-83　Age: 20　Bats: R　Throws: R

YEAR	TM	LG	AGE	AB	H	2B	3B	HR	BB	SO	SB	CS	AVG	OBP	SLG	MLVR	EQBA	EQOBP	EQSLG	EQMLVR	VORP		DEFENSE	
2001	KNE	MDW	18	422	113	19	4	7	37	76	3	0	.268	.330	.382	.018	.206	.255	.295	-.409	-20.0		87-SS	-8
2002	JUP	FSL	19	489	134	43	1	9	38	85	10	1	.274	.338	.421	.128	.236	.280	.370	-.236	-6.0		87-3B	-4
2003	FLA	NL	20	221	54	12	2	5	18	43	3	3	.242	.304	.381	-.136	.249	.307	.406	-.118	.8			

Breakout: 62%　　Improve: 70%　　Collapse: 17%

Signed initially to a big bonus at a time when the Marlins weren't noted for spending money (1999), Cabrera came from Venezuela as a teenaged shortstop. As he filled out and matured, the Marlins moved him to third base in 2002, and he established himself as a top-shelf prospect there. His legs are tree trunks in the making, and at 19 his 43 doubles led the Florida State League. Cabrera will start the season in Double-A. If you're in a keeper league, pick him up.

Luis Castillo 　　　　2B　Born: 12-Sep-75　Age: 27　Bats: B　Throws: R

YEAR	TM	LG	AGE	AB	H	2B	3B	HR	BB	SO	SB	CS	AVG	OBP	SLG	MLVR	EQBA	EQOBP	EQSLG	EQMLVR	VORP		DEFENSE	
2000	FLA	NL	24	539	180	17	3	2	78	86	62	22	.334	.418	.388	.117	.330	.407	.383	.092	47.8		132-2B	-12
2001	FLA	NL	25	534	140	16	10	2	66	90	33	16	.262	.344	.341	-.109	.270	.349	.349	-.110	16.3		131-2B	0
2002	FLA	NL	26	606	185	18	5	2	55	76	48	15	.305	.365	.361	.043	.318	.372	.379	.011	35.9		140-2B	-9
2003	FLA	NL	27	569	157	23	5	2	58	74	43	8	.276	.345	.345	-.091	.284	.348	.368	-.071	17.2			

Breakout: 3%　　Improve: 31%　　Collapse: 26%

His 35-game hitting streak was the most positive publicity the Marlins got in 2003, mostly because there was nothing to interpret, and the organization's flunkeys didn't have to try to spin it or say anything. Over the last three years, Castillo's value as a player has been directly proportional to his ground ball/fly ball ratio:

Year	G/F	EqMLVr
2000	4.74	.092
2001	2.59	-.110
2002	3.39	.011

Although there's an argument that speed players age well, don't be surprised by a steady downward trend as Castillo gradually loses foot speed. Two-tenths of a second off of his home-to-first time will have him hitting about .230.

Ramon Castro — C — Born: 01-Mar-76 — Age: 27 — Bats: R — Throws: R

YEAR	TM	LG	AGE	AB	H	2B	3B	HR	BB	SO	SB	CS	AVG	OBP	SLG	MLVR	EQBA	EQOBP	EQSLG	EQMLVR	VORP	DEFENSE
2000	CLG	PCL	24	218	73	22	0	14	16	38	0	0	.335	.380	.628	.349	.278	.314	.524	.082	17.3	55-C -1
2000	FLA	NL	24	138	33	4	0	2	16	36	0	0	.239	.323	.312	-.252	.243	.316	.321	-.230	.2	41-C 0
2001	CLG	PCL	25	390	131	33	0	27	38	74	1	1	.336	.396	.628	.382	.282	.342	.517	.123	36.9	83-C -1
2002	FLA	NL	26	101	24	4	0	6	14	24	0	0	.238	.330	.455	.059	.243	.333	.476	.014	6.9	23-C 0
2003	FLA	NL	27	166	41	9	0	6	18	35	1	1	.249	.323	.424	-.044	.256	.326	.451	-.021	6.3	

Breakout: 9%   Improve: 28%   Collapse: 36%

Castro sprained his elbow and hit the DL on May 19, and with Mike Redmond grabbing the top backup job in the meantime and Charles Johnson packing his bags, he may be several million dollars lighter for it. Left alone to start, Castro could easily hit 20 bombs in 2003, and with his relative youth that would net him a multiyear contract somewhere. For now, he's behind Redmond on the depth chart.

Juan Encarnacion — CF — Born: 08-Mar-76 — Age: 27 — Bats: R — Throws: R

YEAR	TM	LG	AGE	AB	H	2B	3B	HR	BB	SO	SB	CS	AVG	OBP	SLG	MLVR	EQBA	EQOBP	EQSLG	EQMLVR	VORP	DEFENSE
2000	DET	AL	24	547	158	25	6	14	29	90	16	4	.289	.333	.433	-.028	.301	.336	.455	.042	29.2	133-CF -2
2001	DET	AL	25	417	101	19	7	12	25	93	9	5	.242	.295	.408	-.105	.263	.314	.446	-.044	3.4	106-RF -3
2002	CIN	NL	26	321	89	11	2	16	26	63	9	4	.277	.333	.474	.097	.275	.328	.475	.032	17.5	82-CF 3
2002	FLA	NL	26	263	69	11	3	8	20	50	12	5	.262	.322	.418	.015	.272	.327	.440	-.022	3.7	62-RF -1
2003	FLA	NL	27	497	132	24	4	15	39	93	15	6	.265	.324	.421	-.034	.272	.327	.449	-.009	8.5	

Breakout: 12%   Improve: 46%   Collapse: 17%

It's easy to call Encarnacion's 2002 a breakout season, but he actually played better in 2000 with the tougher park obscuring some of his value. He's not an asset in right field, but with the Wilson trade Encarnacion will be back in center in 2003, where he should be acceptable.

Andy Fox — UT — Born: 12-Jan-71 — Age: 32 — Bats: L — Throws: R

YEAR	TM	LG	AGE	AB	H	2B	3B	HR	BB	SO	SB	CS	AVG	OBP	SLG	MLVR	EQBA	EQOBP	EQSLG	EQMLVR	VORP	DEFENSE
2000	ARI	NL	29	86	18	4	0	1	4	16	2	1	.209	.244	.291	-.478	.207	.225	.299	-.463	-6.2	16-3B 0
2000	FLA	NL	29	164	40	4	2	3	18	37	8	3	.244	.330	.348	-.183	.247	.323	.349	-.175	2.0	29-SS -5
2001	FLA	NL	30	81	15	0	1	3	15	17	1	0	.185	.327	.321	-.214	.195	.331	.341	-.201	.4	11-SS -2
2002	FLA	NL	31	435	109	14	5	4	49	94	31	7	.251	.340	.333	-.074	.266	.348	.358	-.102	13.5	104-SS -13
2003	FLA	NL	32	286	69	11	3	4	31	56	13	4	.242	.321	.335	-.167	.249	.324	.357	-.152	1.0	

Breakout: 9%   Improve: 34%   Collapse: 37%

Fox was stretched from his normal utility role and ended the season as the Marlins starting shortstop. He fit right in with the Marlin philosophy of team speed, but he's not a good defensive player at short, and that hurt the pitching staff all season. He should be returning to the utility role, but if Lowell gets dealt without bringing a third baseman in return, the Marlins could turn to Fox at the hot corner, even if he won't hit enough to carry the position.

Alex Gonzalez — SS — Born: 15-Feb-77 — Age: 26 — Bats: R — Throws: R

YEAR	TM	LG	AGE	AB	H	2B	3B	HR	BB	SO	SB	CS	AVG	OBP	SLG	MLVR	EQBA	EQOBP	EQSLG	EQMLVR	VORP	DEFENSE
2000	FLA	NL	23	385	77	17	4	7	13	77	7	1	.200	.230	.319	-.455	.208	.227	.331	-.413	-19.6	96-SS -5
2001	FLA	NL	24	518	130	36	1	9	31	107	2	2	.251	.306	.376	-.141	.260	.312	.390	-.130	12.4	141-SS -17
2002	FLA	NL	25	151	34	7	1	2	12	32	3	1	.225	.299	.325	-.173	.240	.306	.351	-.210	.3	40-SS 0
2003	FLA	NL	26	286	66	14	2	4	20	53	5	2	.232	.288	.335	-.232	.238	.290	.357	-.220	-4.1	

Breakout: 15%   Improve: 38%   Collapse: 38%

After suffering a dislocated left shoulder on May 19, Gonzalez missed the rest of the season. Over the years the title's been passed back and forth between the two like a live grenade, but at this point it's pretty safe to say that this guy is The Bad Alex Gonzalez. Re-signed for 2003 with the Marlins; he'll be the starting shortstop. If nothing else, it will give the pitching staff a better fielder than Andy Fox.

Adrian Gonzalez   1B   Born: 08-May-82   Age: 21   Bats: L   Throws: L

YEAR	TM	LG	AGE	AB	H	2B	3B	HR	BB	SO	SB	CS	AVG	OBP	SLG	MLVR	EQBA	EQOBP	EQSLG	EQMLVR	VORP	DEFENSE	
2001	KNE	MDW	19	516	161	37	1	17	57	83	5	5	.312	.386	.486	.275	.234	.293	.367	-.217	-15.8	116-1B	5
2002	PME	EAS	20	508	135	34	1	17	54	112	6	3	.266	.346	.437	.075	.229	.294	.377	-.204	-15.2	135-1B	-2
2003	*FLA*	*NL*	*21*	*202*	*49*	*9*	*1*	*6*	*20*	*45*	*3*	*2*	*.243*	*.316*	*.381*	*-.115*	*.250*	*.319*	*.406*	*-.097*	*-3.0*		

Breakout: 36%   Improve: 59%   Collapse: 16%

Gonzalez's career is a coup for the Marlins organization. He looked like a stretch and a signability pick as the first selection in the 2000 draft, but he quickly asserted himself as a legitimately excellent prospect. Gonzalez didn't tear up Double-A, but he played very well for a 20-year-old and displayed projectable power. Surgery to repair torn cartilage in his wrist might cause him to miss spring training, but he should start sneaking into the big league picture by August.

Kevin Hooper   2B/SS   Born: 07-Dec-76   Age: 26   Bats: R   Throws: R

YEAR	TM	LG	AGE	AB	H	2B	3B	HR	BB	SO	SB	CS	AVG	OBP	SLG	MLVR	EQBA	EQOBP	EQSLG	EQMLVR	VORP	DEFENSE			
2000	KNE	MDW	23	457	114	25	6	3	73	83	17	2	.249	.360	.350	.032	.201	.278	.285	-.378	-21.0	120-2B	2		
2001	KNE	MDW	24	65	19	2	0	0	11	13	3	1	.292	.395	.323	.061	.235	.316	.250	-.332	-2.0	17-2B	0		
2001	PME	EAS	24	468	144	19	6	2	59	78	24	12	.308	.393	.387	.130	.266	.342	.336	-.144	9.3	114-2B	1		
2002	CLG	PCL	25	452	130	21	3	2	34	51	17	10	.288	.343	.361	-.093	.244	.297	.305	-.290	-8.5	72-SS	-1	42-2B	3

Make no mistake about it, Hooper isn't a prospect, but remember who his manager is. Given a choice between a useful Freddy Manrique and the inexplicable Jeff Schaefer during his days managing the White Sox, Torborg willingly cooperated in a management scheme to shave Manrique's service time, retaining Schaefer as his utility infielder. Hooper can run a little, and won't embarrass himself afield. He could very easily stick as the utility infielder, especially if Fox is starting somewhere.

Charles Johnson   C   Born: 20-Jul-71   Age: 31   Bats: R   Throws: R

YEAR	TM	LG	AGE	AB	H	2B	3B	HR	BB	SO	SB	CS	AVG	OBP	SLG	MLVR	EQBA	EQOBP	EQSLG	EQMLVR	VORP	DEFENSE	
2000	BAL	AL	28	286	84	16	0	21	32	69	2	0	.294	.365	.570	.245	.309	.371	.604	.324	41.3	77-C	-1
2000	CWS	AL	28	135	44	8	0	10	20	37	0	0	.326	.417	.607	.395	.331	.415	.624	.445	23.7	34-C	1
2001	FLA	NL	29	451	117	32	0	18	38	133	0	0	.259	.323	.450	-.001	.268	.328	.464	.010	30.8	118-C	5
2002	FLA	NL	30	244	53	19	0	6	31	61	0	0	.217	.305	.369	-.109	.229	.309	.398	-.147	5.7	69-C	6
2003	*COL*	*NL*	*31*	*256*	*71*	*16*	*0*	*13*	*30*	*62*	*1*	*1*	*.276*	*.354*	*.501*	*.129*	*.256*	*.330*	*.455*	*-.008*	*10.6*		

Breakout: 8%   Improve: 39%   Collapse: 24%

Johnson's swing comes slower than laughs at a Chevy Chase movie these days. Even pre-humidor, Coors Field was not a panacea for this type of hitter; Howard Johnson and Dale Murphy were both washed-up veterans with lazy bats, and Colorado didn't help them a bit. He's closer to done than to a career rebirth.

Derrek Lee   1B   Born: 06-Sep-75   Age: 27   Bats: R   Throws: R

YEAR	TM	LG	AGE	AB	H	2B	3B	HR	BB	SO	SB	CS	AVG	OBP	SLG	MLVR	EQBA	EQOBP	EQSLG	EQMLVR	VORP	DEFENSE	
2000	FLA	NL	24	477	134	18	3	28	63	123	0	3	.281	.369	.507	.151	.284	.364	.510	.152	33.9	127-1B	12
2001	FLA	NL	25	561	158	37	4	21	50	126	4	2	.282	.349	.474	.100	.290	.354	.486	.108	32.0	147-1B	11
2002	FLA	NL	26	581	157	35	7	27	98	164	19	9	.270	.380	.494	.215	.281	.385	.518	.196	47.5	160-1B	-1
2003	*FLA*	*NL*	*27*	*544*	*147*	*30*	*4*	*25*	*79*	*136*	*13*	*7*	*.270*	*.365*	*.477*	*.109*	*.278*	*.369*	*.507*	*.142*	*27.6*		

Breakout: 8%   Improve: 46%   Collapse: 13%

The Marlins are entering a delicate stretch in their relationship with Lee. He's one of their better players, but the team has first basemen coming out their ears in the minors. The kids aren't ready yet, but unless Lee's willing to re-sign to a short-term deal, the Fish need to sell high on Lee and sign one of the several available temps—David Ortiz would work—to handle first base in 2003.

Mike Lowell   3B   Born: 24-Feb-74   Age: 29   Bats: R   Throws: R

YEAR	TM	LG	AGE	AB	H	2B	3B	HR	BB	SO	SB	CS	AVG	OBP	SLG	MLVR	EQBA	EQOBP	EQSLG	EQMLVR	VORP	DEFENSE	
2000	FLA	NL	26	508	137	38	0	22	54	75	4	0	.270	.350	.474	.058	.274	.344	.481	.068	36.4	131-3B	1
2001	FLA	NL	27	551	156	37	0	18	43	79	1	2	.283	.346	.448	.059	.292	.351	.460	.067	39.0	141-3B	6
2002	FLA	NL	28	597	165	44	0	24	65	92	4	3	.276	.351	.471	.145	.285	.355	.493	.114	47.9	154-3B	2
2003	*FLA*	*NL*	*29*	*558*	*155*	*35*	*1*	*23*	*57*	*85*	*3*	*2*	*.278*	*.347*	*.469*	*.077*	*.285*	*.350*	*.499*	*.109*	*35.3*		

Breakout: 17%   Improve: 56%   Collapse: 5%

Mike Lowell *(continued)*

He batted .330/.388/.542 over the first two months of the season and spent the rest of the year reverting to the mean. Lowell's a Miami native and a solid plus at the hot corner, but the Marlins are looking at trading him for a younger, cheaper model this off-season. With the Red Sox looking to deal Shea Hillenbrand, that's a potential recipe for disaster.

Pat Magness				1B			Born: 19-Jan-78				Age: 25			Bats: L			Throws: R	
YEAR	TM	LG	AGE	AB	H	2B	3B	HR	BB	SO	SB	CS	AVG	OBP	SLG	MLVR	EQBA	EQOBP	EQSLG	EQMLVR	VORP	DEFENSE
2000	UTI	NYP	22	175	54	18	0	5	30	34	2	0	.309	.415	.497	.353	.224	.300	.366	-.211	-5.5	35-1B -3
2001	KNE	MDW	23	227	58	14	0	6	53	41	2	1	.256	.403	.396	.142	.196	.311	.304	-.288	-12.3	13-1B 0
2001	BRV	FSL	23	117	32	7	0	1	16	28	0	0	.274	.366	.359	.079	.238	.303	.320	-.260	-4.1	
2002	JUP	FSL	24	390	114	26	1	16	79	86	2	1	.292	.418	.487	.335	.243	.344	.412	-.052	4.9	93-1B -18
2003	FLA	NL	25	195	48	10	1	6	27	44	2	1	.246	.340	.397	-.052	.252	.343	.422	-.030	.7	

Breakout: 48%   Improve: 74%   Collapse: 10%

Magness was way too old for the FSL. His strikeout-to-walk ratios are the work of a man in complete control of the plate, and if he's ever going to contribute, it wouldn't be a bad idea to skip him up a level and see how he acclimates. There's no room at first in the Marlins chain for this, though.

Jesus Medrano				2B			Born: 11-Sep-78				Age: 24			Bats: R			Throws: R	
YEAR	TM	LG	AGE	AB	H	2B	3B	HR	BB	SO	SB	CS	AVG	OBP	SLG	MLVR	EQBA	EQOBP	EQSLG	EQMLVR	VORP	DEFENSE	
2000	BRV	FSL	21	466	102	18	3	3	48	98	32	8	.219	.299	.290	-.176	.189	.249	.256	-.483	-32.5	112-2B -21	
2001	BRV	FSL	22	454	114	15	2	1	51	81	61	8	.251	.333	.300	-.061	.226	.284	.270	-.374	-19.5	98-2B -12	18-SS 1
2002	PME	EAS	23	414	123	27	6	3	79	82	39	18	.297	.413	.413	.173	.250	.351	.351	-.116	12.2	114-2B -10	
2003	FLA	NL	24	179	43	9	2	2	20	37	9	4	.242	.322	.341	-.158	.249	.325	.363	-.142	.8		

Breakout: 44%   Improve: 69%   Collapse: 16%

Medrano took his place behind Castillo and Quilvio Veras as the next speedy, patient, slap-hitting second-base prospect in the Marlins chain in 2002. He had the year of his life despite moving up to Double-A, and without giving any indication he'd been able to handle Single-A ball, so this year is critical for him. If he retains the gains he's made, he'll have a chance to make Castillo tradable.

Kevin Millar				LF			Born: 24-Sep-71				Age: 31			Bats: R			Throws: R	
YEAR	TM	LG	AGE	AB	H	2B	3B	HR	BB	SO	SB	CS	AVG	OBP	SLG	MLVR	EQBA	EQOBP	EQSLG	EQMLVR	VORP	DEFENSE	
2000	FLA	NL	28	259	67	14	3	14	36	47	0	0	.259	.366	.498	.110	.263	.361	.504	.119	16.0	28-1B 1	13-LF 0
2001	FLA	NL	29	449	141	39	5	20	39	70	0	0	.314	.375	.557	.294	.322	.381	.569	.305	48.0	75-RF -2	13-1B -1
2002	FLA	NL	30	438	134	41	0	16	40	74	0	2	.306	.371	.509	.254	.315	.374	.531	.231	36.5	95-LF -1	
2003	FLA	NL	31	387	109	26	2	16	38	67	1	2	.282	.350	.481	.103	.290	.354	.512	.136	16.7		

Breakout: 7%   Improve: 36%   Collapse: 30%

Millar will play anywhere and get his uniform nice and dirty, but confusing willingness and competence would be a mistake. With the front office talk of a Go-Go Marlins offense in 2003, Millar is as out of place as Pat Boone making a guest appearance on Soul Train. He'd make a pretty good short-term option at DH. The Marlins placed him on waivers; if he clears, he's got a contract waiting for him with the Chunichi Dragons of the Japanese Central League.

Angel Molina				C			Born: 04-Nov-81				Age: 21			Bats: R			Throws: R	
YEAR	TM	LG	AGE	AB	H	2B	3B	HR	BB	SO	SB	CS	AVG	OBP	SLG	MLVR	EQBA	EQOBP	EQSLG	EQMLVR	VORP	DEFENSE
2002	KNE	MDW	20	122	31	3	1	6	11	41	0	0	.254	.326	.443	.120	.206	.259	.357	-.315	-2.6	20-C -4
2003	FLA	NL	21	164	34	5	2	5	15	63	1	3	.205	.280	.349	-.242	.211	.283	.371	-.232	-3.1	

Breakout: 49%   Improve: 67%   Collapse: 24%

Not that it would take much, but he stands a very good chance of being the best-hitting catcher named Molina in professional baseball in 2003. Molina showed fair patience and defense in 2002, and he's got good size, so some power may be in his future.

Abraham Nunez   CF   Born: 05-Feb-77   Age: 26   Bats: B   Throws: R

YEAR	TM	LG	AGE	AB	H	2B	3B	HR	BB	SO	SB	CS	AVG	OBP	SLG	MLVR	EQBA	EQOBP	EQSLG	EQMLVR	VORP	DEFENSE	
2000	BRV	FSL	23	103	20	4	0	1	28	34	11	3	.194	.376	.262	-.089	.174	.313	.239	-.377	-7.5		
2000	PME	EAS	23	221	61	17	3	6	44	64	8	6	.276	.396	.462	.187	.230	.331	.389	-.117	1.1		
2001	PME	EAS	24	467	112	14	9	17	83	155	26	19	.240	.358	.418	.066	.202	.309	.349	-.230	-7.0	134-CF	2
2002	CLG	PCL	25	428	107	24	5	21	51	112	31	6	.250	.331	.477	.014	.212	.288	.402	-.193	-1.7	125-CF	-2
2003	*FLA*	*NL*	*26*	*163*	*37*	*8*	*1*	*5*	*20*	*46*	*5*	*6*	*.228*	*.313*	*.382*	*-.129*	*.235*	*.317*	*.406*	*-.111*	*-.3*		

Breakout: 53%   Improve: 69%   Collapse: 13%

With Juan Pierre in the fold long-term, Nunez is going to have a hard time sneaking onto the major league team. He doesn't make much contact even in Triple-A, and the extra two years tacked onto his age this year really hurt his reasonably expected development.

Eric Owens   LF   Born: 03-Feb-71   Age: 32   Bats: R   Throws: R

YEAR	TM	LG	AGE	AB	H	2B	3B	HR	BB	SO	SB	CS	AVG	OBP	SLG	MLVR	EQBA	EQOBP	EQSLG	EQMLVR	VORP	DEFENSE	
2000	SDP	NL	29	583	171	19	7	6	45	63	29	14	.293	.348	.381	-.047	.302	.346	.393	-.029	9.2	142-OF	7
2001	FLA	NL	30	400	101	16	1	5	29	59	8	6	.253	.303	.335	-.204	.261	.310	.347	-.194	-13.0	88-RF	-3
2002	FLA	NL	31	385	104	15	5	4	31	33	26	9	.270	.325	.366	-.045	.282	.332	.387	-.080	.8	110-LF	-4
2003	*ANA*	*AL*	*32*	*301*	*79*	*14*	*2*	*4*	*21*	*33*	*11*	*4*	*.261*	*.311*	*.355*	*-.122*	*.266*	*.318*	*.366*	*-.141*	*-6.8*		

Breakout: 17%   Improve: 40%   Collapse: 29%

Owens doesn't hit enough to be a good fourth outfielder, he can't field well enough to be a good fifth outfielder, and he'll probably be expensive at either of those positions. After starting out playing second and third base, he hasn't played out of the outfield for two years, so his utility to a major league team is tenuous at best. Signed on with the Angels, where he'll replace Orlando Palmeiro as the guy who pinch-hits for the catchers.

Pablo Ozuna   2B   Born: 25-Aug-74   Age: 28   Bats: R   Throws: R

YEAR	TM	LG	AGE	AB	H	2B	3B	HR	BB	SO	SB	CS	AVG	OBP	SLG	MLVR	EQBA	EQOBP	EQSLG	EQMLVR	VORP	DEFENSE			
2000	PME	EAS	25	464	143	25	6	7	40	55	35	24	.308	.372	.433	.140	.257	.307	.368	-.173	5.1	113-2B	-11		
2002	CLG	PCL	27	261	85	16	1	7	17	37	16	3	.326	.374	.475	.148	.280	.324	.412	-.061	10.5	39-2B	-9	21-RF	-3
2002	FLA	NL	27	47	13	2	2	0	1	3	1	1	.277	.306	.404	-.019	.292	.318	.417	-.054	.9				
2003	*COL*	*NL*	*28*	*171*	*48*	*10*	*1*	*4*	*12*	*23*	*5*	*2*	*.280*	*.331*	*.415*	*-.019*	*.259*	*.309*	*.377*	*-.147*	*.7*				

Breakout: 6%   Improve: 24%   Collapse: 41%

The prospect sheen on Ozuna was already fading, but the extra four years tacked on as he entered the country for spring training finished it off. However, all is not lost; with the trade to Colorado, Ozuna is a strong spring training away from swiping a middle infield spot from an equally fringe guy like Brent Butler, and running with it.

Mike Redmond   C   Born: 05-May-71   Age: 32   Bats: R   Throws: R

YEAR	TM	LG	AGE	AB	H	2B	3B	HR	BB	SO	SB	CS	AVG	OBP	SLG	MLVR	EQBA	EQOBP	EQSLG	EQMLVR	VORP	DEFENSE	
2000	FLA	NL	29	210	53	8	1	0	13	19	0	0	.252	.320	.300	-.265	.263	.317	.310	-.232	.2	67-C	4
2001	FLA	NL	30	141	44	4	0	4	13	13	0	0	.312	.378	.426	.111	.319	.382	.438	.115	13.9	42-C	2
2002	FLA	NL	31	256	78	15	0	2	21	34	0	2	.305	.375	.387	.094	.317	.378	.408	.063	19.7	69-C	9
2003	*FLA*	*NL*	*32*	*221*	*58*	*10*	*1*	*2*	*17*	*25*	*0*	*1*	*.262*	*.321*	*.346*	*-.141*	*.269*	*.324*	*.368*	*-.124*	*2.5*		

Breakout: 4%   Improve: 19%   Collapse: 42%

Redmond and Ramon Castro both made the club out of spring training, but Castro hit the DL with an elbow sprain on May 16. In the interim, the club fell in love with Redmond, and he now stands to grab the lion's share of the playing time with Charles Johnson's departure. If Redmond had timing this good at the plate, he wouldn't need luck to get a major league job. Forced into full-time play, expect his numbers to drop.

Will Smith   LF   Born: 23-Oct-81   Age: 21   Bats: L   Throws: R

YEAR	TM	LG	AGE	AB	H	2B	3B	HR	BB	SO	SB	CS	AVG	OBP	SLG	MLVR	EQBA	EQOBP	EQSLG	EQMLVR	VORP	DEFENSE
2001	KNE	MDW	19	535	150	26	2	16	32	74	4	5	.280	.327	.426	.083	.214	.249	.327	-.372	-36.7	108-LF -10
2002	JUP	FSL	20	549	164	30	12	14	31	75	8	3	.299	.340	.474	.222	.253	.282	.405	-.170	-11.3	121-LF -16
2003	FLA	NL	21	223	54	10	2	5	15	38	3	2	.241	.293	.371	-.170	.247	.296	.395	-.154	-7.1	

Breakout: 32%   Improve: 62%   Collapse: 17%

The Arizona native continued hitting for good power at Jupiter and will make the jump to Double-A in 2003. Picking up about a walk per 10 AB is all that's holding him back from top prospect status. Going by "Bill" would stem the wave of lame headlines that await his arrival in the majors.

Jason Stokes   1B   Born: 23-Jan-82   Age: 21   Bats: R   Throws: R

YEAR	TM	LG	AGE	AB	H	2B	3B	HR	BB	SO	SB	CS	AVG	OBP	SLG	MLVR	EQBA	EQOBP	EQSLG	EQMLVR	VORP	DEFENSE
2001	UTI	NYP	19	130	30	2	1	6	11	48	0	0	.231	.301	.400	.019	.172	.217	.306	-.488	-12.6	
2002	KNE	MDW	20	349	119	25	0	27	47	96	1	1	.341	.426	.645	.585	.258	.325	.485	.026	11.8	86-1B 3
2003	FLA	NL	21	203	47	8	2	8	20	64	2	3	.230	.301	.402	-.122	.237	.304	.428	-.104	-3.6	

Breakout: 21%   Improve: 50%   Collapse: 22%

After a slow start to his career (drafted in 2000, he signed too late to play), Stokes won the Midwest League MVP handily in his first full-season play, despite missing the end of the season with surgery to remove a cyst in his wrist. His monster season puts him on first-base prospect lists, but without another year under his belt he's still on the B-list behind Adrian Gonzalez in the eyes of the organization. Or we thought it did, until the Marlins reportedly put Gonzalez into an attempted three-way trade for Bartolo Colon. Both players should have fine careers wherever each ends up.

Josh Willingham   C/1B   Born: 17-Feb-79   Age: 24   Bats: R   Throws: R

YEAR	TM	LG	AGE	AB	H	2B	3B	HR	BB	SO	SB	CS	AVG	OBP	SLG	MLVR	EQBA	EQOBP	EQSLG	EQMLVR	VORP	DEFENSE	
2000	UTI	NYP	21	205	54	16	0	6	39	55	9	5	.263	.403	.429	.219	.194	.289	.324	-.307	-12.6	24-LF 0	10-2B -2
2001	KNE	MDW	22	320	83	20	2	7	53	85	24	2	.259	.386	.400	.123	.207	.300	.321	-.282	-8.0	80-3B 9	
2002	JUP	FSL	23	376	103	21	4	17	63	88	18	5	.274	.396	.487	.290	.234	.326	.416	-.087	.9	30-1B -1	20-3B -2
2003	FLO	NL	24	192	46	9	1	6	23	51	5	5	.239	.328	.394	-.081	.245	.331	.419	-.060	.3		

Breakout: 44%   Improve: 71%   Collapse: 17%

Willingham has played several positions since being drafted in 2000, but he made his biggest change during the team's instructional league. He'll be shifting to catcher, a position he played in high school, in an attempt to jump-start his career at a position where he isn't blocked. He does a lot of good things offensively, and if he can handle the position he'll be on the fast track.

Preston Wilson   CF   Born: 19-Jul-74   Age: 28   Bats: R   Throws: R

YEAR	TM	LG	AGE	AB	H	2B	3B	HR	BB	SO	SB	CS	AVG	OBP	SLG	MLVR	EQBA	EQOBP	EQSLG	EQMLVR	VORP	DEFENSE
2000	FLA	NL	25	605	160	35	3	31	55	187	36	14	.264	.334	.486	.040	.265	.324	.485	.030	34.9	150-CF 3
2001	FLA	NL	26	468	128	30	2	23	36	107	20	8	.274	.333	.494	.092	.282	.338	.504	.098	35.8	118-CF 1
2002	FLA	NL	27	510	124	22	2	23	58	140	20	11	.243	.331	.429	.031	.254	.335	.452	-.006	23.5	121-CF -5
2003	COL	NL	28	474	139	29	3	28	52	114	20	8	.294	.368	.543	.223	.272	.343	.494	.078	25.3	

Breakout: 11%   Improve: 55%   Collapse: 8%

Wilson's super-sized contract—$27.5 million over the next three years—made him a Rockie, but he's a valuable player who has a great chance to put up superstar numbers in Colorado. Wrist, hammy, knee, and toe injuries did a number on his season with the Marlins; he got plenty of playing time, but generally wasn't at full speed. He'll be healthy for spring training and man center for the Rox in 2003. As we've noted in the past, Coors doesn't just inflate power stats, it deflates strikeouts, which will mean more at-bats for Wilson with balls in play, rattling around in the gaps, and probably pushing him into an All-Star game or two.

Josh Wilson SS Born: 26-Mar-81 Age: 22 Bats: R Throws: R

YEAR	TM	LG	AGE	AB	H	2B	3B	HR	BB	SO	SB	CS	AVG	OBP	SLG	MLVR	EQBA	EQOBP	EQSLG	EQMLVR	VORP	DEFENSE		
2000	UTI	NYP	19	259	89	13	6	3	29	47	9	8	.344	.420	.475	.361	.247	.297	.356	-.216	.2	61-SS -11		
2001	KNE	MDW	20	506	144	28	5	4	28	60	17	11	.285	.327	.383	.029	.219	.252	.297	-.405	-23.2	63-2B -3	49-SS -5	
2002	JUP	FSL	21	398	102	17	1	11	28	67	7	10	.256	.321	.387	.046	.220	.264	.337	-.324	-10.7	103-SS 1		
2002	PME	EAS	21	41	14	3	0	2	2	6	0	1	.341	.372	.561	.356	.293	.326	.463	.029	2.7	12-SS 0		
2003	FLA	NL	22	182	42	8	1	3	14	33	3	2	.232	.292	.344	-.212	.239	.295	.367	-.199	-1.9			

Breakout: 46%   Improve: 66%   Collapse: 20%

Wilson can handle playing shortstop, and that makes him important to the Marlins' future. He's the middle infield prospect that should allow the club to ditch Alex Gonzalez soon. Hell, look at the projection—they wouldn't miss Gonzalez if they cut him tomorrow. Wilson will not be a star, but he's young enough to improve significantly.

PITCHERS

Armando Almanza Born: 26-Oct-72 Age: 30 Bats: L Throws: L

YEAR	TM	LG	AGE	G	GS	IP	H	BB	SO	HR	ERA	EQERA	EQH9	EQBB9	EQSO9	EQHR9	PERA	VORP	STF
2000	FLA	NL	27	67	0	46.3	38	43	46	3	4.86	4.75	7.3	6.6	7.7	0.5	4.67	3.2	-4
2001	FLA	NL	28	52	0	41.0	34	26	45	8	4.83	5.14	7.5	5.2	8.3	1.6	5.10	1.1	-3
2002	FLA	NL	29	51	0	45.7	36	23	57	8	4.33	4.37	7.2	4.0	9.7	1.6	4.41	5.1	11
2003	FLA	NL	30	46	0	41.3	37	24	46	6	4.68	5.20	8.4	4.6	8.9	1.3	5.04	3.0	4

Breakout: 20%   Improve: 47%   Collapse: 38%

In the last three years, Almanza has turned opposing lefty batters into late-model Rickey Henderson—they're hopeless with the bat, but they're always on base because of his really poor control. Almanza's tough fastball has a ton of movement, but until he masters getting it over the plate, he's not going to have a lot of job security.

Denny Bautista Born: 23-Oct-82 Age: 20 Bats: R Throws: R

YEAR	TM	LG	AGE	G	GS	IP	H	BB	SO	HR	ERA	EQERA	EQH9	EQBB9	EQSO9	EQHR9	PERA	VORP	STF
2001	UTI	NYP	18	7	7	39.0	25	6	31	0	2.08	3.87	7.6	2.0	4.0	0.3	2.89	7.1	10
2001	KNE	MDW	18	8	7	39.3	43	14	20	2	4.35	7.20	14.5	4.9	3.0	1.1	6.99	-7.4	-16
2002	JUP	FSL	19	19	15	88.3	80	40	79	6	4.99	6.70	11.9	5.4	6.0	1.6	6.14	-11.8	0

Bautista did his best Pedro Martinez impression in his Jupiter debut, pitching five no-hit innings. That was the highlight of his season, as he was hit hard the rest of the way and landed on the DL with a sore shoulder in late June. He should be healthy and pitching in high-A ball in 2003.

Allen Baxter Born: 06-Jul-83 Age: 20 Bats: R Throws: R

YEAR	TM	LG	AGE	G	GS	IP	H	BB	SO	HR	ERA	EQERA	EQH9	EQBB9	EQSO9	EQHR9	PERA	VORP	STF
2002	KNE	MDW	19	4	4	17.7	19	8	15	0	3.05	6.54	13.4	5.9	5.0	0.3	6.87	-2.0	-3

Baxter was a third round pick in 2001 armed with a good fastball and curveball. Only four games into his 2002 campaign, Baxter was shut down for the season with an elbow ligament strain. He should be back at full strength with Kane County in 2003.

Josh Beckett Born: 15-May-80 Age: 23 Bats: R Throws: R

YEAR	TM	LG	AGE	G	GS	IP	H	BB	SO	HR	ERA	EQERA	EQH9	EQBB9	EQSO9	EQHR9	PERA	VORP	STF
2000	KNE	MDW	20	13	12	59.3	45	15	61	4	2.12	4.10	10.2	2.8	5.9	1.6	4.19	9.2	11
2001	BRV	FSL	21	13	12	65.7	32	15	101	0	1.23	2.42	5.5	2.4	9.0	0.2	2.12	22.5	44
2001	PME	EAS	21	13	13	74.3	50	19	102	8	1.82	3.26	8.1	3.1	8.6	1.5	3.33	18.5	35
2001	FLA	NL	21	4	4	24.0	14	11	24	3	1.50	3.13	5.3	3.8	7.6	1.0	2.89	6.3	30
2002	FLA	NL	22	23	21	107.7	93	44	113	13	4.09	4.35	8.0	3.3	8.3	1.1	4.12	13.8	27
2003	FLA	NL	23	23	18	117.7	103	47	111	12	3.80	4.22	8.1	3.1	7.5	1.0	3.99	18.0	17

Breakout: 10%   Improve: 44%   Collapse: 19%

Josh Beckett *(continued)*

Beckett's got scorching heat, but he needs to be able to throw it without the blister problems he experienced in 2002. Two separate trips to the DL and missed turns in the rotation due to blistering on his middle finger put a damper on his season. Beckett doesn't have a history of blisters, and the injuries kept Torborg from pitching Beckett as hard as he did Burnett, so this could be a blessing in disguise. Look for a full-strength season in 2003, and some enjoyable Beckett-Prior duels down the road.

Brandon Bowe   **Born: 13-Mar-76**   **Age: 27**   **Bats: R**   **Throws: R**

YEAR	TM	LG	AGE	G	GS	IP	H	BB	SO	HR	ERA	EQERA	EQH9	EQBB9	EQSO9	EQHR9	PERA	VORP	STF
2000	KNE	MDW	24	61	0	79.7	73	32	89	4	3.73	5.79	12.0	4.5	6.5	1.2	5.79	-3.6	-8
2001	BRV	FSL	25	42	0	58.0	52	11	45	1	1.55	4.58	10.6	2.1	4.7	0.4	4.50	5.2	-6
2001	PME	EAS	25	9	0	17.3	13	5	10	1	1.56	3.62	9.4	3.7	3.8	0.8	3.53	3.4	-14
2002	PME	EAS	26	45	3	75.0	89	23	53	6	3.72	5.62	13.1	3.4	4.9	1.2	6.13	-1.8	-16

Following a strong 2001 season where Bowe was promoted twice and succeeded at both levels, he had a setback year in 2002. Bowe is a closer without a great fastball, and he lives and dies with his control; it was great in 2001, but only good last year. His chances for a major league career are so-so at best without adding another pitch.

Donnie Bridges   **Born: 10-Dec-78**   **Age: 24**   **Bats: R**   **Throws: R**

YEAR	TM	LG	AGE	G	GS	IP	H	BB	SO	HR	ERA	EQERA	EQH9	EQBB9	EQSO9	EQHR9	PERA	VORP	STF
2000	JUP	FSL	21	11	11	73.3	58	20	66	0	3.19	3.88	8.3	3.0	5.6	0.3	3.76	13.2	19
2000	HAR	EAS	21	19	19	128.0	104	49	84	5	2.39	3.88	9.3	3.9	4.6	0.7	3.85	23.1	8
2001	OTT	INT	22	13	13	55.3	60	43	49	11	7.49	8.53	11.6	8.5	6.4	2.5	8.09	-18.6	-14
2002	HAR	EAS	23	14	13	63.0	63	42	49	7	6.14	7.51	11.8	7.5	5.6	1.8	6.56	-14.1	-13
2002	PME	EAS	23	6	3	15.7	29	18	6	1	13.18	15.11	21.1	13.3	2.8	1.0	13.49	-16.8	-67

He's gone from top pitching prospect to waiver bait in just two years. Bridges's excellent 2000 season came at the cost of his health, and he's fallen so far that he was designated for assignment by the Expos in June. The Marlins claimed him out of sentiment and familiarity. They're hoping he's over some of the emotional problems that dogged him while in the Montreal system and that he'll have at least some mild success in 2003.

Nate Bump   **Born: 24-Jul-76**   **Age: 26**   **Bats: R**   **Throws: R**

YEAR	TM	LG	AGE	G	GS	IP	H	BB	SO	HR	ERA	EQERA	EQH9	EQBB9	EQSO9	EQHR9	PERA	VORP	STF
2000	PME	EAS	23	26	26	149.7	169	49	98	16	4.57	6.08	12.5	3.4	4.5	1.8	6.25	-9.6	-3
2001	PME	EAS	24	11	8	54.7	55	10	41	10	5.27	7.78	12.7	2.3	4.9	2.7	5.81	-13.9	-8
2002	PME	EAS	25	20	20	127.7	110	29	81	5	3.38	4.04	9.2	2.5	4.4	0.6	3.54	20.8	6

Bump is no longer a prospect, but he finally mastered Double-A in 2002. He flashed his usual impressive control without being overpowering in both Portland and the AFL. He'll be in Triple-A in 2003, and needs to hope that it doesn't take him four years to acclimate to the competition there.

A. J. Burnett   **Born: 03-Jan-77**   **Age: 26**   **Bats: R**   **Throws: R**

YEAR	TM	LG	AGE	G	GS	IP	H	BB	SO	HR	ERA	EQERA	EQH9	EQBB9	EQSO9	EQHR9	PERA	VORP	STF
2000	FLA	NL	23	13	13	82.7	80	44	57	8	4.79	4.54	8.9	3.9	5.5	0.8	4.49	8.9	10
2001	FLA	NL	24	27	27	173.3	145	83	128	20	4.05	4.15	7.8	4.0	5.7	1.0	4.10	26.1	9
2002	FLA	NL	25	31	29	204.3	153	90	203	12	3.30	3.46	6.9	3.5	7.8	0.5	3.26	46.4	26
2003	*FLA*	*NL*	*26*	*26*	*25*	*167.7*	*146*	*74*	*149*	*16*	*3.82*	*4.25*	*8.0*	*3.4*	*7.0*	*0.9*	*4.10*	*24.2*	*16*

Breakout: 14%   *Improve: 45%*   *Collapse: 19%*

Burnett's impressive but flawed performance in 2001 was followed up by a very good season last year, and he's assumed the mantle of Marlins ace. How long he'll merit that title is a disturbing question; as a 25-year-old, Burnett pitched a league-leading nine games of more than 120 pitches, and he hit the DL in September with a "bone bruise." Hopefully, Jeff Torborg will realize that Burnett's health is more important to the franchise than a complete-game shutout with the team 10 games back in August, and go easier on him in 2003.

Vic Darensbourg   Born: 13-Nov-70   Age: 32   Bats: L   Throws: L

YEAR	TM	LG	AGE	G	GS	IP	H	BB	SO	HR	ERA	EQERA	EQH9	EQBB9	EQSO9	EQHR9	PERA	VORP	STF
2000	FLA	NL	29	56	0	62.0	61	28	59	7	4.06	4.35	9.0	3.3	7.6	0.9	4.43	7.1	4
2001	FLA	NL	30	58	0	48.7	52	10	33	4	4.25	4.28	10.3	1.8	5.3	0.7	4.21	6.0	-3
2002	FLA	NL	31	42	0	48.3	61	26	33	10	6.15	6.72	11.8	4.3	5.4	1.9	7.31	-7.2	-23
2003	COL	NL	32	37	0	39.0	49	18	26	7	5.74	4.97	10.8	3.4	5.6	1.3	5.15	3.4	-11

Breakout: 17%   Improve: 45%   Collapse: 26%

The longest-tenured Marlin pitcher was unceremoniously dumped on the Rockies as a throw-in on the Charles Johnson trade. Darensbourg has lost a lot of effectiveness since his debut year in 1998, and he's not cheap. With the inexperienced left-handers in the Colorado pen, Darensbourg should become the primary lefty setup man for them in 2003.

Michael Flannery   Born: 20-Sep-79   Age: 23   Bats: R   Throws: R

YEAR	TM	LG	AGE	G	GS	IP	H	BB	SO	HR	ERA	EQERA	EQH9	EQBB9	EQSO9	EQHR9	PERA	VORP	STF
2000	UTI	NYP	20	13	13	70.0	71	20	44	8	4.89	8.58	18.2	4.0	3.7	5.3	7.62	-23.9	-26
2001	KNE	MDW	21	53	0	56.3	58	31	47	5	4.80	8.07	14.3	7.6	5.0	2.0	7.80	-16.8	-28
2002	JUP	FSL	22	58	0	61.0	58	10	44	4	2.21	4.70	12.3	1.9	4.8	1.5	5.20	4.6	-9

Flannery had a very successful season keeping batters off their game in 2002. Unfortunately, there's a high recidivism rate for performance spikes like this, especially with the improved but still so-so peripherals. Flannery will be doing his best to buck this trend with Portland in 2003.

Rob Henkel   Born: 03-Aug-78   Age: 24   Bats: R   Throws: L

YEAR	TM	LG	AGE	G	GS	IP	H	BB	SO	HR	ERA	EQERA	EQH9	EQBB9	EQSO9	EQHR9	PERA	VORP	STF
2002	JUP	FSL	23	14	12	75.3	55	22	82	4	2.51	3.97	9.2	3.4	7.0	1.2	4.09	12.8	18
2002	PME	EAS	23	13	13	70.0	54	27	68	6	3.86	4.25	8.5	4.2	6.7	1.3	3.90	9.8	14

A 2000 third round pick, Henkel pitched well in his first full pro season. He's got good size and an impressive assortment of pitches, but his medical history gives a lot of cause for concern. He lost a year to Tommy John surgery at UCLA, and his delivery is as smooth as Urkel. If he stays healthy, he'll advance quickly. Part of the package sent to the Tigers for Mark Redman.

Gary Knotts   Born: 12-Feb-77   Age: 26   Bats: R   Throws: R

YEAR	TM	LG	AGE	G	GS	IP	H	BB	SO	HR	ERA	EQERA	EQH9	EQBB9	EQSO9	EQHR9	PERA	VORP	STF
2000	PME	EAS	23	27	27	156.3	161	63	113	15	4.66	6.26	11.3	4.1	5.0	1.6	5.78	-13.1	-1
2001	CLG	PCL	24	21	21	118.7	136	43	104	16	5.46	5.09	10.0	3.8	5.6	1.3	5.41	5.5	4
2002	CLG	PCL	25	42	0	53.0	53	32	44	4	4.25	4.96	9.7	6.3	5.8	0.8	4.90	2.5	-14
2002	FLA	NL	25	28	0	30.7	21	16	21	6	4.40	4.23	6.3	4.2	5.4	1.8	4.13	3.9	-13
2003	DET	AL	26	35	0	46.3	50	24	33	6	5.32	5.49	9.4	4.3	6.2	1.2	5.31	1.5	-10

Breakout: 16%   Improve: 49%   Collapse: 20%

Knotts shuttled between Calgary and Florida in 2003, flashing a good fastball and wrestling with his control. His walk numbers weren't in Mitch Williams territory, but they weren't far off, and he doesn't have the goofy ancillaries Wild Thing brought to the table. He'll improve his control but give a few hits back in 2003. With Looper, Nunez, and Spooneybarger on hand, he'll be hard-pressed to stick as a long reliever in the back of the pen. Dealt to the Tigers, where he'll get a longer look.

Graeme Lloyd   Born: 09-Apr-67   Age: 36   Bats: L   Throws: L

YEAR	TM	LG	AGE	G	GS	IP	H	BB	SO	HR	ERA	EQERA	EQH9	EQBB9	EQSO9	EQHR9	PERA	VORP	STF
2001	MON	NL	34	84	0	70.3	74	21	44	6	4.35	4.20	9.6	2.5	4.8	0.7	4.17	9.2	-8
2002	MON	NL	35	41	0	30.7	41	8	17	5	5.86	6.12	12.6	2.1	4.5	1.5	6.29	-2.5	-19
2002	FLA	NL	35	25	0	26.3	26	11	20	1	4.45	4.27	9.2	3.3	6.0	0.4	4.20	3.2	-1
2003	FLA	NL	36	63	0	54.0	57	18	38	5	4.20	4.66	9.8	2.6	5.6	0.9	4.54	6.0	-6

Breakout: 22%   Improve: 48%   Collapse: 23%

Having been gulled once into coming to play for the man in Canada, Lloyd doesn't like playing for Jeff Loria much, and he was none too pleased when he was traded to the Marlins in the Cliff Floyd deal. He should save some indignation for his agents, who failed to submit a list of teams he couldn't be traded to within the deadline, negating his limited no-trade clause. He'll surface somewhere, hopefully with a team that Loria can't possibly wangle a partial share of.

Braden Looper   Born: 28-Oct-74   Age: 28   Bats: R   Throws: R

YEAR	TM	LG	AGE	G	GS	IP	H	BB	SO	HR	ERA	EQERA	EQH9	EQBB9	EQSO9	EQHR9	PERA	VORP	STF
2000	FLA	NL	25	73	0	67.3	71	36	29	3	4.41	4.78	9.9	3.9	3.5	0.4	4.58	4.5	-19
2001	FLA	NL	26	71	0	71.0	63	30	52	8	3.55	3.84	8.4	3.6	5.7	0.9	4.16	12.1	-7
2002	FLA	NL	27	78	0	86.0	73	28	55	8	3.14	3.43	8.0	2.6	5.1	0.9	3.64	18.6	-5
2003	FLA	NL	28	50	0	61.3	61	25	41	6	3.95	4.39	9.2	3.2	5.3	0.9	4.54	7.9	-9

Breakout: 17%   Improve: 50%   Collapse: 22%

The closer job was wide open after Antonio Alfonseca's departure, but two blown saves by April 7 didn't do Looper's case any favors. Once he hit his stride, he grabbed the job with a 2.05 ERA in the last four months of the season. Looper doesn't have a prototypical closer's strikeout rates, but he's the closest thing the Marlins have and it'll be an upset if he doesn't have the job in 2003.

Oswaldo Mairena   Born: 30-Jun-74   Age: 29   Bats: L   Throws: L

YEAR	TM	LG	AGE	G	GS	IP	H	BB	SO	HR	ERA	EQERA	EQH9	EQBB9	EQSO9	EQHR9	PERA	VORP	STF
2000	NRW	EAS	26	35	0	32.3	29	11	30	0	2.79	4.69	9.6	3.4	6.3	0.3	4.09	2.5	-2
2000	IOW	PCL	26	11	0	14.7	13	2	4	1	4.90	3.86	8.5	1.2	2.0	0.8	3.13	2.5	-20
2001	PME	EAS	27	22	0	34.3	27	8	27	3	1.57	4.47	9.7	2.9	5.1	1.3	3.77	3.5	-10
2001	CLG	PCL	27	31	0	39.3	52	13	44	4	7.56	6.15	11.4	3.4	7.1	1.0	6.01	-3.4	-4
2002	CLG	PCL	28	25	0	29.0	39	13	19	2	4.97	6.30	12.9	4.7	4.6	0.8	6.28	-3.0	-22
2002	FLA	NL	28	31	0	33.7	38	12	21	7	5.34	5.75	10.7	2.9	5.0	2.0	6.04	-1.4	-19
2003	FLA	NL	29	35	0	43.0	50	20	29	5	5.01	5.56	10.9	3.6	5.3	1.1	5.68	1.9	-14

Breakout: 11%   Improve: 34%   Collapse: 35%

Platoon splits are real, but they don't affect everyone equally. Your lefty specialist is the guy you want to count on against Jim Thome and Ryan Klesko, but there are plenty of left-handers out there who aren't qualified to pitch against these guys, or anyone else in a major league uniform. Being left-handed doesn't make you any more valuable if you can't get anyone out. There are plenty of right-handers who'll be happy to fill that role.

Blaine Neal   Born: 06-Apr-78   Age: 25   Bats: L   Throws: R

YEAR	TM	LG	AGE	G	GS	IP	H	BB	SO	HR	ERA	EQERA	EQH9	EQBB9	EQSO9	EQHR9	PERA	VORP	STF
2000	BRV	FSL	22	41	0	54.3	40	24	65	1	2.15	4.95	8.3	5.0	7.5	0.4	4.16	2.6	7
2001	PME	EAS	23	54	0	53.3	43	21	45	1	2.36	4.34	9.7	4.9	5.4	0.3	3.89	6.2	-6
2002	CLG	PCL	24	29	0	31.0	27	15	26	2	2.90	3.50	8.4	5.0	5.8	0.7	3.75	6.5	-5
2002	FLA	NL	24	32	0	33.0	32	14	33	1	2.73	3.66	9.0	3.4	7.9	0.3	4.06	6.3	13
2003	FLA	NL	25	42	1	57.7	54	30	50	4	3.88	4.31	8.6	4.0	6.9	0.7	4.45	8.0	0

Breakout: 15%   Improve: 48%   Collapse: 17%

Most minor league closers in the big leagues have the life expectancy of David Duke at a Black Panthers rally, but Neal pairs a reliable curve with the standard-issue 95-mph fastball to good effect wherever he pitches. His actual performance was better than his peripherals from last year suggest, so he's a good bet to be a productive member of the Marlins bullpen in 2003.

Vladimir Nunez   Born: 15-Mar-75   Age: 28   Bats: R   Throws: R

YEAR	TM	LG	AGE	G	GS	IP	H	BB	SO	HR	ERA	EQERA	EQH9	EQBB9	EQSO9	EQHR9	PERA	VORP	STF
2000	CLG	PCL	25	15	15	89.7	92	38	95	9	4.11	3.77	8.8	3.6	7.5	1.0	4.38	17.3	19
2000	FLA	NL	25	17	12	68.3	88	34	45	12	7.91	7.08	11.8	3.6	5.3	1.4	6.63	-12.1	-8
2001	FLA	NL	26	52	3	92.0	79	30	64	9	2.74	3.43	8.2	2.8	5.4	0.8	3.64	20.1	-2
2002	FLA	NL	27	77	0	97.7	80	37	73	8	3.41	3.53	7.7	3.0	5.9	0.8	3.57	20.1	-1
2003	FLA	NL	28	36	6	68.3	68	27	49	7	4.20	4.66	9.2	3.1	5.6	1.0	4.61	6.7	-5

Breakout: 14%   Improve: 42%   Collapse: 27%

Nunez pulled ahead early in the closer race with the Marlins, but his six blown saves by the All-Star break got him kicked off the island, and he didn't record a save after July 21. He's probably better suited to a less restrictive role in any case, since he's effective in multi-inning appearances and is good for 100 innings a season. He'll be pitching setup in 2003.

Kevin Olsen — Born: 26-Jul-76 — Age: 26 — Bats: R — Throws: R

YEAR	TM	LG	AGE	G	GS	IP	H	BB	SO	HR	ERA	EQERA	EQH9	EQBB9	EQSO9	EQHR9	PERA	VORP	STF
2000	BRV	FSL	23	18	18	110.0	93	25	77	2	2.86	4.23	9.6	2.6	4.4	0.4	4.06	15.6	9
2000	PME	EAS	23	9	9	54.0	54	21	47	8	4.83	5.89	11.4	4.0	6.0	2.5	6.01	-2.3	2
2001	PME	EAS	24	26	26	154.7	123	21	144	11	2.68	4.30	9.6	1.7	5.9	1.0	3.36	20.7	17
2002	FLA	NL	25	17	8	55.7	57	31	38	5	4.52	5.05	9.6	4.4	5.4	0.8	5.21	2.6	-5
2002	CLG	PCL	25	8	8	49.0	45	14	25	6	3.86	4.00	9.0	3.0	3.6	1.4	3.83	8.2	-3
2003	FLA	NL	26	21	13	82.3	84	33	55	9	4.26	4.73	9.4	3.1	5.3	1.0	4.74	7.4	-1

Breakout: 15%   Improve: 50%   Collapse: 19%

Olsen started the season in long relief for the Marlins and picked up spot starts as the rotation disintegrated in April. After struggling with his command, and with starters coming off the DL, he was demoted in July. Olsen dropped 15 pounds after 2001, and the difference in mass might have affected his velocity. He'll contend for the swingman spot again in 2003.

Carl Pavano — Born: 08-Jan-76 — Age: 27 — Bats: R — Throws: R

YEAR	TM	LG	AGE	G	GS	IP	H	BB	SO	HR	ERA	EQERA	EQH9	EQBB9	EQSO9	EQHR9	PERA	VORP	STF
2000	MON	NL	24	15	15	97.0	89	34	64	8	3.06	3.13	7.8	2.5	5.2	0.7	3.49	25.6	14
2001	OTT	INT	25	4	4	27.7	27	5	19	4	3.57	4.80	10.1	1.9	4.9	1.8	4.82	2.2	3
2001	MON	NL	25	8	8	42.7	59	16	36	7	6.32	6.38	12.4	3.1	6.4	1.3	6.64	-4.2	5
2002	MON	NL	26	15	14	74.3	98	31	51	14	6.30	6.65	12.3	3.3	5.5	1.7	6.85	-9.5	-7
2002	OTT	INT	26	3	3	20.3	23	2	9	2	3.10	5.06	12.4	1.1	3.5	1.4	5.13	1.0	-2
2002	FLA	NL	26	22	8	61.7	76	14	41	5	3.79	4.94	11.8	1.8	5.4	0.8	5.22	3.6	0
2003	FLA	NL	27	26	16	102.0	111	34	69	11	4.47	4.97	10.0	2.6	5.3	1.0	4.97	6.1	0

Breakout: 10%   Improve: 41%   Collapse: 15%

The Big Tease. Pavano looks very pitcher-ish on the mound, but he's been beaten like the Washington Generals since his pitching elbow was surgically reattached in 2000. With the Marlins, he actually pitched pretty well, especially in a dominant relief stint—a 2.61 ERA over 20 innings—to start his Marlins career. But the Marlins are forgivably stubborn in this case, and he's in the mix for a rotation slot in 2003.

Brad Penny — Born: 24-May-78 — Age: 25 — Bats: R — Throws: R

YEAR	TM	LG	AGE	G	GS	IP	H	BB	SO	HR	ERA	EQERA	EQH9	EQBB9	EQSO9	EQHR9	PERA	VORP	STF
2000	FLA	NL	22	23	22	119.7	120	60	80	13	4.81	4.74	9.2	3.7	5.3	0.9	4.66	10.1	8
2001	FLA	NL	23	31	31	205.0	183	54	154	15	3.69	3.71	8.6	2.2	5.9	0.6	3.46	40.9	19
2002	FLA	NL	24	24	24	129.3	148	50	93	18	4.66	5.42	10.8	3.1	5.7	1.3	5.69	1.2	5
2003	FLA	NL	25	24	21	137.3	134	49	103	14	4.01	4.46	9.0	2.8	5.9	1.0	4.31	17.2	9

Breakout: 16%   Improve: 53%   Collapse: 11%

Penny has been the subject of some interesting postseason talk, where an unnamed NL general manager posited that Penny's got a serious arm problem. The Marlins loudly denounced the rumors, but that's what you do when you've got a pitcher you wouldn't mind trading. It isn't speculation that Penny had a down year in 2002, hitting the DL with biceps inflammation and wrestling with blister problems. With all of the potential buyers suspicious and kicking the tires repeatedly before shrugging and moving on, it looks like Penny will be the #2 starter with Florida in 2003. Assuming his arm doesn't fall off.

Nate Robertson — Born: 03-Sep-77 — Age: 25 — Bats: R — Throws: L

YEAR	TM	LG	AGE	G	GS	IP	H	BB	SO	HR	ERA	EQERA	EQH9	EQBB9	EQSO9	EQHR9	PERA	VORP	STF
2000	KNE	MDW	22	6	6	17.7	24	6	15	0	5.08	8.83	17.4	3.9	5.0	0.4	8.43	-6.5	-10
2001	BRV	FSL	23	19	19	106.3	95	43	67	3	2.88	5.38	10.8	4.5	3.9	0.7	5.51	1.5	-4
2002	PME	EAS	24	27	27	163.0	156	50	109	12	3.42	4.79	10.5	3.3	4.6	1.1	4.63	12.9	2
2002	FLA	NL	24	6	-1	8.3	15	4	3	3	11.93	11.27	16.9	3.8	2.9	3.4	11.15	-5.4	-49
2003	DET	AL	25	15	10	60.3	74	26	35	6	5.30	5.47	10.7	3.6	5.0	1.0	5.40	2.8	-6

Breakout: 20%   Improve: 54%   Collapse: 19%

Robertson has had problems staying off the trainer's table so far in his career, so it wasn't surprising when he developed some soreness in his pitching shoulder around inning 175 in 2002, and he was shut down in the middle of September. He would have had a tough time cracking the Marlin rotation without a fire sale, but in the wide-open situation in Detroit, anything could happen.

Ryan Snare   Born: 08-Feb-79   Age: 24   Bats: L   Throws: L

YEAR	TM	LG	AGE	G	GS	IP	H	BB	SO	HR	ERA	EQERA	EQH9	EQBB9	EQSO9	EQHR9	PERA	VORP	STF
2001	DYT	MDW	22	21	20	115.0	101	37	118	7	3.05	4.95	10.9	4.2	5.8	1.3	4.98	7.1	8
2002	STO	CLF	23	13	13	82.0	74	18	81	4	3.07	5.42	11.9	2.6	5.4	0.9	4.73	0.8	11
2002	CHT	SOU	23	5	0	6.0	5	3	4	1	3.00	5.32	10.1	5.0	4.5	3.2	5.84	0.0	-28
2002	PME	EAS	23	11	9	55.0	46	19	52	6	3.44	4.54	9.4	3.8	6.5	1.7	4.32	5.8	10

Acquired from the Reds in the Ryan Dempster deal, Snare was a 2nd round pick out of the University of North Carolina in 2000. Pushing into Double-A, he did pretty well. He has decent velocity for a lefty, touching 90 at times, but it's his curve that's his out pitch, and he'll mix in a decent changeup. He'll be an asset long after Dempster's gone through a couple of surgeries. A nice pick-up, and somebody who could force his way into the Fish rotation by the end of the year.

Julian Tavarez   Born: 22-May-73   Age: 30   Bats: L   Throws: R

YEAR	TM	LG	AGE	G	GS	IP	H	BB	SO	HR	ERA	EQERA	EQH9	EQBB9	EQSO9	EQHR9	PERA	VORP	STF
2000	COL	NL	27	51	12	120.0	124	53	62	11	4.42	4.15	9.0	3.2	4.1	0.7	3.83	17.2	-10
2001	CHC	NL	28	34	28	161.3	172	69	107	13	4.52	4.85	9.8	3.6	5.1	0.7	4.78	11.6	0
2002	FLA	NL	29	29	27	153.7	188	74	67	9	5.39	5.73	11.6	3.9	3.5	0.6	5.82	-3.9	-11
2003	FLA	NL	30	27	21	130.3	142	57	72	11	4.67	5.19	10.1	3.4	4.4	0.8	5.18	5.3	-5

Breakout: 8%   Improve: 52%   Collapse: 16%

Ugly peripherals, bad results, with a gift for saying dumb stuff around reporters, and you wonder why the line to sign this guy isn't miles long? Tavarez did perform better after he got over a self-inflicted sore shoulder (he made an emergency start on three days' rest without telling anyone his shoulder hurt), but he's a back-of-the-rotation option at best.

Mike Tejera   Born: 18-Oct-76   Age: 26   Bats: L   Throws: L

YEAR	TM	LG	AGE	G	GS	IP	H	BB	SO	HR	ERA	EQERA	EQH9	EQBB9	EQSO9	EQHR9	PERA	VORP	STF
2001	PME	EAS	24	25	25	141.0	143	41	131	17	3.57	5.90	12.5	3.7	6.1	1.8	5.69	-6.2	3
2002	FLA	NL	25	47	18	139.7	144	60	95	17	4.45	4.78	9.7	3.4	5.4	1.1	5.09	10.6	-4
2003	FLA	NL	26	30	13	86.7	91	37	64	10	4.53	5.04	9.7	3.3	5.8	1.1	5.10	6.6	-3

Breakout: 16%   Improve: 46%   Collapse: 23%

Tejera was thrown into Brad Penny's slot when Penny hit the DL in June and he won four straight starts. By late September, he'd given it all back and been kicked back to the bullpen. It isn't hard to pull for Tejera, who's 5′9″ and looks like he'd blow off the mound in a stiff wind, but his peripherals and control aren't good. He'll be in the mix for a rotation slot in 2003.

Nate Teut   Born: 11-Mar-76   Age: 27   Bats: R   Throws: L

YEAR	TM	LG	AGE	G	GS	IP	H	BB	SO	HR	ERA	EQERA	EQH9	EQBB9	EQSO9	EQHR9	PERA	VORP	STF
2000	WTN	SOU	24	27	21	138.3	133	44	106	13	3.06	5.61	12.6	3.3	5.1	1.7	5.73	-1.8	-2
2001	IOW	PCL	25	29	29	167.0	184	69	125	28	5.12	6.59	11.6	4.6	5.1	1.8	6.32	-20.1	-8
2002	CLG	PCL	26	27	19	116.0	132	52	82	19	5.28	6.12	11.2	4.7	5.0	1.8	5.87	-8.1	-15
2002	FLA	NL	26	2	1	7.3	13	3	4	0	9.86	8.65	16.8	3.3	4.4	0.3	8.03	-2.6	-14
2003	FLA	NL	27	15	8	54.0	57	29	38	7	5.06	5.63	9.8	4.2	5.6	1.2	5.65	0.4	-7

Breakout: 27%   Improve: 56%   Collapse: 21%

Former Cubbie property Teut had a mediocre year with Calgary and Florida in 2002, and he may have reached the limits of his abilities. He's got a wide but shallow repertoire, with no true out pitch. He can pitch a ton of innings, and he's a lefty, so he'll have ample opportunities to take his game to the next level.

Justin Wayne — Born: 16-Apr-79 — Age: 24 — Bats: R — Throws: R

YEAR	TM	LG	AGE	G	GS	IP	H	BB	SO	HR	ERA	EQERA	EQH9	EQBB9	EQSO9	EQHR9	PERA	VORP	STF
2001	JUP	FSL	22	8	7	41.7	31	9	35	0	3.02	4.31	9.1	2.4	5.1	0.3	3.42	5.5	13
2001	HAR	EAS	22	14	14	92.7	87	34	70	4	2.62	4.17	10.4	4.5	4.8	0.6	4.78	13.8	6
2002	HAR	EAS	23	17	17	98.7	74	32	47	7	2.37	4.17	8.7	3.6	3.4	1.1	3.48	14.6	-3
2002	PME	EAS	23	7	7	42.7	43	13	30	3	4.85	5.57	11.0	3.3	4.9	1.1	4.90	-0.3	4
2002	FLA	NL	23	5	5	23.7	22	13	16	3	5.32	5.40	8.7	4.4	5.4	1.2	4.97	0.3	0
2003	FLA	NL	24	17	12	74.3	80	36	49	9	4.99	5.55	9.9	3.7	5.2	1.1	5.34	1.6	-5

Breakout: 11%   Improve: 43%   Collapse: 26%

Former Stanford star hurler Wayne was an important part of the Cliff Floyd deal, returning to the ownership team that drafted him in 2000. After a good start at Portland, Wayne closed out the season in mediocre fashion, apart from making his first major league appearance. He could use some work against Triple-A hitters, but he may not get it.

Dontrelle Willis — Born: 12-Jan-82 — Age: 21 — Bats: L — Throws: L

YEAR	TM	LG	AGE	G	GS	IP	H	BB	SO	HR	ERA	EQERA	EQH9	EQBB9	EQSO9	EQHR9	PERA	VORP	STF
2001	BOI	NWN	19	15	15	93.7	76	19	77	1	2.98	4.88	10.4	2.8	4.0	0.3	3.98	6.5	7
2002	KNE	MDW	20	19	19	127.7	91	21	101	3	1.83	3.14	8.6	2.0	4.5	0.6	3.33	33.6	14
2002	JUP	FSL	20	5	5	30.0	24	3	27	2	1.80	3.52	10.3	1.2	5.9	1.5	3.92	6.6	21
2003	FLA	NL	21	16	13	87.0	85	24	54	6	3.60	4.00	9.1	2.2	4.9	0.7	3.91	13.5	7

Breakout: 10%   Improve: 56%   Collapse: 3%

The Marlins gave up a lot in the Clement-Tavarez deal with the Cubs, but it only took about three starts for Willis to demonstrate that he was the key to the deal for the Marlins. He responded to his new organization with a fantastic end to a great season. Willis's fastball-curve combo is lights-out, and he's appropriately averse to the free pass. He'll hit Double-A, at least, in 2003.

Houston Astros

Although *Baseball Prospectus* tends to focus on front offices when discussing baseball clubs, happily, teams are primarily remembered for their players. Whether it's the Joe Morgan/Johnny Bench-driven Big Red Machine or the Jeff Newman/Mitchell Page burned-out shell Athletics, fans associate certain players with certain teams. For the Astros squads of the last decade, it's obviously the duo on the right side of the infield, Jeff Bagwell and Craig Biggio, both of whom rank among the ten greatest players ever at their position.

Prior to the Killer B's joining forces in 1991, the Astros played into October just three times in their 29-year existence. After filling out the supporting cast and firing their bridesmaid manager, Terry Collins, Houston reached the postseason four times between 1997 and 2001. Baseball will never match football's appeal in The Lone Star State, but Minute Maid Park and the 2.5 million fannies that inhabit it are due in large measure to Bagwell and Biggio.

There's no debate that Bagwell and Biggio were the catalysts for the best stretch of success in franchise history. However, 2002 marked the first time that both had campaigns significantly below their established standard. With Bagwell now 35 years old and Biggio 37, they are both closer to the end of the line than their peaks. The question becomes, are they helping the team as it goes forward?

Bagwell's situation is fairly cut and dried. His performance still places him in the top third of major league first basemen and he shouldn't tail off dramatically for a couple of years. Also, the team doesn't have a good alternative at the ready or even identifiable in its farm system. Rather, Bagwell is hurting the Astros in terms of the opportunity costs of the 5-year, $85 million contract he signed before last season. Deferred payments limit the annual payout to no more than the $10 million owed this year, but also guarantee that his ghost will be haunting the organization when President

Jenna Bush is planning the family's third invasion of Iraq. Bagwell won't be much more than a thinner, G-rated version of Mo Vaughn when his contract expires in 2006, but he can still help the team near-term.

Hoping to extend his career, the Astros moved Biggio out from behind the plate over a decade ago. However, second base might be the next most physically taxing position on the diamond. The pounding and Biggio's advancing age and reckless style have taken their toll. He'll pull down a bigger paycheck this year than any of his keystone peers at $9 million, but at this point in their careers, Pokey Reese would do more to push Houston toward a championship. While Biggio sat out more games last year than at any time since his back-stopping days, acknowledging his diminished skills and giving more of his playing time to Geoff Blum while releasing Morgan Ensberg from the doghouse and stationing him at third base would improve the team on the field. And that was before the Astros signed Jeff Kent in December.

It's not clear whether the Astros really meant to land Kent or if the negotiations were simply intended to make fans believe they had bigger off-season plans than re-signing Alan Zinter to a minor league deal. Kent, though, was hell-bent on getting out of San Francisco and playing closer to his home in Austin. Whatever the motives, Kent accepted Houston's moderate two-year offer, in which most of the $18.2 million is deferred without interest. Out of the blue, the 2000 National League MVP and one of the ten best players in the circuit fell into the Astros' lap.

While the signing should have been cause for rejoicing, it immediately became cause for concern. Kent would be a nifty fit at third base, and has previous experience at the position. His switching positions would upgrade the lineup at both the hot corner and second base, with Blum vacating third base and becoming part of a time-share with Biggio at

---

Astros Prospectus
2002 record: 84–78; Second place, NL Central
Pythagenport Record: 87–75
Runs scored per game: 4.6 (5th in NL)
Runs allowed per game: 4.3 (6th in NL)
Team EqA: .260 (10th in NL)
2002 Batters Age: 30.5 (6th oldest in NL)
2002 Pitchers Age: 27.4 (3rd youngest in NL)
Ballpark: Minute Maid Park; Severe hitters' park; Park Factor of 1.052
2002: Lineup holes and pitching problems, some self-inflicted, kept the Astros behind the Cardinals.
2003: Adding Kent makes for more lineup juggling, but the young pitching should keep the team competitive.

second. Instead, general manager Gerry Hunsicker announced that Kent would remain at second base, with Biggio moving to center field for the final year of his contract.

The decision reduces the Kent signing to a sugar-free brownie: it still looks tasty out of the oven, but when you bite into it, most of the goody goodness has vanished. Sure, Kent will be a huge step up from Biggio at second. On the other hand, Blum doesn't hit enough for an everyday third baseman and Biggio creates serious problems in an outfield that was crowded to begin with. Considering he falls short of the league norm at a weak offensive position like second base, Biggio becomes Brian Hunter minus the defense in center field, and the Astros already are saddled with the original. With Lance Berkman moving to left field, Richard Hidalgo, Daryle Ward, and Jason Lane get stuffed into the remaining outfield corner, though all three will outhit Biggio this season. Berkman, Hidalgo, and Lane have already shown they can handle center field. Ward will probably be dealt by Opening Day, but won't fetch much in return after a disappointing 2002 campaign. Chalk it up as a hidden cost of creating room for Biggio.

Forfeiting a couple of wins to find full-time employment for a local icon wouldn't be a big deal if the 2003 Astros were the new millennium Orioles handing 500 plate appearances to the shell of Cal Ripken while hoping to stay out of the divisional basement. On the contrary, Houston needs to squeeze everything possible out of its personnel to overtake the Cardinals for the NL Central crown.

The Astros have had but one losing season in the last decade. Along with the Bagwell/Biggio core, the primary reason for the continued success is the organization's player development program. Prospects move methodically through the system until clearly ready to help at the major league level, at which point the team carves out room by moving overpriced veterans via trades or free agency, keeping the payroll in check. The front office maintains a low profile, but few teams have done a better job of reloading their 25-man roster in recent years than Houston. Cutting into the playing time of younger, better players, or trading them to placate a fading 37-year-old goes against the philosophy that has been at the foundation of the Astros' success. Out of loyalty, they are essentially kicking away the final, most crucial rung of the developmental ladder.

A larger threat to the last step of the team's player development process lurks in its own dugout. Heading into last season, we were cautiously optimistic about new manager Jimy Williams's willingness to integrate youngsters into the ball club. A year later, Williams's roster construction and lineup combinations over the course of the 2002 season suggest that his preferences don't mesh with the needs of the organization.

Houston opened last season with a shiny new left side of the infield. Shortstop Julio Lugo was receiving post-dated

detention for his playoff gaffes six months earlier, and third baseman Vinny Castilla was wisely allowed to exit as a free agent. Following the organizational script, Adam Everett and Morgan Ensberg moved up from New Orleans to fill their slots.

It's an open question whether Everett should have been awarded the shortstop job. Astro pitchers don't generate enough ground balls to take advantage of his slick glovework, and Minute Maid Park's juiced environment magnifies his offensive inadequacies. Still, Jennifer Lopez's commitments last longer than the 44-at-bat trial Williams allotted Everett before sending him packing.

Unlike Everett, Ensberg doesn't have a glaring weakness in his game, nor were any better options for his position on hand when Williams demoted him. He was just a convenient fall guy for the team's offensive problems, or more accurately, Williams's perceived offensive problems. At the time, Houston was fifth in the league in runs scored and outscoring their opponents 233 to 217. The Astros' 22–29 record resulted from Y2K-style bad luck, but Williams chose to point the finger at the rookie.

If Williams really wanted to wake up the ball club, wouldn't it have been more effective to bench a poor performing veteran, with the added bonus of tangibly improving the lineup? Talking loudly and carrying a limp stick, Brad Ausmus was hitting considerably worse than Ensberg and is a lesser player than his backup, Gregg Zaun. At the minimum, Williams could have kept Ensberg around to hammer lefties in a platoon with Blum rather than giving at-bats to established cipher Jose Vizcaino.

And what was the immediate impact of Williams's decision? Over the next three weeks, the Astros run-scoring fell by a quarter run per game, and the team burrowed to a season-high 10 games below .500, 10 1/2 games out of first place.

Williams eventually found creative ways to include large helpings of Vizcaino in the team's daily diet. Not satisfied with one serving of aged meat, he used disappointing performances by Hidalgo and Ward to pack more into the menu, and by late summer, Hunter and Orlando Merced had also become lineup staples. While all played better than anybody could have anticipated, a three-headed monstrosity of Vizcaino, Hunter, and Merced leading an Astros charge culminating in a playoff berth would have been a bigger shock than the 1980 Winter Olympics' "Miracle on Ice." Certainly, some combination of Hidalgo, Ward, and Lane—recalled in August to collect dust until Merced tweaked a hamstring in mid-September—had a far better chance of going nuts on NL pitching.

All things being equal, a manager's most critical job is handling the pitching staff. Williams did pretty well in that department. None of the starters were overworked, and with the notable exception of Carlos Hernandez, nobody on the staff suffered any serious arm problems. Kirk Saarloos entered the rotation in July and wasn't jerked around despite frequent struggles. Williams also had the stones to finally boot the Astros' $6 million mistake, Dave Mlicki, off the starting staff and went with effective journeyman Peter Munro down the stretch. Houston's young mound corps finished in the top half of the league in ERA while toiling in a hitter's ballpark, and is poised to improve this year.

However, Astros owner Drayton McLane would have you believe things aren't equal in Houston. He claims the ball club operates at a financial disadvantage even though: (1) he bought the Astros in 1992 for $115 million and Forbes now values the franchise at $337 million; (2) it plays in a sparkling cash cow of a ballpark, for which the team paid less than 15% of the construction costs; (3) nearly all of the team's $7.1 million annual rent is covered by the stadium's naming rights, which were re-sold last June for $6 million a year (more than twice what any other MLB team receives). To emphasize his plight, McLane went so far as to halt negotiations with last year's draft picks to ease potential cash-flow problems in the event of a work stoppage. Regardless of where the truth lies, the team payroll isn't going to rise from the middle of the pack, and is currently capped at $65 million.

Because of their limited payroll, much of which is devoured by some unnecessarily large contracts, Houston can only remain competitive by growing their own cheap supply of labor. Consequently, a willingness to commit to young players also becomes a top priority for the Astros' manager. Williams failed to do that when he awarded 22% of the team's at bats to Blum, Vizcaino, Hunter, and Merced. In addition to stunting player development, Williams's infatuation with the quartet limits the club's options for 2003 by committing almost $6 million to little more than four replacement-level players.

The Astros face other challenges to keep a steady stream of talent blossoming on their 25-man roster. McLane's frugality extends downward, forcing the team's player development program to operate with a smaller budget than most other clubs. Along with implementing an outstanding, organization-wide teaching plan, assistant GM Tim Purpura and his gang have compensated by using less-traveled roads to find players. The avenues include extensive prospecting in Venezuela, focusing on drafting college players (including seniors), exploiting the draft-and-follow rules to secure projectable junior college players, and a willingness to look beyond physical size and tools in player evaluation. Naturally, success breeds imitation, and many teams now mine these same sources. Perhaps stemming from the increased competition, the Astros don't have any clear grade-A prospects in the minors for the first time in recent memory. That could change quickly, though, as John Buck, Rodrigo Rosario, Tommy Whiteman, and Fernando Nieve are one breakout season away from ascending to that level.

The Astros' extended run of success is largely a testament to the player development program. Their passion and commitment on that front has enabled them to win divisional battles in the past, and has provided the weapons to challenge for the NL Central crown this year and in the near future. The competition is stiff enough without adding a new enemy: themselves. Misguided loyalties to withering local heroes and an unfounded devotion to veteran mediocrities pose a new danger to the organization. Whether the team's front office recognizes the threat, and how they address it is the greatest question the Astros face as they move forward.

HITTERS

Anthony Acevedo								LF		Born: 05-May-78			Age: 25		Bats: L			Throws: L	
YEAR	TM	LG	AGE	AB	H	2B	3B	HR	BB	SO	SB	CS	AVG	OBP	SLG	MLVR	EQBA	EQOBP	EQSLG	EQMLVR	VORP	DEFENSE
2000	MAR	APL	22	200	59	20	3	5	31	41	7	3	.295	.397	.500	.313	.202	.272	.332	-.326	-13.3	52-LF -7
2001	MIC	MDW	23	429	111	35	4	12	69	130	21	5	.259	.370	.443	.137	.196	.282	.332	-.310	-25.9	103-LF -7
2002	LEX	SAL	24	437	132	28	0	12	62	89	11	8	.302	.390	.449	.235	.227	.296	.347	-.243	-18.2	77-LF -10
2003	HOU	NL	25	151	37	8	1	4	18	37	2	3	.244	.326	.401	-.071	.242	.321	.404	-.101	-3.1	

Breakout: 54%   Improve: 72%   Collapse: 12%

One of many college seniors the Astros have drafted in recent years, Acevedo was voted Lexington's MVP. It's always fun to tote home hardware to show friends and family, but he was three years too old for the Sally League. Acevedo will be thrown into the Double-A deep end this year, and has slightly less chance of drowning than an accused witch in the ducking stool.

Jason Alfaro   3B   Born: 29-Nov-77   Age: 25   Bats: R   Throws: R

YEAR	TM	LG	AGE	AB	H	2B	3B	HR	BB	SO	SB	CS	AVG	OBP	SLG	MLVR	EQBA	EQOBP	EQSLG	EQMLVR	VORP	DEFENSE		
2000	KIS	FSL	22	460	115	20	1	7	25	63	2	6	.250	.290	.343	-.105	.204	.235	.286	-.463	-29.1	113-SS	-2	
2001	ROU	TXS	23	284	69	16	2	2	7	40	2	1	.243	.266	.335	-.219	.211	.230	.292	-.461	-16.9	27-2B	0	18-LF -1
2002	ROU	TXS	24	455	143	36	2	16	50	75	11	9	.314	.395	.508	.316	.269	.333	.443	-.009	21.4	113-3B	2	
2003	HOU	NL	25	209	54	11	1	6	14	33	4	2	.260	.310	.405	-.082	.258	.305	.407	-.113	1.3			

Breakout: 44%   Improve: 66%   Collapse: 13%

After five lackluster campaigns, Alfaro seemed well on his way to being another illustration of a terrific athlete failing as a baseball player. However, under the tutelage of minor league hitting coordinator Pat Roessler, Alfaro harnessed his aggressiveness at the plate, and his batting average and power exploded. Good footwork and an arm so strong that the Astros considered moving him to the mound enable him to play any infield position. If Alfaro can hold onto the huge gains he made last year, he'll have a career.

Brad Ausmus   C   Born: 14-Apr-69   Age: 34   Bats: R   Throws: R

YEAR	TM	LG	AGE	AB	H	2B	3B	HR	BB	SO	SB	CS	AVG	OBP	SLG	MLVR	EQBA	EQOBP	EQSLG	EQMLVR	VORP	DEFENSE	
2000	DET	AL	31	523	139	25	3	7	69	79	11	5	.266	.358	.365	-.097	.277	.362	.383	-.033	27.3	139-C	10
2001	HOU	NL	32	422	98	23	4	5	30	64	4	1	.232	.285	.341	-.263	.233	.285	.341	-.269	-3.9	117-C	14
2002	HOU	NL	33	447	115	19	3	6	38	71	2	3	.257	.324	.353	-.095	.259	.321	.359	-.157	8.9	120-C	8
2003	HOU	NL	34	299	76	15	2	5	29	49	4	2	.253	.322	.361	-.125	.251	.317	.363	-.155	1.4		

Breakout: 26%   Improve: 56%   Collapse: 24%

Like an old-time medicine man, Ausmus peddles the elixirs of veteran leadership and game-calling skills to an Astros organization all too willing to buy. He's an excellent defensive backstop, but his bat has descended to the depths of The Matheny Zone. Last year's flailing included tying Ernie Lombardi's NL record by grounding into 30 double plays, but at least The Schnozz had the excuse of being the slowest player of all time. Ausmus didn't need his Dartmouth education to find the wisdom to exercise his $5.5 million player option for 2003.

Jeff Bagwell   1B   Born: 27-May-68   Age: 35   Bats: R   Throws: R

YEAR	TM	LG	AGE	AB	H	2B	3B	HR	BB	SO	SB	CS	AVG	OBP	SLG	MLVR	EQBA	EQOBP	EQSLG	EQMLVR	VORP	DEFENSE	
2000	HOU	NL	32	590	183	37	1	47	107	116	9	6	.310	.428	.615	.406	.302	.413	.598	.371	78.6	154-1B	5
2001	HOU	NL	33	600	173	43	4	39	106	135	11	3	.288	.400	.568	.293	.285	.395	.561	.274	65.7	158-1B	7
2002	HOU	NL	34	571	166	33	2	31	101	130	7	3	.291	.406	.518	.275	.287	.398	.519	.225	51.1	151-1B	0
2003	HOU	NL	35	476	133	27	3	26	84	103	8	3	.279	.391	.508	.196	.277	.384	.511	.171	28.8		

Breakout: 4%   Improve: 51%   Collapse: 11%

Bagwell's heart can't be questioned. He played 158 games while recovering from off-season shoulder surgery that made it painful to take the field and excruciating to throw the ball. While his output improved as the year went on, his final numbers fell for the third straight season. With $10 million due him this year and McLane's tight payroll purse strings, we've already reached the point where his total package is no more pushing the team toward a championship than away from one. Bagwell was a great player, but it only gets worse from here.

Lance Berkman   OF   Born: 10-Feb-76   Age: 27   Bats: B   Throws: L

YEAR	TM	LG	AGE	AB	H	2B	3B	HR	BB	SO	SB	CS	AVG	OBP	SLG	MLVR	EQBA	EQOBP	EQSLG	EQMLVR	VORP	DEFENSE	
2000	NWO	PCL	24	112	37	4	2	6	31	20	4	4	.330	.479	.563	.497	.289	.424	.491	.233	11.2	26-LF	-2
2000	HOU	NL	24	353	105	28	1	21	56	73	6	2	.297	.395	.561	.263	.291	.380	.551	.243	31.4	86-RF	-4
2001	HOU	NL	25	577	191	55	5	34	92	121	7	9	.331	.434	.620	.462	.326	.425	.608	.431	87.3	152-LF	-5
2002	HOU	NL	26	578	169	35	2	42	107	118	8	4	.292	.406	.578	.351	.287	.398	.574	.299	77.5	143-CF	-4
2003	HOU	NL	27	558	167	35	3	36	101	115	8	3	.299	.409	.565	.314	.297	.402	.568	.291	57.2		

Breakout: 6%   Improve: 44%   Collapse: 11%

His happy-go-lucky demeanor stands out in the Astros' game face wearin', cliché spoutin' clubhouse. Berkman is unusual in other ways, too, moving to the right along the defensive spectrum: from first base at Rice, to left field when he turned pro, to a surprisingly adequate job in center field last year. In another unconventional move, Berkman should really consider giving up switch-hitting. Since joining the league, he's been Stan Musial from the left side (.317/.416/.628) and Stan Javier (.256/.366/.394) from the right. In a non-Bonds world, Berkman would be one of the preseason favorites for NL MVP this year.

Craig Biggio 2B/OF? Born: 14-Dec-65 Age: 37 Bats: R Throws: R

YEAR	TM	LG	AGE	AB	H	2B	3B	HR	BB	SO	SB	CS	AVG	OBP	SLG	MLVR	EQBA	EQOBP	EQSLG	EQMLVR	VORP	DEFENSE	
2000	HOU	NL	34	377	101	13	5	8	61	73	12	2	.268	.392	.393	-.001	.265	.379	.386	-.005	22.2	96-2B	7
2001	HOU	NL	35	617	180	35	3	20	66	100	7	4	.292	.385	.455	.122	.293	.380	.457	.115	56.5	149-2B	-7
2002	HOU	NL	36	577	146	36	3	15	50	111	16	2	.253	.331	.404	-.021	.256	.326	.415	-.072	21.2	138-2B	-11
2003	*HOU*	*NL*	*37*	*424*	*110*	*23*	*2*	*9*	*42*	*77*	*12*	*3*	*.259*	*.334*	*.392*	*-.060*	*.258*	*.328*	*.394*	*-.090*	*8.1*		

Breakout: 3%   Improve: 32%   Collapse: 25%

Batting average is an overrated statistic, but it might be the best offensive indicator of when a player is nearing the end. While Biggio's "old player skills" (walks and power) remained solid last year, his batting average fell to a level not seen since Dan Quayle was entertaining the nation. Biggio hoped for a two-year contract extension through 2005 this past winter, but the Astros want him to play out his current deal so they can see what he has left and gather more data on their other options. After acquiring Jeff Kent, the team announced that it plans to move him to center field. Blech.

Geoff Blum 3B/UT Born: 26-Apr-73 Age: 30 Bats: B Throws: R

YEAR	TM	LG	AGE	AB	H	2B	3B	HR	BB	SO	SB	CS	AVG	OBP	SLG	MLVR	EQBA	EQOBP	EQSLG	EQMLVR	VORP	DEFENSE			
2000	MON	NL	27	343	97	20	2	11	26	60	1	4	.283	.339	.449	-.000	.280	.326	.445	-.009	16.7	48-3B	-4	29-SS	1
2001	MON	NL	28	453	107	25	0	9	43	94	9	5	.236	.316	.351	-.184	.239	.315	.352	-.192	-.5	73-3B	-4	27-LF	0
2002	HOU	NL	29	368	104	20	4	10	49	70	2	0	.283	.368	.440	.110	.282	.364	.446	.062	24.7	93-3B	11		
2003	*HOU*	*NL*	*30*	*293*	*76*	*16*	*2*	*8*	*34*	*55*	*3*	*2*	*.261*	*.342*	*.409*	*-.023*	*.259*	*.336*	*.412*	*-.051*	*5.2*				

Breakout: 10%   Improve: 44%   Collapse: 26%

Blum is a handy guy to have on a 25-man roster. He's versatile, has a decent stick from both sides of the plate and can show his teammates how to safely use the New Basics hair coloring brush. He doesn't have enough sock to be a regular at his best positions (third base and left field), though, which can lead to trouble if he falls into the wrong hands. Jimy Williams plays Dr. Evil at The Juicebox, and while he hasn't used Blum to steal the Sodo Mojo, he did use him as an excuse to run Morgan Ensberg out of town. If Blum gets more than 300 at-bats this year, it's time to call on the International Man of Mystery.

John Buck C Born: 07-Jul-80 Age: 22 Bats: R Throws: R

YEAR	TM	LG	AGE	AB	H	2B	3B	HR	BB	SO	SB	CS	AVG	OBP	SLG	MLVR	EQBA	EQOBP	EQSLG	EQMLVR	VORP	DEFENSE	
2000	MIC	MDW	19	390	110	33	0	10	55	81	2	4	.282	.378	.444	.186	.214	.282	.341	-.287	-5.3	99-C	5
2001	LEX	SAL	20	443	122	24	1	22	37	84	4	9	.275	.348	.483	.218	.214	.268	.373	-.270	-4.0	111-C	9
2002	ROU	TXS	21	448	118	29	3	12	31	93	2	3	.263	.320	.422	.044	.231	.275	.379	-.237	-.2	99-C	-9
2003	*HOU*	*NL*	*22*	*183*	*45*	*9*	*1*	*7*	*16*	*39*	*2*	*1*	*.243*	*.308*	*.408*	*-.093*	*.241*	*.303*	*.411*	*-.124*	*2.1*		

Breakout: 39%   Improve: 65%   Collapse: 12%

Don't be too disappointed with Buck's year at Round Rock—he's very much a work in progress. Big and rangy in a Pudge Fisk sort of way, Buck is still getting his mechanics in order. Unlike most catching prospects, he has a well-rounded game with no glaring weaknesses and should eventually develop 20-home run power, especially if he regains the control of the strike zone he showed in 2000. A good campaign in Triple-A puts him front and center to inherit the backstop job from Ausmus next year. Buck has a few All-Star games in his future, but the first one won't happen until the end of the decade.

Chris Burke 2B Born: 11-Mar-80 Age: 23 Bats: R Throws: R

YEAR	TM	LG	AGE	AB	H	2B	3B	HR	BB	SO	SB	CS	AVG	OBP	SLG	MLVR	EQBA	EQOBP	EQSLG	EQMLVR	VORP	DEFENSE			
2001	MIC	MDW	21	233	70	11	6	3	26	31	21	8	.300	.378	.438	.173	.231	.289	.336	-.270	-3.1	55-SS	-7		
2002	ROU	TXS	22	481	127	19	8	3	39	61	16	15	.264	.332	.356	-.025	.231	.283	.317	-.308	-11.5	94-2B	10	42-SS	-8
2003	*HOU*	*NL*	*23*	*171*	*44*	*8*	*2*	*2*	*14*	*26*	*5*	*2*	*.258*	*.318*	*.371*	*-.115*	*.257*	*.313*	*.373*	*-.145*	*.6*				

Breakout: 48%   Improve: 72%   Collapse: 15%

The Astros' lack of a High-A affiliate hurt Burke's development, as the two-story jump to the Texas League after just 56 games in Low-A proved too steep. He was plainly overmatched at the plate the first half of the season, though on a happier note, the anticipated move from shortstop to second base went off without a hitch. Any plans of Burke turning the deuce in Houston in 2004 will have to be scotched unless he rebounds twice as far as he fell last year. Super-elastic collisions of that magnitude are uncommon.

Brooks Conrad   2B   Born: 16-Jan-80   Age: 23   Bats: B   Throws: R

YEAR	TM	LG	AGE	AB	H	2B	3B	HR	BB	SO	SB	CS	AVG	OBP	SLG	MLVR	EQBA	EQOBP	EQSLG	EQMLVR	VORP		DEFENSE
2001	PTS	NYP	21	232	65	16	5	4	26	52	14	2	.280	.384	.444	.241	.218	.287	.350	-.262	-2.9		58-2B -6
2002	MIC	MDW	22	499	143	25	14	14	62	102	18	8	.287	.373	.477	.237	.221	.288	.370	-.231	-2.1		117-2B -4
2003	HOU	NL	23	189	48	10	2	5	18	44	4	4	.254	.326	.403	-.062	.253	.321	.405	-.092	2.6		

Breakout: 46%   Improve: 66%   Collapse: 14%

Conrad fell to the Astros in the 8th round in 2001 after a disappointing junior year at Arizona State. The switch-hitter generates good power from a compact frame and is the get dirty, aggressive type of player the organization loves. Though Conrad can handle second base defensively, he's probably going to be tried at third base or left field this year to increase his versatility.

Morgan Ensberg   3B   Born: 26-Aug-75   Age: 27   Bats: R   Throws: R

YEAR	TM	LG	AGE	AB	H	2B	3B	HR	BB	SO	SB	CS	AVG	OBP	SLG	MLVR	EQBA	EQOBP	EQSLG	EQMLVR	VORP		DEFENSE
2000	ROU	TXS	24	483	145	34	0	28	92	107	9	12	.300	.420	.545	.336	.246	.344	.445	-.006	24.5		136-3B 11
2001	NWO	PCL	25	316	98	20	0	23	45	60	6	3	.310	.401	.592	.398	.283	.367	.534	.190	35.5		77-3B 4
2002	HOU	NL	26	132	32	7	2	3	18	25	2	0	.242	.346	.394	-.014	.241	.342	.398	-.076	4.0		38-3B -3
2002	NWO	PCL	26	292	84	12	3	7	50	56	9	5	.288	.404	.421	.173	.267	.370	.393	-.012	14.5		77-3B -3
2003	HOU	NL	27	255	67	14	1	11	36	50	6	3	.263	.359	.459	.071	.262	.353	.462	.044	12.3		

Breakout: 16%   Improve: 50%   Collapse: 21%

A preseason darkhorse for Rookie of the Year, Ensberg instead fell victim to Williams's short leash and long memory. He got off to a so-so start, but was still outhitting the Astros' other third base candidates before being scapegoated for the team's hitting woes and demoted in late-May. A grand total of five September at-bats clearly indicates Ensberg is no longer in Houston's plans. He could be had cheap by a ball club looking for a low-cost, effective solution at the hot corner.

Adam Everett   SS   Born: 02-Feb-77   Age: 26   Bats: R   Throws: R

YEAR	TM	LG	AGE	AB	H	2B	3B	HR	BB	SO	SB	CS	AVG	OBP	SLG	MLVR	EQBA	EQOBP	EQSLG	EQMLVR	VORP		DEFENSE
2000	NWO	PCL	23	453	111	25	2	5	75	100	13	4	.245	.365	.342	-.097	.230	.330	.322	-.208	1.3		123-SS 3
2001	NWO	PCL	24	441	110	20	8	5	39	74	24	5	.249	.333	.365	-.103	.234	.308	.342	-.222	-.5		113-SS -9
2002	HOU	NL	25	88	17	3	0	0	12	19	3	0	.193	.297	.227	-.335	.202	.296	.236	-.406	-4.4		31-SS 1
2002	NWO	PCL	25	345	95	16	7	2	24	59	12	3	.275	.333	.380	-.023	.261	.311	.361	-.172	4.1		84-SS 23
2003	HOU	NL	26	187	47	9	2	2	18	33	5	2	.250	.321	.355	-.137	.248	.316	.357	-.167	-.1		

Breakout: 28%   Improve: 50%   Collapse: 21%

Ballplayers are bigger than ever, but the phrase "knock the bat out of his hands" still immediately springs to mind when you see Everett hit. He's a Mark Belanger clone on the left side of second base, with soft hands and silky actions around the keystone, but seems to have misplaced Blade's ability to draw a walk after the 2000 season. With the Pyrite Age of shortstops drawing to a close almost 20 years ago, Everett's time has passed before it ever began.

Richard Hidalgo   RF/CF   Born: 02-Jul-75   Age: 28   Bats: R   Throws: R

YEAR	TM	LG	AGE	AB	H	2B	3B	HR	BB	SO	SB	CS	AVG	OBP	SLG	MLVR	EQBA	EQOBP	EQSLG	EQMLVR	VORP		DEFENSE
2000	HOU	NL	25	558	175	42	3	44	56	110	13	6	.314	.397	.636	.392	.307	.380	.620	.358	79.7		150-CF 12
2001	HOU	NL	26	512	141	29	3	19	54	107	3	5	.275	.363	.455	.067	.275	.358	.453	.055	33.1		144-CF 4
2002	HOU	NL	27	388	91	17	4	15	43	85	6	2	.235	.320	.415	-.036	.237	.318	.421	-.093	-1.7		109-RF 4
2003	HOU	NL	27	414	112	24	2	18	44	85	6	4	.270	.347	.472	.076	.268	.342	.475	.048	10.2		

Breakout: 12%   Improve: 45%   Collapse: 15%

As the *BP2001* cover boy, we tend to view Hidalgo through rose-colored glasses. However, after back-to-back disappointing seasons, it's time to remove them and examine the facts. Much of our Hidalgo hype was due to his youth relative to the leagues in which he played, not his offensive performance in isolation. While age and results are inseparable, he never has remotely approached his 2000 numbers in any of his other 10 professional campaigns. Hidalgo always seems to be playing hurt, so perhaps some of the struggles are caused by injuries. If so, that's simply part of his package. Let's face it, Hidalgo's 2000 season was a fluke. We're always eager to point that out with Darin Erstad, and need to stop treating Hidalgo with kid gloves.

Mike Hill   RF   Born: 30-Sep-76   Age: 26   Bats: R   Throws: R

YEAR	TM	LG	AGE	AB	H	2B	3B	HR	BB	SO	SB	CS	AVG	OBP	SLG	MLVR	EQBA	EQOBP	EQSLG	EQMLVR	VORP	DEFENSE
2000	MIC	MDW	23	198	62	18	4	6	11	43	6	1	.313	.362	.535	.316	.244	.268	.413	-.192	-5.6	42-RF -1
2001	LEX	SAL	24	465	142	31	6	12	48	102	27	9	.305	.384	.475	.279	.239	.299	.374	-.192	-14.2	109-RF -9
2002	ROU	TXS	25	527	149	30	6	14	39	105	14	8	.283	.338	.442	.116	.247	.290	.394	-.176	-13.4	133-RF -8
2003	HOU	NL	26	168	43	9	1	5	13	38	4	3	.258	.314	.426	-.048	.256	.309	.429	-.078	-2.8	

Breakout: 37%   Improve: 66%   Collapse: 24%

The organization loves Hill's down-and-dirty style and sees him as a future fourth outfielder. On a more practical level, Hill is already 26 years old and doesn't have the on-base skills, power, or defensive prowess to merit a big league job, now or in the near future. The number of rubberneckers on the road demonstrates our strange fascination with accidents, but is the fact that Hill poses a threat to outfield walls really enough to warrant serious consideration for a spot on the 25-man roster?

Royce Huffman   1B   Born: 11-Jan-77   Age: 26   Bats: R   Throws: R

YEAR	TM	LG	AGE	AB	H	2B	3B	HR	BB	SO	SB	CS	AVG	OBP	SLG	MLVR	EQBA	EQOBP	EQSLG	EQMLVR	VORP	DEFENSE	
2000	KIS	FSL	23	450	134	32	4	5	84	49	31	4	.298	.415	.420	.219	.242	.338	.350	-.148	5.3	64-3B -4	49-2B -9
2001	ROU	TXS	24	511	158	35	1	4	51	90	13	8	.309	.385	.405	.131	.268	.329	.351	-.147	5.5	126-3B -9	
2002	ROU	TXS	25	522	168	36	3	12	41	70	13	6	.322	.386	.471	.261	.281	.331	.421	-.034	8.3	128-1B -15	
2003	HOU	NL	26	152	39	8	1	3	14	24	4	1	.256	.323	.375	-.103	.255	.317	.378	-.133	-2.6		

Breakout: 14%   Improve: 36%   Collapse: 44%

The franchise knows they will have Bagwell through at least 2006, so it isn't concerned with developing first basemen, instead shunting whoever is handy into that position. It basically amounts to confirming that someone is considered either a non-prospect or a possible utilityman. Even though he was runner-up in the Texas League in batting average, Huffman falls into the first group since he hasn't mastered any position and isn't enough of a slugger for those at which he might someday be adequate defensively.

Brian Hunter   OF   Born: 25-Mar-71   Age: 32   Bats: R   Throws: R

YEAR	TM	LG	AGE	AB	H	2B	3B	HR	BB	SO	SB	CS	AVG	OBP	SLG	MLVR	EQBA	EQOBP	EQSLG	EQMLVR	VORP	DEFENSE
2000	COL	NL	29	200	55	4	1	1	21	31	15	3	.275	.347	.320	-.224	.253	.318	.298	-.252	-8.7	50-OF -2
2001	PHI	NL	30	145	40	6	0	2	16	25	14	3	.276	.348	.359	-.074	.284	.350	.372	-.066	.9	35-OF -1
2002	HOU	NL	31	201	54	16	3	3	16	39	5	0	.269	.329	.423	.013	.271	.326	.429	-.040	7.1	56-CF 0
2003	HOU	NL	32	159	41	8	1	2	15	30	7	2	.260	.324	.371	-.104	.258	.319	.373	-.134	-.6	

Breakout: 13%   Improve: 33%   Collapse: 36%

Hunter returned to the team that originally drafted him and had one of the better years of his career. With thundering elephant Daryle Ward in left and Berkman maxed out in center, you can build a case for carrying Hunter on the roster. However, if Williams continues his September folly of starting Hunter and batting him leadoff, you can make a stronger argument that his hacktastic ways will sabotage the Astros' offense.

Charlton Jimerson   CF   Born: 22-Sep-79   Age: 23   Bats: R   Throws: R

YEAR	TM	LG	AGE	AB	H	2B	3B	HR	BB	SO	SB	CS	AVG	OBP	SLG	MLVR	EQBA	EQOBP	EQSLG	EQMLVR	VORP	DEFENSE
2001	PTS	NYP	21	197	46	12	1	9	18	79	15	4	.234	.304	.442	.098	.180	.229	.337	-.417	-12.3	33-CF -5
2002	LEX	SAL	22	439	100	22	4	14	36	168	34	9	.228	.297	.392	-.021	.178	.226	.307	-.465	-32.0	122-CF -5
2003	HOU	NL	23	158	35	7	1	6	15	67	6	13	.223	.298	.391	-.145	.222	.294	.394	-.177	-4.7	

Breakout: 74%   Improve: 86%   Collapse: 10%

The son of a crack addict mother and an abusive father, Jimerson is as great a human-interest story as he is an athlete. What he isn't right now is a good baseball player, though his physical tools are the best in the system. The Astros won't rush him under any circumstances, but K/BB ratios like this make the climb nearly impossible regardless of the time allotted. Jimerson attended the University of Miami on an academic scholarship, graduating with a degree in computer science. Considering his beginnings, he's a success whether he reaches the majors or not.

Jason Lane   OF   Born: 22-Dec-76   Age: 26   Bats: R   Throws: L

YEAR	TM	LG	AGE	AB	H	2B	3B	HR	BB	SO	SB	CS	AVG	OBP	SLG	MLVR	EQBA	EQOBP	EQSLG	EQMLVR	VORP	DEFENSE		
2000	MIC	MDW	23	511	153	38	0	23	62	91	20	7	.299	.384	.509	.294	.230	.288	.392	-.194	-14.0	88-LF -7	23-1B	0
2001	ROU	TXS	24	526	166	36	2	38	61	98	14	2	.316	.408	.608	.447	.266	.340	.507	.090	24.6	131-LF -6		
2002	NWO	PCL	25	426	116	36	2	15	31	90	13	3	.272	.332	.472	.103	.257	.309	.442	-.064	12.5	98-CF -4		
2002	HOU	NL	25	69	20	3	1	4	10	12	1	1	.290	.380	.536	.258	.286	.367	.543	.205	5.2	27-RF 0		
2003	*HOU*	*NL*	*26*	*235*	*63*	*14*	*1*	*11*	*23*	*48*	*5*	*4*	*.269*	*.337*	*.477*	*.065*	*.267*	*.332*	*.480*	*.036*	*6.2*			

Breakout: 26%   Improve: 56%   Collapse: 17%

Lane's career parallels Berkman's in many ways: drafted as a first baseman out of college, not rushed despite his age, moved to an outfield corner and eventually center field, punishes the ball everywhere he goes. Lane made the trek from New Orleans to Houston three times last year and left a good taste by having his best stint in September. He isn't going to thrash big league pitching like Berkman, but he's definitely ready for a job. And as with Berkman, there's no room at the inn until Hunsicker clears some room on the 25-man roster.

Mark Loretta   INF   Born: 14-Aug-71   Age: 31   Bats: R   Throws: R

YEAR	TM	LG	AGE	AB	H	2B	3B	HR	BB	SO	SB	CS	AVG	OBP	SLG	MLVR	EQBA	EQOBP	EQSLG	EQMLVR	VORP	DEFENSE		
2000	MIL	NL	28	352	99	21	1	7	37	38	0	3	.281	.351	.406	-.041	.280	.343	.401	-.041	16.9	79-SS 15		
2001	MIL	NL	29	384	111	14	2	2	28	46	1	2	.289	.348	.352	-.077	.295	.349	.359	-.078	14.5	48-2B 2	31-3B	-4
2002	MIL	NL	30	217	58	14	0	2	23	32	0	0	.267	.351	.359	-.014	.281	.357	.376	-.049	8.2	44-3B -1		
2002	HOU	NL	30	66	28	4	0	2	9	5	1	1	.424	.493	.576	.614	.418	.487	.582	.604	13.2			
2003	*SDP*	*NL*	*31*	*260*	*66*	*12*	*1*	*2*	*24*	*32*	*1*	*1*	*.254*	*.320*	*.332*	*-.166*	*.266*	*.327*	*.360*	*-.131*	*0.4*			

Breakout: 4%   Improve: 20%   Collapse: 46%

Signed in late August to back up the backups over the final 30 games, Loretta hurt himself again and couldn't finish the season. He would make a dandy utility infielder and emergency starter off the Houston bench, but with Jose Vizcaino under contract and laughably considered Loretta's equal by the Astros' brass, it's not getting serious consideration. A free agent, Loretta signed a one-year deal with San Diego, where he'll be their utility infielder.

Julio Lugo   SS   Born: 16-Nov-75   Age: 27   Bats: R   Throws: R

YEAR	TM	LG	AGE	AB	H	2B	3B	HR	BB	SO	SB	CS	AVG	OBP	SLG	MLVR	EQBA	EQOBP	EQSLG	EQMLVR	VORP	DEFENSE		
2000	NWO	PCL	24	101	33	4	1	3	11	20	12	7	.327	.393	.475	.224	.294	.345	.422	.004	6.0	17-2B 2		
2000	HOU	NL	24	420	119	22	5	10	37	93	22	9	.283	.347	.431	-.020	.277	.332	.424	-.031	20.7	54-SS -9	42-2B	-7
2001	HOU	NL	25	513	135	20	3	10	46	116	12	11	.263	.330	.372	-.114	.261	.325	.367	-.137	11.4	123-SS 1		
2002	HOU	NL	26	322	84	15	1	8	28	74	9	3	.261	.324	.388	-.047	.262	.320	.394	-.108	9.1	78-SS -13		
2003	*HOU*	*NL*	*27*	*391*	*101*	*19*	*3*	*9*	*36*	*82*	*12*	*5*	*.258*	*.324*	*.389*	*-.081*	*.257*	*.319*	*.391*	*-.111*	*5.2*			

Breakout: 8%   Improve: 33%   Collapse: 27%

They've never been happy with Lugo's glovework down in Houston, and his key errors in the 2001 NLDS were the last straw. It's not often the incumbent outplays the challengers in all phases of the game in spring training and loses his job, but it happened to Lugo last March. He got it back only after Everett couldn't toe the Mendoza Line. The Astros need to accept Lugo's shortcomings and recognize he's their best near-term solution at shortstop. Entering his age 27 season, he could surprise some people this year.

David Matranga   2B/SS   Born: 08-Jan-77   Age: 26   Bats: R   Throws: R

YEAR	TM	LG	AGE	AB	H	2B	3B	HR	BB	SO	SB	CS	AVG	OBP	SLG	MLVR	EQBA	EQOBP	EQSLG	EQMLVR	VORP	DEFENSE		
2000	ROU	TXS	23	373	87	14	3	6	48	99	5	5	.233	.347	.335	-.131	.201	.284	.291	-.358	-13.8	112-SS -2		
2001	ROU	TXS	24	387	117	34	2	10	45	91	17	7	.302	.395	.478	.239	.260	.334	.412	-.058	16.0	97-2B 17		
2002	NWO	PCL	25	300	82	15	3	7	27	79	7	2	.273	.345	.413	.045	.259	.321	.393	-.110	8.3	53-2B 5	14-SS	1
2003	*HOU*	*NL*	*26*	*146*	*35*	*8*	*1*	*3*	*14*	*36*	*3*	*2*	*.241*	*.316*	*.374*	*-.125*	*.239*	*.311*	*.377*	*-.156*	*-.1*			

Breakout: 20%   Improve: 38%   Collapse: 34%

There's no reason to shell out $2 million for a utility infielder when Matranga is just half a day's drive down I-10. He flashes good leather on either side of second base, pastes the ball into the gaps and can even run a little bit. Matranga bears a striking physical resemblance to Jeff Frye, and with slightly better plate discipline and an opportunity, could yet carve out a similar career.

Orlando Merced   OF/PH   Born: 02-Nov-66   Age: 36   Bats: L   Throws: R

YEAR	TM	LG	AGE	AB	H	2B	3B	HR	BB	SO	SB	CS	AVG	OBP	SLG	MLVR	EQBA	EQOBP	EQSLG	EQMLVR	VORP	DEFENSE	
2000	ORX	JPL	33	80	18	2	1	2	4	14	0	0	.225	.262	.350	-.240	.222	.241	.346	-.355	-4.3		
2000	NWO	PCL	33	67	18	4	0	1	2	4	0	1	.269	.290	.373	-.186	.254	.265	.343	-.292	-3.7	12-RF	1
2001	HOU	NL	34	137	36	6	1	6	14	32	5	1	.263	.336	.453	.005	.261	.332	.449	-.009	2.5	22-RF	-1
2002	HOU	NL	35	251	72	13	3	6	26	50	4	0	.287	.354	.434	.082	.287	.349	.441	.032	7.1	51-RF	1
2003	HOU	NL	36	175	45	8	1	4	17	35	3	1	.255	.320	.390	-.089	.253	.315	.392	-.120	-4.2		

Breakout: 8%   Improve: 42%   Collapse: 28%

Three years ago, Merced was in Japan trying to salvage a career that appeared to be over and Hidalgo was rocking NL pitching for 89 extra-base hits in what seemed to be a breakout year. Fast-forward two years to last July and Williams was giving Merced the bulk of the at-bats in a shortsighted right field platoon arrangement with Hidalgo. Merced jumped on his unexpected good fortune like a hanging curveball, negotiating a $1.7 million extension for 2003 before the balloon burst. Merced is a nice chess piece off the bench, but when he takes playing time away from younger players, the Astros are shooting themselves in the foot.

Colin Porter   OF   Born: 23-Nov-75   Age: 27   Bats: L   Throws: L

YEAR	TM	LG	AGE	AB	H	2B	3B	HR	BB	SO	SB	CS	AVG	OBP	SLG	MLVR	EQBA	EQOBP	EQSLG	EQMLVR	VORP	DEFENSE	
2000	ROU	TXS	24	435	119	25	5	14	56	130	17	9	.274	.364	.451	.090	.230	.298	.380	-.192	-1.5	112-CF	-1
2001	ROU	TXS	25	100	32	5	5	2	5	25	1	3	.320	.358	.530	.275	.260	.298	.440	-.085	2.4	25-CF	0
2001	NWO	PCL	25	312	74	14	1	7	34	105	11	6	.237	.318	.356	-.154	.218	.292	.329	-.281	-9.2	82-CF	-2
2002	NWO	PCL	26	461	122	30	5	6	46	127	28	7	.265	.331	.390	-.020	.249	.310	.369	-.171	-11.6	113-RF	-6
2003	HOU	NL	27	136	34	8	1	4	14	37	4	4	.250	.322	.401	-.075	.248	.317	.403	-.105	-2.6		

Breakout: 35%   Improve: 59%   Collapse: 23%

Porter is only a marginally better prospect than Gary Huckabay, but he's an example of an outfielder already in the Astros' system who would happily play for the major league minimum and bring the same skills off the bench as Hunter. When McLane bellyaches about losing money, remember there are people in the world making real sacrifices, like scraping by with a BAT VK-40 pre-amplifier instead of a Mark Levinson No. 32, while he has equal or better options available at less cost and management chooses to ignore them.

Todd Self   RF/1B   Born: 09-Nov-78   Age: 24   Bats: L   Throws: R

YEAR	TM	LG	AGE	AB	H	2B	3B	HR	BB	SO	SB	CS	AVG	OBP	SLG	MLVR	EQBA	EQOBP	EQSLG	EQMLVR	VORP	DEFENSE			
2000	AUB	NYP	21	160	31	3	1	1	28	42	10	4	.194	.328	.244	-.144	.149	.238	.190	-.609	-25.1	50-RF	-6		
2001	PTS	NYP	22	261	79	13	4	3	46	61	10	6	.303	.411	.418	.261	.222	.304	.312	-.278	-15.0	55-RF	-3		
2002	MIC	MDW	23	491	152	36	5	12	65	104	10	1	.310	.400	.477	.290	.238	.306	.373	-.181	-14.0	65-RF	2	52-1B	-2
2003	HOU	NL	24	189	47	10	2	5	20	45	3	4	.246	.322	.391	-.090	.244	.317	.394	-.120	-5.7				

Breakout: 45%   Improve: 66%   Collapse: 14%

Self makes the book after being named as an outfielder on the Low Class-A All-Star team. Having needed two years to escape the short-season New York-Penn League, the 15th-rounder out of the University of Louisiana-Monroe was easily the oldest player chosen to the squad. Since Self worked part-time at first base at Michigan, the Astros might just consider him organizational filler. If not, they need to push him hard up the ladder to see what they've got.

Henri Stanley   LF   Born: 15-Dec-77   Age: 25   Bats: L   Throws: L

YEAR	TM	LG	AGE	AB	H	2B	3B	HR	BB	SO	SB	CS	AVG	OBP	SLG	MLVR	EQBA	EQOBP	EQSLG	EQMLVR	VORP	DEFENSE	
2000	MAR	APL	22	165	41	8	6	4	25	37	10	4	.248	.351	.442	.131	.174	.242	.297	-.448	-16.6	44-OF	-6
2001	MIC	MDW	23	400	120	24	12	14	73	84	30	5	.300	.409	.525	.327	.220	.309	.382	-.175	.5	71-CF	-2
2002	ROU	TXS	24	456	143	36	10	16	72	85	14	9	.314	.412	.542	.382	.267	.350	.463	.047	17.0	92-LF	-6
2003	HOU	NL	25	206	54	12	2	7	27	45	5	3	.260	.346	.438	.023	.259	.341	.441	-.006	2.0		

Breakout: 22%   Improve: 52%   Collapse: 18%

Signed as a non-drafted free agent in 2000 after his senior year at Clemson, Stanley didn't even play every day in college. The only person who spotted something was Astros regional scout Brian Keegan, who signed him for $2,500. Two years later, Stanley was one of the best hitters in all of Double-A. It could be because of his age, but he still isn't getting many props as a prospect, either inside or outside the organization. Houston assigned Mike Hill to the AFL while Stanley stayed home, and Texas League managers didn't see fit to list him among the Top 20 prospects in the loop. He plays like a man possessed, his back-to-back seasons of double-digit triples due to running hard out of the box, not blazing speed. Besides his birth certificate, Stanley's only negative is a weak throwing arm, but if he keeps on hitting, that concern will vanish.

Jose Vizcaino INF Born: 26-Mar-68 Age: 35 Bats: B Throws: R

YEAR	TM	LG	AGE	AB	H	2B	3B	HR	BB	SO	SB	CS	AVG	OBP	SLG	MLVR	EQBA	EQOBP	EQSLG	EQMLVR	VORP	DEFENSE				
2000	LAD	NL	32	93	19	2	1	0	10	15	1	0	.204	.288	.247	-.425	.213	.288	.266	-.378	-4.1	14-SS	2			
2000	NYY	AL	32	174	48	8	1	0	12	28	5	7	.276	.323	.333	-.202	.287	.322	.351	-.147	2.9	44-2B	1			
2001	HOU	NL	33	256	71	8	3	1	15	33	3	2	.277	.322	.344	-.158	.275	.319	.345	-.170	3.3	37-SS	-2	12-2B	-3	
2002	HOU	NL	34	406	123	19	2	5	24	40	3	5	.303	.343	.397	.027	.302	.339	.400	-.032	19.0	47-SS	1	22-3B	2	
2003	HOU	NL	35	260	70	12	2	2	18	31	3	2	.270	.318	.354	-.130	.268	.313	.356	-.161	-.8					

Breakout: 6%   Improve: 36%   Collapse: 32%

Applying the same logic that caused Roger Peckinpaugh to be voted AL MVP in 1925, many in the Astros organization considered Vizcaino the MVP of last year's ball club. He did have the best year of his career, but still finished closer to replacement level than league average at shortstop. Vizcaino's veteran know-how isn't limited to on-field exploits—he was savvy enough to wring a $2 million extension for 2003 out of Hunsicker last August. For a team on a limited budget, signing an easily replaceable commodity for seven times the league minimum is a terrible misallocation of resources.

Daryle Ward LF Born: 27-Jun-75 Age: 28 Bats: L Throws: L

YEAR	TM	LG	AGE	AB	H	2B	3B	HR	BB	SO	SB	CS	AVG	OBP	SLG	MLVR	EQBA	EQOBP	EQSLG	EQMLVR	VORP	DEFENSE	
2000	HOU	NL	25	264	68	10	2	20	15	61	0	0	.258	.297	.538	.023	.256	.285	.530	.018	7.2	37-LF	-1
2001	HOU	NL	26	213	56	15	0	9	19	48	0	0	.263	.326	.460	-.001	.260	.323	.460	-.011	4.5	35-LF	-1
2002	HOU	NL	27	453	125	31	0	12	33	82	1	3	.276	.326	.424	.016	.276	.323	.429	-.041	5.4	89-LF	-2
2003	HOU	NL	28	349	94	20	1	15	28	69	1	2	.270	.325	.462	.027	.268	.320	.464	-.003	2.3		

Breakout: 19%   Improve: 54%   Collapse: 19%

Handed the starting left field job after years of waiting patiently, Heavy D didn't exactly put it in a hammerlock. Williams stuck with him longer than expected, primarily because Ward's defense was better than anybody thought possible and his work ethic was outstanding. With the Killer B's becoming less and less menacing, the Astros desperately need Ward to take up some of the slack. While he won't meet the once-lofty expectations, Ward should still do all right, establishing himself as a mirror image of Carlos Lee.

Tommy Whiteman SS Born: 14-Jul-79 Age: 23 Bats: R Throws: R

YEAR	TM	LG	AGE	AB	H	2B	3B	HR	BB	SO	SB	CS	AVG	OBP	SLG	MLVR	EQBA	EQOBP	EQSLG	EQMLVR	VORP	DEFENSE	
2000	AUB	NYP	20	232	58	10	3	1	22	52	7	5	.250	.318	.332	-.024	.188	.231	.255	-.522	-19.3	65-SS	-7
2001	LEX	SAL	21	389	124	26	8	18	34	106	17	13	.319	.384	.566	.404	.242	.292	.425	-.132	8.7	110-SS	-5
2002	ROU	TXS	22	56	10	2	1	0	4	17	1	1	.179	.246	.250	-.357	.158	.207	.246	-.597	-5.4	14-SS	-6
2002	LEX	SAL	22	350	106	29	2	10	36	66	6	6	.303	.376	.483	.262	.228	.282	.370	-.238	-1.8	83-SS	6
2003	HOU	NL	23	171	43	10	1	5	15	40	3	3	.249	.313	.404	-.087	.247	.308	.406	-.117	1.6		

Breakout: 47%   Improve: 69%   Collapse: 11%

Despite an All-Star season with Lexington in 2001, Whiteman returned for most of last season, the victim of a double whammy of having no High-A affiliate and the domino effect caused by Everett's demotion to New Orleans. His output actually dipped slightly, although he did improve his plate discipline. Whiteman's power intrigues the organization and he boosted his star with a tremendous showing in the AFL. Defensively, Whiteman is graceful and has good actions for a shortstop, even though he is Ripken-sized. He'll open as Burke's double play partner in the Texas League, a season that will go a long way toward determining if he can eventually replace Lugo.

Gregg Zaun C Born: 14-Apr-71 Age: 32 Bats: B Throws: R

YEAR	TM	LG	AGE	AB	H	2B	3B	HR	BB	SO	SB	CS	AVG	OBP	SLG	MLVR	EQBA	EQOBP	EQSLG	EQMLVR	VORP	DEFENSE	
2000	KCR	AL	29	234	64	11	0	7	43	34	7	3	.274	.393	.410	.013	.271	.386	.410	.044	17.4	66-C	-5
2001	KCR	AL	30	125	40	9	0	6	12	16	1	2	.320	.380	.536	.252	.328	.387	.552	.297	17.4	31-C	-2
2002	HOU	NL	31	185	41	7	1	3	12	36	1	0	.222	.276	.319	-.244	.225	.274	.332	-.309	-3.4	40-C	-8
2003	HOU	NL	32	162	41	8	1	4	17	27	2	1	.251	.326	.387	-.085	.249	.321	.390	-.115	2.4		

Breakout: 24%   Improve: 44%   Collapse: 30%

The Practically Perfect Backup Catcher was anything but in 2002. Zaun hit poorly, threw out only 11% of would-be base thieves and had a lousy CERA, thanks to being Dave Mlicki's personal catcher. It wasn't until after the season that he revealed he had been playing with a torn flexor tendon in his right elbow. The Astros' player rep, Zaun drew McLane's ire when he made disparaging remarks about the questionable accounting practices of MLB owners. Hunsicker wants to unload the last year of his contract, which is too bad since Zaun would outproduce Ausmus at 20% the cost.

Alan Zinter — 1B/C — Born: 19-May-68 — Age: 35 — Bats: B — Throws: R

YEAR	TM	LG	AGE	AB	H	2B	3B	HR	BB	SO	SB	CS	AVG	OBP	SLG	MLVR	EQBA	EQOBP	EQSLG	EQMLVR	VORP	DEFENSE	
2000	IOW	PCL	32	233	53	12	2	14	39	78	0	0	.227	.343	.476	.003	.201	.298	.419	-.159	-4.2	34-1B -5	11-C -4
2001	NWO	PCL	33	332	88	16	0	19	33	85	1	1	.265	.337	.485	.087	.244	.312	.443	-.068	2.6	48-1B -11	17-C -5
2002	NWO	PCL	34	225	52	14	0	11	22	64	2	0	.231	.300	.440	-.035	.218	.278	.415	-.190	-5.5	58-1B 7	
2002	HOU	NL	34	44	6	2	0	2	0	19	0	0	.136	.136	.318	-.537	.136	.136	.341	-.620	-5.0		
2003	HOU	NL	35	94	21	4	0	4	10	28	1	1	.223	.304	.418	-.101	.222	.299	.421	-.132	-2.3		

Breakout: 32%   Improve: 56%   Collapse: 30%

The critics are unanimous! Of Zinter's major league debut after 13 years in the minors, the *Youngstown Vindicator* wrote, "It's the feel-good story of the year!" On becoming the oldest position player in 40 years to hit his first home run in The Show, the *Amarillo Globe News* raved, "Smashing! A rollicking roller coaster of a career!" However, after watching the infrequent, abbreviated performances for three months, the Astros' review wasn't as positive and they outrighted Zinter back to Triple-A last October.

PITCHERS

Jimmy Barrett — Born: 07-Jun-81 — Age: 22 — Bats: R — Throws: R

YEAR	TM	LG	AGE	G	GS	IP	H	BB	SO	HR	ERA	EQERA	EQH9	EQBB9	EQSO9	EQHR9	PERA	VORP	STF
2000	MAR	APL	19	13	13	66.7	60	32	72	4	4.72	6.94	13.0	6.6	5.3	1.7	7.18	-10.6	-6
2001	MIC	MDW	20	27	25	130.7	122	62	98	12	4.48	6.58	11.9	6.4	4.4	2.0	6.41	-15.7	-13
2002	LEX	SAL	21	27	22	134.3	112	40	131	13	2.81	5.69	12.5	4.0	5.8	2.5	5.16	-2.9	2

While the Astros focus on drafting collegians, occasionally they'll use an early selection on a high school arm they can't resist. The club's third round pick in 1999, Barrett has moved gradually as the coaches worked on refining his mechanics and slowing down his delivery. Last year he turned the corner, showing vastly improved command of a 90-mph fastball, sweeping curve and functional changeup. Barrett is at least a year and a half from debuting in Houston, but was added to the 40-man roster as a precaution since the team has lost talents like Johan Santana and Felix Escalona out of Low-A ball in recent Rule 5 drafts.

Pedro Borbon — Born: 15-Nov-67 — Age: 35 — Bats: L — Throws: L

YEAR	TM	LG	AGE	G	GS	IP	H	BB	SO	HR	ERA	EQERA	EQH9	EQBB9	EQSO9	EQHR9	PERA	VORP	STF
2000	TOR	AL	32	59	0	41.7	45	38	29	5	6.47	5.93	8.5	6.3	5.8	0.9	5.66	-2.5	-19
2001	TOR	AL	33	71	0	53.3	48	12	45	8	3.71	3.64	7.9	1.9	7.2	1.2	3.47	10.3	5
2002	TOR	AL	34	16	0	12.7	12	6	11	3	4.96	5.06	8.2	4.0	7.6	1.9	5.05	0.5	-5
2002	HOU	NL	34	56	0	37.7	41	19	39	7	5.49	5.57	9.7	4.0	8.0	1.6	5.68	-0.8	-2
2003	LAD	NL	35	60	0	41.0	38	21	40	5	4.07	4.72	8.9	3.9	7.6	1.1	4.73	5.4	-1

Breakout: 14%   Improve: 50%   Collapse: 21%

The prototypical one-batter southpaw, Borbon is good at his job, but makes the average right-hander look like Albert Pujols (.308/.404/.561 since 1999). True specialists are unaffordable luxuries in a Jimy Williams bullpen, where all hands are worked to the bone. A free agent, Borbon might have been okay in the American League, but he's made his way back to L.A.

Nelson Cruz — Born: 13-Sep-72 — Age: 30 — Bats: R — Throws: R

YEAR	TM	LG	AGE	G	GS	IP	H	BB	SO	HR	ERA	EQERA	EQH9	EQBB9	EQSO9	EQHR9	PERA	VORP	STF
2000	TOL	INT	27	11	10	52.3	54	17	39	9	4.82	5.44	9.7	2.9	5.7	1.9	5.42	0.4	-2
2000	DET	AL	27	27	0	41.0	39	13	34	4	3.07	2.90	8.0	2.3	7.2	0.7	3.37	11.3	10
2001	HOU	NL	28	66	0	82.3	72	24	75	11	4.16	3.92	7.9	2.4	7.0	1.1	3.61	13.4	4
2002	HOU	NL	29	43	5	78.3	90	29	61	12	4.48	5.09	10.5	3.0	6.1	1.4	5.37	2.8	-5
2003	COL	NL	30	40	7	70.3	81	27	52	13	5.4	4.69	9.9	2.9	6.3	1.3	4.72	8.3	-3

Breakout: 17%   Improve: 41%   Collapse: 27%

Cruz pitched through shoulder fatigue last April, leading to some hideous early-season lines and obscuring the fact that he was essentially the same pitcher he had been in 2001. He fell out of the team's good graces by grousing about his usage patterns, which qualifies as a mutinous act in Astroland. Cruz received the death sentence when he was traded to the Rockies last December.

Octavio Dotel						**Born: 25-Nov-73**				**Age: 29**		**Bats: R**		**Throws: R**			
YEAR	TM	LG	AGE	G	GS	IP	H	BB	SO	HR	ERA	EQERA	EQH9	EQBB9	EQSO9	EQHR9	PERA	VORP	STF
2000	HOU	NL	26	50	16	125.0	127	61	142	26	5.40	4.95	8.5	3.5	8.8	1.6	5.16	7.0	10
2001	HOU	NL	27	61	4	105.0	79	47	145	5	2.66	2.92	6.9	3.7	10.5	0.4	2.92	29.0	29
2002	HOU	NL	28	83	0	97.3	58	27	118	7	1.85	2.02	5.4	2.2	9.5	0.6	2.05	36.3	27
2003	HOU	NL	29	65	0	84.7	67	32	96	9	3.02	3.07	7.2	3.0	9.2	0.9	3.23	22.5	19

Breakout: 17%   Improve: 43%   Collapse: 22%

Quite simply, Dotel is the best relief pitcher in the game today. Besides having a nearly unhittable arsenal, he has shown the ability to toss multi-innings stints and work for days on end. This begs the question of why a team searching for a starting pitcher steadfastly refuses to consider sliding him into the rotation. Regardless of the metric and weighting system used, you can't demonstrate that 100 innings at the end of the game are as valuable as 200 at the beginning. They are as physically taxing, though, which together with Dotel's new older age indicates that he could shoulder the changed workload. While relievers are fungible, quality starting pitchers aren't. Derek Lowe's success last year didn't flip the switch on many lightbulbs, so Dotel's impersonation of 1996 Mariano Rivera will continue until the age of enlightenment arrives.

Tom Gordon						**Born: 18-Nov-67**				**Age: 35**		**Bats: R**		**Throws: R**			
YEAR	TM	LG	AGE	G	GS	IP	H	BB	SO	HR	ERA	EQERA	EQH9	EQBB9	EQSO9	EQHR9	PERA	VORP	STF
2001	CHC	NL	33	47	0	45.3	32	16	67	4	3.38	3.08	6.3	2.9	11.2	0.7	2.84	11.6	31
2002	CHC	NL	34	19	0	23.7	27	10	31	1	3.42	4.57	10.2	3.3	10.1	0.4	5.04	2.1	21
2002	HOU	NL	34	15	0	19.0	15	6	17	2	3.32	3.18	7.2	2.5	7.1	0.9	3.13	4.6	7
2003	CWS	AL	35	47	0	55.0	50	24	57	5	3.57	3.47	8.1	3.6	8.9	0.7	3.53	16.4	15

Breakout: 19%   Improve: 51%   Collapse: 17%

Gordon was reunited with Williams in a late-August deal whose main function was to briefly grab the attention of local sports fans, since the young pitchers surrendered to the Cubs have a better chance of haunting the Astros than Gordon did of being the difference in catching St. Louis. Although he finished the season on the active list for the first time since 1999, the status of his right arm remains a major question. The fact that Gordon wants to close precluded a return to Houston, but by signing him to a contract heavy on incentives, the White Sox could still be richly rewarded.

Carlos Hernandez						**Born: 22-Apr-80**				**Age: 23**		**Bats: B**		**Throws: L**			
YEAR	TM	LG	AGE	G	GS	IP	H	BB	SO	HR	ERA	EQERA	EQH9	EQBB9	EQSO9	EQHR9	PERA	VORP	STF
2000	MIC	MDW	20	22	22	110.7	92	63	115	8	3.82	6.54	11.6	6.5	6.1	1.8	6.00	-12.7	0
2001	ROU	TXS	21	24	23	139.0	115	69	167	11	3.69	5.06	9.5	5.6	7.9	1.2	4.89	6.8	21
2001	HOU	NL	21	3	3	17.7	11	7	17	1	1.02	1.59	5.7	3.3	7.4	0.4	2.32	7.7	34
2002	HOU	NL	22	23	21	111.0	112	61	93	11	4.38	4.58	9.1	4.3	6.5	0.9	4.81	11.4	13
2003	HOU	NL	23	20	16	102.3	106	60	93	13	5.11	5.20	9.4	4.5	7.4	1.1	5.24	7.5	9

Breakout: 13%   Improve: 38%   Collapse: 26%

Last year's handling of Hernandez can charitably be referred to as "tough love." After partially tearing his rotator cuff in a baserunning mishap late in 2001, Hernandez admitted not being 100% in spring training, but opened the campaign in the rotation anyway. He pitched hurt all season, sidelined three times with shoulder problems before being diagnosed with nerve impingement and rotator cuff tendonitis. When healthy, there might not be a young southpaw in the league with Hernandez's combination of stuff, poise, and mound presence. As their lone left-handed starter, the Astros desperately want Hernandez in the rotation, but his arm is ticking. As we went to press, Hernandez was due to see Dr. James Andrews after shoulder MRIs showed a suspected rotator cuff tear. While the good doctor and his peers have made great progress in treating elbow injuries, this type of shoulder injury could deal a crushing blow to Hernandez's otherwise promising career.

Brad Lidge Born: 23-Dec-76 Age: 26 Bats: R Throws: R

YEAR	TM	LG	AGE	G	GS	IP	H	BB	SO	HR	ERA	EQERA	EQH9	EQBB9	EQSO9	EQHR9	PERA	VORP	STF
2000	KIS	FSL	23	8	8	41.7	28	15	46	3	2.81	3.81	8.1	4.1	7.0	1.6	3.85	7.9	14
2001	ROU	TXS	24	5	5	26.0	21	7	42	1	1.73	2.97	8.8	3.0	10.3	0.6	3.59	7.3	42
2002	ROU	TXS	25	5	0	11.0	9	3	18	0	2.45	3.82	8.4	2.8	10.9	0.3	3.52	1.9	35
2002	NWO	PCL	25	24	19	111.7	83	47	110	9	3.38	4.61	8.7	4.6	7.1	1.0	3.88	11.0	10
2002	HOU	NL	25	6	1	8.7	12	9	12	0	6.21	6.62	12.2	8.0	10.6	0.2	7.39	-1.2	8
2003	HOU	NL	26	17	11	75.0	70	37	71	8	4.09	4.16	8.5	3.8	7.6	0.9	4.38	11.4	14

Breakout: 20%   *Improve: 52%*   *Collapse: 20%*

If you've ever owned a Jaguar XKE with the V-12, you understand the hope and despair associated with a cranky, high-performance piece of machinery. The organization coddled Lidge through 131.1 innings last year, a total that exceeded his previous four professional seasons combined. Lidge's extreme brittleness prevents him from carrying a starter's workload or recovering quickly enough to survive Williams's typical reliever usage. It's worth creating a unique role for his hard fastball and untouchable slider: regularly scheduled multi-inning relief appearances. Lidge could prepare for them like a start and they also would give his overworked bullpen mates needed days off. Don't bet on it happening.

Wade Miller Born: 13-Sep-76 Age: 26 Bats: R Throws: R

YEAR	TM	LG	AGE	G	GS	IP	H	BB	SO	HR	ERA	EQERA	EQH9	EQBB9	EQSO9	EQHR9	PERA	VORP	STF
2000	NWO	PCL	23	16	15	105.3	95	38	81	6	3.68	4.17	9.3	3.3	5.7	0.7	4.16	15.6	14
2000	HOU	NL	23	16	16	105.0	104	42	89	14	5.14	4.40	8.5	2.9	6.7	1.0	4.26	12.9	19
2001	HOU	NL	24	32	32	212.0	183	76	183	31	3.40	3.77	7.8	3.0	6.6	1.2	3.84	40.9	18
2002	HOU	NL	25	26	26	164.7	151	62	144	14	3.28	3.54	8.3	3.0	6.9	0.8	3.75	36.0	20
2003	HOU	NL	26	26	25	160.7	155	60	136	18	4.02	4.10	8.7	2.9	6.8	0.9	4.11	26.1	17

Breakout: 16%   *Improve: 50%*   *Collapse: 17%*

Miller didn't get rolling until June because of a pinched nerve in his neck, but still finished in the NL top 10 in Support-Neutral W/L. He comes at batters with a heavy, mid-90s two-seamer, mixing it with a curve and slider, either of which are good enough to be out pitches. The icing on the cake is that he's never been sidelined with arm problems. The time has come for Hunsicker to get Miller's signature on a long-term contract, because guaranteed money is going to be lighter on McLane's wallet than taking him to arbitration the next three years.

Dave Mlicki Born: 08-Jun-68 Age: 35 Bats: R Throws: R

YEAR	TM	LG	AGE	G	GS	IP	H	BB	SO	HR	ERA	EQERA	EQH9	EQBB9	EQSO9	EQHR9	PERA	VORP	STF
2000	DET	AL	32	24	21	119.3	143	44	57	17	5.58	4.92	10.1	2.7	4.2	1.1	5.02	7.7	-4
2001	DET	AL	33	15	15	81.0	118	41	48	19	7.33	7.32	12.6	4.2	5.0	1.9	7.94	-16.3	-14
2001	HOU	NL	33	19	14	86.7	85	33	49	18	5.09	5.08	8.8	3.2	4.3	1.7	4.96	4.0	-9
2002	HOU	NL	34	22	16	86.0	101	34	57	11	5.34	5.53	10.7	3.2	5.2	1.1	5.40	-0.4	-4
2003	MIL	NL	35	21	13	80.0	89	32	52	11	4.97	5.40	10.3	3.1	5.1	1.2	5.31	2.8	-6

Breakout: 12%   *Improve: 49%*   *Collapse: 22%*

The best thing about Mlicki's 2002 season was that when it was over, the Astros could take his $6.2 million salary off the books. Mlicki actually had decent stuff early in his career, but has decayed into a junkballer with spotty control, as gruesome a twosome as Michael Jackson and Lisa Marie Presley. Any team that signs him has no clue what they're doing, which makes Kansas City or Milwaukee likely destinations. Bingo.

Peter Munro Born: 14-Jun-75 Age: 28 Bats: R Throws: R

YEAR	TM	LG	AGE	G	GS	IP	H	BB	SO	HR	ERA	EQERA	EQH9	EQBB9	EQSO9	EQHR9	PERA	VORP	STF
2000	SYR	INT	25	10	10	61.7	52	25	45	1	2.48	3.55	8.8	3.7	5.7	0.2	3.34	13.4	14
2000	TOR	AL	25	9	3	25.7	38	16	16	1	5.95	6.08	11.9	4.4	5.2	0.3	6.21	-1.8	-7
2000	OKL	PCL	25	5	5	31.0	27	14	15	3	4.65	4.42	8.5	4.1	3.6	1.1	4.31	3.7	-6
2001	OKL	PCL	26	33	8	88.7	89	43	73	12	4.67	5.59	10.2	5.3	5.5	1.5	5.70	-1.5	-15
2002	NWO	PCL	27	19	13	94.3	68	15	73	3	2.39	3.43	8.4	1.7	5.6	0.4	2.64	21.6	14
2002	HOU	NL	27	19	14	80.7	89	23	45	5	3.57	4.10	10.2	2.3	4.5	0.6	4.25	12.5	0
2003	HOU	NL	28	20	14	87.7	98	34	57	10	4.56	4.64	10.1	3.0	5.2	1.0	4.78	10.1	0

Breakout: 10%   *Improve: 36%*   *Collapse: 24%*

Just when Munro was getting to know every groundskeeper in Triple-A on a first-name basis, he gained control of his curveball and cut his walk rate nearly in half. Credit Hunsicker for not pulling another Mlicki-sized boner when Houston needed a starter at the All-Star break, instead recalling Munro from New Orleans. Job security will be tough to come by after leaving five mph on the operating table in 1999, but Munro is very capable of filling Cruz's role in the bullpen and supplying the Astros with 110 sturdy innings as a spot starter and long reliever.

Roy Oswalt   Born: 29-Aug-77   Age: 25   Bats: R   Throws: R

YEAR	TM	LG	AGE	G	GS	IP	H	BB	SO	HR	ERA	EQERA	EQH9	EQBB9	EQSO9	EQHR9	PERA	VORP	STF
2000	KIS	FSL	22	8	8	45.3	52	11	47	1	2.98	4.77	12.5	2.7	6.5	0.5	6.14	3.7	19
2000	ROU	TXS	22	19	18	129.7	106	22	141	5	1.94	3.23	9.0	1.6	7.2	0.6	3.08	32.8	32
2001	NWO	PCL	23	5	5	31.0	32	6	34	4	4.35	5.30	10.9	2.1	7.4	1.5	5.13	0.7	22
2001	HOU	NL	23	28	20	141.7	126	24	144	13	2.73	3.01	8.2	1.4	7.8	0.7	3.07	39.1	32
2002	HOU	NL	24	35	34	233.0	215	62	208	17	3.01	3.32	8.4	2.1	7.1	0.7	3.39	56.5	26
2003	HOU	NL	25	34	32	212.3	205	57	189	21	3.54	3.60	8.8	2.1	7.2	0.8	3.59	47.6	23

Breakout: 21%   *Improve: 51%*   *Collapse: 17%*

Let's see. An explosive 95-mph fastball that he can make sink or ride. A curveball thrown from the same arm slot with 20 mph of separation that drops three feet. Maddux-like command. Absolutely fearless and loves to pitch inside. Cuts a huge mound presence despite his small size. Sounds a lot like Pedro Martinez, and it's not an overstatement to compare Oswalt to him. The only thing that could stand between Oswalt and future Cy Young awards is injury. Williams managed Pedro in Boston, learned his lesson and did a good job protecting his latest ace until a vain September push to secure win number 20. The Astros' pennant hopes are directly tied to Oswalt's health.

Tony Pluta   Born: 28-Oct-82   Age: 20   Bats: R   Throws: R

YEAR	TM	LG	AGE	G	GS	IP	H	BB	SO	HR	ERA	EQERA	EQH9	EQBB9	EQSO9	EQHR9	PERA	VORP	STF
2001	LEX	SAL	18	26	26	132.3	107	86	138	7	3.20	6.61	12.2	9.7	5.9	1.3	6.77	-16.2	-8
2002	MIC	MDW	19	28	28	143.0	155	83	120	18	5.92	9.27	17.0	8.3	5.4	3.6	8.71	-59.8	-21

After a marvelous debut in 2001, logic said that Pluta would dominate the Midwest League following a lateral move to Michigan. Umm...no. It's not unusual for a young hurler's command of the curveball to come and go, but Pluta pretty much lost the feel for it all season. A one-pitch starter is as effective as a one-armed paperhanger, and the repeated beatings caused Pluta to lose confidence. Mark it down as another one of the hazards attached to high school pitchers. Pluta has an extremely high ceiling, but right now he's a mess. It will be interesting to see what approach the Astros use to try to return him from the brink.

Brandon Puffer   Born: 05-Oct-75   Age: 27   Bats: R   Throws: R

YEAR	TM	LG	AGE	G	GS	IP	H	BB	SO	HR	ERA	EQERA	EQH9	EQBB9	EQSO9	EQHR9	PERA	VORP	STF
2000	ASH	SAL	24	14	0	14.3	19	11	15	3	8.18	11.99	19.3	10.5	6.1	5.3	11.58	-10.5	-62
2000	KIS	FSL	24	18	0	21.3	18	11	26	0	1.27	3.97	9.1	5.8	7.6	0.3	4.92	3.3	2
2001	ROU	TXS	25	56	0	82.7	52	35	91	4	2.07	3.10	7.1	4.7	7.2	0.8	3.23	21.0	3
2002	NWO	PCL	26	11	0	15.0	8	4	13	1	1.80	2.58	6.3	2.8	6.2	0.8	2.28	4.7	2
2002	HOU	NL	26	55	0	69.0	67	38	48	3	4.43	4.42	8.8	4.4	5.5	0.4	4.24	7.4	-8
2003	HOU	NL	27	36	2	49.3	52	26	38	6	4.97	5.06	9.6	4.1	6.1	0.9	5.06	3.7	-8

Breakout: 16%   *Improve: 37%*   *Collapse: 32%*

It's hard not to pull for an Indy league refugee who rode buses for eight years and completely revamped his delivery to reach The Show. Right-handed batters struggled with Puffer's sidearm motion (.234/.289/.309), but he steered clear of lefties, walking 27 of the 100 that he faced. While teams have grown to accept and even embrace lopsided platoon splits from southpaws, most haven't followed suit with northpaws. Puffer will be on the bubble this spring; improved command of his changeup would help his chances immensely.

Chad Qualls — Born: 17-Aug-78 — Age: 24 — Bats: R — Throws: R

YEAR	TM	LG	AGE	G	GS	IP	H	BB	SO	HR	ERA	EQERA	EQH9	EQBB9	EQSO9	EQHR9	PERA	VORP	STF
2001	MIC	MDW	22	26	26	162.0	149	31	125	8	3.72	5.07	10.9	2.5	4.3	1.0	4.62	7.8	5
2002	ROU	TXS	23	29	29	163.0	174	67	142	9	4.36	6.16	11.8	4.5	6.1	1.0	6.12	-11.9	6

Qualls discovered that while just having a low-90s sinker and brutal slider in your holster is enough to scare off Low-A hitters, your bullets have to find the target to succeed in Double-A. Even though he fired 163 high-pitch innings during the regular season, the Astros sent him to the AFL because they wanted to further etch his new smoothed-out delivery into his muscle memory. Qualls should get at least a cup of coffee this year, probably in the bullpen, where his lack of a reliable off-speed pitch is less likely to cause harm.

Santiago Ramirez — Born: 15-Aug-78 — Age: 24 — Bats: R — Throws: R

YEAR	TM	LG	AGE	G	GS	IP	H	BB	SO	HR	ERA	EQERA	EQH9	EQBB9	EQSO9	EQHR9	PERA	VORP	STF
2000	AUB	NYP	21	20	9	53.0	36	39	57	3	4.25	7.23	10.6	9.6	5.8	2.4	6.22	-10.4	-21
2000	MIC	MDW	21	23	0	29.7	27	32	22	6	6.06	11.35	15.5	13.5	4.8	5.4	10.44	-19.7	-63
2001	LEX	SAL	22	45	0	79.3	69	28	85	2	3.63	6.40	12.1	5.0	5.7	0.6	5.51	-9.0	-7
2002	ROU	TXS	23	33	0	63.3	45	26	73	3	2.56	3.63	7.8	4.4	7.9	0.9	3.79	12.3	12
2002	NWO	PCL	23	18	0	21.3	17	11	15	2	3.38	4.78	9.6	5.7	5.2	1.2	4.63	1.4	-14
2003	*HOU*	*NL*	*24*	*14*	*2*	*27.0*	*28*	*17*	*26*	*4*	*5.54*	*5.63*	*9.3*	*4.9*	*7.7*	*1.1*	*5.40*	*0.5*	*-1*

Breakout: 24%   Improve: 49%   Collapse: 14%

Ramirez and sidekick Miguel Saladin, products of the Astros' Dominican program, were discovered to be older than listed last year. Although Saladin did most of the closing at Round Rock, his prospect sheen is almost gone since he is pushing 30. Ramirez has the more promising future, especially after the diminutive right-hander learned to tame his big breaking slider, adding a pitch with a wrinkle to his live fastball and changeup mix. Both pitchers were placed on the 40-man roster after the season, and either could secure a spot in the bullpen with a lights-out spring.

Tim Redding — Born: 12-Feb-78 — Age: 25 — Bats: R — Throws: R

YEAR	TM	LG	AGE	G	GS	IP	H	BB	SO	HR	ERA	EQERA	EQH9	EQBB9	EQSO9	EQHR9	PERA	VORP	STF
2000	KIS	FSL	22	24	24	154.7	125	57	170	5	2.68	4.42	9.0	4.2	6.9	0.7	4.41	18.6	20
2000	ROU	TXS	22	5	5	26.0	14	22	22	4	3.46	4.97	6.6	8.1	5.6	2.2	4.73	1.5	-7
2001	ROU	TXS	23	14	14	90.7	64	25	113	5	2.18	3.41	7.9	3.1	8.0	0.9	3.20	21.1	31
2001	NWO	PCL	23	6	6	37.7	22	19	42	4	4.54	4.49	6.2	5.5	7.4	1.2	3.44	4.3	18
2001	HOU	NL	23	13	9	55.7	62	24	55	11	5.49	5.74	10.0	3.6	7.5	1.6	5.69	-1.6	12
2002	HOU	NL	24	18	14	73.3	78	35	63	10	5.40	5.41	9.6	3.8	6.7	1.2	5.13	0.7	7
2002	NWO	PCL	24	11	7	38.0	32	13	50	6	5.21	5.83	9.8	3.7	9.4	2.0	4.77	-1.5	18
2003	*HOU*	*NL*	*25*	*22*	*16*	*107.0*	*102*	*51*	*100*	*13*	*4.54*	*4.62*	*8.6*	*3.7*	*7.5*	*1.0*	*4.44*	*11.3*	*13*

Breakout: 19%   Improve: 53%   Collapse: 20%

Redding fluctuates between dominant and dreadful, with little time in between. All of his problems stem from inconsistent command of a darting, mid-90s fastball. It's unclear if his lack of a September recall was due to rotator cuff tendonitis or because the organization has grown frustrated with him. Redding's fly-ball tendencies, Minute Maid Park, and the Astros' lumbering outfielders are a poor combination. He could blossom with a change of scenery, although Hunsicker probably wouldn't get equal value in return.

Shane Reynolds — Born: 26-Mar-68 — Age: 35 — Bats: R — Throws: R

YEAR	TM	LG	AGE	G	GS	IP	H	BB	SO	HR	ERA	EQERA	EQH9	EQBB9	EQSO9	EQHR9	PERA	VORP	STF
2000	HOU	NL	32	22	22	131.0	150	45	93	20	5.22	4.89	9.9	2.5	5.6	1.2	5.02	9.0	6
2001	HOU	NL	33	28	28	182.7	208	36	102	24	4.33	4.55	10.5	1.7	4.3	1.1	4.66	19.4	3
2002	HOU	NL	34	13	13	74.0	80	26	47	13	4.86	5.07	9.9	2.8	5.0	1.6	5.15	3.6	0
2003	*HOU*	*NL*	*35*	*18*	*15*	*93.7*	*105*	*30*	*60*	*13*	*4.72*	*4.80*	*10.2*	*2.5*	*5.1*	*1.2*	*4.80*	*9.5*	*2*

Breakout: 11%   Improve: 43%   Collapse: 22%

Reynolds's decline traces back to 2000, when a degenerative disc problem deteriorated to where he began receiving an epidural before each start. Facing permanent nerve damage, he finally had surgery last June. Back surgery isn't the kiss of death it once was, especially with a fitness freak like Reynolds. The Astros chose not to pick up his option for this season, and instead signed him to an incentive-laden, one-year contract. A return to his 1999 form is not out of the question.

Jeriome Robertson   Born: 30-Mar-77   Age: 26   Bats: L   Throws: L

YEAR	TM	LG	AGE	G	GS	IP	H	BB	SO	HR	ERA	EQERA	EQH9	EQBB9	EQSO9	EQHR9	PERA	VORP	STF
2000	KIS	FSL	23	5	5	29.0	28	5	13	1	4.66	5.72	10.8	2.0	2.8	0.8	4.73	-0.7	-4
2000	ROU	TXS	23	11	10	61.0	62	18	30	8	4.13	6.12	12.0	2.9	3.4	2.0	5.51	-4.2	-10
2000	NWO	PCL	23	9	9	49.7	64	23	27	10	7.06	8.12	13.9	4.3	4.1	2.5	8.26	-14.4	-17
2001	ROU	TXS	24	57	0	73.7	89	21	72	10	3.91	6.22	14.1	3.3	6.5	2.2	7.17	-6.9	-10
2002	NWO	PCL	25	27	27	180.0	160	45	114	13	2.55	4.28	10.5	2.7	4.6	0.9	4.09	24.5	5
2002	HOU	NL	25	11	1	9.7	13	5	6	4	6.49	7.83	12.2	4.1	4.9	3.7	8.69	-2.6	-36
2003	*HOU*	*NL*	*26*	*14*	*10*	*58.7*	*69*	*25*	*39*	*8*	*5.40*	*5.50*	*10.6*	*3.2*	*5.3*	*1.2*	*5.38*	*2.2*	*-4*

Breakout: 13%   Improve: 46%   Collapse: 19%

Returned to the rotation after a year of working out of the bullpen, Robertson ended up being voted the Most Valuable Pitcher in the PCL. The University of Washington product is all about command, yielding more than three walks per nine innings only once since Houston picked him in the 24th round in 1995. One of the Astros' few lefties, Robertson will be first in line for a starting audition in Kissimmee if Hernandez isn't ready to go, but it says here that his success is a figment of pitcher-friendly Zephyr Field (2.1 runs per game allowed at home versus 4.1 on the road).

Rodrigo Rosario   Born: 14-Dec-77   Age: 25   Bats: R   Throws: R

YEAR	TM	LG	AGE	G	GS	IP	H	BB	SO	HR	ERA	EQERA	EQH9	EQBB9	EQSO9	EQHR9	PERA	VORP	STF
2000	AUB	NYP	22	14	14	75.7	67	32	67	3	3.45	6.25	12.6	5.4	4.7	1.7	6.17	-6.3	-6
2001	LEX	SAL	23	30	21	147.0	105	36	131	8	2.14	4.85	10.4	3.5	4.7	1.3	4.21	10.4	0
2002	ROU	TXS	24	26	23	130.3	106	59	94	5	3.11	4.64	8.9	4.9	5.0	0.7	4.50	12.4	0
2003	*HOU*	*NL*	*25*	*14*	*9*	*57.3*	*65*	*32*	*39*	*7*	*5.35*	*5.45*	*10.3*	*4.3*	*5.5*	*1.0*	*5.45*	*2.4*	*-5*

Breakout: 18%   Improve: 50%   Collapse: 22%

You could have flipped a coin over Rosario or Kirk Saarloos being Round Rock's best starter through the end of last May. From that point on, Saarloos continued to dominate while Rosario's numbers plummeted. Rosario posted a 4.15 ERA over his final 75 innings, with a significant increase in walks and decrease in strikeouts. Arm pain caused the struggles, though nothing turned up when Houston's team physician examined him in mid-July. The Astros claim he is now 100% healthy. If that's true, Rosario should quickly re-establish himself in New Orleans, as he has filthy stuff, keeps the ball down, and knows how to pitch.

Kirk Saarloos   Born: 23-May-79   Age: 24   Bats: R   Throws: R

YEAR	TM	LG	AGE	G	GS	IP	H	BB	SO	HR	ERA	EQERA	EQH9	EQBB9	EQSO9	EQHR9	PERA	VORP	STF
2001	LEX	SAL	22	22	0	30.7	18	7	40	1	1.17	3.10	8.1	3.1	6.7	0.7	3.09	7.8	8
2002	ROU	TXS	23	13	13	83.3	48	21	82	1	1.40	2.41	6.0	2.7	6.7	0.2	2.36	28.6	28
2002	NWO	PCL	23	4	2	16.0	12	2	19	1	2.25	3.14	8.5	1.3	8.4	0.8	2.85	4.1	32
2002	HOU	NL	23	17	17	85.3	100	27	54	12	6.01	5.56	10.7	2.5	5.0	1.3	5.25	-0.5	3
2003	*HOU*	*NL*	*24*	*23*	*18*	*111.7*	*115*	*41*	*88*	*14*	*4.52*	*4.60*	*9.3*	*2.8*	*6.3*	*1.1*	*4.44*	*13.8*	*8*

Breakout: 8%   Improve: 36%   Collapse: 34%

Dazzle your etymologist friends with this nugget: Saarloos is the first player in big league history to have a pair of double vowels in his last name. Even cooler is that he shows signs of becoming a fixture in Houston's rotation. Saarloos moved out of the bullpen last year and shot through the system despite a fastball that only runs in the mid-80s. However, all of his pitches have good movement and he keeps batters off stride with pinpoint command and an uncanny knack for changing speeds. It's not surprising that he wore down late in the season since he'd never before approached 185 innings. There's a debate as to whether Saarloos can thrive with a fastball that's a few ticks south of average. Put us down squarely on the side that believes his minor league dominance portends success in the majors.

Manny Santillan   Born: 20-Aug-79   Age: 23   Bats: R   Throws: R

YEAR	TM	LG	AGE	G	GS	IP	H	BB	SO	HR	ERA	EQERA	EQH9	EQBB9	EQSO9	EQHR9	PERA	VORP	STF
2000	MAR	APL	20	19	0	22.7	21	24	20	1	4.76	10.07	14.0	15.7	4.7	1.4	10.50	-11.8	-53
2001	LEX	SAL	21	38	7	96.7	83	43	90	4	3.54	6.73	12.5	6.5	5.1	1.0	6.05	-14.0	-12
2002	LEX	SAL	22	14	14	96.0	73	28	76	4	2.06	4.42	10.7	3.9	4.6	1.1	4.12	11.6	5

A converted catcher, Santillan stood second in the South Atlantic League in ERA before a stress fracture in his elbow ended his season. Like most position players who take the mound, Santillan has difficulty with any pitch that requires finesse, but has good command of a low-90s fastball, which the organization rightly believes is the key to success for any hurler.

Ricky Stone   Born: 28-Feb-75   Age: 28   Bats: R   Throws: R

YEAR	TM	LG	AGE	G	GS	IP	H	BB	SO	HR	ERA	EQERA	EQH9	EQBB9	EQSO9	EQHR9	PERA	VORP	STF
2000	ABQ	PCL	25	48	7	120.3	146	42	75	9	4.94	5.50	11.5	3.1	4.5	0.8	5.26	-1.0	-10
2001	NWO	PCL	26	51	8	95.3	98	27	78	8	3.59	4.89	10.9	3.1	5.5	1.0	5.06	5.7	-7
2002	HOU	NL	27	78	0	77.3	78	34	63	9	3.61	4.31	9.1	3.5	6.4	1.0	4.61	9.2	-4
2003	HOU	NL	28	50	0	55.0	59	24	41	7	4.70	4.78	9.8	3.4	6.0	1.0	4.90	5.4	-7

Breakout: 13%   Improve: 43%   Collapse: 28%

Stone's improved changeup enabled him to survive the spring training shakedown and make the cut as the last pitcher on the roster. The sinkerballer parlayed the opportunity and Williams's heavy bullpen usage into a place in the record books, tying Tim Burke's NL rookie mark of 78 appearances. It's a well-known fact that you can't squeeze water from a Stone, so Williams shouldn't attempt to expand his role this season.

Billy Wagner   Born: 25-Jul-71   Age: 31   Bats: L   Throws: L

YEAR	TM	LG	AGE	G	GS	IP	H	BB	SO	HR	ERA	EQERA	EQH9	EQBB9	EQSO9	EQHR9	PERA	VORP	STF
2000	HOU	NL	28	28	0	27.7	28	18	28	6	6.17	5.39	8.4	4.6	7.8	1.7	5.70	-0.0	-5
2001	HOU	NL	29	64	0	62.7	44	20	79	5	2.73	2.62	6.4	2.7	9.6	0.6	2.57	19.2	24
2002	HOU	NL	30	70	0	75.0	51	22	88	7	2.52	2.52	6.2	2.3	9.2	0.8	2.52	23.8	22
2003	HOU	NL	31	70	0	74.0	61	24	83	8	2.92	2.97	7.5	2.5	9.0	0.9	3.20	20.5	19

Breakout: 34%   Improve: 51%   Collapse: 15%

There's no trickery involved with Wagner. He challenges hitters with high cheese, wins most of the battles and the ones he loses often result in memorable home runs. Since he doesn't have a backup plan, when his fastball drops a few mph, the jig is up. That and his $8 million a year contract through 2004 means that Wagner's status needs to be constantly evaluated, not just in isolation, but in a team context. As long as he's pushing triple digits and the Astros are contenders, you can make a fragile case for having him on the roster. However, if Wagner or the team starts to sink, he should be the first chit tossed overboard.

Los Angeles Dodgers

The Dodgers go into the 2003 season with exactly one bat in their lineup that scares you, a rotation full of injury-prone question marks, little wiggle room beneath a luxury tax threshold they vow not to cross, and a farm system that will offer little or no help for at least two more years. And they still could be contenders. After all, the club has faced the same circumstances the last two years. Each time, Jim Tracy has pushed the Dodgers into a September pennant race. Why? Better than perhaps any manager in baseball, Tracy puts his players in the best position for them to succeed.

Talent-wise, the Giants and Diamondbacks have outgunned the Dodgers in each of the past two seasons. Shawn Green's a great player, but he's no Barry Bonds—plus there's been no one close to Jeff Kent in the Dodger lineup to support Green. Kevin Brown was once an all-world pitcher, but he's now an injured shell of his old self, and nowhere near either member of the Diamondbacks' dynamic duo of Randy Johnson and Curt Schilling. The organization has also been one of the worst in the game at producing hitting prospects over the last several years. And yet, Tracy's Dodgers have battled into September in each of his two seasons, winning a combined 178 games.

If you've read *BP* long enough, you've likely read this refrain or something like it: "Every manager in baseball could benefit from playing a few hundred games of Strat-O-Matic." Tracy regularly played the game growing up, and in several ways, it shows: The manner in which he's leveraged platoons and job-sharing arrangements are hallmarks of a great Strat player. But you can't use index cards and a 20-sided die to manage the real-life Dodgers. Tracy's job means he deals with real people, with real egos, real expectations, facing real issues of injury, ineffectiveness, and self-doubt. He's connected on every curveball thrown his way, if not whacking them out of the park, at least spraying line drives into the gap.

We outlined some of Tracy's successes in last year's Dodgers chapter. He helped rescue Paul Lo Duca, giving the catcher a chance to pull himself from the brink of minor league lifer status to All-Star level. He managed his bullpen well. He dealt with a diverse group of players, keeping everyone on an even keel from wire to wire.

What did he do in 2002? With little to lean on talent-wise, Tracy turned a 30-year-old retread in Dave Roberts and a 35-year-old has-been in Marquis Grissom into one of the better center field situations in the league by platooning them. After Cesar Izturis, anointed shortstop of the future, flopped as a left-handed batter, Tracy split playing time, squeezing every drop of offense out of Punch and Judy backup Alex Cora while giving each player enough work to keep his defense sharp.

Paul Quantrill and Matt Herges looked like early favorites to fill the closer role in the spring, with prospect Eric Gagne part of a gulag of pitchers vying for the fifth starter's spot. But while Gagne, not far removed from Tommy John surgery, had struggled at times with consistency and endurance as a starter, he looked positively Eck-tastic in the bullpen. By Opening Day, Herges had been shipped to Gagne's hometown of Montreal, and the kid had reclaimed the role he once held with the Canadian National Team, scaring the bejeezus out of opposing hitters with his hit-me-if-you-can four-seam fastball. In general, we frown on turning would-be 200-inning starters into 80-inning, three-out specialists. But Gagne completely dominated the league in his new role, turning more than a third of all Dodger games into eight-inning affairs. As team orthopedic consultant Dr. Frank Jobe said during an in-season interview, "It's no coincidence he started throwing 98 miles an hour, when before he might have thrown 93. Having his arm repaired helped, but so did knowing he only had to throw 20 pitches, instead of 100 or more."

Dodgers Prospectus

2002 record: 92–70; Third place, NL West

Pythagenport Record: 89–73

Runs scored per game: 4.4 (9th in NL)

Runs allowed per game: 4.0 (3rd in NL)

Team EqA: .264 (6th in NL)

2002 Batters Age: 30.2 (8th oldest in NL)

2002 Pitchers Age: 31.4 (2nd oldest in NL)

Ballpark: Dodger Stadium; Severe pitchers' park; Park Factor .919

2002: Jim Tracy squeezed blood from the gravel on the roster, keeping them in contention.

2003: Youth movement/mediocrity eradication program should improve offense and keep the Dodgers in the mix.

On top of Gagne's performance, Tracy coaxed a fringe Cy Young–worthy season out of Odalis Perez, another young pitcher with a checkered past of injuries and periodic ineffectiveness. When Perez threw back-to-back starts of 129 and 116 pitches in April, the first one in Coors Field, pitcher abuse protestors readied for a daring midnight rescue of Perez and his arm. But Tracy eased back the throttle, permitting only seven more starts all year above 100 pitches, and only three above 110. Perez's obscenely fine control, 38 walks in 222.3 innings, didn't hurt either.

The good tidings end there. The Dodgers' lineup features that one impact hitter in Green. The starting rotation is not only littered with injury risks, most of them are also wildly overpaid. The farm system is virtually bare at the upper levels, with 2001's best upper-level hitting prospect regressing from a poor gloveman with speed and a power bat to a poor, plodding gloveman who may not hit enough to carry the first base or corner outfield slot he's now forced to play. A decent source of pitching prospects heading into last season, a pair of ill-advised deadline deals stripped away just about every valuable arm above A-ball.

So we're looking at an aging team with offensive holes all over the field, still fighting through huge salary commitments, with next to nothing coming from the farm for at least two or three years, owned by a media conglomerate that's trying to get out of the business, run by a general manager with a mixed track record. On the plus side, there's Green, Perez, Gagne, a few kids in A-ball, ample media-generated revenue, and an idyllic ballpark that packs in hordes of fans, whether in a pennant race or a lost season. And Tracy.

It may be tough convincing Dodger fans that a 92-win team needs a major facelift if it plans to compete in 2003 and beyond. That doesn't mean general manager Dan Evans needs to blow up the team, sell Green for cash and magic beans and start from scratch. But at least half the lineup, a chunk of the rotation and much of the bullpen and bench should be turned over to produce a team that won't require mountains of managerial mojo to contend in the next couple of years. Beyond that, the Dodgers will need to completely reinvent their farm system (more on that in a minute).

Luckily for Evans, Fox has deep pockets and a willingness to empty them when needed as long as it's still around. Coming into the off-season, Evans also had an army of salary albatrosses coming off the books:

- Mark Grudzielanek was set to give the team one last year of nothing at $5.5 million before a $500,000 buyout would punt him off the roster.

- Eric Karros's agent saved the often-parochial Dodgers from reaching a stand-off with its all-time home run hitter by forging a $1 million buyout clause that would spare a playing time-based vesting clause in Karros's

contract. Eight million painful dollars would be doled out this year, saving $9 million in 2004.

- Brian Jordan demanded a trade, the Dodgers found no takers, so the marriage will likely last one more year at $9 million before Jordan gets a $2.5 million golden parachute to go away.

- Andy Ashby "earns" $8 million for one more year before yet another option gets dropped by the team.

- Hideo Nomo will make $7.25 million in 2003 before the Dodgers weigh an $8 million 2004 option with a $1.5 million buyout.

That's $37.75 million in salary ready to come off the books after this season. Evans couldn't wait that long, opting to send Grudzielanek, Karros, and $2 million cash to the Cubs for Todd Hundley and Chad Hermansen. The trade shaves more than $7 million off the 2003 payroll. But it also adds another $6.5 million to a 2004 roster that will still include overpaid setup men Paul Quantrill and Paul Shuey, not to mention the obscene salary numbers for Brown and Darren Dreifort through 2005.

Nevertheless, Dodger fans had to be excited after seeing a trade clear up that much cash for this season. Evans would surely take the saved proceeds and parlay them into a contract for Kent or Cliff Floyd, right? Not exactly. Kent and Floyd signed elsewhere, and Evans was forced to tab 39-year-old Fred McGriff to be a one-year solution at first base. Even after the Hundley deal, the Dodgers butted so close to the $117 million luxury tax limit they had just enough money left to spend on a second-tier bat and a left-handed reliever. With McGriff on board to provide less than they need until a solution presents itself next year, the Dodgers should expect another year of inadequate offense, unless Beltre turns into Mike Schmidt overnight.

So Tracy will have to make filet mignon out of horse meat for at least one more year. What then to do with all the cash that funnels in after this season? The Dodgers need bats and lots of 'em. Roberts is a nice stopgap solution, but the team needs a consistent on-base threat to anchor the top of the lineup. The Dodgers, like about 25 other teams, should be pounding on Allard Baird's door, hoping to land the soon-to-be-expensive Carlos Beltran.

In the middle of the lineup, they need another bat to pair with Green. Chin-Feng Chen looked like he could be the guy for a while, but didn't impress anyone in 2002; he's fading as a prospect. Miguel Tejada's a free agent at the end of the year. He'd make a nifty right-handed thumper to bookend Green, especially given Izturis' hitting struggles.

If Dodgers fans want a scapegoat, they need look no further than the team's draftniks, authors of some awful performances in recent years. Teams continue to draft scads of high school pitchers, hoping the countless spectacular failures of same were all a big fluke. Or maybe they just choose to ignore the truckloads of data that suggest picking high school pitchers in the high rounds of the amateur draft is akin to taking a nap in the number two lane of the 405 freeway—you're lucky if you only get maimed.

The Dodgers have proven themselves to be champions of wishful thinking. In 2001, they expended four of their top five picks on high school pitchers—apparently the liquor store had run out of lottery tickets. Before the 2002 season the team tapped Logan White to be the third director of scouting in the last three years. White made noise about drafting a polished college hitter among the Dodgers top three picks—all in the top 51 thanks to the sandwich picks gained from losing Chan Ho Park.

Keeping with recent Dodger Tradition—there's a phrase that doesn't mean much anymore—the team chucked its plans and tapped three high school pitchers with its first three picks anyway. They at least had the good sense to develop top pick James Loney as a first baseman, cultivating the offensive side of his high school career. Still, seven of the Dodgers' first eight picks were high schoolers, five of those pitchers (not including Loney).

It's possible one or more of the kids the Dodgers picked could pan out. But at the end of the day, they're all just that—kids. Their immature arms will be subject to absurdly high injury risk, their young minds struggling to deal with the rigors of professional baseball in a podunk town miles from home. This just weeks after fumbling with a boutonniere and rented tux. Hell, calculus class.

Maybe one day, teams like the Dodgers will see the light and stop wasting dozens of picks and millions of dollars searching in vain for the next Nolan Ryan. Until then, Evans will have to pay the piper. Thanks to shoddy player development, the farm system is loaded with tools freaks who have little idea how to play baseball. The pitching picture looked slightly better for a while, until Evans jettisoned four of his best arms in foolish 2002 deadline deals.

You'd hope the Dodgers could at least follow the example of teams like the Cardinals, Giants, and Red Sox. All three have squeezed very little out of their farm systems in the last few years, but all have contended with strong major league cores and a smattering of trades with the few prospects they've had. Unfortunately, the Dodgers don't have Bonds, Kent, Garciaparra, Manny, Pedro, Pujols, and Edmonds. They most certainly don't have anything close to this year's Giants' young pitching stable of Williams, Foppert, Ainsworth, and Bonser.

Evans could still blow it all up, raze the major league roster and start from scratch, but good luck convincing the backers of "girls club" on the virtue of patience and well thought out ideas. All of which means the Dodgers will have to spend like crazy to contend in the NL West, even when matched against the aging Giants and Diamondbacks, the still-building Padres and the aimless Rockies. They'll have to be some of the best dollars ever spent at Chavez Ravine. Even Jim Tracy runs out of good rolls eventually.

HITTERS

Reggie Abercrombie   RF   Born: 15-Jul-80   Age: 22   Bats: R   Throws: R

YEAR	TM	LG	AGE	AB	H	2B	3B	HR	BB	SO	SB	CS	AVG	OBP	SLG	MLVR	EQBA	EQOBP	EQSLG	EQMLVR	VORP	DEFENSE
2000	GRF	PIO	19	220	60	7	1	2	22	66	32	8	.273	.360	.341	-.080	.186	.227	.232	-.563	-20.8	52-CF -7
2001	WNC	SAL	20	486	110	17	3	10	19	154	44	11	.226	.273	.335	-.078	.194	.227	.293	-.474	-51.4	121-RF -19
2002	VRO	FSL	21	526	145	23	13	10	27	158	41	17	.276	.322	.426	.077	.225	.256	.355	-.311	-33.0	124-RF -11
2002	JAX	SOU	21	4	1	0	0	0	0	1	1	0	.250	.250	.250	-.300	.250	.250	.250	-.461	-.3	
2003	LAD	NL	22	194	43	8	2	4	13	64	6	11	.219	.275	.335	-.263	.230	.282	.360	-.237	-12.8	

Breakout: 63%   Improve: 77%   Collapse: 13%

Looks like a baseball player. Of course if looks were everything, Brooke Burke would be pulling down her 5th Oscar this year. Big, strong, and fast, Abercrombie's one of several tools fiends in the Dodger system. He's also the most glaring example of the Dodgers' inability to teach patience to their hitting prospects. The organization compounds the problem by rewarding players like Abercrombie with various Player of the Day, Week, Fortnight, Month, and Year awards. The Dodgers need to start teaching players like Abercrombie how to convert tools into skills, or consider drafting more polished players. We'd suggest doing both, but baby steps still beat inertia. Converted from right field to center this year, Abercrombie has shown the same tendencies in the field as he had at the plate: good tools—a strong arm and promising range—and poor results.

Luke Allen   RF   Born: 04-Aug-78   Age: 24   Bats: L   Throws: R

YEAR	TM	LG	AGE	AB	H	2B	3B	HR	BB	SO	SB	CS	AVG	OBP	SLG	MLVR	EQBA	EQOBP	EQSLG	EQMLVR	VORP	DEFENSE
2000	SAN	TXS	21	339	90	15	5	7	40	71	14	5	.265	.345	.401	.003	.232	.291	.354	-.240	-4.9	86-3B -13
2001	JAX	SOU	22	486	141	32	6	16	42	111	13	3	.290	.348	.479	.173	.252	.299	.416	-.124	-6.4	118-RF -3
2002	LVG	PCL	23	501	165	28	3	12	56	77	4	6	.329	.399	.469	.192	.282	.348	.403	-.027	6.1	129-RF -2
2002	LAD	NL	23	7	1	1	0	0	2	3	0	0	.143	.333	.286	-.184	.143	.333	.286	-.289	-.3	
2003	LAD	NL	24	215	54	11	2	6	21	41	3	3	.253	.322	.399	-.074	.266	.331	.429	-.034	-.7	

Breakout: 20%   Improve: 57%   Collapse: 15%

A non-drafted free agent, Allen's scratched his way up the organizational ladder with some success. He reversed a troubling trend in strike zone judgment last year, ratcheting his walks back up to nearly one every 10 times up, making better contact and reviving his prospectdom. He still needs to show more power to be considered a viable threat for a starting corner outfield job. At worst, Allen's an infinitely better bench option than the Shawon Dunstons of the world.

Willy Aybar   3B   Born: 09-Mar-83   Age: 20   Bats: B   Throws: R

YEAR	TM	LG	AGE	AB	H	2B	3B	HR	BB	SO	SB	CS	AVG	OBP	SLG	MLVR	EQBA	EQOBP	EQSLG	EQMLVR	VORP	DEFENSE
2000	GRF	PIO	17	266	70	15	1	4	36	45	5	5	.263	.351	.372	-.056	.172	.224	.243	-.560	-25.2	64-3B 1
2001	WNC	SAL	18	431	102	25	2	4	43	64	7	9	.237	.310	.332	-.020	.194	.251	.276	-.449	-31.7	118-3B 8
2002	VRO	FSL	19	372	80	18	2	11	69	54	15	8	.215	.342	.363	-.011	.173	.273	.297	-.386	-22.1	106-3B -4
2003	LAD	NL	20	189	43	8	1	5	21	33	3	2	.227	.306	.366	-.162	.238	.314	.394	-.129	.1	

Breakout: 80%   Improve: 88%   Collapse: 7%

Aybar's made a steady climb up the ladder since nabbing a $1.4 million bonus before his 17th birthday. The Dodgers would do well to let him master the Florida State League before subjecting him to that Double-A jump. Still growing into his body, scouts love his strong wrists, which they expect will produce ample power as Aybar matures. Two big positives: a walk every 6.5 times up at Vero Beach, and an unchanged birth certificate, no mean feat for a Dominican wannabe phenom these days.

Adrian Beltre   3B   Born: 07-Apr-79   Age: 24   Bats: R   Throws: R

YEAR	TM	LG	AGE	AB	H	2B	3B	HR	BB	SO	SB	CS	AVG	OBP	SLG	MLVR	EQBA	EQOBP	EQSLG	EQMLVR	VORP	DEFENSE
2000	LAD	NL	21	510	148	30	2	20	56	80	12	5	.290	.363	.475	.113	.297	.361	.486	.126	44.4	135-3B 7
2001	LAD	NL	22	475	126	22	4	13	28	82	13	4	.265	.313	.411	-.060	.277	.322	.426	-.047	18.5	122-3B -4
2002	LAD	NL	23	587	151	26	5	21	37	96	7	5	.257	.306	.426	.011	.273	.316	.458	-.015	26.4	151-3B 1
2003	LAD	NL	24	542	145	28	4	18	46	86	10	3	.268	.328	.434	-.007	.282	.336	.467	.040	24.7	

Breakout: 12%   Improve: 49%   Collapse: 14%

Of all the surprising numbers above, the name under "TEAM" may be the most eye-opening. A full season removed from a dicey appendectomy, Beltre's rebound on the road to uberstardom seemed a foregone conclusion. Instead, his .238/.289/.359 first half challenged Chino's cow pastures for the title of biggest stink in the L.A. area. The Dodgers stayed patient with him, balking on a Scott Rolen swap while praying for a second-half rebound to fuel their playoff drive. Mission largely accomplished: .281/.319/.509 after the break. If Beltre rediscovers the second-year patience that netted him a walk every 10 times up, he could still be a lineup anchor. The number next to "Age" offers hope.

Jolbert Cabrera   UT   Born: 08-Dec-72   Age: 30   Bats: R   Throws: R

YEAR	TM	LG	AGE	AB	H	2B	3B	HR	BB	SO	SB	CS	AVG	OBP	SLG	MLVR	EQBA	EQOBP	EQSLG	EQMLVR	VORP	DEFENSE	
2000	CLE	AL	27	175	44	3	1	2	8	15	6	4	.251	.292	.314	-.325	.253	.286	.322	-.282	-7.9	49-OF -3	
2001	CLE	AL	28	287	75	16	3	1	16	41	10	4	.261	.314	.348	-.149	.279	.329	.376	-.104	-1.1	46-OF -4	14-2B -1
2002	BUF	INT	29	91	26	5	0	0	9	10	4	2	.286	.356	.341	-.017	.272	.341	.315	-.171	.2	13-CF 0	
2002	CLE	AL	29	72	8	1	0	0	5	13	1	1	.111	.179	.125	-.742	.139	.203	.153	-.737	-12.0	21-OF -2	
2002	LVG	PCL	29	102	35	8	1	2	14	18	2	3	.343	.427	.500	.293	.287	.366	.426	.042	3.4	23-LF -1	
2002	LAD	NL	29	12	4	1	0	0	2	2	0	0	.333	.429	.417	.262	.333	.429	.500	.296	1.4		
2003	LAD	NL	30	144	35	7	1	1	13	21	3	1	.243	.309	.332	-.192	.255	.317	.357	-.161	-2.8		

Breakout: 24%   Improve: 50%   Collapse: 35%

A better option than the artist formerly known as Jeff Reboulet, Cabrera gives the Dodgers a decent utilityman for 2003. They'll need at least one more legitimate bat to contend this year. If they get it and it's a tight race, Tracy's steady hand and a solid bench laced with useful players like Cabrera could be difference makers.

Chin-Feng Chen   1B   Born: 28-Oct-77   Age: 25   Bats: R   Throws: R

YEAR	TM	LG	AGE	AB	H	2B	3B	HR	BB	SO	SB	CS	AVG	OBP	SLG	MLVR	EQBA	EQOBP	EQSLG	EQMLVR	VORP	DEFENSE	
2000	SAN	TXS	22	516	143	27	3	6	61	131	23	15	.277	.357	.376	-.003	.240	.300	.326	-.257	-24.0	125-LF	-6
2001	VRO	FSL	23	235	63	15	3	5	28	56	2	0	.268	.361	.421	.116	.217	.285	.350	-.267	-11.7	11-LF	1
2001	JAX	SOU	23	224	70	16	2	17	41	65	5	4	.313	.423	.629	.497	.262	.356	.524	.137	15.1	48-LF	-3
2002	LVG	PCL	24	511	145	26	4	26	58	160	1	0	.284	.357	.503	.127	.244	.312	.427	-.090	.7	93-1B	-10
2002	LAD	NL	24	5	0	0	0	0	1	3	0	0	.000	.167	.000	-.880	.200	.333	.200	-.375	-.3		
2003	*LAD*	*NL*	*25*	*182*	*44*	*10*	*1*	*7*	*18*	*51*	*3*	*3*	*.240*	*.312*	*.413*	*-.084*	*.253*	*.320*	*.444*	*-.044*	*-.6*		

Breakout: 27%   Improve: 61%   Collapse: 20%

Uh-oh. Chen failed to take a step forward in Triple-A, finishing a dismal seventh in EqA among Las Vegas hitters with more than 300 plate appearances. Making matters worse, the Dodgers have all given up on Chen in the outfield, his one game in left with the big club last year notwithstanding. Though he's still got a little time to turn it around, Chen's gone from a potential star to a poor-fielding plodder who doesn't hit enough to justify his spot at the far end of the defensive spectrum. That's a harsh statement on a Dodgers farm system struggling to churn out big league hitters.

Alex Cora   SS   Born: 18-Oct-75   Age: 27   Bats: L   Throws: R

YEAR	TM	LG	AGE	AB	H	2B	3B	HR	BB	SO	SB	CS	AVG	OBP	SLG	MLVR	EQBA	EQOBP	EQSLG	EQMLVR	VORP	DEFENSE			
2000	ABQ	PCL	24	110	41	8	3	0	7	10	5	3	.373	.420	.500	.281	.318	.356	.430	.057	7.3	30-SS	-3		
2000	LAD	NL	24	353	84	18	6	4	26	53	4	1	.238	.303	.357	-.217	.246	.301	.372	-.186	3.0	97-SS	-8		
2001	LAD	NL	25	405	88	18	3	4	31	58	0	2	.217	.286	.306	-.292	.233	.297	.325	-.268	-5.6	118-SS	-11		
2002	LAD	NL	26	258	75	14	4	5	26	38	7	2	.291	.371	.434	.157	.308	.381	.466	.143	25.3	51-SS	1	20-2B	-1
2003	*LAD*	*NL*	*27*	*254*	*66*	*13*	*2*	*4*	*23*	*37*	*4*	*2*	*.260*	*.329*	*.371*	*-.095*	*.273*	*.337*	*.399*	*-.056*	*7.0*				

Breakout: 11%   Improve: 35%   Collapse: 36%

Take the best computer program you can find, mate it with the wisdom of the world's greatest psychic, and even that love child will still be wrong from time to time in this business. Why? Sh . . . er, stuff happens. Two causes of said stuff: small sample size and the fate of balls in play. Alex Cora went from everyday shortstop to part-time player, digging in just 293 times last year. Combine that nugget with a contact hitter who challenges the defense to make plays, and occasionally you get a 74-point spike in batting average, and related gains everywhere else. The Dodgers will still give Cesar Izturis every chance to be their starting shortstop for the next five years, meaning Cora will either be gone or in a utility role by Opening Day.

Victor Diaz   3B   Born: 10-Dec-81   Age: 21   Bats: R   Throws: R

YEAR	TM	LG	AGE	AB	H	2B	3B	HR	BB	SO	SB	CS	AVG	OBP	SLG	MLVR	EQBA	EQOBP	EQSLG	EQMLVR	VORP	DEFENSE			
2002	SGA	SAL	20	349	122	26	2	10	27	69	20	6	.350	.412	.521	.431	.275	.318	.417	-.069	11.0	62-3B	-12	11-2B	1
2002	JAX	SOU	20	152	32	7	0	4	7	42	7	5	.211	.259	.336	-.187	.188	.217	.312	-.471	-14.2	26-1B	-1		
2003	*LAD*	*NL*	*21*	*218*	*49*	*9*	*1*	*5*	*15*	*55*	*5*	*6*	*.225*	*.283*	*.346*	*-.230*	*.236*	*.291*	*.372*	*-.201*	*-6.2*				

Breakout: 18%   Improve: 40%   Collapse: 21%

A draft-and-follow 37th round pick in 2000, Diaz's progress stalled last year when the Dodgers got too aggressive with him. Jumped two levels, Diaz struggled against Double-A pitching after showing great bat speed and intriguing power in the Gulf Coast League in 2001 and again in the Sally League for much of last year. He could really use an off-season or two of rugged conditioning to get into shape. As is, his suspect defense and bulk have all but silenced hopes of keeping him at second or third base.

Shawn Green   RF   Born: 10-Nov-72   Age: 30   Bats: Throws: L

YEAR	TM	LG	AGE	AB	H	2B	3B	HR	BB	SO	SB	CS	AVG	OBP	SLG	MLVR	EQBA	EQOBP	EQSLG	EQMLVR	VORP	DEFENSE	
2000	LAD	NL	27	610	164	44	4	24	90	121	24	5	.269	.370	.472	.102	.277	.368	.489	.124	34.8	148-RF	3
2001	LAD	NL	28	619	184	31	4	49	72	107	20	4	.297	.375	.598	.343	.307	.382	.616	.355	77.6	159-RF	1
2002	LAD	NL	29	582	166	31	1	42	93	112	8	5	.285	.388	.558	.344	.306	.402	.606	.370	74.2	156-RF	8
2003	*LAD*	*NL*	*30*	*551*	*154*	*31*	*2*	*33*	*80*	*105*	*11*	*4*	*.279*	*.373*	*.525*	*.191*	*.293*	*.382*	*.565*	*.253*	*41.4*		

Breakout: 7%   Improve: 55%   Collapse: 6%

A team's best-paid player tends to shoulder the bulk of the blame when others fall short of expectations. This is often patently unfair. Shawn Green hangs with Kevin Brown at the top of the Dodgers' payroll list. Few players anywhere can hang with Green on the field. Like A-Rod, Green more than earns his ample keep. A durable player in top shape, it's a good bet you'll read a similar comment as he wraps up Year Six of his contract, in 2006.

Marquis Grissom CF Born: 17-Apr-67 Age: 36 Bats: R Throws: R

YEAR	TM	LG	AGE	AB	H	2B	3B	HR	BB	SO	SB	CS	AVG	OBP	SLG	MLVR	EQBA	EQOBP	EQSLG	EQMLVR	VORP	DEFENSE	
2000	MIL	NL	33	595	145	18	2	14	39	99	20	10	.244	.290	.351	-.268	.242	.279	.350	-.263	-13.0	133-CF	3
2001	LAD	NL	34	448	99	17	1	21	16	107	7	5	.221	.251	.404	-.221	.233	.262	.425	-.194	-1.8	108-CF	0
2002	LAD	NL	35	343	95	21	4	17	22	68	5	1	.277	.324	.510	.175	.293	.334	.545	.162	30.4	81-CF	-1
2003	SFG	NL	36	265	64	12	2	8	16	53	5	2	.243	.289	.396	-.141	.255	.296	.436	-.093	.4		

Breakout: 12% Improve: 41% Collapse: 27%

Give credit where credit's due, the Dodgers got more out of a Grissom/Dave Roberts platoon than even their moms would have thought possible. Grissom hit 293/354/617 (!) in 133 at-bats vs. lefties, making a nifty power-hitting complement to Roberts, the speedy on-base threat. A free agent, Grissom angled for a full-time job somewhere, a frightening proposition given his declining defense and ineffectiveness against northpaws. The Giants obliged with a $4.5 million deal, dooming Grissom to two more years in a stats-crushing pitchers' park.

Mark Grudzielanek 2B Born: 30-Jun-70 Age: 33 Bats: R Throws: R

YEAR	TM	LG	AGE	AB	H	2B	3B	HR	BB	SO	SB	CS	AVG	OBP	SLG	MLVR	EQBA	EQOBP	EQSLG	EQMLVR	VORP	DEFENSE	
2000	LAD	NL	30	617	172	35	6	7	45	81	12	3	.279	.337	.389	-.072	.287	.335	.402	-.049	27.4	145-2B	1
2001	LAD	NL	31	539	146	21	3	13	28	83	4	4	.271	.320	.393	-.067	.284	.329	.410	-.051	24.1	130-2B	-2
2002	LAD	NL	32	536	145	23	0	9	22	89	4	1	.271	.303	.364	-.070	.290	.317	.393	-.093	16.7	132-2B	-3
2003	CHC	NL	33	400	104	19	2	6	21	59	4	2	.259	.300	.363	-.156	.266	.303	.381	-.146	.9		

Breakout: 7% Improve: 29% Collapse: 39%

You might be a fan of Joe Thurston. Maybe you're not yet sold on Joe Thurston. Maybe you wouldn't know Joe Thurston from Thurston Howell. You could even argue Joe Thurston has a similar skill set to Grudzielanek's: useful when he hits for a high average, scary when he doesn't. But check Grudzielanek's OBPs the last four years: 377, 335, 317, 300. It's time to see what Joe Thurston can do. He should get his chance after Grudzielanek and Eric Karros landed in Wrigley for Todd Hundley, a nod to an off-season rife with NBA-style, mind-numbing, salary-cap trades. For the Cubs, Grudz doesn't offer much: If he beats out Bobby Hill, that's bad news, and he can't really play anywhere but second, so he's effectively useless as well as overpriced for a utility infielder.

Joel Guzman SS Born: 24-Nov-84 Age: 18 Bats: R Throws: R

YEAR	TM	LG	AGE	AB	H	2B	3B	HR	BB	SO	SB	CS	AVG	OBP	SLG	MLVR	EQBA	EQOBP	EQSLG	EQMLVR	VORP	DEFENSE	
2002	GRF	PIO	17	151	38	8	2	3	18	54	5	3	.252	.331	.391	-.035	.164	.221	.250	-.560	-12.8	41-SS	1
2003	LAD	NL	18	161	38	6	2	5	14	55	3	6	.238	.300	.402	-.118	.250	.308	.432	-.080	2.4		

Breakout: 100% Improve: 100% Collapse: 0%

Cross your fingers. The Dodgers outbid 20 teams to sign Guzman to a $2.25 million bonus in July 2001. He saw his first professional action in Great Falls, where he committed 16 errors in 43 games on patchy Pioneer League fields. He held his own with the bat, though he still needs to work on recognizing breaking pitches. A five-tool talent at 6' 4", 200 pounds, the Dodgers hope he'll develop the power scouts expect from him. Projecting a player this young is damn near impossible. He'll be tested once he graduates from Sally League pitching to the Florida State League.

Dave Hansen PH Born: 24-Nov-68 Age: 34 Bats: L Throws: R

YEAR	TM	LG	AGE	AB	H	2B	3B	HR	BB	SO	SB	CS	AVG	OBP	SLG	MLVR	EQBA	EQOBP	EQSLG	EQMLVR	VORP	DEFENSE			
2000	LAD	NL	31	121	35	6	2	8	26	32	0	1	.289	.415	.570	.338	.301	.415	.585	.355	17.8				
2001	LAD	NL	32	140	33	10	0	2	32	29	0	1	.236	.378	.350	-.038	.257	.392	.375	-.000	4.3	20-1B	-3	16-3B	2
2002	LAD	NL	33	120	35	6	0	2	14	22	1	0	.292	.366	.392	.091	.315	.380	.419	.081	7.1				
2003	SDP	NL	34	102	27	5	0	3	18	21	1	0	.261	.370	.395	.005	.273	.378	.428	.053	3.5				

Breakout: 22% Improve: 53% Collapse: 27%

Listing Hansen as anything other than a pinch hitter is wishcasting at this point. Would he have outhit Eric Karros at first base? Sure. But he's never been given the chance, and opted to move two hours down I-5 rather than wait for a shot with Karros off to Chicago. Signed by the Padres, he'll fill the Dave Magadan role with gusto.

Phil Hiatt — LF — Born: 01-May-69 — Age: 34 — Bats: R — Throws: R

YEAR	TM	LG	AGE	AB	H	2B	3B	HR	BB	SO	SB	CS	AVG	OBP	SLG	MLVR	EQBA	EQOBP	EQSLG	EQMLVR	VORP	DEFENSE		
2000	CSP	PCL	31	507	157	36	1	36	63	149	14	2	.310	.391	.598	.287	.258	.327	.492	.039	18.0	116-1B	2	
2001	LVG	PCL	32	436	144	29	5	44	52	109	6	4	.330	.408	.722	.533	.277	.352	.588	.234	49.3	85-3B -2	15-1B -2	
2001	LAD	NL	32	50	12	3	0	2	3	19	0	0	.240	.283	.420	-.123	.255	.296	.431	-.105	.4			
2002	LVG	PCL	33	355	108	14	2	23	42	88	1	2	.304	.379	.549	.246	.259	.330	.460	.001	8.0	37-LF -2	33-1B -3	
2003	CHC	NL	34	99	23	4	1	5	12	28	2	1	.237	.320	.437	-.039	.244	.324	.459	-.023	1.0			

Breakout: 15%   Improve: 48%   Collapse: 36%

As long as Phil Hiatt keeps mashing the ball, we'll keep writing about him. As the years pass, his ability to handle more challenging positions like third base wanes, and with it some of his value. But he can still DH or share a first-base job for several teams. You'd run out of fingers pretty fast counting the number of stiffs who made millions being the devil a GM knew while Hiatt bided his time in Triple-A. Signed by the Cubs, he'll continue mashing from the cleanup spot in Iowa.

Koyie Hill — C — Born: 09-Mar-79 — Age: 24 — Bats: B — Throws: R

YEAR	TM	LG	AGE	AB	H	2B	3B	HR	BB	SO	SB	CS	AVG	OBP	SLG	MLVR	EQBA	EQOBP	EQSLG	EQMLVR	VORP	DEFENSE	
2000	YAK	NWN	21	251	65	13	1	2	25	47	0	7	.259	.326	.343	.006	.196	.237	.262	-.496	-20.4	15-3B	2
2001	WNC	SAL	22	498	150	20	2	8	49	82	21	12	.301	.372	.398	.192	.247	.301	.326	-.250	-2.2	91-C -1	
2002	JAX	SOU	23	468	127	25	1	11	76	88	5	3	.271	.373	.400	.111	.238	.319	.362	-.171	8.2	114-C -3	
2003	LAD	NL	24	169	38	8	1	3	16	33	2	1	.226	.296	.343	-.211	.238	.303	.369	-.181	-.5		

Breakout: 30%   Improve: 52%   Collapse: 25%

Hill played third base at Wichita State before the Dodgers bumped him to catcher in 2001. He's flashed a strong arm and good instincts despite his inexperience behind the plate. He started the year on fire, hitting safely in 30 of his first 31 games. Hill then fell into a nasty slump as his pitch recognition wavered. He righted himself, finishing the year as the Dodgers' second-best positional prospect behind James Loney. A walk every seven times up and developing doubles power in his jump to Double-A bode well for Hill's future.

Tyler Houston — 3B — Born: 17-Jan-71 — Age: 32 — Bats: L — Throws: R

YEAR	TM	LG	AGE	AB	H	2B	3B	HR	BB	SO	SB	CS	AVG	OBP	SLG	MLVR	EQBA	EQOBP	EQSLG	EQMLVR	VORP	DEFENSE		
2000	MIL	NL	29	284	71	15	0	18	17	72	2	1	.250	.292	.493	-.051	.248	.283	.490	-.050	3.4	30-1B -3	23-3B	1
2001	MIL	NL	30	235	68	7	0	12	18	62	0	0	.289	.343	.472	.082	.294	.346	.475	.082	17.6	56-3B -4		
2002	MIL	NL	31	255	77	15	2	7	14	41	1	0	.302	.348	.459	.142	.312	.350	.481	.115	20.0	60-3B -7		
2002	LAD	NL	31	65	13	5	1	0	2	21	0	0	.200	.224	.308	-.334	.212	.235	.348	-.371	-4.5	11-1B -1		
2003	PHI	NL	32	204	52	10	1	7	14	45	1	1	.255	.305	.407	-.092	.261	.307	.428	-.079	1.8			

Breakout: 9%   Improve: 35%   Collapse: 40%

Acquired from Milwaukee for Ben Diggins and Shane Nance before the deadline, Houston became a spare part when the slumping Adrian Beltre got his groove back. The bigger question was why the Dodgers chased players who'd offer marginal upgrades at best like Houston and Paul Shuey. Guys like Diggins, Nance, Ricardo Rodriguez, and Francisco Cruceta may not amount to much, but given the Dodgers' lack of minor league depth, you'd think they'd have yielded more than a bridge partner for Dave Hansen and a functional reliever. He'll remain in a reserve role as a Phillie, probably replacing Jeremy Giambi in Bowa's mind as their top pinch-hitter.

Cesar Izturis — SS — Born: 10-Feb-80 — Age: 23 — Bats: B — Throws: R

YEAR	TM	LG	AGE	AB	H	2B	3B	HR	BB	SO	SB	CS	AVG	OBP	SLG	MLVR	EQBA	EQOBP	EQSLG	EQMLVR	VORP	DEFENSE		
2000	SYR	INT	20	435	95	16	5	0	20	44	21	11	.218	.254	.278	-.383	.204	.232	.259	-.507	-33.0	130-SS 21		
2001	SYR	INT	21	342	100	16	3	2	10	22	24	9	.292	.314	.374	-.045	.274	.298	.350	-.204	1.2	57-SS 0	24-2B	6
2001	TOR	AL	21	134	36	6	2	2	2	15	8	1	.269	.279	.388	-.153	.284	.299	.410	-.106	3.5	31-2B 7		
2002	LAD	NL	22	439	102	24	2	1	14	39	7	7	.232	.256	.303	-.264	.257	.276	.337	-.277	-6.5	110-SS -2		
2003	LAD	NL	23	375	92	18	3	3	19	36	11	3	.245	.283	.328	-.241	.258	.291	.353	-.213	-4.2			

Breakout: 24%   Improve: 61%   Collapse: 24%

Another instance where Jim Tracy turned lemons into lemonade. OK, maybe just Country Time that's sat in the back of your pantry for too long, but it still beats sucking on a wedge for an hour. A dreadful three-month stretch with the stick knocked Izturis from Opening Day starting shortstop to the bum end of a platoon with Alex Cora by July. There was method to Tracy's sanity—265 OPS points difference between righty-swinging and lefty-swinging Izturis. Given his promising glovework and lack of better options, the Dodgers will give Izturis every chance to improve his power and patience at the dish.

Brian Jordan   LF   Born: 29-Mar-67   Age: 36   Bats: R   Throws: R

YEAR	TM	LG	AGE	AB	H	2B	3B	HR	BB	SO	SB	CS	AVG	OBP	SLG	MLVR	EQBA	EQOBP	EQSLG	EQMLVR	VORP	DEFENSE	
2000	ATL	NL	33	489	129	26	0	17	38	80	10	2	.264	.323	.421	-.084	.264	.314	.420	-.081	-.6	130-RF	9
2001	ATL	NL	34	560	165	32	3	25	31	88	3	2	.295	.338	.496	.115	.299	.341	.502	.117	29.5	144-RF	8
2002	LAD	NL	35	471	134	27	3	18	34	86	2	2	.285	.341	.469	.151	.300	.350	.502	.134	27.5	115-LF	2
2003	LAD	NL	36	374	97	18	2	13	26	65	3	1	.260	.310	.419	-.062	.273	.318	.451	-.019	.8		

Breakout: 5%   Improve: 32%   Collapse: 30%

The third-best player in the Sheffield trade, maybe the fourth-best when all's said and done. Plenty of hand-wringers fretted over the Dodgers' likely offensive downgrade from Sheffield to Jordan. Their worrying proved well-founded as Jordan put up pedestrian numbers while missing more games than usual, even for him. Jordan exercised his right to demand a trade after the World Series, but rescinded it after they brought in McGriff. Given Jordan's enormous contract and age, it was unlikely anyone would have taken the bait, unless Steve Phillips got an itch.

Eric Karros   1B   Born: 04-Nov-67   Age: 35   Bats: R   Throws: R

YEAR	TM	LG	AGE	AB	H	2B	3B	HR	BB	SO	SB	CS	AVG	OBP	SLG	MLVR	EQBA	EQOBP	EQSLG	EQMLVR	VORP	DEFENSE	
2000	LAD	NL	32	584	146	29	0	31	63	122	4	3	.250	.327	.459	-.013	.256	.323	.472	.002	15.8	148-1B	12
2001	LAD	NL	33	438	103	22	0	15	41	101	3	1	.235	.305	.388	-.130	.247	.313	.408	-.113	-2.1	111-1B	10
2002	LAD	NL	34	524	142	26	1	13	37	74	4	2	.271	.326	.399	.019	.289	.338	.430	-.002	13.0	131-1B	25
2003	CHC	NL	35	368	92	18	1	11	31	66	4	2	.249	.310	.396	-.101	.256	.313	.416	-.088	-4.2		

Breakout: 7%   Improve: 44%   Collapse: 20%

Saying Karros improved from 2001 is damning with faint praise. Plagued by a chronic bad back and bum left shoulder, he still stayed just healthy enough to play 142 games, often while hobbled. Karros turned in a good season defensively but remains an offensive liability who's not getting any better with age. Now a Cub, he might be useful as the lesser half of a quasi-platoon with Hee Seop Choi, giving the young Korean slugger a chance to settle in at first base. Might.

Mike Kinkade   UT   Born: 06-May-73   Age: 30   Bats: R   Throws: R

YEAR	TM	LG	AGE	AB	H	2B	3B	HR	BB	SO	SB	CS	AVG	OBP	SLG	MLVR	EQBA	EQOBP	EQSLG	EQMLVR	VORP	DEFENSE			
2000	BIN	EAS	27	317	116	24	3	10	35	39	18	7	.366	.443	.555	.454	.305	.367	.472	.125	32.2	64-C	6	14-3B	-2
2000	ROC	INT	27	55	20	5	0	1	11	11	0	1	.364	.478	.509	.443	.339	.438	.464	.268	6.2				
2001	BAL	AL	28	160	44	5	0	4	14	31	2	1	.275	.345	.381	-.021	.298	.366	.410	.028	4.9	26-LF	-2		
2002	LAD	NL	29	50	19	5	0	2	4	10	1	0	.380	.483	.600	.636	.404	.495	.654	.697	11.2				
2002	LVG	PCL	29	287	98	22	6	11	29	49	6	2	.341	.436	.575	.405	.292	.372	.493	.150	17.0	48-LF	-2	11-3B	0
2003	LAD	NL	30	215	58	12	1	7	19	40	3	2	.271	.340	.431	.012	.285	.349	.464	.060	6.3				

Breakout: 9%   Improve: 33%   Collapse: 26%

He may have never chased Jerry Rice down the field after a crossing pattern, but Kinkade could probably do a decent Brian Jordan impression if ever needed for an extended stretch. As is, he'll settle for an understudy role. A scrap heap pickup from Baltimore last off-season, the Dodgers waited until July to call him up. Handy at the outfield and infield corners, Kinkade should have a bench job waiting for him in 2003.

Chad Kreuter   C   Born: 26-Aug-64   Age: 38   Bats: B   Throws: R

YEAR	TM	LG	AGE	AB	H	2B	3B	HR	BB	SO	SB	CS	AVG	OBP	SLG	MLVR	EQBA	EQOBP	EQSLG	EQMLVR	VORP	DEFENSE	
2000	LAD	NL	35	212	56	13	0	6	54	48	1	0	.264	.418	.410	.103	.270	.416	.423	.116	23.2	67-C	5
2001	LAD	NL	36	191	41	11	1	6	41	52	0	0	.215	.356	.377	-.059	.230	.365	.398	-.040	11.7	62-C	3
2002	LAD	NL	37	95	25	5	0	2	10	31	1	0	.263	.340	.379	.009	.286	.351	.408	-.012	5.7	29-C	2
2003	TEX	AL	38	110	26	6	0	3	14	30	1	0	.234	.322	.372	-.098	.236	.327	.377	-.130	1.2		

Breakout: 11%   Improve: 30%   Collapse: 57%

With Paul Lo Duca entrenched at catcher, Kreuter saw his playing time drop sharply in 2002. His known commodity sheen aside, there's no reason to pay a player like Kreuter a $1.2 million option at this stage of his career, even if your owner's rich enough to shut down half of Alaska for a Bachelorettes-themed romp. Dave Ross at ¼ the cost would have been a far better choice for 2003 after the Dodgers bought out Kreuter's contract. Todd Hundley at two years, $12.5 million? The price of axing the team's pricey, punchless right side of the infield. Picked up by the Rangers, where he could reprise his old role as Chan Ho Park's personal receiver.

Paul Lo Duca   C   Born: 12-Apr-72   Age: 31   Bats: R   Throws: R

YEAR	TM	LG	AGE	AB	H	2B	3B	HR	BB	SO	SB	CS	AVG	OBP	SLG	MLVR	EQBA	EQOBP	EQSLG	EQMLVR	VORP	DEFENSE	
2000	ABQ	PCL	28	279	98	27	3	4	33	14	8	5	.351	.424	.513	.280	.294	.357	.430	.037	19.0	45-C 0	
2000	LAD	NL	28	65	16	2	0	2	6	8	0	2	.246	.310	.369	-.180	.258	.310	.379	-.151	1.5	17-C 4	
2001	LAD	NL	29	460	147	28	0	25	39	30	2	4	.320	.380	.543	.301	.335	.391	.568	.335	74.1	85-C 7	23-1B 0
2002	LAD	NL	30	580	163	38	1	10	34	31	3	1	.281	.332	.402	.040	.299	.343	.434	.022	38.6	129-C 0	
2003	*LAD*	*NL*	*31*	*496*	*137*	*30*	*1*	*12*	*41*	*34*	*3*	*1*	*.277*	*.336*	*.414*	*-.015*	*.291*	*.345*	*.445*	*.032*	*23.3*		

Breakout: 8%   Improve: 35%   Collapse: 29%

In last year's book, we wrote: "His fundamental skills are very good, so there's no reason to believe he won't perform as well as the projection above indicates." So what went wrong? Maybe not as much as you'd think. Lo Duca's home runs plunged from 25 to 10, but his doubles spiked to 38 from 28, suggesting bad luck more than sudden skill erosion. Lo Duca's still a solid hitter for a catcher—he rarely walks, rarely strikes out and drives the ball into the ample Dodger Stadium gaps. He has worked hard to become an asset behind the plate too. The victim of two late-season fades in a row, the Dodgers hope Todd Hundley can soak up enough starts to keep Lo Duca fresh into September.

James Loney   1B   Born: 07-May-84   Age: 19   Bats: L   Throws: L

YEAR	TM	LG	AGE	AB	H	2B	3B	HR	BB	SO	SB	CS	AVG	OBP	SLG	MLVR	EQBA	EQOBP	EQSLG	EQMLVR	VORP	DEFENSE
2002	GRF	PIO	18	170	63	22	3	5	25	18	5	4	.371	.457	.624	.590	.237	.297	.391	-.174	-3.3	41-1B -4
2002	VRO	FSL	18	67	20	6	0	0	6	10	0	0	.299	.356	.388	.092	.235	.288	.324	-.286	-3.5	12-1B 3
2003	*LAD*	*NL*	*19*	*202*	*53*	*13*	*2*	*5*	*20*	*31*	*3*	*2*	*.262*	*.332*	*.420*	*-.024*	*.275*	*.341*	*.452*	*.021*	*3.4*	

Breakout: 70%   Improve: 75%   Collapse: 11%

Given the awful success rate teams have had in drafting high school pitchers in the high rounds of the amateur draft, you had to squirm when the Dodgers made a tall lefty out of Elkins High in Texas the 19th overall pick in 2002. Fortunately, Tommy Lasorda introduced Loney as a first baseman that day—we haven't heard of him as a pitcher since. Good thing, given the pain he inflicted on Pioneer League pitching, rolling up 22 doubles, five homers, and 25 walks in a few weeks' work at Great Falls. Called up to the full-season Florida State League, Loney held his own, hitting .299 in 17 games in Vero Beach, a neat trick for a kid just flipping through his prom pictures. There's talk of moving him to Double-A some time in 2003—if he can shake off a late-season wrist injury and keep progressing—which would be equally amazing. Loney's a line-drive hitter with emerging power, a good eye and a solid glove. It's early, but he's already the best prospect in the organization. Start getting excited.

Dave Roberts   CF   Born: 31-May-72   Age: 31   Bats: L   Throws: L

YEAR	TM	LG	AGE	AB	H	2B	3B	HR	BB	SO	SB	CS	AVG	OBP	SLG	MLVR	EQBA	EQOBP	EQSLG	EQMLVR	VORP	DEFENSE
2000	BUF	INT	28	462	135	16	3	13	59	68	39	11	.292	.375	.424	.094	.270	.342	.395	-.059	14.9	118-CF 1
2001	AKR	EAS	29	64	13	5	0	0	9	8	4	0	.203	.311	.281	-.183	.182	.276	.258	-.427	-4.5	12-CF -1
2001	BUF	INT	29	241	73	12	4	0	18	44	17	6	.303	.356	.386	.057	.283	.335	.365	-.105	-1.1	56-LF -1
2002	LAD	NL	30	422	117	14	7	3	48	51	45	10	.277	.354	.365	.024	.300	.370	.396	.018	22.7	104-CF 4
2003	*LAD*	*NL*	*31*	*360*	*92*	*16*	*4*	*3*	*35*	*52*	*22*	*6*	*.256*	*.325*	*.349*	*-.133*	*.269*	*.334*	*.375*	*-.097*	*3.2*	

Breakout: 8%   Improve: 43%   Collapse: 25%

Tip o' the cap to Dan Evans and friends. Roberts' power might best be described as Doug Flynn-erated, but he still churned out a valuable season. He can go get 'em at a level rivaling most NL center fielders not named Andruw. He pieced together enough walks, bunt hits, and other pesky leadoff man shenanigans to get himself into his most dangerous position, on base. Basestealing may be pooh-poohed in this era of Earl Weaver offense, but it's a valuable weapon when you swipe at an 82% clip. The Dodgers hope Roberts rebounds after wearing down at the end of his first year as a major league regular.

Dave Ross   C   Born: 19-Mar-77   Age: 26   Bats: R   Throws: R

YEAR	TM	LG	AGE	AB	H	2B	3B	HR	BB	SO	SB	CS	AVG	OBP	SLG	MLVR	EQBA	EQOBP	EQSLG	EQMLVR	VORP	DEFENSE
2000	SBR	CLF	23	191	49	11	1	7	17	43	3	2	.257	.321	.435	.031	.206	.243	.351	-.354	-5.8	42-C 11
2000	SAN	TXS	23	67	14	2	1	3	9	17	1	0	.209	.312	.403	-.098	.176	.259	.338	-.358	-2.3	21-C -2
2001	JAX	SOU	24	246	65	13	1	11	34	72	1	1	.264	.376	.459	.166	.232	.319	.406	-.115	8.5	68-C 0
2002	LVG	PCL	25	293	87	16	2	15	35	86	1	1	.297	.389	.519	.212	.254	.335	.443	-.018	16.0	87-C 3
2002	LAD	NL	25	10	2	1	0	1	2	4	0	0	.200	.385	.600	.307	.200	.378	.600	.213	1.0	
2003	*LAD*	*NL*	*26*	*167*	*38*	*9*	*1*	*6*	*17*	*45*	*3*	*2*	*.230*	*.311*	*.404*	*-.103*	*.242*	*.319*	*.435*	*-.065*	*4.6*	

Breakout: 24%   Improve: 52%   Collapse: 24%

Dave Ross (continued)

Lo Duca, the next generation? Ross has progressed nicely through the minors, getting better at each level. He's driving the ball more consistently since learning to keep his weight back longer and after bulking up. His pitch selection is far from perfect, but it's improving. He won't embarrass himself defensively either. After declining the option on Chad Kreuter, the Dodgers could have penciled Ross in for the backup catcher's job had they not picked up two years of Todd Hundley. Tough break for Ross, who's a sleeper waiting for an opportunity.

Wilkin Ruan   CF   **Born: 18-Sep-78**   **Age: 24**   **Bats: R**   **Throws: R**

YEAR	TM	LG	AGE	AB	H	2B	3B	HR	BB	SO	SB	CS	AVG	OBP	SLG	MLVR	EQBA	EQOBP	EQSLG	EQMLVR	VORP	DEFENSE
2000	CPF	SAL	21	574	165	29	10	0	24	75	64	10	.287	.325	.373	.034	.229	.252	.301	-.394	-31.2	129-CF -3
2001	JUP	FSL	22	293	83	8	2	2	10	35	25	14	.283	.314	.345	-.010	.245	.263	.299	-.366	-13.7	69-CF -2
2001	HAR	EAS	22	117	29	7	0	0	3	18	6	0	.248	.279	.308	-.199	.222	.255	.274	-.430	-7.8	28-CF 1
2002	JAX	SOU	23	324	82	16	6	3	17	33	23	3	.253	.307	.367	-.045	.234	.266	.347	-.298	-9.6	74-CF -1
2002	LVG	PCL	23	153	50	7	3	0	2	17	12	0	.327	.335	.412	.003	.287	.296	.360	-.184	-.2	38-CF 1
2002	LAD	NL	23	11	3	1	0	0	0	2	0	0	.273	.273	.364	-.121	.273	.273	.455	-.096	.1	
2003	LAD	NL	24	184	44	8	2	1	8	25	6	3	.239	.277	.323	-.264	.251	.284	.347	-.237	-5.2	

Breakout: 39%   Improve: 62%   Collapse: 18%

Ruan might soon become the best late-inning defensive sub in all of baseball. He gets a great jump on the ball, runs like a gazelle, and guns down more unsuspecting victims than a crack shot paintballer at a Fielder family reunion. If the Dodgers ever lost their minds and gave this guy 150 starts, hop a plane to Vegas with your life savings in hand and bet it all on a new DiSars champ.

Joe Thurston   2B   **Born: 29-Sep-79**   **Age: 23**   **Bats: L**   **Throws: R**

YEAR	TM	LG	AGE	AB	H	2B	3B	HR	BB	SO	SB	CS	AVG	OBP	SLG	MLVR	EQBA	EQOBP	EQSLG	EQMLVR	VORP	DEFENSE	
2000	SBR	CLF	20	551	167	31	8	4	56	61	43	25	.303	.385	.410	.135	.242	.293	.332	-.261	-5.9	110-SS 6	28-2B -4
2001	JAX	SOU	21	544	145	25	7	7	48	65	20	18	.267	.339	.377	.003	.232	.289	.331	-.276	-9.1	121-2B -16	12-SS -1
2002	LVG	PCL	22	587	196	39	13	12	25	60	22	9	.334	.373	.506	.207	.289	.325	.438	-.013	27.9	118-2B 5	17-SS -2
2002	LAD	NL	22	13	6	1	0	0	0	1	0	0	.462	.462	.538	.643	.462	.462	.615	.698	2.6		
2003	LAD	NL	23	232	61	12	2	4	17	28	6	2	.261	.319	.378	-.102	.274	.327	.407	-.063	5.9		

Breakout: 17%   Improve: 51%   Collapse: 18%

The Dodgers love Thurston. Scouts love him, his coaches love him, even the ice-cream vendor slips him a cone from time to time. A .334 average, 64 extra-base hits, and 22 steals in Triple-A before your 23rd birthday tends to foster that kind of adoration. Thurston's talented enough to fare well in the minors by hacking at the first good pitch he sees. But 25 walks in 631 plate appearances won't cut it once he leaves generous Cashman Field for stingy Dodger Stadium. Broken record alert: Thurston's a great example of the Dodgers' glaring weakness in player development. Rather than working with hitters on waiting for a pitch to drive, they're taught to be aggressive, to a fault. He'll get his chance with Grudzielanek now a Cub. Expect a rough ride until he flunks out of the Randall Simon School of Hitting.

PITCHERS

Victor Alvarez — Born: 08-Nov-76 — Age: 26 — Bats: L — Throws: L

YEAR	TM	LG	AGE	G	GS	IP	H	BB	SO	HR	ERA	EQERA	EQH9	EQBB9	EQSO9	EQHR9	PERA	VORP	STF
2000	VRO	FSL	23	4	4	22.7	17	11	20	6	5.15	6.43	12.0	6.1	6.2	6.4	6.37	-2.3	-21
2000	SAN	TXS	23	11	8	48.3	44	30	43	3	3.91	5.55	9.8	5.9	5.8	0.9	5.69	-0.3	-1
2001	JAX	SOU	24	8	8	45.0	27	7	40	1	1.20	2.25	7.1	1.7	5.5	0.3	2.26	16.3	21
2001	LVG	PCL	24	20	20	118.0	115	41	94	12	4.27	4.31	8.9	3.7	5.2	1.0	4.24	15.7	6
2002	LVG	PCL	25	34	15	122.7	132	39	106	11	4.69	4.83	10.3	3.3	6.0	1.0	4.63	8.7	2
2002	LAD	NL	25	4	1	10.3	9	2	7	1	4.37	4.37	9.0	1.6	5.5	1.0	3.59	1.2	3
2003	LAD	NL	26	18	8	55.7	54	25	42	6	4.26	4.95	9.2	3.5	5.9	1.0	4.89	4.5	-2

Breakout: 15%   Improve: 41%   Collapse: 29%

Signed as a non-drafted free agent in 1997, Alvarez has passed a slew of pitchers with shinier pedigrees over the last few years. He split his time in Las Vegas between starting and bullpen work, posting a strikeout-to-walk ratio of nearly 3 to 1. The Dodgers gave him a start in garbage time at the end of last season. They should give him a shot at more than that in 2003, given all the question marks in the rotation. He could be reasonably effective in the fifth starter's role, if handed the chance.

Andy Ashby — Born: 11-Jul-67 — Age: 35 — Bats: R — Throws: R

YEAR	TM	LG	AGE	G	GS	IP	H	BB	SO	HR	ERA	EQERA	EQH9	EQBB9	EQSO9	EQHR9	PERA	VORP	STF
2000	ATL	NL	32	15	15	98.0	103	23	55	12	4.13	4.17	9.9	1.8	4.6	1.0	4.12	14.5	6
2000	PHI	NL	32	16	16	101.3	113	38	51	17	5.69	5.57	10.2	2.8	4.1	1.4	5.14	-0.7	-5
2001	LAD	NL	33	2	2	11.7	14	1	7	2	3.85	4.50	11.5	0.7	4.7	1.5	5.35	1.3	5
2002	LAD	NL	34	30	30	181.7	179	65	107	20	3.91	4.96	10.3	3.0	4.8	1.1	4.79	11.0	1
2003	LAD	NL	35	26	24	154.0	161	52	90	20	4.27	4.95	9.9	2.6	4.5	1.2	5.05	10.6	0

Breakout: 7%   Improve: 41%   Collapse: 23%

When healthy, Ashby's a slightly above-average starter who can give you seven good innings on a sunny day. As is, Ashby's health presents dual problems this year. If he breaks down like he did in 2001, the Dodgers will get minimal return for their $8 million. If he tosses 168.1 innings, Ashby's option kicks in at $8.5 million for 2004. That's a lot of kibble for a guy whose last good season came a year before "Who Let the Dogs Out" delighted music critics worldwide. If only the Dodgers had slapped a leash on Kevin Malone's money clip.

Kevin Beirne — Born: 01-Jan-74 — Age: 29 — Bats: L — Throws: R

YEAR	TM	LG	AGE	G	GS	IP	H	BB	SO	HR	ERA	EQERA	EQH9	EQBB9	EQSO9	EQHR9	PERA	VORP	STF
2000	CHR	INT	26	7	7	33.3	39	7	28	3	3.51	4.72	12.3	1.9	6.6	1.0	5.04	2.9	11
2000	CWS	AL	26	29	1	49.7	50	20	41	9	6.70	5.25	8.4	2.9	7.1	1.3	4.35	0.8	1
2001	SYR	INT	27	18	0	28.7	24	3	17	2	1.57	2.68	8.4	1.1	4.2	0.8	3.09	8.6	-4
2002	LVG	PCL	28	22	22	125.7	129	41	88	12	4.15	4.50	9.9	3.4	4.9	1.1	4.44	14.0	0
2002	LAD	NL	28	12	3	29.0	26	17	17	4	3.41	4.70	9.2	4.8	4.7	1.3	5.26	2.4	-16

Journeyman pitcher who can give you quality innings when he hits the strike zone. Beirne was part of the chewing gum and paper clip act the Dodgers used to keep the rotation together late last year as Brown and Ishii fell by the wayside. He didn't embarrass himself, and could have occupied a swingman role in 2003 had the Dodgers not let him bolt for Japan. Man, could this team use some legitimate high-level pitching prospects.

Andrew Brown — Born: 17-Feb-81 — Age: 22 — Bats: R — Throws: R

YEAR	TM	LG	AGE	G	GS	IP	H	BB	SO	HR	ERA	EQERA	EQH9	EQBB9	EQSO9	EQHR9	PERA	VORP	STF
2001	JAM	NYP	20	14	12	64.3	50	31	59	5	3.92	6.74	12.9	7.2	5.2	2.7	6.01	-8.9	-13
2002	VRO	FSL	21	25	24	127.0	97	62	129	13	4.11	5.29	9.9	5.8	6.7	2.2	4.87	3.0	6

A big righty who took a big step forward in 2002. Acquired in the Gary Sheffield trade, Brown looked good in his first year of full-season ball as a starter, using a live fastball to fan a batter an inning. He needs to tighten his control—if he lops off a walk a game he could move quickly through the system. After the great pitching prospect fire sale last year, Brown ranks behind only Joel Hanrahan in the Dodgers arms race.

Kevin Brown　　　Born: 14-Mar-65　Age: 38　Bats: R　Throws: R

YEAR	TM	LG	AGE	G	GS	IP	H	BB	SO	HR	ERA	EQERA	EQH9	EQBB9	EQSO9	EQHR9	PERA	VORP	STF
2000	LAD	NL	35	33	33	230.0	181	47	216	21	2.58	2.90	7.5	1.5	7.7	0.8	2.82	66.6	29
2001	LAD	NL	36	20	19	115.7	94	38	104	8	2.64	3.25	7.7	2.8	7.0	0.6	3.33	29.0	21
2002	LAD	NL	37	17	10	63.7	68	23	58	9	4.80	5.74	11.0	3.0	7.4	1.4	5.47	-1.8	6
2003	LAD	NL	38	23	15	94.7	89	30	78	10	3.65	4.23	9.0	2.5	6.4	1.0	4.30	13.5	9

Breakout: 7%　　Improve: 26%　　Collapse: 23%

After five straight seasons of 230 innings or more, Brown's old injury woes came home to roost. Chronic back problems have caused the most tsuris, though elbow and shoulder problems have crept into the picture. Worse still, Brown's injuries prompted management to throw more money at pitching help before last season, ignoring the multiple offensive holes in the lineup. With four years left on his $105 million contract that takes him through age 41, the Dodgers have dug themselves a deep ditch, which could quickly become a bottomless pit. Root for a full recovery—when healthy, Brown still throws one of the nastiest sinking fastballs you'll ever see.

Giovanni Carrara　　　Born: 04-Mar-68　Age: 35　Bats: R　Throws: R

YEAR	TM	LG	AGE	G	GS	IP	H	BB	SO	HR	ERA	EQERA	EQH9	EQBB9	EQSO9	EQHR9	PERA	VORP	STF
2000	CSP	PCL	32	18	15	96.7	89	30	89	8	3.26	3.13	8.2	2.7	6.6	0.9	3.38	25.4	16
2000	COL	NL	32	8	0	13.3	21	11	15	5	12.86	10.04	12.5	5.6	8.3	2.6	9.24	-6.9	-18
2001	LVG	PCL	33	6	6	29.0	27	9	35	5	3.10	3.54	8.5	3.2	7.8	1.7	4.39	6.3	13
2001	LAD	NL	33	47	3	85.3	73	24	70	12	3.17	3.50	8.0	2.4	6.4	1.2	3.89	18.0	2
2002	LAD	NL	34	63	1	90.7	83	32	56	14	3.27	4.45	9.5	2.9	5.1	1.5	4.73	9.4	-12
2003	LAD	NL	35	43	5	70.3	67	25	50	9	3.85	4.47	9.1	2.8	5.6	1.2	4.63	8.8	-6

Breakout: 18%　　Improve: 55%　　Collapse: 17%

Carrara regressed from his solid 2001 season as his control wavered at times, a troubling sign for a pitcher who already allows plenty of balls in play. He's still a useful, durable pitcher for a team with a complex about its pitching depth. That said, the line for a soft-tossing, right-handed deception artist gets thinner with each passing year.

Omar Daal　　　Born: 01-Mar-72　Age: 31　Bats: L　Throws: L

YEAR	TM	LG	AGE	G	GS	IP	H	BB	SO	HR	ERA	EQERA	EQH9	EQBB9	EQSO9	EQHR9	PERA	VORP	STF
2000	ARI	NL	28	20	16	96.0	127	42	45	17	7.22	6.74	11.8	3.2	3.7	1.4	6.31	-13.3	-15
2000	PHI	NL	28	12	12	71.0	81	30	51	9	4.69	4.85	10.4	3.1	5.8	1.0	5.10	5.2	6
2001	PHI	NL	29	32	32	185.7	199	56	107	26	4.46	4.97	10.4	2.6	4.5	1.2	4.88	11.0	0
2002	LAD	NL	30	39	23	161.3	142	54	105	20	3.91	4.60	9.2	2.8	5.3	1.2	4.26	15.8	0
2003	BAL	AL	31	31	20	122.0	133	41	73	17	4.76	4.96	9.9	2.8	5.1	1.2	4.79	11.1	-3

Breakout: 9%　　Improve: 51%　　Collapse: 17%

Daal's name surfaced in nearly every Dodger mock trade for a hitter from May to July. The Dodgers refused to deal him, an oddly stubborn stance for a pedestrian starter making $4.5 million on a team with multiple dead spots in the lineup. Daal mixed great and awful starts, going 8–3 in starts where he kept the ball in the park, 2–5 when he didn't. Signed to a pointless two-year, $7.5 million deal by the Orioles, who apparently didn't get the memo about baseball's New Economics.

Darren Dreifort　　　Born: 03-May-72　Age: 31　Bats: R　Throws: R

YEAR	TM	LG	AGE	G	GS	IP	H	BB	SO	HR	ERA	EQERA	EQH9	EQBB9	EQSO9	EQHR9	PERA	VORP	STF
2000	LAD	NL	28	32	32	192.7	175	87	164	31	4.16	4.67	8.5	3.3	6.8	1.3	4.56	17.9	11
2001	LAD	NL	29	16	16	94.7	89	47	91	11	5.13	5.22	8.8	4.2	7.4	1.0	4.80	3.0	13

Even the biggest optimist would concede that Dreifort's days as a starter, let alone an effective one, are done. So what can we expect from a pitcher whose best years weren't all that special, coming off a year and a half off the mound, with multiple Tommy John surgeries in the bank? With Eric Gagne around, Dreifort won't get the closer's job once rumored to be his. But he could fare well as a two-pitch setup man if his elbow holds up. The Dodgers would do well to spot him as a pinch hitter on the odd night they're short of bodies, assuming his bat hasn't atrophied. Having a pitcher who can hit as well as your shortstop is a neat little tactical advantage to have, even if it doesn't bode well for your shortstop.

Jonathan Figueroa   Born: 15-Sep-83   Age: 19   Bats: L   Throws: L

YEAR	TM	LG	AGE	G	GS	IP	H	BB	SO	HR	ERA	EQERA	EQH9	EQBB9	EQSO9	EQHR9	PERA	VORP	STF
2002	GRF	PIO	18	7	7	31.7	16	19	48	0	1.42	2.84	6.6	7.8	7.4	0.3	2.82	9.4	16
2002	SGA	SAL	18	8	8	44.3	22	20	57	1	1.42	3.25	6.3	5.7	7.1	0.6	3.23	11.1	21

The Dodgers' Venezuelan connections are bearing fruit. Signed for a $500,000 bonus, Figueroa breezed through the Pioneer League, then mowed down hitters in the Sally League. He's hiked his velocity up to the 90–94 range after hovering in the high-80s when the Dodgers first scouted him. Figueroa fires from a three-quarter delivery that further accentuates his 6'5" frame and long arms. A would-be high school senior in 2002, he already owns good command over his curve. He's got low mileage on his arm, having converted from first base at age 15. The Dodgers should conserve his fresh arm and not rush him through the system.

Eric Gagne   Born: 07-Jan-76   Age: 27   Bats: R   Throws: R

YEAR	TM	LG	AGE	G	GS	IP	H	BB	SO	HR	ERA	EQERA	EQH9	EQBB9	EQSO9	EQHR9	PERA	VORP	STF
2000	ABQ	PCL	24	9	9	55.7	56	15	59	8	3.88	4.50	9.6	2.4	7.7	1.6	4.34	6.2	23
2000	LAD	NL	24	20	19	101.3	106	60	79	20	5.15	5.67	9.7	4.3	6.2	1.6	6.02	-1.9	1
2001	LVG	PCL	25	4	4	23.7	15	8	31	2	1.52	1.81	5.7	3.5	8.4	0.8	2.38	9.7	31
2001	LAD	NL	25	33	24	151.7	144	46	130	24	4.75	4.85	8.9	2.6	6.6	1.3	4.57	10.8	10
2002	LAD	NL	26	77	0	82.3	55	16	114	6	1.97	2.55	6.8	1.6	11.1	0.7	2.49	25.9	36
2003	LAD	NL	27	36	4	66.3	50	19	69	7	2.50	2.91	7.2	2.3	8.1	0.9	3.15	18.4	17

Breakout: 28%   Improve: 57%   Collapse: 10%

Incroyable! After battling Luke Prokopec for the fifth starter job in 2001, Gagne achieved huge success last year after Prokopec left—as a stopper, not a starter. Using a talented pitcher to throw 82 innings instead of 200 won't usually land you on BP's Christmas card list. But Gagne blew hitters away by regularly dialing up fastballs in the high 90s last year, something we hadn't seen before. Was his increased velocity a function of a healthy elbow shaking off the last effects of Tommy John surgery or of his ability to cut loose, knowing he'd only be needed for 20 pitches a game? A little of both, says the research being done on the topic. The Dodgers may start serving poutine with Dodger Dogs if Gagne keeps going at this rate.

Alfredo Gonzalez   Born: 17-Sep-79   Age: 23   Bats: R   Throws: R

YEAR	TM	LG	AGE	G	GS	IP	H	BB	SO	HR	ERA	EQERA	EQH9	EQBB9	EQSO9	EQHR9	PERA	VORP	STF
2001	GRF	PIO	21	11	8	48.0	43	12	56	1	3.56	4.33	9.7	3.3	5.5	0.4	4.19	6.2	10
2002	VRO	FSL	22	17	0	34.3	20	11	47	3	1.57	2.54	7.5	3.7	8.8	1.8	3.00	10.8	19
2002	JAX	SOU	22	13	0	20.0	13	2	18	0	1.35	2.80	8.3	1.0	6.1	0.2	2.11	5.7	14
2002	LVG	PCL	22	14	0	21.7	23	9	23	1	2.90	4.31	10.0	4.3	7.3	0.5	4.51	2.6	9

Given the spotty success rate of even the best starting pitching prospects, it's doubly hard to get excited about relief prospects. But since the Dodgers' cupboard of starters lies empty in the upper levels, guys like Gonzalez make the most likely candidates for major league jobs in the near future. The slightly-built Dominican came out of nowhere, advancing through two levels before landing in the Vegas bullpen after half a season in Great Falls' 2001 rotation. Gonzalez dominated at every level, fanning more than a hitter per inning at each stop. The Dodgers should let him compete for a job this spring.

Joel Hanrahan   Born: 06-Oct-81   Age: 21   Bats: R   Throws: R

YEAR	TM	LG	AGE	G	GS	IP	H	BB	SO	HR	ERA	EQERA	EQH9	EQBB9	EQSO9	EQHR9	PERA	VORP	STF
2000	GRF	PIO	18	12	11	55.0	49	23	40	4	4.75	5.60	11.7	4.7	3.8	1.7	5.18	-0.6	-10
2001	WNC	SAL	19	27	26	144.0	136	55	116	13	3.38	8.15	15.7	5.9	4.7	2.4	7.54	-42.3	-12
2002	VRO	FSL	20	25	25	143.7	129	51	139	11	4.20	5.45	11.1	4.1	6.3	1.6	4.99	0.9	12
2002	JAX	SOU	20	3	3	11.0	15	7	10	2	10.64	13.15	19.3	6.9	6.7	3.8	10.07	-9.3	-20
2003	LAD	NL	21	17	13	75.3	74	39	62	9	4.68	5.43	9.3	4.0	6.4	1.1	5.36	1.5	2

Breakout: 28%   Improve: 64%   Collapse: 8%

Apparently Jim Brower wasn't available. Rumors had Hanrahan headed out at the deadline along with every other sentient minor league being with a functioning arm, but nothing materialized. Good thing. Hanrahan mixes an effective 91–92 mph fastball with a nasty slider and improving changeup. Even when he's struggled with consistency, Hanrahan has maintained his strong strikeout-per-inning rate. With the cupboard nearly bare, the Dodgers need to develop more pitchers like Hanrahan instead of peddling them to the highest bidder. We won't run projections for most A-ball pitchers, but Hanrahan's the best arm in the system by a fair margin.

Craig House   Born: 08-Jul-77   Age: 25   Bats: R   Throws: R

YEAR	TM	LG	AGE	G	GS	IP	H	BB	SO	HR	ERA	EQERA	EQH9	EQBB9	EQSO9	EQHR9	PERA	VORP	STF
2000	SLM	CRL	22	13	0	16.0	7	10	24	0	2.25	2.90	4.7	6.5	8.1	0.3	2.90	4.4	11
2000	CAR	SOU	22	18	0	21.3	14	15	28	0	3.80	4.75	6.9	6.7	8.1	0.3	4.14	1.5	7
2000	COL	NL	22	16	0	13.7	13	17	8	3	7.23	6.34	7.6	8.5	4.3	1.5	6.49	-1.5	-30
2001	CSP	PCL	23	54	0	58.7	50	31	62	4	4.45	3.81	7.3	5.5	6.8	0.7	3.80	10.2	0
2002	JAX	SOU	24	3	0	4.0	3	2	1	1	4.50	6.83	12.2	5.3	1.8	5.2	6.19	-0.6	-59
2002	LVG	PCL	24	19	0	20.7	25	16	25	3	7.39	7.75	11.6	8.0	8.4	1.6	7.32	-5.5	-11

Yes, we admit we have a soft spot for a guy who makes everyone in the park stop what they're doing to watch him, even with the toned-down version of his wacky delivery. Designated for assignment twice last year and still fighting through shoulder problems, House kept his no-contact-allowed approach going, striking out and walking a ton of hitters during his truncated season. Ben Weber didn't establish himself with his funky delivery and nasty stuff until his 30s. House outfunks him and out-nasties him by a wide margin. Light a candle and hope he settles in a lot faster than Weber did.

Kazuhisa Ishii   Born: 09-Sep-73   Age: 29   Bats: Throws: L

YEAR	TM	LG	AGE	G	GS	IP	H	BB	SO	HR	ERA	EQERA	EQH9	EQBB9	EQSO9	EQHR9	PERA	VORP	STF
2000	YKL	JCL	26	29	27	183.0	137	73	210	15	2.61	3.26	6.9	3.7	8.5	0.8	3.44	45.6	27
2001	YKL	JCL	27	27	27	175.0	135	82	173	18	3.39	4.18	7.2	3.9	7.7	1.0	3.96	25.8	18
2002	LAD	NL	28	28	28	154.0	137	106	143	20	4.27	5.56	9.0	5.6	7.4	1.3	5.46	-0.9	5
2003	LAD	NL	29	20	18	121.3	106	71	114	15	4.26	4.95	8.3	4.5	7.3	1.1	5.00	9.3	12

Breakout: 4%   Improve: 38%   Collapse: 22%

There aren't enough data points out there to tell us definitively if recovering from a line drive to the face is more or less diffi-cult than rehabbing from a scoped knee or bone chips in the elbow. Dickie Thon and Tony Conigliaro were never the same after taking fastballs off their skulls, and Rick Ankiel, Mark Wohlers, and Steve Blass can lecture for days on the fragile psyches of even healthy pitchers. What we do know: Ishii was on the verge of losing his rotation spot before getting injured, thanks to his obscene walk totals. With three more years left on his $12.2 million contract plus the $11.25 million paid out to secure Ishii's negotiating rights, this looks like another signing the Dodgers will end up regretting.

Will McCrotty   Born: 23-Jun-79   Age: 24   Bats: R   Throws: R

YEAR	TM	LG	AGE	G	GS	IP	H	BB	SO	HR	ERA	EQERA	EQH9	EQBB9	EQSO9	EQHR9	PERA	VORP	STF
2001	UTI	NYP	22	17	9	63.3	50	24	39	3	4.12	6.05	10.8	5.3	3.3	1.6	5.37	-4.0	-20
2001	WNC	SAL	22	21	0	36.7	24	10	46	2	1.96	4.51	10.0	3.9	6.7	1.3	4.23	3.5	2
2001	VRO	FSL	22	20	0	22.7	22	14	17	3	4.36	6.80	13.8	7.3	4.9	3.2	7.26	-3.6	-32
2002	JAX	SOU	23	43	0	52.7	37	30	57	3	2.39	4.50	9.2	5.7	7.4	1.1	4.29	5.2	0

In only his second year as a professional pitcher after a conversion from catcher, McCrotty struck out more than a batter an inning in relief for Jacksonville. His fastball hits 94, and he's working on spotting his slider. He'll need to refine his control, as high walk totals plagued him throughout the year, all the way to the Arizona Fall League. His curveball remains a work in progress.

Guillermo Mota   Born: 25-Jul-73   Age: 29   Bats: R   Throws: R

YEAR	TM	LG	AGE	G	GS	IP	H	BB	SO	HR	ERA	EQERA	EQH9	EQBB9	EQSO9	EQHR9	PERA	VORP	STF
2000	OTT	INT	26	35	0	63.0	49	31	35	4	2.29	2.68	7.0	4.4	4.2	0.7	3.74	18.9	-13
2000	MON	NL	26	29	0	30.0	27	12	24	3	6.00	4.16	7.6	2.9	6.3	0.8	3.65	4.1	0
2001	MON	NL	27	53	0	49.7	51	18	31	9	5.25	4.85	9.1	3.0	4.8	1.4	4.93	2.9	-16
2002	LVG	PCL	28	20	0	36.7	34	8	38	1	2.94	3.13	8.7	2.2	7.1	0.3	3.09	9.2	12
2002	LAD	NL	28	43	0	60.7	45	27	49	4	4.15	4.33	7.7	3.6	6.6	0.6	3.48	7.1	0
2003	LAD	NL	29	43	3	62.3	58	26	49	6	3.91	4.54	8.9	3.3	6.2	0.9	4.48	7.3	-3

Breakout: 16%   Improve: 42%   Collapse: 22%

Acquired last March with Wilkin Ruan for Matt Herges and Jorge Nunez, a trade that helped no one except a few real estate agents. Like Billy Koch, Mota's main pitch is a hard fastball that's dead straight. Like Koch, he walks too many hitters. Unlike Koch, Mota hasn't posted great strikeout totals in any of his four big league seasons. He also hasn't shown any consistent off-speed pitches in his arsenal. A converted shortstop, the Dodgers can always hope he's a late bloomer. If not, they've at least got a shotblocker for their intramural hoops team.

Hideo Nomo · Born: 31-Aug-68 · Age: 34 · Bats: R · Throws: R

YEAR	TM	LG	AGE	G	GS	IP	H	BB	SO	HR	ERA	EQERA	EQH9	EQBB9	EQSO9	EQHR9	PERA	VORP	STF
2000	DET	AL	31	32	31	190.0	191	89	181	31	4.74	4.20	8.3	3.4	8.2	1.2	4.47	27.5	21
2001	BOS	AL	32	33	33	198.0	171	96	220	26	4.50	3.95	7.2	4.0	9.2	1.1	3.96	34.2	27
2002	LAD	NL	33	34	34	220.3	189	101	193	26	3.39	4.52	8.8	3.7	7.1	1.2	4.46	24.1	13
2003	LAD	NL	34	28	26	170.3	153	76	160	21	4.03	4.67	8.6	3.5	7.3	1.1	4.56	20.3	15

Breakout: 9%   Improve: 46%   Collapse: 19%

A far cry from the rookie flash of eight years ago, Nomo has become a durable, reliable starter who keeps his team in ballgames. When he's right, his splitter still gives hitters fits. Having lost a few miles off his fastball, he's learned to spot it away from trouble. This is the guy a pennant contender signs when it needs an effective innings muncher to back up a pair of aces and a great offense. That the Dodgers had neither last year wasn't Nomo's fault. A batch of unearned runs and a walk total rivaling a July temperature reading in Riverside make an ERA near four a good bet this year, even in pitcher heaven.

Jesse Orosco · Born: 21-Apr-57 · Age: 46 · Bats: R · Throws: L

YEAR	TM	LG	AGE	G	GS	IP	H	BB	SO	HR	ERA	EQERA	EQH9	EQBB9	EQSO9	EQHR9	PERA	VORP	STF
2001	LAD	NL	44	35	0	16.0	17	7	21	3	3.94	4.78	9.8	3.6	9.9	1.5	5.80	1.1	10
2002	LAD	NL	45	56	0	27.0	24	12	22	4	3.00	4.45	9.2	3.6	6.6	1.5	4.82	2.8	-7
2003	SDN	NL	46	91	0	47.3	38	22	46	6	3.70	4.29	7.5	3.7	7.7	1.2	4.34	6.3	1

Breakout: 38%   Improve: 38%   Collapse: 1%

You remember 1979. Landing a man on the moon was a distant dream. Kids swiveled their hips to Hula Hoops and danced the Funky Chicken. An invention called Tele-Vision ushered in a new era of functionally illiterate zombies. It was also the year Jesse Orosco first took the mound in the big leagues, for the Mets. It would be easy to paint him as a washed-up relic, but Orosco has proven himself as a fairly effective one-batter specialist, called in to drive the Abreus, Heltons, and Kleskos of the league nuts with his assortment of floating frisbees. Feel free to set a target age for his retirement. We'll take the over, a bet that looks even sweeter after the Padres signed him to a one-year deal. You can safely ignore that projection, it doesn't really know what to say about a freak of nature.

Odalis Perez · Born: 11-Jun-77 · Age: 26 · Bats: · Throws: L

YEAR	TM	LG	AGE	G	GS	IP	H	BB	SO	HR	ERA	EQERA	EQH9	EQBB9	EQSO9	EQHR9	PERA	VORP	STF
2001	RIC	INT	24	5	5	23.0	23	2	22	1	2.74	3.58	10.1	0.9	6.7	0.5	3.78	4.9	23
2001	ATL	NL	24	24	16	95.3	108	39	71	7	4.91	5.29	11.2	3.5	5.8	0.6	4.97	2.1	4
2002	LAD	NL	25	32	32	222.3	182	38	155	21	3.00	3.57	8.6	1.4	5.7	0.9	3.26	47.8	17
2003	LAD	NL	26	31	29	191.3	182	46	133	19	3.38	3.92	9.1	1.9	5.4	0.9	3.93	34.0	12

Breakout: 11%   Improve: 44%   Collapse: 11%

Saved the staff, something few would have imagined a year ago. Two years removed from elbow surgery after feeling his way back in 2001, Perez exploded on the National League, grabbing the mantle of staff ace and harnessing his talent into a terrific season. His 129-pitch, two-hit shutout at Coors Field in his third start was the kind of knockout performance expected from Kevin Brown, not a 160-pounder who barely made the Opening Day rotation. Perez yielded just a .226 average to opposing hitters, a figure likely to rise this season as a few more balls in play drop in. Still, if he keeps his walk rate anywhere near this low, he'll see continued success, albeit not as quasi-Koufaxian as in 2002. Red flag alert: While Tracy did a reasonable job of watching Perez's pitch counts, anyone who goes from 118 to 222 innings pitched in a span of a year, that close to a major injury, raises the specter of further injury or periods of ineffectiveness going forward.

Brian Pilkington · Born: 17-Sep-82 · Age: 20 · Bats: R · Throws: R

YEAR	TM	LG	AGE	G	GS	IP	H	BB	SO	HR	ERA	EQERA	EQH9	EQBB9	EQSO9	EQHR9	PERA	VORP	STF
2001	GRF	PIO	18	5	2	16.0	19	2	17	2	5.63	6.46	14.5	1.7	5.2	2.7	7.05	-1.8	-6
2002	SGA	SAL	19	20	18	112.3	129	13	78	8	3.45	7.01	15.8	1.6	4.1	1.9	6.91	-18.8	-1
2002	VRO	FSL	19	3	3	19.0	16	3	10	2	2.37	4.25	11.0	1.9	3.5	2.3	4.15	2.6	0

The Dodgers' top pick in the 2001 draft, his first pro season was cut short due to shoulder problems, which required arthroscopic surgery. Pilkington showed great control in 21 combined starts in the Sally League and Florida State League in 2002. But he struck out just over six batters per nine innings, not the kind of dominance you'd want out of a top prospect. Unless his uncle Bert Blyleven bestows his great curve on him, Pilkington's career path looks like Josh Towers's, at best.

Paul Quantrill   Born: 03-Nov-68   Age: 34   Bats: L   Throws: R

YEAR	TM	LG	AGE	G	GS	IP	H	BB	SO	HR	ERA	EQERA	EQH9	EQBB9	EQSO9	EQHR9	PERA	VORP	STF
2000	TOR	AL	31	68	0	83.7	100	25	47	7	4.52	3.96	9.8	2.2	4.9	0.6	4.25	13.2	-5
2001	TOR	AL	32	80	0	83.0	86	12	58	6	3.04	3.19	9.3	1.2	6.0	0.6	3.38	20.2	5
2002	LAD	NL	33	86	0	76.7	80	25	53	1	2.70	4.12	10.9	2.7	5.7	0.1	4.26	10.7	-1
2003	LAD	NL	34	58	0	50.0	54	16	34	4	3.73	4.33	10.2	2.5	5.3	0.7	4.59	8.8	-7

Breakout: 12%   *Improve: 49%*   *Collapse: 25%*

Made for Dodger Stadium. Quantrill's pitches come in three varieties: sink, sinker, and sinkiest. That style helped him maintain a ludicrously low homer rate. His walk rate rose more than twofold, but remained respectable. The Dodgers' improved defense did the rest, handling scads of balls in play. Quantrill's due to make $6.1 million in the last two years of his three-year contract, a remnant of the Gord Ash era of wheee! spending.

Paul Shuey   Born: 16-Sep-70   Age: 32   Bats: R   Throws: R

YEAR	TM	LG	AGE	G	GS	IP	H	BB	SO	HR	ERA	EQERA	EQH9	EQBB9	EQSO9	EQHR9	PERA	VORP	STF
2000	CLE	AL	29	57	0	63.7	51	30	69	4	3.39	2.80	6.6	3.4	9.3	0.5	2.79	18.3	21
2001	CLE	AL	30	47	0	54.3	53	26	70	1	2.82	3.41	7.9	3.9	10.5	0.1	3.68	11.9	26
2002	AKR	EAS	31	2	2	2.0	2	0	3	0	4.50	3.75	12.3	0.8	11.3	0.3	3.40	0.4	37
2002	CLE	AL	31	39	0	37.3	31	10	39	1	2.41	2.25	6.8	2.2	8.9	0.2	2.53	13.0	24
2002	LAD	NL	31	28	0	30.7	25	21	24	2	4.40	5.35	8.3	5.5	6.2	0.6	4.56	0.1	-10
2003	LAD	NL	32	50	0	56.3	46	26	56	4	2.95	3.43	7.9	3.6	7.7	0.7	3.88	12.9	8

Breakout: 10%   *Improve: 39%*   *Collapse: 34%*

A solid seventh- and eighth-inning guy when healthy, he stayed injury-free after coming to L.A., but struggled anyway. Shuey regained his control over the season's last few weeks to help the team, even if it was too little, too late. He's got one more season left on a three-year contract signed with Cleveland to make ditching Ricardo Rodriguez look like a good idea. If it's any consolation, Rodriguez may not even be a top three pitching prospect in the loaded Indians system, even if he was easily the best upper-level arm the Dodgers had. Actually that's no consolation at all. Never mind.

Milwaukee Brewers

A good rule of thumb in consulting is to charge double if your client's a family-run business. It's not enough, but at least it's a start.

Family-run enterprises of all varieties are notoriously problematic. The politics, intrigue, and associated baggage that occur in every business are intensified and magnified when combined with the emotions and relationships that come with every family. Every business would prefer to have some form of a merit-based recognition and development program, where employees do good work, they're recognized and rewarded for it, the company prospers, and the employees' faith in management and the company increases as a result of the success. The larger the enterprise and/or family, the worse things can get. The competent worker who does a great job can only hope to move up to the Tom Hagen role in the company—you can't get promoted into the inner circle because of an accident of birth, while drooling nephews move into upper management. The best interests of the company and the best interests of individual family members don't often align, and the company finishes second in those skirmishes, often undermining the effectiveness and morale of the people in the company, and eventually dragging the organization down into a spiral with a surprisingly low bottom.

Think about it. Does anyone really think that of the six billion people in the world, the single most qualified individual to run Ford Motor Corporation just happens to be Bill Ford? Of course not. There's probably some management savant guy in Burkina Faso who's a lousy farmer, but has a natural ability to put together and execute a brilliant integrated global strategy, but that guy's not going to get the job. Working in or with a family business has a large number of risks and pitfalls that just aren't present in other companies. Other companies do hire nepotistas, but you don't have the damage caused by sleights from years past, bad memories from family gatherings, emotional baggage that could fill a C-141, and the occasional burst of spectacular incompetence that just wouldn't happen if the company in question hadn't hired someone without any qualifications for the job other than the right DNA.

Which brings us to the Milwaukee Brewers.

If you go to the MLB web site, and check out the front office of the Milwaukee Brewers, you'll find Wendy Selig-Prieb is the first name listed. Laurel Prieb's the vice president of marketing. In the past, you may remember relative Randy Levine as one of the chief negotiators for the owners. I don't know if these people are doing a good job. Wendy Selig-Prieb may be the best chair in the country. Laurel Prieb may have the skills of a Virginia Gray, Saatchi, and Steve Jobs put together. But you know what? I know that even if that's true, it's not why they got those positions. They got those positions because of accidents of birth and relationships. And that sends a clear message throughout the organization—that merit doesn't matter.

Is this unfair and personal? It's not personal at all. Here at BP, we don't know these people. We're only looking at what's plainly visible from the outside—how the organization is run in the eyes of the public, and the success they've had on the field. We see the transactions, the managerial decisions, the signings, the arguments on the mound between the pitcher and the manager, and dozens of other signs of discord. We see an organization making decisions based on fear of a strikeout record rather than on what's going to give the team the best chance to win, now and in the future. It's like judging a politician or a business based on their record and their public statements—it's what they choose to put forward. It's what they choose to be judged on.

So what is the record? This organization has hit bottom. There's nowhere else to fall to. Dean Taylor's regime has come to a merciful end, but it never really had a chance. Managers

---

Brewers Prospectus

2002 record: 56–106; Sixth place, NL Central

Pythagenport Record: 61–101

Runs scored per game: 3.9 (16th in NL)

Runs allowed per game: 5.1 (15th in NL)

Team EqA: .253 (14th in NL)

2002 Batters Age: 30.4 (7th oldest in NL)

2002 Pitchers Age: 27.3 (2nd youngest in NL)

Ballpark: Miller Park; Slight pitchers' park; Park Factor .979

2002: An awful, awful team drove fans away from the brand new ballpark they'd paid for.

2003: Front-office changes may be the start of progress, but there's a long way to go for a team with no stars and fewer prospects.

like Lopes, Garner, and Royster were hired without an understanding of their strengths, weaknesses, and styles. Dean Taylor and his team had no clear idea of how the Brewers were going to compete. They couldn't tell good players from bad players. They didn't know how baseball teams go about the business of winning games. Like management in a lot of fields, they focused too much on process and blame, and not enough on the end result. "Work on the fundamentals!" "We've got to do the little things!" "We gotta catch the ball!" Yes, all those things are nice, but too much attention to things like that, and too many homilies about the value of being aggressive and tough can obscure real problems that are far more serious and require attention more urgently. Alex Sanchez can work on the fundamentals all he wants. While he's doing that, other teams are gathering outfielders that do the things that drive success. They get on base. They hit for power. They stay healthy. Other teams and management groups are taking the time to identify the things that actually cause teams to win games, and they're doing those things.

That may sound simple, but it hasn't been done in Milwaukee in some time. In Milwaukee, the management team has been in the unfortunate situation of being surprised by the expected. All the pitchers that couldn't throw strikes or stay healthy in the minors couldn't do it in the majors, either. The mediocre, aging, fragile, expensive outfielder who had one phantom good season went back to being fragile, mediocre, and expensive. The farm system, which hasn't produced a hitter with plate discipline or power in years, still isn't producing any. Where's the outrage? Were these people really surprised they couldn't contend? Were they so focused on getting a new stadium that they thought they could wrap a dogmeat team with a bow, and people would come running from miles around? There was never a plan based on well-defended conviction.

But there is some good news for Brewers fans. The Brewers have hit bottom, and the latest old regime is gone. Doug Melvin has arrived as GM, hired Reid Nichols to help him rebuild the organization, and they've got a semblance of a plan. They're responsible for putting together the Texas system that produced players like Hank Blalock, Mark Teixeira, Travis Hafner, and a bunch of other farmhands that have a good chance to be good ballplayers. Lopes, Garner, and Royster are fading memories, replaced by Atlanta's Ned Yost, who's been watching Bobby Cox for over a decade.

The infrastructure's in place for Milwaukee to build, with proper marketing, planning, and a good team, a steady revenue stream based on attendance. Miller Park is a great place to watch a ball game, has the requisite luxury boxes to bring home the extra bucks, and gives more distant fans the solace that if they drive to the park, they're not going to go home with a rain check. The Brewers also have the good fortune of residing in the NL Central, where any team that wins 25 out of 30 at some point during the season could well win the division. They're behind Houston, Cincinnati, and St. Louis for now, but hey, Pittsburgh and Chicago haven't exactly been run as models of efficiency and forward thinking.

So the Brewers can get a fresh start, and there are a few ballplayers in the minors that could be part of the next contending Milwaukee team. Prince Fielder's an interesting prospect, and there are several live arms that could be actually converted to pitchers with enough time and patience. But it's an uphill battle. There is no culture of winning here. There is no base of successful convictions around which to build a club. It takes a long time to figure out what an organization should do, figure out what's necessary to do it, and then actually implement those changes, measure the results, and tweak things until it works. Between now and the time the Brewers are a strong organization, a lot of people need to have their noses tweaked, and an honest assessment of every part of the organization needs to take place.

The Brewers are never going to have the kind of revenue stream that the Red Sox or Yankees do. There's just not enough advertising revenue in the Midwest to support a media contract of that magnitude. It's simple math. So the Brewers are going to need to do what other financially constricted clubs have done. But those other clubs, like the Twins and A's, have a head start, talented front offices, and have already gone a long way toward building a lasting organization that runs well. Which means Doug Melvin and the Brewers have little time to waste. They need to get busy. Fortunately for them, since there are teams out there doing what the Brewers need to do, the Brewers can learn from the words of Pablo Picasso: "Good artists copy. Great artists steal." The same holds true in business and baseball.

HITTERS

Izzy Alcantara LF Born: 06-May-71 Age: 32 Bats: R Throws: R

YEAR	TM	LG	AGE	AB	H	2B	3B	HR	BB	SO	SB	CS	AVG	OBP	SLG	MLVR	EQBA	EQOBP	EQSLG	EQMLVR	VORP	DEFENSE		
2000	PAW	INT	29	299	92	17	1	29	25	84	2	1	.308	.369	.662	.430	.280	.331	.597	.217	22.6	46-RF -3		
2001	PAW	INT	30	451	134	26	1	36	57	107	9	2	.297	.382	.599	.374	.275	.356	.553	.189	33.3	61-RF 2		
2002	IND	INT	31	410	110	21	2	27	51	88	9	3	.268	.351	.527	.191	.244	.324	.483	.009	11.1	59-LF -3	19-1B -1	
2002	MIL	NL	31	32	8	1	0	2	0	6	0	1	.250	.250	.469	-.046	.250	.250	.469	-.138	-.0			
2003	MIL	NL	32	172	43	8	1	9	20	43	3	3	.251	.332	.473	.037	.257	.334	.491	.045	3.1			

Breakout: 27%   Improve: 50%   Collapse: 22%

Free talent, provided you can accept the associated baggage. He can hit for some power and some average, and a better defender than he gets credit for, but he's got a reputation as an annoying, obnoxious guy, and that matters. If a club has an abject hole at a corner, they could put Alcantara there, pray he didn't start channeling Carl Douglas tunes, and get some reasonable production from him. Sadly, at a point last year, Alcantara was probably the Brewers' best outfield option. Shudder.

Paul Bako C Born: 20-Jun-72 Age: 31 Bats: L Throws: R

YEAR	TM	LG	AGE	AB	H	2B	3B	HR	BB	SO	SB	CS	AVG	OBP	SLG	MLVR	EQBA	EQOBP	EQSLG	EQMLVR	VORP	DEFENSE
2000	FLA	NL	28	161	39	6	1	0	22	48	0	0	.242	.337	.292	-.248	.245	.331	.301	-.226	.4	47-C 0
2000	ATL	NL	28	58	11	4	0	2	5	15	0	0	.190	.254	.362	-.359	.186	.238	.373	-.346	-1.8	18-C 1
2001	ATL	NL	29	137	29	10	1	2	20	34	1	0	.212	.312	.343	-.208	.216	.314	.353	-.207	1.1	46-C 0
2002	MIL	NL	30	234	55	8	1	4	20	46	0	2	.235	.295	.329	-.172	.248	.304	.353	-.206	1.8	65-C -4
2003	CHC	NL	31	170	38	8	1	3	18	40	1	1	.223	.301	.333	-.217	.229	.304	.350	-.211	-1.9	

Breakout: 26%   Improve: 46%   Collapse: 24%

Bako is what he is: an adequate backup who bats lefty for spice. Acquired by the Cubs in their ingenious plot to acquire every solid backup catcher, except that they're already running out of roster room to bring the scheme to fruition. If they don't add anybody else, he should be Damian Miller's caddy.

Ron Belliard 2B Born: 07-Apr-75 Age: 28 Bats: R Throws: R

YEAR	TM	LG	AGE	AB	H	2B	3B	HR	BB	SO	SB	CS	AVG	OBP	SLG	MLVR	EQBA	EQOBP	EQSLG	EQMLVR	VORP	DEFENSE	
2000	MIL	NL	25	571	150	30	9	8	82	84	7	5	.263	.358	.389	-.067	.261	.348	.386	-.067	23.7	148-2B 2	
2001	MIL	NL	26	364	96	30	3	11	35	65	5	2	.264	.337	.453	.022	.268	.338	.458	.020	24.2	94-2B 10	
2002	MIL	NL	27	289	61	13	0	3	18	46	2	3	.211	.260	.287	-.305	.225	.270	.311	-.346	-9.9	41-2B -4	29-3B -6
2003	MIL	NL	28	281	70	15	2	5	29	46	3	2	.250	.325	.373	-.106	.255	.326	.388	-.104	3.2		

Breakout: 25%   Improve: 50%   Collapse: 23%

There were a few moments there when it looked like Belliard might be a very fine ballplayer. As far back as 1997, he put up pretty reasonable numbers, showing the ability to hit for power, average, play defense, and draw walks. Like others in the organization, he's got a bit of a reputation as a tough guy to work with. No one wants to work with pinheads or jerks, but at some point, don't you have to take a look at the surrounding organization, or the selection process, and make an honest assessment of what's going on? Belliard's got the ability to be a productive and successful ballplayer. He's young enough to break out and put up some impressive numbers, but it's probably not going to happen in Milwaukee. A change of scenery might be best for all concerned.

Ryan Christenson Born: 28-Mar-74 Age: 29 Bats: R Throws: R

YEAR	TM	LG	AGE	AB	H	2B	3B	HR	BB	SO	SB	CS	AVG	OBP	SLG	MLVR	EQBA	EQOBP	EQSLG	EQMLVR	VORP	DEFENSE
2000	OAK	AL	26	129	32	2	2	4	19	33	1	2	.248	.349	.388	-.098	.258	.349	.406	-.040	1.6	54-LF -6
2001	SAC	PCL	27	70	12	4	0	1	4	13	2	0	.171	.216	.271	-.542	.157	.203	.243	-.609	-7.4	14-CF -1
2001	TUC	PCL	27	215	62	17	0	6	23	43	5	2	.288	.357	.451	.033	.244	.312	.380	-.156	1.4	57-CF -4
2002	IND	INT	28	260	66	17	2	5	18	28	11	5	.254	.307	.392	-.064	.230	.283	.364	-.243	-4.4	64-CF 8
2002	MIL	NL	28	58	9	4	0	1	5	13	0	0	.155	.222	.276	-.415	.169	.222	.322	-.457	-4.3	16-CF 0

Christenson never developed the power that he flashed during a season long ago in the Oakland organization. He's an acceptable fifth outfielder at this point. He's a defensive sub who can play center pretty well, pinch run for the Fred McGriffs of the world, draw some walks, and hit a few line drives from the right side. He should either be the first guy called up from Triple-A for a championship team, or a 24th/25th man on a lesser club. With the Rangers, he's waiting on injuries.

Daryl Clark　　　3B　Born: 25-Sep-79　Age: 23　Bats: L　Throws: R

YEAR	TM	LG	AGE	AB	H	2B	3B	HR	BB	SO	SB	CS	AVG	OBP	SLG	MLVR	EQBA	EQOBP	EQSLG	EQMLVR	VORP	DEFENSE	
2000	OGD	PIO	20	218	74	12	4	15	67	53	5	4	.339	.498	.638	.590	.203	.323	.369	-.176	.7	35-3B -10	19-1B -10
2001	BLT	MDW	21	501	142	24	2	21	61	135	4	5	.283	.369	.465	.186	.211	.277	.345	-.293	-14.0	120-3B -29	
2002	HDS	CLF	22	340	83	18	2	19	58	117	4	5	.244	.359	.476	.099	.182	.271	.344	-.323	-12.2	50-3B -20	17-LF -3
2003	MIL	NL	23	157	36	7	1	6	21	50	2	2	.231	.327	.395	-.087	.236	.328	.410	-.085	1.7		

Breakout: 61%　　Improve: 80%　　Collapse: 9%

Clark's an extremely bad defensive third baseman. There's just no way to sugarcoat it. Unlike most offensive players in the Brewers' system, Clark can hit, as he amply demonstrated in the Pioneer and Midwest leagues. For a 17th round pick by the Brewers, he's coming along nicely, but the scouts don't much care for him. He needs to work on shortening his stroke so that breaking pitches don't eat him alive at higher levels. Defensively, he's either going to be in the outfield or be a DH. Ground balls and Daryl are seeking mutual restraining orders against each other.

Edgard Clemente　　　　　Born: 15-Dec-75　Age: 27　Bats: R　Throws: R

YEAR	TM	LG	AGE	AB	H	2B	3B	HR	BB	SO	SB	CS	AVG	OBP	SLG	MLVR	EQBA	EQOBP	EQSLG	EQMLVR	VORP	DEFENSE
2000	EDM	PCL	24	87	21	4	1	2	9	23	0	2	.241	.327	.379	-.166	.207	.277	.322	-.327	-5.8	20-RF 0
2000	ANA	AL	24	78	17	2	0	0	0	27	0	1	.218	.228	.244	-.572	.221	.231	.247	-.519	-7.7	19-OF -1
2001	PAW	INT	25	300	74	14	0	12	25	84	2	0	.247	.315	.413	-.013	.234	.297	.398	-.166	1.0	83-CF 2
2002	PAW	INT	26	231	61	12	0	7	14	63	5	0	.264	.309	.407	-.017	.249	.294	.395	-.165	-5.3	58-RF 2
2002	IND	INT	26	142	29	7	2	1	9	37	1	1	.204	.266	.303	-.279	.190	.249	.289	-.437	-9.7	38-CF -1

Another guy with some baggage, some tools, and a faded star. He still strikes out a bunch, and really has nothing to offer except reasonable defense, and the ability to hammer the occasional cripple pitch. He is 27 this year, and sometimes people suddenly recapture some of the spark from earlier in their life. He's got a marquee name, and baseball's pretty forgiving of the past if you can perform today, so anything's possible for Clemente—he just needs to go out and hit like crazy, and do it now.

Jeff Deardorff　　　LF　Born: 14-Aug-78　Age: 24　Bats: R　Throws: R

YEAR	TM	LG	AGE	AB	H	2B	3B	HR	BB	SO	SB	CS	AVG	OBP	SLG	MLVR	EQBA	EQOBP	EQSLG	EQMLVR	VORP	DEFENSE	
2000	MUD	CLF	21	421	103	20	7	10	32	120	7	10	.245	.300	.397	-.050	.198	.228	.324	-.427	-25.9	71-3B 2	28-1B -2
2001	HDS	CLF	22	260	79	18	1	15	22	70	5	4	.304	.365	.554	.260	.224	.273	.405	-.209	-8.4	37-RF -7	30-1B -6
2001	HUN	SOU	22	201	56	11	1	14	13	66	1	1	.279	.329	.552	.231	.240	.279	.471	-.092	-.9	38-RF -1	
2002	HUN	SOU	23	425	108	23	1	19	60	131	13	6	.254	.356	.447	.135	.224	.302	.400	-.161	-8.6	59-LF -4	32-1B 3
2003	MIL	NL	24	181	45	10	1	8	17	52	4	3	.247	.316	.439	-.037	.253	.317	.455	-.032	.1		

Breakout: 60%　　Improve: 77%　　Collapse: 14%

Deardorff showed significant progress during the 2002 season. Instead of madly flailing at breaking pitches down and away, he learned to lay off the stuff that breaks out of the strike zone. The result was an increased walk rate, and more consistent solid contact and power. His strikeout rate is still high, but there's some promise here with the bat, and his willingness to work and learn new positions is a positive. He'll spend the season at Triple-A, and there may be some further adjustments to make there, but he's on a good path. The Brewers made a mistake by not promoting him to Triple-A at some point during the 2002 season, but it's a small loss.

Tony DeRosso　　　3B　Born: 07-Nov-75　Age: 27　Bats: R　Throws: R

YEAR	TM	LG	AGE	AB	H	2B	3B	HR	BB	SO	SB	CS	AVG	OBP	SLG	MLVR	EQBA	EQOBP	EQSLG	EQMLVR	VORP	DEFENSE	
2000	TRN	EAS	24	449	126	28	4	20	45	91	0	1	.281	.353	.494	.188	.246	.302	.432	-.100	10.3	62-3B -5	33-1B -7
2001	HUN	SOU	25	218	51	17	0	6	19	36	0	1	.234	.301	.394	-.060	.211	.261	.350	-.318	-7.9	60-3B -4	
2001	MOB	SOU	25	94	22	5	0	3	9	20	0	0	.234	.321	.383	-.049	.208	.274	.344	-.302	-2.9	15-3B 0	
2002	HDS	CLF	26	103	38	11	2	7	16	20	2	0	.369	.467	.718	.683	.272	.350	.505	.110	7.9	26-3B 1	
2002	ALT	EAS	26	182	35	5	4	8	27	48	2	0	.192	.300	.396	-.091	.171	.260	.348	-.346	-8.0	24-3B 2	

I can't find anyone that knows anything about this guy. No one seems to have heard of him, and the story his lines tell leads to a number of questions. What happened after the 2000 season? Hitting .281/.353/.494 at Trenton would usually call for a promotion. Instead, he got moved around and struggled in the Southern League, before getting sent to High Desert, where he destroyed the pitching. His numbers imply a pretty interesting story, and someone who's at least worth a second look. This is probably some sort of witness protection thing.

Prince Fielder   1B   Born: 09-May-84   Age: 19   Bats: L   Throws: R

YEAR	TM	LG	AGE	AB	H	2B	3B	HR	BB	SO	SB	CS	AVG	OBP	SLG	MLVR	EQBA	EQOBP	EQSLG	EQMLVR	VORP	DEFENSE
2002	OGD	PIO	18	146	57	12	0	10	37	27	3	4	.390	.534	.678	.768	.245	.352	.415	-.032	2.5	34-1B -8
2002	BLT	MDW	18	112	27	7	0	3	10	27	0	0	.241	.320	.384	.015	.191	.246	.313	-.410	-9.3	30-1B -11
2003	MIL	NL	19	208	52	10	1	8	27	52	3	2	.252	.348	.426	.004	.257	.350	.443	.011	2.9	

Breakout: 64%   Improve: 76%   Collapse: 15%

You know the back story. The young man can most definitely mash. He's got an alert batting eye, a quick stroke, and seems to really have a good grasp of the mechanics of his swing. There's going to be a lot of attention paid to his progress, and he's going to face some obstacles that others won't have to deal with, but he appears to absolutely be the real thing with the bat. Defensively, he looks awkward in the field, and it's going to be a struggle for him to become an adept first baseman. He's a surprisingly good athlete, and it wouldn't surprise me if he were to hook up with a conditioning guru, become a Gabe Kapler-like hard body, and end up as an outfielder. No matter what happens, he's going to hit for power.

Brian Foster   Born: 21-Aug-81   Age: 21   Bats: R   Throws: R

YEAR	TM	LG	AGE	AB	H	2B	3B	HR	BB	SO	SB	CS	AVG	OBP	SLG	MLVR	EQBA	EQOBP	EQSLG	EQMLVR	VORP	DEFENSE
2000	OGD	PIO	18	134	29	7	0	2	17	29	2	2	.216	.327	.313	-.231	.133	.197	.200	-.688	-14.3	38-C -5
2001	BLT	MDW	19	123	18	8	0	4	10	55	0	0	.146	.216	.309	-.334	.112	.162	.232	-.726	-15.6	26-C -3
2002	HDS	CLF	20	230	54	9	1	14	20	87	5	0	.235	.302	.465	-.011	.177	.227	.346	-.410	-10.0	60-C -10
2002	HUN	SOU	20	33	8	3	0	0	16	1	2	.242	.265	.333	-.162	.212	.225	.273	-.498	-2.9	

Flailing catcher who's probably going to have to move to another position. His plate discipline is comparable to Helen Keller's, but he's got good bat speed, and hits the ball with authority. He's going to need to shorten his swing, work on his pitch recognition, and either find another position to play or work on his footwork behind the plate.

Keith Ginter   2B/3B   Born: 05-May-76   Age: 27   Bats: R   Throws: R

YEAR	TM	LG	AGE	AB	H	2B	3B	HR	BB	SO	SB	CS	AVG	OBP	SLG	MLVR	EQBA	EQOBP	EQSLG	EQMLVR	VORP	DEFENSE	
2000	ROU	TXS	24	462	154	30	3	26	82	127	24	11	.333	.458	.580	.476	.276	.375	.481	.124	42.7	121-2B -6	
2001	NWO	PCL	25	457	123	31	5	16	61	147	8	6	.269	.383	.464	.145	.249	.348	.426	-.021	26.1	86-2B -4	31-LF -1
2002	NWO	PCL	26	435	115	28	1	12	56	97	3	4	.264	.364	.416	.075	.250	.336	.392	-.089	14.8	56-2B -7	53-3B 6
2002	HOU	NL	26	5	1	1	0	0	2	1	0	0	.200	.500	.400	.229	.200	.491	.400	.186	.5		
2002	MIL	NL	26	76	18	8	0	1	15	14	0	0	.237	.363	.382	.015	.256	.370	.410	.003	4.3	20-3B -2	
2003	HOU	NL	27	272	69	16	1	9	36	64	5	4	.256	.351	.421	.004	.254	.346	.424	-.024	8.8		

Breakout: 13%   Improve: 42%   Collapse: 33%

Ginter may very well be your Opening Day starter at the hot corner. As temps go, there are worse choices. He's got a wee bit of sock, and he'll take a free pass now and again, and he's shown promise moving over to third from second, where his defense consistently got bad marks.

Cristian Guerrero   RF   Born: 12-Jul-80   Age: 22   Bats: R   Throws: R

YEAR	TM	LG	AGE	AB	H	2B	3B	HR	BB	SO	SB	CS	AVG	OBP	SLG	MLVR	EQBA	EQOBP	EQSLG	EQMLVR	VORP	DEFENSE
2000	OGD	PIO	19	255	87	14	4	12	37	42	24	6	.341	.432	.569	.415	.216	.275	.352	-.284	-12.3	57-RF -2
2000	BLT	MDW	19	55	9	4	0	2	1	18	1	0	.164	.193	.345	-.281	.143	.149	.268	-.692	-8.7	14-RF -2
2001	HDS	CLF	20	327	102	18	2	7	18	79	22	11	.312	.350	.443	.096	.235	.265	.333	-.319	-18.8	80-RF -11
2002	HUN	SOU	21	394	88	17	1	8	26	101	21	9	.223	.277	.332	-.156	.204	.238	.311	-.422	-35.2	100-RF -6
2003	MIL	NL	22	161	37	7	1	4	12	40	5	5	.229	.284	.361	-.206	.234	.286	.374	-.208	-8.6	

Breakout: 65%   Improve: 80%   Collapse: 12%

A gifted athlete with power and speed, Guerrero is not making a lot of progress in terms of converting his physical skills into baseball success. He'll spend another season in Double-A, where he can work on taking the proper line to the ball, and limit his propensity to swing at pitches in his eyes.

Bill Hall   SS   Born: 28-Dec-79   Age: 23   Bats: R   Throws: R

YEAR	TM	LG	AGE	AB	H	2B	3B	HR	BB	SO	SB	CS	AVG	OBP	SLG	MLVR	EQBA	EQOBP	EQSLG	EQMLVR	VORP	DEFENSE	
2000	BLT	MDW	20	470	123	30	6	3	18	127	10	11	.262	.290	.370	-.044	.204	.216	.294	-.490	-33.3	130-SS	-6
2001	HDS	CLF	21	346	105	21	6	15	22	78	18	9	.303	.350	.529	.206	.227	.262	.390	-.249	-2.5	89-SS	-10
2001	HUN	SOU	21	160	41	8	1	3	5	46	5	3	.256	.279	.375	-.108	.228	.242	.333	-.368	-6.4	41-SS	0
2002	IND	INT	22	465	106	20	1	4	25	105	17	10	.228	.273	.301	-.257	.211	.257	.282	-.420	-24.6	125-SS	-23
2002	MIL	NL	22	36	7	1	1	1	3	13	0	1	.194	.256	.361	-.222	.216	.256	.405	-.247	-1.1		
2003	MIL	NL	23	182	43	9	2	4	12	45	4	4	.237	.290	.366	-.185	.243	.291	.379	-.186	-1.7		

Breakout: 61%   Improve: 77%   Collapse: 13%

It was a measure of the club's desperation that they tried to foist Bill Hall off as a prospect. Although he's athletic, he has yet to show he can play short, and he's never going to hit outside of a place like High Desert. One of the benefits of Melvin's arrival is that there's no reason for him to observe the obligations of the past regime and stick Hall in front of season ticket holders for 120 games any time soon.

Jeffrey Hammonds   CF   Born: 05-Mar-71   Age: 32   Bats: R   Throws: R

YEAR	TM	LG	AGE	AB	H	2B	3B	HR	BB	SO	SB	CS	AVG	OBP	SLG	MLVR	EQBA	EQOBP	EQSLG	EQMLVR	VORP	DEFENSE	
2000	COL	NL	29	454	152	24	2	20	44	83	14	7	.335	.400	.529	.215	.313	.371	.492	.168	29.0	103-RF	1
2001	MIL	NL	30	174	43	11	1	6	14	42	5	3	.247	.318	.425	-.064	.250	.317	.432	-.069	5.3	43-CF	1
2002	MIL	NL	31	448	115	26	5	9	52	86	4	5	.257	.337	.397	.004	.268	.342	.419	-.027	18.6	105-CF	-1
2003	MIL	NL	32	329	87	17	2	9	33	65	5	3	.263	.333	.410	-.033	.269	.335	.426	-.027	3.9		

Breakout: 17%   Improve: 46%   Collapse: 25%

I have a friend whose fantasy team name is always "A Dead Horse." In that tradition, we at BP would like to remind everyone what an incredibly bad signing this was, and how bad the internal disease of the organization must be to ever sign such a contract. Hammonds was (a) coming off of a rare healthy season, (b) exiting his prime, and (c) coming from the greatest hitting environment in the history of the world. Since signing that theee-year, $22 million deal, Hammonds has had basically one full season of at-bats over two years, during which he's hit a whopping .252/.329/.405. Depending on how much bad luck the Brewers are in for, he could do something like play 129 games, all after April 20th, and hit .301 with 31 HR, 109 RBI, and 44 walks. That's probably a considerably worse scenario than another year of injuries and mediocrity. God would truly have to hate the Brewers to submit them to that fate, because they'd probably feel obligated to re-sign him at that point.

James Hardy   SS   Born: 19-Aug-82   Age: 20   Bats: R   Throws: R

YEAR	TM	LG	AGE	AB	H	2B	3B	HR	BB	SO	SB	CS	AVG	OBP	SLG	MLVR	EQBA	EQOBP	EQSLG	EQMLVR	VORP	DEFENSE	
2001	OGD	PIO	18	125	31	5	0	2	15	12	1	2	.248	.329	.336	-.146	.159	.215	.214	-.623	-12.9	35-SS	2
2002	HDS	CLF	19	335	98	19	1	6	19	38	9	3	.293	.332	.409	.007	.222	.250	.306	-.395	-14.2	79-SS	16
2002	HUN	SOU	19	145	33	7	0	1	9	19	1	2	.228	.273	.297	-.209	.209	.235	.277	-.473	-9.5	37-SS	3
2003	MIL	NL	20	202	48	8	1	5	12	28	3	2	.236	.283	.358	-.207	.241	.285	.371	-.210	-2.6		

Breakout: 74%   Improve: 84%   Collapse: 9%

There are some things to like here. Hardy's a tremendous and graceful athlete, with great range and a powerful arm at shortstop. He hit for some average at High Desert, with a few doubles as a teaser for more power in the future. He didn't walk a lot, but he put the ball in play, and wasn't fooled by occasions when he wasn't thrown fastballs. Hardy's young enough to develop his offensive skills, and he plays defense well enough that he'll probably be a talented SS in the majors. He's not going to be Alex Rodriguez, but Hardy could turn into a very good ballplayer.

Lenny Harris   PH   Born: 28-Oct-64   Age: 38   Bats: L   Throws: R

YEAR	TM	LG	AGE	AB	H	2B	3B	HR	BB	SO	SB	CS	AVG	OBP	SLG	MLVR	EQBA	EQOBP	EQSLG	EQMLVR	VORP	DEFENSE	
2000	ARI	NL	35	85	16	1	1	1	3	5	5	0	.188	.216	.259	-.594	.186	.205	.256	-.575	-8.6	17-3B	-2
2000	NYM	NL	35	138	42	6	3	3	17	17	8	1	.304	.381	.457	.126	.314	.381	.464	.146	12.9	15-3B	-5
2001	NYM	NL	36	135	30	5	1	0	8	9	3	2	.222	.266	.274	-.378	.234	.276	.292	-.356	-8.2		
2002	MIL	NL	37	197	60	8	2	3	14	17	4	1	.305	.357	.411	.092	.318	.365	.433	.077	8.6	13-LF	0
2003	CHC	NL	38	112	28	5	1	1	8	10	2	0	.254	.306	.343	-.177	.261	.309	.360	-.168	-2.5		

Breakout: 14%   Improve: 37%   Collapse: 37%

Parlayed a few key hits and affability into an aura that's given him a nice little career. Harris has been a prolific pinch hitter, and he's good enough to be in that role, with all it entails. He might want to find a greener pasture and find a contending team with which to ply his trade. His torn quadriceps at the end of last season might have been the curtain for Lenny, but he's a spring training NRI with the Cubs, and you know how Dusty loves veterans.

Corey Hart   3B   Born: 24-Mar-82   Age: 21   Bats: R   Throws: R

YEAR	TM	LG	AGE	AB	H	2B	3B	HR	BB	SO	SB	CS	AVG	OBP	SLG	MLVR	EQBA	EQOBP	EQSLG	EQMLVR	VORP	DEFENSE	
2000	OGD	PIO	18	216	62	9	1	2	13	27	6	0	.287	.333	.366	-.096	.188	.205	.244	-.591	-23.6	53-1B -10	
2001	OGD	PIO	19	262	89	18	1	11	26	47	14	1	.340	.403	.542	.345	.221	.268	.345	-.305	-13.5	60-1B -10	
2002	HDS	CLF	20	393	113	26	10	22	37	101	24	11	.288	.356	.573	.258	.214	.267	.415	-.214	-2.5	47-3B -10	43-1B -2
2002	HUN	SOU	20	94	25	3	0	2	7	16	3	2	.266	.343	.362	.012	.240	.286	.333	-.274	-2.1	19-3B -5	
2003	*MIL*	*NL*	*21*	*223*	*55*	*10*	*2*	*6*	*17*	*49*	*5*	*5*	*.245*	*.304*	*.389*	*-.124*	*.250*	*.306*	*.404*	*-.123*	*-1.2*		

Breakout: 45%   Improve: 75%   Collapse: 16%

Hart's probably miscast as a 3B, but has a good skill set for future development, and isn't the typical corner infielder tweener lummox. He runs well, moves athletically, and has legitimate power to all fields. As he fills out a bit, he's likely to start turning some of those doubles into home runs. His strike zone judgment needs work, and if he can turn that corner, he could be a serious power threat in the majors.

Jose Hernandez   SS/3B   Born: 14-Jul-69   Age: 33   Bats: R   Throws: R

YEAR	TM	LG	AGE	AB	H	2B	3B	HR	BB	SO	SB	CS	AVG	OBP	SLG	MLVR	EQBA	EQOBP	EQSLG	EQMLVR	VORP	DEFENSE	
2000	MIL	NL	30	446	109	22	1	11	41	125	3	7	.244	.316	.372	-.185	.242	.304	.369	-.188	.1	89-3B -2	33-SS 0
2001	MIL	NL	31	542	135	26	2	25	39	185	5	4	.249	.302	.443	-.067	.255	.305	.450	-.062	23.4	143-SS 0	
2002	MIL	NL	32	525	151	24	2	24	52	188	3	5	.288	.356	.478	.168	.295	.359	.499	.139	50.8	147-SS 18	
2003	*COL*	*NL*	*33*	*357*	*97*	*18*	*2*	*16*	*35*	*103*	*3*	*3*	*.271*	*.339*	*.467*	*.056*	*.251*	*.316*	*.424*	*-.076*	*7.0*		

Breakout: 9%   Improve: 30%   Collapse: 31%

Bill James has done a lot of work in baseball analysis, much of it good, some of it not. But one of the most insightful things he ever pointed out is that teams tend to take out their frustration on their best players. In no case is that more true than with Hernandez and the Brewers. Hernandez is a very good defensive shortstop. He gets to a ton of balls, has a great arm, a quick release, and the baseball instincts that Derek Jeter gets credit for. He's a ballplayer. In addition, he's a pretty darn good hitter. He hits for some noteworthy power. But . . . wait for it . . . he strikes out a lot. Would it be good if he struck out less? Sure. But as has happened in the past, once a player gets close to breaking the single season record for strikeouts, that player gets yanked, ostensibly to "protect" him. What a load of crap. Royster and the Brewers were at best foolish, and at worst cowardly. Hernandez was their best player in 2002, and they sat him down, therefore reducing their chance to win ball games, because of ACCOUNTING. That's what baseball stats really are—just a form of accounting to describe what happened on the field, just like consolidated financial statements and statements of cash flows are for businesses. They sabotaged their chances to win games because they were afraid of passing some arbitrary mark with no more meaning than a cuneiform rune. Pathetic. He'll end up playing more third than short for the Rockies, a waste of a good shortstop.

Geoff Jenkins   LF   Born: 21-Jul-74   Age: 28   Bats: L   Throws: R

YEAR	TM	LG	AGE	AB	H	2B	3B	HR	BB	SO	SB	CS	AVG	OBP	SLG	MLVR	EQBA	EQOBP	EQSLG	EQMLVR	VORP	DEFENSE
2000	MIL	NL	25	512	155	36	4	34	33	135	11	1	.303	.362	.588	.267	.302	.351	.583	.254	45.7	130-LF 2
2001	MIL	NL	26	397	105	21	1	20	36	120	4	2	.264	.338	.474	.053	.270	.339	.486	.063	16.8	104-LF 7
2002	MIL	NL	27	243	59	17	1	10	22	60	1	2	.243	.321	.444	.030	.251	.323	.466	-.011	5.0	63-LF 4
2003	*MIL*	*NL*	*28*	*329*	*86*	*19*	*1*	*14*	*32*	*82*	*4*	*2*	*.263*	*.334*	*.461*	*.033*	*.268*	*.336*	*.478*	*.042*	*6.4*	

Breakout: 11%   Improve: 38%   Collapse: 24%

Jenkins suffered a very nasty injury that ended his season just as he was starting to break out of a long funk. Jenkins swings hard and often, and occasionally makes contact and sends the ball a long way. He's a left fielder with a pretty good throwing arm. His injury was certainly gruesome to see, and it was surprising and gratifying to hear that it was a dislocation rather than a break, but I'm not certain whether or not that's necessarily a good thing. Either way, our wishes for a quick and full recovery go out to him—he's a player you pay to see. Thirty more walks a year, and he'd be an excellent player you'd pay to see. He's been heading in that direction the last two years, but injuries have derailed him.

Kade Johnson　　　　　　　C　　Born: 28-Sep-78　　Age: 24　　Bats: R　　Throws: R

YEAR	TM	LG	AGE	AB	H	2B	3B	HR	BB	SO	SB	CS	AVG	OBP	SLG	MLVR	EQBA	EQOBP	EQSLG	EQMLVR	VORP	DEFENSE		
2000	OGD	PIO	21	98	31	7	0	10	14	20	2	1	.316	.422	.694	.552	.206	.269	.423	-.205	-1.6			
2001	HDS	CLF	22	370	94	21	1	21	35	118	9	2	.254	.341	.486	.092	.194	.257	.361	-.321	-7.8	48-C	-9	15-LF -2
2002	HDS	CLF	23	123	34	8	3	5	11	39	0	2	.276	.355	.512	.166	.203	.262	.374	-.287	-6.1	21-LF	-4	

What is it with the Brewers drafting college players that they KNOW can hit, and then sending them to the Pioneer League? Is building confidence more important than learning? "Hey, Dean, this guy hit about .480 in Division I ball, homered every other at-bat against 21-year-old scholarship pitching, and slugged 3.300 during his senior year. Where should we send him?" "Send him to Ogden. Let's see if he can hit 17-year-olds with shaky breaking stuff." "Hey, he can. Cool." Johnson's a second round pick from the 1999 draft who hasn't hit for power yet, but has a cannon for an arm. He may eventually end up as a right-handed Greg Myers type.

Dave Krynzel　　　　　　　CF　　Born: 07-Nov-81　　Age: 21　　Bats: L　　Throws: L

YEAR	TM	LG	AGE	AB	H	2B	3B	HR	BB	SO	SB	CS	AVG	OBP	SLG	MLVR	EQBA	EQOBP	EQSLG	EQMLVR	VORP	DEFENSE	
2000	OGD	PIO	18	131	47	8	3	1	16	23	8	4	.359	.447	.489	.338	.234	.283	.312	-.314	-4.0	30-CF	-2
2001	BLT	MDW	19	141	43	1	1	1	9	28	11	5	.305	.364	.348	.040	.239	.283	.275	-.363	-6.6	32-CF	-3
2001	HDS	CLF	19	383	106	19	5	5	27	122	34	17	.277	.331	.392	-.031	.209	.250	.293	-.420	-22.2	89-CF	-3
2002	HDS	CLF	20	365	98	13	12	11	64	100	29	17	.268	.393	.460	.150	.195	.292	.332	-.290	-10.8	93-CF	-7
2002	HUN	SOU	20	129	31	2	3	2	4	30	13	5	.240	.269	.349	-.136	.221	.231	.328	-.402	-7.2	30-CF	-2
2003	MIL	NL	21	198	46	9	2	4	19	51	6	5	.233	.308	.361	-.161	.238	.310	.375	-.161	-2.4		

Breakout: 55%　　Improve: 77%　　Collapse: 11%

Krynzel took a big step forward with the bat in 2002, improving his plate discipline and power dramatically. He's got great speed, his swing's considerably shorter than in 2001, and he's learning how to play. He could turn into a nice prospect here during the next year or so. If he can retain 50% of his gains in the first half of next season, then move forward on a normal development path, Krynzel could be a very nice ballplayer.

Robert Machado　　　　　　C　　Born: 03-Jun-73　　Age: 30　　Bats: R　　Throws: R

YEAR	TM	LG	AGE	AB	H	2B	3B	HR	BB	SO	SB	CS	AVG	OBP	SLG	MLVR	EQBA	EQOBP	EQSLG	EQMLVR	VORP	DEFENSE	
2000	TAC	PCL	27	330	99	20	0	9	28	43	1	5	.300	.360	.442	.066	.270	.316	.400	-.101	11.1	70-C	8
2001	IOW	PCL	28	180	51	11	0	8	11	36	0	0	.283	.332	.478	.057	.251	.300	.425	-.110	5.9	44-C	2
2001	CHC	NL	28	135	30	10	0	2	7	26	0	0	.222	.266	.341	-.295	.228	.270	.353	-.285	-1.8	38-C	2
2002	CHC	NL	29	58	16	4	0	1	5	11	0	0	.276	.333	.397	.018	.288	.344	.424	-.000	3.6	15-C	4
2002	MIL	NL	29	153	39	10	1	2	12	30	0	0	.255	.313	.373	-.070	.269	.321	.391	-.105	5.3	43-C	1
2003	MIL	NL	30	232	58	11	1	5	17	42	1	1	.250	.306	.373	-.139	.256	.307	.388	-.138	1.6		

Breakout: 14%　　Improve: 38%　　Collapse: 28%

Generic MLB catcher, noteworthy for good technique behind the plate. I don't know that I'd play him over Casanova on a regular basis, but spending a lot of time thinking about things like that is probably not a good use of anyone's time, including Ned Yost. If you're burning your brainpower on something like that, you've got bigger problems.

Chris Morris　　　　　　　CF　　Born: 01-Jul-79　　Age: 24　　Bats: B　　Throws: R

YEAR	TM	LG	AGE	AB	H	2B	3B	HR	BB	SO	SB	CS	AVG	OBP	SLG	MLVR	EQBA	EQOBP	EQSLG	EQMLVR	VORP	DEFENSE	
2000	NWJ	NYP	21	182	31	2	1	0	50	48	42	12	.170	.357	.192	-.150	.152	.284	.173	-.530	-20.1	50-CF	-5
2001	PEO	MDW	22	480	141	11	9	2	83	101	111	24	.294	.399	.367	.132	.241	.324	.303	-.240	-8.4	132-CF	-17
2002	POT	CRL	23	422	105	17	2	0	58	92	55	19	.249	.348	.299	-.067	.206	.284	.249	-.412	-27.1	113-CF	-6
2002	BLT	MDW	23	14	5	2	0	0	1	3	1	0	.357	.400	.500	.365	.286	.333	.429	-.015	.4		
2003	MIL	NL	23	160	36	5	2	1	19	38	9	4	.227	.313	.307	-.226	.232	.315	.319	-.229	-4.1		

Breakout: 45%　　Improve: 71%　　Collapse: 14%

Blazingly fast center fielder acquired from the Cardinals. Morris can run, slap the ball, and draw walks. His lack of power is so extreme that it's questionable if he'll develop into a poor man's Brett Butler, but he has some upside. Somewhere along the line, though, you really need to hit the ball over an outfielder's head. With some progress, he could do enough on the offensive side to be a starter in the bigs.

Brad Nelson   1B   Born: 23-Dec-82   Age: 20   Bats: L   Throws: R

YEAR	TM	LG	AGE	AB	H	2B	3B	HR	BB	SO	SB	CS	AVG	OBP	SLG	MLVR	EQBA	EQOBP	EQSLG	EQMLVR	VORP	DEFENSE
2002	BLT	MDW	19	417	124	38	2	17	34	86	4	1	.297	.356	.520	.280	.230	.274	.400	-.210	-12.4	103-1B -14
2002	HDS	CLF	19	102	26	11	0	3	12	28	0	0	.255	.333	.451	.035	.194	.252	.340	-.359	-6.8	26-1B 3
2003	MIL	NL	20	219	52	11	2	7	18	54	2	4	.238	.299	.399	-.124	.243	.300	.415	-.123	-5.1	

Breakout: 61%   Improve: 76%   Collapse: 20%

Nelson has hit well so far. He's taken well to the world of wooden bats, and hits hard line drives with some backspin to all fields. He could develop into a legitimate 40 HR guy if everything breaks his way. He will have to increase his selectivity, and he's got a lot of work to do on defense.

Johnny Raburn   SS   Born: 16-Feb-79   Age: 24   Bats: B   Throws: R

YEAR	TM	LG	AGE	AB	H	2B	3B	HR	BB	SO	SB	CS	AVG	OBP	SLG	MLVR	EQBA	EQOBP	EQSLG	EQMLVR	VORP	DEFENSE	
2000	BOI	NWN	21	280	71	12	4	0	54	72	28	3	.254	.378	.325	.034	.191	.277	.249	-.433	-15.7	33-SS -3	22-3B -1
2001	CDR	MDW	22	235	74	2	1	0	63	43	37	7	.315	.469	.332	.207	.256	.378	.272	-.164	3.7	51-2B -17	13-SS -3
2002	HDS	CLF	23	66	14	3	1	0	7	13	5	1	.212	.288	.288	-.278	.164	.222	.224	-.593	-6.3	14-2B -4	
2002	RCU	CLF	23	448	131	20	5	1	77	88	35	19	.292	.400	.366	.093	.228	.314	.287	-.289	-8.6	57-SS -17	45-2B -5
2003	MIL	NL	24	155	36	6	1	1	20	31	6	3	.234	.323	.317	-.191	.239	.325	.329	-.192	-1.2		

Breakout: 35%   Improve: 62%   Collapse: 20%

Middle infield prospect with a solid batting eye, great speed, and less power than Raffy Belliard. Scouts don't like his arm much, but he's got some skills. He can hit for a little average, runs like the wind, and doesn't swing at bad balls. Might have a career as a supersub and pinch runner, but he's going to have to give pitchers some reason not to just throw the ball down the middle of the plate.

Jim Rushford   RF   Born: 24-Mar-74   Age: 29   Bats: L   Throws: L

YEAR	TM	LG	AGE	AB	H	2B	3B	HR	BB	SO	SB	CS	AVG	OBP	SLG	MLVR	EQBA	EQOBP	EQSLG	EQMLVR	VORP	DEFENSE	
2000	DUL	NTH	26	289	95	16	3	12	25	32	13	5	.329	.390	.529	.294	.254	.298	.411	-.131	.0		
2001	HDS	CLF	27	259	94	22	2	14	38	35	3	3	.363	.454	.625	.534	.263	.337	.448	-.000	5.8	38-LF -3	26-1B 9
2001	HUN	SOU	27	187	64	16	1	7	23	22	3	2	.342	.428	.551	.429	.286	.359	.464	.081	8.5	45-RF 0	
2002	HUN	SOU	28	19	4	1	0	0	2	5	1	0	.211	.286	.263	-.240	.158	.238	.211	-.579	-2.3		
2002	IND	INT	28	405	128	33	3	7	45	41	0	2	.316	.394	.464	.217	.289	.364	.431	.047	13.7	85-RF -1	
2002	MIL	NL	28	77	11	2	0	1	6	9	0	0	.143	.214	.208	-.521	.154	.222	.231	-.587	-10.4	20-RF -1	
2003	TEX	AL	29	241	64	14	1	7	24	33	2	1	.267	.336	.419	.006	.269	.341	.424	-.020	-0.2		

Breakout: 21%   Improve: 48%   Collapse: 24%

Attack of the free talent. I don't know exactly why the Brewers didn't give him a shot. All he's done for the past few years is hit for average, power, and draw walks. If you go get a guy from the independent leagues to fill out the roster of one of your minor league clubs, and he slaps the competition upside the head like a redheaded stepchild, and he keeps doing that at higher and higher levels, why don't you give him a shot in the majors? Inexplicably non-tendered by the Brewers, for whom he'd probably be the best outfield option. He's solid injury insurance in Texas.

Alex Sanchez   CF   Born: 26-Aug-76   Age: 26   Bats: L   Throws: L

YEAR	TM	LG	AGE	AB	H	2B	3B	HR	BB	SO	SB	CS	AVG	OBP	SLG	MLVR	EQBA	EQOBP	EQSLG	EQMLVR	VORP	DEFENSE
2000	ORL	SOU	23	86	25	2	1	0	1	13	2	6	.291	.307	.337	-.056	.253	.257	.299	-.373	-6.2	19-LF -1
2000	DUR	INT	23	446	130	18	3	2	30	66	52	20	.291	.343	.359	-.049	.274	.315	.336	-.192	-1.4	106-CF -4
2001	IND	INT	24	335	105	14	5	1	22	44	27	8	.313	.359	.394	.077	.292	.338	.372	-.083	8.4	73-CF -6
2001	MIL	NL	24	68	14	3	2	0	5	13	6	2	.206	.260	.309	-.361	.203	.257	.319	-.373	-3.7	13-CF -1
2002	MIL	NL	25	394	114	10	7	1	31	62	37	14	.289	.344	.358	-.013	.297	.348	.367	-.067	11.7	100-CF 3
2003	MIL	NL	26	419	115	18	5	1	30	60	31	8	.273	.325	.349	-.124	.279	.326	.362	-.122	1.5	

Breakout: 8%   Improve: 35%   Collapse: 19%

Alex Sanchez is a good baseball player. He can hit for average, play good defense, and run. That being said, if your MLB club is running him to the outfield every day, you're in deep trouble. Sanchez just doesn't have the power to be a productive major league regular. His lack of plate discipline means he needs to hit .320 to have a reasonable on-base percentage, and he's not going to hit .320 very often. Looking at the 25th man on your roster and seeing Alex Sanchez is a good thing. Looking at your second outfielder and seeing Alex Sanchez should immediately cause hives.

Richie Sexson 1B Born: 29-Dec-74 Age: 28 Bats: R Throws: R

YEAR	TM	LG	AGE	AB	H	2B	3B	HR	BB	SO	SB	CS	AVG	OBP	SLG	MLVR	EQBA	EQOBP	EQSLG	EQMLVR	VORP	DEFENSE			
2000	CLE	AL	25	324	83	16	1	16	25	96	1	0	.256	.317	.460	-.062	.261	.314	.472	-.009	6.1	45-LF	0	25-1B	-3
2000	MIL	NL	25	213	63	14	0	14	34	63	1	0	.296	.400	.559	.277	.294	.390	.551	.262	21.6	56-1B	7		
2001	MIL	NL	26	598	162	24	3	45	60	178	2	4	.271	.343	.547	.169	.275	.345	.554	.173	45.6	155-1B	8		
2002	MIL	NL	27	570	159	37	2	29	70	136	0	0	.279	.366	.504	.208	.287	.367	.524	.180	43.5	150-1B	13		
2003	MIL	NL	28	508	133	27	2	28	58	133	1	2	.262	.342	.489	.082	.268	.344	.507	.093	17.9				

Breakout: 8%   Improve: 38%   Collapse: 16%

Sexson's a lanky first baseman with underrated defense. Lots of power in a relatively long swing, and probably the favorite Brewer of the faithful right now. He's gotten better at the plate, and could do something along the lines of .290/.380/.550 one of these years over 650 PA. Probably won't be part of the next successful Milwaukee ball club, though. He's coming up for free agency after next season, and both parties will have better options available when that happens.

Matt Stairs RF Born: 27-Feb-68 Age: 35 Bats: L Throws: R

YEAR	TM	LG	AGE	AB	H	2B	3B	HR	BB	SO	SB	CS	AVG	OBP	SLG	MLVR	EQBA	EQOBP	EQSLG	EQMLVR	VORP	DEFENSE			
2000	OAK	AL	32	476	108	26	0	21	78	122	5	2	.227	.337	.414	-.100	.237	.341	.434	-.033	5.4	90-RF	1		
2001	CHC	NL	33	340	85	21	0	17	52	76	2	3	.250	.361	.462	.068	.257	.363	.471	.073	17.1	68-1B	-1	17-LF	1
2002	MIL	NL	34	270	66	15	0	16	36	50	2	0	.244	.350	.478	.121	.255	.353	.498	.090	12.5	66-RF	0		
2003	PIT	NL	35	201	50	11	1	9	30	44	1	1	.247	.350	.442	.023	.247	.346	.456	.013	2.1				

Breakout: 18%   Improve: 51%   Collapse: 25%

Wonder Hamster moves on. Played pretty well in his role last season, filling in for nasty injuries and against particular right-handers. His swing resembles a golf swing more than a baseball swing, and he still doesn't leave anything behind when he takes his rips. He's still got some plate discipline and some power, but he's more of an endgame Hail Mary now than someone you want out there on a regular basis, even in a platoon role. Now that he's a Pirate, he should become a lunch bucket hero in the Steel City.

Ryan Thompson LF Born: 04-Nov-67 Age: 35 Bats: R Throws: R

YEAR	TM	LG	AGE	AB	H	2B	3B	HR	BB	SO	SB	CS	AVG	OBP	SLG	MLVR	EQBA	EQOBP	EQSLG	EQMLVR	VORP	DEFENSE	
2000	COH	INT	32	326	93	23	3	23	27	72	10	3	.285	.344	.586	.262	.262	.310	.537	.077	13.8	79-LF	4
2000	NYY	AL	32	50	13	3	0	3	5	12	0	1	.260	.339	.500	.059	.280	.346	.520	.132	2.8	16-LF	0
2001	CLG	PCL	33	300	93	26	0	19	14	65	4	3	.310	.343	.587	.209	.262	.297	.486	-.018	5.3	77-OF	-6
2001	OTT	INT	33	85	14	4	0	2	3	22	0	2	.165	.202	.282	-.424	.165	.208	.271	-.557	-10.3	15-RF	0
2002	IND	INT	34	273	80	12	3	12	11	46	0	4	.293	.330	.491	.135	.267	.305	.451	-.050	2.7	62-LF	-3
2002	MIL	NL	34	137	34	9	2	8	7	38	1	0	.248	.295	.518	.091	.259	.298	.540	.058	5.1	34-LF	-1
2003	MIL	NL	35	163	39	8	1	7	10	39	2	2	.240	.289	.426	-.104	.246	.290	.442	-.102	-2.9		

Breakout: 18%   Improve: 45%   Collapse: 26%

At one time an overrated prospect, Thompson suffered a wicked torn hamstring in September of last season. He can still hit lefties pretty well, and if he's healthy, he'll be bouncing around looking for a fourth OF job/Shawon Dunston gig, but there aren't many of those to be had.

Eric Young 2B Born: 18-May-67 Age: 36 Bats: R Throws: R

YEAR	TM	LG	AGE	AB	H	2B	3B	HR	BB	SO	SB	CS	AVG	OBP	SLG	MLVR	EQBA	EQOBP	EQSLG	EQMLVR	VORP	DEFENSE	
2000	CHC	NL	33	607	180	40	2	6	63	39	54	7	.297	.370	.399	-.000	.297	.361	.399	.003	35.7	144-2B	0
2001	CHC	NL	34	603	168	43	4	6	42	45	31	14	.279	.335	.393	-.050	.283	.336	.397	-.057	26.3	136-2B	2
2002	MIL	NL	35	496	139	29	3	3	39	38	31	11	.280	.340	.369	-.012	.291	.346	.384	-.051	21.6	119-2B	-6
2003	MIL	NL	36	373	103	21	2	3	31	29	19	3	.276	.335	.371	-.075	.282	.337	.385	-.071	10.2		

Breakout: 9%   Improve: 45%   Collapse: 25%

Pretty much the definition of a generic second baseman. You know what Eric Young's going to give you, and it's considerably more in rotisserie than in real life, which is another good reason to look down upon roto. He'll be back to hitting some doubles and turning double plays for a dead end team next year. The space time continuum seldom sees something quite as bland as Eric Young playing for the 2003 Brewers. When the Brewers come to town, opposing teams will be using the "Hey, we've gotta play somebody" tagline in their ads.

PITCHERS

Mike Adams   Born: 29-Jul-78   Age: 24   Bats: R   Throws: R

YEAR	TM	LG	AGE	G	GS	IP	H	BB	SO	HR	ERA	EQERA	EQH9	EQBB9	EQSO9	EQHR9	PERA	VORP	STF
2001	OGD	PIO	22	23	0	32.0	26	6	44	4	2.81	3.68	10.7	2.5	6.8	2.6	4.15	6.0	0
2002	BLT	MDW	23	11	0	15.3	13	2	21	1	2.94	4.11	10.2	1.6	7.7	1.6	4.16	2.2	11
2002	HDS	CLF	23	10	0	14.0	9	7	23	2	2.57	3.86	7.4	5.7	8.6	2.3	3.87	2.4	4
2002	HUN	SOU	23	13	0	18.7	14	12	17	3	3.37	6.33	9.9	6.5	6.2	3.2	5.86	-2.0	-21

Showed promise at three levels, maintaining good peripherals. With two good pitches to work off of, Adams could be in the mix as a potential bullpen guy as early as next year, provided he can keep finding the strike zone.

Mike Buddie   Born: 12-Dec-70   Age: 32   Bats: R   Throws: R

YEAR	TM	LG	AGE	G	GS	IP	H	BB	SO	HR	ERA	EQERA	EQH9	EQBB9	EQSO9	EQHR9	PERA	VORP	STF
2000	COH	INT	29	6	6	30.0	34	20	16	8	7.50	8.30	11.1	6.0	4.1	3.0	8.11	-9.3	-33
2000	IND	INT	29	30	0	58.3	40	29	39	4	2.62	3.52	7.2	4.5	5.2	0.8	3.28	12.0	-8
2001	IND	INT	30	27	0	46.7	36	25	31	4	2.31	3.44	7.7	5.7	4.7	1.0	4.30	10.1	-18
2001	MIL	NL	30	31	0	41.7	34	17	22	2	3.88	3.87	8.1	3.5	4.2	0.4	3.24	7.0	-11
2002	OTT	INT	31	29	0	42.0	34	23	18	2	4.07	5.23	9.0	6.2	3.4	0.7	4.40	0.7	-28
2002	MIL	NL	31	25	0	39.7	46	21	28	5	4.53	5.67	11.1	4.3	5.6	1.2	6.02	-1.3	-13
2003	*MIL*	*NL*	*32*	*35*	*2*	*50.7*	*52*	*28*	*32*	*6*	*4.86*	*5.27*	*9.6*	*4.3*	*5.0*	*1.0*	*5.37*	*1.6*	*-16*

Breakout: 14%   Improve: 50%   Collapse: 18%

Roster filler. Six stops in three years, six negative "stuff" scores. There's no reason that Buddie has a job over a hundred guys all over the minors. It's just luck. Life isn't a meritocracy, there is no Santa Claus, bad things happen to good people, and the people who've been jerks to you aren't going to pay for it down the road. That is all.

Jose Cabrera   Born: 24-Mar-69   Age: 34   Bats: Throws:

YEAR	TM	LG	AGE	G	GS	IP	H	BB	SO	HR	ERA	EQERA	EQH9	EQBB9	EQSO9	EQHR9	PERA	VORP	STF
2000	NWO	PCL	31	12	0	15.3	15	5	12	0	2.94	3.89	10.0	2.9	5.8	0.3	4.03	2.5	-1
2000	HOU	NL	31	52	0	59.3	74	17	41	10	5.92	5.18	10.8	2.1	5.5	1.3	5.48	1.3	-8
2001	ATL	NL	32	55	0	59.3	52	25	43	5	2.88	3.91	8.7	3.6	5.7	0.7	3.79	9.7	-5
2002	MIL	NL	33	50	11	103.3	131	36	61	23	6.80	7.07	12.2	2.8	4.8	2.1	6.76	-18.7	-20
2003	*MIL*	*NL*	*34*	*41*	*7*	*70.3*	*76*	*25*	*42*	*9*	*4.70*	*5.10*	*10.1*	*2.7*	*4.8*	*1.1*	*5.04*	*3.8*	*-11*

Breakout: 6%   Improve: 51%   Collapse: 15%

Ooo. Them's good eatin'. Jose Cabrera's World Whiplash Tour '02 was painful to watch, as he was taken deep by pretty much anyone with a bat. His velocity and movement were both absent, and hitters broke into spontaneous knife fights for the opportunity to get up the plate and leave Bud Selig's signature indented on their bats. He'll be hard-pressed to find a lot of opportunities after that performance, instead calling around for an NRI.

Mike DeJean   Born: 28-Sep-70   Age: 32   Bats: R   Throws: R

YEAR	TM	LG	AGE	G	GS	IP	H	BB	SO	HR	ERA	EQERA	EQH9	EQBB9	EQSO9	EQHR9	PERA	VORP	STF
2000	CSP	PCL	29	12	0	14.3	15	4	12	0	2.52	2.54	9.1	2.4	5.9	0.2	3.35	4.5	3
2000	COL	NL	29	54	0	53.3	54	30	34	9	4.90	4.55	8.6	4.0	5.0	1.2	4.57	4.9	-15
2001	MIL	NL	30	75	0	84.3	75	39	68	4	2.78	3.64	8.7	3.9	6.3	0.4	3.71	16.3	0
2002	MIL	NL	31	68	0	75.0	66	39	65	7	3.12	3.89	8.3	4.2	6.9	0.9	4.28	12.4	-1
2003	*MIL*	*NL*	*32*	*48*	*0*	*55.0*	*53*	*26*	*44*	*6*	*3.82*	*4.15*	*9.0*	*3.7*	*6.3*	*0.9*	*4.62*	*8.5*	*-4*

Breakout: 16%   Improve: 46%   Collapse: 27%

His encounter session with Jerry Royster was a nice little exclamation point to a lost season in Cheeseland. His ERA has consistently been lower than one would expect based on his peripheral numbers. He's under contract next year for $1.7 million, because there's nothing a team going nowhere needs more than an adequate, expensive closer.

Valerio de los Santos   Born: 06-Oct-72   Age: 30   Bats: L   Throws: L

YEAR	TM	LG	AGE	G	GS	IP	H	BB	SO	HR	ERA	EQERA	EQH9	EQBB9	EQSO9	EQHR9	PERA	VORP	STF
2000	MIL	NL	27	66	2	73.7	72	33	70	15	5.13	5.03	9.0	3.3	7.6	1.6	4.88	3.0	0
2002	IND	INT	29	2	0	2.0	1	1	5	0	0.00	2.06	4.5	5.0	16.4	0.2	2.03	0.7	60
2002	MIL	NL	0	51	0	57.7	42	26	38	4	3.12	0.00	0.0	0.0	0.0	0.0	0.00	34.5	0
2003	MIL	NL	30	44	0	46.0	44	21	37	6	4.37	4.74	8.9	3.5	6.4	1.1	4.63	4.8	-5

Breakout: 16%   Improve: 50%   Collapse: 26%

One of those who came down with a sudden case of old last year, after coming back from Tommy John surgery. De los Santos has good stuff, and he'll go on as long as his control holds out. If his command and movement are back, there's no reason he can't be the same pitcher he was before the surgery, or possibly better. If his K rate perks back up, he'll be fine. If not, he could be in Triple-A to stay pretty quickly.

Ben Diggins   Born: 13-Jun-79   Age: 24   Bats: R   Throws: R

YEAR	TM	LG	AGE	G	GS	IP	H	BB	SO	HR	ERA	EQERA	EQH9	EQBB9	EQSO9	EQHR9	PERA	VORP	STF
2001	WNC	SAL	22	21	21	105.7	88	48	79	5	3.58	7.40	13.3	6.9	4.2	1.2	6.43	-22.3	-14
2002	VRO	FSL	23	20	19	114.0	103	41	101	8	3.63	5.24	11.1	4.2	5.8	1.5	4.99	3.3	5
2002	HUN	SOU	23	7	7	37.7	26	15	34	0	1.91	3.67	7.7	3.9	5.9	0.3	3.23	7.7	15
2002	MIL	NL	23	5	5	24.0	28	18	15	4	8.63	7.96	10.9	5.9	4.9	1.5	7.05	-6.5	-12
2003	MIL	NL	24	17	13	78.0	83	40	59	10	5.32	5.77	9.9	3.9	6.0	1.1	5.47	-0.8	0

Breakout: 10%   Improve: 51%   Collapse: 16%

Big tall guy with the ability to throw a good fastball and slider, but Diggins has a hard time holding it all together mechanically. If he does, he's probably more likely to end up in the bullpen than the rotation, as he's really only got two pitches, and he has a hard enough time controlling his mechanics as it is. No matter what, he's going to be considerably better if he can learn to change speeds effectively, and that's still some time off. He shouldn't have been called up last year.

Jayson Durocher   Born: 18-Aug-74   Age: 28   Bats: R   Throws: R

YEAR	TM	LG	AGE	G	GS	IP	H	BB	SO	HR	ERA	EQERA	EQH9	EQBB9	EQSO9	EQHR9	PERA	VORP	STF
2000	MOB	SOU	25	27	0	30.3	26	12	43	4	2.08	3.93	10.4	3.9	9.1	2.3	5.43	4.9	4
2000	LVG	PCL	25	31	0	40.0	44	25	38	2	4.95	5.02	9.8	5.4	6.7	0.5	5.23	1.6	-5
2001	OKL	PCL	26	31	0	39.7	34	23	52	5	4.99	5.53	8.6	6.3	8.7	1.4	5.02	-0.7	-2
2002	IND	INT	27	20	0	26.3	19	15	39	3	2.74	3.79	7.4	6.2	11.4	1.5	4.03	4.6	17
2002	MIL	NL	27	39	0	48.0	27	21	44	3	1.88	2.53	5.3	3.5	7.2	0.6	2.42	15.2	9
2003	MIL	NL	28	42	0	52.7	44	30	54	6	3.99	4.33	7.8	4.4	8.1	0.9	4.40	7.0	5

Breakout: 19%   Improve: 52%   Collapse: 20%

Great stuff, great randomness in where it arrives. Durocher needs to tighten up his mechanics a little bit, as major league hitters (and, well, minor league hitters) aren't going to help out much going forward. Fun to watch, and a good bet to have streaks of great effectiveness with unbelievably frustrating rough spots for the foreseeable future.

Nelson Figueroa   Born: 18-May-74   Age: 29   Bats: B   Throws: R

YEAR	TM	LG	AGE	G	GS	IP	H	BB	SO	HR	ERA	EQERA	EQH9	EQBB9	EQSO9	EQHR9	PERA	VORP	STF
2000	SWB	INT	26	8	8	50.0	50	11	35	9	3.78	5.74	11.1	2.1	5.6	2.2	5.15	-1.3	1
2000	TUC	PCL	26	17	16	112.0	101	28	78	9	2.81	3.19	8.6	2.2	5.1	0.9	3.22	28.8	10
2000	ARI	NL	26	3	3	15.7	17	5	7	4	7.45	5.90	9.5	2.3	3.6	2.0	5.34	-0.7	-13
2001	SWB	INT	27	13	12	87.3	74	18	74	6	2.47	4.28	9.4	2.2	6.1	0.9	3.61	11.8	15
2001	PHI	NL	27	19	13	89.0	95	37	61	8	3.94	4.53	10.4	3.6	5.4	0.7	4.82	9.5	1
2002	IND	INT	28	6	6	39.7	39	13	25	2	3.63	4.50	9.8	3.6	4.9	0.7	4.24	4.4	3
2002	MIL	NL	28	30	11	93.0	96	37	51	18	5.03	5.64	9.9	3.2	4.4	1.8	5.47	-1.9	-15
2003	PIT	NL	29	23	14	90.7	99	35	57	10	4.54	4.73	9.8	3.0	5.1	1.1	4.86	9.2	-3

Breakout: 15%   Improve: 44%   Collapse: 23%

A journeyman pitcher who's been successful enough to warrant an extended look in a rotation. He's never impressed the radar gun or the scouts very much, but he's been able to take the mound and get guys out. Could end up putting together a nice three- or four-year stretch at the back end of a rotation and making a few bucks as an innings eater. Not a bad pickup by Dave Littlefield as bargain-shopping goes; he might crack the Pirates' rotation.

Chad Fox
Born: 03-Sep-70   Age: 32   Bats: R   Throws: R

YEAR	TM	LG	AGE	G	GS	IP	H	BB	SO	HR	ERA	EQERA	EQH9	EQBB9	EQSO9	EQHR9	PERA	VORP	STF
2001	MIL	NL	30	65	0	66.7	44	36	80	6	1.89	2.73	6.3	4.5	9.2	0.7	3.12	19.6	15
2002	HUN	SOU	31	3	0	5.3	5	2	7	0	0.00	3.29	10.1	3.5	8.4	0.3	4.52	1.2	13
2002	MIL	NL	31	3	0	4.7	6	5	3	0	5.74	6.60	11.8	8.2	4.9	0.2	7.41	-0.6	-28

He of the nasty stuff spent most of the year injured. First, his elbow caved a bit, and then his cuff. He's been moved off the 40-man roster, and it's not clear where he'll be, how healthy he'll be, or what role he'll have. It looks like the Red Sox, who knows, and setup man.

Ray King
Born: 15-Jan-74   Age: 29   Bats: L   Throws: L

YEAR	TM	LG	AGE	G	GS	IP	H	BB	SO	HR	ERA	EQERA	EQH9	EQBB9	EQSO9	EQHR9	PERA	VORP	STF
2000	IND	INT	26	29	0	25.7	26	12	20	1	3.50	5.42	10.4	4.2	6.0	0.4	4.69	-0.1	-8
2000	MIL	NL	26	36	0	28.7	18	10	19	1	1.25	2.17	6.2	2.6	5.4	0.3	2.00	10.2	1
2001	MIL	NL	27	82	0	55.0	49	25	49	5	3.60	3.91	8.6	3.9	6.9	0.7	3.99	9.0	0
2002	IND	INT	28	1	1	1.0	1	1	1	0	0.00	6.31	9.1	10.1	7.1	0.3	6.15	-0.1	-21
2002	MIL	NL	28	76	0	65.0	61	24	50	5	3.05	3.75	9.0	3.0	6.2	0.7	4.01	11.8	-1
2003	*ATL*	*NL*	*29*	*65*	*0*	*59.0*	*57*	*25*	*46*	*5*	*3.68*	*3.94*	*8.9*	*3.3*	*6.3*	*0.8*	*4.28*	*10.6*	*-2*

Breakout: 17%   Improve: 44%   Collapse: 18%

Lefty out of the pen, but beware. His ERAs have run consistently stronger than one would expect given his peripherals. Could become suddenly flammable, particularly if asked to expand the role he plays in the pen. Dealt to Atlanta for Wes Helms and John Foster, where he won't really replace Mike Remlinger as much as he'll keep doing what he does as a situational lefty.

Curt Leskanic
Born: 02-Apr-68   Age: 35   Bats: R   Throws: R

YEAR	TM	LG	AGE	G	GS	IP	H	BB	SO	HR	ERA	EQERA	EQH9	EQBB9	EQSO9	EQHR9	PERA	VORP	STF
2000	MIL	NL	32	73	0	77.3	58	51	75	7	2.56	3.13	7.0	4.8	7.6	0.7	3.60	19.3	4
2001	MIL	NL	33	70	0	69.3	63	31	64	11	3.64	4.32	8.6	3.8	7.1	1.3	4.54	8.2	-2
2002	HUN	SOU	34	3	0	3.0	4	2	2	0	3.00	8.00	15.1	6.7	4.5	0.3	8.31	-0.9	-33
2002	IND	INT	34	5	1	6.7	5	1	7	0	1.34	1.96	7.2	1.6	7.9	0.2	2.22	2.6	20

Suffering chronic pain in his shoulder, Leskanic has elected not to go through with career-ending surgery, and will instead try to pitch through it. Good luck to him. Major League Baseball isn't easy, and undertaking an unnatural motion like that with weakened physiology and noteworthy pain will make it that much tougher. In all probability, he's done, but root for him anyway.

Brian Mallette
Born: 19-Jan-75   Age: 28   Bats: R   Throws: R

YEAR	TM	LG	AGE	G	GS	IP	H	BB	SO	HR	ERA	EQERA	EQH9	EQBB9	EQSO9	EQHR9	PERA	VORP	STF
2000	MUD	CLF	25	50	0	71.0	52	52	94	6	3.30	5.72	9.4	7.3	7.6	1.8	5.77	-2.7	-13
2001	HUN	SOU	26	44	0	55.0	43	23	71	4	1.96	3.64	9.0	4.5	8.0	1.1	4.40	10.6	2
2001	IND	INT	26	12	0	17.0	10	8	23	2	1.06	2.82	5.8	4.9	9.4	1.4	3.30	4.8	11
2002	IND	INT	27	45	0	45.3	39	17	50	4	2.78	3.74	8.7	4.1	8.5	1.1	3.98	8.3	6
2002	MIL	NL	27	5	0	5.0	7	3	5	3	10.80	10.89	12.7	4.6	7.6	5.4	11.02	-3.1	-39

A little case of nerves there, or so it appears. Mallette's been successful throughout his minor league career, and despite his advanced age, he's actually a pretty decent middle relief prospect. After his little stint in Milwaukee, he may have to go back to Triple-A and prove it again, but Mallette could be an inexpensive and effective reliever for any number of teams.

Shane Nance   Born: 07-Sep-77   Age: 25   Bats: L   Throws: L

YEAR	TM	LG	AGE	G	GS	IP	H	BB	SO	HR	ERA	EQERA	EQH9	EQBB9	EQSO9	EQHR9	PERA	VORP	STF
2000	YAK	NWN	22	12	9	58.0	41	22	66	1	2.48	4.42	9.3	4.3	5.4	0.6	4.37	6.9	7
2001	VRO	FSL	23	21	0	48.0	28	21	63	3	2.63	3.74	7.6	4.8	8.0	1.4	3.27	8.7	10
2001	JAX	SOU	23	28	0	45.3	31	17	44	4	1.59	3.70	8.5	4.1	6.1	1.4	3.87	8.5	-1
2002	LVG	PCL	24	37	0	58.3	58	26	53	5	4.17	4.73	9.5	4.6	6.3	1.0	4.56	4.2	-3
2002	IND	INT	24	9	0	16.7	12	6	10	0	0.00	0.21	7.2	3.9	4.6	0.2	2.67	9.6	0
2002	MIL	NL	24	4	0	6.3	4	4	5	1	4.29	4.12	6.1	5.1	6.4	1.5	3.84	0.9	-4
2003	*MIL*	*NL*	*25*	*23*	*5*	*46.7*	*46*	*24*	*38*	*5*	*4.63*	*5.02*	*9.2*	*4.1*	*6.4*	*0.9*	*5.02*	*2.5*	*-4*

Breakout: 21%   Improve: 46%   Collapse: 25%

Bullpen fodder who could be more if he could conquer his control problems. He'll likely get a chance to make the club in spring training, but it's more likely he'll work in Triple-A to try to gain a little more command and control. It's not as if the Brewers would want to rush someone with great stuff and no control. They might get injured in a series of meaningless games with little to no worthwhile instruction or leadership . . .

Nick Neugebauer   Born: 15-Jul-80   Age: 22   Bats: R   Throws: R

YEAR	TM	LG	AGE	G	GS	IP	H	BB	SO	HR	ERA	EQERA	EQH9	EQBB9	EQSO9	EQHR9	PERA	VORP	STF
2000	MUD	CLF	19	18	18	77.3	43	87	117	0	4.19	5.62	6.5	10.8	8.3	0.3	5.34	-1.0	9
2000	HUN	SOU	19	10	10	50.7	35	47	57	2	3.73	5.94	7.7	9.0	7.0	0.7	5.76	-2.5	5
2001	HUN	SOU	20	21	21	106.7	94	52	149	6	3.46	5.15	10.0	5.2	8.6	0.9	5.12	4.2	26
2001	IND	INT	20	4	4	24.0	10	9	26	1	1.50	1.96	4.0	3.9	7.5	0.5	1.82	9.5	33
2002	IND	INT	21	5	5	19.3	20	12	18	4	5.13	6.79	11.1	7.0	7.4	2.8	6.77	-2.8	0
2002	MIL	NL	21	12	12	55.3	56	44	47	10	4.72	5.96	9.4	6.3	6.6	1.7	6.47	-2.8	4
2003	*MIL*	*NL*	*22*	*19*	*15*	*86.3*	*74*	*67*	*86*	*9*	*4.72*	*5.12*	*8.0*	*6.0*	*7.9*	*0.9*	*5.15*	*6.1*	*7*

Breakout: 11%   Improve: 57%   Collapse: 29%

Ball eight. Ball twelve. Everyone knows the story. Health-wise, everyone seems to think he's OK, and the inflammation in his shoulder apparently wasn't structural in nature. That remains to be seen, but the bigger question is why Neugebauer is even in the majors. If you're walking 21 batters in 43 Triple-A innings, you probably should be trying to figure out how to stop doing that, rather than hangin' with Dave Stewart and practicing your glare.

Takaki Nomura   Born: 10-Jan-69   Age: 34   Bats: L   Throws: L

YEAR	TM	LG	AGE	G	GS	IP	H	BB	SO	HR	ERA	EQERA	EQH9	EQBB9	EQSO9	EQHR9	PERA	VORP	STF
2000	YOM	JCL	31	24	0	22.0	18	8	21	5	6.75	6.35	7.7	3.4	7.2	2.1	4.98	-2.4	-8
2001	YOM	JCL	32	40	0	37.0	47	12	34	4	4.72	5.75	11.9	2.7	7.2	1.1	6.22	-1.5	-2
2002	IND	INT	33	31	0	33.0	38	11	23	4	5.73	6.56	11.7	3.6	5.4	1.6	5.78	-4.3	-18
2002	MIL	NL	33	21	0	13.7	11	18	9	2	8.54	7.89	7.3	10.1	5.0	1.3	6.76	-3.8	-42

Y'know, you can't find pitchers this good over here. You need to import them.

Jimmy Osting   Born: 07-Apr-77   Age: 26   Bats: R   Throws: L

YEAR	TM	LG	AGE	G	GS	IP	H	BB	SO	HR	ERA	EQERA	EQH9	EQBB9	EQSO9	EQHR9	PERA	VORP	STF
2000	MYR	CRL	23	4	4	23.0	25	5	17	0	3.13	6.38	15.6	2.6	4.5	0.3	6.09	-2.2	4
2000	GRN	SOU	23	11	11	71.3	67	29	52	6	2.65	5.26	11.3	4.1	4.8	1.5	5.43	1.9	0
2000	REA	EAS	23	10	9	56.7	53	26	31	1	2.38	4.36	10.7	4.7	3.8	0.3	4.79	7.2	-1
2001	MOB	SOU	24	18	18	97.7	85	42	69	6	3.59	4.90	10.1	4.7	4.4	0.9	4.78	6.6	-3
2001	POR	PCL	24	5	5	25.3	41	10	15	5	9.60	10.33	17.1	4.4	4.1	2.2	9.91	-13.6	-25
2002	IND	INT	25	22	22	126.7	115	38	112	7	3.48	4.04	9.0	3.2	6.8	0.7	3.77	20.6	17
2002	MIL	NL	25	3	3	12.0	18	10	7	3	7.50	8.95	14.1	6.6	4.6	2.3	9.67	-4.6	-31
2003	*MIL*	*NL*	*26*	*16*	*12*	*75.7*	*78*	*37*	*58*	*8*	*4.72*	*5.12*	*9.6*	*3.8*	*6.0*	*0.9*	*5.03*	*4.5*	*3*

Breakout: 17%   Improve: 49%   Collapse: 20%

Yeah, the stint in Milwaukee wasn't pretty, but don't give up on Osting just yet. He's shown promise, good stuff, and reasonable peripherals in the past, when he was with the Atlanta organization, and he looked pretty good in Indianapolis. May have been a case of nerves. He'll get another opportunity to show his stuff next season.

Ruben Quevedo — Born: 05-Jan-79 — Age: 24 — Bats: R — Throws: R

YEAR	TM	LG	AGE	G	GS	IP	H	BB	SO	HR	ERA	EQERA	EQH9	EQBB9	EQSO9	EQHR9	PERA	VORP	STF
2000	IOW	PCL	21	13	13	74.7	68	31	77	7	4.22	4.15	8.6	3.7	7.4	1.1	4.28	11.2	25
2000	CHC	NL	21	21	15	88.0	96	54	65	21	7.47	6.81	9.6	4.4	5.8	1.9	6.28	-12.9	0
2001	IOW	PCL	22	22	22	141.7	124	48	150	13	2.99	4.08	9.0	3.7	7.1	1.0	4.05	22.4	22
2001	MIL	NL	22	10	10	56.7	56	30	60	9	4.60	5.07	9.3	4.4	8.1	1.3	5.19	2.7	23
2002	IND	INT	23	1	1	2.0	1	1	3	0	0.00	2.12	4.6	5.0	10.7	0.2	2.06	0.8	35
2002	MIL	NL	23	26	25	139.0	159	68	93	28	5.76	6.47	10.9	3.9	5.3	1.9	6.39	-14.9	-2
2003	MIL	NL	24	25	19	116.7	117	56	91	16	4.90	5.32	9.3	3.7	6.2	1.2	5.13	4.2	2

Breakout: 14%   Improve: 41%   Collapse: 20%

The ex-Cub showed a few moments of promise, but overall, it was not a fantastic season. Often criticized for his lack of conditioning, but a bigger concern is his lack of control. Quevedo has the stuff to be absolutely dominating, but lacks the command to take advantage of it. In a different organization, he'd probably still be getting time in the minors.

Glendon Rusch — Born: 07-Nov-74 — Age: 28 — Bats: L — Throws: L

YEAR	TM	LG	AGE	G	GS	IP	H	BB	SO	HR	ERA	EQERA	EQH9	EQBB9	EQSO9	EQHR9	PERA	VORP	STF
2000	NYM	NL	25	31	30	190.7	196	44	157	18	4.01	4.00	9.7	1.7	6.7	0.8	3.96	31.9	21
2001	NYM	NL	26	33	33	179.0	216	43	156	23	4.63	5.23	11.7	2.1	6.8	1.1	5.42	5.5	13
2002	MIL	NL	27	34	34	210.7	227	76	140	30	4.70	5.18	10.4	2.9	5.3	1.3	5.19	7.6	2
2003	MIL	NL	28	30	28	177.3	184	54	126	20	4.12	4.47	9.7	2.4	5.6	1.0	4.51	20.8	9

Breakout: 8%   Improve: 55%   Collapse: 10%

Rosy-cheeked innings eater, but Rusch is probably still capable of being better than that. He's got great control, middling stuff, and he appeared to have gained some of his velocity back that we saw on occasion in 2000 and earlier. Could help a number of major league clubs, and a pretty good bet to continue being a good rotation filler—an undervalued contribution.

Ben Sheets — Born: 18-Jul-78 — Age: 24 — Bats: R — Throws: R

YEAR	TM	LG	AGE	G	GS	IP	H	BB	SO	HR	ERA	EQERA	EQH9	EQBB9	EQSO9	EQHR9	PERA	VORP	STF
2000	HUN	SOU	21	13	13	72.0	55	25	60	4	1.88	3.41	8.7	3.4	5.3	1.0	4.15	16.8	12
2000	IND	INT	21	14	13	81.7	77	31	59	4	2.86	4.13	9.8	3.5	5.6	0.6	4.10	12.5	16
2001	IND	INT	22	2	2	10.7	14	3	6	0	3.36	5.12	12.6	3.0	3.9	0.2	5.88	0.5	1
2001	MIL	NL	22	25	25	151.3	166	48	94	23	4.76	5.31	10.6	2.7	4.9	1.3	5.09	3.3	7
2002	MIL	NL	23	34	34	216.7	237	70	170	21	4.15	4.65	10.5	2.6	6.3	0.9	4.81	20.6	17
2003	MIL	NL	24	29	28	188.3	189	63	139	20	4.01	4.35	9.4	2.6	5.8	0.9	4.37	25.7	11

Breakout: 22%   Improve: 52%   Collapse: 13%

Check out the discrepancy between the ERA and PERA columns. Sheets's reputation has always run a little bit hotter than his performance metrics. He's never had the big strikeout numbers or great control you look for in a top-flight pitcher, but Sheets has a bit of a halo. He's still only 24, and his numbers did look pretty good during the 2002 season. If he can retain the strikeout rate and gain about 10% more control, he can become a very special pitcher. The odds of that aren't hugely promising, though.

Luis Vizcaino — Born: 06-Aug-74 — Age: 28 — Bats: — Throws:

YEAR	TM	LG	AGE	G	GS	IP	H	BB	SO	HR	ERA	EQERA	EQH9	EQBB9	EQSO9	EQHR9	PERA	VORP	STF
2000	SAC	PCL	25	33	2	48.3	48	21	41	4	5.03	5.11	10.1	3.9	6.3	1.0	4.73	1.6	-4
2000	OAK	AL	25	12	0	19.3	25	11	18	2	7.46	6.23	10.8	4.0	7.9	0.8	5.76	-1.8	4
2001	SAC	PCL	26	27	0	42.0	35	10	56	5	2.14	2.88	8.1	2.5	8.7	1.2	3.63	11.7	15
2001	OAK	AL	26	36	0	36.7	38	12	31	8	4.66	4.86	9.3	2.8	7.1	1.8	5.02	2.1	-2
2002	MIL	NL	27	76	0	81.3	55	30	79	6	2.99	2.97	6.4	3.0	7.7	0.7	2.78	21.8	11
2003	MIL	NL	28	52	0	58.3	52	24	55	6	3.74	4.05	8.3	3.2	7.5	0.9	4.11	9.2	5

Breakout: 24%   Improve: 41%   Collapse: 23%

Hard thrower who's likely to be breathing down DeJean's neck for the closer's job. His other pitches really aren't world beaters, and he's had a tendency in the past to get beaten on his second pitch. If he sticks to the fastball and can spot it a little better, he could really be outstanding. As it is, he's a very solid reliever who'll probably be the primary setup man. If he had a changeup that worked, he'd be horrifying.

Montreal Expos

An eroded fan base. Nonexistent media coverage. Apathy from local businesses. Contempt from other teams forced to boot the bills. The looming end of the Expos in Montreal. More than 30 years of good will flushed down the toilet. The game of owner hot potato from Charles Bronfman to Claude Brochu and the consortium to Jeffrey Loria to Major League Baseball has caused all that damage.

Yet as the Expos grope for a last shot at glory before their move, it's the on-field impact of ownership and front office instability that's hurt the most. They have almost no young talent coming up, none to trade for immediate help, and little to look forward to even if Bud Selig drags his feet for another few years. The end result? No matter where they end up, the Expos will likely be non-contenders for the foreseeable future. That MLB forced Omar Minaya to slash as much as $15 million worth of payroll this off-season only makes the situation more dire, unless Minaya pulls one of the greatest magic acts in recent memory.

As *BP* went to press, the Expos' general manager had shuffled through trade offers from some 20 teams. His performance at the winter meetings spoke volumes. While GMs like Beane, Sabean, Epstein, Ricciardi, and even Phillips came in with a plan, Minaya turned the weekend into a circus. Granted, chopping that much salary while keeping a reasonable core intact isn't easy. But running willy-nilly from offer to offer, deciding on none and watching his leverage vanish as teams chose alternate routes to fill out their rosters left Minaya likely to get three quarters for his buck.

The 15 minutes of giddiness over possibly landing *BP 2002* Cover Boy Adam Dunn aside, Expos fans should expect a team similar to last year's version once Minaya gets done whittling down to his $40 million limit. Vladimir Guerrero should be back for the final year of his five-year contract, his last before hitting the free agent market. As much as exoduses by other bygone Expos stars hurt, Vlad's will sting the most.

Guerrero's not only one of baseball's best talents, he's arguably the most exciting player in the game. He may cost the team a few runs a year with his extreme aggressiveness on the basepaths and in the field, but man is he fun to watch. If ever a city wanted to build or rebuild a fan base under new ownership, Vlad would be a perfect centerpiece. The smart money says MLB's clown act will drag on, making it tough for a new owner to re-up Guerrero at season's end.

Rock-solid Jose Vidro should also be back, with two years left until he can test free agent waters. Brad Wilkerson came of age last year, tapping into his power potential while getting on base and even playing a passable center field in a pinch. After those three, the Expos' attack is rife with question marks. Orlando Cabrera and Michael Barrett don't look like impact offensive players at this stage, and both could be gone by Opening Day as the team looks for cheaper options.

Minaya has tried to handcuff Fernando Tatis to one of his two aces for offensive help, with little interest. With his $6.75 million salary, chronic injuries, and bouts with doughiness, Tatis has become a 500-pound weight around the Expos' shoulders—literally.

Subtracting one of the team's top two starters might not work out too badly, given the Expos' pitching depth, the club's biggest strength. Even a small drop-off from 2002 would still mean a very good season from Bartolo Colon if he stays. If Colon goes, Javier Vazquez should still be one of the league's elite pitchers, assuming his workloads haven't caught up to him. Tomo Ohka made Jim Beattie's legacy look a little better with a breakthrough season last year. Tony Armas, while still inconsistent, looks safe enough as a slightly above-average innings-eater if nothing else. Between Sun-Woo Kim, Zach Day, and several other young arms, the back of the rotation could be effective too. A young, cheap bullpen proved decent last year and will be younger, cheaper, and hopefully better with Day or Kim set to take over for departed arsonist Matt

Expos Prospectus

2002 record: 83–79; Second place, NL East

Pythagenport Record: 83–79

Runs scored per game: 4.5 (6th in NL)

Runs allowed per game: 4.4 (8th in NL)

Team EqA: .262 (7th in NL)

2002 Batters Age: 28.5 (4th youngest in NL)

2002 Pitchers Age: 27.9 (6th youngest in NL)

Ballpark: Olympic Stadium; Neutral park; Park Factor of 1.008

2002: Left for dead by Loria and his carrion-eaters, the abandoned franchise stood up and made a run at contention.

2003: With baseball unwilling to end the farce, everyone must endure another year of silliness.

Herges. Wilton Guerrero's gone, so the bench gets better by default.

All that's left is for Minaya to leverage as many young, cheap bats as he can out of Colon or Vazquez. If he can dump Tatis in the process, everyone else probably stays. If he can't, some combination of Cabrera, Barrett, and Armas could become ex-Expos. What Minaya makes out of the whole mess could decide his long-term future as a major league GM.

As the last remnants of the post–Kevin Malone, mostly dry farm system get their suitcases ready, Expos fans can look to the past as an outlet for their anger. The years leading up to and immediately following Bronfman's 1991 departure marked the best period of drafting and player development the Expos had enjoyed since the late '70s and early '80s, when the system popped out Gary Carter, Andre Dawson, Tim Raines, and other Expo stars. Those late '80s and early '90s seasons lacked continuity at the top, same as today. Murray Cook, Dave Dombrowski, and Dan Duquette all rose to the rank of Expos GM, then bolted for greener pastures.

But even as GMs skipped town, core development people remained in place. Gary Hughes ran the scouting operation for years. When he left, a solid group of scouts, player-development staff, and coaches remained behind. They drafted and nurtured Larry Walker, Delino Deshields, and Marquis Grissom. They helped identify Moises Alou, John Wetteland, and Pedro Martinez as worthy targets, and later signed and developed Ugueth Urbina, Vladimir Guerrero, and Jose Vidro.

Brochu and the cheapskate consortium would eventually change all that. The group became hell-bent on squeezing every nickel it could out of the franchise. Free agent signings and big-ticket trades went from rare to unthinkable. After the 1994 season, Brochu ordered Malone to sell off the team's stars for whatever he could get in the span of a week. The nonexistent returns for Walker, Grissom, and Wetteland sent the organization into a tailspin.

Without adding outside help, a team needs to do everything in its power to build from within. Instead, ownership did the opposite. Draft picks were targeted based on signability instead of ability. The pay raises and competitive salaries needed to keep and attract the best scouts and talent evaluators never materialized, chasing away the very people so desperately needed to uncover hidden gems.

Expos minor league coaches and instructors also started leaving for greener pastures, and why not? Even those reasonably compensated didn't want to deal with uncertainty at every level. Would the big club move next year? Would the minor league affiliates drop their ties to the Expos? Few stuck around long enough to find out.

Two losses in the last two years exemplify the Expos' inability to retain their talent, on-field or off. As a few patient hitters began to spring up from the mass of minor league hackers, much of the credit went to director of player development Tony LaCava. Promoted to the position in 2001, LaCava helped change several organizational mandates. Though the Expos weren't as stringent in promoting plate discipline as say, Oakland—the A's won't let any player win a Player of the Week or Player of the Month award without walking at least once every 10 times up—LaCava met with instructors at all levels, stressing the virtue of a keen batting eye. He also tightened the Expos' approach to developing young pitchers. Managers and pitching coaches were taught to enforce strict pitch count limits on the Expos' youngest arms in an effort to curtail injuries. As pitchers mature and progress through the system, they're able to gradually extend their workloads, building up to a major league promotion if all goes well.

Owner Jeffrey Loria bailed for Florida after the 2001 season as part of a chain that rescued John Henry from Wayne Huzienga's stranglehold on Marlins revenue and parachuted him into Boston. The legal mess that followed shoved LaCava out the door to Cleveland, where he became a cross-checker. He's since moved on to become special assistant to Blue Jays GM J. P. Ricciardi, and the Expos have had to fill another hole.

Tim Leiper lasted a year longer. He progressed to one step away from the majors, climbing the ladder in the Expos' system all the way to manager at Triple-A Ottawa. The organization spoke highly of his leadership abilities, and players enjoyed playing for him. Despite a Leiper-led 2002 record of 80–61, Ottawa management chose to swap affiliation at the end of the year, linking up with the Orioles. Years of Expo management's failing to develop exciting prospects, mixed with indifference over signing minor league free agents to help Ottawa and the big club, drove the Lynx away. Those failures spelled the end for Leiper too, as he bolted for Boston's Class-A Sarasota team rather than move to the Expos' new Triple-A home in Edmonton. Because of these symptomatic setbacks and other more minor mishaps, the Expos can all but count on a lousy farm system for the next few years, barring a series of replenishing trades or rapid ascension by college draft picks.

It's against this backdrop that the Expos enter the 2003 season, absolutely, positively their last in Montreal—maybe. Here's what we do know: the Expos will play a large chunk of their home games a long way from Montreal. It's not the first time this has happened—the Expos spent the last month of the 1991 season on the road after a huge concrete chunk fell off Olympic Stadium.

By moving 22 games out of Montreal to Puerto Rico in 2003, Selig has ripped a chunk out of the Expos' dwindling credibility. The move could generate up to $10 million in additional revenue according to some estimates, though the odds of any surplus going toward player acquisitions instead of the 29 owners' pockets are roughly slim and none. Meanwhile, rather than work to find stable, intelligent ownership in the meantime, Selig will continue to hang everyone out to dry. The fans of Montreal, already treated to a sky-high list of embarrassments over the last decade, now get kicked in their collective shins again. Here's one fun scenario to consider: The Expos' last 2003 home games are slated for Puerto Rico. The team somehow overcomes the disadvantages of its grueling travel schedule and unfamiliar surroundings to land in a dead heat for first place in mid-September. The long-suffering fans of Montreal smell playoffs. Sorry folks, you'll have to fly 2,000 miles to cheer your team on for their final home games.

The fans of Washington, D.C., and the myriad other suggested Expo relocation sites will likewise suffer through another frustrating season. Like a drooling 16-year-old pining for the class tease, Washington fans smile and take repeated episodes of flirting, then rejection from the Lords of Baseball. Financier Fred Malek heads the list of qualified owners ready to build a stadium and cultivate a new franchise in D.C. He'll have to wait in line with the rest of the world, as Selig and his cronies continue their determined efforts to bad-mouth the sport and poor-mouth over salaries instead of addressing the most pressing of baseball's current humiliations.

With all that on the table, 2003 promises to be nothing if not interesting for Expos fans. Last year, Minaya operated under a different set of circumstances than perhaps any general manager in history, facing what he thought was a lame-duck season under MLB's stewardship before new owners bought the team and moved it out of Montreal. This prompted Minaya to raze what remained of the farm system and overpay for Bartolo Colon, without worrying about future consequences. That said, you'd have to go back 13 years to find a sensation that compared to Colon's last season, when the Expos traded three prospects—one of them Randy Johnson— for top lefty Mark Langston.

Minaya will surely want to make his bones again this year with the Expos' future and his own still very much in doubt. If he can maneuver through the off-season well enough to get the team back to the edges of a pennant race, look for more in-season fireworks as the Expos make what may be their final desperate grab at a playoff spot. Why the hell not? If you're going to go out, go out with a bang.

HITTERS

Scott Ackerman — C — Born: 23-Apr-79 — Age: 24 — Bats: R — Throws: R

YEAR	TM	LG	AGE	AB	H	2B	3B	HR	BB	SO	SB	CS	AVG	OBP	SLG	MLVR	EQBA	EQOBP	EQSLG	EQMLVR	VORP	DEFENSE	
2000	CPF	SAL	21	210	59	8	0	8	12	35	1	2	.281	.320	.433	.104	.216	.244	.338	-.365	-7.0	47-C	3
2000	JUP	FSL	21	182	51	5	0	2	15	22	1	0	.280	.338	.341	-.008	.238	.282	.292	-.342	-4.9	44-C	-14
2001	JUP	FSL	22	324	81	12	1	3	25	52	1	4	.250	.304	.321	-.079	.213	.251	.279	-.436	-16.9	66-C	-6
2002	BRV	FSL	23	217	64	11	2	7	14	39	1	0	.295	.341	.461	.196	.247	.280	.395	-.193	2.5	37-C	1
2002	HAR	EAS	23	17	4	0	0	0	0	2	0	0	.235	.235	.235	-.406	.235	.235	.235	-.521	-1.6		
2002	OTT	INT	23	31	8	1	0	2	0	8	0	0	.258	.258	.484	.008	.258	.258	.452	-.141	.7	10-C	0
2003	MON	NL	24	165	39	8	1	4	12	31	2	1	.237	.288	.364	-.190	.237	.286	.370	-.212	-1.7		

Breakout: 40%   Improve: 62%   Collapse: 20%

De-fault, the two sweetest words in the English language! Homer Simpson rip-off, or Scott Ackerman's reason for being? The big catcher could sneak his way into a spare catcher's job in the next year or two, with Michael Barrett likely to be traded before he gets too expensive and nothing but tumbleweeds behind Brian Schneider. He's worked hard to become a respectable catch-and-throw guy, but remains a non-hitter, in the minors, the Arizona Fall League, or anywhere else. Of course Mike Matheny's won everlasting love and a starting gig from Tony LaRussa with basically the same profile, so there's always hope.

Jeff Bailey — 1B — Born: 19-Nov-78 — Age: 24 — Bats: R — Throws: R

YEAR	TM	LG	AGE	AB	H	2B	3B	HR	BB	SO	SB	CS	AVG	OBP	SLG	MLVR	EQBA	EQOBP	EQSLG	EQMLVR	VORP	DEFENSE			
2000	BRV	FSL	21	458	113	19	3	14	50	116	3	3	.247	.330	.393	.027	.206	.268	.336	-.326	-27.6	38-1B	-8	14-C	-2
2001	PME	EAS	22	432	104	28	2	13	64	136	7	2	.241	.349	.405	.038	.209	.305	.351	-.231	-16.7	91-1B	-9	12-LF	-2
2002	HAR	EAS	23	309	87	17	1	13	63	78	3	3	.282	.419	.469	.238	.237	.352	.397	-.061	3.0	69-1B	-1	12-C	-1
2003	MON	NL	24	190	46	9	1	6	24	49	3	3	.243	.335	.406	-.051	.244	.331	.413	-.070	-1.6				

Breakout: 28%   Improve: 61%   Collapse: 17%

Any position player who's shown any skill at any level of the Expos organization gets a plug in the next few pages—it's that dire. Bailey got on base 42% of the time last year in Double-A, so he makes the cut. Signed by the Expos out of the Marlins organization, Bailey cut down his strikeouts and raised his walks last season, though his power remains lukewarm for a first baseman. He's done some catching, so he could have some value down the road as a utility guy who can hit a little, or a right-handed Mark Grace Lite if everything broke right. The Harrisburg Senators web site lists his boyhood hero as George "The Animal" Steele. Hmmm, an unheralded on-base fiend who idolized a guy with a green tongue growing up. Yup, we've got a new BP favorite.

Michael Barrett   C   Born: 22-Oct-76   Age: 26   Bats: R   Throws: R

YEAR	TM	LG	AGE	AB	H	2B	3B	HR	BB	SO	SB	CS	AVG	OBP	SLG	MLVR	EQBA	EQOBP	EQSLG	EQMLVR	VORP	DEFENSE		
2000	OTT	INT	23	120	43	7	0	2	13	10	1	0	.358	.430	.467	.303	.331	.389	.430	.127	10.5	24-3B	-1	
2000	MON	NL	23	271	58	15	1	1	23	35	0	1	.214	.278	.288	-.402	.212	.268	.289	-.388	-14.9	46-3B -10		24-C -5
2001	MON	NL	24	472	118	33	2	6	25	54	2	1	.250	.291	.367	-.203	.252	.292	.368	-.205	3.8	125-C	-15	
2002	MON	NL	25	376	99	20	1	12	40	65	6	3	.263	.336	.418	.025	.270	.337	.432	-.017	21.8	106-C	-4	
2003	*MON*	*NL*	*26*	*312*	*80*	*17*	*1*	*7*	*27*	*46*	*5*	*2*	*.258*	*.320*	*.388*	*-.089*	*.258*	*.317*	*.395*	*-.109*	*4.6*			

Breakout: 19%   Improve: 48%   Collapse: 25%

Though much has been made of his 1999 rookie season and the promise it offered for the future, Barrett has mostly been a hitter who looks good when a few more balls drop in for hits, mediocre when they don't. After ringing up 53 extra-base hits in Harrisburg in 1998, Barrett's gotten by largely on his knack for slapping pitches to the opposite field. His .348/.418/.638 April offered a world of hope, then faded from view as the year wore on and his production waned. Barrett may be a few small adjustments away from breaking through. Whether the Expos want to wait on the talented catcher who can't bring himself to pull the ball enough to be dangerous is another matter. The Expos had a great trade match with Texas staring them in the face, but John Hart blinked and overpaid for Einar Diaz instead, making another year of Barrett likely, at a non-bargain price.

Peter Bergeron   CF   Born: 09-Nov-77   Age: 25   Bats: L   Throws: R

YEAR	TM	LG	AGE	AB	H	2B	3B	HR	BB	SO	SB	CS	AVG	OBP	SLG	MLVR	EQBA	EQOBP	EQSLG	EQMLVR	VORP	DEFENSE
2000	MON	NL	22	518	127	25	7	5	58	100	11	13	.245	.321	.349	-.208	.243	.311	.345	-.207	-4.0	124-CF -1
2001	OTT	INT	23	206	49	5	3	0	20	42	15	7	.238	.308	.291	-.186	.230	.296	.282	-.331	-8.4	49-CF -3
2001	MON	NL	23	375	79	11	4	3	28	87	10	7	.211	.275	.285	-.369	.212	.273	.286	-.382	-21.3	89-CF 3
2002	MON	NL	24	123	23	3	2	0	22	44	10	3	.187	.310	.244	-.283	.200	.315	.256	-.341	-5.6	30-CF -1
2002	OTT	INT	24	340	99	9	4	1	39	65	7	7	.291	.366	.350	.028	.277	.348	.334	-.128	-3.8	92-LF -7
2003	*MON*	*NL*	*25*	*325*	*80*	*15*	*3*	*2*	*37*	*67*	*11*	*5*	*.247*	*.327*	*.332*	*-.157*	*.247*	*.324*	*.338*	*-.178*	*-7.6*	

Breakout: 24%   Improve: 51%   Collapse: 22%

Whatever promise Bergeron showed as a 21-year-old center fielder in San Antonio is all but gone. Granted, the trade that unloaded Mark Grudzielanek and Carlos Perez to L.A. for a bushel of prospects would have been addition solely by subtraction. But Bergeron looked like a speedy fly-catcher with nice on-base skills at the time, a solid candidate for the starting center field and leadoff batter jobs. He's gotten progressively worse since then, looking completely lost at the plate. Barring a huge turnaround, you'll likely never see his name in this book again.

Bergeron's the first of several fringe outfield prospects to be profiled in this chapter. If that doesn't entice you, feel free to skip ahead to the pitchers' section, where you'll find fifth starter/swingmen prospects aplenty. Have we mentioned the Expos' farm system sucks?

Orlando Cabrera   SS   Born: 02-Nov-74   Age: 28   Bats: R   Throws: R

YEAR	TM	LG	AGE	AB	H	2B	3B	HR	BB	SO	SB	CS	AVG	OBP	SLG	MLVR	EQBA	EQOBP	EQSLG	EQMLVR	VORP	DEFENSE
2000	MON	NL	25	422	100	25	1	13	25	28	4	4	.237	.281	.393	-.229	.237	.271	.392	-.222	-.4	107-SS 7
2001	MON	NL	26	626	173	41	6	14	43	54	19	7	.276	.327	.428	-.030	.275	.325	.426	-.043	30.7	159-SS 30
2002	MON	NL	27	563	148	43	1	7	48	53	25	7	.263	.323	.380	-.046	.270	.325	.394	-.092	18.4	151-SS 5
2003	*MON*	*NL*	*28*	*492*	*133*	*30*	*2*	*10*	*40*	*47*	*14*	*4*	*.269*	*.326*	*.396*	*-.060*	*.270*	*.323*	*.403*	*-.078*	*11.7*	

Breakout: 15%   Improve: 47%   Collapse: 22%

Cabrera's 2001 season set up perfectly for a trade. His Gold Glove was legit, as he posted one of the best defensive seasons ever for a shortstop. With no better options on hand though, he batted cleanup for much of the year, racking up 96 RBI through little more than opportunity. Brandon Phillips more than held his own in each step up the minor league ladder, despite being one of the younger players in every league he hopped through. With Cabrera due to become expensive and a

Orlando Cabrera *(continued)*

near shoo-in to regress offensively, sucking up a year of fill-ins at short while waiting a year for Phillips, all the while banking a solid hitting prospect or two for a barren farm system seemed a great option.

It didn't happen. A year later, shortstop has gone from a position of strength to "damn, are we screwed." Cabrera regressed as expected with the bat, but also gave up a ton of defensive value, thanks largely to a nasty back injury. The Expos must decide whether carrying an average offensive shortstop (at best) with potentially debilitating back problems is worth the $4 million or more Cabrera will make in arbitration. Shuffling Phillips off to the Indians has left them with few alternate options, short of a mish-mash of Jose Macias, Jamey Carroll, and friends that won't win any beauty contests.

Ron Calloway RF Born: 04-Sep-76 Age: 26 Bats: L Throws: L

YEAR	TM	LG	AGE	AB	H	2B	3B	HR	BB	SO	SB	CS	AVG	OBP	SLG	MLVR	EQBA	EQOBP	EQSLG	EQMLVR	VORP	DEFENSE
2000	JUP	FSL	23	530	147	24	6	6	55	89	34	14	.277	.350	.379	-1.000	.000	.000	.000	.000	-1.0	
2001	HAR	EAS	24	279	92	22	4	9	24	46	25	7	.330	.389	.534	-1.000	.000	.000	.000	.000	-1.0	
2001	OTT	INT	24	239	63	12	0	10	16	64	11	1	.264	.326	.439	-1.000	.000	.000	.000	.000	-1.0	
2002	OTT	INT	25	447	118	21	5	14	44	89	16	12	.264	.338	.427	.064	.247	.318	.407	-.105	-3.6	122-RF -1
2003	MON	NL	26	159	41	8	1	5	16	33	5	3	.258	.329	.413	-.041	.258	.326	.421	-.060	-.6	

Breakout: 30%   Improve: 54%   Collapse: 23%

A year after he came out of nowhere to fight his way into the fringes of discussion for the Expos' center field job, Calloway remains a player with extra-base power, good speed, and poor baseball instincts. Despite his athleticism, he's not a particularly good defensive player at a corner outfield spot, let alone center. He's made little progress in his effort to control the strike zone. Even his poor stolen base success rate bodes ill for his ability to turn tools into skills. Of course these are the Expos, so Calloway would deserve a fifth outfielder's job with a decent spring.

Jamey Carroll 3B Born: 18-Feb-74 Age: 29 Bats: R Throws: R

YEAR	TM	LG	AGE	AB	H	2B	3B	HR	BB	SO	SB	CS	AVG	OBP	SLG	MLVR	EQBA	EQOBP	EQSLG	EQMLVR	VORP	DEFENSE			
2000	HAR	EAS	26	169	49	5	3	0	12	13	8	2	.290	.337	.355	-.035	.253	.291	.312	-.287	-4.4	33-3B	5		
2000	OTT	INT	26	349	97	17	2	2	33	32	6	3	.278	.344	.355	-.066	.261	.315	.332	-.206	.9	58-2B	-11	25-3B	-3
2001	OTT	INT	27	267	64	8	2	0	18	41	5	5	.240	.293	.285	-.222	.230	.281	.274	-.373	-11.0	27-2B	-4	23-SS	1
2002	HAR	EAS	28	9	4	0	0	0	3	0	0	0	.444	.583	.444	.582	.333	.500	.333	.203	1.0				
2002	OTT	INT	28	421	118	19	2	8	37	39	6	10	.280	.343	.392	.037	.265	.326	.372	-.125	7.3	81-3B	16	27-2B	9
2002	MON	NL	28	71	22	5	3	1	4	12	1	0	.310	.347	.507	.205	.306	.342	.514	.144	6.0	13-3B	-2		
2003	MON	NL	29	294	73	13	2	3	26	37	5	2	.249	.313	.334	-.179	.249	.310	.340	-.200	-4.7				

Breakout: 12%   Improve: 37%   Collapse: 28%

As part of Omar Minaya's deadline shuffling, the Expos bid farewell to Mike Mordecai, one of the longest-lasting Expos of the last decade with four and a half years of loyal service. Of course, you only trade Mike Mordecai when you have Mike Mordecai Jr. waiting in the wings. Like Mordecai, Carroll has no pop, little patience or speed, and enough sound glovework, moxie, and golly-gee-whiz-does-that-little-guy-hustle in him to last for half a decade or more in Expoland. Carroll and Willie Bloomquist could have waged a great small sample size death match last September. You'd have to favor Bloomquist, but Carroll may have been scrappy enough to knock him out with a steel chair, or at least a corked Youppi! doll.

Matt Cepicky LF Born: 10-Nov-77 Age: 25 Bats: L Throws: R

YEAR	TM	LG	AGE	AB	H	2B	3B	HR	BB	SO	SB	CS	AVG	OBP	SLG	MLVR	EQBA	EQOBP	EQSLG	EQMLVR	VORP	DEFENSE
2000	JUP	FSL	22	536	160	32	7	5	24	64	32	13	.299	.331	.412	.094	.249	.272	.351	-.270	-23.9	105-LF -8
2001	HAR	EAS	23	459	121	23	8	19	21	97	5	12	.264	.299	.473	.059	.225	.260	.397	-.244	-19.3	102-LF 0
2002	HAR	EAS	24	419	116	25	2	16	33	94	7	1	.277	.333	.461	.093	.235	.282	.393	-.201	-11.9	79-LF -1
2002	MON	NL	24	74	16	3	0	3	4	21	0	0	.216	.256	.378	-.193	.227	.256	.400	-.246	-2.9	12-LF 0
2003	MON	NL	25	195	48	10	1	6	15	42	3	3	.248	.303	.409	-.098	.248	.300	.416	-.118	-4.5	

Breakout: 39%   Improve: 62%   Collapse: 17%

Frank Robinson raved about Cepicky seemingly every other day after his call-up. It must have been the cool, refreshing breeze of his prodigious whiffs. Like Vladimir Guerrero, Cepicky swings hard at everything that moves. That's the last time he'll ever be compared to Vladimir Guerrero, unless you count both men's ability to effectively exchange carbon dioxide and oxygen. With every year that passes, it becomes clearer Cepicky will never learn the strike zone enough to be anything resembling an effective big league hitter. Spare outfielders we'd rather see make the club over Cepicky: Ron Calloway, Val Pascucci, Terrmel Sledge, Herm Winningham.

Endy Chavez — CF — Born: 07-Feb-78 — Age: 25 — Bats: L — Throws: L

YEAR	TM	LG	AGE	AB	H	2B	3B	HR	BB	SO	SB	CS	AVG	OBP	SLG	MLVR	EQBA	EQOBP	EQSLG	EQMLVR	VORP	DEFENSE	
2000	SLU	FSL	22	433	129	20	2	1	47	48	38	16	.298	.367	.360	.062	.245	.299	.302	-.289	-12.4	106-CF	-5
2001	WIC	TXS	23	168	50	6	1	1	16	13	11	6	.298	.359	.363	.011	.247	.301	.306	-.279	-4.4	42-CF	0
2001	OMA	PCL	23	104	35	6	0	0	0	13	4	3	.337	.337	.394	-.008	.301	.301	.350	-.179	.0	20-CF	-1
2001	KCR	AL	23	77	16	2	0	0	3	8	0	2	.208	.237	.234	-.487	.221	.250	.247	-.479	-7.5	22-LF	-1
2002	OTT	INT	24	405	139	28	5	4	33	37	21	13	.343	.393	.467	.273	.318	.369	.437	.090	30.0	101-CF	0
2002	MON	NL	24	125	37	8	5	1	5	16	3	5	.296	.323	.464	.095	.299	.321	.465	.029	6.5	35-CF	2
2003	MON	NL	25	302	84	17	3	3	26	35	8	3	.277	.336	.382	-.057	.277	.332	.389	-.075	3.6		

Breakout: 16%   Improve: 46%   Collapse: 22%

Omar Minaya's waiver wire pick-up ended a three-month odyssey that took Chavez from Kansas City to Detroit to the Mets, then north of the border. Though Wil Cordero, Andres Galarraga, and Troy O'Leary brought more name value, Chavez is the only one of the four who could have a future. Chavez won the International League batting title in Ottawa last year while handling center field respectably. Called up to the big club, he fared well, grabbing just enough playing time as the starting center fielder to at least hint at future success. Chavez should get first crack at the job on Opening Day, unless the Expos have three great prospects and $100 million lying under a rock in Verdun for a Carlos Beltran trade. We'd like Chavez's long-term outlook a lot better if he'd add 30 walks a season.

Wil Cordero — LF — Born: 03-Oct-71 — Age: 31 — Bats: R — Throws: R

YEAR	TM	LG	AGE	AB	H	2B	3B	HR	BB	SO	SB	CS	AVG	OBP	SLG	MLVR	EQBA	EQOBP	EQSLG	EQMLVR	VORP	DEFENSE			
2000	PIT	NL	28	348	98	24	3	16	25	58	1	2	.282	.337	.506	.071	.277	.323	.500	.061	13.6	65-LF	-4		
2000	CLE	AL	28	148	39	11	2	0	7	18	0	0	.264	.310	.365	-.207	.272	.310	.374	-.148	-2.1	38-LF	2		
2001	CLE	AL	29	268	67	11	1	4	22	50	0	0	.250	.316	.343	-.159	.265	.330	.366	-.126	-2.6	34-LF	-2	20-1B	-1
2002	CLE	AL	30	18	4	0	0	0	0	3	0	0	.222	.222	.222	-.499	.278	.278	.278	-.348	-.9				
2002	MON	NL	30	143	39	9	0	6	17	26	2	0	.273	.358	.462	.126	.276	.359	.476	.089	6.8	24-LF	-1		
2003	MON	NL	31	177	46	10	1	5	16	31	1	1	.260	.326	.402	-.059	.261	.323	.409	-.078	-2.0				

Breakout: 22%   Improve: 37%   Collapse: 33%

Miscast in Montreal, Cordero could still help a championship team as a pinch hitter and occasional DH against lefties. The Expos tried to get more out of him, platooning him with Troy O'Leary in left field. Though Cordero may have been the best the Expos could have done under Omar Minaya's tight schedule and limited budget, the less you see of him in the field, the better. That's a far cry from long-ago expectations, but still a lot better than signing a limited veteran like say, Cordero, to a three-year, $9 million contract. The one-year, $600,000 re-up with the Spos won't hurt anyone, unless Minaya decides to test the limits of the Peter Principle and give Cordero the vacant first-base job.

Andres Galarraga — 1B — Born: 18-Jun-61 — Age: 42 — Bats: R — Throws: R

YEAR	TM	LG	AGE	AB	H	2B	3B	HR	BB	SO	SB	CS	AVG	OBP	SLG	MLVR	EQBA	EQOBP	EQSLG	EQMLVR	VORP	DEFENSE	
2000	ATL	NL	39	494	149	25	1	28	36	126	3	5	.302	.369	.526	.188	.299	.356	.524	.174	35.8	120-1B	-5
2001	SFG	NL	40	156	45	12	1	7	13	49	0	3	.288	.355	.513	.187	.306	.367	.538	.220	13.4	34-1B	-5
2001	TEX	AL	40	243	57	16	0	10	18	68	1	0	.235	.311	.424	-.078	.247	.319	.453	-.039	3.4	24-1B	-1
2002	MON	NL	41	292	76	12	0	9	30	81	2	2	.260	.347	.394	.011	.267	.348	.412	-.027	5.4	72-1B	-8
2003	MON	NL	42	154	37	7	0	5	14	41	1	1	.240	.314	.378	-.126	.240	.310	.384	-.146	-4.2		

Breakout: 8%   Improve: 35%   Collapse: 40%

After a long, at times illustrious career, here's hoping Galarraga hangs them up rather than come back for another season. His bat's about three beats too slow, and he's nowhere near the acrobat he used to be around the bag. As great a run as he had in his 10 seasons between Expos gigs, Montreal fans never got to see him at his best, after he'd opened his stance and before age caught up with him. Still, Galarraga brought his trademark smile and enthusiasm back for his comeback tour, and the city won't forget him, even when the team's long gone.

Vladimir Guerrero　　　　　RF　　Born: 09-Feb-76　　Age: 27　　Bats: R　　Throws: R

YEAR	TM	LG	AGE	AB	H	2B	3B	HR	BB	SO	SB	CS	AVG	OBP	SLG	MLVR	EQBA	EQOBP	EQSLG	EQMLVR	VORP	DEFENSE
2000	MON	NL	24	571	197	28	11	44	58	74	9	10	.345	.413	.664	.512	.338	.398	.650	.468	86.3	139-RF -6
2001	MON	NL	25	599	184	45	4	34	60	88	37	16	.307	.379	.566	.280	.301	.370	.554	.242	54.8	157-RF -2
2002	MON	NL	26	614	206	37	2	39	84	70	40	20	.336	.420	.593	.453	.329	.410	.589	.386	77.6	151-RF -1
2003	MON	NL	27	582	184	37	4	34	71	78	30	7	.316	.393	.569	.316	.316	.389	.579	.307	52.8	

Breakout: 8%　　Improve: 42%　　Collapse: 10%

Four more years! Four more years! The mayor of Montreal, San Juan, and any other city he'll play in gets his freedom after the 2003 season, unless the Expos' front office mounts a miracle 11th-hour rally. It's a wonder he's made it this long. The below-market, five-year, $28 million contract Guerrero signed at the end of the 1998 season kept him in an Expos uniform longer than you'd have the right to expect, given the rate of attrition of other Expo stars of recent vintage in Montreal. One cruel twist of MLB owning the Expos: Omar Minaya won't be allowed to sign Vlad until a new ownership group is in place, and by then it'll probably be too late. Yet he probably won't be free to strike up a bidding war for Vlad's services that could net the Expos enough young talent to restock their barren farm system.

We often stress the importance of hitters working walks when a pitcher won't give in. Guerrero bumped his walks up to a career high last year, but intentional and semi-intentional walks fueled most of that increase. Vlad is what he is and he's not likely to ever change. He also may be one of the very few players to get away with swinging at everything. Few hitters in the sport's history can match his hand–eye coordination, not to mention his obscene plate coverage. For a power hitter, he rarely strikes out. He's also strong enough to turn sliders eight inches off the plate or at his shoe tops into 400-foot smashes. Bank on this—Guerrero's plate discipline can stagnate for the rest of his career, and he'll still put up big numbers for the next seven to 10 years. If Alfonso Soriano tries the same tack, his OBPs won't look appreciably different than Rey Sanchez's. That's how unique Vlad's talents are.

Wilton Guerrero　　　　　Sibling　　Born: 24-Oct-74　　Age: 28　　Bats: B　　Throws: R

YEAR	TM	LG	AGE	AB	H	2B	3B	HR	BB	SO	SB	CS	AVG	OBP	SLG	MLVR	EQBA	EQOBP	EQSLG	EQMLVR	VORP	DEFENSE
2000	MON	NL	25	288	77	7	2	2	19	41	8	1	.267	.313	.326	-.243	.269	.305	.328	-.226	-10.7	56-LF -3
2001	LOU	INT	26	227	69	14	2	0	12	30	12	5	.304	.342	.383	.029	.284	.321	.362	-.135	4.6	33-2B -8
2001	CIN	NL	26	142	48	5	1	1	3	17	5	2	.338	.352	.408	.035	.336	.349	.399	.014	8.5	12-SS -4
2002	CIN	NL	27	78	19	1	1	0	6	13	2	1	.244	.298	.282	-.241	.253	.298	.291	-.302	-3.4	
2002	MON	NL	27	62	12	1	0	0	1	19	5	0	.194	.206	.210	-.522	.206	.206	.238	-.590	-6.8	
2003	CIN	NL	28	80	20	3	1	0	4	13	3	1	.250	.290	.307	-.255	.253	.290	.318	-.265	-3	

Breakout: 5%　　Improve: 27%　　Collapse: 47%

Would Wilton Guerrero have made the big leagues if his name were Wilton Copelovich? He's got one of the worst batting eyes in baseball, no power, and a brutal glove at every position on the diamond. It has to be some deluded hope that he can somehow tap into 1/10th of Vlad's ability, right? Actually, Wilton puts the bat on the ball and can slap singles reasonably well. So maybe it's just the misguided views of the talent evaluators and managers who value those sorts of things. Vlad will need a new bridge partner after the Expos released Wilton, a move that will have zero effect on the Guerrero with talent.

Scott Hodges　　　　　3B　　Born: 26-Dec-78　　Age: 24　　Bats: L　　Throws: R

YEAR	TM	LG	AGE	AB	H	2B	3B	HR	BB	SO	SB	CS	AVG	OBP	SLG	MLVR	EQBA	EQOBP	EQSLG	EQMLVR	VORP	DEFENSE
2000	JUP	FSL	21	422	129	32	1	14	49	66	8	2	.306	.382	.486	.273	.249	.309	.402	-.127	6.8	104-3B 3
2001	HAR	EAS	22	305	84	11	2	5	25	56	3	2	.275	.330	.374	-.011	.239	.291	.323	-.279	-7.7	73-3B -2
2002	HAR	EAS	23	526	143	35	2	9	63	102	2	2	.272	.353	.397	.037	.232	.300	.343	-.238	-6.8	130-3B -2
2003	MON	NL	24	168	41	9	1	4	17	33	2	2	.247	.320	.388	-.097	.247	.317	.395	-.117	.5	

Breakout: 40%　　Improve: 63%　　Collapse: 26%

It's starting to look grim for Hodges. That's a shame, since the Expos could really use a good, young third baseman once Fernando Tatis leaves at the end of this year, or earlier. Hodges got a mulligan for a 2001 season marred by severe problems with colitis. Having recovered and regained much of the 30 pounds he'd dropped, Hodges still couldn't duplicate even the modest success he had at Jupiter in 2000. He made 25 errors in 130 games and showed little over-the-fence power. He did slug 35 doubles, which offers some hope. The Expos' system is filled with dilemmas like Hodges: players who haven't mastered the level they're at, who need to move up to have a shot at a big league career.

Jose Macias CF/2B Born: 25-Jan-72 Age: 31 Bats: B Throws: R

YEAR	TM	LG	AGE	AB	H	2B	3B	HR	BB	SO	SB	CS	AVG	OBP	SLG	MLVR	EQBA	EQOBP	EQSLG	EQMLVR	VORP	DEFENSE			
2000	TOL	INT	28	130	30	5	0	0	17	17	2	3	.231	.324	.269	-.249	.214	.298	.244	-.387	-7.5	20-CF -2			
2000	DET	AL	28	173	44	3	5	2	18	24	2	0	.254	.328	.364	-.165	.267	.333	.378	-.102	4.9	26-2B 1	17-3B -1		
2001	DET	AL	29	488	131	24	6	8	32	54	21	6	.268	.317	.391	-.067	.291	.340	.428	.001	23.9	82-3B 10	28-CF 1		
2002	DET	AL	30	107	25	4	0	0	8	13	3	2	.234	.293	.271	-.277	.269	.324	.306	-.220	-.1	16-2B 0			
2002	MON	NL	30	231	59	17	1	7	13	44	5	6	.255	.298	.429	-.028	.256	.295	.440	-.093	5.0	37-CF -1	19-3B -3		
2003	*MON*	*NL*	*31*	*269*	*68*	*13*	*3*	*4*	*22*	*39*	*7*	*3*	*.253*	*.311*	*.366*	*-.138*	*.253*	*.308*	*.373*	*-.158*	*-1.7*				

Breakout: 11%   Improve: 43%   Collapse: 29%

One of a truckload of players to age two years or more before the 2002 season, not that Macias was within five years of being a prospect anyway. The Expos grabbed him from Detroit for Chris Truby, completing a trade cycle that started with Geoff Blum being shipped to Houston to post a career year as an Astro. Macias is a useful utility player who holds his own with five or six different gloves. Lacking power and patience and being unlikely to improve this late in the game, he shouldn't be an option for any starting job. Between Fernando Tatis's injuries, Orlando Cabrera's trade-inducing salary, and Endy Chavez's question marks, he may get one anyway. If that happens, Vladimir Guerrero would need to stand on his head to make this a top offense. Granted, Vlad would probably whack 80 extra-base hits while on his *cabeza* anyway.

Henry Mateo 2B/SS Born: 14-Oct-76 Age: 26 Bats: B Throws: R

YEAR	TM	LG	AGE	AB	H	2B	3B	HR	BB	SO	SB	CS	AVG	OBP	SLG	MLVR	EQBA	EQOBP	EQSLG	EQMLVR	VORP	DEFENSE	
2000	HAR	EAS	23	530	152	25	11	5	58	97	48	16	.287	.364	.404	.072	.248	.309	.353	-.196	2.7	130-2B -1	
2001	OTT	INT	24	500	134	14	12	5	33	89	47	14	.268	.322	.374	-.035	.255	.307	.358	-.188	3.5	116-2B -7	
2002	OTT	INT	25	285	73	10	6	5	18	53	15	6	.256	.307	.386	-.048	.243	.293	.372	-.204	.9	53-2B 11	22-SS -5
2002	MON	NL	25	23	4	0	1	0	2	6	2	0	.174	.240	.261	-.399	.174	.240	.304	-.443	-1.8		
2003	*MON*	*NL*	*26*	*160*	*40*	*7*	*2*	*2*	*13*	*29*	*6*	*2*	*.250*	*.312*	*.356*	*-.151*	*.251*	*.309*	*.363*	*-.172 -.4*			

Breakout: 18%   Improve: 43%   Collapse: 28%

If someone makes a giant mistake and lets Mateo make the team next year, he'd be best used in the Herb Washington role—pinch runner only. Mateo's fast, and that's about it. He lacks on-base skills, has no power, and can't field shortstop well enough to be a competent utility infielder. When a player makes you pine for the return of Tomas de la Rosa, that's when you know you're screwed.

Troy O'Leary LF Born: 04-Aug-69 Age: 33 Bats: L Throws: L

YEAR	TM	LG	AGE	AB	H	2B	3B	HR	BB	SO	SB	CS	AVG	OBP	SLG	MLVR	EQBA	EQOBP	EQSLG	EQMLVR	VORP	DEFENSE
2000	BOS	AL	30	513	134	30	4	13	44	76	0	2	.261	.322	.411	-.110	.271	.324	.429	-.044	5.6	128-LF 4
2001	BOS	AL	31	341	82	16	6	13	25	73	1	3	.240	.302	.437	-.062	.254	.314	.468	-.021	5.8	87-LF 4
2002	OTT	INT	32	86	29	6	0	3	7	15	0	1	.337	.387	.512	.321	.310	.362	.483	.137	5.3	20-LF -2
2002	MON	NL	33	273	78	12	2	3	34	47	1	2	.286	.371	.377	.047	.295	.373	.388	.008	7.1	65-LF -2
2003	*CHC*	*NL*	*33*	*233*	*59*	*11*	*2*	*6*	*23*	*43*	*1*	*1*	*.252*	*.321*	*.388*	*-.092*	*.260*	*.324*	*.407*	*-.078*	*-3*	

Breakout: 13%   Improve: 42%   Collapse: 30%

Getting a .371 OBP and minimal power out of the primary left fielder may have been the best Omar Minaya could have hoped for, given the eternity it took Major League Baseball to get its collective butts in gear and decide on the Expos situation last year. Signed to a minor league deal just before Opening Day, O'Leary didn't embarrass himself upon his early May call-up, chipping in some timely hits when given the chance. With the Cubs, he'll serve as a pinch hitter and inadequate Alou insurance.

Val Pascucci RF Born: 17-Nov-78 Age: 24 Bats: R Throws: R

YEAR	TM	LG	AGE	AB	H	2B	3B	HR	BB	SO	SB	CS	AVG	OBP	SLG	MLVR	EQBA	EQOBP	EQSLG	EQMLVR	VORP	DEFENSE	
2000	CPF	SAL	21	69	22	4	0	3	16	15	5	0	.319	.447	.507	.399	.233	.341	.384	-.102	-.5	19-RF -1	
2000	JUP	FSL	21	405	115	30	2	14	66	98	14	6	.284	.398	.472	.257	.234	.324	.394	-.121	-4.9	90-RF -10	
2001	HAR	EAS	22	476	116	17	1	21	65	114	8	8	.244	.348	.416	.049	.211	.302	.356	-.229	-21.4	111-RF -6	15-1B -4
2002	HAR	EAS	23	459	108	14	1	27	93	115	2	0	.235	.379	.447	.114	.202	.321	.380	-.166	-11.6	101-RF -6	17-1B -5
2003	*MON*	*NL*	*24*	*188*	*46*	*8*	*1*	*8*	*26*	*47*	*2*	*2*	*.246*	*.343*	*.425*	*-.010*	*.247*	*.340*	*.433*	*-.027*	*-.8*		

Breakout: 43%   Improve: 77%   Collapse: 9%

Val Pascucci *(continued)*

Drafted out of the University of Oklahoma in 1999, where he toiled mostly as a pitcher, Pascucci has developed a keen batting eye, a skill which has offered hope for his development. But his long swing has severely stunted his progress. Pascucci slugged 27 homers in Harrisburg last year after repeating the level, at a riper age than most Eastern League prospects. If you're going to own two skills, power and patience are as good as it gets. But Pascucci's game is so limited elsewhere, he looks like little more than a useful boom-or-bust pinch hitter or fill-in corner outfielder with no range. If the Expos could combine Pascucci's batting eye with Matt Cepicky's athleticism and throw in each player's power, you'd have something there.

Brian Schneider   **C**   **Born: 26-Nov-76**   **Age: 26**   **Bats: L**   **Throws: R**

YEAR	TM	LG	AGE	AB	H	2B	3B	HR	BB	SO	SB	CS	AVG	OBP	SLG	MLVR	EQBA	EQOBP	EQSLG	EQMLVR	VORP	DEFENSE	
2000	OTT	INT	23	238	59	22	3	4	16	42	1	0	.248	.295	.416	-.089	.233	.270	.392	-.226	.5	59-C	0
2000	MON	NL	23	115	27	6	0	0	7	24	0	1	.235	.279	.287	-.391	.233	.264	.293	-.379	-4.4	33-C	-6
2001	OTT	INT	24	338	93	27	1	6	27	55	2	0	.275	.336	.414	.046	.262	.319	.397	-.105	11.5	89-C	9
2002	MON	NL	25	207	57	19	2	5	21	41	1	2	.275	.342	.459	.100	.281	.343	.471	.059	16.0	56-C	6
2003	MON	NL	26	184	48	12	1	4	17	33	2	2	.260	.325	.400	-.064	.260	.322	.407	-.083	3.9		

Breakout: 10%   *Improve: 28%*   *Collapse: 38%*

A better option than all the Brad Ausmii out there, with or without accounting for salary. For the Expos' purposes, Schneider's a better-fielding catcher than Michael Barrett, with a bat that at least looked comparable in limited playing time. With payroll concerns all over the roster, Barrett may get shipped out, opening the starting job for Schneider. Paired with a veteran righty hitter, catcher could remain a plus position for the Expos, especially if Schneider converts a few of those ample doubles into homers.

Terrmel Sledge   **CF**   **Born: 18-Mar-77**   **Age: 26**   **Bats: L**   **Throws: L**

YEAR	TM	LG	AGE	AB	H	2B	3B	HR	BB	SO	SB	CS	AVG	OBP	SLG	MLVR	EQBA	EQOBP	EQSLG	EQMLVR	VORP	DEFENSE	
2000	LNC	CLF	23	384	130	22	7	11	72	49	35	11	.339	.463	.518	.377	.244	.340	.381	-.101	-2.4	72-RF	-3
2001	HAR	EAS	24	448	124	22	6	9	51	72	30	8	.277	.362	.413	.091	.242	.318	.362	-.170	-9.6	117-1B	-10
2002	HAR	EAS	25	396	119	18	6	8	55	70	11	8	.301	.402	.437	.186	.256	.341	.373	-.102	8.2	92-CF	2
2002	OTT	INT	25	80	21	5	2	1	11	15	1	1	.263	.359	.412	.077	.244	.331	.402	-.089	-.0	16-LF	-2
2003	MON	NL	26	174	45	9	2	3	20	31	4	2	.259	.342	.392	-.046	.260	.338	.399	-.064	1.2		

Breakout: 28%   *Improve: 54%*   *Collapse: 27%*

Here's what happens when you flip through new owners and front offices every other year and neglect the farm system. You get a 26-year-old corner outfielder/first baseman with negligible power as your best hitting prospect. Sledge has a good eye, good speed, and enough glove to provide a half-decent option as a spare outfielder, or a semi-regular center fielder if no better options emerge. He won't hit enough to carry a corner outfield spot, let alone first base, even if he might be the best candidate the Expos have after the Lee Stevens/Andres Galarraga/Sideshow Bob mess last season. Well, Joe Vitiello's the best candidate, but management would sooner paint the turf a delightful mauve than give the most obvious choice a shot.

Fernando Tatis   **3B**   **Born: 01-Jan-75**   **Age: 28**   **Bats: R**   **Throws: R**

YEAR	TM	LG	AGE	AB	H	2B	3B	HR	BB	SO	SB	CS	AVG	OBP	SLG	MLVR	EQBA	EQOBP	EQSLG	EQMLVR	VORP	DEFENSE	
2000	STL	NL	25	324	82	21	1	18	57	94	2	3	.253	.381	.491	.107	.252	.369	.485	.098	26.8	74-3B	0
2001	MON	NL	26	145	37	9	0	2	16	43	0	0	.255	.345	.359	-.105	.259	.340	.367	-.110	3.3	34-3B	-10
2002	BRV	FSL	27	17	4	1	0	0	3	4	0	0	.235	.409	.294	.048	.222	.332	.278	-.267	-.7		
2002	MON	NL	27	381	87	18	1	15	35	90	2	2	.228	.307	.399	-.073	.236	.307	.420	-.116	7.2	92-3B	-9
2003	MON	NL	28	294	73	17	1	11	35	72	2	1	.249	.335	.424	-.023	.249	.332	.431	-.041	6.7		

Breakout: 27%   *Improve: 59%*   *Collapse: 18%*

Tatis was unlike any third baseman in baseball in 1999. Just 24, he was a short, powerfully built dynamo, stuffed with power, patience, and athleticism. He then spent nearly half the next season on the shelf, drawing rips from Tony LaRussa for his poor work ethic and attitude. Still, the Expos looked to have a steal when they flipped Dustin Hermanson, his bloated contract and plummeting peripherals, along with Steve Kline to St. Louis for Tatis and Britt Reames. A team with no viable third baseman since Tim Wallach circa 1990 had to take the risk. Don't hold your breath waiting for a happy ending. Two years of an often overweight, chronically injured Tatis has set his $6.75 million salary in 2003 up as a Lee Stevens-sized albatross, only worse. As of press time Tatis had made Omar Minaya's quest to shave $15 million off the payroll while getting quality in return a Herculean task.

Jose Vidro — 2B — Born: 27-Aug-74 — Age: 28 — Bats: B — Throws: R

YEAR	TM	LG	AGE	AB	H	2B	3B	HR	BB	SO	SB	CS	AVG	OBP	SLG	MLVR	EQBA	EQOBP	EQSLG	EQMLVR	VORP	DEFENSE
2000	MON	NL	25	606	200	51	2	24	49	69	5	4	.330	.382	.540	.260	.326	.369	.534	.240	75.2	147-2B -3
2001	MON	NL	26	486	155	34	1	15	31	49	4	1	.319	.372	.486	.169	.321	.370	.488	.169	51.9	116-2B -10
2002	MON	NL	27	604	190	43	3	19	60	70	2	1	.315	.379	.490	.234	.319	.379	.502	.202	66.5	147-2B 6
2003	MON	NL	28	555	170	37	2	20	51	62	4	1	.306	.367	.486	.157	.307	.363	.495	.144	43.2	

Breakout: 4%   Improve: 38%   Collapse: 15%

One of the steadiest offensive talents in all of baseball, Vidro has greatly improved his defense, raising his game from its already impressive All-Star status. Several Expos infielders credited 2001 infield instructor Perry Hill for their improvement that year. Vidro meanwhile struggled in 2001, then took a big step forward with the leather in 2002 with Hill gone. Maybe it just took a year for Hill's instruction to kick in with Vidro. Or maybe the results belie Hill's reputation.

Being a great general manager takes more than plucking choice plums off the scrap heap and being the guy who never gets stuck with the Neifi Perez end of a trade. Teams would do well to apply objective analysis instead of cronyism when hiring pitching, hitting, fielding, and baserunning coaches. Other than a few members of the Mazzone congregation, there's little consensus on who makes a good hire, both at the major league and especially the minor league level. Saying the players and not the coaches make all the difference is a cop-out. Teams could save millions of dollars by employing pitching coaches who'd keep arms healthy. They could win a handful more games every year by tapping hitting coaches who'd tell young players more than the standard tripe about staying aggressive. Here's hoping more GMs get hired for their ability to address such issues instead of their membership in the buddy system. The game will be better for it.

Joe Vitiello — 1B — Born: 11-Apr-70 — Age: 33 — Bats: R — Throws: R

YEAR	TM	LG	AGE	AB	H	2B	3B	HR	BB	SO	SB	CS	AVG	OBP	SLG	MLVR	EQBA	EQOBP	EQSLG	EQMLVR	VORP	DEFENSE
2000	LVG	PCL	30	274	96	31	0	11	27	59	2	0	.350	.413	.584	.366	.296	.348	.494	.115	14.4	62-1B -1
2000	SDP	NL	30	52	13	3	0	2	10	9	0	0	.250	.371	.423	.023	.264	.371	.434	.043	2.1	10-1B -3
2001	ORX	JPL	31	407	112	21	0	22	36	125	0	0	.275	.334	.489	.089	.263	.308	.462	-.032	10.6	
2002	OTT	INT	32	431	142	34	0	16	39	58	1	0	.329	.394	.520	.333	.308	.370	.492	.161	30.7	100-1B -4
2003	MON	NL	33	157	42	9	1	6	15	31	1	1	.269	.336	.444	.019	.269	.332	.452	.002	1.9	

Breakout: 7%   Improve: 35%   Collapse: 28%

Check out that 2002 line and you'll see why we're writing about a slow-footed first baseman going on 33. Somewhere along the line, Vitiello got branded a Quadruple-A player. He's never lasted long enough in the Show to prove he can handle regular duty. But with the decaying corpse of Lee Stevens and a game but washed-up Andres Galarraga trying to handle the first-base job, Vitiello smacked International League pitching all last year and never got a chance to even sniff the big leagues. Translations aren't perfect, and no one could guarantee Vitiello's success if promoted. But choosing a player based solely on name value is a nifty way to throw away 20 runs a year. No team can afford to do that on a regular basis, least of all the Expos.

Brad Wilkerson — OF/1B — Born: 01-Jun-77 — Age: 26 — Bats: L — Throws: L

YEAR	TM	LG	AGE	AB	H	2B	3B	HR	BB	SO	SB	CS	AVG	OBP	SLG	MLVR	EQBA	EQOBP	EQSLG	EQMLVR	VORP	DEFENSE	
2000	HAR	EAS	23	229	77	36	2	6	42	38	8	4	.336	.447	.590	.483	.279	.374	.494	.143	15.3	56-LF -1	
2000	OTT	INT	23	212	53	11	1	12	45	60	5	4	.250	.388	.481	.157	.227	.349	.440	-.018	4.6	62-LF -5	
2001	OTT	INT	24	233	63	10	0	12	60	68	12	5	.270	.426	.468	.253	.251	.393	.436	.076	11.8	55-LF -2	
2001	MON	NL	24	117	24	7	2	1	17	41	2	1	.205	.306	.325	-.256	.203	.304	.331	-.263	-6.1	33-LF -1	
2002	MON	NL	25	507	135	27	8	20	81	161	7	8	.266	.373	.469	.154	.269	.370	.483	.112	28.2	111-OF -3	20-1B 5
2003	MON	NL	26	441	117	25	4	18	71	122	8	7	.266	.371	.465	.100	.267	.367	.474	.086	18.0		

Breakout: 20%   Improve: 51%   Collapse: 19%

Minor league hitting instructors urged him to be more aggressive. Jeff Torborg benched him for the withered remains of Mark Smith. He once mistakenly ordered sautéed boot in a downtown bistro (OK, made that one up). Still, Wilkerson overcame all those obstacles, and flourished last year in an organization that avoids patient hitters like the plague. He'd always reached base at a healthy clip thanks to his solid batting eye. What's more exciting is his emerging power—the 47 doubles he hit between Double-A and Triple-A in 2000 started flying over the fence last year. This is why we constantly harp about the virtue of plate discipline. A talented hitter who learns to control the strike zone can wait for his pitch, crush it, and produce runs in bunches. If the fat pitch never comes, walks are a happy by-product. The Expos should decide soon whether Wilkerson's future lies in left field or first base. He'll hit at either position.

PITCHERS

Tony Armas Jr.   Born: 29-Apr-78   Age: 25   Bats: R   Throws: R

YEAR	TM	LG	AGE	G	GS	IP	H	BB	SO	HR	ERA	EQERA	EQH9	EQBB9	EQSO9	EQHR9	PERA	VORP	STF
2000	OTT	INT	22	4	4	19.0	22	4	12	3	3.79	4.98	10.9	1.9	4.8	1.8	5.69	1.1	2
2000	MON	NL	22	17	17	95.0	74	50	59	10	4.36	3.50	6.5	3.8	4.9	0.8	3.49	21.2	8
2001	MON	NL	23	34	34	196.7	180	91	176	18	4.03	4.03	8.2	3.8	6.8	0.7	4.00	32.2	19
2002	MON	NL	24	29	29	164.3	149	78	131	22	4.44	4.57	8.3	3.8	6.3	1.2	4.49	17.1	10
2003	MON	NL	25	28	25	160.7	151	69	131	18	4.18	4.34	8.6	3.3	6.5	1.0	4.25	22.7	12

Breakout: 17%   Improve: 53%   Collapse: 12%

He's all that's left of the horror that was the Pedro Martinez trade, so why not rub it in with maddening year-to-year swings? Armas took a big step up in 2001, hiking his strikeouts, lowering his walks and homers, and throwing 34 healthy starts. Last year? Walks and homers back up, strikeouts and starts back down. Armas has a load of talent without a clear idea of what to do with it. By contrast Tomo Ohka's stuff looks relatively pedestrian, yet he went out and made other teams look silly throughout last season, just by pitching smart. Armas has been somewhat lucky on balls in play over the last three years too. If his walks and homers stay up, one of these years he'll post an ERA over five; if he ever figures it all out, he'll look like Tim Hudson—our money's on the former. He'll get expensive soon, so the Expos hope the leap happens now.

Jim Brower   Born: 29-Dec-72   Age: 30   Bats: R   Throws: R

YEAR	TM	LG	AGE	G	GS	IP	H	BB	SO	HR	ERA	EQERA	EQH9	EQBB9	EQSO9	EQHR9	PERA	VORP	STF
2000	BUF	INT	27	16	15	101.3	99	24	68	7	3.11	4.05	9.9	2.2	5.2	0.8	4.07	16.3	9
2000	CLE	AL	27	17	11	62.0	80	31	32	11	6.24	5.55	10.5	3.6	4.4	1.3	5.90	-0.4	-13
2001	CIN	NL	28	46	10	129.3	119	60	94	17	3.97	4.19	8.2	3.9	5.6	1.0	4.27	17.9	-4
2002	CIN	NL	29	22	0	39.3	38	10	24	2	3.89	3.76	9.1	2.1	4.9	0.5	3.44	7.1	-1
2002	MON	NL	29	30	0	41.0	39	22	33	5	4.83	4.77	8.8	4.3	6.3	1.1	4.82	2.8	-7
2003	MON	NL	30	34	7	63.3	65	26	47	7	4.15	4.31	9.4	3.2	6.0	1.0	4.56	9.2	-3

Breakout: 19%   Improve: 53%   Collapse: 17%

Say this about Omar Minaya. When he sees a hole, he's not afraid to go fill it, even if it means indirectly admitting he goofed the first time. Acquiring Brower for Bruce Chen was one of three such circular deals made by Minaya last season. The Cliff Floyd merry-go-round looks like a wash for now, though the way the two deals unfolded left Expos fans scratching their heads. The other two exchanges—Geoff Blum to Chris Truby to Jose Macias and Scott Strickland to Bruce Chen (and Dicky Gonzalez) to Jim Brower were net losses, though minor ones.

Not that the Expos were the first team to quickly grow tired of Bruce Chen's act. Hell, they were the fourth NL East team alone to do so. Still, getting a fungible reliever like Brower at the end of the chain didn't garner any Executive of the Year votes, especially when Brower's ERA jumped by a run in Montreal. Then again, a moderate 2003 rebound for Brower wouldn't be too far-fetched. Raise your hand if you knew Joey Eischen would pitch like Randy Myers in his prime last year.

Ron Chiavacci   Born: 05-Sep-77   Age: 25   Bats: R   Throws: R

YEAR	TM	LG	AGE	G	GS	IP	H	BB	SO	HR	ERA	EQERA	EQH9	EQBB9	EQSO9	EQHR9	PERA	VORP	STF
2000	JUP	FSL	22	28	26	158.0	145	59	131	12	3.65	5.46	10.8	4.3	5.3	1.8	5.74	0.7	2
2001	HAR	EAS	23	25	25	147.3	137	76	161	12	3.97	5.81	10.5	6.4	7.0	1.2	5.61	-5.0	8
2002	HAR	EAS	24	35	10	111.7	105	65	98	6	4.27	6.18	10.6	6.4	6.2	0.8	5.33	-9.1	-6

After leading the Eastern League in strikeouts and walks his first time through, the horizontally challenged Chiavacci saw his strikeout rate dip while his walks ticked up as he repeated the level in 2002. Reduced to just 10 starts and 25 relief appearances last year, his future may be in the pen, where he can focus on his fastball and knee-buckling curve. No truth to the rumor he ate Harrisburg's mascot last season, despite appearances.

Bartolo Colon   Born: 24-May-73   Age: 30   Bats: Throws: R

YEAR	TM	LG	AGE	G	GS	IP	H	BB	SO	HR	ERA	EQERA	EQH9	EQBB9	EQSO9	EQHR9	PERA	VORP	STF
2000	CLE	AL	27	30	30	188.0	163	98	212	21	3.88	3.39	7.0	3.7	9.6	0.8	3.48	44.2	33
2001	CLE	AL	28	34	34	222.3	220	90	201	26	4.09	3.71	7.9	3.3	7.4	0.9	4.23	44.3	19
2002	CLE	AL	29	16	16	116.3	104	31	75	11	2.55	2.63	7.3	2.2	5.6	0.8	3.22	37.2	15
2002	MON	NL	29	17	17	117.0	115	39	74	9	3.31	3.85	9.2	2.7	5.1	0.7	4.06	21.5	8
2003	CWS	AL	30	29	29	193.0	189	68	139	25	3.91	3.81	8.7	2.9	6.2	1.0	3.95	43.3	13

Breakout: 12%   Improve: 50%   Collapse: 14%

You could forgive Expos fans for getting excited over Colon's arrival last June, even if the team never got past the fringes of the playoff hunt. Adding a championship-caliber player in the middle of a pennant race was something the Expos hadn't done since Bush the Elder's administration. Giving up Brandon Phillips, Cliff Lee, and Brady Sizemore for at most a year and a half of Eau de Colon may come back to haunt the Expos one day, perhaps soon. Most fans who saw Colon pitch at the Big O last year would have made the deal 100 more times anyway. Armed with a devastating high-90s fastball, Colon blew away hitters with gusto. He'd often chuck the rest of his repertoire and throw 80% fastballs or more in a given game. Even more amazingly, he'd go from 95-mph heaters in the early innings to 98 by the ninth, getting nastier as the game went on. He'll dazzle White Sox fans in '03, now that the Expos jettisoned Colon as part of the MLB-ordered payroll purge.

Zach Day — Born: 15-Jun-78 — Age: 25 — Bats: R — Throws: R

YEAR	TM	LG	AGE	G	GS	IP	H	BB	SO	HR	ERA	EQERA	EQH9	EQBB9	EQSO9	EQHR9	PERA	VORP	STF
2000	GRB	SAL	22	13	13	85.3	72	31	101	6	1.90	4.54	10.5	4.5	6.2	1.7	5.29	9.1	10
2000	TAM	FSL	22	7	7	34.3	33	15	36	2	4.20	6.74	11.6	5.1	6.8	1.4	6.07	-4.7	7
2000	AKR	EAS	22	8	8	46.0	38	21	43	1	3.52	4.54	8.9	4.6	6.3	0.4	4.17	4.9	16
2001	AKR	EAS	23	22	22	136.7	123	45	94	8	3.09	4.96	10.4	4.1	4.4	0.9	4.83	8.3	1
2001	OTT	INT	23	6	5	26.7	38	8	15	2	7.42	7.95	14.5	3.2	4.0	0.9	7.38	-7.3	-10
2002	OTT	INT	24	17	16	90.0	77	32	68	5	3.50	4.62	9.3	4.0	6.0	0.8	4.05	8.8	9
2002	MON	NL	24	19	2	37.3	28	15	25	3	3.62	3.66	7.0	3.2	5.3	0.7	3.17	7.3	0
2003	MON	NL	25	18	12	73.7	78	35	56	9	4.87	5.05	9.6	3.6	6.0	1.0	4.87	5.9	1

Breakout: 20%   Improve: 48%   Collapse: 23%

Day mixes a heavy fastball, burrowing sinker, and slurve to generate oodles of ground balls. Paired with great strikeout rates in 2000, you could almost see shades of Kevin Brown if you squinted really hard. His K rates have fallen off sharply since then, conjuring up images of a less successful, right-handed Kirk Rueter. Scouty types still think his clean motion and solid repertoire could translate into success in the middle of a rotation, or higher. The Expos would do well to keep breaking Day in as a reliever, bumping him to high-leverage situations if he succeeds. If he can add a strikeout and shave a walk per nine innings off his record, he'd set up well as a member of the 2004 rotation.

Scott Downs — Born: 17-Mar-76 — Age: 27 — Bats: L — Throws: L

YEAR	TM	LG	AGE	G	GS	IP	H	BB	SO	HR	ERA	EQERA	EQH9	EQBB9	EQSO9	EQHR9	PERA	VORP	STF
2000	CHC	NL	24	18	18	94.0	117	37	63	13	5.17	5.35	11.4	2.9	5.4	1.1	5.67	1.6	4
2002	BRV	FSL	26	7	0	9.0	7	2	7	0	3.00	3.90	9.4	2.6	5.0	0.3	3.50	1.5	-5
2002	OTT	INT	26	17	0	23.3	31	3	15	6	5.79	9.01	15.2	1.5	5.2	3.6	7.81	-9.4	-28

The last link to the Jim Beattie "why do we need to give this guy a physical, anyway?" era, Downs had his second Tommy John surgery last year and won't be a factor until 2004, if ever. Granted, Rondell White didn't do much after his liberation from Montreal, but pitching prospects are as dicey a proposition as making kissy faces upon check-in at Rikers, and Downs had little upside to begin with. Those tired axioms about pitching being 93.7% of the game do more than annoy. They can take over decision makers' brains, prompting them to make desperately stupid choices.

Tim Drew — Born: 31-Aug-78 — Age: 24 — Bats: R — Throws: R

YEAR	TM	LG	AGE	G	GS	IP	H	BB	SO	HR	ERA	EQERA	EQH9	EQBB9	EQSO9	EQHR9	PERA	VORP	STF
2000	AKR	EAS	21	9	9	52.0	41	15	22	1	2.42	3.80	8.6	2.9	2.9	0.3	3.39	9.9	1
2000	BUF	INT	21	16	16	95.0	122	31	53	12	5.87	6.85	13.1	3.0	4.4	1.5	6.65	-14.2	0
2001	BUF	INT	22	18	18	108.0	115	27	75	13	3.92	5.49	11.2	2.7	5.0	1.5	5.39	0.2	6
2001	CLE	AL	22	8	6	35.0	51	16	15	9	7.97	7.74	11.7	3.7	3.5	2.0	7.77	-8.7	-18
2002	BUF	INT	23	15	15	96.3	96	23	43	6	3.27	4.85	10.6	2.7	3.5	0.8	4.35	7.0	0
2002	OTT	INT	23	13	13	84.7	77	24	29	5	2.87	4.44	10.0	3.2	2.7	0.8	4.17	10.0	-5
2002	MON	NL	23	7	1	16.0	12	2	10	1	2.81	3.18	7.1	1.0	5.1	0.6	2.35	4.0	8
2003	MON	NL	24	15	10	61.0	72	24	32	9	5.42	5.62	10.7	3.0	4.2	1.2	5.36	1.5	-10

Breakout: 17%   Improve: 45%   Collapse: 33%

No wonder the Indians get so much ink for their stable of left-handed pitching prospects. The righties were all dealt to the Expos. Unfortunately for the Expos, Cliff Lee's future looks a lot brighter than Tim Drew's. Owner of a solid slider and adequate fastball, Drew has to be just right to be successful. Drew's next couple of years could be limited to 11th-man status, especially with so many back-of-the-rotation candidates from Double-A on up knocking on the door.

Joey Eischen — Born: 25-May-70 — Age: 33 — Bats: L — Throws: L

YEAR	TM	LG	AGE	G	GS	IP	H	BB	SO	HR	ERA	EQERA	EQH9	EQBB9	EQSO9	EQHR9	PERA	VORP	STF
2000	OTT	INT	30	10	9	59.3	55	22	34	8	3.64	4.27	8.5	3.3	4.3	1.5	4.70	8.1	-3
2001	OTT	INT	31	34	1	52.3	42	11	54	6	2.24	3.44	8.2	2.2	7.3	1.4	3.67	11.3	5
2001	MON	NL	31	24	0	29.7	29	16	19	4	4.85	4.69	8.7	4.5	4.9	1.1	4.87	2.3	-16
2002	OTT	INT	32	11	0	14.0	8	3	15	0	0.00	2.68	6.0	2.3	8.2	0.2	1.92	4.2	19
2002	MON	NL	32	59	0	53.7	43	18	51	1	1.34	2.35	7.4	2.7	7.5	0.2	2.83	18.1	13
2003	*MON*	*NL*	*33*	*55*	*0*	*52.7*	*50*	*20*	*44*	*6*	*3.61*	*3.75*	*8.7*	*3.0*	*6.6*	*0.9*	*4.09*	*10.5*	*1*

Breakout: 18%   Improve: 49%   Collapse: 24%

Exhibit 7,296 in why you don't hand out three-year, $10 million contracts to middle relievers. Twenty-nine other teams could have grabbed Eischen in 2001. All 29 passed. So Eischen kicked around Ottawa for a while, just as he'd done in Albuquerque, Adirondack, and other exotic locales. Called up in May, he went nuts, finishing the year as the Expos' best reliever and one of the best in the league. This after Jim Beattie snatched Scott Stewart off the scrap heap before the 2001 season, finding the Expos their eventual closer for the price of some fax paper and a couple of phone calls. Not all cheap pickups blossom the way Eischen and Stewart did. But the obsession with signing the Rheal Cormiers of the world to big contracts after a low-ERA season or two instead of grabbing lesser-known arms with comparable or better peripherals borders on insanity.

Dicky Gonzalez — Born: 21-Dec-78 — Age: 24 — Bats: R — Throws: R

YEAR	TM	LG	AGE	G	GS	IP	H	BB	SO	HR	ERA	EQERA	EQH9	EQBB9	EQSO9	EQHR9	PERA	VORP	STF
2000	BIN	EAS	21	26	25	147.7	130	36	138	14	3.84	4.61	9.6	2.5	6.4	1.5	4.07	14.7	19
2001	NOR	INT	22	17	16	96.0	96	20	70	10	3.09	4.60	10.8	2.3	5.3	1.3	4.84	9.6	10
2001	NYM	NL	22	16	7	59.0	72	17	31	4	4.88	5.10	12.1	2.5	4.2	0.6	5.21	2.4	-1
2002	NOR	INT	23	1	1	5.0	6	2	7	1	3.60	5.59	12.4	4.3	10.7	2.7	7.42	-0.0	26
2002	OTT	INT	23	22	22	119.7	137	33	72	10	3.76	5.88	12.5	3.1	4.8	1.2	5.71	-5.0	1
2003	*MON*	*NL*	*24*	*17*	*12*	*72.7*	*82*	*27*	*49*	*9*	*4.93*	*5.12*	*10.2*	*2.9*	*5.4*	*1.1*	*4.96*	*5.1*	*0*

Breakout: 15%   Improve: 55%   Collapse: 24%

He's a standby option if Sun-Woo Kim and Zach Day can't fill the back end of the rotation. A soft-tosser who knows how to pitch, Gonzalez probably needs to rip off a big hot streak to impress and land something resembling a secure major league job. As bullpens head toward increased specialization, the job of effective long-relief man has gone the way of the dodo bird, replaced by mop-up artists and retreads. Gonzalez could make a good living in that role if the Expos wanted to revive it.

Bryan Hebson — Born: 12-Mar-76 — Age: 27 — Bats: R — Throws: R

YEAR	TM	LG	AGE	G	GS	IP	H	BB	SO	HR	ERA	EQERA	EQH9	EQBB9	EQSO9	EQHR9	PERA	VORP	STF
2000	HAR	EAS	24	29	29	171.3	175	66	90	23	4.57	6.60	12.5	4.1	3.8	2.3	6.01	-20.8	-14
2001	HAR	EAS	25	26	8	75.0	78	19	54	12	4.44	6.11	12.0	3.2	4.6	2.3	6.08	-5.5	-17
2002	HAR	EAS	26	38	3	94.3	60	24	75	5	1.72	2.60	7.2	2.8	5.5	0.8	2.54	29.4	2
2002	OTT	INT	26	5	0	9.3	8	3	11	0	4.84	4.78	8.9	3.5	9.0	0.2	3.51	0.6	18
2003	*MON*	*NL*	*27*	*16*	*5*	*38.7*	*42*	*17*	*28*	*6*	*4.86*	*5.04*	*9.9*	*3.3*	*5.8*	*1.3*	*5.14*	*2.9*	*-6*

Breakout: 25%   Improve: 53%   Collapse: 23%

Like Ron Chiavacci, Hebson repeated Double-A, switching to the bullpen in the process. Unlike Chiavacci, he kicked Eastern League butt doing it. Hebson hiked his strikeout totals and slashed his hit and homer rates. Pat Collins put up similarly solid numbers in his final conversion to relief at Harrisburg and could crack the big club on Hebson's heels or even shoot ahead of him given the two years he has on him. If relief pitching depth were the mark of a great farm system, the Expos could start loading up on party hats and streamers.

Matt Herges — Born: 01-Apr-70 — Age: 33 — Bats: L — Throws: R

YEAR	TM	LG	AGE	G	GS	IP	H	BB	SO	HR	ERA	EQERA	EQH9	EQBB9	EQSO9	EQHR9	PERA	VORP	STF
2000	LAD	NL	30	59	4	110.7	100	40	75	7	3.17	3.53	8.7	2.7	5.5	0.5	3.60	23.0	0
2001	LAD	NL	31	75	0	99.3	97	46	76	8	3.44	4.02	9.3	3.9	5.9	0.7	4.63	15.0	-5
2002	MON	NL	32	62	0	64.7	80	26	50	10	4.03	5.26	11.5	3.2	6.1	1.4	6.13	0.9	-10
2003	*PIT*	*NL*	*33*	*45*	*0*	*55.3*	*59*	*22*	*38*	*6*	*4.00*	*4.13*	*9.6*	*3.1*	*5.5*	*1.0*	*4.70*	*8.7*	*-7*

Breakout: 20%   Improve: 51%   Collapse: 26%

Last year, we noted Herges "takes great advantage of Dodger Stadium; if (he) ever signs anywhere else, his career could definitely explode into a froth of run scoring." So why couldn't Omar Minaya see this? Not that Herges cost much—Wilkin Ruan and Guillermo Mota won't be missed. Still, his bullpen blow-ups happened at the worst possible time, when the Expos were on the edges of the playoff hunt. This made Herges his fair share of enemies, even though a decent finish made his numbers respectable; but even then, did they (ERA 4.03, PERA 6.13)? He's Pittsburgh's problem now, after Dave Littlefield inexplicably traded a decent prospect in Chris Young to get a prime non-tender candidate.

Mike Hinckley   Born: 05-Oct-82   Age: 20   Bats: R   Throws: L

YEAR	TM	LG	AGE	G	GS	IP	H	BB	SO	HR	ERA	EQERA	EQH9	EQBB9	EQSO9	EQHR9	PERA	VORP	STF
2002	VER	NYP	19	16	16	91.7	60	30	66	4	1.37	3.25	8.7	4.7	3.9	1.4	4.03	23.0	0

"Token pitching prospect that everyone loves who's still miles from the majors" alert! Hinckley did a nice job in his first year out of high school, showing decent command in short-season Vermont. You'd like to see a gaudier strikeout rate, but organization types think it'll come as his changeup matures into a strong number two pitch for his live, low-90s fastball. The Expos' main concerns for Hinckley should be honing a repeatable delivery and steering him clear of dangerous workloads. The Florida State League's generous parks and weak hitters should mean another shiny ERA next year, so focus on Hinckley's peripherals and pitch counts to see where he's headed.

Josh Karp   Born: 21-Sep-79   Age: 23   Bats: R   Throws: R

YEAR	TM	LG	AGE	G	GS	IP	H	BB	SO	HR	ERA	EQERA	EQH9	EQBB9	EQSO9	EQHR9	PERA	VORP	STF
2002	BRV	FSL	22	7	7	45.3	31	11	43	1	1.59	2.96	8.3	2.8	6.0	0.5	3.20	12.8	22
2002	HAR	EAS	22	16	16	86.7	83	34	69	6	3.84	5.31	10.9	4.3	5.6	1.1	4.88	1.9	6
2003	MON	NL	23	13	10	61.7	67	29	48	7	4.98	5.16	9.9	3.7	6.3	1	5.12	4.1	4

Breakout: 13%   Improve: 45%   Collapse: 30%

An enigma to college scouts during his days at UCLA, the Expos say Karp has eagerly soaked up instruction since the June 2001 draft. He's steered clear of serious injury so far—last year's owie turned out to be just tendonitis. Karp's fastball and slurve are major league quality, but it's his cutting, sinking circle changeup that pays the bills. After being pushed through High-A ball, Double-A, and the Arizona Fall League last year, the Expos would do well to give Karp at least one more full season in the minors to tighten his mechanics. Starting his service time clock before he's ready with a slew of fourth- and fifth-starter types already around won't help anyone except Karp's accountant.

Sun-Woo Kim   Born: 04-Sep-77   Age: 25   Bats: R   Throws: R

YEAR	TM	LG	AGE	G	GS	IP	H	BB	SO	HR	ERA	EQERA	EQH9	EQBB9	EQSO9	EQHR9	PERA	VORP	STF
2000	PAW	INT	22	26	25	134.3	170	42	116	17	6.03	6.76	12.9	2.9	6.7	1.5	6.42	-18.8	12
2001	PAW	INT	23	19	14	89.0	93	27	79	10	5.36	5.36	10.1	3.2	6.2	1.4	5.36	1.3	7
2001	BOS	AL	23	20	2	41.7	54	21	27	1	5.83	5.07	10.9	4.2	5.4	0.2	5.43	1.6	-2
2002	OTT	INT	24	7	7	43.7	29	16	28	2	1.24	3.19	7.3	4.1	5.1	0.6	3.03	11.2	9
2002	PAW	INT	24	8	8	45.3	34	16	37	4	3.18	3.81	7.6	3.9	6.3	1.2	3.62	8.5	13
2002	BOS	AL	24	15	2	29.0	34	7	18	5	7.45	5.98	10.5	2.0	5.5	1.4	5.19	-1.8	-4
2002	MON	NL	24	4	3	20.3	18	7	11	0	0.89	1.79	8.3	2.8	4.3	0.2	3.13	8.4	9
2003	MON	NL	25	22	13	80.0	82	32	59	9	4.43	4.59	9.3	3.1	5.9	0.9	4.57	8.5	2

Breakout: 19%   Improve: 54%   Collapse: 9%

After a good season capped by three decent starts for the Expos late last year, Kim holds the inside track for a spot in the 2003 rotation, especially with Masato Yoshii gone and either Bartolo Colon or Javier Vazquez likely to leave for salary reasons. When he's on, Kim mixes a fastball, curve, slider, and change, pitching to both sides of the plate effectively. He'll sometimes drop down with two strikes to give hitters a different look, a tack that's worked well for him. The Expos hope the animosity between Kim and Tomo Ohka from their days together in Pawtucket won't be a problem. If it is, they'll be forced to step in the ring with Scott Stewart and T. J. Tucker as penance, and we know that won't end well.

Luke Lockwood — Born: 21-Jul-81 — Age: 21 — Bats: L — Throws: L

YEAR	TM	LG	AGE	G	GS	IP	H	BB	SO	HR	ERA	EQERA	EQH9	EQBB9	EQSO9	EQHR9	PERA	VORP	STF
2000	VER	NYP	18	2	2	12.0	12	1	8	1	2.25	5.20	17.3	1.1	3.8	3.8	6.21	0.4	-5
2000	CPF	SAL	18	9	9	48.0	49	20	33	3	4.50	7.19	12.8	5.3	3.7	1.5	7.02	-9.0	-13
2000	JUP	FSL	18	3	3	14.0	24	5	2	3	10.93	12.83	23.8	4.6	1.0	5.6	13.23	-11.4	-60
2001	CLN	MDW	19	26	26	163.3	152	49	114	8	2.70	5.69	11.8	4.0	4.0	1.0	5.18	-3.4	0
2002	BRV	FSL	20	26	26	147.0	155	38	86	13	3.37	6.15	14.2	3.1	4.0	2.1	6.38	-10.5	-5

With Cliff Lee traded, Rich Rundles and Eric Good coming off injuries, and Michael Hinckley just getting started, Lockwood holds the title of best lefty in the system, at least for now. Like Rundles, Lockwood deals a moving fastball in the high-80s. He's learned to pitch inside, mixing a curveball and change to keep hitters honest. Lockwood already toils on the edge with his low strikeout rates. He needs to master his two-seam, sinking fastball to induce a ton of grounders, or else the pitches he grooved in the Florida State League will go flying over Eastern League fences in 2003.

Julio Manon — Born: 10-Jun-73 — Age: 30 — Bats: L — Throws: R

YEAR	TM	LG	AGE	G	GS	IP	H	BB	SO	HR	ERA	EQERA	EQH9	EQBB9	EQSO9	EQHR9	PERA	VORP	STF
2000	HAR	EAS	27	14	4	31.3	32	8	25	7	5.18	6.73	13.2	2.7	5.8	3.9	6.31	-4.5	-22
2001	HAR	EAS	28	10	7	52.0	50	16	44	6	3.12	4.92	10.9	3.8	5.4	1.6	5.35	3.3	-3
2001	OTT	INT	28	15	14	84.0	71	34	67	11	3.11	4.24	8.8	4.3	5.7	1.6	4.71	11.8	0
2002	HAR	EAS	29	6	6	39.0	37	4	51	3	3.00	3.87	10.5	1.1	8.9	1.2	3.83	7.1	34
2002	OTT	INT	29	28	13	105.3	83	45	81	8	3.50	4.50	8.7	4.8	6.1	1.0	4.07	11.4	-1
2003	MON	NL	30	14	7	41.7	46	20	35	7	5.08	5.27	10.1	3.8	6.8	1.4	5.25	4.1	-1

Breakout: 19%   Improve: 51%   Collapse: 25%

Manon has pitched well as a starter and in relief in Double-A, Triple-A, and the winter leagues over the last two seasons. Domestic disputes and other off-field troubles have prevented him from taking the next step. Demoted to Harrisburg last year to give him time to straighten himself out and to make room for pitchers acquired in trades, Manon posted an outrageous line of 51 strikeouts to four walks in 39 innings. He may have been a 29-year-old at Double-A at the time, but the organization was happy to see him thrive in a playoff atmosphere. He could be another Brendan Donnelly if the Expos give him a clean shot at a bullpen job.

Tomokazu Ohka — Born: 18-Mar-76 — Age: 27 — Bats: R — Throws: R

YEAR	TM	LG	AGE	G	GS	IP	H	BB	SO	HR	ERA	EQERA	EQH9	EQBB9	EQSO9	EQHR9	PERA	VORP	STF
2000	PAW	INT	24	19	19	130.7	111	23	78	15	2.96	3.75	8.8	1.6	4.7	1.3	3.51	25.5	9
2000	BOS	AL	24	13	12	69.3	70	26	40	7	3.12	3.24	8.7	2.7	5.0	0.8	3.75	17.4	9
2001	PAW	INT	25	8	8	42.0	55	9	33	5	5.57	6.96	12.6	2.3	5.5	1.4	6.71	-6.8	0
2001	BOS	AL	25	12	11	52.3	69	19	37	7	6.20	5.77	11.1	3.0	5.9	1.1	5.92	-1.6	2
2001	MON	NL	25	10	10	54.7	65	10	31	8	4.77	4.63	10.7	1.5	4.4	1.2	4.96	5.3	2
2002	MON	NL	26	32	31	192.7	194	45	118	19	3.18	3.92	9.4	1.9	4.9	0.9	4.04	33.9	8
2003	MON	NL	27	27	24	149.0	164	42	91	19	4.44	4.60	10.1	2.2	4.9	1.1	4.65	16.0	4

Breakout: 7%   Improve: 38%   Collapse: 13%

Looking back, former GM Jim Beattie's trade record rates as pretty spotty. Rondell White for Scott Downs was one of several deals that saw Beattie reach for mediocre talent and obsess over pitching, all the while watching the minor league supply of hitting prospects turn to dust. Though Beattie again chose pitching by tapping Ohka and A-ball lefty Rich Rundles in his 2001 trade of closer Ugueth Urbina, it's hard to argue with the results. Ohka broke through last season, establishing himself as an aggressive, efficient pitcher who takes the ball every fifth day and goes after hitters. He'll need to keep his walks and homers down to be effective with those low strikeout totals, something he's shown he can do in the past. If Rundles never throws a major league pitch, the Expos still got a steal.

Britt Reames   Born: 19-Aug-73   Age: 29   Bats: R   Throws: R

YEAR	TM	LG	AGE	G	GS	IP	H	BB	SO	HR	ERA	EQERA	EQH9	EQBB9	EQSO9	EQHR9	PERA	VORP	STF
2000	ARK	TXS	26	8	8	39.7	46	18	39	4	6.12	6.84	12.6	4.4	6.5	1.5	6.52	-5.9	-2
2000	MEM	PCL	26	13	13	75.0	55	20	77	2	2.28	2.79	7.8	2.4	7.6	0.3	2.56	22.6	28
2000	STL	NL	26	8	7	40.7	30	23	31	4	2.87	3.55	6.9	4.1	6.1	0.8	3.38	8.8	8
2001	OTT	INT	27	8	8	54.0	47	13	38	4	3.50	4.18	8.9	2.6	5.0	0.9	3.85	8.0	7
2001	MON	NL	27	41	13	95.0	101	48	86	16	5.59	5.55	9.4	4.2	6.9	1.3	5.43	-1.0	-3
2002	OTT	INT	28	7	7	42.0	31	14	26	3	2.79	4.11	8.2	3.7	4.9	1.0	3.48	6.5	3
2002	MON	NL	28	42	6	68.0	70	38	76	8	5.03	5.32	9.4	4.4	8.7	1.1	5.23	0.8	6
2003	MON	NL	29	26	11	72.7	72	35	66	8	4.31	4.47	9.0	3.7	7.2	1.0	4.50	10.0	6

Breakout: 19%   Improve: 52%   Collapse: 18%

How many trades in the last 10 years have busted so badly for both teams, given the expectations involved? Fernando Tatis went from a middle-of-the-lineup masher at a premium position entering his prime to an injury-prone malcontent and a giant salary albatross. Dustin Hermanson went from snarling staff workhorse to a lame chuck-and-ducker. Reames has sunk from stretch run and playoff hero to a batting practice pitcher with great stuff and no ability to command it. Granted, Tatis suffered through injuries and a bad clubhouse rap, Hermanson had shown signs of decline and Reames had struggled through arm problems and periodic ineffectiveness in the minors before the deal was made. But the notion of a lefty setup man being the prize of the deal should rankle both teams. And Steve Kline was one of the few Expos of recent years to actually get comfortable in Montreal, marrying a French Canadian and buying a home in the city's East End.

Ottawa pitching coach Randy St. Claire helped straighten out Reames's mechanics, leading to a second straight year of Triple-A success and a call-up to Montreal. Reames struck out over a batter an inning with the big club but walked too many hitters and again struggled with command, giving up copious homers and other smashes. The Expos can only hope Reames is a late bloomer. It's hard to give up on one of the prettiest curveballs in the game.

Rich Rundles   Born: 03-Jun-81   Age: 22   Bats: L   Throws: L

YEAR	TM	LG	AGE	G	GS	IP	H	BB	SO	HR	ERA	EQERA	EQH9	EQBB9	EQSO9	EQHR9	PERA	VORP	STF
2001	AUG	SAL	20	19	19	115.0	109	10	94	5	2.43	5.17	12.1	1.2	4.2	1.0	5.15	4.3	8
2001	CLN	MDW	20	4	4	27.0	26	3	20	0	2.33	4.53	11.4	1.4	4.1	0.3	4.13	2.9	11
2002	BRV	FSL	21	12	11	57.3	66	16	31	5	4.08	7.28	15.5	3.4	3.7	2.1	7.18	-11.3	-12

Scouts and pitching instructors like to highlight the difference between control and command. Rundles shows exceptional control, putting the ball over the plate with amazing consistency for a pitcher so young. He hasn't yet mastered spotting the ball properly within the strike zone though, showing a lack of command. A tall, lean lefty, Rundles fools hitters with his changeup, just as they're expecting an explosive fastball that never comes. Topping out at 88 mph, he lives on the outside corner against right-handed hitters.

Though the minor league system has sprung holes everywhere, coaches have done a good job of adhering to pitch counts and yanking pitchers before the innings totals pile too high. That wasn't quite what the Expos had in mind when they had to shut Rundles down with a sore elbow after just 11 starts. They're hoping an off-season of rehab will do the trick. Rundles won't want to hear the words "Tommy John" unless he gets promoted to Triple-A to work with the real McCoy.

Dan Smith   Born: 15-Sep-75   Age: 27   Bats: R   Throws: R

YEAR	TM	LG	AGE	G	GS	IP	H	BB	SO	HR	ERA	EQERA	EQH9	EQBB9	EQSO9	EQHR9	PERA	VORP	STF
2000	PAW	INT	24	24	21	124.7	134	41	70	15	4.84	5.51	11.0	3.0	4.4	1.4	5.32	-0.1	-3
2001	BUF	INT	25	21	16	106.0	110	44	68	17	4.50	6.11	11.2	4.5	4.7	2.0	6.18	-7.3	-13
2002	OTT	INT	26	14	14	83.3	71	18	61	10	3.24	4.30	9.5	2.4	5.8	1.7	4.07	11.2	7
2002	MON	NL	26	33	0	46.7	34	21	34	6	3.47	3.48	6.7	3.6	5.8	1.2	3.51	9.9	-5
2003	MON	NL	27	19	10	64.0	69	27	44	10	4.91	5.09	9.8	3.3	5.5	1.3	5.14	4.3	-5

Breakout: 22%   Improve: 44%   Collapse: 24%

As much as we tout the value of educated guesses on minor league free agents vs. multimillionaire setup men, the Expos' luck with their bullpen reached absurd levels last year. Smith and fellow one-time rejects Scott Stewart and Joey Eischen carried the bullpen, pummeling the combination of high draft choice T. J. Tucker and veteran trade acquisitions Matt Herges and Jim Brower. Given Smith's spotty track record, the Expos would gladly settle for a mild step back in 2003.

Seung Song Born: 29-Jun-80 Age: 23 Bats: R Throws: R

YEAR	TM	LG	AGE	G	GS	IP	H	BB	SO	HR	ERA	EQERA	EQH9	EQBB9	EQSO9	EQHR9	PERA	VORP	STF
2000	LOW	NYP	20	13	13	72.7	63	20	93	1	2.60	5.15	11.4	3.4	6.5	0.6	5.26	2.9	19
2001	AUG	SAL	21	14	14	75.0	56	18	79	3	2.04	4.28	9.6	3.3	5.4	0.9	4.30	10.2	11
2001	SAR	FSL	21	8	8	48.3	28	18	56	1	1.68	2.54	5.9	3.9	6.8	0.5	2.95	15.9	27
2002	HAR	EAS	22	1	1	5.0	5	0	5	0	0.00	3.92	11.4	0.8	7.2	0.3	3.20	0.9	31
2002	TRN	EAS	22	21	21	108.7	106	37	116	11	4.39	5.11	10.1	3.6	7.3	1.6	5.35	4.8	16
2003	MON	NL	23	14	9	59	62	27	50	8	4.99	5.18	9.6	3.5	6.7	1.1	4.88	3.6	6

Breakout: 15%   Improve: 31%   Collapse: 28%

Acquired with Sun-Woo Kim in the second Cliff Floyd deal, Song could be a solid big league starter down the road if he can dodge the arm problems that have bothered him on and off through parts of his career. He struck out more than a batter an inning in Double-A Trenton while bothered by elbow pain through much of the year. The Expos then shut him down with a sore shoulder after five innings in Harrisburg. When healthy, Song brings a darting fastball and hard curve to the mound, along with an improving changeup. If you're tired of caveats, think about this: We could write "there's no such thing as a pitching prospect" for every arm under 25, leave it at that, and be right the vast majority of the time.

Scott Stewart Born: 14-Aug-75 Age: 27 Bats: R Throws: L

YEAR	TM	LG	AGE	G	GS	IP	H	BB	SO	HR	ERA	EQERA	EQH9	EQBB9	EQSO9	EQHR9	PERA	VORP	STF
2000	NOR	INT	24	53	1	72.0	80	18	57	3	3.50	4.62	11.4	2.3	6.1	0.5	4.67	6.1	3
2001	MON	NL	25	62	0	47.7	43	13	39	5	3.77	3.41	8.1	2.3	6.3	0.8	3.49	10.4	2
2002	MON	NL	26	67	0	64.0	49	22	67	4	3.09	3.44	7.0	2.7	8.2	0.6	2.96	13.8	14
2003	MON	NL	27	62	0	64.3	64	24	56	6	4.03	4.18	9.0	2.8	7.0	0.8	4.16	10.2	4

Breakout: 10%   Improve: 32%   Collapse: 30%

Manna from scrap heap heaven. As deft a trade as Urbina for Ohka and Rundles was in 2001, it looked even better when Stewart filled Urbina's void with a lights-out performance as head of the 2002 bullpen committee. Stewart keeps the ball in the park, rarely walks anyone, and can punch a guy out when he needs to. He's young, cheap, durable, and reliable. If the Orioles can pay Buddy Groom more than $3 million a year to pitch through age 39, Stewart's worth what, $68 kajillion? A lot of whatever imaginary note Syd Thrift's face is on anyway.

T. J. Tucker Born: 20-Aug-78 Age: 24 Bats: R Throws: R

YEAR	TM	LG	AGE	G	GS	IP	H	BB	SO	HR	ERA	EQERA	EQH9	EQBB9	EQSO9	EQHR9	PERA	VORP	STF
2000	HAR	EAS	21	8	8	45.0	33	17	24	7	3.60	4.78	9.5	4.0	3.8	2.7	4.33	3.6	-6
2001	HAR	EAS	22	13	13	82.0	77	37	57	10	3.73	5.61	10.9	5.7	4.5	1.8	5.84	-1.0	-5
2001	OTT	INT	22	14	14	84.0	68	33	63	11	3.11	4.76	8.5	4.2	5.4	1.6	4.47	7.0	6
2002	MON	NL	23	57	0	61.3	69	31	42	5	4.11	4.95	10.4	4.0	5.4	0.7	5.33	2.9	-7
2003	MON	NL	24	48	0	50.7	55	26	37	7	5.28	5.48	9.9	4.0	5.9	1.2	5.36	1.7	-12

Breakout: 21%   Improve: 53%   Collapse: 18%

Along with Scott Stewart, Tucker formed a Burly Boys combination that whupped NL hitters through the season's first couple of months. Frank Robinson's ride-the-hot-hand bullpen plan took its toll as the season wore on though, hurting Tucker more than any other pitcher. Regular shellings turned into whispers of a dead arm and eventually a trip to the DL with a strained back. The skills are there, but Tucker needs both a deft bullpen handler and a trip to Jenny Craig to stay successful over long stretches. The Expos do have a deep stable of bullpen candidates if he falters again.

Claudio Vargas Born: 19-May-79 Age: 24 Bats: R Throws: R

YEAR	TM	LG	AGE	G	GS	IP	H	BB	SO	HR	ERA	EQERA	EQH9	EQBB9	EQSO9	EQHR9	PERA	VORP	STF
2000	BRV	FSL	21	24	23	145.3	126	44	143	10	3.28	5.10	10.7	3.5	6.4	1.6	4.95	6.5	15
2000	PME	EAS	21	3	2	15.0	16	6	13	1	3.60	5.98	11.5	4.0	5.9	1.1	5.73	-0.8	8
2001	PME	EAS	22	27	27	159.0	122	67	151	25	4.19	5.79	9.8	5.4	6.2	2.3	4.92	-5.0	4
2002	HAR	EAS	23	8	8	33.0	38	9	34	2	4.64	5.74	12.8	3.0	7.2	0.9	5.55	-0.9	13
2002	CLG	PCL	23	17	16	76.3	88	35	61	18	6.72	7.01	11.5	4.8	5.6	2.6	6.56	-12.8	-9

Vargas is the anti-Jamie Moyer. Hitting 85 on the radar gun's a coup for Moyer, yet his late release point makes his fastball sneak up on hitters, jamming them into weak grounders. Vargas can hit 96 on a gun, but his early release point makes his fastball look considerably slower, leading to tateriffic results. He's mostly a one-pitch pitcher for now, which may kill his shot at a big league starter's job. The Expos are working on refining his delivery and teaching Vargas a slider in the hopes of grooming an effective starter or future closer.

Javier Vazquez								**Born: 25-Jul-76**			**Age: 26**		**Bats: R**		**Throws: R**			
YEAR	TM	LG	AGE	G	GS	IP	H	BB	SO	HR	ERA	EQERA	EQH9	EQBB9	EQSO9	EQHR9	PERA	VORP	STF
2000	MON	NL	23	33	33	217.7	247	61	196	24	4.05	3.87	9.8	2.0	7.1	0.9	4.51	39.5	25
2001	MON	NL	24	32	32	223.7	197	44	208	24	3.42	3.24	7.9	1.6	7.1	0.9	3.20	56.3	27
2002	MON	NL	25	34	34	230.3	243	49	179	28	3.91	4.31	9.9	1.7	6.2	1.1	4.37	30.6	16
2003	MON	NL	26	30	30	203.3	200	48	159	23	3.65	3.78	9.0	1.8	6.3	1.0	3.72	40.6	17

Breakout: 15%   Improve: 54%   Collapse: 12%

Time for a chart:

2002	IP	K/9	BB/9	HR/9	ERA
Vazquez	230.3	7.0	1.9	1.1	3.91
Colon	233.3	5.7	2.7	0.8	2.93

The difference in home run and walk rates comes close to evening out, all other things being equal. So what made Colon the staff ace and Vazquez the staff disappointment? Vazquez yielded a batting average of .302 on balls in play that weren't hit for home runs, Colon .281. Think that's a consistently repeatable skill? Go back one year and you'll have your answer. Vazquez posted better peripheral numbers than Colon across the board in 2001, allowing fewer homers and walks per nine innings while striking out a few more batters. But the two pitchers' balls in play stats were reversed. Result? Vazquez's 3.42 ERA beats Colon's 4.09 by a comfortable margin—factor in park and league effects and Vazquez still beats Colon.

Evaluating pitchers based on three true outcomes, home runs allowed, walks allowed, and strikeouts, is your best bet for making accurate future predictions of pitchers' performance, whether you're running a $100 million big league payroll or a two-bit roto team. By those measures, Vazquez has bested Colon in each of the last three seasons. Some argued Vazquez wasn't fully healthy last year; Expo Nation's still holding its breath hoping his high inning totals at a young age don't come back to haunt him. If he's healthy, and Omar Minaya trades Colon and keeps Vazquez this off-season, the fans won't be disappointed.

Masato Yoshii								**Born: 20-Apr-65**			**Age: 38**		**Bats: R**		**Throws: R**			
YEAR	TM	LG	AGE	G	GS	IP	H	BB	SO	HR	ERA	EQERA	EQH9	EQBB9	EQSO9	EQHR9	PERA	VORP	STF
2000	COL	NL	35	29	29	167.3	201	53	88	32	5.86	5.09	10.4	2.3	4.2	1.4	4.93	7.7	-3
2001	MON	NL	36	42	11	113.0	127	26	63	18	4.78	4.69	10.1	1.9	4.3	1.3	4.87	9.5	-9
2002	MON	NL	37	31	20	131.3	143	32	74	15	4.11	4.50	10.2	2.0	4.5	1.1	4.60	14.4	-1
2003	MON	NL	38	26	15	92.3	105	25	50	11	4.52	4.69	10.4	2.1	4.4	1.0	4.72	9.0	-5

Breakout: 18%   Improve: 45%   Collapse: 14%

Yoshii was your typical functional fifth starter last season, throwing five innings a start, giving up two or three runs, six hits and a walk while striking out two or three batters. On good days, same line, six innings. Yoshii made only $300,000 last year, making him a handy player for the Montreal Wal-Marts. He had surgery at the end of the year to repair a torn labrum and minor rotator cuff fraying in his non-pitching shoulder. His arbitration-eligible status, more than his injury, prompted the Expos to release him, and rather than get shorted on his next offer as he was in 2001, Yoshii elected to go back to Japan.

New York Mets

To a lot of historians looking back, the Byzantine emperor Justinian was nuts. Made of spare time, as is generally imperial fashion, he thought it would be neat to reform the Roman Empire, having grown disgruntled by the notion that previous generations had lost it. He didn't have much to achieve this goal beyond coin, but he really, really wanted it. So he summoned up the eunuch Belisarius, told him to go out and buy an army, and then go reconquer the Roman Empire. And armed with cash, a mission, and gumption, Belisarius very nearly did it. In the long run, Justinian ran out of cash, and the means to win simply could not be bought without an unachievable investment in organizational improvement. Plus, relying on all sorts of free talent, the barbarians had significantly better depth; they were bound to win in the long run, as they did, but not before things were made very interesting for a few decades.

So thinking on that, you can sort of appreciate Steve Phillips's position over the last few years. Courtesy of the shared desire of Lords Doubleday and Wilpon, Phillips has had the money to spend, and ambitious goals to strive for, but he hasn't had a whole lot of infrastructure to rely upon. He's been told to win, and given only one really useful tool—cash—to achieve that victory. And like mosquito hunting with hammers, where you will kill what you catch but can't always count on getting something useful out of the exercise, Phillips has spent, boldly and bravely, pursuing the quest his masters have set for him.

Certainly, since taking over in mid-1997 with the ouster of Joe McIlvaine, going into 2002 Phillips had achieved quite a bit. Inheriting an organization that had squandered its best pitching assets in Dallas Green's reign of madness and ruin, saddled with an old lineup, and with very little young talent on hand, Phillips has had to play an extended shell game to preserve himself while fielding a competitive team. Check out table 1 to see what he finished each season with, to get a sense of the turnover.

Life isn't easy when you're in the Braves' division, but armed with cash and really only inheriting one young star in Edgardo Alfonzo, Phillips stayed in motion, constantly introducing mutations to a semi-competitive roster, and reshaping the team to try and achieve the relevance that escaped the Mets for most of the 90s. As plans go, only two things were certain: Alfonzo would play somewhere, and Rey Ordonez would play short. Look at the list, though, and you can see that he secured certain working parts, which allowed him to address other problems. He added Al Leiter and Mike Piazza for dimes on the dollar. He grabbed Rick Reed cheaply off of the scrap heap, and Reed was one of the rotation's few constants.

And with the happy accident in 2000, when the Mets didn't have to see the Braves and instead drew a NLCS match-up against a Cardinals team woefully unprepared to face quality left-handed pitching, his well-aged confections made the World Series once, tying him with well-regarded peers like Kevin Towers and Brian Sabean. He did it with a controversial manager he inherited and didn't really work well with, and without much he could count on from his farm system beyond bargaining chips.

Longtime *BP* readers will recognize we conducted a similar exercise with the Indians a couple of years ago, to illustrate a very similar problem. Having fallen short time and again, Phillips kept going to the well, and wound up trading downward and/or taking worse risks in a scramble to secure the slender bragging rights he'd already earned. After a tremendously disappointing 2001 season, going into 2002 Phillips decided he couldn't tear down and rebuild, and instead stocked the Mets lineup and rotation with high-risk, dubious-yield veterans.

Mets Prospectus

2002 record: 75–86; Fifth place; NL East

Pythagenport Record: 79–82

Runs scored per game: 4.3 (13th in NL)

Runs allowed per game: 4.4 (7th in NL)

Team EqA: .258 (11th in NL)

2002 Batters Age: 31.2 (3rd oldest in NL)

2002 Pitchers Age: 30.9 (5th oldest in NL)

Ballpark: Shea Stadium; Severe pitchers' park; Park Factor .935

2002: Heavy investments in weak starting pitchers, punchless sluggers and a past-prime Alomar sank the team.

2003: Concerned that people have already forgotten last season, they plan on doing a historical re-enactment of 2002, but at least Reyes and Heilman will arrive.

Table 1. The Phillips Era Cores, September 1997–2002

Position	1997	1998	1999	2000	2001	2002
C	Hundley	Piazza	Piazza	Piazza	Piazza	Piazza
1B	Olerud	Olerud	Olerud	Zeile	Zeile	Vaughn
2B	Baerga	Baerga	Alfonzo	Alfonzo	Alfonzo	Alomar
3B	Alfonzo	Alfonzo	Ventura	Ventura	Ventura	Alfonzo
SS	Ordonez	Ordonez	Ordonez	Ordonez	Ordonez	Ordonez
LF	Gilkey	Phillips	Henderson	Agbayani	Agbayani	Cedeno
CF	McRae	McRae	Hamilton	Payton	Payton	Perez
RF	Everett	Huskey	Cedeno	D, Bell	Lawton	Burnitz
#1 Starter	B. J. Jones	Leiter	Leiter	Leiter	Leiter	Leiter
#2 Starter	Reed	Reed	Reed	Reed	Appier	Astacio
#3 Starter	Mlicki	B. J. Jones	Hershiser	Hampton	Trachsel	Trachsel
#4 Starter	Reynoso	Nomo	Rogers	Rusch	Rusch	Thomson
Finish	88–74/3rd	88–74/2nd	97–66/2nd	94–68/2nd	82–80/3rd	75–86/5th

In the rotation, he added Pedro Astacio, Shawn Estes, and Jeff D'Amico. None of them arrived without large, easily readable warning labels. It didn't take much to haul Estes in, but he hasn't been particularly special since 1997. Signing Astacio as a free agent was a worthwhile risk since it was an incentive-laden deal, but it had to be, considering everyone knew Astacio would be pitching with a partially torn labrum in his throwing shoulder. Depending on your point of view, D'Amico's fame has either been mostly achieved or left on the surgeon's table.

The offensive additions weren't very inspiring either. Jeromy Burnitz was old and doubtful to age well, while D'Amico's fame has mostly been achieved in surgery manuals. Mo Vaughn might have patched one hole in the lineup, but it cost the Mets Kevin Appier, a stronger starter than most of Phillips's rotation patches, and Vaughn was coming off of a season wiped out by injury, and with persistent questions about his health, girth, and joie de vivre. Since his brilliant 1999, free agent Roger Cedeno had exasperated the Astros and Tigers.

The final deal to fill out the lineup was the high-stakes pickup of Roberto Alomar. Like the Vaughn or Burnitz deals, Phillips had to pay to acquire, and he was getting Alomar when his value was at its highest. Unfortunately, it also came with the expectation that they'd be acquiring the 2000 or 2001 edition of one of the game's greatest second basemen. Instead, as you can normally expect from players in their mid-30s, they got somebody who was getting old.

By way of explanation, Phillips claimed he was changing team chemistry for the better, adding aggressive players while deleting veterans he identified as too laid back, singling out Robin Ventura and Todd Zeile. The quietly effective regulars, guys like Ventura and Olerud and Benny Agbayani (and even the noisily effective semi-regulars like Rickey Henderson or Tony Phillips) had been phased out and replaced by guys like Tsuyoshi Shinjo, and the Mets' offense went from a unit that relied on walks and power to one that could rely on very little beyond wishful thinking.

The Mets spent the first four months of 2002 basically puttering around .500, hoping things would get better. Still hoping to shoot for the wild card and at least build on the 2001 setback, Phillips added John Thomson from the Rockies to help shore up a rotation that had not been improved by the winter's acquisitions. D'Amico had predictably struggled, while Estes had only added an equally predictable adequacy. Nevertheless, with a 10–0 win on the last day of July, the Mets were 55–51 and 4.5 games behind the Dodgers for the wild card. Although the Giants were also between them and the goal, the Mets weren't irrelevant, not yet.

Unfortunately, puttering around .500 was as good as this team would get. On August 1, the Mets' most effective starter to that point, Astacio, lost a pitcher's duel with Houston's Roy Oswalt. Opening a four-game set against the Snakes before hitting the road, the Mets lost all four. No problem, they were off to Milwaukee, they'd get back to .500. They won the opening game against the Cardinals to get back to 58–57, a bad spot, but not impossible. Then they lost 12 consecutive games, not particularly close games, and long before Labor Day, they were as dead as Julius Caesar.

To his credit, in the panic surrounding the collapse, Phillips essentially took his medicine. Despite the potential temptations of near-contention at the end of July, he didn't deal any of his top prospects, notably holding onto Aaron Heilman. Indeed, given the relative modesty of his maneuvering at the end of July, you could infer that Phillips felt he'd already done his best, and that this team would be allowed to sink on its own lack of merit.

Which brings us to the present, and trying to sort out if the last two seasons have been the Mets' "wilderness years," or if they've got further down to go. Complicating the situation is the parallel decline of the Braves from juggernaut to mere contender. Ever the opportunist, Phillips has to balance the opportunities of the present with the responsibilities to the future. Because while doing what he could to keep the Mets in contention over the last six years, Phillips has quietly started to build something more lasting. Where once the Mets were the most moribund system in baseball, the farm is finally starting to yield something more than filler to use in barter for the next stretch-drive pickup.

For starters, the system is packed with pitching, which is what you need, since the fates hang over young pitchers like seagulls in those horrific nature films about how newly hatched sea turtles die in the thousands while only a few live to reach the open sea. At Norfolk in particular, you'll have a crowded rotation picture in 2003, with Heilman, Mike Bacsik, Jae Seo, Pat Strange, Jason Middlebrook, Tyler Walker, and Phil Seibel all in the picture. Barring any surprises, Heilman will be in the rotation by August, while any of the others could win the fifth slot in the rotation in camp and do a decent job if the Mets don't haul in another graybeard. Behind them, you've got a bunch of live arms, and while few will survive, some will, and others will be useful bargaining chits. And below them all, the Mets can invest some measure of hope that lefty flamethrower Scott Kazmir, nabbed in the 2002 draft, will be among the survivors.

The organization is also starting to develop some promising position players. Jose Reyes has undoubtedly already come to your attention; he has a legitimate shot at being one of the game's best shortstops, and even if he falls well short of that, he could be the best in organization history easily enough. While the Mets will let Rey Sanchez hold the big league job at short in 2003, Reyes should be able to force his way into the picture before the end of the season. Beyond Reyes, the Mets have an outstanding tandem almost ready for Double-A: third baseman David Wright and catcher Justin Huber. If both survive the jump to Double-A, they'll start entering the big league picture before the end of 2004. Beyond them, the Mets have also developed a gaggle of outfielders who, if not star-caliber, will all at least have value as fourth outfielders or in trade.

Overall, the player development plan seems to be a more effective variation on what has served the Cardinals so well in the past: focus on cranking out a couple of stars, and settle for stocking the rest of the system with organizational soldiers. Reyes, Huber, Wright, Kazmir, and Heilman all have star potential. The relative absence of greatness in the rest of the system is less of a handicap than some prospect mavens make it out to be.

The dilemma is that while the Mets have already fallen into the 75- to 85-win range, the threshold for what it takes to contend in the NL East is coming down to 85 wins. Acknowledging that, Phillips hasn't given up on contending while nursing the player development program. Signing up Tom Glavine, Cliff Floyd, and even Sanchez are all significant upgrades on the players they're replacing. Unfortunately, they'll have to play alongside the mistakes of the recent past, and hope that Alomar, Burnitz, and Cedeno improve while Vaughn and Piazza age gracefully. They still need to find a third baseman, which is fine as long as they avoid giving up any of the system's real talent to get a two-year fill-in pending Wright's potential arrival.

Call it a weeding-out (or outing weed), but the Mets will be shaking up the roster. Phillips finally got to discard the mercurial Valentine, and replace him with the more amiable, patient Art Howe, in the traditional exchange of bad cop to good cop. Elsewhere, they can choose to rehabilitate the image of some (coming soon to a *People* cover near you: "Grant Roberts: He's Off of Drugs, and High on Life!"), but some overdue culling has already been done. Ordonez has finally been excused, a year early. If either Burnitz or Cedeno fail in the early going of 2003, Phillips won't have the same flexibility with his payroll to do things as creative as paying Ordonez to be a Devil Ray forever. However, even if he has to eat salary, Phillips has assembled a possibly passable platoon to man center as a contingency in case Cedeno can't handle the position, bringing Shinjo back as the right-handed half of a platoon with Timo Perez.

Now that Wilpon has bought out Doubleday, the Mets' situation tracks the Indians' in another way, with an owner bearing considerable debt and harboring high expectations. Fortunately for Phillips and perhaps also the Mets, the division's getting weaker, and the core talent and especially the top prospects he has to sift through are generally better than what many teams have to play with. Unless the Phillies go crazy right now, the Mets should be on the fringes of contention. The real danger, either of having to strip down or trying to contend and rebuild simultaneously, won't happen for at least another year, but that's where the real problem lies, beyond 2003. The Mets' aging major league core could very easily be used up by the time the team's homegrown talent is ready to move into place. Assuming Phillips survives that long, he might not have the money to buy the right supporting cast for his first generation of homegrown stars. If Phillips can change gears and run that sort of team, and survive his owner's inevitable displeasure, it'll be the start of a stronger Mets organization, one built on more than need and expense, but instead on organic strength.

HITTERS

Edgardo Alfonzo　　3B　Born: 08-Nov-73　Age: 29　Bats: R　Throws: R

YEAR	TM	LG	AGE	AB	H	2B	3B	HR	BB	SO	SB	CS	AVG	OBP	SLG	MLVR	EQBA	EQOBP	EQSLG	EQMLVR	VORP		DEFENSE
2000	NYM	NL	26	544	176	40	2	25	95	70	3	2	.324	.429	.542	.353	.330	.426	.552	.360	91.2		138-2B -2
2001	NYM	NL	27	457	111	22	0	17	51	62	5	0	.243	.326	.403	-.069	.253	.332	.421	-.055	21.1		115-2B -5
2002	NYM	NL	28	490	151	26	0	16	62	55	6	0	.308	.394	.459	.235	.323	.401	.487	.222	55.5		129-3B 13
2003	SFG	NL	29	449	124	25	2	13	59	60	5	1	.276	.364	.427	.048	.289	.372	.470	.110	30.6		

Breakout: 10%　　Improve: 48%　　Collapse: 16%

For years, Alfonzo had to be the Mets' other great hitter, giving Mike Piazza a worthwhile complement in a lineup that essentially tended to depend too heavily on the two of them. While that projection looks initially nasty, keep in mind, he's moving to Pac Bell, and everything looks smaller in the shadow of his 2000 peak season. It is sort of a shame that he's going from one tough hitting environment to another, however. After the past couple of years, he's taken to conditioning to keep his back problems under control. However, if he's moving back to second (to get Pedro Feliz into the lineup, laughably), that won't help Alfonzo stay healthy over a full season.

Roberto Alomar　　2B　Born: 05-Feb-68　Age: 35　Bats: B　Throws: R

YEAR	TM	LG	AGE	AB	H	2B	3B	HR	BB	SO	SB	CS	AVG	OBP	SLG	MLVR	EQBA	EQOBP	EQSLG	EQMLVR	VORP	DEFENSE
2000	CLE	AL	32	610	189	40	2	19	64	82	39	4	.310	.381	.475	.124	.314	.380	.484	.173	57.8	148-2B 3
2001	CLE	AL	33	575	193	34	12	20	80	71	30	6	.336	.420	.541	.354	.355	.439	.575	.442	100.9	146-2B -3
2002	NYM	NL	34	590	157	24	4	11	57	83	16	4	.266	.332	.376	-.012	.281	.342	.402	-.041	27.5	137-2B -13
2003	NYM	NL	35	478	132	24	3	10	53	64	16	3	.277	.351	.401	-.007	.287	.357	.429	.028	25.2	

Breakout: 5%　　Improve: 30%　　Collapse: 21%

Alomar started cold, but everyone clucked and said he was just adjusting to the league. Then he stayed cold: Before the All-Star break, he hit .268/.332/.381, then .263/.331/.371 after. More troubling still, he started to get overpowered at the plate, something we haven't really seen since the late 80s, if even then. Everybody gets old, even the great ones. If there's a silver lining, at least he didn't hit well enough to win the Gold Glove, not that this gives you any hope for the electorate. He's in the walk year of his contract, but he's at his lowest point since 1998. Don't invest.

Chris Basak　　SS　Born: 06-Dec-78　Age: 24　Bats: R　Throws: R

YEAR	TM	LG	AGE	AB	H	2B	3B	HR	BB	SO	SB	CS	AVG	OBP	SLG	MLVR	EQBA	EQOBP	EQSLG	EQMLVR	VORP	DEFENSE		
2000	PTS	NYP	21	249	87	18	4	0	26	36	32	12	.349	.417	.454	.362	.269	.312	.358	-.169	3.4	57-SS 0		
2001	SLU	FSL	22	472	110	19	4	4	47	125	30	9	.233	.309	.316	-.097	.202	.256	.278	-.432	-27.3	118-SS 3		
2002	BIN	EAS	23	377	96	18	3	4	38	94	19	14	.255	.326	.350	-.089	.211	.272	.292	-.376	-15.7	70-SS 4	15-2B	4
2002	NOR	INT	23	60	13	1	1	0	3	14	5	0	.217	.254	.267	-.325	.200	.250	.250	-.484	-4.2	13-2B -4		
2003	NYM	NL	24	143	33	7	1	2	12	35	5	4	.232	.295	.335	-.219	.241	.300	.358	-.199	-1.7			

Breakout: 56%　　Improve: 74%　　Collapse: 18%

An organizational zit, Basak is about to be pinched between Rey Sanchez's one-year rental from above, and Jose Reyes pushing up from below. Acknowledging the inevitable, the Mets had him play some second and third last summer, cinching his future as a utility infielder. The first choice would be to go without one, instead keeping hitters like McEwing or Scutaro or Russ Johnson around as infield reserves.

Craig Brazell　　1B　Born: 10-May-80　Age: 23　Bats: L　Throws: R

YEAR	TM	LG	AGE	AB	H	2B	3B	HR	BB	SO	SB	CS	AVG	OBP	SLG	MLVR	EQBA	EQOBP	EQSLG	EQMLVR	VORP	DEFENSE
2000	CMB	SAL	20	406	98	28	0	8	15	82	3	3	.241	.284	.369	-.065	.188	.214	.293	-.504	-41.9	77-1B -15
2001	CMB	SAL	21	331	102	25	5	19	15	74	0	3	.308	.348	.586	.386	.238	.268	.446	-.149	-4.7	56-1B -7
2002	SLU	FSL	22	402	107	25	3	16	13	78	2	1	.266	.299	.463	.104	.223	.243	.390	-.288	-18.7	100-1B -1
2002	BIN	EAS	22	130	40	8	0	6	1	28	0	2	.308	.343	.508	.191	.256	.279	.426	-.143	-1.5	28-1B -7
2003	NYM	NL	23	207	49	10	1	7	10	48	1	2	.238	.281	.394	-.161	.247	.286	.421	-.136	-5.2	

Breakout: 47%　　Improve: 75%　　Collapse: 13%

The Mets keep comparing Brazell to Rico Brogna, as if this was somehow a good thing or that you'd somehow want the new Rico Brogna at first base. However, Brazell did have a very good AFL in 2002, pounding seven home runs and drawing almost as many walks (9) as he did during the entire regular season (14). In most organizations, he'd be just another minor league slugger, but the Mets are shallow, and he did belt 22 home runs at age 22. He'll need to thrive and not just survive at Double-A this year if he's going to have a career.

Jeromy Burnitz RF Born: 15-Apr-69 Age: 34 Bats: L Throws: R

YEAR	TM	LG	AGE	AB	H	2B	3B	HR	BB	SO	SB	CS	AVG	OBP	SLG	MLVR	EQBA	EQOBP	EQSLG	EQMLVR	VORP	DEFENSE	
2000	MIL	NL	31	564	131	29	2	31	99	121	6	4	.232	.360	.456	.006	.232	.350	.452	.004	12.9	149-RF	1
2001	MIL	NL	32	562	141	32	4	34	80	150	0	4	.251	.349	.504	.101	.256	.351	.511	.105	29.9	148-RF	2
2002	NYM	NL	33	479	103	15	0	19	58	135	10	7	.215	.313	.365	-.094	.235	.324	.402	-.109	-4.3	121-RF	-1
2003	NYM	NL	34	329	75	15	1	13	48	84	6	3	.228	.331	.400	-.075	.236	.336	.428	-.047	-2.7		

Breakout: 24%   Improve: 65%   Collapse: 18%

Say what you want about Dean Taylor, but he didn't trade Burnitz a moment too soon. With the best of intentions, Burnitz tried, hustled, struggled, and died through all six months of the season, like a fly on the windscreen stuck in a feedback loop. He can reach that projection, but let's face it, in today's game, he's an old man with problems making contact in a tough place to hit. Adding Floyd should move him out of the heart of the order, and he can almost be a marginal asset hitting seventh or lower in a lineup.

Roger Cedeno OF Born: 16-Aug-74 Age: 28 Bats: B Throws: R

YEAR	TM	LG	AGE	AB	H	2B	3B	HR	BB	SO	SB	CS	AVG	OBP	SLG	MLVR	EQBA	EQOBP	EQSLG	EQMLVR	VORP	DEFENSE	
2000	HOU	NL	25	259	73	2	5	6	43	47	25	11	.282	.384	.398	.001	.273	.368	.385	-.022	4.8	60-OF	-2
2001	DET	AL	26	523	153	14	11	6	36	83	55	15	.293	.340	.396	-.001	.312	.361	.426	.054	31.7	106-CF	-10
2002	NYM	NL	27	511	133	19	2	7	42	92	25	4	.260	.319	.346	-.079	.277	.331	.371	-.109	-2.7	113-LF	-4
2003	NYM	NL	28	427	112	17	5	5	42	72	24	6	.262	.330	.360	-.107	.272	.336	.385	-.079	-2.0		

Breakout: 11%   Improve: 43%   Collapse: 20%

Some relationships are easy, and you fall into them with the comfort level you have with an old shoe or a favorite chair. Other relationships are high-maintenance, and require endless amounts of catering and nudging and hoping and fearing, and even then, they don't always work out so well. To date, Cedeno has been a major disappointment to just about every team he's ever played for, and in almost every season he's played in. Nothing seems to set him at ease, not money, not fame, and not a less stressful position than center. The one moment when he finally looked like he was worth the attention that people like us have given him over the years was 1999, with a lot of credit going to Rickey Henderson for taking an interest and helping Cedeno focus on what it takes to lead off. Since then, Cedeno's gotten hurt, annoyed his employers, and struggled. It might be worth hauling in Rickey for a shot at redeeming Cedeno and making the relationship work, because as is, he's almost certainly going to have to go back to center with Cliff Floyd moving into left.

McKay Christensen CF Born: 14-Aug-75 Age: 27 Bats: L Throws: L

YEAR	TM	LG	AGE	AB	H	2B	3B	HR	BB	SO	SB	CS	AVG	OBP	SLG	MLVR	EQBA	EQOBP	EQSLG	EQMLVR	VORP	DEFENSE	
2000	CHR	INT	24	337	89	13	2	6	32	51	28	6	.264	.330	.368	-.092	.245	.298	.345	-.231	-4.6	81-CF	-5
2001	CHR	INT	25	273	75	15	6	7	30	52	17	3	.275	.351	.451	.106	.256	.330	.422	-.055	9.2	67-CF	-1
2001	LVG	PCL	25	57	14	2	1	1	5	11	3	1	.246	.317	.368	-.189	.196	.270	.304	-.371	-2.9	15-CF	-2
2002	NYM	NL	26	3	1	0	0	0	1	1	0	0	.333	.500	.333	.268	.333	.500	.333	.203	.3		
2002	NOR	INT	26	377	107	23	6	5	26	72	20	13	.284	.341	.416	.071	.267	.322	.395	-.099	8.1	80-CF	-3
2003	PHI	NL	27	164	43	9	1	3	15	33	6	4	.259	.328	.386	-.077	.266	.330	.407	-.065	2.3		

Breakout: 26%   Improve: 52%   Collapse: 26%

Christensen opened the season as the Mets' fifth outfielder, but with Timo Perez and Jay Payton around, he wasn't going to force his way any higher up the depth chart. If a team is looking for some decent defense and a pinch-runner, he might yet stick in that role with somebody, but that's a lot less than was expected from the one-time first round pick.

Brady Clark Born: 18-Apr-73 Age: 30 Bats: R Throws: R

YEAR	TM	LG	AGE	AB	H	2B	3B	HR	BB	SO	SB	CS	AVG	OBP	SLG	MLVR	EQBA	EQOBP	EQSLG	EQMLVR	VORP	DEFENSE	
2000	LOU	INT	27	487	148	41	6	16	72	51	12	8	.304	.403	.511	.266	.275	.363	.464	.079	20.4	131-RF	-2
2001	LOU	INT	28	167	44	5	1	2	18	17	6	2	.263	.356	.341	-.029	.253	.335	.329	-.175	-4.5	46-RF	2
2001	CIN	NL	28	129	34	3	0	6	22	16	4	1	.264	.375	.426	.041	.267	.372	.427	.038	4.8	26-LF	-1
2002	LOU	INT	29	109	33	7	0	1	3	9	0	2	.303	.333	.394	.029	.284	.318	.367	-.134	-1.2	25-LF	0
2002	CIN	NL	29	66	10	3	0	0	6	9	1	2	.152	.233	.197	-.507	.164	.231	.224	-.574	-7.5		
2002	NYM	NL	29	12	5	1	0	0	1	2	0	0	.417	.462	.500	.509	.417	.462	.500	.446	1.8		
2003	NYM	NL	30	93	22	5	0	2	10	12	2	1	.243	.322	.354	-.141	.252	.327	.378	-.117	-2.0		

Breakout: 19%   Improve: 49%   Collapse: 29%

Clark finally managed to escape the Reds as he was being swamped by their wave of outfield talent, only to have to come into the Mets' camp this year already having to compete with two other solid fourth outfield candidates in Raul Gonzalez and Timo Perez, and that was before the Mets decided to blow money on bringing back Tsuyoshi Shinjo's sorry ass. If he makes it, Clark will have to settle for a pinch-hitting role, and then only if the Mets make a point of not scaring up some extra lefty bat for the bench.

Enrique Cruz   3B/SS   Born: 21-Nov-81   Age: 21   Bats: R   Throws: R

YEAR	TM	LG	AGE	AB	H	2B	3B	HR	BB	SO	SB	CS	AVG	OBP	SLG	MLVR	EQBA	EQOBP	EQSLG	EQMLVR	VORP		DEFENSE		
2000	KNG	APL	18	223	56	14	0	9	26	56	19	7	.251	.337	.435	.081	.175	.226	.293	-.486	-17.5		40-3B	4	19-SS -1
2000	CMB	SAL	18	157	29	12	0	1	25	44	1	3	.185	.301	.280	-.182	.146	.228	.226	-.584	-16.2		41-SS -15		
2001	CMB	SAL	19	438	110	20	2	9	59	106	33	7	.251	.348	.368	.068	.201	.276	.299	-.363	-22.2		102-3B -11		21-SS -6
2002	SLU	FSL	20	467	136	21	2	6	32	76	33	16	.291	.339	.383	.073	.245	.279	.324	-.298	-12.9		103-3B -9		21-SS -6
2003	MIL	NL	21	193	45	8	1	4	17	41	5	4	.233	.300	.355	-.184	.238	.301	.369	-.185	-2.9				

Breakout: 51%   *Improve: 70%*   *Collapse: 12%*

Cruz was nabbed by the Brewers through the Rule 5 draft, where they're entertaining ideas about keeping him around to play short or third. He's still extremely raw afield, but by the standard that he can probably outhit Neifi Perez right now, he's ready. Trying to make the jump from A-ball, he'll do nothing to dispel the notion that the only things that come out of Florida with real teeth are the reptiles.

Jeff Duncan   OF   Born: 09-Dec-78   Age: 24   Bats: L   Throws: L

YEAR	TM	LG	AGE	AB	H	2B	3B	HR	BB	SO	SB	CS	AVG	OBP	SLG	MLVR	EQBA	EQOBP	EQSLG	EQMLVR	VORP	DEFENSE
2000	PTS	NYP	21	186	45	3	5	2	34	46	20	3	.242	.371	.344	.081	.192	.278	.278	-.392	-11.7	50-CF -3
2001	CMB	SAL	22	318	69	16	8	3	46	97	41	3	.217	.322	.346	-.015	.182	.262	.290	-.413	-21.7	83-CF -12
2002	CMB	SAL	23	150	59	13	3	4	18	34	15	3	.393	.468	.600	.629	.290	.350	.445	.042	5.2	25-OF -5
2002	SLU	FSL	23	102	35	5	0	2	24	15	10	1	.343	.472	.451	.380	.278	.388	.361	-.013	2.3	29-LF -2
2003	NYM	NL	24	181	44	9	2	4	20	44	7	6	.244	.324	.371	-.115	.254	.329	.397	-.088	-1.5	

Breakout: 36%   *Improve: 59%*   *Collapse: 17%*

A rangy, athletic outfielder drafted out of Arizona State in 2000, Duncan shows you bits and pieces that might make you think he's the next Brett Butler, assuming you've lost a contact or something. Sure, he walks and runs, but he was old for the Sally League, has nothing that resembles what you'd call power, and seems more of another product from the organization's patented (read: unsaleable in any yard sale) Jason Tyner mold.

Danny Garcia   2B   Born: 12-Apr-80   Age: 23   Bats: R   Throws: R

YEAR	TM	LG	AGE	AB	H	2B	3B	HR	BB	SO	SB	CS	AVG	OBP	SLG	MLVR	EQBA	EQOBP	EQSLG	EQMLVR	VORP		DEFENSE	
2001	BRO	NYP	21	56	18	2	0	1	4	10	3	2	.321	.387	.411	.204	.228	.276	.298	-.351	-2.0		14-2B -2	
2001	CMB	SAL	21	103	31	12	1	2	15	18	7	3	.301	.419	.495	.350	.229	.320	.385	-.144	2.2		30-2B -4	
2002	SLU	FSL	22	432	118	34	5	4	53	77	13	6	.273	.372	.403	.132	.230	.302	.347	-.230	-1.7		105-2B -18	17-SS -8
2003	NYM	NL	23	180	44	10	2	3	17	37	4	3	.246	.319	.377	-.114	.255	.324	.404	-.087	3.1			

Breakout: 44%   *Improve: 70%*   *Collapse: 13%*

Garcia's a second baseman, so he's automatically referred to as a scrapper because he hustles and pegs doubles. He also played a bit of outfield in college at Pepperdine, and he may need that sort of versatility. He's gunning for a Craig Counsell kind of career, and he'll need Counsell's luck to make it as a semi-regular. Either that, or he'll have to crib some notes from Marco Scutaro on how to endure until you get your shot. Still, there's plenty to like, hitting for power in Florida isn't easy, and he'll take a walk.

Raul Gonzalez   CF   Born: 27-Dec-73   Age: 29   Bats: R   Throws: R

YEAR	TM	LG	AGE	AB	H	2B	3B	HR	BB	SO	SB	CS	AVG	OBP	SLG	MLVR	EQBA	EQOBP	EQSLG	EQMLVR	VORP	DEFENSE
2000	IOW	PCL	26	241	64	13	1	4	21	20	5	5	.266	.330	.378	-.133	.237	.285	.336	-.274	-12.7	60-RF -3
2001	LOU	INT	27	539	161	39	1	11	64	70	6	8	.299	.374	.436	.147	.278	.350	.407	-.021	23.1	136-CF -4
2002	LOU	INT	28	432	144	27	2	13	61	59	9	8	.333	.421	.495	.327	.305	.389	.459	.144	37.7	108-CF -6
2002	CIN	NL	28	23	6	1	0	0	2	5	2	0	.261	.320	.304	-.163	.261	.320	.304	-.235	-.6	
2002	NYM	NL	28	81	21	2	0	3	4	17	2	2	.259	.294	.395	-.055	.277	.302	.434	-.071	.3	19-OF 1
2003	NYM	NL	29	202	52	10	1	4	21	31	4	2	.258	.331	.378	-.083	.268	.337	.404	-.055	2.8	

Breakout: 13%   *Improve: 35%*   *Collapse: 32%*

Raul Gonzalez *(continued)*

How hard up were the Mets for simply adequate outfield help last season? They needed to acquire both Gonzalez and Brady Clark from the Reds for Shawn Estes. Sure, the Reds weren't going to have to give up that much in the first place, but why get outfielders you could sign as minor league free agents? That's the sort of situation where you may as well get randomly selected live arms, on the off chance that one of them works out. Gonzalez and Clark are never going to be the kinds of players you couldn't just replace with somebody else from Triple-A.

Justin Huber C Born: 01-Jul-82 Age: 21 Bats: R Throws: R

YEAR	TM	LG	AGE	AB	H	2B	3B	HR	BB	SO	SB	CS	AVG	OBP	SLG	MLVR	EQBA	EQOBP	EQSLG	EQMLVR	VORP	DEFENSE
2001	KNG	APL	19	159	50	11	1	7	17	42	4	2	.314	.423	.528	.394	.218	.283	.358	-.259	-1.1	46-C 0
2002	CMB	SAL	20	330	96	22	2	11	45	81	1	2	.291	.412	.470	.290	.227	.310	.370	-.185	4.5	69-C -5
2002	SLU	FSL	20	100	27	2	1	3	11	18	0	0	.270	.376	.400	.132	.233	.306	.350	-.216	.5	23-C -4
2003	NYM	NL	20	209	47	8	1	5	18	54	2	2	.226	.299	.344	-.204	.234	.304	.368	-.184	-1.0	

Breakout: 23%   Improve: 43%   Collapse: 30%

Huber might achieve what neither Vance Wilson or Jason Phillips will get clean shots at doing, which is move Piazza to first. If he survives the jump to Double-A, he might be able to claim a job for keeps by 2005. His receiving skills get good marks, but he doesn't have a cannon behind the plate; of course life with Piazza has probably gotten the Mets used to not having a catcher who can squelch the running game. Coachable and enthusiastic in what you might interpret as the characteristic gung-ho Aussie style that Alan Moorehead so carefully documented following the Desert Rats around North Africa.

Mark Johnson 1B Born: 17-Oct-67 Age: 35 Bats: L Throws: L

YEAR	TM	LG	AGE	AB	H	2B	3B	HR	BB	SO	SB	CS	AVG	OBP	SLG	MLVR	EQBA	EQOBP	EQSLG	EQMLVR	VORP	DEFENSE	
2000	NOR	INT	32	315	85	21	1	17	67	54	14	2	.270	.406	.505	.239	.252	.372	.467	.079	14.3	33-RF -2	37-1B -3
2001	NOR	INT	33	152	48	15	0	8	22	20	2	1	.316	.409	.572	.408	.293	.381	.535	.224	14.4	40-1B 8	
2001	NYM	NL	33	118	30	6	1	6	16	31	0	2	.254	.343	.475	.071	.264	.350	.488	.079	6.1	13-1B -1	
2002	NYM	NL	34	51	7	4	0	1	9	18	0	0	.137	.267	.275	-.331	.154	.279	.308	-.368	-4.0	10-1B 0	
2002	NOR	INT	34	270	70	17	1	14	32	53	1	0	.259	.346	.485	.149	.244	.327	.462	-.015	6.1	41-1B 6	33-LF -1

One of Valentine's *gaijins*, Johnson's slowing bat and lack of a position other than first really cut into his usefulness. He has trouble getting around on anything with any velocity, which pretty much limits him to spot starts against right-handed junkballers and pinch-hitting against low-end middle relievers. He could make it back, but the odds are similar to those of Korn playing the Mormon Tabernacle.

Wayne Lydon OF Born: 17-Apr-81 Age: 22 Bats: R Throws: R

YEAR	TM	LG	AGE	AB	H	2B	3B	HR	BB	SO	SB	CS	AVG	OBP	SLG	MLVR	EQBA	EQOBP	EQSLG	EQMLVR	VORP	DEFENSE
2000	KNG	APL	19	172	35	4	1	3	24	47	35	6	.203	.305	.291	-.187	.146	.210	.208	-.646	-21.7	52-CF -3
2001	KNG	APL	20	98	18	7	0	0	11	35	15	1	.184	.266	.255	-.251	.137	.193	.186	-.714	-14.7	25-CF -2
2001	BRO	NYP	20	57	14	1	1	0	7	18	10	1	.246	.348	.298	-.036	.186	.260	.237	-.487	-4.7	16-CF -1
2002	CMB	SAL	21	473	139	9	5	0	54	104	87	13	.294	.371	.334	.063	.237	.294	.270	-.349	-32.7	116-LF -11
2003	NYM	NL	22	197	44	8	2	2	18	54	9	10	.221	.293	.305	-.268	.230	.298	.326	-.252	-12.0	

Breakout: 73%   Improve: 84%   Collapse: 13%

With an organization-high 87 steals, Lydon is the current king of the Mets' gaggle of outfielders who run and scamper and slap instead of thumping and mashing and scoring. Beyond Lydon and Jeff Duncan, they've also got Angel Pagan and Ron Acuna. A little more variety in the organization's taste in outfield prospects would help, because most of these guys will wind up like McKay Christensen. Still, having a lot of these guys around is sort of like the outfield equivalent of having lots of live arms in the organization: bundle a bunch of them and get good stuff for the stretch drive, because odds are most of them will never haunt you a la Willie McGee/Bob Sykes.

Joe McEwing UT Born: 19-Oct-72 Age: 30 Bats: R Throws: R

YEAR	TM	LG	AGE	AB	H	2B	3B	HR	BB	SO	SB	CS	AVG	OBP	SLG	MLVR	EQBA	EQOBP	EQSLG	EQMLVR	VORP	DEFENSE	
2000	NOR	INT	27	171	44	10	2	5	16	34	7	3	.257	.321	.427	-.016	.243	.296	.399	-.160	.9	16-CF -1	11-3B 1
2000	NYM	NL	27	153	34	14	1	2	5	29	3	1	.222	.252	.366	-.324	.232	.251	.374	-.289	-7.9	23-LF 0	12-3B 0
2001	NYM	NL	28	283	80	17	3	8	17	57	8	5	.283	.345	.449	.064	.295	.352	.469	.085	13.4	40-LF -1	16-3B 1
2002	NYM	NL	29	196	39	8	1	3	9	50	4	4	.199	.245	.296	-.316	.221	.261	.332	-.337	-12.9	24-RF 0	14-SS -3
2003	NYM	NL	30	162	39	8	1	4	11	34	4	2	.238	.291	.369	-.178	.247	.296	.394	-.155	-3.2		

Breakout: 27%   Improve: 54%   Collapse: 23%

A standard-issue utility man, which means you shouldn't get too bent out of shape if he doesn't hit; his playing time is far too sporadic to let you form much of a judgment. He's a 25th man, and you know what they say, he's scrappier than a bulldog. Or a really angry goat. One that's eaten hot chili peppers.

Rey Ordonez — SS — Born: 11-Jan-71 — Age: 32 — Bats: R — Throws: R

YEAR	TM	LG	AGE	AB	H	2B	3B	HR	BB	SO	SB	CS	AVG	OBP	SLG	MLVR	EQBA	EQOBP	EQSLG	EQMLVR	VORP	DEFENSE	
2000	NYM	NL	29	133	25	5	0	0	17	16	0	0	.188	.280	.226	-.485	.200	.280	.237	-.440	-8.2	39-SS	-1
2001	NYM	NL	30	461	114	24	4	3	34	43	3	2	.247	.300	.336	-.207	.258	.309	.352	-.191	3.5	136-SS	5
2002	NYM	NL	31	460	117	25	2	1	24	46	2	2	.254	.294	.324	-.157	.272	.306	.349	-.192	3.2	128-SS	7
2003	TBA	AL	32	307	76	15	1	3	21	34	1	1	.246	.297	.329	-.189	.252	.305	.343	-.203	-3.4		

Breakout: 25%   Improve: 42%   Collapse: 33%

Now that St. Rey the Overrated is no longer in New York, does this mean no more tedious "just so" assertions that Ordonez is the greatest defensive shortstop this side of Old Testament God? No more Ordonez-specific "well, who needs hitting anyway" comments? Well, not quite, the Mets still have a shortstop named Rey with a great defensive rep and light offensive contributions. Except this year, when Flushing denizens claim they've got the best glove at short in baseball, it'll be worth listening to. And this other Rey? Well, if he comes up with some superficial, phony angle, maybe he can get the wrong Quaid to play him in a movie too.

Timo Perez — CF — Born: 08-Apr-75 — Age: 28 — Bats: L — Throws: L

YEAR	TM	LG	AGE	AB	H	2B	3B	HR	BB	SO	SB	CS	AVG	OBP	SLG	MLVR	EQBA	EQOBP	EQSLG	EQMLVR	VORP	DEFENSE	
2000	NOR	INT	25	291	104	17	5	6	16	25	13	7	.357	.397	.512	.326	.329	.360	.473	.138	23.5	70-CF	3
2001	NOR	INT	26	192	69	10	2	6	12	18	15	2	.359	.403	.526	.386	.342	.384	.500	.232	16.8	45-OF	-3
2001	NYM	NL	26	239	59	9	1	5	12	25	1	6	.247	.289	.356	-.203	.255	.295	.370	-.194	-7.7	61-RF	2
2002	NYM	NL	27	444	131	27	6	8	23	36	10	6	.295	.333	.437	.097	.312	.345	.468	.088	30.4	110-CF	2
2003	NYM	NL	28	406	115	21	3	7	25	39	10	4	.284	.328	.409	-.029	.294	.334	.437	.005	9.8		

Breakout: 4%   Improve: 21%   Collapse: 28%

The trade of Jay Payton forced him into the everyday lineup, which wasn't the end of the world, but since the revelation that Perez is two years older, what you see is all you're going to get. With Floyd now manning left field, Perez will still get playing time in center or right at the expense of Burnitz and Cedeno. He's the only legitimate center fielder of the three.

Jason Phillips — C — Born: 27-Sep-76 — Age: 26 — Bats: R — Throws: R

YEAR	TM	LG	AGE	AB	H	2B	3B	HR	BB	SO	SB	CS	AVG	OBP	SLG	MLVR	EQBA	EQOBP	EQSLG	EQMLVR	VORP	DEFENSE	
2000	SLU	FSL	23	297	82	21	0	6	23	19	1	1	.276	.345	.407	.076	.226	.274	.342	-.294	-4.5	71-C	7
2000	BIN	EAS	23	98	38	4	0	0	7	9	0	0	.388	.439	.429	.295	.337	.376	.367	.017	6.8	24-C	1
2001	BIN	EAS	24	317	93	21	0	11	31	25	0	1	.293	.365	.464	.164	.251	.316	.393	-.125	9.7	81-C	1
2001	NOR	INT	24	66	20	2	0	2	7	8	0	0	.303	.370	.424	.142	.294	.351	.412	.001	4.4	15-C	1
2002	NOR	INT	25	323	91	22	1	13	24	29	1	0	.282	.335	.477	.140	.266	.319	.456	-.019	18.7	80-C	-2
2002	NYM	NL	25	19	7	0	0	1	1	1	0	0	.368	.429	.526	.443	.400	.452	.550	.483	3.1		
2003	NYM	NL	26	167	41	8	0	4	14	19	2	1	.246	.309	.380	-.127	.256	.314	.406	-.100	3.1		

Breakout: 14%   Improve: 44%   Collapse: 31%

Phillips's misfortune is that while the Mets would love to have a catcher who could let them move Piazza to first base, it won't be him. Because of nimble footwork and a snappy release, he controls the running game well, and he has decent power. He'll make a great backup or part-timer, but that isn't enough to get him 300 at-bats on a team that needs all the offense it can get. Right around now would be a great time to find another Ed Hearn buyer.

Mike Piazza — C — Born: 04-Sep-68 — Age: 34 — Bats: R — Throws: R

YEAR	TM	LG	AGE	AB	H	2B	3B	HR	BB	SO	SB	CS	AVG	OBP	SLG	MLVR	EQBA	EQOBP	EQSLG	EQMLVR	VORP	DEFENSE	
2000	NYM	NL	31	482	156	26	0	38	58	69	4	2	.324	.400	.614	.412	.328	.396	.623	.412	86.7	113-C	-4
2001	NYM	NL	32	503	151	29	0	36	67	87	0	2	.300	.385	.573	.321	.310	.391	.587	.332	84.0	120-C	-16
2002	NYM	NL	33	478	134	23	2	33	57	82	0	3	.280	.361	.544	.273	.293	.368	.572	.255	64.1	109-C	-20
2003	NYM	NL	34	418	114	21	1	24	51	74	0	1	.273	.355	.499	.126	.284	.361	.534	.170	37.2		

Breakout: 6%   Improve: 31%   Collapse: 14%

Mike Piazza (*continued*)

So what if he's turning into SuperSimba? Is that so bad? Like Ted Simmons, he isn't much of a catcher: he can't throw, and he's not a good receiver or plate blocker. Also like Simba, his pitchers don't complain about him. And it isn't like you've got a pitch-back in the lineup as well as on the field. However, it may have taken his first full season where he didn't hit .300 to convince the Mets that they might have to protect their investment over the next three years, and try to start letting Piazza play some first before converting him entirely. Once Mo Vaughn waddles out of town, consider it done.

Prentice Redman   **OF**   **Born: 23-Aug-79**   **Age: 23**   **Bats: R**   **Throws: R**

YEAR	TM	LG	AGE	AB	H	2B	3B	HR	BB	SO	SB	CS	AVG	OBP	SLG	MLVR	EQBA	EQOBP	EQSLG	EQMLVR	VORP	DEFENSE
2000	CMB	SAL	20	497	129	19	1	3	52	90	26	10	.260	.333	.320	-.044	.205	.259	.254	-.458	-49.5	122-OF -15
2001	SLU	FSL	21	495	129	18	1	9	42	91	29	8	.261	.326	.356	-.004	.223	.269	.312	-.348	-34.2	118-LF -9
2002	BIN	EAS	22	491	139	35	2	11	59	112	43	9	.283	.370	.430	.106	.242	.314	.371	-.166	-10.2	115-OF -6
2003	NYM	NL	23	180	43	9	1	4	17	41	5	4	.239	.308	.368	-.149	.248	.313	.393	-.125	-4.1	

Breakout: 43%   *Improve: 71%*   *Collapse: 13%*

Tike's kid brother, Prentice was noted for a history of second-half fades until last season, when he finally hit well down the stretch. He still needs to pick up certain skill sets: he hasn't learned how to hammer lefty junk, and he gets everything in the air, frustrating people who want to see him take better advantage of his speed. As you can see, he's a bit of a tweener: he can't really play center, but he doesn't have the power you expect from a corner. That said, he's turned himself into a decent prospect. If he keeps improving, he'll be opening eyes in major league front offices soon enough.

Jose Reyes   **SS**   **Born: 11-Jun-83**   **Age: 20**   **Bats: B**   **Throws: R**

YEAR	TM	LG	AGE	AB	H	2B	3B	HR	BB	SO	SB	CS	AVG	OBP	SLG	MLVR	EQBA	EQOBP	EQSLG	EQMLVR	VORP	DEFENSE
2000	KNG	APL	17	132	33	3	3	0	20	37	10	4	.250	.361	.318	-.035	.169	.242	.213	-.564	-12.4	35-SS 2
2001	CMB	SAL	18	407	125	22	15	5	18	71	30	10	.307	.340	.472	.228	.243	.269	.377	-.243	-2.6	108-SS 1
2002	SLU	FSL	19	288	83	10	11	6	30	35	31	13	.288	.357	.462	.199	.236	.289	.384	-.199	1.4	69-SS 5
2002	BIN	EAS	19	275	79	16	8	2	16	42	27	11	.287	.331	.425	.042	.244	.280	.360	-.245	-1.9	63-SS -7
2003	NYM	NL	20	217	54	10	2	4	19	37	9	5	.248	.310	.375	-.130	.257	.316	.401	-.104	3.3	

Breakout: 58%   *Improve: 70%*   *Collapse: 19%*

You run out of superlatives after a while, but 19-year-olds who play a great short, smack more than 50 extra-base hits, steal nearly 60 bases... well, skip silly accusations about New York bias, he's one of the best prospects in baseball. After a great year in the Sally League as the youngest regular in full-season baseball, Reyes responded to 'show me again' questions with a vengeance. He thrived as a leadoff hitter, flashes the hands, arm, and range to be a plus shortstop, and had a nice cameo in the Futures Game, rapping a key triple. His thigh injury suffered in winter ball is not supposed to be serious. Barring one of the AL greats coming over to the senior circuit, he'll be the best shortstop in both the National League and New York within four years.

Marco Scutaro   **2B**   **Born: 30-Oct-75**   **Age: 27**   **Bats: R**   **Throws: R**

YEAR	TM	LG	AGE	AB	H	2B	3B	HR	BB	SO	SB	CS	AVG	OBP	SLG	MLVR	EQBA	EQOBP	EQSLG	EQMLVR	VORP	DEFENSE	
2000	BUF	INT	24	425	117	20	5	5	61	53	9	6	.275	.378	.381	.028	.256	.344	.353	-.123	10.7	109-2B -7	18-SS -6
2001	IND	INT	25	495	146	29	3	11	62	83	11	11	.295	.384	.432	.154	.273	.356	.404	-.018	26.6	116-2B -19	
2002	NOR	INT	26	354	113	22	6	7	30	61	7	8	.319	.376	.475	.234	.297	.352	.447	.055	25.9	48-2B -8	25-SS 1
2002	NYM	NL	26	36	8	0	1	1	0	11	0	1	.222	.222	.361	-.254	.222	.222	.389	-.330	-1.7		
2003	NYM	NL	27	205	53	10	1	4	22	36	4	2	.257	.333	.371	-.091	.267	.338	.396	-.063	5.0		

Breakout: 9%   *Improve: 29%*   *Collapse: 40%*

The Brewers and Indians didn't appreciate him, but it looks like the Mets do. They flat out know he's a ballplayer. Maybe it was the success with Joe McEwing, but a guy who never says die at the plate and proves willing to move around the diamond is a far better option as a utility infielder than somebody like Jorge Velandia. Scutaro would be an improvement over at least a half dozen teams' starters at second.

Esix Snead
Born: 07-Jun-76 **Age: 27** **Bats: B** **Throws: R**

YEAR	TM	LG	AGE	AB	H	2B	3B	HR	BB	SO	SB	CS	AVG	OBP	SLG	MLVR	EQBA	EQOBP	EQSLG	EQMLVR	VORP	DEFENSE
2000	POT	CRL	24	493	116	14	3	1	72	98	109	35	.235	.341	.282	-.108	.206	.281	.249	-.419	-33.0	131-CF -8
2001	NHV	EAS	25	520	121	21	6	1	44	115	64	23	.233	.307	.302	-.149	.212	.277	.274	-.390	-31.1	132-CF 0
2002	BIN	EAS	26	401	101	9	6	3	45	72	66	18	.252	.336	.327	-.104	.220	.289	.289	-.341	-17.3	115-CF -4
2002	NYM	NL	26	13	4	0	0	1	1	4	4	3	.308	.357	.538	.289	.308	.357	.538	.206	1.1	
2003	NYN	NL	27	133	31	5	1	1	13	27	7	4	.231	.305	.313	-.230	.240	.310	.335	-.212	-3.0	

Breakout: 56%   *Improve: 74%*   *Collapse: 18%*

Faster than the Lorax, but not quite as cool, Snead's about as likely to steal only seven bases if he sticks in the majors long enough to get 133 at-bats as Pamela Anderson is to appear on the cover of next year's book. Not that any of this is a good idea. If he's up, it'll be because he's going to pinch-run a lot, which means more than seven steals. Think he's a ballplayer? Put it this way: Snead was the first guy to win back-to-back stolen base titles in the Eastern League since Gary Varsho. You think that's a good thing?

John Valentin
INF **Born: 18-Feb-67** **Age: 36** **Bats: R** **Throws: R**

YEAR	TM	LG	AGE	AB	H	2B	3B	HR	BB	SO	SB	CS	AVG	OBP	SLG	MLVR	EQBA	EQOBP	EQSLG	EQMLVR	VORP	DEFENSE	
2001	BOS	AL	34	60	12	2	0	1	9	8	0	0	.200	.314	.283	-.261	.217	.326	.317	-.230	-0.2	16-SS -1	
2002	NYM	NL	35	208	50	15	0	3	22	37	0	0	.240	.342	.356	-.039	.258	.349	.390	-.062	8.8	15-SS 2	13-1B -2
2003	NYM	NL	36	153	35	7	0	4	18	28	0	1	.231	.317	.352	-.160	.239	.322	.376	-.137	-1.1		

Breakout: 21%   *Improve: 38%*   *Collapse: 34%*

In almost the exact opposite of the prodigal son story, 2002 was the year that the Mets and Red Sox took a look at each other's former star infielder, and both were put to work. The Mets came out ahead: Despite a bum shoulder, Valentin was a useful spot starter around the infield, while Carlos Baerga was a singles-hitting DH. Valentin's fragility will be a handicap if he tries to do anything more than hold onto a reserve role, but there are worse options.

Mo Vaughn
1B **Born: 15-Dec-67** **Age: 35** **Bats: L** **Throws: R**

YEAR	TM	LG	AGE	AB	H	2B	3B	HR	BB	SO	SB	CS	AVG	OBP	SLG	MLVR	EQBA	EQOBP	EQSLG	EQMLVR	VORP	DEFENSE
2000	ANA	AL	32	614	167	31	0	36	79	181	2	0	.272	.368	.498	.108	.281	.371	.516	.169	41.8	142-1B -1
2002	NYM	NL	34	487	126	18	0	26	59	145	0	1	.259	.351	.456	.120	.275	.359	.487	.103	26.6	123-1B -8
2003	NYM	NL	35	360	88	16	1	17	42	100	1	1	.244	.328	.433	-.027	.253	.334	.463	.005	4.4	

Breakout: 10%   *Improve: 35%*   *Collapse: 24%*

Presumably after shaking off the cobwebs of a lost year, Vaughn did hit .270/.360/.520 after the All-Star break, with 16 home runs. You might interpret that as a reason to think Vaughn's going to be a big asset in 2003, but the future is rarely kind to gravity's larger targets. George Scott, Boog Powell, and Cecil Fielder were all big boppers, and they all flamed out by the time they turned 35, and they all shared a famous capacity to indulge various appetites. Captain Obvious alert: It has apparently just come to the attention of the right honorable Fred Wilpon that Mo Vaughn is undertall, and he's not happy about it. Where was the interdepartmental memo on this?

Matt Watson
LF **Born: 05-Sep-78** **Age: 24** **Bats: L** **Throws: R**

YEAR	TM	LG	AGE	AB	H	2B	3B	HR	BB	SO	SB	CS	AVG	OBP	SLG	MLVR	EQBA	EQOBP	EQSLG	EQMLVR	VORP	DEFENSE
2000	JUP	FSL	21	137	24	5	2	0	18	23	4	3	.175	.276	.241	-.297	.149	.228	.213	-.600	-18.7	18-LF -3
2001	JUP	FSL	22	446	147	33	4	5	63	45	17	9	.330	.419	.455	.323	.275	.344	.387	-.063	3.1	101-LF 2
2002	BIN	EAS	23	437	122	26	2	10	39	52	12	8	.279	.342	.416	.042	.234	.287	.355	-.245	-18.0	101-LF -5
2003	NYM	NL	24	164	40	9	1	3	15	24	3	2	.246	.312	.367	-.139	.255	.318	.392	-.113	-3.5	

Breakout: 31%   *Improve: 60%*   *Collapse: 16%*

Part of the swag from the Mets' April trade with the Expos, and notionally the least of the three players acquired (the others were Scott Strickland and Phil Seibel). Watson survived the jump to Double-A, but didn't exactly thrive, and usually managed to get eaten up by good heat at the plate. Since he doesn't have the power to be an offensive asset as an outfield regular, he's basically gunning for a Darren Bragg type of career.

Ty Wigginton · 3B · Born: 11-Oct-77 · Age: 25 · Bats: R · Throws: R

YEAR	TM	LG	AGE	AB	H	2B	3B	HR	BB	SO	SB	CS	AVG	OBP	SLG	MLVR	EQBA	EQOBP	EQSLG	EQMLVR	VORP	DEFENSE			
2000	BIN	EAS	22	453	129	27	3	20	24	107	5	5	.285	.324	.490	.118	.241	.270	.415	-.188	3.4	64-2B	-10	48-3B	-3
2001	NOR	INT	23	260	65	12	0	7	27	66	3	3	.250	.325	.377	-.033	.238	.309	.366	-.185	.3	36-3B	-13	20-2B	-2
2002	NOR	INT	24	383	115	26	3	6	43	50	5	3	.300	.372	.431	.153	.284	.353	.412	-.004	19.6	46-3B	-12	31-2B	1
2002	NYM	NL	24	116	35	8	0	6	8	19	2	1	.302	.357	.526	.265	.319	.366	.563	.269	13.8	10-3B	-1	12-2B	-1
2003	NYM	NL	25	260	67	14	1	8	23	47	5	2	.257	.319	.408	-.064	.266	.325	.437	-.033	5.9				

Breakout: 23%   Improve: 54%   Collapse: 29%

You need to give Wigginton some benefit of the doubt for his lousy 2001 season. He was playing through bone chips in his throwing elbow, which prevented him from throwing or swinging properly (although it's worth asking: why then was he playing?). Originally coming up when John Valentin broke down, he kept doing enough nice little things that he managed to keep getting playing time now and again. He's sort of the default option at third if the Mets don't add anybody. Given that he'll probably hit .280 with a wee bit of power if he's in the lineup every day, he wouldn't be dramatically dissimilar in impact than oft-rumored trade target Shea Hillenbrand.

Vance Wilson · C · Born: 17-Mar-73 · Age: 30 · Bats: R · Throws: R

YEAR	TM	LG	AGE	AB	H	2B	3B	HR	BB	SO	SB	CS	AVG	OBP	SLG	MLVR	EQBA	EQOBP	EQSLG	EQMLVR	VORP	DEFENSE	
2000	NOR	INT	27	400	104	23	1	16	24	65	11	6	.260	.321	.443	.008	.243	.291	.417	-.144	9.3	97-C	0
2001	NOR	INT	28	228	56	14	0	6	12	34	0	1	.246	.309	.386	-.051	.238	.293	.381	-.195	2.5	63-C	-1
2001	NYM	NL	28	57	17	3	0	0	2	16	0	1	.298	.344	.351	-.065	.310	.351	.362	-.059	2.7	19-C	1
2002	NYM	NL	29	163	40	7	0	5	5	32	0	1	.245	.301	.380	-.074	.265	.311	.410	-.100	5.5	48-C	7
2003	NYM	NL	30	179	42	8	1	4	10	33	1	1	.237	.287	.358	-.200	.246	.292	.383	-.178	-.6		

Breakout: 17%   Improve: 35%   Collapse: 35%

A slightly better receiver than Jason Phillips, which is why he's up and holding a big league bench job while Phillips keeps his slightly better bat fresh by playing every day in the International League. Once Wilson hits arbitration eligibility, he's gone, unless he can learn to settle if he wants to sit still, or hope to make just as much while moving around.

David Wright · 3B · Born: 20-Dec-82 · Age: 20 · Bats: R · Throws: R

YEAR	TM	LG	AGE	AB	H	2B	3B	HR	BB	SO	SB	CS	AVG	OBP	SLG	MLVR	EQBA	EQOBP	EQSLG	EQMLVR	VORP	DEFENSE	
2001	KNG	APL	18	116	35	7	0	4	16	29	9	1	.302	.396	.466	.270	.207	.276	.306	-.351	-5.4	33-3B	-2
2002	CMB	SAL	19	496	132	30	2	11	76	114	21	5	.266	.369	.401	.128	.207	.284	.317	-.320	-17.9	120-3B	-10
2003	NYM	NL	20	205	47	9	2	5	21	52	5	4	.231	.307	.365	-.160	.240	.312	.390	-.137	-.7		

Breakout: 61%   Improve: 75%   Collapse: 16%

A supplemental first round choice in 2001, Wright was considered one of the best high school players in the draft. Tip your cap, the scouts were absolutely right about him. "Hard-nosed" is used to describe every element of his game. At the hot corner, he's relatively mobile at third, covering the line or moving to his left equally well. As a hitter, he's already showing good power and patience, and he runs well. If he keeps progressing while moving up to St. Lucie and the difficult hitting environment of the Florida State League, he'll be one of the best third-base prospects in the game.

PITCHERS

Pedro Astacio   Born: 28-Nov-69   Age: 33   Bats: R   Throws: R

YEAR	TM	LG	AGE	G	GS	IP	H	BB	SO	HR	ERA	EQERA	EQH9	EQBB9	EQSO9	EQHR9	PERA	VORP	STF
2000	COL	NL	30	32	32	196.3	217	77	193	32	5.27	4.59	9.4	2.8	7.7	1.2	4.47	20.0	19
2001	COL	NL	31	22	22	141.0	151	50	125	21	5.49	4.84	9.3	2.9	6.7	1.1	4.43	10.4	13
2001	HOU	NL	31	4	4	28.7	30	4	19	1	3.14	3.19	9.9	1.2	5.2	0.3	3.36	7.4	17
2002	NYM	NL	32	31	31	191.7	192	63	152	32	4.79	5.10	9.7	2.7	6.4	1.6	5.11	8.6	8
2003	NYM	NL	33	27	25	161.3	155	54	128	18	3.96	4.48	9.0	2.6	6.2	1.1	4.40	19.1	12

Breakout: 13%   Improve: 52%   Collapse: 14%

The numbers look uglier than the value he gave the Mets last year, because he gave up six or more runs in seven of his last nine starts, after the Mets ceased to matter. Before that, he'd given them 16 quality starts in 22 outings. Unfortunately, his melt-down was a symptom of something more troubling. Astacio pitched through last season with a partially torn labrum. You can understand why the Mets apparently can't get rid of him fast enough, and why they're also almost certainly stuck with him.

Mike Bacsik   Born: 11-Nov-77   Age: 25   Bats: L   Throws: L

YEAR	TM	LG	AGE	G	GS	IP	H	BB	SO	HR	ERA	EQERA	EQH9	EQBB9	EQSO9	EQHR9	PERA	VORP	STF
2000	KIN	CRL	22	11	11	65.0	72	8	56	4	4.57	6.27	13.7	1.4	5.0	1.4	6.07	-5.5	8
2000	AKR	EAS	22	11	11	71.3	61	15	44	3	2.78	3.71	9.5	2.1	4.3	0.7	3.66	14.2	10
2000	BUF	INT	22	5	5	29.0	31	7	9	7	5.59	6.38	11.4	2.3	2.5	2.9	6.07	-2.8	-16
2001	AKR	EAS	23	4	4	27.3	21	3	19	2	1.98	3.33	8.7	1.3	4.3	1.0	3.36	6.6	11
2001	BUF	INT	23	21	20	121.3	115	25	81	13	3.26	4.43	10.0	2.2	4.8	1.3	4.43	14.5	7
2002	NOR	INT	24	25	14	108.3	134	25	75	13	3.74	5.43	12.8	2.5	5.4	1.6	6.40	0.6	0
2002	NYM	NL	24	11	9	55.7	63	19	30	8	4.36	5.23	11.1	2.8	4.4	1.4	5.70	1.6	-3
2003	NYM	NL	25	18	12	73.0	81	23	45	10	4.56	5.17	10.4	2.4	4.9	1.2	5.20	4.9	-3

Breakout: 16%   Improve: 46%   Collapse: 25%

A throw-in from the Tribe in the Alomar deal, Bacsik is one of those guys who people really want to see succeed, but you have to wonder if it's just going to be Dave Fleming redux, without the highlights. He's never going to overawe anyone, having already been condemned to the finesse lefty toolkit, but with Rey Sanchez at short behind him, he might end up looking pretty sweet in short doses. He'll compete for the last slot in the rotation.

Heath Bell   Born: 29-Sep-77   Age: 25   Bats: R   Throws: R

YEAR	TM	LG	AGE	G	GS	IP	H	BB	SO	HR	ERA	EQERA	EQH9	EQBB9	EQSO9	EQHR9	PERA	VORP	STF
2000	SLU	FSL	22	48	0	60.0	43	21	75	4	2.55	3.99	8.8	4.0	8.0	1.5	3.96	9.3	9
2001	BIN	EAS	23	43	0	61.3	82	19	55	13	6.02	7.99	15.0	3.9	5.7	3.0	8.57	-17.8	-21
2002	BIN	EAS	24	24	0	38.0	22	6	49	0	1.18	1.69	5.9	1.7	8.6	0.2	1.61	15.6	29
2002	NOR	INT	24	22	0	31.7	38	9	28	2	4.26	5.36	12.0	3.1	6.8	0.8	5.85	0.1	1

An odd choice for the Mets to have added to their 40-man roster. Bell is a minor league closer with marginal velocity, decent command, and no real out pitch. After getting slapped around in the Eastern League the first time around, he was a man among boys in 2002. He might yet make it to the majors, but he's not going to rack up saves.

Armando Benitez   Born: 03-Nov-72   Age: 30   Bats: R   Throws: R

YEAR	TM	LG	AGE	G	GS	IP	H	BB	SO	HR	ERA	EQERA	EQH9	EQBB9	EQSO9	EQHR9	PERA	VORP	STF
2000	NYM	NL	27	76	0	76.0	39	38	106	10	2.61	2.66	4.6	3.6	10.9	1.1	2.56	23.0	27
2001	NYM	NL	28	73	0	76.3	59	40	93	12	3.77	4.01	7.2	4.4	9.3	1.3	4.20	11.6	10
2002	NYM	NL	29	62	0	67.3	46	25	79	8	2.27	3.08	6.5	3.0	9.3	1.1	3.25	17.2	17
2003	NYM	NL	30	53	0	55.7	44	24	62	7	3.52	3.99	7.4	3.3	8.8	1.1	3.82	9.9	12

Breakout: 18%   Improve: 34%   Collapse: 27%

Far and away the best reliever the Mets have (shiny new Stanton or no), and wasted in single-inning dribs and drabs that depend on the lineup to actually build a lead first. Unfortunately, like putting lipstick on a pig, there just isn't much point to paying a closer $6 or $7 million to pitch on a last-place club. If the Mets struggle early, Phillips should move quickly to make Benitez somebody else's amply compensated white elephant.

P. J. Bevis   Born: 28-Jul-80   Age: 22   Bats: R   Throws: R

YEAR	TM	LG	AGE	G	GS	IP	H	BB	SO	HR	ERA	EQERA	EQH9	EQBB9	EQSO9	EQHR9	PERA	VORP	STF
2000	MSO	PIO	19	14	14	83.7	92	22	63	4	3.33	6.00	13.9	3.0	4.0	1.1	5.78	-4.6	0
2001	YAK	NWN	20	12	0	14.0	9	7	22	0	0.64	2.18	8.0	6.7	7.6	0.3	4.20	5.0	7
2001	ELP	TXS	20	14	0	16.7	11	6	19	2	2.16	2.31	6.3	3.9	7.1	1.7	3.12	5.7	8
2002	ELP	TXS	21	49	0	63.7	50	29	62	3	2.83	3.65	8.1	4.8	6.6	0.8	3.81	12.2	4
2002	BIN	EAS	21	4	0	7.0	5	3	14	0	1.29	2.13	7.2	4.4	13.1	0.2	2.91	2.5	55

Pitching well in El Paso is one of the hardest things a minor league pitcher can be asked to do, and Bevis was sharp and kept the ball in the yard. He dials his fastball into the mid-90s and changes speeds on his curve well, throwing from an arm slot that makes it hard to pick anything up. The Snakes blow it again, and the Mets wind up with a hard-throwing Aussie who could be ready to join the big league bullpen before the end of the season.

Jaime Cerda   Born: 26-Oct-78   Age: 24   Bats: L   Throws: L

YEAR	TM	LG	AGE	G	GS	IP	H	BB	SO	HR	ERA	EQERA	EQH9	EQBB9	EQSO9	EQHR9	PERA	VORP	STF
2000	PTS	NYP	21	20	1	47.0	33	6	51	0	0.57	2.63	8.8	1.5	5.4	0.3	3.45	14.5	9
2001	SLU	FSL	22	28	0	55.7	40	12	56	3	0.97	2.57	8.6	2.3	6.1	1.2	3.54	17.4	7
2001	BIN	EAS	22	12	0	20.3	17	6	22	1	3.10	3.75	8.7	3.5	6.6	0.7	3.84	3.7	7
2002	BIN	EAS	23	14	0	31.7	21	10	33	0	2.27	2.56	6.9	3.3	7.0	0.2	2.39	9.9	16
2002	NOR	INT	23	12	0	21.0	10	7	17	0	0.43	1.51	4.7	3.6	6.2	0.2	1.83	9.0	10
2002	NYM	NL	23	32	0	25.7	22	14	21	0	2.45	3.19	8.2	4.4	6.5	0.2	3.80	6.3	4
2003	NYM	NL	24	29	8	63.7	57	27	52	5	3.51	3.97	8.4	3.3	6.4	0.8	4.16	11.3	2

Breakout: 16%   Improve: 44%   Collapse: 16%

What you're seeing is Cerda's entire pro career, and yes, it adds up to a career minor league ERA of 1.35. He's already survived Tommy John surgery, and he's throwing a nasty sinker that comes in just over 90. To mix things up he'll include a decent slider and a good cutter. He hasn't had problems spanking right-handed hitters, so he doesn't need to be shoe-horned into the situational lefty role. Instead, he can be a plain old quality reliever, like Jesse Orosco was. You know, back when the rest of us were learning to use stone tools.

Mike Cox   Born: 03-Nov-78   Age: 24   Bats: L   Throws: L

YEAR	TM	LG	AGE	G	GS	IP	H	BB	SO	HR	ERA	EQERA	EQH9	EQBB9	EQSO9	EQHR9	PERA	VORP	STF
2000	PTS	NYP	21	14	12	61.7	43	30	81	3	2.48	5.33	10.6	6.2	7.0	2.1	5.56	1.2	4
2001	BRO	NYP	22	13	7	52.7	40	41	73	2	2.90	7.67	12.2	11.7	7.9	1.3	6.82	-12.8	-7
2001	CMB	SAL	22	15	0	32.3	27	19	40	1	4.46	6.63	10.8	8.4	6.6	0.7	6.45	-4.5	-10
2002	CMB	SAL	23	33	1	58.3	33	54	92	3	5.25	6.89	7.6	12.3	9.1	1.3	5.63	-9.7	-9
2002	SLU	FSL	23	4	0	5.7	7	11	11	1	14.21	16.66	18.4	26.0	14.5	4.5	15.70	-7.1	-48

Cox is just here as a statistical freak. Look at that: in 64 IP, he allowed 40 hits, walked 65, and struck out 103. He hit 15 batters, but tossed only four wild pitches. He doesn't throw hard, so it's hard to explain what's going on here beyond these lefty hijinks. There's no indication that he's a latter-day Tommy Byrne, and simply choosing not to pitch to the people (a whole lot of people) that he doesn't care to face. No, he isn't a prospect, but as long as you're behind the screen, you might get a kick out of watching him pitch.

Jeff D'Amico   Born: 27-Dec-75   Age: 27   Bats: R   Throws: R

YEAR	TM	LG	AGE	G	GS	IP	H	BB	SO	HR	ERA	EQERA	EQH9	EQBB9	EQSO9	EQHR9	PERA	VORP	STF
2000	MIL	NL	24	23	23	162.3	143	46	101	14	2.66	3.17	8.6	2.1	5.1	0.7	3.17	42.1	14
2001	MIL	NL	25	10	10	47.3	60	16	32	11	6.09	7.37	12.1	2.9	5.3	1.9	6.65	-9.8	-7
2002	NYM	NL	26	29	22	145.7	152	37	101	20	4.94	5.07	10.2	2.1	5.6	1.3	4.88	88.9	4
2003	PIT	NL	27	24	18	112.3	119	34	73	14	4.54	4.73	9.5	2.3	5.2	1.2	4.50	9.4	2

Breakout: 14%   Improve: 44%   Collapse: 14%

On the one hand, he was only brought in as the team's fifth starter, but despite his track record for repeated breakdowns, Phillips noted how special he'd been in 2000, as if that was likely to happen again. After running off quality starts in eight of his first 10 games, it even began to seem like a reasonable proposition. Then came the little breakdowns, the declining endurance, and heightened frustration as the team didn't contend. One of baseball's most massive pitchers won't be back with the Mets, but the Pirates are willing to take their chances.

John Franco — Born: 17-Sep-60 — Age: 42 — Bats: L — Throws: L

YEAR	TM	LG	AGE	G	GS	IP	H	BB	SO	HR	ERA	EQERA	EQH9	EQBB9	EQSO9	EQHR9	PERA	VORP	STF
2000	NYM	NL	39	62	0	55.7	46	26	56	6	3.39	3.71	7.6	3.4	8.0	0.9	3.74	10.3	8
2001	NYM	NL	40	58	0	53.3	55	19	50	8	4.05	4.61	9.8	3.0	7.2	1.2	5.00	4.6	0

Franco is still talking about his comeback, and was testing his Tommy John'd elbow in January. He's generally the face you associate with this team, but with Stanton signed and Cerda on hand, you have to wonder if he'll be worth the roster spot. He probably won't be back until the middle of the season.

Jeremy Griffiths — Born: 22-Mar-78 — Age: 25 — Bats: R — Throws: R

YEAR	TM	LG	AGE	G	GS	IP	H	BB	SO	HR	ERA	EQERA	EQH9	EQBB9	EQSO9	EQHR9	PERA	VORP	STF
2000	CMB	SAL	22	26	26	128.7	120	39	138	12	4.34	6.00	11.6	3.8	5.6	2.3	5.96	-7.1	0
2001	SLU	FSL	23	23	20	132.0	126	35	95	9	3.75	5.46	11.7	3.0	4.5	1.6	5.45	0.6	0
2001	BIN	EAS	23	2	2	13.0	8	4	12	0	0.69	2.45	6.3	3.7	5.6	0.2	2.39	4.4	19
2002	BIN	EAS	24	27	26	152.7	157	54	126	12	3.89	5.13	11.2	3.9	5.7	1.2	5.10	6.3	5

The Mets love their pitchers big, and Griffiths is another one of their six-and-a-half-foot-tall behemoths. He's not exactly a right-handed junkballer, since he does reach the 90s, but he throws a little bit of everything. His stock went up considerably after a great AFL in 2002.

Mark Guthrie — Born: 22-Sep-65 — Age: 37 — Bats: R — Throws: L

YEAR	TM	LG	AGE	G	GS	IP	H	BB	SO	HR	ERA	EQERA	EQH9	EQBB9	EQSO9	EQHR9	PERA	VORP	STF
2000	CHC	NL	34	19	0	18.7	17	10	17	1	4.81	4.24	8.3	3.9	7.2	0.4	3.79	2.4	3
2000	TBY	AL	34	34	0	32.0	33	18	26	4	4.50	4.38	8.7	4.1	7.0	0.9	4.49	3.6	-1
2000	TOR	AL	34	23	0	20.7	20	9	20	3	4.78	3.99	7.7	3.1	8.2	1.1	3.95	3.2	8
2001	OAK	AL	35	54	0	52.3	49	20	52	7	4.47	4.53	8.5	3.2	8.4	1.1	4.06	4.9	8
2002	NYM	NL	36	68	0	48.0	35	19	44	3	2.44	2.91	7.0	3.2	7.3	0.6	3.18	13.2	7
2003	*CHC*	*NL*	*37*	*61*	*0*	*43.7*	*41*	*18*	*44*	*5*	*3.76*	*4.15*	*8.7*	*3.2*	*7.9*	*0.9*	*4.28*	*7.8*	*6*

Breakout: 29%   Improve: 46%   Collapse: 38%

Although Guthrie pitched in 68 games, and that seems like a lot, he also warmed up in several games as a decoy, as Bobby Valentine angled to be extra clever. He's never really been a true situational lefty. As a one-time starter, he's actually pretty even in terms of getting right- and left-handed batters out. Nevertheless, he did get enough game action to have his best season in years, and he was easily the best thing in the Mets pen not named Armando Benitez.

Aaron Heilman — Born: 12-Nov-78 — Age: 24 — Bats: R — Throws: R

YEAR	TM	LG	AGE	G	GS	IP	H	BB	SO	HR	ERA	EQERA	EQH9	EQBB9	EQSO9	EQHR9	PERA	VORP	STF
2001	SLU	FSL	22	7	7	38.3	26	13	39	0	2.35	3.37	7.5	3.6	6.0	0.3	3.31	9.1	19
2002	BIN	EAS	23	17	17	96.7	85	28	97	7	3.82	4.29	9.5	3.1	6.9	1.1	3.93	13.1	19
2002	NOR	INT	23	10	7	49.3	42	16	35	3	3.29	3.89	8.6	3.6	5.5	0.8	3.95	8.8	8
2003	*NYM*	*NL*	*24*	*15*	*11*	*73.0*	*68*	*30*	*61*	*7*	*3.92*	*4.44*	*8.7*	*3.2*	*6.6*	*0.9*	*4.41*	*9.2*	*10*

Breakout: 16%   Improve: 44%   Collapse: 17%

The Mets' first round choice in 2001, Heilman should be ready to step into the rotation this spring or summer. There's a lot to like. He's got good mechanics, throws hard, never seems to get shaken up, and if he perfects his splitter, he'll have command of four pitches in a sinker-slider repertoire. He did carry a heavy workload in college, which brings up the one thing you can't like about him, since he's a Domer, and it's hard to like anything associated with Notre Dame. The time when Heilman will be a very good third starter is close at hand.

Scott Kazmir — Born: 24-Jan-84 — Age: 19 — Bats: L — Throws: L

YEAR	TM	LG	AGE	G	GS	IP	H	BB	SO	HR	ERA	EQERA	EQH9	EQBB9	EQSO9	EQHR9	PERA	VORP	STF
2002	BRO	NYP	18	5	5	18.0	5	7	34	0	0.50	1.81	3.5	5.2	9.6	0.3	1.73	7.4	36

By happy accident, Kazmir fell to the 15th pick of the 2002 draft after being named Baseball America's High School Player of the Year. The expectation was that he'd want one of Jupiter's moons as a signing bonus, and instead he settled for only a couple of million. Kazmir comes at you again and again with heat that gives everyone the willies, a slider he's mastering, and a changeup he already knows how and when to spot. He's on the fast track, and one of the few people below High-A worth noting this early.

Bob Keppel
Born: 11-Jun-82   Age: 21   Bats: R   Throws: R

YEAR	TM	LG	AGE	G	GS	IP	H	BB	SO	HR	ERA	EQERA	EQH9	EQBB9	EQSO9	EQHR9	PERA	VORP	STF
2000	KNG	APL	18	8	6	29.0	31	13	29	1	6.83	9.05	15.6	6.3	5.0	1.0	7.66	-11.5	-13
2001	CMB	SAL	19	26	20	124.3	118	25	87	6	3.11	5.68	12.1	2.8	3.6	1.1	5.74	-2.6	-4
2002	SLU	FSL	20	27	26	152.0	162	43	109	13	4.32	6.13	13.1	3.3	4.7	1.9	6.38	-10.6	0

A supplemental first round choice in 2000, Keppel has been pushed hard, and he's still very raw. Nevertheless, he's survived. It almost goes without saying that he throws hard, but he hasn't mastered his breaking stuff yet; his slider doesn't consistently bite, and his curve can tumble. He's still learning, but he hasn't been clobbered yet.

Satoru Komiyama
Born: 15-Sep-65   Age: 37   Bats: R   Throws: R

YEAR	TM	LG	AGE	G	GS	IP	H	BB	SO	HR	ERA	EQERA	EQH9	EQBB9	EQSO9	EQHR9	PERA	VORP	STF
2000	YKO	JCL	34	26	24	161.3	166	37	108	24	3.96	4.64	9.8	2.2	5.1	1.4	4.87	15.4	4
2001	YKO	JCL	35	24	24	148.7	150	30	74	9	3.03	3.87	9.7	1.7	4.0	0.6	3.94	27.0	5
2002	NYM	NL	36	25	0	43.3	53	12	33	7	5.61	6.11	11.9	2.3	6.1	1.6	6.10	-3.5	-6
2002	NOR	INT	36	17	6	44.3	27	9	43	4	1.42	2.30	6.3	2.2	7.5	1.2	2.56	15.5	14
2003	*NYM*	*NL*	*37*	*27*	*6*	*56.3*	*62*	*17*	*39*	*7*	*4.23*	*4.79*	*10.3*	*2.3*	*5.4*	*1.2*	*4.93*	*5.6*	*-5*

Breakout: 8%   Improve: 35%   Collapse: 36%

The "Greg Maddux of Japan" turned out to be the Greg Maddux of the greater Norfolk metropolitan area, although to be fair, the Mets didn't really give him an extended opportunity. But when you don't throw hard, you're old, and you don't fool anybody, even your manager's idiosyncratic affection for Japanese imports peters out. A team like the Brewers or D-Rays could do worse than taking a chance with him.

Al Leiter
Born: 23-Oct-65   Age: 37   Bats: L   Throws: L

YEAR	TM	LG	AGE	G	GS	IP	H	BB	SO	HR	ERA	EQERA	EQH9	EQBB9	EQSO9	EQHR9	PERA	VORP	STF
2000	NYM	NL	34	31	31	208.0	176	76	200	19	3.20	3.46	7.9	2.7	7.7	0.8	3.45	47.3	25
2001	NYM	NL	35	29	29	187.3	178	46	142	18	3.32	3.89	9.2	2.1	5.9	0.8	3.86	33.6	14
2002	NYM	NL	36	33	33	204.3	194	69	172	23	3.48	4.47	9.2	2.7	6.7	1.1	4.44	23.5	15
2003	*NYM*	*NL*	*37*	*28*	*25*	*163.3*	*157*	*51*	*129*	*17*	*3.73*	*4.22*	*9.0*	*2.4*	*6.2*	*1.0*	*4.23*	*23.8*	*13*

Breakout: 17%   Improve: 45%   Collapse: 15%

Leiter's in New York, he's a local, and he's a stand-up guy, so he assumes a larger place on the stage than his performance would really make you think he deserves. Last year, he definitely showed his age; 20 unearned runs make his ERA look superficially neato, but he was hardly the staff ace. If anything, Astacio was over the first four months, before his meltdown. As he's gotten older, Leiter's gotten more subtle, relying more and more on a cut fastball; the days when he was credited with being able to throw a pork chop past a wolf are pretty well gone. The trends generally aren't positive, so don't expect him to suddenly bounce back to where he was in 1998 or 2000.

Jason Middlebrook
Born: 26-Jun-75   Age: 28   Bats: R   Throws: R

YEAR	TM	LG	AGE	G	GS	IP	H	BB	SO	HR	ERA	EQERA	EQH9	EQBB9	EQSO9	EQHR9	PERA	VORP	STF
2000	MOB	SOU	25	24	24	120.0	133	52	75	15	6.15	7.84	13.6	4.5	4.1	2.2	7.30	-31.1	-21
2001	MOB	SOU	26	10	9	52.7	36	9	51	1	1.20	2.50	7.6	1.8	5.9	0.3	2.53	17.6	19
2001	POR	PCL	26	15	15	90.3	86	23	66	5	3.29	4.02	9.8	2.8	4.9	0.6	4.04	14.9	7
2001	SDP	NL	26	4	3	19.3	18	10	10	6	5.13	5.60	8.3	4.3	4.0	2.6	6.37	-0.2	-21
2002	POR	PCL	27	10	7	36.7	42	13	32	6	5.64	7.49	13.0	3.9	6.4	2.1	6.60	-8.2	-10
2002	SDP	NL	27	12	2	35.3	31	15	28	1	5.10	4.13	8.1	3.4	6.3	0.3	3.79	5.1	6
2002	NOR	INT	27	5	5	23.7	13	1	22	1	2.66	2.24	5.4	0.5	7.0	0.6	1.63	8.6	28
2002	NYM	NL	27	3	3	16.0	13	7	14	1	3.94	3.88	7.8	3.5	7.0	0.6	3.69	2.9	16
2003	*NYM*	*NL*	*28*	*19*	*11*	*71.7*	*74*	*29*	*52*	*9*	*4.34*	*4.91*	*9.6*	*3.1*	*5.7*	*1.1*	*4.79*	*7.2*	*0*

Breakout: 19%   Improve: 45%   Collapse: 22%

For those of you who remember the bitterly fought waiver wire war of 1996, waged by the Reds and the Royals for the services of the generally nondescript Tim Pugh, we give you the Mets v. Padres scrum over Middlebrook. The two teams claimed him back and forth in 2000, and the Mets finally got him back in trade in 2002. As if his season wasn't interesting enough, consistent with a past riddled with injuries, he fought off back trouble, a groin strain, and shoulder tendonitis, and despite all of that, still managed to pitch pretty well. He throws in the low 90s, gets a couple of different breaks on his slider, and mixes in his change effectively. If he can stay healthy, he's the most ready internal option for the fifth slot in the rotation and could do well with it, but he's almost never completely healthy.

Matt Peterson | Born: 11-Feb-82 | Age: 21 | Bats: R | Throws: R

YEAR	TM	LG	AGE	G	GS	IP	H	BB	SO	HR	ERA	EQERA	EQH9	EQBB9	EQSO9	EQHR9	PERA	VORP	STF
2001	BRO	NYP	19	6	6	33.3	26	14	19	0	1.62	4.86	11.9	6.1	3.2	0.3	4.91	2.4	-8
2001	CMB	SAL	19	18	14	79.3	87	29	72	9	4.99	7.78	15.4	5.4	5.0	2.7	8.51	-20.1	-14
2002	CMB	SAL	20	26	26	137.7	109	61	153	13	3.86	5.81	11.0	5.9	6.5	2.4	5.62	-4.7	3
2002	SLU	FSL	20	1	1	6.0	5	2	5	0	1.50	3.90	9.4	3.8	5.4	0.3	4.14	1.1	15

More of a small forward than another one of the Mets' offensive tackles who happens to pitch, the 6′5″ Peterson is another hard thrower with a solid curve and developing change. A high school pitcher selected in the second round in 2000, he exemplifies the pros and the cons of such a selection: he's projectable, looks good, seems talented, and could blow out a joint (hmmm, perhaps not the right word in this organization) before he reaches Norfolk.

Steve Reed | Born: 11-Mar-66 | Age: 37 | Bats: R | Throws: R

YEAR	TM	LG	AGE	G	GS	IP	H	BB	SO	HR	ERA	EQERA	EQH9	EQBB9	EQSO9	EQHR9	PERA	VORP	STF
2000	CLE	AL	34	57	0	56.0	58	21	39	7	4.34	3.90	8.5	2.7	6.0	0.9	3.96	9.2	-2
2001	CLE	AL	35	32	0	27.3	22	10	21	3	3.63	2.94	6.4	3.0	6.4	0.9	3.21	7.4	1
2001	ATL	NL	35	39	0	31.0	30	13	25	3	3.48	4.39	9.5	3.6	6.3	0.8	4.32	3.4	-4
2002	SDP	NL	36	40	0	41.0	33	10	36	2	1.98	2.44	7.4	2.0	7.0	0.5	3.06	13.4	11
2002	NYM	NL	36	24	0	26.0	23	4	14	0	2.08	2.55	8.7	1.3	4.4	0.2	2.85	8.2	0
2003	COL	NL	37	55	0	49.0	54	16	36	6	4.15	3.59	9.5	2.5	6.2	0.9	4.03	11.1	-1

Breakout: 21%   Improve: 45%   Collapse: 28%

OK, you want to talk about freaky platoon swings? Reed went from a 2001 season where all lefties hit .519/.620/.904 (long past the point some people would just have him intentionally walk all of them) to .181/.258/.217. Not consistently a side-armer but someone who usually comes at you from that angle, he's still had his most success over the past several seasons as a situational right-hander, but it looks like he was more effective using his curve and slider and changing his arm angles this past year. A longtime BP favorite, he can continue to be a nice veteran bit part for the right (low) price.

Grant Roberts | Born: 13-Sep-77 | Age: 25 | Bats: R | Throws: R

YEAR	TM	LG	AGE	G	GS	IP	H	BB	SO	HR	ERA	EQERA	EQH9	EQBB9	EQSO9	EQHR9	PERA	VORP	STF
2000	NOR	INT	22	25	25	157.3	154	63	115	6	3.38	4.40	10.0	3.7	5.7	0.4	4.41	19.3	15
2001	NOR	INT	23	30	6	67.7	80	19	54	4	4.52	6.15	12.6	3.0	5.8	0.7	5.82	-5.4	-1
2001	NYM	NL	23	16	0	26.0	24	8	29	2	3.81	3.80	8.9	2.6	8.7	0.6	3.75	4.6	23
2002	BIN	EAS	24	1	1	1.0	0	0	1	0	0.00	0.11	0.1	0.5	6.3	0.2	0.11	0.6	19
2002	NYM	NL	24	34	0	45.0	43	16	31	3	2.20	3.31	9.3	2.9	5.5	0.6	4.20	10.3	0
2003	NYM	NL	25	37	2	54.0	53	21	41	5	3.78	4.28	9.1	3.0	5.9	0.8	4.38	7.2	-3

Breakout: 20%   Improve: 50%   Collapse: 15%

Smokey had to be shut down early with a bit of shoulder tendonitis, but the Mets made the right decision to move him into the pen. He's consistently in the low 90s with his heat, which has great movement, but his other pitches have always come up short. Assuming they forgive him his past indiscretions—and heck, they forgave Steve Phillips his, and tolerated Bobby Valentine, right?—he should continue to be an asset in the bullpen.

Phil Seibel | Born: 28-Jan-79 | Age: 24 | Bats: L | Throws: L

YEAR	TM	LG	AGE	G	GS	IP	H	BB	SO	HR	ERA	EQERA	EQH9	EQBB9	EQSO9	EQHR9	PERA	VORP	STF
2001	JUP	FSL	22	29	21	134.3	144	28	88	12	3.95	6.82	14.7	2.4	4.2	2.2	6.53	-19.8	-8
2002	BIN	EAS	23	28	25	149.7	147	49	114	17	3.97	5.25	10.9	3.6	5.3	1.7	5.03	4.2	2

Yes, you can be a crafty, battling lefty before you turn 24. Seibel doesn't throw hard, but he's got a good curve and change. He came over as part of the bounty from placing Bruce Chen on his fourth different NL East team; how much longer can the Marlins resist? Anyway, most guys like this don't grow up to be Greg Hibbard, let alone Jamie Moyer, but every once in a while, one does. Seibel got used in relief in the AFL. Considering the Mets' wealth in lefty relief, that might have been a useful bit of showcasing.

Jae Seo   Born: 24-May-77   Age: 26   Bats: R   Throws: R

YEAR	TM	LG	AGE	G	GS	IP	H	BB	SO	HR	ERA	EQERA	EQH9	EQBB9	EQSO9	EQHR9	PERA	VORP	STF
2001	SLU	FSL	24	6	5	25.3	21	6	19	2	3.56	4.78	10.3	2.6	4.6	1.8	4.56	2.0	-4
2001	BIN	EAS	24	12	10	60.3	44	11	47	3	1.94	2.72	7.6	2.2	4.8	0.7	2.91	18.6	10
2001	NOR	INT	24	9	9	47.3	53	6	25	4	3.42	4.84	12.1	1.4	3.8	1.1	5.12	3.5	0
2002	BIN	EAS	25	1	0	5.0	5	1	6	1	5.40	5.80	11.9	2.3	8.7	3.1	5.40	-0.2	13
2002	NOR	INT	25	26	24	128.7	145	22	87	14	3.99	5.34	11.6	1.9	5.3	1.5	5.42	2.3	2
2002	NYM	NL	25	1	0	1.0	0	0	1	0	0.00	0.38	0.0	0.4	7.6	0.1	0.38	0.6	28
2003	NYM	NL	26	14	8	54.3	59	16	35	7	4.34	4.91	10.3	2.2	5.1	1.1	4.76	6.0	-1

Breakout: 14%   Improve: 48%   Collapse: 25%

The bad news is that Seo has lost a lot of velocity since having surgery on his elbow in 1999. The good news is that he got a lot sharper in 2002 once the Mets broke him of his ritual of not eating the day of his start. He's still in the low 90s, mixes in a splitter that makes him tough on lefties looking for something to drive, and usually tries to finish hitters off with his changeup. He's probably never going to be much more than an adequate fifth starter, but that's a higher upside than some people felt Cory Lidle had not so long ago.

Pat Strange   Born: 23-Aug-80   Age: 22   Bats: R   Throws: R

YEAR	TM	LG	AGE	G	GS	IP	H	BB	SO	HR	ERA	EQERA	EQH9	EQBB9	EQSO9	EQHR9	PERA	VORP	STF
2000	SLU	FSL	19	19	13	88.0	78	32	77	4	3.58	5.79	10.5	4.2	5.6	1.0	4.96	-2.9	5
2000	BIN	EAS	19	10	10	55.3	62	30	36	2	4.56	5.86	11.7	5.5	4.4	0.6	6.18	-2.2	-1
2001	BIN	EAS	20	26	24	153.3	171	52	106	18	4.87	6.38	12.2	4.2	4.4	1.6	6.39	-15.0	-2
2002	NOR	INT	21	29	25	165.0	165	59	109	12	3.82	4.91	10.2	3.9	5.1	1.0	5.01	10.8	8
2002	NYM	NL	21	5	0	8.0	6	1	4	0	1.13	1.75	7.5	1.0	4.2	0.2	2.22	3.2	5
2003	NYM	NL	22	12	8	56.7	61	28	39	7	5.05	5.72	10.1	3.9	5.4	1.1	5.54	0.2	-4

Breakout: 11%   Improve: 46%   Collapse: 28%

A big guy with a full-effort delivery and doubtful mechanics, Strange nevertheless manages to not be a power pitcher. He's more a sinker-slider guy with a plus changeup, generating a goodly number of ground ball outs. He could have a nice Walt Terrell sort of career if he avoids too many mechanical breakdowns and continues to improve command of his slider, which is less than some scouts hope for, and more than some statheads expect.

Scott Strickland   Born: 26-Apr-76   Age: 27   Bats: R   Throws: R

YEAR	TM	LG	AGE	G	GS	IP	H	BB	SO	HR	ERA	EQERA	EQH9	EQBB9	EQSO9	EQHR9	PERA	VORP	STF
2000	MON	NL	24	49	0	48.0	38	16	48	3	3.00	2.66	6.8	2.4	7.9	0.5	2.75	14.5	18
2001	MON	NL	25	77	0	81.3	67	41	85	9	3.21	3.67	7.3	4.2	7.9	0.9	3.79	15.4	7
2002	MON	NL	26	1	0	1.0	0	0	2	0	0.00	0.27	0.0	0.4	15.1	0.1	0.27	0.6	72
2002	NYM	NL	26	68	0	67.7	61	33	67	7	3.59	4.30	8.6	3.9	7.9	1.0	4.57	8.1	3
2003	NYM	NL	27	57	0	78.3	66	33	73	7	3.30	3.74	7.9	3.3	7.3	0.9	3.98	14.6	5

Breakout: 19%   Improve: 51%   Collapse: 15%

Strickland can get recklessly aggressive with his fastball, leading to the Aurelio Lopez–style Senor Smoke moments of two varieties, either inspired mitt-popping strikeouts or jacktastic smites that crash into the bleachers harder than Skylab. His success and struggles are intimately related to his platoon split, since he doesn't have something off-speed to freeze lefties with.

John Thomson   Born: 01-Oct-73   Age: 29   Bats: R   Throws: R

YEAR	TM	LG	AGE	G	GS	IP	H	BB	SO	HR	ERA	EQERA	EQH9	EQBB9	EQSO9	EQHR9	PERA	VORP	STF
2001	CSP	PCL	27	12	12	68.0	74	13	52	6	3.31	3.47	9.2	2.0	4.9	0.9	4.16	15.4	7
2001	COL	NL	27	14	14	93.7	84	25	68	15	4.03	3.75	7.9	2.2	5.6	1.2	3.45	18.3	11
2002	COL	NL	28	21	21	127.3	136	27	76	21	4.88	4.70	9.6	1.7	4.7	1.4	4.29	11.4	4
2002	NYM	NL	28	9	9	54.3	65	17	31	7	4.31	6.16	11.7	2.6	4.6	1.3	5.83	-4.0	-2
2003	TEX	AL	29	27	25	161.0	187	40	92	24	4.97	4.75	10.1	2.0	5.0	1.1	4.50	17.9	6

Breakout: 13%   Improve: 50%   Collapse: 18%

That's right, Thomson came over from Coors Field and pitched worse despite lowering his ERA. Nevertheless, on the year, he gave his team quality starts in half of his 30 times out (two were blown after the sixth). The two months as a Met must have left him missing the dangerous life, since he returned to Texas and a hitter's park. That projection seems about right; his road ERA over the last three years is 4.52, and he'll be in the DH league now.

Steve Trachsel — Born: 31-Oct-70 — Age: 32 — Bats: R — Throws: R

YEAR	TM	LG	AGE	G	GS	IP	H	BB	SO	HR	ERA	EQERA	EQH9	EQBB9	EQSO9	EQHR9	PERA	VORP	STF
2000	TBY	AL	29	23	23	137.7	160	49	78	16	4.58	4.34	9.9	2.6	4.9	0.9	4.49	17.8	5
2000	TOR	AL	29	11	11	63.0	72	25	32	10	5.29	4.59	9.3	2.9	4.4	1.2	4.80	6.4	-1
2001	NYM	NL	30	28	28	173.7	168	47	144	28	4.46	4.57	9.2	2.3	6.4	1.4	4.49	18.0	12
2002	NYM	NL	31	30	30	173.7	170	69	105	16	3.37	4.46	9.5	3.2	4.9	0.9	4.64	20.2	2
2003	NYM	NL	32	28	24	154.7	158	56	99	17	4.24	4.80	9.6	2.8	5.0	1.1	4.82	12.2	2

Breakout: 10%   Improve: 40%   Collapse: 16%

Word to the wise: do NOT take a baseball-disinterested friend or date to a game where Steve Trachsel is scheduled to pitch. You see, there's slow, and slug slow, and frozen slug crushed beneath a sprinting glacier slow, and then there's Trachsel slow, that unit of time where the passage of every moment has the mind-gnawing tedium of a Super Bowl halftime show. We're not saying that keeping the Mets and Trachsel out of prime-time postseason broadcasts is a national priority, but it probably is in the best interests of baseball. As long as the commissioner is coming up with lame ways to make the All-Star game useful, he'll probably look into this next.

Tyler Walker — Born: 15-May-76 — Age: 27 — Bats: R — Throws: R

YEAR	TM	LG	AGE	G	GS	IP	H	BB	SO	HR	ERA	EQERA	EQH9	EQBB9	EQSO9	EQHR9	PERA	VORP	STF
2000	BIN	EAS	24	22	22	121.0	82	55	111	3	2.75	3.40	7.0	4.5	6.2	0.4	3.12	28.3	14
2000	NOR	INT	24	5	5	26.3	29	9	17	0	2.40	3.60	11.3	3.1	5.0	0.2	4.61	5.6	8
2001	SLU	FSL	25	4	4	15.7	19	3	11	0	8.03	7.91	13.7	2.1	4.3	0.3	6.30	-4.2	-7
2001	BIN	EAS	25	4	3	22.3	9	13	13	1	0.40	1.65	4.3	7.1	3.7	0.6	2.48	9.5	-7
2001	NOR	INT	25	8	8	40.3	34	8	35	7	4.02	4.95	9.3	2.1	6.2	2.2	4.44	2.5	6
2002	NOR	INT	26	28	25	142.0	152	38	109	13	3.99	4.99	10.9	2.9	6.0	1.2	5.26	8.0	4
2002	NYM	NL	26	5	1	10.7	11	5	7	3	5.89	6.32	9.7	3.7	5.2	2.7	6.62	-1.1	-22
2003	NYM	NL	27	17	11	73.7	72	30	53	8	4.18	4.73	9.2	3.2	5.7	1.0	4.75	6.3	2

Breakout: 16%   Improve: 49%   Collapse: 18%

Walker's been dinged up the last couple of years, requiring shoulder surgery in 2001, and having his knee 'scoped after 2002. But considering he's an ex-catcher, are we surprised that he needs to be patched up? He's still mastering off-speed stuff, but spins a nice curve and generally flirts with 90. He wasn't tremendously effective last year, but he might carve out a job as a swingman and middle reliever.

Dave Weathers — Born: 25-Sep-69 — Age: 33 — Bats: R — Throws: R

YEAR	TM	LG	AGE	G	GS	IP	H	BB	SO	HR	ERA	EQERA	EQH9	EQBB9	EQSO9	EQHR9	PERA	VORP	STF
2000	MIL	NL	30	69	0	76.3	73	32	50	7	3.07	3.70	9.1	3.1	5.3	0.7	3.92	14.2	-6
2001	MIL	NL	31	52	0	57.7	37	25	46	3	2.03	2.51	6.3	3.7	6.2	0.4	2.56	18.4	2
2001	CHC	NL	31	28	0	28.3	28	9	20	3	3.18	3.52	9.1	2.7	5.5	0.9	4.23	5.8	-5
2002	NYM	NL	32	71	0	77.3	69	36	61	6	2.91	3.96	8.6	3.7	6.3	0.7	4.28	12.2	-3
2003	NYM	NL	33	55	0	60.7	58	27	45	6	3.80	4.30	9.0	3.4	5.8	0.9	4.59	8.2	-6

Breakout: 10%   Improve: 46%   Collapse: 23%

In the interests of maintaining competitive balance in the NL East, the Mets apparently felt obligated to provide matching funds to compete with the Phillies' wacky "Burn Bucks!" campaign to keep every reliever everywhere employed. Stormy just happened to be the beneficiary in this case. He's adequate, but it isn't hard to scare up adequate, and it's usually a lot cheaper than Weathers.

Philadelphia Phillies

For most of their history the Philadelphia Phillies have been one of the clearest examples of what can happen when a franchise is perpetually mishandled. Their streak of 30 losing seasons in 31 years between 1918 and 1948 will hopefully never be matched by any team, but the past two decades have not been much better, with the team only posting three winning seasons since 1984. However, despite some of the downright bizarre and destructive moves the team has made over the past few years, there is truly cause for hope among Phillies fans. The 2003 Phillies look like a team with enormous talent and potential. While there are still warning signs of things that could go wrong, through a combination of good planning and good fortune, Ed Wade has built a legitimate championship contender.

Any consideration of the talent the Phillies have must start with the middle of the lineup. Last season Pat Burrell took enormous strides forward, living up to the potential he showed as the number one overall draft pick in 1998. Bobby Abreu continued to be the best anonymous player in the majors. In the off-season the Phillies added Jim Thome to form one of, if not the strongest middle of a lineup of any team in the majors. Using Clay Davenport's Equivalent Runs as a metric, last season Thome was the third-best hitter in the American League while Abreu and Burrell were seventh and 11th, respectively, in the National League. While a few other teams had two players near that level, no one had three. Thome May slide a little bit from the career highs he established last year, but his average production level still leaves him among the elite players in the game. Burrell is still in his mid-20s, so some additional improvement is quite possible. As a result, the Phillies could very well wind up with three batters in a row with on-base percentages over .400 and slugging percentages over .500, a prospect sure to give many pitchers sleepless nights.

That said, there still are five other position players needed to fill out the lineup, and there the outlook for the Phillies becomes substantially cloudier. Last season, even with Abreu and Burrell in the middle of the lineup, the Phillies were only eighth in the NL in runs scored, a fact which is due almost entirely to their lousy production with runners in scoring position. Indeed, using equivalent runs as a metric again, no team in 2002 underperformed their expected scoring level as badly as the Phillies did; they got runners on, but they were unable to drive them in. While bad luck was certainly a factor, this is also a reflection of the wide spread in talent in the Phillies lineup last year. When you rely on the likes of Travis Lee and Marlon Anderson to drive in runs, you are going to leave a lot of runners on base. The strength of the other positions in the lineup will go a long way toward determining whether the Phillies will score enough runs to be a top team.

There are mixed signs on that front. While the signing of Thome removes one of the gigantic holes in the lineup, there are other spots to worry about. For all the hype that surrounded his signing, David Bell is not a top-notch player and his performance last year only represents a minor upgrade over Anderson's efforts. Furthermore, Bell's near the age where players of his caliber can often decline rapidly. The four-year, $17 million signing could very easily turn into a dud.

The same could be said about the catcher position, where Mike Lieberthal was signed to a four-year extension. When he's been healthy, Lieberthal has been one of the best catchers in the NL over the past few years, but he's only made it through a full season without serious injury twice in the last five years. If he were to be injured again, he would most likely be replaced by Todd Pratt who is a perfectly respectable second catcher but is unlikely to produce enough as an everyday starter. Even if he does stay healthy, Lieberthal's a sub-par hitter vs. righties who'd do better in a semi-platoon with a Greg Myers type.

A third question mark is center field. While it won't be hard to improve on the wretched offensive performance of Doug Glanville, it remains to be seen whether the Phillies will stick with rookie Marlon Byrd if he starts slowly. If they don't, they're likely to use Ricky Ledee as a replacement and he's not much of an upgrade, even compared to Glanville the cipher.

Creating even more uncertainty is the lurking menace in the dugout. Larry Bowa has already run one all-star out of town after making Scott Rolen's life absolutely miserable, and there is no shortage of future targets. One particular concern has to be Jimmy Rollins, who regressed substantially last year. While Bowa has correctly identified that Rollins must improve his on-base skills to be an asset to the team, he's shown nothing to indicate he knows how to instill those skills. Instead of talking about the need for Rollins to improve his batting eye and draw more walks, he is talking about having Rollins bunt more and hit more ground balls to use his speed to get on base, just like Bowa did in his playing days. This conveniently ignores the reality that Bowa was an offensive liability for his entire playing career, just like most slap hitters are. If Rollins pays too much attention to Bowa's advice it could short-circuit what was a promising career and prove once again to Phillies fans that "Bowa" is a four letter word.

Putting it all together, the Phillies will field a lineup that will certainly score plenty of runs if everything goes right. But they missed an opportunity during the relatively slow free agent market this off-season to make some sanely priced acquisitions which would have helped considerably. Signing Ray Durham or Edgardo Alfonzo would have done far more to help the team than signing David Bell. If the Phillies find themselves in a close pennant race this fall, that missed opportunity could come back to haunt them.

As with the lineup, the pitching staff provides plenty of cause for optimism, but also considerable cause for concern. The rotation was already set up well at the end of last season with four talented, young starters. That rotation was substantially strengthened by John Schuerholz's infantile temper tantrum about baseball economics, which handed Kevin Millwood to the Phillies for some shiny rocks and pretty tinsel.

In Millwood, Randy Wolf, and Vicente Padilla, the Phillies have three starters who were among the top 30 starters in the majors last year who are all under 30 years old. The decision to hire Joe Kerrigan as pitching coach could also be a good move. Though he's made his bones by boosting the careers of second-chance pitchers, Kerrigan also knows how to manage a staff. Brett Myers and Brandon Duckworth should hopefully benefit from his guidance. In the longer term the Phillies have done a good job of establishing a steady stream of young pitchers coming through the minors, so they have options should openings arise in the rotation.

Those options may very well be needed due to the team's recent past. While the 2002 Phillies used their pitchers fairly sensibly, the long arm of Terry Francona's mismanagement of pitchers may still come back to haunt them. One victim of Francona's heavy workload fell by the wayside last season as Robert Person struggled for most of the year before finally revealing shoulder problems, which resulted in season-ending surgery. While the final tear occurred in 2002, the bulk of the damage was likely done in 1999 and 2000 when Person was ridden hard.

The other pitcher who was badly overworked by Francona is Randy Wolf, who has since become the ace of the Phillies staff. While he has managed to avoid serious injury so far, the damage from overwork tends to be cumulative, so he may still be on his way to Tommy John surgery. New acquisition Kevin Millwood has a history of shoulder problems, and while he seemed to have fully recovered from them last season, it's not unreasonable to wonder if he is a time bomb as well. While the Phillies have the depth to compensate in the long run for any injuries that might derail Wolf or Millwood, the short-term outlook is not as good and such injuries would derail a pennant chase.

The system's depth could also benefit the big league bullpen. The Phillies have struggled for years to assemble a consistent pen; Ed Wade's attempts have resembled a Wall Street investment banker's explanations of why analysts don't face a conflict of interest, namely somewhere between desperate and pathetic. In particular Wade has become obsessed with the need for proven veterans in the bullpen. Over the past few years he's brought in Jose Mesa, Ricky Bottalico, and Rheal Cormier as expensive free agents, traded young pitchers for Turk Wendell, Dennis Cook, and Dan Plesac, then inexplicably took Mike Timlin in the trade that sent Scott Rolen to the Cardinals. Only Plesac and Mesa have helped the Phils much.

Far cheaper and more effective than the veteran train wrecks in the bullpen were pitchers such as David Coggin and Carlos Silva, converted starters who didn't fit into the rotation but who were good enough to be worth keeping around. In 2001 Cliff Politte had filled a similar role for the team on the rare occasions that Larry Bowa deigned to use him; after he was traded to Toronto for Plesac, Politte picked up right where he left off. There's a lesson begging to be learned here, one that should have been slammed home by seeing Anaheim win the World Series with their low-rent bullpen: high-priced relievers are not worth the risk.

The Phillies have options in their system. They'd be better off trying to fill the last few bullpen slots with effective Triple-A relievers such as Cary Hiles, Elio Serrano, and Jeremy Wedel and starters who can't crack the rotation like Eric Junge,

Ryan Madson, and Joe Roa. Not all of them will pan out of course, but since they all lack big contracts and in most cases have options available, they can easily be shuttled back and forth while the team finds someone who will be effective. That flexibility is missing when you're stuck with the contracts of a Cormier or a Wendell. Wade has learned enough that he has not added more long-term contracts to the bullpen this off-season, but some of the past mistakes are still being touted as the answer for this season.

The organization deserves its share of credit for what it's done over the past few years. Thanks largely to assistant GM and former scouting director Mike Arbuckle, they've rebuilt their farm system from the vast wasteland it was half a dozen years ago into one of the game's best. Though Ed Wade's made plenty of blunders, his fleecing of Millwood from the Braves sets the team's pitching staff up nicely going forward. The Phillies have given themselves a real chance at competing, a substantial step up from the likes of the Brewers and Tigers, in whose company they dwelled just a few years ago.

Given the relative mediocrity of their division, the Phillies should contend for division titles over the next couple of years, and this is a core of what could be a dominant team over the next five seasons. They've picked a good time to make their move, getting fans excited just before they move into their posh new stadium; the new park will offer a vastly better lease than they've had at the Vet, further helping the cause.

The key questions: Have the Phillies learned enough to avoid surrounding their core with the same old dregs that have doomed them to futility in recent years? The Lieberthal contract says they've still got plenty to learn. And can they overcome a key weakness in Larry Bowa? Last year's Jeremy Giambi/Travis Lee fiasco says they might not, unless Wade signs enough Thomes to ensure even Bowa can't botch things. We'll find out soon enough. The Phillies could strike gold, or develop an uncanny resemblance to the White Sox clubs of the past few years, destined to wind up as a hallmark of missed opportunities.

HITTERS

Bob Abreu   RF   Born: 11-Mar-74   Age: 29   Bats: L   Throws: R

YEAR	TM	LG	AGE	AB	H	2B	3B	HR	BB	SO	SB	CS	AVG	OBP	SLG	MLVR	EQBA	EQOBP	EQSLG	EQMLVR	VORP	DEFENSE
2000	PHI	NL	26	576	182	42	10	25	100	116	28	8	.316	.418	.554	.323	.311	.406	.544	.297	62.1	151-RF 2
2001	PHI	NL	27	588	170	48	4	31	106	137	36	14	.289	.399	.543	.277	.290	.397	.544	.260	60.1	153-RF -4
2002	PHI	NL	28	572	176	50	6	20	104	117	31	12	.308	.417	.521	.341	.318	.421	.543	.327	64.7	147-RF -2
2003	PHI	NL	29	536	155	35	5	22	96	110	26	8	.290	.399	.499	.208	.297	.402	.526	.236	40.9	

Breakout: 6%   Improve: 37%   Collapse: 13%

Abreu is the same player he's been for several years. He hits for average, knows the strike zone, has good power, and can gain a few runs with his speed on the basepaths. In short, exactly the sort of player who can help a team a lot more than is commonly realized. After the Scott Rolen fiasco, the Phillies wised up and signed Abreu to a lucrative five-year extension. He's worth it.

Marlon Anderson   2B   Born: 06-Jan-74   Age: 29   Bats: L   Throws: R

YEAR	TM	LG	AGE	AB	H	2B	3B	HR	BB	SO	SB	CS	AVG	OBP	SLG	MLVR	EQBA	EQOBP	EQSLG	EQMLVR	VORP	DEFENSE
2000	SWB	INT	26	397	121	18	8	8	39	43	24	10	.305	.374	.451	.149	.284	.343	.419	-.012	21.1	94-2B -3
2000	PHI	NL	26	162	37	8	1	1	12	22	2	2	.228	.282	.309	-.356	.227	.272	.307	-.347	-5.7	40-2B 0
2001	PHI	NL	27	522	153	30	2	11	35	74	8	5	.293	.340	.421	.012	.298	.343	.430	.015	33.0	134-2B 5
2002	PHI	NL	28	539	139	30	6	8	42	71	5	1	.258	.317	.380	-.045	.270	.324	.403	-.081	18.3	129-2B -6
2003	TBY	AL	29	489	131	27	3	10	38	65	6	2	.268	.323	.398	-.041	.275	.332	.415	-.043	14.4	

Breakout: 13%   Improve: 48%   Collapse: 16%

Anderson's 2001 season now looks like a career year instead of a breakthrough year. His lousy on-base percentage makes him a hole in the lineup, and while his softball shortfielder approach to second-base defense is novel, it's not that effective. After signing David Bell, the Phillies moved Placido Polanco to second so Anderson's days were numbered. Like a lot of people on the lam and looking to catch a break, he'll be playing in major league baseball's equivant of Indy ball in Tampa Bay. He might take Brent Abernathy's job.

Pat Burrell   LF   Born: 10-Oct-76   Age: 26   Bats: R   Throws: R

YEAR	TM	LG	AGE	AB	H	2B	3B	HR	BB	SO	SB	CS	AVG	OBP	SLG	MLVR	EQBA	EQOBP	EQSLG	EQMLVR	VORP	DEFENSE		
2000	SWB	INT	23	143	42	15	1	4	32	36	1	1	.294	.423	.497	.279	.274	.387	.459	.114	8.4	29-LF	-1	10-1B 0
2000	PHI	NL	23	408	106	27	1	18	63	139	0	0	.260	.360	.463	.040	.260	.352	.462	.043	16.2	56-1B	-6	40-LF 0
2001	PHI	NL	24	539	139	29	2	27	70	162	2	1	.258	.349	.469	.064	.265	.352	.478	.070	24.7	132-LF	-6	
2002	PHI	NL	25	586	165	39	2	37	89	153	1	0	.282	.379	.544	.291	.290	.382	.568	.268	57.1	154-LF	-7	
2003	PHI	NL	26	548	148	32	2	31	89	146	3	3	.271	.375	.503	.159	.277	.377	.530	.184	32.5			

Breakout: 12%   Improve: 47%   Collapse: 10%

Now we see why he was such a highly touted prospect. Freed from the "guidance" of Richie Hebner, Burrell improved every aspect of his offensive game to become one of the top hitters in the league. While his defense in left is at best average, that's a vast improvement from his early days out there. An MVP-caliber season is quite possible for 2003.

Marlon Byrd   CF   Born: 30-Aug-77   Age: 25   Bats: R   Throws: R

YEAR	TM	LG	AGE	AB	H	2B	3B	HR	BB	SO	SB	CS	AVG	OBP	SLG	MLVR	EQBA	EQOBP	EQSLG	EQMLVR	VORP	DEFENSE
2000	PIE	SAL	22	515	159	29	13	17	51	110	41	5	.309	.382	.515	.313	.235	.286	.394	-.192	-14.0	103-LF 0
2001	REA	EAS	23	510	161	22	8	28	52	93	32	5	.316	.391	.555	.357	.274	.341	.478	.059	33.7	133-CF -3
2002	SWB	INT	24	538	160	37	7	15	46	98	15	1	.297	.365	.476	.191	.277	.341	.450	.022	27.8	129-CF -12
2003	PHI	NL	25	314	84	18	2	11	28	61	8	5	.268	.333	.449	.021	.274	.335	.473	.039	12.4	

Breakout: 23%   Improve: 60%   Collapse: 19%

The hype around Byrd has some people expecting him to immediately match the production of Abreu and Burrell, which is a highly unfair burden to put on a rookie. It's still reasonable to expect Byrd to be a solid player with moderate power and good understanding of the strike zone. That alone will represent a huge upgrade for the Phillies in center field.

Travis Chapman   3B   Born: 05-Jun-78   Age: 25   Bats: R   Throws: R

YEAR	TM	LG	AGE	AB	H	2B	3B	HR	BB	SO	SB	CS	AVG	OBP	SLG	MLVR	EQBA	EQOBP	EQSLG	EQMLVR	VORP	DEFENSE
2000	BAT	NYP	22	174	55	10	2	1	12	24	0	1	.316	.383	.414	.214	.236	.272	.320	-.323	-5.8	45-3B 2
2001	CLR	FSL	23	329	101	22	0	4	44	39	3	1	.307	.406	.410	.201	.254	.326	.343	-.173	1.4	88-3B -2
2002	REA	EAS	24	478	144	35	1	15	54	77	3	1	.301	.394	.473	.227	.258	.331	.408	-.071	14.8	105-3B -1
2003	DET	AL	25	198	50	11	1	4	15	32	2	1	.254	.312	.382	-.089	.263	.324	.412	-.071	3.1	

Breakout: 26%   Improve: 56%   Collapse: 17%

Chapman has consistently shown a good batting eye as he moved through the minors, but this season he suddenly developed considerable power. He managed to do this with one of the goofiest stances you'll ever see. Imagine Craig Counsell's stretch, add in a front foot that looks like a ballet dancer standing "en pointe" and you get the basic idea. It's hard to argue with the results. He's wound up in Detroit after foolishly being left unprotected for the Rule 5 draft. If he gets a chance to play he could surprise some, and he has a shot at the job at third.

Nate Espy   1B   Born: 24-Apr-78   Age: 25   Bats: R   Throws: R

YEAR	TM	LG	AGE	AB	H	2B	3B	HR	BB	SO	SB	CS	AVG	OBP	SLG	MLVR	EQBA	EQOBP	EQSLG	EQMLVR	VORP	DEFENSE
2000	PIE	SAL	22	452	141	32	2	21	101	105	7	0	.312	.442	.531	.409	.231	.334	.393	-.105	-1.2	128-1B -3
2001	CLR	FSL	23	470	134	31	2	11	88	90	6	2	.285	.404	.430	.206	.230	.324	.355	-.176	-10.7	124-1B -17
2002	REA	EAS	24	517	138	28	2	14	73	83	18	1	.267	.365	.410	.073	.230	.312	.357	-.196	-14.1	136-1B -16
2003	PHI	NL	25	183	45	10	1	5	22	36	3	1	.247	.332	.394	-.068	.253	.334	.415	-.055	-.6	

Breakout: 39%   Improve: 67%   Collapse: 16%

Espy continues to be a solid hitter as he works his way up through the minor league system and the Phillies continue to try and discount him as a prospect. At one point last season they claimed that he was most likely going to wind up as a DH because of a weak throwing arm, which seems an odd claim for a first baseman. Espy won't be a star player, but for a team with a hole at first base, he would be a reasonable cheap alternative. He could also be a useful bench player.

Johnny Estrada   C   Born: 27-Jun-76   Age: 27   Bats: B   Throws: R

YEAR	TM	LG	AGE	AB	H	2B	3B	HR	BB	SO	SB	CS	AVG	OBP	SLG	MLVR	EQBA	EQOBP	EQSLG	EQMLVR	VORP	DEFENSE	
2000	REA	EAS	24	356	105	18	0	12	10	20	1	0	.295	.322	.447	.078	.258	.273	.395	-.198	3.2	83-C	6
2001	SWB	INT	25	131	38	13	0	0	5	6	0	0	.290	.321	.389	.000	.273	.308	.371	-.155	2.6	30-C	2
2001	PHI	NL	25	298	68	15	0	8	16	32	0	0	.228	.277	.359	-.243	.236	.282	.369	-.234	.1	79-C	0
2002	SWB	INT	26	434	121	27	0	11	26	53	1	0	.279	.327	.417	.037	.263	.311	.398	-.118	12.7	112-C	-1
2003	ATL	NL	27	160	40	8	0	4	11	20	1	1	.251	.302	.386	-.128	.254	.302	.400	-.132	1.6		

Breakout: 23%   Improve: 49%   Collapse: 25%

Estrada returned to Triple-A with Mike Lieberthal having the rare healthy season, and promptly got the organization excited with a hot start. As the season wore on his offense returned to the same mediocre level seen in years past. He'll make a fine backup, but he's not going to be a starter for a championship team. Not that the Braves are likely to find out, since flipping Kevin Millwood for Estrada is a nifty way to crush a team's championship hopes.

Jeremy Giambi   1B/DH   Born: 30-Sep-74   Age: 28   Bats: L   Throws: L

YEAR	TM	LG	AGE	AB	H	2B	3B	HR	BB	SO	SB	CS	AVG	OBP	SLG	MLVR	EQBA	EQOBP	EQSLG	EQMLVR	VORP	DEFENSE			
2000	OAK	AL	25	260	66	10	2	10	32	61	0	0	.254	.342	.423	-.057	.264	.345	.442	.007	5.4	42-RF	-1		
2001	OAK	AL	26	371	105	26	0	12	63	83	0	1	.283	.393	.450	.146	.300	.408	.483	.206	28.4	35-RF	-4		
2002	OAK	AL	27	157	43	7	0	8	27	40	0	0	.274	.390	.471	.170	.291	.406	.513	.234	13.9	34-LF	-1		
2002	PHI	NL	27	156	38	10	0	12	52	54	0	1	.244	.435	.538	.332	.255	.439	.559	.313	20.3	18-1B	-1	15-RF	-2
2003	BOS	AL	28	270	69	15	1	12	47	66	0	0	.257	.370	.448	.090	.263	.379	.470	.099	9.8				

Breakout: 5%   Improve: 33%   Collapse: 33%

Dumped by Oakland in one of the strangest deals you'll ever see, Giambi rotted on the Phillies' bench thanks to Larry Bowa's unwillingness to try to outscore the opposing team. Giambi's natural position is designated hitter, since he's a brutal fielder at any position. That said, Bowa's reluctance to use him last season bordered on the inexplicable. Travis Lee's bat was an unmitigated disaster with little to make you think it would get any better any time soon and Giambi scorched the ball whenever he got a chance. Giambi's been traded to the Red Sox for Josh Hancock, so the Phillies turned John Mabry into a Giambi rental and a nondescript minor league pitcher. Boston will appreciate his offensive skills and put them to far greater use.

Doug Glanville   CF   Born: 25-Aug-70   Age: 32   Bats: R   Throws: R

YEAR	TM	LG	AGE	AB	H	2B	3B	HR	BB	SO	SB	CS	AVG	OBP	SLG	MLVR	EQBA	EQOBP	EQSLG	EQMLVR	VORP	DEFENSE	
2000	PHI	NL	29	637	175	27	6	8	31	76	31	8	.275	.310	.374	-.171	.275	.301	.373	-.164	2.5	141-CF	3
2001	PHI	NL	30	634	166	24	3	14	19	91	28	6	.262	.288	.375	-.176	.269	.293	.385	-.166	2.1	150-CF	8
2002	PHI	NL	31	422	105	16	3	6	25	57	19	2	.249	.294	.344	-.142	.261	.301	.364	-.187	-.9	100-CF	0
2003	TEX	AL	32	356	91	17	2	5	16	48	12	4	.256	.291	.362	-.151	.258	.295	.366	-.187	-4.9		

Breakout: 9%   Improve: 37%   Collapse: 25%

Glanville is one of the most interesting people in the major leagues. Unfortunately, his baseball skills are substantially less interesting. His batting average has dropped consistently for three straight seasons. Combine that decline with his lack of power and inability to take a walk and you've got trouble. After inexplicably staying in the starting lineup most of last season he finally lost his job this off-season, signing with the Rangers. Texas doesn't have many viable alternatives, so the Metroplex may get more than its share of Glanville's popgun production.

Dave Hollins   1B   Born: 25-May-66   Age: 37   Bats: B   Throws: R

YEAR	TM	LG	AGE	AB	H	2B	3B	HR	BB	SO	SB	CS	AVG	OBP	SLG	MLVR	EQBA	EQOBP	EQSLG	EQMLVR	VORP	DEFENSE	
2000	ROC	INT	34	70	19	2	0	0	9	12	1	0	.271	.362	.300	-.108	.268	.340	.282	-.222	-.6	10-3B	0
2001	BUF	INT	35	316	86	25	2	16	45	79	0	0	.272	.375	.516	.230	.254	.348	.483	.060	13.9	16-1B	-3
2002	PHI	NL	36	17	2	0	0	0	0	3	0	1	.118	.167	.118	-.733	.176	.216	.176	-.667	-2.1		
2003	PHI	NL	37	89	19	4	0	2	15	23	1	1	.217	.342	.333	-.146	.222	.344	.351	-.139	-2.3		

Breakout: 8%   Improve: 41%   Collapse: 34%

The Phillies made many bizarre moves in 2002, but putting Hollins on the 40-man roster was by far the most indefensible. His production certainly didn't justify it, and his tough guy act only served to infuriate people in the clubhouse.

Ricky Ledee   **OF**   **Born: 22-Nov-73**   **Age: 29**   **Bats: L**   **Throws: L**

YEAR	TM	LG	AGE	AB	H	2B	3B	HR	BB	SO	SB	CS	AVG	OBP	SLG	MLVR	EQBA	EQOBP	EQSLG	EQMLVR	VORP	DEFENSE	
2000	NYY	AL	26	191	46	11	1	7	26	39	7	3	.241	.335	.419	-.081	.253	.340	.442	-.011	3.8	43-LF	2
2000	CLE	AL	26	63	14	2	1	2	8	9	0	0	.222	.310	.381	-.213	.226	.314	.387	-.155	-1.1	18-LF	1
2000	TEX	AL	26	213	50	6	3	4	25	50	6	3	.235	.318	.347	-.240	.237	.312	.355	-.195	-6.4	54-RF	0
2001	TEX	AL	27	242	56	21	1	2	23	58	3	3	.231	.306	.351	-.184	.244	.318	.376	-.150	-4.5	61-RF	-3
2002	PHI	NL	28	203	46	13	1	8	35	50	1	2	.227	.343	.419	.027	.237	.349	.444	-.005	9.8	44-CF	-1
2003	PHI	NL	29	164	40	8	1	5	22	38	2	2	.245	.338	.400	-.053	.251	.340	.420	-.040	1.2		

Breakout: 31%   Improve: 51%   Collapse: 29%

After hanging around forever as a much-hyped prospect, Ledee seems to have found a role as a useful fourth outfielder. While he was better than Glanville last year, a good team shouldn't ask for more than a bench role out of Ledee.

Travis Lee   **1B**   **Born: 26-May-75**   **Age: 28**   **Bats: L**   **Throws: L**

YEAR	TM	LG	AGE	AB	H	2B	3B	HR	BB	SO	SB	CS	AVG	OBP	SLG	MLVR	EQBA	EQOBP	EQSLG	EQMLVR	VORP	DEFENSE			
2000	ARI	NL	25	224	52	13	0	8	25	46	5	1	.232	.309	.397	-.182	.227	.296	.391	-.183	-6.7	54-RF	1	15-1B	-1
2000	PHI	NL	25	180	43	11	1	1	40	33	3	0	.239	.383	.328	-.115	.238	.375	.326	-.109	-.7	43-1B	10		
2001	PHI	NL	26	555	143	34	2	20	71	109	3	4	.258	.346	.434	.012	.265	.350	.446	.022	19.0	153-1B	-4		
2002	PHI	NL	27	536	142	26	2	13	54	104	5	3	.265	.332	.394	.003	.276	.339	.415	-.032	9.0	135-1B	10		
2003	PHI	NL	28	443	114	24	2	13	54	85	5	2	.258	.341	.408	-.029	.264	.343	.429	-.014	3.4				

Breakout: 14%   Improve: 50%   Collapse: 16%

Even before they signed Jim Thome, it was time for the Phillies to give up on Lee. Not only is he not developing as a hitter, his one reliable skill from the past, his batting eye, seems to be deteriorating. He is a good defensive first baseman, but that doesn't come close to making up for the hole he creates in the lineup.

Mike Lieberthal   **C**   **Born: 18-Jan-72**   **Age: 31**   **Bats: R**   **Throws: R**

YEAR	TM	LG	AGE	AB	H	2B	3B	HR	BB	SO	SB	CS	AVG	OBP	SLG	MLVR	EQBA	EQOBP	EQSLG	EQMLVR	VORP	DEFENSE	
2000	PHI	NL	28	389	108	30	0	15	40	53	2	0	.278	.354	.470	.055	.278	.345	.469	.057	30.9	99-C	3
2001	PHI	NL	29	121	28	8	0	2	12	21	0	0	.231	.316	.347	-.181	.236	.316	.358	-.184	1.8	33-C	0
2002	PHI	NL	30	476	133	29	2	15	38	58	0	1	.279	.350	.443	.111	.292	.356	.467	.086	39.0	122-C	1
2003	PHI	NL	31	351	91	20	1	11	31	48	1	1	.260	.328	.415	-.039	.266	.330	.437	-.025	13.2		

Breakout: 8%   Improve: 41%   Collapse: 32%

Lieberthal returned from a gruesome knee injury to have an excellent 2002 season and was rewarded by a lengthy, expensive contract extension. That extension is an awful gamble. Very few everyday catchers retain their effectiveness past the age of 30 and Lieberthal has already demonstrated that he is injury-prone and a lousy hitter against righties. A few weeks after the season ended Lieberthal had surgery to repair a torn meniscus in his knee. Expect other problems to follow.

Anderson Machado   **SS**   **Born: 25-Jan-81**   **Age: 22**   **Bats: B**   **Throws: R**

YEAR	TM	LG	AGE	AB	H	2B	3B	HR	BB	SO	SB	CS	AVG	OBP	SLG	MLVR	EQBA	EQOBP	EQSLG	EQMLVR	VORP	DEFENSE	
2000	CLR	FSL	19	417	102	19	7	1	54	103	32	18	.245	.331	.331	-.074	.197	.265	.272	-.425	-24.0	118-SS	-8
2001	CLR	FSL	20	272	71	5	8	5	31	66	23	9	.261	.345	.393	.062	.215	.277	.333	-.307	-6.5	82-SS	2
2001	REA	EAS	20	101	15	2	0	1	12	25	5	2	.149	.239	.198	-.440	.136	.219	.184	-.662	-12.6	30-SS	1
2002	REA	EAS	21	450	113	24	3	12	72	118	40	11	.251	.357	.398	.033	.217	.306	.348	-.228	-1.2	122-SS	10
2003	PHI	NL	22	196	47	8	2	6	21	49	7	5	.240	.316	.397	-.096	.245	.319	.417	-.085	3.7		

Breakout: 60%   Improve: 82%   Collapse: 7%

Machado's walk rate increased substantially last year as he made the jump to Double-A and improved his defense. That's an impressive combination. He may not be as good as the hype around him, but he's much closer than he was before and he's still very young with lots of time to improve. If Jimmy Rollins continues to struggle, Machado may get a chance to replace him in 2004.

Jason Michaels   CF   Born: 04-May-76   Age: 27   Bats: R   Throws: R

YEAR	TM	LG	AGE	AB	H	2B	3B	HR	BB	SO	SB	CS	AVG	OBP	SLG	MLVR	EQBA	EQOBP	EQSLG	EQMLVR	VORP	DEFENSE
2000	REA	EAS	24	437	129	30	4	10	28	87	7	4	.295	.342	.451	.115	.255	.290	.393	-.171	.9	111-CF -2
2001	SWB	INT	25	418	109	19	3	17	37	126	11	3	.261	.333	.443	.068	.247	.314	.424	-.089	-.0	97-LF -3
2002	PHI	NL	26	105	28	10	3	2	13	33	1	1	.267	.353	.476	.148	.280	.363	.495	.126	8.5	14-CF -1
2003	PHI	NL	27	134	33	7	1	4	14	35	2	2	.245	.318	.393	-.095	.251	.320	.414	-.083	-.5	

Breakout: 9%   Improve: 28%   Collapse: 46%

Michaels made an excellent transition to a bench player role last year, providing what little power off the bench the Phillies had. Given that he was also competent defensively in center field, he really should have played more in lieu of Glanville. He's a decent short-term contingency plan if Byrd turns out to be not quite ready.

Jorge Padilla   RF   Born: 11-Aug-79   Age: 23   Bats: R   Throws: R

YEAR	TM	LG	AGE	AB	H	2B	3B	HR	BB	SO	SB	CS	AVG	OBP	SLG	MLVR	EQBA	EQOBP	EQSLG	EQMLVR	VORP	DEFENSE
2000	PIE	SAL	20	413	126	24	8	11	26	89	8	4	.305	.349	.482	.224	.232	.263	.372	-.269	-20.2	94-RF -2
2001	CLR	FSL	21	358	93	13	2	16	40	73	23	6	.260	.346	.441	.123	.215	.277	.371	-.255	-17.2	92-RF -6
2002	REA	EAS	22	484	124	30	2	7	40	77	32	11	.256	.327	.370	-.049	.225	.281	.325	-.305	-28.5	122-RF -2
2003	PHI	NL	23	162	40	8	1	5	14	34	4	3	.246	.315	.399	-.091	.252	.317	.420	-.079	-2.8	

Breakout: 56%   Improve: 76%   Collapse: 12%

The Phillies continue to tout Padilla as a prospect, keeping him on the 40-man roster, but his offense would have been barely acceptable for a shortstop, let alone a corner outfielder. If they can't sucker a team into trading for him, the roster spot is better used elsewhere.

Tomas Perez   UT   Born: 29-Dec-73   Age: 29   Bats: B   Throws: R

YEAR	TM	LG	AGE	AB	H	2B	3B	HR	BB	SO	SB	CS	AVG	OBP	SLG	MLVR	EQBA	EQOBP	EQSLG	EQMLVR	VORP	DEFENSE	
2000	SWB	INT	26	279	82	16	2	10	16	48	4	1	.294	.337	.473	.110	.274	.307	.445	-.049	9.8	54-3B -1	14-SS 2
2000	PHI	NL	26	140	31	7	1	1	11	30	1	1	.221	.278	.307	-.369	.220	.267	.312	-.353	-5.0	40-SS -7	
2001	PHI	NL	27	135	41	7	1	3	7	22	0	1	.304	.347	.437	.057	.307	.348	.445	.054	9.8	18-2B 1	
2002	PHI	NL	28	212	53	13	1	5	21	40	1	0	.250	.321	.392	-.031	.264	.329	.417	-.057	8.7	32-2B 0	12-3B -2
2003	PHI	NL	29	206	53	10	1	5	17	37	1	1	.258	.318	.390	-.090	.264	.320	.411	-.078	3.7		

Breakout: 8%   Improve: 31%   Collapse: 25%

For the past two years Perez has been a very solid utility infielder and should be one for a few more years. As long as the Phillies don't get foolish thinking he's more than that or that he is irreplaceable (and therefore worth a large contract) he's useful to have on the team.

Placido Polanco   2B/3B   Born: 10-Oct-75   Age: 27   Bats: R   Throws: R

YEAR	TM	LG	AGE	AB	H	2B	3B	HR	BB	SO	SB	CS	AVG	OBP	SLG	MLVR	EQBA	EQOBP	EQSLG	EQMLVR	VORP	DEFENSE	
2000	STL	NL	24	323	102	12	3	5	16	26	4	4	.316	.350	.418	.003	.314	.340	.412	-.002	17.8	38-2B 3	26-3B 2
2001	STL	NL	25	564	173	26	4	3	25	43	12	3	.307	.343	.383	-.031	.313	.346	.392	-.022	25.4	88-3B 17	34-SS 7
2002	PHI	NL	26	206	61	13	1	4	14	14	2	2	.296	.353	.427	.107	.310	.360	.452	.088	14.4	53-3B 11	
2002	STL	NL	26	342	97	19	1	5	12	27	3	1	.284	.316	.389	-.026	.294	.322	.403	-.066	10.4	66-3B 10	10-SS -1
2003	PHI	NL	27	490	138	24	3	5	24	37	6	2	.282	.319	.376	-.089	.289	.322	.396	-.077	7.9		

Breakout: 2%   Improve: 21%   Collapse: 38%

Placido Polanco represented only a small defensive drop-off when he replaced Scott Rolen at third base in August. His offense was a very different story. The combination makes him an average third baseman at best. Bell's signing moves Polanco to second, where he will be a minor upgrade over Anderson. He's not a liability, but the Phillies shouldn't hesitate to replace him if a better option comes along.

Todd Pratt   C   Born: 09-Feb-67   Age: 36   Bats: R   Throws: R

YEAR	TM	LG	AGE	AB	H	2B	3B	HR	BB	SO	SB	CS	AVG	OBP	SLG	MLVR	EQBA	EQOBP	EQSLG	EQMLVR	VORP	DEFENSE
2000	NYM	NL	33	160	44	6	0	8	22	31	0	0	.275	.380	.463	.105	.284	.378	.469	.120	16.0	47-C 3
2001	NYM	NL	34	80	13	5	0	2	15	36	1	0	.163	.309	.300	-.283	.183	.314	.329	-.256	-.5	21-C -4
2001	PHI	NL	34	93	19	3	0	2	19	25	0	0	.204	.345	.301	-.197	.211	.347	.316	-.192	1.2	28-C -3
2002	PHI	NL	35	106	33	11	0	3	24	28	2	0	.311	.455	.500	.374	.321	.458	.523	.362	18.5	33-C -2
2003	PHI	NL	36	175	41	9	0	4	32	45	2	1	.233	.362	.363	-.065	.238	.364	.382	-.053	5.6	

Breakout: 2%   Improve: 20%   Collapse: 49%

In 2001 Todd Pratt appeared to be in the decline phase of his career, but he returned to form in 2002. At his age the end is probably close, but he likely bought a few more years of pension-building service time with his performance. Given how undervalued he was early in his career, it's hard to begrudge him that. At least for 2003, he'll be the Phillies' backup.

Nick Punto — SS — Born: 08-Nov-77 — Age: 25 — Bats: B — Throws: R

YEAR	TM	LG	AGE	AB	H	2B	3B	HR	BB	SO	SB	CS	AVG	OBP	SLG	MLVR	EQBA	EQOBP	EQSLG	EQMLVR	VORP	DEFENSE
2000	REA	EAS	22	456	116	15	4	5	69	71	33	10	.254	.355	.338	-.048	.222	.304	.299	-.296	-9.7	116-SS -1
2001	SWB	INT	23	463	106	19	5	1	68	114	33	9	.229	.328	.298	-.146	.222	.314	.289	-.289	-9.1	119-SS 20
2002	SWB	INT	24	443	120	12	5	1	76	84	42	8	.271	.380	.327	.004	.258	.360	.315	-.142	9.4	115-SS 14
2003	PHI	NL	25	181	44	8	2	1	25	35	8	3	.242	.337	.332	-.142	.248	.340	.350	-.134	1.7	

Breakout: 26%   Improve: 56%   Collapse: 19%

Punto has an interesting skill set, being a solid defensive shortstop whose sole offensive strength is a good batting eye. A smart team will find a Dave Magadan role for him. If that's going to happen, it should soon, as Punto enters his prime.

Jimmy Rollins — SS — Born: 27-Nov-78 — Age: 24 — Bats: B — Throws: R

YEAR	TM	LG	AGE	AB	H	2B	3B	HR	BB	SO	SB	CS	AVG	OBP	SLG	MLVR	EQBA	EQOBP	EQSLG	EQMLVR	VORP	DEFENSE
2000	SWB	INT	21	470	129	28	11	12	49	55	24	7	.274	.345	.457	.084	.257	.317	.429	-.068	18.6	130-SS 5
2000	PHI	NL	21	53	17	1	1	0	2	7	3	0	.321	.345	.377	-.061	.321	.345	.358	-.068	2.1	11-SS -2
2001	PHI	NL	22	656	180	29	12	14	48	108	46	8	.274	.326	.419	-.032	.281	.331	.426	-.027	34.6	155-SS -5
2002	PHI	NL	23	637	156	33	10	11	54	103	31	13	.245	.308	.380	-.071	.257	.315	.404	-.107	18.2	148-SS -1
2003	PHI	NL	24	651	176	34	8	14	59	93	33	7	.270	.333	.413	-.025	.277	.336	.434	-.010	28.9	

Breakout: 18%   Improve: 53%   Collapse: 15%

A seemingly disastrous sophomore season for Rollins wasn't all bad. He failed to show any development in his game early in the season and was awful in the second half. But Rollins hiked his walk rate a bit and smacked 54 extra-base hits, just one less than he collected in his supposedly stellar rookie season. Bowa has made suggestions about Rollins bunting more and slapping at pitches for infield hits. Since Rollins's line drive power is his primary offensive strength, this is a recipe for disaster.

Chase Utley — 3B/2B — Born: 17-Dec-78 — Age: 24 — Bats: L — Throws: R

YEAR	TM	LG	AGE	AB	H	2B	3B	HR	BB	SO	SB	CS	AVG	OBP	SLG	MLVR	EQBA	EQOBP	EQSLG	EQMLVR	VORP	DEFENSE
2000	BAT	NYP	21	153	47	13	1	2	18	23	5	3	.307	.387	.444	.252	.222	.276	.329	-.311	-3.8	34-2B 2
2001	CLR	FSL	22	467	120	25	2	16	37	88	19	8	.257	.328	.422	.071	.214	.262	.355	-.307	-11.2	114-2B -4
2002	SWB	INT	23	464	122	39	1	17	46	89	8	3	.263	.355	.461	.127	.247	.332	.438	-.036	18.4	123-3B -22
2003	PHI	NL	24	184	45	10	1	6	18	38	4	2	.242	.318	.399	-.089	.248	.320	.420	-.077	2.9	

Breakout: 30%   Improve: 57%   Collapse: 21%

The attempt to become a third baseman did not go well for Utley. By the end of the season he had managed to raise his defense from atrocious to bad, but the Phillies wised up and moved him back to his original position at second base. Matching his second-base defense from 2000 and 2001 with his 2002 offense produces a decent but not spectacular player. If he can build on his strengths he'll be a reasonable cheap part to plug into the lineup in 2004, helping to support the big three. Like any team, the Phillies need players like Utley instead of wasting money on the David Bells of the world.

Eric Valent — RF — Born: 04-Apr-77 — Age: 26 — Bats: L — Throws: L

YEAR	TM	LG	AGE	AB	H	2B	3B	HR	BB	SO	SB	CS	AVG	OBP	SLG	MLVR	EQBA	EQOBP	EQSLG	EQMLVR	VORP	DEFENSE	
2000	REA	EAS	23	469	121	22	5	22	70	89	2	3	.258	.360	.467	.133	.222	.306	.404	-.149	-9.5	122-RF 1	
2001	SWB	INT	24	448	122	30	2	21	49	105	0	1	.272	.354	.489	.172	.256	.332	.464	.007	10.0	90-RF 0	23-1B 0
2002	SWB	INT	25	546	137	34	2	9	49	94	0	2	.251	.314	.370	-.068	.237	.299	.355	-.220	-20.3	118-RF 2	21-1B -6
2003	PHI	NL	26	159	39	9	1	4	16	31	2	1	.245	.317	.396	-.094	.251	.319	.417	-.083	-2.8		

Breakout: 33%   Improve: 58%   Collapse: 29%

If you want to argue that a premature call-up can damage a player's future, Valent is a good Exhibit A. On track to be at worse a solid bench player through mid-2001, he suffered through a horrendous stint in the majors and hasn't recovered. Both his pitch selection and power declined precipitously last year. His only hope to resurrect his career may be to get a fresh start elsewhere.

PITCHERS

Terry Adams — Born: 06-Mar-73 — Age: 30 — Bats: R — Throws: R

YEAR	TM	LG	AGE	G	GS	IP	H	BB	SO	HR	ERA	EQERA	EQH9	EQBB9	EQSO9	EQHR9	PERA	VORP	STF
2000	LAD	NL	27	66	0	84.3	80	39	56	6	3.52	4.27	9.1	3.4	5.4	0.6	4.17	10.4	-6
2001	LAD	NL	28	43	22	166.3	172	54	141	9	4.33	4.35	9.9	2.8	6.6	0.5	4.30	20.8	10
2002	PHI	NL	29	46	19	136.7	132	58	96	9	4.35	4.77	9.4	3.4	5.6	0.6	4.34	10.6	0
2003	PHI	NL	30	36	16	105.0	102	43	79	8	3.92	4.30	9.0	3.1	6.0	0.7	4.27	14.3	3

Breakout: 13%   Improve: 55%   Collapse: 15%

Signed to be a starter, Terry Adams was extremely ineffective in that role. Once the Phillies moved him to the bullpen, he returned to what he has been, a very effective setup man. The starter experiment was one worth trying, but it seems clear that Adams's value is as a reliever.

Ricky Bottalico — Born: 26-Aug-69 — Age: 33 — Bats: L — Throws: R

YEAR	TM	LG	AGE	G	GS	IP	H	BB	SO	HR	ERA	EQERA	EQH9	EQBB9	EQSO9	EQHR9	PERA	VORP	STF
2000	KCR	AL	30	62	0	72.7	65	41	56	12	4.83	4.20	7.6	4.1	6.6	1.2	3.94	9.5	-3
2001	PHI	NL	31	66	0	67.0	58	25	57	11	3.90	4.27	8.2	3.2	6.6	1.3	4.18	8.3	-3
2002	PHI	NL	32	30	0	27.3	33	13	24	3	4.62	5.79	11.7	3.8	7.0	1.0	6.09	-1.2	-5
2003	PHI	NL	33	43	0	43	42	19	34	5	4.26	4.67	9.0	3.5	6.3	1.1	4.76	4.4	-6

Breakout: 17%   Improve: 49%   Collapse: 22%

After being barely acceptable in 2001, Ricky Bottalico led the parade of veteran reliever disasters in the 2002 Phillies bullpen before going down to season-ending surgery. He should have entered the point of his career where he won't get another guaranteed contract, but the Phillies inexplicably offered him arbitration.

Taylor Bucholz — Born: 13-Oct-81 — Age: 21 — Bats: R — Throws: R

YEAR	TM	LG	AGE	G	GS	IP	H	BB	SO	HR	ERA	EQERA	EQH9	EQBB9	EQSO9	EQHR9	PERA	VORP	STF
2001	LWD	SAL	19	28	26	176.7	165	57	136	8	3.36	6.58	13.1	4.7	4.2	1.1	6.52	-21.2	-3
2002	CLR	FSL	20	23	23	158.7	140	51	129	11	3.29	5.01	11.3	3.8	5.4	1.5	4.85	8.7	8
2002	REA	EAS	20	4	4	23.0	29	6	17	5	7.43	8.69	15.8	3.0	5.4	3.5	7.74	-8.1	-4
2003	PHI	NL	21	17	14	83	88	39	57	9	4.71	5.16	9.8	3.7	5.5	1.0	5.22	4.0	0

Breakout: 10%   Improve: 61%   Collapse: 13%

The Phillies have a wealth of good young pitchers working their way up through the system and Bucholz is one of them. The perpetual concern is their workload; Robinson Tejada went down with an injury last year and Bucholz has thrown a lot of innings. If he survives this season (most likely at Double-A) Bucholz may wind up as trade bait in July, given the logjam in the system.

Dave Coggin — Born: 30-Oct-76 — Age: 26 — Bats: R — Throws: R

YEAR	TM	LG	AGE	G	GS	IP	H	BB	SO	HR	ERA	EQERA	EQH9	EQBB9	EQSO9	EQHR9	PERA	VORP	STF
2000	CLR	FSL	23	6	5	33.7	25	13	26	1	2.67	3.94	8.6	4.4	4.9	0.7	3.78	5.8	5
2000	REA	EAS	23	7	7	42.0	49	13	30	5	4.93	6.86	14.1	3.3	5.1	2.1	6.66	-6.3	-1
2000	SWB	INT	23	9	9	45.7	35	33	27	2	4.33	5.48	8.3	6.6	4.6	0.5	4.41	0.1	-5
2000	PHI	NL	23	5	5	27.0	35	12	17	2	5.33	5.79	11.9	3.2	5.0	0.6	5.57	-0.9	4
2001	SWB	INT	24	15	15	97.3	93	31	53	6	3.05	4.77	10.8	3.5	4.0	0.8	4.55	7.9	0
2001	PHI	NL	24	17	17	95.0	99	39	62	7	4.17	4.57	10.2	3.5	5.1	0.6	4.55	9.9	6
2002	PHI	NL	25	38	7	77.0	65	51	64	4	4.68	4.72	8.1	5.3	6.6	0.5	4.33	6.1	-1
2003	PHI	NL	26	26	11	74.3	71	39	55	7	4.36	4.78	8.9	4.0	5.8	0.8	4.74	6.2	-3

Breakout: 16%   Improve: 55%   Collapse: 15%

After spending most of the season as a useful member of the bullpen, Coggin made an emergency start in August when the Phillies wisely decided not to risk Randy Wolf on a chilly rainy evening. Unfortunately Coggin wound up with a torn labrum out of the deal. The team is optimistic that he'll be ready by April, but given that Coggin has had injury problems before you have to wonder how long it'll be before he breaks down for good.

Rheal Cormier
Born: 23-Apr-67 **Age: 36** **Bats: L** **Throws: L**

YEAR	TM	LG	AGE	G	GS	IP	H	BB	SO	HR	ERA	EQERA	EQH9	EQBB9	EQSO9	EQHR9	PERA	VORP	STF
2000	BOS	AL	33	64	0	68.3	74	17	43	7	4.61	4.12	9.4	1.8	5.5	0.8	3.74	9.6	-1
2001	PHI	NL	34	60	0	51.3	49	17	37	5	4.21	4.39	9.3	2.8	5.7	0.8	4.04	5.6	-5
2002	PHI	NL	35	54	0	60.0	61	32	49	6	5.25	5.55	9.8	4.3	6.5	0.9	5.19	-1.1	-7
2003	PHI	NL	36	51	0	50.0	49	21	40	5	3.94	4.32	9.0	3.3	6.3	0.8	4.45	7.4	-3

Breakout: 24%   Improve: 48%   Collapse: 20%

Yet another example of why signing relievers to long-term contracts is foolish. Cormier struggled all year long, losing his role as the principle left-handed setup man in large part because lefty batters started hitting him better than righties. Cormier's still under contract through next year, so unless the Phillies break form, he'll take up roster space again.

Brandon Duckworth
Born: 23-Jan-76 **Age: 27** **Bats: B** **Throws: R**

YEAR	TM	LG	AGE	G	GS	IP	H	BB	SO	HR	ERA	EQERA	EQH9	EQBB9	EQSO9	EQHR9	PERA	VORP	STF
2000	REA	EAS	24	27	27	165.0	145	52	178	17	3.16	4.96	10.4	3.2	7.5	1.7	4.61	10.0	18
2001	SWB	INT	25	22	20	147.0	122	36	150	14	2.63	4.00	9.2	2.7	7.4	1.2	3.83	24.5	21
2001	PHI	NL	25	11	11	69.0	57	29	40	2	3.52	3.61	8.2	3.6	4.5	0.2	3.24	14.5	7
2002	PHI	NL	26	30	29	163.0	167	69	167	26	5.41	5.62	9.8	3.4	8.1	1.5	5.32	-2.1	14
2003	PHI	NL	27	26	23	153.3	145	59	137	17	4.19	4.59	8.8	3.0	7.1	1.0	4.39	16.5	16

Breakout: 14%   Improve: 49%   Collapse: 13%

Duckworth followed up his excellent 2001 season with a lackluster 2002, yielding a ton of homers and hand-wringing. The official team line is that his mechanics were still solid, it was merely a matter of shaky confidence. While that may be part of it, it's also likely Duckworth needs to learn how to adjust to big league hitters. Last year we predicted Duckworth would blossom into an excellent pitcher. That strikeout rate means we're not changing our minds now. As good a bet to take a big step forward this season as anyone in this book.

Gavin Floyd
Born: 27-Jan-83 **Age: 20** **Bats: R** **Throws: R**

YEAR	TM	LG	AGE	G	GS	IP	H	BB	SO	HR	ERA	EQERA	EQH9	EQBB9	EQSO9	EQHR9	PERA	VORP	STF
2002	LWD	SAL	19	27	27	166.0	119	64	140	13	2.77	5.34	11.1	5.3	5.0	2.1	4.95	3.0	0
2003	PHI	NL	20	10	9	59.3	55	41	40	11	5.39	5.91	8.6	5.3	5.3	1.8	5.82	-2.7	-9

Breakout: 0%   Improve: 71%   Collapse: 7%

He's got a long way to go, but Floyd has so far lived up to the hype. The fact that he pitched a no-hitter and still lost is typical of the way his season went. He pitched well, but his support was lackluster. All the standard caveats about young pitchers apply, but Floyd has star potential if his arm holds up.

Eric Junge
Born: 05-Jan-77 **Age: 26** **Bats: R** **Throws: R**

YEAR	TM	LG	AGE	G	GS	IP	H	BB	SO	HR	ERA	EQERA	EQH9	EQBB9	EQSO9	EQHR9	PERA	VORP	STF
2000	SBR	CLF	23	29	24	158.0	159	53	116	8	3.36	5.87	13.4	3.5	4.4	1.1	5.53	-6.6	-1
2001	JAX	SOU	24	27	27	164.0	143	56	116	19	3.46	5.61	11.1	3.8	4.6	1.8	5.17	-1.9	-3
2002	SWB	INT	25	29	29	180.7	170	67	126	16	3.54	4.97	10.2	4.1	5.5	1.2	4.77	10.7	3
2002	PHI	NL	25	4	1	12.7	14	5	11	0	1.42	3.28	10.8	3.2	7.0	0.2	4.47	3.1	13
2003	PHI	NL	26	17	11	69.3	73	33	51	8	4.89	5.36	9.8	3.7	5.8	1.0	5.23	2.3	-1

Breakout: 18%   Improve: 48%   Collapse: 17%

Picked up from the Dodgers in exchange for Omar Daal, Eric Junge was a solid pitcher at Triple-A for most of the year until he started to wear down a little at the end of the season. Has the potential to be a back-of-the-rotation innings-eater for a few years. If he ever picks up a fan club along the lines of the Wolf Pack, the Junge Frankensteins would be a great name for it.

Seung Lee
Born: 02-Jun-79 **Age: 24** **Bats: R** **Throws: R**

YEAR	TM	LG	AGE	G	GS	IP	H	BB	SO	HR	ERA	EQERA	EQH9	EQBB9	EQSO9	EQHR9	PERA	VORP	STF
2001	BAT	NYP	22	4	4	20.0	31	4	14	3	7.65	14.18	26.3	3.2	4.3	5.6	12.13	-19.3	-37
2002	LWD	SAL	23	23	22	147.3	132	46	112	8	3.24	6.29	13.2	4.3	4.5	1.5	5.68	-12.9	-3
2002	CLR	FSL	23	3	3	19.0	6	2	16	0	0.00	0.90	3.7	1.2	5.2	0.2	0.87	9.7	26
2003	PHI	NL	24	13	8	53	63	24	34	7	5.40	5.92	11.0	3.4	5.1	1.2	5.98	-1.3	-8

Breakout: 18%   Improve: 57%   Collapse: 13%

Seung Lee *(continued)*

Signed out of Korea in early 2001, Lee's been hampered by injuries for most of his professional career. Once he started pitching though he made rapid progress, impressing in the Arizona Fall League with a nasty slider. Lee's primary injury problem has been his back—his time off may preserve precious mileage on his arm.

Ryan Madson — Born: 28-Aug-80 — Age: 22 — Bats: L — Throws: R

YEAR	TM	LG	AGE	G	GS	IP	H	BB	SO	HR	ERA	EQERA	EQH9	EQBB9	EQSO9	EQHR9	PERA	VORP	STF
2000	PIE	SAL	19	21	21	135.7	113	45	123	5	2.59	5.63	11.8	4.3	4.9	0.9	4.82	-1.9	6
2001	CLR	FSL	20	22	21	117.7	137	49	101	4	3.90	7.12	13.9	4.7	5.3	0.8	7.02	-21.1	2
2002	REA	EAS	21	26	26	171.3	150	53	132	11	3.20	4.55	10.2	3.4	5.4	1.0	4.11	18.2	13
2003	PHI	NL	22	14	9	60.7	66	36	44	1	4.71	5.17	10.1	4.6	5.7	0.1	5.10	2.4	1

Breakout: 11%   Improve: 47%   Collapse: 24%

Madson's slowly but steadily improved his control as he's climbed the organizational ladder. At age 21 he more than held his own last year in Double-A. Madson could use an additional pitch, but he has the time to develop one. His biggest problem down the road may be finding an opening in a rotation chock full of young talent.

Hector Mercado — Born: 29-Apr-74 — Age: 29 — Bats: L — Throws: L

YEAR	TM	LG	AGE	G	GS	IP	H	BB	SO	HR	ERA	EQERA	EQH9	EQBB9	EQSO9	EQHR9	PERA	VORP	STF
2000	LOU	INT	26	47	5	77.0	69	48	67	2	3.04	3.80	8.6	5.6	6.6	0.3	4.51	13.8	-3
2000	CIN	NL	26	12	0	14.0	12	8	13	2	4.50	4.38	8.0	4.2	7.4	1.1	4.11	1.6	0
2001	LOU	INT	27	12	0	13.3	12	6	13	0	1.35	2.74	9.1	4.8	6.9	0.2	4.10	3.9	0
2001	CIN	NL	27	56	0	53.0	55	30	59	6	4.08	4.58	9.2	4.7	8.4	0.9	5.01	4.7	3
2002	SWB	INT	28	26	0	33.3	22	12	43	2	1.62	2.66	7.0	3.9	10.0	0.8	2.99	10.1	21
2002	PHI	NL	28	31	3	39.0	32	25	40	2	4.62	4.59	7.8	5.1	8.0	0.5	4.13	3.6	4
2003	PHI	NL	29	38	4	61.0	54	34	62	5	3.98	4.37	8.1	4.4	8.1	0.8	4.46	8.2	6

Breakout: 14%   Improve: 41%   Collapse: 22%

Mercado throws hard, and he is left-handed. As you'd expect, he gets lots of chances as a result, despite shaky control. He'll likely keep bouncing from team to team as he gets those chances. Unless he suddenly chops two walks per nine frames, he'll never be consistent.

Jose Mesa — Born: 22-May-66 — Age: 37 — Bats: R — Throws: R

YEAR	TM	LG	AGE	G	GS	IP	H	BB	SO	HR	ERA	EQERA	EQH9	EQBB9	EQSO9	EQHR9	PERA	VORP	STF
2000	SEA	AL	34	66	0	80.7	89	41	84	11	5.35	5.00	9.6	3.7	9.0	1.0	5.01	3.4	10
2001	PHI	NL	35	71	0	69.3	65	20	59	4	2.34	3.58	9.2	2.5	6.7	0.5	3.55	13.9	5
2002	PHI	NL	36	74	0	75.7	65	39	64	5	2.97	3.70	8.3	4.1	6.7	0.6	4.06	14.1	0
2003	PHI	NL	37	60	0	60.3	56	27	53	5	3.42	3.75	8.5	3.5	7.0	0.8	4.23	13.1	2

Breakout: 28%   Improve: 55%   Collapse: 16%

Mesa's control deteriorated dramatically in the second half of last season, making him nowhere near as effective as he'd been in 2001. Given that many observers believe he's several years older than he claims—his oldest son was born in 1979—Mesa should be near the end of the line. He could implode any time now.

Brett Myers — Born: 17-Aug-80 — Age: 22 — Bats: R — Throws: R

YEAR	TM	LG	AGE	G	GS	IP	H	BB	SO	HR	ERA	EQERA	EQH9	EQBB9	EQSO9	EQHR9	PERA	VORP	STF
2000	PIE	SAL	19	27	27	175.3	165	69	140	7	3.18	6.77	13.4	5.2	4.4	1.0	5.94	-24.6	-1
2001	REA	EAS	20	26	23	156.0	156	43	130	21	3.87	5.71	11.7	3.4	5.4	1.9	5.89	-3.6	6
2002	SWB	INT	21	19	19	128.0	121	20	97	9	3.59	4.52	10.0	1.7	5.9	0.9	3.93	14.0	21
2002	PHI	NL	21	12	12	72.0	73	29	34	11	4.25	5.10	9.9	3.3	3.8	1.5	5.19	3.2	0
2003	PHI	NL	22	19	17	106.3	119	41	68	13	4.85	5.32	10.4	3.0	5.0	1.2	5.31	3.4	0

Breakout: 12%   Improve: 40%   Collapse: 21%

In terms of raw stuff, Myers can hold his own with any pitcher in the majors, armed with a darting fastball and nasty curve. What he needs to develop now is consistency and the ability to adjust when he doesn't have his best stuff. At this point when he struggles he tends to react by trying to throw even harder, usually with poor results. If Joe Kerrigan can get through to him, he could be frighteningly good within a couple years.

Franklin Nunez Born: 18-Jan-77   Age: 26   Bats: R   Throws: R

YEAR	TM	LG	AGE	G	GS	IP	H	BB	SO	HR	ERA	EQERA	EQH9	EQBB9	EQSO9	EQHR9	PERA	VORP	STF
2000	CLR	FSL	23	23	14	112.0	112	57	81	4	3.62	5.96	11.7	5.9	4.7	0.8	6.04	-5.9	-7
2001	REA	EAS	24	39	14	110.0	107	51	112	9	4.42	6.62	11.2	5.8	6.6	1.2	5.93	-14.2	-6
2002	SWB	INT	25	4	4	17.0	9	12	16	2	3.18	4.03	6.1	7.9	7.4	1.6	3.81	2.8	0
2003	PHI	NL	26	10	6	38.3	40	24	32	5	5.19	5.69	9.7	5.0	6.5	1.2	5.85	1.1	-3

Breakout: 12%   Improve: 32%   Collapse: 22%

Nunez throws hard, but has yet to show any consistent control. He was out most of this season with a bad shoulder, but the Phillies were already souring on him because he seemed uninterested in working on improving his control. Removed from the 40-man roster, he was claimed by the Mets on waivers, but he's unlikely to ever be an effective big league pitcher unless he encounters an industrious pitching coach who can straighten him out.

Vicente Padilla Born: 27-Sep-77   Age: 25   Bats: R   Throws: R

YEAR	TM	LG	AGE	G	GS	IP	H	BB	SO	HR	ERA	EQERA	EQH9	EQBB9	EQSO9	EQHR9	PERA	VORP	STF
2000	TUC	PCL	22	12	3	18.3	22	8	22	2	4.43	4.83	11.2	3.8	8.6	1.2	5.59	1.2	14
2000	ARI	NL	22	27	0	35.0	32	10	30	0	2.31	2.48	8.3	2.1	6.9	0.2	2.70	11.3	17
2000	PHI	NL	22	28	0	30.3	40	18	21	3	5.35	6.24	12.1	4.3	5.5	0.8	6.31	-2.9	-8
2001	PHI	NL	23	23	0	34.0	36	12	29	1	4.24	4.54	10.4	3.0	6.7	0.2	4.13	3.2	9
2001	SWB	INT	23	16	16	81.7	64	11	75	8	2.42	3.62	8.8	1.5	6.6	1.2	3.26	17.1	21
2002	PHI	NL	24	32	32	206.0	198	53	128	16	3.28	3.90	9.4	2.1	5.0	0.7	3.90	36.7	12
2003	PHI	NL	25	32	29	188.3	186	54	131	18	3.66	4.01	9.1	2.2	5.5	0.9	4.08	31.6	11

Breakout: 14%   Improve: 55%   Collapse: 10%

Once Padilla learned how to consistently use his different release points he started making opposing batters look foolish. After pitching quite a few innings in winter ball, he wore down late in the season. To their credit the Phillies took extra precautions in how they used him. Unless a hidden injury suddenly pops up he should make the Curt Schilling trade look as good as it can over the next few years.

Robert Person Born: 08-Jan-69   Age: 34   Bats: R   Throws: R

YEAR	TM	LG	AGE	G	GS	IP	H	BB	SO	HR	ERA	EQERA	EQH9	EQBB9	EQSO9	EQHR9	PERA	VORP	STF
2000	PHI	NL	31	28	28	173.3	144	95	164	13	3.64	3.52	7.5	4.0	7.5	0.6	3.57	38.2	20
2001	PHI	NL	32	33	33	208.3	179	80	183	34	4.19	4.40	8.2	3.2	6.8	1.3	4.17	25.6	12
2002	PHI	NL	33	16	16	87.7	79	51	61	13	5.44	5.62	8.7	4.7	5.5	1.4	5.11	-1.1	-3
2003	PHI	NL	34	19	15	101.0	95	48	78	12	4.56	5.00	8.7	3.7	6.1	1.1	4.73	6.4	5

Breakout: 16%   Improve: 46%   Collapse: 21%

Person has been nursing a fragile shoulder for the past few years and last year it finally caught up to him. He tried to pitch through it in his walk year, which only made it worse. A 34-year-old pitcher coming off major shoulder surgery is not likely to get a significant contract offer, nor should he. Person might sneak in one more good season, but his brief days as a rotation anchor are done.

Dan Plesac Born: 04-Feb-62   Age: 41   Bats: L   Throws: L

YEAR	TM	LG	AGE	G	GS	IP	H	BB	SO	HR	ERA	EQERA	EQH9	EQBB9	EQSO9	EQHR9	PERA	VORP	STF
2000	ARI	NL	38	62	0	40.0	34	26	45	4	3.15	4.07	7.4	4.6	8.8	0.8	3.99	5.8	7
2001	TOR	AL	39	62	0	45.3	34	24	68	4	3.58	3.26	6.5	4.4	12.4	0.7	3.19	10.7	33
2002	TOR	AL	40	19	0	13.3	11	6	14	1	3.38	3.16	7.2	3.8	9.1	0.6	3.27	3.3	16
2002	PHI	NL	40	41	0	23.0	16	12	27	5	4.70	4.62	6.6	4.1	9.2	2.0	4.32	1.9	4
2003	PHI	NL	41	79	0	43.3	36	21	49	5	3.63	3.98	7.7	3.8	9.0	1.1	3.97	8.4	10

Breakout: 20%   Improve: 52%   Collapse: 32%

Yet another veteran reliever of the sort Ed Wade loves, Plesac looked respectable last year, unlike most of his over-30 bullpen mates. How his modest success earned Plesac a $2 million deal for 2003 will remain one of the great mysteries of life. Really old by non-Orosco standards, Plesac's been reduced to a specialist's role. Meanwhile his trade counterpart Cliff Politte will give the Jays plenty of effective relief work at a fraction of the price. Did the Phillies' Triple-A pitchers collectively run over Ed Wade's dog? All of his dogs? Rough up his paper boy? There's no logical explanation for his aversion to non-geezers in the big league bullpen.

Joe Roa — Born: 11-Oct-71 — Age: 31 — Bats: R — Throws: R

YEAR	TM	LG	AGE	G	GS	IP	H	BB	SO	HR	ERA	EQERA	EQH9	EQBB9	EQSO9	EQHR9	PERA	VORP	STF
2000	AKR	EAS	28	19	14	103.0	91	38	59	7	3.41	4.95	10.0	3.8	4.0	1.2	4.62	6.2	-7
2001	PME	EAS	29	7	7	36.0	36	3	26	2	3.00	5.19	12.0	1.0	4.6	0.8	4.24	1.3	5
2001	CLG	PCL	29	19	19	124.0	134	12	81	16	3.92	3.72	9.3	1.0	4.2	1.3	4.15	24.6	5
2002	SWB	INT	30	17	17	111.0	83	16	74	4	1.86	2.79	7.9	1.6	5.2	0.5	2.67	33.5	16
2002	PHI	NL	30	14	11	71.3	78	13	35	11	4.04	4.67	10.8	1.5	4.0	1.5	4.93	6.5	-3
2003	PHI	NL	31	21	16	98.7	107	26	56	13	4.23	4.64	10.0	2.1	4.5	1.2	4.60	11.3	-2

Breakout: 16%   Improve: 47%   Collapse: 24%

Roa is a perfect example of how a team can cheaply fill out its pitching staff. A minor league free agent who put up gaudy numbers in the International League, he got a chance in the majors and did a solid job for two months. He's not likely to continue that success after getting tonked his second time through the league. Not that it's likely to happen, if a team offered the Phillies a legitimate player for Roa, they should trade him immediately.

Jose Santiago — Born: 05-Nov-74 — Age: 28 — Bats: R — Throws: R

YEAR	TM	LG	AGE	G	GS	IP	H	BB	SO	HR	ERA	EQERA	EQH9	EQBB9	EQSO9	EQHR9	PERA	VORP	STF
2000	OMA	PCL	25	11	0	17.0	19	3	14	2	3.18	4.44	11.6	1.6	6.2	1.4	4.85	1.8	0
2000	KCR	AL	25	45	0	69.0	70	26	44	7	3.91	3.76	8.8	2.8	5.6	0.7	3.58	12.4	0
2001	KCR	AL	26	20	0	29.3	40	9	15	2	6.76	5.77	12.1	2.6	4.4	0.5	5.21	-1.3	-12
2001	PHI	NL	26	53	0	62.3	66	13	28	3	3.61	3.87	10.6	1.8	3.6	0.4	3.87	10.5	-10
2002	PHI	NL	27	42	0	47.0	56	15	30	7	6.70	6.35	11.6	2.6	5.2	1.4	5.83	-5.1	-14
2002	SWB	INT	27	22	0	28.0	28	7	21	0	1.29	3.35	10.4	2.7	5.8	0.2	4.00	6.3	0
2003	CLE	AL	28	38	0	49.3	59	16	29	6	4.91	4.83	10.7	2.6	5.1	0.9	4.83	5.9	-9

Breakout: 18%   Improve: 45%   Collapse: 28%

Santiago was a prime example of reliever flakiness last year. Coming off a solid 2001 season he started 2002 in terrible form. Demoted to Triple-A, he found his stuff again, and was a key part of Scranton's run at an International League title. Removed from the Phils' 40-man roster at the end of the year, he declared free agency. The Indians quickly signed him, and they should have a useful back-of-the-bullpen guy on their hands.

Elio Serrano — Born: 04-Dec-78 — Age: 24 — Bats: R — Throws: R

YEAR	TM	LG	AGE	G	GS	IP	H	BB	SO	HR	ERA	EQERA	EQH9	EQBB9	EQSO9	EQHR9	PERA	VORP	STF
2000	PIE	SAL	21	38	0	67.3	67	15	56	5	2.27	6.33	14.6	2.9	4.6	1.9	5.94	-7.1	-13
2001	CLR	FSL	22	17	1	35.3	34	7	22	0	3.31	4.76	11.2	2.2	3.8	0.3	4.37	2.5	-6
2001	REA	EAS	22	30	0	37.3	22	9	30	3	2.90	3.39	6.8	2.9	5.0	1.1	2.81	8.2	-2
2002	SWB	INT	23	43	0	71.0	64	17	45	6	2.92	4.46	9.7	2.7	5.0	1.1	4.08	7.3	-4
2003	PHI	NL	24	19	3	34.3	37	12	23	4	4.54	4.98	10.0	2.8	5.3	1.1	4.88	2.8	-8

Breakout: 18%   Improve: 50%   Collapse: 24%

Instead of throwing good money and good prospects around in search of veteran relievers, the Phillies would be better served giving guys like Serrano a shot. He's been quietly getting the job done at every level he's pitched. The difference between Serrano's skills now and Mike Williams's skills before he became a "proven closer" are negligible, so he'd be a cheap gamble worth taking.

Carlos Silva — Born: 23-Apr-79 — Age: 24 — Bats: R — Throws: R

YEAR	TM	LG	AGE	G	GS	IP	H	BB	SO	HR	ERA	EQERA	EQH9	EQBB9	EQSO9	EQHR9	PERA	VORP	STF
2000	CLR	FSL	21	26	24	176.3	229	26	82	7	3.57	6.79	15.1	1.7	3.0	0.9	6.70	-25.2	-3
2001	REA	EAS	22	28	28	180.0	197	27	100	20	3.90	5.81	12.6	1.9	3.6	1.6	5.82	-6.1	-2
2002	PHI	NL	23	68	0	84.0	88	22	41	4	3.21	4.03	10.3	2.2	4.0	0.5	4.14	12.6	-7
2003	PHI	NL	24	52	3	74.7	89	21	38	7	4.45	4.88	11.0	2.2	4.0	0.9	4.88	7.0	-14

Breakout: 12%   Improve: 62%   Collapse: 20%

With Silva, Larry Bowa took a page from Earl Weaver's methods—this being one of the few times you'll ever see those two managers mentioned in the same sentence with any congruence. Silva was a hard-throwing starter in the Phillies' minor league system that Bowa put in his bullpen as a long reliever for the year, with the thought of eventually returning him to the rotation. Silva's control remained excellent, and he significantly cut down on his home runs allowed, two needed improvements if he hopes to survive with a low strikeout rate. Unless he develops a good strikeout pitch Silva's likely to be a useful spare part for a few years but not much else.

Bud Smith   Born: 23-Oct-79   Age: 23   Bats: L   Throws: L

YEAR	TM	LG	AGE	G	GS	IP	H	BB	SO	HR	ERA	EQERA	EQH9	EQBB9	EQSO9	EQHR9	PERA	VORP	STF
2000	ARK	TXS	20	18	18	108.7	93	27	102	5	2.32	3.27	9.1	2.4	6.2	0.7	3.46	27.0	24
2000	MEM	PCL	20	9	8	54.3	40	15	34	4	2.15	3.83	8.1	2.5	4.7	0.9	2.93	10.1	13
2001	MEM	PCL	21	17	17	108.0	114	28	78	6	2.75	4.01	10.6	2.8	4.8	0.6	4.62	17.9	12
2001	STL	NL	21	16	14	84.7	79	24	59	12	3.83	4.45	9.3	2.4	5.5	1.2	4.07	9.9	13
2002	STL	NL	22	11	10	48.0	67	22	22	4	6.94	7.43	14.0	3.8	3.7	0.8	6.76	-10.3	-10
2002	MEM	PCL	22	6	6	38.0	33	13	34	1	2.13	3.58	9.7	3.7	6.4	0.3	3.75	8.1	22
2002	SWB	INT	22	3	3	17.3	21	6	11	0	4.16	5.57	12.7	3.9	5.0	0.3	5.55	-0.1	7
2003	PHI	NL	23	19	16	98.3	107	39	66	10	4.74	5.19	10.1	3.1	5.3	1.0	5.02	6.0	2

Breakout: 12%   Improve: 41%   Collapse: 27%

Smith had been with the Phillies for only a couple weeks after the Scott Rolen trade when he was shut down with what was thought to be tendonitis. The Phillies soon discovered bigger problems and sent Smith under the knife, where he had a minor tear in his shoulder repaired. Given his struggles last year, it looks like the Phils got damaged goods. Smith has a ton of talent, but there are now serious doubts surrounding his future.

Evan Thomas   Born: 14-Jun-74   Age: 29   Bats: R   Throws: R

YEAR	TM	LG	AGE	G	GS	IP	H	BB	SO	HR	ERA	EQERA	EQH9	EQBB9	EQSO9	EQHR9	PERA	VORP	STF
2000	SWB	INT	26	29	27	171.0	163	50	127	17	3.53	4.62	10.4	2.7	5.9	1.2	4.45	16.8	8
2001	SWB	INT	27	19	18	104.0	123	36	74	14	5.28	7.34	13.4	3.9	5.3	1.7	6.65	-21.2	-9
2002	SWB	INT	28	22	20	113.0	106	37	75	6	3.90	4.97	10.0	3.6	5.2	0.7	4.33	6.7	1
2003	TOR	AL	29	13	9	54.3	66	23	35	8	5.43	5.26	10.6	3.4	5.6	1.1	5.26	5.0	-2

Breakout: 18%   Improve: 37%   Collapse: 30%

Good teams find places to use players like Thomas. Coming off shoulder surgery, he spent most of the season regaining his velocity while still demonstrating the ability to mix pitches and speeds effectively. Thomas stands less than six feet tall and the Phils aren't anywhere near as open-minded as the Astros in giving such pitchers a shot. Toronto signed him as a minor league free agent; they'll get a cheap, useful pitcher out of the deal.

Mike Timlin   Born: 10-Mar-66   Age: 37   Bats: R   Throws: R

YEAR	TM	LG	AGE	G	GS	IP	H	BB	SO	HR	ERA	EQERA	EQH9	EQBB9	EQSO9	EQHR9	PERA	VORP	STF
2000	BAL	AL	34	37	0	35.0	37	15	26	6	4.89	4.71	8.8	3.1	6.4	1.3	4.80	2.6	-5
2000	STL	NL	34	25	0	29.7	30	20	26	2	3.33	3.97	9.3	4.9	6.9	0.5	4.78	4.7	-2
2001	STL	NL	35	67	0	72.7	78	19	47	6	4.09	4.63	10.8	2.3	5.1	0.7	4.29	6.1	-6
2002	STL	NL	36	42	1	61.0	48	7	35	9	2.51	3.25	8.0	1.0	4.7	1.4	3.07	14.5	-3
2002	PHI	NL	36	30	0	35.7	27	7	15	6	3.78	3.80	7.4	1.6	3.4	1.6	3.37	6.3	-16
2003	BOS	AL	37	50	0	52.7	60	14	29	7	4.32	4.29	9.9	2.2	4.8	1.2	4.51	9.8	-10

Breakout: 18%   Improve: 48%   Collapse: 26%

The most inexplicable part of the Scott Rolen trade, Timlin had one of his periodic solid seasons. Even so, he wasn't worth what he was paid and he was never likely to re-sign with the team. Ed Wade's fetish with veteran relievers badly burned the team here; even with a farm system as thin as the Cardinals, the Phillies would have been better off trying to get another young player instead of Timlin. The Red Sox signed him to a one-year deal, hoping Timlin can duplicate his 2002 success.

Turk Wendell   Born: 19-May-67   Age: 36   Bats: L   Throws: R

YEAR	TM	LG	AGE	G	GS	IP	H	BB	SO	HR	ERA	EQERA	EQH9	EQBB9	EQSO9	EQHR9	PERA	VORP	STF
2000	NYM	NL	33	77	0	82.7	60	41	73	9	3.59	3.54	6.6	3.6	7.0	0.9	3.37	16.9	2
2001	NYM	NL	34	49	0	51.3	42	22	41	8	3.51	4.11	7.7	3.6	6.2	1.3	4.16	7.2	-6
2001	PHI	NL	34	21	0	15.7	21	12	15	4	7.45	8.02	12.4	6.3	7.2	2.0	8.57	-4.6	-23

Yet another overpaid veteran reliever in the Phillies bullpen, Wendell finally admitted that his elbow problems were serious and required surgery. He missed all of 2002, and even if he pitches in 2003, he's not likely to be very effective. Thanks to his goofy contract, he'll likely take up a roster spot anyway.

Randy Wolf — Born: 22-Aug-76 — Age: 26 — Bats: L — Throws: L

YEAR	TM	LG	AGE	G	GS	IP	H	BB	SO	HR	ERA	EQERA	EQH9	EQBB9	EQSO9	EQHR9	PERA	VORP	STF
2000	PHI	NL	23	32	32	206.3	210	83	160	25	4.36	4.31	9.3	2.9	6.2	1.0	4.37	27.4	16
2001	PHI	NL	24	28	25	163.0	150	51	152	15	3.70	4.02	8.9	2.7	7.3	0.8	3.77	26.8	24
2002	PHI	NL	25	31	31	210.7	172	63	172	23	3.20	3.55	7.9	2.4	6.6	1.0	3.53	45.8	19
2003	PHI	NL	26	29	28	186.0	171	58	152	19	3.49	3.83	8.5	2.4	6.5	0.9	3.84	35.4	17

Breakout: 16%   Improve: 56%   Collapse: 9%

Just plain fun to watch. Wolf has four different pitches, all with different movements and speeds, and he now has the control to use all of them effectively. The Tanana-esque 68-mph slow curve he throws often makes batters look obscenely foolish. After a case of elbow tendonitis in the spring, Wolf was among the best pitchers in the majors in the second half. If he stays healthy, and with a good chance at a whole lot of runs being scored for him, a Cy Young isn't out of the question.

Pete Zamora — Born: 13-Aug-75 — Age: 27 — Bats: L — Throws: L

YEAR	TM	LG	AGE	G	GS	IP	H	BB	SO	HR	ERA	EQERA	EQH9	EQBB9	EQSO9	EQHR9	PERA	VORP	STF
2000	REA	EAS	24	43	7	101.3	105	45	94	6	4.09	5.95	11.9	4.6	6.5	1.0	5.73	-5.9	-3
2001	SWB	INT	25	45	6	89.0	64	41	79	7	2.93	4.07	8.2	5.0	6.5	1.0	3.82	13.3	-2
2002	SWB	INT	26	55	0	62.0	63	29	32	2	3.48	5.02	10.8	5.2	4.1	0.4	5.10	2.5	-22
2003	NYM	NL	27	23	0	23.3	26	14	16	2	5.15	5.83	10.3	4.6	5.4	1.0	5.81	0.0	-17

Breakout: 20%   Improve: 38%   Collapse: 29%

In a typical case of roster mismanagement, the Phillies kept Zamora on the 40-man roster all season but never called him up to the majors. He could be marginally useful as a lefty out of the bullpen, but he's hardly a unique property, so unless he's in the majors there's no point in wasting the roster spot on him. They finally removed him in the off-season, and the Mets picked him up. With Mike Stanton and Jaime Cerda likely to be the team's lefty tandem, and with John Franco healing up, Zamora's only going to spend another summer in the International League.

Pittsburgh Pirates

The Pirates endured yet another losing season in 2002—their tenth in a row—falling further toward the precipice of hopelessness that could doom the franchise for the rest of the decade if it doesn't right the ship soon. Not coincidentally, the start of this horrendous losing streak tracks with the loss of Barry Bonds to free agency after the 1992 season.

History is, needless to say, full of twists and turns that defy prediction and that make even the retrospective jobs of scholars quite difficult. Trying to ascertain the causes of long-term trends is frequently frustrating, as many different factors are operating at any given time, some of them in concert, some of them in conflict. Sorting out these myriad elements and assigning primary responsibility to any one of them is not nearly as simple as it might seem. Occasionally though, the exact place and time of a watershed event can be affixed with certainty. Sometimes, the cause is a single action whose consequences are so far-reaching that they overwhelm all other factors. Once in a while, a single, incredibly wrong-headed mistake can ruin an institution, a company, or a ball club.

Such was the magnitude of a pair of decisions made by the Pittsburgh Pirates in 1991–92. While signing Andy Van Slyke to a budget-busting contract extension and the subsequent failure to re-sign Barry Bonds might seem like separate events, they were really flip sides of the same coin.

In contrast, letting Bobby Bonilla go was a smart move. Though Bonilla was both good and popular, he wasn't worth anywhere near the record amount of money the Mets were throwing at him. Trading stars like John Smiley was also defensible, even if the fans didn't understand it at the time. Failing to retain the services of the best player on the planet was, plainly and simply, idiotic. Squandering a similar amount of treasure on a hardworking but hardly brilliant white guy like Van Slyke to compensate for the expected departure of Bonds was suicidal. Bonds ultimately turned down a five-year, $25 million offer from the Pirates to test

free agency, but by then it was a foregone conclusion. Tragically, Pittsburgh earlier had the opportunity to sign Bonds to a long-term deal at a lower salary if they didn't take him to arbitration. When the team refused, a bitter arbitration hearing ensued, and the Pirates then threw their money down a rat hole by re-upping Van Slyke.

One of the unspoken but likely reasons contributing to the Bonds debacle was the fear among many major league executives that MLB's largely white fan base wouldn't respond enthusiastically to a team that was "too black." Pittsburgh was perceived as a blue-collar town that fit the profile perfectly. No one can be sure of course if that fear contributed to letting Bonds walk, but it certainly seems suspicious. That Van Slyke was club president Carl Barger's favorite player didn't help, either.

Presumably, one of the reasons for this fear was the memory of the 1970s. Did you know that, on September 1, 1971, the Pirates became the first team in major league history to field an all-minority lineup? (Rennie Stennett, 2B; Gene Clines, CF; Roberto Clemente, RF; Willie Stargell, LF; Manny Sanguillen, C; Dave Cash, 3B; Al Oliver, 1B; Jackie Hernandez, SS; and Dock Ellis, P.) The Pirates' 1971 and 1979 World Championship clubs didn't set any attendance records, to be sure, but many other baseball clubs struggled to draw well in the 1970s, including teams in much bigger markets and including championship clubs that were "whiter."

If a commemorative coin were struck to represent the history of the Pirates since 1992, the obverse side would feature the wreckage of the NL Eastern Division championship Pirates' teams of the early 1990s, symbolized by Bonds and his MVP trophies' flight to the Giants. The reverse side of the coin would commemorate Pittsburgh's spiral downward into the ranks of the perennially downtrodden, symbolized by the fantastically rich yet increasingly hapless Van Slyke. New ownership and a beautiful new ballpark haven't been enough

---

Pirates Prospectus

2002 record: 72–89; Fourth place, NL Central

Pythagenport Record: 71–90

Runs scored per game: 4.0 (15th in NL)

Runs allowed per game: 4.5 (10th in NL)

Team EqA: .245 (16th in NL)

2002 Batters Age: 28.1 (2nd youngest in NL)

2002 Pitchers Age: 28 (7th youngest in NL)

Ballpark: PNC Park; Slight hitters' park; Park Factor of .1.024

2002: Progress is progress; the team is working its way through the scar tissue.

2003: Continued pain and potentially the first winning season in recent memory.

to remove the "Quadruple-A" label slapped on the struggling Bucs in the mid-1990s.

The 2001–02 PNC Pirates were a paradigm of how settling for "the best you can afford" is a great way to perpetuate the problem. Second-tier free agents are rarely worth the substantial investment that they require; third-tier free agents are almost never worth a gamble unless they come incredibly cheap.

Aside from their miserable play on the field, the Pirates' management committed an unforgivable gaffe off the field that was completely avoidable; they insulted their fans after their embarrassing 2001 season by raising prices. This miscalculation certainly contributed to the 27% drop in attendance in PNC's sophomore season, a drop exceeded only by Miller Park among the new ballparks opened since 1989 by existing clubs. The team's damage control efforts were not adequate either. Instead of acknowledging their mistake and rolling back prices, the Pirates merely admitted to having made a mistake and promised not to raise prices the next year. The team was clueless: not only was this empty promise too little, too late, it was also not linked to real hope of putting a contending club on the field anytime soon. The opening of a new ballpark is an opportunity that comes along only once in a generation. Fumbling that golden opportunity is akin to digging your own grave. Building a contending club whose emergence will coincide with the opening of that new ballpark is hard work, but figuring out that you shouldn't alienate your customers by charging more for a disappointing and inferior product is a no-brainer.

In order to rebuild a club in the dire straits that the Buccos have been in for the past decade, management must either have a lot of courage, be prepared to take a lot hits in the press, be prepared to lose money in the short term, or be able to draw upon a well of good will built up over the years. Since 1992, the Pirates have rarely had the courage or been willing to pay the price to make the long-term moves that would change their future, and now they're paying the long-term price of their short-term thinking.

A well-chronicled procession of incompetent general managers has been a major factor in Pittsburgh's descent into hopelessness. Larry Doughty, Ted Simmons, and Cam Bonifay all had difficult jobs to do, but all of them committed major mistakes that made a bad situation even worse. Since 1988, when Doughty replaced Syd Thrift, the Pirates have seen one of the worst strings of general managers in recent history. All three men had their supporters, and all had a litany of reasons why they couldn't keep the Pirates in contention or return them to respectability. Is it too harsh to blame executives like Doughty and Bonifay, both of whom can claim to have been hamstrung by their ownership and their budgets?

No way. When small-market teams like the Pirates contend or win, the suits in the front office are more than eager to take the credit. When a winning club's president, vice president, or general manager turns down the inevitable "Executive of the Year Award" after a surprising year, or when they return a hefty portion of their six- or seven-figure paychecks because they couldn't do their job properly with one hand tied behind their back by ownership, then maybe they should escape responsibility. Until then, they should be judged on their results. Even if you want to temper judgment based on a fair measurement of their resources, they should not be excused from judgment simply because they didn't have all of the advantages of their richer or larger-market competitors.

One of the reasons things look so bad in the Steel City is the fallout from the false spring of '97. The 1997 "pennant race" in the weak NL Central was deceptive, as the Pirates simply hung close enough to be within mathematical contention of the leader in a very weak division. Pittsburgh never rose above .500 in the last month of 1997, and it was never more than two games above .500 in the second half. The Bucs' final record of 79–83 was certainly an improvement, but it hardly represented convincing evidence that the team had a bright future.

Pittsburgh's late-season collapse in 1998 caused the team to blame its supposedly disappointing younger players and to overcompensate by spending money on washed-up veterans. The financial legacy of these moves (especially the Kevin Young and Pat Meares contracts) continues to haunt the Pirates to this day. Fortunately, the Pirates lucked out on Wil Cordero, another unexplainable signing that was obviated by Cleveland's amorous pursuit of the veteran mediocrity. The Young contract sucked up the money needed to sign Jon Lieber, who was therefore dumped on the Cubs for a virtually worthless Brant Brown. To cap it all off, the signings of Derek Bell and Meares were two of the worst signings in recent history.

Since the early 1990s, though the Pirates have managed to trade their big-salaried veterans for lots of other organizations' prospects, the talent crop from Pittsburgh's own drafts has been meager. Furthermore, the Pirates have failed to develop much of the young talent that they reaped from trades and from having favorable draft positions, as one after another of the club's highly touted prospects stalled or crashed and burned.

Given the ridiculous bias in favor of veteran leadership that exists in the big leagues, it isn't that hard to trade veteran deadwood and their extravagant salaries for inexpensive prospects. Maybe people shouldn't give so much credit to Randy Smith and Dave Dombrowski and other GMs who perform brilliantly in Act One of rebuilding a team (kicking ass and taking names while cleaning out the previous administration's dry rot), but who crash and burn in Act Two (scouting, drafting, and developing their own talent) or in Act Three (assembling a winning team from these disparate sources of talent).

A case in point is Bonifay's tenure in Pittsburgh. Check out the kudos Bonifay was receiving in 1997, then take a look at the results five years down the road:

> In a series of seven trades between July and December of 1996, Cam acquired 17 prospects in an effort to strengthen an already promising player development system. The moves that Bonifay and his staff made in the past year received national notice as *Baseball America* recognized the Pirates as having the best minor league system in all of baseball prior to the season, and *USA Today* named the Pirates its organization of the year in September of '97.
>
> — 1998 Pirates media guide.

The long-term impact of those seven deals Bonifay made in 1996 was a helluva lot less than implicitly promised (by the team) or expected (by the fans and media). Only a few of these acquisitions made a difference; none made the major difference between winning and losing. In fact, most of the players acquired by Bonifay never even played for the Bucs. The Darwin-for-Loiselle deal helped for a while, as did the Neagle-for-Schmidt deal, but the team later dealt the disappointing and injury-prone Schmidt and the underrated John Vander Wal (stolen from San Diego in 2000) to the Giants in 2001. That disastrous deal netted a total of four games from Armando Rios and Ryan Vogelsong before they were both felled by career-threatening injuries.

The blockbuster deal, Bonifay's big-game trophy, was a nine-player trade with Toronto. Another salary dump by the Pirates, it gained them a lot of raw talent that ultimately yielded very little production. Two of the players sent to the Jays, Orlando Merced and Dan Plesac, remain in the majors as veteran role players, still the types of players the Pirates can't afford. On Pittsburgh's side of the ledger, Abraham Nunez has become a utility infielder after failing miserably as a regular, Jose Silva has already washed out, and Jose Pett, Mike Halpern, and Brandon Cromer never made it. Only Craig Wilson still has a chance to make the trade look better for the Pirates.

The greatest trade Bonifay made was clearly kidnapping franchise cornerstone Brian Giles from the Indians for Ricardo Rincon. That heist was of the magnitude a small-market team like Pittsburgh needs to make to change its fortunes, taking advantage of a needy and wealthy (and temporarily insane) contender. Regrettably, Bonifay turned right around and gave Lieber away a month later, showing that temporary insanity and desperation worked both ways.

More damaging than the lack of production from players acquired in trades was Bonifay's inability to develop the young players he drafted. Bonifay's first round picks from 1993–2001, in chronological order, were outfielder Charles Peterson, shortstop Mark Farris, shortstop Chad Hermansen, pitcher Kris Benson, outfielder-pitcher J. J. Davis, pitcher Clint Johnson, pitcher Bobby Bradley, pitcher Sean Burnett, and pitcher John VanBenschoten. It's too early to write off the disappointing Davis and too early to tell about the last three pitchers, but otherwise, only Benson has made any impact. Bonifay's background was in scouting, so the organization's failure to develop quality youngsters was especially troubling. Considering that Benson was the #1 pick in 1996, and that four of the others were top-10 picks, and that fifth round pick but first round talent J. R. House stalled at Double-A, and will now miss a year or more due to injuries, the meager haul from those drafts looks even worse.

One of the problems with Pittsburgh's top hitting prospects is that few of them started out with any idea of the strike zone. While that's not necessarily uncommon, the biggest problem is that none of these guys were taught plate discipline in the Pirates system. Players with obvious talent (Peterson, Hermansen, Davis, Kevin Haverbusch, and many others), have seen their careers broken because of execrable command of the strike zone. Even guys who have reached the majors such as Rob Mackowiak, Aramis Ramirez, Tony Alvarez, and Tike Redman exhibit an almost pathological aversion to working the count. Many of them also strike out far too much for hitters that don't consistently produce power.

Currently, the tattered Pittsburgh organization is banking on the future of House, shortstop Jose Castillo, and the pitching trio of Burnett, VanBenschoten, and Bradley. While those players' futures are promising, all of them except House were in the low minors last year, and House and Bradley have struggled to stay healthy. In other words, most of them have a long way to go before they can help out the major league club.

After taking the reins in mid-2001, GM Dave Littlefield cleaned house, replacing the big wheels in the scouting and player development departments. Only time will tell if his efforts will work, but the Bucs certainly needed to overhaul their player development system from top to bottom.

HITTERS

Tony Alvarez　OF　Born: 10-May-78　Age: 25　Bats: R　Throws: R

YEAR	TM	LG	AGE	AB	H	2B	3B	HR	BB	SO	SB	CS	AVG	OBP	SLG	MLVR	EQBA	EQOBP	EQSLG	EQMLVR	VORP	DEFENSE
2000	HIC	SAL	22	442	126	25	4	15	39	93	52	21	.285	.363	.462	.190	.220	.271	.357	-.283	-20.9	101-LF -6
2001	LYN	CRL	23	93	32	4	0	2	7	11	7	3	.344	.390	.452	.285	.281	.324	.375	-.113	-.6	19-LF -4
2001	ALT	EAS	23	254	81	16	1	6	9	30	17	11	.319	.359	.461	.210	.278	.315	.402	-.093	-.3	61-LF -3
2002	ALT	EAS	24	507	161	37	1	15	27	71	29	18	.318	.363	.483	.224	.273	.308	.418	-.087	12.0	118-CF -8
2002	PIT	NL	24	26	8	2	0	1	3	5	1	0	.308	.379	.500	.238	.308	.379	.500	.188	2.3	
2003	PIT	NL	25	229	62	13	1	6	14	36	7	4	.271	.318	.416	-.046	.271	.314	.429	-.058	2.5	

Breakout: 26%　　Improve: 55%　　Collapse: 19%

Alvarez's mark is that he hits for average, finishing second in the Eastern League last year in his second year in Altoona. A line-drive hitter, he rarely walks and is not a very good basestealer. If he doesn't hit .300 or develop some over-the-fence power (unlikely), he's not going to help. He's been in pro ball since he was 17, but still is inconsistent and prone to mistakes on defense. Having played both second and third in the past, a utility role is the best he can aspire to.

Mike Benjamin　INF　Born: 22-Nov-65　Age: 37　Bats: R　Throws: R

YEAR	TM	LG	AGE	AB	H	2B	3B	HR	BB	SO	SB	CS	AVG	OBP	SLG	MLVR	EQBA	EQOBP	EQSLG	EQMLVR	VORP	DEFENSE	
2000	PIT	NL	34	233	63	18	2	2	12	45	5	4	.270	.315	.391	-.149	.268	.300	.387	-.151	2.2	26-3B 1	21-SS 2
2002	PIT	NL	36	120	18	2	1	0	7	31	0	4	.150	.203	.183	-.578	.165	.210	.207	-.641	-14.0	20-3B -5	11-SS -1

Benjamin won the lottery in the fall of 1998, receiving an astonishing long-term contract from the Pirates because the team had panicked after 22-year-old prospect Abraham Nunez made seven errors in 23 games at shortstop while hitting a buck-ninety-two in a September trial. After missing all of 2001 with elbow trouble, Benji came back and played the role of the dog to the hilt in his swan song in Pittsburgh.

Adrian Brown　CF　Born: 07-Feb-74　Age: 29　Bats: B　Throws: R

YEAR	TM	LG	AGE	AB	H	2B	3B	HR	BB	SO	SB	CS	AVG	OBP	SLG	MLVR	EQBA	EQOBP	EQSLG	EQMLVR	VORP	DEFENSE
2000	PIT	NL	26	308	97	18	3	4	29	34	13	1	.315	.374	.432	.061	.311	.362	.427	.057	19.4	75-CF -3
2002	NAS	PCL	28	184	62	7	1	3	23	18	22	6	.337	.411	.435	.230	.310	.377	.396	.039	5.8	45-RF -4
2002	PIT	NL	28	208	45	10	2	1	19	34	10	6	.216	.285	.298	-.251	.219	.283	.310	-.325	-8.1	52-CF -3
2003	BOS	AL	29	246	64	12	2	3	20	33	11	4	.263	.320	.363	-.094	.268	.329	.381	-.100	0.0	

Breakout: 19%　　Improve: 57%　　Collapse: 16%

The Pirates thought Brown had arrived after he cleared the wondrous .300 mark in 2000 while stealing 13 bases in 14 attempts, but he lost most of 2001 to various injuries, and never got untracked last year. Released at season's end, signed by Tampa Bay, then claimed by Boston in the fourth round of the Rule 5 draft, he'll likely never get another chance to play regularly. At best, he's a decent reserve outfielder who can play center field. Brown hasn't yet taken full advantage of his speed or his natural power and is yet another poster child for a chronic lack of development at the high levels of the Bucs' system.

Jose Castillo　SS　Born: 19-Mar-81　Age: 22　Bats: R　Throws: R

YEAR	TM	LG	AGE	AB	H	2B	3B	HR	BB	SO	SB	CS	AVG	OBP	SLG	MLVR	EQBA	EQOBP	EQSLG	EQMLVR	VORP	DEFENSE
2000	HIC	SAL	19	529	158	32	8	16	29	107	16	12	.299	.347	.480	.205	.226	.257	.368	-.290	-9.0	121-SS -16
2001	LYN	CRL	20	485	119	20	7	7	21	94	23	10	.245	.289	.359	-.036	.206	.241	.308	-.419	-25.8	117-SS -9
2002	LYN	CRL	21	503	151	25	2	16	49	95	27	14	.300	.375	.453	.203	.238	.297	.369	-.204	1.9	128-SS 16
2003	PIT	NL	22	205	50	10	1	5	17	42	5	3	.245	.310	.380	-.126	.245	.307	.392	-.140	1.0	

Breakout: 51%　　Improve: 74%　　Collapse: 14%

Bothered by a wrist injury at the end of 2001, Castillo did well in his second year at Lynchburg. He doubled his walks and displayed plus range and a strong arm though he still struggled on defense, making 33 errors. Castillo clearly has the tools to progress quickly in the high minors; the question is whether the Bucs have the proper people in place to mentor him.

Humberto Cota   C   Born: 07-Feb-79   Age: 24   Bats: R   Throws: R

YEAR	TM	LG	AGE	AB	H	2B	3B	HR	BB	SO	SB	CS	AVG	OBP	SLG	MLVR	EQBA	EQOBP	EQSLG	EQMLVR	VORP	DEFENSE
2000	ALT	EAS	21	429	112	20	1	8	21	80	6	4	.261	.300	.368	-.076	.235	.262	.334	-.323	-9.7	90-C -21
2001	NAS	PCL	22	377	112	22	2	14	25	74	7	2	.297	.354	.477	.124	.270	.322	.429	-.048	19.0	84-C -10
2002	NAS	PCL	23	404	108	27	1	9	31	106	5	8	.267	.327	.406	-.018	.246	.299	.371	-.192	4.6	81-C -7
2002	PIT	NL	23	17	5	1	0	0	1	4	0	0	.294	.333	.353	-.047	.294	.333	.353	-.118	.1	
2003	PIT	NL	24	212	52	11	1	5	18	46	3	2	.246	.309	.379	-.129	.246	.305	.391	-.143	1.4	

Breakout: 17%   Improve: 41%   Collapse: 24%

In two years at Triple-A Nashville, Cota has displayed line-drive power and a lack of plate discipline, the broken record of the Pirates' organization. The question is whether he can play defense well enough to be a backup in the majors. He does not throw particularly well, but is mobile and has good hands. With Keith Osik now out of the picture, Cota should earn some big-league meal money in 2003, but he has a pretty low ceiling.

J. J. Davis   RF   Born: 25-Oct-78   Age: 24   Bats: R   Throws: R

YEAR	TM	LG	AGE	AB	H	2B	3B	HR	BB	SO	SB	CS	AVG	OBP	SLG	MLVR	EQBA	EQOBP	EQSLG	EQMLVR	VORP	DEFENSE
2000	LYN	CRL	21	485	118	36	1	20	52	171	9	4	.243	.322	.445	.075	.199	.254	.361	-.323	-32.8	119-RF -17
2001	ALT	EAS	22	228	57	13	3	4	21	79	2	5	.250	.319	.386	-.007	.221	.283	.345	-.275	-12.7	58-RF -1
2002	ALT	EAS	23	348	100	17	3	20	33	101	7	4	.287	.354	.526	.240	.249	.303	.455	-.064	1.1	100-RF -6
2002	PIT	NL	23	10	1	0	0	0	0	4	0	0	.100	.182	.100	-.734	.100	.171	.100	-.884	-1.8	
2003	PIT	NL	24	197	49	11	2	7	19	61	3	4	.248	.319	.427	-.047	.248	.316	.440	-.059	-2.8	

Breakout: 49%   Improve: 73%   Collapse: 16%

The 2002 season was seen as Davis's last chance after a poor performance the previous year, especially with questions about his preparation and commitment. Repeating at Altoona, the #6 pick in the 1997 draft showed some power and cut down on his strikeouts. Davis still doesn't make enough contact to hit in the big leagues, but he now has earned another year to prove he could make an impact with his bat. Davis has a very strong arm and wanted to convert to pitching after 2001, but the Bucs wouldn't let him. The jury is still out on that decision.

Ryan Doumit   Born: 03-Apr-81   Age: 22   Bats: B   Throws: R

YEAR	TM	LG	AGE	AB	H	2B	3B	HR	BB	SO	SB	CS	AVG	OBP	SLG	MLVR	EQBA	EQOBP	EQSLG	EQMLVR	VORP	DEFENSE
2000	WPT	NYP	19	246	77	15	5	2	23	33	2	2	.313	.381	.439	.251	.232	.274	.335	-.300	-4.4	44-C -4
2001	HIC	SAL	20	148	40	6	0	2	10	32	2	1	.270	.333	.351	.027	.217	.264	.283	-.402	-6.6	22-C -2
2002	HIC	SAL	21	258	83	14	1	6	18	40	3	5	.322	.384	.453	.238	.245	.287	.352	-.242	-.5	27-C -7

A second round pick in 1999, Doumit played just 48 games due to back trouble in 2001 and only 68 last season after surgery to fix a broken index finger on his throwing hand. He did hit .322 and showed above-average defensive skills, which got him added to the 40-man roster in November. A small player for a catcher, Doumit could replace Cota as the ML backup-in-waiting if he can stay healthy.

Christopher Duffy   CF   Born: 20-Apr-80   Age: 23   Bats: B   Throws: L

YEAR	TM	LG	AGE	AB	H	2B	3B	HR	BB	SO	SB	CS	AVG	OBP	SLG	MLVR	EQBA	EQOBP	EQSLG	EQMLVR	VORP	DEFENSE
2001	WPT	NYP	21	221	70	12	4	1	33	33	30	5	.317	.443	.421	.302	.240	.325	.322	-.213	-2.1	60-CF -2
2002	LYN	CRL	22	539	162	27	5	10	33	101	22	7	.301	.354	.425	.138	.243	.284	.353	-.248	-9.3	126-CF -5
2003	PIT	NL	23	182	45	9	2	4	14	38	5	3	.248	.310	.377	-.128	.248	.306	.389	-.143	-1.1	

Breakout: 38%   Improve: 66%   Collapse: 15%

Duffy successfully made the leap from short-season ball to High-A last year, but he might as well be wearing a black eye patch when he bats to signify that he is afflicted by the Pirates' prospect syndrome. He has a standard skill set: line-drive power, speed, and the ability to hit for average. What he lacks—surprise, surprise—is enough plate discipline to turn those skills into meaningful production by laying off marginal deliveries and taking walks until he forces pitchers to give him better pitches to hit. Duffy has the opportunity in front of him to play center field in Pittsburgh, but he has only one more year to mature before he joins the legions of undifferentiated 25-year-old mediocre prospects lurking in the high minors.

Brian Giles   OF   Born: 20-Jan-71   Age: 32   Bats: L   Throws: L

YEAR	TM	LG	AGE	AB	H	2B	3B	HR	BB	SO	SB	CS	AVG	OBP	SLG	MLVR	EQBA	EQOBP	EQSLG	EQMLVR	VORP	DEFENSE
2000	PIT	NL	29	559	176	37	7	35	114	69	6	0	.315	.437	.594	.398	.308	.423	.581	.370	75.0	154-OF -2
2001	PIT	NL	30	576	178	37	7	37	90	67	13	6	.309	.406	.590	.359	.306	.401	.583	.337	74.3	149-LF -11
2002	PIT	NL	31	497	148	37	5	38	135	74	15	6	.298	.454	.622	.486	.296	.447	.623	.448	83.7	143-LF -5
2003	PIT	NL	32	472	141	31	4	25	100	70	13	3	.298	.422	.540	.300	.298	.417	.557	.300	47.8	

Breakout: 4%   Improve: 40%   Collapse: 13%

The player who single-handedly has kept the Pirates' offense worthy of the term *major league* (OK, just barely, but that's not Giles's fault) had another outstanding season in 2002. His four seasons with Pittsburgh have been notable not only for their excellence but also for their consistency. What more could you ask from a power hitter? Many callers have tried to pry Giles away from the Pirates; but the team has so far been properly reluctant to deal the one hitter they can build around.

Kevin Haverbusch   OF   Born: 16-Jun-76   Age: 27   Bats: R   Throws: R

YEAR	TM	LG	AGE	AB	H	2B	3B	HR	BB	SO	SB	CS	AVG	OBP	SLG	MLVR	EQBA	EQOBP	EQSLG	EQMLVR	VORP	DEFENSE
2000	ALT	EAS	24	140	39	3	1	5	11	15	2	2	.279	.340	.421	.075	.246	.292	.380	-.192	-.1	31-3B -12
2001	ALT	EAS	25	153	40	10	2	2	5	23	1	2	.261	.294	.392	-.032	.232	.266	.348	-.297	-3.3	22-2B -1
2001	NAS	PCL	25	147	49	7	2	7	4	34	3	1	.333	.376	.551	.311	.301	.341	.500	.117	7.8	19-LF -3
2002	ALT	EAS	26	130	38	7	0	5	4	21	4	2	.292	.319	.462	.103	.260	.279	.405	-.170	-2.7	17-LF 1
2002	NAS	PCL	26	94	26	5	1	2	3	18	3	1	.277	.327	.415	.001	.255	.296	.394	-.158	-1.6	21-LF -3

Injuries and lack of any progress in learning how to hit have essentially destroyed Haverbusch's career. He returned to Double-A for a fourth season in 2002 before finally earning a promotion to Triple-A and hasn't much time left to move up. Part of the problem is that Haverbusch rarely walks, doesn't steal bases, and only occasionally hits for power, but hey, he's a Pittsburgh prospect. What did you expect?

J. R. House   C   Born: 11-Nov-79   Age: 23   Bats: R   Throws: R

YEAR	TM	LG	AGE	AB	H	2B	3B	HR	BB	SO	SB	CS	AVG	OBP	SLG	MLVR	EQBA	EQOBP	EQSLG	EQMLVR	VORP	DEFENSE	
2000	HIC	SAL	20	420	146	29	1	23	46	91	1	2	.348	.419	.586	.483	.254	.310	.431	-.081	16.0	77-C -2	
2001	ALT	EAS	21	426	110	25	1	11	37	103	1	1	.258	.325	.399	.025	.233	.292	.361	-.228	.8	88-C -12	11-1B -1
2002	ALT	EAS	22	91	24	6	0	2	13	21	0	0	.264	.356	.396	.049	.226	.308	.344	-.224	.3	20-C -1	

The Pirates' best prospect lost most of 2002 to abdominal and elbow injuries that required three surgeries, the last being the familiar Tommy John operation in September. Despite his problems, he remains the Bucs' catcher of the future since he can hit for power and average and throw well. House will miss most or all of 2003; that's a big blow to his future and an even bigger blow to the Bucs' future.

Adam Hyzdu   OF   Born: 06-Dec-71   Age: 31   Bats: R   Throws: R

YEAR	TM	LG	AGE	AB	H	2B	3B	HR	BB	SO	SB	CS	AVG	OBP	SLG	MLVR	EQBA	EQOBP	EQSLG	EQMLVR	VORP	DEFENSE
2000	ALT	EAS	28	514	149	39	2	31	94	102	3	7	.290	.407	.554	.364	.249	.347	.477	.045	19.7	131-OF -3
2001	NAS	PCL	29	261	76	17	2	11	17	68	1	3	.291	.335	.498	.114	.263	.306	.443	-.063	.9	58-RF 4
2001	PIT	NL	29	72	15	1	0	5	4	18	0	1	.208	.260	.431	-.202	.219	.258	.438	-.194	-2.3	16-RF -1
2002	NAS	PCL	30	243	59	17	0	10	29	59	1	2	.243	.324	.436	-.003	.224	.298	.394	-.177	-6.7	57-RF -3
2002	PIT	NL	30	155	36	6	0	11	21	44	0	0	.232	.328	.484	.071	.236	.325	.497	.022	8.7	41-CF 1
2003	PIT	NL	31	210	52	12	1	9	24	52	2	2	.247	.326	.438	-.022	.247	.323	.452	-.033	.9	

Breakout: 33%   Improve: 55%   Collapse: 27%

Lots of people have been rooting for Hyzdu, who has been playing pro ball since 1990. A competitive and intelligent player, Hyzdu has power to all fields but is pretty much a mistake hitter. Nevertheless, he did have his moments in 2002, most of them in July, when he batted .379 with five long balls. After that, he slumped terribly in the last two months. A power bat is an asset to have on any bench; too bad for Hyzdu that he's stuck on the Pirates' pine.

Jason Kendall   C   Born: 26-Jun-74   Age: 29   Bats: R   Throws: R

YEAR	TM	LG	AGE	AB	H	2B	3B	HR	BB	SO	SB	CS	AVG	OBP	SLG	MLVR	EQBA	EQOBP	EQSLG	EQMLVR	VORP	DEFENSE	
2000	PIT	NL	26	579	185	33	6	14	79	79	22	12	.320	.415	.470	.193	.312	.399	.459	.168	64.6	143-C -2	
2001	PIT	NL	27	606	161	22	2	10	44	48	13	14	.266	.336	.358	-.117	.266	.332	.358	-.133	17.3	123-C -12	26-LF -4
2002	PIT	NL	28	545	154	25	3	3	49	29	15	8	.283	.352	.356	-.019	.289	.352	.367	-.066	24.7	132-C 3	
2003	PIT	NL	29	506	142	27	3	5	51	41	12	3	.280	.351	.374	-.039	.280	.348	.386	-.051	16.3		

Breakout: 7%   Improve: 49%   Collapse: 14%

Kendall's offensive drop-off is alarming. He's stopped taking walks, he no longer hits for power, and he doesn't run as well as he did before his ankle injury despite being a top-of-the-order hitter. Obviously, his career is in crisis in tandem with the Pirates' budget: it's not Kendall's defense that has kept him in the majors, and the Bucs would love to unload his $10 million/year contract. That'll be tough, with both his ironclad no-trade clause and struggles to get on base and hit the ball with authority clouding the picture. Lloyd McClendon is planning on using Kendall as a leadoff hitter in 2003; maybe that will force him to start taking some pitches again.

Ron Mackowiak — UT — Born: 20-Jun-76 — Age: 27 — Bats: L — Throws: R

YEAR	TM	LG	AGE	AB	H	2B	3B	HR	BB	SO	SB	CS	AVG	OBP	SLG	MLVR	EQBA	EQOBP	EQSLG	EQMLVR	VORP	DEFENSE		
2000	ALT	EAS	24	526	156	33	4	13	22	96	18	5	.297	.336	.449	.123	.264	.291	.407	-.142	9.8	68-2B -3	33-RF -2	
2001	NAS	PCL	25	118	31	5	0	4	7	39	1	1	.263	.304	.407	-.103	.237	.280	.364	-.244	-5.3	13-RF -2		
2001	PIT	NL	25	214	57	15	2	4	15	52	4	3	.266	.323	.411	-.067	.264	.319	.412	-.083	-.4	37-RF 0	18-2B -2	
2002	PIT	NL	26	385	94	22	0	16	42	120	9	3	.244	.329	.426	.009	.249	.328	.441	-.038	4.0	80-RF 1	22-3B -1	
2003	*PIT*	*NL*	*27*	*348*	*90*	*20*	*2*	*11*	*30*	*87*	*9*	*5*	*.258*	*.322*	*.425*	*-.038*	*.258*	*.318*	*.438*	*-.050*	*1.7*			

Breakout: 23%   Improve: 53%   Collapse: 23%

A hustling "can-do" guy from Chicago, Mackowiak performed far better in 2002 than anyone could have anticipated. This doesn't mean that he was especially good—Mackowiak really only looks good in a Pittsburgh context. Nor should he have been playing regularly, especially in center field, where he started 37 times. He's probably won himself a roster spot for a few seasons, but if he ends up taking time away from prospects who are ready to jump to The Show, someone should be canned.

Pat Meares — Insurance Scam — Born: 06-Sep-68 — Age: 34 — Bats: R — Throws: R

YEAR	TM	LG	AGE	AB	H	2B	3B	HR	BB	SO	SB	CS	AVG	OBP	SLG	MLVR	EQBA	EQOBP	EQSLG	EQMLVR	VORP	DEFENSE
2000	PIT	NL	31	462	111	22	2	13	36	91	1	0	.240	.306	.381	-.201	.239	.295	.378	-.194	2.9	118-SS 5
2001	PIT	NL	32	270	57	11	1	4	10	45	0	2	.211	.245	.304	-.403	.213	.245	.309	-.406	-13.9	70-2B -3

After conflicting medical opinions about Meares's hand injury, a bizarre farce ensued between the Pirates and Meares last year that could have served as the plot line on an episode of the Sopranos. Meares actually filed a grievance in September, claiming he was healthy enough to play and wanting to be released so he could find another team. Even if his hand really was healthy, the Pirates could have claimed that Meares was so delusional that it wasn't safe to allow him near sharp objects again, never mind on a baseball field. A negotiated settlement ensued: Meares will get his 3,750,000 clams in 2003 that he never deserved, and the club will keep him as a phantom on its roster to collect the insurance money on his contract.

Abraham Nunez — 2B/SS — Born: 16-Mar-76 — Age: 27 — Bats: B — Throws: R

YEAR	TM	LG	AGE	AB	H	2B	3B	HR	BB	SO	SB	CS	AVG	OBP	SLG	MLVR	EQBA	EQOBP	EQSLG	EQMLVR	VORP	DEFENSE	
2000	NAS	PCL	24	351	97	11	1	3	36	46	20	5	.276	.345	.339	-.137	.256	.310	.312	-.247	-2.7	77-SS 6	
2000	PIT	NL	24	91	20	1	0	1	8	14	0	0	.220	.283	.264	-.428	.217	.265	.272	-.415	-4.7	18-SS -1	
2001	PIT	NL	25	301	79	11	4	1	28	53	8	2	.262	.327	.336	-.166	.263	.327	.336	-.175	3.7	37-SS 5	38-2B -6
2002	PIT	NL	26	253	59	14	1	2	27	44	3	4	.233	.312	.320	-.165	.238	.313	.332	-.224	-.6	39-2B 10	17-SS -1
2003	*PIT*	*NL*	*27*	*233*	*59*	*11*	*2*	*2*	*22*	*38*	*5*	*2*	*.255*	*.321*	*.342*	*-.150*	*.255*	*.318*	*.353*	*-.165*	*-.3*		

Breakout: 24%   Improve: 54%   Collapse: 23%

After putting on some weight and losing his speed, Nunez has seen his chances to play regularly evaporate—he'd already shown an inability to hit for power or average (even if he does take some pitches) plus a knack for crucial errors. Now a utility infielder, but a limited one. Even though he switch-hits and is a good bunter, he's helpless against lefties and not much better facing righties.

Keith Osik — Born: 22-Oct-68 — Age: 34 — Bats: R — Throws: R

YEAR	TM	LG	AGE	AB	H	2B	3B	HR	BB	SO	SB	CS	AVG	OBP	SLG	MLVR	EQBA	EQOBP	EQSLG	EQMLVR	VORP	DEFENSE
2000	PIT	NL	31	123	36	6	1	4	14	11	3	0	.293	.387	.455	.099	.285	.373	.447	.082	10.6	19-C -1
2001	PIT	NL	32	120	25	4	0	2	13	24	1	0	.208	.301	.292	-.306	.215	.304	.298	-.301	-2.3	32-C -1
2002	PIT	NL	33	100	16	3	0	2	6	25	0	0	.160	.215	.250	-.467	.168	.214	.277	-.536	-7.8	21-C -1

The Bucs finally decided to release Osik following his dreadful 2002 performance. He's what he has always been, a light-hitting hustler with some defensive skills. Now that he's 34 and looking for a job, Osik has to hope that something terrible happens to Tom Prince, Todd Pratt, Roberto Machado, Chad Kreuter, or Joe Girardi. As we went to press Osik was close to signing a minor league deal with the Brewers, where his lack of skills would fit perfectly.

Aramis Ramirez — 3B — Born: 25-Jun-78 — Age: 25 — Bats: — Throws:

YEAR	TM	LG	AGE	AB	H	2B	3B	HR	BB	SO	SB	CS	AVG	OBP	SLG	MLVR	EQBA	EQOBP	EQSLG	EQMLVR	VORP	DEFENSE	
2000	NAS	PCL	22	167	59	12	2	4	11	26	2	1	.353	.407	.521	.328	.319	.361	.470	.125	13.6	40-3B	-5
2000	PIT	NL	22	254	65	15	2	6	10	36	0	0	.256	.297	.402	-.177	.254	.283	.402	-.172	1.1	58-3B	-10
2001	PIT	NL	23	603	181	40	0	34	40	100	5	4	.300	.352	.536	.188	.300	.350	.533	.178	61.7	154-3B	-7
2002	PIT	NL	24	522	122	26	0	18	29	95	2	0	.234	.284	.387	-.125	.241	.285	.402	-.178	1.4	116-3B	-8
2003	PIT	NL	25	524	141	30	2	19	33	85	3	2	.270	.318	.445	-.006	.270	.315	.460	-.017	14.8		

Breakout: 10%   Improve: 35%   Collapse: 18%

Bothered by an ankle sprain for much of the season, Ramirez's poor performance in 2002, in a season when he should have had been establishing himself as a star, helped sink the Pirates' ship. While Ramirez has one of the strongest arms in the game, his overall defense leaves something to be desired. Off-season reports from winter ball said Ramirez had lost the extra pounds he put on during 2002; a svelte, healthy, and productive Ramirez is critical to Pittsburgh's hope of impersonating a bona fide major league team in 2003.

Tike Redman — Born: 10-Mar-77 — Age: 26 — Bats: L — Throws: L

YEAR	TM	LG	AGE	AB	H	2B	3B	HR	BB	SO	SB	CS	AVG	OBP	SLG	MLVR	EQBA	EQOBP	EQSLG	EQMLVR	VORP	DEFENSE	
2000	NAS	PCL	23	506	132	24	11	4	32	73	24	18	.261	.309	.375	-.167	.235	.270	.337	-.303	-16.4	113-CF	-4
2001	NAS	PCL	24	398	121	18	10	3	24	37	21	7	.304	.350	.422	.042	.276	.319	.383	-.115	6.9	94-CF	-1
2001	PIT	NL	24	125	28	4	1	1	4	25	3	5	.224	.248	.296	-.400	.222	.246	.294	-.420	-8.1	35-CF	3
2002	NAS	PCL	25	311	84	9	4	2	21	24	16	7	.270	.318	.344	-.121	.249	.293	.316	-.279	-8.1	74-CF	-4

The 5-foot-11, 166-pound outfielder spent all season at Nashville, failing to convince anyone that he should be called up to the majors. The Pirates dumped him in December. One would think that guys like Redman who can't generate any power but who have real speed would understand that their ticket to a six-figure salary and first-class hotels would be to get on base enough and run up steal totals. Ah, but that would imply that they have a clue, or that someone with a clue on the coaching staff would hammer the message into their heads.

Pokey Reese — 2B — Born: 10-Jun-73 — Age: 30 — Bats: R — Throws: R

YEAR	TM	LG	AGE	AB	H	2B	3B	HR	BB	SO	SB	CS	AVG	OBP	SLG	MLVR	EQBA	EQOBP	EQSLG	EQMLVR	VORP	DEFENSE			
2000	CIN	NL	27	518	132	20	6	12	45	86	29	3	.255	.322	.386	-.157	.252	.309	.381	-.154	8.4	128-2B	19		
2001	CIN	NL	28	428	96	20	2	9	34	82	25	4	.224	.286	.343	-.264	.223	.283	.341	-.280	-7.1	74-SS	-5	48-2B	-1
2002	PIT	NL	29	421	111	25	0	4	41	81	12	1	.264	.333	.352	-.069	.269	.334	.361	-.123	10.5	113-2B	6		
2003	PIT	NL	30	372	92	19	2	6	34	69	13	3	.248	.314	.362	-.142	.248	.310	.373	-.157	1.1				

Breakout: 18%   Improve: 49%   Collapse: 19%

Given Reese's limited offensive capabilities—a result of a serious lack of bat speed and patience—the 2002 season was a good one for him. This doesn't mean he's an acceptable hitter, of course. Defensively, he's got a good arm, good hands, and outstanding range. Reese missed two weeks with a strained hamstring but did bat .285 after the All-Star break, a change from his usual late-season fade. If he has a good first half in 2003, Littlefield should be working the phones trying to move Reese for a prospect who can really help the club down the road.

Armando Rios — RF — Born: 13-Sep-71 — Age: 31 — Bats: L — Throws: L

YEAR	TM	LG	AGE	AB	H	2B	3B	HR	BB	SO	SB	CS	AVG	OBP	SLG	MLVR	EQBA	EQOBP	EQSLG	EQMLVR	VORP	DEFENSE	
2000	SFG	NL	28	233	62	15	5	10	31	43	3	2	.266	.352	.502	.112	.274	.351	.519	.133	13.7	65-RF	-3
2001	SFG	NL	29	316	82	17	3	14	34	73	3	2	.259	.331	.465	.051	.272	.341	.485	.066	12.5	86-RF	-1
2002	PIT	NL	30	208	55	11	0	1	16	39	1	1	.264	.320	.332	-.118	.270	.321	.341	-.175	-5.5	49-RF	3
2003	PIT	NL	31	191	49	10	1	4	21	38	3	1	.255	.330	.391	-.071	.255	.326	.403	-.084	-3.2		

Breakout: 19%   Improve: 36%   Collapse: 33%

Expected to provide punch after his acquisition from San Francisco in the 2001 Jason Schmidt trade, Rios immediately blew out his left knee. Last season, he re-injured the knee and was phenomenally unproductive when he did play. Rather than take him to arbitration, the Pirates released him in November. His stock has hit rock bottom but, if healthy, Rios could still make a cheap, useful part-time player for someone.

Carlos Rivera — 1B Born: 10-Jun-78 Age: 25 Bats: L Throws: L

YEAR	TM	LG	AGE	AB	H	2B	3B	HR	BB	SO	SB	CS	AVG	OBP	SLG	MLVR	EQBA	EQOBP	EQSLG	EQMLVR	VORP	DEFENSE	
2000	LYN	CRL	22	233	63	17	0	5	6	34	0	1	.270	.295	.408	.008	.221	.234	.336	-.384	-17.1	56-1B	0
2001	ALT	EAS	23	389	91	30	0	10	13	71	0	2	.234	.261	.388	-.111	.211	.239	.348	-.363	-27.4	95-1B	1
2002	ALT	EAS	24	494	149	28	2	22	27	75	1	1	.302	.348	.500	.210	.263	.298	.435	-.089	.9	112-1B	4
2003	PIT	NL	25	198	50	10	1	6	12	35	2	2	.252	.299	.409	-.102	.252	.295	.422	-.115	-3.8		

Breakout: 39%   Improve: 57%   Collapse: 25%

The 24-year-old first baseman repeated at Double-A Altoona in 2002 and this time had a good season, resulting in his being added to the ML roster in October. However, Rivera's lack of patience didn't improve much, and first basemen with his profile don't often climb the ladder successfully (see Cruz, Ivan).

Craig Wilson — RF/1B Born: 30-Nov-76 Age: 26 Bats: R Throws: R

YEAR	TM	LG	AGE	AB	H	2B	3B	HR	BB	SO	SB	CS	AVG	OBP	SLG	MLVR	EQBA	EQOBP	EQSLG	EQMLVR	VORP	DEFENSE			
2000	NAS	PCL	23	396	112	24	2	33	44	121	1	2	.283	.389	.604	.335	.254	.341	.537	.121	38.2	65-C	-8	27-1B	-2
2001	PIT	NL	24	158	49	3	1	13	15	53	3	1	.310	.394	.589	.340	.312	.391	.587	.334	19.5	18-1B	1		
2002	PIT	NL	25	368	97	16	1	16	32	116	2	3	.264	.356	.443	.089	.271	.354	.458	.051	12.5	61-RF	1	29-1B	2
2003	PIT	NL	26	373	97	19	2	20	35	106	3	4	.259	.338	.476	.057	.259	.334	.491	.048	8.1				

Breakout: 6%   Improve: 29%   Collapse: 31%

Just when the Pirates should have been penciling Wilson in for 500 at-bats to see what he can really do, the team went out and traded for Randall Simon in November and then signed Matt Stairs in December. Wilson's decent plate discipline was augmented by taking 21 plunkings from opposing pitchers. He's not good defensively at any position, but is certainly adequate enough to play first or right. With good power to all fields, Wilson is a valuable player who has years of hitting ahead of him, if only the Bucs would let him.

Jack Wilson — SS Born: 29-Dec-77 Age: 25 Bats: R Throws: R

YEAR	TM	LG	AGE	AB	H	2B	3B	HR	BB	SO	SB	CS	AVG	OBP	SLG	MLVR	EQBA	EQOBP	EQSLG	EQMLVR	VORP	DEFENSE	
2000	ARK	TXS	22	343	101	20	8	6	36	59	2	3	.294	.370	.452	.110	.248	.304	.379	-.169	4.5	88-SS	10
2000	ALT	EAS	22	139	35	7	2	1	14	17	1	3	.252	.329	.353	-.057	.225	.282	.317	-.314	-3.5	30-SS	1
2001	NAS	PCL	23	103	38	6	1	1	9	13	2	2	.369	.430	.476	.331	.337	.391	.423	.126	9.8	24-SS	4
2001	PIT	NL	23	390	87	17	1	3	16	70	1	3	.223	.256	.295	-.387	.224	.256	.298	-.393	-18.5	98-SS	5
2002	PIT	NL	24	527	133	22	4	4	37	74	5	2	.252	.306	.332	-.149	.258	.307	.343	-.208	1.5	133-SS	8
2003	PIT	NL	25	460	119	23	3	5	33	65	5	3	.260	.313	.358	-.140	.260	.310	.369	-.155	.9		

Breakout: 31%   Improve: 57%   Collapse: 19%

Wilson is a sort of experiment in keeping a living example of a shortstop from the 1950s or 1960s alive in a plastic bubble. Producing a level of offense that might have been acceptable decades ago when the Mark Belanger model was still in fashion, Wilson plays outstanding defense and has led the NL in sacrifices both of his seasons in the league. On the other side of the equation, he sucks up wads of at-bats and does nothing with them. He's young enough to improve somewhat with the bat if he got good coaching; maybe new hitting coach Gerald Perry (who came over from Seattle) can help.

Kevin Young — 1B Born: 16-Jun-69 Age: 34 Bats: R Throws: R

YEAR	TM	LG	AGE	AB	H	2B	3B	HR	BB	SO	SB	CS	AVG	OBP	SLG	MLVR	EQBA	EQOBP	EQSLG	EQMLVR	VORP	DEFENSE	
2000	PIT	NL	31	496	128	27	0	20	32	96	8	3	.258	.313	.433	-.098	.257	.301	.429	-.097	-.2	119-1B	-8
2001	PIT	NL	32	449	104	33	0	14	42	119	15	11	.232	.313	.399	-.129	.232	.309	.395	-.149	-6.8	119-1B	14
2002	PIT	NL	33	468	115	26	1	16	50	101	4	6	.246	.324	.408	-.023	.249	.323	.420	-.076	2.6	130-1B	2
2003	PIT	NL	34	293	71	16	1	10	28	64	6	3	.243	.314	.403	-.090	.243	.310	.416	-.104	-4.5		

Breakout: 21%   Improve: 56%   Collapse: 25%

For some reason, the Pirates appeared to be surprised by Young's terrible drop-off at the plate. Instead, they should have been surprised that he ever hit as well as he did in 1998–99. Young has put on weight and slowed down and as a result has lost much of his range and defensive value. He retains some pull power and will get some platoon at-bats but will probably spend most of his time riding the pine and watching Randall Simon.

Walter Young　　　　1B　Born: 18-Feb-80　Age: 23　Bats: L　Throws: R

YEAR	TM	LG	AGE	AB	H	2B	3B	HR	BB	SO	SB	CS	AVG	OBP	SLG	MLVR	EQBA	EQOBP	EQSLG	EQMLVR	VORP		DEFENSE
2000	WPT	NYP	20	92	17	4	0	2	1	26	0	0	.185	.202	.293	-.264	.151	.154	.237	-.722	-14.5		18-1B -6
2001	WPT	NYP	21	232	67	10	1	13	19	43	1	1	.289	.355	.509	.280	.213	.260	.377	-.281	-11.5		44-1B -10
2002	HIC	SAL	22	492	164	34	2	25	36	102	2	6	.333	.396	.563	.408	.247	.291	.418	-.140	-5.4		75-1B -14

Last season was Young's fourth in pro ball and easily his best, as he led the Hickory club in nearly every important offensive category. However, higher-level pitchers will probably exploit Young's overanxiousness and long swing; he needs to be more patient and wait for better pitches. In addition, he is very, very large (300 pounds or more) and will probably always struggle with his weight.

PITCHERS

Jimmy Anderson　　　Born: 22-Jan-76　Age: 27　Bats: L　Throws: L

YEAR	TM	LG	AGE	G	GS	IP	H	BB	SO	HR	ERA	EQERA	EQH9	EQBB9	EQSO9	EQHR9	PERA	VORP	STF
2000	NAS	PCL	24	2	2	13.0	18	4	7	0	4.15	5.37	14.3	2.8	4.0	0.3	6.17	0.2	1
2000	PIT	NL	24	27	26	144.0	169	58	73	13	5.25	4.77	10.3	2.9	4.0	0.7	4.88	11.7	0
2001	PIT	NL	25	34	34	206.3	232	83	89	15	5.10	4.70	10.2	3.4	3.3	0.6	4.78	18.5	-4
2002	PIT	NL	26	28	25	140.7	167	63	47	20	5.44	5.97	11.5	3.6	2.7	1.3	5.87	-7.3	-20
2003	CIN	NL	27	29	21	129.3	146	49	59	14	4.84	5.18	10.4	2.9	3.7	1.0	5.13	4.3	-10

Breakout: 11%　Improve: 52%　Collapse: 9%

The Pirates gave Anderson 89 major league starts to prove himself, showing great patience in a guy with mediocre control, no strikeout pitch, and a big league weight problem. Finally, after his third straight plus-5 ERA campaign, Pittsburgh released him during the winter meetings. Anderson had the prototypical marginal lefty's skills: deceptive delivery, average-minus fastball, average slider, average splitter, and a plus turned-over change. He might have been able to turn those skills into a league-average ERA in Pittsburgh; it's possible but not likely he can do that with the Reds.

Bronson Arroyo　　　Born: 24-Feb-77　Age: 26　Bats: R　Throws: R

YEAR	TM	LG	AGE	G	GS	IP	H	BB	SO	HR	ERA	EQERA	EQH9	EQBB9	EQSO9	EQHR9	PERA	VORP	STF
2000	NAS	PCL	23	13	13	88.7	82	25	52	7	3.65	4.45	9.8	2.6	4.4	0.9	4.01	10.4	6
2000	PIT	NL	23	20	12	71.7	88	36	50	10	6.40	5.98	10.5	3.6	5.5	1.1	5.78	-4.0	-1
2001	NAS	PCL	24	9	9	66.3	63	15	49	6	3.94	4.62	9.8	2.5	5.0	1.0	4.26	6.5	8
2001	PIT	NL	24	24	13	88.3	99	34	39	12	5.10	4.97	10.1	3.2	3.4	1.1	5.17	5.0	-12
2002	NAS	PCL	25	22	21	143.0	126	28	116	10	2.96	3.83	9.1	2.1	5.7	0.9	3.66	26.6	15
2002	PIT	NL	25	9	4	27.0	30	15	22	1	4.00	4.95	10.5	4.4	6.5	0.3	5.00	1.6	3
2003	PIT	NL	26	17	11	69.0	73	25	48	7	4.56	4.75	9.6	2.8	5.6	1.0	4.61	5.9	2

Breakout: 13%　Improve: 42%　Collapse: 19%

Arroyo is basically a right-hander with a marginal left-hander's repertoire (see above). He has a good attitude, decent control, and a usable sinker, but he doesn't have enough of anything to be successful in the rotation. (His career ERA in 29 starts is 5.66.) If he gets a little stronger Arroyo could have a career as a middle reliever/spot starter. If he were 5-foot-11 instead of 6-foot-5, he wouldn't get as many chances.

Joe Beimel　　　Born: 19-Apr-77　Age: 26　Bats: L　Throws: L

YEAR	TM	LG	AGE	G	GS	IP	H	BB	SO	HR	ERA	EQERA	EQH9	EQBB9	EQSO9	EQHR9	PERA	VORP	STF
2000	LYN	CRL	23	18	18	120.7	111	44	82	6	3.36	4.85	10.8	4.0	3.9	1.1	5.28	8.8	-2
2000	ALT	EAS	23	10	10	62.7	72	21	28	8	4.16	6.51	13.1	3.5	3.1	2.2	7.09	-7.0	-15
2001	PIT	NL	24	42	15	115.3	131	49	58	12	5.23	4.99	10.2	3.6	3.9	0.8	5.13	6.0	-12
2002	PIT	NL	25	53	8	85.3	88	45	53	9	4.64	5.21	9.8	4.2	4.9	1.0	5.02	2.0	-13
2003	PIT	NL	26	33	7	64.7	69	31	41	7	4.98	5.19	9.6	3.7	5.1	1.0	5.01	3.0	-11

Breakout: 19%　Improve: 57%　Collapse: 19%

After bombing out as a starter with the Bucs in 2001 (which should have been expected; he was 1–6 at Double-A in 2000), Beimel was recast last season as a situational lefty. In that limited role, he pitched well, struggling only when shifted to the rotation to replace the injured Dave Williams. Returning to the bullpen, he had a hard time adjusting but managed to pull himself together in September. He has enough of a fastball for that role but still needs help with his command.

Kris Benson — Born: 07-Nov-74 — Age: 28 — Bats: R — Throws: R

YEAR	TM	LG	AGE	G	GS	IP	H	BB	SO	HR	ERA	EQERA	EQH9	EQBB9	EQSO9	EQHR9	PERA	VORP	STF
2000	PIT	NL	25	32	32	217.7	206	86	184	24	3.84	3.65	8.2	2.9	6.7	0.9	3.86	44.9	18
2002	PIT	NL	27	25	25	130.3	152	50	79	18	4.70	5.50	11.2	3.1	4.9	1.3	5.52	0.1	-3
2003	PIT	NL	28	22	19	126.0	131	47	93	14	4.36	4.54	9.4	2.9	5.9	1.1	4.54	15.3	8

Breakout: 10%   Improve: 51%   Collapse: 18%

Benson underwent Tommy John elbow ligament replacement surgery on May 22, 2001. Less than a year later, the hardworking righty was back with the Pirates. His first four starts were nothing to write home about, but from June through the end of the season, Benson was 9–3 with a 3.92 ERA. Both his two-seam and four-seam fastballs have good movement and velocity, and he has a plus slider. If Benson fully regains command of his knee-buckling curve and stays healthy, he can be the Bucs' rotation anchor.

Brian Boehringer — Born: 08-Jan-70 — Age: 33 — Bats: R — Throws: R

YEAR	TM	LG	AGE	G	GS	IP	H	BB	SO	HR	ERA	EQERA	EQH9	EQBB9	EQSO9	EQHR9	PERA	VORP	STF
2000	SDP	NL	30	7	3	15.7	18	10	9	4	5.73	7.68	10.6	4.6	4.6	2.1	7.20	-3.9	-28
2001	NYY	AL	31	22	0	34.7	35	12	33	3	3.11	3.71	8.7	2.9	8.0	0.7	4.10	6.4	11
2001	SFG	NL	31	29	0	34.3	32	17	27	4	4.20	4.99	8.9	4.2	6.1	1.0	4.84	1.5	-8
2002	PIT	NL	32	70	0	79.7	65	33	65	5	3.39	3.49	7.8	3.3	6.5	0.6	3.33	16.7	2
2003	PIT	NL	33	55	0	65.3	65	29	51	7	4.25	4.43	8.9	3.4	6.3	0.9	4.47	8.0	-3

Breakout: 13%   Improve: 46%   Collapse: 23%

After spending the previous seven years as a spot starter and long reliever, Boehringer made a career-high 70 appearances as a setup pitcher for Pittsburgh. He did what he was supposed to do—get righties out and keep the ball in the park—and as a result cashed in after the season with a multiyear deal. A sinker/slider specialist, Boehringer could be traded for prospects down the stretch if he can reprise his 2002 effectiveness.

Bobby Bradley — Born: 15-Dec-80 — Age: 22 — Bats: R — Throws: R

YEAR	TM	LG	AGE	G	GS	IP	H	BB	SO	HR	ERA	EQERA	EQH9	EQBB9	EQSO9	EQHR9	PERA	VORP	STF
2000	HIC	SAL	19	14	14	82.7	62	21	118	3	2.29	3.91	8.5	3.0	7.2	0.8	3.78	14.7	27
2001	LYN	CRL	20	9	9	49.0	44	20	46	3	3.12	5.78	11.0	5.5	5.4	1.4	5.84	-1.5	1

Bradley, a first round pick in 1999, has pitched just 29 games since signing. In early 2001, he came up lame and underwent Tommy John surgery. He's got a fastball and change, but a big bending curve is his top pitch, a problematic situation for a guy with a rebuilt elbow and questionable work habits. Bradley will likely start 2003 in the Carolina League; the Pirates need to give him plenty of time to develop and not be tempted to rush him up the ladder.

Sean Burnett — Born: 17-Sep-82 — Age: 20 — Bats: L — Throws: L

YEAR	TM	LG	AGE	G	GS	IP	H	BB	SO	HR	ERA	EQERA	EQH9	EQBB9	EQSO9	EQHR9	PERA	VORP	STF
2001	HIC	SAL	18	26	26	161.3	164	33	134	11	2.62	5.47	13.1	2.9	4.3	1.5	6.20	0.6	2
2002	LYN	CRL	19	26	26	155.3	118	33	96	4	1.80	3.69	8.9	2.7	3.9	0.6	3.41	31.3	8
2003	PIT	NL	20	17	15	92.3	97	28	54	10	4.03	4.20	9.5	2.4	4.7	1.0	4.39	13.4	3

Breakout: 22%   Improve: 58%   Collapse: 0%

A dominating year in the Carolina League kept Burnett on everyone's top prospects list. He excelled at keeping the ball down, allowing only four homers in 26 starts. Burnett has an outstanding change and has added a plus curve, but he'll need to tack a little more velocity onto his low-90s fastball if he is going to be a big winner in the majors. At least two years away in the best of circumstances.

Adrian Burnside   Born: 15-Mar-77   Age: 26   Bats: R   Throws: L

YEAR	TM	LG	AGE	G	GS	IP	H	BB	SO	HR	ERA	EQERA	EQH9	EQBB9	EQSO9	EQHR9	PERA	VORP	STF
2000	SAN	TXS	23	17	17	93.0	73	55	82	6	2.90	4.50	8.4	5.6	5.8	1.0	4.80	10.4	4
2001	ALT	EAS	24	6	6	32.3	28	14	32	3	3.62	5.39	10.1	5.4	6.4	1.4	5.39	0.4	3
2001	JAX	SOU	24	13	12	67.7	44	30	67	6	2.66	4.15	8.1	4.8	6.2	1.4	3.92	10.2	6
2002	ALT	EAS	25	32	23	130.7	120	67	122	18	4.54	6.08	11.1	5.7	6.7	2.2	5.97	-8.6	-8

A 6-foot-3 southpaw who hails from Australia, Burnside joined his fourth organization in November when the Tigers acquired him for Randall Simon. Burnside has a good fastball, which he will use to all parts of the plate, and complements it with a slider. While he hasn't yet mastered a change-of-speed pitch and needs some help with command, he's got enough stuff to contribute to Detroit in a relief role within the next two years.

Josh Fogg   Born: 13-Dec-76   Age: 26   Bats: R   Throws: R

YEAR	TM	LG	AGE	G	GS	IP	H	BB	SO	HR	ERA	EQERA	EQH9	EQBB9	EQSO9	EQHR9	PERA	VORP	STF
2000	BIR	SOU	23	27	27	192.3	190	44	136	7	2.57	4.82	11.8	2.3	4.6	0.7	5.16	14.6	7
2001	CHR	INT	24	40	16	114.7	129	30	89	19	4.79	6.20	11.9	2.8	5.6	2.0	6.02	-9.4	-7
2001	CWS	AL	24	11	0	13.3	10	3	17	0	2.03	2.00	6.7	1.9	10.7	0.2	1.98	5.0	41
2002	PIT	NL	25	33	33	194.3	199	69	113	28	4.35	4.86	9.9	2.9	4.7	1.3	4.75	13.9	1
2003	*PIT*	*NL*	*26*	*25*	*21*	*130.3*	*146*	*47*	*80*	*17*	*4.87*	*5.07*	*10.1*	*2.8*	*5.0*	*1.2*	*5.03*	*8.0*	*0*

Breakout: 9%   *Improve: 41%*   *Collapse: 12%*

Stolen from the White Sox, Fogg was the league's surprise starter during the first half. He was 9–6 with a 3.56 ERA before the All-Star break because he was challenging hitters, changing speeds, and keeping the ball around the plate. Unfortunately, he fell apart in August and September and ended the season on a major down note. Left-handed hitters lit him up, and Fogg will need to use his changeup to combat that problem.

Mike Gonzalez   Born: 23-May-78   Age: 25   Bats: R   Throws: L

YEAR	TM	LG	AGE	G	GS	IP	H	BB	SO	HR	ERA	EQERA	EQH9	EQBB9	EQSO9	EQHR9	PERA	VORP	STF
2000	LYN	CRL	22	12	10	56.0	57	34	53	6	4.66	7.11	12.8	6.8	5.5	2.4	7.61	-10.0	-12
2001	LYN	CRL	23	14	2	30.7	28	7	32	3	2.93	5.55	11.6	3.1	5.9	2.2	5.53	-0.4	-6
2001	ALT	EAS	23	14	14	87.3	81	36	66	5	3.71	5.24	10.6	5.2	4.9	0.9	5.41	2.6	0
2002	ALT	EAS	24	16	16	85.3	77	47	82	4	3.80	5.20	10.3	6.1	6.7	0.7	5.17	2.9	6

Injuries have hampered Gonzalez's progress. Last year, he tore up his left knee in June and thus made only 16 starts for Altoona. However, he was 8–4 with a 3.80 ERA, showing a good sinker/slider combination. He shone in the Arizona Fall League for the second straight year, where his velocity was reported to be in the high-90s. With the Pirates perpetually scrambling for healthy starters, Gonzalez could move up quickly even though his stuff is more suited for relief, unless he develops a good change or split.

John Grabow   Born: 04-Nov-78   Age: 24   Bats: L   Throws: L

YEAR	TM	LG	AGE	G	GS	IP	H	BB	SO	HR	ERA	EQERA	EQH9	EQBB9	EQSO9	EQHR9	PERA	VORP	STF
2000	ALT	EAS	21	24	24	145.3	145	65	109	10	4.34	5.70	10.8	4.5	5.1	1.2	5.89	-3.1	5
2001	LYN	CRL	22	7	7	36.7	42	26	35	3	6.38	9.51	15.0	10.2	5.8	2.0	9.25	-16.3	-20
2001	ALT	EAS	22	10	10	50.7	30	39	42	1	3.37	4.77	6.8	9.7	5.4	0.3	4.31	4.1	-4
2002	ALT	EAS	23	28	27	146.3	181	47	97	10	5.48	7.07	14.3	3.6	4.7	1.1	6.70	-25.5	-3

Last year was another disappointing one for the lefty, a third-rounder who at one time was one of the organization's best hopes. Grabow was healthy after losing much of 2001 while recovering from surgery, but he continues to struggle to get the ball over and was hammered in Altoona for a horrendous 5.47 ERA. Blessed with a good change and a nice feel for pitching, Grabow hasn't turned his gifts into results. After being designated for assignment over the winter, he should get another chance in a different organization.

Matt Guerrier
Born: 02-Aug-78 Age: 24 Bats: R Throws: R

YEAR	TM	LG	AGE	G	GS	IP	H	BB	SO	HR	ERA	EQERA	EQH9	EQBB9	EQSO9	EQHR9	PERA	VORP	STF
2000	WNS	CRL	21	30	0	34.7	25	12	35	0	1.30	3.67	7.7	3.6	5.5	0.3	3.55	6.6	1
2000	BIR	SOU	21	23	0	23.3	17	12	19	1	2.70	4.76	8.7	5.1	5.2	0.8	4.65	1.6	-8
2001	BIR	SOU	22	15	15	98.7	85	32	75	8	3.10	4.88	9.8	3.5	4.7	1.3	5.05	6.9	4
2001	CHR	INT	22	12	12	81.3	75	18	43	7	3.54	4.30	9.7	2.4	3.8	1.1	4.05	10.9	4
2002	NAS	PCL	23	27	26	157.0	154	47	130	20	4.59	5.28	10.3	3.2	5.9	1.6	5.03	3.9	9
2003	PIT	NL	24	14	10	61.7	65	26	45	7	4.80	5.00	9.4	3.2	5.9	1.1	4.81	4.4	2

Breakout: 21%   Improve: 50%   Collapse: 21%

A closer in the low minors, Guerrier was converted to starting in 2001 in the White Sox organization, and came to Pittsburgh in a March deal that sent Damaso Marte to Chicago. Spending 2002 at Nashville, Guerrier dropped his first six starts before turning his season around, finishing 7–12. With only 53 pro starts under his belt, he will need another season in Triple-A before he's anywhere near ready to take on big league hitters. His solid mix of fastball, slider, and curve offers hope.

Mike Lincoln
Born: 10-Apr-75 Age: 28 Bats: R Throws: R

YEAR	TM	LG	AGE	G	GS	IP	H	BB	SO	HR	ERA	EQERA	EQH9	EQBB9	EQSO9	EQHR9	PERA	VORP	STF
2000	SLC	PCL	25	12	12	74.3	72	16	37	4	3.88	3.59	9.0	1.9	3.6	0.6	3.33	15.8	4
2000	MIN	AL	25	8	4	20.7	36	13	15	10	10.87	9.45	13.3	4.3	6.0	3.4	10.44	-9.1	-27
2001	NAS	PCL	26	18	13	91.7	90	25	71	10	3.44	4.60	10.2	3.0	5.2	1.2	4.75	9.1	0
2001	PIT	NL	26	31	0	40.3	34	11	24	3	2.68	3.07	7.6	2.3	4.6	0.6	3.05	10.3	-4
2002	PIT	NL	27	55	0	72.3	80	27	50	7	3.11	4.26	10.6	3.0	5.6	0.9	4.87	9.0	-6
2002	NAS	PCL	27	10	0	14.7	14	2	15	0	1.22	2.24	9.6	1.4	7.1	0.2	3.34	5.1	15
2003	PIT	NL	28	38	2	54.3	62	21	36	7	4.50	4.69	10.3	3.1	5.4	1.2	5.12	6.0	-10

Breakout: 12%   Improve: 37%   Collapse: 26%

A failure as a starter with the Twins, Lincoln has gotten his act together as a middle reliever in Pittsburgh. His 2001–02 performance should ensure future employment. However, there is a very real danger of overexposure—neither his minus fastball nor his slider is anything special.

Josias Manzanillo
Born: 16-Oct-67 Age: 35 Bats: R Throws: R

YEAR	TM	LG	AGE	G	GS	IP	H	BB	SO	HR	ERA	EQERA	EQH9	EQBB9	EQSO9	EQHR9	PERA	VORP	STF
2000	NAS	PCL	32	15	0	23.3	19	6	23	0	2.70	3.13	8.4	2.3	7.3	0.2	2.77	5.8	13
2000	PIT	NL	32	43	0	58.7	50	32	39	6	3.37	3.28	7.3	3.9	5.2	0.8	3.79	13.7	-7
2001	PIT	NL	33	71	0	79.7	60	26	80	4	3.39	2.89	6.8	2.7	7.7	0.4	2.64	22.1	13
2002	NAS	PCL	34	15	1	20.3	18	2	14	3	2.66	3.46	9.3	1.0	4.9	1.8	3.95	4.4	-7
2002	PIT	NL	34	13	0	13.0	20	5	4	5	7.62	8.47	14.7	3.1	2.5	3.6	9.25	-4.5	-51

After his surprisingly successful 2001, Manzanillo found no one interested in him as a free agent, so he had to crawl back to the Pirates and sign a minor league deal (he couldn't return to the Bucs until May 1). The last of Manzanillo's nine lives appears to have expired in 2002, as the well-traveled righty reliever was released in August after missing the middle of the season recovering from surgery to remove bone chips in his right elbow. It's possible he'll get a look-see from another team in the spring, but a real stretch to believe he'll make another comeback.

Tony McKnight
Born: 29-Jun-77 Age: 26 Bats: L Throws: R

YEAR	TM	LG	AGE	G	GS	IP	H	BB	SO	HR	ERA	EQERA	EQH9	EQBB9	EQSO9	EQHR9	PERA	VORP	STF
2000	ROU	TXS	23	6	6	32.0	39	10	24	4	4.78	6.77	14.1	3.1	5.1	1.9	6.83	-4.5	-2
2000	NWO	PCL	23	19	19	118.3	129	36	63	10	4.56	5.31	11.4	2.8	4.0	1.0	5.33	2.6	0
2000	HOU	NL	23	6	6	35.0	35	9	23	4	3.86	3.83	8.7	1.9	5.3	0.9	3.78	6.5	14
2001	NWO	PCL	24	18	18	92.7	104	24	61	10	4.76	6.08	11.9	2.9	4.5	1.2	5.79	-5.9	-3
2001	HOU	NL	24	3	3	18.0	21	3	10	4	4.00	4.53	10.8	1.4	4.3	1.8	5.38	2.0	2
2001	PIT	NL	24	12	12	69.3	88	21	36	15	5.19	5.60	11.3	2.5	4.0	1.7	6.27	-0.7	-5
2002	NAS	PCL	25	30	28	175.3	198	45	120	22	5.24	5.93	11.9	2.7	4.9	1.5	5.79	-8.3	-1
2003	PIT	NL	26	14	10	56.0	66	20	34	7	5.10	5.31	10.6	2.7	4.9	1.2	5.15	3.5	-5

Breakout: 17%   Improve: 51%   Collapse: 25%

Tony McKnight *(continued)*

Given the Bucs' shortage of starting pitching, they seemed awfully hasty in outrighting McKnight late in spring training 2002. However, their judgment was confirmed, as McKnight didn't pitch well at Triple-A. He is now drifting into the sea of high-minors pitchers who might not get another chance in the majors. McKnight could still surprise a bit, as his career has been stalled by numerous injuries, but there's not much upside for him anymore.

Brian Meadows   Born: 21-Nov-75   Age: 27   Bats: R   Throws: R

YEAR	TM	LG	AGE	G	GS	IP	H	BB	SO	HR	ERA	EQERA	EQH9	EQBB9	EQSO9	EQHR9	PERA	VORP	STF
2000	SDP	NL	24	22	22	124.7	150	50	53	24	5.34	5.91	11.5	3.0	3.5	1.6	6.29	-5.6	-10
2000	KCR	AL	24	11	10	71.7	84	14	26	8	4.77	4.22	10.3	1.5	3.2	0.8	3.89	10.2	1
2001	KCR	AL	25	10	10	50.3	73	12	21	12	6.98	6.72	12.6	2.0	3.5	1.9	6.63	-6.8	-13
2001	OMA	PCL	25	18	18	105.0	143	20	74	21	6.17	7.26	14.1	2.1	4.7	2.2	7.40	-20.5	-6
2002	NAS	PCL	26	23	22	126.3	132	26	98	15	4.28	5.21	11.0	2.2	5.5	1.5	5.01	4.1	3
2002	PIT	NL	26	11	11	62.7	62	14	31	7	3.88	4.20	9.7	1.8	4.0	1.0	3.95	9.1	1
2003	*PIT*	*NL*	*27*	*18*	*12*	*77.0*	*91*	*23*	*45*	*10*	*4.80*	*5.00*	*10.6*	*2.3*	*4.7*	*1.2*	*5.06*	*5.3*	*-3*

Breakout: 17%   Improve: 46%   Collapse: 22%

After making 22 starts at Triple-A, Meadows was promoted to Pittsburgh and made his first start on August 1. In his 11 appearances for the Bucs, he did what he always does, changing speeds, throwing his fastball and curve for strikes, and eating innings. Because he displayed four average pitches last year and worked both sides of the plate, Meadows might get another 20 starts to see if his 2002 performance represented real improvement or was just a fluke.

Roberto Novoa   Born: 15-Aug-79   Age: 23   Bats: R   Throws: R

YEAR	TM	LG	AGE	G	GS	IP	H	BB	SO	HR	ERA	EQERA	EQH9	EQBB9	EQSO9	EQHR9	PERA	VORP	STF
2001	WPT	NYP	21	14	13	79.7	76	20	55	4	3.39	7.39	14.5	3.7	3.8	1.7	6.39	-16.7	-7
2002	HIC	SAL	22	10	10	42.7	61	15	29	2	5.48	9.40	19.2	4.8	4.1	1.2	9.16	-18.5	-18
2002	WPT	NYP	22	12	12	66.7	62	8	56	4	3.64	6.52	14.1	1.8	4.7	2.1	5.37	-7.5	1

A raw talent with a big fastball, 2002 was Novoa's third season in pro ball. It was also the year that he added two years to his age in the wave of Dominican visa catch-ups. After going 1–5 in 10 starts at Hickory, he was demoted back to Williamsport in the New York-Penn League. Novoa went 8–3 after the demotion, overmatching the short-season kids—now we know why—and earning him a Rule 5 ticket to the Motor City.

Al Reyes   Born: 10-Apr-71   Age: 32   Bats: R   Throws: R

YEAR	TM	LG	AGE	G	GS	IP	H	BB	SO	HR	ERA	EQERA	EQH9	EQBB9	EQSO9	EQHR9	PERA	VORP	STF
2000	BAL	AL	29	13	0	13.0	13	11	10	2	6.92	5.64	8.1	6.0	6.5	1.1	5.61	-0.4	-14
2000	ABQ	PCL	29	30	0	38.7	33	21	39	5	3.72	4.37	8.1	4.8	7.3	1.4	4.28	4.3	-4
2001	LVG	PCL	30	19	0	29.3	24	10	37	3	3.38	3.23	7.4	3.6	8.1	1.0	3.37	7.0	9
2001	LAD	NL	30	19	0	25.7	28	13	23	3	3.85	5.03	10.3	4.3	6.9	1.0	5.66	1.0	-4
2002	NAS	PCL	31	43	0	66.7	40	22	90	5	2.70	2.93	6.1	3.4	9.4	0.9	2.66	18.2	19
2002	PIT	NL	31	15	0	17.0	9	7	21	1	2.65	2.46	5.1	3.3	9.8	0.5	2.09	5.5	25
2003	*PIT*	*NL*	*32*	*32*	*4*	*51.0*	*44*	*23*	*54*	*5*	*3.51*	*3.66*	*7.8*	*3.4*	*8.5*	*0.9*	*3.83*	*10.6*	*13*

Breakout: 21%   Improve: 45%   Collapse: 18%

Believe it or not, Reyes has appeared in the majors in each of the last eight seasons. In 2002, it was for Pittsburgh, his fourth big league club. Reyes's best pitch is his changeup; he's really just a stopgap, but there are worse pitchers in plenty of big league bullpens. The Pirates liked him enough to sign him to a split contract for 2003.

Duaner Sanchez   Born: 14-Oct-79   Age: 23   Bats: R   Throws: R

YEAR	TM	LG	AGE	G	GS	IP	H	BB	SO	HR	ERA	EQERA	EQH9	EQBB9	EQSO9	EQHR9	PERA	VORP	STF
2000	SBN	MDW	20	28	28	165.3	152	54	121	6	3.65	5.42	11.3	3.6	4.2	0.9	5.37	1.6	2
2001	LNC	CLF	21	10	10	59.0	65	18	49	7	4.58	6.24	11.7	3.6	4.3	2.0	6.11	-4.8	-2
2001	ELP	TXS	21	13	13	70.3	92	25	41	5	6.79	6.14	11.9	3.8	3.6	1.0	6.59	-5.0	-6
2002	ELP	TXS	22	31	0	35.7	31	13	37	1	3.03	4.14	8.7	3.9	7.0	0.5	3.82	4.9	7
2002	TUC	PCL	22	4	0	5.3	6	1	9	1	6.79	6.10	11.1	1.9	11.7	2.1	5.24	-0.4	34
2002	ARI	NL	22	6	0	3.7	3	5	4	1	4.86	5.99	7.1	10.5	8.3	2.4	7.60	-0.3	-14
2002	NAS	PCL	22	20	0	22.7	23	11	20	2	4.76	5.41	10.6	5.2	6.3	1.1	5.56	-0.1	-5
2002	PIT	NL	22	3	0	2.3	3	2	2	1	15.65	12.16	11.6	6.6	6.5	3.8	9.66	-1.7	-30
2003	PIT	NL	23	25	0	32.0	36	16	24	4	5.1	5.3	10.2	4.0	6.0	1.1	5.32	1.9	-9

Breakout: 13%   Improve: 45%   Collapse: 26%

After coming over from Arizona in exchange for Mike Fetters on July 6, Sanchez pitched 20 ineffective games at Nashville before joining the Bucs in September for three appearances. Not highly regarded, he is a smallish control pitcher with an average fastball, but he could help the Pirates if he can keep his pitches down.

Scott Sauerbeck   Born: 09-Nov-71   Age: 31   Bats: R   Throws: L

YEAR	TM	LG	AGE	G	GS	IP	H	BB	SO	HR	ERA	EQERA	EQH9	EQBB9	EQSO9	EQHR9	PERA	VORP	STF
2000	PIT	NL	28	75	0	75.7	76	61	83	4	4.04	4.14	8.5	5.6	8.4	0.4	4.90	10.4	4
2001	PIT	NL	29	70	0	62.7	61	40	79	4	5.60	4.87	8.6	5.2	9.5	0.5	4.58	3.6	10
2002	PIT	NL	30	78	0	62.7	50	27	70	4	2.30	3.05	7.5	3.4	8.8	0.6	3.28	16.2	15
2003	PIT	NL	31	64	0	50.7	44	26	54	4	3.44	3.58	7.9	4.0	8.6	0.7	3.98	10.5	10

Breakout: 11%   Improve: 50%   Collapse: 20%

Rebounding from a poor 2001, Sauerbeck showed again how freely available talent can benefit a team as well as how little such things matter to an organization with the gaping holes the Pirates have. Taken from the Mets in the December 1998 Rule 5 draft, he has been a mainstay of the Pittsburgh bullpen ever since. Sauerbeck posted his best performance ever last season, mixing his fine curve, changing speeds, and delivering from a variety of motions and arm angles. A prime candidate for a mid-season trade to a contender, or maybe even a deal before Opening Day.

Chris Spurling   Born: 28-Jun-77   Age: 26   Bats: R   Throws: R

YEAR	TM	LG	AGE	G	GS	IP	H	BB	SO	HR	ERA	EQERA	EQH9	EQBB9	EQSO9	EQHR9	PERA	VORP	STF
2000	TAM	FSL	23	34	0	57.0	50	22	55	1	3.79	5.22	10.0	4.4	6.1	0.4	4.86	1.0	-1
2000	LYN	CRL	23	9	0	18.3	8	3	17	1	0.98	1.53	5.2	1.7	5.2	1.1	1.74	7.8	5
2001	ALT	EAS	24	34	15	121.7	133	28	63	9	3.11	5.26	12.6	2.9	3.3	1.1	5.98	2.8	-14
2002	ALT	EAS	25	51	0	70.0	54	12	60	8	2.19	3.38	9.2	1.9	6.0	1.8	3.60	15.6	-1

A former Yankees' farmhand, Spurling nailed down 20 saves for Altoona in his second year in Double-A and was rewarded by being selected by the Braves in the December Rule 5 draft. Lacking a distinctive fastball, thriving instead on control and breaking pitches, he might be a helpful reliever at the back end of the Atlanta pen.

Salomon Torres   Born: 11-Mar-72   Age: 31   Bats: R   Throws: R

YEAR	TM	LG	AGE	G	GS	IP	H	BB	SO	HR	ERA	EQERA	EQH9	EQBB9	EQSO9	EQHR9	PERA	VORP	STF
2002	NAS	PCL	30	26	24	162.3	169	39	136	12	3.83	4.76	10.8	2.5	5.9	0.9	4.73	13.4	10
2002	PIT	NL	30	5	5	30.0	28	13	12	2	2.70	3.62	9.1	3.5	3.2	0.6	3.99	6.3	-4
2003	PIT	NL	31	18	13	82.0	90	32	55	8	4.35	4.53	9.9	3.0	5.4	1.0	4.81	10.0	2

Breakout: 17%   Improve: 45%   Collapse: 22%

One of the oddest stories of 2002 was the return of the once-promising Torres, who hung it up in 1997 to pitch for the Jehovah's Witnesses. After a brief appearance in Korea during 2001, he inked a contract with Pittsburgh in January 2002 and made 26 appearances for Nashville, posting an 8–5 record. The Pirates promoted him on September 3. While his five appearances in Bucs' garb made for a nice feel-good piece, it's not likely that his current mix of pitches will make him an effective starter. Torres no longer throws with his old bite, and his control probably won't be good enough to survive with his diminished stuff.

John VanBenschoten | Born: 14-Apr-80 | Age: 23 | Bats: R | Throws: R

YEAR	TM	LG	AGE	G	GS	IP	H	BB	SO	HR	ERA	EQERA	EQH9	EQBB9	EQSO9	EQHR9	PERA	VORP	STF
2001	WPT	NYP	21	9	9	25.7	23	10	19	0	3.50	6.65	12.7	5.6	4.1	0.4	6.01	-3.3	-14
2002	HIC	SAL	22	27	27	148.0	119	62	145	6	2.80	5.12	10.6	5.5	5.6	1.0	4.75	6.3	4

If the Pirates have one blue-chip mound prospect, it's VanBenschoten. As a two-way college player at Kent State (outfielder and closer), he led Division I in 2001 with 31 homers, and the 2001 first round pick would have been drafted by other teams as a hitter. He started slowly in the Sally League last season but then won eight of his last 10 decisions en route to an 11–4 campaign. VanBenschoten's fastball is as good as anyone's in the system, including Kris Benson's, plus he has a slider and is developing an off-speed pitch. There is some concern about overwork, but the Pirates limited him to 148 innings in 2002. If he passes his test in High-A in 2003, he could be fast-tracked to Pittsburgh. If he stumbles badly on the mound, there's still time to let him return to hitting.

Ron Villone | Born: 16-Jan-70 | Age: 33 | Bats: L | Throws: L

YEAR	TM	LG	AGE	G	GS	IP	H	BB	SO	HR	ERA	EQERA	EQH9	EQBB9	EQSO9	EQHR9	PERA	VORP	STF
2000	CIN	NL	30	35	23	141.0	154	78	77	22	5.43	5.80	10.4	4.1	4.4	1.2	5.34	-4.9	-12
2001	COL	NL	31	22	6	46.7	56	29	48	6	6.36	5.87	10.3	5.1	7.6	0.9	5.64	-2.2	-1
2001	HOU	NL	31	31	6	68.0	77	24	65	12	5.56	5.56	10.3	3.0	7.3	1.4	5.39	-1.0	1
2002	PIT	NL	32	45	7	93.0	95	34	55	8	5.81	5.26	9.9	3.0	4.8	0.8	4.34	1.7	-9
2003	PIT	NL	33	32	9	69.0	74	30	45	8	4.92	5.13	9.7	3.3	5.3	1.1	4.93	3.7	-9

Breakout: 12%   Improve: 39%   Collapse: 29%

The Pirates used Villone as a lefty long reliever and occasional starter in 2002. He missed two weeks in August with a sore elbow as he slogged through an ineffective season. He still throws hard, and he still has little idea how to control his fastball. The Bucs were his eighth club in eight years, and they won't be his last as he became a free agent after the season. Some guys, and some teams, never learn.

Ryan Vogelsong | Born: 22-Jul-77 | Age: 25 | Bats: R | Throws: R

YEAR	TM	LG	AGE	G	GS	IP	H	BB	SO	HR	ERA	EQERA	EQH9	EQBB9	EQSO9	EQHR9	PERA	VORP	STF
2000	SHV	TXS	22	27	27	155.3	153	69	147	15	4.23	5.62	11.2	4.3	6.3	1.4	5.44	-2.0	10
2001	FRE	PCL	23	10	10	58.0	35	18	53	6	2.79	2.69	6.0	3.3	6.0	1.1	2.37	18.1	18
2001	SFG	NL	23	13	0	28.7	29	14	17	5	5.64	6.06	9.6	4.1	4.6	1.5	5.73	-2.2	-13
2001	NAS	PCL	23	6	6	31.7	26	15	33	2	3.97	4.50	8.5	5.2	7.0	0.7	4.13	3.5	14
2002	LYN	CRL	24	4	4	15.7	19	7	20	0	8.03	8.79	13.9	5.7	8.3	0.3	7.02	-5.7	7
2002	ALT	EAS	24	8	8	43.7	47	10	35	5	5.56	6.40	12.7	2.6	5.7	1.8	5.70	-4.3	3

The 2001 trade that sent Jason Schmidt and John Vander Wal to the Giants for Armando Rios and Vogelsong hasn't turned out well for Pittsburgh, to put it mildly. Vogelsong suffered a torn right elbow ligament in 2001 and underwent surgery that September. Vogelsong missed most of 2002, making 12 rehab starts in the minors. When he was healthy, he had four solid pitches including a mid-90s fastball, but it will probably be another year before he comes all the way back, if he ever does.

Kip Wells | Born: 21-Apr-77 | Age: 26 | Bats: R | Throws: R

YEAR	TM	LG	AGE	G	GS	IP	H	BB	SO	HR	ERA	EQERA	EQH9	EQBB9	EQSO9	EQHR9	PERA	VORP	STF
2000	CHR	INT	23	12	12	62.0	67	27	38	10	5.37	6.31	11.6	4.0	4.8	1.9	5.90	-5.5	-5
2000	CWS	AL	23	20	20	98.7	126	58	71	15	6.02	5.94	10.6	4.2	6.1	1.1	5.98	-4.8	5
2001	CHR	INT	24	4	4	25.3	26	8	24	2	3.56	4.83	10.6	3.4	6.7	1.0	4.87	1.9	16
2001	CWS	AL	24	40	20	133.3	145	61	99	14	4.79	4.95	9.6	3.8	6.3	0.8	4.76	7.8	4
2002	PIT	NL	25	33	33	198.3	197	71	134	21	3.59	4.38	9.6	2.9	5.4	1.0	4.32	24.8	8
2003	PIT	NL	26	30	26	157.3	165	64	111	18	4.49	4.68	9.4	3.1	5.7	1.0	4.74	15.4	5

Breakout: 8%   Improve: 44%   Collapse: 10%

Wells doesn't have an outstanding pitch, but he can get to the mid-90s with his sinking fastball, though his comfort zone is lower. He also has an average curve and average slider, but he lacks a change or split to keep hitters off-balance. When Wells keeps the ball down consistently, he can win. He anchored a mediocre Pirates staff in 2002; despite an 8–2 record at the end of May, Wells captured just four games afterward, though he pitched nearly as well in the second half as he did in the first.

Dave Williams — Born: 12-Mar-79 — Age: 24 — Bats: L — Throws: L

YEAR	TM	LG	AGE	G	GS	IP	H	BB	SO	HR	ERA	EQERA	EQH9	EQBB9	EQSO9	EQHR9	PERA	VORP	STF
2000	HIC	SAL	21	24	24	170.0	145	39	193	14	2.96	4.49	10.4	2.8	5.9	1.9	4.84	19.2	13
2000	LYN	CRL	21	2	2	11.0	18	3	8	2	6.55	9.54	21.9	3.2	4.5	4.2	11.48	-4.9	-19
2001	ALT	EAS	22	9	8	58.7	45	12	39	8	2.61	3.88	9.0	2.5	4.2	2.0	4.29	10.6	2
2001	NAS	PCL	22	2	2	10.7	9	5	6	3	3.36	5.45	9.0	5.2	3.8	3.1	6.15	0.1	-17
2001	PIT	NL	22	22	18	114.0	100	45	57	15	3.71	3.78	7.8	3.3	3.8	1.1	3.93	21.7	0
2002	PIT	NL	23	9	9	43.3	38	24	33	9	4.99	5.32	8.3	4.4	6.0	1.9	5.05	0.9	2
2003	PIT	NL	24	17	13	80.7	81	37	61	12	4.85	5.05	9.0	3.5	6.1	1.4	4.97	4.8	2

Breakout: 24%   Improve: 52%   Collapse: 15%

The Pirates have been high on Williams ever since he led the Sally League in strikeouts in 2000, but he hasn't yet proven he's ready for prime time. Williams pitched just 11 times above Class A before his 2001 promotion. Last season he suffered a torn labrum in his left shoulder and underwent season-ending surgery in July. Williams is not expected back until late this season at the earliest, but he's young enough to have a good chance at making a full comeback and gaining the requisite experience to be a big league starter. That is, if he can overcome his torn labrum, as close to a death sentence injury for a pitcher as there is in today's game.

Mike Williams — Born: 29-Jul-68 — Age: 34 — Bats: R — Throws: R

YEAR	TM	LG	AGE	G	GS	IP	H	BB	SO	HR	ERA	EQERA	EQH9	EQBB9	EQSO9	EQHR9	PERA	VORP	STF
2000	PIT	NL	31	72	0	72.0	56	40	71	8	3.50	3.48	6.6	4.0	7.7	0.9	3.51	15.2	5
2001	PIT	NL	32	40	0	41.7	39	21	43	6	3.67	3.99	8.2	4.2	7.8	1.1	4.59	6.4	2
2001	HOU	NL	32	25	0	22.3	21	14	16	3	4.04	4.36	8.5	5.2	5.5	1.1	4.95	2.5	-16
2002	PIT	NL	33	59	0	61.3	54	21	43	6	2.94	3.73	8.5	2.8	5.6	0.9	3.66	11.2	-3
2003	PIT	NL	34	50	0	52.7	50	23	42	5	3.95	4.11	8.6	3.3	6.5	1.0	4.27	8.7	-2

Breakout: 15%   Improve: 50%   Collapse: 21%

Is it a sinker, slider, splitter, or a scuffball? Whatever Williams uses to get hitters out, he did it again in 2002. His 46 saves ranked third among big league pitchers, an impressive statistic for a guy whose club won just 72 games. Now would be the ideal time to trade Williams, who is both cheap and effective, but the Pirates don't seem to want to go that route. Too bad. Turning 35 this year, he's not going to get any better and an injury could reduce his value to zero. The Bucs don't have the luxury of keeping a veteran closer when their needs are so great.

St. Louis Cardinals

Over the years, we've found various and sundry reasons to criticize the three leading figures in the Cardinals organization. Manager Tony LaRussa, pitching coach Dave Duncan, and General Manager Walt Jocketty have all been fired on in this space. Criticizing them does nothing to minimize the role that all three have played in creating the popular conception within the game that St. Louis is a destination of choice for the ballplayer looking for contention, fan appreciation, and a nice city to bring his family to. But having helped to create that kind of competitive advantage, the Cardinals nevertheless managed to squander Mark McGwire's glorious final few seasons. The division titles of 1996 and 2000 had produced humiliating defeats at the hands of the Braves and Mets, and the wild card of 2001 had seen the Cardinals fall beneath the same 1-2 steamroller that the Diamondbacks used to crush all opposition that October. So if you were frustrated with the Cardinals and their big three and the organization's near misses, it would have been perfectly understandable. But in 2002, all three men were critical to the organization in the way they played their parts, helping a team that had no end of excuses for falling short to get as far as the NLCS. None of them had fallen so far as to need anything as dramatic as redemption, but if 2002 wasn't a year in which the Cardinals won it all, it was a season that could give everyone reason to appreciate strengths that often get short shrift from publications like this one.

The National League has had a gaggle of the same contenders or near-contenders for the last five or six years, each with their own strengths and weaknesses. Of the group, arguably only the Braves and the Astros have done a good job of developing self-renewing organizational engines for contention, the Braves obviously more successfully, while the Astros swing between divisional dynasty, a strong also-ran, and a retooled contender. But they're both old-fashioned

---

Cardinals Prospectus

2002 record: 97–65; First place, NL Central; Lost to Giants in Championship Series

Pythagenport Record: 96–66

Runs scored per game: 4.9 (2nd in NL)

Runs allowed per game: 4 (4th in NL)

Team EqA: .267 (3rd in NL)

2002 Batters Age: 29.4 (7th youngest in NL)

2002 Pitchers Age: 31.1 (4th oldest in NL)

Ballpark: Busch Stadium; Neutral Park; Park Factor of .992

2002: Team overcame adversity and injuries to win division with a blend of superstars and scrappers.

2003: Fragile core of star talent and LaRussa's obsessions make team a question mark.

---

contenders. Beyond them, we've had the five spendthrifts, relying predominantly on their ability to acquire top-shelf veteran talent to go toe-to-toe, all basically having to keep a wary eye on each other to count how many teams have a shot at 90 wins and a wild card if they can't win their own divisions. The Giants have been in this boat for years, and finally made it pay off with a trip to the big dance. Up until the last couple of seasons, the Mets have flirted with it. The Diamondbacks and the Dodgers have fought this war with different degrees of success, the Snakes winning it all, while the Dodgers seem stuck in a perennial wallflower role. And finishing the quintet, generally trailing the Astros, you'll find the Cardinals. All five treat their organizational talent as feeders for their drives at contention, and all of them tend to be as friskily acquisitive every winter as a thirty-something divorcee. In such a tight situation, management decisions can have a significant winnowing effect, separating the winners from the also-rans.

This year, however, several things happened that unsettled this particular logjam. Certainly, the Mets rolling over and the Astros mismanaging their opportunity created shots for others. But beyond all of that, the Cardinals were struck by an appalling tragedy with the death of Darryl Kile. And you can call it kismet or fate or the unknowable, unpredictable nature of people and how they respond in a bad spot, but it provided an object lesson for why the game is just something you see on the diamond, and character is something you can too easily overlook in people.

A man's strength, character, reputation, his achievements and perceived lack of same, these can all become props with which a critic can beat that man about the head. In our post-sarcastic, post-ironic readiness to laugh at life's straight men, it has been too easy to mock Tony LaRussa's heart-on-his-sleeve overt seriousness. LaRussa is often accused of being a failed motivator, an uninspiring martinet, and a rigidly self-important tactical micro-manager. If, as a man once said, "people as they age become a parody of things they once believed in," then perhaps we have been quick to parody Tony LaRussa as a manager in our readiness to consign him to yesterday's news and the shifting sands of history. Then again, LaRussa never had to rise to an occasion like this. But just as suddenly as Kile was gone in a time when life and the world take on a seriousness that makes the frothy, greedy, insipid '90s seem like a distant memory, a serious man was no longer a laughing matter.

But just as this was a year that reminded us about LaRussa's strengths, it was also one that reflected well on his oft-criticized pitching coach, Dave Duncan. The loyalty between the two men stretches back to the Winning Ugly White Sox of 1983, and in a season where Kile's death exacerbated the problems the Cardinals were having with their rotation, that commitment was rewarded as the two cobbled together enough of a pitching staff to win. Duncan's career has often been marked by veteran starters getting their careers back in order, and also by young pitchers who didn't quite make it. It is perhaps too easy to focus on the latter. After all, pitchers and injuries go together like Anna Nicole Smith and laughter; you wish they didn't, but you just can't help it. While Alan Benes and Rick Ankiel are big what-ifs, it would be hard to chalk up Ankiel's failings to Duncan, and Matt Morris has bounced back from Tommy John to acedom. Duncan and the Cardinals have had outstanding success with veteran starters, reinforcing Duncan's reputation as a coach who works effectively with veteran starters. In the recent past, Pat Hentgen, Woody Williams, Kent Bottenfield, Dustin Hermanson, Darryl Kile, and Garrett Stephenson have all come in with reputations on the wane, and you'd have to say all of them came out the better for working with Duncan.

The challenge that 2002 provided was a season-long exercise in crisis management in the Cardinals' rotation. While you can't automatically connect Duncan and success (causation's slippery, after all), clearly the Cards were good enough. This wasn't a season with remarkable veteran seasons as much as it was the triumph of the walking wounded, with a no-name journeyman thrown in for good measure. When the season opened, Ankiel was already out, Williams and Stephenson were both less than entirely healthy, and Andy Benes was coming off of a year with an ERA of 7.38. Despite such inauspicious beginnings, Williams was tremendous when he was healthy enough to pitch, not bad for a guy who ten years ago was perceived as an organizational soldier and the Blue Jays' 11th pitcher. In early May, virtual nobody Jason Simontacchi came up to fill in for a rotation already denuded of Benes and Stephenson, and surprised everybody by rattling off five wins and seven good starts in his first seven. After Kile's death, Andy Benes bounced back from what looked like

the certain end to give the Cardinals a game, gimpy asset down the stretch. The failures and the patches were a season-long trial, as Duncan and LaRussa tried patching the rotation with Bud Smith (who flopped), Bud Pearce (far too soon), and out of desperation, journeymen Travis Smith and Luther Hackman. Not all of the patches worked well, but to take and hold a lead with these sorts of problems in the rotation was no easy feat.

Which is where we have to give credit to GM Walt Jocketty, because as often as it might have been easy for this team to quit or its leadership to be assailed by doubt, Jocketty had a remarkable season by any estimation. With a farm system virtually bare of prospects worthy of the name, Jocketty managed to acquire two of the best stretch-drive pickups available. Hoping to reinforce a thoroughly worked pen, he picked up Rick White and later Jeff Fassero when their value was at its lowest. Lacking many homegrown prospects, he could instead rent a few to play for higher stakes. Using Luis Garcia, one of the players gotten from the Red Sox for Dustin Hermanson, he acquired Chuck Finley from the Indians. Taking advantage of the Phillies' self-inflicted distaste for Scott Rolen, he got the best player available at the end of July without having to give up anything resembling a blue chipper: a beat-up Bud Smith, plus journeymen Placido Polanco and Mike Timlin. You can argue that Jocketty took advantage of the changing economic circumstances of the game, but it isn't like he makes the rules, he just exploits them. If the Indians or Phillies didn't want to keep their players and take their eventual draft picks (acknowledging that the status of compensation picks were up in the air with the labor situation coming to a head), you can't blame Jocketty. He had a slender hand to play, and he played it masterfully, giving the Cards two key players for the stretch. And even then, rather than sit still when the rotation's cast remained in doubt, he cobbled together an ad hoc package of suspects to send to the Brewers for Jamey Wright.

As we know, in the end it wasn't enough. Although you could argue the problem was self-inflicted, the Cardinals' lack of depth hurt them in the playoffs. They could hardly replace an injured Rolen and have a bench with which to attack every offensive opportunity at the same time, not that wondering when LaRussa might use Miguel Cairo was going to make Dusty Baker or Bob Brenly lose sleep. In a season where so much had been achieved in the face of so many setbacks, it was disappointing to see the Cardinals incapable of putting their best foot forward, losing several tight playoff games.

Looking forward, however, it's hard not to like their short-term chances to remain in the same competitive niche they've held for the last three years. The Astros haven't gotten their ducks lined up in the last couple of seasons, and the Cubs and Reds, while not far off, are both still early on in their individual rebuilds; the Pirates and Brewers will continue to provide important giveaway scheduling dates for the Cardinals' marketing department.

Acknowledging that they were caught short in terms of pitching depth last summer, Jocketty has been aggressive about hauling in veteran retread candidates. He's traded for Brett Tomko, and hauled in Chris Carpenter, Joey Hamilton, and even Cal Eldred. Those are the more famous names, but he's also brought in some nifty long shots in Kiko Calero and Carlos Chantres; neither is exactly likely to be the next Simontacchi, but who thought there'd be a first edition? Barring further additions, behind the front pair of Matt Morris and Woody Williams, you've got Tomko pretty much locked into the third slot. That's a risk, but Tomko's generally acknowledged as a smart pitcher who has somehow managed to do less with more. If Duncan really is a miracle worker, it'd be hard to find him a more promising veteran vessel than Tomko. The fourth and fifth slots are open to Simontacchi, Carpenter (who's like Tomko, only more so), Hamilton, Stephenson, and Eldred. Picking won't be easy, but at least they have more options this spring. Lingering in the background are the eventual arrival of Jimmy Journell, and Ankiel represents the same wild card he's been for the last two years.

The offense will have the benefit of a full season from Scott Rolen. The greater issue is whether they'll ever get a full season from J. D. Drew, and which Edgar Renteria they get this summer. With Tino Martinez, Mike Matheny, and Fernando Vina all trundling deep into the decline phases of their careers, they're going to need all the offensive help they can get from the offensive core of Albert Pujols, Jim Edmonds, and Rolen, plus 130 games out of Drew and another strong year from Renteria. Without that, they're so dependent on their frontline hitters that if any of them fail or suffer a season-ending injury, Jocketty will almost certainly have to wait until the end of July before he can really take advantage of another financially desperate trading partner. The Astros will be running with the Cardinals all summer, but they can afford injuries that would send the Cards into a tailspin.

If there's an organizational disappointment for 2002, it's the failure to browbeat and bully either the city of St. Louis or the Missouri legislature into funding a new stadium. Politicians armed with the positive example of the Giants building their own stadium could afford to scoff at the Cardinals' threatened move across the river to East St. Louis, away from their fan base and into a location they'd have to fortify to have a shot at retaining even a fraction of their season ticket holders. So now the Cardinals are looking at arranging private funding for a downtown park, which, while it might create jealousy of the Reds or Brewers and their sweet stadium swindles, doesn't instantly convey competitiveness to the organization. The challenge for Jocketty will be continuing to provide a contender to inspire the private investors through 2006 in a way that the last three years failed to win any friends in political circles.

HITTERS

Rick Asadoorian   CF   Born: 23-Jul-80   Age: 22   Bats: R   Throws: R

YEAR	TM	LG	AGE	AB	H	2B	3B	HR	BB	SO	SB	CS	AVG	OBP	SLG	MLVR	EQBA	EQOBP	EQSLG	EQMLVR	VORP	DEFENSE
2001	AUG	SAL	20	406	86	13	6	6	47	139	13	4	.212	.300	.318	-.081	.174	.241	.261	-.499	-36.3	96-CF -3
2002	PEO	MDW	21	445	118	12	11	8	44	96	14	8	.265	.341	.396	.089	.211	.267	.322	-.345	-19.4	137-CF 2
2003	STL	NL	22	186	42	7	2	3	16	51	4	4	.225	.291	.342	-.221	.230	.293	.357	-.221	-5.3	

Breakout: 65%   Improve: 78%   Collapse: 14%

Part of the package from the Red Sox received for Dustin Hermanson, so if he turns out to be anything, the Cardinals come out even further ahead. Asadoorian is your basic assemblage of tools: he's a good flycatcher in center, he has a great arm, and he runs well. The Cardinals worked hard to get him to cut down his strikeouts, and his offensive game improved across the boards. He still has decent patience. If he takes another step forward in 2003, he could end up with a big league career.

Shaun Boyd   2B   Born: 15-Aug-81   Age: 21   Bats: R   Throws: R

YEAR	TM	LG	AGE	AB	H	2B	3B	HR	BB	SO	SB	CS	AVG	OBP	SLG	MLVR	EQBA	EQOBP	EQSLG	EQMLVR	VORP	DEFENSE
2000	JCY	APL	18	152	40	9	0	2	10	22	6	5	.263	.317	.362	-.053	.170	.200	.235	-.622	-16.7	40-CF -5
2001	PEO	MDW	19	277	78	12	2	5	33	42	20	3	.282	.360	.394	.098	.224	.285	.315	-.311	-7.3	79-2B 7
2002	PEO	MDW	20	520	163	36	5	12	54	78	32	7	.313	.382	.471	.281	.249	.302	.380	-.171	6.1	127-2B -19
2003	STL	NL	21	229	57	10	1	6	20	39	6	3	.248	.312	.382	-.118	.254	.313	.399	-.113	2.5	

Breakout: 46%   Improve: 74%   Collapse: 8%

The Cardinals aren't always quick about picking positions for their farmhands. A 2000 1st rounder or no, they didn't treat Boyd any differently, wrestling with a choice between shortstop, center field, or second. They're now adamant that it'll be second for the duration. He could move up quickly; his 2001 season was shortened by a broken cheekbone, and his repeat engagement in the Midwest League was a near-complete success, his 40 errors excepted.

Miguel Cairo   2B   Born: 04-May-74   Age: 29   Bats: R   Throws: R

YEAR	TM	LG	AGE	AB	H	2B	3B	HR	BB	SO	SB	CS	AVG	OBP	SLG	MLVR	EQBA	EQOBP	EQSLG	EQMLVR	VORP	DEFENSE			
2000	TBY	AL	26	375	98	18	2	1	29	34	28	7	.261	.318	.328	-.239	.271	.318	.340	-.182	3.1	97-2B	3		
2001	IOW	PCL	27	123	37	7	1	3	8	11	3	4	.301	.348	.447	.060	.268	.311	.398	-.114	3.3	25-2B	-5		
2001	CHC	NL	27	123	35	3	1	2	16	21	2	1	.285	.367	.374	-.012	.288	.369	.384	-.010	6.4	22-3B	-2		
2002	STL	NL	28	184	46	9	2	2	13	36	1	1	.250	.310	.353	-.107	.262	.316	.374	-.144	-2.6	11-LF	-2	12-2B	-2
2003	*STL*	*NL*	*29*	*144*	*37*	*7*	*1*	*1*	*12*	*21*	*3*	*1*	*.255*	*.316*	*.345*	*-.157*	*.260*	*.317*	*.360*	*-.153*	*-1.4*				

Breakout: 4%   *Improve: 29%*   *Collapse: 37%*

Rarely was so much wishful thinking expended on such an odd, unworthy vessel. The Cardinals wish and sometimes pretend that Cairo is as good as Placido Polanco, but he isn't. He doesn't hit, and as he showed in the playoffs, he's really only an emergency third baseman—if he plays anywhere other than second, he's trouble. Why the Cardinals set up their postseason roster to carry Cairo and Wilson Delgado, and not anyone who could hit, is one of those little annoying areas where you wish that Jocketty would reign in LaRussa's fascination with players about as good as LaRussa was.

Mike Coolbaugh   INF   Born: 05-Jun-72   Age: 31   Bats: R   Throws: R

YEAR	TM	LG	AGE	AB	H	2B	3B	HR	BB	SO	SB	CS	AVG	OBP	SLG	MLVR	EQBA	EQOBP	EQSLG	EQMLVR	VORP	DEFENSE			
2000	COH	INT	28	387	105	28	0	23	67	96	6	3	.271	.383	.522	.219	.247	.346	.474	.038	27.6	54-SS	-7	27-2B	-1
2001	IND	INT	29	347	93	24	3	10	39	92	3	2	.268	.350	.441	.089	.252	.329	.416	-.068	11.3	79-3B	12	15-SS	4
2001	MIL	NL	29	70	14	6	0	2	5	16	0	0	.200	.273	.371	-.255	.211	.278	.380	-.243	-1.1	15-3B	0		
2002	MEM	PCL	30	411	100	20	1	29	51	126	9	3	.243	.340	.509	.126	.225	.310	.463	-.060	14.7	107-3B	10		
2002	STL	NL	30	12	1	0	0	0	1	3	0	0	.083	.154	.083	-.810	.167	.231	.167	-.650	-1.6				
2003	*PHI*	*NL*	*31*	*196*	*45*	*10*	*1*	*8*	*24*	*55*	*4*	*2*	*.228*	*.317*	*.404*	*-.094*	*.233*	*.319*	*.425*	*-.083*	*2.7*				

Breakout: 25%   *Improve: 50%*   *Collapse: 36%*

As an example of the kind of player that the Cardinals could have had on their postseason roster, someone who can play third with grace and short in a pinch, and who can do a wee bit of mashing, we present Mike Coolbaugh. A long swing probably keeps him from being the kind of guy you want on your bench, since he probably wouldn't cash in many pinch-hitting opportunities, but if something bad happens to your starting third baseman or shortstop, who do you want in the lineup? A second baseman who can't do more than paste a single, or somebody who can actually start? Coolbaugh's too old to have a real future. In an infield where you needed to have a spot-starter at least twice a week, he'd be handy, but that isn't the Cardinals.

Ivan Cruz   1B   Born: 03-May-68   Age: 35   Bats: L   Throws: L

YEAR	TM	LG	AGE	AB	H	2B	3B	HR	BB	SO	SB	CS	AVG	OBP	SLG	MLVR	EQBA	EQOBP	EQSLG	EQMLVR	VORP	DEFENSE	
2000	NAS	PCL	32	121	38	11	0	7	15	26	0	0	.314	.394	.579	.346	.281	.349	.512	.127	7.4	26-1B	2
2001	HNS	JCL	33	239	56	5	0	14	25	62	0	0	.234	.307	.431	-.009	.237	.306	.452	-.072	4.0		
2002	MEM	PCL	34	461	129	27	0	35	49	96	0	0	.280	.353	.566	.264	.255	.321	.510	.051	18.6	121-1B	-2
2002	STL	NL	34	14	5	0	0	1	1	3	0	0	.357	.400	.571	.432	.357	.400	.571	.381	1.8		
2003	*SLN*	*NL*	*35*	*110*	*25*	*5*	*0*	*5*	*11*	*27*	*1*	*1*	*.230*	*.302*	*.424*	*-.092*	*.235*	*.304*	*.443*	*-.086*	*-1.3*		

Breakout: 11%   *Improve: 41%*   *Collapse: 39%*

After leading the minor leagues in home runs, you'd think the Cardinals could have found a way to cram Cruz onto their postseason roster. Instead, they wanted to have Cairo, Wilson Delgado, and Mike Difelice all present and accounted for. You never know when you're going to need a third catcher in the postseason, after all. Of course, you can't pinch-hit for your starting catcher and keep Marrero in the outfield and use that third catcher if you don't have anyone to pinch-hit with in the first place. At this point, Cruz would push Tino for the job in a fair fight, not that one's coming.

Wilson Delgado   INF   Born: 15-Jul-72   Age: 30   Bats: B   Throws: R

YEAR	TM	LG	AGE	AB	H	2B	3B	HR	BB	SO	SB	CS	AVG	OBP	SLG	MLVR	EQBA	EQOBP	EQSLG	EQMLVR	VORP		DEFENSE			
2000	KCR	AL	27	83	22	1	0	0	6	17	1	1	.265	.315	.277	-.333	.268	.310	.280	-.286	-1.4		19-2B	8		
2001	OMA	PCL	28	255	63	11	2	4	16	43	8	3	.247	.294	.353	-.222	.224	.268	.314	-.346	-8.5		40-2B	-6	17-3B	-4
2002	MEM	PCL	29	365	95	19	2	7	23	54	2	5	.260	.309	.381	-.090	.240	.286	.349	-.252	-3.2		94-SS	15		
2002	STL	NL	29	20	4	2	0	2	0	6	0	0	.200	.200	.600	.008	.200	.200	.600	-.083	.2					
2003	STL	NL	30	139	33	6	1	2	10	25	2	1	.236	.287	.341	-.222	.241	.289	.356	-.222	-2.3					

Breakout: 39%   Improve: 60%   Collapse: 24%

There are equally bad-hitting utility infielders floating around, to be sure, but Delgado can definitely handle short. Choosing between Delgado and Cairo for the postseason roster should have been an "either-or" proposition, not an "and." You spend all season getting to the postseason; why hurt your chances with choices like these?

Mike Difelice   C   Born: 28-May-69   Age: 34   Bats: R   Throws: R

YEAR	TM	LG	AGE	AB	H	2B	3B	HR	BB	SO	SB	CS	AVG	OBP	SLG	MLVR	EQBA	EQOBP	EQSLG	EQMLVR	VORP		DEFENSE	
2000	TBY	AL	31	204	49	13	1	6	12	40	0	0	.240	.282	.402	-.216	.246	.282	.419	-.156	4.0		58-C	-4
2001	TBY	AL	32	149	31	5	1	2	8	39	1	1	.208	.263	.295	-.342	.228	.282	.329	-.295	-2.3		45-C	2
2002	STL	NL	33	174	40	11	0	4	17	42	0	0	.230	.302	.362	-.122	.237	.304	.384	-.170	3.0		49-C	2
2003	KCA	AL	34	142	34	8	1	4	11	33	0	0	.236	.294	.375	-.141	.233	.294	.372	-.198	-1.1			

Breakout: 34%   Improve: 62%   Collapse: 23%

First added to be the sweet-swinging backup to Mike Matheny, Difelice has now moved on to the Royals, where he'll partner up with Brent Mayne to create the most feeble platoon in the major leagues.

J. D. Drew   RF   Born: 20-Nov-75   Age: 27   Bats: L   Throws: R

YEAR	TM	LG	AGE	AB	H	2B	3B	HR	BB	SO	SB	CS	AVG	OBP	SLG	MLVR	EQBA	EQOBP	EQSLG	EQMLVR	VORP		DEFENSE	
2000	STL	NL	24	407	120	17	2	18	67	99	17	9	.295	.402	.479	.167	.289	.388	.469	.142	25.4		115-RF	-5
2001	STL	NL	25	375	121	18	5	27	57	75	13	3	.323	.417	.613	.433	.326	.418	.616	.432	57.2		100-RF	1
2002	STL	NL	26	424	107	19	1	18	57	104	8	2	.252	.352	.429	.065	.259	.352	.449	.025	11.6		100-RF	1
2003	STL	NL	27	416	115	21	2	20	63	94	10	4	.275	.373	.479	.129	.281	.375	.500	.146	20.2			

Breakout: 6%   Improve: 45%   Collapse: 15%

This year's breakdown? Tendonitis in both knees. He's already having significant joint trouble before 30? Is he going to break out, or did he already do it in 2001? It looks like PECOTA doesn't care for his odds, and at this point, I can't say I disagree. Drew's a very useful player, but let's not bring up Fred Lynn. Fred Lynn was great first and hurt early. Drew has only been very good and pretty much hurt all along. If this winter's relatively new microsurgery procedure rejuvenates the dead tendon in his left knee, chalk it up to another modern medical miracle. Hope for it, because Cardinals fans deserve to see Drew play a full season, and it's pretty certain that he'd enjoy himself.

Chris Duncan   1B   Born: 05-May-81   Age: 22   Bats: L   Throws: R

YEAR	TM	LG	AGE	AB	H	2B	3B	HR	BB	SO	SB	CS	AVG	OBP	SLG	MLVR	EQBA	EQOBP	EQSLG	EQMLVR	VORP		DEFENSE	
2000	PEO	MDW	19	450	115	34	0	8	36	111	1	2	.256	.319	.384	.026	.205	.242	.313	-.410	-37.5		85-1B	-22
2001	POT	CRL	20	168	30	6	0	3	10	47	4	4	.179	.229	.268	-.269	.152	.196	.228	-.646	-24.7		47-1B	0
2001	PEO	MDW	20	297	91	23	2	13	36	55	13	3	.306	.387	.529	.336	.235	.297	.397	-.167	-5.8		78-1B	-27
2002	PEO	MDW	21	487	132	25	4	16	44	118	5	5	.271	.340	.437	.147	.217	.267	.352	-.299	-25.9		114-1B	-14
2003	STL	NL	22	183	40	8	1	5	18	49	2	2	.220	.295	.360	-.195	.225	.296	.376	-.194	-7.6			

Breakout: 56%   Improve: 74%   Collapse: 15%

The Cardinals are maintaining their optimism about their pitching coach's son, pointing out that Duncan had a good second half, but this was his third year in the Midwest League, and nobody makes the majors for being invited to join the Peoria Knights of Columbus. He's still got significant problems commanding the strike zone, but he's young enough to master them. And his defense? Well, at least it can only improve. But if he doesn't make it to High-A and thrive this year, they can't afford to be so sanguine about his chances.

Jim Edmonds   CF   Born: 27-Jun-70   Age: 33   Bats: L   Throws: L

YEAR	TM	LG	AGE	AB	H	2B	3B	HR	BB	SO	SB	CS	AVG	OBP	SLG	MLVR	EQBA	EQOBP	EQSLG	EQMLVR	VORP	DEFENSE
2000	STL	NL	30	525	155	25	0	42	103	167	10	3	.295	.416	.583	.335	.292	.406	.573	.315	76.5	136-CF 3
2001	STL	NL	31	500	152	38	1	30	93	136	5	5	.304	.417	.564	.344	.306	.416	.567	.338	79.8	131-CF 2
2002	STL	NL	32	476	148	31	2	28	86	134	4	3	.311	.425	.561	.397	.316	.424	.575	.373	74.6	130-CF 6
2003	STL	NL	33	424	116	23	2	22	76	115	6	3	.274	.387	.495	.170	.280	.389	.517	.189	37.1	

Breakout: 1%   Improve: 26%   Collapse: 15%

As much as Edmonds is one of those signature players you love to watch play because he's reeeally good, there has to be something a little frustrating to see the Angels actually reach the World Series first, let alone win the damned thing. Beyond his two weeks on the DL, Edmonds started 132 games, but he wasn't really that broken-down this year. Other than missing 15 starts earlier in the year to injury, he was rested for six more in September, and spead out over the year, LaRussa sat him against some of the usual left-handed suspects (Randy Johnson, Al Leiter, Shawn Estes twice, etc.). If LaRussa can continue to spare him now and again, Edmonds's chances of avoiding another 1999-style breakdown are decent. Given his style of play and his advancing age, Edmonds is going to need his manager to do exactly that.

John Gall   1B   Born: 02-Apr-78   Age: 25   Bats: R   Throws: R

YEAR	TM	LG	AGE	AB	H	2B	3B	HR	BB	SO	SB	CS	AVG	OBP	SLG	MLVR	EQBA	EQOBP	EQSLG	EQMLVR	VORP	DEFENSE	
2000	NWJ	NYP	22	259	62	10	0	2	25	37	16	5	.239	.309	.301	-.065	.190	.233	.245	-.531	-30.4	58-1B -5	12-3B -1
2001	PEO	MDW	23	205	62	23	0	4	16	18	0	3	.302	.364	.473	.228	.234	.281	.364	-.244	-8.0	43-1B -5	
2001	POT	CRL	23	319	101	25	0	4	24	40	5	6	.317	.370	.433	.210	.255	.300	.359	-.201	-9.1	44-1B -5	28-3B -5
2002	NHV	EAS	24	526	166	45	3	20	38	75	4	1	.316	.364	.527	.293	.273	.315	.455	-.021	10.2	93-1B -7	17-3B -5
2003	STL	NL	25	203	52	11	1	5	14	31	3	2	.255	.306	.394	-.107	.261	.308	.411	-.101	-3.1		

Breakout: 26%   Improve: 54%   Collapse: 19%

"Stones" might have had a future if he'd been put at third or moved out to left, but as things stand now, Gall is running down the exciting Russ Morman career path, trapped in an almost-major league universe populated by Myron Noodleman and Mike Veeck. It sounds nicer than it is. Gall hit into 26 twin-killings, so as contact guys go, he's dangerous to both teams with a runner at first.

Reid Gorecki   CF   Born: 22-Dec-80   Age: 22   Bats: R   Throws: R

YEAR	TM	LG	AGE	AB	H	2B	3B	HR	BB	SO	SB	CS	AVG	OBP	SLG	MLVR	EQBA	EQOBP	EQSLG	EQMLVR	VORP	DEFENSE
2002	NWJ	NYP	21	274	77	8	13	8	20	57	22	11	.281	.334	.493	.229	.206	.243	.365	-.335	-11.4	70-CF -2

Gorecki was the team's 13th round pick from the University of Delaware, coming out after a junior season where he led the Colonial Athletic Association in runs scored. Look at the triples, steals, and position, and you think he can lead off. But he's flashed enough power that at this point it would be premature to slot him for anything beyond being one of the more promising hitters in a shallow system.

Dee Haynes   LF   Born: 22-Feb-78   Age: 25   Bats: R   Throws: R

YEAR	TM	LG	AGE	AB	H	2B	3B	HR	BB	SO	SB	CS	AVG	OBP	SLG	MLVR	EQBA	EQOBP	EQSLG	EQMLVR	VORP	DEFENSE
2000	NWJ	NYP	22	243	62	18	4	7	16	53	4	1	.255	.304	.449	.134	.196	.225	.344	-.406	-20.2	63-LF -11
2001	POT	CRL	23	417	121	24	3	13	14	82	5	1	.290	.330	.456	.168	.241	.270	.387	-.228	-16.5	77-RF -2
2002	NHV	EAS	24	504	157	29	4	21	25	67	3	2	.312	.357	.510	.256	.273	.306	.447	-.049	5.0	122-LF -8
2003	STL	NL	25	202	52	11	1	6	11	36	2	2	.256	.300	.419	-.083	.262	.302	.437	-.076	-2.4	

Breakout: 35%   Improve: 58%   Collapse: 21%

One of the more advanced hitters in the organization, Haynes isn't really a prospect. He's consistently caught fishing on the outside corner, he isn't a good fielder, and he didn't turn heads in the Arizona Fall League.

Gabe Johnson   3B   Born: 21-Sep-79   Age: 23   Bats: R   Throws: R

YEAR	TM	LG	AGE	AB	H	2B	3B	HR	BB	SO	SB	CS	AVG	OBP	SLG	MLVR	EQBA	EQOBP	EQSLG	EQMLVR	VORP	DEFENSE	
2000	PEO	MDW	20	197	31	8	0	4	13	91	1	2	.157	.224	.259	-.337	.134	.170	.223	-.714	-24.8	31-C -5	19-3B -1
2001	PEO	MDW	21	134	30	10	4	2	16	49	1	1	.224	.316	.403	.002	.174	.244	.312	-.424	-8.6	33-3B -7	
2001	POT	CRL	21	281	53	14	0	4	21	113	2	3	.189	.252	.281	-.213	.163	.213	.247	-.581	-29.8	83-3B -10	
2002	PEO	MDW	22	516	128	32	0	26	57	153	6	6	.248	.325	.461	.139	.198	.256	.364	-.316	-17.5	120-3B -6	
2003	STL	NL	23	182	39	8	1	6	17	65	2	3	.214	.287	.363	-.208	.218	.288	.379	-.208	-4.2		

Breakout: 71%   Improve: 77%   Collapse: 15%

Gabe Johnson *(continued)*

A high school catcher drafted in the 3rd round in 1998, Johnson got pushed up the chain a bit too quickly, getting hurt and struggling behind the plate. Johnson got his first serious playing time and was moved to third for good in 2001, and it seems to have paid off. He finally put something together in 2002, posting a nifty little season as Peoria's top slugger. The Chiefs had their best season ever, and smacked down Lansing in the playoffs, including a cliching Game Four where they scored eight runs in the top of the 9th to take an 11–10 lead and win. Whether his poor defensive reputation is something that will change once he doesn't have to throw in Chris Duncan's general direction remains to be seen.

Eli Marrero C Born: 17-Nov-73 Age: 29 Bats: R Throws: R

YEAR	TM	LG	AGE	AB	H	2B	3B	HR	BB	SO	SB	CS	AVG	OBP	SLG	MLVR	EQBA	EQOBP	EQSLG	EQMLVR	VORP	DEFENSE			
2000	STL	NL	26	102	23	3	1	5	9	16	5	0	.225	.307	.422	-.148	.233	.298	.427	-.125	3.0	29-C	4		
2001	STL	NL	27	203	54	11	3	6	15	36	6	3	.266	.317	.438	-.034	.267	.317	.442	-.041	10.9	52-C	-1		
2002	STL	NL	28	397	104	19	1	18	40	72	14	2	.262	.330	.451	.064	.270	.333	.473	.034	12.8	84-OF	3	26-C	-5
2003	STL	NL	29	412	108	20	3	15	39	74	13	5	.262	.328	.435	-.010	.268	.330	.454	.000	10.6				

Breakout: 17%   Improve: 52%   Collapse: 11%

Marrero finally had a full season where he lived up to the promise that has always been held out for him, but he did getting most of his playing time in the outfield. A study we really need to get around doing is seeing how much people's hitting improves once they have fewer defensive responsibilities at an easier position. It's an intuitive argument, and we have plenty of subjective and anecdotal information, from Tony Phillips to Mickey Tettleton; you can argue about guys like Ron Gant and Danny Tartabull, certainly, just like you can argue about Mickey Mantle's days as a shortstop. Anyway, it would be worth carving out the time to see if there's anything to quantify what might just be a shared stathead instinct. At any rate, Marrero finally blossomed, and while it's nice to speculate he could have hit this well catching 100 times a year, the obvious risk is that his past health issues prevent him from taking on that kind of workload. If this means that LaRussa winds up with the best possible variation on his well-worked Scott Hemond super-utility theme, then it's still a source of strength. It also won't stop us from wishing...

Tino Martinez 1B Born: 07-Dec-67 Age: 35 Bats: L Throws: R

YEAR	TM	LG	AGE	AB	H	2B	3B	HR	BB	SO	SB	CS	AVG	OBP	SLG	MLVR	EQBA	EQOBP	EQSLG	EQMLVR	VORP	DEFENSE	
2000	NYY	AL	32	569	147	37	4	16	52	74	4	1	.258	.329	.422	-.074	.270	.334	.443	-.007	12.8	144-1B	1
2001	NYY	AL	33	589	165	24	2	34	42	89	1	2	.280	.330	.501	.117	.298	.350	.538	.183	42.1	142-1B	6
2002	STL	NL	34	511	134	25	1	21	58	71	3	2	.262	.340	.438	.065	.269	.342	.456	.025	16.5	135-1B	17
2003	STL	NL	35	380	100	20	1	14	38	57	3	1	.264	.333	.437	.001	.270	.335	.456	.012	5.5		

Breakout: 14%   Improve: 55%   Collapse: 12%

It's only going to get worse, unfortunately. As much as he's a good guy in a city that loves its ballplayers, it's only going to get worse, unfortunately. His bat speed is slowing, and he's been reduced to lunging at off-speed stuff. He's still nimble around the bag, but that's not what the Cardinals are paying him for. Since Tino placed the call, do you think Jocketty regrets picking up the phone that day?

Mike Matheny C Born: 22-Sep-70 Age: 32 Bats: R Throws: R

YEAR	TM	LG	AGE	AB	H	2B	3B	HR	BB	SO	SB	CS	AVG	OBP	SLG	MLVR	EQBA	EQOBP	EQSLG	EQMLVR	VORP	DEFENSE	
2000	STL	NL	29	417	109	22	1	6	32	96	0	0	.261	.320	.362	-.181	.262	.312	.362	-.168	7.4	113-C	18
2001	STL	NL	30	381	83	12	0	7	28	76	0	1	.218	.278	.304	-.325	.223	.282	.312	-.322	-9.2	110-C	11
2002	STL	NL	31	315	77	12	1	3	32	49	1	3	.244	.318	.317	-.144	.253	.322	.331	-.198	3.0	87-C	6
2003	STL	NL	32	241	56	10	1	3	21	43	1	1	.233	.299	.321	-.230	.239	.300	.336	-.230	-4.1		

Breakout: 20%   Improve: 48%   Collapse: 28%

He's about as respected a pro as you'll find without being able to hit. At the plate, he's about as much of a noncontributor as a player can be. His defense helps, but you can't help but think that Matheny's combination of extraordinary toughness on the field and good works off of it aren't the basic reason why LaRussa and company make do. In a perfect world, good citizenship would be enough, but the diamond demands a different kind of perfection.

Keith McDonald   C   Born: 08-Feb-73   Age: 30   Bats: R   Throws: R

YEAR	TM	LG	AGE	AB	H	2B	3B	HR	BB	SO	SB	CS	AVG	OBP	SLG	MLVR	EQBA	EQOBP	EQSLG	EQMLVR	VORP	DEFENSE	
2000	MEM	PCL	27	266	70	15	0	5	28	59	0	2	.263	.340	.376	-.108	.236	.297	.341	-.244	-.6	71-C	3
2001	MEM	PCL	28	333	87	22	1	11	24	60	1	0	.261	.315	.432	-.051	.237	.286	.389	-.197	3.3	86-C	-3
2002	MEM	PCL	29	267	72	20	0	12	15	55	1	2	.270	.325	.479	.086	.249	.294	.442	-.098	9.5	78-C	0
2003	CHC	NL	30	124	29	6	0	4	10	26	2	1	.236	.294	.386	-.151	.243	.297	.405	-.141	1.0		

Breakout: 24%   Improve: 54%   Collapse: 19%

When the Cubs decided that they had a catching problem they needed to fix, they fixed it with a vengeance. Not only have they dumped both Hundley and Girardi, they've brought in Damian Miller, Paul Bako, and Keith McDonald. All three of them are better than Girardi and Hundley, to be sure, but they can't keep all of them, let alone keep all three and go a-hunting for wild I-Rod in the bargain bin.

Chad Meyers   CF/2B?   Born: 08-Aug-75   Age: 27   Bats: R   Throws: R

YEAR	TM	LG	AGE	AB	H	2B	3B	HR	BB	SO	SB	CS	AVG	OBP	SLG	MLVR	EQBA	EQOBP	EQSLG	EQMLVR	VORP	DEFENSE			
2000	IOW	PCL	24	301	81	10	0	2	43	41	34	15	.269	.370	.322	-.130	.236	.321	.286	-.272	-4.8	60-2B	-16	15-OF	-2
2000	CHC	NL	24	52	9	2	0	0	3	11	1	0	.173	.232	.212	-.624	.189	.230	.226	-.564	-5.8				
2001	IOW	PCL	25	446	134	31	5	9	58	72	27	9	.300	.411	.453	.182	.268	.367	.402	-.004	26.4	101-2B	-18	19-RF	-1
2002	SAC	PCL	26	54	11	0	0	1	12	10	0	0	.204	.358	.259	-.205	.182	.324	.236	-.355	-3.3				
2002	MEM	PCL	26	358	96	19	1	8	51	54	43	9	.268	.389	.394	.081	.253	.356	.371	-.077	10.3	57-CF	-3	18-2B	2
2003	SEA	AL	27	164	40	8	1	3	18	27	7	2	.243	.329	.362	-.094	.257	.347	.390	-.063	3.6				

Breakout: 27%   Improve: 54%   Collapse: 25%

It only seems like he's been around forever, but Meyers hasn't turned 28 yet. He's still flipping back and forth between center and second, playing whichever position the team he's with needs filled. He's a decent spare part as a pinch hitter and pinch-runner, and with the Mariners he'd be an improvement on guys like Gipson or Bloomquist.

Yadier Molina   C   Born: 13-Jul-82   Age: 20   Bats: R   Throws: R

YEAR	TM	LG	AGE	AB	H	2B	3B	HR	BB	SO	SB	CS	AVG	OBP	SLG	MLVR	EQBA	EQOBP	EQSLG	EQMLVR	VORP	DEFENSE	
2001	JCY	APL	18	158	41	11	0	4	12	23	1	1	.259	.324	.405	.051	.174	.217	.273	-.532	-12.6	42-C	5
2002	PEO	MDW	19	393	110	20	0	7	21	36	2	7	.280	.333	.384	.074	.224	.258	.313	-.368	-13.2	103-C	14
2003	STL	NL	20	194	45	7	1	5	12	27	1	1	.233	.286	.351	-.214	.238	.287	.367	-.213	-2.1		

Breakout: 62%   Improve: 75%   Collapse: 11%

Yes, he's the third catching brother of the Flying Molinas. Yes, look at the name, look at the cringe, let your suspicions rise up, and then take some reassurance: he was drafted out of Puerto Rico, so he really ought to be 20 going on 21. Like both Ben and Jose, he's quick on his feet behind the plate, but he may be the best gun of the bunch. Better still, he showed a little bit of pop, so he might end up being the best Molina in every way.

John Nelson   SS   Born: 03-Mar-79   Age: 24   Bats: R   Throws: R

YEAR	TM	LG	AGE	AB	H	2B	3B	HR	BB	SO	SB	CS	AVG	OBP	SLG	MLVR	EQBA	EQOBP	EQSLG	EQMLVR	VORP	DEFENSE	
2001	NWJ	NYP	22	252	60	16	3	8	35	76	14	3	.238	.338	.421	.123	.184	.255	.323	-.382	-13.7	59-CF	-7
2002	PEO	MDW	23	481	132	28	5	16	54	123	16	3	.274	.351	.453	.185	.218	.275	.362	-.269	-6.5	129-SS	-7
2003	STL	NL	24	179	41	8	1	5	18	53	4	5	.228	.300	.378	-.155	.233	.302	.395	-.152	-.5		

Breakout: 61%   Improve: 76%   Collapse: 12%

A shortstop at the University of Kansas before he was picked in 2001, the Cardinals tried moving him to center, but then thought better of it and returned him to short. He was named the best defensive shortstop in the Midwest League in *Baseball America*'s polls, but that could have been a sympathy vote for the guy who had to play with Chris Duncan's stone hands at first, and flanked by Shaun Boyd (40 errors) and Gabe Johnson (29 more). In this organization, he's flirting with prospect status, but he was a big program player in the Midwest League. If he's going to have a career, he'll have to move up quickly.

Eduardo Perez   PH   Born: 11-Sep-69   Age: 33   Bats: R   Throws: R

YEAR	TM	LG	AGE	AB	H	2B	3B	HR	BB	SO	SB	CS	AVG	OBP	SLG	MLVR	EQBA	EQOBP	EQSLG	EQMLVR	VORP	DEFENSE			
2000	MEM	PCL	30	277	80	12	3	19	43	48	10	3	.289	.386	.560	.268	.259	.341	.493	.066	11.9	33-1B	-1	21-3B	0
2000	STL	NL	30	91	27	4	0	3	5	19	1	0	.297	.354	.440	.025	.304	.344	.446	.046	3.3	19-1B	2		
2002	STL	NL	32	154	31	9	0	10	17	36	0	0	.201	.293	.455	-.037	.205	.294	.474	-.090	-.6	25-RF	1		
2003	STL	NL	33	148	35	7	0	7	17	33	1	1	.234	.317	.433	-.053	.239	.319	.452	-.045	-.4				

Breakout: 18%   Improve: 53%   Collapse: 27%

Eduardo Perez (continued)

Perez is a perfect example of what you can do with free talent. Perez can hurt lefties (.271/.354/.643 in 2002) and play either infield or outfield corner in a pinch. And since he cost half as much as Bobby Bonilla did in 2001, there was no part of going with Perez that didn't make sense. He may get sucked into more starts at first than would be wise as Tino's decay slips into its more advanced stages, but Perez can continue to be a nifty platoon mate for somebody.

Albert Pujols   LF/3B   Born: 16-Jan-80   Age: 23   Bats: R   Throws: R

YEAR	TM	LG	AGE	AB	H	2B	3B	HR	BB	SO	SB	CS	AVG	OBP	SLG	MLVR	EQBA	EQOBP	EQSLG	EQMLVR	VORP		DEFENSE		
2000	PEO	MDW	20	395	128	32	6	17	38	37	2	4	.324	.390	.565	.424	.253	.295	.440	-.096	9.8	103-3B	12		
2000	POT	CRL	20	81	23	8	1	2	7	8	1	1	.284	.341	.481	.180	.229	.264	.398	-.232	-.9	21-3B	4		
2001	STL	NL	21	590	194	47	4	37	69	93	1	3	.329	.407	.610	.421	.333	.408	.616	.426	88.2	69-OF	-1	54-3B	4
2002	STL	NL	22	590	185	40	2	34	72	69	2	4	.314	.396	.561	.361	.321	.398	.580	.346	69.1	87-LF	1	33-3B	0
2003	STL	NL	23	609	187	42	2	34	75	79	4	3	.307	.385	.553	.274	.314	.387	.577	.299	58.4				

Breakout: 5%   Improve: 44%   Collapse: 13%

If there's something unfair, it's that Pujols was labeled a defensive liability at third. He wasn't Terry Pendleton (or Scott Rolen for that matter), but he was effective enough. The point isn't particularly relevant now, of course. Assuming anyone still believes that Pujols is 23 and not around 27, you should have seen an attractive if mature-looking Mrs. Pujols in last year's *Sports Illustrated* swimsuit edition. Whatever his actual age, Pujols will be an asset with the Cardinals for the next four years, whether he divulges his age to the organization and signs a multiyear deal or not. He should achieve that projection handily.

Edgar Renteria   SS   Born: 07-Aug-75   Age: 27   Bats: R   Throws: R

YEAR	TM	LG	AGE	AB	H	2B	3B	HR	BB	SO	SB	CS	AVG	OBP	SLG	MLVR	EQBA	EQOBP	EQSLG	EQMLVR	VORP	DEFENSE	
2000	STL	NL	24	562	156	32	1	16	63	77	21	13	.278	.351	.423	-.020	.274	.339	.417	-.031	28.9	140-SS	-3
2001	STL	NL	25	493	128	19	3	10	39	73	17	4	.260	.318	.371	-.131	.265	.321	.377	-.128	12.5	128-SS	4
2002	STL	NL	26	544	166	36	2	11	49	57	22	7	.305	.367	.439	.145	.312	.370	.455	.112	47.1	144-SS	-10
2003	STL	NL	27	507	140	27	3	11	47	60	17	4	.276	.340	.407	-.017	.282	.342	.425	-.007	22.0		

Breakout: 7%   Improve: 33%   Collapse: 19%

Just as there's lingering doubt about how old Pujols is, there's still some wondering if Renteria isn't really a year younger than advertised. Good luck getting anyone from the '97 Marlins to talk about it, however. Regardless, the good news is that Renteria put up another campaign to remind everyone that while he briefly slipped into A-Gonz territory for part of one season, the gains he made in the second half of 2001 were more descriptive, and he's still one of the best shortstops in the National League.

Kerry Robinson   OF   Born: 03-Oct-73   Age: 29   Bats: L   Throws: L

YEAR	TM	LG	AGE	AB	H	2B	3B	HR	BB	SO	SB	CS	AVG	OBP	SLG	MLVR	EQBA	EQOBP	EQSLG	EQMLVR	VORP	DEFENSE	
2000	COH	INT	26	437	139	17	9	0	41	40	37	18	.318	.379	.398	.085	.292	.343	.367	-.080	11.2	102-CF	-1
2001	STL	NL	27	186	53	6	1	1	12	20	11	2	.285	.335	.344	-.118	.287	.335	.351	-.122	-1.7	52-LF	-1
2002	STL	NL	28	181	47	7	4	1	11	29	7	4	.260	.302	.359	-.107	.266	.304	.375	-.162	-3.4	43-LF	-2
2003	STL	NL	29	157	42	7	2	1	12	21	6	2	.267	.322	.342	-.141	.273	.323	.357	-.137	-3.1		

Breakout: 8%   Improve: 29%   Collapse: 30%

Rather than carry a lefty pinch hitter who could mash or at least rope a few doubles, the Cards gave nostalgia buffs another spin with a token '85 model Cardinal. It's okay, there was a time I though that the Scorpions' *Love at First Sting* was the greatest album ever. Well, hold on a sec, sometimes it pays not to grow up, that was one of the greatest albums ever. So sure, if the Cardinals want to carry a low-wattage pinch-runner and twelve pitchers and three catchers, well, that's okay. Nobody should have to give up their inner child if they don't want to.

Scott Rolen   3B   Born: 04-Apr-75   Age: 28   Bats: R   Throws: R

YEAR	TM	LG	AGE	AB	H	2B	3B	HR	BB	SO	SB	CS	AVG	OBP	SLG	MLVR	EQBA	EQOBP	EQSLG	EQMLVR	VORP	DEFENSE	
2000	PHI	NL	25	483	144	32	6	26	51	99	8	1	.298	.371	.551	.222	.296	.361	.547	.212	52.8	125-3B	11
2001	PHI	NL	26	554	160	39	1	25	74	127	16	5	.289	.385	.498	.195	.296	.387	.510	.203	63.3	148-3B	22
2002	PHI	NL	27	375	97	21	4	17	52	68	5	2	.259	.361	.472	.148	.269	.365	.493	.116	30.8	96-3B	3
2002	STL	NL	27	205	57	8	4	14	20	34	3	2	.278	.354	.561	.263	.287	.356	.579	.239	23.1	55-3B	13
2003	STL	NL	28	537	149	31	4	27	70	104	11	4	.277	.365	.502	.150	.284	.367	.524	.168	44.0		

Breakout: 6%   Improve: 50%   Collapse: 12%

Among the various slanders that "unnamed (Philly) sources" fired off at Rolen as he left town were accusations that he couldn't lead or rise to the occasion the way a star is supposed to. What, having already gotten little enough for him, they felt obligated to give him that much more incentive to make them look like idiots? Rolen remains what he's always been, a superb player, a plus defender, a patient hitter, and a power source. If he wound up being more Doug DeCinces than Mike Schmidt, that's hardly a bad thing. Freed from the sniping cronies and the unfair expectations, he's primed to rip 70–80 extra-base hits.

So Taguchi Import Born: 02-Jul-69 Age: 34 Bats: R Throws: R

YEAR	TM	LG	AGE	AB	H	2B	3B	HR	BB	SO	SB	CS	AVG	OBP	SLG	MLVR	EQBA	EQOBP	EQSLG	EQMLVR	VORP	DEFENSE
2000	ORX	JPL	31	509	142	26	3	8	55	80	9	2	.279	.353	.389	.008	.270	.327	.379	-.110	3.1	
2001	ORX	JPL	32	453	127	21	6	8	43	88	6	0	.280	.343	.406	-.008	.269	.318	.387	-.116	2.0	
2002	NHV	EAS	33	107	33	10	0	1	9	15	3	1	.308	.378	.430	.173	.275	.328	.385	-.096	2.3	26-CF 0
2002	MEM	PCL	33	304	75	17	0	5	13	44	6	3	.247	.289	.352	-.179	.233	.269	.328	-.319	-11.0	84-CF 1
2002	STL	NL	33	15	6	0	0	0	2	1	1	0	.400	.471	.400	.337	.400	.471	.400	.293	1.7	

Fire up the Ellis Valentine comeback, the Cardinals are paying a cool million per year for a player who seems to have one tool, a strong outfield arm. If he had some other skills that separated him from a couple of hundred other minor league outfielders, they didn't show up this year. So what's the most hip/clever thing Valentine could do? Claim to be a Russian amateur? That would be an extra-zesty bit of foreign flavor, that's gotta be worth hundreds of thousands of dollars these days.

Fernando Vina 2B Born: 16-Apr-69 Age: 34 Bats: L Throws: R

YEAR	TM	LG	AGE	AB	H	2B	3B	HR	BB	SO	SB	CS	AVG	OBP	SLG	MLVR	EQBA	EQOBP	EQSLG	EQMLVR	VORP	DEFENSE
2000	STL	NL	31	487	146	24	6	4	36	36	10	8	.300	.381	.398	.019	.298	.368	.394	.010	29.0	115-2B 14
2001	STL	NL	32	631	191	30	8	9	32	35	17	7	.303	.358	.418	.043	.309	.358	.427	.048	45.1	145-2B -1
2002	STL	NL	33	622	168	29	5	1	44	36	17	11	.270	.336	.338	-.070	.283	.342	.354	-.107	17.2	144-2B -6
2003	STL	NL	34	506	139	25	3	3	33	32	12	2	.275	.330	.354	-.107	.281	.331	.369	-.101	8.2	

Breakout: 6%   Improve: 25%   Collapse: 32%

Vina's not a bad guy to have, but if you're paying him $4–5 million, as the Cardinals have had to in the last couple of years, you're paying too much. That's not an indictment of Vina as much as an acknowledgment that there are plenty of people who can crank out OBPs in the .330–.350 range and play a decent second base. Vina's getting old, and losing little slivers of ability with age. Like Mickey Morandini, he could be one of those guys whose contract runs out after his career does. Nevertheless, right now, he's still legitimately one of the game's best bunters, as opposed to being reputed to be a great bunter because he's asked to bunt a lot.

PITCHERS

Rick Ankiel Born: 19-Jul-79 Age: 23 Bats: L Throws: L

YEAR	TM	LG	AGE	G	GS	IP	H	BB	SO	HR	ERA	EQERA	EQH9	EQBB9	EQSO9	EQHR9	PERA	VORP	STF
2000	STL	NL	20	31	30	175.0	137	90	194	21	3.50	3.79	7.2	3.7	8.8	1.0	3.57	33.3	35
2001	STL	NL	21	6	6	24.0	25	25	27	7	7.13	8.14	9.6	8.5	8.4	2.3	8.06	-7.0	2
2001	JCY	APL	21	14	14	87.7	42	18	158	1	1.33	2.32	5.7	2.8	6.9	0.3	2.01	31.0	32

Rick Ankiel the Hitter

YEAR	TM	LG	AGE	AB	H	2B	3B	HR	BB	SO	SB	CS	AVG	OBP	SLG	MLVR	EQBA	EQOBP	EQSLG	EQMLVR	VORP	DEFENSE
2001	JCY	APL	21	105	30	7	0	10	11	26	0	0	.286	.364	.638	.418	.194	.247	.398	-.289	-4.5	

On any college campus anywhere, you can see ghosts. Not the paranormal kind, but the kind that's 18 and away from home and reacting to newfound responsibilities and pleasures and challenges. All sorts of people operate poorly in the free-form environment college offers to raging minds, hormones, and beerbellies. Even kids with a world of talent flop, try, drift out of school . . . and then they don't really leave. They just haunt the scene of their failure, waiting and wondering what comes next. Welcome to the Ankiel Zone. He's still here. He's still talented. And who knows what comes next?

After missing the entire season with elbow tendonitis, the Cardinals say that they might look at him in a relief role this spring. It's just as well that they already have Kline and Fassero for lefty situational and late-inning situations. Ankiel will be better off getting multi-inning assignments and situations where he doesn't inherit baserunners. If you're an optimist, you can hope that if he shows that he's under control in those situations, he may yet work his way back into the rotation. If you're a pessimist, you'll note that some former athletes warn that once you start thinking too much about what you're doing as you're doing it, you're never the same.

Andy Benes   Born: 20-Aug-67   Age: 35   Bats: R   Throws: R

YEAR	TM	LG	AGE	G	GS	IP	H	BB	SO	HR	ERA	EQERA	EQH9	EQBB9	EQSO9	EQHR9	PERA	VORP	STF
2000	STL	NL	32	30	27	166.0	174	68	137	30	4.88	5.01	9.7	3.0	6.6	1.5	5.01	9.0	8
2001	STL	NL	33	27	19	107.3	122	61	78	30	7.38	7.64	10.9	4.8	5.6	2.3	7.05	-25.6	-17
2002	STL	NL	34	18	17	97.0	80	51	64	10	2.78	4.19	8.2	4.3	5.3	1.0	4.12	14.1	1

Went out in a blaze of glory, with his best bud at his side and the Bolivian Army waiting for them armed to the teeth, and then Newman says to Redford...oops, at any rate, let's just say Benes went down fighting. Unlike his stretch drive performance for the Mariners in 1995, Benes was desperately needed for the Cardinals in August and September. After reconsidering an early decision to retire with knee trouble that was never going to go away, he gave the Cards a dozen starts down the stretch where he gave up as many as three runs only once, and finishing the year with a game effort against the Giants in the NLCS. And then, rather than being carried off on his shield or waiting for them to mail it to him, he said "enough." It was a hell of a career, and he'll be missed.

B. R. Cook   Born: 02-Mar-78   Age: 25   Bats: R   Throws: R

YEAR	TM	LG	AGE	G	GS	IP	H	BB	SO	HR	ERA	EQERA	EQH9	EQBB9	EQSO9	EQHR9	PERA	VORP	STF
2000	PEO	MDW	22	18	18	97.7	90	52	83	7	3.68	7.09	12.0	6.0	5.0	1.8	6.84	-17.2	-8
2000	POT	CRL	22	8	8	42.3	48	27	23	3	5.53	8.69	14.7	7.4	3.3	1.6	8.22	-15.0	-26
2001	POT	CRL	23	8	8	50.3	35	12	36	2	2.86	4.43	8.6	3.2	4.0	0.9	3.53	6.0	3
2001	NHV	EAS	23	20	20	121.7	115	37	84	11	3.99	5.60	10.6	3.8	4.4	1.3	5.29	-1.3	-1
2002	NHV	EAS	24	28	28	163.3	180	65	111	14	4.57	6.66	12.6	4.4	4.8	1.4	6.43	-21.0	-5

Cook isn't going to be mistaken for a prospect, but unlike so many of the Cardinals' more highly touted young pitchers, he's still standing. He has good command of a pretty ordinary sinker-slider-change combo, but he isn't going to overpower anybody. If he improves his command, he could wind up getting his big score the way Kevin Jarvis or Tanyon Sturtze did, but those guys tend to be the exceptions.

Mike Crudale   Born: 03-Jan-77   Age: 26   Bats: R   Throws: R

YEAR	TM	LG	AGE	G	GS	IP	H	BB	SO	HR	ERA	EQERA	EQH9	EQBB9	EQSO9	EQHR9	PERA	VORP	STF
2000	PEO	MDW	23	38	0	50.7	40	16	45	2	2.31	4.10	9.6	3.5	5.0	0.9	4.52	7.2	-8
2000	POT	CRL	23	21	0	25.7	31	11	28	3	4.55	8.23	16.0	4.9	6.5	2.6	8.27	-8.1	-19
2001	NHV	EAS	24	62	0	80.3	76	22	85	7	3.25	5.35	10.4	3.3	6.6	1.3	5.11	0.3	-2
2002	MEM	PCL	25	13	0	14.7	10	5	16	1	1.84	2.87	7.7	3.6	7.8	0.8	3.06	4.1	9
2002	STL	NL	25	49	1	52.7	43	14	47	3	1.88	2.69	8.2	2.2	7.2	0.5	3.03	15.8	13
2003	*STL*	*NL*	*26*	*50*	*0*	*59.7*	*56*	*22*	*50*	*6*	*3.68*	*4.00*	*8.8*	*2.8*	*6.6*	*0.9*	*4.19*	*9.5*	*1*

Breakout: 17%   Improve: 51%   Collapse: 15%

Some people get called throwbacks because they take their profession seriously. Crudale isn't that kind of throwback. Effectively dropped into Timlin's setup role in the pen after being yo-yo'd between Memphis and St. Louis in the first three months of the year, Crudale took the mound and simply reared back and fired, claiming he didn't have time out there to think about scouting reports or who he was throwing to. That's fun, but it also isn't a recipe for long-term success. With the departure of Veres, he'll be sharing the primary setup duties with Kline, so hopefully he can avoid a tough second pass through the league. His fastball still doesn't have much movement, and relief role or no, he's going to need something to fool people once in a while.

Matt Duff   Born: 06-Oct-74   Age: 28   Bats: R   Throws: R

YEAR	TM	LG	AGE	G	GS	IP	H	BB	SO	HR	ERA	EQERA	EQH9	EQBB9	EQSO9	EQHR9	PERA	VORP	STF
2000	ALT	EAS	25	47	0	55.0	50	36	61	1	3.93	5.62	9.4	6.5	7.5	0.3	5.61	-1.5	-5
2002	POT	CRL	27	4	0	4.3	4	1	7	0	0.00	0.26	9.8	2.8	9.9	0.3	3.98	2.4	26
2002	NHV	EAS	27	47	0	65.0	38	21	91	3	1.38	2.43	6.3	3.4	9.4	0.7	2.68	21.3	20
2002	MEM	PCL	27	4	0	4.7	2	4	3	1	1.91	3.48	5.7	9.7	4.9	2.8	4.47	1.0	-40
2002	STL	NL	27	7	0	5.7	3	8	4	0	4.74	4.96	5.1	10.9	5.4	0.2	4.56	0.3	-29
2003	*STL*	*NL*	*28*	*27*	*3*	*44.0*	*37*	*25*	*43*	*4*	*3.69*	*4.02*	*7.7*	*4.3*	*7.8*	*0.8*	*4.20*	*7.1*	*6*

Breakout: 23%   Improve: 39%   Collapse: 21%

The man from Alligator, Mississippi, is a former Frontier Leaguer and later a Northern Leaguer. The Frontier League got him to the Pirates, the Northern League to the Eastern League All-Star game, and a brief spin with the Cardinals. Taking a flyer on an indy leaguer is exactly the sort of thing the Cardinals should be doing to fill out the organization, and Duff has a chance to make the team next spring given their relative shortage of experienced right-handed relievers.

Jeff Fassero — Born: 05-Jan-63 — Age: 40 — Bats: L — Throws: L

YEAR	TM	LG	AGE	G	GS	IP	H	BB	SO	HR	ERA	EQERA	EQH9	EQBB9	EQSO9	EQHR9	PERA	VORP	STF
2000	BOS	AL	37	38	23	130.0	153	50	97	16	4.78	4.48	10.0	2.8	6.5	0.9	4.70	14.5	5
2001	CHC	NL	38	82	0	73.7	66	23	79	6	3.42	3.53	8.2	2.6	8.2	0.7	3.57	15.1	13
2002	CHC	NL	39	57	0	51.0	65	22	44	5	6.18	6.01	11.5	3.4	6.8	0.9	6.24	-3.6	-6
2002	STL	NL	39	16	0	18.0	16	5	12	4	3.00	4.03	8.8	2.3	5.4	2.1	4.57	2.7	-11
2003	STL	NL	40	47	0	41.3	51	23	41	6	4.98	5.43	11.4	4.2	7.9	1.2	5.07	6.0	-1

Breakout: 14%   Improve: 34%   Collapse: 26%

Fassero spent an inordinate amount of time struggling with pitching from the stretch last year, which you can't live with from someone who's moved on to situational relief work in his golden years. The solution? He gave up, pitching from a full windup full-time. It'll be interesting to see if this is something that Duncan addresses in camp, because striving to fulfill their need to go through every old lefty in the quest to replace the long-gone Rick Honeycutt, the Cards have already re-signed Fassero. They'd already cycled through both Tony Fossas and Jesse Orosco.

Chuck Finley — Born: 26-Nov-62 — Age: 40 — Bats: L — Throws: L

YEAR	TM	LG	AGE	G	GS	IP	H	BB	SO	HR	ERA	EQERA	EQH9	EQBB9	EQSO9	EQHR9	PERA	VORP	STF
2000	CLE	AL	37	34	34	218.0	211	101	189	23	4.17	3.65	7.9	3.3	7.4	0.8	3.76	44.9	20
2001	CLE	AL	38	22	22	113.7	131	35	96	14	5.54	4.71	9.3	2.5	7.0	1.0	4.80	10.0	14
2002	CLE	AL	39	18	18	105.3	114	48	91	6	4.44	3.97	8.9	3.7	7.4	0.5	4.36	18.0	19
2002	STL	NL	39	14	14	85.3	69	30	83	7	3.80	4.11	8.0	2.9	7.8	0.8	3.38	13.2	24
2003	STL	NL	40	28	25	153.3	146	66	138	14	3.78	4.12	8.9	3.3	7.1	0.8	3.90	30.0	16

Breakout: 9%   Improve: 63%   Collapse: 4%

Finley still throws hard on his better days, and still has a nifty splitter (hey, aren't throwing those supposed to ruin a guy's career?). After coming over, he gave the Cards the six innings and three runs for a quality start ten times in 14 games (with two QSs being lost after the 6th), and shutting out the Snakes into the 7th in the divisional series. The Cardinals took a hard line with him in winter negotiations, which was unfortunate for both parties. Like a lot of free agents this winter, Finley overplayed his hand. He should have taken what the Cardinals offered, because there aren't that many rotation slots on contenders available. Meanwhile, the Cards are going into the season counting on a lot of ciphers in the rotation. Nobody's going to give him another three-year deal again, and that's not the end of the world.

Luther Hackman — Born: 10-Oct-74 — Age: 28 — Bats: R — Throws: R

YEAR	TM	LG	AGE	G	GS	IP	H	BB	SO	HR	ERA	EQERA	EQH9	EQBB9	EQSO9	EQHR9	PERA	VORP	STF
2000	MEM	PCL	25	21	21	119.7	134	36	66	11	4.74	5.87	12.2	2.8	4.2	1.1	5.27	-4.9	-3
2001	MEM	PCL	26	16	0	22.7	21	1	12	2	2.78	3.26	9.3	0.5	3.5	1.0	3.46	5.3	-9
2001	STL	NL	26	35	0	35.7	28	14	24	7	4.29	4.56	7.7	3.4	5.3	1.6	4.05	3.3	-13
2002	STL	NL	27	43	6	81.0	90	39	46	7	4.11	5.36	11.1	3.9	4.6	0.8	5.35	0.5	-15
2003	SDP	NL	28	29	8	63	70	28	39	7	4.75	5.51	10.5	3.5	4.8	1.1	5.66	1.3	-13

Breakout: 10%   Improve: 42%   Collapse: 29%

Whether by design or accident, the Cardinals cut loose both of the pitchers who came over with Darryl Kile from the Rockies. Hackman was dealt to the Cardinals for Brett Tomko, while Dave Veres was allowed to leave and become a Cub. Hackman can get into the 90s, but he doesn't have good command, and has always managed to struggle in every opportunity he's been given. Although some scouts like him, he's probably just going to be no more than staff filler again.

Dan Haren — Born: 17-Sep-80 — Age: 22 — Bats: R — Throws: R

YEAR	TM	LG	AGE	G	GS	IP	H	BB	SO	HR	ERA	EQERA	EQH9	EQBB9	EQSO9	EQHR9	PERA	VORP	STF
2001	NWJ	NYP	20	12	8	52.3	47	8	57	6	3.10	6.37	15.1	2.3	6.1	4.1	6.41	-5.1	-1
2002	PEO	MDW	21	14	14	101.7	89	12	89	6	1.95	4.76	12.2	1.5	5.2	1.6	4.58	8.4	13
2002	POT	CRL	21	14	14	92.0	90	19	82	8	3.62	5.16	11.8	2.6	5.8	2.0	5.09	3.5	12

A 2001 2nd round pick out of Pepperdine, Haren had a great summer, but that's what's supposed to happen to a guy from a top program pitching in the Midwest League. He's got a lively fastball that gets into the low 90s that he uses aggressively to set up his spiky slider. If he's having trouble with a hitter, he'll spring a splitter on them; he throws a polished change as well. The organization loves him for his ferocity, but he hasn't seen Double-A yet. If he makes it there, he'll become one of the people everyone will ask after at next summer's trade deadline.

Jason Isringhausen — Born: 07-Sep-72 — Age: 30 — Bats: R — Throws: R

YEAR	TM	LG	AGE	G	GS	IP	H	BB	SO	HR	ERA	EQERA	EQH9	EQBB9	EQSO9	EQHR9	PERA	VORP	STF
2000	OAK	AL	27	66	0	69.0	67	32	57	6	3.78	3.80	8.2	3.4	7.2	0.7	3.80	12.1	4
2001	OAK	AL	28	65	0	71.3	54	23	74	5	2.65	2.92	6.9	2.7	8.8	0.6	2.68	19.5	19
2002	STL	NL	29	60	0	65.3	46	18	68	0	2.48	2.87	7.0	2.2	8.4	0.2	2.26	18.2	20
2003	STL	NL	30	57	0	60.3	50	21	62	5	2.98	3.24	7.8	2.7	8.1	0.7	3.33	15.0	13

Breakout: 20%   Improve: 49%   Collapse: 21%

A top shelf closer at the top of his game, Izzy will continue to be as much of an asset as an ace closer can be. His sinker was almost impossible to lift out of the infield last year, and he complements it with a nice curve, although he still doesn't get it over for strikes to lefties as often as you'd like. It also wasn't a perfect season in that he had elbow and shoulder soreness at different times during the year. Neither ailment is supposed to be anything major for 2003, but LaRussa likes to keep his closer for the 9th inning alone, and those kinds of yips won't encourage anyone to think of expanding his role into the 8th.

He's another product of one of the innumerable little colleges named after Lewis and Clark, but again, not the one in Oregon, so he's not a former classmate of Monica Lewinsky. Are her fifteen minutes up yet, or will she eventually be as forgotten as Warren Harding's molls?

Tyler Johnson — Born: 07-Jun-81 — Age: 22 — Bats: B — Throws: L

YEAR	TM	LG	AGE	G	GS	IP	H	BB	SO	HR	ERA	EQERA	EQH9	EQBB9	EQSO9	EQHR9	PERA	VORP	STF
2001	JCY	APL	20	9	9	40.7	26	21	58	1	2.65	4.62	8.3	7.6	5.9	0.6	4.41	4.0	2
2001	PEO	MDW	20	3	3	13.7	14	10	15	1	3.94	7.45	12.3	9.7	6.3	1.6	8.51	-3.0	-10
2002	PEO	MDW	21	22	18	121.3	96	42	132	7	2.00	4.70	11.2	4.5	6.5	1.6	4.93	10.7	12

Johnson was a 2000 JuCo draft-and-follow who works in the high 80s and low 90s, relying heavily on a sharp slider. Or, your basic 1970s-style power lefty, from the land before Big Unit. He's shown great command so far; he lost a no-hitter last summer on a line drive that struck a walked batter with two outs in the ninth. Remember the name, in case he survives.

Kevin Joseph — Born: 01-Aug-76 — Age: 26 — Bats: R — Throws: R

YEAR	TM	LG	AGE	G	GS	IP	H	BB	SO	HR	ERA	EQERA	EQH9	EQBB9	EQSO9	EQHR9	PERA	VORP	STF
2000	SHV	TXS	23	27	16	102.7	116	48	71	8	5.17	6.37	12.9	4.6	4.7	1.2	6.33	-10.1	-10
2001	SJO	CLF	24	9	0	13.3	12	1	15	0	3.38	4.59	10.6	0.9	5.8	0.3	3.52	1.2	6
2001	SHV	TXS	24	24	0	33.3	31	13	27	1	2.43	3.88	10.3	4.4	5.3	0.5	4.62	5.5	-7
2001	MEM	PCL	24	12	0	12.0	8	11	6	2	6.75	6.35	7.1	10.3	3.5	1.9	5.56	-1.3	-46
2002	MEM	PCL	25	31	0	35.7	37	11	14	2	1.76	4.22	12.0	3.4	2.9	0.7	4.86	4.6	-23
2002	STL	NL	25	11	0	11.0	16	6	2	1	4.91	6.92	14.5	4.5	1.5	0.9	7.41	-1.9	-41

Part of the package that the Cardinals received for Jason Christiansen, Joseph pumps gas in the high 90s. You've heard the story before, though: no command, little movement, and lots of high-velocity projectiles screaming around the diamond and rocketing to the gaps. He'll keep getting looks, because some people trust speed guns more than results.

Jimmy Journell — Born: 29-Dec-77 — Age: 25 — Bats: R — Throws: R

YEAR	TM	LG	AGE	G	GS	IP	H	BB	SO	HR	ERA	EQERA	EQH9	EQBB9	EQSO9	EQHR9	PERA	VORP	STF
2000	NWJ	NYP	22	13	1	32.0	12	24	39	0	1.97	3.72	4.0	8.8	6.0	0.3	3.72	6.0	-6
2001	POT	CRL	23	26	26	151.0	121	42	156	8	2.50	4.72	10.0	3.7	5.8	1.2	4.46	13.2	10
2002	NHV	EAS	24	10	10	66.7	50	18	66	3	2.70	3.51	8.2	2.9	6.8	0.7	3.38	14.8	22
2002	MEM	PCL	24	7	7	36.7	38	18	32	3	3.68	5.50	11.7	5.3	6.4	1.0	5.68	0.0	3

Journell would show up on a few prospect lists if anyone had any confidence he was healthy and would stay that way. Between Tommy John surgery in 1999 and a further surgery to remove bone chips in January 2002, there have been enough caution flags thrown up that nobody really knows what to expect, and shoulder soreness in July last season only added to the whispering campaign. Mercifully, the Cardinals didn't put him in the spotlight, pitching in Darryl Kile's vacated rotation slot when they had the opportunity. While he can throw in the mid-90s and smoke batters with his slider, there's no way anybody knows what to expect. He's the best prospect in the organization, and he could be in the rotation or on the 60-day DL by September.

Steve Kline   Born: 22-Aug-72   Age: 30   Bats: B   Throws: L

YEAR	TM	LG	AGE	G	GS	IP	H	BB	SO	HR	ERA	EQERA	EQH9	EQBB9	EQSO9	EQHR9	PERA	VORP	STF
2000	MON	NL	27	83	0	82.3	88	27	64	8	3.50	3.57	9.2	2.4	6.1	0.8	4.24	16.6	0
2001	STL	NL	28	89	0	75.0	53	29	54	3	1.80	2.52	7.2	3.3	5.7	0.3	2.66	23.8	0
2002	STL	NL	29	66	0	58.3	54	21	41	3	3.40	3.99	9.3	2.9	5.7	0.5	3.77	9.0	-2
2003	STL	NL	30	59	0	52.7	50	21	42	4	3.49	3.80	8.8	3.1	6.3	0.7	4.17	10.2	-1

Breakout: 14%   Improve: 47%   Collapse: 18%

In another testament to his ever-ready cachet, Kline missed 28 games with a stint on the DL, and still finished with 66 appearances. In other words, if he'd been healthy, he would have topped 80 games again. Now that the Cardinals have lost a few veteran relievers, it might not be a bad idea for him to slip into a more traditional setup role, giving him more complete innings in the 7th and 8th, and lowering his total number of appearances.

Scotty Layfield   Born: 13-Sep-76   Age: 26   Bats: R   Throws: R

YEAR	TM	LG	AGE	G	GS	IP	H	BB	SO	HR	ERA	EQERA	EQH9	EQBB9	EQSO9	EQHR9	PERA	VORP	STF
2000	PEO	MDW	23	53	0	54.3	65	40	50	4	5.14	9.70	15.7	8.5	5.5	1.9	10.04	-26.1	-36
2001	POT	CRL	24	47	0	53.7	36	18	66	1	1.84	3.53	8.0	4.4	6.8	0.4	3.54	11.0	2
2002	NHV	EAS	25	58	0	65.0	54	24	63	5	2.35	4.08	9.3	4.0	6.7	1.2	4.45	9.4	-3

A former college infielder, Layfield has adapted to pitching, picking up velocity in the last couple of years. He relies on good low 90s heat to set up a power slider. The pitches are nice enough, but he showed a good-sized platoon split in the Eastern League, which means the slider could still use some work if he's going to keep lefties honest. Still, the opportunity to make the team with a good camp is there.

Matt Morris   Born: 09-Aug-74   Age: 28   Bats: R   Throws: R

YEAR	TM	LG	AGE	G	GS	IP	H	BB	SO	HR	ERA	EQERA	EQH9	EQBB9	EQSO9	EQHR9	PERA	VORP	STF
2000	STL	NL	25	31	0	53.0	53	17	34	3	3.57	3.69	9.5	2.4	5.2	0.5	3.65	10.0	0
2001	STL	NL	26	34	34	216.3	218	54	185	13	3.16	3.95	10.1	2.2	6.7	0.5	3.76	37.4	21
2002	STL	NL	27	32	32	210.3	210	64	171	16	3.42	4.23	10.0	2.5	6.6	0.7	4.13	29.8	17
2003	STL	NL	28	28	26	174.7	174	51	139	14	3.56	3.88	9.2	2.3	6.3	0.7	4.01	31.4	17

Breakout: 8%   Improve: 51%   Collapse: 6%

An ace starter at the top of his game, he also gave the Cardinals two great postseason starts, making it four out of five times he's pitched well enough to win, and come away with only one win. Morris's moving fastball is one of the toughest pitches in the league, and so is his curve, so what's not to like? The Tommy John surgery is in the far-distant past, and his one stint on the DL was because of a hamstring strain. That projection is overly modest, he should continue to roll in 2003.

Chris Narveson   Born: 20-Dec-81   Age: 21   Bats: L   Throws: L

YEAR	TM	LG	AGE	G	GS	IP	H	BB	SO	HR	ERA	EQERA	EQH9	EQBB9	EQSO9	EQHR9	PERA	VORP	STF
2000	JCY	APL	18	12	12	55.0	57	25	63	7	3.27	6.97	14.7	6.3	5.7	3.4	8.14	-9.0	-13
2001	PEO	MDW	19	8	8	50.0	32	11	53	3	1.98	2.93	7.2	2.8	5.8	1.2	3.24	14.3	19
2001	POT	CRL	19	11	11	66.7	52	13	53	4	2.56	4.36	9.8	2.6	4.5	1.3	4.07	8.5	8
2002	JCY	APL	20	6	6	18.3	23	6	16	2	4.92	7.39	17.2	4.4	4.5	2.6	8.48	-3.8	-19
2002	PEO	MDW	20	9	9	42.3	49	8	36	5	4.47	7.99	17.8	2.6	5.4	3.4	7.71	-11.7	-6

One of the almost-unique qualities of the Cardinals organization is that if you're a top prospect, you can tear up your elbow, and chances are, you're still one of the organization's top prospects, because they don't come up with too many prospects to start off with. A healthy Narveson could throw four pitches for strikes, and could get his heat into the low 90s. He showed flashes of that Narveson last summer, his first back since having Tommy John surgery in July 2001. This year, assuming he's sound, he should take a step forward.

Rhett Parrott   Born: 12-Nov-79   Age: 23   Bats: R   Throws: R

YEAR	TM	LG	AGE	G	GS	IP	H	BB	SO	HR	ERA	EQERA	EQH9	EQBB9	EQSO9	EQHR9	PERA	VORP	STF
2001	NWJ	NYP	21	11	11	45.7	45	28	58	3	4.92	8.85	15.5	9.3	7.3	2.4	9.06	-17.0	-10
2002	POT	CRL	22	19	19	113.0	91	41	82	6	2.71	4.25	9.4	4.6	4.7	1.2	4.29	15.8	3
2002	NHV	EAS	22	9	9	66.0	53	13	38	3	2.86	3.70	8.8	2.1	4.0	0.7	3.46	13.2	8
2003	STL	NL	23	13	10	58.3	64	31	40	7	5.21	5.68	10.2	4.1	5.5	1.1	5.67	0.4	-4

Breakout: 12%   Improve: 52%   Collapse: 20%

Rhett Parrott *(continued)*

The fashionable comparison he draws is to Brad Radke, except Radke had sharper control and a great changeup, and Parrott throws hard and is still trying to sort out whether he wants to rely on a curve or slider as his major breaking pitch, and not being as sharp as you'd like with either. That's not to say Parrott is a bum, but sometimes these scouty comparisons make you wonder. Although the Cardinals are relying heavily on retreads going into camp, he'll probably have to spend a full year in the minors, both to prove he can succeed in a full season in Double- or Triple-A, and because he doesn't have to be added to the 40-man until after the 2003 season.

Justin Pope   Born: 08-Nov-79   Age: 23   Bats: B   Throws: R

YEAR	TM	LG	AGE	G	GS	IP	H	BB	SO	HR	ERA	EQERA	EQH9	EQBB9	EQSO9	EQHR9	PERA	VORP	STF
2001	NWJ	NYP	21	15	15	69.3	64	14	66	6	2.60	6.73	14.7	3.0	5.3	3.1	6.56	-9.4	-4
2002	PEO	MDW	22	12	12	78.3	48	12	72	3	1.38	3.06	8.4	1.9	5.3	1.0	2.87	21.3	17

The organization likes his businesslike approach to the game, and he's coming off of a good AFL campaign. None of his pitches are especially overpowering, but he knows how to pitch (his father was his pitching coach in high school), mixing a low 90s fastball with a well-spotted change and slider. He missed a couple of months with an injured triceps, but started and finished strong; the injury only really cost him a shot to move up the chain quickly. In 2003, he's expected to pitch his way up to Double-A, at which point he'll be on the fringes of the big league picture.

Jason Simontacchi   Born: 13-Nov-73   Age: 29   Bats: R   Throws: R

YEAR	TM	LG	AGE	G	GS	IP	H	BB	SO	HR	ERA	EQERA	EQH9	EQBB9	EQSO9	EQHR9	PERA	VORP	STF
2001	EDM	PCL	27	32	18	143.3	192	23	83	21	5.34	6.15	12.8	1.7	3.8	1.5	6.45	-10.7	-11
2002	MEM	PCL	28	6	6	42.3	44	5	28	2	2.34	3.92	11.7	1.3	4.8	0.6	4.13	7.4	11
2002	STL	NL	28	24	24	143.3	134	54	72	18	4.02	4.69	9.4	3.1	4.1	1.2	4.41	13.0	-2
2003	STL	NL	29	22	17	109.0	126	38	60	15	4.96	5.40	10.8	2.7	4.3	1.2	5.31	5.5	-6

Breakout: 12%   *Improve: 40%*   *Collapse: 28%*

How often does a team get a guy out of nowhere to toss 15 quality starts in 24 starts? Simontacchi doesn't throw hard (of course), so he was particularly dependent on his defense. That doesn't bode well for his future. Proud veteran of Italian national Olympic team, his Cinderella story has been squashed as flat as if the lady's stepsisters were Claudia Schiffer and Fairuza Balk now that the Cardinals have hauled in Chris Carpenter, Joey Hamilton, and Brett Tomko. He'll have to fight to win the fourth or fifth slot in the rotation, but he's been going uphill all along, and he got here anyway.

Travis Smith   Born: 07-Nov-72   Age: 30   Bats: R   Throws: R

YEAR	TM	LG	AGE	G	GS	IP	H	BB	SO	HR	ERA	EQERA	EQH9	EQBB9	EQSO9	EQHR9	PERA	VORP	STF
2000	HUN	SOU	27	27	24	154.3	141	37	113	13	3.73	5.19	10.7	2.4	4.7	1.5	4.95	5.3	0
2001	ROU	TXS	28	29	22	160.3	154	26	85	7	3.09	4.71	10.8	1.8	3.5	0.7	4.22	13.9	-1
2002	MEM	PCL	29	16	13	85.7	76	14	62	7	2.31	3.68	10.1	1.8	5.2	1.0	3.70	17.3	9
2002	STL	NL	29	12	10	54.0	69	20	32	10	7.17	7.34	12.7	3.0	4.8	1.8	6.62	-11.1	-12
2003	STL	NL	30	22	13	84.0	91	26	50	11	4.35	4.74	10.0	2.4	4.7	1.2	4.81	8.6	-4

Breakout: 22%   *Improve: 53%*   *Collapse: 21%*

Right-handed junkballers aren't a famous subset, and short right-handed junkballers basically need extraordinary luck or a lot of trouble in the big league rotation to finally get a shot. Smith had the requisite four pitches he can throw for strikes, he's 5′10″, and the Cardinals had that trouble. So up he came, and as emergency starters go, Smith was about what you expected, 2001 Texas League ERA title or no. He battled, he got belted around, and he went back to Memphis.

Gene Stechschulte   Born: 12-Aug-73   Age: 29   Bats: R   Throws: R

YEAR	TM	LG	AGE	G	GS	IP	H	BB	SO	HR	ERA	EQERA	EQH9	EQBB9	EQSO9	EQHR9	PERA	VORP	STF
2000	MEM	PCL	26	41	0	47.7	38	18	37	4	2.45	3.32	8.6	3.4	5.8	1.0	3.61	10.9	-5
2000	STL	NL	26	20	0	25.7	24	17	12	6	6.30	6.46	8.4	4.8	3.7	1.9	5.61	-3.1	-31
2001	STL	NL	27	67	0	70.0	71	30	51	10	3.86	5.00	10.0	3.7	5.7	1.2	4.94	3.0	-10
2002	STL	NL	28	29	0	32.0	27	17	21	4	4.78	5.18	8.4	4.3	5.3	1.2	4.39	0.7	-14
2002	MEM	PCL	28	10	0	10.0	8	2	7	0	1.80	2.78	9.0	2.2	5.0	0.2	2.80	2.9	-1
2003	STL	NL	29	44	0	40.7	42	20	30	5	4.50	4.90	9.5	3.8	5.9	1.1	4.99	4.6	-10

Breakout: 23%   *Improve: 45%*   *Collapse: 27%*

Stechschulte melted down, but in his defense he was complaining of a stiff arm, and was diagnosed with tendonitis in both his elbow and shoulder. Signing Al Levine is a pretty good indicator that the Cards aren't counting on him to win a job as a long reliever, but with the departures of Veres and Hackman, jobs are there for the taking. If Stechschulte's arm is sound and he has a good camp, he could get some keen hold stats.

Garrett Stephenson   Born: 02-Jan-72   Age: 31   Bats: R   Throws: R

YEAR	TM	LG	AGE	G	GS	IP	H	BB	SO	HR	ERA	EQERA	EQH9	EQBB9	EQSO9	EQHR9	PERA	VORP	STF
2000	STL	NL	28	32	31	200.3	209	63	123	31	4.49	4.59	9.8	2.3	5.0	1.3	4.53	20.3	4
2002	STL	NL	30	12	10	45.0	48	25	34	4	5.40	5.72	10.6	4.5	6.1	0.8	5.35	-1.1	-2
2003	STL	NL	31	23	14	89.7	96	36	64	10	4.50	4.90	9.9	3.2	5.7	1.0	4.96	8.2	0

Breakout: 12%   Improve: 49%   Collapse: 32%

Like Rick Ankiel, Stephenson hasn't really been a part of the Cardinals since their playoff run in 2000. It's worth asking if the Cardinals kept pushing him out there too soon, as he broke down in April (the back), came back in May and was back on the DL by the end of the month (officially for the hamstring, which required surgery to remove dead tissue, but he was also having shoulder trouble), and then he was finally "back" at the end of August, but he wasn't ready to really contribute even then. He's been re-signed, and he'll have a shot at the fourth or fifth slot in the rotation, but there's little indication that he can pitch and stay healthy, or that he's got much left.

Nick Stocks   Born: 27-Aug-78   Age: 24   Bats: R   Throws: R

YEAR	TM	LG	AGE	G	GS	IP	H	BB	SO	HR	ERA	EQERA	EQH9	EQBB9	EQSO9	EQHR9	PERA	VORP	STF
2000	PEO	MDW	21	25	24	150.0	133	52	118	4	3.78	5.72	10.7	3.8	4.5	0.6	5.23	-3.6	4
2001	NHV	EAS	22	16	15	82.0	89	33	63	10	5.16	6.85	12.4	5.1	5.0	1.8	6.94	-12.3	-7
2002	NWJ	NYP	23	7	7	22.0	28	13	24	0	5.73	10.15	19.1	9.3	6.5	0.4	9.81	-11.4	-19
2002	PEO	MDW	23	1	1	8.0	6	1	3	0	2.25	3.72	9.7	1.6	2.1	0.3	3.28	1.6	0
2002	POT	CRL	23	3	3	15.7	18	6	11	3	5.73	8.61	16.0	5.3	4.9	4.7	8.07	-5.4	-25

Stocks has been a huge disappointment. He's had back and elbow trouble, and he was obviously not 100% in the Arizona Fall League. At this point, you might have to add him to the pile of scragged Cardinal minor league hurlers.

Dave Veres   Born: 19-Oct-66   Age: 36   Bats: R   Throws: R

YEAR	TM	LG	AGE	G	GS	IP	H	BB	SO	HR	ERA	EQERA	EQH9	EQBB9	EQSO9	EQHR9	PERA	VORP	STF
2000	STL	NL	33	71	0	75.7	65	25	67	6	2.85	3.13	8.1	2.4	7.1	0.6	3.17	18.9	8
2001	STL	NL	34	71	0	65.7	57	28	61	12	3.70	4.46	8.4	3.6	7.2	1.5	4.45	6.7	-2
2002	STL	NL	35	71	0	82.7	67	39	68	12	3.48	4.24	8.0	3.8	6.6	1.4	4.18	10.5	-4
2003	CHC	NL	36	56	0	57.7	53	25	49	8	3.74	4.13	8.6	3.4	6.7	1.2	4.58	9.4	-3

Breakout: 23%   Improve: 46%   Collapse: 16%

After rescuing Veres from the Rockies, they got three nice little years out of him, after which the Cardinals chose discretion over nostalgia (and an option worth more than $5 million), letting Veres become a Cub for a couple of million. While he's a useful enough utility reliever, equally comfortable in long relief or closing, on a hot day in Wrigley, don't be surprised to see a few of his splitters rattling around on Waveland Avenue, spite fence or no.

Rick White   Born: 23-Dec-68   Age: 34   Bats: R   Throws: R

YEAR	TM	LG	AGE	G	GS	IP	H	BB	SO	HR	ERA	EQERA	EQH9	EQBB9	EQSO9	EQHR9	PERA	VORP	STF
2000	TBY	AL	31	44	0	71.3	57	26	47	7	3.41	2.98	6.9	2.7	5.8	0.7	2.77	19.0	2
2000	NYM	NL	31	22	0	28.3	26	12	20	2	3.82	4.00	8.6	3.1	5.7	0.6	3.82	4.3	-2
2001	NYM	NL	32	55	0	69.7	71	17	51	7	3.87	4.54	9.9	2.1	5.7	0.8	4.24	6.5	-2
2002	COL	NL	33	41	0	40.7	49	18	27	4	6.19	5.65	10.7	3.5	5.2	0.8	5.13	-1.2	-13
2002	STL	NL	33	20	0	22.0	13	3	14	0	0.82	1.65	6.1	1.1	5.3	0.2	1.55	9.1	8
2003	STL	NL	34	48	0	47.3	48	18	35	5	4.26	4.65	9.5	2.9	5.8	0.9	4.46	6.0	-6

Breakout: 13%   Improve: 41%   Collapse: 28%

A nice cheap stretch drive pickup for the Cards, the amazing thing being that nobody picked White up before he cleared waivers. Apparently everyone couldn't overlook that bad numbers in Coors don't tell you a whole lot about whether or not a guy can pitch; in 23.2 Coors innings, he gave 20 runs, and everywhere else, he gave up three runs per nine. Whether the Cardinals picked him up because he was old enough, or because they kept in mind he still throws in the 90s and usually keeps the ball on the ground, it was worthwhile. However, he pretty much gets sole credit for losing Game Four in the NLCS, and Cardinals fans don't forget.

Woody Williams   Born: 19-Aug-66   Age: 36   Bats: R   Throws: R

YEAR	TM	LG	AGE	G	GS	IP	H	BB	SO	HR	ERA	EQERA	EQH9	EQBB9	EQSO9	EQHR9	PERA	VORP	STF
2000	SDP	NL	33	23	23	168.0	152	54	111	23	3.75	3.94	8.6	2.4	5.4	1.2	4.02	29.2	8
2001	SDP	NL	34	23	23	145.0	170	37	102	28	4.97	5.54	11.0	2.2	5.5	1.6	5.92	-0.6	2
2001	STL	NL	34	11	11	75.0	54	19	52	7	2.28	2.92	7.2	2.2	5.5	0.8	2.69	21.5	14
2002	STL	NL	35	17	17	103.3	84	25	76	10	2.53	3.20	8.2	2.0	6.0	0.9	3.21	26.5	16
2003	STL	NL	36	22	18	116.7	112	34	87	15	3.63	3.95	8.9	2.3	5.9	1.1	4.15	20.6	10

Breakout: 16%   Improve: 41%   Collapse: 10%

Talk about a season of what-ifs. After returning from the DL the first time, Woody made quality starts in ten of his eleven games; the other game was one run allowed in five innings. Who needs Greg Maddux? The problem was that he hurt himself three times with the same rib cage strain, which considering how some of the other injured pitchers were handled, makes you wonder if they were trying a bit too hard to get him on the mound instead of letting him heal entirely. Williams might be a little older than your usual Duncan success story, but you can't argue with the results. After being rewarded with a two-year, $14.9 million contract, it looks like he bluffed the Cardinals into bigger money by talking about going to Houston; given his career, should anyone feel confident he'd do this well anywhere else?

Blake Williams   Born: 22-Feb-79   Age: 24   Bats: R   Throws: R

YEAR	TM	LG	AGE	G	GS	IP	H	BB	SO	HR	ERA	EQERA	EQH9	EQBB9	EQSO9	EQHR9	PERA	VORP	STF
2000	NWJ	NYP	21	6	6	28.3	20	9	25	1	1.59	3.31	8.7	3.8	4.4	1.5	4.54	6.9	0
2001	POT	CRL	22	17	17	107.3	82	30	92	12	2.43	5.14	10.5	3.8	5.0	2.6	4.78	4.4	0
2002	NWJ	NYP	23	2	2	5.3	2	1	8	1	1.70	3.20	9.5	2.8	8.5	6.5	2.92	1.4	-1

A big guy who throws in the mid-90s, Williams was selected by the Reds in the Rule 5 draft. Bouncing back from Tommy John surgery, he's supposed to be fully healthy, and throwing hard could make him useful out of the pen; it remains to be seen whether he'll still have command of his nasty breaking stuff. Jumping from A-ball to the majors is going to be tough, so don't be surprised if he's back with the Cardinals and pitching in Double-A in 2003.

Jamey Wright   Born: 24-Dec-74   Age: 28   Bats: R   Throws: R

YEAR	TM	LG	AGE	G	GS	IP	H	BB	SO	HR	ERA	EQERA	EQH9	EQBB9	EQSO9	EQHR9	PERA	VORP	STF
2000	MIL	NL	25	26	25	164.7	157	88	96	12	4.10	4.30	9.1	3.9	4.7	0.6	4.11	22.0	3
2001	MIL	NL	26	33	33	194.7	201	98	129	26	4.90	5.37	10.0	4.3	5.2	1.1	5.19	2.9	-1
2002	MIL	NL	27	19	19	114.3	115	63	69	15	5.35	5.54	9.6	4.4	4.8	1.2	5.33	-0.4	-5
2002	STL	NL	27	4	3	15.0	15	12	8	2	4.80	5.76	9.8	6.4	4.3	1.2	6.11	-0.4	-22
2003	STL	NL	28	22	18	113.0	113	59	78	12	4.73	5.15	9.3	4.0	5.5	1.0	5.17	5.8	0

Breakout: 12%   Improve: 54%   Collapse: 17%

Although Wright started off the season recovering from elbow surgery and shoulder tendonitis, he bounced back in time to have a nice August, just in time to make him a tad more expensive for the Cardinals to acquire. At this point, it's worth wondering if Wright will ever get his struggles ironed out, or if he'll just wind up being the sphinx without a riddle. You'd hope that coming to the Cardinals and working with Dave Duncan would help, but he didn't get that much exposure. Wright still has good stuff, and if he can hook up with a Gullett or Duncan or Ruhle to coach him, and tackle his temper, he could finally turn the corner. You can say that about a lot of guys, naturally.

San Diego Padres

The Padres' 2002 season didn't go exactly as planned. At the start of the year, they looked poised to compete and possibly win the NL West. They had a bunch of talented young players, including a raft of live arms, a possible Rookie of the Year in Sean Burroughs, and a solid if shallow offensive core, centered on the likes of Nevin, Klesko, and Kotsay. Besides those core guys, there were a collection of talented role-players on hand, including some analyst favorites, a couple of older outfielders who could reasonably be expected to help, and a bullpen with some question marks, anchored by a proven closer with borderline Hall of Fame credentials. They weren't the Yankees, but no one else in the division was a lock to win 100 games, or even 90. Arizona was old. The Dodgers were flailing around under the weight of some bad contracts yet to expire and a bunch of injured pitchers, and the Giants' off-season moves consisted of picking up outfielders that couldn't get on base, and still had Barry Bonds and the 4 lineup holes. The Padres had a shot. They were young and everything had to break right, but they had a shot.

Of course, it didn't turn out that way. Barry Bonds, Randy Johnson, and Curt Schilling were all absurdly good, the Padres ran into the injuries, glitches, and pitfalls that pop up every year, and they sank out of contention early before completely collapsing and winning only eight games in September. Injuries hit the Padres fairly hard. Phil Nevin went down with a broken arm, causing him to miss a big chunk of a season and robbing him of his strength when he finally returned. Kevin Jarvis's elbow surgery took him out for the season in July. Only two Padre pitchers logged enough innings to qualify for the ERA title. Overall, 2002 wasn't a season the Padre fans, players, or front office will want to spend a whole lot of time dwelling on.

That's because they'll want to focus on an incredibly bright future. The Padre farm system is jam-packed with talent. They've got pitchers, they've got hitters, they've even got some hitters that can play positions other than the corners. The Padre talent acquisition and development system is among the very best in baseball, and the dividends are about to arrive. Kevin Towers and the rest of the Padre front office understand why teams win baseball games, and they've set up their organization to crank out ballplayers that do precisely those things. The Padres have been very successful drafting college hitters with power and plate discipline, including probably the best four-pack of hitters in any organization—Xavier Nady, Tagg Bozied, Jake Gautreau, and Khalil Greene. That's not even counting Sean Burroughs, who, after a rough year, is still young enough to be a Grade-A prospect.

On the mound, there's a gobload of young pitchers with great stuff, and more important, great performance histories that correlate tremendously well with expected future success. It's entirely possible that by the end of the 2003 season, the Padres could have one of the best rotations in baseball, and they could also be the youngest. Jake Peavy's a #1 waiting to happen, Oliver Perez has already demonstrated that he can be dominant, and if Dennis Tankersley can overcome some of his on- and off-field difficulties, the trio could be among the best in baseball, challenging Boston, Arizona, and Oakland. If Adam Eaton's back and healthy, and that appears to be the case, he could be at full strength and tremendously effective, particularly in the second half of the season. Towers and company understand that strikeout rate for a pitcher is a tremendous predictor of future ERA, and the farm system screams it. At every stop, the Padres have a coterie of relievers that strike out more than a guy per inning, and they've usually got either a great fastball or some sort of devastating breaking pitch or changeup. Unlike many organizations that haven't yet figured that out, the Padres let the strikeouts guide them to the stuff, rather than the other way around. Removes a level of abstraction and error from the process. This is a smart organization.

Padres Prospectus

2002 record: 66–96; Fourth place, NL West

Pythagenport Record: 65–97

Runs scored per game: 4.1 (14th in NL)

Runs allowed per game: 5.0 (14th in NL)

Team EqA: .257 (12th in NL)

2002 Batters Age: 29.6 (8th youngest in NL)

2002 Pitchers Age: 27.7 (4th youngest in NL)

Ballpark: Qualcomm Stadium; Severe pitchers' park; Park Factor of .920

2002: Injuries led to an ugly stumble for an organization and team on the way up.

2003: Kevin Towers has to sort out the pieces of the lineup and hope for better health this season.

The Padres enter the 2003 season with a team full of young veterans, a stocked farm system, and a look reminiscent of the 2000 Oakland A's. So what do they need to do to begin a similar run?

Don't overwork the young pitchers. On occasion, Bruce Bochy has had a history of working young starters (like Adam Eaton) too hard. The Padres have truly great pitching prospects, but they're all young, and they shouldn't have to withstand some sort of Dallas Greeneesque trial by fire. They won't survive it, and that's not an indictment of their fortitude or anything—it's simply a result of the nature of throwing overhand. They need to be babied. Quick hooks, and lots of them. That means a deep bullpen, or at least a willingness to use relievers for extended outings. It's going to cost the Padres some platoon advantages, and the occasional tactically useful pinch hitter, but it's a small and necessary price to pay.

Thank the Baltimore Orioles. Not that the Padres were tempted, but the Orioles signed noted albatross Deivi Cruz, preventing him from taking the field for the Padres again. Cruz was predictably awful, but due to a combination of factors, played 151 games for the Padres in 2002. No team has ever won a title with Deivi Cruz playing over 150 games for them, and no team ever will. Brrrr.

Keep Sean Burroughs in the lineup. He'll hit, and it'll be this year.

Find some depth. The Padres got hurt badly by injuries, and they're sure to happen again. Stocking up on freely available talent like Jim Rushford, Mario Valdez, and the like will help dramatically. If one of the corner guys gets hurt, the Padres need to have someone available to drop in there for quick production, without putting undue pressure or expectations on the Nady/Bozied cohort. The Padres are going to need good options available in Triple-A. The injuries are going to happen, and they need to be ready.

Find a reliable swingman. One thing missing from the club is a guy who can make a few emergency starts, pitch long relief, and do so at a level suggesting he could handle more. If Ramiro Mendoza were healthy, he'd be a good free agent pickup. (He's not, and we're not suggesting it—that's the KIND of guy we're talking about.)

Find a left fielder. A platoon partner for Buchanan would probably do, and if you can find one for Trammell, too, all the better.

The NL West isn't standing still. The Giants have Bonds, and had a surprisingly great off-season, picking up two guys who get on base, hit for power, and are pretty much stathead dreams in Ray Durham and Edgardo Alfonzo. Rich Aurilia will probably be better, and Russ Ortiz was overrated. They're a very good club. Arizona still has Schilling and Johnson, but fortunately hamstrung themselves by moving Durazo for Elmer Dessens. Los Angeles still has Jim Tracy and a bunch of expensive question marks to go with a depleted farm system. The Padres do not have an easy time ahead of them. They have the curse and the benefit of active and worthy opponents.

Starting in 2004, the Padres should be in a considerably better situation. Their new downtown ballpark opens, and revenue is expected to increase dramatically, allowing them greater flexibility in discretionary expenses like salaries and player development. A raft of talented kids reminiscent of Oakland's wave should be arriving on a regular basis, and filling in a couple of the very serious holes in the Padre lineup. If your 2002 shortstop is Deivi Cruz, and your 2004 shortstop is Khalil Greene, who will likely be the best in the National League, that's an improvement that'll cause abdominal cramps among your competitors. Add in the arrival of Jake Gautreau at second, and you've probably got the National League's best infield in 2005 or so, with Xavier Nady or Tagg Bozied picking up the slack at first base.

The Dodgers, Giants, and Diamondbacks are all on the beach working on sand castles, and the Padres are the wave that's about to break and demolish all their hard work. It's the best-run organization in the National League, and the fruit of all the planning and hard work is just about to arrive. This is not an organization that's set up a team to win before a brief window closes. This is a team that's going to be competitive all the time, and change as needed from year to year. It's going to be a lot of fun to watch for a very long time.

HITTERS

Joshua Barfield 2B Born: 17-Dec-82 Age: 20 Bats: R Throws: R

YEAR	TM	LG	AGE	AB	H	2B	3B	HR	BB	SO	SB	CS	AVG	OBP	SLG	MLVR	EQBA	EQOBP	EQSLG	EQMLVR	VORP	DEFENSE			
2001	IDA	PIO	18	277	86	15	4	4	16	54	12	4	.310	.355	.437	.106	.209	.239	.293	-.442	-14.9	40-2B	-4	23-SS	-9
2002	FTW	MDW	19	536	164	22	3	8	26	105	26	8	.306	.343	.403	.139	.250	.276	.333	-.288	-10.1	128-2B	-7		
2002	LEL	CLF	19	23	2	0	0	0	1	4	0	0	.087	.125	.087	-.858	.087	.125	.087	-1.004	-4.9				
2003	SDP	NL	20	214	50	9	2	4	12	45	5	4	.233	.280	.342	-.236	.244	.286	.371	-.205	-3.2				

Breakout: 59%   Improve: 67%   Collapse: 19%

Barfield has lots to learn. He's not going to have his dad's arm or power, but looks like he has a knack for hitting for average, and he's expected to be a good glove man at second base. Obviously, he's got a long way to go in terms of plate discipline, but he's got some physical tools, and he's showing some ability. Let's see how he does in a full season in the Cal League.

Kevin Barker Born: 26-Jul-75 Age: 27 Bats: L Throws: L

YEAR	TM	LG	AGE	AB	H	2B	3B	HR	BB	SO	SB	CS	AVG	OBP	SLG	MLVR	EQBA	EQOBP	EQSLG	EQMLVR	VORP	DEFENSE			
2000	IND	INT	24	286	56	10	1	11	52	76	0	1	.196	.322	.353	-.165	.183	.292	.328	-.302	-16.6	73-1B	5		
2000	MIL	NL	24	100	22	5	0	2	20	21	1	0	.220	.355	.330	-.180	.218	.341	.337	-.173	-2.3	28-1B	-3		
2001	HUN	SOU	25	232	75	16	1	8	35	51	0	2	.323	.414	.504	.329	.275	.352	.433	.016	7.7	57-1B	1		
2001	IND	INT	25	159	30	5	0	4	20	40	0	0	.189	.283	.296	-.256	.180	.269	.286	-.405	-14.2	30-RF	1	16-1B	5
2002	POR	PCL	26	390	98	14	1	14	46	70	1	1	.251	.335	.400	-.022	.232	.307	.371	-.186	-9.8	106-1B	4		
2002	SDP	NL	26	19	3	0	0	0	1	6	1	0	.158	.200	.158	-.600	.211	.250	.211	-.534	-1.9				

Patient corner type with some power, and a tendency to go into slumps longer than an episode of "The Mind of the Married Man." Barker's chance for a career is fading fast. He's going to need to light it up this season to have any chance of a career as a 24th/25th man. It wouldn't hurt him to hit .290 with power and patience.

Jason Bay OF Born: 20-Sep-78 Age: 24 Bats: R Throws: R

YEAR	TM	LG	AGE	AB	H	2B	3B	HR	BB	SO	SB	CS	AVG	OBP	SLG	MLVR	EQBA	EQOBP	EQSLG	EQMLVR	VORP	DEFENSE	
2000	VER	NYP	21	135	41	5	0	2	11	25	17	4	.304	.361	.385	.144	.237	.271	.309	-.340	-8.4	13-LF	0
2001	CLN	MDW	22	318	115	20	4	13	48	62	15	2	.362	.451	.572	.512	.268	.340	.424	-.024	4.5	78-RF	6
2001	JUP	FSL	22	123	24	4	1	1	18	26	10	3	.195	.308	.268	-.168	.180	.260	.250	-.472	-13.5	35-RF	-2
2002	SLU	FSL	23	261	71	12	2	9	34	54	22	2	.272	.367	.437	.167	.229	.299	.373	-.200	-7.8	67-LF	-9
2002	BIN	EAS	23	107	31	4	2	4	15	23	13	3	.290	.392	.477	.205	.241	.326	.398	-.106	-.9	24-RF	-2
2002	MOB	SOU	23	81	25	5	2	4	13	22	4	2	.309	.411	.568	.402	.253	.337	.482	.038	2.8	19-OF	-2
2003	SDP	NL	24	186	46	8	1	5	18	41	7	4	.246	.317	.392	-.097	.258	.325	.425	-.055	-1.4		

Breakout: 37%   Improve: 69%   Collapse: 11%

Bay has a chance to be a very good outfielder. He does a little bit of everything: he can hit for some power and average, plays pretty good defense, and has some speed. If he can take a step forward in one part of his game, he could end up with an outside shot at a job as a major league regular. He could jump out very quickly, and is young enough to have a career like a healthy Rusty Greer or so. A good sleeper, and a nice guy for the Pads to have in the organization.

Tagg Bozied 1B Born: 24-Jul-79 Age: 23 Bats: R Throws: R

YEAR	TM	LG	AGE	AB	H	2B	3B	HR	BB	SO	SB	CS	AVG	OBP	SLG	MLVR	EQBA	EQOBP	EQSLG	EQMLVR	VORP	DEFENSE	
2001	sxf	NTH	21	228	70	17	0	6	13	34	3	2	.307	.360	.461	.155	.235	.281	.358	-.252	-.4		
2002	LEL	CLF	22	282	84	23	1	15	35	60	3	4	.298	.381	.546	.319	.233	.297	.420	-.136	-2.9	64-1B	-4
2002	MOB	SOU	22	234	50	14	0	9	16	43	1	0	.214	.270	.389	-.106	.189	.225	.353	-.397	-17.8	57-1B	-6
2003	SDP	NL	23	183	42	8	1	6	17	43	2	3	.228	.301	.381	-.151	.239	.308	.413	-.115	-3.9		

Breakout: 51%   Improve: 73%   Collapse: 7%

A classic masher. Scouts think Bozied is going to be a classic power hitter, and he's got a quick, vicious stroke, and part of San Diego's endless supply of "They're on the left end of the defensive spectrum for a reason" hitters. He hasn't gotten the same press as Xavier Nady, but he might end up being the superior hitter. In the Arizona Fall League, he flashed serious power, banging 12 home runs in 41 games. He'll be hulking to the plate in a major league stadium near you by 2005.

Brian Buchanan   OF   Born: 21-Jul-73   Age: 29   Bats: R   Throws: R

YEAR	TM	LG	AGE	AB	H	2B	3B	HR	BB	SO	SB	CS	AVG	OBP	SLG	MLVR	EQBA	EQOBP	EQSLG	EQMLVR	VORP	DEFENSE	
2000	SLC	PCL	26	364	108	20	1	27	41	75	5	1	.297	.373	.580	.229	.251	.315	.483	-.001	6.5	73-RF	-4
2000	MIN	AL	26	82	19	3	0	1	8	22	0	2	.232	.308	.305	-.316	.235	.304	.309	-.275	-4.1	17-RF	-1
2001	MIN	AL	27	197	54	12	0	10	19	58	1	1	.274	.344	.487	.097	.289	.359	.518	.160	12.2	34-RF	-2
2002	MIN	AL	28	135	34	5	1	5	6	33	2	1	.252	.294	.415	-.088	.267	.311	.444	-.049	.9	20-RF	0
2002	SDP	NL	28	92	27	5	0	6	9	26	0	1	.293	.363	.543	.295	.316	.374	.589	.316	11.0		
2003	SDP	NL	29	161	40	8	1	7	15	43	1	1	.246	.315	.434	-.047	.257	.322	.470	-.000	1.0		

Breakout: 9%   Improve: 35%   Collapse: 31%

Squeezed out by a numbers game in Minnesota, Buchanan's not a bad guy to have around. He can hit the ball over the fence, play better defense than he appears to, and hits lefties pretty well. Lot of guys like this are available, but Buchanan does it all pretty well.

Sean Burroughs   3B   Born: 12-Sep-80   Age: 22   Bats: L   Throws: R

YEAR	TM	LG	AGE	AB	H	2B	3B	HR	BB	SO	SB	CS	AVG	OBP	SLG	MLVR	EQBA	EQOBP	EQSLG	EQMLVR	VORP	DEFENSE			
2000	MOB	SOU	19	392	114	29	4	2	58	45	6	8	.291	.386	.401	.145	.256	.330	.356	-.146	4.7	106-3B	-6		
2001	POR	PCL	20	394	127	28	1	9	37	54	9	2	.322	.386	.467	.190	.290	.350	.419	.005	20.9	96-3B	6		
2002	POR	PCL	21	179	54	16	2	2	21	16	1	0	.302	.384	.447	.173	.280	.351	.412	-.011	10.2	29-2B	2	14-3B	-1
2002	SDP	NL	21	192	52	5	1	1	12	30	2	0	.271	.317	.323	-.103	.294	.335	.350	-.119	3.4	37-3B	-5		
2003	SDP	NL	22	313	88	19	1	6	34	39	5	1	.280	.353	.405	.004	.293	.362	.439	.053	16.4				

Breakout: 26%   Improve: 62%   Collapse: 19%

After their 2002 seasons, it might seem like this guy and Hank Blalock dropped off the face of the earth. Don't believe it. Burroughs can still rake, the power's eventually going to increase, and if there's anything to worry about, it's the declining walk rate, not anything more mysterious than that. His rotator cuff injury wasn't as bad as all that, and the surgery went exceptionally well. He'll start the season at third base, and two years from now, the 2002 glitch season will be a fading memory.

Bernie Castro   2B   Born: 14-Jul-79   Age: 23   Bats: B   Throws: R

YEAR	TM	LG	AGE	AB	H	2B	3B	HR	BB	SO	SB	CS	AVG	OBP	SLG	MLVR	EQBA	EQOBP	EQSLG	EQMLVR	VORP	DEFENSE	
2001	STA	NYP	21	57	20	1	0	0	11	12	8	3	.351	.464	.368	.269	.250	.342	.267	-.248	-.5	14-2B	-2
2001	GRB	SAL	21	389	101	15	7	1	54	67	67	20	.260	.351	.342	.041	.212	.284	.280	-.368	-16.7	96-2B	-10
2002	MOB	SOU	22	419	109	13	3	0	52	67	53	20	.260	.346	.305	-.070	.234	.299	.278	-.329	-12.6	105-2B	3
2003	SDP	NL	23	166	39	6	1	1	17	29	8	3	.234	.308	.303	-.238	.245	.315	.328	-.209	-2.0		

Breakout: 49%   Improve: 67%   Collapse: 22%

Castro is an extreme ground ball hitter with a good batting eye and a tendency to suddenly move at 25 mph. He's learning how to play the infield, and making progress on that front. If he can do a little something to occasionally lift the ball, and increase his strength a little, Castro could be a very interesting player. He puts the ball in play and runs, which is a great strategy with his kind of speed, especially if you only swing at pitches in the strike zone. It doesn't work as well if you have the speed of say, a John Olerud. This is a big season coming up for Castro—the next 750 PA will go a long way toward determining his career path.

Cesar Crespo   UT   Born: 23-May-79   Age: 24   Bats: B   Throws: R

YEAR	TM	LG	AGE	AB	H	2B	3B	HR	BB	SO	SB	CS	AVG	OBP	SLG	MLVR	EQBA	EQOBP	EQSLG	EQMLVR	VORP	DEFENSE			
2000	PME	EAS	21	482	124	21	6	9	77	118	41	15	.257	.362	.382	.017	.220	.306	.332	-.248	-9.3	112-CF	-9	16-2B	-4
2001	POR	PCL	22	273	71	18	3	8	39	66	23	3	.260	.355	.436	.030	.236	.325	.391	-.121	7.3	32-2B	1	22-RF	0
2001	SDP	NL	22	153	32	6	0	4	25	50	6	2	.209	.320	.327	-.199	.224	.331	.346	-.178	1.7	27-2B	-6	13-CF	0
2002	POR	PCL	23	322	83	17	2	9	50	78	21	7	.258	.363	.407	.043	.238	.333	.372	-.130	7.9	34-2B	2	26-OF	0
2002	SDP	NL	23	29	5	2	0	0	3	6	3	2	.172	.250	.241	-.387	.200	.250	.300	-.415	-2.1				
2003	SDP	NL	24	177	42	9	1	4	25	43	8	5	.239	.335	.373	-.095	.250	.343	.405	-.055	3.5				

Breakout: 36%   Improve: 65%   Collapse: 15%

A potential supersub, as long as everything goes well. Castro has some power, can play anywhere defensively if he has to, and has a good batting eye. There's a lot here to like, even if he's never going to be a star. If he can lay off the fastball two inches up out of the zone, he'd be a lot better off. Of course, that's true for everyone, but with Crespo, it may be a requisite for career survival.

Deivi Cruz — SS — Born: 06-Nov-72 — Age: 30 — Bats: R — Throws: R

YEAR	TM	LG	AGE	AB	H	2B	3B	HR	BB	SO	SB	CS	AVG	OBP	SLG	MLVR	EQBA	EQOBP	EQSLG	EQMLVR	VORP	DEFENSE
2000	DET	AL	27	583	176	46	5	10	13	43	1	4	.302	.322	.449	-.011	.313	.325	.470	.057	37.6	150-SS 4
2001	DET	AL	28	414	106	28	1	7	17	46	4	1	.256	.292	.379	-.139	.274	.311	.411	-.091	13.3	102-SS -16
2002	SDP	NL	29	514	135	28	2	7	22	58	2	3	.263	.297	.366	-.085	.281	.310	.395	-.110	14.0	129-SS -11
2003	BAL	AL	30	394	103	23	1	9	16	44	2	1	.262	.294	.392	-.102	.275	.307	.415	-.086	7.2	

Breakout: 16%   Improve: 54%   Collapse: 21%

This was not his best season. He aged three years, hit like you would expect a post-peak Deivi Cruz to hit, and his once impressive defense looked more like Howard Johnson at shortstop than Ozzie Smith. Had people known about his real age several years ago, well-meaning teams would have saved a lot of money. On his merits, Cruz is a Triple-A player (or an Oriole) at this point. There's really no need to let him go out there in the majors, except perhaps as a backup infielder, and even then, there are usually better options.

Kory DeHaan — CF — Born: 16-Jul-76 — Age: 26 — Bats: L — Throws: R

YEAR	TM	LG	AGE	AB	H	2B	3B	HR	BB	SO	SB	CS	AVG	OBP	SLG	MLVR	EQBA	EQOBP	EQSLG	EQMLVR	VORP	DEFENSE
2000	SDP	NL	23	103	21	7	0	2	5	39	4	2	.204	.241	.330	-.404	.219	.241	.352	-.349	-7.3	30-RF -1
2001	MOB	SOU	24	159	47	8	2	4	22	27	12	4	.296	.388	.447	.184	.252	.330	.387	-.106	-1.4	40-RF -1
2001	POR	PCL	24	304	77	9	5	7	20	71	12	9	.253	.304	.385	-.145	.227	.278	.339	-.290	-9.0	80-CF 4
2002	POR	PCL	25	442	125	31	14	2	31	96	23	9	.283	.342	.430	.059	.262	.314	.397	-.115	7.6	117-CF 2
2002	SDP	NL	25	11	1	0	0	0	0	6	0	0	.091	.091	.091	-.920	.182	.182	.182	-.730	-1.6	
2003	SDP	NL	26	171	42	9	2	3	14	38	6	4	.248	.309	.377	-.129	.260	.316	.408	-.090	.2	

Breakout: 38%   Improve: 63%   Collapse: 21%

DeHaan needs to have a few things break his way to have a major league career. For starters, he has to hit for a good average to have much value, as he has little power or plate discipline. Defensively, he's better than scouts give him credit for, and may be good enough to carry a light bat as a fourth outfielder. He's extremely vulnerable to pitches in: his hands come out of his swing early, and pitchers are taking advantage of that and working him in. He clearly needs to make some adjustments.

Omar Falcon — C — Born: 01-Sep-82 — Age: 20 — Bats: R — Throws: R

YEAR	TM	LG	AGE	AB	H	2B	3B	HR	BB	SO	SB	CS	AVG	OBP	SLG	MLVR	EQBA	EQOBP	EQSLG	EQMLVR	VORP	DEFENSE
2001	IDA	PIO	18	107	20	5	0	5	33	50	0	1	.187	.396	.374	.003	.124	.268	.230	-.501	-8.3	32-C -8
2002	IDA	PIO	19	185	42	12	0	9	36	100	1	1	.227	.364	.438	.063	.147	.240	.279	-.489	-12.3	46-C -2
2002	LEL	CLF	19	5	0	0	0	0	2	4	0	0	.000	.286	.000	-1.000	.000	.286	.000	-.745	-1.0	

Is there a way you can not love this guy? He's got some pop, has a name that absolutely demands that he eventually make the majors, and he clearly leaves nothing in the bag when he takes a rip. Strikeouts accounted for 70% of his outs in the Pioneer League. At least the walk totals are also high. If someone like Ichiro Suzuki struck out 70% of the time he made an out, that would be 307 punch-outs for the year. We haven't seen him up against a good changeup; there's a possibility he might just spontaneously combust or something.

Ron Gant — LF — Born: 02-Mar-65 — Age: 38 — Bats: R — Throws: R

YEAR	TM	LG	AGE	AB	H	2B	3B	HR	BB	SO	SB	CS	AVG	OBP	SLG	MLVR	EQBA	EQOBP	EQSLG	EQMLVR	VORP	DEFENSE
2000	PHI	NL	35	343	87	16	2	20	36	73	5	4	.254	.326	.487	.006	.251	.315	.486	.003	8.5	84-LF 0
2000	ANA	AL	35	82	19	3	1	6	20	18	1	2	.232	.382	.512	.115	.235	.380	.531	.162	5.8	19-LF 0
2001	COL	NL	36	171	44	8	2	8	24	56	3	1	.257	.349	.468	.008	.246	.335	.439	-.030	2.8	43-LF -2
2001	OAK	AL	36	81	21	5	1	2	11	24	2	0	.259	.348	.420	.010	.272	.366	.444	.054	4.0	
2002	SDP	NL	37	309	81	14	1	18	36	59	4	6	.262	.343	.489	.159	.278	.353	.527	.151	20.1	74-LF -1
2003	SDP	NL	38	194	46	9	1	7	24	47	2	2	.236	.322	.405	-.078	.247	.330	.440	-.036	-.3	

Breakout: 12%   Improve: 37%   Collapse: 38%

It's been a long time since Gant was a young, error-prone second baseman for the Braves, so it was nice to see him have a nifty little season in a part-time role. He wasn't hideous in the outfield, hit lefties pretty well, and did what he was asked. If he wants to play another season, he's worth the roster spot and the risk, but probably not in San Diego. He can still get around on a high fastball, but has become more of a guess hitter, which is natural for a 37-year-old not named Barry Bonds.

Jake Gautreau   2B   Born: 14-Nov-79   Age: 23   Bats: L   Throws: R

YEAR	TM	LG	AGE	AB	H	2B	3B	HR	BB	SO	SB	CS	AVG	OBP	SLG	MLVR	EQBA	EQOBP	EQSLG	EQMLVR	VORP	DEFENSE	
2001	EUG	NWN	21	178	55	19	0	6	22	47	1	1	.309	.397	.517	.337	.223	.290	.370	-.226	-1.8	44-3B	2
2002	LEL	CLF	22	371	106	20	1	10	42	86	2	3	.286	.361	.426	.114	.227	.284	.338	-.279	-6.1	87-2B	-6
2003	SDP	NL	23	157	36	7	1	4	14	40	1	2	.228	.296	.364	-.182	.239	.303	.394	-.147	-.1		

Breakout: 43%   Improve: 61%   Collapse: 13%

Lots of hype and expectations surround Gautreau. His defense at second base is spotty but getting better, and he's done a reasonable job of avoiding the dangers inherent in playing the position. He has a quick bat, good mechanics, solid plate discipline, and plenty of time to pull it all together. His arm's a little weak when forced to release the ball quickly, but he's playing second base. He's going to be a good one, and he'll make Tulane alums proud. Well, as proud as they can be, I guess, having graduated from Tulane. Could be worse. Could be Brown.

Richard Gomez   OF   Born: 19-Jul-76   Age: 26   Bats: R   Throws: R

YEAR	TM	LG	AGE	AB	H	2B	3B	HR	BB	SO	SB	CS	AVG	OBP	SLG	MLVR	EQBA	EQOBP	EQSLG	EQMLVR	VORP	DEFENSE	
2000	LAK	FSL	23	455	126	20	10	8	50	102	48	8	.277	.359	.418	.102	.223	.286	.344	-.270	-22.1	115-LF	-10
2001	ERI	EAS	24	346	93	21	2	14	25	75	26	7	.269	.346	.462	.120	.236	.300	.402	-.154	-5.8	90-LF	-6
2002	POR	PCL	25	334	79	15	2	11	25	74	13	5	.237	.299	.392	-.109	.220	.276	.362	-.266	-17.1	93-RF	-4

Yes, he's not young, but Gomez has a shot at a career, and will get to the point where he can help a club. He runs very well, hits hard line drives, and won't kill you with the glove. He could help a club a year down the road in a platoon or right-handed pinch-hitting role. On the down side, he has a clichéd, horrible time against breaking stuff, a la Pedro Cerrano. A 10% bump in average and plate discipline, and Gomez's chance of having a career increases dramatically.

Wiki Gonzalez   C   Born: 17-May-74   Age: 29   Bats: R   Throws: R

YEAR	TM	LG	AGE	AB	H	2B	3B	HR	BB	SO	SB	CS	AVG	OBP	SLG	MLVR	EQBA	EQOBP	EQSLG	EQMLVR	VORP	DEFENSE	
2000	SDP	NL	26	284	66	15	1	5	30	31	1	2	.232	.312	.345	-.217	.242	.311	.360	-.187	3.8	76-C	5
2001	SDP	NL	27	160	44	6	0	8	11	28	2	0	.275	.337	.463	.066	.288	.345	.485	.089	14.0	37-C	-1
2002	LEL	CLF	28	53	18	8	0	1	12	3	0	0	.340	.493	.547	.513	.255	.378	.418	.028	3.9	13-C	-1
2002	SDP	NL	28	164	36	8	1	1	27	24	0	0	.220	.333	.299	-.135	.238	.347	.327	-.163	3.3	50-C	-2
2003	SDP	NL	29	195	49	11	0	4	26	28	1	1	.250	.341	.373	-.079	.262	.349	.404	-.038	7.0		

Breakout: 28%   Improve: 54%   Collapse: 24%

Yeah, I can see why you'd want to pick up Mike Rivera. Wiki's got a little pop, but he's stretched as a starter. He's not going to post an .800 OPS in anything near full-time play, and his skills are really best suited to a backup role.

Khalil Greene   SS   Born: 21-Oct-79   Age: 23   Bats: R   Throws: R

YEAR	TM	LG	AGE	AB	H	2B	3B	HR	BB	SO	SB	CS	AVG	OBP	SLG	MLVR	EQBA	EQOBP	EQSLG	EQMLVR	VORP	DEFENSE	
2002	EUG	NWN	22	37	10	1	0	0	5	6	0	0	.270	.400	.297	.069	.231	.303	.231	-.387	-2.6		
2002	LEL	CLF	22	183	58	9	1	9	12	33	0	0	.317	.372	.525	.297	.254	.292	.416	-.135	3.7	37-SS	-3
2003	SDP	NL	23	160	38	7	1	4	12	32	2	1	.235	.299	.359	-.179	.246	.306	.389	-.145	.7		

Breakout: 25%   Improve: 52%   Collapse: 17%

So far, so good. Greene was the coveted middle infielder in the draft among the enlightened front offices, and Towers picked first. Greene's defense has been better than some expected, and he looked fully adapted and acclimated to the pro game in the Cal League. He's going to need a year of seasoning, but he could be up for a cup of coffee this season, and might compete for the starting shortstop job at the start of next season. He and Jose Reyes may well be the Nomar and Derek of the National League very soon. Or perhaps the Nomar and Miguel.

Pete Incaviglia   Thunderstick of Yore   Born: 02-Apr-64   Age: 39   Bats: R   Throws: R

YEAR	TM	LG	AGE	AB	H	2B	3B	HR	BB	SO	SB	CS	AVG	OBP	SLG	MLVR	EQBA	EQOBP	EQSLG	EQMLVR	VORP	DEFENSE
2001	Nwk	ATL	37	142	55	9	0	8	14	19	2	0	.387	.446	.620	.591	.315	.362	.503	.171	.1	
2002	POR	PCL	38	41	5	1	0	0	4	16	0	0	.122	.200	.146	-.695	.122	.200	.146	-.756	-7.0	

And thus, the comeback trail endeth. Thanks for the memories, Pete. Interesting how closely the careers of Incaviglia and Canseco began and ended. Who can forget Incaviglia jogging out to play center field in Arlington? I'm certain whoever was on the mound can't.

Ben Johnson RF Born: 18-Jun-81 Age: 22 Bats: R Throws: R

YEAR	TM	LG	AGE	AB	H	2B	3B	HR	BB	SO	SB	CS	AVG	OBP	SLG	MLVR	EQBA	EQOBP	EQSLG	EQMLVR	VORP	DEFENSE	
2000	FTW	MDW	19	109	21	6	2	3	7	25	0	3	.193	.261	.367	-.124	.152	.190	.295	-.567	-14.0	29-RF	1
2000	PEO	MDW	19	330	80	22	1	13	53	78	17	6	.242	.356	.433	.132	.194	.273	.348	-.307	-21.7	87-RF	-7
2001	LEL	CLF	20	503	139	35	6	12	54	141	22	7	.276	.359	.441	.129	.224	.286	.354	-.255	-23.2	131-RF	-13
2002	MOB	SOU	21	456	110	23	4	10	65	127	11	9	.241	.340	.375	-.000	.209	.284	.335	-.294	-26.8	123-RF	-9
2003	SDP	NL	22	184	41	8	2	5	19	50	3	4	.225	.302	.364	-.173	.236	.309	.395	-.138	-6.5		

Breakout: 47%   Improve: 68%   Collapse: 14%

Yes, the strikeouts are high, but the tools are all there. Johnson has power and speed, his throwing arm is solid, and he's still only 22 years old this season. He's not on anyone's top prospects lists, but it's entirely possible that he could put together a very nice season and start getting a lot of attention. Check in on him in August to see how his strikeout rate is doing. If it's down even a little bit, expect him to have enough to make it as a major league regular, especially if everything else he can do is on display.

Gene Kingsale OF Born: 20-Aug-76 Age: 26 Bats: B Throws: R

YEAR	TM	LG	AGE	AB	H	2B	3B	HR	BB	SO	SB	CS	AVG	OBP	SLG	MLVR	EQBA	EQOBP	EQSLG	EQMLVR	VORP	DEFENSE		
2000	BAL	AL	23	88	21	2	1	0	2	14	1	2	.239	.256	.284	-.433	.250	.258	.307	-.361	-3.8	23-CF	-2	
2001	ROC	INT	24	244	49	12	2	0	26	44	16	2	.201	.283	.266	-.282	.202	.276	.266	-.408	-20.9	57-OF	-1	
2001	TAC	PCL	24	215	63	14	4	3	8	25	12	4	.293	.327	.437	.012	.262	.298	.393	-.151	1.5	51-CF	0	
2002	TAC	PCL	25	188	49	15	3	6	15	30	10	3	.261	.319	.468	.039	.238	.293	.423	-.136	-3.1	44-RF	-2	
2002	SEA	AL	25	3	2	0	0	0	0	0	0	0	.667	.667	.667	1.457	.667	.667	.667	1.435	1.1			
2002	SDP	NL	25	216	60	10	3	2	20	47	9	2	.278	.347	.380	.032	.297	.360	.410	.017	5.3	63-RF	-2	
2003	DET	AL	26	289	75	16	3	4	22	50	10	5	.260	.317	.379	-.082	.269	.328	.409	-.063	-1.3	34%69%		18%

Breakout: 34%   Improve: 69%   Collapse: 18%

A better player than he's gotten credit for, especially from the likes of us. Kingsale still has great wheels, and can play a legitimate center field, but he's also developed some extra-base power, and has become a very efficient basestealer. He's been cast down to the 6th circle, and will spend the 2003 season in Comerica Park, tracking down the fly balls of the damned. Well, maybe it won't be quite that dramatic, but he will be in Detroit at the insistence of new manager Alan Trammell.

Ryan Klesko 1B/OF Born: 12-Jun-71 Age: 32 Bats: L Throws: L

YEAR	TM	LG	AGE	AB	H	2B	3B	HR	BB	SO	SB	CS	AVG	OBP	SLG	MLVR	EQBA	EQOBP	EQSLG	EQMLVR	VORP	DEFENSE		
2000	SDP	NL	29	494	140	33	2	26	91	81	23	7	.283	.396	.516	.229	.292	.395	.531	.241	49.2	123-1B	-1	
2001	SDP	NL	30	538	154	34	6	30	88	89	23	4	.286	.390	.539	.273	.302	.401	.566	.309	64.8	137-1B	-11	
2002	SDP	NL	31	540	162	39	1	29	76	86	6	2	.300	.390	.537	.333	.315	.399	.572	.329	63.9	108-1B	-11	20-RF -1
2003	SDP	NL	32	504	141	31	3	23	79	83	13	3	.280	.379	.486	.152	.294	.388	.527	.213	36.2			

Breakout: 3%   Improve: 38%   Collapse: 14%

After floundering for a few years, Klesko's become one of the most consistently good offensive players in the game, reminiscent of Fred McGriff during his peak. He's not a great defender anywhere, but it's not as if he's a black hole in the field. Where he used to be a dead fish against lefties, he hit them at about an .850 OPS last season, and he no longer needs to be platooned. People are always surprised at his speed—despite his size, Klesko is not a slow guy by any means. He'll be back at first base for the Padres this season through 2006, as part of a very nasty middle of the order.

Mark Kotsay CF Born: 02-Dec-75 Age: 27 Bats: L Throws: L

YEAR	TM	LG	AGE	AB	H	2B	3B	HR	BB	SO	SB	CS	AVG	OBP	SLG	MLVR	EQBA	EQOBP	EQSLG	EQMLVR	VORP	DEFENSE	
2000	FLA	NL	24	530	158	31	5	12	42	46	19	9	.298	.350	.443	.039	.299	.342	.446	.038	16.4	135-RF	5
2001	SDP	NL	25	406	118	29	1	10	48	58	13	5	.291	.368	.441	.106	.303	.379	.462	.129	35.7	106-CF	3
2002	SDP	NL	26	578	169	27	7	17	59	89	11	9	.292	.361	.452	.165	.313	.375	.487	.168	53.7	140-CF	-1
2003	SDP	NL	27	515	146	28	4	13	57	70	11	3	.283	.356	.429	.044	.296	.364	.465	.097	28.8		

Breakout: 4%   Improve: 42%   Collapse: 13%

Kotsay has developed into a very fine all-around ballplayer. He can do a little bit of everything—hit for average, power, draw a few walks, play good defense. What he can do a lot of really well is throw. Kotsay has a gun for an arm, and he's one of those guys who's just fun to watch throw, like Ichiro or Vlad. All in all, he's a solid building block for a club considering his position and age. The Padres have locked him in with a long-term contract through the 2006 season for $5.5 million annually, which is probably a very good deal for both sides.

Tom Lampkin C Born: 04-Mar-64 Age: 39 Bats: L Throws: R

YEAR	TM	LG	AGE	AB	H	2B	3B	HR	BB	SO	SB	CS	AVG	OBP	SLG	MLVR	EQBA	EQOBP	EQSLG	EQMLVR	VORP	DEFENSE	
2000	SEA	AL	36	103	26	6	1	7	9	17	0	0	.252	.330	.534	.088	.262	.334	.563	.153	9.9	23-C	1
2001	SEA	AL	37	204	46	10	0	5	18	41	1	0	.225	.310	.348	-.160	.249	.328	.390	-.108	6.5	56-C	2
2002	SDP	NL	38	281	61	10	1	10	38	59	4	2	.217	.317	.367	-.079	.236	.329	.399	-.103	10.2	78-C	-2
2003	SDP	NL	39	168	37	7	1	5	21	36	2	1	.223	.314	.356	-.164	.234	.322	.385	-.129	1.8		

Breakout: 29%   Improve: 44%   Collapse: 31%

Despite his struggles, Lampkin has been a good backup or platoon catcher to have. He hits from the left side with some pop and discipline, has a good reputation for working with pitchers, and he won't kill you by letting everyone run wild.

Ray Lankford LF Born: 05-Jun-67 Age: 36 Bats: L Throws: L

YEAR	TM	LG	AGE	AB	H	2B	3B	HR	BB	SO	SB	CS	AVG	OBP	SLG	MLVR	EQBA	EQOBP	EQSLG	EQMLVR	VORP	DEFENSE	
2000	STL	NL	33	392	99	16	3	26	70	148	5	6	.253	.371	.508	.112	.249	.360	.497	.095	20.9	93-LF	-1
2001	STL	NL	34	264	62	18	3	15	44	105	4	2	.235	.348	.496	.074	.239	.350	.500	.073	12.9	74-LF	-3
2001	SDP	NL	34	125	36	10	1	4	18	40	6	0	.288	.386	.480	.189	.297	.394	.500	.202	10.6	28-LF	0
2002	SDP	NL	35	205	46	7	1	6	30	61	2	2	.224	.329	.356	-.066	.243	.342	.395	-.079	.5	53-LF	-4
2003	SDP	NL	36	169	38	7	1	6	28	57	4	2	.228	.340	.394	-.067	.238	.349	.427	-.026	.7		

Breakout: 23%   Improve: 53%   Collapse: 23%

The decline came on pretty quickly, augured by a stratospheric strikeout rate. It was kind of surprising, as Lankford's skill set wasn't indicative of an Alvin Davis-like collapse, but the injuries and age took their toll. Lankford has always been one of the really classy guys in the game, and maybe he'll catch on somewhere, but any team that picks him up would probably be taking on a bad risk. His hamstring may still not be 100%, and even if it is, there's a lot to stay away from here.

Paul McAnulty 1B Born: 24-Feb-81 Age: 22 Bats: L Throws: R

YEAR	TM	LG	AGE	AB	H	2B	3B	HR	BB	SO	SB	CS	AVG	OBP	SLG	MLVR	EQBA	EQOBP	EQSLG	EQMLVR	VORP	DEFENSE	
2002	IDA	PIO	21	235	89	29	0	8	49	43	7	2	.379	.493	.604	.613	.238	.327	.383	-.127	-1.9	55-1B	0
2003	SDP	NL	22	172	40	8	1	5	22	42	3	3	.231	.321	.374	-.123	.242	.329	.405	-.085	-2.3		

Breakout: 27%   Improve: 48%   Collapse: 23%

I'd say Mr. McAnulty doesn't have much left to demonstrate in the Pioneer League. An ox of a first baseman from Long Beach State, McAnulty has a potent, well-crafted swing, and a physique and look that evokes images of former Dodger farmhand Brian Traxler. He's already polished from years of college competition; it'll be interesting to see how he plays against more challenging foes. If he lights up the Midwest and/or California leagues, the Padres may have themselves a real find, and another body cluttering their pool of potential sluggers.

Donaldo Mendez SS Born: 07-Jun-78 Age: 25 Bats: R Throws: R

YEAR	TM	LG	AGE	AB	H	2B	3B	HR	BB	SO	SB	CS	AVG	OBP	SLG	MLVR	EQBA	EQOBP	EQSLG	EQMLVR	VORP	DEFENSE	
2000	MIC	MDW	22	370	100	17	0	2	33	68	39	10	.270	.353	.332	-.001	.222	.272	.275	-.394	-16.3	100-SS	14
2001	SDP	NL	23	118	18	2	1	1	5	37	1	2	.153	.206	.212	-.615	.168	.217	.235	-.587	-11.4	36-SS	-11
2002	MOB	SOU	24	224	49	16	0	4	19	53	15	5	.219	.297	.344	-.120	.197	.251	.316	-.393	-10.0	55-SS	3
2002	POR	PCL	24	217	47	9	1	6	14	63	11	4	.217	.283	.350	-.212	.205	.258	.333	-.351	-7.6	59-SS	-1
2003	SDP	NL	25	154	33	6	1	3	11	40	5	4	.213	.276	.326	-.275	.223	.283	.353	-.248	-3.9		

Breakout: 68%   Improve: 79%   Collapse: 15%

What would constitute a "breakout" for Donaldo Mendez's bat? A Rey Sanchez-lite year? Mendez fields the ball fairly well, but he can't hit. That he's seen the light of the majors is something of an accident of history, and represents more of a fluke than a trend. He might be able to grab a job eventually as a pinch hitter and defensive sub on a team with bad infielders, but he's never going to be a regular, and you can't swing a dead cat without hitting eight or ten guys with comparable skill sets. Mrow.

Xavier Nady LF Born: 14-Nov-78 Age: 24 Bats: R Throws: R

YEAR	TM	LG	AGE	AB	H	2B	3B	HR	BB	SO	SB	CS	AVG	OBP	SLG	MLVR	EQBA	EQOBP	EQSLG	EQMLVR	VORP	DEFENSE	
2001	LEL	CLF	22	524	158	38	1	26	62	109	6	0	.302	.386	.527	.308	.239	.304	.413	-.129	-4.5	109-1B	-6
2002	LEL	CLF	23	169	47	6	3	13	28	40	2	0	.278	.384	.580	.346	.216	.301	.438	-.117	.7		
2002	POR	PCL	23	315	89	12	1	10	20	60	0	1	.283	.331	.422	.028	.262	.305	.391	-.140	-4.4	53-LF	-2
2003	SDP	NL	24	169	43	8	1	5	16	35	2	2	.254	.322	.412	-.057	.266	.330	.447	-.012	.9		

Breakout: 32%   Improve: 65%   Collapse: 17%

Another of Kevin Towers's collection of corner ballplayers that can flat-out hit. Nady's got a real bat, and he'll probably get a chance to come up to San Diego and hit at the first injury to one of the oxen on the major league roster. He's a prototypical right-handed power hitter with a pretty reasonable batting eye, and a reputation for being a quick learner. He's not going to set the world on fire defensively, but he'll have enough of a bat so he won't have to.

Phil Nevin   **3B/LF**   **Born: 19-Jan-71**   **Age: 32**   **Bats: R**   **Throws: R**

YEAR	TM	LG	AGE	AB	H	2B	3B	HR	BB	SO	SB	CS	AVG	OBP	SLG	MLVR	EQBA	EQOBP	EQSLG	EQMLVR	VORP	DEFENSE	
2000	SDP	NL	29	538	163	34	1	31	59	121	2	0	.303	.376	.543	.255	.311	.375	.556	.264	67.3	137-3B -16	
2001	SDP	NL	30	546	167	31	0	41	71	147	4	4	.306	.390	.588	.362	.316	.396	.604	.370	88.1	137-3B 2	
2002	SDP	NL	31	407	116	16	0	12	38	87	4	0	.285	.348	.413	.084	.301	.359	.443	.065	27.5	65-3B -4	32-1B -5
2003	SDP	NL	32	417	112	21	1	17	47	94	4	2	.267	.343	.446	.033	.280	.351	.484	.085	22.1		

Breakout: 4%   *Improve: 34%*   *Collapse: 26%*

Nevin is going to be moving to left field to accommodate Burroughs's development. The Padres have the potential to be a very good team right away, but they need Nevin to stay healthy and productive. We don't know how well he's likely to play in left field, but if he's able to take the field, he'll likely hit enough and field enough to push the Pads toward a division title. They're going to need a lot of breaks, and a return to 2000–2001 form by Nevin would be a big one to start with.

Ben Risinger   **3B**   **Born: 25-Nov-77**   **Age: 25**   **Bats: R**   **Throws: R**

YEAR	TM	LG	AGE	AB	H	2B	3B	HR	BB	SO	SB	CS	AVG	OBP	SLG	MLVR	EQBA	EQOBP	EQSLG	EQMLVR	VORP	DEFENSE	
2000	FTW	MDW	22	159	28	4	0	0	15	31	0	1	.176	.268	.201	-.331	.159	.212	.177	-.680	-19.8	28-2B 0	13-3B 3
2000	RCU	CLF	22	50	13	4	0	2	6	13	0	0	.260	.351	.460	.110	.216	.266	.373	-.273	-1.8		
2001	LEL	CLF	23	351	88	16	0	1	32	86	2	5	.251	.336	.305	-.110	.204	.263	.249	-.457	-24.0	39-3B 1	37-C -1
2002	MOB	SOU	24	466	134	26	0	3	40	62	1	2	.288	.359	.363	.043	.255	.303	.327	-.240	-6.2	95-3B -9	14-C -3
2003	SDP	NL	25	154	34	6	1	2	11	28	2	1	.223	.282	.314	-.274	.234	.289	.341	-.247	-4.6		

Breakout: 52%   *Improve: 68%*   *Collapse: 16%*

Some plate discipline, some signs of power, and the willingness to play catcher to make the majors. That's a start. Risinger will likely spend the season at Triple-A, possibly experimenting as a supersub. There are very few clubs couldn't use a guy who can play anywhere and hit somewhere near the league average. Risinger might be able to get there, but it's going to be an uphill climb.

Mark Sweeney   **PH**   **Born: 26-Oct-69**   **Age: 33**   **Bats: L**   **Throws: L**

YEAR	TM	LG	AGE	AB	H	2B	3B	HR	BB	SO	SB	CS	AVG	OBP	SLG	MLVR	EQBA	EQOBP	EQSLG	EQMLVR	VORP	DEFENSE
2000	IND	INT	30	55	28	8	0	2	10	8	0	0	.509	.585	.764	1.120	.455	.524	.673	.841	14.9	
2000	MIL	NL	30	73	16	6	0	1	12	18	0	0	.219	.337	.342	-.201	.216	.325	.351	-.188	-1.1	
2001	IND	INT	31	404	116	34	1	6	56	71	3	1	.287	.377	.421	.120	.267	.352	.396	-.041	5.2	49-LF 0
2001	MIL	NL	31	89	23	3	1	3	12	23	2	1	.258	.347	.416	-.015	.256	.343	.422	-.031	1.5	16-LF -1
2002	SDP	NL	32	65	11	3	0	1	4	19	0	0	.169	.217	.262	-.424	.185	.232	.308	-.448	-5.2	

Sweeney was once good enough to be a member of the Ken Phelps All-Star Team. He's been hampered by muscle pulls, and has been released by the Padres. A club with no good options at first base or in one of its outfield corners could do worse than to give him an NRI to training camp, and a lot of clubs could do worse for a pinch hitter. He can still probably hit if he's healthy, and a couple hundred at-bats with some power and plate discipline is more than certain clubs are getting from the corner spots. Inexplicable, but true.

Bubba Trammell   **RF**   **Born: 06-Nov-71**   **Age: 31**   **Bats: R**   **Throws: R**

YEAR	TM	LG	AGE	AB	H	2B	3B	HR	BB	SO	SB	CS	AVG	OBP	SLG	MLVR	EQBA	EQOBP	EQSLG	EQMLVR	VORP	DEFENSE
2000	TBY	AL	28	189	52	11	2	7	21	30	3	0	.275	.354	.466	.038	.283	.356	.481	.097	9.1	35-LF -1
2000	NYM	NL	28	56	13	2	0	3	8	19	1	0	.232	.328	.429	-.076	.246	.328	.439	-.043	.5	14-RF -1
2001	SDP	NL	29	490	128	20	3	25	48	78	2	2	.261	.332	.467	.051	.271	.339	.487	.065	19.3	122-RF 2
2002	SDP	NL	30	403	98	16	1	17	53	71	1	3	.243	.336	.414	.033	.261	.346	.447	.013	9.8	90-RF -5
2003	SDP	NL	31	328	83	16	1	13	39	60	2	1	.253	.336	.427	-.016	.265	.344	.462	.032	4.5	

Breakout: 21%   *Improve: 52%*   *Collapse: 26%*

Bubba Trammell *(continued)*

An off year, partially because of lingering knee problems. Trammell has been rumored to be on the trading block, but the Padres haven't found a deal they like, so for now he's back with the Padres for the 2003 season, and he's under contract for another year beyond that. He's expendable because of the large number of players with similar skill sets in the system, but it's unlikely Towers will be able to get out from under his salary without taking some dog of a contract in return. If healthy and playing full-time, he'll outhit that projection, and is a pretty reasonable candidate to show a power spike.

Ramon Vazquez — 2B/SS — Born: 21-Aug-76 — Age: 26 — Bats: L — Throws: R

YEAR	TM	LG	AGE	AB	H	2B	3B	HR	BB	SO	SB	CS	AVG	OBP	SLG	MLVR	EQBA	EQOBP	EQSLG	EQMLVR	VORP	DEFENSE			
2000	NHV	EAS	23	405	116	25	4	8	52	76	1	6	.286	.370	.427	.132	.249	.317	.377	-.147	7.7	123-SS	6		
2001	TAC	PCL	24	466	140	28	1	10	76	84	9	7	.300	.400	.429	.141	.271	.363	.385	-.033	23.8	127-SS	18		
2002	SDP	NL	25	423	116	21	5	2	45	79	7	2	.274	.345	.362	.002	.294	.359	.389	-.017	22.5	62-2B	4	31-SS	1
2003	*SDP*	*NL*	*26*	*376*	*96*	*18*	*3*	*5*	*43*	*65*	*7*	*3*	*.255*	*.334*	*.359*	*-.105*	*.268*	*.342*	*.389*	*-.066*	*9.4*				

Breakout: 5%   Improve: 38%   Collapse: 22%

Vazquez was kind of considered the lesser of two options in the Seattle chain, so the Padres were able to get him, and he's worked out very well. Defensively, he's become a very steady and reliable glove with pretty good range. With the bat, he's hitting for average, a little pop, and drawing some walks. It's not inconceivable that given the opportunity to play every day, he could be the best of a mixed lot at shortstop in the NL this coming season, depending on where Rich Aurilia plays, and which incarnation of Edgar Renteria takes the field. Of course, that's also assuming that Vazquez isn't playing second instead.

PITCHERS

Brad Baker — Born: 06-Nov-80 — Age: 22 — Bats: R — Throws: R

YEAR	TM	LG	AGE	G	GS	IP	H	BB	SO	HR	ERA	EQERA	EQH9	EQBB9	EQSO9	EQHR9	PERA	VORP	STF
2000	AUG	SAL	19	27	27	137.7	125	55	126	3	3.07	5.68	11.5	5.0	4.9	0.5	5.68	-2.7	1
2001	SAR	FSL	20	24	23	120.0	132	64	103	8	4.72	6.74	12.4	5.8	5.2	1.5	7.55	-16.5	-5
2002	SAR	FSL	21	12	12	61.3	53	25	65	4	2.79	4.54	10.6	4.7	6.9	1.4	5.05	6.6	14
2002	MOB	SOU	21	12	12	64.3	47	45	57	5	4.48	5.39	8.7	6.9	5.9	1.5	4.98	0.8	2

Baker's one of those guys who could flounder for years, then suddenly put it together and become very nasty. He's got a great fastball and plus curve, but has trouble with his command, which isn't unusual for a 21-year-old. He'll likely start the season in Double-A, and may have one of those seasons where his ERA's over six for the first half, then around 2.00 with everything in gear in the second half. He's got a high upside and lots of time, but he's also got a lot to learn. Check back late in the year. If things are going great, then he's a great prospect. If they're not, he could be a great prospect in *BP 2005*.

Cliff Bartosh — Born: 05-Sep-79 — Age: 23 — Bats: L — Throws: L

YEAR	TM	LG	AGE	G	GS	IP	H	BB	SO	HR	ERA	EQERA	EQH9	EQBB9	EQSO9	EQHR9	PERA	VORP	STF
2000	FTW	MDW	20	50	4	77.0	50	44	94	6	3.04	5.70	9.0	6.4	7.0	1.9	4.98	-2.5	-4
2001	LEL	CLF	21	38	0	45.7	42	12	66	2	1.58	4.82	11.1	3.1	7.6	0.8	4.72	2.8	11
2001	MOB	SOU	21	20	0	22.7	20	13	20	5	3.96	6.50	11.1	6.4	5.7	3.5	6.88	-2.8	-22
2002	MOB	SOU	22	62	0	70.7	54	32	70	4	3.18	4.34	8.8	4.5	6.6	1.1	4.09	8.2	0

Bartosh's stuff is basically some percentage of Barry Zito's. He's got a gigantic curveball that lefties might as well just take, and a variety of other pitches he uses to set it up, including a generic fastball. He's got enough stuff so he'll eventually make the majors as a lefty specialist, and he'll probably be a pretty good one. He'll start the season in Triple-A.

Jason Boyd — Born: 23-Feb-73 — Age: 30 — Bats: R — Throws: R

YEAR	TM	LG	AGE	G	GS	IP	H	BB	SO	HR	ERA	EQERA	EQH9	EQBB9	EQSO9	EQHR9	PERA	VORP	STF
2000	CLR	FSL	27	6	3	11.3	11	4	12	0	2.39	4.58	10.6	4.0	6.6	0.3	4.81	1.1	0
2000	SWB	INT	27	11	2	15.7	8	14	10	0	1.72	2.79	5.6	8.1	4.9	0.2	3.30	4.6	-18
2000	PHI	NL	27	30	0	34.3	39	24	32	2	6.56	5.97	10.3	5.0	7.3	0.5	5.38	-2.2	-3
2001	SWB	INT	28	52	0	59.3	44	22	66	4	1.97	3.69	8.2	4.0	8.0	0.8	3.55	11.1	6
2002	SDP	NL	29	23	0	28.3	33	15	18	6	7.95	7.68	10.8	4.2	5.0	2.0	7.07	-7.2	-26
2002	POR	PCL	29	19	0	26.0	19	7	22	2	1.04	2.56	8.3	2.9	6.1	1.0	3.17	8.1	0
2002	PAW	INT	29	9	0	16.0	13	9	15	3	3.94	4.92	8.8	6.3	7.5	2.6	5.47	0.8	-14
2003	*SDP*	*NL*	*30*	*32*	*3*	*45.0*	*45*	*26*	*42*	*5*	*4.67*	*5.41*	*9.4*	*4.4*	*7.2*	*1.1*	*5.19*	*2.5*	*-3*

Breakout: 13%   Improve: 43%   Collapse: 22%

All over the place. Boyd looked horrific with the Padres, and unhittable in Portland. High upsides and semi-electric stuff are nice to have, but there's something to be said for predictability in a reliever. Boyd's going to have to earn another shot with two or three consecutive solid months in Triple-A.

Mike Bynum — Born: 20-Mar-78 — Age: 25 — Bats: L — Throws: L

YEAR	TM	LG	AGE	G	GS	IP	H	BB	SO	HR	ERA	EQERA	EQH9	EQBB9	EQSO9	EQHR9	PERA	VORP	STF
2000	RCU	CLF	22	21	21	126.0	101	51	129	4	3.00	4.09	8.8	3.9	5.7	0.6	4.10	19.8	14
2000	MOB	SOU	22	6	6	34.0	31	16	27	2	2.91	4.78	10.7	4.7	5.1	1.0	5.46	2.7	3
2001	MOB	SOU	23	16	15	84.3	90	35	69	14	5.02	7.12	12.9	4.6	5.3	2.6	6.97	-15.2	-9
2002	MOB	SOU	24	6	5	33.0	17	7	29	0	0.82	1.85	5.7	2.0	5.7	0.2	1.74	13.4	22
2002	POR	PCL	24	7	7	41.0	36	7	35	6	3.51	4.83	10.0	1.8	6.1	1.8	4.15	3.1	13
2002	SDP	NL	24	14	3	27.3	33	15	17	3	5.27	5.64	11.2	4.4	4.9	1.0	6.57	-0.6	-13
2003	SDP	NL	25	20	11	73.0	77	31	53	9	4.67	5.42	10.0	3.3	5.7	1.2	5.44	2.0	-3

Breakout: 10%   Improve: 51%   Collapse: 20%

If Bynum has a career, it'll be off of his slider, which is great. In Mobile, he looked like he was throwing his changeup more effectively, so maybe he's ready to take a big step forward. His fastball's not great, but if the change is working, the fastball's enough, and his slider's outstanding. Bynum needs a full year in Triple-A; after that, everyone will know more.

Clay Condrey — Born: 19-Nov-75 — Age: 27 — Bats: R — Throws: R

YEAR	TM	LG	AGE	G	GS	IP	H	BB	SO	HR	ERA	EQERA	EQH9	EQBB9	EQSO9	EQHR9	PERA	VORP	STF
2000	RCU	CLF	24	18	0	20.7	18	7	21	1	3.48	4.25	9.8	3.3	5.7	1.0	4.43	2.6	-5
2000	MOB	SOU	24	35	0	43.7	41	20	25	4	5.35	6.47	11.3	4.7	3.8	1.6	5.93	-5.3	-28
2001	MOB	SOU	25	27	0	33.7	33	15	21	1	4.54	6.48	11.1	4.8	3.9	0.5	5.25	-4.1	-23
2001	POR	PCL	25	39	0	53.0	63	13	45	7	4.75	6.59	12.4	2.7	5.7	1.5	6.06	-7.1	-11
2002	POR	PCL	26	25	23	133.7	128	40	73	12	3.50	4.85	10.9	3.3	4.0	1.1	4.62	9.7	-6
2002	SDP	NL	26	9	3	26.7	20	8	16	1	1.69	2.54	6.8	2.4	4.8	0.4	2.92	8.6	3
2003	SDP	NL	27	17	10	62.7	69	26	37	7	4.75	5.51	10.4	3.3	4.6	1.1	5.50	0.9	-9

Breakout: 15%   Improve: 46%   Collapse: 21%

Well, that idea worked out pretty well, but I still don't understand how. That 3.50 ERA in Portland was probably something of a miracle and fluke, based on the iffy peripheral numbers. If Condrey can keep up that kind of success with that strikeout rate, he's a magician. It doesn't happen very often. It does occasionally, but the better bet is for a significant slide. Certainly, he's earned a longer look.

Eric Cyr — Born: 11-Feb-79 — Age: 24 — Bats: R — Throws: L

YEAR	TM	LG	AGE	G	GS	IP	H	BB	SO	HR	ERA	EQERA	EQH9	EQBB9	EQSO9	EQHR9	PERA	VORP	STF
2000	FTW	MDW	21	9	6	32.7	28	15	31	2	4.68	6.37	11.5	5.2	5.6	1.5	5.87	-3.2	-4
2001	LEL	CLF	22	21	16	100.7	68	24	131	1	1.61	3.32	8.0	2.8	6.7	0.2	2.87	24.3	24
2002	MOB	SOU	23	14	14	72.3	62	34	65	6	3.24	5.37	10.2	4.7	6.1	1.6	4.95	1.1	4
2002	POR	PCL	23	9	2	14.3	14	10	11	0	3.15	5.21	11.0	7.7	5.6	0.3	5.36	0.4	-12
2002	SDP	NL	23	5	0	6.0	6	6	4	0	10.50	7.45	8.9	7.7	5.1	0.2	6.03	-1.4	-19

Cyr's fastball is average, but he spots it well, and it's enough to leave batters slack-jawed at the sight of his curveball. He could probably use a full season in the rotation at Triple-A to see how well he's pulled everything together, and how he handles the workload. That said, his curveball is really that outstanding, and there's no substitute for a well-placed fastball, so there's no reason Cyr can't be successful in the bigs. He may end up as a super setup man or something, depending on how the rest of his repertoire comes together.

Adam Eaton — Born: 23-Nov-77 — Age: 25 — Bats: R — Throws: R

YEAR	TM	LG	AGE	G	GS	IP	H	BB	SO	HR	ERA	EQERA	EQH9	EQBB9	EQSO9	EQHR9	PERA	VORP	STF
2000	MOB	SOU	22	10	10	57.0	47	18	58	3	2.68	4.20	9.5	3.1	6.5	0.9	4.23	8.3	19
2000	SDP	NL	22	22	22	135.0	134	61	90	14	4.13	4.34	9.5	3.3	5.4	0.9	4.62	17.5	12
2001	SDP	NL	23	17	17	116.7	108	40	109	20	4.32	4.58	8.6	2.9	7.2	1.4	4.66	12.0	20
2002	SDP	NL	24	6	6	33.3	28	17	25	5	5.41	4.82	7.6	4.0	5.9	1.4	4.75	2.5	5
2003	SDP	NL	25	15	13	86.3	84	36	65	9	4.29	4.97	9.2	3.3	5.9	1.0	4.83	6.2	7

Breakout: 16%   Improve: 51%   Collapse: 21%

Adam Eaton (continued)

Command hasn't returned to Eaton since the injury, but everything else looked pretty reasonable. It may take all of this season for him to get back to full health and confidence. If he can do that, he's going to be outstanding. If not, he's still young enough to spend some time and learn how to pitch without the same stuff he had before. Tommy John surgery pretty much qualifies as a miracle, doesn't it?

Jeremy Fikac — Born: 08-Apr-75 — Age: 28 — Bats: R — Throws: R

YEAR	TM	LG	AGE	G	GS	IP	H	BB	SO	HR	ERA	EQERA	EQH9	EQBB9	EQSO9	EQHR9	PERA	VORP	STF
2000	RCU	CLF	25	61	0	75.0	46	24	101	2	1.80	2.51	6.6	3.0	7.4	0.5	2.64	23.9	10
2001	MOB	SOU	26	53	0	68.7	54	20	75	3	1.97	3.25	8.8	3.1	6.7	0.7	3.62	16.3	2
2001	SDP	NL	26	23	0	26.3	15	5	19	2	1.37	2.02	5.3	1.6	5.6	0.6	1.99	9.8	5
2002	MOB	SOU	27	3	0	3.0	5	0	0	0	3.00	5.47	21.2	1.0	0.0	0.3	7.67	-0.0	-38
2002	SDP	NL	27	65	0	69.0	74	34	66	13	5.48	6.14	9.9	3.9	7.5	1.8	6.24	-5.8	-7
2003	OAK	AL	28	43	1	58.7	60	23	45	8	4.80	4.80	9.1	3.2	6.5	1.2	4.52	6.9	-3

Breakout: 16%   Improve: 42%   Collapse: 27%

A control freak without tremendous stuff. Fikac will have a shot at a bullpen job a few more times in his career, but what the Padres saw last year wasn't particularly impressive. He needs to have his main pitch going and spotting where he wants it in the strike zone to be effective. He may get to work on that in Triple-A, though the A's may want more than that from him after picking him up.

Bryan Gaal — Born: 17-Dec-76 — Age: 26 — Bats: R — Throws: R

YEAR	TM	LG	AGE	G	GS	IP	H	BB	SO	HR	ERA	EQERA	EQH9	EQBB9	EQSO9	EQHR9	PERA	VORP	STF
2001	FTW	MDW	24	23	0	32.3	20	4	42	0	1.95	2.29	6.7	1.5	6.9	0.3	2.26	11.1	15
2001	LEL	CLF	24	35	0	47.0	37	17	50	3	3.64	5.36	10.0	4.4	5.7	1.2	4.44	0.1	-10
2002	LEL	CLF	25	32	0	34.7	28	9	45	3	2.59	4.54	9.9	3.0	6.9	1.5	4.13	3.2	-2
2002	MOB	SOU	25	32	0	36.7	40	11	32	1	2.94	4.84	12.2	3.0	5.8	0.5	5.27	2.2	-4

A good candidate to fill out the back of the pen, either late this year or early next year. Gaal keeps the ball down, spots it well, and his peripheral numbers support the low ERAs. I'd rather give him the ball for $300,000 than give it to Todd Van Poppel for multiple millions. The results probably wouldn't be too different.

Trevor Hoffman — Born: 13-Oct-67 — Age: 35 — Bats: R — Throws: R

YEAR	TM	LG	AGE	G	GS	IP	H	BB	SO	HR	ERA	EQERA	EQH9	EQBB9	EQSO9	EQHR9	PERA	VORP	STF
2000	SDP	NL	32	70	0	72.3	61	11	85	7	2.99	3.23	8.1	1.1	9.5	0.8	2.95	17.3	26
2001	SDP	NL	33	62	0	60.3	48	21	63	10	3.43	3.79	7.3	2.9	8.0	1.4	3.95	10.7	6
2002	SDP	NL	34	61	0	59.3	52	18	69	2	2.73	3.15	8.1	2.4	9.2	0.3	3.45	14.7	22
2003	SDP	NL	35	57	0	56.3	48	19	61	5	2.89	3.36	8.0	2.6	8.5	0.9	3.51	14.9	15

Breakout: 26%   Improve: 57%   Collapse: 19%

Another year, a few more saves. It gets to the point where you've really got several changeups, each varying in velocity from the others. He doesn't have the great stuff he used to, but hitters still can't get a read on the ball as it leaves his hand. Responsible for more stuck front feet than gum on the sidewalk in August. Fun to watch him pitch, but he does occasionally leave a ball right in the happy zone, and most Padre fans can see it happen before it actually occurs. Coming off shoulder surgery, there's a good chance he won't be ready for Opening Day, which prompted the Pads to sign Jay Witasick, Jaret Wright, and others.

Ben Howard — Born: 15-Jan-79 — Age: 24 — Bats: R — Throws: R

YEAR	TM	LG	AGE	G	GS	IP	H	BB	SO	HR	ERA	EQERA	EQH9	EQBB9	EQSO9	EQHR9	PERA	VORP	STF
2000	RCU	CLF	21	32	19	107.3	88	111	150	8	6.37	7.53	9.4	10.0	7.8	1.5	7.22	-24.4	-3
2001	LEL	CLF	22	18	18	101.7	86	32	107	4	2.83	4.66	10.4	3.8	5.6	0.7	4.42	9.5	11
2001	MOB	SOU	22	7	5	30.0	17	15	29	3	2.40	3.60	6.7	5.3	6.0	1.5	3.54	6.3	4
2002	MOB	SOU	23	6	6	33.0	26	16	30	2	2.18	3.96	9.1	4.8	6.1	1.1	4.39	5.7	9
2002	POR	PCL	23	11	7	45.0	47	15	25	10	6.20	7.53	12.3	3.7	4.1	2.9	6.44	-10.2	-19
2002	SDP	NL	23	3	2	10.7	13	14	10	4	9.25	9.96	10.9	10.1	7.1	3.5	11.15	-5.3	-28
2003	SDP	NL	24	15	9	58.7	59	36	48	8	5.29	6.13	9.5	4.8	6.3	1.4	6.11	-2.9	-6

Breakout: 16%   Improve: 53%   Collapse: 15%

Howard has serious control problems to accompany serious velocity. His main problem is that he's still learning the skill of creating and maintaining a repeatable pitching motion. He has had flashes of success when he simplified his delivery, and if he ever puts it all together, he could be simply devastating. He'll spend another year in the minors trying to identify some mechanics that work for him, and learning how to always go back to those on every pitch. People think it's easy, but it requires a great deal of discipline, concentration, and learning.

Kevin Jarvis — Born: 01-Aug-69 — Age: 33 — Bats: R — Throws: R

YEAR	TM	LG	AGE	G	GS	IP	H	BB	SO	HR	ERA	EQERA	EQH9	EQBB9	EQSO9	EQHR9	PERA	VORP	STF
2000	CSP	PCL	30	7	7	39.0	18	13	18	1	0.69	1.06	4.1	3.0	3.3	0.3	1.19	19.3	5
2000	COL	NL	30	24	19	115.0	138	33	60	26	5.95	5.36	10.3	2.1	4.1	1.7	5.08	1.7	-7
2001	SDP	NL	31	32	32	193.3	189	49	133	37	4.80	4.77	9.1	2.2	5.3	1.6	4.84	15.8	4
2002	SDP	NL	32	7	7	35.0	36	10	24	5	4.37	4.69	9.6	2.3	5.5	1.4	5.00	3.2	3
2003	SDP	NL	33	16	11	71.0	74	22	42	10	4.54	5.26	9.9	2.4	4.7	1.3	4.90	4.4	-4

Breakout: 7%   Improve: 36%   Collapse: 34%

Elbow surgery ended Jarvis's season early. He's under contract through 2004, and has been rumored in every potential trade out of San Diego, including one to the Royals. He should remain a crafty right-hander without great stuff, but someone who can hopefully eat some innings and give his team a chance to win. That said, signing him long-term was not Kevin Towers's most shining moment.

Bobby J. Jones — Born: 10-Feb-70 — Age: 33 — Bats: R — Throws: R

YEAR	TM	LG	AGE	G	GS	IP	H	BB	SO	HR	ERA	EQERA	EQH9	EQBB9	EQSO9	EQHR9	PERA	VORP	STF
2000	NYM	NL	30	27	27	154.7	171	49	85	25	5.06	5.02	10.4	2.4	4.5	1.4	5.13	8.3	-1
2001	SDP	NL	31	33	33	195.0	250	38	113	37	5.12	6.13	12.2	1.7	4.5	1.6	6.31	-13.5	-2
2002	SDP	NL	32	19	18	108.0	134	21	60	20	5.50	5.65	11.7	1.6	4.5	1.8	6.21	-1.8	-3
2003	SDP	NL	33	20	17	110.0	125	27	60	16	4.74	5.50	10.7	1.9	4.3	1.4	5.21	4.6	-3

Breakout: 19%   Improve: 38%   Collapse: 35%

This is the one that you definitely don't want to suddenly appear at your favorite team's training camp. Nondescript right-hander, Jones will likely bounce from team to team looking to hook up as an emergency starter. In his old age, he's got a broad repertoire of pitches, none of them particularly effective.

Bobby M. Jones — Born: 11-Apr-72 — Age: 31 — Bats: R — Throws: L

YEAR	TM	LG	AGE	G	GS	IP	H	BB	SO	HR	ERA	EQERA	EQH9	EQBB9	EQSO9	EQHR9	PERA	VORP	STF
2000	NOR	INT	28	22	21	133.3	122	58	100	13	4.32	4.84	9.5	4.0	5.8	1.1	4.64	9.8	4
2000	NYM	NL	28	11	1	21.7	18	14	20	2	4.15	4.24	7.6	4.7	7.3	0.8	4.18	2.8	2
2002	NOR	INT	30	13	6	40.3	42	15	35	4	4.02	5.90	10.7	4.1	6.7	1.3	5.52	-1.9	-3
2002	NYM	NL	30	12	0	17.0	20	11	11	3	5.29	6.53	11.3	5.2	5.1	1.7	7.16	-2.2	-25
2002	SDP	NL	30	4	2	9.7	10	7	7	1	6.49	6.03	9.5	5.8	5.7	1.0	6.13	-0.6	-15
2003	SDP	NL	31	25	9	62.3	61	30	48	6	4.31	5.00	9.2	3.8	6.1	0.9	5.01	3.4	-3

Breakout: 19%   Improve: 57%   Collapse: 16%

This one at least strikes some guys out, and throws from the left side. With age, he's leaning more and more toward becoming a strict lefty specialist, a role that he could probably fill successfully for some time.

Brian Lawrence — Born: 14-May-76 — Age: 27 — Bats: R — Throws: R

YEAR	TM	LG	AGE	G	GS	IP	H	BB	SO	HR	ERA	EQERA	EQH9	EQBB9	EQSO9	EQHR9	PERA	VORP	STF
2000	MOB	SOU	24	21	21	126.7	99	28	119	6	2.42	3.70	9.0	2.2	6.0	0.8	3.61	25.4	18
2000	LVG	PCL	24	8	8	46.7	48	7	46	6	1.93	2.85	9.4	1.3	7.1	1.4	3.91	13.8	25
2001	POR	PCL	25	9	8	45.0	42	17	42	3	3.80	4.75	9.6	4.1	6.2	0.7	4.42	3.8	7
2001	SDP	NL	25	27	15	114.7	107	34	84	10	3.45	3.95	8.8	2.5	5.7	0.7	3.96	19.5	8
2002	SDP	NL	26	35	31	210.0	230	52	149	16	3.69	4.21	10.2	2.0	5.7	0.7	4.71	30.1	12
2003	SDP	NL	27	30	27	175.0	177	50	121	16	3.83	4.44	9.6	2.2	5.4	0.9	4.43	21.0	9

Breakout: 8%   Improve: 41%   Collapse: 9%

Lawrence has become the mainstay of the rotation on the strength of his command. He doesn't have overpowering stuff, but he works the edges, changes speeds, drops down effectively, and it's rare to see someone stand up against him and look comfortable in the box. He probably can't maintain his ERA under 4.00 on a regular basis, but he can probably be right around there for the foreseeable future. Lawrence does an especially good job surprising batters with the right pitch for the knockout, creating the fun you and I get watching an angry hitter storm back to the dugout.

Mike Nicolas — Born: 05-Sep-79 — Age: 23 — Bats: R — Throws: R

YEAR	TM	LG	AGE	G	GS	IP	H	BB	SO	HR	ERA	EQERA	EQH9	EQBB9	EQSO9	EQHR9	PERA	VORP	STF
2001	FTW	MDW	21	54	0	62.7	44	34	70	4	3.44	5.00	8.6	7.1	6.3	1.4	4.93	2.6	-9
2001	LEL	CLF	21	8	0	12.0	11	5	15	2	5.25	7.01	12.3	5.1	6.8	3.1	6.61	-2.2	-10
2002	LEL	CLF	22	65	0	77.3	49	42	121	4	2.91	4.26	7.6	6.2	8.2	0.9	3.80	9.6	7

Nicolas is a Dominican right-hander with electric movement and improving control. If he's got 50% of his control, hitters can't touch him. He struck out 14 batters per nine innings in the Cal League in 2002; Double-A hitters will get their crack at him this season. If he stays healthy, he's 18 months from being an outstanding closer prospect. We generally don't put much stock in stuff like that, but numbers like this demand a readjustment of perception.

Jake Peavy — Born: 31-May-81 — Age: 22 — Bats: R — Throws: R

YEAR	TM	LG	AGE	G	GS	IP	H	BB	SO	HR	ERA	EQERA	EQH9	EQBB9	EQSO9	EQHR9	PERA	VORP	STF
2000	FTW	MDW	19	26	25	133.7	107	53	164	6	2.89	5.36	10.4	4.4	7.0	1.1	4.97	2.1	16
2001	LEL	CLF	20	19	19	105.3	76	33	144	6	3.08	4.40	8.9	3.7	7.2	1.0	3.76	12.9	23
2001	MOB	SOU	20	5	5	28.0	19	12	44	3	2.57	3.69	7.8	4.5	9.6	1.6	3.94	5.6	36
2002	MOB	SOU	21	14	14	80.3	65	30	89	4	2.80	3.91	9.2	3.6	7.3	0.9	4.01	14.2	25
2002	SDP	NL	21	17	17	97.7	106	33	90	11	4.51	4.87	10.1	2.7	7.3	1.1	5.22	6.9	25
2003	SDP	NL	22	23	20	129.7	124	54	121	14	4.16	4.83	9.0	3.3	7.3	1.0	4.74	11.1	15

Breakout: 7%   Improve: 36%   Collapse: 21%

Peavy owns an above-average fastball, which combined with good command of three pitches and an understanding of how to pitch make him one of the very best young pitchers in baseball. People not only rave about his stuff and ability to pitch, but also his maturity and level-headedness. Barring an injury, there's no limit to how good Peavy can be. He will probably be in the rotation to start the season, but if he's at Triple-A for a few starts, it's nothing to worry about. From subjective perception to stuff to performance analysis to health, there's no reason not to like Peavy's chances of being a #1 starter.

Oliver Perez — Born: 15-Aug-81 — Age: 21 — Bats: L — Throws: L

YEAR	TM	LG	AGE	G	GS	IP	H	BB	SO	HR	ERA	EQERA	EQH9	EQBB9	EQSO9	EQHR9	PERA	VORP	STF
2000	IDA	PIO	18	5	5	24.3	24	9	27	1	4.07	5.88	12.3	4.1	5.8	1.0	5.58	-1.0	7
2001	FTW	MDW	19	19	19	101.3	84	43	98	9	3.46	5.19	10.3	5.6	5.5	1.9	5.60	3.5	0
2001	LEL	CLF	19	9	9	53.0	45	25	62	4	2.72	5.43	10.8	5.8	6.3	1.4	5.41	0.4	9
2002	LEL	CLF	20	9	8	48.7	36	24	66	0	1.85	3.48	8.6	5.7	7.2	0.3	3.85	10.9	22
2002	MOB	SOU	20	4	4	23.0	11	16	34	1	1.17	2.31	5.4	6.7	9.6	0.8	3.21	8.2	37
2002	SDP	NL	20	16	15	90.0	71	48	94	13	3.50	3.98	7.1	4.2	8.1	1.4	4.48	15.2	27
2003	SDP	NL	21	21	19	115.0	104	65	111	12	4.32	5.01	8.5	4.4	7.5	1.0	5.14	6.6	12

Breakout: 17%   Improve: 44%   Collapse: 15%

I had seen notes that showed Perez's fastball at 90 mph, but it sure looked better than that to me. He supports it with a tremendous changeup and tight curveball, giving him three quality pitches to work with. Perez is mature beyond his years in terms of working hitters with speed changes; somewhere, his changeup against Reggie Sanders just hit the glove. San Diego might be the only club with better and younger front-line starting pitching than Oakland. These guys are that good.

Mark Phillips — Born: 30-Dec-81 — Age: 21 — Bats: L — Throws: L

YEAR	TM	LG	AGE	G	GS	IP	H	BB	SO	HR	ERA	EQERA	EQH9	EQBB9	EQSO9	EQHR9	PERA	VORP	STF
2000	IDA	PIO	18	10	10	37.0	35	24	37	2	5.35	7.71	12.0	7.2	5.2	1.3	6.73	-9.1	-12
2001	EUG	NWN	19	4	4	21.7	16	9	19	1	3.73	4.93	9.3	5.7	4.3	1.2	4.78	1.4	-3
2001	FTW	MDW	19	5	5	30.7	19	14	27	1	2.64	3.75	7.1	5.8	4.9	0.7	3.74	6.0	6
2001	LEL	CLF	19	5	5	28.0	19	14	34	0	2.57	3.80	8.3	6.0	6.4	0.3	3.72	5.3	16
2002	LEL	CLF	20	28	26	148.3	123	94	156	9	4.19	5.87	10.2	7.5	5.7	1.1	5.53	-6.1	0

A hard-throwing lefty who's going to have to spend time on mechanics and control. You can be effective in the low minors without good control, but as you move up and people lay off the burners outside the strike zone, you can get lit up in a hurry. Phillips is one of Kevin Towers's endless supply of young guys with good fastballs. Just like the A's teach plate discipline mercilessly, the Padres preach the gospel of changing speeds, and draft enough guys with good fastballs to keep a stream of promising young arms flowing toward the big club. It's a good plan.

Dennis Tankersley | Born: 24-Feb-79 | Age: 24 | Bats: R | Throws: R

YEAR	TM	LG	AGE	G	GS	IP	H	BB	SO	HR	ERA	EQERA	EQH9	EQBB9	EQSO9	EQHR9	PERA	VORP	STF
2000	AUG	SAL	21	15	15	75.3	73	32	74	4	4.06	6.90	12.8	5.5	5.3	1.3	6.62	-11.7	-2
2000	FTW	MDW	21	12	12	66.3	48	25	87	5	2.85	4.73	9.8	4.2	7.5	1.8	4.64	5.7	20
2001	LEL	CLF	22	9	8	52.3	29	12	68	1	0.52	1.84	6.6	2.7	6.7	0.3	2.26	21.3	29
2001	MOB	SOU	22	13	13	69.7	44	24	89	6	2.07	3.61	7.3	3.6	7.8	1.3	3.26	14.7	26
2001	POR	PCL	22	3	3	14.3	16	8	16	2	6.92	7.89	11.7	6.1	7.6	1.6	6.79	-3.8	6
2002	MOB	SOU	23	10	10	50.7	47	21	56	1	3.02	4.59	10.2	4.0	7.2	0.4	4.60	5.2	19
2002	POR	PCL	23	9	9	51.0	43	30	51	6	3.88	5.85	9.6	6.4	7.2	1.5	5.15	-2.0	8
2002	SDP	NL	23	17	9	51.3	59	40	39	10	8.07	7.56	10.5	6.1	5.9	1.8	7.66	-11.9	-13
2003	SDP	NL	24	17	12	78.7	77	44	71	10	4.83	5.60	9.2	4.4	7.0	1.2	5.55	1.6	4

Breakout: 12%   Improve: 46%   Collapse: 21%

He's good, but is he Ed Sprague good? Tankersley's available pitches are a fastball in the 94 range and a nasty slider, mixed in with an occasional curveball for show. He's got the stuff and peripherals you like to see, but there are concerns that he occasionally tips his pitches, and there are rumors of coachability and maturity issues. Then again, I think most everyone's had some coachability and maturity issues from time to time. If he can avoid distractions and focus on the field, there's no reason to expect Tankersley to be anything except a formidable part of a nasty rotation in San Diego for years to come. That is, unless Kevin Towers feels like he absolutely has to acquire Mike Blowers from some senior league. How do Red Sox fans stand it?

Brian Tollberg | Born: 16-Sep-72 | Age: 30 | Bats: R | Throws: R

YEAR	TM	LG	AGE	G	GS	IP	H	BB	SO	HR	ERA	EQERA	EQH9	EQBB9	EQSO9	EQHR9	PERA	VORP	STF
2000	LVG	PCL	27	13	13	76.3	72	11	60	5	2.83	2.88	8.6	1.3	5.7	0.7	3.03	22.3	18
2000	SDP	NL	27	19	19	118.0	126	35	76	13	3.58	4.43	10.3	2.2	5.3	0.9	4.58	14.1	8
2001	SDP	NL	28	19	19	117.3	133	25	71	15	4.30	4.62	10.8	1.8	4.7	1.1	5.07	11.5	4
2002	SDP	NL	29	12	11	61.7	88	19	33	11	6.13	6.86	13.5	2.5	4.3	1.7	7.54	-9.3	-12
2003	SDP	NL	30	18	14	90.7	102	27	53	11	4.42	5.13	10.6	2.3	4.6	1.2	5.28	4.7	-2

Breakout: 14%   Improve: 47%   Collapse: 19%

Well, that didn't work out particularly well. Tollberg gets by on control and ground balls to the infield, but he got the ball up a lot last year, as hitters just sat back and let stuff go by if it looked like it was going to be below their belt. Tollberg has some adjustments to make, and may have to develop a better changeup in order to keep his job. It's raining live young arms in this organization, and Tollberg's gotta come up with an umbrella pretty fast if he wants to avoid the Mickey Callaway career path. The Pads brought him back with a minor league invite. If healthy, he could take some innings in case Perez and Peavy need more seasoning or a few starts off to avoid overuse.

Brett Tomko | Born: 07-Apr-73 | Age: 30 | Bats: R | Throws: R

YEAR	TM	LG	AGE	G	GS	IP	H	BB	SO	HR	ERA	EQERA	EQH9	EQBB9	EQSO9	EQHR9	PERA	VORP	STF
2000	SEA	AL	27	32	8	92.3	92	40	59	12	4.68	4.56	8.9	3.2	5.6	1.0	4.25	9.1	-1
2001	TAC	PCL	28	19	18	127.0	124	25	117	12	4.04	4.86	10.2	2.1	6.2	1.0	4.34	9.1	13
2001	SEA	AL	28	11	4	34.7	42	15	22	9	5.19	6.94	11.6	3.7	5.5	2.2	6.87	-5.7	-16
2002	SDP	NL	29	32	32	204.3	212	60	126	31	4.49	4.69	9.6	2.4	4.9	1.5	5.15	18.5	2
2003	STL	NL	30	28	26	167.7	174	54	108	23	4.40	4.80	9.7	2.5	5.1	1.2	4.73	13.2	4

Breakout: 9%   Improve: 43%   Collapse: 14%

Hey, thanks! If you have any others you want to throw our way, please let us know! Tomko wasn't dominating, but he did gobble up 200 pretty generic innings, something that would be of value on pretty much every club in the majors. The Cardinals thought so, and were just as happy this year as the Padres were last to take Tomko in a minor deal, this time moving for Luther Hackman and a PTBNL. It was a better return than the nothing the Pads would have received had they non-tendered him as planned, but still a pretty unimpressive haul, New Economics or not.

J. J. Trujillo   Born: 09-Oct-75   Age: 27   Bats: R   Throws: R

YEAR	TM	LG	AGE	G	GS	IP	H	BB	SO	HR	ERA	EQERA	EQH9	EQBB9	EQSO9	EQHR9	PERA	VORP	STF
2000	FTW	MDW	24	63	0	74.7	39	25	85	3	1.33	2.90	6.8	3.6	6.4	1.0	2.89	20.6	0
2001	LEL	CLF	25	23	0	29.0	20	13	31	1	1.86	3.60	8.5	5.4	5.6	0.6	3.89	5.7	-10
2001	MOB	SOU	25	43	0	51.0	44	20	44	1	2.65	4.47	9.6	4.2	5.3	0.3	4.23	5.2	-8
2002	MOB	SOU	26	31	0	41.0	25	12	49	1	0.66	1.62	6.8	2.8	7.8	0.5	2.51	17.1	14
2002	POR	PCL	26	18	1	27.0	30	8	28	2	4.33	5.75	12.3	3.2	7.5	0.9	5.36	-1.1	1
2002	SDP	NL	26	4	0	2.7	4	6	3	1	10.00	12.40	13.6	17.3	8.6	3.5	15.68	-2.1	-71

Front foot. Repeatedly and without fail. Trujillo's a finesse righty who throws a lot like Doug Jones. Changeups and sliders away, and then the occasional sneaky fastball, maybe at 83–88 mph, on the inside half when no one's looking for it. He's worked this formula hard, and he's been successful with it. He's a candidate for the middle of the bullpen if he can get everything together in Triple-A to start the season. It's very strange to see guys swing and miss late on 84-mph fastballs, but Trujillo makes it happen.

Brandon Villafuerte   Born: 17-Dec-75   Age: 27   Bats: R   Throws: R

YEAR	TM	LG	AGE	G	GS	IP	H	BB	SO	HR	ERA	EQERA	EQH9	EQBB9	EQSO9	EQHR9	PERA	VORP	STF
2000	TOL	INT	24	46	6	87.7	112	49	85	7	6.67	6.59	11.7	4.9	7.3	0.9	6.88	-11.4	-2
2001	OKL	PCL	25	38	0	63.7	63	26	65	4	2.83	3.93	9.9	4.4	6.8	0.7	4.71	10.3	0
2002	POR	PCL	26	47	0	58.0	43	22	54	2	2.02	3.47	8.2	4.1	6.6	0.4	3.26	12.3	1
2002	SDP	NL	26	31	0	32.0	29	12	25	2	1.41	2.43	8.4	3.0	6.2	0.6	4.02	10.5	1
2003	SDP	NL	27	35	0	46.0	46	22	38	4	4.03	4.67	9.4	3.8	6.4	0.9	4.99	4.9	-4

Breakout: 14%   *Improve: 52%*   *Collapse: 22%*

So the Rangers had no use for a bullpen guy who was right around a strikeout per inning, cost the major league minimum, and didn't have a history of antisocial behavior, huh? Whatever. Villafuerte was rescued from the Ranger organization and responded by keeping his breaking pitches down in the zone, mixing in a fastball, and executing a plan against each hitter. He did a very nice job in the Padre pen, and he's renewable for another year after this. A great pickup by the Padres, and a great illustration of the state of the two franchises.

San Francisco Giants

S ure, the Giants will be just fine without Dusty Baker. Like Speed 2 was just fine without Keanu Reeves. Like the Jackson Five was just fine without Michael. Like Fantasy Island was just fine without Tattoo. Like Baseball Prospectus was just fine without Keith Law. Wait, forget I mentioned that last one.

Success breeds complacency, and in the wake of the Giants' 2002 dream run, it's easy for San Francisco fans and media to expect more of the same. It's easy to believe that last year's NL Championship was the result of the inherent quality of the organization as a whole, and that no single member of the franchise was irreplaceable. Maybe that explains the relative lack of outcry in the Bay Area when the Giants announced in December that they would not make Baker a formal offer to return as manager in 2003.

But Baker was not just a replaceable cog in the Giants' machine. You can't just plug in another manager and expect the organization to run as efficiently as it did last year. Aside from Barry Bonds, no one person has played as pivotal a role to the Giants' success since 1993 as Dusty Baker. And this is not because of the near meaningless "Dusty maintains the peace in the clubhouse" and "Dusty is a players' manager" assertions you read in the newspapers. This is because of something concrete and observable: Players seem to play better under Baker than under other managers. Much better.

During the Dusty Baker era, Giant position players have a remarkable record for career years, career peaks, and career turnarounds. Player after player has joined the Giants and immediately begun exceeding all reasonable expectations at the plate. Under Baker, replacement-level mediocrities have become useful regulars, useful regulars have become superstars, and superstars have become gods.

Consider just the players in the 2002 postseason lineup. All but one, Rich Aurilia, came to the Giants with significant

---

Giants Prospectus

2002 record: 95–66; Second place, NL West; Lost to Angels in World Series

Pythagenport Record: 98–63

Runs scored per game: 4.9 (2nd in NL)

Runs allowed per game: 3.8 (2nd in NL)

Team EqA: .283 (1st in NL)

2002 Batters Age: 32.8 (oldest in NL)

2002 Pitchers Age: 29.3 (5th oldest in NL)

Ballpark: Pac Bell Park; Severe pitchers' park; Park Factor of .920

2002: How far can one historically amazing player carry a team? About 95 wins if Kent is around too.

2003: Team needs hitters around Bonds and improved pitching, adds the first through free agency and looking to the farm for the second.

---

previous major league experience, so we can easily compare their established pre-Baker performance levels to what they achieved under Baker. In table 1, the "Pre-Baker" column shows their average rate of offensive performance in the three years prior to joining the Giants. (The number three was chosen arbitrarily to get a sense of established performance level, not cooked to get a particular result.) The "With Baker" column shows the average rate of offensive performance for all of that player's years with the Giants. To measure offensive performance, we'll use the PRO+ stat from *Total Baseball* (calculated slightly differently from how they do it there). PRO+ is just park-adjusted OPS divided by league-wide OPS. So, for example, David Bell's pre-Giants 97 PRO+ means his park-adjusted OPS was 3% worse than the league in 1999–2001, and his 113 with the Giants means he was 13% better than the league last year.

All the players in the Giants playoff lineup have performed better under Baker than their established performance level would predict. That's impressive, but the magnitude of these jumps is even more amazing. With the exception of Reggie Sanders, these guys performed not just better, but way better under Baker. The longtime Giants—Bonds, Kent, Snow, and Santiago—are all on completely different levels than they were pre-Giants. Bonds's three best seasons by PRO+, and eight of his best nine, came under Baker, despite the fact that he showed a little hitting ability before 1993. Kent went from solid regular with the Mets and Indians to MVP with the Giants. And Snow and Santiago both came out of nowhere to produce individual seasons that ranked them near the top of the league at their positions.

But the guys on the 2002 roster only tell part of the story. After all, Baker has a 10-year record, with lots of player movement during that time. Let's expand the set of guys we're looking at to cover all of Baker's tenure. Table 2 presents the

Table 1.

Player	PRO+ Pre-Baker	PRO+ With Baker	Change
J. T. Snow	94	114	+20
Jeff Kent	110	129	+19
David Bell	97	113	+16
Kenny Lofton	97	112	+15
Barry Bonds	147	161	+14
Benito Santiago	91	105	+14
Reggie Sanders	114	115	+1

Table 2.

Player	PRO+ Pre-Baker	PRO+ With Baker	Change
Ellis Burks	110	137	+27
Mark Carreon	96	115	+19
Bobby Estalella	96	112	+16
Brent Mayne	91	107	+16
Matt Williams	115	130	+15
Darryl Hamilton	91	104	+13
Mark Lewis	95	106	+11
Royce Clayton	86	93	+7
Glenallen Hill	108	112	+4
Stan Javier	101	104	+3
Charlie Hayes	96	98	+2
Kirk Manwaring	92	93	+1
Jose Vizcaino	94	95	+1
Darren Lewis	92	92	0
Tsuyoshi Shinjo	102	98	-4
Willie McGee	111	106	-5
Robby Thompson	112	105	-7
Will Clark	128	116	-12
Average (Both tables)			+8

same before-and-after measurements for every player who was a regular under Dusty Baker at some point during his managerial career (at least 350 plate appearances in one season) and who had some pre-Baker major league experience.

Ellis Burks's production at the plate exploded when he joined the Giants in mid-1998. He put up a career-high PRO+ of 133 in 1999, and then he beat that mark with a 146 the following year. And he was one of several Giants to put up his best numbers at an advanced age. Matt Williams not only had the best four individual seasons of his career the four years he spent under Dusty Baker, he produced those four years at a level that was miles above anything he was able to achieve before or since. Mark Carreon, Brent Mayne, Darryl Hamilton—the list of guys who played over their offensive heads for Dusty Baker's Giants is long.

Baker is no miracle worker, and not everyone who plays for him explodes like Burks, Kent, and company. But just as

telling as the long list of overperformers under Baker is the scarcity of underperformers. Even the few guys with minus signs by their names above have mitigating stories behind them. Robby Thompson, for instance, had his career year under Baker, but then began an injury-plagued decline. You have to go back 10 seasons to a single off year by Will Clark before he left for Texas as a free agent, to find the lone unambiguous example of a hitter underperforming under Dusty Baker.

Baker's record with offensive breakthroughs doesn't just apply to players with previous major league experience; he's gotten the most out of homegrown products as well. The Giants haven't had a top hitting prospect since Matt Williams, but that hasn't stopped Baker from producing several good players and one MVP candidate from the system. Rich Aurilia was a middling prospect in the Rangers and Giants systems, projecting at best to be a decent major league regular. He certainly gave no indication then of the kind of hitting ability he's displayed since 1999 with the Giants, particularly when he had one of the best shortstop seasons of all time in 2001. Marvin Benard has exceeded expectations. Same with Bill Mueller. Heck, Baker managed to get three fine years out of Armando Rios, of all people.

Of course, there's no way to prove that this solid stream of breakout seasons is due entirely or even mostly to Baker. Maybe Brian Sabean has an eye for players who are about to improve. Maybe batting coach Gene Clines (departed with Baker to Chicago) is a genius at fixing and improving swings. Maybe Barry Bonds's aura rubs off on his teammates. Maybe Giants hitters have gone through a 10-year period of extraordinarily good luck. There might be some small element of truth to any or all of those, but the biggest common denominator behind these performances is Baker. He's the one who's been with the club for all of them, who interacts closely with the entire team on a daily basis, and whose job it is to get the most out of his players.

How does he do it? You hear lots of theories, but no one knows for sure, and we can't pretend to have any definitive answers here. What we can do is point out the three main characteristics of Baker's managerial style: loyalty, loyalty, and loyalty. Baker decides on the players he likes and the roles he wants to use them in, and then he sticks with those decisions. He doesn't tinker, sitting a player after every 1-for-20 stretch. Veterans under Baker rarely face the threat of losing their jobs to a younger player. Sometimes Baker's unbending devotion to his chosen players can be maddening to Giants fans, as when he gave a hapless Shawn Dunston significant playing time and a postseason roster spot last year. But overall Baker's loyalty has got to instill confidence in his regulars, and that confidence could be finding its way to the plate.

Baker's record with pitching is not as spectacular, but it is just as distinctive. He has never had the magic with pitching staffs that, for example, Cox/Mazzone or LaRussa/Duncan have had. Far from it. Nevertheless, his pitching staffs have always been characterized by two positive features: dependability and health.

Take his starting rotations. Baker doesn't play the conventional game of jerking guys out of the rotation because of a few rough outings, another example of his aforementioned loyalty. And because he's managed to keep his starters unusually healthy over the years, he generally hasn't had to mess with his rotations for injury reasons either. The result can be seen in table 3, showing the teams with the most 30+ start pitchers per season during the past ten years.

Table 3.

Team	Avg. 30+ Start Pitchers
Braves	3.3
GIANTS	2.9
Astros	2.7
Diamondbacks	2.6
Dodgers	2.6

Baker hasn't had starters as good as Atlanta's, Houston's, Arizona's, and Los Angeles' over the past decade, but he's taken the guys he had, kept them healthy, and reliably sent them out there every fifth day. That may not always be the optimal way to run a starting rotation (see the Livan Hernandez comment), but if nothing else it minimizes the number of starts from replacement-level injury call-ups and middle relievers that can wreck a rotation's overall numbers.

So now that they've let their heart-and-soul manager get away, the Giants must be doomed to the second division for the foreseeable future, right? Not necessarily. Losing Baker hurts, but there are still quite a few positive signs for the Giants in the near term.

First, their farm system is in better shape than it's been in years. The high minors are brimming with top-flight pitching talent, with four of the top 30 pitchers on John Sickels's end-season prospects list: Jesse Foppert (#1), Jerome Williams (#13), Kurt Ainsworth (#16), and Boof Bonser (#26). BP's own Top 40 Prospects list at the back of this book grades them even more favorably, placing Williams (#5), Foppert (#13), and Ainsworth (#19) among the top 20 prospects in all of baseball, pitchers or otherwise.

And former University of Washington and LSU masher Todd Linden emerged last year as the best Giants hitting prospect in a decade. Granted, that's a little like being named "best actor in an Ed Wood film," but trust us, he's good.

Second, Felipe Alou is the perfect manager to move some of this farm talent to the major league level. While Baker's infatuation with veterans is legendary, Alou's reputation is built on his work with young players, especially young pitchers. In Montreal, Alou oversaw the development of Pedro Martinez, John Wetteland, Ken Hill, Kirk Rueter, Ugueth Urbina, and Javier Vazquez, among other successful hurlers. The question mark facing Alou is not whether he can work with the Giants' young pitching talent, but whether he can repeat his Montreal success with what will still be a largely veteran team.

Third, whatever we may have said about him in the past, Sabean has shown repeatedly over the past couple of seasons that he's become a top-flight GM. In adding the final pieces to last year's championship team, he did a fine job buying low, getting Bonds, Sanders, Bell, and Lofton with bargain contracts (Bonds and Sanders) or low trade cost (Bell and Lofton). He's accomplished more of the same this off-season, adding Ray Durham and Edgardo Alfonzo for less than what some inferior players are getting.

Fourth, they still have the best player on this or any other planet. After Barry Bonds broke the single-season home run record and obliterated the season SLG mark in 2001, then won a batting title and obliterated the season OBP mark in 2002, it's hard to believe he would merely set his sights on something as mundane as passing Willie Mays on the all-time home run list in 2003. We can't say what superhuman feats he has planned for this year—Earl Webb's doubles record? A stolen base title? A Cy Young Award?—but the Barry Bonds Show should be a draw whether the Giants contend or not.

It'll be a fun ride the next few years in The Park Formerly Known As Pac Bell as the Bonds era comes to a close. It's just a shame for Giants fans that it will no longer be the Bonds/Baker era.

HITTERS

Rich Aurilia　　　SS　Born: 02-Sep-71　Age: 31　Bats: R　Throws: R

YEAR	TM	LG	AGE	AB	H	2B	3B	HR	BB	SO	SB	CS	AVG	OBP	SLG	MLVR	EQBA	EQOBP	EQSLG	EQMLVR	VORP	DEFENSE	
2000	SFG	NL	28	509	138	24	2	20	54	90	1	2	.271	.341	.444	.012	.279	.340	.456	.030	34.7	136-SS	11
2001	SFG	NL	29	636	206	37	5	37	47	83	1	3	.324	.370	.572	.339	.336	.381	.592	.356	98.9	143-SS	8
2002	SFG	NL	30	538	138	35	2	15	37	90	1	2	.257	.309	.413	-.003	.274	.320	.445	-.026	26.5	126-SS	2
2003	SFG	NL	31	514	137	28	2	18	41	81	1	2	.266	.323	.431	-.021	.279	.330	.475	.038	26.1		

Breakout: 7%　　Improve: 34%　　Collapse: 32%

Aurilia's subpar 2002—his worst season ever as a full-time player—was largely the result of the bone chips in his elbow that put him on the DL in May and affected his swing much of the year. He did show a flash of the old, healthy Aurilia with a .293/.351/.475 September and a .265/.311/.588 postseason, against good pitching in both cases. He's a good bet to rebound and be the NL's best-hitting shortstop in 2003.

David Bell　　　3B/2B　Born: 14-Sep-72　Age: 30　Bats: R　Throws: R

YEAR	TM	LG	AGE	AB	H	2B	3B	HR	BB	SO	SB	CS	AVG	OBP	SLG	MLVR	EQBA	EQOBP	EQSLG	EQMLVR	VORP	DEFENSE			
2000	SEA	AL	27	454	112	24	2	11	42	66	2	3	.247	.319	.381	-.158	.263	.327	.406	-.077	12.5	78-3B	2	39-2B	-3
2001	SEA	AL	28	470	122	28	0	15	28	59	2	1	.260	.305	.415	-.056	.281	.328	.450	.002	22.0	123-3B	23		
2002	SFG	NL	29	552	144	29	2	20	54	80	1	2	.261	.337	.429	.069	.277	.347	.463	.051	34.7	125-3B	9	11-2B	-2
2003	PHI	NL	30	422	111	23	2	14	41	62	1	1	.263	.331	.424	-.019	.269	.334	.446	-.003	14.3				

Breakout: 12%　　Improve: 50%　　Collapse: 19%

No one—except maybe a guy who works in the Phillies payroll department—would consider David Bell an elite player, but he played a pivotal role in the pennant race fortunes of not one but two teams in 2002. The losers were the Mariners, whose "upgrade" at third base to Jeff Cirillo may have cost them a chance to hang with the Angels down the stretch. The winners were the Giants, who got solid production out of a position that had been a complete black hole the previous year under Russ Davis and Pedro Feliz. As a bonus, Bell filled in capably at every other infield position as well. He'll be a valuable, if overpaid, piece of the Phillies' puzzle next year.

Marvin Benard　　　OF　Born: 20-Jan-70　Age: 33　Bats: L　Throws: L

YEAR	TM	LG	AGE	AB	H	2B	3B	HR	BB	SO	SB	CS	AVG	OBP	SLG	MLVR	EQBA	EQOBP	EQSLG	EQMLVR	VORP	DEFENSE	
2000	SFG	NL	30	560	147	27	6	12	63	97	22	7	.263	.343	.396	-.060	.272	.343	.409	-.036	22.1	127-CF	5
2001	SFG	NL	31	392	104	19	2	15	29	66	10	5	.265	.322	.439	.002	.282	.335	.464	.036	22.7	87-CF	-4
2002	SFG	NL	32	123	34	9	2	1	7	26	5	1	.276	.321	.407	.023	.294	.330	.437	-.001	2.7	24-OF	0
2003	SFG	NL	33	194	51	10	2	3	16	35	6	2	.261	.321	.384	-.090	.274	.329	.423	-.039	1.7		

Breakout: 14%　　Improve: 44%　　Collapse: 26%

It's an indication of Giants followers' expectations during the Dusty Baker era that Marvin Benard can be termed an "underperforming hitter," as he was recently by a Giants beat writer. Benard had seasons at age 27 and 28 that were better than anyone could have expected, given his minor league performance. He's come down from that peak, but last year, at age 32, he still hit like an average center fielder. Fans of any other team would thank their lucky stars they got as much out of him as they did. But for Giants fans, any scrub who doesn't transform into an All-Star is an underperformer. I suspect he'll continue to underperform as he approaches his mid-30s.

Barry Bonds　　　LF　Born: 24-Jul-64　Age: 38　Bats: L　Throws: L

YEAR	TM	LG	AGE	AB	H	2B	3B	HR	BB	SO	SB	CS	AVG	OBP	SLG	MLVR	EQBA	EQOBP	EQSLG	EQMLVR	VORP	DEFENSE	
2000	SFG	NL	35	480	147	28	4	49	117	77	11	3	.306	.445	.688	.567	.314	.444	.705	.572	97.9	122-LF	0
2001	SFG	NL	36	476	156	32	2	73	177	93	13	3	.328	.517	.863	.916	.343	.524	.902	.953	174.9	117-LF	-1
2002	SFG	NL	37	403	149	31	2	46	198	47	9	2	.370	.584	.799	.955	.393	.595	.860	1.038	168.0	114-LF	-1
2003	SFG	NL	38	412	135	30	1	43	155	69	7	1	.329	.515	.719	.666	.344	.527	.792	.776	111.4		

Breakout: 18%　　Improve: 44%　　Collapse: 19%

Here are the top consecutive-year home run collapses in history (minimum 600 PAs each season):

Rank	Player	Years	HR Yr 1	HR Yr 2	Drop
1	Brady Anderson	1996–97	50	18	32
2	Luis Gonzalez	2001–02	57	28	29
3	Roger Maris	1961–62	61	33	28
4	BARRY BONDS	2001–02	73	46	27
T5	Andre Dawson	1987–88	49	24	25
T5	Carl Yastrzemski	1970–71	40	15	25

It's not surprising that most of these guys suffered huge drops in overall production the year their home runs fell off. That's because most of these guys didn't manage to counteract their homer decline with 21 more singles and 21 more walks, all while using up 66 fewer outs. That Barry Bonds did these things and arguably improved on his amazing 2001 season is, well, amazing.

Shawon Dunston   **UT**   **Born: 21-Mar-63**   **Age: 40**   **Bats: R**   **Throws: R**

YEAR	TM	LG	AGE	AB	H	2B	3B	HR	BB	SO	SB	CS	AVG	OBP	SLG	MLVR	EQBA	EQOBP	EQSLG	EQMLVR	VORP	DEFENSE
2000	STL	NL	37	216	54	11	2	12	6	47	3	1	.250	.280	.486	-.084	.248	.267	.486	-.084	.2	42-LF 0
2001	SFG	NL	38	186	52	10	3	9	2	32	3	1	.280	.295	.511	.072	.291	.304	.529	.086	8.2	37-OF -2
2002	SFG	NL	39	147	34	5	0	1	3	33	1	0	.231	.252	.286	-.297	.253	.267	.320	-.322	-8.4	24-OF -1
2003	SFG	NL	40	103	23	4	0	3	3	24	1	1	.226	.253	.357	-.266	.237	.259	.394	-.228	-4.7	

Breakout: 21%   *Improve: 39%*   *Collapse: 53%*

While at a particularly dismal Giants game during the most injury-riddled low point of the 2002 season, I remarked to my neighbor that having Feliz and Dunston batting in the 7 and 8 spots meant the Giants essentially had three consecutive pitchers in the lineup. I now realize that may have been unfair... to Giant pitchers. Russ Ortiz outhit Dunston by a fair amount, and Livan Hernandez was better at the plate as well. Dunston's improbable home run in game 6 of the World Series very nearly brought him the ring he's been missing throughout his long career. It'd be a good high point to go out on.

Jason Ellison   **CF**   **Born: 04-Apr-78**   **Age: 25**   **Bats: R**   **Throws: R**

YEAR	TM	LG	AGE	AB	H	2B	3B	HR	BB	SO	SB	CS	AVG	OBP	SLG	MLVR	EQBA	EQOBP	EQSLG	EQMLVR	VORP	DEFENSE
2000	SLO	NWN	22	300	90	15	2	0	29	45	13	7	.300	.375	.363	.105	.225	.267	.277	-.400	-16.4	70-CF 0
2001	HAG	SAL	23	494	144	38	3	8	71	68	19	15	.291	.391	.429	.217	.223	.301	.332	-.256	-10.7	129-CF 0
2002	SJO	CLF	24	322	87	13	0	5	25	37	9	9	.270	.327	.357	-.044	.217	.258	.284	-.413	-19.2	79-CF -2
2002	FRE	PCL	24	196	61	8	1	3	21	28	16	3	.311	.389	.408	.087	.277	.345	.364	-.092	4.6	49-CF 3
2003	SFG	NL	25	152	37	7	1	1	13	23	4	2	.244	.305	.334	-.195	.255	.313	.368	-.154	-1.1	

Breakout: 50%   *Improve: 73%*   *Collapse: 13%*

Ellison jumped straight from A to Triple-A in mid-season, and his numbers jumped too, roughly back to where they were his first two pro seasons. He's a little guy who projects as a fourth outfielder, occasional leadoff guy, and decent defensive sub in center field. In other words, Marvin Benard's heir apparent.

Pedro Feliz   **3B**   **Born: 27-Apr-77**   **Age: 26**   **Bats: R**   **Throws: R**

YEAR	TM	LG	AGE	AB	H	2B	3B	HR	BB	SO	SB	CS	AVG	OBP	SLG	MLVR	EQBA	EQOBP	EQSLG	EQMLVR	VORP	DEFENSE
2000	FRE	PCL	23	503	150	34	2	33	30	94	1	1	.298	.340	.571	.176	.257	.289	.483	-.042	18.7	119-3B 10
2001	SFG	NL	24	220	50	9	1	7	10	50	2	1	.227	.267	.373	-.226	.241	.278	.393	-.204	-.9	56-3B -14
2002	SFG	NL	25	146	37	4	1	2	6	27	0	0	.253	.283	.336	-.158	.275	.299	.362	-.184	.2	34-3B 0
2003	SFG	NL	26	196	47	10	1	5	11	37	2	1	.240	.284	.374	-.181	.252	.291	.412	-.136	-.3	

Breakout: 23%   Improve: 48%   Collapse: 34%

Heralded as the Giants third baseman of the future after his 33 HR season at homer-happy Fresno three years ago, Feliz showed a little pop in his extended major league tryout in 2001, but nothing else. Last year, it was just the "nothing else." He may never get the playing time to prove otherwise, but it's looking more and more like 2000 will go down as his career year.

Tom Goodwin   CF   Born: 27-Jul-68   Age: 34   Bats: L   Throws: R

YEAR	TM	LG	AGE	AB	H	2B	3B	HR	BB	SO	SB	CS	AVG	OBP	SLG	MLVR	EQBA	EQOBP	EQSLG	EQMLVR	VORP	DEFENSE	
2000	COL	NL	31	317	86	8	8	5	50	76	39	7	.271	.372	.394	-.075	.252	.348	.364	-.103	6.7	83-CF	0
2000	LAD	NL	31	211	53	3	1	1	18	41	16	3	.251	.310	.289	-.294	.262	.310	.304	-.255	-4.3	55-CF	6
2001	LAD	NL	32	286	66	8	5	4	23	58	22	8	.231	.288	.336	-.239	.244	.299	.351	-.221	-3.4	70-CF	-1
2002	FRE	PCL	33	62	14	3	1	0	8	8	3	2	.226	.314	.306	-.242	.194	.275	.258	-.424	-4.2	16-CF	0
2002	SFG	NL	33	154	40	5	2	1	14	25	16	2	.260	.321	.338	-.082	.285	.339	.373	-.085	.1	41-OF	0
2003	CHC	NL	34	136	33	5	2	1	15	26	10	3	.246	.322	.331	-.169	.253	.325	.348	-.160	-1.8		

Breakout: 19%   Improve: 60%   Collapse: 12%

Goodwin got a handful of high-profile hits during the Giants' stretch run, and after each one of them the Bay Area airwaves were filled with giddy reminders that his $3.25 million salary was being paid by the arch-rival Dodgers. The Dodgers front office showed a good grasp of the concept of sunk costs when they jettisoned the replacement-level Goodwin, but it couldn't have been fun to have that ridiculous contract repeatedly waved in their faces.

Edwards Guzman   C   Born: 11-Sep-76   Age: 26   Bats: L   Throws: R

YEAR	TM	LG	AGE	AB	H	2B	3B	HR	BB	SO	SB	CS	AVG	OBP	SLG	MLVR	EQBA	EQOBP	EQSLG	EQMLVR	VORP	DEFENSE			
2000	FRE	PCL	23	421	118	24	1	6	17	43	1	5	.280	.316	.385	-.164	.241	.265	.330	-.319	-11.0	31-2B	-5	28-C	-6
2001	FRE	PCL	24	72	26	3	2	0	4	3	0	1	.361	.395	.458	.184	.310	.347	.394	-.019	4.2	11-C	-3		
2001	SFG	NL	24	115	28	6	0	3	5	16	0	0	.243	.275	.374	-.197	.256	.287	.393	-.176	1.8	15-C	1		
2002	FRE	PCL	25	390	116	22	0	5	16	26	1	3	.297	.325	.392	-.059	.259	.287	.342	-.247	-1.3	36-C	1	23-3B	2

In the spring training battle for the backup catcher spot, the Giants went with Yorvit Torrealba's youth over Guzman's versatility, a decision that turned out very well for them. Guzman went to Fresno and had his ordinary year: decent defense at multiple positions, coupled with a replacement-level bat. He's likely to play the same role in 2003, waiting in the wings in case Santiago or Torrealba hits the skids or the DL.

Joe Jester   2B   Born: 17-Jul-78   Age: 24   Bats: R   Throws: R

YEAR	TM	LG	AGE	AB	H	2B	3B	HR	BB	SO	SB	CS	AVG	OBP	SLG	MLVR	EQBA	EQOBP	EQSLG	EQMLVR	VORP	DEFENSE	
2000	SJO	CLF	21	429	113	13	4	8	69	75	24	8	.263	.386	.368	.056	.218	.301	.307	-.293	-8.8	104-2B	-6
2001	SJO	CLF	22	295	75	17	2	7	35	77	20	5	.254	.357	.397	.050	.209	.283	.328	-.306	-7.1	73-2B	-1
2001	SHV	TXS	22	150	48	14	2	6	12	33	4	1	.320	.382	.560	.351	.272	.323	.477	.024	9.6	40-2B	1
2002	SHV	TXS	23	359	100	20	2	11	29	66	14	5	.279	.336	.437	.103	.244	.289	.392	-.182	3.2	86-2B	-7
2003	SFG	NL	24	169	40	9	1	4	15	35	5	3	.238	.304	.365	-.160	.250	.311	.402	-.116	1.8		

Breakout: 40%   Improve: 71%   Collapse: 18%

Jester isn't a great prospect, but he deserves more attention than he gets, at least among the Giant farm system's weak collection of position players. He's a converted college shortstop who's turned into a good defensive second baseman. He's got some power, some plate discipline, and some speed. If he adds a few more homers to his ledger this year in Fresno, or if he rediscovers the terrific batting eye he demonstrated in San Jose, he could be a pretty good utility infielder for the Giants starting in 2004.

Jeff Kent   2B   Born: 07-Mar-68   Age: 35   Bats: R   Throws: R

YEAR	TM	LG	AGE	AB	H	2B	3B	HR	BB	SO	SB	CS	AVG	OBP	SLG	MLVR	EQBA	EQOBP	EQSLG	EQMLVR	VORP	DEFENSE			
2000	SFG	NL	32	587	196	41	7	33	90	107	12	9	.334	.430	.596	.455	.340	.427	.608	.452	112.1	142-2B	5		
2001	SFG	NL	33	607	181	49	6	22	65	96	7	6	.298	.376	.507	.226	.317	.390	.538	.269	82.0	129-2B	11	23-1B	-3
2002	SFG	NL	34	623	195	42	2	37	52	101	5	1	.313	.370	.565	.356	.329	.379	.598	.353	92.0	142-2B	12		
2003	HOU	NL	35	549	167	34	3	30	61	86	6	2	.304	.377	.544	.247	.302	.371	.547	.221	53.2				

Breakout: 1%   Improve: 24%   Collapse: 19%

BP's Michael Wolverton wrote an article for ESPN.com in early September that stacked Kent's 2002 against history's great second base seasons, and found that Kent was on track to have one of the elite seasons ever at that position. Kent finished slow, so his season fell a little short of that lofty territory projected in the article, but it was a historically great season nevertheless. Using the metric used in that article, Kent's 2002 was bettered by only nine second basemen in history (Hornsby many times; Morgan, Lajoie, and Gehringer twice each; and Biggio, Collins, Lazzeri, Robinson, and Kent himself once each). "Two of the top 20 second base seasons of all time" is a pretty good top bullet for a Hall of Fame resume. Gone to Houston, he'll be teammates with a second baseman who has an even better Hall of Fame resume.

Todd Linden   RF   Born: 30-Jun-80   Age: 23   Bats: B   Throws: R

YEAR	TM	LG	AGE	AB	H	2B	3B	HR	BB	SO	SB	CS	AVG	OBP	SLG	MLVR	EQBA	EQOBP	EQSLG	EQMLVR	VORP	DEFENSE
2002	SHV	TXS	22	392	123	26	2	12	61	101	9	5	.314	.422	.482	.317	.270	.359	.424	.012	10.0	108-RF -4
2002	FRE	PCL	22	100	25	2	1	3	20	35	2	0	.250	.380	.380	-.009	.218	.334	.337	-.187	-2.9	28-LF 1
2003	SFG	NL	23	222	55	10	2	5	26	64	5	4	.247	.332	.382	-.085	.258	.340	.420	-.035	-1.4	

Breakout: 20%   Improve: 49%   Collapse: 22%

The Giants' system is rightly lampooned for its lack of position player prospects, but Todd Linden is the one diamond among the coal. Concerns about an allegedly cocky attitude may have caused him to fall in the draft (he was picked 41st overall in 2001), but the Giants above all organizations understand that a homer hit by a prima donna counts just as much as one hit by a choirboy. There were also some legitimate issues about his plate discipline in college, but Linden addressed those by drawing walks at a very healthy rate of one per seven plate appearances in his pro debut. His power is likely to improve over the next few years, and if it does, he's got the makings of a star.

Kenny Lofton   CF   Born: 31-May-67   Age: 36   Bats: L   Throws: L

YEAR	TM	LG	AGE	AB	H	2B	3B	HR	BB	SO	SB	CS	AVG	OBP	SLG	MLVR	EQBA	EQOBP	EQSLG	EQMLVR	VORP	DEFENSE
2000	CLE	AL	33	543	151	23	5	15	79	72	30	7	.278	.374	.422	.007	.282	.372	.430	.054	32.0	135-CF 2
2001	CLE	AL	34	517	135	21	4	14	47	69	16	8	.261	.325	.398	-.062	.276	.340	.423	-.019	21.1	123-CF -5
2002	CWS	AL	35	352	91	20	6	8	49	51	22	8	.259	.349	.418	.013	.274	.364	.446	.055	22.4	86-CF 4
2002	SFG	NL	35	180	48	10	3	3	23	22	7	3	.267	.353	.406	.068	.286	.368	.438	.061	11.7	41-CF 3
2003	SFG	NL	36	392	102	19	4	7	50	58	19	5	.260	.344	.381	-.055	.272	.353	.420	-.003	14.3	

Breakout: 21%   Improve: 62%   Collapse: 6%

A shrewd pickup by Brian Sabean. The Lofton deadline deal plugged two huge holes (center field and leadoff hitter) with one player, and Sabean did it without giving up any of the system's top prospects. Lofton can still play a decent center field, although he isn't as good as the 2002 defensive ratings above suggest.

Trey Lunsford   C   Born: 25-May-79   Age: 24   Bats: R   Throws: R

YEAR	TM	LG	AGE	AB	H	2B	3B	HR	BB	SO	SB	CS	AVG	OBP	SLG	MLVR	EQBA	EQOBP	EQSLG	EQMLVR	VORP	DEFENSE
2000	SLO	NWN	21	215	58	9	0	3	30	40	1	0	.270	.379	.353	.079	.203	.272	.275	-.403	-9.3	58-C 1
2001	HAG	SAL	22	396	94	19	0	5	45	89	10	5	.237	.323	.323	-.038	.189	.254	.259	-.469	-25.2	108-C 0
2002	SJO	CLF	23	51	13	3	0	1	3	5	2	0	.255	.321	.373	-.043	.212	.254	.308	-.390	-2.0	15-C 0
2002	SHV	TXS	23	210	59	13	0	1	29	42	5	2	.281	.379	.357	.063	.250	.328	.324	-.198	2.2	62-C -3
2002	FRE	PCL	23	57	10	0	0	2	6	15	0	0	.175	.266	.281	-.394	.158	.233	.263	-.520	-4.4	18-C 1
2002	SFG	NL	23	3	2	1	0	0	0	1	0	0	.667	.667	1.000	-1.000	.667	.667	.000	.228	-1.0	
2003	SFG	NL	24	162	35	7	1	3	16	36	2	1	.214	.288	.314	-.268	.224	.295	.346	-.235	-2.7	

Breakout: 49%   Improve: 63%   Collapse: 24%

One of the few players to play at A, Double-A, Triple-A, and the majors last year, Lunsford showed a decent stick at Double-A, where he stayed the longest. He may never develop the power he would need to become a major league starting catcher, but his defense is strong enough to make him a decent backup or platoon partner. He could see some time with the Giants this year as an injury fill-in.

Ramon Martinez   INF   Born: 10-Oct-72   Age: 30   Bats: R   Throws: R

YEAR	TM	LG	AGE	AB	H	2B	3B	HR	BB	SO	SB	CS	AVG	OBP	SLG	MLVR	EQBA	EQOBP	EQSLG	EQMLVR	VORP	DEFENSE	
2000	SFG	NL	27	189	57	13	2	6	15	22	3	2	.302	.356	.487	.133	.307	.354	.500	.145	18.4	26-SS 2	17-2B -5
2001	SFG	NL	28	391	99	18	3	5	38	52	1	2	.253	.327	.353	-.118	.268	.337	.373	-.101	9.4	64-3B -2	31-2B 7
2002	SFG	NL	29	181	49	10	2	4	14	26	2	0	.271	.337	.414	.056	.290	.348	.446	.040	12.1	32-SS -4	
2003	CHC	NL	30	211	54	11	1	4	19	29	2	1	.257	.323	.384	-.090	.264	.326	.403	-.076	3.9		

Breakout: 5%   Improve: 27%   Collapse: 41%

This is what a utility guy should be. He plays a decent second and third and is passable at short. He wields a pretty good stick for an infielder, with league average power and plate discipline. When he's asked to do too much, as he was in 2001 when he was made the everyday third baseman, he can hurt the team. But as a backup and occasional injury replacement, where he can get a high percentage of platoon-advantage PAs, he's a big asset.

Damon Minor   1B   Born: 05-Jan-74   Age: 29   Bats: L   Throws: L

YEAR	TM	LG	AGE	AB	H	2B	3B	HR	BB	SO	SB	CS	AVG	OBP	SLG	MLVR	EQBA	EQOBP	EQSLG	EQMLVR	VORP	DEFENSE
2000	FRE	PCL	26	482	140	27	1	30	87	97	0	0	.290	.400	.537	.217	.246	.342	.452	.000	13.0	128-1B -11
2001	FRE	PCL	27	406	125	22	3	24	44	83	1	1	.308	.382	.554	.243	.264	.335	.465	.021	13.5	100-1B -4
2002	FRE	PCL	28	29	15	6	1	0	5	5	0	0	.517	.588	.793	1.163	.429	.515	.643	.744	7.2	
2002	SFG	NL	28	173	41	6	0	10	24	34	0	0	.237	.337	.445	.071	.253	.344	.483	.052	7.0	37-1B -4
2003	SFG	NL	29	207	50	10	1	8	29	43	1	1	.242	.338	.413	-.038	.254	.346	.455	.016	3.2	

Breakout: 13%   Improve: 38%   Collapse: 30%

Minor's 2002 is a cautionary tale for Mark Bellhorn or any other "unproven" Cub who needs Dusty Baker to let him establish himself. After Minor took over for the struggling J. T. Snow and mashed the ball for a couple of months, it only took a mini-slump—most likely just bad luck—for Baker to ditch him in favor of the veteran Snow. Minor even suffered the indignity of being left off the postseason roster in favor of such offensive powerhouses as Tom Goodwin and Shawon Dunston. He isn't a great long-term solution at first, but he does represent a potent left-handed bat as he goes through his peak these next few years.

Bill Mueller   3B   Born: 17-Mar-71   Age: 32   Bats: B   Throws: R

YEAR	TM	LG	AGE	AB	H	2B	3B	HR	BB	SO	SB	CS	AVG	OBP	SLG	MLVR	EQBA	EQOBP	EQSLG	EQMLVR	VORP	DEFENSE
2000	SFG	NL	29	560	150	29	4	10	52	62	4	2	.268	.337	.388	-.082	.276	.335	.401	-.059	19.6	136-3B -1
2001	CHC	NL	30	210	62	12	1	6	37	19	1	1	.295	.408	.448	.171	.302	.410	.460	.180	23.6	56-3B -1
2002	CHC	NL	31	353	94	19	4	7	51	41	0	0	.266	.359	.402	.062	.280	.367	.424	.035	21.7	98-3B -4
2002	SFG	NL	31	13	2	0	0	0	1	1	0	0	.154	.214	.154	-.577	.231	.286	.231	-.422	-.9	
2003	BOS	AL	32	329	89	18	2	6	38	38	1	0	.269	.346	.390	-.013	.275	.355	.409	-.012	10.5	

Breakout: 7%   Improve: 33%   Collapse: 20%

Mueller started slowly after spending April on the DL for knee surgery, but he was back to his usual self in the second half, hitting .279/.378/.447 after the break. It's not clear why the Giants gave up a decent relief prospect (Jeff Verplancke) to get him in September, knowing he wouldn't be available for the postseason roster. He basically sat on the bench for the month, but it made for a nice prodigal son story. If the troublesome left knee, which also cost him most of 2001, is healthy, Mueller stands to be an above-average third baseman for at least a couple more years. That's a big if.

Lance Niekro   1B   Born: 29-Jan-79   Age: 24   Bats: R   Throws: R

YEAR	TM	LG	AGE	AB	H	2B	3B	HR	BB	SO	SB	CS	AVG	OBP	SLG	MLVR	EQBA	EQOBP	EQSLG	EQMLVR	VORP	DEFENSE	
2000	SLO	NWN	21	196	71	14	4	5	11	25	2	0	.362	.408	.551	.455	.263	.283	.409	-.155	1.6	32-3B -1	
2001	SJO	CLF	22	163	47	11	0	3	4	14	4	2	.288	.305	.411	.012	.233	.247	.325	-.367	-7.1	32-3B 1	
2002	SHV	TXS	23	297	92	20	1	4	7	32	0	2	.310	.330	.424	.103	.271	.285	.378	-.190	-7.2	48-1B -3	26-3B -7
2003	SFG	NL	24	168	41	9	1	3	7	22	2	1	.244	.276	.355	-.220	.255	.282	.391	-.179	-5.0		

Breakout: 25%   Improve: 54%   Collapse: 21%

He invariably shows up on lists of the top players in the Giants system, so we have to include his numbers here so you can see for yourself: Despite the second round draft pick status and the Hall of Fame name, Lance Niekro is not a prospect. If he ever does make it to the majors, he'll be a perpetual contender for the DiSars.

Cody Ransom   Born: 17-Feb-76   Age: 27   Bats: R   Throws: R

YEAR	TM	LG	AGE	AB	H	2B	3B	HR	BB	SO	SB	CS	AVG	OBP	SLG	MLVR	EQBA	EQOBP	EQSLG	EQMLVR	VORP	DEFENSE
2000	SHV	TXS	24	459	92	21	2	7	40	141	9	3	.200	.265	.301	-.351	.176	.220	.265	-.536	-39.6	128-SS -17
2001	FRE	PCL	25	469	113	21	6	23	44	137	17	2	.241	.306	.458	-.085	.208	.271	.388	-.248	-3.9	133-SS 3
2002	FRE	PCL	26	449	93	18	4	13	47	151	6	4	.207	.287	.352	-.245	.178	.251	.303	-.420	-24.6	132-SS 0
2002	SFG	NL	26	3	2	0	0	0	1	1	0	0	.667	.750	.667	1.395	.667	.800	.667	1.371	1.8	

Ransom has always had major league defensive ability. The question is still whether his swing-for-the-fences approach at the plate will produce as much offense as, say, Rey Ordonez. It's a valiant attempt at the Three True Outcomes philosophy, and when it results in a homer for every six strikeouts (2001), he looks like a potential major leaguer. When it results in a homer for every 12 strikeouts (last year), he doesn't. Time is running out.

Reggie Sanders — RF — Born: 01-Dec-67 — Age: 35 — Bats: R — Throws: R

YEAR	TM	LG	AGE	AB	H	2B	3B	HR	BB	SO	SB	CS	AVG	OBP	SLG	MLVR	EQBA	EQOBP	EQSLG	EQMLVR	VORP	DEFENSE
2000	ATL	NL	32	340	79	23	1	11	32	78	21	4	.232	.302	.403	-.176	.233	.293	.405	-.165	-7.1	85-LF -3
2001	ARI	NL	33	441	116	21	3	33	46	126	14	10	.263	.339	.549	.143	.258	.333	.537	.112	22.7	113-RF 2
2002	SFG	NL	34	505	126	23	6	23	47	121	18	6	.250	.328	.455	.080	.269	.340	.497	.079	20.4	127-RF 0
2003	SFG	NL	35	361	89	18	3	14	36	87	13	5	.246	.318	.431	-.045	.257	.326	.474	.011	3.5	

Breakout: 10%   Improve: 45%   Collapse: 20%

For the second year in a row, signing Sanders to a low-risk, one-year contract paid big dividends to the team that got him. And for the second year in a row, Sanders's team rewarded his fine play with a heartfelt "Thanks for the memories" before showing him the door. Not that we can blame the Giants, Diamondbacks, or any other team for taking a skeptical attitude towards Sanders's future—35-year-olds with chronic injury histories are generally not the safest bets. Even when Sanders declines to the point of not being a viable everyday player, he'll be a great platoon partner; he absolutely mashes lefties.

Benito Santiago — C — Born: 09-Mar-65 — Age: 38 — Bats: R — Throws: R

YEAR	TM	LG	AGE	AB	H	2B	3B	HR	BB	SO	SB	CS	AVG	OBP	SLG	MLVR	EQBA	EQOBP	EQSLG	EQMLVR	VORP	DEFENSE
2000	CIN	NL	35	252	66	11	1	8	19	45	2	2	.262	.316	.409	-.130	.257	.303	.399	-.136	6.5	68-C 5
2001	SFG	NL	36	477	125	25	4	6	23	78	5	4	.262	.299	.369	-.145	.278	.313	.393	-.110	15.6	119-C 0
2002	SFG	NL	37	478	133	24	5	16	27	73	4	2	.278	.320	.450	.084	.294	.330	.482	.064	36.1	117-C -1
2003	SFG	NL	38	316	76	15	2	6	18	52	3	2	.241	.284	.356	-.204	.253	.291	.392	-.162	.7	

Breakout: 7%   Improve: 19%   Collapse: 46%

We came down hard on Santiago in this spot last year, concluding with "The Giants desperately need a real catcher." We're not sure if it was boiling rage over that comment, or the Dusty Baker/Ellis Burks Elixir of Youth™, but Santiago was a real catcher and much more in 2002. He was at or near the top of a weak field of NL catchers in combined offensive and defensive performance, along with Lieberthal, Piazza, and Kendall. At the risk of giving him more bulletin board material, we'll go out on a limb and predict he won't do it again at age 38.

Deivis Santos — OF — Born: 09-Feb-80 — Age: 23 — Bats: L — Throws: L

YEAR	TM	LG	AGE	AB	H	2B	3B	HR	BB	SO	SB	CS	AVG	OBP	SLG	MLVR	EQBA	EQOBP	EQSLG	EQMLVR	VORP	DEFENSE	
2001	HAG	SAL	21	520	151	27	3	12	25	91	16	10	.290	.328	.423	.124	.226	.256	.331	-.345	-33.1	122-1B -8	
2002	SHV	TXS	22	407	127	33	5	3	18	42	4	4	.312	.349	.440	.155	.273	.299	.389	-.146	-6.1	69-LF -4	38-1B -2
2002	FRE	PCL	22	88	25	3	1	3	2	14	4	0	.284	.300	.443	-.041	.253	.270	.391	-.213	-2.6	23-1B 5	
2003	SFG	NL	23	197	50	10	2	3	11	31	3	2	.252	.295	.367	-.165	.264	.302	.404	-.120	-4.3		

Breakout: 49%   Improve: 70%   Collapse: 11%

Santos skipped over San Jose and had a good year in the Texas League, finishing seventh in the league in batting average, 16th in slugging average, and sixth in doubles. He could develop more power in the next year or two, but with his walk rates, he's no threat to ever appear on the leader boards of any league in OBP. He projects as a fourth outfielder at best. When you write about the Giants farm system, you tend to use that sentence a lot.

Tsuyoshi Shinjo — CF — Born: 28-Jan-72 — Age: 31 — Bats: R — Throws: R

YEAR	TM	LG	AGE	AB	H	2B	3B	HR	BB	SO	SB	CS	AVG	OBP	SLG	MLVR	EQBA	EQOBP	EQSLG	EQMLVR	VORP	DEFENSE
2000	HNS	JCL	28	511	142	23	1	28	32	93	15	5	.278	.322	.491	.088	.267	.314	.480	.008	20.0	
2001	NYM	NL	29	400	107	23	1	10	25	70	4	5	.268	.322	.405	-.054	.280	.331	.423	-.032	6.2	115-OF 2
2002	SFG	NL	30	362	86	15	3	9	24	46	5	0	.238	.296	.370	-.098	.257	.308	.405	-.119	5.6	106-CF 1
2003	NYM	NL	31	297	74	15	2	8	24	48	5	2	.250	.310	.397	-.100	.260	.315	.424	-.072	2.4	

Breakout: 24%   Improve: 52%   Collapse: 18%

The winner of the annual Deion Sanders Award, given to the player whose media attention outstrips his on-field performance by the greatest margin. Shinjo wants to play every day, but his best chance of helping a team is as a platoon partner and defensive sub. Signed by the Mets, who might use him as the right side of a banjo-hitting center field platoon, given their lack of other options.

J. T. Snow   1B   Born: 26-Feb-68   Age: 35   Bats: B   Throws: L

YEAR	TM	LG	AGE	AB	H	2B	3B	HR	BB	SO	SB	CS	AVG	OBP	SLG	MLVR	EQBA	EQOBP	EQSLG	EQMLVR	VORP	DEFENSE
2000	SFG	NL	32	536	152	33	2	19	66	129	1	3	.284	.374	.459	.105	.292	.371	.472	.119	32.1	145-1B -2
2001	SFG	NL	33	285	70	12	1	8	55	81	0	0	.246	.375	.379	.005	.259	.384	.403	.022	10.1	78-1B 0
2002	SFG	NL	34	422	104	26	2	6	59	90	0	0	.246	.348	.360	-.013	.267	.360	.394	-.029	7.7	113-1B -7
2003	SFG	NL	35	272	66	14	1	7	39	64	1	1	.245	.342	.375	-.078	.256	.350	.413	-.028	.9	

Breakout: 19%   *Improve: 52%*   *Collapse: 20%*

A highly respected baseball writer suggested to me recently that J. T. Snow's fielding—especially his ability to receive throws—means so much to the Giants infield that he's a big asset despite his problems at the plate. Whether that claim is true or not, it's a good reminder to us sabermetric types that there are plenty of areas of baseball that remain unmeasured, like first basemen's receiving ability. Still, we can measure hitting, and Snow's punchless work at the plate was worth about 14 runs less than an average first baseman last year. It would take a lot of scoops at first to make up 14 runs.

Tony Torcato   LF   Born: 25-Oct-79   Age: 23   Bats: L   Throws: R

YEAR	TM	LG	AGE	AB	H	2B	3B	HR	BB	SO	SB	CS	AVG	OBP	SLG	MLVR	EQBA	EQOBP	EQSLG	EQMLVR	VORP	DEFENSE
2000	SJO	CLF	20	490	159	37	2	7	41	62	19	4	.324	.384	.451	.220	.263	.299	.368	-.184	.5	104-3B -16
2001	SJO	CLF	21	258	88	21	2	2	17	40	9	3	.341	.391	.461	.266	.272	.309	.368	-.158	-4.6	14-LF -2
2001	SHV	TXS	21	147	43	9	1	1	9	15	0	1	.293	.350	.388	.036	.257	.299	.338	-.231	-5.5	36-LF 1
2001	FRE	PCL	21	150	48	8	1	2	2	20	0	1	.320	.329	.427	-.020	.279	.293	.367	-.185	-3.8	34-LF 2
2002	FRE	PCL	22	490	142	23	3	13	29	65	4	6	.290	.332	.429	-.001	.251	.291	.372	-.202	-14.5	118-LF -4
2003	SFG	NL	23	208	54	12	1	4	14	31	3	2	.258	.309	.374	-.126	.270	.316	.412	-.078	-1.9	

Breakout: 32%   *Improve: 61%*   *Collapse: 18%*

Torcato has drawn praise from *USA Today* for being "one of the best pure hitters in the minor leagues." Translation: he may someday hit an empty .300 in the majors. Okay, that's a bit harsh, he did develop a little home run power last year, and he's still young enough to develop more. But without any batting eye to speak of, and without any special defensive ability, he's a poor man's Reggie Jefferson rather than a major league star.

Yorvit Torrealba   C   Born: 19-Jul-78   Age: 24   Bats: R   Throws: R

YEAR	TM	LG	AGE	AB	H	2B	3B	HR	BB	SO	SB	CS	AVG	OBP	SLG	MLVR	EQBA	EQOBP	EQSLG	EQMLVR	VORP	DEFENSE
2000	SHV	TXS	21	398	114	21	1	4	34	55	2	3	.286	.352	.374	-.026	.248	.292	.325	-.269	-3.7	102-C 0
2001	FRE	PCL	22	394	108	23	3	8	19	65	2	3	.274	.314	.409	-.113	.237	.275	.350	-.274	-4.1	107-C 1
2002	SFG	NL	23	136	38	10	0	2	14	20	0	0	.279	.355	.397	.071	.300	.367	.429	.059	10.5	44-C 0
2003	SFG	NL	24	226	55	13	1	3	19	33	1	1	.245	.307	.348	-.173	.257	.314	.383	-.130	2.3	

Breakout: 11%   *Improve: 37%*   *Collapse: 26%*

The unsung hero of the 2002 Giants. No one said word one about Torrealba's performance all year, but when all was said and done he probably should have been part of the Rookie of the Year discussion. The list of catchers with as many plate appearances as Torrealba who hit better (measured by EQA) is awfully short: Posada, Piazza, Rodriguez, Lieberthal, and Redmond. That's it. While 150 plate appearances doesn't wipe out seven years of so-so play in the minors, you also can't completely ignore that kind of hitting from a 23-year-old with a good defensive rep in his first major league season. He could have a nice career in front of him.

Carlos Valderrama   OF   Born: 30-Nov-77   Age: 25   Bats: R   Throws: R

YEAR	TM	LG	AGE	AB	H	2B	3B	HR	BB	SO	SB	CS	AVG	OBP	SLG	MLVR	EQBA	EQOBP	EQSLG	EQMLVR	VORP	DEFENSE
2000	BAK	CLF	22	435	137	21	5	13	39	96	54	11	.315	.377	.476	.219	.249	.287	.380	-.200	-11.9	109-LF -6
2001	SHV	TXS	23	159	49	12	2	1	18	29	11	5	.308	.379	.428	.151	.261	.324	.360	-.149	1.3	36-CF 0
2002	SJO	CLF	24	299	94	19	6	15	34	60	14	5	.314	.384	.569	.379	.248	.303	.441	-.084	3.9	
2002	SHV	TXS	24	135	33	3	1	4	10	23	4	0	.244	.306	.370	-.060	.219	.267	.336	-.320	-6.8	
2003	SFG	NL	25	194	49	10	1	5	15	39	5	4	.252	.309	.393	-.106	.264	.316	.433	-.055	.1	

Breakout: 40%   *Improve: 67%*   *Collapse: 13%*

The torn rotator cuff that ended Valderrama's 2001 shaped his 2002 as well. The shoulder left him unable to play the field, and NL organizations eschew the DH above A-ball, so Valderrama spent most of the year DHing in San Jose. There he destroyed California League pitching, but he was repeating the level and old for the league, so take those numbers with a big grain of salt. This year will give us a better sense of where his offense and defense stand after the injury. Best guess right now is that he'll be—you guessed it—a fourth outfielder.

PITCHERS

Kurt Ainsworth — Born: 09-Sep-78 — Age: 24 — Bats: R — Throws: R

YEAR	TM	LG	AGE	G	GS	IP	H	BB	SO	HR	ERA	EQERA	EQH9	EQBB9	EQSO9	EQHR9	PERA	VORP	STF
2000	SHV	TXS	21	28	28	158.0	138	63	130	12	3.30	4.57	9.9	3.9	5.5	1.1	4.42	16.4	11
2001	FRE	PCL	22	27	26	149.0	139	54	157	22	5.07	5.12	9.1	3.9	6.9	1.5	4.48	6.3	16
2002	FRE	PCL	23	20	19	116.0	101	43	119	7	3.41	3.85	8.7	3.9	7.2	0.7	3.51	21.3	22
2002	SFG	NL	23	6	4	25.7	22	12	15	1	2.10	3.46	8.8	3.8	4.8	0.4	3.95	5.8	4
2003	SFG	NL	24	18	13	87.0	81	39	75	8	4.02	4.70	8.6	3.5	6.8	1.0	4.67	8.5	9

Breakout: 17%   Improve: 51%   Collapse: 13%

If Ainsworth's reputation prior to 2002 was that of a polished safe bet with a relatively low ceiling, he dispelled that last year in two ways. First, by improving in nearly every category in his second go-round at Fresno. Second, by having some success at the major league level, albeit in too short an audition (see Ryan Jensen). He should be in the Giants rotation to stay starting this year.

Boof Bonser — Born: 14-Oct-81 — Age: 21 — Bats: R — Throws: R

YEAR	TM	LG	AGE	G	GS	IP	H	BB	SO	HR	ERA	EQERA	EQH9	EQBB9	EQSO9	EQHR9	PERA	VORP	STF
2000	SLO	NWN	18	10	9	33.0	21	29	41	2	6.00	7.66	9.7	10.4	6.2	1.9	6.10	-7.9	-17
2001	HAG	SAL	19	27	27	134.0	91	61	178	7	2.49	4.50	9.2	6.4	7.0	1.2	4.66	15.0	12
2002	SHV	TXS	20	5	5	24.3	30	14	23	3	5.56	7.51	14.8	6.5	6.8	2.4	8.38	-5.4	-1
2002	SJO	CLF	20	23	23	128.3	89	70	139	9	2.88	4.64	9.4	6.5	6.0	1.3	4.44	12.3	6

Life imitates art. Boof Bonser is Nuke LaLoosh, right down to the classic baseball name. Granted, I never saw him bean a mascot, but Bonser is the stereotypical youngster with a big frame, blazing stuff, and little idea where it's going. His star dimmed a bit in 2002, partly because he made no progress on his control, but he's still young and still has that million-dollar arm. His second try against Double-A hitters this year will tell us a lot.

Matt Cain — Born: 01-Oct-84 — Age: 19 — Bats: R — Throws: R

Cain was the Giants' first round pick (25th overall) out of Houston High School in Germantown, Tennessee. He has a live arm, but many observers were surprised at how high he was taken, even those who don't believe in a hard-and-fast rule of avoiding high school pitchers. Cain struggled with his command in the handful of innings he threw in the Arizona Rookie League, walking 11 with four hit batters and three wild pitches in 19 1/3 innings. The Giants' sixth round pick and another high schooler, lefty Jesse English, was much more impressive in Arizona, striking out 68 and walking 18 in 47 innings.

Jason Christiansen — Born: 21-Sep-69 — Age: 33 — Bats: R — Throws: L

YEAR	TM	LG	AGE	G	GS	IP	H	BB	SO	HR	ERA	EQERA	EQH9	EQBB9	EQSO9	EQHR9	PERA	VORP	STF
2000	PIT	NL	30	44	0	38.0	28	25	41	2	4.97	3.68	6.2	4.6	8.3	0.4	3.23	7.2	9
2000	STL	NL	30	21	0	10.0	13	2	12	1	5.40	5.55	12.2	1.5	9.7	0.8	5.04	-0.2	18
2001	STL	NL	31	30	0	19.3	15	10	19	4	4.66	4.78	7.4	4.3	7.5	1.7	4.43	1.3	-4
2001	SFG	NL	31	25	0	17.0	14	5	12	1	1.59	2.39	8.0	2.5	5.5	0.5	3.29	5.6	0
2002	SFG	NL	32	6	0	5.0	6	2	1	1	5.40	6.49	12.2	3.3	1.6	2.0	6.85	-0.6	-43

Christiansen missed almost the whole year because of Tommy John surgery in May, and his absence was keenly felt by the Giants in the first half of the season. His timetable for return is up in the air at press time; he hopes to be on the Opening Day active roster, but don't bet on it.

Jeff Clark — Born: 06-May-80 — Age: 23 — Bats: R — Throws: R

YEAR	TM	LG	AGE	G	GS	IP	H	BB	SO	HR	ERA	EQERA	EQH9	EQBB9	EQSO9	EQHR9	PERA	VORP	STF
2001	HAG	SAL	21	27	27	148.0	152	15	131	18	3.65	6.67	14.7	1.5	4.8	2.8	6.47	-19.2	0
2002	SJO	CLF	22	21	21	140.0	118	18	129	10	2.06	3.89	11.2	1.5	5.0	1.3	3.83	25.1	14
2002	SHV	TXS	22	6	6	35.7	45	2	20	5	5.04	6.54	15.1	0.6	4.0	2.7	6.71	-4.1	-2

As a 20th round pick out of junior college with a 3.65 ERA in his only full pro season, Clark was barely on the radar screen last April. That changed in a hurry with his 2002 performance in the California League, where he lapped the field for the ERA crown and was named the league's Pitcher of the Year. Clark uses his terrific curve and his pinpoint control—check out the K:BB ratios—to keep hitters off balance and work deep into games. In any other organization he'd be drawing raves; with the Giants, he's so far down the organizational depth chart he's still having trouble getting noticed.

Scott Eyre Born: 30-May-72 Age: 31 Bats: L Throws: L

YEAR	TM	LG	AGE	G	GS	IP	H	BB	SO	HR	ERA	EQERA	EQH9	EQBB9	EQSO9	EQHR9	PERA	VORP	STF
2000	CHR	INT	28	47	0	48.0	33	20	46	1	3.00	3.41	7.2	3.8	7.4	0.2	2.67	10.5	7
2000	CWS	AL	28	13	1	19.0	29	12	16	3	6.63	6.66	12.6	4.5	7.1	1.1	7.34	-2.6	-8
2001	SYR	INT	29	62	2	79.3	67	26	96	8	3.18	3.99	8.5	3.5	8.5	1.2	4.02	12.3	8
2001	TOR	AL	29	17	0	15.7	15	7	16	1	3.44	3.50	8.4	3.7	8.6	0.5	3.77	3.3	12
2002	TOR	AL	30	49	3	63.3	69	29	51	4	4.98	4.57	9.5	3.8	7.0	0.5	4.47	5.8	1
2002	SFG	NL	30	21	0	11.3	11	7	7	0	1.59	4.23	9.9	5.1	5.0	0.2	4.70	1.4	-14
2003	SFG	NL	31	55	0	58.7	55	27	54	4	3.68	4.30	8.8	3.6	7.2	0.7	4.61	7.8	2

Breakout: 11%   Improve: 50%   Collapse: 21%

Another of Brian Sabean's mini-coups in 2002. After suffering through Aaron Fultz's ineffectiveness for the first half of the year, the Giants were desperate for another lefty out of the pen to go with Chad Zerbe. For the cost of a waiver wire claim, Sabean nabbed a good one in Eyre, who gave them solid work down the stretch and during the postseason. Signed by the Giants to a one-year deal, he has a key role in the pen at least until Christiansen returns, and possibly beyond that.

Jesse Foppert Born: 10-Jul-80 Age: 22 Bats: R Throws: R

YEAR	TM	LG	AGE	G	GS	IP	H	BB	SO	HR	ERA	EQERA	EQH9	EQBB9	EQSO9	EQHR9	PERA	VORP	STF
2001	SLO	NWN	20	14	14	70.0	35	23	88	7	1.93	3.49	7.8	4.6	6.2	2.5	3.12	15.7	9
2002	SHV	TXS	21	11	11	61.3	44	21	74	3	2.79	3.75	7.9	3.7	8.3	0.9	3.50	12.0	32
2002	FRE	PCL	21	14	14	79.0	71	35	109	12	3.99	4.54	9.1	4.6	9.6	1.7	4.53	8.5	34
2003	SFG	NL	22	16	11	66.7	57	32	67	8	4.11	4.80	8.0	3.7	7.9	1.3	4.59	5.8	12

Breakout: 17%   Improve: 48%   Collapse: 22%

By mowing down Double-A and Triple-A batters to the tune of 11.7 Ks per nine innings in his first full professional season, Foppert skyrocketed up the minor league lists to become the top pitching prospect in baseball. Strengthening his case is the fact that he did essentially the same thing in 2001, albeit in the Northwest League. He's snuck up on people because he only converted to pitching one year before he was drafted. But he's got terrific mechanics, throws in the low 90s, and mixes four above-average pitches well. It'd be nice to see him cut down on the gopher balls, but Pac Bell Park or whatever they plan to call it should help with that. He's a front-line major league starter waiting to happen.

Aaron Fultz Born: 04-Sep-73 Age: 29 Bats: L Throws: L

YEAR	TM	LG	AGE	G	GS	IP	H	BB	SO	HR	ERA	EQERA	EQH9	EQBB9	EQSO9	EQHR9	PERA	VORP	STF
2000	SFG	NL	26	58	0	69.3	67	28	62	8	4.68	4.62	9.1	3.0	7.2	1.0	4.44	5.9	2
2001	SFG	NL	27	66	0	71.0	70	21	67	9	4.56	4.77	9.4	2.5	7.3	1.1	4.57	4.8	3
2002	SFG	NL	28	43	0	41.3	47	19	31	4	4.79	5.67	11.6	3.8	6.1	1.0	5.84	-1.3	-10
2002	FRE	PCL	28	17	0	22.7	18	11	22	1	3.17	3.45	8.0	5.1	6.8	0.5	3.36	4.9	-1
2003	TEX	AL	29	40	0	43.3	49	18	33	6	4.91	4.69	9.9	3.5	6.6	1.1	4.78	6.4	-4

Breakout: 21%   Improve: 46%   Collapse: 22%

Don't read too much into Fultz's 2002 decline. Yes, he was genuinely awful at the beginning of the year before being sent down, but that stretch covered only 34 innings. He pitched very well in Fresno after the demotion, and was terrific in September after being called back up to the Giants. Chances are he'll regain his 2000–2001 form and be a reliable situational lefty again in 2003. Signed with Texas, where lefty relievers go to die.

Ryan Hannaman Born: 28-Aug-81 Age: 21 Bats: L Throws: L

YEAR	TM	LG	AGE	G	GS	IP	H	BB	SO	HR	ERA	EQERA	EQH9	EQBB9	EQSO9	EQHR9	PERA	VORP	STF
2001	SLO	NWN	19	3	3	13.0	8	8	19	1	2.08	5.16	9.3	8.9	7.5	2.0	4.86	0.5	3
2002	HAG	SAL	20	24	24	131.7	129	46	145	9	2.80	5.10	12.0	4.5	6.2	1.7	6.01	5.9	9

Minor league specialist John Sickels is high on Hannaman, and it's easy to see why. A fourth round pick in the 2000 draft, Hannaman dominated Sally League hitters last year, striking out 9.9 hitters per game and recording more than three Ks for each walk. He's a big lefty with a fastball in the mid-90s and a growing level of composure and smarts on the mound. As with any 21-year-old pitcher, Hannaman's main goal in life right now is to avoid being on a first-name basis with Dr. Frank Jobe.

Brad Hennessey						Born: 07-Feb-80			Age: 23		Bats: R		Throws: R		
YEAR	TM	LG	AGE	G	GS	IP	H	BB	SO	HR	ERA	EQERA	EQH9	EQBB9	EQSO9	EQHR9	PERA	VORP	STF
2001	SLO	NWN	21	9	9	34.0	28	11	22	1	2.38	4.40	11.2	4.5	3.2	0.7	4.67	4.2	-11

A first round pick (25th overall) in 2001, Hennessey missed the first two-thirds of the season recovering from off-season surgery to remove a benign tumor from his back. Just when he had started throwing again in August, it was discovered that the tumor had grown back, and he went through another surgery to remove the second one. You read about devastating injuries that threaten and end young careers every day, but somehow it seems more tragic when the problem isn't the result of the risks of playing the game. Here's hoping we see him back on the mound in 2003.

Livan Hernandez						Born: 20-Feb-75			Age: 28		Bats: R		Throws: R		
YEAR	TM	LG	AGE	G	GS	IP	H	BB	SO	HR	ERA	EQERA	EQH9	EQBB9	EQSO9	EQHR9	PERA	VORP	STF
2000	SFG	NL	25	33	33	240.0	254	73	165	22	3.75	4.32	10.2	2.3	5.6	0.8	4.45	31.6	12
2001	SFG	NL	26	34	34	226.7	266	85	138	24	5.24	5.63	11.4	3.2	4.8	0.9	5.72	-3.1	0
2002	SFG	NL	27	33	33	216.0	233	71	134	19	4.38	5.24	11.1	2.7	5.1	0.9	5.04	6.4	4
2003	SFG	NL	28	29	28	180.0	185	59	117	14	4.06	4.75	9.6	2.6	5.1	0.8	4.63	14.3	6

Breakout: 16% Improve: 53% Collapse: 8%

Here's the dirty little secret about Livan Hernandez: He's never been all that good. He's given up runs at a park-adjusted rate 9% higher than league average over his career, the worst rate of any full-time starter over that period. His reputation as a promising or dependable starter over the years has been built more on luck than on performance: friendly parks, strong offenses, Cuban mystique, Eric Gregg's bizarre strike zone, and Dusty Baker's extreme loyalty. Many have been predicting a Hernandez collapse based on overuse, but to borrow the old joke, if Livan Hernandez collapsed, how could you tell?

Ryan Jensen						Born: 17-Sep-75			Age: 27		Bats: R		Throws: R		
YEAR	TM	LG	AGE	G	GS	IP	H	BB	SO	HR	ERA	EQERA	EQH9	EQBB9	EQSO9	EQHR9	PERA	VORP	STF
2000	FRE	PCL	24	26	26	135.3	167	63	114	18	5.79	6.02	11.1	4.1	6.0	1.4	6.21	-7.7	1
2001	FRE	PCL	25	20	17	106.0	97	34	95	11	3.48	3.93	8.9	3.4	5.9	1.1	3.93	18.5	8
2001	SFG	NL	25	10	7	42.3	44	25	26	5	4.26	5.06	9.9	5.0	4.8	1.0	5.77	2.0	-9
2002	SFG	NL	26	32	30	171.7	183	66	105	21	4.51	5.51	10.9	3.2	5.0	1.2	5.42	-0.1	-2
2003	SFG	NL	27	26	20	126.3	135	52	82	14	4.57	5.34	9.9	3.2	5.1	1.2	5.43	3.0	-3

Breakout: 7% Improve: 36% Collapse: 20%

It's hard to make sense of Sabean and Baker's decision to keep Jensen in the rotation all year instead of Ainsworth. Ainsworth has more raw talent, a better track record in the minors, and better performance in spring training and April when both were with the Giants. The decision "worked," in the sense that the Giants powerhouse offense generally scored runs faster than Jensen could give them up. Jensen would be valuable to a lot of teams as a fifth starter and long reliever, but he should not be permitted to stand in the way of the Giants' young guns.

Noah Lowry						Born: 10-Oct-80			Age: 22		Bats: L		Throws: L		
YEAR	TM	LG	AGE	G	GS	IP	H	BB	SO	HR	ERA	EQERA	EQH9	EQBB9	EQSO9	EQHR9	PERA	VORP	STF
2001	SLO	NWN	20	8	7	25.0	26	8	28	2	3.60	7.69	14.7	4.6	5.7	2.1	6.87	-6.1	-8
2002	SJO	CLF	21	15	12	58.7	38	20	62	4	2.15	4.19	8.7	4.0	5.7	1.2	3.39	8.5	7

One of the Giants' two first round picks in 2001, Lowry missed much of 2002 with shoulder tendonitis. But there was plenty to like when he was healthy, from the low ERA to the fine strikeout and walk numbers behind it. He's a hard-throwing lefty with a better-than-average changeup and a decent curve. He'll start the year in the Norwich rotation, where his primary objective is to stay healthy.

Joe Nathan   Born: 22-Nov-74   Age: 28   Bats: R   Throws: R

YEAR	TM	LG	AGE	G	GS	IP	H	BB	SO	HR	ERA	EQERA	EQH9	EQBB9	EQSO9	EQHR9	PERA	VORP	STF
2000	FRE	PCL	25	3	3	14.3	15	7	9	4	4.41	5.17	9.8	4.3	4.5	3.0	6.42	0.5	-17
2000	SFG	NL	25	20	15	93.3	89	63	61	12	5.21	5.60	8.9	4.9	5.2	1.1	5.34	-1.1	-5
2001	SHV	TXS	26	21	7	62.3	73	37	33	11	6.93	8.65	14.3	7.0	3.6	2.9	8.43	-22.1	-46
2001	FRE	PCL	26	10	10	46.3	63	33	21	13	7.78	9.44	13.8	7.9	3.1	3.0	9.30	-20.2	-49
2002	FRE	PCL	27	31	25	146.3	167	74	117	20	5.60	6.27	11.7	5.4	5.7	1.6	6.05	-12.6	-10
2003	SFN	NL	28	18	12	70.7	70	44	48	9	5.10	5.96	9.2	4.9	5.4	1.3	5.93	-2.1	-11

Breakout: 24%   Improve: 54%   Collapse: 21%

Nathan continued his comeback from shoulder surgery in 2000, with a year that was impressive only relative to the year before. He was never a great prospect, even before the shoulder woes, but he could be a serviceable innings-eater in middle relief. He's been mentioned as a candidate to take over Jay Witasick's role in the bullpen.

Robb Nen   Born: 28-Nov-69   Age: 33   Bats: R   Throws: R

YEAR	TM	LG	AGE	G	GS	IP	H	BB	SO	HR	ERA	EQERA	EQH9	EQBB9	EQSO9	EQHR9	PERA	VORP	STF
2000	SFG	NL	30	68	0	66.0	37	19	92	4	1.50	2.05	5.3	2.1	11.1	0.5	1.96	24.4	37
2001	SFG	NL	31	79	0	77.7	58	22	93	6	3.01	3.14	7.1	2.4	9.2	0.7	3.00	19.3	21
2002	SFG	NL	32	68	0	73.7	64	20	81	2	2.20	3.10	8.8	2.2	8.9	0.3	3.32	18.7	21
2003	SFG	NL	33	57	0	62.0	51	17	60	4	2.49	2.91	7.7	2.1	7.6	0.7	3.12	17.0	13

Breakout: 32%   Improve: 45%   Collapse: 32%

With Nen passing the 300 saves mark last year and moving up to 11th on the all-time career saves list, is he also moving up to elite status in more meaningful measures of pitching performance—those measuring run prevention? Not yet. Nen has prevented around 100 runs above an average pitcher in his career, good for only 24th on the list of full-time relievers, and in a tight pack with a bunch of other contemporary closers like Jeff Montgomery, Roberto Hernandez, Troy Percival, and Armando Benitez. He needs another three to five dominant years to reach the inner circle of all-time relievers, and historically closers tend to suffer quick collapses. The declining strikeout rate is another strike against him, no pun intended.

Russ Ortiz   Born: 05-Jun-74   Age: 29   Bats: R   Throws: R

YEAR	TM	LG	AGE	G	GS	IP	H	BB	SO	HR	ERA	EQERA	EQH9	EQBB9	EQSO9	EQHR9	PERA	VORP	STF
2000	SFG	NL	26	33	32	195.7	192	112	167	28	5.01	5.25	9.1	4.2	6.8	1.2	5.26	5.5	8
2001	SFG	NL	27	33	33	218.7	187	91	169	13	3.29	3.75	8.2	3.5	6.0	0.5	3.79	42.6	12
2002	SFG	NL	28	33	33	214.3	191	94	137	15	3.61	4.33	9.1	3.6	5.2	0.7	4.25	28.0	5
2003	ATL	NL	29	28	26	165.3	164	73	114	17	4.30	4.57	9.1	3.4	5.5	0.9	4.59	18.1	6

Breakout: 5%   Improve: 42%   Collapse: 17%

Ortiz may have regressed a little from his breakthrough 2001, but the Giants aren't complaining about what he gave them: a solid start every fifth day from the beginning of April to the end of October, plus the best hitting of any pitcher in the league. The declining strikeout rate isn't a good sign for those who expect him to take another step up in the near future. Neither is his eyebrow-raising 2002 workload: 4,017 pitches in the regular- and post-seasons, by far a career high, and second in the majors only to Randy Johnson. On the other hand, joining the Cox/Mazzone pitching factory in Atlanta is usually a good sign for any pitcher.

Felix Rodriguez   Born: 09-Sep-72   Age: 30   Bats: Throws:

YEAR	TM	LG	AGE	G	GS	IP	H	BB	SO	HR	ERA	EQERA	EQH9	EQBB9	EQSO9	EQHR9	PERA	VORP	STF
2000	SFG	NL	27	76	0	81.7	65	42	95	5	2.64	3.36	7.5	3.7	9.2	0.5	3.54	18.3	17
2001	SFG	NL	28	80	0	80.3	53	27	91	5	1.68	2.29	6.3	2.8	8.7	0.5	2.67	27.6	19
2002	SFG	NL	29	71	0	69.0	53	29	58	5	4.17	4.23	7.8	3.4	6.8	0.7	3.59	8.8	1
2003	SFG	NL	30	59	0	54.3	46	23	53	5	3.37	3.94	7.9	3.3	7.6	0.9	4.06	9.8	5

Breakout: 15%   Improve: 41%   Collapse: 29%

Rodriguez had a famously bipolar season: runs galore in April through July, almost none in August through October. You'd think that his low 2002 strikeout rate would mostly come from his poor first half, but you'd be wrong. It was when he stopped trying to throw every pitch 150 mph, bringing his strikeouts down but also getting his walks under control, that he turned it around last year. It remains to be seen whether Dave Righetti can help him rediscover his 2001 form, where he combined good control with the devastating out pitch.

Kirk Rueter   Born: 01-Dec-70   Age: 32   Bats: L   Throws: L

YEAR	TM	LG	AGE	G	GS	IP	H	BB	SO	HR	ERA	EQERA	EQH9	EQBB9	EQSO9	EQHR9	PERA	VORP	STF
2000	SFG	NL	29	32	31	184.0	205	62	71	23	3.96	4.75	10.8	2.5	3.2	1.1	5.13	15.4	-7
2001	SFG	NL	30	34	34	195.3	213	66	83	25	4.42	5.02	10.6	2.9	3.3	1.1	5.33	10.5	-8
2002	SFG	NL	31	33	33	203.7	204	54	76	22	3.23	4.47	10.4	2.2	3.1	1.1	4.59	23.4	-5
2003	SFG	NL	32	28	25	157.0	172	48	66	19	4.29	5.01	10.2	2.4	3.3	1.3	5.14	9.6	-9

Breakout: 13%   Improve: 46%   Collapse: 23%

We're sure to read a handful of stories this year about Rueter reuniting with his former manager Felipe Alou. Looking at the numbers doesn't show a big difference in Rueter's pitching between Alou and Baker. Park-adjusted, he allowed runs at a rate 3% better than league average under Alou, and 1% worse than average under Baker. And that's not surprising. No manager is going to teach Rueter to throw 95. You just sit back, watch him move his junk around, and hope he keeps it in the strike zone. He's the kind of pitcher that will collapse suddenly and without warning some year.

Jason Schmidt   Born: 29-Jan-73   Age: 30   Bats: R   Throws: R

YEAR	TM	LG	AGE	G	GS	IP	H	BB	SO	HR	ERA	EQERA	EQH9	EQBB9	EQSO9	EQHR9	PERA	VORP	STF
2000	PIT	NL	27	11	11	63.3	71	41	51	6	5.40	5.14	9.6	4.6	6.2	0.7	5.34	2.6	5
2001	PIT	NL	28	14	14	84.0	81	28	77	11	4.61	4.22	8.6	2.8	7.0	1.0	4.14	12.0	17
2001	SFG	NL	28	11	11	66.3	57	33	65	2	3.39	3.88	8.3	4.2	7.6	0.3	3.84	12.0	21
2002	SLO	NWN	29	9	0	12.3	12	8	13	0	4.39	7.64	13.8	8.9	5.7	0.4	7.38	-3.1	-31
2002	FRE	PCL	29	2	2	12.0	11	2	12	0	3.00	3.06	9.0	1.7	6.9	0.2	2.74	3.3	27
2002	SFG	NL	29	29	29	185.3	148	73	196	15	3.45	4.05	8.0	3.2	8.5	0.8	3.70	30.0	27
2003	SFG	NL	30	27	25	163.7	142	66	152	12	3.45	4.03	8.1	3.1	7.3	0.8	3.95	26.4	20

Breakout: 13%   Improve: 47%   Collapse: 6%

Jason Schmidt *looooves* pitching in Pac Bell Park. Loves it. Secure with the park's cavernous outfield dimensions, he's increasingly challenging hitters to catch up to his high fastball, and the result is usually a lazy fly or a strikeout—Schmidt sported the majors' fifth-lowest G/F ratio in 2001, and the fifth-best strikeout rate. If he can keep his right arm from falling off—always the big "if" with Schmidt—and can tone down the "Hit this!" machismo a bit away from San Fran, he could step up to become one of the NL's premiere pitchers this year.

Erick Threets   Born: 04-Nov-81   Age: 21   Bats: L   Throws: L

YEAR	TM	LG	AGE	G	GS	IP	H	BB	SO	HR	ERA	EQERA	EQH9	EQBB9	EQSO9	EQHR9	PERA	VORP	STF
2001	SJO	CLF	19	14	14	59.3	49	40	60	2	4.25	6.48	10.3	8.3	5.5	0.6	5.72	-6.4	-6
2001	HAG	SAL	19	12	0	24.0	13	9	32	1	0.75	2.60	7.3	5.2	6.9	0.9	3.31	7.4	8
2002	SJO	CLF	20	26	0	28.3	23	28	43	2	6.68	8.79	10.9	12.0	8.5	1.3	7.06	-10.7	-12

When Threets had success in the bullpen after being demoted to Hagerstown in 2001, the thought was that he had found his niche and was set to rocket through the system. Never mind. Threets really can throw 100 mph. He also can't throw a strike to save his life. He's still young enough that there's a chance he'll learn.

Jeff Urban   Born: 25-Jan-77   Age: 26   Bats: R   Throws: L

YEAR	TM	LG	AGE	G	GS	IP	H	BB	SO	HR	ERA	EQERA	EQH9	EQBB9	EQSO9	EQHR9	PERA	VORP	STF
2001	SHV	TXS	24	27	27	156.7	178	32	117	16	3.91	6.10	13.0	2.3	4.9	1.6	5.91	-10.4	1
2002	FRE	PCL	25	35	14	103.0	114	36	72	9	3.41	4.70	11.2	3.7	4.9	1.0	4.94	8.7	-7

The soft-tossing lefty continued his comeback from a torn labrum in 2000, posting a low ERA at Fresno, albeit with mediocre peripherals. The Giants converted him to relief in mid-season, and he could settle into a major league role as a long reliever and spot starter. He should be on a few Fresno-SFO flights this year.

Jerome Williams   Born: 04-Dec-81   Age: 21   Bats: R   Throws: R

YEAR	TM	LG	AGE	G	GS	IP	H	BB	SO	HR	ERA	EQERA	EQH9	EQBB9	EQSO9	EQHR9	PERA	VORP	STF
2000	SJO	CLF	18	23	19	125.7	89	48	115	6	2.94	3.75	7.9	3.7	5.1	1.0	3.74	24.4	10
2001	SHV	TXS	19	23	23	130.0	116	34	84	14	3.95	5.35	10.4	3.0	4.3	1.7	4.59	2.2	1
2002	FRE	PCL	20	28	28	160.7	140	50	130	16	3.58	4.16	8.9	3.3	5.7	1.1	3.63	24.0	15
2003	SFG	NL	21	16	13	79.7	76	35	58	7	4.01	4.69	8.9	3.4	5.7	1.0	4.66	7.4	3

Breakout: 7%   Improve: 51%   Collapse: 14%

Jerome Williams *(continued)*

Entering 2002 as the Giants' top prospect, all Williams did was improve his strikeout rate, his home run rate, and his ERA from the previous year, all while he was the youngest regular starter in Triple-A. Despite that, the buzz surrounding Williams from some media outlets has quieted down a little. The reason? Mostly that his W/L record was only 6–11. Even in this day and age, the silly convention of assigning wins and losses to pitchers corrupts player evaluation. He was pulled from the Arizona Fall League due to elbow soreness; the Giants say he'll be fine for spring training, but just hearing "elbow soreness" in conjunction with "20-year-old pitcher" is enough to make you cringe, but not even minor elbow soreness dims his luster. So he's an injury risk. He's a pitcher; we already knew that.

Jay Witasick — Born: 28-Aug-72 — Age: 30 — Bats: R — Throws: R

YEAR	TM	LG	AGE	G	GS	IP	H	BB	SO	HR	ERA	EQERA	EQH9	EQBB9	EQSO9	EQHR9	PERA	VORP	STF
2000	KCR	AL	27	22	14	89.3	109	38	67	15	5.95	5.47	10.3	3.1	6.5	1.2	5.09	0.1	3
2000	SDP	NL	27	11	11	60.7	69	35	54	9	5.63	6.04	10.7	4.2	7.1	1.2	6.10	-3.6	6
2001	SDP	NL	28	31	0	38.7	31	15	53	3	1.86	3.34	7.5	3.2	10.5	0.6	3.48	8.8	26
2001	NYY	AL	28	32	0	40.3	47	18	53	5	4.69	5.33	10.0	3.7	10.9	1.0	5.44	0.2	20
2002	SFG	NL	29	44	0	68.3	58	21	54	3	2.37	3.27	8.7	2.5	6.4	0.4	3.46	16.0	6
2003	*SDP*	*NL*	*30*	*36*	*5*	*62.3*	*59*	*24*	*57*	*6*	*3.72*	*4.31*	*8.9*	*3.0*	*7.2*	*1.0*	*4.51*	*9.1*	*5*

Breakout: 17%   Improve: 47%   Collapse: 30%

Witasick put together his best year yet in 2002, producing the top Adjusted Runs Prevented total in a remarkably deep Giants bullpen. Future Witasick teams—like his new employer, the Padres—may want to think twice about adding him to the postseason roster though. Yankee fans watching Witasick struggle against the Angels in the World Series suffered painful flashbacks to his shellacking at the hands of the Diamondbacks in the previous Fall Classic. His 6.75 ERA last October actually lowered his career postseason ERA, to a staggering 15.70.

Tim Worrell — Born: 05-Jul-67 — Age: 36 — Bats: R — Throws: R

YEAR	TM	LG	AGE	G	GS	IP	H	BB	SO	HR	ERA	EQERA	EQH9	EQBB9	EQSO9	EQHR9	PERA	VORP	STF
2000	CHC	NL	33	54	0	62.0	60	24	52	7	2.47	3.27	8.8	2.8	6.7	0.9	4.05	14.5	2
2001	SFG	NL	34	73	0	78.3	71	33	63	4	3.45	3.89	8.8	3.6	6.3	0.4	4.00	13.0	0
2002	SFG	NL	35	80	0	72.0	55	30	55	3	2.25	3.29	7.7	3.4	6.2	0.4	3.36	16.7	0
2003	*SFG*	*NL*	*35*	*61*	*0*	*54.7*	*48*	*23*	*43*	*4*	*3.19*	*3.73*	*8.2*	*3.2*	*6.2*	*0.8*	*4.10*	*11.0*	*-2*

Breakout: 23%   Improve: 56%   Collapse: 15%

Worrell has been a solid reliever for several years now, but his managers seriously need to reconsider how they use him. Last year was the fifth season in a row he was worse than average at handling inherited runners. Since 1998, Worrell has inherited 187 runners. Average pitching would have allowed 63 of those 187 to score, but Worrell allowed 78 of them home, and left another four runs on the bases for his successors to deal with. After park adjustments, he has allowed 20 more inherited runners to score than an average reliever would have, easily the worst record with inherited runners in the majors over the past five seasons. They've got to stop bringing him in with runners on base.

Chad Zerbe — Born: 27-Apr-72 — Age: 31 — Bats: L — Throws: L

YEAR	TM	LG	AGE	G	GS	IP	H	BB	SO	HR	ERA	EQERA	EQH9	EQBB9	EQSO9	EQHR9	PERA	VORP	STF
2000	SHV	TXS	28	9	9	38.7	37	9	34	1	2.33	3.56	10.6	2.2	5.9	0.4	3.91	8.4	10
2000	FRE	PCL	28	17	11	81.3	94	17	41	5	4.32	4.19	10.4	1.8	3.6	0.7	4.36	11.7	-2
2001	FRE	PCL	29	17	0	25.3	28	9	17	2	3.56	4.95	10.8	3.9	4.5	0.8	4.91	1.2	-16
2001	SFG	NL	29	27	1	39.0	41	10	22	3	3.92	4.58	10.2	2.2	4.4	0.7	4.44	3.5	-9
2002	SFG	NL	30	50	0	56.3	52	21	26	3	3.04	4.15	9.5	3.1	3.8	0.5	4.10	7.7	-14
2003	*SFG*	*NL*	*31*	*54*	*0*	*53.0*	*55*	*21*	*30*	*4*	*3.95*	*4.62*	*9.7*	*3.1*	*4.4*	*0.8*	*4.85*	*5.5*	*-15*

Breakout: 16%   Improve: 45%   Collapse: 27%

Zerbe was the Giants' one lefty reliever in 2002 who maintained a respectable ERA all year, but a pitcher with the low strikeout rates shown above isn't likely to keep his ERA respectable for long. Zerbe also hasn't shown any special ability to handle left-handed hitters in his brief major league career; lefties have hit .299/.349/.374 off of him, a little better than righties .238/.300/.385.

Introducing PECOTA

by Nate Silver

What a forecasting system should tell us, how it can do it, and what we're going to do about it.

> We still carry the historical baggage of a Platonic heritage that seeks sharp essences and definite boundaries. . . . This Platonic heritage, with its emphasis in clear distinctions and separated immutable entities, leads us to view statistical measures of central tendency wrongly, indeed opposite to the appropriate interpretation in our actual world of variation, shadings, and continua. In short, we view means and medians as the hard "realities," and the variation that permits their calculation as a set of transient and imperfect measurements of this hidden essence. . . .
>
> But all evolutionary biologists know that variation itself is nature's only irreducible essence. Variation is the hard reality, not a set of imperfect measures for a central tendency. Means and medians are the abstractions.
>
> — Stephen Jay Gould[1]

This excerpt, stolen from one of the greatest statheads of them all, was written three years after its author had learned that he suffered from abdominal mesothelioma, a rare form of cancer. Gould had discovered that the median survival rate associated with his cancer was eight months; he would go on to live another 20 years.

Devoid of the sentimentality that normally pervades any discussion of such subjects, Gould's article is a treatise on the limitations of using statistical analysis to make predictions about the fate of any one individual. We turn to statistics for certainty in a chaotic world; we expect them to provide definitive answers. In so doing, we both overstate and undersell their potential.

All of this might seem like a strange way to introduce a new projection system. Projections, if you'll indulge me the analogy, are the fortune tellers of the sabermetric carnival, mixing a few well-practiced tricks with a dash of folk wisdom, telling you something you already ought to know, and expecting you to pay (in our case, $21.95) for the privilege. We tell you Troy Glaus is gonna hit 40 homers next year, and if he doesn't, well, we're no more responsible for that than for your failure to meet your soul mate in the cotton candy line.

What we ought to be doing isn't telling fortunes at all, but providing advice. We ought to tell you that you're more likely to meet your dream girl if you straighten your tie, shave your six o'clock stubble, and avoid starting the discussion with a critique of Derek Jeter's range factor. We also ought to tell you that, in spite of doing all these things, there's still a good chance that you might spend the night curled up with the *Spice* network.

That sort of advice is what the PECOTA[2] system tries to provide. Its foundation is a pair of interrelated premises:

- Variation, to paraphrase Gould, is the hard reality underlying the statistical performance of baseball players;
- Both the scope and the direction of this variation are themselves predictable, and predicting them provides valuable information.

Variation, in other words, isn't something that a projection system should seek to avoid, but something that it should seek to embrace.

The Comparable Players Approach

The mechanism by which PECOTA attempts to model variance is via the explicit identification of comparable baseball players. The idea that identifying similar players can provide insight into a given player's future has existed informally since the dawn of sabermetrics, and has been given new life in recent years by Bill James's *The Politics of Glory*, in which he introduced similarity scores, and the web site http://baseball-reference.com, which has popularized them.

---

1. This text originally appeared in Gould's article "The Median Isn't the Message," *Discover,* June 1985. It has been reprinted in full at numerous places on the Internet, including: http://www.cancerguide.org/median_not_msg.html.

2. PECOTA stands for Pitcher Empirical Comparison and Optimization Test Algorithm. It is our hope that, like TCBY and N*SYNC, the acronym will become sufficiently popular that nobody can remember what it actually denotes.

Clay Davenport's "Wilton" projection system, which appeared in previous editions of *Baseball Prospectus,* also considered comparable players as an element of its hitter forecasts.

PECOTA strives to apply this method systematically. While similar in spirit to the James similarity scores, the PECOTA scores differ in a number of meaningful ways:

- The PECOTA scores are based on a weighted average of the prior three years of performance, although career length is also considered.
- The PECOTA scores are based primarily on rate statistics, rather than raw totals, although quantity of playing time and usage patterns are also considered, especially for pitchers.
- The database that PECOTA uses is park and league normalized.
- PECOTA attempts to account for the interaction effects between various performance metrics differently.
- The PECOTA scores are derived in such a way that emphasizes prospective similarity, rather than retrospective similarity.

The latter two considerations are the more important, and require further explanation.

Interaction Effects

The James scores are derived by means of subtraction; one point is subtracted for each difference of 20 stolen bases, another point is subtracted for each difference of two home runs, and so on. Although PECOTA also starts from a perfect score representing two identical players, and deducts points based on their differences, the means by which it does so is different.

Figure 1 presents an idealized rendering of PECOTA's methodology. Suppose that we are interested in assessing the similarity of Magglio Ordonez to two other players in our database, Dale Murphy and Darrin Erstad, and that we are considering only two characteristics in order to do so, Power and Average. Erstad has similar Average to Ordonez, but considerably less Power; Murphy has somewhat more Power, but somewhat less Average.

If we plot these characteristics on a plane, it is evident that the distance between Murphy and Ordonez is less than that between Erstad and Ordonez; Murphy is the more similar player. The James scores understate the dissimilarity between Ordonez and Erstad by summing along the sides of the sides of the triangle, rather than along its hypotenuse.

Figure 1. Schematic Illustration of PECOTA Similarity Algorithm

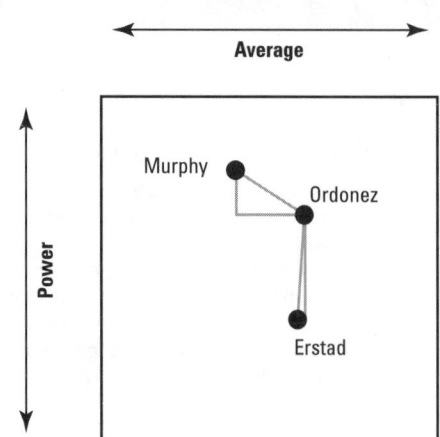

The upshot of this is that the PECOTA scores punish a player more for being very dissimilar with respect to any one characteristic; therefore it is hoped that PECOTA is better equipped to model the interaction effects between multiple characteristics.[3]

Prospective vs. Retrospective Similarity

In *The Politics of Glory,* James applied his similarity scores to assess the suitability of a particular player for the Hall of Fame by means of comparison with his historical peers. The emphasis of the PECOTA system is somewhat different. It is not designed to assess the productivity of a given player retrospectively, but to predict his performance going forward.

As a result, PECOTA weights the various components of the similarity score differently, based on their relative predictive value.[4] Batters' strikeouts are not very heavily emphasized in the James scores, and appropriately so, because the marginal impact of a strikeout on run production is minimal. However, my research indicates that strikeout rate is relatively important as a predictor of *future* productivity; therefore it is weighted as such by PECOTA. Another example is PECOTA's use of a player's height and weight in assessing similarity. Except to a eugenicist, these factors should be of no importance whatsoever in comparing the suitability of two players for the Hall of Fame. They are of some importance in predicting a player's future development, and so PECOTA considers them.

---

3. Although the example provided involves only two dimensions, the distance between two points in a plane, as an application of the Pythagorean theorem, can be extrapolated in n dimensions.

4. The weights that PECOTA employs were derived via analysis of variance (ANOVA).

An example: Ray Durham

By comparing the most similar players as determined by PECOTA with those determined under the James method, we observe that the two approaches often lead to dramatically different results as seen in tables 1 and 2.

Table 1. Most Similar Players to Ray Durham, per PECOTA

1. Don Buford
2. Bill Doran
3. Harold Reynolds
4. Jose Offerman
5. Chuck Knoblauch
6. Luis Alicea
7. Lou Whitaker
8. Tim Raines
9. Roy White
10. Tommy Harper

Table 2. Most Similar Players to Ray Durham, per James Similarity Scores[5], PECOTA Rank in Parenthesis

1. Joe Morgan (NR)
2. Lou Whitaker (7)
3. Juan Samuel (36)
4. Paul Molitor (67)
5. Craig Biggio (18)
6. Tony Cuccinello (N/A)
7. Chuck Knoblauch (5)
8. Carlos Baerga (N/A)
9. Gil McDougald (34)
10. Red Kress (N/A)

Two players, Chuck Knoblauch and Lou Whitaker, are common to both lists; another James comp, Craig Biggio, is in PECOTA's top twenty. Two others on the James list, Tony Cuccinello and Red Kress, are not eligible in PECOTA because these players completed their age 30 seasons prior to WWII.[6] Another, Carlos Baerga, is also ineligible because of different conventions the two systems use in comparing player ages.[7] The four others illustrate various points about the two systems, and deserve further explanation:

- **Joe Morgan.** Morgan was a historically great player whom Ray Durham has little business being compared to; PECOTA does not consider him to be one of Durham's 100 best comparables. Though both players were of similar body type and had a diversity of offensive skills, Morgan's batting average, adjusted for his park and league context, was a standard deviation better than Durham's, and his isolated power and walk rate were close to two standard deviations better. The high score under the James system results from failing to account for the difference in the run environments in which they played.
- **Juan Samuel.** The James score underestimates the importance of plate discipline, especially as reflected in Samuel's strikeout rate. Moreover, it gives Samuel too much credit for being a productive player early in his career; he was not much like Ray Durham by age 30.
- **Paul Molitor.** Molitor was primarily a designated hitter even at age 30, which PECOTA holds against him. On the other hand, he hit for a far superior batting average relative to his league. Durham and Molitor had similar counting stats through age 30, but were not highly similar players.
- **Gil McDougald.** Although they were of similar overall value, McDougald had a different body type than Durham's, and considerably less speed.

PECOTA selects as Durham's best comparables a gaggle of short switch-hitters with good speed, good plate discipline, and average power. The comparables themselves are similar players to one another; there is no list on which the names Joe Morgan and Juan Samuel should appear alongside one another.

Forecasting Risk

By evaluating the performance of his comparables, PECOTA is able to develop a robust idea about the potential performances that a given player might exhibit. Figure 2 presents Robin Ventura's PECOTA forecast for 2003, as measured by his EQA. The thick, dark line indicates Ventura's potential outcomes; these are compared against a normal distribution on EQA for all major league players ("Norm"), and a straight, dashed line representing the EQA of a replacement-level third baseman ("Replace").

---

5. Reprinted from http://www.baseball-reference.com.

6. World War II was chosen as a cutoff point for two reasons. First, self-evident differences in the game which cannot be well accounted for by statistical adjustments, most notably desegregation and advances in conditioning and medical care. Second, the effects of players going to war are themselves difficult to account for.

7. PECOTA determines age comparability by constructing a 182-game interval on either side of a player's date of birth, rather than using "baseball age" as under the James approach. Baerga was already out of the majors by the season that PECOTA matches to Ray Durham's age-30 year.

Figure 2. EQA Outcomes for Robin Ventura

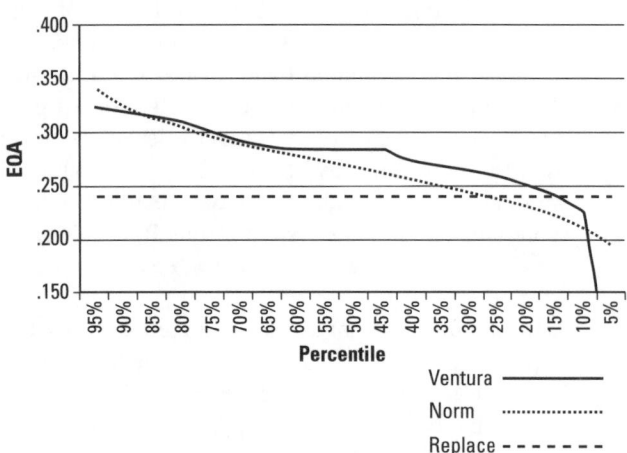

As can be observed from the figure, Ventura's probability distribution is highly asymmetric. There is a meaningful chance, roughly 10%, that he will undergo a sudden and dramatic collapse; players such as Dick McAullife and Willie Jones, whom the PECOTA system considers to be reasonably similar to Ventura, suffered such a fate at age 35. On the other hand, Ventura is more than 80% likely to be superior to a replacement-level performer, and in most of those cases, will be significantly better than that.

If confronted with a forecast such as this one, a major league executive would be able to make a more informed decision about what to do with Ventura: Bring him back for another season, but make sure that there are adequate hedges in place in case of a marked collapse.[8]

Pitchers

Forecasting a range of outcomes is particularly helpful when evaluating pitchers. A lot of analysts, including my colleagues at Baseball Prospectus, have been reluctant to publish pitcher forecasts at all, and understandably so. Pitchers exhibit demonstrably greater variance in their year-to-year performance than do hitters, especially as measured by ERA.

PECOTA "solves" this problem by representing this range of outcomes appropriately. Even an established pitcher has a very wide range on his ERA distribution. Take Andy Pettitte, for example. PECOTA estimates that there is a 50% chance that his ERA will be between 3.41 and 4.54—and a 50% chance that it will be outside this range. Although the perceptual difference between the two figures is great, the reality is

that such apparently large differences in ERA can emerge as the result of very small variances in a pitcher's peripheral statistics, defense, and luck.

At the same time, the fact that ERA is inherently volatile does not render a pitching forecast meaningless. A pitcher with a wide range of outcomes centered around a 3.00 ERA is a substantially better investment than a pitcher with a wide range of outcomes centered around a 4.00 ERA, even though the 4.00 ERA pitcher will *appear* to be better in a substantial number of individual seasons. In other words, it is not that pitcher performance is "unpredictable," but that the large variance in their performance needs to be made part of their forecasts.

The PECOTA forecasts can also be used to compare two players. Figure 3 presents one such comparison, Russ Ortiz against Damian Moss, that should be near and dear to John Schurholtz' heart:[9]

PECOTA concludes that Ortiz is likely to be the better pitcher, but the difference increases markedly as we move from left to right along the graph. Moss, probably by virtue of his very high walk rate, has more downside risk; he has roughly a 35% chance of producing an ERA in excess of 5.50, versus a 15% chance for Ortiz. The extent to which Schurholtz would be willing to pay a premium for Ortiz would depend on the composition of the rest of his roster; having an adequate replacement in tow for Moss might enable him to spend scarce resources in other places.

Thus, PECOTA is designed to provide a representation of a player's expected performance that accounts not only for his mean or median performance, but also for the variance (risk) around this mean. Oftentimes, this variance can be

Figure 3. ERA Outcomes for Russ Ortiz and Damian Moss

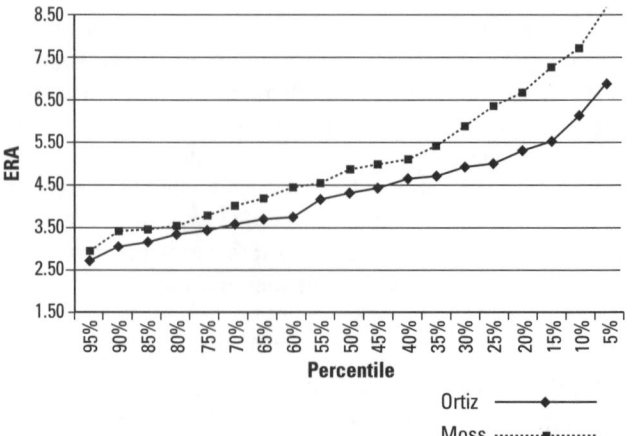

---

8. By signing Ventura to a one-year contract and Todd Zeile as his backup, this is in fact what the Yankees have done.

9. For purposes of comparison, both pitchers have been projected in Turner Field.

meaningfully different for two different players, even if their mean level of projected performance is similar. This is not to suggest that risk is always to be avoided; there are plausible circumstances under which a major league team might prefer to be risk loving. Nevertheless, a forecasting tool that allows it to objectively assess risk would be of value in almost any situation.

A Problem of Representation

Having emphasized the importance of forecasting variance, it will come as something of a disappointment that the forecasts in this book are presented as single lines of projected performance. Interesting as they might be, neither I, nor my colleagues, want a book completely dominated by projections. We do have a fully fledged version of a player's PECOTA, including charts such as those presented for Ventura, Ortiz, and Moss, available on our premium web site.

We feel the best way to represent a player given this constraint is by printing his weighted mean forecast.[10] The alternative would be to present a median forecast (e.g., the 50th percentile). Although the two sets of projections will generally be quite close, the mean forecast accounts for all of the data points within a player's probability distribution. The mean forecast will be less favorable than the median for a player with downside risk (such as Moss), but more favorable for a player with upside risk.

In addition to the forecast line, PECOTA generates for each player a series of three metrics, called Breakout, Improve, and Collapse, which assess the likelihood of change from the player's previously established level of performance. In particular:

- **Breakout** is the percent chance that a given hitter's productivity, as measured by equivalent runs per plate appearance (EQR/PA), will improve by at least 20% above his baseline level of performance.[11] For pitchers, it is the percent chance that his PERA will improve by at least 20% relative to his baseline.[12] High breakout scores are an indicator of upside risk.
- **Collapse** is the mirror image of breakout, and represents downside risk. For hitters, Collapse is the percent

chance that his EQR/PA will decline by at least 20%, and for pitchers, the chance that his PERA will increase by at least 25%.[13]

- **Improve** is the percent chance that a given hitter's EQR/PA, or a given pitcher's PERA, will improve *at all* relative to his baseline. It measures, quite simply, how likely a player is likely to be better than he has been in the past. A player who is expected to perform just the same as has in the past will have an Improve rating equal to 50%.

Thus, for each player, a Breakout/ Improve/ Collapse (BIC) triplet is presented. A player with substantial downside risk might have a BIC triplet on the order of 5%/35%/25%. This indicates that he has a 35% chance to improve upon his baseline—and therefore a 65% chance to decline. Moreover, his Collapse score of 25% indicates that there is a one-in-four chance that his performance will decline *substantially*.

Beware the Ugueto Effect

Although Breakout and Collapse scores can be a lot of fun, there is one critical fact that must be kept in mind when evaluating them. That is, they measure change *relative to a player's previously established level of performance.*

For this reason, a high Breakout score can create a falsely optimistic picture for a player who has a very poor performance record. My colleagues and I have dubbed this phenomenon the Ugueto Effect. It is far easier for a player like Luis Ugueto, who would produce about 40 EQR over a full season, to improve upon that figure by 20% than it is for Alex Rodriguez; as a result, his Breakout score is likely to be higher. This does not mean that Ugueto is a player you'd want anywhere near your roster; he's very likely to display some improvement, but very unlikely to be a hitter of major league caliber, as the rest of his projection line will reflect. For this reason, Breakout and Collapse scores are most valuable when comparing players of roughly the same age and underlying performance level.

But Does It Work?

Ultimately, every projection system makes use of essentially the same data: the indelible record of performance of previous

---

10. In calculating the weighted mean forecast, an adjustment is made based upon the number of plate appearances or innings pitched that each comparable player accumulates. Absent this adjustment, the negative impact of poor performances would be overstated, as poor performances are almost always associated with reduced playing time; they don't hurt the team quite as much as good performances help it.

11. I am using the term "baseline" here without an adequate explanation; basically, the baseline is a three-year weighted average with luck removed. For a fuller description, please read on to the Technical Appendix.

12. PERA is used in place of ERA because it is more subject to factors within the pitcher's immediate control.

13. 25% is used instead of 20% because of the non-linearity of ERA. Even with this adjustment, most pitchers have a Collapse rate that exceeds their Breakout rate.

ballplayers. What counts is how this data is best put to use. I have found that the interaction effects between different player attributes are sufficiently complex that they cannot be well accounted for through regression and averaging alone. Making explicit use of comparable players is my way of solving the puzzle; it may not be the only way, but I'm a believer, and I hope to pick up a few converts along the way.

It should go without saying that ultimate proof of PECOTA's effectiveness will come on the playing field. In developing PECOTA, I tested it on virtually every major league pitcher and hitter using their numbers through 2001, and it performed very well in forecasting their 2002 statistics. After the 2003 season is consigned to history, we'll be able to conduct an objective comparison of PECOTA against other forecasting systems.

It's also worth thinking about what kind of information a forecasting system provides us with. Accuracy matters, but so too does a system's ability to differentiate between various types of players, and identify which of those players are most likely to undergo substantial changes in their value. On that account, I think PECOTA holds up well.

To take one example—the Giants' middle infield for next season includes two 30-year-old players, Ray Durham and Rich Aurilia, who have been of roughly equal value over the course of the past three seasons. However, PECOTA regards the set of skills that Durham possesses to be substantially more likely to age gracefully than are Aurilia's. This is evident when evaluating their BIC metric as shown in table 3.

Table 3.

	Breakout	Improve	Collapse
Durham	10%	49%	12%
Aurilia	7%	34%	32%

Aurilia is nearly three times more likely than Durham to see a dramatic decline in his performance. Since PECOTA uses as many as 100 comparable players to generate its forecasts, it is unlikely that result would emerge from random variance alone. Rather, the comparable players approach allows it to identify particular combinations of attributes that have a meaningful impact on player development.

Completing the Circle and Other Pretensions

One of the virtues of a forecasting system that presents a *range* of expected outcomes is that it freely admits its fallibility. There is no such thing as a perfect forecast.

I believe that PECOTA does an excellent job of using the information available to it. In spite of that, the range of outcomes it describes for any particular player is often quite

large. Much of this variance is the result of luck. As Brady Anderson or the folks at Dom DeLuise's local Old Country Buffet can tell you, crazy things can happen when you go to the plate 650 times.

I do not mean to suggest, however, that the variance is entirely related to luck. On the contrary, some of this variance results from a variety of factors that PECOTA is *not* able to measure directly. This includes such sabermetrically incorrect attributes as work ethic, intelligence, coaching, innate athletic ability, and so on. Stephen Jay Gould discussed something similar in the article that I referenced at the beginning of this essay. He knew that the median survival time for people with his form of cancer was eight months; he also knew that he possessed certain advantages that the "average" cancer patient did not: He was younger at the time of diagnosis than most of the other patients, he had access to world-class medical care, a network of friends and family to support him, and so on.

Some of what PECOTA is *not* very adept at measuring can be made up for by good scouting. In fact, because it acknowledges the limitations of statistical analysis, I believe that the PECOTA system is better equipped to work in *conjunction* with scouting evaluations than other kinds of forecasts. PECOTA can tell us that hitters who are statistically similar to Adrian Gonzalez have a 36% chance of a breakout in their age 21 season. A scout can tell us whether there's anything in particular about Adrian Gonzalez—a perfect swing, an insatiable desire to better himself, a fondness for In-N-Out burgers—that makes him more or less likely than his comparable group to achieve that degree of improvement. The two kinds of information can serve to check-and-balance one another. Lots of players are touted as breakout candidates, but not all of them are.

Technical Appendix

Thus far, I have deliberately skimmed over some of the technical considerations in how a PECOTA forecast is generated. Although this section will not provide a comprehensive description of PECOTA's inner workings, it should at least provide a reasonable explication of how the system operates.

In essence, PECOTA operates in three related steps:

1. Generation of a Baseline forecast.
2. Identification of comparable players.
3. Creation of a forecast range based on comparable player performances.

Generation of the Baseline Forecast

The first step of the PECOTA forecast does not differ that greatly from the techniques employed by most other forecasting models. A Baseline forecast is developed based on the player's previous three seasons of performance. Both major league and (translated) minor league performances are considered.[14]

One way in which the PECOTA Baseline is somewhat distinguished from those generated by other systems is the degree to which it accounts for interaction effects between various statistical categories. For example, doubles have a positive influence on home runs, stolen bases have a positive influence on singles, and so on; it turns out that there are tons of statistically meaningful interactions such as these. PECOTA employs a technique known as seemingly unrelated regression in order to account for these.[15]

The Baseline forecast is also significant in that it attempts to remove luck from a forecast line. For example, a player who hit .310, but with a poor batting eye and unimpressive speed indicators, is probably not really a .310 hitter; it's more likely that he's a .290 hitter who had a few balls bounce his way. A more extreme and much discussed example is a pitcher's hit rate on balls in play; luck and defense account for the majority of variance in this statistic. Different elements of the batting and pitching lines are more subject to luck than are others, and the Baseline forecast does its best to account for this before it begins to compare players.

Identification of Comparable Players

I have already spent some time describing how PECOTA's comparability algorithm works. It compares each pitcher against a database of roughly 10,000 pitcher seasons since World War II, and each hitter against a database of about 15,000 player seasons since World War II. The database also contains about 5,000 translated minor league hitter seasons (1998–2002) that are used in combination with the major league database in order to evaluate hitting prospects. Players are compared only against others of the same age.

PECOTA considers three broad categories of attributes in determining comparability:

- **Production metrics** such as isolated power, batting average, speed scores, walk and strikeout rates for hitters, and strikeout rates, walk rates, and home run rates for pitchers. These elements constitute the bulk of the similarity score.
- **Usage metrics** such as career length, plate appearances, total batters faced, batters faced per game, and so on.

The usage categories are relatively more important for pitchers.

- **Phenotypic** attributes such as handedness, height, and weight. Fielding position, which has quite an important effect on player development, also belongs here.[16]

In most cases, the database is large enough to provide a meaningfully large set of appropriate comparables. When it isn't, the program is designed to "cheat" by expanding its tolerance for dissimilar players until a reasonable sample size is reached. There's a trade-off, in other words, between the precision that PECOTA requires in identifying comparables, and the size of the comparables set. I believe that PECOTA generally does a good job of balancing the two, with a handful of notable exceptions. Jesse Orosco has a forecast I wouldn't bet money on, simply because there's hardly anyone left at his age to compare him to. Similarly, very young players (18- and 19-year-olds) have relatively small comparable sets, which we hope to improve upon as we add additional minor league seasons to the database. PECOTA does the best it can with a player like Barry Bonds, identifying Ted Williams, Hank Aaron, and the rest of the inner circle Hall of Famers as comparables, but it is important to keep in mind that no player has achieved anything like what Bonds has in his late 30s. The best we can do is an educated guess, with the emphasis on guess.

Creation of the Forecast Range

The final step is really a combination of the previous two: PECOTA evaluates how the comparable players perform relative to their baselines in order to estimate how the player it is projecting will perform relative to his baseline.

This sounds relatively straightforward, and for the most part, it is. The complicated part is matching up the peripheral statistics with a player's overall level of productivity. In order to accomplish this, one statistic serves as an indexing key around which the other elements of a player's line are derived—equivalent runs are used for hitters, and runs allowed for pitchers.

PECOTA runs a series of regressions within the set of comparable data in order to estimate how changes in peripheral statistics are related to changes in the indexing key. For example, if it first estimates that Pat Burrell will

---

14. The previous three years of data are weighted based on playing time, and more recent seasons are weighted more heavily. In addition, for certain statistics such as hitters' walks, major league statistics are weighted more heavily than minor league statistics.

15. For the somewhat less geeky among us, the advantage of seemingly unrelated regression is that it is designed to estimate many different parameters at once—in this case, all the components of a batting or pitching line. In any given plate appearance, batting or pitching outcomes are mutually exclusive—a player who hits a double cannot draw a walk in the same at-bat. For this reason, it is advantageous to work with all elements of a statistical line simultaneously as this technique facilitates.

16. PECOTA doesn't require that a comparable hitter play the same defensive position; it is a factor that is evaluated along with many others, and assigned a relatively substantial weight. Consideration is also given to the "similarity" between two positions; for example, a shortstop will be compared to a second baseman before he is compared to a left fielder.

account for 100 runs next year, it then tries to determine what home run total, walk total, and so on are most likely to be associated with a 100-run season. After all the peripheral statistics have been estimated, the final step is an iterative process which seeks to ensure that this set of statistics adds up to the run productivity that it purports to. The peripheral statistics are tweaked incrementally until an appropriate result has been achieved.

PECOTA also differs from other systems in that playing time is endogenous to the forecast. That is, it doesn't pre-impose any particular amount of playing time, but seeks to estimate it from a player's usage history and his other attributes, just as it does the other elements of the forecast.[17] I am convinced that this is the "right" way to do things. It is possible to do a pretty good job of estimating playing time based solely on a player's track record; since playing time constitutes part of his value, to fail to do so means that we have thrown away a lot of useful information. Of course, there are exceptions—Erubiel Durazo is likely to exceed his playing time forecast, simply because he has escaped to an organization that better appreciates his talent. But reductions in playing time are as routine a part of aging as reductions in rate statistics, and the forecasts take this into account.

Implications and Innuendos

I'll conclude this piece with a series of declarative statements that represent some of the things that I've learned in developing PECOTA. For now, you'll have to take me at my word; expect the proof to come to a web site near you soon.

1. Position has a significant effect on hitter career paths. Players at more difficult defensive positions don't age as well, and second basemen do especially poorly.

2. The extent to which young hitters display variability in their performance is understated; no hitting prospect is foolproof.

3. Batting average is subject to considerably greater regression to the mean than other elements of offensive performance.

4. Strikeout rate has a meaningful impact on hitter development, although the impact isn't always negative.

5. Different player attributes should be considered in combination with one another. For example, players with both speed and power age very well, but players with one and not the other often age poorly.

6. Players who have established a very high level of performance are unlikely to display demonstrable improvement, regardless of age. Conversely, the players who are most likely to exhibit dramatic improvement are often those who have the most to improve upon.

7. It is questionable to call any pitcher a breakout candidate. We know how important strikeout and walk rates are in driving success; there is no class of pitchers likely to markedly improve upon its previously established level of performance in these categories as a matter of course.

8. All else being equal, pitchers with high walk rates display greater volatility in their performance, both upside and downside.

9. Innings pitched totals are often easier to predict than ERA, even in the absence of specific information about how a pitcher's manager regards him.

10. A pitcher's height and handedness, and a batter's height, weight, and handedness, are meaningful elements to consider when assessing his development. For example, short hitters have trouble developing power, while tall hitters struggle with plate discipline.

---

17. An exception is made in the case of minor league prospects, whose playing time is deliberately inflated some in order to provide a reasonable basis for evaluation.

The Medhead Manifesto

by Will Carroll and Dr. William Carroll

On the simplest level, medheads aren't any different in their basic goals than statheads: we aim to provide information. In this case, we're seeking to bring a greater understanding of the art and science of sports medicine to sports fans. While practitioners toil in relative obscurity—quick, name the three best trainers in MLB—their impact on the game is unquestionable. Last year's Fall Classic matched up a team that was kept healthy all year (the Angels) and another that was nursed back to full health (the Giants). Teams fell by the wayside as injuries to key players took them down, whittled away at depth, and as pitchers faded under heavy workloads. Yet not once did we hear an announcer or sportswriter in the mainstream credit Ned Bergert or Stan Conte. Even the most knowledgeable fans cannot usually identify their team's assistant trainer, someone who could have more impact on their team than the manager or middle reliever.

Injuries and injury history remain very important to the game, both on the field and off, yet strangely enough, they do not get analyzed or used as much as performance or scouting metrics. As players and owners bickered throughout last year's near-strike, mind-bending numbers about player salaries and operating losses were bandied about. One of the more significant numbers seldom discussed was the salary lost to injury. When a player such as Albert Belle or Kevin Brown goes down to injury, the loss is not only to the team on the field, but also to the team's financial ledger. When a team loses ten percent or more of its payroll, the opportunity cost expands as well. Add insurance costs, and it becomes clear that teams could save enormous sums by concentrating on keeping their players healthy, and not signing players with significant injury risk to large, long-term contracts in the first place.

According to baseball's own figures, baseball teams have lost over $200 million over the last six years to salaries paid to players unable to perform on the field. Remembering that the owners and players were never this far apart in their negotiations, simply reducing injury costs could be the most significant financial move the owners could make, while reducing injuries would clearly be in the interest of players. There is no clearer win-win situation in sports. However, there is no central database of player injuries, no organized study of how to reduce injuries, and little or no recognition for the teams that have made significant strides in reducing injuries. As a result, while there are a few teams with a clear advantage over every other team in this area, that advantage is rarely recognized.

Throughout the history of baseball, teams have considered injury risk and injury history when making signings, but the lack of hard data has made signings of players with injury risks and injury histories relative gambles where the odds are unknown. When signing a Woody Williams or a Tom Glavine, any general manager worth his salary must look not only at performance, but also at age and at injury history. As metrics are developed and the art and science of sports medicine in baseball develops, it will be interesting to see where the statheads and the medheads merge.

Sports Medicine 101

According to the insurance industry, there are two broad classifications of injuries in baseball, but defining them is very difficult. The classifications—preventable and non-preventable injuries—leave much room for debate. While a traumatic injury that is the result of a collision or freak accident is clearly non-preventable, stating without question that something such as a torn rotator cuff is "preventable" is very difficult, and places an enormous responsibility on the team's medical staff. Until better measures are found on preventing injuries, especially with pitchers, I prefer to classify injuries as traumatic and fatigue-based. If an organization is suffering through a high percentage of fatigue-based injuries, such as labrum tears or ulnar collateral ligament ruptures, it should have to acknowledge that there is a problem, and then take a hard look at every factor that could have created this situation, from its medical staff to player conditioning to on-field management. As better tools are developed, it is hoped that fatigue-based injuries can be reduced. Even a five or ten percent reduction in these injuries would have an astounding effect on baseball, giving the first teams to find this magic bullet an advantage unlike any other in baseball.

According to figures from the Under the Knife Injury Database, five injuries result in nearly fifty percent of all lost playing time. While these injuries are discussed amongst fans and fantasy owners, few have a clear understanding of what these injuries actually entail. The "Big Five" are the ulnar collateral ligament (UCL) rupture, SLAP Lesion (commonly known as a labrum tear), meniscus tears, hamstring strains, and calcaneal tendon strains.

The **UCL rupture** will be skipped here due to space constraints, as well as the relative wealth of knowledge that already exists about the timeline of the injury and its rehabilitation following "Tommy John" surgery.

The **SLAP Lesion** (Superior Labrum Anterior Posterior) is an overuse syndrome injury commonly associated with overhead activities, such as the throwing motion in baseball. Technically, the anatomical structure that makes the SLAP lesion possible is the origin of the tendon of the long head of the biceps muscle and the way it hooks over the head of the humerus (the bone of the upper arm that makes up part of the shoulder joint). If the arm is forcibly bent inward at the shoulder as it is in the throwing motion, the humerus acts as a lever and tears the biceps tendon and the labrum. The lining of the shoulder joint from the glenoid cavity is torn in a front-to-back fashion, hence the name SLAP—the superior aspect of the labrum is torn from anterior to posterior.

Usually the signs and symptoms involve the athlete either complaining of pain or instability in the shoulder while throwing. This condition worsens when the athlete puts his arm into the "cocked position" ready to throw. Some athletes with this condition may experience pain while doing overhead weight lifting and some have reported actually hearing a clicking sound in the shoulder when attempting to throw.

Unfortunately this condition is seldom discovered until the damage to the labrum is already done. Athletic trainers and physicians utilize a clinical test called the shoulder impingement test to clinically identify this condition. The test is performed by stabilizing the rear of the athlete's shoulder, extending his elbow and passively forward flexing the arm. If the test is positive for a SLAP lesion, the athlete will experience pain near the end of the range of motion. If this test is positive, usually an MRI will be done to confirm the diagnosis.

If the damage to the labrum is not significant, withholding the athlete from activity and prescribing anti-inflammatory medications may treat the condition. Stretching and stabilization exercises can be utilized under supervision when the pain lessens. It is extremely important that the athlete not return to sports-specific activity (such as throwing) until the pain has entirely disappeared.

If the labrum is significantly torn, the only viable treatment for someone who wants to continue to be active in the sport is a surgery in which the surgeon arthroscopically reattaches the torn labrum. After the surgery, it is very important that the athlete undergoes supervised rehabilitation designed to both strengthen the shoulder muscles and gain flexibility in the joint. Unlike the generally more positive

outcomes that result from Tommy John surgery, only a small percentage of players of those that suffer significant labral tears are able to successfully return to anywhere near their previous level of performance. Most often, players that are able to come back lose significant velocity, are forced to alter their mechanics, creating further injury risk, and often re-tear the labrum. Recent cases such as Mike Sirotka and Mariners prospect Ryan Anderson come to mind as typical.

Meniscal injuries are very common in sports activities. Commonly called torn cartilage, these injuries are normally caused by a rotational movement of the knee while the foot is planted. To fully understand this injury, it is important to understand what the meniscus is and what it is designed to do. The meniscus is a piece of soft tissue (cartilage) that lines the joint between the femur (bone of the upper leg) and the tibia (bone in the front part of the lower leg) at the knee joint. There are two of these structures, the medial meniscus and the lateral meniscus. They are designed for shock absorption within the knee joint and to add rotational stability to the knee. Twenty years ago, when the cartilage was torn as the result of an injury, it was not uncommon for the surgeon to remove the entire cartilage. Now, with the perfection of arthroscopic surgery (a less invasive technique), surgeons are able to remove the torn part of the meniscus and save the remaining part of the cartilage to perform at least part of its original function. The meniscus has a poor blood supply; therefore, if a portion of it is torn, it will not heal the way other parts of the body such as muscles or ligaments heal.

Due to the positional aspect of the mechanism of injury to the cartilage, there is virtually no way to prevent this injury. Maintaining strength in the quadriceps muscles (muscles in the front of the thigh) and the hamstring muscles (muscles in the back of the thigh) will add strength and stability to the knee joint and lessen the chances of injury to the knee, but, given the right amount of force or a trauma causing rotation of the knee, the meniscus is still very much at risk.

Symptoms of a torn meniscus include unexplained swelling, clicking, locking, and the sensation of the knee "giving way." Descending a staircase can be very difficult and dangerous because of the "giving way" factor associated with the torn meniscus.

Once a diagnosis of torn meniscus is made and verified by a diagnostic MRI, the only treatment for someone who wishes to remain active is surgery to remove the damaged part of the meniscus. The surgery is relatively uneventful and can even be done on an outpatient basis, but the key to successful return is the rehabilitation. The period of rehabilitation involves strengthening the quadriceps and hamstrings to provide better secondary stabilization of the knee joint. The strength of these muscles will continue to be of great importance to the individual for as long as he/she wishes to be able to use the knee in activities of daily living without pain. For the active athlete, the great advance of arthroscopic surgery for a meniscal tear is that the period of being withheld from activity is relatively short. Highly conditioned athletes with excellent muscle tone in the quadriceps and hamstrings has been able to return to contact sports in as little as 1–2 weeks with little or no effect on the player's function.

The meniscus may also be injured in combination with other structures, such as a sprain of a ligament. The difference in recovery time following one of these combination injuries is a greater amount of lost playing time while the ligament heals.

The **hamstrings** are the large muscles in the back of the thigh. These muscles are very important in baseball because of their dynamic nature. It is the contraction of these muscles that enable the player to go from a standing start to full speed in a matter of seconds. This explosive stop-start running pattern can often cause a strain (tearing) of the hamstring muscles or their tendons. The mechanism of injury is often the overstretching of the muscles, causing either minor tearing or a complete rupture of the muscle or its tendinous attachment. This injury most commonly occurs in explosive situations where a player goes from rest to maximum exertion, such as the batter running to first base, a player attempting to steal a base, or an outfielder chasing a sharply hit line drive.

Hamstring strains often occur at the beginning of an activity, primarily due to improper warm-up, or in the late innings of a game when fatigue of the muscle can be a contributing factor. If these muscles are not properly evaluated or diagnosed and do not receive proper treatment, a buildup of inflexible scar tissue may form causing the hamstrings to be more prone to re-injury.

Prevention of hamstring injuries begins with the conditioning program. It is very important not to let the ratio of quadriceps (muscles in the front of the thigh) to hamstring strength become too great. Although the quadriceps are always going to be stronger, allowing the ratio to become too great will create a muscle imbalance that will put the hamstrings at a greater risk for injury. A good weight-training program must include both quadriceps and hamstring strengthening. The second part of the continuing conditioning program for the hamstring muscles is proper flexibility training. Obviously, the use of creatine supplements places additional risks on the muscle for injury, usually due to increased skeletal muscle compartment pressure. Unless the creatine supplement user is superhydrated (far beyond the perceived need for fluids triggered by the thirst reflex), hamstring muscle dysfunction and injury can occur.

Treatment of hamstrings will involve rest, ice, range-of-motion exercises, and exercises to strengthen the muscles. It is extremely important that the athlete has full, pain-free range of motion of the hamstrings and be able to run both forward and backward without limping before he is allowed to return to activity. If these prevention and treatment steps are carefully followed, the hamstring strain will not become chronic and the buildup of scar tissue will be minimized. Recovery from a hamstring strain depends almost entirely on the severity of the injury and the physical condition of the athlete prior to injury. Even after a return, due to the scarring and changes within the muscle, the player becomes much more susceptible to future hamstring injuries and can often lose some speed and flexibility due to the scarring and changes within the muscle.

The **calcaneal tendon,** commonly known as the Achilles tendon, is subject to strain in baseball during such activities as running across first base and foot-first slides. The calcaneal tendon, which aids in such activities as running and jumping, is the prime flexor of the foot. The mechanism of injury for this structure is what is normally termed "forced extension of the foot," where the toes bend back in the direction of your shin.

Tendon and ligament strains are classified by severity as Grades I, II, or III. To better understand this system, picture a climbing rope. If the rope is slightly frayed, but suffers no loss of function that would be the equivalent of a Grade I strain. If the rope were cut less than half of its diameter, it would lose some of its function and would be the equivalent of a Grade II strain. If the rope were cut more than half of its diameter, it would lose most or all of its function and would be the equivalent of a Grade III strain. Grade I strains of the calcaneal tendon will present mild pain, little or no swelling, and no loss of function. Grade II strains of this structure will present moderate pain, swelling, and some loss of function. Grade III strains will be accompanied by severe pain, swelling, and observable loss of function.

Evaluation of a calcaneal tendon injury is fairly easy using the Thompson Test. To perform this test, the athlete is placed facedown, and the examiner lifts the lower leg. The examiner then squeezes the calf muscle. If the foot points downward as a result of the squeeze, the calcaneal tendon is intact and functional. If the foot fails to point, the integrity of the calcaneal tendon has been disrupted. One should always examine the noninjured limb first, because this will serve as a point of reference for what is normal for this individual. If the calcaneal tendon is significantly torn, there is little alternative for the active athlete to surgical repair. Grade I and II strains usually respond well to treatment and rest. To actively prevent a calcaneal tendon strain, the athlete has to stretch the tendon. Depending on the severity of the injury, the timeline for return is anywhere from one week to six months. Surgical re-attachment is usually successful, but most players will lose some spring and explosion, so players who rely on speed as a major part of their game will be more affected by such injury, while players like Edgar Martinez see little change in their effectiveness.

Applying the Lessons

Looking both back to 2002 and ahead to 2003, I think we can see many injuries that could be described as inevitable and only a few that were truly totally unexpected. While there is no way to predict the occurrence of traumatic injuries, it is possible to predict the effect on performance over time in the case of chronic injuries.

Two outfielders, J. D. Drew and Ken Griffey, make excellent examples of how the chronic nature of an injury can impact a career. Both were young phenoms who are now too old to get by on mere athletic talent, and are seeing their talent and performance sucked away by the injury vampire. Drew played the entire 2002 season while suffering with patellar tendonitis, an injury Cardinals fans should be all too familiar with. Patellar tendonitis ended the career of Mark McGwire, but after surgery and the removal of necrotic (dead) tissue in his knee, Drew should be able to return at some point in the 2003 season. Drew was often compared to Mickey Mantle early in his career; like Mantle, he will need to overcome chronic leg problems to reach his potential. Looking at comparable injuries in the database, it is likely that Drew will be able to re-establish himself as a solid corner outfielder, perhaps relying less on speed while developing more power.

For Griffey, the chronic knee and hamstring problems have affected him more than any other superstar of the modern era. His insistence on playing center contributes to the persistent problem, and there are continued whispers that Griffey, having reached the pinnacle of the sport on natural talent, has neither the work ethic nor self-awareness to keep himself in peak physical condition. By playing in the field, particularly center, Griffey makes it more likely that he will re-injure a hamstring that is now almost as much scar as muscle. A move to first base or at least a corner outfield slot would be advisable, but again, Griffey seems unlikely to make such a move. While Griffey still retains many of the tools that made him a star, he is following a career path that will lead him out of the game much earlier than many expected, and is unlikely to play in many more than 120 games in any given season from here on out.

When traumatic injuries occur, there are several factors that need to be taken into account in assessing the chances of players coming back 100 percent. For example, both B. J. Surhoff and Alex Escobar suffered virtually the exact same injury (a ruptured ACL) last season. Sometimes observers automatically jump to the conclusion that the younger and

better athlete has the better shot at returning to the same level. Certainly, youth and athleticism are advantages. But a player like Surhoff has far more experience at keeping himself in peak condition in order to maintain his hold on a major league job. Sometimes the player who has learned to work hard to keep himself in shape has an advantage in making the adjustments necessary to come back from this sort of injury over a younger player who has been relying more on his natural athletic abilities. So it's really necessary to look at the entire situation in making any kind of assessment on how individual players will recover from these traumatic injuries.

The ugliest injuries of the season happened in Milwaukee, where the Brewers lost not one, but two players to impact-based ankle injuries. Geoff Jenkins was by far the more dramatic, with a dislocation, but Alex Sanchez's injury will have the larger long-term effect on his career. Jenkins should follow the path of Moises Alou and Jason Kendall in returning to baseball around six months post-injury. Since Jenkins's game did not rely on foot speed, he should adjust quickly to any minor loss of mobility. Sanchez, on the other hand, relied almost entirely on his speed, both in the field and at bat. While he should be able to return, the loss of speed he is likely to face may make the difference between his being a tolerable major leaguer and a forgotten Triple-A player.

Pitchers with back injuries should always raise a red flag, and both Kevin Brown and Shane Reynolds should have two or three red flags flapping in the breeze. Brown's back injury did help his injured elbow by enforcing rest. Unfortunately, his attempted comeback well ahead of any reasonable timetable for recovering, showed that the Dodgers are unable to control Brown's almost-suicidal (in career terms) drive to play. While it may be inspiring to see someone so willing to play through pain, allowing your biggest on-field investment to risk his future when there is nothing on the line isn't just futile, it's stupid. While the injuries Brown and Reynolds had were not identical, they are similar, and allow a good point for comparison. The Dodgers allowed Brown to come back because they believed they had a shot late in the season and had no replacements ready within the organization. The Astros, on the other hand, played comparatively poorly all season, and had a wealth of arms that they were willing and able to plug into Reynolds's starting slot. Reynolds is a free agent, but due to the quick surgery and extended rehab, a team might find him to be a bargain. Although Brown is clearly the better pitcher, he's also become the bigger risk.

Shoulder injuries are becoming the most dreaded injuries for pitchers. Where elbow problems, such as bone spurs or even ligament ruptures, can be repaired in "easy" and predictable fashion, injuries such as torn labrums and rotator cuffs are much more difficult to predict. Oddly, injuries to pitchers seem to happen in packs. Several years ago, it seemed every Braves pitcher was facing Tommy John surgery. For the last two years, the Mariners and Blue Jays have had epidemics of injuries. At the major league level, the Yankees have had their most important pitchers both dealing with arm injuries. Mariano Rivera was publicly stalked over the last half of the season as he attempted to return from what is now known to be a torn rotator cuff. His struggles show the wear he has put on that shoulder and the way the Yanks constructed their bullpen in the previous winter gives many the idea that the Yanks saw the injury coming. In their rotation, the Yankees expected dings and missed starts from their older pitchers (Clemens, Wells, and Hernandez), but the elbow injury to Andy Pettitte had the greatest impact to the team and caused them to deal for Jeff Weaver. Pettitte has probably pitched a significant portion of his career with an elbow that would be considered less than healthy medically, but that is also true of many other pitchers, some of whom will pitch effectively for years. Pettitte was able to return from similar struggles several years ago, and has never been significantly overused. In Rivera's case, the outlook is a bit more worrisome. He was not able to overcome the injury and return effectively, yet there was no surgery to correct the problem. While it is possible to rehabilitate an injury without surgical intervention—Pedro Martinez comes to mind—it is a red flag, especially for someone with the mechanical problems Rivera has.

While it is impossible in this format to cover all the players that I feel are at an increased risk of losing performance due to injury, here are some "quick hits" on players that could have the most impact:

Matt Lawton: Out until the All-Star break after having his shoulder not only misdiagnosed, but mistreated, at least according to Lawton's agent. Lawton will probably have a 2003 very similar to his injury-plagued 2002.

Juan Gonzalez: The type of thumb injury that ended Gonzalez's season is a type likely to recur. While rest will help, it will likely force Buck Showalter to spot him more often, cutting down on his plate appearances and overall value.

Ivan Rodriguez: Pudge's injuries may help him much in the way that injuries rejuvenated the career of Carlton Fisk. He's at an age where most catchers begin to feel the toll of the position, but in essence, he's had a year off over the last couple of seasons. His back cleared up when he lost weight, and it appeared to really jar him when he initially suffered the injury. I saw him shortly after and he was in great shape. While his arm doesn't have the same value it once did and he's always been overvalued, Rodriguez shouldn't be much of an injury concern next year. That said, catchers are always more likely to have unexpected injuries, as Ivan did a few years back when Mo Vaughn broke his thumb.

Edgardo Alfonzo: Back injuries are always likely to recur, but Alfonzo appeared to find himself. He's probably never going to regain the mobility and flexibility to play up the middle, but Alfonzo is still much better than David Bell. Even when GMs do take injury into account, they often overemphasize the negatives.

Scott Rolen: His shoulder injury may have ruined the Cards' postseason, but Rolen should have no problems with it going forward. His back is a bit of a concern, but the Cards felt that he would be fine away from the cement of the Vet, signing him to a long-term deal after a full team physical.

Bernie Williams: Ideally, Bernie could move to an outfield corner and spare his deteriorating shoulders and legs. Signing Godzilla could allow Bernie to do this, but the Yanks seem to like Bernie out near the monuments for some reason. Williams is the type of player that will slowly erode from great to good, much as Paul O'Neill did.

Barry Larkin: Fans are cheering his routine plays, which speak to the brilliance of his earlier career and the capacity for unconditional love from Cincinnati fans. Of his many injuries, the hamstring problems are the most serious, but Larkin is simply aging beyond his ability to play his position, and doesn't seem to have the skills to move to another and retain any value.

Joe Mays: His surgery came late, after coming back to help his team head into the playoffs. It's unclear how much damage is in the shoulder or how much he was hurt by the comeback, if at all. The Twins have had slightly more medical problems ever since firing longtime trainer Dick Martin.

Robb Nen: Nen was handled well through the playoffs, but this is a specialty of Stan Conte. Shoulder surgery is never a great thing, but between Conte and Alou, Nen should be in the same situation he was last year—used sparingly and watched closely.

Edgar Martinez: His age is a concern, but if Edgar was going to hurt anything, it would be his legs. He was robbed of any speed by a knee injury years ago, but remains a dangerous hitter. There's no reason to expect that he won't continue to be one for another year. His surgery was a very new procedure, and it's unclear if the surgery will have any long-term impact one way or another.

Roger Clemens: Clemens is following the Nolan Ryan career path, assuming it's staked out well enough for someone else to follow it. Clemens is pitching well at an age most veteran pitchers are looking into careers in television or coaching, but is getting to a point where he'll need special attention and/or extended rest between starts. With their pitching depth, the Yankees remain the perfect situation for him. When Clemens breaks down, it will start with his legs.

Troy Glaus: Surgery to remove a nerve sounds much more serious than it actually is. I'm told Glaus isn't as stiff at third as he looked in the World Series, but mobility isn't a core skill for this masher. I still think he'll move across the diamond soon, a la Jim Thome.

A. J. Burnett: One of the oddest injuries of the year was also greatly misunderstood. In essence, Burnett had a freak occurrence in his elbow that makes him no more or less likely to be injured. In fact, the time away from Torborg's overuse may have helped. Don't let rumors or innuendo keep you away from a dominant pitcher.

Mark Prior: People really panicked when Prior had high pitch counts. They shouldn't have, but that's another discussion. His hamstring gave the Cubs an excuse to shelve him at the end of a lost season. Prior could be the next Clemens and has no worries—arm or hamstring—coming into the 2003 season.

Chan Ho Park: Park had hamstring problems, and in pitchers, this is seldom a long-term concern. Most of the blame was dropped on former pitching coach Oscar Acosta, and Orel Hershiser put Park back on his prior conditioning program. It seemed to work, and there's no medical reason Park shouldn't pitch well, though there are plenty of other reasons.

There are also six pitchers not on this list that I am watching very closely due to a combination of age, usage patterns, loss of velocity over the season, and biomechanical inefficiencies. It is a very inexact science to predict injury—note that Randy Johnson and Livan Hernandez should be on about their last legs by many measures—but I am concerned about Roy Oswalt, Jason Jennings, C. C. Sabathia, Damian Moss, and Francisco Rodriguez for the upcoming season. While some will likely have no problems at all, each of these pitchers has key indicators for a traumatic breakdown.

Will Carroll is the editor of "Under the Knife," a recurring column on Baseball Prospectus focused on baseball injuries. Called "remarkable" by Peter Gammons and "the best" by Lee Sinins, UTK has succeeded in bringing sports medicine to the attention of the baseball fan.

Dr. William Carroll is professor of Human Performance and Exercise Science and director of the Athletic Training Education Program at the University of Mobile and serves on the UTK Medical Advisory Board.

The New Combined Bargaining Agreement

by Doug Pappas

The issues that would dominate negotiations for the ninth collective bargaining agreement (CBA) between Major League Baseball (MLB) and the Major League Baseball Players Association (MLBPA) were apparent before the ink was dry on the eighth CBA. That agreement, signed in November 1996, gave the owners greater revenue sharing and a luxury tax—but not the one thing they wanted most, meaningful restraints on player salaries. MLB would try again in 2002.

Like all baseball labor negotiations since 1975, when arbitrator Peter Seitz limited the reserve clause to one year, the 1993–96 talks centered on MLB's demands for givebacks from the MLBPA. Having tried and failed to obtain a hard salary cap, the owners turned to indirect ways to reduce spending by the wealthiest teams, in the form of greater revenue sharing and a "luxury tax" on the highest-payroll clubs.

When fully implemented, the 1996 CBA provided for all teams to contribute 20% of their local revenue, net of stadium expenses, into a common pool. Three-fourths of the money in the pool was then divided equally among all the clubs, with the last quarter distributed proportionally among the low-revenue franchises. This formula created a perverse incentive when several owners, notably Minnesota's Carl Pohlad, realized that they could make more money by doing nothing to promote their product and fielding the cheapest possible team than by investing in marketing and better players.

The luxury tax was adopted as a self-limiting experiment, applicable only to the 1997 through 1999 seasons. In theory the luxury tax would check high-spending clubs by imposing a 35% tax (34% in 1999) on clubs whose payrolls exceeded $51 million in 1997, $55 million in 1998, or $58.9 million in 1999. But the effect of the tax was greatly weakened by two modifications demanded by the MLBPA: It was limited to the five highest-payroll clubs, and as salaries rose, the tax threshold became the midpoint between the fifth and sixth highest payrolls.

These limitations soon came into play. According to MLB's own financial disclosures, MLB's revenue doubled between 1996 and 2001, and owners with more money to spend invested it in their players. When the CBA was signed in 1996, the average club took in $63.4 million and only three teams paid their players more than $50 million. Three years later, the average club grossed $92 million and nine payrolls topped $70 million.

As a result, by 1998, the luxury tax threshold was $15.5 million above the figure set by the CBA, which meant that each of the five highest-paying clubs was saving more than $5 million in luxury tax. From 1997 to 1999, the luxury tax collected just $30 million, two-thirds from the Orioles and Yankees, before vanishing altogether in 2000. Thus, as the owners looked toward the next negotiations, one of their goals was to reinstate the luxury tax on a permanent basis, at a higher rate and with fewer loopholes.

Their other main goal was greater revenue sharing. This had been their most contentious issue in 1993–94, when large-, middle-, and small-market clubs fought one another for more than a year over the proper formula, but the subsequent consolidation of authority behind commissioner Bud Selig effectively resolved this dispute.

Selig's Milwaukee Brewers played in MLB's smallest market. The commissioner needed little persuading that his own club's pathetic performance—the Brewers last made the playoffs in 1982, and last finished above .500 in 1992—was caused by a revenue imbalance. After all, the alternative explanation was that he and his daughter had mismanaged the club for two decades. As the 2001–02 labor talks continued, Selig's incessant "small markets can't compete" rhetoric led to much unintentional hilarity as he resolutely refused to accept that the Athletics and Twins could win their divisions despite payrolls $10 million below the Brewers'. So long as Bud Selig controlled the owners' negotiating team, increased revenue sharing and a stronger luxury tax would be among MLB's principal goals.

The 1996 CBA gave the owners a powerful new tool for attaining these goals. Although all previous CBAs had expired on December 31, the 1996 CBA provided that it would expire on October 31 (or the last day of the World Series, if later). The importance of this seemingly innocuous change, barely mentioned in press accounts of the time, becomes clear when one considers the interaction of labor law and the baseball calendar.

American labor law provides that after a collective bargaining agreement expires, the parties to the expired agreement continue to operate under its terms until one of four things happens: the workers strike, management locks them out, the parties agree on a new CBA, or the parties bargain to an impasse. If the parties bargain to an impasse, management can impose the terms of its most recent offer, forcing the workers either to strike or to operate under management's terms until a new agreement is reached. An "impasse, then imposition" strategy would give the owners considerable leverage, but only if they could negotiate to an impasse before the players could strike.

Leverage in baseball negotiations is determined by the calendar. Early in the year it belongs to the owners, who can declare a signing freeze or lock out the players at little or no cost to themselves. The players' leverage grows as the regular season progresses, peaking in September, when a strike would threaten MLB's postseason TV money. After the World Series, the owners immediately regain the upper hand going into November and December, the months in which players file for free agency and clubs must tender the next season's contracts.

Thus by advancing the expiration date of the CBA from December 31 to before the date when players could file for free agency, the owners gained the opportunity to force a showdown with the players on their terms. If MLB could negotiate to an impasse before the old CBA expired, they could force the MLBPA to choose between two unpalatable alternatives: Operate under the terms of the owners' proposal during the 2001–02 off-season, or make the best deal possible under the circumstances. Either way, the owners would likely end up with more favorable terms than if they let the CBA expire.

First the owners needed to formulate a proposal—ideally, one which could be sold to the players, and the public, as something more than their own self-interested pleading. Toward this end commissioner Selig appointed a "Blue Ribbon Panel on Baseball Economics," charged with examining "the question of whether Baseball's current economic system has created a problem of competitive balance in the game."

A glance at the Blue Ribbon Panel's membership made clear that the answer to this question was a foregone conclusion. The panel consisted of 12 baseball insiders and four "independent members," all of whom had long-standing ties to MLB. It had no representatives from the MLBPA and no truly independent members. Nor was there much doubt that the Blue Ribbon Panel would recommend "solving" the "problem" through exactly the steps favored by the commissioner. Indeed, although Selig denied any role in the panel's work, Murray Chass of the *New York Times* reported that "three people with close ties to management said that Selig reviewed various drafts of the report and sent it back for stiffer recommendations."

Those recommendations, issued amidst great fanfare in July 2000, included:

- The sharing of 40 to 50% of local revenues, up from 20% under the old CBA;
- A 50% "competitive balance tax" on all payrolls above $84 million, with all clubs "encouraged" (but not required) to maintain a minimum payroll of $40 million; and
- Draft modifications intended to reduce wealthy teams' advantage, such as requiring foreign players to go through the draft, eliminating compensation picks, limiting draftees' ability to hold out or re-enter the draft another year, giving more picks to bad teams, and allowing clubs to trade draft picks.

Significantly, the Blue Ribbon Panel did not propose a salary cap. This inflammatory demand, which had triggered the 1994–95 strike, was off the table even before negotiations began. Nor did the panel endorse some owners' calls for contraction of two or more clubs, instead asserting that the problem of teams in weak markets could be addressed through "strategic franchise relocation" to better markets.

Sure enough, when talks about a new CBA began, quietly and informally, in March 2001, the owners focused on the need for greater revenue sharing, a meaningful luxury tax, and a worldwide amateur draft. Between March and June 2001, Paul Beeston, MLB's president and chief operating officer, and chief labor lawyer Rob Manfred met two dozen times with Donald Fehr and Gene Orza of the MLBPA. Selig abruptly ended these talks in late June, apparently afraid that Beeston was giving away too much to the players.

As Beeston was a moderate on labor issues who enjoyed a good working relationship with the MLBPA, the collapse of these unpublicized talks did not bode well for subsequent negotiations. But there were no further negotiations in 2001. The owners had become distracted by the "need" to contract by two teams before the 2002 season. The solution rejected by the Blue Ribbon Panel just one year before was now an obsession.

MLB's farcical attempt to contract the Twins and Expos infuriated the players, the public, and Congress. It ultimately led to a three-team game of musical owners involving the Expos, Marlins, and Red Sox, and the embarrassing disclosure that Selig himself had flagrantly violated MLB's conflict of interest rules by accepting an undisclosed loan from Twins owner Carl Pohlad. And most importantly for the labor talks, it cost the owners their bargaining leverage with the MLBPA.

When the CBA expired after the 2001 World Series, the owners were in no position to declare an impasse. Not only had they themselves broken off talks five months before, but the owners admitted that even if they could unilaterally eliminate franchises, they still had to bargain with the MLBPA over the effects of contraction, such as the dispersal of players on the affected teams. The MLBPA's grievance over contraction further complicated matters by distracting both sides' labor lawyers. The 2001–02 off-season passed with no luxury tax and no changes in the owners' revenue-sharing formula, and on Opening Day 2002, player salaries were 5.2% higher than the year before.

The multi-front battles over contraction left MLB in no condition to pick a fight with the players. When the labor talks resumed on January 9, 2002, Selig pledged that the owners would not lock out the players if an agreement was not reached before spring training camps opened. Noting that Selig's promise did not extend to the 2002–03 off-season, the MLBPA declined to make a similar no-strike pledge.

MLB's opening offer closely tracked the Blue Ribbon Panel report. Selig proposed a worldwide draft, 50% sharing of local revenues, and a 50% luxury tax on the amounts of payrolls above $98 million. This luxury tax threshold was $14 million higher than proposed by the Blue Ribbon Panel in 2000, but would have had a comparable effect when payroll increases since 2000 were taken into account.

For the MLBPA, changes in the amateur draft were easy to accept. The union doesn't represent draftees, and most of the money saved by the owners would likely flow back to the players in the form of higher salaries. The MLBPA also had no philosophical objection to increased revenue sharing. The luxury tax was another matter; as Donald Fehr explained, "Our view is that players aren't luxuries." In addition, the players claimed that the combination of a 50% luxury tax on high payrolls and 50% local revenue sharing would turn the luxury tax threshold into a de facto salary cap.

The parties also differed over the distribution of revenue sharing money. The 1996 CBA adopted a "split pool" system in which 75% of the money paid into the common pool was divided equally among all the clubs and the remaining 25% was distributed unequally among the clubs with below-average revenue, with the lowest-revenue franchises receiving the most. The split-pool system funneled the most money to the neediest teams—but with no requirement that the recipients reinvest it in their clubs, it also encouraged them to turn revenue sharing into a straight subsidy by pocketing the money. The two teams targeted for contraction were the worst offenders: In 2000, the Twins' revenue sharing receipts exceeded their major league payroll by $5 million, while in 2001 the Expos received $28.5 million in revenue sharing, but less than $10 million from all local revenue sources combined.

With George Steinbrenner particularly critical of such abuses, the owners proposed eliminating the split-pool system in favor of a "straight pool" distribution, with all clubs receiving an equal amount from the revenue sharing pool. But this, in turn, required a much higher level of revenue sharing to redistribute the same amount of money. Although the owners' proposal called for a 150% increase in revenue sharing, from 20% to 50%, their own calculations showed

that if the pool were redistributed on a straight-pool basis, the amount of shared revenue would increase by just 52%, from $166 million to $253 million. The players, who were then suggesting 22.5% revenue sharing with split-pool distribution, could have matched this effect by increasing their proposed percentage to 31%.

The owners' straight-pool formula furthered their agenda in another way, though not one they cared to discuss openly. An economically rational club will spend additional money on players only to the extent it anticipates getting that money back in the form of increased revenue. Since revenue sharing compels the club to turn over a certain percentage of this increase to its competitors, it's the functional equivalent of a tax on local revenues. The higher the tax/revenue sharing rate goes, the lower the payoff for spending more money on players, and the less likely that the money will be spent. Thus the straight-pool formula was better for the owners precisely *because* its inefficiency required a higher percentage of shared revenues to transfer the desired amount.

By Opening Day, the course the negotiations would take was clear. Unlike in 1994, the owners and players were arguing over details, not pursuing wholly inconsistent visions of the future, so a deal was attainable. The players would control the timing of the inevitable showdown. Content to negotiate indefinitely while operating under the terms of the 1996 CBA, they would strike rather than allow the owners to declare an impasse or impose a signing freeze after the season. In both 1985 and 1994, the MLBPA had set a mid-August strike date to give the parties time to reach agreement without endangering the postseason. After this strategy failed so spectacularly in 1994, some hard-line players favored striking the day after the close of the 2002 regular season: the baseball equivalent of a poker player opening with the maximum bet and daring his opponents to call.

Either way, as of April the strike date was months away, so neither side had any pressing reason to yield on the key issues. Instead MLB and the MLBPA occupied themselves with lesser issues, and the owners added the kind of pie-in-the-sky demands made largely so their eventual withdrawal could be hailed as a "concession." These included a $100 million fund to be disbursed at the commissioner's sole discretion; the right to release players after exchanging arbitration figures; and a central "information bank" in the commissioner's office to which all offers to free agents would be reported, a virtual invitation to collusion. The parties moved incrementally closer on revenue sharing and swapped proposals regarding the draft, while agreeing to postpone discussion of the luxury tax until later in the process.

In June, a once-minor issue assumed much greater significance. Early in the talks, MLB had asked the players to accept random drug testing for steroids, but never pressed the point until public outcry over admissions of steroid use by former MVPs Jose Canseco and Ken Caminiti forced the issue to the center of the negotiating table. Neither side wanted it there. Though many players wanted to clear their names against suspicions of steroid use, the MLBPA had historically opposed random testing, while MLB's interests (like those of the NFL) were best served through impressive-sounding tests that weren't actually likely to catch violators. Indeed, the testing plan eventually adopted was immediately ridiculed as a sham by drug testing authorities in amateur sports.

After passing up several opportunities to set a strike date, the MLBPA's executive board voted on August 16 to walk out if no agreement had been reached by August 30. Not coincidentally, the vote was taken shortly after the negotiators focused for the first time on the contours of a luxury tax. They remained far apart on the details, though: under the MLBPA's August 16 proposal, the Yankees would owe just over $20 million over the duration of the CBA if they maintained their payroll at its 2002 level, while under MLB's plan, they would pay a tax of more than $122 million.

The negotiators' differences gradually narrowed. First MLB and the MLBPA agreed to appoint a committee to study the draft, then they shook hands on a drug testing program. The major holdup remained the luxury tax. As the strike deadline approached, former commissioner Fay Vincent opined that the owners' bankers wouldn't let them hold out for long, while Padres owner John Moores vowed to cancel the 2002 and 2003 seasons if necessary "for us to get a deal that brings sanity back to the game." The *New York Times* estimated that a season-ending strike would cost the owners and players a collective $1 billion.

As the parties moved incrementally closer on the luxury tax, dozens of reporters spent the night of August 29 camped outside the MLB and MLBPA offices on Park Avenue, watching negotiators shuttle back and forth. A deal was announced less than two hours before the first game would have been affected. The last sticking point was whether the new CBA would expire on October 31 or December 31: The parties compromised on December 19, 2006, the last day before club owners must tender contracts for the 2007 season, and fans across America reaffirmed plans to spend their Labor Day weekend at the ballpark of their choice.

Here are the key terms of the new CBA:

Duration: Five years, 2002–2006. Agreement is retroactive to start of 2002 season and expires December 19, 2006.

Local Revenue Sharing: Rises from 20% under the 1996–2001 CBA to 34%, net of ballpark expenses. Revenue sharing money divided equally among all teams, using the owners' straight-pool formula. The memorandum of understanding between the players and owners provides that

"each club shall use its revenue-sharing payments to improve its performance on the field." The document doesn't define this standard and says only that the commissioner "has the authority to enforce this provision."

Central Fund Revenue Sharing: $72.2 million (based on 2001 revenue figures) taken from clubs which are net payers in the local revenue sharing plan and given to those who are net receivers. This money is paid and disbursed in proportion to a club's distance from the average. Central fund revenue sharing is intended to ensure that the desired amount of revenue will be transferred in each season, regardless of fluctuations in the distribution of local revenues. It will be phased in at the 60% level in 2003, 80% in 2004, and 100% in 2005 and 2006.

Discretionary Fund: $10 million from central fund to be placed within the commissioner's control, to be allocated at his discretion.

Luxury Tax Threshold: No luxury tax in 2002; thresholds of $117 million in 2003, $120.5 million in 2004, $128 million in 2005, $136.5 million in 2006. Luxury tax expires on the final day of the 2006 season, so if the parties play under the terms of the expired agreement in 2007, there will be no luxury tax. For luxury tax purposes, payrolls are defined to include salaries plus earned bonuses for all players on the 40-man roster, plus a fixed amount per team in benefits and related expenses. All multiyear contracts are valued at their average annual value regardless of the actual payout in a specific season.

Luxury Tax Rates:

2002: No tax

2003: 17.5%

2004: 22.5% for first-time payers, 30% for second-time payers

2005: 22.5% for first-timers, 30% for second-timers, 40% for third-timers

2006: No tax for first-timers; 30% for second-timers; 40% for third- and fourth-timers.

Luxury tax money to be used for player benefits, an industry growth fund, or player development in countries lacking organized high school baseball.

Minimum Salary: $300,000 in 2003 and 2004, with two-year cost of living adjustment in 2005 and one-year COLA in 2006. As of 2003, minor leaguers on split contracts must receive at least $50,000/year while in the minors, up from $40,500 under previous CBA.

Amateur Draft: Rules for a proposed worldwide draft to be established by a jointly appointed committee. Committee will decide whether international players will be included and whether clubs will be allowed to trade draft picks, and will determine the number of rounds. Although early reports said that compensation picks for free agent signings had been eliminated, this issue was ultimately thrown into the mix for the committee, with the compensation formula left intact for the 2002–03 off-season.

Contraction: Clubs agree to maintain 30 teams through 2006. They may elect to eliminate two teams for the 2007 season; if they do, they must notify the players by July 1, 2006. Players agree that if they do, they will not argue before the NLRB that contraction is a mandatory subject of collective bargaining. If owners elect to contract in 2007, their July 1, 2006, notice does not have to tell the players which teams will be contracted.

Discipline: Same as current system: suspended players to receive full salary.

Salary arbitration: Same as under prior CBA.

Club debt: Cannot exceed 10 times EBIDTA (earnings before interest, depreciation, taxes and amortization), except that clubs which have moved into new parks within the past 10 years can have debt equal to 15 times EBIDTA. Three-year grace period, at the end of which the commissioner must choose between this debt limitation formula and the old "60/40" rule. "Debt" defined to exclude money owed to players on long-term contracts.

Interleague play: Expressly reauthorized for the duration of the CBA.

Drug testing: Random testing of all players for illegal steroids in 2003. Half of the players will be tested once during spring training, the other half once during the regular season. If 5% of players test positive, mandatory random testing during the next two seasons; if 2.5% or fewer test positive in consecutive years, mandatory random testing ceases, replaced by survey testing. The first time a player tests positive, he is placed in a treatment program; the second through fifth positive tests bring suspensions of 15 days, 25 days, 50 days and one year, all without pay. No random testing for other illegal drugs, or for legal drugs such as androstenedione. Testing for reasonable cause at any time, with "reasonable cause" determined by a joint labor-management committee.

Penalties for other drug offenses: Players convicted of possessing hard drugs face suspensions of 15–30 days for a first offense, 30–90 days for a second, with an automatic one-year suspension for a third conviction, a two-year suspension for a fourth. Players convicted of selling or distributing hard drugs will be suspended 60–90 days and fined $100,000 for a first offense, suspended two years for a second offense. Marijuana use and possession is punishable by fines, but no suspensions. These penalties don't apply to players who come forward and seek treatment, who receive their full salary for the first 30 days of treatment, half salary for the next 30 days.

Benefits: Clubs' contribution increased from $70 million in 2002 to $114–$115 million.

Expense allowances: Annual cost of living increases for spring training, meal, and other expense allowances.

Injury rehabilitation: Players with less than five years of major league service can be sent to a club's spring training facility for rehabilitation; however, each day starting with the 11th counts toward the maximum length for rehabilitation assignments (30 days for pitchers, 20 days for others).

Second opinions: Clubs will pay for players' transportation expenses if they seek a second medical opinion anywhere in the country. Formerly the country was divided into three regions; players paid for their own transportation if they went outside their region to seek the second opinion.

Contract tenders: All contract tenders to unsigned players on 40-man rosters will be made by the commissioner's office instead of by individual teams.

Waivers: Additional round of waivers added: current waiver period of Nov. 11–30th day of season is split in two, with the first period ending February 15 and the second beginning February 16.

So what effect will the new CBA have on player salaries and competitive balance? Ironically, the relatively uncontroversial increase in revenue sharing, which the owners could have won without a nasty, season-threatening confrontation, will do more for small-market teams than the luxury tax, which in its final form may as well be called the "Yankees tax."

Increasing the percentage of shared local revenue from 20% to 34% means that high-revenue clubs will pay much more into the common pool, while the switch from a split-pool to a straight-pool distribution plan will give more of this money to moderately low-revenue clubs, less to the Expos. In his September 6 column on ESPN.com, Jayson Stark ran the numbers: Based on 2001 revenues, the Yankees would pay an additional $16 million into the pool, with the Mariners contributing $10 million, the Mets $9 million, and the Red Sox $8 million. The biggest net gainers would be the Brewers (surprise!) and Pirates, each of whom would receive $5.9 million more than under the old formula, and the Athletics, who would get an extra $4.4 million.

Even with no luxury tax, the new revenue sharing formula would have driven down the payrolls of the highest-revenue teams. Not only will they have less money to spend, but the new formula also reduces their incentive to spend it. Whether their cutbacks will be offset by payroll increases on the part of low-revenue teams remains to be seen. At one point the owners proposed a minimum payroll requirement to force recipients to spend their money. The MLBPA rejected the idea; the players are as philosophically opposed to minimum payrolls as they are to maximum payrolls. Early signs are not promising: For every Carl Pohlad, who has boosted his budget to keep the young Twins together, there's a Carl Lindner, who won't increase the Reds' payroll even as the team prepares to open a new ballpark in 2003.

The owners, however, pinned their salary-reduction hopes on a stronger luxury tax. As previously noted, the luxury tax in the last CBA proved ineffectual. Because MLB's gross revenue doubled in five years, salaries and the tax threshold rose far higher than anticipated. The new CBA attempted to close these loopholes by adopting fixed annual tax thresholds, which could theoretically be paid by an unlimited number of teams.

If revenue and salaries were to increase at the same rate during the new CBA, the luxury tax could affect a dozen teams, many of which would owe eight-figure annual luxury tax bills. But there's good reason to believe that revenue won't rise so fast under the new CBA. Indeed, it's unlikely to rise fast enough for the luxury tax to affect anyone but the Yankees.

According to MLB's 2001 financial disclosures, 62% of industry revenue comes from two sources: "regular season game receipts" (ticket sales) and "other local operating revenue" (luxury boxes, premium seats, parking, advertising, and concessions). These sources of income will almost certainly grow at a much slower rate under the new CBA.

From 1996 to 2001, the years of the last CBA, attendance at major league games increased by about 20%. (It then fell about 6% in 2002, due in large part to the scheduling and marketing chaos caused by contraction and fans' fears of another work stoppage.) This modest growth was accompanied, however, by record ticket price increases. According to the annual "Fan Cost Index" survey conducted by *Team Marketing Report*, the cost of the average ticket to a major league game jumped 62% between 1996 and 2002, from $11.32 to $18.31. Such increases, running about three times the inflation rate, are highly unlikely to continue.

Moreover, during the last CBA attendance and other local revenue streams were boosted by a wave of new stadium construction. Seven clubs (Atlanta, Detroit, Houston, Milwaukee, Pittsburgh, San Francisco, and Seattle) opened new ballparks between 1997 and 2001. The 1998 expansion to Arizona and Tampa Bay, and the continued popularity of recently opened parks in Baltimore, Cleveland, Colorado, and Texas, also contributed mightily to MLB's coffers.

By contrast, between 2003 and 2006 only Cincinnati, Philadelphia, San Diego, and possibly St. Louis will move into new facilities. And as the Tigers, Brewers, and Pirates are learning to their sorrow, casual fans may visit a new ballpark once or twice, but they won't become regular patrons without a quality team to watch. Among the teams playing in parks opened since 1991, only Arizona, San Francisco, and Seattle—three of the four most successful teams in this group over the past two seasons—have avoided steep declines in attendance. The combination of fewer new parks, the erosion of the novelty factor at recently opened parks, and an economy considerably weaker than the late 1990s boom years should limit the growth of ticket and luxury box revenues during the new CBA.

Under the circumstances, MLB will be fortunate to grow half as quickly during the next CBA as it did under the last. This would translate to a 40% revenue increase over four years. If this growth were evenly distributed among the teams, and if salaries kept pace, eight teams would be affected by the luxury tax.

But this is too simplistic. Revenue growth won't be distributed equally. It will go primarily to the clubs whose fortunes suddenly improve, or who move into new parks (or new cities, in the case of the Expos). None of the eight highest-payroll clubs fall into either of these categories. In addition, all eight enjoyed well above-average revenues, which means that the new revenue sharing formula will cost them millions of dollars each year.

For 2003, the two clubs most likely to experience huge revenue jumps are the surprise world champion Anaheim Angels, whose 2002 payroll was $40 million below the 2003 luxury tax threshold, and the Cincinnati Reds, the new tenants of the Great American Ballpark, whose 2002 payroll was $55 million below the tax threshold. The luxury tax is irrelevant to them, and to the other 16 clubs who finished 2002 more than $34 million below the tax threshold. No rational spending plan could possibly boost their payrolls to a level affected by the luxury tax.

If the 2003 luxury tax had been in place for the 2002 season, only three teams would have paid the tax. A 17.5% tax on 2002 payrolls over $117 million would have cost the Los Angeles Dodgers $300,000, the Texas Rangers $2.5 million, and the New York Yankees $9.5 million. In addition to the millions the new revenue sharing formula will cost these clubs, a quirk of the luxury tax computation makes them unlikely to be counted as having raised their payrolls.

These and many other clubs signed many of their highest-paid players to back-loaded contracts, in which the player's salary rises over the course of the contract. But since the luxury tax formula values all multiyear contracts at their average annual value no matter how the money is distributed, even as the club's actual outlay for player salary increases, the value of these contracts will remain the same. Except for the Yankees, whose 2002 payroll for luxury tax purposes was $58 million over the threshold (and $45 million higher than anyone else's), no team need worry that the luxury tax will discourage them from making roster decisions on sound baseball principles.

"Sound baseball principles"... there's the catch. One of the first principles of sound baseball management, applicable to all teams regardless of their revenue, is not to waste money by paying top dollar for replacement-level performance. Well-run teams fill their benches with low-salaried reserves and their lineups with young, relatively inexpensive talent. Badly run teams can spend over $100 million without acquiring a pitching staff (Texas) or an outfield (New York

Mets). When Oakland can remain $51 million below the luxury tax threshold after winning 298 games over three seasons and locking up its three young starting pitchers through 2005, any club which blunders across that threshold through poor roster management should consider the payment a form of stupidity tax.

In the end, though, the greatest downward pressure on player salaries will come not from the CBA, but from advances in baseball management. The new generation of sabermetrically oriented general managers, led by Billy Beane of Oakland and including J. P. Ricciardi of Toronto and Theo Epstein of Boston, understands that by the time most players accrue enough service time to file for free agency, they're poor investments because their skills have already begun to fade. They know that perfectly adequate reserves and middle relievers are often available on the waiver wire or among six-year minor league free agents, and know how to interpret minor league statistics to separate true prospects from trade bait.

As more of these GMs are hired, and more Brady Andersons and Greg Vaughns are replaced by better players earning a tenth as much, the rate of increase in player salaries will slow. Well-run organizations don't need the threat of a luxury tax to appreciate moves which make the club both better and cheaper. Meanwhile, a badly run organization will continue to pay $5 million or more to the likes of Jeffrey Hammonds, Marquis Grissom, Mark Loretta, and Jaime Navarro, only to have its principal owner whine that its years of failure confirm that "small markets can't compete." The problem isn't small markets—it's small minds.

Top 40 Prospects

by Rany Jazayerli

The paradigm shifted this winter. The concept of the free cost of replacement-level talent finally reached the inner sanctum of baseball front offices everywhere. The idea of paying seven-figure salaries for guaranteed adequacy has evaporated and left behind a legacy of perfectly competent major league players settling for non-guaranteed contracts and non-roster invitations. Now that the tipping point in baseball's economic structure has been reached, it remains to be seen how the ripples of this sea change will affect the sport in other ways. Regarding the future of the minor leagues, it is clear that this brave new world is a great boon—and an equally great burden.

On the one hand, the mass efflux of non-star players onto the waiver wire and into the free agent market has opened job opportunities for dozens, if not hundreds, of qualified minor leaguers happy to do a veteran's job for a rookie's pay. Small-market teams are coming to the realization that while the cost of proven mediocrity is prohibitive, unproven mediocrity is available to any team willing to invest its priorities, if not its capital, in its minor league system. Prospects that otherwise might not get the opportunity to showcase their skills are suddenly favored over established major leaguers who haven't gotten the memo that the salary structure of the late 1990s and early 2000s is dead. The Royals, for instance, might enter the season with as many as eight rookies—none of them top prospects—on their roster, because they have correctly (if belatedly) recognized that even second-tier prospects can contribute to the win column as much as the veterans whose jobs they are taking, while making smaller contribution to the payroll.

Not so fast. The flip side of the coin is that, as the demand for veterans declines, so eventually will their contract demands. This is no across-the-board decline; the economics of supply and demand are keeping superstar salaries in the eight-figure range even while their somewhat less gifted—and far, far more replaceable—brethren see their salaries slashed in half or even more. This off-season, Jim Thome signed for over $14 million a year, which if not quite Delgado-like in its generosity, represented a marginal market correction. Meanwhile, Brad Fullmer, the very profile of the productive, proven hitter who took home multiyear, megamillion dollar contracts in previous years, was non-tendered by the Angels and re-signed for $1 million, barely a quarter of his 2002 salary.

How does this hurt the minor leagues? Simple: if you can sign a productive, proven, low-risk hitter on the open market for $1 million, what's the point in investing in your farm system to produce players who might, if they develop according to expectations, turn out to be as valuable as Brad Fullmer? In the short-term, opportunities might arise for youngsters while veterans with inflated expectations receive the market's cold shoulder. But eventually an equilibrium will be reached and middle-class veterans will come to accept their new role in baseball's economic structure on a reduced financial plane. And when that happens, just as the savings a team can collect from playing a rookie over a veteran will decline, so too will the incentive to gamble on the rookie. And just as we see in the NFL and NBA today, the ability to sift through the dustbin of freely available talent will become as important to an organization's long-term success as the ability to draft amateur players and develop them in the minor leagues.

Already, we have seen the Cardinals in recent years essentially abandon the idea of developing organizational talent, focusing instead on identifying and nurturing only their premium players—Rick Ankiel, J. D. Drew, Albert Pujols—using their Grade B prospects only as currency in trade for other established stars (Jim Edmonds, Scott Rolen), and filling out the rest of their roster through judicious use of the second-tier free agent market. This idea will only catch on in the new economic climate. Just as the game's salary structure becomes more and more stratified, with the superstars of the game earning a greater and greater fraction of their team's payrolls, so too may the development of minor leaguers become a less egalitarian process. Teams will focus all their efforts on developing superstars, players so extraordinary that not even arbitration will prevent them from being underpaid for at least their first six years, at the exclusion of less remarkable prospects who will only be let loose to the vagaries of free agency the minute they become arbitration-eligible.

The best illustration of this new paradigm is, as you might expect, the Yankees, who operate under the mantra that if you can't help us today, we're not going to wait for you to help us tomorrow. The Yankees see even their highest draft picks only as chits to acquire stars that other teams can't afford, whether it's Jeff Weaver (for a package that included 2001 first-rounder John-Ford Griffin and second-rounder Jason

Arnold) or Chuck Knoblauch (for a package that included 1996 first-rounder Eric Milton and 1994 first-rounder Brian Buchanan). Nick Johnson, the best player the Yankees have developed in the past five years, could have been on a plane to Montreal this winter as fast as Omar Minaya could say "Bartolo Colon." For George Steinbrenner, it's not enough to be a prospect who could be a superstar one day—it's only enough to be a prospect who can be a superstar *today*. Which is to say, a player who's not really a prospect at all, but rather an established major leaguer who, by simple accident of geography, hasn't actually played in the major leagues yet.

And when such a "prospect" comes along, get out of the way. A woman scorned hath no fury like Steinbrenner when he doesn't get what he wants. Ladies and gentlemen, I present to you Hideki Matsui and Jose Contreras, who were collectively guaranteed $53 million before they ever tried on a major league uniform.

It's a brave new world, all right. Which is why it's so comforting that for all the uncertainty regarding the future of the minor leagues, at least one thing hasn't changed at all. For the second straight year, the *Baseball Prospectus* Prospect of the Year plays third base for the Texas Rangers. That his identity has changed is testimony that the Rangers have one very difficult—if exceedingly pleasant—decision to make. Hank Blalock, our #1 prospect a year ago, may compare favorably to a young George Brett, the second-greatest third baseman of all time. Unfortunately for him, Mark Teixeira compares favorably to a young, switch-hitting Mike Schmidt, who happens to be the reason why Brett isn't the greatest third baseman of all time. A competition this fierce could be solved by a position change. But if the Rangers are paying attention to the new paradigm in baseball, they'll do what the Yankees would do—trade one of them for an emerging superstar whose very greatness has priced him out of his current team's future.

1.	Mark Teixeira		3B	Texas Rangers		Age 22
	AVG	OBP	SLG	EqA	Defense	
2002	.254	.327	.495	.271	3B: -6	

The short story on Teixeira is, to quote Joe Sheehan from his newsletter: "He's not very fast. His name is hard to spell. His feet touch the ground when he walks. That sums up the downside." The long story on Teixeira is: That really does sum up his downside. Teixeira has been a major league-caliber hitter since his sophomore year of college, and has spent the last two seasons polishing his defense, a task accomplished so successfully that it is Blalock, not Teixeira, who has to worry most about a position switch. But it's on offense where he really shines. Teixeira has that rarest of gifts: the ability to hit with light-tower power from both sides of the plate. He

also commands the strike zone like Patton controlled the Third Army, and could hit .300 if his Shirley Temple was spiked with enough cough syrup to cure anthrax. What I'm trying to say is, Teixeira can mash.

Teixeira does have a pair of non-insignificant injuries in his past—a severely sprained ankle that took a chunk out of his final college season, and a ruptured elbow tendon which initially looked like it might sideline him for all of 2002. Instead, he was out barely two months and came back in plenty of time to put the fear of God in pitchers throughout the Florida State and Texas leagues. So he's a fast healer to boot. Like we said: There really is no downside.

2.	Hideki Matsui		RF	New York Yankees		Age 29
	AVG	OBP	SLG	EqA	Defense	
2001	.314	.441	.597	.336	CF: N/A	
2002	.319	.451	.668	.353	CF: N/A	

A physical and stylistic comp for Brian Giles, "Godzilla" could be a .280/.370/.500 hitter on this side of the Pacific, and legitimately call it an off-year. As a lumbering power hitter with little foot speed, he's the complete opposite of Ichiro Suzuki, and while he's not likely to garner the attention the 2001 AL MVP did with his slap hitting and base stealing, Matsui will put more runs on the board than Ichiro did. Given the sorry state of AL corner outfielders, Matsui should be a legitimate All-Star selection. He might even be an MVP candidate, and unlike Ichiro, he might actually deserve to win. No conditional clause here: He is, no question, an absolute bargain at $7 million a year.

3.	Jose Reyes		SS	New York Mets		Age 20
	AVG	OBP	SLG	EqA	Defense	
2001	.243	.269	.377	.216	SS: +4	
2002	.236	.280	.378	.222	SS: 0	

The Mets' best prospect since Edgardo Alfonzo is similar to Fonzie in many ways, and unlike Alfonzo, will reach the majors without being moved off of shortstop. Reyes can drive the ball—53 extra-base hits in two good pitchers' environments as a 19-year-old—run (58 steals in 79 attempts) and field. He's a year away, with just a half-season of Double-A under his belt, and enough deterioration in his strike-zone judgment in that time to cause some concern. But his combination of age, positional value, and offensive potential gives him arguably the highest upside of any player on this list. The Rey Sanchez deal is a sign that the Mets understand Reyes isn't quite ready, but that when he is they don't want his path blocked by anyone more imposing than, say, Rey Sanchez. Reyes projects as Edgar Renteria on the low end, Barry Larkin on the high end.

4. Victor Martinez   C   Cleveland Indians   Age 24

	AVG	OBP	SLG	EqA	Defense
2001	.273	.328	.414	.247	C: -4
2002	.283	.350	.488	.277	C: -3

Martinez built on his out-of-nowhere 2001 season to be named the Eastern League MVP, his second straight league MVP award. He's shown a complete offensive game, hitting for power and average and showing remarkable contact ability for a man with his power. As a general rule, bet on success for a player with as many extra-base hits (in Martinez's case, 62) as strikeouts. He may be a victim of Nichols's Law of Catcher Defense, as criticism of his glovework is growing with each 900 OPS he posts. Don't be concerned if Martinez loses out to Josh Bard in March; he ought to be the regular by mid-season. Long-term, he should be the middle-of-the-order threat that Sandy Alomar was supposed to be for the Indians a decade ago.

5. Jose Contreras   RHP   New York Yankees   Age "31"

No Professional Record

How does a man who has yet to throw his first pitch as a professional rank as the best pitching prospect in the game? It's not that hard, when you've been the best amateur pitcher in the world for several years. It's pretty simple when, in the last three major international tournaments, you've gone 7–0 with a 0.59 ERA and 66 Ks in 61 innings. It's downright easy when you throw three nasty pitches (fastball, slider, splitter) with both command and deception. Contreras is not the second coming of Rene Arocha. He's not the new Rolando Arrojo. Not even Orlando Hernandez was considered in such high regard in international circles as Contreras is. The only concerns Contreras has are the long history of heavy workloads for the greater glory of Fidel Castro and the proletariat, and an age of 31 Cuban years, which converts to up to 35 years on the Gregorian calendar. He might not last as long as some other players on this list, but for 2003 he should give his fellow Yankee import serious competition for Rookie of the Year honors.

6. Brandon Phillips   2B/SS   Cleveland Indians   Age 22

	AVG	OBP	SLG	EqA	Defense
2001	.242	.302	.390	.237	SS: +4
2002	.265	.308	.437	.249	SS: -2

No team did more to upgrade its farm system in 2002 than the Indians, and no player contributed more to that improvement than Phillips, who was just part of the impressive booty captured from the Expos in exchange for Bartolo Colon. Phillips built on his impressive 2001 campaign by adding power (18 homers is power, when it comes from a 21-year-

old middle infielder), and had little difficulty adjusting to a change in both organization and position. With Omar Vizquel entrenched at shortstop, the Indians sent Phillips to the AFL to work on his second base play, and he was named the league's best defensive infielder. For Indian fans still smarting over the loss of their best pitcher (Colon) and hitter (Thome) in the past year, Phillips and Martinez make for a nice anesthetic.

7. Hee Choi   1B   Chicago Cubs   Age 23

	AVG	OBP	SLG	EqA	Defense
2001	.205	.288	.369	.223	1B: +5
2002	.248	.356	.447	.270	1B: -10

Hitter. Choi has been a monster at every level, and after a huge AFL performance seems ready to be a Carlos Delgado-type player in the major leagues. There's been some scouty muttering that he can't handle hard stuff up and in, and that he can't hit left-handers, but everything in his performance record, capped off by a monster campaign in the Arizona Fall League, indicates a player who can hit .280 with power and walks right now, and who should routinely flirt with a four-figure OPS at his peak. His defense has improved considerably, and is now an asset. If Dusty Baker is half as willing to let rookies play as he claims he is, then Eric Karros better start shopping for a nice pair of pom-poms.

8. Jerome Williams   RHP   San Francisco Giants   Age 21

	H/9	BB/9	K/9	ERA	PERA
2001	10.4	3.0	4.3	5.34	4.59
2002	8.9	3.3	5.7	4.16	3.63

Yes, Jerome Williams really is the best non-Cuban-refugee pitching prospect in baseball. No, I am not hallucinating. Williams is a former sandwich pick and has always been well thought of in scouting circles as a perfectly respectable future #2 starter. So why am I throwing caution to the wind here? Because the closer you look, the better Williams appears. Drafted at 17, he has been among the youngest players at his classifications for his entire career. A 3.59 ERA—even in the PCL—doesn't look that impressive, until you consider that Williams was just 20 years old. Since 1990, just one 20-year-old pitcher has thrown at least 120 innings in Triple-A with a lower ERA than Williams: Pedro Martinez.

Most pitching prospects as precocious as Williams would have been overused to some degree, but his 161 innings were a career high, and he has never averaged even six innings a start. Moreover, he's an efficient pitcher, with preternatural control for one so young, further limiting his pitch counts. He is even more mature off the field than on it, maturity forced upon him by having a father who is wheelchair-bound and a mother who died of breast cancer at the beginning of the 2001 season. With only one more level to jump, and with the spacious confines of Pac Bell Park to buffer him even then, Williams could be one of the best rookie pitchers in the NL this season and still only scratch the surface of his potential.

9. Joe Mauer   C   Minnesota Twins   Age 20

	AVG	OBP	SLG	EqA	Defense
2001	.274	.343	.333	.238	C: -3
2002	.236	.307	.311	.214	C: +11

The fourth catcher in history to be drafted #1 overall, Mauer has so far played like he has no idea that the previous three draftees caught a total of nine major league games combined. (And let's not even get into the history of high school catchers taken in the first round.) It helps that, unlike Mike Ivie, Steve Chilcott, and Danny Goodwin, Mauer is a hitter first and a catcher second. He's no slouch behind the plate, mind you. He's tremendously athletic, possesses an above-average arm, and gets great marks for his leadership skills. More importantly, though, he has a picture-perfect line drive swing rarely associated with a backstop. He also possesses eerie command of the strike zone for someone so young: how many teenagers can draw 61 walks against just 42 strikeouts? His lack of power would be more of a concern if he wasn't just 19 years old.

If there's one red flag regarding Mauer, it's that at 6'4", his height may work against him. A lifetime of repetitive squatting and standing is not easy on the knees, which may explain why none of the best catchers in history stood taller than 6'3". Ivan Rodriguez is 5'9"; Yogi Berra was 5'7" in his playing days, and might be shorter than Michael J. Fox by now.

10. Chris Snelling   CF/RF   Seattle Mariners   Age 21

	AVG	OBP	SLG	EqA	Defense
2001	.266	.329	.389	.243	LF: -3
2002	.261	.328	.437	.262	OF: 0

If only he can stay healthy. The Thunder from Down Under is in danger of becoming the Canberra Cripple, or at least the Australian version of Fred Lynn. (Disclaimer: he's not actually from Canberra.) In 2000, he missed half the season when he broke his hand crashing into an outfield wall, then missed time with a strained wrist. (He also hit .305 with power as the youngest hitter in the Midwest League.) In 2001, the only season he's played in so much as 75 games, he battled through a stress fracture in his ankle. (He also won the California League batting title while still in his teens.) In

2002, he missed the first month of the season with a broken thumb diving for a catch, then tore his ACL in early June and missed the rest of the season. (In between, he hit .326 in Double-A before making his major league debut at age 20.) Some of his injuries are the result of overaggressive play, some are just the result of bad luck, but none of them have taken away his ability to rake like no other kid his age can. The list of people who can hit major league pitching before they can hit the bar scene is a very short one, and Snelling's on it. If only he can stay healthy.

11. Jason Stokes   1B   Florida Marlins   Age 21

	AVG	OBP	SLG	EqA	Defense
2001	.172	.217	.306	.176	N/A
2002	.258	.325	.485	.264	1B: +4

Despite his billing as one of the best power-hitting prospects ever out of high school, concerns about signability and a lack of other skills allowed Stokes to slide into the second round in 2000. The lesson, as always: major league teams are penny-wise and pound-foolish. After back trouble limited his playing time and effectiveness in 2001, Stokes officially went live last season, plastering frozen ropes all around the Midwest League. If power really is the last skill to develop, it's scary to think what a 20-year-old who slugged .645 (despite a painful cyst in his left wrist, which was removed after the season) is going to do when he develops his. The Marlins have placed Stokes on their list of untouchables, a list more telling for who didn't make it: Adrian Gonzalez, who was the first pick in the draft the same year and occupies his own spot on this list.

12. Rich Harden   RHP   Oakland Athletics   Age 21

	H/9	BB/9	K/9	ERA	PERA
2001	8.9	7.1	6.7	5.21	4.86
2002	8.2	5.3	7.5	3.99	3.97

Think Tim Hudson, and think soon, because Harden is coming on like a freight train. A late-round draft-and-follow who played outfield growing up in Canada, all Harden has done as a pro is whiff 287 batters in 227 innings, with just nine homers allowed. Like Hudson, he's not particularly tall (just 6'1") but throws a hard, heavy fastball. He also changes speeds exceptionally well. Sure, his slider is still in its rudimentary stages, but cut the kid some slack—he just turned 21. Perhaps most importantly, he's in an organization that has done such a good job of keeping their young pitchers healthy and effective that we may have to adjust our slogan to, "There's no such thing as a pitching prospect . . . unless he pitches for Oakland." At the rate Harden is progressing, while other contenders are attempting to bolster their squads at the trading deadline, the A's may get their biggest addition from within.

13. Jesse Foppert   RHP   San Francisco Giants   Age 22

	H/9	BB/9	K/9	ERA	PERA
2001	7.8	4.6	6.2	3.49	3.12
2002	8.5	4.2	9.0	4.16	4.09

If you had spent a week in Fresno last August, as consolation you could have witnessed the most prospect-laden rotation of the new millennium. Foppert, who attended the University of San Francisco before the Giants drafted him in the second round in 2001, was overpowering the Pacific Coast League by mid-2002 and is considered by many to be the best pitching prospect in the game. Tempering our enthusiasm is that he's only been a pitcher for about three years, and is still learning both his craft and how to get through a full season. He also hasn't had to make the inevitable adjustments that come with struggling on the mound; expect him to go through a rough patch at some point in 2003, and emerge as an even better pitcher. The Giants' pitching depth, and Brian Sabean's history of using his farm system to trade for major leaguers, make it likely that Foppert will start his career with another team.

14. Marlon Byrd   CF   Philadelphia Phillies   Age 25

	AVG	OBP	SLG	EqA	Defense
2001	.274	.341	.478	.273	CF: -1
2002	.275	.327	.451	.263	CF: -12

What a novel concept: a top minor league prospect who spent a full year in Double-A *and* a full year in Triple-A! At 25, Byrd lacks the limitless potential label that shadows many a prospect, but the upside for a team with playoff aspirations is that he is ready, like, yesterday. Last season was as close to an off-year as Byrd's internal metronome will allow; he's hit between .296 and .316 in all four pro seasons, with OBPs ranging from .362 to .386. He has scored between 103 and 108 runs three years running. After almost having a leg amputated following a freak injury in college, he has never been on the disabled list as a pro. He is a career 96-for-111 (86%) on stolen base attempts. Like I said, he's ready, so ready that with the Braves as vulnerable as they've been since Kuwait was still the 19th Province, the Phillies aren't hesitating in the slightest to hand Byrd the center field job. Nor should they.

15. Michael Cuddyer   RF   Minnesota Twins   Age 24

	AVG	OBP	SLG	EqA	Defense
2001	.250	.333	.482	.267	3B: +2
2002	.269	.329	.506	.271	RF: -2

Raw power, especially from the right side, is something the Twins have lacked for years. Cuddyer provides it in spades, so much so that he was the Twins' regular right fielder in the playoffs last year and goes into 2003 with an impressive amount of job security for a rookie breaking in on a squad that includes Torii Hunter, Jacque Jones, Bobby Kielty, and Dustan Mohr. While he won't hit for a high average or walk a ton—at least not right away—he is the perfect fit for these Twins: a 30-homer candidate on a six-figure salary for the next three years. Since coming into baseball as a third baseman, Cuddyer has adjusted well to right field, where his strong arm is an asset and his footwork isn't a liability.

16. Shin-Soo Choo   CF   Seattle Mariners   Age 20

	AVG	OBP	SLG	EqA	Defense
2002	.230	.312	.359	.232	CF: -5

They might not have made a play for Hideki Matsui, but make no mistake about it: the Mariners are still clearly the Lords of the Pacific Rim, and come 2005 could employ an outfield that's one-third Australian (Snelling), one-third Japanese (Ichiro), and one-third Korean, thanks to Choo. The Mariners signed Choo for $1.3 million after he dominated international competition as much with his arm (winning a pair of games against Team USA) as with his bat. Choo has hit .300 at every minor league stop the last two years, and his 19 triples in that time is testimony to both his speed and his power potential. That he walked 79 times last season augurs well for his chances to tap into that power. It's unlikely he'll sniff the coffee-drenched air of Safeco Field this year, but we could have said that about Snelling a year ago. And unlike Snelling, Choo isn't likely to tear something the moment he arrives in Seattle.

17. Aaron Heilman   RHP   New York Mets   Age 24

	H/9	BB/9	K/9	ERA	PERA
2001	7.5	3.6	6.0	3.37	3.31
2002	9.2	3.3	6.4	4.11	3.94

This highly polished right-hander, who returned to Notre Dame for his senior season rather than sign with the Twins in 2000, will be the second impact pitcher (after Mark Prior) from the 2001 draft. Heilman keeps everything down, allowing just 10 home runs in 184 professional innings. His performance record calls to mind a young Kevin Brown. Physically mature at 24, with a pretty good workload and health record, Heilman is as close to being a pitching prospect can get to being a safe pick, and should be pitching well in the majors by late summer.

18. Brendan Harris   3B   Chicago Cubs   Age 22

	AVG	OBP	SLG	EqA	Defense
2001	.207	.291	.328	.214	2B: +5
2002	.267	.312	.448	.251	3B: +2

Two years ago, we took a gamble by ranking a little-known prospect—lets call him X—on the basis of an excellent year as a third baseman in A-ball the year after he was drafted. Brendan Harris is also a little-known prospect, drafted in 2001, who had an excellent year as a third baseman in A-ball. The similarities between the two players don't stop there. Compare their numbers:

Prospect	AB	H	D	T	HR	BB	K	AVG/OBP/SLG
X	490	154	41	7	19	46	47	.314/.378/.543
Harris	478	157	39	7	15	45	62	.328/.389/.533

X was just 20 years old that season; Harris was 21 last year. X had better defensive numbers, while Harris split time between third and second base. On the other hand, Harris was a classification higher than X, and was voted the best defensive third baseman in his league. He also had a higher EqA (.251 to .238) than X, who happens to be Albert Pujols.

We're not saying that Harris is destined to break into the Cubs' lineup in spring training and go on to post one of the most prolific rookie seasons in history. We are saying that he's worthy of a Top 20 ranking, and that he's the greatest sleeper prospect in the game.

19. Kurt Ainsworth   RHP   San Francisco Giants   Age 24

	H/9	BB/9	K/9	ERA	PERA
2001	9.1	4.0	7.0	5.17	4.59
2002	8.7	3.8	6.8	3.76	3.59

The best-kept secret in the minor leagues is the pitching depth of the San Francisco Giants. Kurt Ainsworth was the fifth-best pitching prospect in the minors last year, yet he's only #3 in the Giants' pecking order. Boof Bonser, their fourth-best, received consideration for this list as well. Ainsworth made the Giants' Opening Day rotation last season, only to be banished to the minors in favor of Ryan Jensen despite a 1.69 ERA in his first three starts. Maybe the Giants were concerned about his 5.07 ERA in Triple-A in 2001, even though Ainsworth's peripheral numbers were outstanding. Sure enough, with only slight improvement in his hit and walk rates, his ERA in Fresno last year dropped to 3.41. Ainsworth has struck out 276 batters in 265 innings the last two years in the PCL, and has no business whatsoever returning to the minors again. With five established major league starters along with Williams, Foppert, and Ainsworth, the Giants seem nearly as determined as the Yankees to prove that you can, in fact, have too much pitching.

20. Travis Hafner   1B   Cleveland Indians   Age 26

	AVG	OBP	SLG	EqA	Defense
2001	.236	.336	.453	.262	1B: 0
2002	.298	.397	.489	.298	1B: -1

All he does is hit, and that's just fine by us. Hafner's OBPs the last four years: .387, .447, .396, and a minor league-high .463 last season. His slugging averages: .546, .580, .545, and .559. So what if he's 26, the oldest minor leaguer on this list? Hafner is ready to join the upper echelon of major league first basemen right now, and thanks to John Hart he'll get that chance—in Cleveland, where Indians fans will miss Jim Thome a lot less than they think they will. He's a similar player to the Diamondbacks' Lyle Overbay, but Hafner's the better hitter, a few months younger, and has the clearer opportunity this season. He suffered a minor wrist injury in winter ball, which is only worth mentioning because he has a history of wrist problems. If healthy, Hafner projects as a souped-up version of Paul Sorrento: not a superstar in the making, but a key part of the Tribe's lineup for years to come.

21. Francisco Rodriguez   RHP   Anaheim Angels   Age 21

	H/9	BB/9	K/9	ERA	PERA
2001	13.4	5.9	6.9	7.14	7.60
2002	7.3	3.4	10.3	2.89	2.92

And to think, on October 1st there was actually some discussion as to whether Rodriguez, on account of having one of the most impressive minor league relief seasons since Armando Benitez was leaving ash and brimstone in his wake, deserved to become the first reliever ever to crack the BP Top 40. A month later, he had accumulated more postseason wins than Sandy Koufax, and with the nickname K-Rod, had become the first pitcher since Dwight Gooden to assimilate the strikeout into his very identity.

To say he deserves the nickname would be an egregious understatement; Rodriguez struck out 41 batters in the first 24.1 innings of his major league career, most of them thrown in the crucible of the postseason against the best teams in baseball. If those innings were of the regular-season variety, he would have set the major league record for the highest strikeout ratio (15.16 per nine innings) of any pitcher with more than 10 innings. (As it is, his 13 Ks in 5.2 regular-season innings is the record for anyone with more than two innings pitched.) We don't know whether the Angels will gamble on making him a starter again, or settle for making him the best setup man in baseball. We do know that he's good. Of course, unless you spent all of last October in Myanmar, you knew that already.

22. Joe Borchard   CF Chicago White Sox   Age 24

	AVG	OBP	SLG	EqA	Defense
2001	.262	.336	.449	.259	CF: -8
2002	.244	.319	.458	.256	CF: 0

He's a former collegiate quarterback and possible first round NFL pick who gave up football to play baseball full-time, and unlike Drew Henson, it looks like Borchard made the right decision. His numbers dipped a bit from 2001, and he still strikes out too much, but Borchard is a tremendous athlete with excellent power from both sides of the plate and solid plate discipline for someone who routinely whiffs more than once a game. If anything, the fact that Borchard has played as well as he has despite all the Ks is a good prognostic sign; he's hit .426 and .398 the past two seasons when he makes contact, meaning he needs only to make better contact to take a quantum leap forward. He projects best in right field as a switch-hitting Tim Salmon clone, but if the White Sox are daring they'll sacrifice some range in center to let Borchard play between Ordonez and Carlos Lee, and make a run at the Hundred Homer Outfield.

23. Scott Hairston   2B   Arizona Diamondbacks   Age 23

	AVG	OBP	SLG	EqA	Defense
2001	.228	.289	.376	.222	2B: +1
2002	.256	.320	.453	.257	2B: -14

He's the younger brother of an established major leaguer, he plays second base, and despite next to no publicity he has emerged as one of the most intriguing power-laden second-base prospects in the game. Amazingly enough, he's not Marcus Giles. Since he was drafted in the third round in 2001, Hairston has put up numbers (last year, he hit .345 with 46 doubles, 22 homers, and 63 walks) that would make most left fielders green with envy. Which is important, because that may be his final destination if the Diamondbacks get antsy over his sometimes shaky defense. Whether he can weather the storm and be the new Jeff Kent, or whether he has to bite the bullet and become the next Ron Gant, Hairston is one of the more underrated prospects in baseball. Which means there's a very good chance that the Diamondbacks will trade him away before he gets the opportunity to establish himself. Their loss.

24. Adrian Gonzalez   1B   Florida Marlins   Age 21

	AVG	OBP	SLG	EqA	Defense
2001	.234	.293	.367	.221	1B: +8
2002	.229	.294	.377	.225	1B: 0

In the 2000 draft, the Marlins took Gonzalez and Jason Stokes with their first two picks, one of the better double-dip bonanzas of the modern draft era. (It's far from the best, however; in 1998, the Reds parlayed their first two picks into Austin Kearns and Adam Dunn.) While Stokes has passed him in the hearts and minds of the Marlins front office, a case can be made that Gonzalez is still the better prospect. His .266 average last season comes with a strong alibi: He was one of the youngest hitters in Double-A, and had jumped two levels from the Midwest League, where Stokes—who is four months older—played. Gonzalez is also a world-class defensive first baseman. He may start the season slowly after off-season surgery to repair torn cartilage in his wrist (what is it with first base prospects and wrist injuries?) but long-term,

the Keith Hernandez comparisons we made in last year's book still apply.

25. Jason Arnold   RHP   Toronto Blue Jays   Age 24

	H/9	BB/9	K/9	ERA	PERA
2001	7.5	3.1	5.8	3.06	2.65
2002	8.8	3.6	6.6	4.09	3.97

Normally, getting traded twice in six months would send up red flags about a prospect. In Arnold's case, it's a sign of just how much first the A's (who dealt Carlos Pena and Jeremy Bonderman to get a package that included Arnold) and Blue Jays (who snagged him for shortstop prospect Felipe Lopez) wanted him. Arnold is a converted reliever who throws everything hard and down, helping him keep the ball in the park—he has allowed just seven homers in 221 innings in his pro career. His performance in the pitchers' hell of Midland—a 2.33 ERA in 58 innings—eradicated any lingering doubts that he wasn't list-worthy. The Blue Jays don't want to rush him (why else would they sign Tanyon Sturtze?), but given the holes in their rotation, they won't leave Arnold in Triple-A a moment longer than necessary this year.

26. John Patterson   RHP   Arizona Diamondbacks   Age 25

	H/9	BB/9	K/9	ERA	PERA
2001	10.4	4.1	3.9	5.75	6.22
2002	9.6	3.5	6.6	4.73	4.83

Nearly seven years after being one of the 1996 draft's "loophole" free agents, John Patterson is finally a top prospect. After losing most of two seasons to Tommy John surgery, Patterson was dominant in the PCL last season even as he worked his way back to 100%, then put together several good starts to help the D-Backs hold onto the NL West. Patterson used a good fastball and curve to strike out 135 batters in 143 innings last year, and goes into the season as the Snakes' #4 starter. With the Diamondbacks into Year 3 of the Johnson & Schilling & then God Willing Plan, Patterson could have the most impact on a pennant race of anyone on this list.

27. Casey Kotchman   1B   Anaheim Angels   Age 20

	AVG	OBP	SLG	EqA	Defense
2002	.221	.308	.356	.226	1B: +4

Some players are said to have been cut from the same cloth. Kotchman and Adrian Gonzalez were cut from the same stitch. Like Gonzalez, Kotchman is a celebrated high school player from a baseball family (Kotchman's dad is a longtime coach with the Angels) who plays terrific defense at first base, knows the strike zone, hits line drives all over the field, and has emerging left-handed power. Kotchman is a year younger than Gonzalez and a year behind him on the development curve, and his 2002 season is, statistically speaking, a dead ringer for Gonzalez's 2001 campaign. Has anyone seen the two of them together at the same time? Given that they play for the Marlins and Angels, we may never be able to prove that they are not, in fact, the same person.

28. Rocco Baldelli   CF   Tampa Bay Devil Rays   Age 21

	AVG	OBP	SLG	EqA	Defense
2001	.201	.242	.321	.192	CF: -4
2002	.265	.288	.429	.240	CF: -6

He's more raw than the oysters on the half shell served in his native New England. He hit .216 and .249 in his first two pro seasons. He played in 23 games in Triple-A last season without accepting a single handout from a moundsman. For God's sake, he plays for the Devil Rays. So how on Earth was Baldelli named *Baseball America*'s Minor League Player of the Year? Because he has more tools than you'd find in Al Borland's garage, and in 2002 he showed more than just an inkling of how to use them. Baldelli was promoted twice in-season, reaching Triple-A before his 21st birthday, and shined in the AFL last fall. While he hasn't figured out plate discipline to this point, he seemed to have figured out just about every other phase of the game last year. His package of power and speed has evoked comparisons to Jose Canseco, which we suppose is meant as a compliment. Tampa Bay badly needs to resist the temptation to disturb him from his apprenticeship in Durham this season, because the plaudits aside, he's still far from a sure thing. After all, he plays for the Devil Rays.

29. Miguel Cabrera   3B   Florida Marlins   Age 20

	AVG	OBP	SLG	EqA	Defense
2001	.206	.255	.295	.189	SS: -6
2002	.236	.280	.370	.219	3B: -2

The key numbers? Forty-three and 19. Cabrera hit 43 doubles at the age of 19 in the Florida State League, which is what a stock market analyst might call a leading indicator; those doubles will almost certainly roll over into home runs over time. Those numbers replace the number by which he had been known, 1.9 million, which was the dollar amount of his Venezuelan record signing bonus. Obviously, the scouts like him too. He's officially a third baseman now, after coming into the system as a shortstop, and he's made the transition well. He'll leap to the Eastern League in 2003, and could make trading Mike Lowell a good idea for the Marlins as early as next winter.

30. Justin Morneau   1B   Minnesota Twins   Age 22

	AVG	OBP	SLG	EqA	Defense
2001	.243	.298	.408	.239	1B: +3
2002	.256	.308	.412	.240	1B: -12

Morneau can be forgiven for dropping a tick in our rankings—he was our #29 prospect last year—given that he developed an intestinal infection last spring and lost 20 pounds. He recovered quickly enough that, while making the jump to Double-A, he hit 16 homers for the second straight year. No one likes his defense; the ex-catcher moved to first base even before the Twins drafted Joe Mauer, and compared to Doug Mientkiewicz he's positively maladroit. But as long as we're pulling out the thesaurus, compared to Morneau, Mientkiewicz is (pick one:) sickly, flaccid, or—my favorite—nebbish. With another year of physical development and a healthy colon, Morneau is primed for a 30-homer season and should emerge this year as one of the best power-hitting prospects in the game.

31. Wilson Betemit   SS   Atlanta Braves   Age 21

	AVG	OBP	SLG	EqA	Defense
2001	.251	.293	.397	.231	SS: +4
2002	.231	.297	.352	.220	SS: -19

A terrible season from a former top prospect, both in terms of performance—look at those defensive numbers—and attitude. A year after ranking #5 on these pages, Betemit hit just .245 with little power and less range afoot, prompting rumors of a move to third base, if not left field. There are some mitigating factors here: Betemit struggled with back and foot injuries early in the year, hitting .198 during the first half of the season, .292 in the second half. And as hard as it is to believe for a player entering his seventh pro season, Betemit is just 21, as he signed at age 14 (!) in violation of MLB rules, not to mention child labor laws. Most 20-year-old prospects who hit .245 in Triple-A are called phenoms, not disappointments. If Betemit gets his head on straight, he'll still be a big part of the Braves future.

32. Cliff Lee   LHP   Cleveland Indians   Age 24

	H/9	BB/9	K/9	ERA	PERA
2001	10.3	4.8	7.5	5.22	5.06
2002	8.3	4.3	7.4	4.14	3.96

Only the second-best player the Indians acquired for Bartolo Colon—and the third man, Grady Sizemore, might make this list next season—Lee is a four-pitch left-hander who may have been the best pitcher in the Eastern League last year. He made batters miss with his excellent movement, although he struggled with command of that movement at Triple-A and in a brief stint in Cleveland. Lee is emblematic of an Indians' farm system that, suddenly, might be the deepest in baseball. He'd be best served by tasting a little more success at Buffalo before being dropped into the Indians' rotation, but even so, with apologies to Mike Gosling and Scott Kazmir, he's the best left-handed pitching prospect in the game.

33. Hanley Ramirez   SS   Boston Red Sox   Age 19

	AVG	OBP	SLG	EqA	Defense
2002	.263	.290	.384	.222	SS: -6

Just when it looked like the Red Sox had the weakest farm system in baseball, Hanley Ramirez arrived on our shores. In his first season on American soil, Ramirez was named the best prospect in both the Gulf Coast League (where he hit .341) and the New York-Penn League (.371), with power, speed, and defense. And hey, 20 walks in 261 at-bats is a fine start for an 18-year-old who couldn't walk off the island. Ramirez is the long-term replacement for Nomar Garciaparra, and while he's at least two seasons from the majors, he's already the Sox's best prospect, and the second-best pure shortstop prospect in baseball.

34. Justin Huber   C   New York Mets   Age 20

	AVG	OBP	SLG	EqA	Defense
2001	.206	.251	.344	.207	C: +1
2002	.224	.288	.372	.229	C: -8

Huber's promising stat line hides a big first-half/second-half split, as he wore down in his first full year of minor league ball. Just 20 last year, he showed maturity both at the plate, with a good walk rate and K/BB ratio, and behind the plate, where his work with pitchers drew raves. He has two questions to answer this year: will the Australian-born catcher hang in against Double-A pitching, and can he withstand the rigors of a full season behind the plate without wearing down. The Mets are hoping that Mike Piazza can hang on behind the plate for two more years, which should be just long enough to hand over the reins to one of the few prospects worthy of being his successor.

35. Clint Nageotte   RHP   Seattle Mariners   Age 22

	H/9	BB/9	K/9	ERA	PERA
2001	11.9	4.3	7.0	5.58	5.58
2002	11.3	4.8	7.0	6.11	5.35

The most relevant statistic in determining a pitcher's future potential is strikeouts. Last season, Clint Nageotte led the minor leagues in strikeouts. Any questions? Nageotte also ranked sixth in the minors in Ks in 2001, and has rung up 401 batters in just 317 innings the past two years. Yet he receives little mention among the game's best pitching prospects, and is lost in the shadow of fellow Mariner Rafael Soriano (who, by virtue of spending two months on the major league roster last spring, lost both his rookie eligibility and a spot on this list).

Perhaps Nageotte is ignored because of his 4.54 ERA last season—in a great hitters' league, and more importantly, despite peripheral numbers that suggest an ERA a full run lower. As discussed with Kurt Ainsworth, when a pitcher's ERA

is out of line with the rest of his performance, bet on the ERA to be influenced by the peripherals the following year, not the other way around. Nageotte will likely move to Double-A this year, and in the pitcher-friendly environment of San Antonio, his strikeout rate will likely not be the only eye-catching number that he'll put up. He's as good a candidate as anyone to be the best pitching prospect in baseball a year from now.

36. Juan Rivera   OF   New York Yankees   Age 24

	AVG	OBP	SLG	EqA	Defense
2001	.280	.318	.499	.263	RF: +5
2002	.294	.332	.454	.261	OF: -5

The presence of the #2 guy on this list blocks Rivera, who spent most of the winter being offered in trade. Rivera can hit for average and power, and his strong arm makes him a good defensive right fielder. He's never walked enough though, and his strike zone judgment has regressed over the past couple of years. Besides, these are the Yankees, who don't have the time to wait for Nick Johnson to erupt into stardom, let alone Rivera. There's a thin line that separates Raul Mondesi's career from Jose Guillen's, and right now Rivera is straddling it.

37. Khalil Greene   SS   San Diego Padres   Age 22

	AVG	OBP	SLG	EqA	Defense
2002	.246	.281	.384	.225	SS: -2

The first college hitter selected in the 2002 draft did exactly what you'd expect from the first college hitter selected in the draft: after a 10-game tune-up in the Northwest League, he reported to High-A ball and immediately established himself as one of the best hitters in the league. A shortstop throughout his collegiate career, Greene hardly resembles the major league prototype, but thanks to Cal Ripken, Alex Rodriguez, and others, he fits it well enough that the Padres will give him every opportunity to play there. He has uncommon power for a man of his position, and will hit even if he does have to drop a rung or two on the defensive spectrum. Greene almost certainly will become the best major league hitter ever of the Baha'i faith. We're betting he'll be even better than that.

38. Jayson Werth   CF/RF   Toronto Blue Jays   Age 24

	AVG	OBP	SLG	EqA	Defense
2001	.219	.315	.394	.241	C: +5
2002	.236	.330	.410	.253	OF: -1

Never underestimate the importance of common sense. Werth was a first round draft pick as a high school catcher, and despite flashes of greatness he failed to make an impression on anyone—to the point where the Orioles traded him to Toronto for John Bale. Until that is, someone in the Blue

Jays organization looked at Werth's lanky, 6′5″, 210-pound physique and thought, "gee, he really doesn't look like a catcher." He didn't look like a catcher because he wasn't one—he was a speedy center fielder trapped behind the plate for reasons not easily divined. Freed from the shackles of the tools of ignorance, Werth stole a career-high 25 bases and so impressed the Blue Jays with his defensive play that they didn't think twice about letting Jose Cruz go. He's not the second coming of Dale Murphy—for one thing, he'll play right field as long as the Jays have Vernon Wells in center—but he's also a lot more than Eli Marrero redux.

39. Joey Thurston   2B   Los Angeles Dodgers   Age 23

	AVG	OBP	SLG	EqA	Defense
2001	.232	.289	.331	.210	2B: -14
2002	.292	.318	.446	.256	2B: +6

If the Dodgers' new second baseman seems out of place on this list, it's because he adheres to the old-school theory of prospectdom. While other BP prospects embrace the Three True Outcomes, Joey Ballgame is the shining example of the ideal middle-infield prospect—circa 1976. He hits for a high average, but his power is more to the gaps than the bleachers, and his idea of commanding the strike zone is to put the ball in play. Hey, just because his philosophy is old-fashioned doesn't mean it can't work for him. He's a similar all-around player to the man he is replacing in L.A., Mark Grudzielanek. But at age 23, and with a reputation as a scrappy over achiever, he projects more like a Dodger second baseman of slightly older vintage: Steve Sax. Preferably without the yips.

40. Bobby Jenks   RHP Anaheim Angels   Age 22

	H/9	BB/9	K/9	ERA	PERA
2001	11.0	8.4	5.9	7.06	7.06
2002	8.6	8.2	6.0	5.49	5.33

From the makers of "Nick Neugebauer" comes the long-awaited sequel, "Bobby Jenks: the Anaheim Enigma." Jenks throws very, very, VERY hard—one of the few pitchers in the game with legitimate triple-digit velocity—and his curveball is, like the women advertised in most of the spam that shows up in my e-mail box, barely legal. But if Jenks knows where the ball is headed, he ain't telling. He allowed nearly as many walks (90) as hits (99) in 123 innings last year, and has consistently averaged a strikeout an inning throughout his career. A terrific AFL campaign (1.08 ERA in 42 IP, 54 Ks vs. just 17 walks) has the Angels excited that he's more likely to blow up, as the kids say these days, than to blow out. Sure he's a gamble, but then that's why he's at the bottom of this list instead of the top.

Honorable Mention

Bobby Basham, RHP, Cincinnati Reds: An unheralded seventh round pick out of the University of Richmond in 2001, Basham had a ridiculous 97–9 strikeout-to-walk ratio last season in the Midwest League, then proved he wasn't just beating up on youngsters by doing the same thing in the AFL. He throws hard and he throws strikes, and he's one of the most underrated pitching prospects in the game.

Jeremy Bonderman, RHP, Detroit Tigers: The A's first round pick in 2001 is doing his best to make the Tigers' trade of Jeff Weaver look a lot better than most analysts—myself included—thought at first blush. Just 19, with no pro experience, he was challenged with a placement in the California League and was borderline spectacular before he was acquired by the Tigers as the PTBNL in the Weaver deal. Could be one of the best pitching prospects in baseball a year from now; standard disclaimers about A-ball pitchers apply.

Tagg Bozied, Jake Gautreau, and Xavier Nady, hitters, San Diego Padres: These three hitters were all drafted as third basemen out of college, but have since dispersed around the diamond, Nady to the outfield, Bozied to first, and Gautreau to second. All three can rake, and Bozied and Nady have monster power potential (Bozied led the AFL in homers). The same logjam that has started to form in the Padres' rotation could soon manifest itself in the lineup as well. We should all have such problems.

Kevin Cash, C, Toronto Blue Jays: Arguably the most unlikely catching prospect since Mike Piazza, Cash was a third baseman at Florida State—and went undrafted—when he was forced into emergency duty as a catcher in the Cape Cod League, and promptly nailed a pair of baserunners. Impressed, the Blue Jays signed him, and three years later his defense has moved Josh Phelps to first base and Jayson Werth to the outfield. His plate discipline needs to be tightened up, but if he can hit even a little, he'll play.

Jack Cust and Brad Hawpe, mashers, Colorado Rockies: When you (1) play for the Rockies and (2) can hit in any time zone, you're a prospect even if you're as defensively limited as Jack Cust, a poor first baseman forced to toil as a horrible left fielder, or Brad Hawpe, a poor first baseman forced to toil as a poor first baseman. The Rockies would never think of trading Todd Helton away, but teams with lesser first basemen ought to be reminded that one man's trash is another man's treasure.

Prince Fielder, 1B, Milwaukee Brewers: Cecil's son apparently didn't realize he was playing in the minors, because his numbers in rookie ball—.390 with a .531 OBP and a .678 slugging average—look like they were put up against high school pitching. His power potential exceeds even that of his father at the same age; unfortunately, so does his girth. There hasn't been a guy with this much to gain from losing weight since Jared from Subway.

Gavin Floyd, RHP, Philadelphia Phillies: The Phillies' first pick (#4 overall) in 2001 has done nothing so far to prove the adage that drafting a high school pitcher in the first round is, more or less, suicidal. The Phillies love his lethal fastball-curveball combination; we like his 119 hits allowed in 166 innings and his 140-64 strikeout-to-walk ratio. There are no question marks about his talent or aptitude, just the usual question marks about his choice of position.

Ken Harvey, 1B, Kansas City Royals: Four-seventy-nine. The hefty hit machine struggled for the first time as a pro, batting just .277 in Triple-A as he adjusted to a new batting stance, but Harvey hit .479 in the Arizona Fall League. Four-seventy-nine. Without bringing any other outstanding skill to the table, Harvey must hit .300 to be of value in the major leagues, but he might do just that—as soon as this year.

Brandon Larson, 3B, Cincinnati Reds: A surprise first round pick out of LSU in 1997, Larson was the quintessential collegiate hitter bust—until last season, when he started attending the Church of Plate Discipline. Larson not only doubled his walk rate, he hit .340 with a home run every 12 at-bats in the International League, then outhit incumbent third baseman Aaron Boone—now second baseman Aaron Boone—during a September call-up. If the conversion takes, he'll be one of the best rookies in the NL this season.

Todd Linden, LF, San Francisco Giants: Drafted in the supplemental first round in 2001 after an up-and-down collegiate career, Linden settled down in his first pro season to post a combined .411 OBP between Double-A and Triple-A. The Giants are pretty happy with their current left fielder, but if Linden taps into the power potential that scouts and analysts alike perceive, they'll open up a spot for him somewhere.

James Loney, 1B, Los Angeles Dodgers: The surprise of the 2002 draft so far, Loney was scouted by most teams as a pitcher, but after the Dodgers drafted him in the first round, he tore up the Pioneer League by hitting .371 with 22 doubles in 47 games and more walks than strikeouts. Just as impres-

sively, he held his own in the High-A Florida State League, a pitcher's haven, hitting .299 in 17 games with good plate discipline. A broken wrist—is this some sort of hazing ritual among first-base prospects?—kept him from becoming the first player ever to play in the AFL the fall after graduating high school. At the rate he's going, pretty soon pitchers throughout baseball will be cursing the Dodgers for not seeing what everyone else saw.

Miguel Olivo, C, Chicago White Sox: The strong-armed catcher is doing his best to justify being traded straight up to the White Sox for Dan Quisenberry Jr. . . . er, Chad Bradford. Olivo hit .306 in his second go-round in Double-A, and shook up the Catchers' Guild by stealing 29 bases and leading the Southern League with 10 triples. If he doesn't become obsessed with being the new John Wathan, he could be significantly better.

Adam Wainwright, RHP, Atlanta Braves: What would a top prospect list be without a Braves' pitcher? Wainwright is the torch-bearer for a group that includes Macay McBride, Matt Belisle, Zach Miner, and the usual cadre of live arms that get churned out of the Braves' organization like they came off an assembly line. If you want to know who's the real deal and who's just a pretender, just wait and see which pitchers the Braves keep and which ones they trade away.

David Wright, 3B, New York Mets: The Mets have no depth to their minor league system, but their upper crust—Reyes, Heilman, Huber, Wright, and Scott Kazmir—ranks with the best in the game. Wright is a Scott Rolen clone who showed across-the-board skills—.266 average, 43 extra-base hits, 76 walks, 21 steals—as a 19-year-old in his first full season. And unlike Michael Cuddyer—the last Scott Rolen clone to pass through the minors—Wright's defense shouldn't require a position change.

Kevin Youkilis, 3B, Boston Red Sox: Our annual homage to an unheralded on-base machine goes to Kevin Youkilis, whose OBPs since he was drafted in 2001 read .512, .433, .422, and in Double-A, .462. There's not much here aside from OBP; Youkilis has little power and his defense evokes fond memories of Butch Hobson. If he can keep reaching base 45% of the time, he'll get a chance to man Boston's hot corner if his defense evokes memories of Roger Dorn in *Major League.*

Team Name Key and Park Factors

by Clay Davenport

Code	Team	2002 Park Factor	League	Code	Team	2002 Park Factor	League	Code	Team	2002 Park Factor	League
ABE	Aberdeen	1000	SAL	DUR	Durham	977	INT	MID	Midland	1047	TEX
AKR	Akron	980	EAS	DYT	Dayton	1026	MDW	MIL	Milwaukee	978	NL
ALT	Altoona	976	EAS	EDM	Edmonton	991	PCL	MIN	Minnesota	1027	AL
ANA	Anaheim	1017	AL	ELP	El Paso	1088	TEX	MOB	Mobile	1021	SOU
ARI	Arizona	1034	NL	ERI	Erie	1043	EAS	MOD	Modesto	969	CAL
ARK	Arkansas	1006	TEX	FKU	Fukuoka	966	JPL	MON	Montreal	1005	Limbo
ASH	Asheville	1105	SAL	FLA	Florida	965	NL	MYR	Myrtle Beach	919	CAR
ATL	Atlanta	995	NL	FRD	Frederick	1016	CAR	NAS	Nashville	922	INT
AUG	Augusta	993	SAL	FRE	Fresno	1040	PCL	NBR	New Britain	990	EAS
BAK	Bakersfield	988	CAL	FTM	Ft. Myers	953	FLA	NHV	New Haven	955	EAS
BAL	Baltimore	961	AL	FTW	Ft. Wayne	954	MDW	NIP	Nippon Ham	1034	JPL
BIN	Binghamton	1052	EAS	GRB	Greensboro	1026	SAL	NOR	Norfolk	963	INT
BIR	Birmingham	922	SOU	GRN	Greenville	1020	SOU	NRW	Norwich	967	EAS
BLT	Beloit	1028	MDW	HAG	Hagerstown	1024	SAL	NWO	New Orleans	880	PCL
BOS	Boston	999	AL	HAR	Harrisburg	1025	EAS	NYM	NY Mets	935	NL
BOW	Bowie	994	EAS	HDS	High Desert	1090	CAL	NYY	NY Yankees	1002	AL
BRV	Brevard County	958	FLA	HIC	Hickory	1048	SAL	OAK	Oakland	1016	AL
BUF	Buffalo	1003	INT	HNS	Hanshin	979	JCL	OKL	Oklahoma	952	PCL
BUR	Burlington (IA)	1006	MDW	HOU	Houston	1043	NL	OMA	Omaha	961	PCL
CAR	Carolina	1019	SOU	HRO	Hiroshima	1055	JCL	ORL	Orlando	985	SOU
CDR	Cedar Rapids	977	MDW	HUN	Huntsville	989	SOU	ORX	Orix	1028	JPL
CGA	Columbus (GA)	1009	SAL	IND	Indianapolis	1038	INT	OSA	Osaka	980	JPL
CHB	Chiba	1001	JPL	IOW	Iowa	964	PCL	OTT	Ottawa	963	INT
CHC	Chicago Cubs	957	NL	JAX	Jacksonville	991	SOU	PAW	Pawtucket	982	INT
CHR	Charlotte (NC)	1008	INT	JUP	Jupiter	940	FLA	PCH	Charlotte (FL)	997	FLA
CHT	Chattanooga	999	SOU	KAN	Kannapolis	986	SAL	PEO	Peoria	976	MDW
CHU	Chunichi	933	JCL	KCR	Kansas City	1078	AL	PHI	Philadelphia	961	NL
CIN	Cincinnati	1036	NL	KIN	Kinston	979	CAR	PIT	Pittsburg	1014	NL
CLE	Cleveland	1023	AL	KNE	Kane County	980	MDW	PME	Portland (ME)	1018	EAS
CLG	Calgary	1087	PCL	LAD	Los Angeles	918	NL	POR	Portland (OR)	913	PCL
CLN	Clinton	1000	MDW	LAK	Lakeland	1015	FLA	POT	Potomac	1043	CAR
CLR	Clearwater	1020	FLA	LEL	Lake Elsinore	959	CAL	QUD	Quad Cities	1027	MDW
CMB	Columbia	983	SAL	LEX	Lexington	1011	MDW	RCU	Rancho Cucamonga	982	CAL
COH	Columbus (OH)	1006	INT	LNC	Lancaster	1098	CAL	REA	Reading	1012	EAS
COL	Colorado	1118	NL	LNS	Lansing	1018	MDW	RIC	Richmond	1000	INT
CSC	Charleston (SC)	997	SAL	LOU	Louisville	1002	INT	ROC	Rochester	995	INT
CSP	Colorado Springs	1088	PCL	LVG	Las Vegas	1067	PCL	ROU	Round Rock	968	TEX
CWS	Chicago W. Sox	1037	AL	LWD	Lakewood	925	SAL	SAC	Sacramento	971	PCL
CWV	Charleston (WV)	1002	SAL	LYN	Lynchburg	1037	CAR	SAN	San Antonio	909	TEX
DAY	Daytona	1020	FLA	MCN	Macon	1001	SAL	SAR	Sarasota	1016	FLA
DEL	Delmarva	928	SAL	MEM	Memphis	916	PCL	SAV	Savannah	946	SAL
DET	Detroit	973	AL	MIC	Michigan	1026	MDW	SBN	South Bend	1019	MDW

Code	Team	2002 Park Factor	League	Code	Team	2002 Park Factor	League	Code	Team	2002 Park Factor	League
SBR	San Bernardino	953	CAL	SWB	Scranton/Wilkes-Barre	984	INT	VIS	Visalia	1002	CAL
SDP	San Diego	921	NL					VRO	Vero Beach	1059	FLA
SEA	Seattle	937	AL	SYR	Syracuse	1035	INT	WIC	Wichita	983	TEX
SEI	Seibu	1007	JPL	TAC	Tacoma	946	PCL	WIL	Wilmington	979	CAR
SFG	San Francisco	921	NL	TAM	Tampa	936	FLA	WIS	Wisconsin	992	MDW
SGA	South Georgia	937	SAL	TBY	Tampa Bay	1002	AL	WMI	Western Michigan	935	MDW
SHV	Shreveport	967	TEX	TEN	Tennessee	1059	SOU	WNS	Winston-Salem	1001	CAR
SJO	San Jose	943	CAL	TEX	Texas	1044	AL	WTN	West Tennessee	975	SOU
SLC	Salt Lake City	1048	PCL	TOL	Toledo	1023	INT	YKL	Yakult	977	JCL
SLM	Salem (VA)	1002	CAR	TOR	Toronto	1024	AL	YKO	Yokohama	1032	JCL
SLU	St. Lucie	1002	FLA	TRN	Trenton	976	EAS	YOM	Yomiuri	1005	JCL
STL	St. Louis	986	NL	TUC	Tucson	1051	PCL				
STO	Stockton	890	CAL	TUL	Tulsa	987	TEX				

Index

The following is an alphabetical index of the players in *Baseball Prospectus 2003*. Davenport Translations for players not listed here can be found at http://www.baseballprospectus.com.

Biographies

Jeff Bower lives in Seattle, Washington, with his wife, Vivian; son, Harrison; and catahoula, Bella. He works as an automation engineer in microelectronics for a Northwest OEM. Any thoughts he had of being a big league manager were scotched as a teen when his squad lost by 128 runs in a 24-hour wiffleball game.

Will Carroll joins BP after exploding into baseball writing with "Under the Knife," known as "baseball's best source for injury info." His knowledge of injuries comes from his background in sports medicine and from having nearly every injury a baseball player can possibly have. Will also serves as the host of "Baseball Prospectus Radio." He lives in Indianapolis and will someday finish his novel about Steve Dalkowski.

Clay Davenport is a meteorologist living in Bowie, Maryland, with his wife of six months, Susan, and her two cats. Outside of the day job and baseball, he picks up a ridiculous amount of trivial knowledge from God knows where and tosses it back out in bars. Or at least he used to.

Ted Fischer (a.k.a. Valentine) was first introduced to the Red Sox during the magical, frustrating 1986 campaign. He survived the rec.sport.baseball Internet flame wars with few serious burns, and in the process gained a deep respect for the intricacies of baseball analysis. Holding degrees in mathematics and computer science from Yale and Cornell, he is happily employed as a high school math teacher.

Gary Gillette grew up as a persecuted Tigers fan in Pennsylvania, then matriculated at Michigan State University—where he learned to love the National Pastime and despise Sparky Anderson, Domino's Pizza, and the benighted management of baseball franchises. A longtime contributor to *Total Baseball*, he is the erstwhile proprietor of The Baseball Workshop and baseball commentator for several National Public Radio stations.

Jeff Hildebrand is a visiting assistant professor of mathematics at Bates College in Maine. Despite currently living in the middle of Red Sox Nation, he has yet to be swayed from his lifelong support for the Phillies. In a sign of incipient loss of sanity, he is one of the few people who will not be gleefully happy to see the Vet fall to the wrecking ball next year.

Gary Huckabay is the founder of Baseball Prospectus. He received his MBA from the University of California, Davis. He lives in Concord, California, with his wife, Kathy, several furry quadrupeds, too many Monterey Pines, a couple of computers with excessively bloated statistical packages installed, and a large number of woodworking tools.

Rany Jazayerli is a senior dermatology resident at Henry Ford Hospital in Detroit, and has found bossing around cowering medical students to be a great stress breaker, allowing him to savor the joys of fatherhood when he comes home to see his daughter, Cedra, born December 23rd. He expects to relocate to the Chicago area in time for next year's bio.

Chris Kahrl is one of the four men that Gary Huckabay tabbed to found BP. He is the sports editor at Brassey's, where he's had the good fortune to publish a number of sports titles aimed at seamheads like you. As a former honor scholar at the University of Chicago, this happy turn of events means that he's now familiar with what it means to be a failed prospect. Out of sensitivity to Jonah, he tries not to let his D.C. location inspire too vocal a "Move the Expos NOW!" boosterism.

Jonah Keri is a journalist, covering the stock market for a major daily financial newspaper. He lives in Los Angeles with his ridiculously amazing wife Angèle and cat Oreo, who's an awful exterminator. He's considered BP's David Eckstein for his boundless enthusiasm. Jonah will gladly take golf and pickup hoops in L.A.'s 80-degree January splendor over the blizzards back home in Montreal.

Mat Olkin is a writer and copyeditor for *USA Today Sports Weekly*. He contributes to the *STATS Inc. Scouting Notebook* and the *Fantasy Baseball Index*, and pens his own annual book, the *Baseball Examiner*. He enjoys spending time with his wife Laura and their four horses, and trying not to think about Alex Sanchez or Bill Hall.

Doug Pappas is chairman of SABR's Business of Baseball Committee. He practices law during the week, haunts the New York Public Library's microfilm room on Saturdays and writes about what he has found on Sundays. He hopes to finish his web site before the new CBA expires.

Dave Pease lives in San Diego with his girlfriend and two cats and works for a wireless communications company. His interests include old-school gangsta rap, Coen brothers movies, and watching Ryan Klesko hit 48 bombs with the Padres in 2004.

Keith Scherer is a JAG for the United States Air Force. His enthusiasm for conflict is the product of a childhood spent as a White Sox fan in Cubs territory on Chicago's northwest side, but nevertheless, he harbors a lifelong admiration for Lee Elia, the last Cub to tell the truth about the Cubs or their fans. He currently resides in South Dakota, downrange from Derek Zumsteg's kaleidoscopic misanthropy.

Nate Silver lives six blocks from Wrigley Field and shares a birthday with Billy Jo Robidoux. In addition to his work with BP, he works as an economist for a large, monolithic firm. A graduate of the University of Chicago, Nate is committed to debunking his alma matter's reputation for catering to undersexed misanthropes, especially after his third vodka tonic.

Michael Wolverton has been writing and crunching numbers for Baseball Prospectus since 1996. He has degrees from two college baseball powerhouses, Rice and Stanford (although admittedly Wayne Graham and Mark Marquess have a little more to do with the success of those programs than he does). He lives in the San Francisco Bay Area with his wife, Cindy, and sons Scott, 6, and Mark, 3.

Keith Woolner abandoned Silicon Valley for greener pastures back east this year, but remembered to take his wife, Kathy, and new son Sagan along with him. He holds undergraduate degress in mathematics, computer science, and management from M.I.T., a master's degree in decision analysis from Stanford University, and works in product management for SAS. Einstein said that God does not play dice, but Keith is pretty sure that he was in a Strat-O-Matic league with Him a few years back, and apologizes for trading Phil Plantier to Him for Barry Bonds.

Derek Zumsteg lives and drinks on Seattle's Eastside with his lovely, talented, and (as you would guess) patient wife, Jill, alongside their cat, a black Volvo 850, and thousands of good books. Like all Seattle pitchers, he tore something painful in his shoulder while throwing, but his employer refuses to have Dr. Andrews take a look at it.

Dedications

I want to dedicate my contributions to everyone at the John Muir Medical Center, as well as Bramson, Plutzik, Mahler, and Birkhauser (BPMB) in Walnut Creek, California. The professionalism and compassion demonstrated by everyone at John Muir is something we can all strive for, and the generosity and support demonstrated by BPMB is enough to restore one's faith in humanity. You can't be surrounded by better people if you're unlucky enough to be in a car accident. It's just not possible.

— Gary Huckabay

To the men it is my pleasure to call partners and friends here at BP, particularly to Jonah and the yeoman work he did in helping prepare this year's book, and Dave for the years of thankless labor on the web site.

— Chris Kahrl

To my wife, Angèle, who surreptitiously planned our low-budget honeymoon to Atlanta to see the Expos, despite my "objections"; witnessed a Pedro Martinez nine-inning perfect game without me and kept score on lined paper; and saved me from punting baseball for good after the fiasco of 1994. Also to the Maple Ridge Boys, the best group of baseball fans you'll ever meet.

— Jonah Keri

Jose Reyes
a Floyd
S Hairston